Baseball America DIRECTORY 2003

Your Definitive Guide To The Game

Detailed Information on Baseball in All Leagues at All Levels!

Majors
Minors
Independent
International
College
Amateur

Published by Baseball America
Durham, North Carolina

Baseball America DIRECTORY 2003

EDITOR
Allan Simpson

ASSOCIATE EDITOR
Geoff Wilson

ASSISTANT EDITORS
J.J. Cooper
Mark Derewicz
Will Lingo

PRODUCTION DIRECTOR
Phillip Daquila

PRODUCTION ASSISTANTS
Matthew Eddy
Linwood Webb

ACCOUNT EXECUTIVE
Keith Dangel

SERVICE DIRECTORY MANAGER
Cliff Gardner

Baseball America Inc.

PRESIDENT
Catherine Silver

PUBLISHER
Lee Folger

EDITOR
Allan Simpson

MANAGING EDITOR
Will Lingo

DESIGN & PRODUCTION DIRECTOR
Phillip Daquila

COVER PHOTOS
Jose Vidro by Morris Fostoff; Kevin Towers by Larry Goren;
Fifth Third Field, Toledo, by David Cantor

Distributed by Simon & Schuster.

For additional copies, send US $17.95 each plus $7 shipping per order to
Baseball America, P.O. Box 2089, Durham NC 27702.

TABLE OF CONTENTS

MAJOR LEAGUES

MINOR LEAGUES

INDEPENDENT LEAGUES

OTHER LEAGUES/ORGANIZATIONS

2003–2004 CALENDAR

2003

March

Sun	Mon	Tue	Wed	Thu	Fri	Sat
						1
2	3	4	5	6	7	8
9	10	11	12	13	14	15
16	17	18	19	20	21	22
23	24	25	26	27	28	29
30	31					

April

Sun	Mon	Tue	Wed	Thu	Fri	Sat
		1	2	3	4	5
6	7	8	9	10	11	12
13	14	15	16	17	18	19
20	21	22	23	24	25	26
27	28	29	30			

May

Sun	Mon	Tue	Wed	Thu	Fri	Sat
				1	2	3
4	5	6	7	8	9	10
11	12	13	14	15	16	17
18	19	20	21	22	23	24
25	26	27	28	29	30	31

June

Sun	Mon	Tue	Wed	Thu	Fri	Sat
1	2	3	4	5	6	7
8	9	10	11	12	13	14
15	16	17	18	19	20	21
22	23	24	25	26	27	28
29	30					

July

Sun	Mon	Tues	Wed	Thur	Fri	Sat
		1	2	3	4	5
6	7	8	9	10	11	12
13	14	15	16	17	18	19
20	21	22	23	24	25	26
27	28	29	30	31		

August

Sun	Mon	Tue	Wed	Thu	Fri	Sat
					1	2
3	4	5	6	7	8	9
10	11	12	13	14	15	16
17	18	19	20	21	22	23
24	25	26	27	28	29	30
31						

September

Sun	Mon	Tue	Wed	Thu	Fri	Sat
	1	2	3	4	5	6
7	8	9	10	11	12	13
14	15	16	17	18	19	20
21	22	23	24	25	26	27
28	29	30				

October

Sun	Mon	Tue	Wed	Thu	Fri	Sat
			1	2	3	4
5	6	7	8	9	10	11
12	13	14	15	16	17	18
19	20	21	22	23	24	25
26	27	28	29	30	31	

November

Sun	Mon	Tue	Wed	Thu	Fri	Sat
						1
2	3	4	5	6	7	8
9	10	11	12	13	14	15
16	17	18	19	20	21	22
23	24	25	26	27	28	29
30						

December

Sun	Mon	Tue	Wed	Thu	Fri	Sat
	1	2	3	4	5	6
7	8	9	10	11	12	13
14	15	16	17	18	19	20
21	22	23	24	25	26	27
28	29	30	31			

2004

January

Sun	Mon	Tue	Wed	Thu	Fri	Sat
				1	2	3
4	5	6	7	8	9	10
11	12	13	14	15	16	17
18	19	20	21	22	23	24
25	26	27	28	29	30	31

February

Sun	Mon	Tue	Wed	Thu	Fri	Sat
1	2	3	4	5	6	7
8	9	10	11	12	13	14
15	16	17	18	19	20	21
22	23	24	25	26	27	28
29						

March

Sun	Mon	Tue	Wed	Thu	Fri	Sat
	1	2	3	4	5	6
7	8	9	10	11	12	13
14	15	16	17	18	19	20
21	22	23	24	25	26	27
28	29	30	31			

April

Sun	Mon	Tue	Wed	Thu	Fri	Sat
				1	2	3
4	5	6	7	8	9	10
11	12	13	14	15	16	17
18	19	20	21	22	23	24
25	26	27	28	29	30	

EVENTS CALENDAR

March 2003 – February 2004

MARCH

1—Opening Day: Chinese Professional Baseball League.

15—Opening Day: China League.

18—Opening Day: Mexican League.

25—Opening Day: American League (Oakland vs. Seattle in Tokyo, two-game series through March 26).

28—Opening Day: Japan Central League, Japan Pacific League.

30—Opening Day: American League (Texas at Anaheim).

31—Opening Day: American League (Cleveland at Baltimore, Boston at Tampa Bay, Chicago at Kansas City, Minnesota at Detroit, New York at Toronto).

31—Opening Day: National League (Los Angeles at Arizona, Montreal at Atlanta, Chicago at New York, Pittsburgh at Cincinnati, Philadelphia at Florida, Milwaukee at St. Louis, San Francisco at San Diego).

U.S. Cellular Field, site of the 2003 major league all-star game

APRIL

1—Opening Day: National League (Colorado at Houston).

3—Opening Day: International League, Pacific Coast League, Eastern League, Southern League, Texas League, California League, Florida State League, Midwest League, South Atlantic League.

4—Opening Day: Carolina League.

5—Opening Day: Korean Baseball Organization.

11—Montreal Expos vs. New York Mets in San Juan, P.R. (first of 22 Expos games in Puerto Rico)

14—National Classic High School Tournament at Fullerton, Calif. (through April 17).

MAY

1—Opening Day: Atlantic League.

7—Opening Day: Central League.

14—Perfect Game Top Prospect Predraft Showcase, Cedar Rapids, Iowa.

17—Junior College Division III World Series at Batavia, N.Y. (through May 23).

21—Opening Day: Canadian Baseball League.

22—Opening Day: Northeast League.

23—Opening Day: Frontier League.

23—Opening Day: Northern League.

23—NCAA Division III World Series at Appleton, Wis. (through May 27).

23—NAIA World Series at Lewiston, Idaho (through May 30).

24—NCAA Division II World Series at Montgomery, Ala. (through May 31).

24—Junior College World Series at Grand Junction, Colo. (through May 31).

24—Junior College Division II World Series at Millington, Tenn. (through May 31).

30—Opening Day: Arizona-Mexico League.

30—Opening Day: Southeastern League.

30—NCAA Division I Regionals at campus sites (through June 1).

30—Opening Day: Coastal Plain League, Southern Collegiate League.

JUNE

1—Opening Day: Venezuelan Summer League.

1—Opening Day: Atlantic Collegiate League, California Coastal Collegiate League, Pacific International League.

2—Opening Day: Northwoods League.

3—Amateur free agent draft (through June 4).

3—Opening Day: Central Illinois Collegiate League.

3—First Interleague games (Anaheim vs. Montreal at San Juan, Baltimore at Houston, Boston at Pittsburgh, Chicago White Sox at Arizona, Cleveland at Colorado, Detroit at San Diego, Kansas City at Los Angeles, Minnesota at San Francisco, New York Yankees at Cincinnati, Oakland at Florida, Seattle at Philadelphia, Tampa Bay at Chicago Cubs, Texas at Atlanta, Toronto at St. Louis)

6—Opening Day: Clark Griffith Collegiate League, Valley League.

6—NCAA Division I Super Regionals at campus sites (through June 9).

7—Opening Day: Dominican Summer League.

7—Opening Day: New England Collegiate League.

9—Opening Day: Jayhawk League.

9—Opening Day: Alaska League.

10—Opening Day: New York Collegiate League.

12—Opening Day: Great Lakes League.

13—56th College World Series at Omaha (through June 22/23).

13—Opening Day: Cape Cod League.

13—Perfect Game national showcase at Lincoln, Neb. (through June 15).

14—Florida State League all-star game at Fort Myers, Fla.

14—Opening Day: Florida Collegiate Instructional League.

15—USA Baseball junior Tournament of Stars at Joplin,

Mo. (through June 23).

16—Texas League all-star game at Wichita, Kansas.

16—Opening Day: Appalachian League.

16—Hall of Fame Game at Cooperstown (Philadelphia Phillies vs. Tampa Bay Devil Rays).

17—Midwest League all-star game at Grand Rapids, Mich.

17—Opening Day: New York-Penn League, Northwest League, Pioneer League.

18—Sunbelt Classic Baseball Series at Dale/ Seminole/Shawnee/ Tecumseh, Okla. (through June 23).

19—Opening Day: Gulf Coast League.

20—USA Baseball Junior Olympic Championships at Jupiter, Fla., and Tucson (through June 28).

21—USA Baseball college team trials at Durham, N.C. (through June 27).

23—Opening Day: Arizona League.

24—California League/Carolina League all-star game at Rancho Cucamonga, Calif.

24—South Atlantic League all-star game at Lexington, Ky.

JULY

7—Perfect Game World Wood Bat Championship at Marietta, Ga. (through July 13).

8—Southern League all-star game at Jacksonville, Fla.

9—Atlantic League all-star game at Nashua, N.H.

13—5th All-Star Futures Game at U.S. Cellular Field, Chicago.

14—COPABE Pan Am Championship at Willemstad, Curacao (through July 24).

14—Central League all-star game at Edinburg, Texas.

15—74th Major League All-Star Game at U.S. Cellular Field, Chicago.

15—Japan All-Star Game I at Osaka Dome.

16—Triple-A all-star game at Memphis.

16—Eastern League all-star game at New Britain, Conn.

16—Frontier League All-Star Game at Sauget, Ill.

16—Japan All-Star Game II at Chiba.

22—Northern League all-star game at Lincoln, Neb.

23—European Olympic Qualifier (qualifier for 2004 Olympics) at Rotterdam/Haarlem, Netherlands (through July 27).

26—Cape Cod League all-star game at Falmouth, Mass.

27—Hall of Fame induction ceremonies, Cooperstown.

30—East Coast Professional Baseball Showcase at Wilmington, N.C. (through Aug. 2).

AUGUST

1—End of major league trading period without waivers.

1—Pan American Games at Santo Domingo, Dominican Republic (through Aug. 15).

1—Connie Mack World Series at Farmington, N.M. (through Aug. 7).

2—National Baseball Congress World Series at Wichita (through Aug. 16).

4—Area Code Games at Long Beach (through Aug. 9).

8—IBAF World Youth Championship at Kaohsiung, Taiwan (through Aug. 17).

9—Babe Ruth 16-18 World Series at Weimar, Texas. (through Aug. 16).

9—Pony League World Series at Washington, Pa. (through Aug. 16).

15—Little League World Series at Williamsport, Pa. (through Aug. 24).

16—Babe Ruth 13-15 World Series at Williston, N.D. (through Aug. 23).

22—American Legion World Series at Bartlesville, Okla. (through Aug. 26).

31—Postseason major league roster eligibility frozen.

SEPTEMBER

1—Major league roster limits expanded from 25 to 40.

28—Major league season ends.

30—Major league Division Series begin.

30—Opening Day: Arizona Fall League.

OCTOBER

1—Beginning of major league trading period without waivers.

4—Baseball America/Perfect Game 16-and-under Wood Bat Championship at Fort Myers, Fla. (through Oct. 6).

4—All Africa Games (qualifier for 2004 Olympics) at Abuja, Nigeria (through Oct. 10).

7—Major league Championship Series begin.

12—XXXV World Cup at Havana, Cuba (through Oct. 25).

18—World Series begins.

18—Japan Series begins at home of Pacific League champion.

24—Baseball America/Perfect Game World Wood Bat Championship at Jupiter, Fla. (through Oct. 27).

30—Pan American Championship (qualifier for 2004 Olympics) at Panama City, Panama (through Nov. 11).

31—Asian Championship (qualifier for 2004 Olympics) at Sapporo, Japan (through Nov. 7).

NOVEMBER

20—Filing date, 40-man major league winter rosters.

DECEMBER

4—National High School Baseball Coaches Association convention at Albuquerque, N.M. (through Dec. 7).

12—101st annual Winter Meetings at New Orleans (through Dec. 15).

15—Rule 5 major league/minor league drafts.

JANUARY 2004

2—American Baseball Coaches Association convention at San Antonio (through Jan. 5).

2—Perfect Game World Underclassmen Showcase at Fort Myers, Fla. (through Jan. 4).

9—Perfect Game World Showcase at Fort Myers, Fla. (through Jan. 11).

10—NCAA National Convention at Nashville (through Jan. 12).

FEBRUARY

1—Caribbean Series at Dominican Repubilc (through Feb. 8).

BASEBALL AMERICA

ESTABLISHED 1981

PRESIDENT: Catherine Silver

PUBLISHER: Lee Folger

EDITOR: Allan Simpson

MANAGING EDITOR: Will Lingo
EXECUTIVE EDITOR: Jim Callis
SENIOR WRITERS: John Manuel, Alan Schwarz
NEWS EDITOR: J.J. Cooper
ASSOCIATE EDITORS: Josh Boyd, Geoff Wilson
ONLINE EDITOR: Will Kimmey
ASSISTANT EDITOR: Alan Matthews

DESIGN AND PRODUCTION DIRECTOR: Phillip Daquila
PRODUCTION ASSISTANTS: Matthew Eddy, Linwood Webb

CUSTOMER SERVICE: Ronnie McCabe, Demetris Burns, Shirley McCabe
customerservice@baseballamerica.com

ADVERTISING SALES
ACCOUNT EXECUTIVE: Keith Dangel
MARKETPLACE MANAGER: Cliff Gardner
P.O. Box 2089, Durham, NC 27702
Phone: (800) 845-2726; **FAX:** (919) 682-2880

BUSINESS STAFF
ECONOMIST: Bill Porter
MANAGER, FINANCE: Cara Callanan
FINANCIAL ADMINISTRATOR: Leon Lashway
LEGAL COUNSEL: Mike Ring

BASEBALL AMERICA INC.

Mailing Address: P.O. Box 2089, Durham, NC 27702
Street Address: 201 West Main Street, Suite 201, Durham, NC 27701
Telephone: (919) 682-9635 • **Toll-Free:** (800) 845-2726
FAX: (919) 682-2880
Website: BaseballAmerica.com

BASEBALL AMERICA, the nation's most complete all-baseball magazine, publishes 26 issues a year. Subscription rates are US $61.95 for one year, $97.90 for two years. Call or write for non-U.S. addresses.

BASEBALL AMERICA PUBLICATIONS

2003 Almanac: A comprehensive look at the 2002 season, featuring major and minor league statistics and commentary; 480 pages. **$15.95** ($18.95 spiral bound)

2003 Prospect Handbook: Detailed scouting reports and biographical sketches on 900 of the top prospects in the minor leagues; 512 pages. **$21.95**

2003 Super Register: A complete record, with biographical information, of every player who played professional baseball in 2002; 704 pages. **$59.95**

2003 Directory: Names, addresses, phone numbers, major and minor league schedules—vital to baseball insiders and fans; 384 pages. **$17.95** ($20.95 spiral bound)

2003 Great Parks: The Baseball America Calendar. **$12.95**

All prices in US funds. Add $7 to order for shipping and handling. Allow four weeks for delivery.

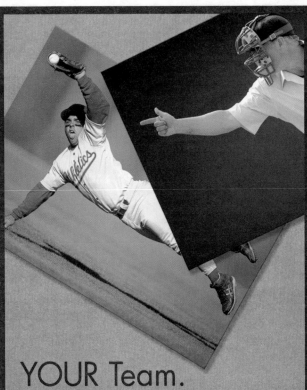

BASEBALL AMERICA
2002 AWARD WINNERS

MAJOR LEAGUES

Player of the Year
Alex Rodriguez, ss, Rangers
Executive of the Year
Billy Beane, Athletics
Rookie of the Year
Eric Hinske, 3b, Blue Jays
Roland Hemond Award (Contributions to Scouting and Player Development)
Buck O'Neil
Lifetime Achievement Award
Frank Robinson

MINOR LEAGUES

Organization of the Year
Minnesota Twins
Player of the Year
Rocco Baldelli, of, Devil Rays (Bakersfield/California, Orlando/Southern, Durham/International)
Manager of the Year
John Russell, Twins (Edmonton/Pacific Coast)
Executive of the Year
Randy Mobley, International League
Team of the Year
Akron Aeros, Indians/Eastern
Bob Freitas Awards (Best Minor League Operations)
Triple-A: Memphis Redbirds (Pacific Coast)
Double-A: Chattanooga Lookouts (Southern)
Class A: Fort Myers Miracle (Florida State)
Short-season: Ogden Raptors (Pioneer)
Classification Players of the Year
Triple-A: Joe Thurston, 2b, Dodgers (Las Vegas/Pacific Coast)
Double-A: Victor Martinez, c, Indians (Akron/Eastern)
High Class A: Rocco Baldelli, of, Devil Rays (Bakersfield/California)
Low Class A: Jason Stokes, 1b, Marlins (Kane County/Midwest)
Short-season: Andy Sisco, rhp, Cubs (Boise/Northwest)
Rookie: Ryan Shealy, 1b, Rockies (Casper/Pioneer)

JEFFREY CAMARATI
Baseball America's Minor League Player of the Year
Devil Rays prospect Rocco Baldelli

LARRY GOREN
Baseball America's Major League Player of the Year
Rangers shortstop Alex Rodriguez

INDEPENDENT LEAGUES

Player of the Year
Bobby Madritsch, lhp, Winnipeg (Northern)

WINTER LEAGUES

Player of the Year
Arnie Munoz, lhp, Aguilas (Dominican Republic)/White Sox

COLLEGES

Player of the Year
Khalil Greene, ss, Clemson
Coach of the Year
Augie Garrido, Texas
Freshman of the Year
Stephen Drew, ss, Florida State

AMATEUR/YOUTH LEAGUES

Summer Player of the Year (College players)
Brad Sullivan, rhp, Team USA
Youth Player of the Year (High school and younger)
Delmon Young, of, Camarillo, Calif.
Ripken Baseball Youth Coach of the Year
Donnie Warner, Lexington, Ky.

HIGH SCHOOLS

Player of the Year
Scott Kazmir, lhp, Cypress Falls HS, Houston
National Champion (Baseball America/National High School Baseball Coaches Association poll)
Elkins HS, Missouri City, Texas

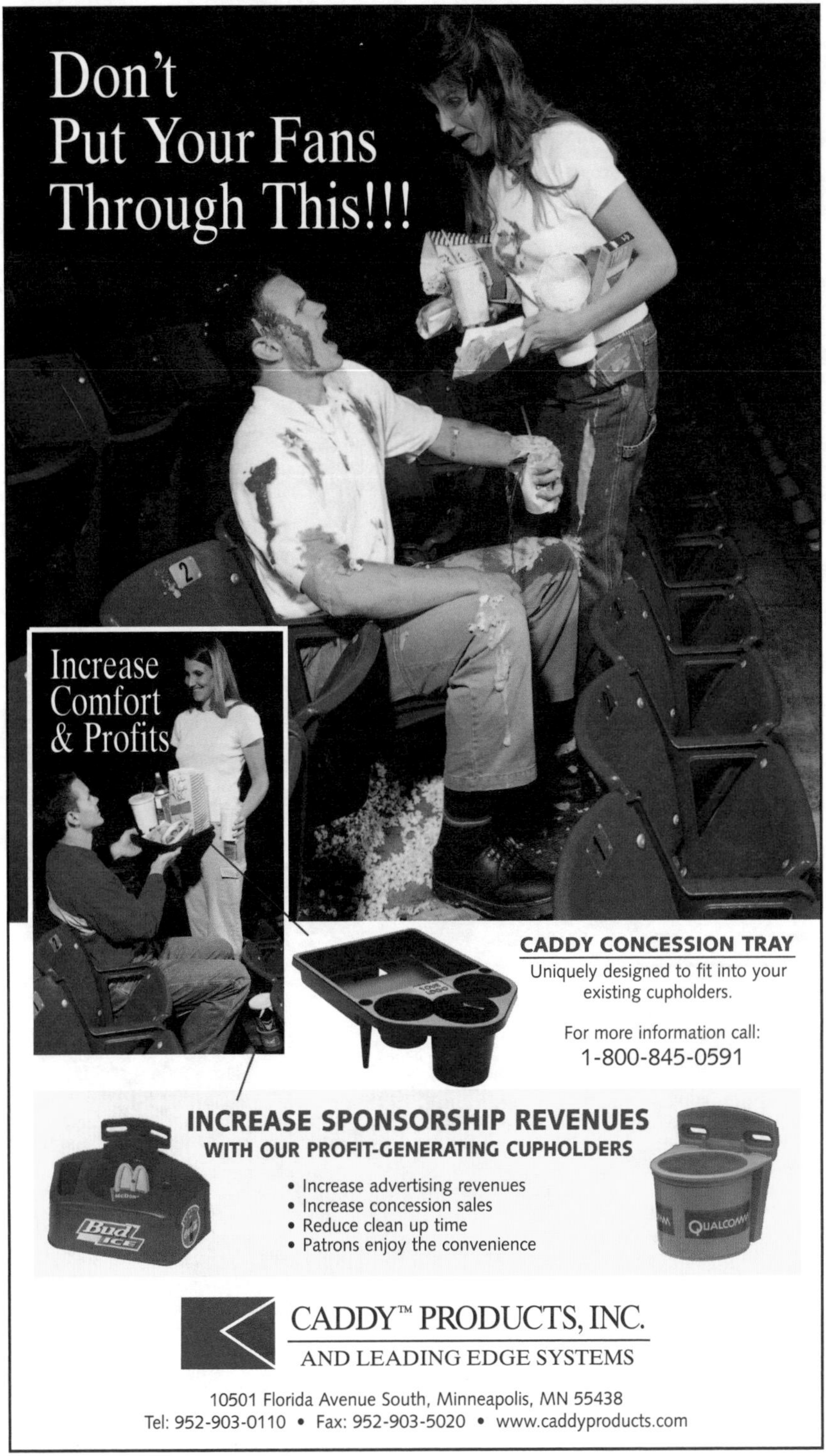
Don't Put Your Fans Through This!!!
Increase Comfort & Profits
CADDY CONCESSION TRAY
Uniquely designed to fit into your existing cupholders.
For more information call:
1-800-845-0591
INCREASE SPONSORSHIP REVENUES
WITH OUR PROFIT-GENERATING CUPHOLDERS
• Increase advertising revenues
• Increase concession sales
• Reduce clean up time
• Patrons enjoy the convenience
Bud ICE
QUALCOMM
CADDY™ PRODUCTS, INC.
AND LEADING EDGE SYSTEMS
10501 Florida Avenue South, Minneapolis, MN 55438
Tel: 952-903-0110 • Fax: 952-903-5020 • www.caddyproducts.com

TRAVEL INFO
TOLL-FREE NUMBERS & WEBSITES

AIRLINES

Aeromexico	aeromexico.com	800-237-6639
Air Canada	aircanada.com	800-361-2159
Airtran Airways	airtran.com	800-247-8726
Alaska Airlines	alaskaair.com	800-426-0333
Aloha Airlines	alohaairlines.com	800-227-4900
America West	americawest.com	800-235-9292
American Airlines	aa.com	800-433-7300
Continental Airlines	continental.com	800-525-0280
Delta Air Lines	delta.com	800-221-1212
Japan Air Lines	jal.co.jp/e/	800-525-3663
Korean Air	koreanair.com	800-438-5000
Northwest Airlines	nwa.com	800-225-2525
Olympic Airways	olympic-airways.gr	800-223-1226
Qantas Airways	qantas.com	800-227-4500
Southwest Airlines	southwest.com	800-435-9792
United Airlines	ual.com	800-864-8331
U.S. Airways	usairways.com	800-428-4322

CAR RENTALS

Alamo	goalamo.com	800-732-3232
Avis	avis.com	800-331-1212
Budget	budget.com	800-527-0700
Dollar	dollar.com	800-800-4000
Enterprise	enterprise.com	800-325-8007
Hertz	hertz.com	800-654-3131
National	nationalcar.com	800-227-7368
Thrifty	thrifty.com	800-367-2277

HOTELS/MOTELS

Best Western	bestwestern.com	800-528-1234
Choice Hotels	choicehotels.com	800-424-6423
Clarion	choicehotels.com	800-221-2222
Comfort Inn	choicehotels.com	800-221-2222
Courtyard by Marriott	marriott.com	800-321-2211
Days Inn	daysinn.com	800-325-2525
Doubletree Hotels	doubletree.com	800-424-2900
Econo Lodge	choicehotels.com	800-424-4777
Embassy Suites	embassy-suites.com	800-362-2779
Fairfield (Marriott)	fairfieldinn.com	800-228-2800
Hampton Inn	hampton-inn.com	800-426-7866
Hilton Hotels	hilton.com	800-445-8667
Holiday Inn/ Holiday Inn Express	sixcontinentshotels.com	800-465-4329
Howard Johnson	hojo.com	800-654-2000
Hyatt Hotels	hyatt.com	800-228-9000
La Quinta	laquinta.com	800-531-5900
Marriott Hotels	marriott.com	800-228-9290
Omni Hotels	omnihotels.com	800-843-6664
Quality Inn	choicehotels.com	800-221-2222
Radisson Hotels	radisson.com	800-333-3333
Ramada Inns	ramada.com	800-228-2828
Red Lion	redlion.com	800-547-8010
Red Roof Inns	redroof.com	800-843-7663
Renaissance Hotels	renaissancehotels.com	800-468-3571
Residence Inn	marriott.com	800-331-3131
Rodeway Inn	choicehotels.com	800-228-2000
Sheraton Hotels	sheraton.com	800-325-3535
Sleep Inn	choicehotels.com	800-221-2222
Super 8 Motels	super8.com	800-800-8000
TraveLodge	travelodge.com	800-578-7878
Westin Hotels	starwood.com/westin	800-228-3000
Wyndham Hotels	wyndham.com	800-996-3426

RAIL

Amtrak	amtrak.com	800-872-7245

WHAT'S NEW IN 2003

MAJOR LEAGUES

■ BALLPARKS

Cincinnati: Great American Ball Park.

■ SPRING TRAINING

Rangers and Royals move from Florida to shared complex in Surprise, Ariz.

MINOR LEAGUES

Triple-A

Calgary (Pacific Coast) moves to Albuquerque (Albuquerque Isotopes).

■ AFFILIATION CHANGES

Expos move from Ottawa (IL) to Edmonton (PCL).
Orioles move from Rochester (IL) to Ottawa (IL).
Twins move from Edmonton (PCL) to Rochester (IL).

Double-A

Shreveport (Texas) moves to Frisco (Frisco RoughRiders).

■ BALLPARKS

Frisco (Texas): Dr Pepper/Seven Up Ballpark
Jacksonville (Southern): The Baseball Grounds of Jacksonville.

■ AFFILIATION CHANGES

Blue Jays move from Tennessee (SL) to New Haven (EL).
Cardinals move from New Haven (EL) to Tennessee (SL).
Giants move from Shreveport (TL) to Norwich (EL).
Marlins move from Portland (EL) to Carolina (SL).
Rangers move from Tulsa (TL) to Frisco (TL).
Red Sox move from Trenton (EL) to Portland (EL).
Rockies move from Carolina (SL) to Tulsa (TL).
Yankees move from Norwich (EL) to Trenton (EL).

Class A

Charlotte (Florida State) moves to Palm Beach (Palm Beach Cardinals).
Columbus (South Atlantic) moves to Eastlake (Lake County Captains).
Macon (South Atlantic) moves to Rome (Rome Braves).

■ NAME CHANGES

Michigan Battle Cats (Midwest) become Battle Creek Yankees.
San Bernardino Stampede (California) become Inland Empire 66ers.

■ BALLPARKS

Lake County (South Atlantic): Eastlake Ballpark.
Rome (South Atlantic): Floyd County Stadium.

■ AFFILIATION CHANGES

Astros move from Michigan (MWL) to Salem (CL).
Athletics move from Visalia (CAL) to Kane County (MWL).
Cardinals move from Potomac (CL) to Palm Beach (FSL).
Expos move from Clinton (MWL) to Savannah (SAL).
Marlins move from Kane County (MWL) to Greensboro (SAL).
Rangers move from Savannah (SAL) to Clinton (MWL).
Rangers move from Charlotte (FSL) to Stockton (CAL).
Reds move from Stockton (CAL) to Potomac (CL).
Rockies move from Salem (CL) to Visalia (CAL).
Yankees move from Greensboro (SAL) to Battle Creek (MWL).

Short-Season

Medicine Hat (Pioneer) moves to Helena (Helena Brewers).
Rangers and Royals leave Gulf Coast League.
Royals add two teams in Arizona League.

■ BALLPARK

Missoula (Pioneer): Missoula Civic Stadium.

■ NICKNAME CHANGES

Great Falls (Pioneer) from Dodgers to White Sox.
Pulaski (Appy) from Rangers to Blue Jays.

■ AFFILIATION CHANGES

Blue Jays move from Medicine Hat (PL) to Pulaski (Appy).
Brewers move from Ogden (PL) to Helena (PL).
Dodgers move from Great Falls (PL) to Ogden (PL).
Rangers move from Pulaski (Appy) to Spokane (NWL).
Royals move from Spokane (NWL) to Arizona League.

INDEPENDENT LEAGUES

Adirondack (Northeast) moves to Bangor.
Albany-Colonie (Northeast) replaced by North Shore.
Arizona-Mexico League will begin play with four teams in 2003.
Canton (Frontier) moves to Columbia (Mid-Missouri).
Central League adds Shreveport and Coastal Bend.
Dubois County (Frontier) moves to Kenosha.
Duluth-Superior (Northern) moves to Kansas City.
Johnstown (Frontier) moves to Florence.
Northern League Central and Northern League East did not renew their affiliation agreement. The Northern League East becomes the Northeast League.
Southeastern League adds Houma and Macon.
Western League will not play in 2003.

FOREIGN/WINTER LEAGUES

Canadian League will begin play with eight teams in 2003.
International Baseball League-Australia ceases operations.
Probeis (Panama) ceases operations.
Taiwan Major League ceases operations; two teams absorbed into Chinese Professional Baseball League

COLLEGE

Super-regional round of NCAA Division I tournament staggered, with half played June 6-8 and half played June 7-9. All games to be televised by ESPN.
College World Series format moves to best-of-three championship series between bracket winners, June 21-23. All games to be televised by ESPN.

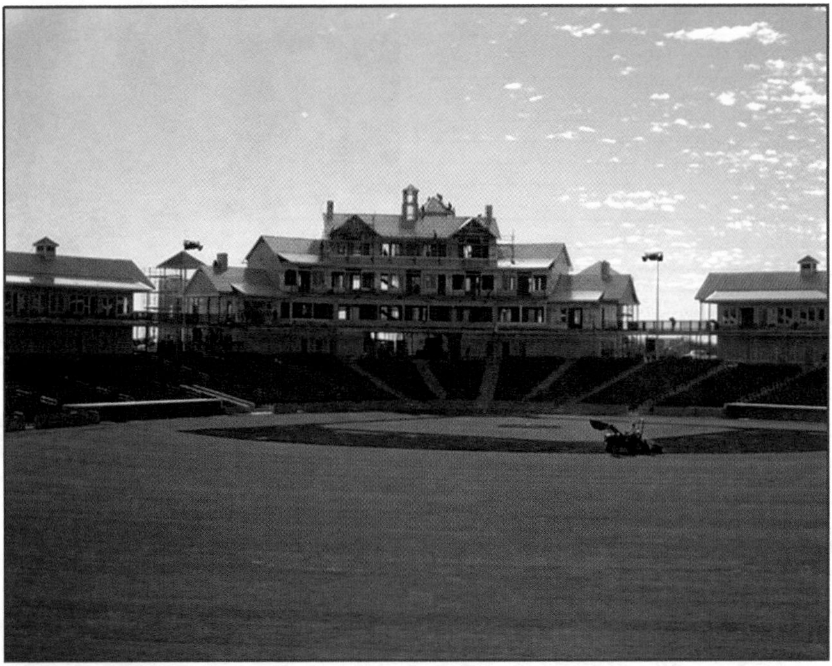

Texas League addition
Dr Pepper/Seven Up Ballpark, new home of the Frisco RoughRiders

2003 DRAFT ORDER

The order of selection for the 2003 first-year player draft (Rule 4), scheduled for June 3-4, includes at least five compensation picks between the first and second rounds for Type A free agents lost after the 2002 season.

It is possible that one additional pick will be authorized, depending on whether the Orioles sign their first-round pick prior to the closed period, which begins May 28. The Orioles retained the rights to lefthander Adam Loewen, the fourth overall pick in the 2002 draft, who did not sign and elected to attend Chipola (Fla.) Junior College. Loewen is eligible to sign with the Orioles once his season is complete. If the Orioles do not sign Loewen, they would be entitled to compensation in the form of a draft pick after the first five compensation selections have been made. The Orioles would gain the 36th overall selection.

Teams are awarded compensation in the form of draft picks based on the type of free agent involved. A team losing a Type A free agent gets the first-round pick of the team that signs the player, as well as a supplemental pick. A team losing a Type B free agent receives only the signing team's top pick. In both cases, a team selecting in the top half of the draft rotation cannot lose its first-round pick. The loss of a Type C free agent provides a team a pick between the second and third rounds.

Following is the order of selection for the first round and supplemental rounds, along with adjustments in the second, third, fourth and fifth rounds.

FIRST ROUND

	Club	Pick From	For (Type)
1.	Devil Rays		
2.	Brewers		
3.	Tigers		
4.	Padres		
5.	Royals		
6.	Cubs		
7.	Orioles		
8.	Pirates		
9.	Rangers		
10.	Rockies		
11.	Indians		
12.	Mets		
13.	Blue Jays		
14.	Reds		
15.	White Sox		
16.	Marlins		
17.	Red Sox		
18.	Indians	Phillies	Jim Thome (A)
19.	Diamondbacks	Mariners	Greg Colbrunn (B)
20.	Expos		
21.	Twins		
22.	Giants	Astros	Jeff Kent (A)
23.	Angels		
24.	Dodgers		
25.	Athletics		
26.	Athletics	Giants	Ray Durham (A)
27.	Yankees		
28.	Cardinals		
29.	Diamondbacks		
30.	Royals	Braves	Paul Byrd (B)

SUPPLEMENTAL FIRST ROUND

	Club	
31.	Indians	Jim Thome
32.	Athletics	Ray Durham
33.	Giants	Jeff Kent
34.	Braves	Tom Glavine
35.	Braves	Mike Remlinger
36.	*Orioles	Adam Loewen

No. 1 pick from the 2002 draft
Pittsburgh's Bryan Bullington

SECOND ROUND

	Club	Pick From	For (Type)
42.	Braves	Cubs	Mike Remlinger (A)
48.	Braves	Mets	Tom Glavine (A)
54.	Giants	Phillies	David Bell (B)

* Provisional selection

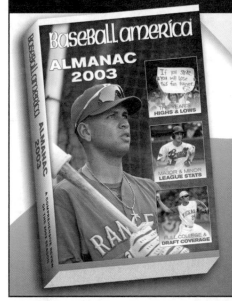

BASEBALL INFORMATION

BASEBALL TERMINOLOGY

■ Roster Limits

Major league rosters may include 40 players until Opening Day, when the number must be reduced to 25. The number returns to 40 on Sept. 1. The minimum number of active players maintained by each club throughout the season is 24.

■ Trading Regulations

The trading deadline is July 31. Trades may be made with any other major league club in the period from the end of the season through July 31 (midnight) without waivers.

■ Disabled Lists

There are two disabled lists, 15-day and 60-day. Players may be disabled retroactively, up to a maximum of 10 days, beginning with the day after the last day they played. A player on the 15-day DL may be shifted to the 60-day DL at any time. Players may be assigned to a minor league club for injury rehabilitation for a maximum of 20 days (30 days for pitchers).

15-day. There is no limit on the number of players per club.

60-day. There is no limit on the number of players per club, but it may be used only when a club is at the maximum of 40 players. Players carried on this list do not count against a club's control limit of 40 players. If a player is transferred to this list after Aug. 1, he must remain through the end of the season and postseason.

■ Options

When a player is on a major league club's 40-man roster and in the minor leagues, he is on "optional assignment." Players have three options and may be sent up and down as many times as the club chooses within those seasons but will only be charged with one option per season. When a player is "out of options," it means he's been on a 40-man roster during at least three different seasons and in his fourth pro season or later, he will have to clear irrevocable waivers in order to be sent down.

■ Waivers

If a player placed on major league waivers is not claimed by another team within two business days after waivers have been requested, then the player has "cleared waivers," and the team has secured waivers for the remainder of the waiver period. The team then can do one of two things:

1. Send him to the minors.
2. Trade him to another team, even if the trading deadline has passed, or do nothing at all.

Note: Any trades involving a 40-man roster player from July 31 to the end of the season may only involve players who have cleared major league waivers. If a player does not clear waivers—he is claimed by another team or teams—the club requesting waivers may withdraw the waiver request. If the club does not withdraw the waiver request, the player's contract is assigned as follows:

a. If only one claim is entered, the player's contract is assigned to the claiming club.

b. If more than one club in the same league makes claims, the club currently lower in the standings gets the player.

c. If clubs in both leagues claim the player, preference shall always go to the club in the same league as the club requesting waivers.

■ Designated for Assignment

This rule allows a club to open a roster spot for up to 10 days while waiting for a player to clear waivers.

Recalled vs. Contract Purchased

If a player is on the 40-man roster, he is "recalled." If not, then his contract is purchased from the minor league team. A player must be added to the 40-man roster when his contract is purchased.

■ Free agency

Six years of major league service are required to be eligible for free agency. A player has 15 days from the first day after the World Series to file for free agency.

By Dec. 7, a player's former club must offer to arbitrate or it becomes ineligible to sign the player. By Dec. 19, the player must accept the club's offer or on Jan. 9 the former club becomes ineligible to sign the player.

Six-year free agent (minor leagues). A player is eligible for free agency if he has played all or part of seven seasons in the major or minor leagues and is not placed on a major league team's 40-man roster as of Oct. 15.

■ Salary Arbitration

Three years of major league service are required for eligibility. A player with at least two years but less than three years of major league service will also be eligible if he ranks in the top 17 percent in total service in the class of players who have at least two but less than three years of major league service, however accumulated, but with at least 86 days of service accumulated during the immediately preceding season.

■ Rule 5 Draft

A player not on a major league 40-man roster as of Nov. 20 is eligible for the Rule 5 draft if:

1. The player was 18 or younger when he first signed a pro contract and this is the fourth Rule 5 draft since he signed.
2. The player was 19 or older when he first signed a pro contract and this is the third Rule 5 draft since he signed.

ITEMS OF INTEREST

■ Consecutive Game Hitting Streak

A consecutive game hitting streak shall not be terminated if all the player's plate appearances (one or more) result in a base on balls, hit-by-pitch, defensive interference or a sacrifice bunt. The streak shall terminate if the player has a sacrifice fly and no hit.

■ Consecutive Games Played Streak

A consecutive games played streak shall be extended if the player plays one-half inning on defense, or if he completes a time at bat by reaching base or being put out.

■ Major League Service

A full year of service in the major leagues constitutes 172 days.

■ Rookie Qualifications

A player shall be considered a rookie if:

1. He does not have more than 130 at-bats or 50 innings pitched in the major leagues during a previous season or seasons and,
2. He has not accumulated more than 45 days on a major league roster during the 25-player limit, excluding time on the disabled list.

■ Save Rule

A pitcher shall be credited with a save when he meets the following three conditions:

1. He is the finishing pitcher in a game won by his club, and
2. He is not the winning pitcher, and
3. He qualifies under one of the following conditions:
   a. he enters the game with a lead of no more than three runs and pitches for at least one inning, or
   b. he enters the game with the potential tying run either on base, at bat or on deck, or
   c. he pitches effectively for at least three innings.

Blown save. When a relief pitcher enters a game in a save situation and departs with the save situation no longer in effect because he has given up the lead, he is charged with a blown save.

■ Qualifying Marks

Batting Championship. Major leagues—To qualify, a player must have a minimum of 502 plate appearances (3.1 plate appearances for each of the scheduled 162 games). Minor leagues—To qualify, a player must have accumulated 2.7 plate appearances for each scheduled game.

Earned Run Average. Major leagues—To qualify, a pitcher must have at least 162 innings pitched and have the lowest ERA. Minor leagues—To qualify, a pitcher must have pitched a number of innings at least .8 times the number of scheduled games.

Fielding Average. To qualify as a leader at the positions of first base, second base, third base, shortstop and outfield, a player must have appeared in a minimum of two-thirds of his team's games. For catcher, a player must have appeared in a minimum of one half of his team's games. For pitcher, the player with the highest average and the greatest number of total chances qualifies as the leader.

HOW TO FIGURE

■ Batting Average

Divide the number of hits by the number of at-bats (H/AB).

■ Earned Run Average

Multiply the number of earned runs by nine; take that number and divide it by the number of innings pitched (ER x 9/IP).

■ Slugging Percentage

Divide the total bases of all safe hits by the total of times at bat. At-bats do not include walks, sacrifices, hit-by-pitches or times awarded first base because of interference or obstruction (TB/AB).

■ On-Base Percentage

Add the total number of hits, walks and number of times hit by pitches and divide by the total of at-bats, walks, hit-by-pitches and sacrifice flies (H+BB+HBP/AB+BB+HBP+SF).

■ Fielding Percentage

Divide the total number of putouts and assists by total chances—putouts, assists and errors (PO+A/PO+A+E).

■ Winning Percentage

Divide the number of games won by the total games won and lost (W/W+L).

■ Magic Number

Determine the number of games yet to be played, add one, and then subtract the number of games ahead in the loss column of the standings from the closest opponent.

DRIVING DIRECTIONS

AMERICAN LEAGUE STADIUMS

EDISON INTERNATIONAL FIELD, ANAHEIM

Highway 57 (Orange Freeway) to Orangewood exit, west on Orangewood, stadium on west side of Orange Freeway.

CAMDEN YARDS, BALTIMORE

From the north and east on I-95, take I-395 (exit 53), downtown to Russell Street; from the south or west on I-95, take exit 52 to Russell Street North.

FENWAY PARK, BOSTON

Massachusetts Turnpike (I-90) to Prudential exit (stay left), right at first set of lights, right on Dalton Street, left on Boylston Street, right on Ipswich Street.

U.S. CELLULAR FIELD, CHICAGO

Dan Ryan Expressway (I-90/94) to 35th Street exit.

JACOBS FIELD, CLEVELAND

From south, I-77 North to East Ninth Street exit, to Ontario Street; From east, I-90/Route 2 west to downtown, remain on Route 2 to East Ninth Street, left to stadium.

COMERICA PARK, DETROIT

I-75 to Grand River exit, follow service drive east to stadium, located off Woodward Avenue.

KAUFFMAN STADIUM, KANSAS CITY

From north or south, take I-435 to stadium exits. From east or west, take I-70 to stadium exits.

METRODOME, MINNESOTA

I-35W south to Washington Avenue exit or I-35W north to Third Street exit. I-94 East to I-35W north to Third Street exit or I-94 West to Fifth Street exit.

YANKEE STADIUM, NEW YORK

From I-95 North, George Washington Bridge to Cross Bronx Expressway to exit 1C; Major Deegan South (I-87) to exit G (161st Street); I-87 North to 149th or 155th Streets; I-87 South to 161st Street.

NETWORK ASSOCIATES COLISEUM, OAKLAND

From I-880, take either the 66th Avenue or Hegenberger Road exit.

SAFECO FIELD, SEATTLE

I-5 or I-90 to Fourth Avenue South exit.

TROPICANA FIELD, TAMPA BAY

I-275 South to St. Petersburg, exit 11, left onto Fifth Avenue, right onto 16th Street.

THE BALLPARK IN ARLINGTON, TEXAS

From I-30, take Ballpark Way exit, south on Ballpark Way; From Route 360, take Randol Mill exit, west on Randol Mill.

SKYDOME, TORONTO

From west, take QEW/Gardiner Expressway eastbound and exit at Spadina Avenue, north on Spadina one block, right on Bremner Boulevard. From east, take Gardiner Expressway westbound and exit at Spadina Avenue, north on Spadina one block, right on Bremner Boulevard.

NATIONAL LEAGUE STADIUMS

BANK ONE BALLPARK, ARIZONA

I-10 to Seventh Street exit, turn south; I-17 to Seventh Street, turn north.

TURNER FIELD, ATLANTA

I-75/85 northbound/southbound, take exit 246 (Fulton Street); I-20 westbound, take exit 58A (Capitol Avenue); I-20 eastbound, take exit 56B (Windsor Street), right on Windsor Street, left on Fulton Street.

WRIGLEY FIELD, CHICAGO

I-90/94 to Addison Street exit, follow Addison five miles to ballpark. One mile west of Lakeshore Drive, exit at Belmont going northbound, exit at Irving Park going southbound.

GREAT AMERICAN BALL PARK, CINCINNATI

I-75 southbound, take Second Street exit. Ballpark is located off Second Street at Main Street. I-71 southbound, take Third Street exit, right on Broadway. I-75/I-71 northbound, take Second Street exit—far right lane on Brent Spence Bridge. Ballpark is located off Second Street at Main Street.

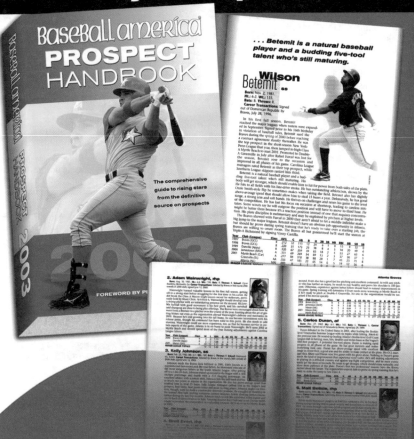

COORS FIELD, COLORADO

I-70 to I-25 South to exit 213 (Park Avenue) or 212C (20th Street); I-25 to 20th Street, east to park.

PRO PLAYER STADIUM, FLORIDA

From south, Florida Turnpike extension to stadium exit; From north, I-95 to I-595 West to Florida Turnpike to stadium exit; From west, I-75 to I-595 to Florida Turnpike to stadium exit; From east, Highway 826 West to NW 27th Avenue, north to Dan Marino Blvd., right to stadium.

MINUTE MAID FIELD, HOUSTON

From I-10 East, take Smith Street (exit 769A), left at Texas Ave., 0.6 miles to park at corner of Texas Ave. and Crawford St.; from I-10 West, take San Jacinto St. (exit 769B), right on Fannin St., left on Texas Ave., 0.3 miles to park; From Hwy. 59 North: take Gray Ave./Pierce Ave. exit, 0.3 miles on Gray St. to Crawford St., one mile to park.

DODGER STADIUM, LOS ANGELES

I-5 to Stadium Way exit, left on Stadium Way, right on Academy Road, left to Stadium Way to Elysian Park Avenue, left to stadium; I-110 to Dodger Stadium exit, left on Stadium Way, right on Elysian Park Avenue; US 101 to Alvarado exit, right on Sunset, left on Elysian Park Avenue.

MILLER PARK, MILWAUKEE

From airport/south, I-94 West to Madison exit, to stadium.

OLYMPIC STADIUM, MONTREAL

From New England, take I-87 North from Vermont to Quebec Highway 15 to the Jacques Cartier Bridge, exit left, right on Sherbrooke. From upstate New York, take I-81 North to Trans Canada Highway 401, east to Quebec Highway 20, north to Highway 40 to Boulevard Pie IX exit south to stadium. Access by subway from downtown Montreal to Pie IX Metro station.

SHEA STADIUM, NEW YORK

From Bronx and Westchester, take Cross Bronx Expressway to Bronx-Whitestone Bridge, then take bridge to Whitestone Expressway to Northern Boulevard/Shea Stadium exit. From Brooklyn, take Eastbound BQE to Eastbound Grand Central Parkway. From Long Island, take either Northern State Parkway or LIE to Westbound Grand Central Parkway. From northern New Jersey, take George Washington Bridge to Cross Bronx Expressway. From Southern New Jersey, take any of bridge crossings to Verazzano Bridge, and then take either Belt Parkway or BQE to Grand Central Parkway.

VETERANS STADIUM, PHILADELPHIA

I-95 or I-76 to Broad Street exit.

PNC PARK, PITTSBURGH

From south, I-279 through Fort Pitt Tunnel, make left off bridge to Fort Duquesne Bridge, cross Fort Duquesne Bridge, follow signs to PNC Park. From north, I-279 to PNC Park (exit 12, left lane), follow directions to parking.

BUSCH STADIUM, ST. LOUIS

From Illinois, take I-55 South, I-64 West, I-70 West or US 40 West across the Mississippi River (Poplar Street Bridge) to Busch Stadium exit. In Missouri, take I-55 North, I-64 East, I-70 East, I-44 East or US 40 East to downtown St. Louis and Busch Stadium exit.

QUALCOMM STADIUM, SAN DIEGO

From downtown, Route 163 North to Friars Road, east to stadium. From north, I-15 South to Friars Road, west to stadium, or I-805 South to Route 163 South to Friars Road, west to stadium. From east, I-8 West to I-15 North to Friars Road, west to stadium. From west, I-8 East to Route 163 North to Friars Road, east to stadium.

PACIFIC BELL PARK, SAN FRANCISCO

From Peninsula/South Bay, I-280 north (or U.S. 101 north to I-280 north) to Mariposa Street exit, right on Mariposa, left on Third Street. From East Bay (Bay Bridge), I-80/Bay Bridge to Fifth Street exit, right on Fifth Street, right on Folsom Street, right on Fourth Street, continue on Fourth Street to parking lots (across bridge). From North Bay (Golden Gate Bridge), U.S. 101 south/Golden Gate Bridge to Downtown/Lombard Street exit, right on Van Ness Ave., left on Golden Gate Ave., right on Hyde Street and across Market Street to Eighth Street, left on Bryant Street, right on Fourth Street.

MAJOR LEAGUES

MAJOR LEAGUE BASEBALL

Mailing Address: 245 Park Ave., New York, NY 10167. **Telephone:** (212) 931-7800. **Website:** www.mlb.com.

Commissioner: Allan H. "Bud" Selig.

Senior Executive Assistant to Commissioner: Lori Keck. **Administrative Assistant to Commissioner:** Sandy Ronback. **Office Assistant:** Lisa Steinman. **Supervisor, Security:** Earnell Lucas. **Supervisor, Security/Investigations:** Tom Christopher.

President/Chief Operating Officer: Bob DuPuy.

Executive Vice President, Baseball Operations: Sandy Alderson. **Executive VP, Administration:** John McHale. **Executive VP, Labor Relations/Human Resources:** Robert Manfred. **Executive VP, Business:** Tim Brosnan.

Bud Selig

Baseball Operations

Senior VP, Baseball Operations: Jimmie Lee Solomon. **VP, Baseball Operations/Administration:** Ed Burns. **Senior Director, Major League Operations:** Roy Krasik. **Manager, Baseball Operations:** Jeff Pfeifer.

Manager, Waivers/Major League Records: Brian Small. **Senior Manager, Minor League Operations:** Sylvia Lind.

VP, International Baseball Operations: Lou Melendez. **Manager, Dominican Operations:** Rafael Perez.

Bob DuPuy

VP, On-Field Operations: Bob Watson.

VP, Umpiring: Ralph Nelson. **Director, Umpire Administration:** Tom Lepperd. **Director, Umpire Medical Services:** Mark Letendre. **Special Assistant, Umpiring:** Marty Springstead. **Umpiring Supervisors:** Rich Garcia, Jim McKean, Steve Palermo, Frank Pulli, Rich Rieker, Marty Springstead.

Director, Arizona Fall League: Steve Cobb.

Director, Major League Scouting Bureau: Frank Marcos. **Assistant Director, Scouting Bureau:** Rick Oliver.

Security, Facilities

Senior Vice President, Security/Facilities: Kevin Hallinan. **Director, Security Investigations:** Marty Maquire. **Senior Manager, Facilities Operations:** Linda Pantell. **Manager, Security Operations:** Paul Padilla. **Manager, Investigations:** Leroy Hendricks.

General Administration

Senior Vice President, Chief Financial Officer: Jonathan Mariner. **VP, Accounting/Treasurer:** Bob Clark. **Senior Director:** Kathleen Lyons. **Senior Manager, Royalty/Administration:** Geary Sellers.

Senior VP/General Counsel: Tom Ostertag. **Senior Manager, Records:** Charlyne Sanders.

Senior VP/General Counsel: Ethan Orlinsky. **Deputy General Counsel:** Domna Candido, Jennifer Cohane. **Senior Counsel, Productions/Advertising:** Elizabeth Scott. **Director, Quality Control:** Peggy O'Neill-Janosik.

VP, Information Technologies: Julio Carbonell. **Manager, Operations/Technical Support:** Peter Surhoff. **Manager, Software Development:** John Moran.

Senior Director, Baseball Assistance Team: Jim Martin.

VP, Educational Programming: Sharon Robinson.

VP/General Counsel, Labor Relations: Frank Coonelly. **Deputy General Counsel, Labor:** Jennifer Gefsky. **Manager, Salary/Contract Administration:** John Ricco.

VP, Strategic Planning for Recruitment/Diversity: Wendy Lewis. **Senior Manager, Diverse Business Partners:** Hanh Pham. **Director, Recruitment:** Denise Males. **Director, Office Services:** Donna Hoder.

VP, Human Resources: Ray Scott. **Manager, Benefits/HRIS:** Diane Cuddy.

Sandy Alderson

Public Relations

Telephone: (212) 931-7878. **FAX:** (212) 949-5654.

Senior Vice President, Public Relations: Rich Levin. **Director, PR Operations:** Patrick Courtney.

Senior Manager, Marketing: Carole Coleman. **Manager, Business Information Systems:** Robert Doelger. **Specialist, Business Information Systems:** John Blundell. **Manager, Properties/International:** Kathleen Fineout. **Manager, Media Relations:** Matt Gould. **PR Specialists:** Matt Burton, Carmen Tiso.

Baseball Historian: Jerome Holtzman.

Coordinators, PR: Dominick Balsamo, Paige Novack. **Senior Administrative Assistant:** Heather Flock. **Administrative Assistant:** Adriana Arcia.

Licensing

Senior Vice President, Licensing: Howard Smith.

Senior Director, Adult Wearables/Authentics: Steve Armus. **Senior Director, Home/Hard Goods/Toys:** Karen Donohue. **Senior Director, New Technology/New Business:** Carol Ann Dunn. **VP, Collectibles/Cooperstown:** Colin

Hagen. **Director, Licensing/Minor Leagues:** Eliot Runyon.

Senior Manager, Apparel Retail: Adam Blinderman. **Director, Authentics:** Dennis Nolan.

VP, Publishing/Photographs: Don Hintze. **Editor, Publishing/Photographs:** Mike McCormick. **Art Director, Publications:** Faith Matorin. **Manager, MLB Photographs:** Rich Pilling.

Senior VP, Special Events: Marla Miller. **Directors, Special Events:** Morgan Littlefield, Brian O'Gara. **Managers, Special Events:** Eileen Buser, Christine Buckley, Joe Fitzgerald, Carolyn Taylor.

Sales, Marketing

VP, Corporate Sales: Justin Johnson.

Senior VP, Broadcasting: Chris Tully. **VP, Broadcast Administration/Operations:** Bernadette McDonald. **Director, Distribution Development:** Susanne Hilgefort.

VP, Community Affairs: Tom Brasuell.

VP, Advertising/Marketing: Jacqueline Parkes. **Managers, Advertising:** Karen Clark, Robin Jaffe. **Manager, Promotions:** Colleen LeMay.

Creative Director, Design Services: Anne Occi.

Club Relations

Vice President, Club Relations/Scheduling: Katy Feeney. **Coordinator, Club Relations/Scheduling:** Paul Kuo. **Senior Administrative Assistant, Club Relations/Scheduling:** Raxel Concepcion.

VP, Club Relations: Phyllis Merhige. **Coordinator, Club Relations:** Michael Teevan. **Senior Administrative Assistant, Club Relations:** Angelica Cintron.

Major League Baseball Productions

Office Address: 75 Ninth Ave., New York, NY 10011. **Telephone:** (212) 931-7777. **FAX:** (212) 931-7788.

Vice President/Executive Producer: Dave Gavant.

Senior Coordinating Producer: David Check. **Senior Manager Producer, Field Productions:** Steve Fortunato. **Managing Producer:** Adam Schlackman. **Senior Producer:** Jeff Spaulding. **Senior Writer:** Jeff Scott.

Director, Productions/Operations: Shannon Valine. **Manager, Stock Footage:** Dina Panto. **Manager, Videotape Library:** Frank Caputo.

International Business Operations

Mailing Address: 245 Park Ave., 30th Floor, New York, NY 10167. **Telephone:** (212) 931-7500. **FAX:** (212) 949-5795.

Senior Vice President, International Operations: Paul Archey. **VP, International Licensing/Sponsorship:** Shawn Lawson-Cummings.

Director, Broadcast Sales: Italo Zanzi. **Director, Latin American Marketing:** Sara Loarte. **Senior Director, Market Development/Events:** Jim Small. **Director, Australian Operations:** Thomas Nicholson. **Director, European Operations:** Clive Russell. **Senior Manager, Market Development/Events:** James Pearce. **Executive Producer, MLB International:** Russell Gabay.

MLB Advanced Media (MLB.com)

Office Address: 75 Ninth Ave., 5th Floor, New York, NY 10011. **Telephone:** (212) 485-3444. **FAX:** (212) 485-3456.

Chief Executive Officer: Bob Bowman.

Senior Vice President, Chief Marketing Officer: Holly Arnowitz, **VP, Ticketing:** Laura Baumans. **VP, Multi-Media:** Jane Buford. **VP, Human Resources:** Jennifer Caputo.

Senior VP/Chief Technical Officer: Joe Choti. **VP, Chief Financial Officer:** Jeff D'Onofrio. **Senior VP, Corporate Communications:** Jim Gallagher. **Senior VP, E-Commerce:** Noah Garden. **Senior VP/Editor-In-Chief, mlb.com:** Dinn Mann. **VP, Design:** Deck Rees.

VP/General Counsel: Michael Mellis, **VP, Sponsorship:** Mark Sage.

Umpires

Ted Barrett (Gilbert, AZ), Wally Bell (Boardman, OH), Joe Brinkman (Cocoa, FL), C.B. Bucknor (Brooklyn, NY), Mark Carlson (Channahon, IL), Gary Cederstrom (Minot, ND), Eric Cooper (Johnston, IA), Derryl Cousins (Hermosa Beach, CA), Terry Craft (Bradenton, FL), Jerry Crawford (Tiera Verde, FL), Fieldin Culbreth (Inman, SC), Phil Cuzzi (Nutley, NJ), Kerwin Danley (Los Angeles, CA), Gary Darling (Phoenix, AZ), Gerry Davis (Appleton, WI), Dana DeMuth (Gilbert, AZ), Laz Diaz (Kissimmee, FL), Mike DiMuro (Chandler, AZ), Bruce Dreckman (Marcus, IA), Doug Eddings (Los Lunas, NM), Paul Emmel (Bradenton, FL), Mike Everitt (Clive, IA), Andy Fletcher (Olive Branch, MS), Marty Foster (Beloit, WI), Bruce Froemming (Mequon, WI), Greg Gibson (Catlettsburg, KY), Brian Gorman (Camarillo, CA), Angel Hernandez (Wellington, FL), John Hirschbeck (Youngstown, OH), Mark Hirschbeck (Shelton, CT), Bill Hohn (Blue Bell, PA), Sam Holbrook (Lexington, KY), Marvin Hudson (Washington, GA), Jim Joyce (Beaverton, OR), Jeff Kellogg (Mattawan, MI), Ron Kulpa (Maryland Heights, MO), Jerry Layne (Winter Haven, FL), Alfonso Marquez (Gilbert, AZ), Randy Marsh (Edgewood, KY), Tim McClelland (West Des Moines, IA), Jerry Meals (Salem, OH), Chuck Meriwether (Nashville, TN), Bill Miller (Aptos, CA), Ed Montague (San Mateo, CA), Paul Nauert (Lawrenceville, GA), Jeff Nelson (Windermere, FL), Brian O'Nora (Canfield, OH), Larry Poncino (Tucson, AZ), Tony Randazzo (Las Cruces, NM), Ed Rapuano (Boca Raton, FL), Rick Reed (Rochester Hills, MI), Mike Reilly (Battle Creek, MI), Charlie Reliford (Ashland, KY), Jim Reynolds (Osprey, FL), Steve Rippley (Fort Lauderdale, FL), Brian Runge (Ramona, CA), Paul Schrieber (Scottsdale, AZ), Dale Scott (Portland, OR), John Shulock (Vero Beach, FL), Tim Timmons (New Albany, OH), Tim Tschida (Turtle Lake, WI), Larry Vanover (Owensboro, KY), Mark Wegner (Plant City, FL), Tim Welke (Kalamazoo, MI), Bill Welke (Marshall, MI), Hunter Wendelstedt (Daytona Beach, FL), Joe West (Ft. Lauderdale, FL), Mike Winters (Poway, CA), Larry Young (Roscoe, IL).

EVENTS

2003 Major League All-Star Game: July 15 at U.S. Cellular Field, Chicago.

2003 World Series: Begins Oct. 18.

AMERICAN LEAGUE

Years League Active: 1901-.
2003 Opening Date: March 25. **Closing Date:** Sept. 28.
Regular Season: 162 games.
Division Structure: East—Baltimore, Boston, New York, Tampa Bay, Toronto. **Central**—Chicago, Cleveland, Detroit, Kansas City, Minnesota. **West**—Anaheim, Oakland, Seattle, Texas.
Playoff Format: Three division champions and second-place team with best record meet in best-of-5 Division Series. Winners meet in best-of-7 League Championship Series.
All-Star Game: July 15 at U.S. Cellular Field, Chicago (AL vs. National League).
Roster Limit: 25, through Aug. 31 when rosters expand to 40.
Brand of Baseball: Rawlings.
Statistician: Elias Sports Bureau, 500 Fifth Ave., New York, NY 10110.

STADIUM INFORMATION

		Dimensions				
City	Stadium	LF	CF	RF	Capacity	2002 Att.
Anaheim	Edison International	365	406	365	45,050	2,305,547
Baltimore	Camden Yards	333	410	318	48,876	2,682,439
Boston	Fenway Park	310	390	302	33,871	2,650,862
Chicago	U.S. Cellular Field	300	400	335	44,321	1,676,911
Cleveland	Jacobs Field	325	405	325	43,863	2,616,940
Detroit	Comerica Park	346	422	330	40,000	1,503,623
Kansas City	Kauffman Stadium	330	400	330	40,529	1,323,036
Minnesota	Humphrey Metrodome	343	408	327	48,678	1,924,473
New York	Yankee Stadium	318	408	314	57,545	3,465,807
Oakland	Network Assoc. Coliseum	330	400	367	43,662	2,169,811
Seattle	Safeco Field	331	405	326	45,600	3,542,938
Tampa Bay	Tropicana Field	315	407	322	45,200	1,065,742
Texas	Ballpark in Arlington	334	400	325	49,166	2,352,397
Toronto	SkyDome	328	400	328	50,516	1,637,900

NATIONAL LEAGUE

Years League Active: 1876-.
2003 Opening Date: March 31. **Closing Date:** Sept. 28.
Regular Season: 162 games.
Division Structure: East—Atlanta, Florida, Montreal, New York, Philadelphia. **Central**—Chicago, Cincinnati, Houston, Milwaukee, Pittsburgh, St. Louis. **West**—Arizona, Colorado, Los Angeles, San Diego, San Francisco.
Playoff Format: Three division champions and second-place team with best record meet in best-of-5 Division Series. Winners meet in best-of-7 League Championship Series.
All-Star Game: July 15 at U.S. Cellular Field, Chicago (NL vs. American League).
Roster Limit: 25, through Aug. 31 when rosters expand to 40.
Brand of Baseball: Rawlings.
Statistician: Elias Sports Bureau, 500 Fifth Ave., New York, NY 10110.

STADIUM INFORMATION

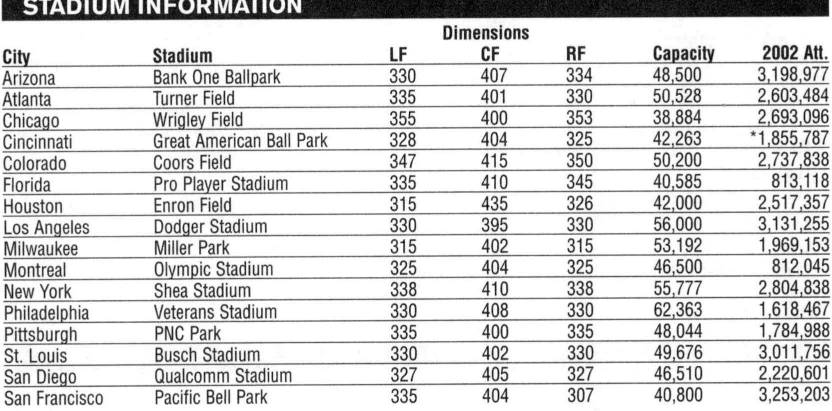

		Dimensions				
City	Stadium	LF	CF	RF	Capacity	2002 Att.
Arizona	Bank One Ballpark	330	407	334	48,500	3,198,977
Atlanta	Turner Field	335	401	330	50,528	2,603,484
Chicago	Wrigley Field	355	400	353	38,884	2,693,096
Cincinnati	Great American Ball Park	328	404	325	42,263	*1,855,787
Colorado	Coors Field	347	415	350	50,200	2,737,838
Florida	Pro Player Stadium	335	410	345	40,585	813,118
Houston	Enron Field	315	435	326	42,000	2,517,357
Los Angeles	Dodger Stadium	330	395	330	56,000	3,131,255
Milwaukee	Miller Park	315	402	315	53,192	1,969,153
Montreal	Olympic Stadium	325	404	325	46,500	812,045
New York	Shea Stadium	338	410	338	55,777	2,804,838
Philadelphia	Veterans Stadium	330	408	330	62,363	1,618,467
Pittsburgh	PNC Park	335	400	335	48,044	1,784,988
St. Louis	Busch Stadium	330	402	330	49,676	3,011,756
San Diego	Qualcomm Stadium	327	405	327	46,510	2,220,601
San Francisco	Pacific Bell Park	335	404	307	40,800	3,253,203

*Attendance for Cinergy Field in 2002

ANAHEIM ANGELS

Telephone, Address

Office Address: Edison International Field of Anaheim, 2000 Gene Autry Way, Anaheim, CA 92806. **Mailing Address:** P.O. Box 2000, Anaheim, CA 92803. **Telephone:** (714) 940-2000. **FAX:** (714) 940-2001. **Website:** www.angelsbaseball.com.

Ownership

Operated by: The Walt Disney Company.

Chairman, Chief Executive Officer: Michael Eisner. **President:** Jay Rasulo.

Executive Counsel: Bruce Carter.

Michael Eisner

BUSINESS OPERATIONS

Senior Vice President, Business Operations: Kevin Uhlich. **Administrative Assistant:** Leslie Flammini.

Finance, Administration

Vice President, Finance/Administration: Andy Roundtree. **Administrative Assistant:** Meta Maynard.

Director, Finance: Molly Taylor. **Senior Financial Analyst:** Amy Langdale. **Manager, Information Services:** Al Castro. **Senior Network Engineer:** Neil Farris. **Senior End User Computing Analyst:** Phil Alger. **Senior Customer Support Analyst:** David Yun. **Assistant Controllers:** Cris Fisher, Melody Martin. **Accountants:** Lorelei Largey, Jean Ouyang, Rosanna Sitzman.

Senior Travel Consultant: Chantelle Ball.

Director, Human Resources: Jenny Price. **Assistant, Human Resources:** Lidia Argomaniz.

Marketing, Sales

Director, Advertising Sales: Richard McClemmy. **Manager, Sponsorship Services:** Jennifer Carnahan. **Managers, Advertising Sales:** Paul LaFerla, Bill Pedigo, Sam Piccione. **Administrative Assistant:** Janine Schunk.

Director, Ticket Sales/Customer Service: Steve Shiffman. **Director, Marketing/Promotions:** Robert Alvarado. **Manager, Suites/Guest Relations:** Lynda Nelson. **Senior Marketing Representative:** Jennifer Randall. **Marketing Representative:** Joel Hobson. **Account Executives:** Dan Carnahan, Lisa Gaspar, Mike Kirby, Damon Roschke, Keith Rowe.

Senior Group Sales Account Executive: Joe Furmanski. **Group Sales Account Executives:** Scott Booth, Ryan Redmond, Angel Rodriguez. **Marketing/Database Manager:** Veronica Tarnofsky. **Telemarketing Supervisor:** Chad Franzen. **Executive Secretary, Marketing/Promotions:** Monica Campanis. **Executive Secretary, Sales:** Pat Lissy.

Manager, Entertainment: Peter Bull. **Producer, Video/Scoreboard Operations:** Robert Castillo. **Associate Producer, Video/Scoreboard Operations:** David Tsuruda.

Public Relations, Communications

Telephone: (714) 940-2014. **FAX:** (714) 940-2205.

Vice President, Communications: Tim Mead. **Administrative Assistant:** Trish Pene.

Manager, Baseball Information: Larry Babcock. **Manager, Media Services:** Nancy Mazmanian. **Manager, Publications:** Doug Ward.

Director, Publicity/Broadcasting: Jay Lucas. **Manager, Community Development:** Matt Bennett. **Manager, Publicity/Broadcasting:** Aaron Tom. **Community Relations Assistant:** Kevin Vann. **Traveling Secretary/Media Representative:** Tom Taylor.

Speakers' Bureau: Bobby Grich, Clyde Wright.

Ballpark Operations

Director, Ballpark Operations: John Drum. **Manager, Facility Services:** Mike McKay. **Assistant Operations Manager:** Sam Maida.

Manager, Security: Keith Cleary. **Manager, Field/Ground Maintenance:** Barney Lopas. **Purchasing Specialist:** Ron Sparks. **Office Specialist:** Linda Fitzgerald. **Warehouse Coordinator:** Suzanne Peters. **Receptionist:** Jeannette Radillo.

PA Announcer: David Courtney. **Official Scorer:** Ed Munson. **Organist:** Peggy Duquesnel.

Ticketing

Manager, Ticket Operations: Sheila Brazelton. **Assistant Ticket Manager:** Susan Weiss. **Supervisor, Ticketing:** Eric Challman. **Ticketing Representative:** Clancy Holligan, Kim Weaver.

Travel, Clubhouse

Clubhouse Manager: Ken Higdon. **Assistant Clubhouse Manager:** Keith Tarter. **Visiting Clubhouse Manager:** Brian Harkins.

Senior Video Coordinator: Diego Lopez. **Video Coordinator:** Ruben Montano.

General Information

Home Dugout: Third Base. **Playing Surface:** Grass.

Team Colors: Red, dark red, blue and silver.

Player Representative: Scott Schoeneweis.

Bill Stoneman

BASEBALL OPERATIONS

Vice President, General Manager: Bill Stoneman.

Assistant GM: Ken Forsch. **Special Assistants to GM:** Preston Gomez, Gary Sutherland. **Executive Secretary, Scouting/General Manager:** Laura Fazioli.

Manager, Baseball Operations: Abe Flores.

Major League Staff

Manager: Mike Scioscia.

Coaches: Bench—Joe Maddon; Pitching—Bud Black; Batting—Mickey Hatcher; First Base—Alfredo Griffin; Third Base—Ron Roenicke; Bullpen—Orlando Mercado; Bullpen Catcher—Steve Soliz.

Medical, Training

Medical Director: Dr. Lewis Yocum. **Team Physician:** Dr. Craig Milhouse.

Head Athletic Trainer: Ned Bergert. **Athletic Trainer:** Rick Smith.

Physical Therapist: Brian Scherr. **Strength/Conditioning Coach:** Brian Grapes. **Administrative Assistant:** Chris Titchenal.

Mike Scioscia

Player Development

Telephone: (714) 940-2031. **FAX:** (714) 940-2203.

Director, Player Development: Tony Reagins. **Executive Secretary, Player Development:** Maria Arellano.

Field Coordinator: Bruce Hines. **Roving Instructors:** Mike Butcher (pitching), Trent Clark (strength/conditioning), Howie Gershberg (pitching/special assignment), Geoff Hostettor (trainer coordinator), Bill Lachemann (catching/special assignment), Bobby Mitchell (outfield/baserunning/bunting), Bobby Ramos (catching), Ty Van Burkleo (hitting).

Farm System

Class	Farm Team	League	Manager	Coach	Pitching Coach
AAA	Salt Lake	Pacific Coast	Mike Brumley	Jim Eppard	Rich Bombard
AA	Arkansas	Texas	Tyrone Boykin	Wes Clements	Keith Comstock
High A	Rancho Cucamonga	California	Bobby Meacham	Todd Takayoshi	Zeke Zimmerman
Low A	Cedar Rapids	Midwest	Todd Claus	James Rowson	Erik Bennett
Rookie	Provo	Pioneer	Tom Kotchman	Kevin Ham	Kernan Ronan
Rookie	Mesa	Arizona	Brian Harper	Bobby Magallanes	Jack Uhey
Rookie	Angels	Dominican	Charlie Romero	Edgal Rodriguez	Santos Alcala

Scouting

Telephone: (714) 940-2038. **FAX:** (714) 940-2203.

Director, Scouting: Donny Rowland.

Advance Scout: John Van Ornum (Bass Lake, CA).

Major League Scouts: Jay Hankins (Greenwood, MO), Jon Neiderer (Johnstown, PA), Rich Schlenker (Walnut Creek, CA), Moose Stubing (Villa Park, CA), Dale Sutherland (La Crescenta, CA).

National Crosscheckers: Guy Mader (Tewksbury, MA), Hank Sargent (Palm Harbor, FL). **Regional Supervisors:** West—Tom Davis (Ripon, CA). Midwest—Ron Marigny (Houston, TX). East—Marc Russo (Mooresville, NC).

Area Scouts: Brian Bridges (Naperville, IL), John Burden (Fairfield, OH), Tom Burns (Harrisburg, PA), Arnold Cochrane (Ponce, PR), Tim Corcoran (La Verne, CA), Jeff Crane (Tuscaloosa, AL), Bobby DeJardin (San Clemente, CA), Kevin Ham (El Paso, TX), Tom Kotchman (Seminole, FL), Dan Lynch (Marlboro, MA), Chris McAlpin (Huntersville, NC), Chad MacDonald (Arlington, TX), Mike Powers (Houston, TX), Scott Richardson (Vacaville, CA), Jeff Scholzen (Hurricane, UT), Mike Silvestri (Davie, FL), Jack Uhey (Vancouver, WA).

Don Rowland

International Supervisor: Clay Daniel (Jacksonville, FL).

International Scouts: Amador Arias (Venezuela), Luis Cuevas (Dominican Republic), Felipe Gutierrez (Mexico), Tak Kawamoto (Japan), Alex Messier (Canada), Leo Perez (Dominican Republic), Carlos Porte (Venezuela), Dennys Suarez (Venezuela), Ramon Valenzuela (Dominican Republic), Grant Weir (Australia).

ARIZONA DIAMONDBACKS

Jerry Colangelo

Telephone, Address

Office Address: Bank One Ballpark, 401 E. Jefferson St., Phoenix, AZ 85004. **Mailing Address:** P.O. Box 2095, Phoenix, AZ 85001. **Telephone:** (602) 462-6500. **FAX:** (602) 462-6599. **Website:** www.azdiamondbacks.com.

Ownership

Operated by: AZPB Limited Partnership.

Chairman of the Board: Jerry Colangelo.

Executive Committee: Bill Andrew, Evy Chipman, Mike Chipman, George Getz, Jon Held, Dale Jensen, Ken Kendrick, Bob Lavinia, Mel Shultz.

BUSINESS OPERATIONS

President: Richard Dozer. **Assistant to President:** Michelle Libonati.

General Counsel: Tom O'Malley.

Director, Human Resources: Peter Wong.

Finance

Senior Vice President, Finance: Tom Harris. **VP, Information Systems:** Bill Bolt. **Controller:** Michelle Johnson. **Assistant Controller:** Barbara Ragsdale. **Office Manager:** Pat Perez.

Marketing, Sales

Senior Vice President, Marketing/Sales: Scott Brubaker. **VP, Corporate Sales:** Mark Fernandez. **VP, Broadcasting:** Scott Geyer.

Director, Hispanic Marketing: Richard Saenz. **Tucson Operations Manager:** Jack Donovan. **Senior Director, Marketing/Communications:** Mike Malo. **Assistant, Marketing:** Melanie Mitchell.

Community Affairs

Director, Community Affairs: Karen Couch. **Senior Manager, Community Affairs:** Veronica Zendejas.

Public Relations, Communications

Telephone: (602) 462-6519. **FAX:** (602) 462-6527.

Director, Public Relations: Mike Swanson. **Manager, Publications:** Joel Horn. **Assistant to Director:** David Pape. **Media Coordinator:** Susan Webner. **Assistants, Media Relations:** Jeff Munn, Casey Wilcox.

Stadium Operations

President: Bob Machen. **General Manager:** Paige Peterson.

Vice President, Facilities Management: Alvan Adams. **VP, Event Services:** Russ Amaral. **VP, Security:** George Bevans. **Director, Suite Services:** Diney Mahoney. **Director, Ballpark Attractions:** Charlene Vazquez-Inzunza. **Assistant Managers, Guest Relations:** Kim Brown, Bryan White. **Director, Event Operations:** Jim Bochenek.

Head Groundskeeper: Grant Trenbeath.

PA Announcer: Jeff Munn. **Official Scorer:** Rodney Johnson.

Ticketing

Telephone: (602) 514-8400. **FAX:** (602) 462-4141.

Senior Vice President, Ticket Operations/Special Services: Dianne Aguilar.

VP, Sales/Group and Season Tickets: Rob Kiese. **Director, Ticket Operations:** Darrin Mitch.

Travel, Clubhouse

Director, Team Travel: Roger Riley. **Visitors Clubhouse:** Bob Doty.

General Information

Home Dugout: Third Base. **Playing Surface:** Grass.

Team Colors: Purple, copper and turquoise.

Player Representative: Craig Counsell.

Joe Garagiola Jr.

BASEBALL OPERATIONS

Telephone: (602) 462-6500. **FAX:** (602) 462-6599.

Vice President, General Manager: Joe Garagiola Jr.

Assistant GM: Sandy Johnson. **Director, Baseball Operations:** Bob Miller. **Business Manager, Baseball Operations:** Craig Bradley. **Assistant to GM:** Valerie Dietrich.

Major League Staff

Manager: Bob Brenly.

Coaches: Bench—Glenn Sherlock; Pitching—Chuck Kniffin; Batting—Dwayne Murphy; First Base—Robin Yount; Third Base—Eddie Rodriguez; Bullpen—Mark Davis.

Medical, Training

Club Physicians: Dr. Michael Lee, Dr. Roger McCoy.

Head Trainer: Paul Lessard. **Assistant Trainer:** Dave Edwards. **Strength and Conditioning Coach:** David Page.

Bob Brenly

Minor Leagues

Telephone: (602) 462-4400. **FAX:** (602) 462-6425.

Director, Player Development: Tommy Jones. **Administrative Assistant, Player Development/Scouting:** Lisa Ventresca.

Field Coordinator: Ron Hassey. **Coordinators:** Dennis Lewallyn (pitching), Damon Berryhill (catching), Chip Hale (infield), Lee Tinsley (outfield), Rick Schu (hitting).

Head Trainer/Rehabilitation Coordinator: Greg Latta. **Tucson Complex Coordinator:** Bob Bensinger. **Rehabilitation Coach**: John Denny.

Farm System

Class	Farm Team	League	Manager	Coach	Pitching Coach
AAA	Tucson	Pacific Coast	Al Pedrique	Jack Howell	Mike Parrott
AA	El Paso	Texas	Scott Coolbaugh	Lorenzo Bundy	Claude Osteen
High A	Lancaster	California	Mike Aldrete	Damon Mashore	Mel Stottlemyre Jr.
Low A	South Bend	Midwest	Von Hayes	Hector De la Cruz	Dan Carlson
Short season	Yakima	Northwest	Bill Plummer	Jay Gainer	Jeff Pico
Rookie	Missoula	Pioneer	Tony Perezchica	Jason Bates	Wellington Cepeda
Rookie	Diamondbacks	Dominican	Juan Ballara	Melvin Gomez	Ernesto Borbon

Scouting

Telephone: (602) 462-6520. **FAX:** (602) 462-6421.

Director, Scouting: Mike Rizzo. **Scouting Assistant:** Michele Copes.

Advance Scout: Mike Paul (Tucson, AZ).

Major League Scouts: Mack Babitt (Richmond, CA), Bryan Lambe (North Massapequa, NY), Jim Marshall (Paradise Valley, AZ).

Special Assignment Scout: Phil Rizzo (Rolling Meadows, IL).

Professional Scouts: Bill Earnhart (Point Clear, AL), Doug Gassaway (Blum, TX), Mike Piatnik (Winter Haven, FL), Mike Sgobba (Scottsdale, AZ).

National Supervisor: Kendall Carter (Scottsdale, AZ).

Regional Supervisors: East—Ed Durkin (Safety Harbor, FL); Central—Kris Kline (Scottsdale, AZ); West—Charles Scott (Novato, CA).

Mike Rizzo

Scouts: Mark Baca (Temecula, CA), Ray Blanco (Miami, FL), Fred Costello (Livermore, CA), Trip Couch (Sugar Land, TX), Mike Daughtry (St. Charles, IL), Ed Gustafson (Tacoma, WA), Scott Jaster (Midland, MI), Steve Kmetko (Phoenix, AZ), Hal Kurtzman (Van Nuys, CA), Greg Lonigro (Connellsville, PA), Steve McAllister (Chillicothe, IL), Howard McCullough (Greenville, NC), Matt Merullo (Madison, CT), Mike Valarezo (Cantonment, FL), Luke Wrenn (Lakeland, FL).

Latin America Supervisor: Junior Noboa (Santo Domingo, DR). **Coordinator, Mexico:** Mike Sgobba (Scottsdale, AZ). **Scout, Mexico:** Jack Pierce (Leon Guanajunato, Mexico).

ATLANTA BRAVES

Stan Kasten

Telephone, Address

Office Address: 755 Hank Aaron Dr., Atlanta, GA 30315. **Mailing Address:** P.O. Box 4064, Atlanta, GA 30302. **Telephone:** (404) 522-7630. **FAX:** (404) 614-1392. **Website:** www.atlantabraves.com.

Ownership

Operated by: Atlanta National Baseball Club, Inc. **Owner:** AOL Time Warner.

Chairman: Bill Bartholomay.

Board of Directors: Henry Aaron, Bill Bartholomay, Bobby Cox, Stan Kasten, Rubye Lucas, Terry McGuirk, John Schuerholz, M.B. Seretean, Ted Turner.

President: Stan Kasten. **Senior Vice President/Assistant to President:** Henry Aaron.

BUSINESS OPERATIONS

Senior Vice President, Administration: Bob Wolfe. **Team Counsel:** John Cooper.

Finance

Vice President, Controller: Chip Moore.

Marketing, Sales

Senior Director, Promotions/Civic Affairs: Miles McRea. **Director, Ticket Sales:** Paul Adams. **Director, Community Relations/Braves Foundation:** Cara Maglione. **Director, Corporate Sales:** Jim Allen.

Public Relations, Communications

Telephone: (404) 614-1556. **FAX:** (404) 614-1391.

Director, Public Relations: Jim Schultz.

Manager, Media Relations: Glen Serra. **Administrative Assistant:** Anne McAlister. **Assistants, Public Relations:** Adam Liberman, Meagan Swingle.

Stadium Operations

Director, Stadium Operations/Security: Larry Bowman. **Field Director:** Ed Mangan.

PA Announcer: Bill Bowers. **Official Scorers:** Mark Frederickson, Mike Stamus, Tony Schiavone.

Director, Audio-Video Operations: Jennifer Berger.

Ticketing

Telephone: (800) 326-4000. **FAX:** (404) 614 -2480.

Director, Ticket Operations: Ed Newman.

Travel, Clubhouse

Director, Team Travel/Equipment Manager: Bill Acree. **Visiting Clubhouse Manager:** John Holland.

General Information

Home Dugout: First Base. **Playing Surface:** Grass.

Team Colors: Red, white and blue.

Player Representative: Unavailable.

John Schuerholz

BASEBALL OPERATIONS

Telephone: (404) 522-7630. **FAX:** (404) 614-3308.

Executive Vice President, General Manager: John Schuerholz.

VP/Assistant GM: Frank Wren. **Special Assistant to GM/Player Development:** Jose Martinez. **Executive Assistant:** Melissa Stone.

Major League Staff

Manager: Bobby Cox.

Coaches: Dugout—Pat Corrales; Pitching—Leo Mazzone; Batting—Terry Pendleton; First Base—Glenn Hubbard; Third Base—Fredi Gonzalez; Bullpen—Bobby Dews.

Medical, Training

Director, Medical Services: Dr. Joe Chandler.

Trainer: Jeff Porter. **Assistant Trainer:** Jim Lovell. **Strength and Conditioning Coach:** Frank Fultz.

Bobby Cox

Player Development

Telephone: (404) 522-7630. **FAX:** (404) 614-1350.

Director, Player Personnel: Dayton Moore. **Assistant, Player Personnel**: Tyrone Brooks. **Assistant Director, Player Development:** Marco Paddy. **Administrative Assistants:** Lena Burney, Chris Rice.

Baseball Operations Assistant: Matt Price.

Coordinator, Instruction: Chino Cadahia. **Roving Instructors:** Rick Adair (pitching), Jim Beauchamp (outfield), Rafael Belliard (infield), Phil Falco (strength and conditioning), Otis Nixon (baserunning), Franklin Stubbs (hitting).

Farm System

Class	Farm Team	League	Manager	Coach	Pitching Coach
AAA	Richmond	International	Pat Kelly	Rick Albert	Guy Hansen
AA	Greenville	Southern	Brian Snitker	Mel Roberts	Mike Alvarez
High A	Myrtle Beach	Carolina	Randy Ingle	Jack Maloof	Bruce Dal Canton
Low A	Rome	South Atlantic	Rocket Wheeler	Bobby Moore	Kent Willis
Rookie	Danville	Appalachian	Kevin McMullan	Billy Best	Jim Czajkowski
Rookie	Kissimmee	Gulf Coast	Ralph Henriquez	S. Lezcano/J. Saul	D. Botelho/G. Luckert
Rookie	Braves I	Dominican	Jose Mota	Tommy Herrera	Lester Straker
Rookie	Braves II	Dominican	Diego Herrera	Jose Villar	Juan Rojas

Scouting

Telephone: (404) 614-1354. **FAX:** (404) 614-1350.

Director, Scouting: Roy Clark. **Administrative Assistants:** Dixie Keller, Matt Price.

Advance Scout: Bobby Wine (Norristown, PA).

Special Assignment Scouts: Dick Balderson (Atlanta, GA), Jim Fregosi (Tarpon Springs, FL), Duane Larson (Knoxville, TN), Chuck McMichael (Grapevine, TX), Scott Nethery (Houston, TX), Paul Snyder (Murphy, NC). **Professional Scouts:** Rod Gilbreath (Lilburn, GA), Bob Wadsworth (Westminster, CA)

National Crosschecker: John Flannery (Austin, TX), Tim Conroy (Monroeville, PA). **Regional Supervisors:** Hep Cronin (Cincinnati, OH), Paul Faulk (Raleigh, NC), Kurt Kemp (Vancouver, WA).

Roy Clark

Area Supervisors: Mike Baker (Santa Ana, CA), Daniel Bates (Oklahoma City, OK), Billy Best (Holly Springs, NC), Stu Cann (Bradley, IL), Sherard Clinkscales (Indianapolis, IN), Al Goetz (Lawrenceville, GA), Ralph Garr Jr. (Missouri City, TX), J Harrison (Antelope, CA), Robert Lucas (Atlanta, GA), Darryl Monroe (Kansas City, MO), Alex Morales (Lake Worth, FL), J.J. Picollo (Mt. Laurel, NJ), John Ramey (Murrieta, CA), Charlie Smith (Austin, TX), John Stewart (Granville, NY), Don Thomas (Baton Rouge, LA), Terry Tripp (Shawnee, OK).

International Supervisors: Phil Dale (Victoria, Australia), Courtland Hall (Germany), Julian Perez (Levittown, PR).

International Scouts: Roberto Aquino (Dominican Republic), Neil Burke (Australia), Richard Castro (Venezuela), Jeremy Chou (Taiwan), Edgar Fernandez (Venezuela), Jose Pedro Flores (Venezuela), Bill Froberg (Netherlands), Carlos Garcia (Colombia), Ruben Garcia (Venezuela), Lonnie Goldberg (Canada), Rafael Jozefa (Netherlands Antilles), David Latham (Japan), Jason Lee (Korea), Jose Leon (Venezuela), Luis Martinez (Venezuela), Luis Ortiz (Panama), Hiroyuki Oya (Japan), Rolando Petit (Venezuela), Elvis Pineda (Dominican Republic), Manuel Samaniego (Mexico), Miguel Teran (Colombia), Raymond Tew (South Africa), Marvin Throneberry (Nicaragua), Carlos Torres (Venezuela).

BALTIMORE ORIOLES

Peter Angelos

Telephone, Address

Office Address: 333 West Camden St., Baltimore, MD 21201. **Telephone:** (410) 685-9800. **FAX:** (410) 547-6272. **E-Mail Address:** fanservi@opacy.com. **Website:** www.theorioles.com.

Ownership

Operated by: The Baltimore Orioles Limited Partnership, Inc.
Chairman/Chief Executive Officer: Peter G. Angelos.

BUSINESS OPERATIONS

Vice Chairman, Community Projects/Public Affairs: Thomas Clancy.
Vice Chairman, Chief Operating Officer: Joe Foss.
Executive Vice President: John Angelos.
VP/Special Liaison to Chairman: Lou Kousouris.
General Legal Counsel: Russell Smouse.
Director, Human Resources: Lisa Tolson. **Director, Information Systems:** James Kline.

Finance

Vice President, Chief Financial Officer: Robert Ames.
Controller: Edward Kabernagel.

Marketing, Sales

Director, Corporate Sponsorship/Sales: Ron Brown.

Public Relations, Communications

Telephone: (410) 547-6150. **FAX:** (410) 547-6272.
Executive Director, Communications: Spiro Alafassos.
Director, Public Relations: Bill Stetka. **Manager, Baseball Information**: Kevin Behan. **Manager, Communications**: Monica Pence. **Administrative Assistant, Public/Community Relations:** Shannon Obaker.
Director, Community Relations: Julie Wagner. **Coordinator, Community Relations**: Jennifer Steier.
Director, Publishing/Creative Media: Jessica Fisher.

Ballpark Operations

Director, Ballpark Operations: Roger Hayden**. Manager, Event Operations**: Doug Rosenberger.
Director, Concession Operations: Robert Gallion.
Head Groundskeeper: Al Capitos.
PA Announcer: Dave McGowan. **Official Scorers**: Jim Henneman, Marc Jacobsen.

Fan, Ticket Services

Telephone: (410) 547-6600. **FAX:** (410) 547-6270.
Director, Sales: Matt Dryer. **Assistant Director, Sales:** Mark Hromalik.
Director, Fan/Ticket Services: Don Grove. **Ticket Manager**: Audrey Brown**. Systems Inventory Manager**: Steve Kowalski.

Travel, Clubhouse

Traveling Secretary: Phil Itzoe. **Equipment Manager (Home):** Jim Tyler. **Equipment Manager (Road):** Fred Tyler. **Umpires, Field Attendant**: Ernie Tyler.

General Information

Home Dugout: First Base. **Playing Surface**. Grass.
Team Colors: Orange, black and white.
Player Representative: Jason Johnson.

Jim Beattie

BASEBALL OPERATIONS

Telephone: (410) 547-6121. **FAX:** (410) 547-6271.

Executive Vice President, Baseball Operations: Jim Beattie. **VP, Baseball Operations:** Mike Flanagan.

Director, Baseball Administration: Ed Kenney Jr. **Executive Assistant to VP, Baseball Operations:** Ann Lange.

Major League Staff

Manager: Mike Hargrove.

Coaches: Bench—Sam Perlozzo; Pitching—Mark Wiley; Batting—Terry Crowley; First Base—Rick Dempsey; Third Base—Tom Trebelhorn; Bullpen—Elrod Hendricks.

Medical, Training

Club Physician: Dr. William Goldiner. **Club Physician, Orthopedics**: Dr. Charles Silberstein.

Head Athletic Trainer: Richie Bancells. **Assistant Athletic Trainer**: Brian Ebel. **Strength/Conditioning Coach**: Tim Bishop.

Mike Hargrove

Minor Leagues

Telephone: (410) 547-6120. **FAX:** (410) 547-6298.

Director, Minor League Operations: Doc Rodgers. **Assistant Director, Minor League Operations:** Tripp Norton. **Assistant, Minor League Operations**: Kevin Ibach.

Medical Coordinator: Dave Walker. **Strength/Conditioning Coach**: Pat Hedge. **Assistant Strength/Conditioning Coach**: Chris Dunaway. **Facilities Coordinator**: Jaime Rodriguez. **Camp Coordinator**: Len Johnston.

Roving Instructors: Moe Drabowsky (Florida pitching), Andy Etchebarren (catching), Bien Figueroa (infield), Dave Schmidt (pitching), Dave Stockstill (hitting), Jack Voigt (outfield/baserunning).

Farm System

Class	Farm Team	League	Manager	Coach	Pitching Coach
AAA	Ottawa	International	Gary Allenson	Dave Cash	Steve McCatty
AA	Bowie	Eastern	Dave Trembley	Butch Davis	Dave Schuler
High A	Frederick	Carolina	Tom Lawless	Moe Hill	Scott McGregor
Low A	Delmarva	South Atlantic	Stan Hough	Don Werner	Larry McCall
Short season	Aberdeen	New York-Penn	Joe Almaraz	G. Kendall/C. Landrum	Doc Watson
Rookie	Bluefield	Appalachian	Don Buford	H. Meulens/L. Johnston	Andre Rabouin
Rookie	Sarasota	Gulf Coast	Jesus Alfaro	J. Tanner/M. Felder	Larry Jaster
Rookie	Orioles	Dominican	Salvador Ramirez	Unavailable	Miguel Jabalara

Scouting

Telephone: (410) 547-6187. **FAX:** (410) 547-6298.

Director, Scouting: Tony DeMacio.

Administrative Assistants: Marcy Zerhusen, Brian Hopkins.

Advance Scout: Deacon Jones (Sugar Land, TX).

Professional Scouts: Larry Himes (Mesa, AZ), Bruce Kison (Bradenton, FL), Curt Motton (Baltimore, MD), Tim Thompson (Lewistown, PA), Fred Uhlman Sr. (Baltimore, MD).

National Crosschecker: Shawn Pender (Drexel Hill, PA).

Regional Crosscheckers: Central—Deron Rombach (Arlington, TX), West—Dave Blume (Elk Grove, CA).

Tony DeMacio

Full-Time Scouts: Joe Almaraz (San Antonio, TX), Bill Bliss (Gilbert, AZ), Ralph Garr Jr. (Missouri City, TX), John Gillette (Kirkland, WA), Troy Hoerner (Naperville, IL), Jim Howard (Clifton Park, NY), Dave Jennings (Daphne, AL), Ray Krawczyk (Lake Forest, CA), Gil Kubski (Huntington Beach, CA), Lamar North (Rossville, GA), Nick Presto (West Palm Beach, FL), Harry Shelton (Ocoee, FL), Ed Sprague (Lodi, CA), Marc Tramuta (Elkridge, MD), Mike Tullier (River Ridge, LA), Dominic Viola (Oklahoma City, OK), Marc Ziegler (Columbus, OH).

Director, Latin American Scouting: Carlos Bernhardt (San Pedro de Macoris, D.R.).

Supervisor, Central/South America, Lesser Antilles: Jesus Halabi (Aruba).

International Scouts: Rob Derksen (Pacific Rim), Ubaldo Heredia (Venezuela), Salvador Ramirez (Dominican Republic), Arturo Sanchez (Venezuela), Brett Ward (Australia).

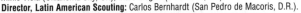

BOSTON RED SOX

Larry Lucchino

Telephone, Address

Office Address: Fenway Park, 4 Yawkey Way, Boston, MA 02215. **Telephone:** (617) 267-9440. **FAX:** (617) 375-0944. **Website:** www.redsox.com.

Ownership

Principal Owner: John Henry. **Chairman:** Tom Werner. **Vice Chairmen:** David Ginsberg, Les Otten

President/Chief Executive Officer: Larry Lucchino. **Director:** George Mitchell.

BUSINESS OPERATIONS

Chief Legal Officer, NESV: Lucinda Treat. **Vice President, Club Counsel:** Elaine Steward. **Staff Counsel:** Jennifer Flynn. **Law Clerk:** Judy Liu.

Executive Vice President, Business Affairs: Mike Dee. **Executive VP, Public Affairs:** Dr. Charles Steinberg. **Executive Assistant to President/Chief Executive Officer:** Fay Scheer. **Special Assistants to President/CEO:** Jonathan Gilula, Jeremy Kapstein. **Executive Assistants:** Barbara Bianucci, Jeanne Bill, Lorraine Leong.

Finance

Vice President, Chief Financial Officer: Robert Furbush.

Director, Human Resources/Office Administration: Michele Julian. **Administrative Assistant:** Adis Benitez. **Director, Information Technology:** Steve Conley. **Manager, Information Technology:** Clay Rendon. **Senior Systems Analyst:** Randy George.

Sales, Marketing

Vice President, Sales/Corporate Partnerships: Sam Kennedy. **Director, Corporate Partnerships:** Joseph Januszewski. **Manager, Sponsor Services:** Troup Parkinson. **Coordinator, Sponsor Services:** Laura Reff. **Senior Manager, Season/Group Sales:** Corey Bowdre. **Senior Manager, Premium Sales:** Sean Curtin. **Manager, Suite/Premium Seating Sales:** Todd McDonald. **Account Executives:** Kimberly Cameron, Tyler Fairchild, Jordan Kogler.

Director, Advertising/Ballpark Entertainment: Jeffrey Goldenberg. **Manager, Ballpark Events:** Marcita Thompson. **Manager, Scoreboard/Video Production:** Daniel Kischel. **Manager, Ballpark Entertainment:** Richard Subrizio.

Vice President, Planning/Development: Janet Marie Smith. **Coordinator, Planning/Development:** Paul Hanlon.

Community Relations

Manager, Community Athletic Programs: Ron Burton Jr. **Manager, Community Relations:** Vanessa Leyvas.

Media Relations

Director, Media Relations: Kevin Shea. **Director, Communications:** Glenn Geffner. **Coordinator, Media Relations:** Peter Chase. **Media Relations Assistant/Credentials:** Meghan McClure. **Media Relations Assistants:** Christopher Mearn, Mark Rogoff.

Vice President, Publications/Archives: Richard Bresciani. **Executive Consultant, Public Affairs:** Lou Gorman. **Director, Publications:** Debbie Matson. **Manager, Special Writing Projects:** Ann Marie Starzyk. **Manager, Publications/Archives:** Rod Oreste. **Coordinator, Alumni/Archives:** Pam Ganley.

Stadium Operations

Vice President, Stadium Operations: Joe McDermott.

Superintendent, Park/Maintenance: Joe Mooney. **Director, Grounds:** David Mellor. **Assistant Director, Grounds:** Charles Brunetti. **Stadium Operations Staff:** Greg Arrington, Albert Forester, Bob Levin.

Director, Facilities Management: Tom Queenan. **Manager, Property Maintenance:** John Caron.

Director, Fan/Neighborhood Services: Sarah McKenna.

Senior Vice President, Fenway Affairs: Larry Cancro. **Manager, Fenway Affairs:** Dan Lyons. **Administrator, Fenway Affairs:** Debbie McIntyre.

PA Announcer: Ed Brickley. **Official Scorers:** Bruce Guindon, Dave O'Hara, Charles Scoggins.

Ticket Services, Operations

Telephone: (617) 267-1700, (617) 482-4769, (877) REDSOX-9. **FAX:** (617) 236-6640.

Director, Ticket Services/Operations: Charles Steedman. **Director, Ticket Services/Information:** Michael Schetzel. **Director, Ticket Operations:** Richard Beaton Jr. **Manager, Season Ticket Services:** Joseph Matthews. **Manager, Group/Premium Services:** Carole Alkins. **Manager, Ticket Services:** Marcell Saporita.

Travel, Clubhouse

Traveling Secretary: Jack McCormack. **Administrative Assistant:** Jean MacDougall. **Equipment Manager/Clubhouse Operations:** Joseph Cochran. **Visiting Clubhouse Manager:** Thomas McLaughlin. **Video/Advance Scouting Coordinator:** William Broadbent.

General Information

Home Dugout: First Base. **Playing Surface:** Grass.
Team Colors: Navy blue, red and white.
Player Representative: Trot Nixon.

Theo Epstein

BASEBALL OPERATIONS

Telephone: (617) 267-9440. **FAX:** (617) 236-6649.

Senior Vice President, General Manager: Theo Epstein.

VP, Baseball Operations: Mike Port. **Assistant GM:** Joshua Byrnes. **Special Assistant to GM/Scouting:** Bill Lajoie. **Special Assistant to GM/Player Development:** Craig Shipley. **Special Assistant to GM:** Lee Thomas. **Baseball Operations Assistant:** Jed Hoyer.

Major League Staff

Manager: Grady Little.

Coaches: Bench—Jerry Narron; Pitching—Tony Cloninger; Batting—Ron Jackson; First Base—Dallas Williams; Third Base—Mike Cubbage; Bullpen—Euclides Rojas.

Medical, Training

Medical Director: Dr. William Morgan.

Head Trainer: Jim Rowe. **Assistant Trainer/Rehab Coordinator:** Chris Correnti. **Assistant Trainer:** Chang Lee.

Player Development

Telephone: (617) 267-9440. **FAX:** (617) 236-6695.

Director, Player Development: Ben Cherington. **Director, Minor League Administration:** Raquel Ferreira. **Administrative Assistant, Scouting/Player Development:** Victor Cruz. **Player Development Consultants:** Dick Berardino, Dwight Evans, Tommy Harper, Felix Maldonado, Frank Malzone, Bob Tewksbury.

Coordinator, Florida Operations: Todd Stephenson. **Minor League Equipment Manager:** Mike Stelmach.

Roving Instructors/Coordinators: Luis Aguayo (infield), Orv Franchuk (hitting coordinator), Glenn Gregson (pitching coordinator), Lynn Jones (outfield/baserunning), Johnny Pesky (special assignment), Jim Rice (instructor), Victor Rodriguez (hitting instructor), John Sanders (catching), Charlie Wagner (special assignment), Carl Yastrzemski (instructor), Jim Young (medical). **Coordinator, Latin Field:** Nelson Norman.

STEVE MOORE
Grady Little

Farm System

Class	Farm Team	League	Manager	Coach	Pitching Coach
AAA	Pawtucket	International	Buddy Bailey	U.L. Washington	Mike Griffin
AA	Portland	Eastern	Ron Johnson	Mark Budaska	Bob Kipper
High A	Sarasota	Florida State	Tim Leiper	Chad Epperson	Ace Adams
Low A	Augusta	South Atlantic	Russ Morman	John Malzone	Dave Tomlin
Short season	Lowell	New York-Penn	Jon Deeble	Randy Phillips	Darryl Milne
Rookie	Fort Myers	Gulf Coast	Ralph Treuel	Walter Miranda	Alan Mauthe
Rookie	Red Sox	Dominican	Nelson Paulino	Cesar Hernandez	Jose Sosa

Scouting

Director, Amateur Scouting: David Chadd. **Assistant Director, Amateur Scouting:** James Orr.

Director, International Scouting: Louie Eljaua. **Assistant Director, Professional/International Scouting:** Thomas Moore. **Advance Scouting Coordinator:** Galen Carr.

Major League Scouts: Tom Mooney (Pittsfield, MA), Jerry Stephenson (Fullerton, CA). **Pro Scouts:** Rene Mons (Manchester, NH), Gary Rajsich (Wilsonville, OR), Matt Sczesny (Deer Park, NY). **Special Assignment Scout:** Mark Wasinger (El Paso, TX).

National Crosscheckers: Ray Crone Jr. (Cedar Hill, TX), Curtis Dishman (San Juan Capistrano, CA). **Regional Crosscheckers:** Murray Cook (Washington, DC), Dave Finley (San Diego, CA).

Area Scouts: John Booher (Vancouver, WA), Grant Brittain, Edwin Correa (Carolina, PR), John DiPuglia (Pembroke Pines, FL), Rob English (Duluth, GA), Ray Fagnant (East Granby, CT), Danny Haas (Paducah, KY), Matt Haas (Cincinnati, OH), Ernie Jacobs (Wichita, KS), Wally Komatsubara (Aiea, HI), Dan Madsen, Joe Mason (Millbrook, AL), Darryl Milne (Denver, CO), Jim Robinson (Mansfield, TX), Ed Roebuck (Lakewood, CA), Fay Thompson (Vallejo, CA), Jim Woodward (Claremont, CA), Jeff Zona (Mechanicsville, VA).

David Chadd

Consulting Scouts: Pat Anderson (Pine Bluff, AR), Walter Atkins (Guntersville, AL), Buzz Bowers (East Orleans, MA), Kelvin Bowles (Rocky Mount, VA), Cucho Rodriguez (San Juan, PR), Dick Sorkin (Potomac, MD), Terry Sullivan (Lagrange, LA), Dick Wilson (Sun Valley, NV).

CHICAGO CUBS

Andy MacPhail

Telephone, Address

Office Address: Wrigley Field, 1060 W. Addison St., Chicago, IL 60613. **Telephone:** (773) 404-2827. **FAX:** (773) 404-4129. **E-Mail Address:** cubs@cubs.com. **Website:** www.cubs.com.

Ownership

Operated by: Chicago National League Ball Club, Inc. **Owner:** Tribune Company.
Board of Directors: Dennis Fitzsimmons, Andy MacPhail.
President, Chief Executive Officer: Andy MacPhail.

BUSINESS OPERATIONS

Executive Vice President, Business Operations: Mark McGuire.

Director, Information Systems/Special Projects: Carl Rice. **PC Systems Analyst:** Sean True. **Senior Legal Counsel/Corporate Secretary:** Crane Kenney. **Executive Secretary, Business Operations:** Gayle Finney. **Director, Human Resources:** Jenifer Surma.

Finance

Controller: Jodi Reischl. **Manager, Accounting:** Terri Lynn. **Payroll Administrator:** Mary Jane Iorio. **Senior Accountant:** Angela Boone.

Marketing, Broadcasting

Vice President, Marketing/Broadcasting: John McDonough.

Director, Promotions/Advertising: Jay Blunk. **Manager, Cubs Care/Community Relations:** Rebecca Polihronis. **Coordinator, Marketing/Community Affairs:** Mary Dosek. **Manager, Mezzanine Suites:** Louis Artiaga. **Manager, Special Events/Player Relations:** Annie Fitzgerald

Media Relations, Publications

Telephone: (773) 404-4191. **FAX:** (773) 404-4129.

Director, Media Relations: Sharon Pannozzo. **Manager, Media Information:** Chuck Wasserstrom. **Assistant, Media Relations:** Samantha Newby.

Director, Publications: Lena McDonagh. **Manager, Publications:** Jim McArdle. **Editorial Specialist, Publications:** Michael Huang. **Senior Graphic Designer:** Juan Alberto Castillo. **Graphic Design Specialist:** Joaquin Castillo. **Photographer:** Stephen Green.

Stadium Operations

Director, Stadium Operations: Paul Rathje.

Manager, Event Operations/Security: Mike Hill. **Coordinator, Event Operations/Security:** Julius Farrell. **Head Groundskeeper:** Roger Baird. **Facility Supervisor:** Bill Scott. **Coordinator, Office Services:** Randy Skocz. **Coordinator, Stadium Operations:** Danielle Alexa. **Switchboard Operator:** Brenda Morgan.

PA Announcer: Paul Friedman. **Official Scorers:** Bob Rosenberg, Don Friske.

Ticketing

Telephone: (773) 404-2827. **FAX:** (773) 404-4014.

Director, Ticket Operations: Frank Maloney. **Assistant Director, Ticket Sales:** Brian Garza. **Assistant Director, Ticket Services:** Joe Kirchen. **Vault Room Supervisor:** Cherie Blake.

Travel, Clubhouse

Traveling Secretary: Jimmy Bank.
Home Clubhouse Manager: Tom Hellmann. **Visiting Clubhouse Manager:** Dana Noeltner.

General Information

Home Dugout: Third Base. **Playing Surface:** Grass.
Team Colors: Royal blue, red and white.
Player Representative: Unavailable.

Jim Hendry

BASEBALL OPERATIONS

Telephone: (773) 404-2827. **FAX:** (773) 404-4111.

Vice President/General Manager: Jim Hendry. **Executive Assistant to President/GM:** Arlene Gill.

Director, Baseball Operations: Scott Nelson. **Assistant, Baseball Operations:** Brian Williams.

Special Assistant to President: Billy Williams. **Special Assistants to GM:** Keith Champion, Gary Hughes, Ken Kravec, Ed Lynch.

Major League Staff

Manager: Dusty Baker.

Coaches: Dugout—Dick Pole; Pitching—Larry Rothschild; Batting—Gary Matthews; First Base—Gene Clines; Third Base—Wendell Kim; Bullpen—Juan Lopez.

Dusty Baker

Medical, Training

Team Physicians: Dr. Stephen Adams, Dr. Michael Schafer.

Head Trainer: David Tumbas. **Assistant Trainer:** Sandy Krum. **Strength/Conditioning Coordinator:** Tim Buss.

Player Development

Telephone: (773) 404-4035. **FAX:** (773) 404-4147.

Director, Player Development/Latin American Operations: Oneri Fleita. **Coordinator, Minor League Operations:** Patti Kargakis.

Field Coordinator: Dave Bialas. **Coordinator:** Lester Strode (pitching).

Equipment Manager: Michael Burkhart. **Minor League Medical Coordinator:** Greg Keuter.

Roving Instructors: John Cangelosi (outfield/baserunning), Jeff Huson (infield), Scott Servais (catching), Danny Stinnett (strength/conditioning), Ritchie Zisk (hitting).

Farm System

Class	Farm Team	League	Manager	Coach	Pitching Coach
AAA	Iowa	Pacific Coast	Mike Quade	Pat Listach	Jerry Reuss
AA	West Tenn	Southern	Bobby Dickerson	Von Joshua	Alan Dunn
High A	Daytona	Florida State	Rick Kranitz	Trey Forkerway	Tom Pratt
Low A	Lansing	Midwest	Julio Garcia	Mike Micucci	Mike Anderson
Short season	Boise	Northwest	Steve McFarland	Tom Beyers	David Haas
Rookie	Mesa	Arizona	Carmelo Martinez	Ricardo Medina	Rick Tronerud
Rookie	Cubs	Dominican	Ramon Caraballo	L. Vals/P. Cabrera	Leo Hernandez
Rookie	Cubs	Venezuela	Franklin Font	None	Julio Figueroa

Scouting

Telephone: (773) 404-2827. **FAX:** (773) 404-4147.

Director, Scouting: John Stockstill. **Administrative Assistant:** Patricia Honzik.

Advance Scout: Bob Didier (Federal Way, WA). **Major League Scouts:** Bill Harford (Chicago, IL). **Professional Scouts:** Joe Housey (Hollywood, FL), Mark Servais (LaCrosse, WI).

Special Assignment Scouts: Gene Handley (Huntington Beach, CA), Spider Jorgensen (Cucamonga, CA), Demie Manieri (South Bend, IN), Glen Van Proyen (Lisle, IL).

National Crosschecker: Brad Kelley (Glendale, AZ). **Regional Crosscheckers:** Mark Adair (Florissant, MO), Mike Soper (Tampa, FL).

John Stockstill

Full-Time Scouts: Billy Blitzer (Brooklyn, NY), Jim Crawford (Columbus, MS), Steve Fuller (Brea, CA), Al Geddes (Canby, OR), Steve Hinton (Sacramento, CA), Sam Hughes (Smyrna, GA), Brian Milner (Edgecliff Village, TX), Fred Petersen (Long Beach, CA), Rolando Pino (Pembroke Pines, FL), Pat Portugal (Cookeville, TN), Steve Riha (Houston, TX), Tom Shafer (Overland Park, KS), Mitch Sokol (Phoenix, AZ), Billy Swoope (Norfolk, VA), Jose Trujillo (Puerto Rico), Stan Zielinski (Winfield, IL).

International Scouts: Hector Ortega (Venezuela), Jose Serra (Dominican Republic).

CHICAGO WHITE SOX

Telephone, Address

Office Address: 333 W. 35th St., Chicago, IL 60616. **Telephone:** (312) 674-1000. **FAX:** (312) 674-5116. **Website:** www.whitesox.com.

Jerry Reinsdorf

Ownership

Operated by: Chicago White Sox, Ltd.

Chairman: Jerry Reinsdorf. **Vice Chairman:** Eddie Einhorn.

Board of Directors: Fred Brzozowski, Robert Judelson, Judd Malkin, Robert Mazer, Allan Muchin, Jay Pinsky, Larry Pogofsky, Lee Stern, Sanford Takiff, Burton Ury, Charles Walsh.

General Counsel: Allan Muchin.

BUSINESS OPERATIONS

Executive Vice President: Howard Pizer.

Special Assistant to Chairman: Dennis Gilbert. **Director, Information Services:** Don Brown.

Director, Human Resources: Moira Foy. **Assistant to Chairman:** Anita Fasano. **Administrator, Human Resources:** Leslie Gaggiano.

Finance

Vice President, Administration/Finance: Tim Buzard. **Director, Finance:** Bill Waters. **Accounting Manager:** Julie O'Shea.

Marketing, Sales

Senior VP, Marketing/Broadcasting: Rob Gallas. **Director, Marketing/Broadcasting:** Bob Grim. **Manager, Promotions/Marketing Services:** Sharon Sreniawski. **Manager, Scoreboard Operations/Production:** Jeff Szynal. **Manager, Broadcasting/Marketing Services:** Jo Simmons. **Manager, Sponsorship Sales:** Ryan Gribble. **Marketing Account Executives:** Dale Song, Gail Tucker. **Coordinator, Sponsorship Sales:** Stephanie Brewer. **Coordinator, Promotions/Marketing Services:** Amy Gullick. **Sponsorship Sales Administrator:** Percy Thornbor.

Director, Ticket Sales: Jim Muno. **Coordinator, Suite Sales:** Debbie Theobald. **Manager, Ticket Sales:** Tom Sheridan.

Director, Advertising/Community Relations: Christine O'Reilly. **Director, Marketing Communications:** Amy Kress. **Manager, Design Services:** Nicole Stack. **Manager, Community Relations:** Nicole Arceneaux. **Coordinator, Publications:** Kyle White. **Coordinator, Community Relations:** Danielle Disch. **Administrator, Community Relations:** Stephanie Carew.

Public Relations

Telephone: (312) 674-5300. **FAX:** (312) 674-5116.

Director, Public Relations: Scott Reifert. **Assistant Director, Media Relations:** Bob Beghtol. **Manager, Corporate Communications:** Katie Kirby. **Coordinator, Media Relations:** Eric Phillips. **Coordinator, Public Relations:** Vivian Stalling.

Stadium Operations

Vice President, Stadium Operations: Terry Savarise. **Director, Park Operations:** David Schaffer. **Director, Guest Services/Diamond Suite Operations:** Julie Taylor.

Head Groundskeeper: Roger Bossard.

PA Announcer: Gene Honda. **Official Scorers:** Bob Rosenberg, Don Friske, Scott Reed.

Ticketing

Telephone: (312) 674-1000. **FAX:** (312) 674-5102.

Director, Ticket Operations: Bob Devoy. **Manager, Ticket Operations:** Mike Mazza. **Manager, Ticket Accounting Administration:** Ken Wisz.

Travel, Clubhouse

Manager, Team Travel: Ed Cassin. **Equipment Manager, Clubhouse Operations:** Vince Fresso. **Visiting Clubhouse:** Gabe Morell. **Umpires Clubhouse:** Joey McNamara.

Major League Computer Scouting Analyst: Mike Gellinger. **Video Coordinator:** Andy Glogowski. **Assistant Video Coordinator:** Daniel Zien.

General Information

Home Dugout: Third Base. **Playing Surface:** Grass.

Team Colors: Black, white and silver.

Player Representative: Unavailable.

Ken Williams

BASEBALL OPERATIONS

Senior Vice President/General Manager: Ken Williams. **Assistant GM:** Rick Hahn. **Executive Advisor to GM:** Roland Hemond. **Special Assistant to GM:** Dave Yoakum. **Executive Assistant to GM:** Nancy Nesnidal.

Senior Director, Player Personnel: Duane Shaffer. **Director, Baseball Operations Systems:** Dan Fabian. **Assistant Director, Baseball Operations Systems:** Andrew Pinter. **Assistant, Baseball Operations:** J.J. Lally.

Major League Computer Scouting Analyst: Mike Gellinger. **Video Coordinator:** Andy Glogowski. **Assistant Video Coordinator:** Daniel Zien.

Major League Staff

Manager: Jerry Manuel.

Coaches: Bench—Joe Nossek; Pitching—Don Cooper; Hitting—Gary Ward; First Base—Rafael Santana; Third Base—Bruce Kimm; Bullpen—Art Kusnyer.

Medical, Training

Senior Team Physician: Dr. James Boscardin. **Head Trainer:** Herm Schneider. **Assistant Trainer:** Brian Ball. **Director, Conditioning:** Steve Odgers.

Jerry Manuel

Player Development

Telephone: (312) 674-1000. **FAX:** (312) 674-5105.

Director, Player Development: Bob Fontaine. **Assistant Director, Player Development:** Brian Porter.

Director, Minor League Administration: Grace Zwit. **Coordinator, Minor League Administration:** Kathy Potoski. **Manager, Clubhouse/Equipment:** Dan Flood.

Director, Instruction: Jim Snyder.

Roving Instructors/Coordinators: Kirk Champion (pitching), Mike Lum (hitting), Daryl Boston (outfield), Nick Leyva (infield), Tommy Thompson (catching), Chris Cron (bunting), Allen Thomas (conditioning), Trung Cao (conditioning assistant). **Coordinator, Minor League Trainers/Rehabilitation:** Scott Takao.

Farm System

Class	Farm Team	League	Manager	Coach	Pitching Coach
AAA	Charlotte	International	Nick Capra	Greg Walker	Curt Hasler
AA	Birmingham	Southern	Wally Backman	Gregg Ritchie	Juan Nieves
High A	Winston-Salem	Carolina	Razor Shines	Ken Dominguez	J.R. Perdew
Low A	Kannapolis	South Atlantic	John Orton	Brandon Moore	Sean Snedeker
Rookie	Great Falls	Pioneer	Chris Cron	Mark Haley	Richard Dotson
Rookie	Bristol	Appalachian	Jerry Hairston	R. Long/C. DeMidio	Bill Kinneberg
Rookie	White Sox	Dominican	Unavailable	Unavailable	Unavailable

Scouting

Telephone: (312) 674-1000. **FAX:** (312) 451-5105.

Vice President, Free Agent/Major League Scouting: Larry Monroe. **Scouting Director:** Doug Laumann (Florence, KY).

Professional Scouts: Joe Butler (Temecula, CA), Larry Maxie (Upland, CA), Gary Pellant (Chandler, AZ), Billy Scherrer (Grand Island, NY), Daraka Shaheed (Vallejo, CA), Bill Young (Long Beach, CA).

National Crosschecker: Ed Pebley (Brigham City, UT). **Regional Supervisors:** East Coast—John Tumminia (Newburgh, NY), West Coast—Rick Ingalls (Long Beach, CA), Midwest—Paul Provas (Arlington, TX), Southwest—Derek Valenzuela (Temecula, CA).

Doug Laumann

Full-Time Area Scouts: Rico Cortes (Plant City, FL), Alex Cosmidis (Raleigh, NC), Curt Daniels (Vancouver, WA), Nathan Durst (Villa Park, IL), Chuck Fox (Glen Rock, NJ), Larry Grefer (Park Hills, KY), Matt Hattabaugh (Westminster, CA), Nick Hostetler (Atlanta, GA), Warren Hughes (Mobile, AL), George Kachigian (Coronado, CA), John Kazanas (Phoenix, AZ), Jose Ortega (Fort Lauderdale, FL), Alex Slattery (Maumelle, AR), Keith Staab (College Station, TX), Adam Virchis (Modesto, CA).

Part-Time Scouts: Tom Butler (East Rancho Dominguez, CA), Javier Centeno (Guaynabo, PR), E.J. Chavez (El Paso, TX), John Doldoorian (Whitinsville, MA), James Ellison (Georgetown, TX), Jack Jolly (Murfreesboro, TN), Reggie Lewis (Elkton, MD), Glen Murdock (Livonia, MI), Howard Nakagama (Salt Lake City, UT), Al Otto (Schaumburg, IL), Mike Paris (Boone, IA), Ralph Reyes (Miami, FL), Mike Shirley (Anderson, IN), Larry Silveira (Gardenerville, NV).

Latin American Coordinator: Miguel Ibarra (Panama).

International Scouts: Roberto Espinoza (Venezuela), Denny Gonzalez (Dominican Republic).

CINCINNATI REDS

John Allen

Telephone, Address

Office Address: 100 Main St., Cincinnati, OH 45202. **Telephone:** (513) 765-7000. **FAX:** (513) 765-7342. **Website:** www.cincinnatireds.com.

Ownership

Operated by: The Cincinnati Reds, Inc.

Ownership Group: Gannett Co. Inc., Carl Lindner, Mrs. Louis Nippert, William Reik Jr., Marge Schott, George Strike.

Chief Executive Officer: Carl Lindner. **Chief Operating Officer:** John Allen. **Executive Assistant to Chief Operating Officer:** Joyce Pfarr.

BUSINESS OPERATIONS

General Counsel: James Evans. **Secretary Counsel:** Karl Grafe.

Finance

Senior Director, Finance and Administration/Controller: Anthony Ward. **Accounting Manager:** Samantha Bailey. **Payroll Supervisor:** Brian Koniak. **Payroll Accountant:** Ayanna Goddard. **Staff Accountant:** Jason Randolph. **Accounts Payable:** Dion Burnett. **Accounting Clerk:** Srey Pic.

Human Resources Manager: Stephanie Dicks.

Administrator, Business/Broadcasting: Ginny Kamp.

Marketing, Sales

Director, Marketing: Cal Levy. **Director, Corporate Marketing:** Brad Blettner. **Manager, Media/Advertising:** Jennifer Black. **Manager, Corporate Service:** Molly Mott. **Director, Promotions/Entertainment:** Amy Schneider.

Director, Season/Group Operations: Pat McCaffrey. **Director, Sales:** Jenny Gardner. **Manager, Group Tickets Operations:** Brad Callahan. **Manager, Season Tickets Operations:** Cyndi Strzynski. **Senior Account Executive:** Jodi Czanik. **Account Executives:** Chris Herrell, Ryan Niemeyer, Ryan Rizzo. **Manager, Suite/Premium Service:** Libbie Williams. **Coordinator, Riverfront Club/Sales:** Maya Wadleigh.

Manager, Merchandise: Amy Hafer. **Manager, Dugout Shop:** Dena Holland. **Manager, Game Day Merchandise:** Scott Wick. **Assistant Manager, Dugout Shop:** Brian Stoehr. **Merchandise Inventory Control Clerk:** John Rieder. **Merchandise Accounting Assistant:** Shelley Haas.

Public Relations, Communications

Telephone: (513) 765-7800. **FAX:** (513) 765-7180.

Director, Media Relations: Rob Butcher. **Assistant Director, Media Relations:** Michael Vassallo. **Coordinator, Media Relations:** Larry Herms. **Assistant, Media Relations:** Jamie Ramsey.

Director, Communications/Community Relations: Michael Ringering. **Assistant Director, Communications:** Ralph Mitchell. **Manager, Community Relations:** Lorrie Platt. **Coordinator, Communications:** Erin Vernon. **Assistant, Communications:** Dann Stupp.

Ballpark Operations

Senior Director, Ballpark Operations: Declan Mullin. **Assistant Director, Ballpark Operations:** Mike Maddox. **Chief Engineer:** Roger Smith. **Superintendent, Ballpark Operations:** Bob Harrison. **Assistant, Ballpark Operations:** Colleen Brown.

Head Groundskeeper: Doug Gallant. **Assistant Groundskeeper:** Jon Phelps. **Supervisor, Grounds:** Matthew Williams.

Ticketing

Telephone: (513) 765-7400. **FAX:** (513) 765-7119.

Director, Ticket Operations: John O'Brien. **Assistant Director, Ticket Operations:** Ken Ayer. **Coordinator, Ticket Operations:** Hallie Kinney. **Ticket Operations Accountant:** Jim Hall. **Ticket Operations Assistant:** Kevin Barnhill.

Travel, Clubhouse

Traveling Secretary: Gary Wahoff.

Senior Clubhouse/Equipment Manager: Bernie Stowe. **Reds Clubhouse/Equipment Manager:** Rick Stowe. **Visiting Clubhouse Manager:** Mark Stowe.

General Information

Home Dugout: First Base. **Playing Surface:** Grass.

Team Colors: Red, white and black.

Player Representative: Ryan Dempster.

Jim Bowden

BASEBALL OPERATIONS

Telephone: (513) 765-7700. **FAX:** (513) 765-7799.

General Manager: Jim Bowden.

Assistant GM: Brad Kullman. **Special Assistant to GM/Senior Advisor, Player Development:** Johnny Almaraz. **Senior Special Assistant to GM/Advance Scout:** Gene Bennett. **Special Assistants to GM:** Larry Barton Jr., Al Goldis. **Special Consultants to GM:** Johnny Bench, Ken Griffey Sr. **Special Consultant:** Bob Zuk. **Executive Assistant to GM:** Lois Schneider. **Coordinator Research/Development:** Jim Thrift. **Assistant, Baseball Administration:** Geoff Silver.

Major League Staff

Manager: Bob Boone.

Coaches: Dugout—Ray Knight; Hitting—Tom Robson; Pitching—Don Gullett; First Base—Jose Cardenal; Third Base-Tim Foli; Bullpen—Tom Hume.

Medical, Training

Medical Director: Dr. Tim Kremchek.

Head Trainer: Mark Mann. **Assistant Trainer:** Lonnie Soloff. **Assistant Trainer:** Nick Kenney. **Strength and Conditioning Coach:** Carlo Alvarez.

Bob Boone

Player Development

Director, Player Development: Tim Naehring. **Assistant to Director, Player Development:** Grant Griesser. **Senior Advisor:** Chief Bender. **Administrative Coordinator, Player Development:** Lois Hudson.

Roving Coordinators: Freddie Benavides (infield), Sammy Ellis (pitching), Rod McCray (outfield/baserunning), Leon Roberts (hitting). **Roving Hitting Instructors:** Mike Easler, Jim Hickman.

Director, Dominican Player Development: Jose Baez.

General Manager, Gulf Coast League: Trish Bardi. **Minor League Medical Coordinator:** Mark Farnsworth. **Strength/Conditioning Coordinator:** Unavailable. **Equipment Manager:** Tim Williamson.

Farm System

Class	Farm Team	League	Manager	Coach(es)	Pitching Coach
AAA	Louisville	International	Dave Miley	Adrian Garrett	Mack Jenkins
AA	Chattanooga	Southern	Phillip Wellman	G. Grall/A. Powell	Bill Moloney
High A	Potomac	Carolina	Jayhawk Owens	Jamie Dismuke	Larry Pierson
Low A	Dayton	Midwest	Donnie Scott	Billy White	Jaime Garcia
Rookie	Billings	Pioneer	Rick Burleson	Jay Sorg	Ed Hodge
Rookie	Sarasota	Gulf Coast	Edgar Caceres	B. Williams/M. Davalillo	Jeff Gray
Rookie	Reds	Dominican	Frank Laureano	Victor Franco	Manuel Solano
Rookie	Reds	Venezuela	Jose Villa	Unavailable	Unavailable

Scouting

Telephone: (513) 765-7000. **FAX:** (513) 765-7799.

Assistant General Manager/Director, Scouting: Leland Maddox. **Director, Scouting Administration:** Wilma Mann. **Scouting/Administrative Assistant:** Paul Pierson.

Professional Scouts: Jason Angel (Glen Allen, VA), Jeff Barton (Higley, AZ), Gregory McClain (Oakland, CA), Bip Roberts (San Ramon, CA), Michael Williams (Valley Village, CA).

Regional Crosscheckers: East—Jim Thrift (Sarasota, FL); Central—Jim Gonzales (San Antonio, TX); West—Butch Baccala (Weimar, CA).

Scouting Supervisors: Terry Abbott (Orlando, FL), Jeff Barton (Higley, AZ), Howard Bowens (Tacoma, WA), John Brickley (Melrose, MA), Rex De la Nuez (Burbank, CA), Jerry Flowers (Baton Rouge, LA), Jimmy Gonzales (San Antonio, TX), Mike Keenan (Chicago, IL), Craig Kornfeld (Rancho Santa Margarita, CA), Steve Kring (Charlotte, NC), Steve Mondile (Wenonah, NJ), Tom Severtson (Denver, CO), Perry Smith (Charlotte, NC), Brian Wilson (Albany, TX), Greg Zunino (Cape Coral, FL).

Leland Maddox

Director, International Scouting: Jorge Oquendo (Aguadilla, PR).

International Scouts: Oswaldo Alvarez (Mexico), Kevin Carcamo (Panama), Felix Delgado (Venezuela), Orlando Granda (Brazil), Michael Hartman (Oak Park, MI), Tony Jordan (Charlotte, NC), Min Lee (Korea), Victor Mateo (Dominican), Rafael Nava (Venezuela), Juan Rodriquez (Colombia).

CLEVELAND INDIANS

Telephone, Address

Office Address: Jacobs Field, 2401 Ontario St., Cleveland, OH 44115. **Telephone:** (216) 420-4200. **FAX:** (216) 420-4396. **Website:** www.indians.com.

Ownership

Owner, President: Larry Dolan.

Vice President, General Counsel: Paul Dolan.

BUSINESS OPERATIONS

Executive Vice President, Business: Dennis Lehman. **Senior Director, Human Resources:** Sara Lehrke.

Manager, Spring Training: Jerry Crabb.

Finance

Senior Vice President, Finance/Chief Financial Officer: Ken Stefanov.

Controller: Sarah Taylor. **Senior Director, Information Systems:** Dave Powell. **Director, Planning, Analysis/Reporting:** Rich Dorffer. **Manager, Accounting:** Karen Menzing.

Larry Dolan

Marketing, Merchandising

Vice President, Sales: Jon Starrett. **Director, Corporate Marketing:** Chris Previte. **VP, Marketing/Broadcasting:** Valerie Arcuri. **Manager, Publications/Graphic Design:** Bernadette Repko. **Manager, Brand Development/Special Events:** Dan Foust. **Manager, Broadcast Operations:** Steve Warren. **Manager, Promotions/Broadcasting:** Alex Slemc.

VP, Merchandising/Licensing: Jayne Churchmack. **Merchandise Manager:** Carol Schultz. **Buyers, Retail:** Iris Delgado, Karen Fox. **Retail Controller:** Marjorie Ruhl. **District Managers:** Joanne Kahr, Marie Patten.

Public Relations, Communications

Telephone: (216) 420-4350. **FAX:** (216) 420-4396.

Vice President, Public Relations: Bob DiBiasio.

Director, Media Relations: Bart Swain. **Manager, Media Relations/Administration:** Susie Giuliano. **Manager, Media Relations:** Curtis Danburg. **Coordinator, Media Relations:** Jeff Sibel. **Press Box Supervisor:** John Krepop.

Coordinator, Public Relations: Angela Brdar.

Director, Community Relations: Latisha James. **Director, Cleveland Indians Charities:** Melissa Zapanta. **Coordinator, Cleveland Indians Charities:** Stephanie Hierro. **Manager, Community Relations:** John Carter.

Stadium Operations

Vice President, Ballpark Operations: Jim Folk. **Manager, Ballpark Operations:** Mike DeCore. **Manager, Building Maintenance:** Chris Donahoe. **Manager, Field Maintenance:** Brandon Koehnke. **Manager, Safety Services:** Greg Baeppler.

PA Announcers: Duane Robinson, Bob Tayak. **Official Scorers:** Hank Kozloski, Rick Rembielak, Chuck Murr.

Ticketing

Telephone: (216) 420-4240, (216) 420-4487. **FAX:** (216) 420-4481.

Director, Ticket Services: Michael Thom. **Manager, Ticket System/Development:** Gail Liebenguth. **Manager, Public Sale:** Susan Leslie. **Manager, Vault/Processing:** Ann Gaertner. **Director, Ticket Sales:** Jim Willits. **Manager, Ticket Sales:** Larry Abel.

Travel, Clubhouse

Director, Team Travel: Mike Seghi.

Home Clubhouse/Equipment Manager: Tony Amato. **Assistant Home Clubhouse/Equipment Manager:** Tommy Foster. **Visiting Clubhouse Manager:** Cy Buynak. **Manager, Equipment Acquisition/Distribution:** Jeff Sipos.

General Information

Home Dugout: Third Base. **Playing Surface:** Grass.

Team Colors: Navy blue, red and silver.

Player Representative: John McDonald.

Mark Shapiro

BASEBALL OPERATIONS

Telephone: (216) 420-4200. **FAX:** (216) 420-4321.

Executive Vice President, General Manager: Mark Shapiro. **Assistant GMs:** Chris Antonetti, Neal Huntington.

Director, Player Personnel: Steve Lubratich. **Special Advisor, Baseball Operations:** Karl Kuehl. **Special Assistants, Baseball Operations:** Tim Belcher, Robby Thompson.

Director, Baseball Administration: Wendy Hoppel. **Executive Administrative Assistants, Baseball Operations:** Marlene Lehky, Barbara Lessman. **Senior Coordinator, Baseball Systems:** Dan Mendlik. **Sport Psychologist/Director, Psychological Services:** Dr. Charles Maher.

Major League Staff

Manager: Eric Wedge.

Coaches: Bench—Buddy Bell; Pitching—Mike Brown; Batting—Eddie Murray; First Base—Jeff Datz; Third Base—Joel Skinner; Bullpen—Luis Isaac.

Medical, Training

Medical Director: Dr. Louis Keppler.

Head Trainer: Paul Spicuzza. **Assistant Trainer:** Rick Jameyson. **Strength/Conditioning Coach:** Tim Maxey. **Director, Rehabilitation:** Jim Mehalik.

Eric Wedge

Player Development

Telephone: (216) 420-4308. **FAX:** (216) 420-4321.

Director, Player Development: John Farrell. **Assistant Director, Player Development:** Ross Atkins. **Administrative Assistant:** Joan Pachinger. **Coordinator, Cultural Development:** Lino Diaz.

Sport Psychology Assistant: John Couture. **Nutrition Consultant:** Jackie Berning.

Field Coordinator: Tim Tolman. **Coordinators:** Al Bumbry (outfield/baserunning), Johnny Goryl (defense), Joe Hughes (strength/conditioning), Dave Miller (pitching), Derek Shelton (hitting).

Field Coordinator, Latin America: Minnie Mendoza. **Field Coordinator, Venezuela:** Rouglas Odor.

Farm System

Class	Farm Team	League	Manager	Coach	Pitching Coach
AAA	Buffalo	International	Marty Brown	Carlos Garcia	Carl Willis
AA	Akron	Eastern	Brad Komminsk	Mike Sarbaugh	Terry Clark
High A	Kinston	Carolina	Torey Lovullo	Lou Frazier	Steve Lyons
Low A	Lake County	South Atlantic	Luis Rivera	Wayne Kirby	Tony Arnold
Short-Season	Mahoning Valley	New York-Penn	Ted Kubiak	Chris Bando	Ken Rowe
Rookie	Burlington	Appalachian	Rouglas Odor	Jack Mull	Ruben Niebla
Rookie	Indians I	Dominican	Felix Fermin	J. Urena/V.Veras	Juan Jimenez
Rookie	Indians	Venezuelan	Henry Centeno	Jose Stela	Angel Hernandez

Scouting

Telephone: (216) 420-4309. **FAX:** (216) 420-4321.

Assistant GM, Scouting Operations: John Mirabelli. **Assistant Director, Scouting:** Brad Grant.

Director, Professional Scouting/Major League Scout: DeJon Watson (Phoenix, AZ). **Assistant Director, Professional Scouting:** Mike Hazen.

Professional Scouts: Rodney Davis (Glendale, AZ), Robyn Lynch (Randolph, NJ), Dave Malpass (Huntington Beach, CA), Don Poplin (Norwood, NC), Jonathan Story (Melbourne, FL).

Special Assignment Scout: Chuck Tanner (New Castle, PA).

National Crosschecker: Jim Olander (Tucson, AZ). **Free-Agent Supervisors:** Southeast—Jerry Jordan (Kingsport, TN). Northeast—Chuck Ricci (Myersville, MD). Midwest—Ken Stauffer (Katy, TX). West Coast—Paul Cogan (Rocklin, CA).

John Mirabelli

Full-Time Area Scouts: Doug Baker (Fallbrook, CA), Scott Barnsby (Hermitage, TN), Keith Boeck (Chandler, AZ), Henry Cruz (Fajardo, PR), Mike Daly (Kansas City, MO), Jim Gabella (Deltona, FL), Chris Jefts (Redondo Beach, CA), Don Lyle (Sacramento, CA), Bob Mayer (Somerset, PA), Scott Meaney (Humble, TX), Tim Moore (Greenville, NC), Les Pajari (Duluth, MN), Phil Rossi (Jessup, PA), Matt Ruebel (Oklahoma City, OK), Bill Schudlich (Dearborn, MI), Jason Smith (Long Beach, CA), Shawn Whalen (Vancouver, WA).

Director, International Scouting: Rene Gayo. **Director, Dominican Operations:** Winston Llenas (Dominican Republic) **Latin America Supervisors:** Luis Aponte (Venezuela), Josue Herrera (Dominican Republic), Nelson Davila (Dominican Republic).

COLORADO ROCKIES

Telephone, Address

Office Address: 2001 Blake St., Denver, CO 80205. **Telephone:** (303) 292-0200. **FAX:** (303) 312-2116. **Website:** www.coloradorockies.com.

Ownership

Operated by: Colorado Rockies Baseball Club, Ltd.

Chairman, Chief Executive Officer: Jerry McMorris. **Vice Chairmen:** Charles Monfort, Richard Monfort. **Executive Assistant to Vice Chairmen:** Patricia Penfold.

BUSINESS OPERATIONS

President: Keli McGregor. **Executive Assistant to President:** Terry Douglass.

Senior Vice President, Business Operations: Greg Feasel. **Assistant to Senior VP:** Marcia McGovern.

Senior Director, Personnel/Administration: Elizabeth Stecklein. **Director, Information Systems:** Bill Stephani.

Finance

Senior VP/Chief Financial Officer: Hal Roth. **Assistant to Senior VP/Chief Financial Officer:** Tammy Vergara.

Jerry McMorris

VP, Finance: Michael Kent. **Senior Director, Accounting:** Gary Lawrence. **Payroll Administrator:** Phil Emerson. **Accountants:** Jane Stammer, Matt Vinnola. **Assistant, Finance Department:** Janet Glant.

Marketing, Sales

Senior Director, Corporate Sales: Marcy English Glasser. **Account Executives:** Shayne Cotner, William Kreidler, Derrek Patrick, Paula Swanson-Dorr. **Coordinator, Corporate Sales:** Kari Anderson.

Senior Director, Promotions/Broadcasting: Alan Bossart. **Assistant to Senior Director, Promotions/Broadcasting:** Kathy Wilson.

Coordinator, Promotions: Jason Fleming. **Coordinator, Broadcasting/Video Services:** Brian Ives. **Assistant, Broadcasting/Video Services:** Dan Storey.

Senior Director, Community/Retail Operations: Jim Kellogg. **Assistant to Senior Director, Community/Retail Operations:** Kelly Hall. **Manager, Community Affairs:** Stacy Schafer. **Coordinator, Community Affairs:** Antigone Vigil. **Coordinator, Publications:** Mike Kennedy. **Manager, Coors Field Receiving/Distribution Center:** Steve Tomlinson.

Public Relations, Communications

Telephone: (303) 312-2325. **FAX:** (303) 312-2319.

Senior Director, Communications/Public Relations: Jay Alves. **Assistant to Senior Director, Communications/Public Relations:** Irma Thumim.

Coordinators, Communications/Public Relations: Billy Witter, Brendan McNicholas.

Stadium Operations

Vice President, Ballpark Operations: Kevin Kahn.

Director, Coors Field Administration/Development: Dave Moore. **Manager, Ballpark Services:** Mary Beth Benner. **Director, Guest Services:** Steven Burke. **Scheduling/Payroll Assistant:** Katie Kraskey.

Director, Security: Don Lyon. **Director, Engineering/Facilities:** James Wiener. **Manager, Engineering:** Randy Carill. **Manager, Facilities:** Dan Olsen. **Manager, Youth Sports Development:** Sean McGraw.

Head Groundskeeper: Mark Razum. **Assistant Head Groundskeeper:** Jose Gonzalez.

PA Announcer: Kelly Burnham. **Official Scorers:** Dave Einspahr, Jack Rose.

Ticketing

Telephone: (303) 762-5437, (800) 388-7625. **FAX:** (303) 312-2115.

Vice President, Ticket Operations/Sales: Sue Ann McClaren. **Senior Director, Ticket Operations/Development:** Kevin Fenton. **Director, Ticket Operations/Finances:** Kent Hakes. **Assistant Director, Vault:** Scott Donaldson. **Manager, Ticket Processing:** Eric O'Leary.

Senior Director, Ticket Sales/Advertising: Jill Roberts. **Coordinator, Advertising:** Angela Keenan. **Director, Ticket Services/Spring Training Business Operations:** Chuck Javernick. **Director, Group Sales:** Jeff Spector. **Director, Season Tickets:** Jeff Benner. **Assistant Director, Ticket Services:** Cindy Ibarra. **Supervisor, Ticket Services:** Michael Bishop.

Travel, Clubhouse

Director, Major League Operations: Paul Egins.

Clubhouse/Equipment Manager: Dan McGinn. **Visiting Clubhouse Manager:** Keith Schulz. **Video Coordinator:** Mike Hamilton.

General Information

Home Dugout: First Base. **Playing Surface:** Grass.
Team Colors: Purple, black and silver.
Player Representative: Unavailable.

Dan O'Dowd

BASEBALL OPERATIONS

Telephone: (303) 292-0200. **FAX:** (303) 312-2320.

Executive Vice President/General Manager: Dan O'Dowd. **Assistant to Executive VP/GM:** Adele Armagost. **Director, Baseball Administration:** Thad Levine.

Major League Staff

Manager: Clint Hurdle.

Coaches: Bench—Jamie Quirk; Pitching—Bob Apodaca; Hitting—Duane Espy; First Base—Dave Collins; Third Base—Sandy Alomar Sr.; Bullpen—Rick Mathews; Strength—Brad Andress.

Medical, Training

Medical Director: Dr. Richard Hawkins. **Club Physicians:** Dr. Michael Curtin, Dr. Allen Schreiber, Dr. Douglas Wyland. **Physical Therapist:** Mike Allen.

Head Trainer: Tom Probst. **Assistant Trainer:** Keith Dugger. **Rehabilitation Coordinator:** Scott Gehret.

Clint Hurdle

Player Development

Telephone: (303) 292-0200. **FAX:** (303) 312-2320.

Director, Player Personnel: Bill Geivett. **Assistant Director, Player Development:** Marc Gustafson. **Assistant to Director, Player Development:** Jody Ross.

Roving Instructors: Mike Gallego (infield), Scott Gehret (rehab), Jimmy Johnson (hitting), Brian Jordan (strength/conditioning), Fred Kendall (catching), Jim Wright (pitching).

Farm System

Class	Farm Team	League	Manager	Coach	Pitching Coach
AAA	Colorado Springs	Pacific Coast	Rick Sofield	Alan Cockrell	Bob McClure
AA	Tulsa	Texas	Marv Foley	Theron Todd	Bo McLaughlin
High A	Visalia	California	Stu Cole	Don Reynolds	Jim Bennett
Low A	Asheville	South Atlantic	Joe Mikulik	Darron Cox	Mike Arner
Short season	Tri-City	Northwest	Ron Gideon	Fred Ocacio	Mike Snyder
Rookie	Casper	Pioneer	P.J. Carey	Tony Diaz	Richard Palacios
Rookie	Rockies	Dominican	Mauricio Gonzalez	Edison Lora	Pablo Paredes
Rookie	Rockies	Venezuela	Maurio Mendez	Unavailable	Dilson Torres

Scouting

Telephone: (303) 292-0200. **FAX:** (303) 312-2320.

Director, Scouting: Bill Schmidt. **Assistant Director:** Coley Brannon.

Special Assistants to General Manager: Pat Daugherty (Aurora, CO), Marcel Lachemann (Penryn, CA), Kasey McKeon (Stoney Creek, NC).

Major League Scout: Will George (Woolwich Township, NJ). **Professional Scouts:** Mike Berger (Oakmont, PA), Jack Gillis (Sarasota, FL), Joe McDonald (Lakeland, FL), Art Pontarelli (Cranston, RI), Tom Wheeler (Martinez, CA).

Special Assignment Scouts: Dave Holliday (Coalgate, OK), Terry Wetzel (Overland Park, KS).

National Crosschecker: Danny Montgomery (Charlotte, NC). **Regional Supervisors:** Midwest—Ty Coslow (Louisville, KY); West—Bo Hughes (Sherman Oaks, CA); Northeast—Mike Garlatti (Edison, NJ).

Bill Schmidt

Full-Time Area Scouts: Todd Blyleven (Orange, CA), John Cedarburg (Fort Myers, FL), Scott Corman (Lexington, KY), Dar Cox (Frisco, TX), Mike Day (Dallas, GA), Jeff Edwards (Houston, TX), Billy Eppler (Los Alamitos, CA), Mike Ericson (Glendale, AZ), Orsino Hill (Des Moines, IA), Bert Holt (Visalia, CA), Greg Hopkins (Beaverton, OR), Damon Iannelli (Brandon, MS), Jay Matthews (Charlotte, NC), Sean O'Connor (Natick, MA), Jorge de Posada (Rio Piedras, PR), Ed Santa (Powell, OH), Gary Wilson (Sacramento, CA).

Scouts: Norm DeBriyn (Fayetteville, AR), Don Lindeberg (Anaheim, CA), Dave McQueen (Bossier City, LA).

Director, Latin America Operations: Rolando Fernandez. **Coordinator, Pacific Rim Scouting:** Kent Blasingame (Fountain Hills, AZ).

International Scouts: Phil Allen (Australia), Dario Arias (Dominican Republic), Francisco Cartaya (Venezuela), Felix Feliz (Dominican Republic), Cristobal Giron (Panama), Jorge Moreno (Dominican Republic).

DETROIT TIGERS

Telephone, Address

Office Address: 2100 Woodward Ave., Detroit, MI, 48201. **Telephone:** (313) 471-2000. **FAX:** (313) 471-2138. **Website:** www.detroittigers.com.

Ownership

Operated by: Detroit Tigers, Inc.

Owner: Mike Ilitch.

President, Chief Executive Officer: Dave Dombrowski. **Special Assistants to President:** Al Kaline, Willie Horton. **Executive Assistant to President/CEO:** Patricia McConnell.

Senior Vice President: Jim Devellano.

Mike Ilitch

BUSINESS OPERATIONS

Senior Vice President, Business Affairs: Jim Stapleton.

Senior Vice President, Marketing/Communications: Mike Veeck.

Executive Assistant to Senior VPs, Business Affairs/Marketing and Communications: Tamara Mitin.

Finance

Vice President, Chief Financial Officer: Steve Quinn. **Assistant to VP, Finance/CFO:** Peggy Bacarella.

Director, Finance: Jennifer Orow. **Manager, Accounting/Finance:** Karla Felton.

Senior Director, Information Technology: Cole Stewart. **Director, Human Resources:** Lara Juras.

Senior Manager, Payroll Administration: Maureen Kraatz. **Payroll/Human Resources Clerk:** Stephanie Duchane.

Mail Services: Paul Kustra. **Switchboard Operator:** Janet Ware.

Marketing, Communications

Vice President, Public Affairs/Strategic Planning: Elaine Lewis.

Director, Community Relations: Celia Bobrowsky. **Coordinator, Community Relations:** Corey Bell.

Sales, Marketing

Vice President, Sales/Service: Michael Dietz.

Manager, Corporate Sales: John Wolski. **Account Executive:** Jim Spadafore. **Corporate Sales Coordinator:** Jill Chamberlain.

Director, Marketing: Ellen Hill-Zeringue. **Coordinator, Marketing:** Ed Sanchez.

Director, Promotions/In-Game Entertainment: Joel Scott. **Coordinator, Promotions/Special Events:** Eli Bayless.

Vice President, Corporate Suite Sales and Services/Hospitality: Charles Jones. **Manager, Suite Sales/Service:** Scot Pett.

Director, Fantasy Camps: Jerry Lewis. **Coordinator, Fantasy Camps:** Paige Grzelak.

Media Relations, Communications

Telephone: (313) 471-2114. **FAX:** (313) 471-2138.

Senior Director, Communications: Cliff Russell. **Manager, Media Relations:** Jim Anderson. **Coordinator, Media Relations:** Brian Britten. **Media Relations Assistant:** Rick Thompson. **Media Relations/Broadcast Manager:** Molly Light.

Park Operations

Vice President, Park Operations: John Pettit.

Head Groundskeeper: Heather Nabozny. **Senior Managers, Park Operations:** Jodi Engler, Ed Goward. **Manager, Park Operations:** Jason Warzecha. **Managers, Ballpark Services:** Allan Carrise, DuShawn Brandy. **Manager, Event Staff Operations:** Sue Gerten.

Scoreboard/Video Producer: Scott Fearncombe.

Ticketing

Telephone: (313) 471-2255.

Vice President, Ticket Sales/Service: Bob Raymond.

Manager, Ticket Sales: Steve Fox. **Manager, Group Sales:** Dwain Lewis.

Senior Director, Ticket Services: Ken Marchetti. **Administrator, Ticket Systems:** Sandra Sobotka.

Travel, Clubhouse

Traveling Secretary: Bill Brown

Manager, Home Clubhouse: Jim Schmakel. **Assistant Manager, Visiting Clubhouse:** John Nelson. **Clubhouse Assistant:** Tyson Steele.

Ballpark Video Operations: Jeremy Kelch.

General Information

Home Dugout: Third Base. **Playing Surface:** Grass.

Team Colors: Navy blue, orange and white.

Player Representative: Damion Easley.

Dave Dombrowski

BASEBALL OPERATIONS

Telephone: (313) 471-2096. **FAX:** (313) 471-2099.

General Manager: Dave Dombrowski.

Vice President/Assistant GM: Al Avila. **Special Assistant to GM:** Al Hargesheimer. **Administrative Assistant to GM/Assistant GM:** Eileen Surma.

VP, Player Personnel: Scott Reid.

Director, Baseball Administration: Dave Miller. **Assistant, Baseball Operations/Foreign Affairs:** Ramon Pena. **Assistant, Baseball Operations:** Mike Smith. **International Liaison/Instructor:** Joe Alvarez.

VP/Baseball Legal Counsel: John Westhoff.

Major League Staff

Manager: Alan Trammell.

Coaches: Bench—Kirk Gibson; Pitching—Bob Cluck; Batting—Bruce Fields; First Base—Mick Kelleher; Third Base—Juan Samuel; Bullpen—Lance Parrish.

Medical, Training

Team Physicians: Dr. Kyle Anderson, Dr. David Collon, Dr. Michael Workings. **Director, Medical Services/Head Athletic Trainer:** Kevin Rand. **Assistant Athletic Trainer:** Steve Carter. **Administrative Assistant, Training/Conditioning:** Barbara McNulty. **Strength/Conditioning Coach:** Dennie Taft.

Alan Trammell

Player Development

Telephone, Detroit: (313) 471-2096. **FAX:** (313) 471-2099. **Telephone, Florida Operations:** (863) 686-8075. **FAX:** (863) 688-9589.

Director, Player Development: Steve Boros. **Director, Minor League Operations:** Rick Bennett. **Administrative Assistant, Minor Leagues:** Audrey Zielinski.

Field Coordinator: Glenn Ezell. **Roving Instructors:** Keith Burns (strength/conditioning), Bill Freehan (catching), Gene Roof (outfield/baserunning), Rafael Landestoy (infield), Jon Matlack (pitching), Brian Peterson (performance enhancement), Tom Runnells (hitting), Doug Teter (medical coordinator).

Farm System

Class	Farm Team	League	Manager	Coach	Pitching Coach
AAA	Toledo	International	Larry Parrish	Leon Durham	Jeff Jones
AA	Erie	Eastern	Kevin Bradshaw	Matt Martin	Britt Burns
High A	Lakeland	Florida State	Gary Green	Basilio Cabrera	Joe Boever
Low A	West Michigan	Midwest	Phil Regan	Barbaro Garbey/Brent Gates	A.J. Sager
Short season	Oneonta	New York-Penn	Randy Ready	Joe Alvarez	Bill Monbouquette
Rookie	Lakeland	Gulf Coast	Howard Bushong	Scott Makarewicz	Greg Sabat
Rookie	Tigers	Dominican	Felix Nivar	M. de la Mota/F. Peniche	Marcos Aguasivas

Scouting

Telephone: (313) 471-2098. **FAX:** (313) 471-2099.

Director, Scouting: Greg Smith. **Administrative Assistant, Scouting:** Gwen Keating.

Major League Scouts: Scott Bream (Phoenix, AZ), Dick Egan (Phoenix, AZ), Al Hargesheimer (Arlington Heights, IL), Mike Russell (Gulf Breeze, FL), Jeff Wetherby (Wesley Chapel, FL).

National Crosschecker: Rob Guzik (Latrobe, PA). **Regional Supervisors:** Southeast—Steve Williams (Raleigh, NC). Northeast—Pat Murtaugh (Lafayette, IN). Midwest—Bob Cummings (Oak Lawn, IL). West—Jeff Malinoff (Lopez, WA).

Area Scouts: Bill Buck (Manassas, VA), Vaughn Calloway (Detroit, MI), Jerome Cochran (South Holland, IL), Tim Grieve (Katy, TX), Mike Herbert (Chicago, IL), Tom Hinkle (Atascadero, CA), Joe Hodges (Rockwood, TN), Lou Laslo (Maumee, OH), Mark Monahan (Saline, MI), Steve Nichols (Mount Dora, FL), Frank Paine (Hartsdale, NY), Brian Reid (Phoenix, AZ), Derrick Ross (Newington, CT), Reuben Smiley (Los Angeles, CA), Steve Taylor (Shawnee, OK), Clyde Weir (Portland, MI), Rob Wilfong (San Dimas, CA), Gary York (Rome, GA), Harold Zonder (Louisville, KY).

Greg Smith

Assistant, Baseball Operations/Foreign Affairs: Ramon Pena (Dominican Republic).

FLORIDA MARLINS

Telephone, Address

Office Address: Pro Player Stadium, 2267 Dan Marino Blvd. Miami, FL 33056. **Telephone:** (305) 626-7400. **FAX:** (305) 626-7428. **Website:** www.floridamarlins.com.

Ownership

Chairman, Chief Executive Officer/Managing General Partner: Jeffrey Loria. **Vice Chairman:** Joel Mael.

President: David Samson. **Executive Assistant to President:** Beth McConnville.

Special Assistants to President: Andre Dawson, Tony Perez.

Jeffrey Loria

BUSINESS OPERATIONS

Director, Human Resources: Ana Hernandez. **Administrator, Benefits:** Ruby Mattei. **Manager, Business Information Systems:** Ken Strand. **Manager, Telecommunications:** Sam Mora.

Office Services: Karl Heard. **Senior Receptionist:** Kathy Lanza. **Receptionist:** Christina Fredericks.

Finance

Senior Vive President, Chief Financial Officer: Michel Bussiere. **VP, Finance:** Susan Jaison. **Executive Assistant to VP, Finance:** Robin Deffler.

Manager, Accounting: Barry LaChance. **Administrator, Payroll:** Carolina Calderon. **Senior Staff Accountant:** Nancy Hernandez.

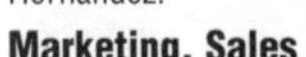

Marketing, Sales

Vice President, Sales: Sean Flynn.

Manager, Hispanic Sales/Marketing: Juan Martinez. **Manager, Marlins en Miami Store:** Alberto Calimano.

Vice President, Sales: Dale Hendricks. **Executive Assistant to VP/Sales:** Liza Rodriguez. **Director, Corporate Sales:** Brendan Cunningham. **Coordinator, Corporate Sales:** Rachel Bell. **Corporate Sales Executives:** Hector Nolasco, Kraig O'Barski, Anthony Tome. **Corporate Sales Assistant:** Judy Cavanaugh.

Manager, Executive Affairs: Michelle Azel. **Manager, Community Affairs:** Angela Smith. **Coordinator, Community Affairs:** Bruce Thompson. **Community Affairs Assistant:** Jennifer Smith.

Executive Director, Florida Marlins Community Foundation: Nancy Olson. **Foundation Assistant:** Kelly Semrad.

Media Relations, Communications

Telephone: (305) 626-7429. **FAX:** (305) 626-7302.

Vice President, Communications/Broadcasting: P.J. Loyello.

Director, Media Relations: Steve Copses. **Coordinator, Media Information:** Andrew Feirstein. **Administrative Assistant, Media Relations:** Maria Armella. **Director, Broadcasting:** Suzanne Rayson. **Coordinator, Broadcasting:** Alex Bentley.

Stadium Operations

Director, Creative Services/In-Game Entertainment: Leslie Riguero. **Manager, In-Game Entertainment:** Gary Levy. **Creative Services Coordinator:** Robert Vigon. **Producer, Game Presentation:** Matt Hagood. **Production Assistant:** Wayne Ricker. **Video Archivist:** Chris Myers. **Organist:** Lowery Ballew.

PA Announcer: Dick Sanford. **Official Scorer:** Ron Jernick.

Ticketing

Telephone: (305) 930-4487. **FAX:** (305) 626-7432.

Director, Season/Group Sales: Pat McNamara. **Manager, Season/Group Sales:** Marty Mulford.

Account Executives: Bob Eckert, Jeremy Fullerton, Orestes Hernandez, David Krakower, Jose Ramos, Darren Ressler. **Customer Service Manager:** Spencer Linden. **Customer Service Representative:** David Argote.

Travel, Clubhouse

Director, Team Travel: Bill Beck. **Video Coordinator:** Cullen McRae.

Equipment Manager: John Silverman. **Assistant Equipment Manager:** Mark Brown. **Visiting Clubhouse Manager:** Bryan Greenberg. **Assistant Clubhouse Attendant:** Michael Hughes. **Assistant, Visiting Clubhouse:** Michael King.

General Information

Home Dugout: First Base. **Playing Surface:** Grass.
Team Colors: Teal, black and white.
Player Representative: Mike Lowell.

Larry Beinfest

BASEBALL OPERATIONS

Telephone: (305) 626-7400.

Senior Vice President, General Manager: Larry Beinfest. **Vice President, Assistant GM:** Mike Hill.

Senior VP/Director, International Operations: Fred Ferreira. **Vice President, Player Personnel:** Dan Jennings. **Special Assistant to GM/Professional Scout:** Orrin Freeman.

Manager, Baseball Information Systems: David Kuan. **Executive Assistant, Baseball Operations:** Rita Filbert.

Major League Staff

Manager: Jeff Torborg.

Coaches: Dugout—Jeff Cox; Pitching—Brad Arnsberg; Batting—Bill Robinson; First Base—Perry Hill; Third Base—Ozzie Guillen; Bullpen—Pierre Arsenault.

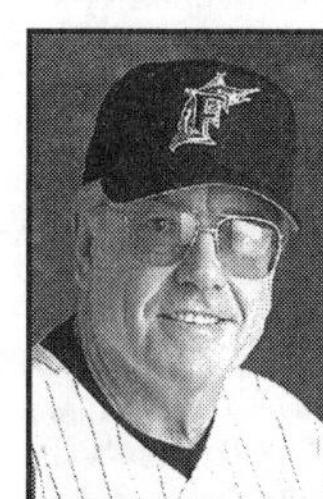
Jeff Torborg

Medical, Training

Club Physician: Dr. Daniel Kanell. **Head Trainer:** Sean Cunningham. **Assistant Trainer:** Mike Kozak. **Strength/Conditioning Coach:** Dale Torborg.

Player Development

VP, Player Development and Scouting/Assistant General Manager: Jim Fleming.

Director, Player Development: Marc DelPiano. **Executive Assistant, Player Development/Scouting:** Yobanna Coll. **Assistant, Baseball Operations:** Brian Chattin. **Director, Minor League Operations/Scouting Administration:** Cheryl Evans.

Field Coordinator: Doug Davis. **Coordinators:** Paul Fournier (strength/conditioning, rehabilitation), John Mallee (hitting), Wayne Rosenthal (pitching), Randy Whisler (infield). **Equipment Manager:** Mark Brown.

Farm System

Class	Farm Team	League	Manager	Coach	Pitching Coach
AAA	Albuquerque	Pacific Coast	Dean Treanor	Matt Stark	Gary Buckels
AA	Carolina	Southern	Tracy Woodson	Matt Raleigh	Tom Signore
A	Jupiter	Florida State	Luis Dorante	Paul Sanagorski	Gil Lopez
A	Greensboro	South Atlantic	Steve Phillips	Tom Donovan	Scott Mitchell
Short season	Jamestown	New York-Penn	Benny Castillo	Brian Hyde	Reid Cornelius
Rookie	Jupiter	Gulf Coast	Tim Cossins	Johnny Rodriguez	Jeff Schwarz
Rookie	Marlins	Dominican	Unavailable	Unavailable	Unavailable

Scouting

Telephone: (305) 626-7400. **FAX:** (305) 626-7294.

Director, Scouting: Stan Meek (Norman, OK). **Assistant Director, Scouting:** Gregg Leonard.

Major League Scout: Tommy Thompson (La Mesa, CA). **Advance Scout:** Joe Moeller (Manhattan Beach, CA).

National Crosschecker: Joe Jordan (Blanchard, OK). **Regional Crosscheckers:** East—Mike Cadahia (Miami Springs, FL); Central—Dennis Cardoza (Denton, TX); West—Scott Goldby (Yuba City, CA).

Area Scouts: Alex Agostino (St. Bruno, Quebec), Matt Anderson (Williamsport, PA), Carlos Berroa (San Juan, PR), Darrell Brown (Edmond, OK), John Cole (Lake Forest, CA), Robby Corsaro (Adelanto, CA), David Crowson (College Station, TX), Dave Dangler (Northport, AL), Hal DeBerry (Richland, WA), Scot Engler (Aurora, IL), John Hughes (Walnut Creek, CA), John Martin (Tampa, FL), Joel Matthews (Concord, NC), Bob Oldis (Iowa City, IA), Steve Payne (Barrington, RI), Joel Smith (Macon, GA), Scott Stanley (Phoenix, AZ).

Stan Meek

Assistant Director, International Operations: Randy Kierce. **International Supervisors:** Carlos Acosta (Venezuela), Jesus Campos (Dominican Republic), A.B. Jesurun (Europe).

International Scouts: Wilmer Adrian (Venezuela), Evelio Areas (Nicaragua), Greg Burrows (Bahamas), Aristides Bustamonte (Panama/Costa Rica), Nelson Castro (Venezuela), Terry Chinnery (British West Indies), Enrique Constante (Dominican Republic), Nathan Davison (Australia), Scott Dawes, (Australia), Rene Garcia (Venezuela), Carlos Guzman (Guatemala), Ton Hofstede (Holland), Go Ikeda (Japan/Korea/Taiwan), Brian Lombard (South Africa), Roberto Marquez (Venezuela), Pedro Martinez (Venezuela), Willie Marugo (Colombia), Spencer Mills (Netherlands), Romulo Oliveros (Venezuela), Rene Picota (Panama), Carlos Rivero (Venezuela), Carlos Sanchez (Venezuela), Craig Stoves (Australia), Jaime Torres (Venezuela), Francis Wanga (Bonaire).

HOUSTON ASTROS

Drayton McLane

Telephone, Address

Office Address: Minute Maid Park, Union Station, 501 Crawford, Suite 400, Houston, TX 77002. **Mailing Address:** P.O. Box 288, Houston, TX 77001. **Telephone:** (713) 259-8000. **FAX:** (713) 259-8981. **E-Mail Address:** fanfeedback@astros.mlb.com. **Website:** www.astros.com.

Ownership

Operated by: McLane Group, LP.

Chairman, Chief Executive Officer: Drayton McLane.

Board of Directors: Drayton McLane, Bob McClaren, Sandy Sanford, Webb Stickney.

BUSINESS OPERATIONS

President, Business Operations: Pam Gardner. **Executive Assistants:** Eileen Colgin, Tracy Faucette.

Finance

Senior Vice President, Finance: Unavailable.

Accounts Receivable: Mary Ann Bell. **Accounts Payable:** Irene Dumenil. **Manager, Payroll:** Ruth Kelly.

Marketing, Sales

Vice President, Sales/Broadcasting: Jamie Hildreth. **VP, Market Development:** Rosi Hernandez. **VP, Marketing:** Andrew Huang. **Director, Advertising Sales:** Alicia Nevins. **Coordinator, Sales/Promotions:** Yvette Casares. **Manager, Marketing Operations:** Phoenix Mak. **Coordinator, Broadcast Network Traffic:** Christine O'Beirne.

Public Relations, Communications

Telephone: (713) 259-8900. **FAX:** (713) 259-8981.

Senior Vice President, Operations/Communications: Rob Matwick.

Director, Media Relations: Warren Miller. **Assistant Directors, Media Relations:** Lisa Ramsperger, Jimmy Stanton.

VP, Community Development: Marian Harper. **Director, Business Communications:** Todd Fedewa. **Manager, Community Development:** Rita Suchma.

Director, Information Technology: Brad Bourland. **Director, Information Systems Administration:** Doug Swan.

Stadium Operations

Vice President, Special Events: Kala Sorenson. **Senior Director, Engineering:** Bobby Forrest. **Director, Ballpark Entertainment:** Kirby Kander. **Assistant Director, Ballpark Entertainment:** Brock Jessel. **Director, Telecommunications/Broadcast Technology:** Mike Cannon. **Director, Customer Service:** Michael Kenny. **Conference Center/Special Events Sales:** Jill McCormick. **Manager, Minute Maid Park Tours:** Jennifer Ammel. **Manager, Safety/Security:** Chris White.

Director, Field Operations: Darren Seybold. **Assistant Groundskeeper:** Colin Castille.

PA Announcer: Bob Ford. **Official Scorers:** Rick Blount, Ivy McLemore, David Matheson, Trey Wilkinson.

Ticketing

Telephone: (713) 259-8500. **FAX:** (713) 259-8326.

Vice President, Ticket Services: John Sorrentino.

Director, Ticket Operations: Marcia Coronado. **Director, Box Office Operations:** Bill Cannon. **Manager, Sales Support:** Matt Rogers. **Manager, Premium Sales:** Andrea Levine-Spier.

Travel, Clubhouse

Director, Baseball Administration: Barry Waters. **Equipment Manager:** Dennis Liborio. **Assistant Equipment Managers:** Carl Schneider, Butch New. **Visiting Clubhouse Manager:** Steve Perry. **Umpires/Clubhouse Assistant:** Chuck New.

General Information

Home Dugout: First Base. **Playing Surface:** Grass.

Team Colors: Brick red, sand beige and black.

Player Representative: Gregg Zaun.

Gerry Hunsicker

BASEBALL OPERATIONS

Telephone: (713) 259-8000. **FAX:** (713) 259-8600.

President, Baseball Operations: Tal Smith.

General Manager: Gerry Hunsicker. **Director, Baseball Administration:** Barry Waters. **Administrative Assistant:** Beverly Rains.

Major League Staff

Manager: Jimy Williams.

Coaches: Bench—John Tamargo; Pitching—Burt Hooton; Batting—Harry Spilman; First Base—Jose Cruz Sr.; Third Base—Gene Lamont; Bullpen—Mark Bailey.

Medical, Training

Medical Director: Dr. David Lintner.

Head Trainer: Dave Labossiere. **Assistant Trainer:** Rex Jones. **Strength and Conditioning Coach:** Dr. Gene Coleman.

Jimy Williams

Player Development

Telephone: (713) 259-8922. **FAX:** (713) 259-8600.

Assistant General Manager/Director, Player Development: Tim Purpura.

Director, Minor League Administration: David Gottfried. **Minor League Administrator:** Jay Edmiston. **Administrative Assistant:** Monica Shak. **Assistant, Baseball Operations:** Carlos Perez.

Field Coordinator: Tom Wiedenbauer. **Minor League Coordinators:** Dewey Robinson (pitching), Jim Pankovits (defense), Pat Roessler (hitting).

Coordinator, Training/Conditioning: Pete Fagan. **Coordinator, Strength/Conditioning:** Nathan Lucero

Farm System

Class	Farm Team	League	Manager	Coach	Pitching Coach
AAA	New Orleans	Pacific Coast	Chris Maloney	Gary Gaetti	Jim Hickey
AA	Round Rock	Texas	Jackie Moore	S. Berry/S. Owen	Joe Slusarski
High A	Salem	Carolina	John Massarelli	Pete Rancont	Stan Boroski
Low A	Lexington	South Atlantic	Russ Nixon	Gregg Langbehn	Charley Taylor
Short season	Tri-City	New York-Penn	Ivan DeJesus	Brian Dayett	Bill Ballou
Rookie	Martinsville	Appalachian	Jorge Orta	Marc Ronan	Jack Billingham
Rookie	Astros	Dominican	Rafael Ramirez	Rodney Linares	Rick Aponte
Rookie	Astros	Venezuela	Mario Gonzalez	Omar Lopez	Oscar Padron

Scouting

Telephone: (713) 259-8921. **FAX:** (713) 259-8600.

Director, Scouting: David Lakey.

Assistant Director, Scouting: Pat Murphy. **Administrative Assistant, Scouting:** Traci Dearing.

Coordinator, Professional Scouting: Paul Ricciarini (Pittsfield, MA).

Advance Scout: Fred Nelson (Richmond, TX). **Special Assignment Scout:** Bob Skinner (San Diego, CA).

Major League Scouts: Stan Benjamin (Greenfield, MA), Gordy MacKenzie (Fruitland Park, FL), Walt Matthews (Texarkana, TX), Paul Weaver (Phoenix, AZ).

Professional Scouts: Kimball Crossley (Providence, RI), Gene DeBoer (Brandon, WI), Joe Pittman (Columbus, GA), Tom Romenesko (Santee, CA), Scipio Spinks (Houston, TX).

National Supervisor: Joe Robinson (Olivette, MO), Tad Slowik (Arlington Heights, IL).

Regional Supervisors: East—Gerry Craft (St. Clairsville, OH); Southwest/West—Ralph Bratton (Dripping Springs, TX), Southeast/Central—Kevin Burrell (Sharpsburg, GA).

David Lakey

Area Scouts: Chuck Carlson (Orlando, FL), Doug Deutsch (Costa Mesa, CA), Ellis Dungan (Pensacola, FL), James Farrar (Shreveport, LA), David Henderson (Edmond, OK), Brian Keegan (Matthews, NC), Bob King (La Mesa, CA), Mike Maggart (Penn Yan, NY), Jerry Marik (Chicago, IL), Tom McCormack (University City, MO), Mel Nelson (Highland, CA), Rusty Pendergrass (Houston, TX), Bob Poole (Redwood City, CA), Mike Rosamond (Madison, MS), Mark Ross (Tucson, AZ), Nick Venuto (Massillon, OH), Gene Wellman (Danville, CA).

Special Assistant to GM, International Scouting/Development: Andres Reiner. **Coordinator, Venezuela:** Pablo Torrealba. **Director, Dominican Operations:** Julio Linares.

KANSAS CITY ROYALS

Telephone, Address

Office Address: One Royal Way, Kansas City, MO 64129. **Mailing Address:** P.O. Box 419969, Kansas City, MO 64141. **Telephone:** (816) 921-8000. **FAX:** (816) 921-1366. **Website:** www.kcroyals.com.

Ownership

Operated by: Kansas City Royals Baseball Club, Inc.

Chairman/Chief Executive Officer: David Glass. **President:** Dan Glass. **Board of Directors:** Ruth Glass, Don Glass, Dayna Martz, Julia Irene Kauffman, Herk Robinson.

Executive Vice President, Chief Operating Officer: Herk Robinson. **Executive Administrative Assistant:** Ginger Salem.

David Glass

BUSINESS OPERATIONS

Senior Vice President, Business Operations: Mark Gorris. **Executive Administrative Assistant:** Cindy Hamilton.

Finance

Vice President, Finance/Administration: Dale Rohr. **Senior Administrative Assistant:** Janet Milone.

Senior Director/Controller: John Luther. **Manager, Accounting:** Sean Ritchie. **Manager, Ticket Office/Concession Accounting:** Lisa Kresha. **Accounting Coordinators:** Sarah Kosfeld, Shelley Wilson.

Director, Payroll Benefits/Human Resources: Tom Pfannenstiel. **Manager, Human Resources:** Lynne Elder. **Payroll Administrator:** Margaret Willits. **Human Resources Assistant:** Megan Barnes.

Senior Director, Information Systems: Jim Edwards. **Manager, Programming/Systems Analyst:** Becky Randall.

Marketing, Community Relations

Vice President, Sales/Marketing: Charlie Seraphin. **Senior Administrative Assistant:** Emily Rand. **Graphic Designer:** Vic Royal.

Director, Community Relations: Shani Tate. **Coordinator, Community Relations:** Ben Aken.

Senior Director, Sales Development: Mike Phillips. **Director, Corporate Sponsorship Sales:** Michele Kammerer. **Senior Account Executive, Corporate Sponsorship Sales:** Joy Gibson. **Account Executive, Corporate Sponsorship Sales:** Daniel Cooper.

Director, Promotions: Kim Hillix. **Manager, Promotions/Group Sales:** Curt Nelson. **Coordinator, Game Entertainment/Productions:** Chris DeRuyscher. **Mascot Coordinator:** Byron Shores.

Public Relations, Communications

Telephone: (816) 921-8000. **FAX:** (816) 921-5775.

Vice President, Broadcasting/Public Relations: David Witty. **Director, Broadcast Services/Royals Alumni:** Fred White. **Director, Media Relations:** Aaron Babcock. **Manager, Broadcast/Media Services:** Chris Stathos. **Manager, Media Relations:** Lora Grosshans.

Ballpark Operations

Director, Event Operations/Guest Relations: Chris Richardson. **Administrative Assistant:** Velda Valentine.

Director, Groundskeeping/Landscaping: Trevor Vance. **Manager, Groundskeeping:** Unavailable. **Landscape Assistant:** Anthony Bruce.

Manager, Stadium Engineering: Chris Frank. **Supervisor, Stadium Operations Technicians:** Marty Roe.

Director, Stadium Operations: Rodney Lewallen. **Manager, Stadium Administration:** Judy Van Meter. **Coordinator, Telephone Services:** Kathy Butler. **Coordinator, Mail Services:** Larry Garrett.

Manager, Stadium Services: Johnny Williams.

PA Announcer: Dan Hurst. **Official Scorers:** Del Black, Alan Eskew.

Ticketing

Telephone: (816) 921-8000. **FAX:** (816) 504-4144.

Director, Ticket Operations: Lance Buckley. **Director, Ticket Services:** Chris Darr. **Director, Season Ticket Services:** Joe Grigoli. **Coordinator, Season Tickets:** Mary Lee Martino. **Manager, Call Center:** NuKrisha Lee. **Coordinators, Ticket Office:** Betty Bax, Jacque Tschirhart.

Director, Season/Group Ticket Sales: Rick Amos. **Manager, Lancer Program:** Lyndy Luther. **Manager, Group Sales:** Scott Wadsworth. **Account Executives:** Carl Keenan, Jeff Miller, Rachelle Smith.

Travel, Clubhouse

Manager, Team Travel: Jeff Davenport.

Equipment Manager: Mike Burkhalter. **Visiting Clubhouse Manager:** Chuck Hawke.

General Information

Home Dugout: First Base. **Playing Surface:** Grass.

Team Colors: Royal blue and white.

Player Representative: Jason Grimsley.

Allard Baird

BASEBALL OPERATIONS

Telephone: (816) 921-8000. **FAX:** (816) 924-0347.

Senior Vice President/General Manager: Allard Baird.

Senior Advisor to GM: Art Stewart. **Assistant to GM:** Brian Murphy. **Special Assistants to GM:** Pat Jones, Frank White.

Vice President, Baseball Operations: George Brett. **Manager, Baseball Operations:** Jin Wong.

Manager, Major League Operations: Karol Kyte.

Major League Staff

Manager: Tony Pena.

Coaches: Bench—Bob Schaefer; Pitching—John Cumberland; Batting—Jeff Pentland; First Base—Luis Silverio; Third Base—John Mizerock; Bullpen—Tom Gamboa.

Medical, Training

Team Physician: Dr. Steven Joyce. **Associate Physicians:** Dr. Mark Bernhardt, Dr. Dan Gurba, Dr. Thomas Phillips, Dr. Charles Rhoades.

Head Trainer: Nick Swartz. **Assistant Trainer:** Frank Kyte. **Strength/Conditioning Coordinator:** Chris Mihlfeld. **Assistant Strength/Conditioning Coordinator:** Jason Estep.

Tony Pena

Minor Leagues

Telephone: (816) 921-8000. **FAX:** (816) 924-0347.

Assistant General Manager, Player Personnel: Muzzy Jackson. **Manager, Minor League Operations:** Shaun McGinn. **Coordinator, Minor League Operations:** Mindy Torrey.

Supervisor, Field Operations: Joe Jones. **Coordinator, Instruction:** Jeff Garber. **Roving Instructors:** Ron Clark (infield), Andre David (hitting), Jason Estep (strength/conditioning), Dale Gilbert (rehabilitation), Brian Poldberg (catching).

Latin American Strength/Conditioning Coordinator: Ryan Stoneberg. **Minor League Equipment Coordinator:** Johnny O'Donnell.

Farm System

Class	Farm Team	League	Manager	Coach	Pitching Coach
AAA	Omaha	Pacific Coast	Mike Jirschele	Kevin Long	Dave LaRoche
AA	Wichita	Texas	Keith Bodie	Nelson Liriano	Larry Carter
High A	Wilmington	Carolina	Billy Gardner Jr.	Terry Bradshaw	Bill Slack
Low A	Burlington	Midwest	Joe Szekely	Patrick Anderson	Tom Burgmeier
Rookie	Surprise I	Arizona	Kevin Boles	Pookie Wilson	Jose Bautista
Rookie	Surprise II	Arizona	Lloyd Simmons	Tom Poquette	Royal Clayton
Rookie	Royals	Dominican	Julio Bruno	J. Tartabull/M. Garcia	Oscar Martinez

Scouting

Telephone: (816) 921-8000. **FAX:** (816) 924-0347.

Senior Director, Scouting: Deric Ladnier. **Manager, Scouting Administration:** Linda Smith.

Professional Scouts: Brannon Bonifay (Stuart, FL), Louie Medina (Phoenix, AZ), Earl Winn (Bowling Green, KY).

Special Assignment Scouts: Carlos Pascual (Miami, FL), John Wathan (Blue Springs, MO).

Regional Supervisors: Jeff McKay (Walterville, OR), Junior Vizcaino (Wake Forest, NC), Dennis Woody (Pensacola, FL).

Area Supervisors: Bob Bishop (San Dimas, CA), Mike Brown (Chandler, AZ), Jason Bryans (Detroit, MI), Steve Connelly (Massapequa, NY), Albert Gonzalez (Coral Springs, FL), Spencer Graham (Greensboro, NC), Phil Huttmann (Overland Park, KS), Gary Johnson (Costa Mesa, CA), Cliff Pastornicky (Venice, FL), Johnny Ramos (Carolina, PR), Sean Rooney (Caldwell, NJ), Max Semler (Lake City, FL), Chet Sergo (Houston, TX), Greg Smith (Davenport, WA), Keith Snider (Stockton, CA), Gerald Turner (Euless, TX), Brad Vaughn (Griffithville, AR), Jon Weil (Atlanta, GA), Mark Willoughby (Hammond, LA).

Deric Ladnier

Coordinator, Latin America Operations: Albert Gonzalez (Coral Springs, FL). **Dominican Scouting Supervisor:** Pedro Silveiro. **Venezuelan Scouting Supervisor:** Juan Carlos Indriago.

International Scouts: Julio Alcala (Colombia), Wilmer Castillo (Venezuela), Luis Cordoba (Panama), Jose Guarache (Venezuela), Daurys Nin (Dominican Republic), Mike Randall (South Africa), Rafael Vasquez (Dominican Republic).

LOS ANGELES DODGERS

Bob Daly

Telephone, Address

Office Address: 1000 Elysian Park Ave., Los Angeles, CA 90012. **Telephone:** (323) 224-1500. **FAX:** (323) 224-1269. **Website:** www.dodgers.com.

Ownership

Operated by: Los Angeles Dodgers, Inc. **Principal Owner:** News Corp.

Board of Directors: Bob Daly, Bob Graziano, Gary Ehrlich, Sam Fernandez.

Managing Partner/Chairman, Chief Executive Officer: Bob Daly. **President, Chief Operating Officer:** Bob Graziano.

Senior Vice President: Tommy Lasorda. **Senior VP, General Counsel:** Sam Fernandez. **Associate Counsel:** Christine Chrisman. **Secretary, Legal:** Irma Duenas.

BUSINESS OPERATIONS

Human Resources and Administration

Vice President, Human Resources/Administration: David Walkley. **Finance**

Vice President, Chief Financial Officer: Cristine Hurley. **Director, Finance/Accounting:** Amanda Shearer. **Manager, Payroll:** Rebecca Aguilar. **Chief Information Officer/Director, Management Information Systems:** Mike Mularky.

Sales, Advertising, Client Services

Vice President, Sales: Sergio del Prado. **Assistant Director, Group/Season Sales:** Lisa Johnson.

Director, Sponsorship Sales: Jason Klein. **Director, Sponsorship Sales:** Karen Marumoto.

Manager, Advertising/Special Events: Dan Brewster.

Public Relations, Communications

Senior Vice President, Communications: Derrick Hall. **VP, External Affairs:** Tommy Hawkins.

Director, Public Relations: John Olguin. **Assistant Director, Public Relations:** Josh Rawitch. **Manager, Baseball Information:** Dave Tuttle. **Supervisor, Broadcast/Publications:** Paul Gomez.

Director, Community Affairs: Erikk Aldridge. **Director, Community Relations:** Don Newcombe.

Stadium Operations

Vice President, Stadium Operations: Doug Duennes.

Director, Stadium Operations: Lon Rosenberg. **Executive VP, Fox Sports Enterprise:** Gary Ehrlich. **Assistant Director, Stadium Operations:** Charles Taylor. **Assistant Director, Stadium Operations/Turf and Grounds:** Eric Hansen.

PA Announcer: Unavailable. **Official Scorers:** Don Hartack, Gordie Verrell. **Organist:** Nancy Bea Hefley.

Ticketing

Telephone: (323) 224-1471. **FAX:** (323) 224-2609.

Director, Ticket Operations: Billy Hunter. **Director, Special Projects:** Debra Duncan. **Assistant Director, Ticket Operations:** Chris Furmento.

Travel, Clubhouse

Director, Team Travel: Shaun Rachau. **Home Clubhouse Managers:** Dave Dickinson, Mitch Poole. **Visiting Clubhouse Manager:** Jerry Turner.

General Information

Home Dugout: Third Base. **Playing Surface:** Grass.

Team Colors: Dodger blue, red and white.

Player Representative: Unavailable.

Dan Evans

BASEBALL OPERATIONS

Telephone: (323) 224-1500, (323) 224-1463. **FAX:** (323) 224-1269.

Executive Vice President, General Manager: Dan Evans. **VP, Assistant GM:** Kim Ng. **Special Assistant to GM:** Jeff Schugel. **Special Assistant to GM/Advance Scout**: Mark Weidemaier (Tierre Verde, FL).

Senior VP, Baseball Operations: Dave Wallace. **Senior Advisors, Baseball Operations:** Joe Amalfitano, John Boles. **Assistant, Baseball Operations:** A.J. Preller.

Major League Staff

Manager: Jim Tracy.

Coaches: Bench—Jim Riggleman; Pitching—Jim Colborn; Hitting—Jack Clark; First Base—John Shelby; Third Base—Glenn Hoffman; Bullpen—Jim Lett; Coach—Manny Mota.

Medical, Training

Team Physicians: Dr. Frank Jobe, Dr. Michael Mellman, Dr. Ralph Gambardella, Dr. Herndon Harding.

Head Trainer: Stan Johnston. **Assistant Trainer:** Matt Wilson. **Physical Therapist:** Pat Screnar. **Strength/Conditioning Coach:** Todd Clausen. **Muscle Therapist:** Bill Le Seur.

Player Development

Telephone: (323) 224-1431. **FAX:** (323) 224-1359.

Director, Player Development: Bill Bavasi. **Assistant Director, Player Development:** Luchy Guerra. **Player Development Adminstrator:** Chris Haydock. **Administrative Assistant:** Cathy Carey. **Roving Instructor:** Del Crandall.

Vice President, Spring Training/Minor League Facilities: Craig Callan.

Director, Dominican Operations: Pablo Peguero. **Field Coordinator, Dominican Operations:** Luis Montalvo. **Supervisor, Venezuelan Operations:** Camilo Pasqual.

Director, Asian Operations: Acey Kohrogi. **Manager, Japanese Affairs:** Scott Akasaki. **Manager, Korean Affairs:** Curtis Jung. **Manager, Chinese/Taiwanese Affairs:** Vincent Liao.

Field Coordinator: Terry Collins. **Assistant Field Coordinator:** Joe Vavra.

Roving Coordinators: Mark Brewer (pitching), Jon Debus (catching), Rick Honeycutt (pitching), Bob Mariano (hitting), Kevin McNair (physical development), Gene Richards (outfield/baserunning), Jerry Royster (infield), Jason Steere (physical therapy).

Jim Tracy

Farm System

Class	Farm Team	League	Manager	Coach	Pitching Coach
AAA	Las Vegas	Pacific Coast	John Shoemaker	George Hendrick	Shawn Barton
AA	Jacksonville	Southern	Dino Ebel	Pat Harrison	Marty Reed
High A	Vero Beach	Florida State	Scott Little	Brian Traxler	Ken Howell
Low A	South Georgia	South Atlantic	Dann Bilardello	Garey Ingram	Roger McDowell
Rookie	Ogden	Pioneer	Travis Barbary	Juan Bustabad	Tim Kelly
Rookie	Vero Beach	Gulf Coast	Luis Salazar	Tony Harris	George Culver
Rookie	Dodgers I	Dominican	Pedro Mega	Rafael Rijo	Victor Baez
Rookie	Dodgers II	Dominican	Antonio Bautista	Jose Mejia	Hector Eduardo

Scouting

Director, Amateur Scouting: Logan White. **Director, Professional Scouting:** Matt Slater. **Director, International Scouting**: Rene Francisco. **Administrator, Scouting:** Tim Kelly. **Administrator, Baseball Operations:** Ellen Harrigan. **Coordinator, Scouting Operations**: Bill McLaughlin.

Senior Scouting Advisor: Don Welke.

Major League Scouts: Al LaMacchia (San Antonio, TX), Carl Loewenstine (Hamilton, OH).

Professional Scouting Coordinator: Terry Reynolds (Altadena, CA). **Professional Scouts:** Dan Freed (Lexington, IL), Vance Lovelace (Tampa, FL), Ron Rizzi (Joppa, MD).

Special Advisor to Amateur Scouting Director/National Crosschecker: Gib Bodet (San Clemente, CA). **National Crosschecker:** Tim Hallgren (Roanoke, TX).

Regional Supervisors: East—John Barr (Palm City, FL); Midwest—Gary Nickels (Naperville, IL); West Coast—Tom Thomas (Phoenix, AZ).

Logan White

Area Scouts: Doug Carpenter (Jupiter, FL), James Chapman (Delta, B.C.), Bobby Darwin (Cerritos, CA), Scott Groot (Mission Viejo, CA), Mike Hankins (Lee's Summit, MO), Clarence Johns (Hattiesburg, MS), Calvin Jones (Henderson, NV), Hank Jones (Vancouver, WA), Lon Joyce (Spartanburg, SC), John Kosciak (Milford, MA), Marty Lamb (Lexington, KY), Mike Leuzinger (Mansfield, TX), James Merriweather (Los Angeles, CA), Bill Pleis (Parrish, FL), Clair Rierson (Frederick, MD), Mark Sheehy (Sacramento, CA), Chris Smith (Montgomery, TX), Brian Stephenson (Phoenix, AZ), Mitch Webster (Great Bend, KS).

International Scouts: Mike Brito (Mexico), Pat Kelly (Pacific Rim), Camilo Pascual (Venezuela).

MILWAUKEE BREWERS

Ulice Payne

Telephone, Address

Office Address: Miller Park, One Brewers Way, Milwaukee, WI 53214. **Telephone:** (414) 902-4400. **FAX:** (414) 902-4053. **Website:** www.milwaukeebrewers.com.

Ownership

Operated by: Milwaukee Brewers Baseball Club.

Board of Directors: John Canning, Francis Croak, Mitchell Fromstein, Michael Grebe, Wendy Selig-Prieb, Richard Strup, Harris Turer. **Chairman:** Wendy Selig-Prieb.

President, Chief Executive Officer: Ulice Payne, Jr. **Executive Assistant to President:** Diane Valenti.

BUSINESS OPERATIONS

Executive Vice President: Rick Schlesinger; **VP, General Counsel:** Tom Gausden. **Assistant General Counsel:** Eugene Randolph. **Manager, Corporate Partner Services:** Patty Harsch. **Manager, Human Resources:** Mariela Garcia-Danet. **Executive Assistant, Business Operations:** Adela Reeve.

Finance

Senior Vice President, Chief Financial Officer: Bob Quinn Jr. **Director, Purchasing:** Charlotte Tisdale. **Director, Management Information Systems:** Dan Krautkramer. **Systems Administrator:** Tristan Benson.

Manager, Budget/Special Projects: Carol McInnes. **Payroll Coordinator/Accountant:** Brian Krueger. **Staff Accountants:** Wes Seidel, Vicki Wise. **Supervisor, Accounts Receivable/Payable:** Cathy Schwab.

Coordinator, Telecommunications: Tonya Powell.

Corporate Affairs, Sales/Marketing

Vice President, Marketing: Laurel Prieb. **VP, Community/Government Affairs:** Lynn Sprangers.

Directors, Corporate Sales: Matt Groniger, Amy Welch. **Manager, Corporate Sales/Promotions:** Katie Moakley. **Account Executive:** Jaclyn Habeck. **Administrative Assistant, Marketing:** Lisa Brzeski.

Public Relations, Communications

Telephone: (414) 902-4400. **FAX:** (414) 4053.

Director, Publications: Mario Ziino. **Publications Assistant:** Robbin Barnes.

Director, Media Relations: Jon Greenberg. **Assistant Director, Media Relations:** Jason Parry. **Manager, Media Relations:** Nicole Saunches. **Team Photographers:** Scott Paulus, Jill Stolt.

Director, Broadcasting: Tim Van Wagoner. **Manager, Broadcasting:** Aleta Mercer. **Director, Electronic Media Operations:** Mike Jakubowski. **Manager, Audio/Video Productions:** Deron Anderson.

Director, Community Relations: Leonard Peace. **Coordinator, Community Relations:** Patricia Ramirez.

Stadium Operations

Vice President, Stadium Operations: Richard Cox.

Director, Event Services: Steve Ethier. **Director, Grounds:** Gary Vanden Berg. **Manager, Grounds:** Raechal Volkening.

Coordinator, Guest Relations: Kristy Suworoff. **Manager, Stadium Control:** Dave Duernberger. **Director, Ballpark Engineering/Maintenance:** Russ Rutowski. **Electronic Media Engineer:** Walt Grenier. **Supervisor, Warehouse:** Patrick Rogo. **Supervisor, Maintenance:** James Broeker.

PA Announcer: Robb Edwards. **Official Scorers:** Tim O'Driscoll, Wayne Franke.

Ticketing

Telephone: (414) 902-4000. **FAX:** (414) 902-4100.

Vice President, Tickets/Advertising: Dean Rennicke, **Director, Ticket Services:** John Barnes. **Director, Ticket Sales:** Jim Bathey. **Director, Business Development/Suites:** Geoff Campion. **Manager, Season Ticket/Group Sales:** Chris Barlow. **Manager, Business Development/Hospitality:** Mike Harlan. **Administrative Assistant:** Irene Bolton. **Assistant Director, Ticket Services:** Nancy Jorgensen. **Manager, Ticket Services:** Scott Parsons. **Manager, Phone Center/Customer Service:** Glenn Kurylo. **Representative, Ticket Office Support Services:** Diane Schoenfeld. **Senior Account Executives:** Beau Bradle, Billy Friess, Bill Junker, Kara Kabitzke.

Travel, Clubhouse

Director, Team Travel: Dan Larrea.

Director, Clubhouse Operations/Equipment Manager: Tony Migliaccio. **Coordinator, Visiting Clubhouse:** Phil Rozewicz. **Assistant, Home Clubhouse:** Mike Moulder. **Coordinator, Umpires Room:** Duane Lewis.

General Information

Home Dugout: First Base. **Playing Surface:** Grass.

Team Colors: Navy blue, gold and white.

Player Representative: Unavailable.

Doug Melvin

BASEBALL OPERATIONS

Senior Vice President, General Manager: Doug Melvin. **Assistant GM:** Gord Ash.

Senior Special Assistant to GM: Larry Haney (Barboursville, VA). **Special Assistant to GM/Scouting:** Dick Groch (Marysville, MI).

Senior Administrator, Baseball Operations: Barb Stark.

Major League Staff

Manager: Ned Yost.

Coaches: Bench—Rich Dauer. Pitching—Mike Maddux; Batting—Butch Wynegar; First Base—Dave Nelson; Third Base—Rich Donnelly; Bullpen—Bill Castro.

Medical, Training

Head Team Physician: Dr. William Raasch. **Associate Team Physician:** Dr. Angelo Mattalino.

Head Trainer: Roger Caplinger. **Assistant Trainer/Coordinator, Strength and Conditioning:** Dan Wright. **Assistant Trainer:** Paul Anderson.

Ned Yost

Player Development

Telephone: (414) 902-4400. **FAX:** (414) 902-4059.

Special Assistant to GM/Player Development: Reid Nichols. **Assistant Director, Player Development:** Scott Martens. **Administrator, Minor Leagues:** Kate Geenen. **Administrative Assistant:** Amanda Klecker.

Field Coordinator: Ed Sedar. **Coordinators:** Dwight Bernard (pitching), Jim Skaalen (hitting), Richard Stark (trainers), Keith Wilson (strength/conditioning). **Roving Instructor:** Ed Romero (infield). **Equipment Manager:** J.R. Rinaldi. **Performance Enhancement Coordinator:** Dr. Jack Curtis.

Farm System

Class	Farm Team	League	Manager	Coach	Pitching Coach
AAA	Indianapolis	International	Cecil Cooper	Gaylen Pitts	Mike Caldwell
AA	Huntsville	Southern	Frank Kremblas	Sandy Guerrero	Stan Kyles
High A	High Desert	California	Tim Blackwell	Rich Morales	Bill Champion
Low A	Beloit	Midwest	Don Money	Unavailable	Rich Sauveur
Rookie	Helena	Pioneer	Ed Sedar	Andy Tomberlin	Mark Littell
Rookie	Phoenix	Arizona	Hector Torres	George McPherson	Steve Cline
Rookie	Brewers	Dominican	Mike Guerrero	A. Morillo/J. Martinez	Antonio Figueroa

Scouting

Telephone: (414) 902-4400. **FAX:** (414) 902-4059.

Director, Scouting: Jack Zduriencik. **Assistant Director, Scouting:** Tom Flanagan.

Advance Scout: Elanis Westbrooks (Houston, TX). **Special Assignment Scout:** David Wilder (Scottsdale, AZ).

Professional Scouts: Lary Aaron (Atlanta, GA), Hank Allen (Upper Marlboro, MD), Carl Blando (Sarasota, FL), Russ Bove (Apopka, FL), Ken Califano (Brookfield, WI), Dick Hager (Sunnyvale, CA), Alan Regier (Gilbert, AZ).

National Crosschecker: Larry Doughty (Leawood, KS). **Regional Crosscheckers:** Midwest—Tom Allison (Austin, TX); East Coast—Bobby Heck (Apopka, FL); West Coast—Ric Wilson (Chandler, AZ). Latin America—Epy Guerrero (Santo Domingo, DR).

Jack Zduriencik

Area Supervisors: Fernando Arango (Dania, FL), Tony Blengino (Magnolia, NJ), Jeff Brookens (Chambersburg, PA), Jeff Cornell (Lee's Summit, MO), Mike Farrell (Indianapolis, IN), Manolo Hernandez (Moca, PR), Brian Johnson (Avondale, AZ), Harvey Kuenn Jr. (New Berlin, WI), Justin McCray (Davis, CA), Ray Montgomery (Pearland, TX), Brandon Newell (Bellingham, WA), Larry Pardo (Miami, FL), Doug Reynolds (Tallahassee, FL), Corey Rodriguez (Hermosa Beach, CA), Bruce Seid (Aliso Viejo, CA), Jim Stevenson (Tulsa, OK), George Swain (Raleigh, NC).

Scouts: Edward Fastaia (Brooklyn, NY), Dick Foster (Otis, OR), Roger Janeaway (Englewood, OH), John Logan (Milwaukee, WI), Mike Rasdall (Colorado Springs, CO), Brad Stoll (Lawrence, KS).

International Scouts: Richard Clemons (Canada), Chris Miller (South Africa), John Viney (Australia).

MINNESOTA TWINS

Telephone, Address

Office Address: 34 Kirby Puckett Place, Minneapolis, MN 55415. **Telephone:** (612) 375-1366. **FAX:** (612) 375-7480. **Website:** www.twinsbaseball.com.

Ownership

Operated by: The Minnesota Twins.

Owner: Carl Pohlad. **Chairman, Executive Committee:** Howard Fox.

Executive Board: Jerry Bell, Kevin Cattoor, Carl Pohlad, Eloise Pohlad, James Pohlad, Robert Pohlad, William Pohlad, Kirby Puckett.

President, Minnesota Twins: Dave St Peter. **President, Twins Sports Inc:** Jerry Bell

BUSINESS OPERATIONS

Vice President, Operations: Matt Hoy. **VP, Human Resources/Diversity:** Raenell Dorn. **Coordinator, Human Resources:** Leticia Fuentes. **Administrative Assistant to President/Office Manager:** Joan Boeser.

Finance

Chief Financial Officer: Kip Elliott.

Carl Pohlad

Director, Financial Planning: Andy Weinstein. **Director, Financial Reporting:** Michelle Knuesel. **Payroll Manager:** Lori Beasley. **Accountant:** Jerry McLaughlin. **Accounts Payable:** Amy Fong.

Director, Information Systems: Wade Navratil. **Director, Network/Baseball Information Systems:** Jon Avenson. **PC Support Specialist:** Erik Vermeulen. **Programmer/Analyst:** Tony Persio.

Marketing, Sales

Vice President, Corporate Partnerships: Eric Curry.

VP, Marketing: Patrick Klinger. **Account Sales Executives:** Dan Craighead, Jeff Hibicke, Eric Hudson, Mike Leonard, Rob Malec, Chris Malek, Jason Stern. **Marketing Director, Advertising:** Nancy O'Brien. **Manager, Special Projects:** Denise Johnson. **Manager, Game Presentation:** Andy Price. **Manager, Sales Administration:** Beth Vail. **Managers, Corporate Sales:** Chad Jackson, Lori Peterson, Dick Schultz, Mark Zobel. **Manager, Client Services:** Bodie Rykken. **Coordinator, Client Services:** Jordan Gross.

Public Relations, Communications

Telephone: (612) 375-7471. **FAX:** (612) 375-7473.

Manager, Media Relations: Sean Harlin. **Assistant Manager, Media Relations:** Mike Herman. **Coordinator, Baseball Information:** Kristian Connolly.

Director, Communications: Brad Ruiter. **Director, Community Affairs:** Peter Martin. **Coordinator, Community Affairs:** Gloria Westerdahl. **Coordinator, Community Affairs/Youth Baseball:** Bryan Donaldson.

Stadium Operations

Director, Stadium Operations: Dave Horsman. **Manager, Stadium Operations:** Ric Johnson. **Manager, Special Events:** Heidi Sammon. **Manager, Security:** Dick Dugan.

PA Announcer: Bob Casey. **Official Scorer:** Tom Mee.

Ticketing

Telephone: (612) 338-9467, (800) 338-9467. **FAX:** (612) 375-7464.

Director, Ticket Sales: Scott O'Connell.

Director, Ticket Operations: Paul Froehle. **Manager, Box Office:** Mike Stiles. **Supervisor, Ticket Office:** Karl Dedenbach. **Coordinator, Ticket Office:** Mike Johnson. **Manager, Telemarketing:** Patrick Forsland.

Travel, Clubhouse

Traveling Secretary: Remzi Kiratli.

Equipment Manager: Jim Dunn. **Visitors Clubhouse:** Troy Matchan. **Internal Video Specialist:** Nyal Peterson.

General Information

Home Dugout: Third Base. **Playing Surface:** Artificial turf.

Team Colors: Burgundy, navy blue and white.

Player Representative: Denny Hocking.

Terry Ryan

BASEBALL OPERATIONS

Telephone: (612) 375-7484. **FAX:** (612) 375-7417.

Vice President, General Manager: Terry Ryan.

VP, Assistant GM: Bill Smith. **Assistant GM:** Wayne Krivsky. **Special Assistants to GM:** Larry Corrigan, Joe McIlvaine, Tom Kelly.

Director, Baseball Operations: Rob Antony. **Administrative Assistant, Major League Operations:** Juanita Lagos-Benson.

Major League Staff

Manager: Ron Gardenhire.

Coaches: Bench—Steve Liddle; Pitching—Rick Anderson; Batting—Scott Ullger; First Base—Jerry White; Third Base—Al Newman; Bullpen—Rick Stelmaszek.

Ron Gardenhire

Medical, Training

Club Physicians: Dr. Dan Buss, Dr. Veejay Eyunni, Dr. Tom Jetzer, Dr. John Steubs, Dr. Jon Hallberg.

Head Trainer: Jim Kahmann. **Assistant Trainer:** Rick McWane. **Strength and Conditioning Coach:** Randy Popple.

Player Development

Telephone: (612) 375-7488. **FAX:** (612) 375-7417.

Director, Minor Leagues: Jim Rantz. **Administrative Assistant, Minor Leagues:** Colleen Schroeder.

Field Coordinator: Joe Vavra. **Roving Instructors:** Jim Dwyer (hitting), Rick Knapp (pitching).

Farm System

Class	Farm Team	League	Manager	Coach	Pitching Coach
AAA	Rochester	International	Phil Roof	Mike Hart	Bobby Cuellar
AA	New Britain	Eastern	Stan Cliburn	Riccardo Ingram	Stu Cliburn
High A	Fort Myers	Florida State	Jose Marzan	Mike Tosar	Eric Rasmussen
Low A	Quad City	Midwest	Jeff Carter	Floyd Rayford	Gary Lucas
Rookie	Elizabethton	Appalachian	Ray Smith	Jeff Reed	Jim Shellenback
Rookie	Fort Myers	Gulf Coast	Rudy Hernandez	Jon Pont/Milt Cuyler	Steve Mintz
Rookie	Twins	Dominican	Frank Valdez	Maximo Ronbley	Andres Lopez
Rookie	Twins	Venezuela	Nelson Prada	Asdrubal Estrada	Ivan Arteaga

Scouting

Telephone: (612) 375-7477. **FAX:** (612) 375-7417.

Director, Scouting: Mike Radcliff (Overland Park, KS).

Administrative Assistant, Scouting: Brad Steil.

Special Assignment Scouts: Larry Corrigan (Fort Myers, FL), Cal Ermer (Chattanooga, TN), Dale McReynolds (Walworth, WI).

Major League Scout: Bill Harford (Chicago, IL). **Coordinator, Professional Scouting:** Vern Followell (Buena Park, CA). **Advance Scout:** Bob Hegman (Lee's Summit, MO).

Scouting Supervisors: East—Earl Frishman (Greensboro, NC); West—Deron Johnson (Sacramento, CA); Midwest—Joel Lepel (Plato, MN), Mike Ruth (Lee's Summit, MO).

Mike Radcliff

Area Scouts: Kevin Bootay (Sacramento, CA), Ellsworth Brown (Beason, IL), Marty Esposito (Hewitt, TX), Sean Johnson (Chandler, AZ), John Leavitt (Garden Grove, CA), Bill Lohr (Centralia, WA), Bill Mele (El Segundo, CA), Gregg Miller (Chandler, OK), Billy Milos (South Holland, IL), Tim O'Neil (Lexington, KY), Hector Otero (Trujillo Alto, PR), Mark Quimuyog (Lynn Haven, FL), Ricky Taylor (Hickory, NC), Brad Weitzel (Haines City, FL), Jay Weitzel (DuBois, PA), John Wilson (Hackettstown, NJ), Mark Wilson (Lindstrom, MN).

Director, International Scouting: Joe McIlvaine (Tuckahoe, NY).

International Scouts: Renato Anasagasti (Curacao), John Cortese (Italy), Austis Gibbs (Aruba), Gene Grimaldi (Europe), David Kim (South Korea), Jose Leon (Venezuela), Howard Norsetter (Australia, Europe), Yoshi Okamoto (Japan), Jim Ridley (Canada), Johnny Sierra (Dominican Republic), Koji Takahashi (Japan), David Yen (Taiwan).

MONTREAL EXPOS

Tony Tavares

Telephone, Address

Office Address: Olympic Stadium, 4549 Pierre-de-Coubertin Ave., Montreal, Quebec H1V 3N7. **Mailing Address:** P.O. Box 500, Station M, Montreal, Quebec H1V 3P2. **Telephone:** (514) 253-3434. **FAX:** (514) 253-8282. **Website:** www.montrealexpos.com.

Ownership

Operated by: Baseball Expos, LP.

President: Tony Tavares. **Executive Assistant:** Monique Chibok.

BUSINESS OPERATIONS

Executive Vice President, Business Affairs: Claude Delorme.

Sales, Marketing

Director, Ticket Sales: John DiTerlizzi; **Director, Promotions/Special Events:** Gina Hackl. **Director, Administration/Sales and Marketing:** Chantal Dalpe. **Producer, Scoreboard Operations:** Chantal Burnett. **Coordinator, Entertainment:** Jean-Simon Bibeau. **Coordinator, Special Events:** Martine Peters.

Media Relations, Communications

Director, Media Services: Monique Giroux. **Director, Baseball Information:** John Dever. **Coordinator, Media Relations:** Elias Makes. **Administrative Assistant:** Sina Gabrielli.

Stadium Operations

Director, Game Operations: Denis Pare. **General Manager, Space Coast Stadium:** Andy Dunn. **Assistant Director, Game Operations:** Stephane Mercier. **Director, Management Information System:** Yves Poulin. **Manager, Souvenirs:** Peggy O'Leary.

PA Announcer: Marc Leveille. **Official Scorers:** Serge Rivest, Michel Spinelli.

Ticketing

Director, Olympic Stadium Ticket Office: Frederique Brault.

Travel, Clubhouse

Coordinator, Team Travel/Conditioning: Rob McDonald.

Equipment Manager: Mike Wallace. **Visiting Clubhouse:** Matt Rosenthal.

General Information

Home Dugout: First Base. **Playing Surface:** Artificial turf.

Team Colors: Blue, red and white.

Player Representative: Brian Schneider.

Omar Minaya

BASEBALL OPERATIONS

Vice President, General Manager: Omar Minaya.
Assistant GM/Director, Baseball Administration: Tony Siegle. **Assistant to GM:** Dan Lunetta. **Administrative Assistant:** Marcia Schnaar.

Major League Staff

Manager: Frank Robinson.

Coaches: Dugout—Brad Mills; Pitching—Randy St. Claire; Batting—Tom McCraw; First Base/Outfield—Jerry Morales; Third Base/Infield—Manny Acta; Bullpen/Catchers—Bob Natal; Roving—Claude Raymond.

Frank Robinson

Medical, Training

Team Physician: Dr. Michael Thomassin. **Team Orthopedist:** Dr. Larry Coughlin.

Head Trainer: Ron McClain. **Assistant Trainer:** John Adam.

Player Development

Telephone: (514) 253-3434. **FAX:** (514) 253-8282.

Director, Player Development: Adam Wogan. **Assistant Director, Player Development:** Glenn Wilburn. **Coordinator, Minor League Administration:** Nick Manno.

Field Coordinator: Doug Sisson. **Roving Coordinators:** Tim Abraham (training, strength/conditioning), Frank Cacciatore (hitting), Mike McGowan (rehabilitation), Brent Strom (pitching).

Minor League Equipment/Clubhouse Manager: Dan Wallin.

Farm System

Class	Farm Team	League	Manager	Coach	Pitching Coach
AAA	Edmonton	Pacific Coast	Dave Huppert	Jose Castro	Tommy John
AA	Harrisburg	Eastern	Dave Machemer	Art Defreites	Charlie Corbell
High A	Brevard County	Florida State	Doug Sisson	Joe Marchese	Mark Grater
Low A	Savannah	South Atlantic	Joey Cora	Andy Skeels	Reggie Jackson
Short season	Vermont	New York-Penn	Dave Barnett	Steve Allyn	Craig Bjornson
Rookie	Melbourne	Gulf Coast	Bobby Henley	Jose Alguacil	Doug White
Rookie	Expos	Dominican	Unavailable	Elvis Herrera	Franklyn Bravo

Scouting

Director, Amateur Scouting: Dana Brown. **Director, Pro Scouting:** Lee MacPhail IV. **Coordinator, Scouting Operations:** Alex Anthopoulos.

Advance Scout: Jerry Terrell (Blue Springs, MO). **Professional Scouts:** Jack Bloomfield (San Diego, CA), Chris Bourjos (Scottsdale, AZ), Manny Estrada (Brandon, FL), Mike Toomey (Gaithersburg, MD), Rick Williams (St. Petersburg, FL).

National Crosschecker: Paul Tinnell (Cortez, FL). **Regional Crosschecker:** West Coast—Fred Mazuca (Tustin, CA).

Area Scouts: Anthony Arango (Los Angeles, CA), Ray Corbett (College Station, TX), Zack Hoyrst (Hattiesburg, MS), Larry Izzo (Deer Park, NY), Raymond Jackson (Ocala, FL), Doug McMillan (Shingle Springs, CA), Lance Nichols (Dodge City, KS), Delvy Santiago (Vega Alta, PR), Alex Smith (Abingdon, MD).

Dana Brown

Part-Time Scouts: Mike Alberts (Worcester, MA), Leslie Gonzalez (Arlington, TX), Wilmer Reid (Philadelphia, PA).

Director, Latin American Scouting/Development: Ismael Cruz. **Coordinator, Dominican Republic:** Sandi Rosaro.

NEW YORK METS

Telephone, Address

Office Address: 123-01 Roosevelt Ave., Flushing, NY 11368. **Telephone:** (718) 507-6387. **FAX:** (718) 507-6395. **Website:** www.mets.com.

Ownership

Operated by: Sterling Mets, LP.

Board of Directors: Fred Wilpon, Saul Katz, Jeff Wilpon, Marvin Tepper, Arthur Friedman, Michael Katz, David Katz, Tom Osterman, Richard Wilpon, Stuart Sucherman, Steve Greenberg.

Chairman, Chief Executive Officer: Fred Wilpon. **President:** Saul Katz. **Executive Vice President, Chief Operating Officer:** Jeff Wilpon.

BUSINESS OPERATIONS

Senior Vice President, Business Operations: David Howard.

VP, General Counsel: David Cohen.

Finance

Controller: Lenny Labita. **Director, Information Systems:** Dot Pope. **Chief Accountant:** Rebecca Mahadeva.

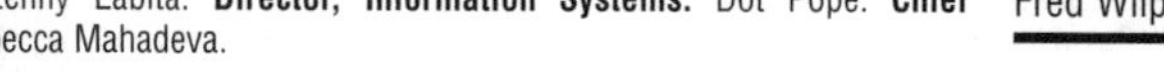

Fred Wilpon

Marketing, Sales

Vice President, Corporate Sales/Services: Paul Danforth.

Director, Marketing: Tina Bucciarelli. **Director, Marketing Productions:** Tim Gunkel.

Director, Promotions: Jim Plummer. **Manager, Publications:** Jill Grabill. **Director, Community Outreach:** Jill Knee. **Coordinator, Community Outreach:** Chris Brown.

Media Relations

Telephone: (718) 565-4330. **FAX:** (718) 639-3619.

Vice President, Media Relations: Jay Horwitz. **Manager, Media Relations:** Shannon Dalton. **Manager, Corporate/Media Services:** Stella Fiore. **Media Relations Specialists:** Dave Campanaro, Chris Tropeano, Ethan Wilson.

Stadium Operations

Vice President, Facilities: Karl Smolarz. **Director, Stadium Operations:** Kevin McCarthy. **Manager, Stadium Operations:** Sue Lucchi.

Manager, Field Operations: Mike Williams.

PA Announcer: Roger Luce. **Official Scorers:** Joe Donnelly, Howie Karpin, Bill Shannon, Jordan Sprechman.

Ticketing

Telephone: (718) 507-8499. **FAX:** (718) 507-6396.

Vice President, Ticket Sales/Services: Bill Ianniciello.

Director, Ticket Operations: Dan DeMato. **Assistant Director, Ticket Sales Development:** Jamie Ozure. **Manager, Corporate Ticket Sales:** Marc Steir. **Director, Group/Ticket Sales Services:** Thomas Fersch. **Manager, Group/Ticket Sales Services:** Mark Phillips.

Travel, Clubhouse

Equipment Manager, Associate Travel Director: Charlie Samuels. **Assistant Equipment Manager:** Vinny Greco. **Visiting Clubhouse Manager:** Tony Carullo. **Video Editor:** Joe Scarola.

General Information

Home Dugout: First Base. **Playing Surface:** Grass.

Team Colors: Blue and orange.

Player Representative: Vance Wilson.

Steve Phillips

BASEBALL OPERATIONS

Telephone: (718) 565-4315. **FAX:** (718) 507-6391.

Senior Vice President, General Manager: Steve Phillips.

Special Assistants to GM: Fred Wright, Harry Minor. **Executive Assistant to GM:** Denise Morris.

Major League Staff

Manager: Art Howe.

Coaches: Dugout—Don Baylor. Batting—Denny Walling; Pitching—Vern Ruhle; First Base/Outfield—Gary Pettis; Third Base/Infield—Matt Galante; Bullpen—Rick Waits.

Medical, Training

Team Physician: Dr. Andrew Rokito. **Associate Team Physician:** Dr. Joe Bosco.

Head Trainer: Scott Lawrenson. **Assistant Trainer:** Mike Herbst. **Coordinator, Strength/Conditioning:** Rick Slate. **Assistant Coordinator, Fitness/Conditioning:** Jose Vazquez.

MARC LEVINE/NY METS

Art Howe

Player Development

Telephone: (718) 565-4302. **FAX:** (718) 205-7920.

Senior Assistant GM/Player Personnel: Jim Duquette. **Director, Minor League Operations:** Kevin Morgan. **Assistant Director, Minor League Operations:** John Fantauzzi. **Assistant, Player Development:** Amy Neal.

Field Coordinator: Guy Conti. **Roving Instructors:** Mickey Brantley (consultant), Chris Chambliss (hitting), Gary Carter (catching), David Howard (infield), Rick Miller (outfield/baserunning), Ray Rippelmeyer (pitching).

Advisor, Minor Leagues: Chuck Hiller. **Training Coordinator:** Bill Wagner. **Coordinator, Strength/Conditioning:** Jason Craig. **Assistant Coordinator, Strength/Conditioning:** Ken Coward. **Equipment Manager:** Kevin Kierst. **Assistant Equipment Manager:** Jack Brenner.

Farm System

Class	Farm Team	League	Manager	Coach	Pitching Coach
AAA	Norfolk	International	Bobby Floyd	Al LeBoeuf	Randy Niemann
AA	Binghamton	Eastern	John Stearns	Edgar Alfonzo	Bobby Ojeda
High A	St. Lucie	Florida State	Ken Oberkfell	Howard Johnson	Dan Warthen
Low A	Capital City	South Atlantic	Tony Tijerina	Donovan Mitchell	Blaine Beatty
Short season	Brooklyn	New York-Penn	Tim Teufel	Roger LaFrancois	Hector Berrios
Rookie	Kingsport	Appalachian	Mookie Wilson	Luis Natera	Rick Mahler
Rookie	Mets	Dominican	Luis Natera	H. Sierra/L. Castro	Orlando Encarnacion
Rookie	Mets	Venezuela	Jesus Tiamo	Leonardo Hernandez	Jesus Hernaiz

Scouting

Telephone: Amateur—(718) 565-4311, Professional—(718) 803-4013. **FAX:** (718) 205-7920.

Assistant GM/Director, Scouting Operations: Gary LaRocque. **Assistant, Professional /International Scouting:** Anne Fairbanks.

Advance Scout: Bruce Benedict (Dunwoody, GA). **Professional Scouts:** Dave Engle (San Diego, CA), Howie Freiling (Apex, NC), Carmen Fusco (Mechanicsburg, PA), Roland Johnson (Newington, CT).

Director, Amateur Scouting: Jack Bowen. **Assistant, Amateur Scouting:** Elizabeth Gadsden.

National Crosscheckers: Paul Fryer (Calabasas, CA), Terry Tripp (Harrisburg, IL). **Regional Supervisors:** West—Bob Minor (Garden Grove, CA); North—Gene Kerns (Hagerstown, MD); South—Joe DelliCarri (Longwood, FL).

MARC LEVINE/NY METS

Jack Bowen

Area Supervisors: Dave Birecki (Peoria, AZ), Quincy Boyd (Plainfield, IL), Erwin Bryant (Lexington, KY), Ty Brown (Ruther Glen, VA), Jon Bunnell (Tampa, FL), Larry Chase (Pearcy, AR), Rodney Henderson (Lexington, KY), Chuck Hensley Jr. (Sacramento, CA), Brian Hunter (Lake Elsinore, CA), Steve Leavitt (Huntington Beach, CA), Dave Lottsfeldt (Richardson, TX), Marlin McPhail (Irmo, SC), Greg Morhardt (South Windsor, CT), Joe Nigro (Staten Island, NY), Claude Pelletier (St. Lazare, Quebec), Jim Reeves (Camas, WA), Junior Roman (San Sebastian, PR), Bob Rossi (Baton Rouge, LA), Joe Salermo (Miami Beach, FL).

NEW YORK YANKEES

George Steinbrenner

Telephone, Address

Office Address: Yankee Stadium, East 161st Street and River Avenue, Bronx, NY 10451. **Telephone:** (718) 293-4300. **FAX:** (718) 293-8431. **Website:** www.yankees.com.

Ownership

Principal Owner: George Steinbrenner. **General Partners:** Harold Steinbrenner, Henry Steinbrenner, Stephen Swindal.

BUSINESS OPERATIONS

President: Randy Levine.
Chief Operating Officer: Lonn Trost.
Vice President: Richard Smith. **VP, Administration:** Sonny Hight.

Finance

Vice President, Chief Financial Officer: Martin Greenspun. **Controller:** Robert Brown.

Marketing, Community Relations

Vice President, Marketing: Deborah Tymon.
Vice President, Corporate/Community Relations: Brian Smith.
Director, Sponsorship Sales/Services: Michael Tusiani.

Media Relations, Publications

Telephone: (718) 579-4460. **FAX:** (718) 293-8414.
Director, Media Relations/Publicity: Rick Cerrone. **Assistant Director, Media Relations/Publicity:** Jason Zillo. **Senior Advisor:** Arthur Richman. **Assistant, Media Relations:** Ben Tuliebitz. **Director, Publications/Multimedia:** Mark Mandrake.

Stadium Operations

Director, Stadium Operations: Kirk Randazzo. **Assistant Director, Stadium Operations:** Doug Behar. **Stadium Superintendent:** Pete Pullara.
Head Groundskeeper: Dan Cunningham. **Scoreboard/Broadcasting Manager:** Mike Bonner.
Director, Concessions/Hospitality: Joel White.
PA Announcer: Bob Sheppard. **Official Scorers:** Bill Shannon, Howie Karpin.

Ticketing

Telephone: (718) 293-6000. **FAX:** (718) 293-4841.
Vice President, Ticket Operations: Frank Swaine.
Senior Director, Ticket Operations: Irfan Kirimca.

Travel, Clubhouse

Traveling Secretary: David Szen.
Equipment Manager: Rob Cucuzza. **Visiting Clubhouse Manager:** Lou Cucuzza Jr.

General Information

Home dugout: First Base. **Playing Surface:** Grass.
Team colors: Navy blue and white.
Player representative: Bernie Williams.

Brian Cashman

BASEBALL OPERATIONS

Telephone: (718) 293-4300. **FAX:** (718) 293-0015.

Senior Vice President/General Manager: Brian Cashman. **VP, Assistant GM:** Jean Afterman.

Senior VP, Baseball Operations: Gordon Blakeley. **VP/Director, Baseball Operations:** John Coppolella.

Director, Baseball Operations: Brian Werner. **Assistant, Baseball Operations:** Trevor Schaffer. **Special Assistants, Baseball Operations:** Frank Howard, Jim Benedict.

VP, Major League Scouting: Gene Michael.

Special Advisory Group: Yogi Berra, Reggie Jackson, Clyde King, Don Mattingly, Dick Williams.

Major League Staff

Manager: Joe Torre.

Coaches: Dugout—Don Zimmer; Pitching—Mel Stottlemyre; Batting—Rick Down; First Base—Lee Mazzilli; Third Base—Willie Randolph; Bullpen—Rich Monteleone. Catching—Gary Tuck.

Joe Torre

Medical, Training

Team Physician, New York: Dr. Stuart Henshon. **Team Physician, Tampa:** Dr. Andrew Boyer.

Head Trainer: Gene Monahan. **Assistant Trainer:** Steve Donohue.

Strength and Conditioning Coach: Jeff Mangold.

Player Development

Florida Complex: 3102 N. Himes Ave., Tampa, FL. 33607. **Telephone:** (813) 875-7569. **FAX**: (813) 873-2302.

Vice President, Minor League Operations: Rob Thomson. **VP, Player Personnel**: Billy Connors.

Head Trainer: Mark Littlefield. **Coordinator, Strength/Conditioning**: Russell Orr. **Equipment Manager:** David Hays. **Clubhouse Manager:** Jack Terry.

Farm System

Class	Farm Club	League	Manager	Coach	Pitching Coach
AAA	Columbus	International	Bucky Dent	H. Cassady/S. Rende	Neil Allen
AA	Trenton	Eastern	Stump Merrill	Steve Braun	Gary Lavelle
High A	Tampa	Florida State	Bill Masse	Joe Breeden	Greg Pavlick
Low A	Battle Creek	Midwest	Mitch Seoane	Ty Hawkins	Steve Renko
Short season	Staten Island	New York-Penn	Andy Stankiewicz	Kevin Higgins	Rick Tomlin
Rookie	Tampa	Gulf Coast	Dan Radison	Bill Mosiello	David Eiland
Rookie	Yankees	Dominican	Humberto Trejo	Freddie Tiburcio	Wilfredo Cordova
Rookie	Yankees	Dominican	Darwin Bracho	Carlos Mota	Jose Duran

Scouting

Telephone: (813) 875-7569. **FAX:** (813) 348-2302.

Vice President, Scouting/Player Development: Lin Garrett.

VP, Pro Scouting: Damon Oppenheimer. **Special Assistant, Pro Scouting:** John Coppolella. **Assistant, Scouting/Baseball Operations:** Stephanie Carapazza.

Advance Scout: Wade Taylor (Orlando, FL).

Professional Scouts: Jim Benedict (Sarasota, FL), Ron Brand (Mesa, AZ), Wayne Britton (Staunton, VA), Joe Caro (Tampa, FL), Bill Emslie (Safety Harbor, FL), Jack Hubbard (Safety Harbor, FL).

Regional Crosscheckers: East—Joe Arnold (Lakeland, FL), Midwest—Tim Kelly (New Lenox, IL), West—Greg Orr (Sacramento, CA).

Lin Garrett

Area Scouts: Mike Baker (Cave Creek, AZ), Brian Barber (Glen Allen, VA), Mark Batchko (Arlington, TX), Steve Boros (Kingwood, TX), Mike Gibbons (Liberty Township, OH), Steve Lemke (Geneva, IL), Tim McIntosh (Stockton, CA), Jeff Patterson (Anaheim, CA), Scott Pleis (Tampa, FL), Cesar Presbott (Bronx, NY), Gus Quattlebaum (Hermosa Beach, CA), Dan Radison (Deerfield Beach, FL), D.J. Svihlik (Birmingham, AL), Steve Swail (Mooresville, NC).

Coordinator, Latin American Scouting: Carlos Rios (Santo Domingo, DR). **Coordinator, Pacific Rim:** John Cox (Redlands, CA).

International Scouts: Ricardo Finol (Venezuela), Luis Gonzalez (Dominican Republic), Karl Heron (Panama), Ricardo Heron (Panama), Rudy Jabalera (Dominican Republic), Jose Luna (Dominican Republic), Victor Mata (Dominican Republic), Tito Quintero (Colombia), Dan Radison (Puerto Rico/Virgin Islands), Hector Rincones (Venezuela), Edgar Rodriguez (Nicaragua), Arquimedes Rojas (Venezuela), Cesar Suarez (Venezuela), Fred Tiburcio (Dominican Republic).

OAKLAND ATHLETICS

Steve Schott

Telephone, Address

Office Address: 7000 Coliseum Way, Oakland, CA 94621. **Telephone:** (510) 638-4900. **FAX:** (510) 562-1633. **Website:** www.oaklandathletics.com.

Ownership

Operated by: Athletics Investment Group LLC (1996).

Co-Owner/Managing Partner: Steve Schott. **Partner/Owner:** Ken Hofmann.

President: Michael Crowley. **Executive Assistant to President:** Carolyn Jones.

BUSINESS OPERATIONS

Finance, Administration

Vice President, Finance: Paul Wong.

Director, Human Resources: Eleanor Yee. **Director, Finance:** Linda Rease. **Payroll Specialist:** Kathy Leviege. **Accounts Payable Specialist:** Lynell Roeber. **Senior Staff Accountant:** Isabelle Mahaffey. **Staff Accountant:** Helga Mahlmann. **Accounts Receivable Specialist**, David Bunnell. **Human Resources/Finance Coordinator:** Unavailable. **Information Systems Manager:** Debbie Dean.

Marketing, Sales

Vice President, Sales/Marketing: David Alioto.

Director, Merchandising/Purchasing: Drew Bruno. **Director, Corporate Advertising Sales:** Franklin Lowe. **Manager, Sales/Marketing:** Lisa Wood.

Manager, Merchandising Operations/Purchasing: Colin Nicholas. **Manager, Merchandise Warehouse:** Doug Heater.

Manager, Spring Training Marketing/Operations: Mike Saverino. **Manager, Creative Services:** Mike Ono. **Account Managers, Corporate Sales:** Tika Belanger, Jill Golden, Kelle Venezia, Susan Weiglein.

Manager, Special Events: Adrienne Carew.

Public Relations, Communications

Telephone: (510) 563-2207. **FAX:** (510) 562-1633.

Vice President, Broadcasting/Communications: Ken Pries.

Director, Public Relations: Jim Young. **Manager, Baseball Information:** Mike Selleck. **Manager, Broadcasting:** Robert Buan. **Media Services/Credentials:** Debbie Gallas. **Manager, Media Relations:** Unavailable.

Manager, Community Relations: Detra Paige. **Coordinator, Broadcasting/Community Relations:** Warren Chu. **Coordinator, Community Relations:** Sharon Floyd.

Director, Stadium Entertainment: Troy Smith. **Director, Multimedia Services:** David Don. **Coordinator, Multimedia Services:** Rick Ruvalcaba. **Coordinator, In-Stadium Entertainment:** Jeff Gass. **Team Photographer:** Michael Zagaris.

Stadium Operations

Vice President, Stadium Operations: David Rinetti.

Director, Stadium Operations: David Avila. **Director, Stadium Services:** Matt Fucile. **Managers, Stadium Services:** Randy Duran. **Manager, Stadium Operations Systems:** Eric Nelson. **Manager, Stadium Operations:** Lesley Nolan. **Coordinator, Stadium Services:** Dave Cochran. **Coordinator, Stadium Operations:** Kristy Ledbetter. **Coordinator, Guest Services:** Unavailable.

Head Groundskeeper: Clay Wood.

PA Announcer: Roy Steele. **Official Scorers:** Chuck Dybdal, Dick O'Connor, Art Santo Domingo.

Ticketing

Director, Ticket Operations: Steve Fanelli.

Manager, Inside Sales: Parker Newton. **Manager, Premium Seating Sales:** Grant Christensen. **Manager, Premium Seating Services:** Dayn Floyd. **Manager, Ticket Operations:** Doug Vanderheyden. **Manager, Ticket Services:** Josh Ziegenbusch. **Area Sales Managers:** Phil Chapman, Brian Ditucci, Mike Fagundes, Craig Kadden, Sean O'Keefe, Mercedes Veloz. **Coordinator, Ticket Operations:** David Adame. **Manager, Box Office:** Cameron Stwart. **Assistant Manager, Box Office:** Anthony Silva. **Coordinator, Box Office:** Patrick Quigney.

Travel, Clubhouse

Director, Team Travel: Mickey Morabito.

Equipment Manager: Steve Vucinich. **Visitors Clubhouse:** Mike Thalblum. **Assistant Equipment Manager:** Brian Davis.

General Information

Home Dugout: Third Base. **Playing Surface:** Grass.

Team Colors: Kelly green and gold.

Player Representative: Unavailable.

Billy Beane

BASEBALL OPERATIONS

Vice President, General Manager: Billy Beane.

Assistant General Manager: Paul DePodesta. **Special Assistants to GM:** Randy Johnson, Matt Keough. **Executive Assistant:** Betty Shinoda.

Director, Baseball Administration: Pamela Pitts. **Assistant, Baseball Operations:** David Forst.

Major League Staff

Manager: Ken Macha.

Coaches: Dugout—Bob Geren; Pitching—Rick Peterson; Batting—Terry Francona; First Base—Thad Bosley; Third Base—Ron Washington; Bullpen—Brad Fischer.

Medical, Training

Ken Macha

Team Physician: Dr. Allan Pont. **Team Orthopedist:** Dr. Jerrald Goldman. **Consulting Orthopedists:** Dr. John Frazier, Dr. Lewis Yocum. **Arizona Team Physician:** Dr. Fred Dicke.

Head Trainer: Larry Davis. **Assistant Trainer:** Steve Sayles.

Player Development

Telephone, Oakland: (510) 638-4900. **FAX:** (510) 563-2376.

Arizona Complex: Papago Park Baseball Complex, 1802 N. 64th St., Phoenix, AZ 85008. **Telephone:** (602) 949-5951. **FAX:** (602) 945-0557.

Director, Player Development: Keith Lieppman. **Assistant Director:** Dave Hudgens.

Director, Minor League Operations: Ted Polakowski.

Roving Instructors: Juan Navarette, Ron Plaza, Ron Romanick (pitching).

Medical Coordinator: Jeff Collins. **Strength and Conditioning:** Chris Lantz.

Farm System

Class	Farm Team	League	Manager	Coach	Pitching Coach
AAA	Sacramento	Pacific Coast	Tony DeFrancesco	Roy White	Curt Young
AA	Midland	Texas	Greg Sparks	Dave Joppie	Craig Lefferts
High A	Modesto	California	Rick Rodriguez	Brian McArn	Scott Emerson
Low A	Kane County	Midwest	Webster Garrison	Eddie Williams	Jim Coffman
Short season	Vancouver	Northwest	Dennis Rogers	Juan Dilone	Ed Vosberg
Rookie	Phoenix	Arizona	Ruben Escalera	Billy Owens	Fernando Arroyo
Rookie	Athletics I	Dominican	Evaristo Lantigua	Tomas Silverio	Expeddy Garcia
Rookie	Athletics II	Dominican	Jose Guillen	L. Martinez/L. Gomez	Nasusel Cabrera

Scouting

Eric Kubota

Telephone: (510) 638-4900. **FAX:** (510) 563-2376.

Director, Scouting: Eric Kubota (Roseville, CA). **Coordinator, Scouting/Player Development:** Danny McCormack.

National Field Coordinator: Chris Pittaro (Robbinsville, NJ).

Advance Scout: Bob Johnson (University Park, FL). **National Crosschecker:** Ron Vaughn (Corona, CA).

Area Scouts: Steve Barningham (Beaverton, OR), Steve Bowden (Cypress, TX), Tom Clark (Shrewsbury, MA), Ruben Escalera (San Juan, PR), Carl Fraticelli (Antioch, CA), Kelly Heath (Cary, NC), Tim Holt (Allen, TX), John Kuehl (Fountain Hills, AZ), Rick Magnante (Van Nuys, CA), Kelcey Mucker (Metairie, LA), Billy Owens (Marietta, GA), Jim Pransky (Bettendorf, IA), Jeremy Schied (Charlotte, NC), Will Schock (Oakland, CA), Rich Sparks (Sterling Heights, MI).

Coordinator, Dominican Republic: Raymond Abreu (Santo Domingo, DR).

International Scouts: Ruben Barradas (Venezuela), Juan Carlos De la Cruz (Dominican Republic), Angel Eusebio (Dominican Republic), Julio Franco (Venezuela), Juan Martinez (Dominican Republic), Fausto Pena (Dominican Republic), Bernardino Rosario (Dominican Republic), Oswaldo Troconis (Venezuela).

PHILADELPHIA PHILLIES

David Montgomery

Telephone, Address

Office Address: Veterans Stadium, 3501 S. Broad St., Philadelphia, PA 19148. **Mailing Address:** P.O. Box 7575, Philadelphia, PA 19101. **Telephone:** (215) 463-6000. **Website:** www.phillies.com.

Ownership

Operated by: The Phillies.

President, Chief Executive Officer: David Montgomery. **Chairman:** Bill Giles.

BUSINESS OPERATIONS

Vice President, General Counsel: Bill Webb.

Chief Communications Officer, New Ballpark: Sharon Swainson. **Director, Business Development:** Joe Giles. **Director, Human Resources:** Terry DeRugeriis.

Finance

Senior Vice President, Chief Financial Officer: Jerry Clothier.

Controller: John Fusco. **Manager, Payroll Services:** Karen Wright. **Director, Information Systems:** Brian Lamoreaux.

Marketing, Promotions

Vice President, Advertising Sales: David Buck.

Manager, Client Services/Alumni Relations: Debbie Nocito. **Manager, National Sales:** Rob MacPherson. **Manager, Advertising Sales:** Scott Nickle. **Director, Events:** Kurt Funk. **Director, Entertainment:** Chris Long.

Director, Broadcasting/Video Services: Rory McNeil. **Manager, Advertising/Internet Services:** Jo-Anne Levy-Lamoreaux.

Public Relations, Communications

Telephone: (215) 463-6000. **FAX:** (215) 389-3050.

Vice President, Public Relations: Larry Shenk.

Director, Media Relations: Leigh Tobin. **Director, Print/Creative Services:** Tina Urban. **Coordinator, Public Relations/Publications:** Christine Negley. **Media Relations Representative:** Greg Casterioto.

Director, Community Relations: Gene Dias. **Speakers' Bureau Representative:** Maje McDonnell. **Community/Fan Development Representative:** Dick Allen.

Stadium Operations

Vice President, Operations/Administration: Michael Stiles.

Director, Facility Management: Mike DiMuzio. **Director, Event Operations:** Eric Tobin. **Operations Assistant/Concessionaire Liaison:** Bruce Leith.

PA Announcer: Dan Baker. **Official Scorers:** Jay Dunn, Bob Kenney, John McAdams.

Ticketing

Telephone: (215) 463-1000. **FAX:** (215) 463-9878.

Vice President, Ticket Operations: Richard Deats.

Director, Ticket Department: Dan Goroff. **Director, Sales:** John Weber. **Director, Group Sales:** Kathy Killian. **Manager, Ticket Technology/Development:** Chris Pohl. **Manager, Premium Seating:** Tom Mashek. **Manager, Phone Center:** Phil Feather.

Travel, Clubhouse

Manager, Equipment/Team Travel: Frank Coppenbarger. **Assistant Equipment Manager:** Dan O'Rourke. **Manager, Visiting Clubhouse:** Kevin Steinhour. **Assistant, Home Clubhouse:** Phil Sheridan.

General Information

Home Dugout: First Base. **Playing Surface:** Artificial turf.
Team Colors: Red, blue and white.
Player Representative: Randy Wolf.

Ed Wade

BASEBALL OPERATIONS

Vice President, General Manager: Ed Wade.

Assistant GM: Ruben Amaro Jr. **Director, Baseball Administration:** Susan Ingersoll. **Computer Analysis:** Jay McLaughlin.

Senior Advisors to GM: Dallas Green, Paul Owens. **Special Assistant to GM:** Charlie Manuel.

Major League Staff

Manager: Larry Bowa.

Coaches: Dugout—Gary Varsho; Pitching—Joe Kerrigan; Batting—Greg Gross; First Base—Tony Scott; Third Base—John Vukovich; Bullpen—Ramon Henderson.

Medical, Training

Director, Medical Services: Dr. Michael Ciccotti. **Assistant Director, Medical Services:** Dr. John McShane.

Head Trainer: Jeff Cooper. **Assistant Trainer:** Mark Andersen. **Conditioning Coordinator:** Scott Hoffman.

Larry Bowa

Player Development

Telephone: (215) 463-6000. **FAX:** (215) 755-9324.

Assistant GM, Scouting/Player Development: Mike Arbuckle.

Director, Minor League Operations: Steve Noworyta. **Assistant to Director, Minor League Operations/Scouting:** Rob Holiday. **Administrative Assistant, Minor Leagues/Scouting:** Mike Ondo.

Advisor, Player Development: Ruben Amaro Sr. **Director, Latin America Operations:** Sal Artiaga. **Director, Florida Operations:** John Timberlake.

Field Coordinator: Bill Dancy. **Coordinators, Instruction:** Mick Billmeyer (catching), Gorman Heimueller (pitching), Don Long (hitting), Ron Oester (infield), Pat Sandora (conditioning), Scott Sheridan (trainers), Milt Thompson (outfield/base running).

Farm System

Class	Farm Team	League	Manager	Coach	Pitching Coach
AAA	Scranton/W-B	International	Marc Bombard	Jerry Martin	Mike Mason
AA	Reading	Eastern	Greg Legg	John Morris	Rod Nichols
High A	Clearwater	Florida State	Roly de Armas	Manny Amador	Rich Dubee
Low A	Lakewood	South Atlantic	Buddy Biancalana	Tony Barron	Ken Westray
Short season	Batavia	New York-Penn	Luis Melendez	Jim Morrison	Warren Brusstar
Rookie	Clearwater	Gulf Coast	Ruben Amaro Sr.	Ramon Aviles	Carlos Arroyo
Rookie	Phillies	Dominican	Sammy Mejia	Domingo Brito	Caesar Mejia
Rookie	Phillies	Venezuela	Rafael DeLima	Silverio Navas	Jose Betancourt

Scouting

Telephone: (215) 952-8204. **FAX:** (215) 755-9324.

Director, Scouting: Marti Wolever (Papillion, NE).

Coordinators, Scouting: Jim Fregosi Jr. (Murrieta, CA), Mike Ledna (Arlington Heights, IL).

Director, Major League Scouts: Gordon Lakey (Barker, TX). **Major League Scout:** Jimmy Stewart (Odessa, FL). **Advance Scout:** Hank King (Limerick, PA).

Professional Scouts: Sonny Bowers (Waco, TX), Ron Hansen (Baldwin, MD), Dean Jongewaard (Fountain Valley, CA), Dick Lawlor (Windsor, CT), Larry Rojas (Clearwater, FL), Del Unser (Dove Canyon, CA).

Regional Supervisors: East—Dean Decillis (Weston, FL); Central—Brian Kohlscheen (Norman, OK); West—Billy Moore (Alta Loma, CA).

Marti Wolever

Area Scouts: Sal Agostinelli (Kings Park, NY), Therron Brockish (Council Bluffs, IA), Darrell Conner (Riverside, CA), Tim Kissner (Mountlake Terrace, WA), Jerry Lafferty (Kansas City, MO), Chip Lawrence (Somerfield, FL), Matt Lundin (Santa Ana, CA), Miguel Machado (Miami Lakes, FL), Paul Murphy (Wilmington, DE), Dave Owen (Cleburne, TX), Scott Ramsay (Rocklin, CA), Gene Schall (Harleysville, PA), Paul Scott (Frisco, TX), Mike Stauffer (Ridgeland MS), Bob Szymkowski (Chicago, IL), Roy Tanner (Charleston, SC).

International Supervisor: Sal Agostinelli (Kings Park, NY).

International Scouts: Tomas Herrera (Mexico), Allen Lewis (Panama, Central America), Jesus Mendez (Venezuela), Wil Tejada (Dominican Republic).

PITTSBURGH PIRATES

Kevin McClatchy

Telephone, Address

Office Address: PNC Park at North Shore, 115 Federal St., Pittsburgh, PA 15212. **Mailing Address:** P.O. Box 7000, Pittsburgh, PA 15212. **Telephone:** (412) 323-5000. **FAX:** (412) 325-4412. **Website:** www.pittsburghpirates.com.

Ownership

Operated by: Pittsburgh Pirates Acquisition, Inc.

Principal Owner: Kevin McClatchy.

Board of Directors: William Allen, Don Beaver, Frank Brenner, Chip Ganassi, Kevin McClatchy, Thomas Murphy Jr., Ogden Nutting.

BUSINESS OPERATIONS

Finance

Vice President, Finance: Jim Plake.

Controller: David Bowman. **Director, Office Services:** Patti Mistick. **Director, Information Technology:** Terry Zeigler.

Marketing, Sales

Vice President, Marketing/Broadcasting: Vic Gregovits.

Director, Ticket Sales/Services: Jim Alexander. **Director, Season Ticket Services:** Gary Remlinger. **Director, Merchandising:** Joe Billetdeaux. **Director, Promotions:** Rick Orienza. **Director, Corporate Sales:** Mike Berry. **Manager, Broadcasting:** Marc Garda.

Communications

Telephone: (412) 325-4976. **FAX:** (412) 325-4413.

Vice President, Communications: Patty Paytas. **VP, Corporate Projects:** Nelson Briles.

Director, Media Relations: Jim Trdinich. **Manager, Media Services:** Dan Hart. **Assistants, Public Relations:** Donna Beltz, Sherry Rusiski, Christine Serkoch.

Director, Player Relations: Kathy Guy. **Director, Community Development:** Wende Torbert.

Alumni Liaison: Sally O'Leary. **In-Game Entertainment:** Eric Wolff, Alex Moser.

Stadium Operations

Vice President, PNC Park Operations/Facilities Management: Dennis DaPra.

Director, Operations: Chris Hunter. **Director, Security/Contract Services:** Jeff Podobnik. **Director, Guest Services:** Brenda Thompson. **Field Maintenance Manager:** Luke Yoder.

PA Announcer: Tim DeBacco. **Official Scorers:** Bob Hertzel, Evan Pattak, Bob Webb, Tony Krizmanich.

Ticketing

Telephone: (800) BUY-BUCS. **FAX:** (412) 325-4404.

Assistant Director, Ticket Services: Mike Weller. **Manager, Ticket Services:** Dave Wysocki.

Travel, Clubhouse

Traveling Secretary: Greg Johnson.

Equipment Manager/Home Clubhouse Operations: Roger Wilson. **Visitors Clubhouse Operations:** Kevin Conrad.

General Information

Home Dugout: Third Base. **Playing Surface:** Grass.

Team Colors: Black, gold, red and white

Player Representative: Kevin Young.

David Littlefield

BASEBALL OPERATIONS

Telephone: (412) 325-4743. **FAX:** (412) 325-4414.

Senior Vice President, General Manager: David Littlefield.

Assistant GM: Roy Smith. **Special Assistants to GM:** Jesse Flores, Jax Robertson, Bill Singer, Doug Strange, Pete Vuckovich.

Coordinator, Baseball Operations: Jon Mercurio. **Baseball Operations Assistant:** Anthony Dennis. **Administrative Assistant, Baseball Operations:** Jeannie Donatelli.

Major League Staff

Manager: Lloyd McClendon.

Coaches: Bench—Pete Mackanin; Pitching—Spin Williams; Batting—Gerald Perry; First Base—Rusty Kuntz; Third Base—John Russell; Bullpen—Bruce Tanner.

Lloyd McClendon

Medical, Training

Medical Director: Dr. Patrick DeMeo. **Team Physician:** Dr. Edwin Snell.

Head Trainer: Brad Henderson. **Assistant Trainers:** Mark Rogow, Mike Sandoval. **Strength/Conditioning Coordinator:** Frank Velasquez.

Minor Leagues

Telephone: (412) 325-4737. **FAX:** (412) 325-4414.

Director, Player Development: Brian Graham. **Administrator, Minor Leagues:** Diane DePasquale.

Coordinator, Instruction: Jeff Banister. **Roving Instructors:** Doug Mansolino (infield), Jeff Manto (hitting), Gary Redus (outfield/baserunning), Gary Ruby (pitching), Ramon Sambo (Latin American field coordinator).

Farm System

Class	Farm Team	League	Manager	Coach	Pitching Coach
AAA	Nashville	Pacific Coast	Trent Jewett	Jay Loviglio	Darold Knowles
AA	Altoona	Eastern	Dale Sveum	John Wehner	Jeff Andrews
High A	Lynchburg	Carolina	Dave Clark	Jeff Livesey	Scott Lovekamp
Low A	Hickory	South Atlantic	Tony Beasley	Matt Winters	Bob Milacki
Short-season	Williamsport	New York-Penn	Andy Stewart	Jeff Branson	Ray Searage
Rookie	Bradenton	Gulf Coast	Woody Huyke	Greg Briley	Miguel Bonilla
Rookie	Pirates	Dominican	Ramon Zapata	Ceciliio Beltre	Leonardo Mejia

Scouting

Telephone: (412) 325-4738. **FAX:** (412) 325-4414.

Director, Scouting: Ed Creech.

Coordinator, Scouting Systems: Sandy Deutsch.

Advance Scout: Chris Lein (Boca Raton, FL).

National Supervisor: Jimmy Lester (Columbus, GA). **Regional Supervisors:** John Green (Conowingo, MD), Scott Littlefield (Long Beach, CA), Mark McKnight (Atlanta, GA).

Area Scouts: Tom Barnard (Houston, TX), Kevin Clouser (Seattle, WA), Joe Ferrone (Santa Clarita, CA), Steve Fleming (Matouca, VA), Mark Germann (Atkins, IA), Duane Gustavson (Columbus, OH), Mike Kendall (Manhattan Beach, CA), Jaron Madison (Vallejo, CA), Jack Powell (Sweetwater, TN), Jim Rough (Oklahoma City, OK), Everett Russell (Monroe, LA), Scott Sharp (Miami, FL), Rob Sidwell (Windermere, FL), Charlie Sullivan (Latham, NY), Ted Williams (Glendale, AZ).

Ed Creech

Director, Dominican Republic: Esteban Beltre. **Director, Venezuela:** Osmin Melendez.

International Scouts: Pastor Melendez (Venezuela), Kuni Ogawa (Far East), Ramon Perez (Dominican Republic), Pete Yarasavich (The Netherlands), Alez Zapata (Panama).

ST. LOUIS CARDINALS

Telephone, Address

Office Address: 250 Stadium Plaza, St. Louis, MO 63102. **Telephone:** (314) 421-3060. **FAX:** (314) 425-0640. **Website:** www.stlcardinals.com.

Ownership

Operated by: St. Louis Cardinals, LP.

General Partner: Bill DeWitt Jr. **Vice Chairman:** Fred Hanser. **Secretary/Treasurer:** Andrew Baur.

President: Mark Lamping.

Senior Administrative Assistant to Chairman: Grace Hale. **Senior Administrative Assistant to President:** Julie Laningham.

Mark Lamping

BUSINESS OPERATIONS

Vice President, Business Development: Bill DeWitt III.

VP, Public Affairs/Employee Relations: Marian Rhodes. **Manager, Office Administration/Human Resources Specialist:** Karen Brown.

Finance

Vice President, Controller: Brad Woods.

Director, Accounting: Deborah Pfaff. **Payroll Manager:** Rex Carter. **Senior Accountant:** Michelle Flach.

Marketing, Sales

Senior Vice President, Sales/Marketing: Dan Farrell. **Administrative Assistant, Corporate Sales:** Gail Ruhling.

Director, Corporate Sales: Thane van Breusegen. **Director, Target Marketing:** Ted Savage. **Corporate Sales Account Executives:** Matt Gifford, Theron Morgan, Tony Simokaitis.

Public Relations, Community Relations

Telephone: (314) 421-3060. **FAX:** (314) 982-7399.

Director, Media Relations: Brian Bartow. **Assistant to Director, Media Relations:** Brad Hainje. **Coordinator, Media Services:** Melody Yount.

Director, Publications: Steve Zesch. **Publications Assistants:** Kerry Hines, Tom Raber.

Vice President, Community Relations: Marty Hendin. **Associate Manager, Community Relations:** Shawn Bertani.

VP/Group Director, Community Outreach and Cardinals Care: Tim Hanser. **Community Outreach Assistant:** Marlene Long.

Stadium Operations

Vice President, Stadium Operations: Joe Abernathy. **Administrative Assistant:** Nan Bommarito.

Director, Stadium Operations: Mike Bertani. **Director, Security/Special Services:** Joe Walsh. **Administrative Assistant, Security:** Hope Baker.

Director, Quality Assurance/Guest Services: Mike Ball. **Coordinator, Operations:** Cindy Richards.

Director, Event Services: Vicki Bryant. **Administrative Assistant, Event Services:** Missy Tobey.

Head Groundskeeper: Bill Findley. **Assistant Head Groundskeeper:** Chad Casella.

PA Announcer: John Ulett. **Official Scorers:** Gary Mueller, Jeff Durbin, Mike Smith.

Ticketing

Telephone: (314) 421-2400. **FAX:** (314) 425-0649.

Vice President, Ticket Operations: Josie Arnold.

Senior Director, Ticket Sales: Joe Strohm.

Manager, Ticket Operations: Kim Kleeschulte. **Manager, Box Office:** Julie Baker. **Director, Season/Premium Ticket Sales:** Mark Murray. **Manager, Season Ticket Sales/Service:** Julia Kelley.

Director, Group Sales: Michael Hall. **Manager, Direct Ticket Sales:** Mary Clare Bena. **Manager, Customer Service/Telephone Operations:** Patti McCormick. **Supervisor, Customer Service:** Marilyn Mathews.

Travel, Clubhouse

Traveling Secretary: C.J. Cherre.

Equipment Manager: Rip Rowan. **Assistant Equipment Manager:** Buddy Bates. **Visiting Clubhouse Manager:** Jerry Risch. **Video Coordinator:** Chad Blair.

General Information

Home Dugout: First Base. **Playing Surface:** Grass.

Team Colors: Red and white.

Player Representative: Steve Kline.

Walt Jocketty

BASEBALL OPERATIONS

Telephone: (314) 425-0687. **FAX:** (314) 425-0648.

Senior Vice President, General Manager: Walt Jocketty. **Assistant GM/Director, Baseball Operations:** John Mozeliak.

VP, Player Personnel: Jerry Walker. **VP/Special Assistant to GM:** Bob Gebhard. **Special Assistants to GM:** Red Schoendienst, Mike Jorgensen. **Senior Executive Assistant to GM:** Judy Carpenter-Barada.

Major League Staff

Manager: Tony La Russa.

Coaches: Bench—Joe Pettini; Pitching—Dave Duncan; Batting—Mitchell Page; First Base—Dave McKay; Third Base—Jose Oquendo; Bullpen—Marty Mason.

Medical, Training

Senior Medical Advisor: Dr. Stan London. **Club Physician:** Dr. George Paletta.

Head Trainer: Barry Weinberg. **Assistant Trainer:** Mark O'Neal.

Tony La Russa

Player Development

Telephone: (314) 425-0628. **FAX:** (314) 425-0638.

Director, Player Development: Bruce Manno. **Director, Minor League Operations:** Scott Smulczenski. **Manager, Baseball Information/Assistant, Player Development:** John Vuch. **Administrative Assistant:** Judy Francis.

Player Development Advisor/Infield Instructor: George Kissell.

Field Coordinator: Bob Humphreys. **Pitching Coordinator:** Mark Riggins. **Hitting Coordinator:** Gene Tenace.

Minor League Equipment Manager: Ernie Moore.

Farm System

Class	Farm Team	League	Manager	Coach	Pitching Coach
AAA	Memphis	Pacific Coast	Tom Spencer	Tommy Gregg	Dyar Miller
AA	Tennessee	Southern	Mark DeJohn	Steve Balboni	Blaise Ilsley
High A	Palm Beach	Florida State	Tom Nieto	Todd Steverson	Rich DeLucia
Low A	Peoria	Midwest	Joe Cunningham	Tony Diggs	Derek Lilliquist
Short season	New Jersey	New York-Penn	Tommy Shields	Ron Warner	Sid Monge
Rookie	Johnson City	Appalachian	Danny Sheaffer	Tom Kidwell	Al Holland
Rookie	Cardinals	Dominican	Unavailable	Unavailable	Unavailable

Scouting

Telephone: (314) 516-0152. **FAX:** (314) 425-0638.

Director, Amateur Scouting: Marty Maier. **Director, Professional Scouting:** Marteese Robinson. **Administrative Assistant, Baseball Operations:** Linda Brauer.

Major League/Special Assignment Scouts: Bing Devine (St. Louis, MO), Marty Keough (Scottsdale, AZ), Mike Jorgensen (St. Louis, MO), Jim Leyland (Pittsburgh, PA), Fred McAlister (Katy, TX), Joe Sparks (Phoenix, AZ), Mike Squires (Kalamazoo, MI).

Professional Scouts: Clark Crist (Tucson, AZ), Bill Harford (Chicago, IL), Jeff Scott (St. Anne, IL).

Special Assignment, Baseball Operations: Chuck Fick (Newbury Park, CA).

National Crosscheckers: Fred McAlister (Katy, TX), Mike Roberts (Kansas City, MO). **Regional Crosscheckers:** Scott Nichols (Richland, MS), Jay North, (Vacaville, CA), Joe Rigoli (Parsippany, NJ), Roger Smith (Eastman, GA).

Marty Maier

Area Supervisors: Randy Benson (Salisbury, NC), Ben Galante (Houston, TX), Steve Gossett (Broken Arrow, OK), Manny Guerra (Las Vegas, NV), Nakia Hill (Granada Hills, CA) Dave Karaff (Hot Springs Village, AR), Scott Melvin (Quincy, IL), Scott Nichols (Richland, MS), Dan Ontiveros (Corona, CA), Tommy Shields (Lititz, PA), Steve Turco (Largo, FL), Dane Walker (Canby, OR).

International Scouts: Enrique Brito (Venezuela), Domingo Carrasquel (Venezuela), Roberto Diaz (Dominican Republic).

SAN DIEGO PADRES

Telephone, Address

Office Address: 8880 Rio San Diego Dr., Suite 400, San Diego, CA 92108. **Mailing Address:** P.O. Box 122000, San Diego, CA 92112. **Telephone:** (619) 881-6500. **FAX:** (619) 497-5339. **E-Mail Address:** comments@padres.com. **Website:** www.padres.com

Ownership

Operated by: Padres, LP.

Principal Owner, Chairman: John Moores. **Vice Chairman:** Charlie Noell. **President/Chief Operating Officer:** Dick Freeman

John Moores

BUSINESS OPERATIONS

Executive Director, Administrative Services: Lucy Freeman.

Finance

Senior Vice President, Finance: Fred Gerson. **Executive Director, Finance:** Steve Fitch. **Director, Information Systems:** Joe Lewis.

Marketing, Sales

Executive Vice President, Business Operations: Steve Violetta.

Manager, Corporate Development: Jim Ballweg. **Assistant Director, Corporate Sponsorships:** Marty Gorsich.

Public Relations, Community Relations

Telephone: (619) 881-6510. **FAX:** (619) 497-5454.

Director, Media Relations: Luis Garcia. **Assistants, Media Relations:** Steve Hoem, Karen Slaton.

Vice President, Community Relations: Michele Anderson.

Director, Padres Foundation: Sue Botos. **Manager, Community Relations:** Nhu Tran.

Stadium Operations

Executive Vice President/Managing Director, Ballpark Operations: Richard Andersen. **VP, Operations:** Mark Guglielmo.

Director, Stadium Operations: Ken Kawachi. **Head Groundskeeper:** Steve Wightman.

PA Announcer: Bob Chandler. **Official Scorers:** Dennis Smythe, Bill Zavestoski.

Ticketing

Telephone: (619) 283-4494. **FAX:** (619) 280-6239.

Vice President, Ticket Sales: Mark Tilson.

Travel, Clubhouse

Director, Team Travel/Equipment Manager: Brian Prilaman. **Home Clubhouse Operations:** Tony Petricca. **Visitors Clubhouse Operations:** David Bacharach.

General Information

Home Dugout: First Base. **Playing Surface:** Grass.

Team Colors: Blue and orange.

Player Representative: Kevin Jarvis.

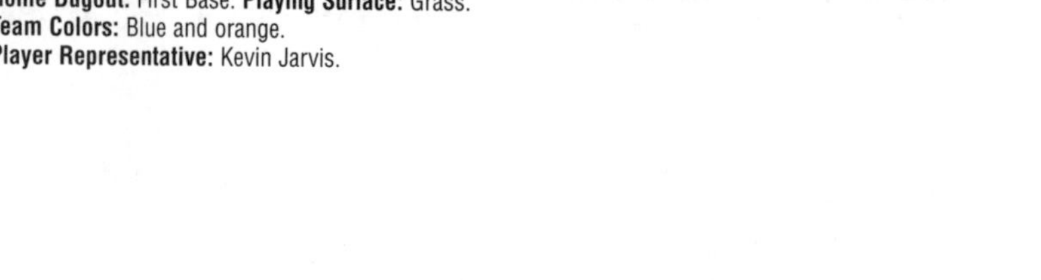

Kevin Towers

BASEBALL OPERATIONS

Telephone: (619) 881-6574. **FAX:** (619) 497-5338.

Executive Vice President, General Manager: Kevin Towers.

Assistant GM: Fred Uhlman Jr. **Special Assistants to GM:** Ken Bracey, Ted Simmons, Randy Smith. **Assistant, Baseball Operations:** Jeff Kingston. **Administrative Assistant:** Herta Bingham.

Major League Staff

Manager: Bruce Bochy.

Coaches: Bench—Tony Muser; Pitching—Greg Booker; Batting—Dave Magadan; First Base—Alan Trammell; Third Base—Rob Picciolo; Bullpen—Darrel Akerfelds.

Bruce Bochy

Medical, Training

Club Physician: Scripps Clinic medical staff.

Head Trainer: Todd Hutcheson. **Assistant Trainer:** Jim Daniel. **Strength and Conditioning Coach:** Bill Henry.

Player Development

Telephone: (619) 881-6519. **FAX:** (619) 497-5338.

Director, Player Development: Tye Waller. **Director, Minor League Operations:** Priscilla Oppenheimer. **Assistant to Director, Player Development:** Juan Lara.

Special Assistant to GM/Field Coordinator: Bill Bryk. **Roving Instructors:** Tom Brown (pitching), Doug Dascenzo (outfield/baserunning), Tony Franklin (infield), Wally Joyner (hitting). **Coordinator, Trainers:** Lance Cacanindin.

Farm System

Class	Farm Team	League	Manager	Coach	Pitching Coach
AAA	Portland	Pacific Coast	Rick Sweet	Rob Deer	Mike Couchee
AA	Mobile	Southern	Craig Colbert	Mike Davis	Darren Balsley
High A	Lake Elsinore	California	Jeff Gardner	Rick Renteria	Gary Lance
Low A	Fort Wayne	Midwest	Gary Jones	Tom Tornincasa	Mike Harkey
Short season	Eugene	Northwest	Roy Howell	Ben Oglivie	Dave Rajsich
Rookie	Idaho Falls	Pioneer	Carlos Lezcano	Jake Molina	Jerry Nyman
Rookie	Padres	Dominican	Pablo Martinez	Jose Mateo	Juan Melo

Scouting

Telephone: (619) 881-6500. **FAX:** (619) 497-5338.

Director, Scouting: Bill Gayton. **Assistant Director, Scouting:** Mike Wickham.

Major League Scouts: Ken Bracey (Morton, IL), Ray Crone (Waxahachie, TX), Moose Johnson (Arvada, CO), Brad Sloan (Brimfield, IL), Gene Thompson (Scottsdale, AZ). **Professional Scouts:** Steve Demeter (Parma, OH), Jimmy Dreyer (Keller, TX), Gail Henley (LaVerne, CA), Ben McLure (Hummelstown, PA), Tom McNamara (Lakewood Ranch, FL), Van Smith (Belleville, IL).

National Crosschecker: Jay Darnell (Plano, TX). **Regional Crosscheckers:** West Coast—Tim McWilliam (San Diego, CA); East Coast—Scott Trcka (Hobart, IN).

Scouting Supervisor, Independent Leagues: Mal Fichman.

Bill Gayton

Full-Time Scouts: Joe Bochy (Plant City, FL), Rich Bordi (Rohnert Park, CA), Jim Bretz (South Windsor, CT), Lane Decker (Piedmont, OK), Bob Filotei (Wilmer, AL), Paul Fletcher (Atlanta, GA), Chris Gwynn (Alta Loma, CA), Dan Huston (Bellevue, WA), Tripp Keister (Wilmington, DE), Jason McLeod (San Diego, CA), Billy Merkel (Columbia, TN), Mike Rikard (Durham, NC), Jeff Stewart (Normal, IL), Jake Wilson (Phoenix, AZ).

Part-Time Scouts: Robert Beattie (Sioux Falls, SD), Bob Buob (Fanwood, NJ), Leroy Dreyer (Brenham, TX), Tony Flood (Mt. Pearl, NL), Robert Gutierrez (Carol City, FL), Rich Hacker (Belleville, IL), Don Hanson (Mandan, ND), Tim Harkness (Courtice, ON), William Killian (Stanwood, MA), Steve Oleschuck (Saint Laurent, QC), Chuck Pierce (Bakersfield, CA), Cam Walker (Centerville, IA), Murray Zuk (Souris, Manitoba).

International Supervisor: Bill Clark (Columbia, MO).

International Scouts: Ray Brown (Oceania/Pacific Islands), Marcial Del Valle (Colombia), Felix Francisco (Dominican Republic), Andres Garcia (Dominican Republic), Elvin Jarquin (Nicaragua), Victor Magdaleno (Venezuela), Franco Martis (The Netherlands), Daniel Mavares (Colombia), Ricardo Montenegro (Panama), Giorgio Moretti (Italy), Ricardo Petit (Venezuela), Robert Rowley (Panama), Jose Salado (Dominican Republic), Trevor Schumm (Australia), Basil Tarasko (Eastern Europe), Modesto Ulloa (Dominican Republic), Yoshiyuki Sano (Japan).

SAN FRANCISCO GIANTS

Peter Magowan

Telephone, Address

Office Address: 24 Willie Mays Plaza, San Francisco, CA 94107. **Telephone:** (415) 972-2000. **FAX:** (415) 947-2800. **Website:** sfgiants.com.

Ownership

Operated by: San Francisco Baseball Associates, LP.

President, Managing General Partner: Peter Magowan.

Senior General Partner: Harmon Burns. **Special Assistant:** Willie Mays. **Senior Advisor:** Willie McCovey.

BUSINESS OPERATIONS

Executive Vice President, Chief Operating Officer: Larry Baer.

Senior VP, General Counsel: Jack Bair. **Vice President, Human Resources:** Joyce Thomas.

Finance

Senior Vice President, Chief Financial Officer: John Yee. **VP, Chief Information Officer:** Bill Schlough. **Director, Management Information Systems:** John Winborn.

VP, Finance: Lisa Pantages.

Marketing, Sales

Senior Vice President, Corporate Marketing: Mario Alioto. **VP, Corporate Sponsorship:** Jason Pearl. **Director, Special Events:** Valerie McGuire. **Manager, Promotions:** Alison Vidal.

Senior VP, Consumer Marketing: Tom McDonald. **Manager, Game Entertainment:** Bryan Srabian. **Director, Client Relations:** Annemarie Hastings. **Director, Sales:** Rob Sullivan. **Manager, Season Ticket Sales:** Craig Solomon.

VP and General Manager, Retail/Tours: Connie Kullberg. **Director, Retail/Tour Operations:** Derik Landry.

Media Relations, Community Relations

Telephone: (415) 972-2448. **FAX:** (415) 947-2800.

Manager, Media Relations: Jim Moorehead. **Manager, Media Services/Broadcasting:** Maria Jacinto. **Manager, Baseball Information:** Blake Rhodes. **Media Relations Assistant:** Matt Hodson.

VP, Publications: Nancy Donati. **VP, Public Affairs:** Staci Slaughter.

Director, Public Affairs: Shana Daum. **Manager, Photography/Archives:** Missy Mikulecky.

Ballpark Operations

Senior Vice President, Ballpark Operations: Jorge Costa. **VP, Guest Services:** Rick Mears.

Senior Director, Ballpark Operations: Gene Telucci. **Director, Maintenance:** Tito Guzman. **Assistant Director, Ballpark Operations:** Bob DeAntoni. **Security Manager:** Tinie Roberson.

Head Groundskeeper: Scott MacVicar.

PA Announcer: Renel Brooks-Moon. **Official Scorers:** Chuck Dybdal, Dick O'Connor, Art Santo Domingo.

Ticketing

Telephone: (415) 972-2000. **FAX:** (415) 947-2500.

Vice President, Ticket Services/Client Relations: Russ Stanley. **Director, Ticket Services:** Devin Lutes. **Director, Luxury Suites:** Amy Quartaroli. **Manager, Ticket Services:** Bob Bisio. **Manager, Ticket Accounting:** Kem Easley. **Manager, Ticket Operations:** Anita Sprinkles. **Special Events Ticket Manager:** Todd Pierce.

Travel, Clubhouse

Director, Travel: Reggie Younger. **Assistant, Travel:** Mike Scardino.

Equipment Manager: Miguel Murphy. **Visitors Clubhouse:** Harvey Hodgerney. **Assistant Equipment Manager:** Richard Cacace.

General Information

Home Dugout: Third Base. **Playing Surface:** Grass.

Team Colors: Black, orange and cream.

Player Representative: Unavailable.

Brian Sabean

BASEBALL OPERATIONS

Telephone: (415) 972-1922. **FAX:** (415) 947-2737.

Senior Vice President, General Manager: Brian Sabean.

VP, Assistant GM: Ned Colletti. **Special Assistant to GM:** Ron Perranoski. **Executive Assistant, Baseball Operations:** Karen Sweeney. **Assistant, Baseball Operations:** Jeremy Shelley.

Major League Staff

Manager: Felipe Alou.

Coaches: Bench—Ron Wotus; Pitching—Dave Righetti; Batting—Joe Lefebvre; First Base—Luis Pujols; Third Base—Gene Glynn; Bullpen—Mark Gardner.

Felipe Alou

Medical, Training

Team Physicians: Dr. Robert Murray, Dr. Gary Fanton.

Medical Director/Head Trainer: Stan Conte. **Assistant Trainer:** Barney Nugent.

Director, Strength/Conditioning: Dave Groeschner.

Player Development

Telephone: (415) 972-1922. **FAX:** (415) 947-2737.

Vice President, Player Personnel: Dick Tidrow.

Director, Player Development: Jack Hiatt. **Director, Minor League Administration:** Bobby Evans. **Special Assistants, Player Personnel:** Bobby Bonds, Jim Davenport, Ted Uhlaender.

Roving Instructors: Will Malerich (traveling), Kirt Manwaring (catching), Lenn Sakata (hitting/bunting/baserunning/infield), Lee Smith (pitching).

Farm System

Class	Farm Team	League	Manager	Coach	Pitching Coach
AAA	Fresno	Pacific Coast	Fred Stanley	Steve Decker	Bert Bradley
AA	Norwich	Eastern	Shane Turner	Willie Upshaw	Ross Grimsley
High A	San Jose	California	Bill Hayes	F.P. Santangelo	Jerry Cram
Low A	Hagerstown	South Atlantic	Mike Ramsey	Willie Aviles	Bob Stanley
Short season	Salem-Keizer	Northwest	Jack Lind	Joe Strain	Trevor Wilson
Rookie	Scottsdale	Arizona	Bert Hunter	Leo Garcia	Maximino Molina
Rookie	Giants	Dominican	Enrique Burgos	Jesus Lazo	Aguedo Vasquez

Scouting

Telephone: (415) 972-1922. **FAX:** (415) 947-2737.

Coordinator, Scouting: Matt Nerland.

Major League Scouts: Bobby Bonds (San Carlos, CA), Jim Davenport (San Carlos, CA), Joe DiCarlo (Ringwood, NJ), Stan Saleski (Dayton, OH), Paul Turco Sr. (Sarasota, FL), Ted Uhlaender (Parshall, CO), Randy Waddill (Valrico, FL), Tom Zimmer (St. Petersburg, FL). **Advance Scout:** Pat Dobson (El Cajon, CA).

Special Assignment Scouts: Dick Cole (Costa Mesa, CA), Larry Osborne (Woodstock, GA).

National Crosschecker: Doug Mapson (Chandler, AZ). **Regional Crosscheckers:** Canada—Steve Arnieri (Barrington, IL); Southwest—Lee Carballo (Westchester, CA); East—Alan Marr (Sarasota, FL); East Coast—Bobby Myrick (Colonial Heights, VA); West Coast—Darren Wittcke (Gresham, OR).

Dick Tidrow

Area Scouts: Billy Castell (El Cerrito, CA); John DiCarlo (Glenwood, NJ), Lee Elder (Martinez, GA), Charlie Gonzalez (Davie, FL), Tom Korenek (Houston, TX), John Shafer (Portland, OR), Joe Strain (Englewood, CO), Todd Thomas (Dallas, TX), Glenn Tufts (Bridgewater, MA), Paul Turco Jr. (Sarasota, FL).

Coordinator, International Operations: Rick Ragazzo (Leona Valley, CA).

International Scouts: Matty Alou (Dominican Republic), Pedro Chavez (Venezuela), Rafel DeLeon (Dominican Republic), Jorge Diaz (Colombia), Philip Elhage (Curacao), Martin Hernandez (Venezuela), Luis Pena (Mexico), Jesus Stephens (Dominican Republic), Alex Torres (Nicaragua), Ciro Villalobos (Venezuela).

SEATTLE MARINERS

Chuck Armstrong

Telephone, Address

Office Address: 1250 First Ave. S., Seattle, WA 98134. **Mailing Address:** P.O. Box 4100, Seattle, WA 98104. **Telephone:** (206) 346-4000. **FAX:** (206) 346-4400. **E-Mail Address:** mariners@seattlemariners.com. **Website:** www.seattlemariners.com.

Ownership

Operated by: Baseball Club of Seattle, LP.

Board of Directors: Minoru Arakawa, John Ellis, Chris Larson, Howard Lincoln, John McCaw, Frank Shrontz, Wayne Perry.

Chairman, Chief Executive Officer: Howard Lincoln. **President, Chief Operating Officer:** Chuck Armstrong.

BUSINESS OPERATIONS

Finance

Executive Vice President, Finance/Ballpark Operations: Kevin Mather.

Controller: Tim Kornegay. **Assistant Controller:** Greg Massey.

VP, Human Resources: Marianne Short. **VP, Technology Servies:** Larry Witherspoon.

Marketing, Sales

Executive Vice President, Business/Operations: Bob Aylward.

VP, Marketing: Kevin Martinez. **Director, Marketing:** Jon Schuller. **Director, Promotions:** Gregg Greene. **Director, Retail Operations:** Jim La Shell. **Manager, Retail Operations:** Jeff Ibach. **Suite Sales:** Moose Clausen.

Baseball Information, Communications

Telephone: (206) 346-4000. **FAX:** (206) 346-4400.

Vice President, Communications: Randy Adamack.

Director, Baseball Information: Tim Hevly. **Administrative Assistant, Baseball Information:** Kelly Munro.

Director, Public Information: Rebecca Hale. **Assistant Director, Baseball Information:** Matt Roebuck. **Manager, Graphic Design:** Carl Morton. **Coordinator, Baseball Information:** Jason Carr. **Coordinator, International Media:** Megan Barrett.

Coordinator, Community Relations: Gina Hasson. **Project Manager, Community Relations:** Sean Grindley.

Ticketing

Telephone: (206) 346-4001. **FAX:** (206) 346-4100.

Director, Ticket Services: Kristin Fortier. **Manager, Ticket Operations:** Connie McKay. **Manager, Group Tickets:** Steve Belling. **Manager, Box Office:** Malcolm Rogel. **Director, Season Tickets/Group Sales:** Bob Hellinger.

Stadium Operations

Vice President, Ballpark Operations: Neil Campbell. **Director, SAFECO Field**: Tony Pereira. **Director, Guest Services/Ballpark Operations:** Kameron Durham.

Head Groundskeeper: Bob Christopherson.

PA Announcer: Tom Hutyler. **Official Scorer:** Terry Mosher.

Travel, Clubhouse

Director, Team Travel: Ron Spellecy.

Clubhouse Manager: Ted Walsh. **Visiting Clubhouse Manager:** Henry Genzale.

Video Coordinator: Carl Hamilton.

General Information

Home Dugout: First Base. **Playing Surface:** Grass.

Team Colors: Northwest green, silver and navy blue.

Player Representative: Unavailable.

Pat Gillick

BASEBALL OPERATIONS

Executive Vice President, General Manager: Pat Gillick.

VP, Baseball Administration: Lee Pelekoudas. **VP, Scouting/Player Development:** Roger Jongewaard.

Special Assignments: Woody Woodward.

Administrator, Baseball Operations: Debbie Larsen. **Coordinator, Baseball Technical Information:** Jim Na.

Major League Staff

Manager: Bob Melvin.

Coaches: Dugout—Rene Lachemann; Pitching—Bryan Price; Batting—Lamar Johnson; First Base—John Moses; Third Base—Dave Myers; Bullpen—Orlando Gomez.

Medical, Training

Medical Director: Dr. Larry Pedegana. **Club Physician:** Dr. Mitchel Storey.

Head Trainer: Rick Griffin. **Assistant Trainer:** Tom Newberg. **Strength/Conditioning Coach:** Allen Wirtala.

Bob Melvin

Player Development

Telephone: (206) 346-4313. **FAX:** (206) 346-4300.

Vice President, Player Development: Benny Looper. **Director, Minor League Administration:** Greg Hunter. **Administrator, Player Development:** Jan Plein.

Coordinator, Minor League Instruction: Mike Goff. **Trainer Coordinator:** Mickey Clarizio.

Roving Instructors: Glenn Adams (hitting), James Clifford (strength/conditioning), Roger Hansen (catching), Buzzy Keller (special assignment), Cal McLish (special assignment), Pat Rice (pitching).

Farm System

Class	Farm Team	League	Manager	Coach	Pitching Coach
AAA	Tacoma	Pacific Coast	Dan Rohn	Gary Thurman	Jim Slaton
AA	San Antonio	Texas	Dave Brundage	Terry Pollreisz	Rafael Chaves
High A	Inland Empire	California	Steve Roadcap	Henry Cotto	Scott Budner
Low A	Wisconsin	Midwest	Daren Brown	Dana Williams	Brad Holman
Short season	Everett	Northwest	Pedro Grifol	Darrin Garner	Gary Wheelock
Rookie	Peoria	Arizona	Scott Steinmann	T. Cruz/A. Bottin	Marcos Garcia
Rookie	Mariners	Dominican	Unavailable	Bienvenido Liriano	Manuel Marrero
Rookie	Mariners	Venezuela	Jose Moreno	Jonathan Arraiz	Luis Hernandez

Scouting

Telephone: (206) 346-4000. **FAX:** (206) 346-4300.

Director, Scouting: Frank Mattox (Peoria, AZ). **Administrator, Scouting:** Hallie Larson.

Advance Scout: Stan Williams (Lakewood, CA).

Director, Professional Scouting: Ken Compton (Cypress, CA).

Major League Scouts: Bob Harrison (Long Beach, CA), Bill Kearns (Milton, MA), Charley Kerfeld (Chico, CA), Steve Pope (Asheville, NC), Tim Schmidt (San Bernardino, CA).

National Crosschecker: Steve Jongewaard (Huntington Beach, CA).

Regional Supervisors: West—Ron Tostenson (El Dorado Hills, CA); East—John McMichen (Treasure Island, FL); Midwest—Carroll Sembera (Shiner, TX); Canada—Wayne Norton (Port Moody, British Columbia).

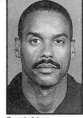

Frank Mattox

Full-Time Scouts: Craig Bell (Charlotte, NC), Joe Bohringer (Claremont, CA), Phil Geisler (Port Orchard, WA), Pedro Grifol (Miami, FL), Mark Leavitt (Maitland, FL), Mark Lummus (Cleburne, TX), Ken Madeja (Novi, MI), David May (Bear, DE), Robert Mummau (Martinsburg, WV), Steve Peck (Scottsdale, AZ), Stacey Pettis (Antioch, CA), Tim Reynolds (Irvine, CA), Alvin Rittman (Memphis, TN), Eric Robinson (Hiram, GA), Kyle Van Hook (Brenham, TX),

Supervisor, Pacific Rim Operations: Ted Heid (Peoria, AZ). **Assistant Director, Professional/International Scouting:** Hide Sueyoshi (Bellevue, WA).

Supervisors, Venezuela/Dominican Republic: Bob Engle (Tampa, FL).

International Scouts: Emilo Carrasquel (Venezuela), Patrick Guerrero (Dominican Republic), Mauro Mazzotti (Italy).

TAMPA BAY DEVIL RAYS

Vince Naimoli

Telephone, Address

Office Address: Tropicana Field, One Tropicana Dr., St. Petersburg, FL 33705. **Telephone:** (727) 825-3137. **FAX:** (727)-825-3111. **Website:** www.devilrays.com.

Ownership

Operated by: Tampa Bay Devil Rays, Ltd.

Ownership: Robert Basham, P.J. Benton, Mark Bostick, Joseph Chlaparty, Mel Danker, Daniel Doyle Sr., Franklin Eck, Florida Progress Corporation, Claude Focardi, Jim Goodmon, Griffin Family Trust, Robert Kleinert, Gary Markel, Arthur Nagle, Vincent Naimoli, Daniel O'Connell, Frank Richardson, Lance Ringhaver, Thomas Sansone, Gus Stavros, Chris Sullivan, Stephen Waters.

Managing General Partner, Chief Executive Officer: Vince Naimoli. **Executive Assistant:** Diane Villanova **Administrative Assistant:** Janda Lucas.

BUSINESS OPERATIONS

Senior Vice President, Administration/General Counsel: John Higgins. **VP, Employee/Guest Relations:** Jose Tavarez. **Benefits Coordinator:** Jennifer Tran.

Finance

Controller: Patrick Smith. **Supervisor, Accounting:** Sandra Faulkner. **Payroll Supervisor:** Debbie Clement. **Director, Business Administration:** Bill Wiener. **Coordinator, Purchasing:** Mike Yodis.

Marketing, Sales

Vice President, Sales: Wayne Hodes, **VP, Marketing:** John Browne. **Administrative Assistant:** Silvia Bynes.

Senior Director, Corporate Sales/Broadcasting: Larry McCabe. **Senior Director, Marketing:** Richard Champion. **Director, Corporate Sales:** Ron Myers. **Director, Promotions/Special Events:** Allen Jernigan. **Director, Sponsorship Coordination:** Kelly Davis. **Director, Event Productions/Entertainment:** John Franzone. **Assistant Event Producer:** Stephanie Renica.

Manager, Broadcast Operations: Kevin Daigle. **Manager, Sponsorship Coordination:** Lauren Miller. **Manger, Marketing/Advertising:** Brian Killingsworth. **Manager, Print/Graphic Production:** Charles Parker. **Graphic Designer/Photo Manager:** Erik Ruiz. **Manager, Video/Graphic Production:** Jason Rundle. **Mascot Coordinator:** Shawn Christopherson.

Public Relations

Telephone: (727) 825-3242. **FAX:** (727) 825-3111.

Vice President, Public Relations: Rick Vaughn. **Assistant to VP, Public Relations:** Carmen Molina.

Director, Media Relations: Chris Costello. **Assistant Director, Media Relations:** Greg Landy.

Director, Community Relations: Liz-Beth Lauck. **Executive Director, Community Development:** Dick Crippen.

Website Manager: Eric Helmer.

Stadium Operations

VP, Operations/Facilities: Rick Nafe. **Administrative Assistant:** Lorra Gillespie. **Building Superintendent:** Scott Kelyman. **Event Manager:** Tom Karac. **Event Coordinator:** Tom Buscemi. **Manager, Suites/Customer Liaison Services:** Cass Halpin. **Booking Coordinator:** Caren Gramley.

Head Groundskeeper: Dan Moeller. **Director, Audio/Visual Services:** Ron Golick.

Ticketing

Director, Ticket Sales: Chris Gargani, **Manager, Group Sales:** Joe Steinberg. **Senior Group Sales Account Executive:** Brian Hunston. **Group Sales Account Executives:** Shannon Follet, Kyle Tadman. **Account Executives, Ticket Sales:** John Hardy, Barry Jones, Dean Quinlan, Seth Truman, Jaret Willi. **Manager, Inside Sales:** Matt DiFebo. **Sales Associates:** Brandon Berrios, Angela Gillissee, Dean Huls, Mike Migliarino, Chris Montiplisar, Jerry Patterson. **Premium/Seat Suite Sales Account Executive:** Jennifer Collins. **Power Hitter Program Coordinator:** John Heffernan. **Manager, Ticket Services:** Eric Weishaar. **Customer Service Representatives:** Kristi Capone, Erin Sullivan. **Director, Ticket Operations:** Robert Bennett. **Assistant Director, Ticket Operations:** Ken Mallory. **Ticket Operations:** Karen Smith.

Travel, Clubhouse

Director, Team Travel: Jeff Ziegler. **Travel Consultant:** Dirk Smith. **Equipment Manager, Home Clubhouse:** Chris Westmoreland. **Visitors Clubhouse:** Guy Gallagher.

General Information

Home Dugout: First Base. **Playing Surface:** FieldTurf.

Team Colors: Black, blue and green.

Player Representative: Unavailable.

Chuck LaMar

BASEBALL OPERATIONS

Senior Vice President, Baseball Operations/General Manager: Chuck LaMar.

Assistant GMs: Bart Braun, Scott Proefrock. **Director, Major League Administration:** Sandy Dengler. **Special Assistants to GM:** Eddie Bane, Hal McRae.

Video Coordinator: Chris Fernandez.

Major League Staff

Manager: Lou Piniella.

Coaches: Bench—John McLaren; Pitching—Chris Bosio; Batting—Lee Elia; First Base—Billy Hatcher; Third Base—Tom Foley; Bullpen—Matt Sinatro.

Lou Piniella

Medical, Training

Medical Director: Dr. James Andrews. **Medical Team Physician:** Dr. Michael Reilly. **Orthopedic Team Physician:** Dr. Koco Eaton.

Head Trainer: Ken Crenshaw. **Assistant Trainer:** Ron Porterfield. **Strength/Conditioning Coach:** Kevin Barr.

Minor Leagues

Telephone: (727) 825-3267. **FAX:** (727) 825-3493.

Director, Player Personnel/Scouting: Cam Bonifay. **Assistant, Player Development:** Mitch Lukevics. **Administrative Assistant, Player Development:** Denise Vega-Smith.

Field Coordinator: Jim Hoff. **Minor League Coordinators:** Paul Harker (medical/rehabilitation), Steve Henderson (hitting), Chuck Hernandez (pitching), Dwight Smith (outfield/baserunning). **Equipment Manager:** Tim McKechney.

Farm System

Class	Farm Team	League	Manager	Coach	Pitching Coach
AAA	Durham	International	Bill Evers	Richie Hebner	Joe Coleman
AA	Orlando	Southern	Charlie Montoyo	Skeeter Barnes	Dick Bosman
High A	Bakersfield	California	Omer Munoz	Ramon Ortiz	Marty DeMerritt
Low A	Charleston, SC	South Atlantic	Mako Oliveras	Steve Livesey	Xavier Hernandez
Short season	Hudson Valley	New York-Penn	Dave Howard	Jorge Robles	Rafael Montalvo
Rookie	Princeton	Appalachian	Jamie Nelson	Manny Castillo	Brad Woodall

Scouting

Telephone: (727) 825-3137. **FAX:** (727) 825-3300.

Assistant to Scouting Director: Nancy Berry.

Major League Scouts: Bart Johnson (Bridgeview, IL), Don Williams (Paragould, AR). **Major League Consultants:** Jerry Gardner (Los Alamitos, CA), George Zuraw (Englewood, FL).

National Scouting Coordinator: R.J. Harrison (Phoenix, AZ).

Regional Scouting Coordinators: Dave Roberts (Portland, OR), Mac Siebert (Molino, FL). **Special Assignment Scout:** Benny Latino (Hammond, LA).

Scouting Supervisors: Rich Aude (Woodland Hills, CA), Jonathan Bonifay (Austin, TX), James Bonnici (Ortonville, MI), Skip Bundy (Birmingham, AL), Rickey Drexler (Oklahoma City, OK), Kevin Elfering (Wesley Chapel, FL), Milt Hill (Marietta, GA), Hank King (Athens, GA), Paul Kirsch (Sherwood, OR), Fred Repke (Carson City, NV), Dale Tilleman (Taber, Alberta), Craig Weissmann (LaCosta, CA), Doug Witt (Glen Burnie, MD), Mike Zimmerman (Brooklyn, NY).

Cam Bonifay

Area Scouts: Tom Couston (Chicago, IL), Joe Murphy (Rock Island, IL).

Director, International Scouting: Rudy Santin (Miami, FL). **International Scout:** Junior Ramirez (Dominican Republic).

TEXAS RANGERS

Tom Hicks

Telephone, Address

Office Address: 1000 Ballpark Way, Arlington, TX 76011. **Mailing Address:** P.O. Box 90111, Arlington, TX 76004. **Telephone:** (817) 273-5222. **FAX:** (817) 273-5110. **Website:** www.texasrangers.com.

Ownership

Owner: Southwest Sports Group, Inc.

Chairman, Chief Executive Officer: Tom Hicks.

President, Chief Operating Officer: Michael Cramer. **Executive Assistant:** Katy Terrill.

Executive Vice President/Chief Financial Officer: Joe Armes. **Executive Assistant:** Genee Darden.

BUSINESS OPERATIONS

Executive Vice President, Business Operations: Rick McLaughlin. **Senior VP, General Counsel:** Casey Coffman. **Executive Assistant:** Judy Southworth.

Assistant Vice President, Human Resources: Terry Turner. **Director, Benefits/Compensation:** Janine Airhart. **Manager, Staffing/Development:** Carla Smith. **Legal Assistant:** Brenda Whittenberg.

Vice President, Information Technology: Steve McNeill. **Director, Application Systems:** Russell Smutzer. **Manager, Systems Administration:** Karl Clark. **Desktop Support Technician:** Greg Garrison. **Desktop/LAN Support:** Bill Jennings.

Finance

Vice President, Finance: Kellie Fischer. **Executive Assistant, Finance:** Carolyn Corbett.

Assistant Controllers: Melissa Embry, Starr Pritchard, Christie Steblein. **Manager, Payroll:** Donna Blaylock.

Marketing, Sales

Executive Vice President, Chief Sales/Marketing Officer: Greg McElroy.

Vice President, Sponsorship Sales: Brad Alberts. **VP, Advertising Sales:** Tom Comerford. **Director, Corporate Sales:** Jim Cochrane. **Director, Advertising Sales:** Grady Raskin. **Director, Broadcasting Sales Services:** Angie Swint. **Manager, Corporate Sales Services:** Ginger Reed. **Corporate Account Executives:** Mark Briggs, Lillian Zars.

Executive VP, Marketing/Entertainment: Chuck Morgan. **Senior Director, Marketing:** Kelly Calvert. **Senior Director, Graphic Design:** Rainer Uhlir. **Director, Events:** Sherry Flow. **Director, Graphic Design:** Michelle Hays. **Director, Marketing:** Kelly Calvert. **Director, Media:** Heidi Leonards. **Creative Director, Media:** Rush Olson.

Assistant Vice President, Merchandising: Todd Grizzle. **Director, Merchandising:** Diane Atkinson. **Manager, Ballpark Retail Operations:** Gary Mayfield. **Inventory Controller:** Gary Peterson.

Public Relations, Communications

Telephone: (817) 273-5203. **FAX:** (817) 273-5110.

Senior Vice President, Communications: John Blake. **Director, Publications:** Kurt Daniels. **Manager, Media Relations:** Rich Rice. **Assistant, Media Relations:** Dustin Morse. **Assistant, Communications:** Jessica Beard.

VP, Community Development/Relations: Norm Lyons. **Director, Community Relations:** Taunee Paur Taylor. **Assistant Director, Community Relations:** Tyler Beckstrom.

Stadium Operations

Vice President, Event Operations/Security: John Hardin. **Senior Director, Customer Service:** Donnie Pordash. **Director, Baseball Programs/Youth Ballpark:** Chris Shabay. **Assistant Director, Security:** Mickey McGovern.

Assistant VP, Facilities Operations: Gib Searight. **Director, Facilities/Special Events Operations:** Kevin Jimison. **Director, Grounds:** Tom Burns. **Director, Maintenance:** Mike Call. **Coordinator, Facility Services:** Duane Arber.

PA Announcer: Chuck Morgan. **Official Scorers:** John Mocek, Steve Weller.

Ticketing

Telephone: (817) 273-5100. **FAX:** (817) 273-5190.

Senior Director, Ticket Operations: Michael Wood. **Director, Ticket Services:** Mike Lentz. **Manager, Ticket Operations:** David Larson. **Coordinator, Ticket Accounting Administration:** Ranae Lewis. **Coordinator, Season/Group Sales:** Jena Tunnell. **Coordinator, Box Office:** Jason Mackey.

VP, Ticket Sales: Kerry Bubolz. **Assistant VP, Luxury Suite Sales:** Paige Jackson. **Manager, Group Sales:** Justin Aglialoro. **Manager, Season Ticket Sales:** Ken Troupe. **Manager, Inside Sales:** Chip Kisabeth.

Travel, Clubhouse

Director, Travel: Chris Lyngos.

Equipment/Home Clubhouse Manager: Zack Minasian. **Assistant Clubhouse Manager:** Dave Bales. **Visiting Clubhouse Manager:** Kelly Terrell. **Video Coordinator:** Josh Frasier.

General Information

Home Dugout: First Base. **Playing Surface:** Grass.

Team Colors: Royal blue and red.

Player Representative: Jeff Zimmerman.

BASEBALL OPERATIONS

John Hart

Telephone: (817) 273-5222. **FAX:** (817) 273-5285.

Executive Vice President, General Manager: John Hart.

Assistant GM, Baseball Operations: Dan O'Brien. **Special Assistants to GM:** Dom Chiti, Jay Robertson. **Senior Advisor to GM:** Tom Giordano.

Director, Major League Administration: Judy Johns. **Assistant, Baseball Operations:** Jon Daniels.

Major League Staff

Manager: Buck Showalter.

Coaches: Dugout—Don Wakamatsu; Pitching—Orel Hershiser; Batting—Rudy Jaramillo; First Base—De Marlo Hale; Third Base—Steve Smith; Bullpen—Mark Connor.

Medical, Training

Team Physician: Dr. John Conway. **Team Internist:** Dr. David Hunter.

Head Trainer/Medical Director: Jamie Reed. **Assistant Trainers:** Greg Harrel, Ray Ramirez. **Director, Strength/Conditioning:** Fernando Montes.

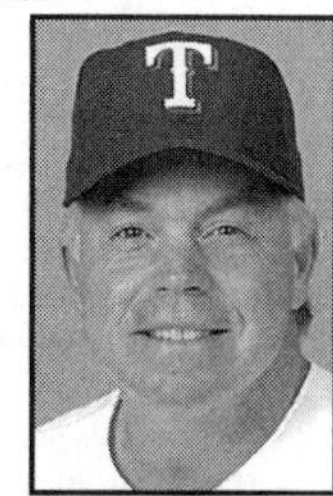
Buck Showalter

Player Development

Telephone: (817) 273-5224. **FAX:** (817) 273-5285.

Assistant General Manager, Player Development/Scouting: Grady Fuson.

Director, Minor League Operations: John Lombardo. **Coordinator, Player Development:** Bob Miscik. **Administrative Assistant:** Margaret Bales.

Roving Instructors: Ralph Dickinson (hitting), Kevin Harmon (medical/conditioning), Greg Riddoch (defense), Lee Tunnell (pitching).

Manager, Minor League Complex Operations: Chris Guth. **Assistant Equipment Manager:** Joe Catalano. **Coordinator, Performance Enhancement:** Don Kalkstein. **Administrative Assistant, Arizona Operations:** Marc Dallman.

Farm System

Class	Farm Team	League	Manager	Coach	Pitching Coach
AAA	Oklahoma	Pacific Coast	Bobby Jones	Bruce Crabbe	Glenn Abbott
AA	Frisco	Texas	Tim Ireland	Paul Carey	Steve Luebber
High A	Stockton	California	Arnie Beyeler	Joe Ayrault	Fred Dabney
Low A	Clinton	Midwest	Carlos Subero	Mike Boulanger	Andy Hawkins
Short season	Spokane	Northwest	Darryl Kennedy	Derek Lee	David Chavarria
Rookie	Surprise	Arizona	Pedro Lopez	B. Jacoby/K. Dattola	Aris Tirado
Rookie	Rangers	Dominican	Fermin Infante	Unavailable	Francisco Saneaux

Scouting

Telephone: (817) 273-5277. **FAX:** (817) 273-5243.

Coordinator, Scouting: Ron Hopkins. **Special Assistant, Scouting Operations:** Dick Bogard. **Assistant, Scouting Operations:** Russ Ardolina. **Assistant, Professional Scouting Operations:** Jeff Wood.

Special Assignment Scouts: Mel Didier (Phoenix, AZ), Rudy Terrasas (Santa Fe, TX). **Professional Scouts:** Toney Howell (Gurnee, IL), Les Parker (Hudson, FL), Ross Sapp (Cherry Valley, CA), Bill Wood (Coppell, TX).

Regional Crosscheckers: Kip Fagg (Gilbert, AZ), Dave Klipstein (Roanoke, TX), Doug Harris (Carlisle, PA).

Area Scouts: John Castleberry (High Point, NC), Jay Eddings (Sperry, OK), Steve Flores (Temecula, CA), Tim Fortugno (Elk Grove, CA), Mark Giegler (Fenton, MI), Mike Grouse (Olathe, KS), Todd Guggiana (Cerritos, CA), Derek Lee (Homewood, IL), Gary McGraw (Gaston, OR), John Poloni (Tarpon Springs, FL), Rick Schroeder (Arizona), Doug Simons (Cumming, GA), Tommy Tanous (Swansea, MA), Randy Taylor (Katy, TX), Frankie Thon (Guaynabo, PR).

Grady Fuson

Part-time Scouts: Mark Harris (Gainesville, VA), Ron Toenjes (Georgetown, TX).

Latin Coordinator: Manny Batista (Vega Alta, PR).

International Scouts: Charlie Currier (Venezuela), Marlon Nava (Venezuela), Jesus Ovalle (Dominican Republic), Rodolfo Rosario (Dominican Republic), Edgar Suarez (Venezuela), Richard Seko (Pacific Rim), Danilo Troncoso (Dominican Republic), Guido Verducci (Italy, Southern Europe).

TORONTO BLUE JAYS

Paul Godfrey

Telephone, Address

Office/Mailing Address: 1 Blue Jays Way, Suite 3200, Toronto, Ontario M5V 1J1. **Telephone:** (416) 341-1000. **FAX:** (416) 341-1250. **E-Mail Address:** bluejay@bluejays.ca **Website:** www.bluejays.com.

Ownership

Operated by: Toronto Blue Jays Baseball Club.
Principal Owner: Rogers Communications, Inc.
President, Chief Executive Officer: Paul Godfrey.

BUSINESS OPERATIONS

Finance

Senior Vice President, Administration/Business Affairs: Lisa Novak. **VP, Finance/Administration:** Susan Brioux. **Controller:** Cathy McNamara-Mackay.

Director, Risk Management: Suzanne Joncas. **Manager, Payroll/Benefits:** Brenda Dimmer. **Manager, Financial Reporting:** Tanya van der Wouden. **Manager, Budgeting/Forecasting:** Sharon Labenski. **Accounting Analyst:** Shari Ralph. **Coordinator, Accounts Receivable:** Marion Sullivan. **Coordinator, Accounts Payable:** Andy Topolie. **Coordinator, Ticket Office Receivables:** Joseph Roach. **Coordinator, General Accounting:** Tony Phung. **Coordinator, Payroll/Benefits:** Lindsey Simonini.

Manager, Human Resources: Sarah Keenan.

Director, Information Technology: Jacques Farand. **Senior Systems Analyst:** Tony Miranda. **Systems Administrator:** Spencer Lui. **Information Systems Support:** Vidal Abad. **Ticket System Administrator:** Darlene Samakese.

Marketing, Sales

Senior Vice President, Marketing/Sales: Paul Allamby.

Director, Consumer Marketing: Jim Bloom. **Manager, Game Entertainment/Promotions:** Tim Sullivan. **Manager, Marketing Communications/Advertising:** Alyssa Berenstein. **Coordinator, Mascot/Youth Outreach:** Brennan Anderson. **Coordinator, Marketing Communications:** Melinn Chaban. **Associate Producer, Game Entertainment:** Deb Belinsky. **Executive Assistant:** Maria Cresswell.

Director, Merchandising: Michael Andrejek. **Manager, Purchasing/Mail Order Operations:** Helen Maunder. **Manager, Retail Operations:** Stephen Tolkunow. **Manager, Stadium Events:** Linda Mykytyshyn. **Manager, Bullpen Store:** Teresa Michalski.

Vice President, Corporate Partnerships/Business Development: Mark Lemmon. **Directors, Corporate Marketing:** Wilna Behr, Robert Mackay. **Manager, Corporate Partnerships:** Jennifer Santamaria. **Interim Manager, Corporate Marketing:** Susan Burrows. **Coordinator, Corporate Marketing:** Honsing Leung. **Executive Assistant:** Darla McKeen.

Media Relations, Communications

Telephone: (416) 341-1301/1303. **FAX:** (416) 341-1250.

Senior Vice President, Communications/External Relations: Rob Godfrey. **VP, Special Projects:** Howard Starkman.

Director, Communications: Jay Stenhouse. **Director, Public Relations:** Will Hill. **Manager, Baseball Information:** Michael Shaw. **Coordinator, Communications:** Leanna England. **Communications Assistant:** Erik Grossman.

Stadium Operations

Director, Stadium Operations: Mario Coutinho. **Manager, Guest Relations:** Paul So. **Office Manager:** Anne Fulford.
Game Security Supervisor: John Booth. **Supervisor, Maintenance/Housekeeping Services:** Mick Bazinet.
PA Announcer: Murray Eldon. **Official Scorers:** Louis Cauz, Doug Hobbs, Neil MacCarl, Joe Sawchuk.

Ticketing

Telephone: (416) 341-1280. **FAX:** (416) 341-1177.

Vice President, Ticket Sales/Service: Steve Smith.

Director, Customer Service: Sheila Cantarutti. **Director, Market Investments:** Felix Paulick.

Manager, Inside Sales: Isabelle Frati. **Manager, Group Sales:** Travis Tinning. **Manager, Customer Service:** Justin McInytre. **Manager, Database/Ticket System:** Doug Barr. **Manager, Special Projects:** Franc Rota. **Assistant Manager, Corporate Sales:** Jason Diplock. **Assistant Manager, Internal Communication/Data Control:** Sandra Wilbur. **Assistant Manager, Ticket System/Database:** Mark Nguyen. **Assistant Manager, Inside Sales:** Paul Fruitman.

Travel, Clubhouse

Manager, Team Travel: Bart Given.

Equipment Manager: Jeff Ross. **Clubhouse Manager:** Kevin Malloy. **Visitors Video Operations:** Robert Baumander.

General Information

Home Dugout: Third Base. **Playing Surface:** Artificial turf.
Team Colors: Blue, red and white.
Player Representative: Vernon Wells.

J.P. Ricciardi

BASEBALL OPERATIONS

Senior Vice President, Baseball Operations/General Manager: J.P. Ricciardi. **Executive Assistant to GM:** Fran Brown.

Vice President, Baseball Operations/Assistant GM: Tim McCleary. **Assistant to GM:** Tony LaCava. **Special Assistants to GM:** Keith Law, Bill Livesey.

Vice Presidents: Bob Mattick, Tim Wilken.

Director, Florida Operations: Ken Carson.

Manager, Amateur Baseball: Kevin Briand. **Executive Assistant, Baseball:** Heather Connolly.

Major League Staff

Manager: Carlos Tosca.

Coaches: Bench—Unavailable; Pitching—Gil Patterson; Batting—Mike Barnett; First Base—John Gibbons; Third Base—Brian Butterfield; Bullpen—Bruce Walton. Bullpen Catcher—Alex Andreopoulos.

Carlos Tosca

Medical, Training

Team Physician: Dr. Ron Taylor. **Head Trainer:** Scott Shannon. **Assistant Trainer:** George Poulis. **Strength/Conditioning Coordinator:** Donovan Santas.

Player Development

Telephone: (416) 341-1228. **FAX:** (416) 341-1245.

Director, Player Development: Dick Scott.

Director, Minor League Operations: Bob Nelson. **Administrative Assistants:** Donna Kuzoff, Angie Van Evera.

Coordinators: Jay Inouye (training), Chris Joyner (strength/conditioning), Merv Rettenmund (hitting), Billy Wardlow (equipment), Ernie Whitt (roving).

Employee Assistance Program Director: Ray Karesky.

Farm System

Class	Farm Team	League	Manager	Coach	Pitching Coach
AAA	Syracuse	International	Omar Malave	Ken Landreaux	Tom Filer
AA	New Haven	Eastern	Marty Pevey	Ken Joyce	Dane Johnson
High A	Dunedin	Florida State	Mike Basso	Gary Cathcart	Rick Langford
Low A	Charleston, W.Va.	South Atlantic	Mark Meleski	Charles Poe	James Keller
Short season	Auburn	New York-Penn	Dennis Holmberg	Dave Pano	Tom Bradley
Rookie	Pulaski	Appalachian	Paul Elliott	Unavailable	Lee Guetterman
Rookie	Blue Jays	Dominican	Juan Bernhardt	Unavailable	Antonio Caceres
Rookie	Blue Jays	Venezuelan	Domingo Carrasquel	Hedbertt Hurtado	Oswald Peraza

Scouting

Telephone: (416) 341-1115, (416) 341-1339. **FAX:** (416) 341-1245.

Director, Scouting: Chris Buckley. **Assistant Director, Scouting:** Mark Snipp. **Coordinators, Scouting Operations:** Jon Lalonde, Charlie Wilson.

Advance Scout: Sal Butera. **Special Assignment Scouts:** Ted Lekas (Worcester, MA), Jeff Taylor (Newark, DE).

National Crosschecker: Mike Mangan (Clermont, FL).

Scouting Supervisors: Charles Aliano (Columbia, SC), Jaymie Bane (Lexington, KY), Andy Beene (Center Point, TX), Bill Byckowski (Georgetown, Ontario), John Ceprini (Massapequa, NY) Don Cowan (Delta, B.C.), Joey Davis (Roseville, CA), Joel Grampietro (Shrewsbury, MA), Ed Heather (Cambridge, Ontario), Tim Huff (Cave Creek, AZ), Walt Jeffries (Paris, Otario), Marty Miller (Chicago, IL), Ty Nichols (Broken Arrow, OK), Demerius Pittman (Corona, CA), Jorge Rivera (Puerto Nuevo, PR), Jim Rooney (Seal Beach, CA), Andrew Tinnish (Tallahassee, FL).

Chris Buckley

Director, Latin America Operations: Tony Arias (Miami, FL). **Scouting Supervisor, Australia:** Greg Wade (Queensland).

MAJOR LEAGUE
SCHEDULES

2002 STANDINGS
SPRING TRAINING

AMERICAN LEAGUE

2002 STANDINGS

EAST	W	L	PCT	GB	Manager(s)	General Manager
New York Yankees	103	58	.640	—	Joe Torre	Brian Cashman
Boston Red Sox	93	69	.574	10½	Grady Little	Mike Port
Toronto Blue Jays	78	84	.481	25½	Buck Martinez/Carlos Tosca	J.P. Ricciardi
Baltimore Orioles	67	95	.414	36½	Mike Hargrove	Syd Thrift
Tampa Bay Devil Rays	55	106	.342	48	Hal McRae	Chuck LaMar

CENTRAL	W	L	PCT	GB	Manager(s)	General Manager(s)
Minnesota Twins	94	67	.584	—	Ron Gardenhire	Terry Ryan
Chicago White Sox	81	81	.500	13½	Jerry Manuel	Ken Williams
Cleveland Indians	74	88	.457	20½	Charlie Manuel/Joel Skinner	Mark Shapiro
Kansas City Royals	62	100	.383	32½	Tony Muser/Tony Pena	Allard Baird
Detroit Tigers	55	106	.342	39	Phil Garner/Luis Pujols	Randy Smith/Dave Dombrowski

WEST	W	L	PCT	GB	Manager	General Manager
Oakland Athletics	103	59	.636	—	Art Howe	Billy Beane
*Anaheim Angels	99	63	.611	4	Mike Scioscia	Bill Stoneman
Seattle Mariners	93	69	.574	10	Lou Piniella	Pat Gillick
Texas Rangers	72	90	.444	31	Jerry Narron	John Hart

*Won wild-card playoff berth

PLAYOFFS: Division Series (best-of-5)—Anaheim defeated New York 3-1; Minnesota defeated Oakland 3-2. **League Championship Series** (best-of-7)—Anaheim defeated Minnesota 4-1.

NATIONAL LEAGUE

2002 STANDINGS

EAST	W	L	PCT	GB	Manager	General Manager
Atlanta Braves	101	59	.631	—	Bobby Cox	John Schuerholz
Montreal Expos	83	79	.512	19	Frank Robinson	Omar Minaya
Philadelphia Phillies	80	81	.497	21½	Larry Bowa	Ed Wade
Florida Marlins	79	83	.488	23	Jeff Torborg	Larry Beinfest
New York Mets	75	86	.466	26½	Bobby Valentine	Steve Phillips

CENTRAL	W	L	PCT	GB	Manager(s)	General Manager(s)
St. Louis Cardinals	97	65	.599	—	Tony La Russa	Walt Jocketty
Houston Astros	84	78	.519	13	Jimy Williams	Gerry Hunsicker
Cincinnati Reds	78	84	.481	19	Bob Boone	Jim Bowden
Pittsburgh Pirates	72	89	.447	24½	Lloyd McClendon	Dave Littlefield
Chicago Cubs	67	95	.414	30	Don Baylor/Bruce Kimm	Andy MacPhail/Jim Hendry
Milwaukee Brewers	56	106	.346	41	Dave Lopes/Jerry Royster	Dean Taylor

WEST	W	L	PCT	GB	Manager(s)	General Manager
Arizona Diamondbacks	98	64	.605	—	Bob Brenly	Joe Garagiola Jr.
*San Francisco Giants	95	66	.590	2½	Dusty Baker	Brian Sabean
Los Angeles Dodgers	92	70	.568	6	Jim Tracy	Dan Evans
Colorado Rockies	73	89	.451	25	Buddy Bell/Clint Hurdle	Dan O'Dowd
San Diego Padres	66	96	.407	32	Bruce Bochy	Kevin Towers

*Won wild-card playoff berth

PLAYOFFS: Division Series (best-of-5)—San Francisco defeated Atlanta 3-2; St. Louis defeated Arizona 3-0. **League Championship Series** (best-of-7)—San Francisco defeated St. Louis 4-1.

WORLD SERIES

(Best-of-7)

Anaheim (American) defeated San Francisco (National) 4-3.

AMERICAN LEAGUE

ANAHEIM ANGELS
Edison International Field

■ **Standard Game Times:** 7:05 p.m.; Sun. 1:05.

MARCH
30 .... Texas

APRIL
1-**2** .... Texas
4-**5**-**6** .... at Oakland
8-9-10 .... at Seattle
11-12-**13** .... Oakland
14-15-16-**17** .... at Texas
18-19-**20** .... Seattle
22-23-24 .... Yankees
25-26-**27** .... Boston
29-30 .... at Cleveland

MAY
1 .... at Cleveland
2-**3**-**4** .... at Toronto
6-7-8 .... Cleveland
9-10-**11** .... Toronto
13-14-15 .... at Yankees
16-**17**-**18** .... at Boston
20-21-22 .... Baltimore
23-24-**25** .... Tampa Bay
27-28 .... at Baltimore
29-30-31 .... at Tampa Bay

JUNE
1 .... at Tampa Bay
3-4-5 .... *#Montreal
6-7-**8** .... *at Florida
9-10-11 .... *Philadelphia
13-14-**15** .... *Mets
16-17-18-**19** .... at Seattle
20-**21**-22 .... *at L.A.
24-25-26 .... Seattle
27-28-**29** .... *L.A.
30 .... Texas

JULY
1-2-3 .... Texas
4-5-**6** .... at Oakland
8-9-**10** .... Kansas City
11-12-**13** .... Minnesota
17-18-19-**20** .... at Balt.
21-**22** .... at Tampa Bay
23-**24** .... at Texas
25-26-**27**-28 .... Oakland
29-30-31 .... Yankees

AUGUST
1-2-**3** .... Toronto
5-6-7 .... at Boston
8-9-**10** .... at Cleveland
11-12-13-14 .... White Sox
15-16-**17** .... Detroit
18-19-20 .... at White Sox
21-22-23-**24** .... at Detroit
26-27-**28** .... Minnesota
29-30-**31** .... at K.C.

SEPTEMBER
1-2-**3** .... at Minnesota
5-6-**7** .... Kansas City
8-9-10-**11** .... at Oakland
12-**13**-**14** .... at Seattle
15-16-17 .... Oakland
19-20-**21** .... at Texas
22-23-**24** .... Seattle
26-27-**28** .... Texas

BALTIMORE ORIOLES
Oriole Park at Camden Yards

■ **Standard Game Times:** 7:05 p.m.; Sat. (April-May) 1:35; Sun. 1:35.

MARCH
31 .... Cleveland

APRIL
2-3 .... Cleveland
4-**5**-**6** .... Boston
8-9-10 .... at Tampa Bay
11-12-13 .... at Boston
15-16-17 .... at Cleveland
18-**19**-**20**-21 .... Tampa Bay
22-23-24 .... White Sox
25-26-**27** .... at Tampa Bay
29-30 .... at Detroit

MAY
1 .... at Detroit
2-**3**-**4** .... Kansas City
5-6-**7** .... Detroit
8-9-10-**11** .... at K.C.
13-14-15 .... at White Sox
16-17-**18** .... Tampa Bay
20-21-22 .... at Anaheim
23-24-**25** .... at Texas
27-28 .... Anaheim
29-30-31 .... Texas

JUNE
1 .... Texas
3-4-5 .... *at Houston
6-**7**-**8** .... *at St. Louis
10-11-12 .... *Cubs
13-14-**15** .... *Milwaukee
17-18-19 .... Toronto
20-21-**22** .... *at Atlanta
23-24-25-26 .... at Toronto
27-28-**29** .... *Philadelphia
30 .... Yankees

JULY
1-**2** .... Yankees
4-5-**6** .... Toronto
8-9-10 .... at Seattle
11-**12**-**13** .... at Oakland
17-18-19-**20** .... Anaheim
21-**22** .... Texas
23-**24** .... at Yankees
25-**26**-**27** .... at Toronto
29-30-31 .... at Minnesota

AUGUST
1-2-**3** .... Boston
4-5-6-**7** .... Minnesota
8-9-**10** .... at Boston
11-12-**13** .... at Tampa Bay
15-16-**17** .... Yankees
19-20-21 .... Tampa Bay
22-**23**-**24**-25 .... at Yankees
26-27-**28** .... at Oakland
29-**30**-**31** .... at Seattle

SEPTEMBER
2-3-4 .... Oakland
5-6-**7** .... Seattle
8-9-**10** .... Boston
12-**13**-**14** .... at Toronto
15-16-17-18 .... Yankees
19-20-**21** .... Toronto
22-23-24-25 .... at Boston
26-**27**-**28** .... at Yankees

BOSTON RED SOX
Fenway Park

■ **Standard Game Times:** 7:05 p.m., (April, Sept.) 6:05; Sat. (April-May) 1:05, (June-Aug) 5:05; Sun. 2:05.

MARCH
31 .... at Tampa Bay

APRIL
1-2-**3** .... at Tampa Bay
4-**5**-**6** .... at Baltimore
8-9-10 .... at Toronto
11-12-**13** .... Baltimore
15-16-17 .... Tampa Bay
18-**19**-**20**-**21** .... Toronto
22-23-24 .... at Texas
25-26-**27** .... at Anaheim
29-30 .... Kansas City

MAY
1 .... Kansas City
2-3-**4** .... Minnesota
5-6-**7** .... at Kansas City
9-10-**11** .... at Minnesota
13-14-15 .... Texas
16-**17**-**18** .... Anaheim
19-20-21 .... Yankees
23-24-**25** .... Cleveland
26-27-28 .... at Yankees
30-**31** .... at Toronto

JUNE
1 .... at Toronto
3-4-5 .... *at Pittsburgh
6-7-**8** .... *at Milwaukee
10-11-12 .... *St. Louis
13-14-**15** .... *Houston
16-17-18-**19** .... at Wh. Sox
20-21-**22** .... *at Phila.
23-24-25-**26** .... Detroit
27-28-**29** .... *Florida

JULY
1-2-3 .... at Tampa Bay
4-**5**-**6**-**7** .... at Yankees
8-9-10 .... at Toronto
11-12-**13** .... at Detroit
17-18-19-**20** .... Toronto
21-22 .... Detroit
23-**24** .... Tampa Bay
25-26-**27** .... Yankees
29-30-31 .... at Texas

AUGUST
1-2-**3** .... at Baltimore
5-6-7 .... Anaheim
8-9-**10** .... Baltimore
11-12-13-**14** .... at Oakland
15-**16**-**17** .... at Seattle
19-20-21 .... Oakland
22-23-**24**-**25** .... Seattle
26-27 .... Toronto
29-30-**31** .... Yankees

SEPTEMBER
2-3 .... at White Sox
5-**6**-**7** .... at Yankees
8-9-**10** .... at Baltimore
12-13-**14** .... White Sox
15-16-17-18 .... T.B.
19-20-**21** .... at Cleveland
22-23-24-25 .... Baltimore
26-27-**28** .... at T.B.

CHICAGO WHITE SOX
U.S. Cellular Field

■ **Standard Game Times:** 7:05 p.m.; Sat. (June-Sept.) 6:05; Sun. 1:05.

MARCH
31 .... at Kansas City

APRIL
2-**3** .... at Kansas City
4-**5**-**6** .... Detroit
7-9-10 .... at Cleveland
11-**12**-**13** .... at Detroit
15-16-**17** .... Kansas City
18-19-**20**-**21** .... Cleveland
22-23-24 .... at Baltimore
25-26-**27** .... Minnesota
29-30 .... Oakland

MAY
1 .... Oakland
2-3-**4** .... Seattle
6-7-**8** .... at Oakland

9-10-**11** .... at Seattle
13-14-15 .... Baltimore
16-17-**18** ... at Minnesota
19-20-21 .... Toronto
23-24-**25** .... Detroit
26-27-28-29 .. at Toronto
30-31 .... at Cleveland

JUNE

1-2 .... at Cleveland
3-4-5 .... *at Arizona
6-7-**8** .... *at Los Angeles
10-11-12 .... *San Fran.
13-14-**15** ...... *San Diego
16-17-18-**19** .... Boston
20-21-22 .... *at Cubs
24-25-**26** ... at Minnesota
27-28-29 .... *Cubs
30 .... Minnesota

JULY

1-2 .... Minnesota
4-5-**6** .... at Tampa Bay
8-9-10 .... at Detroit
11-12-**13** ..... at Cleveland
17-18-19-**20** .... Detroit
21-**22** .... Cleveland
23-24 .... at Toronto
25-26-**27** .... Tampa Bay
29-30-31 .... at K.C.

AUGUST

1-**2-3** .... at Seattle
4-5-**6** .... Kansas City
8-9-**10** .... Oakland
11-12-13-14 .... at Ana.
15-16-17 .... at Texas
18-19-20 .... Anaheim
21-22-23-**24** .... Texas
26-27-**28** .... at Yankees
29-30-**31** .... at Detroit

SEPTEMBER

2-3 .... Boston
5-6-**7** .... Cleveland
8-9-10-**11** ...... Minnesota
12-13-**14** .... at Boston
16-17-18 ... at Minnesota
19-20-**21** ..... Kansas City
22-23-**24** .... Yankees
25-26-27-**28** .... at K.C.

CLEVELAND INDIANS
Jacobs Field

■ **Standard Game Times:** 7:05 p.m.; Sat. 1:05, 7:05; Sun. 1:05.

MARCH

31 .... at Baltimore

APRIL

2-3 .... at Baltimore
4-**5-6** .... at Kansas City
7-9-10 .... White Sox
11-**12-13**-14 .... K.C.
15-16-17 .... Baltimore
18-19-**20-21** .. at Wh. Sox
22-23-24 .... at Seattle
25-**26-27** .... at Oakland
29-30 .... Anaheim

MAY

1 .... Anaheim
2-**3-4** .... Texas
6-7-8 .... at Anaheim
9-10-**11** .... at Texas
13-14-15 .... Seattle
16-**17-18** .... Oakland
19-20-21-22 .... Detroit
23-24-**25** .... at Boston
26-27-28 .... at Detroit
30-31 .... White Sox

JUNE

1-2 .... White Sox
3-4-**5** .... *at Colorado
6-7-**8** .... *at Arizona
10-11-12 ...... *San Diego
13-14-**15** ... *Los Angeles
17-18-**19** .... at Detroit
20-21-**22** .... *at Pitt.
24-25-26 ..... Kansas City
27-28-**29** ...... *Cincinnati
30 .... at Kansas City

JULY

1-2 .... at Kansas City
3-4-5-**6** ...... at Minnesota
8-9-10 .... Yankees
11-12-**13** .... White Sox
17-18-**19-20** .. at Yankees
21-**22** .... at White Sox
23-24 .... Detroit
25-26-**27** .... Minnesota
29-30-**31** .... at Oakland

AUGUST

1-2-3 .... at Texas
5-6-7 .... Seattle
8-9-**10** .... Anaheim
11-12-13-**14** .... at Minn.
15-16-**17**-18 .... T.B.
19-20 .... Minnesota
22-23-**24** ... at Tampa Bay
26-27-28 .... Detroit
29-30-**31** .... Toronto

SEPTEMBER

1-2-3-4 .... at Detroit
5-6-**7** .... at White Sox
9-10-**11** ... at Kansas City
12-13-**14**-15 ... Minnesota
16-17-18 ..... Kansas City
19-20-**21** .... Boston
23-24 .... at Minnesota
26-**27-28** .... at Toronto

DETROIT TIGERS
Comerica Park

■ **Standard Game Times:** 7:05 p.m.; Sat. (April-May) 1:05; Sun. 1:05.

MARCH

31 .... Minnesota

APRIL

2-**3** .... Minnesota
4-5-6 .... at White Sox
8-**9-10** .... Kansas City
11-**12-13** .... White Sox
15-16-17 ... at Minnesota
18-**19-20** .... at K.C.
22-23-**24** .... at Oakland
25-26-**27** .... at Seattle
29-30 .... Baltimore

MAY

1 .... Baltimore
2-**3-4** .... Tampa Bay
5-6-**7** .... at Baltimore
9-10-**11** ..... at Tampa Bay
13-14-15 .... Oakland
16-**17-18** .... Seattle
19-20-21-22 ...... at Cleve.
23-24-**25** .... at White Sox
26-27-28 .... Cleveland
30-**31** .... Yankees

JUNE

1 .... Yankees
3-4-**5** .... *at San Diego
6-**7-8** .... *at San Fran.
10-11-12 ... *Los Angeles
13-14-**15** .... *Colorado
17-18-**19** .... Cleveland
20-21-**22** .... *at Colorado
23-24-25-**26** ... at Boston
27-28-**29** .... *Arizona
30 .... Toronto

JULY

1-2 .... Toronto
3-4-5-**6** .... at Kansas City
8-9-10 .... White Sox
11-12-**13** .... Boston
17-18-19-**20** at White Sox
21-22 .... at Boston
23-24 .... at Cleveland
25-26-**27** ..... Kansas City
29-30-**31** .... at Seattle

AUGUST

1-2-**3** .... at Minnesota
5-6-7 .... Oakland
8-9-**10** .... Minnesota
11-12-13-14 ...... at Texas
15-16-**17** ...... at Anaheim
18-19-20 .... Texas
21-22-23-**24** ..... Anaheim
26-27-28 ..... at Cleveland
29-30-**31** .... White Sox

SEPTEMBER

1-2-3-4 .... Cleveland
5-**6-7** .... at Toronto
9-10-11 .... at Yankees
12-13-**14** ..... Kansas City
16-17-18 .... Toronto
19-**20-21** ... at Minnesota
22-23-24 .... at K.C.
25-26-27-**28** ... Minnesota

KANSAS CITY ROYALS
Kauffman Stadium

■ **Standard Game Times:** 7:05 p.m.; Sat. (April) 1:05, 6:05; Sun. 1:05.

MARCH

31 .... White Sox

APRIL

2-3 .... White Sox
4-5-6 .... Cleveland
8-**9-10** .... at Detroit
11-**12-13**-14 ...... at Cleve.
15-16-**17** .... at White Sox
18-**19-20** .... Detroit
22-23-**24** .... Minnesota
25-**26-27** .... at Toronto
29-30 .... at Boston

MAY

1 .... at Boston
2-**3-4** .... at Baltimore
5-6-**7** .... Boston
8-9-10-**11** .... Baltimore
12-13-14-**15** .... at Minn.
16-17-**18** .... Toronto
20-21-**22** .... at Seattle
23-**24-25** .... at Oakland
27-**28** .... Seattle
29-30-**31** .... Oakland

JUNE

1 .... Oakland
3-4-5 .... *at Los Angeles
6-7-**8** .... *at Colorado
10-11-12 .... *Arizona
13-14-**15** .... *San Fran.
17-18-**19** .... Minnesota
20-21-**22** .... *at St. Louis
24-25-26 ..... at Cleveland
27-28-**29** .... *St. Louis
30 .... Cleveland

JULY

1-2 .... Cleveland
3-4-5-**6** .... Detroit
8-9-**10** .... at Anaheim
11-12-13 .... at Texas
17-18-19-20 .... Seattle
21-22 .... Oakland
23-**24** .... at Minnesota
25-26-**27** .... at Detroit
29-30-31 .... White Sox

AUGUST

1-2-**3** .... Tampa Bay
4-5-**6** .... at White Sox
7-8-9-**10** ... at Tampa Bay
11-12-13 .... Yankees
15-16-**17** .... Minnesota
18-19-**20** .... at Yankees
21-22-23-**24** .... at Minn.
26-27-28 .... Texas
29-30-**31** .... Anaheim

SEPTEMBER

1-2-3 .... at Texas
5-6-**7** .... at Anaheim
9-10-**11** .... Cleveland
12-13-**14** .... at Detroit
16-17-18 ..... at Cleveland
19-20-**21** .... at White Sox
22-23-24 .... Detroit
25-26-27-**28** ... White Sox

MINNESOTA TWINS
Hubert H. Humphrey Metrodome

Standard Game Times: 12:05 p.m., 7:05; Sat 6:05, Sun. 1:05.

MARCH
31 ... at Detroit
APRIL
2-**3** ... at Detroit
4-5-**6** ... Toronto
7-9-**10** ... at Yankees
11-**12**-**13** ... at Toronto
15-16-17 ... Detroit
18-19-20-**21** ... Yankees
22-23-**24** ... at K.C.
25-26-**27** ... at White Sox
29-30 ... Tampa Bay
MAY
1 ... Tampa Bay
2-3-**4** ... at Boston
6-7-8 ... at Tampa Bay
9-10-**11** ... Boston
12-13-14-**15** Kansas City
16-17-**18** ... White Sox
20-**21**-**22** ... at Oakland
23-24-**25** ... at Seattle
27-**28** ... Oakland
29-30-31 ... Seattle
JUNE
1 ... Seattle
3-4-5 ... *at San Francisco
6-7-**8** ... *at San Diego
10-11-12 ... *Colorado
13-14-**15** ... *Arizona
17-18-**19** ... at K.C.
20-21-**22** ... *at Mil.
24-25-**26** ... White Sox
27-28-**29** ... *Milwaukee
30 ... at White Sox
JULY
1-2 ... at White Sox
3-4-5-**6** ... Cleveland
8-9-10 ... at Texas
11-12-**13** ... at Anaheim
17-18-19-**20** ... Oakland
21-22 ... Seattle
23-**24** ... Kansas City
25-26-**27** ... at Cleveland
29-30-31 ... Baltimore
AUGUST
1-2-**3** ... Detroit
4-5-6-**7** ... at Baltimore
8-9-**10** ... at Detroit
11-12-13-**14** ... Cleveland
15-16-**17** ... at K.C.
19-20 ... at Cleveland
21-22-23-**24** ... K.C.
26-27-**28** ... at Anaheim
29-30-**31** ... at Texas
SEPTEMBER
1-2-**3** ... Anaheim
5-**6**-**7** ... Texas
8-9-10-**11** .. at White Sox
12-13-**14**-15 ... at Cleve.
16-17-18 ... White Sox
19-**20**-**21** ... Detroit
23-24 ... Cleveland
25-26-27-**28** ... at Detroit

NEW YORK YANKEES
Yankee Stadium

Standard Game Times: 7:05 p.m.; Sat. (April-May) 1:05, (June-Sept.) 4:05; Sun. 1:05.

MARCH
31 ... at Toronto
APRIL
1-2 ... at Toronto
4-5-**6** ... at Tampa Bay
7-9-10 ... Minnesota
11-**12**-**13** ... Tampa Bay
14-15-16-**17** ... Toronto
18-19-20-**21** at Minnesota
22-23-24 ... at Anaheim
25-26-**27** ... at Texas
29-30 ... Seattle
MAY
1 ... Seattle
2-**3**-**4** ... Oakland
6-7-8 ... at Seattle
9-**10**-**11** ... at Oakland
13-14-15 ... Anaheim
16-**17**-**18** ... Texas
19-20-21 ... at Boston
22-23-**24**-**25** ... Toronto
26-27-28 ... Boston
30-**31** ... at Detroit
JUNE
1 ... at Detroit
3-4-5 ... *at Cincinnati
6-7-**8** ... *at Cubs
10-11-**12** ... *Houston
13-**14**-**15** ... *St. Louis
17-18-**19** ... Tampa Bay
20-**21**-22 ... *at Mets
23-24-25-**26** ... at T.B.
27-**28**-29 ... *Mets
30 ... at Baltimore
JULY
1-**2** ... at Baltimore
4-5-6-7 ... Boston
8-9-10 ... at Cleveland
11-**12**-**13** ... at Toronto
17-18-**19**-**20** ... Cleveland
21-22 ... Toronto
23-**24** ... Baltimore
25-26-**27** ... at Boston
29-30-31 ... at Anaheim
AUGUST
1-**2**-**3** ... at Oakland
5-6-**7** ... Texas
8-**9**-**10** ... Seattle
11-12-13 ... at K.C.
15-16-**17** ... at Baltimore
18-19-**20** ... Kansas City
22-**23**-**24**-25 ... Baltimore
26-27-**28** ... White Sox
29-30-**31** ... at Boston
SEPTEMBER
1-3-4 ... at Toronto
5-**6**-**7** ... Boston
9-10-11 ... Detroit
12-**13**-**14** ... Tampa Bay
15-16-17-18 ... at Balt.
19-20-**21** ... at Tampa Bay
22-23-**24** ... at White Sox
26-**27**-**28** ... Baltimore

OAKLAND ATHLETICS
Network Associates Coliseum

Standard Game Times: Weekday—12:35 p.m., 7:05. Weekend—1:05, 6:05.

MARCH
25-26 ... %Seattle
APRIL
1-2 ... Seattle
4-**5**-**6** ... Anaheim
8-9-**10** ... at Texas
11-12-**13** ... at Anaheim
14-15-16-**17** ... at Seattle
18-**19**-**20** ... Texas
22-23-**24** ... Detroit
25-**26**-**27** ... Cleveland
29-30 ... at White Sox
MAY
1 ... at White Sox
2-**3**-**4** ... at Yankees
6-7-**8** ... White Sox
9-**10**-**11** ... Yankees
13-14-15 ... at Detroit
16-**17**-**18** ... at Cleveland
20-**21**-**22** ... Minnesota
23-**24**-**25** ... Kansas City
27-**28** ... at Minnesota
29-30-**31** ... at K.C.
JUNE
1 ... at Kansas City
3-4-5 ... *at Florida
6-7-**8** ... *at Philadelphia
10-11-**12** ... *Atlanta
13-**14**-**15** ... *Montreal
17-18-**19** ... Texas
20-**21**-**22** ... *San Fran.
23-24-25-26 ... at Texas
27-**28**-**29** ... *at San Fran.
JULY
1-2-**3** ... Seattle
4-5-**6** ... Anaheim
8-**9**-**10** ... Tampa Bay
11-**12**-**13** ... Baltimore
17-18-19-**20** ... at Minn.
21-22 ... at Kansas City
23-24 ... at Seattle
25-26-**27**-28 ... at Ana.
29-30-**31** ... Cleveland
AUGUST
1-**2**-**3** ... Yankees
5-6-7 ... at Detroit
8-9-**10** ... at White Sox
11-12-13-**14** ... Boston
15-**16**-**17** ... Toronto
19-20-21 ... at Boston
22-**23**-**24**-25 ... at Toronto
26-27-**28** ... Baltimore
29-30-**31** ... Tampa Bay
SEPTEMBER
2-3-4 ... at Baltimore
5-6-**7** ... at Tampa Bay
8-9-10-**11** ... Anaheim
12-13-**14** ... at Texas
15-16-17 ... at Anaheim
19-**20**-**21** ... Seattle
22-23-**24** ... Texas
26-27-**28** ... at Seattle

SEATTLE MARINERS
Safeco Field

Standard Game Times: 7:05 p.m., 1:35; Sat. (April-May) 7:05, (June-Sept.) 1:05; Sun. 1:05.

MARCH
25-26 ... %Oakland
APRIL
1-2 ... at Oakland
4-5-**6** ... at Texas
8-9-10 ... Anaheim
11-12-**13** ... Texas
14-15-16-**17** ... Oakland
18-19-**20** ... at Anaheim
22-23-24 ... Cleveland
25-26-**27** ... Detroit
29-30 ... at Yankees
MAY
1 ... at Yankees
2-3-**4** ... at White Sox
6-7-8 ... Yankees
9-10-**11** ... White Sox
13-14-15 ... at Cleveland
16-**17**-**18** ... at Detroit
20-21-**22** ... Kansas City
23-24-**25** ... Minnesota
27-**28** ... at Kansas City
29-30-31 ... at Minnesota
JUNE
1 ... at Minnesota
3-4-5 ... *at Philadelphia
6-7-**8** ... *at Mets
10-11-12 ... *Montreal
13-**14**-**15** ... *Atlanta
16-17-18-**19** ... Anaheim
20-21-**22** ... *at San Diego
24-25-26 ... at Anaheim
27-**28**-**29** ... *San Diego
JULY
1-2-**3** ... at Oakland
4-5-6 ... at Texas

8-9-10 .... Baltimore
11-**12-13** .... Tampa Bay
17-18-19-20 .... at K.C.
21-22 .... at Minnesota
23-24 .... Oakland
25-**26-27**-28 .... Texas
29-30-**31** .... Detroit

AUGUST

1-**2-3** .... White Sox
5-6-7 .... at Cleveland
8-**9-10** .... at Yankees
11-12-13-14 ...... Toronto
15-**16-17** .... Boston
19-20-21 .... at Toronto
22-23-**24-25** ... at Boston
26-27-**28** .... Tampa Bay
29-**30-31** .... Baltimore

SEPTEMBER

2-3-4 .... at Tampa Bay
5-6-**7** .... at Baltimore
9-10-11 .... Texas
12-**13-14** .... Anaheim
15-16-17-**18** ...... at Texas
19-**20-21** .... at Oakland
22-23-**24** ...... at Anaheim
26-27-**28** .... Oakland

TAMPA BAY DEVIL RAYS
Tropicana Field

■ **Standard Game Times:** 7:15 p.m.; Sat. 6:15; Sun. 1:15.

MARCH

31 .... Boston

APRIL

1-2-**3** .... Boston
4-5-**6** .... Yankees
8-9-10 .... Baltimore
11-**12-13** .... at Yankees
15-16-17 .... at Boston
18-**19-20**-21 .... at Balt.
22-23-24 .... Toronto
25-26-**27** .... Baltimore
29-30 .... at Minnesota

MAY

1 .... at Minnesota
2-**3-4** .... at Detroit
6-7-8 .... Minnesota
9-10-**11** .... Detroit
13-14-15 .... at Toronto
16-17-**18** ..... at Baltimore
20-21-**22** .... at Texas
23-24-**25** ...... at Anaheim
27-28 .... Texas
29-30-31 .... Anaheim

JUNE

1 .... Anaheim
3-4-**5** .... *at Cubs
6-7-**8** .... *at Houston
10-11-12 ...... *Cincinnati
13-14-**15** ..... *Pittsburgh
17-18-19 .... at Yankees
20-21-**22** .... *at Florida
23-24-25-**26** ...... Yankees
27-28-**29** .... *Atlanta

JULY

1-2-3 .... Boston
4-5-**6** .... White Sox
8-**9-10** .... at Oakland
11-**12-13** .... at Seattle
17-18-19-**20** .... Texas
21-**22** .... Anaheim
23-**24** .... at Boston
25-26-**27** .... at White Sox
29-30-**31** .... at Toronto

AUGUST

1-2-**3** .... at Kansas City
4-5-**6** .... Toronto
7-8-9-**10** ...... Kansas City
11-12-**13** ....Baltimore
15-16-**17**-18 ...... at Cleve.
19-20-21 ..... at Baltimore
22-23-**24** .... Cleveland
26-27-**28** .... at Seattle
29-30-**31** .... at Oakland

SEPTEMBER

2-3-4 .... Seattle
5-6-**7** .... Oakland
9-10-**11** .... Toronto
12-**13-14** .... at Yankees
15-16-17-18 ... at Boston
19-20-**21** .... Yankees
22-23-24-25 ... at Toronto
26-27-**28** .... Boston

TEXAS RANGERS
The Ballpark at Arlington

■ **Standard Game Times:** 7:05 p.m.; Thurs. (April-May, Sept.) 1:05; Sun. (April-June, Sept.) 1:05.

MARCH

30 .... at Anaheim

APRIL

1-**2** .... at Anaheim
4-5-6 .... Seattle
8-9-**10** .... Oakland
11-12-**13** .... at Seattle
14-15-16-**17** ..... Anaheim
18-**19-20** .... at Oakland
22-23-**24** .... Boston
25-26-**27** .... Yankees
29-30 .... at Toronto

MAY

1 .... at Toronto
2-**3-4** .... at Cleveland
6-7-**8** .... Toronto
9-10-**11** .... Cleveland
13-14-15 .... at Boston
16-**17-18** .... at Yankees
20-21-**22** .... Tampa Bay
23-24-**25** .... Baltimore
27-28 .... at Tampa Bay
29-30-31 ..... at Baltimore

JUNE

1 .... at Baltimore
3-4-**5** .... *at Atlanta
6-7-**8** .... *#Montreal
10-11-12 .... *Mets
13-14-**15** .... *Florida
17-18-**19** .... at Oakland
20-21-**22** .... *Houston
23-24-25-26 ...... Oakland
27-28-**29** .... *at Houston
30 .... at Anaheim

JULY

1-2-3 .... at Anaheim
4-5-6 .... Seattle
8-9-10 .... Minnesota
11-12-13 ..... Kansas City
17-18-19-**20** .... at T.B.
21-**22** .... at Baltimore
23-**24** .... Anaheim
25-**26-27**-28 .... at Seattle
29-30-31 .... Boston

AUGUST

1-2-3 .... Cleveland
5-6-**7** .... at Yankees
8-**9-10** .... at Toronto
11-12-13-14 .... Detroit
15-16-17 .... White Sox
18-19-20 .... at Detroit
21-22-23-**24** ... at Wh. Sox
26-27-28 .... at K.C.
29-30-**31** .... Minnesota

SEPTEMBER

1-2-3 .... Kansas City
5-**6-7** .... at Minnesota
9-10-11 .... at Seattle
12-13-**14** .... Oakland
15-16-17-**18** .... Seattle
19-20-**21** .... Anaheim
22-23-**24** .... at Oakland
26-27-**28** ...... at Anaheim

TORONTO BLUE JAYS
SkyDome

■ **Standard Game Times:** 7:05 p.m.; Sat. (April-May) 1:05, (June-Sept.) 4:05; Sun. 1:05.

MARCH

31 .... Yankees

APRIL

1-2 .... Yankees
4-5-**6** .... at Minnesota
8-9-10 .... Boston
11-**12-13** .... Minnesota
14-15-16-**17** .. at Yankees
18-**19-20-21** ... at Boston
22-23-24 ... at Tampa Bay
25-**26-27** ..... Kansas City
29-30 .... Texas

MAY

1 .... Texas
2-**3-4** .... Anaheim
6-7-**8** .... at Texas
9-10-**11** .... at Anaheim
13-14-**15** .... Tampa Bay
16-17-**18** .... at K.C.
19-20-21 .... at White Sox
22-23-**24-25** ... at Yankees
26-27-28-29 ... White Sox
30-**31** .... Boston

JUNE

1 .... Boston
3-4-5 .... *at St. Louis
6-7-**8** .... *at Cincinnati
10-11-12 ..... *Pittsburgh
13-**14-15** .... *Cubs
17-18-19 ..... at Baltimore
20-21-**22** .... *at Montreal
23-24-25-26 ... Baltimore
27-**28-29** .... *Montreal
30 .... at Detroit

JULY

1-2 .... at Detroit
4-5-**6** .... at Baltimore
8-9-10 .... Boston
11-**12-13** .... Yankees
17-18-19-**20** ... at Boston
21-22 .... at Yankees
23-24 .... White Sox
25-**26-27** .... Baltimore
29-30-**31** .... Tampa Bay

AUGUST

1-2-**3** .... at Anaheim
4-5-**6** .... at Tampa Bay
8-**9-10** .... Texas
11-12-13-14 .... at Seattle
15-**16-17** .... at Oakland
19-20-21 .... Seattle
22-**23-24**-25 ...... Oakland
26-27 .... at Boston
29-30-**31** ..... at Cleveland

SEPTEMBER

1-3-4 .... Yankees
5-**6-7** .... Detroit
9-10-**11** ..... at Tampa Bay
12-**13-14** .... Baltimore
16-17-18 .... at Detroit
19-20-**21** ..... at Baltimore
22-23-24-25 .... T.B.
26-**27-28** .... Cleveland

NOTE: Dates in **bold** indicate afternoon games. All game times are subject to change. Gaps in dates indicate scheduled off days but may be affected by rainouts.

* Interleague Series # At San Juan, P.R. % At Tokyo, Japan

NATIONAL LEAGUE

ARIZONA DIAMONDBACKS
Bank One Ballpark

■ **Standard Game Times:** 6:35 p.m., 7:05; Sun. 1:35.

MARCH
31 ... Los Angeles
APRIL
1-2 ... Los Angeles
4-5-6 ... at Colorado
7-8-**9** ... at Los Angeles
11-12-**13** ... Milwaukee
14-15-16-**17** ... Colorado
18-**19-20** ... at St. Louis
22-23-24 ... at Montreal
25-**26-27** ... at Mets
28-29-30 ... Florida
MAY
1 ... Florida
2-3-**4** ... Atlanta
5-6-**7** ... Philadelphia
9-10-**11** ... at Pittsburgh
13-14-**15** ... at Phila.
16-17-**18** ... Pittsburgh
19-20-21 ... San Francisco
23-24-**25-26** ... San Diego
27-28 ... at San Francisco
30-31 ... at San Diego
JUNE
1-2 ... at San Diego
3-4-5 ... *White Sox
6-7-**8** ... *Cleveland
10-11-12 ... *at K.C.
13-14-**15** ... *at Minn.
17-18-19 ... at Houston
20-21-**22** ... Cincinnati
23-24-**25** ... Houston
27-28-**29** ... *at Detroit
30 ... at Colorado
JULY
1-2-3 ... at Colorado
4-**5**-6 ... at Los Angeles
7-8 ... Colorado
9-**10** ... San Diego
11-**12-13** ... San Francisco
17-18-19-**20** ... at S.D.
21-22-23-**24** ... at S.F.
25-**26-27** ... Los Angeles
28-29-30 ... at Florida
AUGUST
1-2-3 ... at Cubs
5-6-7 ... Montreal
8-9-**10** ... Mets
12-13-14 ... at Cincinnati
15-16-**17-18** ... at Atlanta
19-20-21 ... Cincinnati
22-23-**24** ... Cubs
25-26-27 ... San Diego
29-**30**-31 ... San Francisco
SEPTEMBER
1 ... San Francisco
2-3 ... at San Diego
5-**6-7** ... at San Francisco
8-9-10-11 ... Los Angeles
12-13-**14** ... Colorado
16-17-18 ... at L.A.
19-20-**21** ... at Milwaukee
22-23-**24** ... at Colorado
26-**27-28** ... St. Louis

ATLANTA BRAVES
Turner Field

■ **Standard Game Times:** 7:35 p.m.; Sat. 7:05; Sun. 1:05.

MARCH
31 ... Montreal
APRIL
2-3 ... Montreal
4-5-**6-7** ... Florida
8-9-10 ... at Philadelphia
11-12-**13** ... at Florida
15-16-**17** ... #Montreal
18-19-**20** ... Philadelphia
22-23-24 ... St. Louis
25-26-**27** ... Milwaukee
29-30 ... at Houston
MAY
1 ... at Houston
2-3-**4** ... at Arizona
6-7-8 ... Colorado
9-10-**11** ... San Francisco
12-13-14 ... at L.A.
15-16-17-**18** ... at S.D.
20-21-22 ... at Cincinnati
23-**24-25** ... Mets
26-27-28 ... Cincinnati
30-**31** ... at Mets
JUNE
1 ... at Mets
3-4-**5** ... *Texas
6-7-**8** ... Pittsburgh
10-11-**12** ... *at Oakland
13-**14-15** ... *at Seattle
17-18-**19** ... at Phila.
20-21-**22** ... *Baltimore
24-25-26 ... Philadelphia
27-28-**29** ... *at T.B.
30 ... at Florida
JULY
1-2 ... at Florida
3-4-5-**6** ... Montreal
7-8-**9** ... at Mets
10-11-12-13 ... at Cubs
17-18-**19-20** ... Mets
21-22 ... Cubs
23-**24** ... Florida
25-26-**27**-28 ... at Mont.
29-30-31 ... Houston
AUGUST
1-**2-3** ... Los Angeles
5-6-**7** ... at Milwaukee
8-**9-10** ... at St. Louis
12-13-14 ... San Diego
15-16-**17-18** ... Arizona
19-20-21 ... at San Fran.
22-23-**24** ... at Colorado
26-27-28 ... Mets
29-30-**31** ... at Pittsburgh
SEPTEMBER
1-2-**3** ... at Mets
5-6-**7** ... Pittsburgh
8-9-10-11 ... Philadelphia
12-13-**14** ... at Florida
15-16-**17** ... at Montreal
19-20-**21**-22 ... Florida
23-24 ... Montreal
26-**27-28** ... at Phila.

CHICAGO CUBS
Wrigley Field

■ **Standard Game Times:** 1:20 p.m., 7:05; Thurs. 1:20; Fri. 2:20; Sat. 12:15, 3:05; Sun. 1:20.

MARCH
31 ... at Mets
APRIL
2-**3** ... at Mets
4-**5-6** ... at Cincinnati
7-9-10 ... Montreal
11-12-13 ... Pittsburgh
14-**15-16-17** ... Cincinnati
18-19-**20** ... at Pittsburgh
22-**23-24** ... San Diego
25-**26-27** ... at Colorado
29-30 ... at San Francisco
MAY
1 ... at San Francisco
2-3-4 ... Colorado
5-6-7 ... Milwaukee
9-10-11 ... St. Louis
12-13-14-**15** ... at Mil.
16-**17-18-19** ... at St.L.
20-21-22 ... at Pittsburgh
23-24-**25** ... at Houston
26-27-28 ... Pittsburgh
30-31 ... Houston
JUNE
1 ... Houston
3-4-**5** ... *Tampa Bay
6-7-8 ... *Yankees
10-11-12 ... *at Baltimore
13-**14-15** ... *at Toronto
16-17-18-**19** ... at Cin.
20-21-22 ... *White Sox
24-**25-26** ... Milwaukee
27-28-29 ... *at White Sox
30 ... at Philadelphia
JULY
1-2-3 ... at Philadelphia
4-5-6 ... St. Louis
7-**8-9** ... Florida
10-11-12-13 ... Atlanta
18-19-**20** ... at Florida
21-22 ... at Atlanta
23-**24** ... Philadelphia
25-26-**27** ... at Houston
29-**30-31** ... San Fran.
AUGUST
1-2-3 ... Arizona
5-6-7 ... at San Diego
8-9-**10** ... at Los Angeles
11-12-**13-14** ... Houston
15-16-17 ... Los Angeles
19-20-21 ... at Houston
22-23-**24** ... at Arizona
26-27-28 ... at St. Louis
29-30-31 ... Milwaukee
SEPTEMBER
1-2-3-**4** ... St. Louis
5-6-7 ... at Milwaukee
9-10-**11** ... #Montreal
12-13-14 ... Cincinnati
15-16-**17** ... Mets
19-20-**21** ... at Pittsburgh
23-24-25 ... at Cincinnati
26-27-28 ... Pittsburgh

CINCINNATI REDS
Great American Ball Park

■ **Standard Game Times:** 7:10 p.m.; Sat. (April, Sept.) 1:15; Sun. 1:15.

MARCH
31 ... Pittsburgh
APRIL
2-**3** ... Pittsburgh
4-**5-6** ... Cubs
8-9-10 ... at Houston
11-**12-13** ... Philadelphia
14-**15-16-17** ... at Cubs

18-19-**20** .... #Montreal
22-23-24 .... Los Angeles
25-**26**-**27** .... San Diego
29-30 .... at Colorado

MAY

1 .... at Colorado
2-**3**-**4** .... at San Francisco
5-6-7-**8** .... St. Louis
9-10-**11** .... Milwaukee
13-14-**15** ...... at St. Louis
16-**17**-**18** ... at Milwaukee
20-21-22 .... Atlanta
23-24-**25** .... Florida
26-27-28 .... at Atlanta
30-31 .... at Florida

JUNE

1 .... at Florida
3-4-5 .... *Yankees
6-7-**8** .... *Toronto
10-11-12 .... *at T.B.
13-14-**15** ..... Philadelphia
16-17-18-**19** .... Cubs
20-21-**22** .... at Arizona
24-25-26 ...... at St. Louis
27-**28**-**29** ... *at Cleveland

JULY

1-2-3 .... at Pittsburgh
4-**5**-**6** .... Mets
7-8-9-10 .... at Houston
11-12-**13** ... at Milwaukee
17-18-19-**20** ..... Houston
21-22 .... Milwaukee
23-**24** .... Pittsburgh
25-**26**-**27** .... at Mets
29-30-31 .... Colorado

AUGUST

1-2-**3** .... San Francisco
5-6-7 ...... at Los Angeles
8-9-**10** .... at San Diego
12-13-14 .... Arizona
15-16-**17** .... Houston
19-20-21 .... at Arizona
22-23-**24** ...... at Houston
25-26-27-**28** ... Milwaukee
29-30-**31** .... St. Louis

SEPTEMBER

1-2-3 .... at Milwaukee
5-6-**7** .... at St. Louis
8-9-10-**11** ...... Pittsburgh
12-**13**-**14** .... at Cubs
15-16-17-18 .... at Pitt.
19-20-**21** .... at Phila.
23-24-25 .... Cubs
26-**27**-**28** .... Montreal

COLORADO ROCKIES
Coors Field

■ **Standard Game Times:** 7:05 p.m., 1:05; Sat. (April-May, Sept.) 1:05, (June-Aug.) 6:05; Sun. 1:05.

APRIL

1-2-**3** .... at Houston
4-**5**-**6** .... Arizona
8-9-**10** .... St. Louis
11-12-**13** .... at San Diego
14-15-16-**17** ... at Arizona
18-**19**-**20** .... San Diego
22-23-**24** .... at Phila.
25-**26**-**27** .... Cubs
29-30 .... Cincinnati

MAY

1 .... Cincinnati
2-**3**-**4** .... at Cubs
6-7-8 .... at Atlanta
9-10-**11** .... at Florida
12-13-**14** .... Mets
15-16-**17**-**18** .... Montreal
20-21-**22** .... at L.A.
23-**24**-**25**-**26** ... San Fran.
27-28-**29** .... Los Angeles
30-**31** ... at San Francisco

JUNE

1-2 .... at San Francisco
3-4-**5** .... *Cleveland
6-7-**8** .... *Kansas City
10-11-12 .... *at Minn.
13-14-**15** .... *at Detroit
16-17-18-19 .... S.D.
20-21-**22** .... *Detroit
23-24-25 .... at San Diego
27-28-**29** ... at Pittsburgh
30 .... Arizona

JULY

1-2-3 .... Arizona
4-5-**6** .... at Milwaukee
7-8 .... at Arizona
9-10 .... San Francisco
11-12-**13** .... Los Angeles
17-18-**19**-**20** .... at S.F.
21-22-23-**24** .... at L.A.
25-26-**27** .... Milwaukee
29-30-31 .... at Cincinnati

AUGUST

1-2-**3** .... at Pittsburgh
5-6-**7** .... Philadelphia
8-9-**10** .... Pittsburgh
11-12-13 ...... at Montreal
15-16-**17**-**18** .... at Mets
19-20-21 .... Florida
22-23-**24** .... Atlanta
26-27-**28** .... San Fran.
29-30-31 .... at L.A.

SEPTEMBER

2-**3** .... at San Francisco
5-**6**-**7** .... Los Angeles
9-10-**11** .... at St. Louis
12-13-**14** .... at Arizona
16-17-**18** .... Houston
19-**20**-**21** .... San Diego
23-24-**25** .... Arizona
26-27-**28** .... at San Diego

FLORIDA MARLINS
Pro Player Stadium

■ **Standard Game Times:** 7:05 p.m.; Sat. 6:05; Sun. 1:35.

MARCH

31 .... Philadelphia

APRIL

2-**3** .... Philadelphia
4-5-**6**-**7** .... at Atlanta
8-9-10 .... Mets
11-12-**13** .... Atlanta
14-15-16-**17** ...... at Phila.
18-**19**-**20** .... at Mets
22-23-24 .... Milwaukee
25-26-**27** .... St. Louis
28-29-30 .... at Arizona

MAY

1 .... at Arizona
2-3-**4** .... at Houston
6-7-8 .... San Francisco
9-10-**11** .... Colorado
12-13-14 .... at San Diego
16-17-**18** .... at L.A.
20-21-22 ...... at Montreal
23-24-**25** .... at Cincinnati
26-27-28-29 .... Montreal
30-31 .... Cincinnati

JUNE

1 .... Cincinnati
3-4-5 .... *Oakland
6-7-**8** .... *Anaheim
10-11-**12** ... at Milwaukee
13-14-15 .... *at Texas
16-17-18-19 .... Mets
20-21-**22** ..... *Tampa Bay
24-25-26 .... at Mets
27-28-**29** .... *at Boston
30 .... Atlanta

JULY

1-2 .... Atlanta
4-5-**6** ...... at Philadelphia
7-**8**-**9** .... at Cubs
11-12-**13** ...... at Montreal
18-19-**20** .... Cubs
21-22 .... Montreal
23-**24** .... at Atlanta
25-26-**27** ..... Philadelphia
28-29-30 .... Arizona

AUGUST

1-2-**3** .... Houston
5-6-7 .... at St. Louis
8-9-**10** .... at Milwaukee
11-12-13-**14** .... L.A.
15-16-**17** .... San Diego
19-20-21 ...... at Colorado
22-**23**-**24** ..... at San Fran.
26-27-28 ... at Pittsburgh
29-30-**31** .... Montreal

SEPTEMBER

1 .... Montreal
2-3-**4** .... Pittsburgh
5-6-**7** .... #Montreal
8-9-**10** .... at Mets
12-13-**14** .... Atlanta
16-17-18 .... at Phila.
19-20-**21**-22 .... at Atlanta
23-24-25 ..... Philadelphia
26-27-**28** .... Mets

HOUSTON ASTROS
Minute Maid Park

■ **Standard Game Times:** 7:05 p.m.; Sun. 1:05.

APRIL

1-2-**3** .... Colorado
4-**5**-**6** .... at St. Louis
8-9-10 .... Cincinnati
11-12-**13** .... St. Louis
14-15-16 ..... at San Fran.
17-18-**19**-**20** .... at Mil.
22-23-24 .... at Mets
25-**26**-**27** ...... at Montreal
29-30 .... Atlanta

MAY

1 .... Atlanta
2-3-**4** .... Florida
5-6-7-**8** .... Pittsburgh
9-10-**11** ... at Philadelphia
12-13-14-**15** .... at Pitt.
16-17-**18** ..... Philadelphia
20-21-22 .... St. Louis
23-24-**25** .... Cubs
26-27-28 ...... at St. Louis
30-**31** .... at Cubs

JUNE

1 .... at Cubs
3-4-5 .... *Baltimore
6-7-**8** .... *Tampa Bay
10-11-**12** ..... *at Yankees
13-14-**15** .... *at Boston
17-18-19 .... Arizona
20-21-22 .... *at Texas
23-24-**25** .... at Arizona
27-28-**29** .... *Texas

JULY

1-2-3 .... Milwaukee
4-**5**-**6** .... at Pittsburgh
7-8-9-10 .... Cincinnati
11-12-**13** .... Pittsburgh
17-18-19-**20** .... at Cin.
21-22 .... at Pittsburgh
23-24 .... at Milwaukee
25-26-**27** .... Cubs
29-30-31 .... at Atlanta

AUGUST

1-2-**3** .... at Florida
5-6-7 .... Mets
8-9-**10** .... Montreal
11-12-**13**-**14** ...... at Cubs

15-16-**17** .... at Cincinnati
19-20-21 .... Cubs
22-23-**24** .... Cincinnati
26-27-28 .... L.A.
29-30-**31** .... San Diego
SEPTEMBER
1-2-3 ...... at Los Angeles
5-6-**7** .... at San Diego
8-9-10-**11** ... at Milwaukee
12-13-**14** .... St. Louis
16-17-**18** ...... at Colorado
19-**20**-**21** ...... at St. Louis
22-23-**24** .... San Fran.
25-26-27-**28** ... Milwaukee

LOS ANGELES DODGERS
Dodger Stadium

■ **Standard Game Times:** 7:10 p.m.; Sat. (June-July) 1:10; Sun. 1:10, 5:10.

MARCH
31 .... at Arizona
APRIL
1-2 .... at Arizona
3-4-5-**6** ...... at San Diego
7-8-**9** .... Arizona
10-11-**12**-13 .... at S.F.
15-16-17 .... San Diego
18-19-20 .... San Fran.
22-23-24 .... at Cincinnati
25-26-**27** ... at Pittsburgh
28-29-30 ..... Philadelphia
MAY
1 .... Philadelphia
2-3-**4** .... Pittsburgh
6-7-8 .... at Mets
9-**10**-**11** .... at Montreal
12-13-14 .... Atlanta
16-17-**18** .... Florida
20-21-**22** .... Colorado
23-24-**25** ... at Milwaukee
27-28-**29** ...... at Colorado
30-31 .... Milwaukee
JUNE
1 .... Milwaukee
3-4-5 .... *Kansas City
6-7-**8** .... *White Sox
10-11-12 .... *at Detroit
13-14-**15** ... *at Cleveland
17-18-19 .... San Fran.
20-**21**-22 .... *Anaheim
23-24-25 ..... at San Fran.
27-28-**29** .... *at Anaheim
JULY
1-2-3 .... San Diego
4-**5**-6 .... Arizona
7-8 .... at San Diego
9-10 .... at St. Louis
11-12-**13** ...... at Colorado
17-18-**19**-20 .... St. Louis
21-22-23-**24** .... Colorado
25-**26**-**27** .... at Arizona
29-30-31 .... at Phila.
AUGUST
1-**2**-**3** .... at Atlanta
5-6-7 .... Cincinnati
8-9-**10** .... Cubs
11-12-13-**14** .... at Florida
15-**16**-**17** .... at Cubs
19-20-**21** .... Montreal
22-23-24 .... Mets
26-27-28 ...... at Houston
29-30-31 .... Colorado
SEPTEMBER
1-2-3 .... Houston
5-**6**-**7** .... at Colorado
8-9-10-11 .... at Arizona
12-13-**14** .... San Diego
16-17-18 .... Arizona
19-20-**21** .... San Fran.
22-23-24-25 .... at S.D.
26-**27**-**28** ..... at San Fran.

MILWAUKEE BREWERS
Miller Park

■ **Standard Game Times:** 7:05 p.m.; Thurs. 12:05, 1:05, 7:05; Sun. 1:05.

MARCH
31 .... at St. Louis
APRIL
2-**3** .... at St. Louis
4-5-**6** .... San Francisco
7-9-**10** .... at Pittsburgh
11-12-**13** .... at Arizona
14-15-**16** .... St. Louis
17-18-**19**-**20** ..... Houston
22-23-24 .... at Florida
25-26-**27** .... at Atlanta
29-30 .... Montreal
MAY
1 .... Montreal
2-3-**4** .... Mets
5-6-**7** .... at Cubs
9-10-**11** ...... at Cincinnati
12-13-14-**15** .... Cubs
16-**17**-**18** .... Cincinnati
19-20-**21** .... San Diego
23-24-**25** .... Los Angeles
27-28-**29** .... at San Diego
30-31 ...... at Los Angeles
JUNE
1 .... at Los Angeles
3-4-5 .... at Mets
6-7-**8** .... *Boston
10-11-**12** .... Florida
13-14-**15** ... *at Baltimore
16-17-18-**19** .... St. Louis
20-21-**22** ..... *Minnesota
24-**25**-**26** .... at Cubs
27-28-**29** .... *at Minn.
JULY
1-2-3 .... at Houston
4-5-**6** .... Colorado
7-8-9-**10** .... Pittsburgh
11-12-**13** .... Cincinnati
17-18-19-**20** .... at Pitt.
21-22 .... at Cincinnati
23-24 .... Houston
25-26-**27** ...... at Colorado
29-30-**31** .... at Mets
AUGUST
1-2-**3** .... at Montreal
5-6-**7** .... Atlanta
8-9-**10** .... Florida
12-13-14 .... at Phila.
15-**16**-**17** ... at Pittsburgh
19-20-**21** ..... Philadelphia
22-23-**24** .... Pittsburgh
25-26-27-**28** .... at Cinc.
29-**30**-**31** .... at Cubs
SEPTEMBER
1-2-3 .... Cincinnati
5-6-**7** .... Cubs
8-9-10-**11** .... Houston
12-**13**-**14** ..... at San Fran.
15-16-17-18 .... at St.L.
19-20-**21** .... Arizona
23-24 .... St. Louis
25-26-27-**28** .... at Hou.

MONTREAL EXPOS
Olympic Stadium/Hiram Bithorn Stadium

■ **Standard Game Times:** Montreal—7:05 p.m.; Sun. 1:05. San Juan—7:05 p.m.; Sun. 1:05, 2:05.

MARCH
31 .... at Atlanta
APRIL
2-3 .... at Atlanta
4-**5**-**6** .... at Mets
7-**9**-**10** .... at Cubs
11-12-**13**-**14** .... #Mets
15-16-**17** .... #Atlanta
18-19-**20** ...... #Cincinnati
22-23-24 .... Arizona
25-**26**-**27** .... Houston
29-30 .... at Milwaukee
MAY
1 .... at Milwaukee
2-**3**-**4** .... at St. Louis
6-7-8 .... San Diego
9-**10**-**11** ...... Los Angeles
12-13-**14** ..... at San Fran.
15-16-**17**-**18** ...... at Colo.
20-21-22 .... Florida
23-24-**25** ..... Philadelphia
26-27-28-29 .... at Florida
30-31 ...... at Philadelphia
JUNE
1 .... at Philadelphia
3-4-5 .... *#Anaheim
6-7-**8** .... *#Texas
10-11-12 .... *at Seattle
13-**14**-**15** ..... *at Oakland
17-18-**19** ... at Pittsburgh
20-21-**22** .... *Toronto
23-**24**-**25** .... Pittsburgh
27-**28**-**29** ...... *at Toronto
30 .... at Mets
JULY
1-2 .... at Mets
3-4-5-**6** .... at Atlanta
7-8-9 .... Philadelphia
11-12-**13** .... Florida
17-18-19-**20** ...... at Phila.
21-22 .... at Florida
23-24 .... Mets
25-26-**27**-28 .... Atlanta
29-30-31 .... St. Louis
AUGUST
1-2-**3** .... Milwaukee
5-6-7 .... at Arizona
8-9-**10** .... at Houston
11-12-13 .... Colorado
15-16-**17**-**18** ... San Fran.
19-20-**21** .... at L.A.
22-23-**24** .... at San Diego
25-26-27-**28** .... Phila.
29-30-**31** .... at Florida
SEPTEMBER
1 .... at Florida
2-**3** .... at Philadelphia
5-6-**7** .... #Florida
9-10-**11** .... #Cubs
12-13-**14** .... Mets
15-16-**17** .... Atlanta
18-19-**20**-**21** .... at Mets
23-24 .... at Atlanta
26-**27**-**28** .... at Cincinnati

NEW YORK METS
Shea Stadium

■ **Standard Game Times:** 7:10 p.m.; Sat. 1:10, 1:15, 7:10; Sun. 1:10.

MARCH
31 .... Cubs
APRIL
2-**3** .... Cubs
4-**5**-**6** .... Montreal
8-9-10 .... at Florida
11-12-**13**-**14** ... #Montreal
15-16-17 ... at Pittsburgh
18-**19**-**20** .... Florida
22-23-24 .... Houston
25-**26**-**27** .... Arizona
29-30 .... at St. Louis
MAY
1 .... at St. Louis

2-3-**4** .... at Milwaukee
6-7-8 .... Los Angeles
9-**10-11** .... San Diego
12-13-**14** ...... at Colorado
15-16-**17-18** .... at S.F.
20-21-**22** ..... Philadelphia
23-**24-25** .... at Atlanta
27-28-29 .... at Phila.
30-**31** .... Atlanta

JUNE

1 .... Atlanta
3-4-5 .... Milwaukee
6-7-**8** .... *Seattle
10-11-12 .... *at Texas
13-14-**15** .... *at Anaheim
16-17-18-19 .... at Florida
20-**21**-22 .... *Yankees
24-25-26 .... Florida
27-**28**-29 ..... *at Yankees
30 .... Montreal

JULY

1-2 .... Montreal
4-5-6 .... at Cincinnati
7-8-**9** .... Atlanta
10-11-**12-13** .... Phila.
17-18-**19-20** .... at Atlanta
21-**22** ...... at Philadelphia
23-24 .... at Montreal
25-26-**27** .... Cincinnati
29-30-**31** .... Milwaukee

AUGUST

1-**2-3** .... St. Louis
5-6-7 .... at Houston
8-9-**10** .... at Arizona
12-13-14 .... San Fran.
15-16-**17-18** .... Colorado
19-20-**21** .... at San Diego
22-23-24 .... at L.A.
26-27-28 .... at Atlanta
29-30-**31** ..... Philadelphia

SEPTEMBER

1-2-3 .... Atlanta
4-5-6-**7** ... at Philadelphia
8-9-**10** .... Florida
12-13-**14** ...... at Montreal
15-16-**17** .... at Cubs
18-19-**20-21** .... Montreal
23-24-25 .... Pittsburgh
26-27-**28** .... at Florida

PHILADELPHIA PHILLIES
Veterans Stadium

■ **Standard Game Times:** 7:05 p.m.; Sun. 1:35.

MARCH

31 .... at Florida

APRIL

2-**3** .... at Florida
4-5-6 .... Pittsburgh
8-9-10 .... Atlanta
11-**12-13** .... at Cincinnati
14-15-16-**17** .... Florida
18-19-**20** .... at Atlanta
22-23-**24** .... Colorado
25-26-**27** .... San Fran.
28-29-30 .... at L.A.

MAY

1 .... at Los Angeles
2-3-**4** .... at San Diego
5-6-**7** .... at Arizona
9-10-**11** .... Houston
13-14-**15** .... Arizona
16-17-18 ...... at Houston
20-21-**22** .... at Mets
23-24-**25** ...... at Montreal
27-28-29 .... Mets
30-31 .... Montreal

JUNE

1 .... Montreal
3-4-5 .... *Seattle
6-7-**8** .... *Oakland
9-10-11 ...... *at Anaheim
13-14-**15** .... at Cincinnati
17-18-**19** .... Atlanta
20-21-**22** .... *Boston
24-25-26 .... at Atlanta
27-28-**29** ... *at Baltimore
30 .... Cubs

JULY

1-2-3 .... Cubs
4-5-**6** .... Florida
7-8-9 .... at Montreal
10-11-**12-13** .... at Mets
17-18-19-**20** .... Montreal
21-**22** .... Mets
23-**24** .... at Cubs
25-26-**27** .... at Florida
29-30-31 .... Los Angeles

AUGUST

1-2-2-**3** .... San Diego
5-6-**7** .... at Colorado
8-**9-10** .... at San Fran.
12-13-14 .... Milwaukee
15-16-**17** .... St. Louis
19-20-**21** ... at Milwaukee
22-**23-24** ...... at St. Louis
25-26-27-**28** ..... at Mont.
29-30-**31** .... at Mets

SEPTEMBER

2-**3** .... Montreal
4-5-6-**7** .... Mets
8-9-10-11 ....at Atlanta
12-13-**14** ... at Pittsburgh
16-17-18 .... Florida
19-20-**21** .... Cincinnati
23-24-25 .... at Florida
26-**27-28** .... Atlanta

PITTSBURGH PIRATES
PNC Park

■ **Standard Game Times:** 7:05 p.m.; Thurs. 12:35, 7:05; Sun. 1:35.

MARCH

31 .... at Cincinnati

APRIL

2-**3** .... at Cincinnati
4-5-6 .... at Philadelphia
7-9-**10** .... Milwaukee
11-12-13 .... at Cubs
15-16-17 .... Mets
18-19-**20** .... Cubs
22-23-**24** ... San Francisco
25-26-**27** .... Los Angeles
29-30 .... at San Diego

MAY

1 .... at San Diego
2-3-**4** ...... at Los Angeles
5-6-7-**8** .... at Houston
9-10-**11** .... Arizona
12-13-14-**15** ..... Houston
16-17-**18** .... at Arizona
20-21-22 .... Cubs
23-24-**25** .... St. Louis
26-27-**28** .... at Cubs
30-**31** .... at St. Louis

JUNE

1 .... at St. Louis
3-4-5 .... *Boston
6-7-**8** .... at Atlanta
10-11-12 ...... *at Toronto
13-14-**15** .... *at T.B.
17-18-**19** .... Montreal
20-21-**22** .... *Cleveland
23-**24-25** ...... at Montreal
27-28-**29** .... Colorado

JULY

1-2-3 .... Cincinnati
4-5-**6** .... Houston
7-8-9-**10** .... at Milwaukee
11-12-**13** ...... at Houston
17-18-19-**20** ... Milwaukee
21-22 .... Houston
23-**24** .... at Cincinnati
25-**26-27-28** .... at St.L.
29-30-**31** .... San Diego

AUGUST

1-2-**3** .... Colorado
5-6-**7** .... at San Francisco
8-9-**10** .... at Colorado
11-12-13-**14** .... St. Louis
15-**16-17** .... Milwaukee
19-20-21 ...... at St. Louis
22-23-**24** ... at Milwaukee
26-27-28 .... Florida
29-30-**31** .... Atlanta

SEPTEMBER

2-3-**4** .... at Florida
5-6-**7** .... at Atlanta
8-9-10-**11** ... at Cincinnati
12-13-**14** ..... Philadelphia
15-16-17-18 ... Cincinnati
19-20-**21** .... Cubs
23-24-25 .... at Mets
26-27-28 .... at Cubs

ST. LOUIS CARDINALS
Busch Stadium

■ **Standard Game Times:** 7:10 p.m.; Thurs. (April-May) 12:10; Sat. (April) 1:10, (Aug.) 12:15; Sun. 1:10.

MARCH

31 .... Milwaukee

APRIL

2-**3** .... Milwaukee
4-**5-6** .... Houston
8-9-**10** .... at Colorado
11-12-**13** ...... at Houston
14-15-**16** ... at Milwaukee
18-**19-20** .... Arizona
22-23-24 .... at Atlanta
25-26-**27** .... at Florida
29-30 .... Mets

MAY

1 .... Mets
2-**3-4** .... Montreal
5-6-7-**8** .... at Cincinnati
9-10-11 .... at Cubs
13-14-**15** .... Cincinnati
16-**17-18-19** .... Cubs
20-21-22 ...... at Houston
23-24-**25** ... at Pittsburgh
26-27-28 .... Houston
30-**31** .... Pittsburgh

JUNE

1 .... Pittsburgh
3-4-5 .... *Toronto
6-**7-8** .... *Baltimore
10-11-12 .... *at Boston
13-**14-15** ..... *at Yankees
16-17-18-**19** .... at Mil.
20-21-**22** ... *Kansas City
24-25-26 .... Cincinnati
27-28-**29** .... *at K.C.
30 .... San Francisco

JULY

1-2-**3** .... San Francisco
4-5-6 .... at Cubs
7-**8** .... at San Francisco
9-10 .... Los Angeles
11-12-**13** .... San Diego
17-18-**19**-20 .... at L.A.
21-22-**23** .... at San Diego
25-**26-27-28** ... Pittsburgh
29-30-31 ...... at Montreal

AUGUST

1-**2-3** .... at Mets

5-6-7 .... Florida
8-**9-10** .... Atlanta
11-12-13-**14** .... at Pitt.
15-16-**17** .... at Phila.
19-20-21 .... Pittsburgh
22-**23-24** ..... Philadelphia
26-27-28 .... Cubs
29-30-**31** .... at Cincinnati

SEPTEMBER

1-2-**3-4** .... at Cubs
5-6-**7** .... Cincinnati
9-10-**11** .... Colorado
12-13-**14** ...... at Houston
15-16-17-18 ... Milwaukee
19-**20-21** .... Houston
23-24 .... at Milwaukee
26-**27-28** .... at Arizona

SAN DIEGO PADRES
Qualcomm Stadium

■ **Standard Game Times:** 7:05 p.m.; Thurs. 2:05; Sun. 2.

MARCH

31 .... San Francisco

APRIL

1-2 .... San Francisco
3-4-5-**6** .... Los Angeles
7-8-**9** .... at San Francisco
11-12-**13** .... Colorado
15-16-17 .... at L.A.
18-**19-20** ...... at Colorado
22-**23-24** .... at Cubs
25-**26-27** .... at Cincinnati
29-30 .... Pittsburgh

MAY

1 .... Pittsburgh
2-3-**4** .... Philadelphia
6-7-8 .... at Montreal
9-**10-11** .... at Mets
12-13-14 .... Florida
15-16-17-**18** .... Atlanta
19-20-**21** ... at Milwaukee
23-24-**25-26** ... at Arizona
27-28-**29** .... Milwaukee
30-31 .... Arizona

JUNE

1-2 .... Arizona
3-4-**5** .... *Detroit
6-7-**8** .... *Minnesota
10-11-12 ... *at Cleveland
13-14-**15** ... *at White Sox
16-17-18-19 ...... at Colo.
20-21-**22** .... *Seattle
23-24-25 .... Colorado
27-**28-29** .... *at Seattle

JULY

1-2-3 ...... at Los Angeles
4-5-**6** .... San Francisco
7-8 .... Los Angeles
9-**10** .... at Arizona
11-12-**13** ...... at St. Louis
17-18-19-**20** .... Arizona
21-22-**23** .... St. Louis
25-**26-27** ..... at San Fran.
29-30-**31** ... at Pittsburgh

AUGUST

1-2-2-**3** ... at Philadelphia
5-6-**7** .... Cubs
8-9-**10** .... Cincinnati
12-13-14 .... at Atlanta
15-16-**17** .... at Florida
19-20-**21** .... Mets
22-23-**24** .... Montreal
25-26-27 .... at Arizona
29-30-**31** ...... at Houston

SEPTEMBER

2-3 .... Arizona
5-6-**7** .... Houston
9-10-11 .... San Francisco
12-13-**14** .... at L.A.
15-16-17-**18** .... at S.F.
19-**20-21** ...... at Colorado
22-23-24-25 .... L.A.
26-27-**28** .... Colorado

SAN FRANCISCO GIANTS
Pacific Bell Park

■ **Standard Game Times:** 7:15 p.m.; Thurs. 7:15, 12:35; Sat.-Sun. 1:05.

MARCH

31 .... at San Diego

APRIL

1-2 .... at San Diego
4-5-6 .... at Milwaukee
7-8-9 .... San Diego
10-11-**12**-13 .... L.A.
14-15-16 .... Houston
18-19-20 .... at L.A.
22-23-**24** ... at Pittsburgh
25-26-**27** .... at Phila.
29-30 .... Cubs

MAY

1 .... Cubs
2-**3-4** .... Cincinnati
6-7-8 .... at Florida
9-10-**11** .... at Atlanta
12-13-**14** .... Montreal
15-16-**17-18** .... Mets
19-20-21 .... at Arizona
23-**24-25-26** ...... at Colo.
27-28 .... Arizona
30-**31** .... Colorado

JUNE

1-2 .... Colorado
3-4-5 .... *Minnesota
6-**7-8** .... *Detroit
10-11-12 ... *at White Sox
13-14-**15** .... *at K.C.
17-18-19 .... at L.A.
20-**21-22** ..... *at Oakland
23-24-25 .... Los Angeles
27-**28-29** .... *Oakland
30 .... at St. Louis

JULY

1-2-**3** .... at St. Louis
4-5-**6** .... at San Diego
7-**8** .... St. Louis
9-10 .... at Colorado
11-**12-13** .... at Arizona
17-18-**19-20** .... Colorado
21-22-23-**24** .... Arizona
25-**26-27** .... San Diego
29-**30-31** .... at Cubs

AUGUST

1-2-**3** .... at Cincinnati
5-6-**7** .... Pittsburgh
8-**9-10** .... Philadelphia
12-13-14 .... at Mets
15-16-**17-18** ..... at Mont.
19-20-21 .... Atlanta
22-**23-24** .... Florida
26-27-**28** ...... at Colorado
29-**30**-31 .... at Arizona

SEPTEMBER

1 .... at Arizona
2-**3** .... Colorado
5-**6-7** .... Arizona
9-10-11 ...... at San Diego
12-**13-14** .... Milwaukee
15-16-17-**18** .... S.D.
19-20-**21** .... at L.A.
22-23-**24** ...... at Houston
26-**27-28** .... Los Angeles

NOTE: Dates in **bold** indicate afternoon games. All game times are subject to change. Gaps in dates indicate scheduled off days but may be affected by rainouts.

* Interleague Series # At San Juan, P.R.

INTERLEAGUE SCHEDULE

June 3

#Anaheim vs. Montreal
Baltimore at Houston
Boston at Pittsburgh
Chicago White Sox at Arizona
Cleveland at Colorado
Detroit at San Diego
Kansas City at Los Angeles
Minnesota at San Francisco
New York Yankees at Cincinnati
Oakland at Florida
Seattle at Philadelphia
Tampa Bay at Chicago Cubs
Texas at Atlanta
Toronto at St. Louis

June 4

#Anaheim vs. Montreal
Baltimore at Houston
Boston at Pittsburgh
Chicago White Sox at Arizona
Cleveland at Colorado
Detroit at San Diego
Kansas City at Los Angeles
Minnesota at San Francisco
New York Yankees at Cincinnati
Oakland at Florida
Seattle at Philadelphia
Tampa Bay at Chicago Cubs
Texas at Atlanta
Toronto at St. Louis

June 5

#Anaheim vs. Montreal
Baltimore at Houston
Boston at Pittsburgh
Chicago White Sox at Arizona
Cleveland at Colorado
Detroit at San Diego
Kansas City at Los Angeles
Minnesota at San Francisco
New York Yankees at Cincinnati
Oakland at Florida
Seattle at Philadelphia
Tampa Bay at Chicago Cubs
Texas at Atlanta
Toronto at St. Louis

June 6

Anaheim at Florida
Baltimore at St. Louis
Boston at Milwaukee
Chicago Cubs at New York Yankees
Chicago White Sox at Los Angeles
Cleveland at Arizona
Detroit at San Francisco
Kansas City at Colorado
Minnesota at San Diego
Oakland at Philadelphia
Seattle at New York Mets
Tampa Bay at Houston
#Texas vs. Montreal
Toronto at Cincinnati

June 7

Anaheim at Florida
Baltimore at St. Louis
Boston at Milwaukee
Chicago Cubs at New York Yankees
Chicago White Sox at Los Angeles
Cleveland at Arizona
Detroit at San Francisco
Kansas City at Colorado
Minnesota at San Diego
Oakland at Philadelphia
Seattle at New York Mets
Tampa Bay at Houston
#Texas vs. Montreal
Toronto at Cincinnati

June 8

Anaheim at Florida
Baltimore at St. Louis
Boston at Milwaukee
Chicago Cubs at New York Yankees
Chicago White Sox at Los Angeles
Cleveland at Arizona
Detroit at San Francisco
Kansas City at Colorado
Minnesota at San Diego
Oakland at Philadelphia
Seattle at New York Mets
Tampa Bay at Houston
#Texas vs. Montreal
Toronto at Cincinnati

June 9

Philadelphia at Anaheim

June 10

Arizona at Kansas City
Atlanta at Oakland
Chicago Cubs at Baltimore
Cincinnati at Tampa Bay
Colorado at Minnesota
Houston at New York Yankees
Los Angeles at Detroit
Montreal at Seattle
New York Mets at Texas
Philadelphia at Anaheim
Pittsburgh at Toronto
St. Louis at Boston
San Diego at Cleveland
San Francisco at Chicago White Sox

June 11

Arizona at Kansas City
Atlanta at Oakland
Chicago Cubs at Baltimore
Cincinnati at Tampa Bay
Colorado at Minnesota
Houston at New York Yankees
Los Angeles at Detroit
Montreal at Seattle
New York Mets at Texas
Philadelphia at Anaheim
Pittsburgh at Toronto
St. Louis at Boston
San Diego at Cleveland
San Francisco at Chicago White Sox

June 12

Arizona at Kansas City
Atlanta at Oakland
Chicago Cubs at Baltimore
Cincinnati at Tampa Bay
Colorado at Minnesota
Houston at New York Yankees
Los Angeles at Detroit
Montreal at Seattle
New York Mets at Texas
Pittsburgh at Toronto
St. Louis at Boston
San Diego at Cleveland
San Francisco at Chicago White Sox

June 13

Arizona at Minnesota
Atlanta at Seattle
Chicago Cubs at Toronto
Colorado at Detroit
Florida at Texas
Houston at Boston
Los Angeles at Cleveland
Milwaukee at Baltimore
Montreal at Oakland
New York Mets at Anaheim
Pittsburgh at Tampa Bay
St. Louis at New York Yankees
San Diego at Chicago White Sox
San Francisco at Kansas City

June 14

Arizona at Minnesota
Atlanta at Seattle
Chicago Cubs at Toronto
Colorado at Detroit
Florida at Texas
Houston at Boston
Los Angeles at Cleveland
Milwaukee at Baltimore
Montreal at Oakland
New York Mets at Anaheim
Pittsburgh at Tampa Bay
St. Louis at New York Yankees
San Diego at Chicago White Sox
San Francisco at Kansas City

June 15

Arizona at Minnesota
Atlanta at Seattle
Chicago Cubs at Toronto
Colorado at Detroit
Florida at Texas
Houston at Boston
Los Angeles at Cleveland
Milwaukee at Baltimore
Montreal at Oakland
New York Mets at Anaheim

Pittsburgh at Tampa Bay
St. Louis at New York Yankees
San Diego at Chicago White Sox
San Francisco at Kansas City

June 20

Anaheim at Los Angeles
Baltimore at Atlanta
Boston at Philadelphia
Chicago White Sox at Chicago Cubs
Cleveland at Pittsburgh
Detroit at Colorado
Houston at Texas
Kansas City at St. Louis
Minnesota at Milwaukee
New York Yankees at New York Mets
San Francisco at Oakland
Seattle at San Diego
Tampa Bay at Florida
Toronto at Montreal

June 21

Anaheim at Los Angeles
Baltimore at Atlanta
Boston at Philadelphia
Chicago White Sox at Chicago Cubs
Cleveland at Pittsburgh
Detroit at Colorado
Houston at Texas
Kansas City at St. Louis
Minnesota at Milwaukee
New York Yankees at New York Mets
San Francisco at Oakland
Seattle at San Diego
Tampa Bay at Florida
Toronto at Montreal

June 22

Anaheim at Los Angeles
Baltimore at Atlanta
Boston at Philadelphia
Chicago White Sox at Chicago Cubs
Cleveland at Pittsburgh
Detroit at Colorado
Houston at Texas
Kansas City at St. Louis
Minnesota at Milwaukee
New York Yankees at New York Mets
San Francisco at Oakland
Seattle at San Diego
Tampa Bay at Florida
Toronto at Montreal

June 27

Arizona at Detroit
Atlanta at Tampa Bay
Chicago Cubs at Chicago White Sox
Cincinnati at Cleveland
Florida at Boston
Los Angeles at Anaheim
Milwaukee at Minnesota
Montreal at Toronto
New York Mets at New York Yankees
Oakland at San Francisco
Philadelphia at Baltimore
St. Louis at Kansas City
San Diego at Seattle
Texas at Houston

June 28

Arizona at Detroit
Atlanta at Tampa Bay
Chicago Cubs at Chicago White Sox
Cincinnati at Cleveland
Florida at Boston
Los Angeles at Anaheim
Milwaukee at Minnesota
Montreal at Toronto
New York Mets at New York Yankees
Oakland at San Francisco
Philadelphia at Baltimore
St. Louis at Kansas City
San Diego at Seattle
Texas at Houston

June 29

Arizona at Detroit
Atlanta at Tampa Bay
Chicago Cubs at Chicago White Sox
Cincinnati at Cleveland
Florida at Boston
Los Angeles at Anaheim
Milwaukee at Minnesota
Montreal at Toronto
New York Mets at New York Yankees
Oakland at San Francisco
Philadelphia at Baltimore
St. Louis at Kansas City
San Diego at Seattle
Texas at Houston

At San Juan, P.R.

SPRING TRAINING

ARIZONA/CACTUS LEAGUE

ANAHEIM ANGELS

Major League Club

Complex Address (first year): Diablo Stadium (1993), 2200 W. Alameda, Tempe, AZ 85282. Telephone: (602) 438-4300. FAX: (602) 438-7950. **Seating Capacity:** 9,785. **Location:** I-10 to exit 153B (48th Street), south one mile on 48th Street to Alameda Drive, left on Alameda.

Minor League Clubs

Complex Address: Gene Autry Park, 4125 E. McKellips, Mesa, AZ 85205. Telephone: (480) 830-4137. FAX: (480) 438-7950. **Hotel Address:** Lake View Apartments, 1849 S. Power Rd., Mesa, AZ 85206.

ARIZONA DIAMONDBACKS

Major League Club

Complex Address (first year): Tucson Electric Park (1998), 2500 Ajo Way, Tucson, AZ 85713. Telephone: (520) 434-1400. FAX: (520) 434-1443. **Seating Capacity:** 11,000. **Location:** I-10 to exit 262 (Park Street) or 263 (Kino Street), south to Ajo Way, left (east) on Ajo Way to park.

Hotel Address: Doubletree Suites, 6555 E. Speedway, Tucson, AZ 85710. Telephone: (520) 721-7100.

Minor League Clubs

Complex Address: Kino Veterans Memorial Sportspark, 3600 S. Country Club, Tucson, AZ 85713. Telephone: (520) 434-1400. FAX: (520) 434-1443. **Hotel Address:** Holiday Inn, 181 W. Broadway, Tucson, AZ 85701. Telephone: (520) 624-8711.

CHICAGO CUBS

Major League Club

Complex Address (first year): HoHoKam Park (1979), 1235 N. Center St., Mesa, AZ 85201. Telephone: (480) 668-0500. FAX: (480) 668-4541. **Seating Capacity:** 8,963. **Location:** Main Street (US Highway 60) to Center Street, north 1½ miles on Center Street.

Hotel Address: Best Western Dobson Ranch Inn, 1666 S. Dobson Rd., Mesa, AZ 85202. Telephone: (480) 831-7000.

Minor League Clubs

Complex Address: Fitch Park, 160 E. Sixth Place, Mesa, AZ 85201. Telephone: (480) 668-0500. FAX: (480) 668-4501. **Hotel Address:** Best Western Mezona, 250 W. Main St., Mesa, AZ 85201. Telephone: (480) 834-9233.

CHICAGO WHITE SOX

Major League Club

Complex Address (first year): Tucson Electric Park (1998), 2500 E. Ajo Way, Tucson, AZ 85713. Telephone: (520) 434-1300. FAX: (520) 434-1151. **Seating Capacity:** 11,000. **Location:** I-10 to exit 262 (Park Street) or 263 (Kino Street), south to Ajo Way, left (east) on Ajo Way to park.

Hotel Address: Doubletree Guest Suites, 6555 E. Speedway Blvd., Tucson, AZ 85710. Telephone: (520) 721-7100.

Minor League Clubs

Complex Address: Same as major league club. **Hotel Address:** Ramada Palo Verde, 5251 S. Julian Dr., Tucson, AZ 85706. Telephone: (520) 294-5250.

COLORADO ROCKIES

Major League Club

Complex Address (first year): Hi Corbett Field (1993), 3400 E. Camino Campestre, Tucson, AZ 85716. Telephone: (520) 322-4500. **Seating Capacity:** 9,500. **Location:** I-10 to Broadway exit, east on Broadway to Randolph Park.

Hotel Address: Hilton Tucson East, 7600 Broadway, Tucson, AZ 85710.

Minor League Clubs

Complex Address: Same as major league club. **Hotel Address:** Clarion Hotel, 102 N. Alvernon, Tucson, AZ 85711. Telephone: (520) 795-0330.

KANSAS CITY ROYALS

Major League Club

Complex Address (first year): Surprise Stadium (2003), 15946 N. Bullard Ave., Surprise, AZ 85374. **Telephone:** (623) 266-4400. **FAX:** (623) 266-4584. **Seating Capacity:** 10,700. **Location:** I-10 West to Route 101 North, 101 North to Bell Road, left on Bell for five miles, stadium on left.

Hotel Address: Wingate Inn & Suites, 1188 N. Dysart Rd., Avondale, AZ 85323. Telephone: (623) 547-1313.

Minor League Clubs

Complex/Hotel Address: Same as major league club.

MILWAUKEE BREWERS

Major League Club

Complex Address (first year): Maryvale Baseball Park (1998), 3600 N. 51st Ave., Phoenix, AZ 85031. Telephone: (623) 245-5555. FAX: (623) 247-7404. **Seating Capacity:** 9,000. **Location:** I-10 to exit 139 (51st Ave.), north on 51st Ave.; I-17 to exit 202 (Indian School Road), west on Indian School Road.

Hotel Address: Sheraton Four Points, 10220 N. Metro Parkway East, Phoenix, AZ 85051. Telephone: (623) 997-5900.

Minor League Clubs

Complex Address: Maryvale Baseball Complex, 3805 N. 53rd Ave., Phoenix, AZ 85031. Telephone: (623) 245-5600. FAX: (623) 849-8941. **Hotel Address:** Town Place Suites, 5223 S. Priest Dr., Tempe, AZ 85283. Telephone: (480) 345-7889.

OAKLAND ATHLETICS

Major League Club

Complex Address (first year): Phoenix Municipal Stadium (1982), 5999 E. Van Buren, Phoenix, AZ 85008. Telephone: (602) 225-9400. FAX: (602) 225-9473. **Seating Capacity:** 8,500. **Location:** I-10 to exit 153 (48th Street), HoHoKam Expressway to Van Buren Street (US Highway 60), right on Van Buren; park two miles on right.

Hotel Address: Doubletree Suites Hotel, 320 N. 44th St., Phoenix, AZ 85008. Telephone: (602) 225-0500.

Minor League Clubs

Complex Address: Papago Park Baseball Complex, 1802 N. 64th St., Phoenix, AZ 85008. Telephone: (480) 949-5951. FAX: (480) 945-0557. **Hotel Address:** Fairfield Inn, 5101 N. Scottsdale Rd., Scottsdale, AZ 85251. Telephone: (480) 945-4392.

SAN DIEGO PADRES

Major League Club

Complex Address (first year): Peoria Sports Complex (1994), 8131 W. Paradise Lane, Peoria, AZ 85382. Telephone: (623) 486-7000. FAX: (623) 412-9382. **Seating Capacity:** 10,000. **Location:** I-17 to Bell Road exit, west on Bell to 83rd Ave.

Hotel Address: Comfort Suites, 8473 W. Paradise Lane, Peoria, AZ 85382. Telephone: (623) 334-3993.

Minor League Clubs

Complex Address: Same as major league club.

Hotel Address: Sheraton Crescent, 2620 W. Dunlap Ave., Phoenix, AZ 85021. Telephone: (623) 943-8200.

SAN FRANCISCO GIANTS

Major League Club

Complex Address (first year): Scottsdale Stadium (1981), 7408 E. Osborn Rd., Scottsdale, AZ 85251. Telephone: (480) 990-7972. FAX: (480) 990-2643. **Seating Capacity:** 10,500. **Location:** Scottsdale Road to Osborne Road, east on Osborne ½ mile.

Hotel Address: Courtyard Marriott, 3311 N. Scottsdale Rd., Scottsdale, AZ 85251. Telephone: (480) 429-7785.

Minor League Clubs

Complex Address: Indian School Park, 4289 N. Hayden Road at Camelback Road, Scottsdale, AZ 85251. Telephone: (480) 990-0052. FAX: (480) 990-2349.

Hotel Address: Days Inn, 4710 N. Scottsdale Rd., Scottsdale, AZ 85351. Telephone: (480) 947-5411.

SEATTLE MARINERS

Major League Club

Complex Address (first year): Peoria Sports Complex (1993), 15707 N. 83rd Ave., Peoria, AZ 85382. Telephone: (602) 412-9000. FAX: (602) 412-9382. **Seating Capacity:** 10,000. **Location:** I-17 to Bell Road exit, west on Bell to 83rd Ave.

Hotel Address: 4 Point Sheraton, 10220 N. Metro Parkway, Phoenix, AZ 85051. Telephone: (602) 997-5900.

Minor League Clubs

Complex Address: Peoria Sports Complex (1993), 15707 N. 83rd Ave., Peoria, AZ 85382. Telephone: (602) 412-9000. FAX: (602) 412-9382.

Hotel Address: Hampton Inn, 8408 W. Paradise Lane, Peoria, AZ 85382. Telephone: (623) 486-9918.

TEXAS RANGERS

Major League Club

Complex Address (first year): Surprise Stadium (2003), 15754 N. Bullard Ave., Surprise, AZ 85374. **Telephone:** (623) 266-4600. **FAX:** (623) 266-4639. **Seating Capacity:** 10,714. **Location:** I-10 West to Route 101 North, 101 North to Bell Rd., left at Bell for five miles, stadium on left.

Hotel Address: Windmill Suites at Sun City West, 12545 W. Bell Rd., Surprise, AZ 85374. Telephone: (623) 583-0133.

Minor League Clubs

Complex Address: Same as major league club.

Hotel Address: Hampton Inn, 2000 N. Litchfield Rd., Goodyear, AZ 85338. Telephone: (623) 536-1313

SPRING TRAINING

FLORIDA/GRAPEFRUIT LEAGUE

ATLANTA BRAVES

Major League Club

Stadium Address (first year): Disney's Wide World of Sports Complex (1998), Cracker Jack Stadium, 700 S. Victory Way, Kissimmee, FL 34747. Telephone: (407) 939-2200. **Seating Capacity:** 9,500. **Location:** I-4 to exit 25B (Highway 192 West), follow signs to Magic Kingdom/Wide World of Sports Complex, right on Victory Way.

Hotel Address: World Center Marriott, World Center Drive, Orlando, FL 32821. Telephone: (407) 239-4200.

Minor League Clubs

Complex Address: Same as major league club. Telephone: (407) 939-2232. FAX: (407) 939-2225. **Hotel Address:** Days Suites, 5820 W. Hwy. 92, Kissimmee, FL 34746. Telephone: (407) 396-7900.

BALTIMORE ORIOLES

Major League Club

Complex Address (first year): Fort Lauderdale Stadium (1996), 1301 NW 55th St., Fort Lauderdale, FL 33309. Telephone: (954) 776-1921. FAX: (954) 776-9116. **Seating Capacity:** 8,340. **Location:** I-95 to exit 32 (Commercial Blvd.), West on Commercial, right on Orioles Blvd. (NW 55th Street), stadium on left.

Hotel Address: Sheraton Suites, 555 NW 62nd St., Fort Lauderdale, FL 33309. Telephone: (954) 772-5400.

Minor League Clubs

Complex Address: Twin Lakes Park, 6700 Clark Rd., Sarasota, FL 34241. Telephone: (941) 923-1996. FAX: (941) 922-3751. **Hotel Address:** Ramada Inn Osprey, 1660 S. Tamiami Trail, Sarasota, FL 34229. Telephone: (941) 966-2121.

BOSTON RED SOX

Major League Club

Complex Address (first year): City of Palms Park (1993), 2201 Edison Ave., Fort Myers, FL 33901. Telephone: (239) 334-4799. FAX: (239) 334-6060. **Seating Capacity:** 6,990. **Location:** I-75 to exit 39, three miles west to Tuttle Ave., right on Tuttle to 12th Street, stadium on left.

Hotel Address: Homewood Suites Hotel, 5255 Big Pine Way Fort Myers, FL 33907. Telephone: (239) 275-6000.

Minor League Clubs

Complex Address: Red Sox Minor League Complex, 4301 Edison Ave., Fort Myers, FL 33916. Telephone: (239) 461-4500. FAX: (239) 332-8107. **Hotel Address:** Ramada Inn, 2500 Edwards Drive, Fort Myers, FL 33901. Telephone: (239) 337-0300.

CINCINNATI REDS

Major League Club

Complex Address (first year): Ed Smith Stadium (1998), 12th Street and Tuttle Avenue, Sarasota, FL 34237. Telephone: (941) 955-6501. FAX: (941) 955-6365. **Seating Capacity:** 7,500. **Location:** I-75 to exit 39, west on Fruitville Road (Fla. 780) for four miles, right on Tuttle.

Hotel Address: Marriott Residence Inn, 1040 University Pkwy., Sarasota, FL 34234. Telephone: (941) 358-1468. FAX: (941) 358-0850.

Minor League Clubs

Complex Address: Same as major league club. **Hotel Address:** Wellesley Inn, 1803 N. Tamiami Trail, Sarasota, FL 34234. Telephone: (941) 366-5128.

CLEVELAND INDIANS

Major League Club

Complex Address: Chain O' Lakes Park (1993), Cypress Gardens Blvd. at US 17, Winter Haven, FL 33880. Telephone: (863) 293-5405. FAX: (863) 291-5772. **Seating Capacity:** 7,000. **Location:** US 17 (3rd Street) south through Winter Haven to Cypress Gardens Blvd.

Hotel Address: Holiday Inn, 1150 Third St. SW, Winter Haven, FL 33880. Telephone: (863) 294-4451.

Minor League Clubs

Complex Address/Hotel: Same as major league club.

DETROIT TIGERS

Major League Club

Complex Address (first year): Joker Marchant Stadium (1946), 2301 Lakeland Hills Blvd., Lakeland, FL 33805. Telephone: (863) 686-8075. FAX: (863) 688-9589. **Seating Capacity:** 7,027. **Location:** I-4 to exit 19

(Lakeland Hills Blvd.), left 1½ miles.

Hotel Address: Wellesley Inn, 3520 Hwy. 98 N., Lakeland, FL 33805. Telephone: (863) 859-3399.

Minor League Clubs

Complex/Hotel Address: Tigertown, 2125 N. Lake Ave., Lakeland, FL 33805. Telephone: (863) 686-8075. FAX: (863) 688-9589.

FLORIDA MARLINS

Major League Club

Complex Address (first year): Roger Dean Stadium (2003), 4751 Main St., Jupiter, FL 33458. Telephone: (561) 775-1818. **Seating Capacity:** 7,000. **Location:** I-95 to exit 58, east on Donald Ross Road for ¼ mile.

Hotel Address: Hampton Inn, 401 RCA Blvd., Palm Beach Gardens, FL 33410. Telephone: 561-625-8880. FAX: (561) 625-6766.

Minor League Clubs

Complex Address: Same as major league club.

Hotel Address: Fairfield Inn, 6748 W. Indiantown Road, Jupiter, FL 33458. Telephone: (561) 748-5252.

HOUSTON ASTROS

Major League Club

Complex Address (first year): Osceola County Stadium (1985), 631 Heritage Park Way, Kissimmee, FL 34744. Telephone: (321) 697-3150. FAX: (321) 697-3199. **Seating Capacity:** 5,300. **Location:** From Florida Turnpike South, take exit 244, west on US 192, right on Bill Beck Boulevard; From Florida Turnpike North, take exit 242, west on US 192, right on Bill Beck Blvd.; From I-4, take exit onto 192 East for 12 miles, stadium on left; From 17-92 South, take US 192, left for three miles.

Minor League Clubs

Complex Address: 1000 Bill Beck Blvd., Kissimmee, FL 34744. Telephone: (321) 697-3100. FAX: (321) 697-3195. **Hotel Address:** Four Points Sheraton, 4018 West Vine St. (US 192), Kissimmee, FL 34741. Telephone: (321) 870-2000.

LOS ANGELES DODGERS

Major League Club

Complex Address (first year): Holman Stadium (1948). **Seating Capacity:** 6,500. **Location:** Exit I-95 to Route 60 East, left on 43rd Avenue, right on Aviation Boulevard.

Hotel Address: Dodgertown, 4001 26th St., Vero Beach, FL 32960. Telephone: (772) 569-4900. FAX: (772) 567-0819.

Minor League Clubs

Complex/Hotel Address: Same as major league club.

MINNESOTA TWINS

Major League Club

Complex Address (first year): Lee County Sports Complex/Hammond Stadium (1991), 14100 Six Mile Cypress Pkwy., Fort Myers, FL 33912. Telephone: (239) 768-4282. FAX: (239) 768-4211. **Seating Capacity:** 7,500. **Location:** Exit 21 off I-75, west on Daniels Parkway, left on Six Mile Cypress Parkway.

Hotel Address: Radisson Inn, 12635 Cleveland Ave., Fort Myers, FL 33907. Telephone: (239) 936-4300.

Minor League Clubs

Complex Address/Hotel: Same as major league club.

MONTREAL EXPOS

Major League Club

Complex Address (first year): Space Coast Stadium, 5800 Stadium Parkway, Viera, FL 32940. Telephone: (321) 633-9200. **Seating Capacity:** 7,200. **Location:** I-95 southbound to Fiske Blvd. (exit 74), south on Fiske/Stadium Parkway to stadium; I-95 northbound to State Road #509/Wickham Road (exit 73), left off exit, right on Lake Andrew Drive and follow to complex.

Hotel Address: Melbourne Airport Hilton, 200 Rialto Place, Melbourne, FL 32901. Telephone: (321) 768-0200

Minor League Clubs

Complex Address: Same as major league club. **Hotel Address:** Holiday Inn Cocoa Beach Resort, 1300 N. Atlantic Ave., Melbourne, FL 32940. Telephone: (321) 633-8119.

NEW YORK METS

Major League Club

Complex Address (first year): St. Lucie Sports Complex/Thomas J. White Stadium (1987), 525 NW Peacock Blvd., Port St. Lucie, FL 34986. Telephone: (772) 871-2100. FAX: (772) 878-9802. **Seating Capacity:** 7,347. **Location:** Exit 121 (St. Lucie West Boulevard) off I-95, east ½ mile, left on NW Peacock Boulevard.

Hotel Address: Holiday Inn, 10120 South Federal Hwy., Port St. Lucie, FL 34952. Telephone: (772) 337-2200.

Minor League Clubs

Complex/Hotel Address: Same as major league club. Telephone: (772) 871-2152.

NEW YORK YANKEES

Major League Club

Complex Address (first year): Legends Field (1996), One Steinbrenner Dr., Tampa, FL 33614. Telephone: (813) 875-7753. FAX: (813) 673-3199. **Seating Capacity:** 10,000. **Location:** I-275 to Martin Luther King, west on Martin Luther King to Dale Mabry.

Hotel Address: Radisson Bay Harbor Inn, 770 Courtney Campbell Causeway, Tampa, FL 33607. Telephone: (813) 281-8900.

Minor League Clubs

Complex Address: Yankees Player Development/Scouting Complex, 3102 N. Himes Ave., Tampa, FL 33607. Telephone: (813) 875-7569. FAX: (813) 873-2302. **Hotel Address:** Holiday Inn Express, 4732 N. Dale Mabry, Tampa, FL 33614.

PHILADELPHIA PHILLIES

Major League Club

Complex Address (first year): Jack Russell Memorial Stadium (1955), 800 Phillies Dr., Clearwater, FL 33755. Telephone: (727) 441-9941. FAX: (727) 461-7768. **Seating Capacity:** 6,917. **Location:** US 19 North to Drew Street, west to Greenwood Avenue, north to Seminole Street, right to park.

Hotel: None.

Minor League Clubs

Complex Address: Carpenter Complex, 651 Old Coachman Rd., Clearwater, FL 33765. Telephone: (727) 799-0503. FAX: (727) 726-1793. **Hotel Addresses:** Hampton Inn, 21030 US Highway 19 North, Clearwater, FL 34625. Telephone: (727) 797-8173; Econolodge, 21252 US Highway 19, Clearwater, FL 34625. Telephone: (727) 799-1569.

PITTSBURGH PIRATES

Major League Club

Stadium Address (first year): McKechnie Field

(1969), 17th Ave. West and Ninth St. West, Bradenton, FL 34205. **Seating Capacity:** 6,562. **Location:** US 41 to 17th Ave, west to 9th Street.

Complex/Hotel Address: Pirate City, 1701 27th St. E., Bradenton, FL 34208. Telephone: (941) 747-3031. FAX: (941) 747-9549.

Minor League Clubs

Complex/Hotel Address: Same as major league club.

ST. LOUIS CARDINALS

Major League Club

Complex Address (first year): Roger Dean Stadium (1998), 4795 University Dr., Jupiter, FL 33458. Telephone: (561) 775-1818. FAX: (561) 799-1380. **Seating Capacity:** 6,871. **Location:** I-95 to exit 58, east on Donald Ross Road for ¼ mile.

Hotel Address: Palm Beach Gardens Marriott, 4000 RCA Blvd., Palm Beach Gardens, FL 33410. Telephone: (561) 622-8888.

Minor League Clubs

Complex: Same as major league club. **Hotel:** Doubletree Hotel, 4431 PGA Blvd., Palm Beach Gardens, FL 33410. Telephone: (561) 622-2260.

TAMPA BAY DEVIL RAYS

Major League Club

Stadium Address (first year): Progress Energy Park, Home of Al Lang Field (1998), 180 Second Ave. SE, St. Petersburg, FL 33701. Telephone: (727) 344-3259. FAX: (727) 825-3167. **Seating Capacity:** 6,438. **Location:** I-275 to exit 23C, left on First Street South to Second Avenue South, stadium on right.

Complex/Hotel Address: Devil Rays Spring Training Complex, 7901 30th Ave. N., St. Petersburg, FL 33710. Telephone: (727) 825-3042.

Minor League Clubs

Complex/Hotel Address: Same as major league club.

TORONTO BLUE JAYS

Major League Club

Stadium Address (first year): Dunedin Stadium (1977), 373 Douglas Ave. #A, Dunedin, FL 34698. Telephone: (727) 733-9302. **Seating Capacity:** 5,509. **Location:** From I-275, north on Highway 19, left on Sunset Point Road for four miles, right on Douglas Avenue, stadium one mile on right.

Minor League Clubs

Complex Address: Bobby Mattick Training Facility at Englebert Complex, 1700 Solon Ave., Dunedin, FL 34698. Telephone: (727) 743-8007. **Hotel Address:** Red Roof Inn, 3200 US 19 N., Clearwater, FL 34684. Telephone: (727) 786-2529.

MEDIA
INFO

MEDIA INFORMATION

AMERICAN LEAGUE

ANAHEIM ANGELS

Radio Announcers: English—Darren Chan, Rory Markas, Terry Smith. Spanish—Ivan Lara, Jose Mota. **Flagship Station:** KSPN 710-AM, XPRS 1190-AM (Spanish).

TV Announcers: Rex Hudler, Steve Physioc. **Flagship Stations:** KCAL Channel 9, Fox Sports Net (regional cable).

NEWSPAPERS, Daily Coverage (beat writers): Long Beach Press Telegram, Los Angeles Times (Ross Newhan, Bill Shaikin), Orange County Register (Bill Plunkett, Cheryl Rosenberg), Riverside Press Enterprise (Matt Tresaugue), San Gabriel Valley Tribune (Joe Haakenson), Inland Valley Daily Bulletin.

BALTIMORE ORIOLES

Radio Announcers: Jim Hunter, Fred Manfra, Chuck Thompson. **Flagship Station:** WBAL 1090-AM.

TV Announcers: Jim Palmer, Michael Reghi. **Flagship Stations:** WJZ-TV, WNUV-TV, Comcast SportsNet.

NEWSPAPERS, Daily Coverage (beat writers): Baltimore Sun (Joe Christensen, Roch Kubatko), Washington Post (Dave Sheinin), Washington Times (Duff Durkin), York, Pa., Daily Record (Dan Connolly).

BOSTON RED SOX

Radio Announcers: Joe Castiglione, Jerry Trupiano. **Flagship Station:** WEEI 850-AM.

TV Announcers: WSBK-38—Sean McDonough, Jerry Remy; NESN—Don Orsillo, Jerry Remy. **Flagship Stations:** WSBK-38, New England Sports Network (regional cable).

NEWSPAPERS, Daily Coverage (beat writers): Boston Globe (Bob Hohler, Gordon Edes), Boston Herald (Howard Bryant, Jeff Horrigan, Tony Massarotti, Mike Silverman), Providence Journal (Steve Krasner, Sean McAdam), Worcester Telegram (Bill Ballou, Phil O'Neill), Hartford Courant (Paul Doyle, Dave Heuschkel).

CHICAGO WHITE SOX

Radio Announcers: John Rooney, Ed Farmer. **Flagship Station:** WMVP/ESPN Radio 1000-AM.

TV Announcers: Ken Harrelson, Darrin Jackson. **Flagship Stations:** WGN TV-9, WCIU-TV, FOX Sports Net Chicago (regional cable).

NEWSPAPERS, Daily Coverage (beat writers): Chicago Sun-Times (Doug Padilla), Chicago Tribune, Arlington Heights Daily Herald (Scot Gregor), Daily Southtown (Joe Cowley).

CLEVELAND INDIANS

Radio Announcers: Tom Hamilton, Mike Hegan, Matt Underwood. **Flagship Station:** WTAM 1100-AM.

TV Announcers: Rick Manning, John Sanders, Mike Hegan. **Flagship Station:** Fox Sports Net.

NEWSPAPERS, Daily Coverage (beat writers): Cleveland Plain Dealer (Paul Hoynes), Lake County News-Herald (Jim Ingraham), Akron Beacon-Journal (Sheldon Ocker), Canton Repository (Andy Call).

DETROIT TIGERS

Radio Announcers: Dan Dickerson, Jim Price. **Flagship Station:** WXYT 1270-AM.

TV Announcers: Frank Beckmann, Rod Allen, Mario Impemba. **Flagship Stations:** WKBD-50, Fox Sports Net Detroit (regional cable).

NEWSPAPERS, Daily Coverage (beat writers): Detroit Free Press (John Lowe, Gene Guidi), Detroit News (Tom Gage), Oakland Press (Crystal Evola, Pat Caputo), Booth Newspapers (Danny Knobler), Windsor Star (Jim Parker).

KANSAS CITY ROYALS

Radio Announcers: Ryan Lefebvre, Denny Matthews. **Flagship Station:** KMBZ 980-AM.

TV Announcers: Bob Davis, Paul Splittorff. **Flagship Stations:** Royals Television Network.

NEWSPAPERS, Daily Coverage (beat writers): Kansas City Star (Dick Kaegel, Bob Dutton), MLB.com (Chris Shaeffer, Robert Falkoff).

MINNESOTA TWINS

Radio Announcers: John Gordon, Dan Gladden. **Flagship Station:** WCCO 830-AM.

TV Announcers: Bert Blyleven, Dick Bremer. **Flagship Station:** Unavailable.

NEWSPAPERS, Daily Coverage (beat writers): St. Paul Pioneer Press (Gordon Wittenmyer), Minneapolis Star Tribune (LaVelle Neal).

NEW YORK YANKEES

Radio Announcers: John Sterling, Charley Steiner. **Flagship Station:** WCBS 880-AM.

TV Announcers: Michael Kay, Jim Kaat, Ken Singleton, Paul O'Neill, Fred Hickman, Suzyn Waldman. **Flagship Stations:** YES! Network (Yankees Entertainment & Sports), WCBS-TV, Ch. 2.

NEWSPAPERS, Daily Coverage (beat writers): New York Daily News (Anthony McCarron), New York Post (George King), New York Times (Tyler Kepner), Newark Star-Ledger (Dan Graziano), The Bergen Record (Tom Haudricourt), Newsday (Ken Davidoff), Hartford Courant (Dom Amore), The Journal News (John Delcos).

OAKLAND ATHLETICS

Radio Announcers: Bill King, Ray Fosse, Ken Korach. **Flagship Station:** KFRC 610-AM.

TV Announcers: Ray Fosse, Greg Papa. **Flagship Stations:** KICU, FOX Sports Net (regional cable).

NEWSPAPERS, Daily Coverage (beat writers): San Francisco Chronicle (Susan Slusser), Oakland Tribune (Mark Saxon), Contra Costa Times (Rick Hurd), Sacramento Bee (Jim Van Vliet), San Jose Mercury-News (Laurence

Miedema), Santa Rosa Press Democrat (Jeff Fletcher).

SEATTLE MARINERS

TV/Radio Announcers: Ron Fairly, Dave Henderson, Dave Niehaus, Rick Rizzs, Dave Valle.

Flagship Stations: KOMO 1000-AM (radio), FOX Sports Net Northwest (TV).

NEWSPAPERS, Daily Coverage (beat writers): Seattle Times (Bob Finnigan, Bob Sherwin), Seattle Post-Intelligencer (John Hickey), Tacoma News Tribune (Larry LaRue), The Everett Herald (Kirby Arnold), Kyodo News (Keizo Konishi), Nikkan Sports (Mamoru Shikama), MLB.com (Jim Street).

TAMPA BAY DEVIL RAYS

Radio Announcers: Paul Olden, Charlie Slowes. **Flagship Station:** WFLA 970-AM.

TV Announcers: DeWayne Staats, Joe Magrane. **Flagship Stations:** PAX-TV Fox SportsNet (regional cable).

NEWSPAPERS, Daily Coverage (beat writers): St. Petersburg Times (Marc Topkin), Tampa Tribune (Carter Gaddis), Bradenton Herald (Roger Mooney), Port Charlotte Sun-Herald (John Fineran), Lakeland Ledger (Dick Scanlan), Sarasota Herald-Tribune (Chris Anderson).

TEXAS RANGERS

Radio Announcers: Eric Nadel, Vince Cotroneo, Eleno Ornelas (Spanish), Edgar Lopez (Spanish). **Flagship Station:** KRLD 1080-AM, KESS 1270-AM (Spanish).

TV Announcers: Josh Lewin, Tom Grieve. **Flagship Stations:** KDFI, KDFW, Fox Sports Southwest (regional cable).

NEWSPAPERS, Daily Coverage (beat writers): Dallas Morning News (Sean Horgan, Ken Daley), Fort Worth Star-Telegram (T.R. Sullivan, Carlos Mendez), MLB.com (Jesse Sanchez).

TORONTO BLUE JAYS

Radio Announcers: Tom Cheek, Jerry Howarth. **Flagship Station:** The Fan 590-AM.

TV Announcers: Sportsnet—Rob Faulds, John Cerutti, Tom Candiotti. TSN—Rod Black, Pat Tabler. **Flagship Stations:** Rogers Sports Net (cable), CBC, TSN.

NEWSPAPERS, Daily Coverage (beat writers): Toronto Sun (Mike Rutsey, Bob Elliott, Mike Ganter), Toronto Star (Geoff Baker, Richard Griffin, Alan Ryan, Mark Zwolinski), Globe and Mail (Larry Millson, Jeff Blair).

NATIONAL LEAGUE

ARIZONA DIAMONDBACKS

Radio Announcers: English—Thom Brennaman, Jeff Munn, Greg Schulte, Victor Rojas; Spanish—Miguel Quintana, Oscar Soria, Richard Saenz. **Flagship Stations:** KTAR 620-AM (English), KSUN 1400-AM (Spanish).

TV Announcers: Thom Brennaman, Steve Lyons, Jim Traber, Joe Garagiola, Greg Schulte. **Flagship Stations:** KTVK-TV 3, FOX Sports Net Arizona (regional cable). **Spanish TV Announcers:** Freddy Morales, Oscar Soria. **Spanish Flagship Station:** MAS-Arizona.

Newspapers, Daily Coverage (beat writers): Arizona Republic (Mark Gonzales), Tribune Newspapers (Ed Price), Arizona Daily Star (Jack Magruder), Tucson Citizen (Ken Brazzle).

ATLANTA BRAVES

Radio Announcers: Skip Caray, Don Sutton, Joe Simpson, Pete Van Wieren. **Flagship Station:** WSB 750-AM.

TV Announcers: TBS—Skip Caray, Pete Van Wieren, Don Sutton, Joe Simpson; Fox Sports Net—Bob Rathbun, Tom Paciorek. **Flagship Stations:** TBS (national cable); Fox Sports Net South, Turner South (regional cable).

NEWSPAPERS, Daily Coverage (beat writers): Atlanta Journal-Constitution: (Dave O'Brien), Morris News (Bill Zack).

CHICAGO CUBS

Radio Announcers: Pat Hughes, Ron Santo. **Flagship Station:** WGN 720-AM.

TV Announcers: Chip Caray, Steve Stone. **Flagship Stations:** WGN Channel 9 (national cable), Fox Sports Net Chicago (regional cable), WCIU-TV Channel 26 (local).

NEWSPAPERS, Daily Coverage (beat writers): Chicago Tribune (Paul Sullivan, Phil Rogers), Chicago Sun-Times (Mike Kiley), Arlington Daily Herald (Bruce Miles), Daily Southtown (Jeff Vorva).

CINCINNATI REDS

Radio Announcers: Mary Brennaman, Joe Nuxhall. **Flagship Station:** WLW 700-AM.

TV Announcers: George Grande, Chris Welsh. **Flagship Station:** Fox Sports Net (regional cable).

NEWSPAPERS, Daily Coverage (beat writers): Cincinnati Enquirer (John Fay), Cincinnati Post (Tony Jackson), Dayton Daily News (Hal McCoy), Columbus Dispatch (Jim Massie).

COLORADO ROCKIES

Radio Announcers: Jack Corrigan, Jeff Kingery. **Flagship Station:** KOA 850-AM.

TV Announcers: Drew Goodman, George Frazier. **Flagship Station:** KTVD Channel 20 (UPN), Fox Sports Net (regional cable).

NEWSPAPERS, Daily Coverage (beat writers): Rocky Mountain News (Tracy Ringolsby, Jack Etkin), Denver Post (Troy Renck, Mike Klis), Boulder Daily Camera (Barney Hutchinson).

FLORIDA MARLINS

Radio Announcers: English—Jon Sciambi, Dave Van Horne. Spanish—Felo Ramirez, Yiky Quintana. **Flagship Stations:** WQAM 560-AM, WQBA 1140-AM (Spanish).

TV Announcers: Len Kasper, Tommy Hutton. **Flagship Stations:** PAX TV, Fox Sports Net (regional cable).

NEWSPAPERS, Daily Coverage (beat writers): Miami Herald (Kevin Baxter, Clark Spencer), Fort Lauderdale Sun-Sentinel (Mike Berardino, Juan Rodriguez), Palm Beach Post (Joe Capozzi). Spanish—El Nuevo Herald (Jorge Ebro).

HOUSTON ASTROS

Radio Announcers: English—Alan Ashby, Milo Hamilton; Spanish—Francisco Ernesto Ruiz, Alex Trevino. **Flagship Station:** KTRH 740-AM (English).

TV Announcers: Bill Brown, Jim Deshaies, Bill Worrell. **Flagship Station:** Fox Sports Net (regional cable).

NEWSPAPERS, Daily Coverage (beat writers): Houston Chronicle (Jesus Ortiz, Richard Justice), Beaumont Enterprise (Paula Hunt), Port Arthur News (Tom Halliburton), The Herald Coaster (Bill Hartman), MLB.com (Alyson Footer, Jim Molony).

LOS ANGELES DODGERS

Radio Announcers: English—Vin Scully, Rick Monday, Ross Porter; Spanish—Jaime Jarrin, Pepe Yniguez. **Flagship Stations:** KFWB 980-AM, KWKW 1330-AM (Spanish).

TV Announcers: Vin Scully, Rick Monday, Ross Porter. **Flagship Station:** KCOP Channel 13, Fox Sports Net 2 (regional cable).

NEWSPAPERS, Daily Coverage (beat writers): Los Angeles Times (Ross Newhan, Jason Reid), South Bay Daily Breeze (Bill Cizek), Los Angeles Daily News (Brian Dohn), Orange County Register (Robert Kuwada), Riverside Press-Enterprise (Andrew Baggarly), La Opinion (Carlos Alvarado).

MILWAUKEE BREWERS

Radio Announcers: Bob Uecker, Jim Powell. **Flagship Station:** WTMJ 620-AM.

TV Announcers: Bill Schroeder, Daron Sutton. **Flagship Station:** Fox Sports Net, WCGV Channel 24.

NEWSPAPERS, Daily Coverage (beat writers): Milwaukee Journal Sentinel (Drew Olson).

MONTREAL EXPOS

Radio Announcers: English—Elliott Price, Terry Haig. French—Jacques Doucet, Marc Griffin. **Flagship Stations:** TEAM 990-AM (English), CKAC 730-AM (French).

NEWSPAPERS, Daily Coverage (beat writers): English—Montreal Gazette (Stephanie Myles, Jack Todd, Pat Hickey). French—Canadian Press (Michel Lajeunesse, Richard Milo), La Presse (Alexandre Pratt, Pierre Ladouceur), Le Journal de Montreal (Serge Touchette, Daniel Cloutier).

NEW YORK METS

Radio Announcers: Gary Cohen, Ed Coleman, Bob Murphy, Ted Robinson. **Flagship Station:** WFAN 660-AM.

TV Announcers: Fran Healy, Keith Hernandez, Ralph Kiner, Matt Loughlin, Dave O'Brien, Ted Robinson, Howie Rose, Tom Seaver. **Flagship Stations:** WPIX-TV, Fox Sports New York (regional cable), Madison Square Garden (regional cable).

NEWSPAPERS, Daily Coverage (beat writers): New York Times (Rafael Hermoso), New York Daily News, New York Post (Mike Morrisey), Newsday (Dave Lennon), Newark Star-Ledger (Dave Waldstein), The Bergen Record (Pete Caldera), The News Journal (Pete Abraham).

PHILADELPHIA PHILLIES

Radio Announcers: Larry Andersen, Scott Graham, Harry Kalas, Chris Wheeler. **Flagship Station:** WPEN 950-AM.

TV Announcers: Larry Andersen, Harry Kalas, Chris Wheeler. **Flagship Stations:** WPSG UPN-57, Comcast SportsNet (regional cable).

NEWSPAPERS, Daily Coverage (beat writers): Philadelphia Inquirer (Bob Brookover, Jim Salisbury), Philadelphia Daily News (Paul Hagen, Marcus Hayes), Bucks County Courier Times (Randy Miller), Camden Courier-Post (Kevin Roberts), Delaware County Times (Dennis Deitch), Wilmington News-Journal (Edward de la Fuente), Trenton Times (Chris Edwards).

PITTSBURGH PIRATES

Radio Announcers: Steve Blass, Greg Brown, Lanny Frattare, Bob Walk. **Flagship Station:** KDKA 1020-AM.

TV Announcers: Steve Blass, Greg Brown, Lanny Frattare, Bob Walk. **Flagship Station:** Fox Sports Net Pittsburgh (regional cable).

NEWSPAPERS, Daily Coverage (beat writers): Pittsburgh Post-Gazette (Bob Dvorchak), Pittsburgh Tribune-Review (Joe Rutter), Beaver County Times (John Perrotto).

ST. LOUIS CARDINALS

Radio Announcers: Mike Shannon, Wayne Hagin. **Flagship Station:** KMOX 1120-AM.

TV Announcers: Joe Buck , Al Hrabosky, Dan McLaughlin. **Flagship Stations:** KPLR Channel 11, Fox Sports Midwest (regional cable).

NEWSPAPER, Daily Coverage (beat writers): St. Louis Post-Dispatch (Joe Strauss, Rick Hummel), Belleville, Ill., News-Democrat (Joe Ostermeier, David Wilhelm).

SAN DIEGO PADRES

Radio Announcers: Jerry Coleman, Ted Leitner. **Flagship Station:** KOGO 600-AM.

TV Announcers: Matt Vasgersian, Rick Sutcliffe, Mark Grant. **Flagship Stations:** KUSI TV-9/51, Channel 4 Padres (cable).

NEWSPAPERS, Daily Coverage (beat writers): San Diego Union-Tribune (Tom Krasovic, Bill Center), North County Times (Shaun O'Neill, John Maffei).

SAN FRANCISCO GIANTS

Radio Announcers: Mike Krukow, Duane Kuiper, Jon Miller, Joe Angel. **Flagship Station:** KNBR 680-AM.

TV Announcers: FOX—Mike Krukow, Duane Kuiper; KTVU—Mike Krukow, Jon Miller. **Flagship Stations:** KTVU-TV 2, FOX Sports Net (regional cable).

NEWSPAPERS, Daily Coverage (beat writers): San Francisco Chronicle (Henry Schulman), San Jose Mercury News (Dan Brown), Contra Costa Times (Joe Roderick), Sacramento Bee (Nick Peters), Oakland Tribune (Josh Suchon), Santa Rosa Press Democrat (Jeff Fletcher).

NATIONAL MEDIA INFORMATION

BASEBALL STATISTICS

ELIAS SPORTS BUREAU INC.

Official Major League Statistician

Mailing Address: 500 Fifth Ave., Suite 2140, New York, NY 10110. **Telephone:** (212) 869-1530. **FAX:** (212) 354-0980. **Website:** www.esb.com.

President: Seymour Siwoff.

Executive Vice President: Steve Hirdt. **Vice President:** Peter Hirdt. **Data Processing Manager:** Chris Thorn.

SPORTSTICKER-BOSTON

Official Minor League Statistician

Mailing Address: Boston Fish Pier, West Bldg. #1, Suite 302, Boston, MA 02210. **Telephone:** (617) 951-0070. **FAX:** (617) 737-9960.

Director, Minor League Operations: Jim Keller. **Assistant Director, Minor League Operations:** Michael Walczak. **Director, Special Projects:** Jay Virshbo. **Programmer Analysts:** John Foley, Walter Kent. **Senior Bureau Manager:** Don Goss. **Bureau Managers:** Bryan Evans, Will Morin, Brian Rabuffetti, Marshall Wright. **Associate Bureau Manager:** Jon Mailloux. **Senior Editor:** Joe Barbieri. **Editor:** Matt Santillo.

Historical Consultant: Bill Weiss.

STATS INC.

Mailing Address: 8130 Lehigh Ave., Morton Grove, IL 60053. **Telephone:** (847) 583-2100. **FAX:** (847) 470-9160. **Website:** biz.stats.com.

President: Alan Leib. **Senior Vice President, Sales:** Jim Capuano. **Senior VP:** Steve Byrd. **Vice Presidents:** Arthur Ashley, Bob Schur. **Assistant VP, Technical Operations:** Jeff Smith. **Director, Sports Operations:** Allan Spear. **Manager, Sales:** Greg Kirkorsky. **Manager, Baseball Operations:** Jeff Chernow.

TELEVISION NETWORKS

ESPN/ESPN2

- Baseball Tonight
- Sunday Night Baseball
- Monday Night Baseball
- Wednesday Night Doubleheaders
- Wednesday Afternoon Baseball
- Home Run Derby and other all-star programming
- Opening Day

Mailing Address, ESPN Connecticut: ESPN Plaza, Bristol, CT 06010. **Telephone:** (860) 766-2000. **FAX:** (860) 766-2213. **Website:** www.espn.com.

Mailing Address, ESPN New York: 77 W. 66th St., New York, NY 10023. **Telephone:** (212) 456-7777. **FAX:** (212) 456-2930.

President: George Bodenheimer.

Executive Vice President, Production/Technical Operations: Steve Anderson. **Executive VP, Administration:** Ed Durso. **Executive VP, Programming and Production:** Mark Shapiro.

Senior Vice President, Executive Editor: John Walsh. **Senior VP, Programming:** Len Deluca. **Director, Programming:** Mike Ryan.

Senior Vice President, Remote Production: Jed Drake. **Coordinating Producer, Remote Production:** Tim Scanlan.

Senior Vice Presidents, Co-Managing Editors/Studio Production: Bob Eaton, Norby Williamson.

Senior Coordinating Producer, Baseball Tonight: Jay Levy.

ESPN.com/Vice President, Executive Editor: John Marvel.

ESPN Classic/Executive Producer: Jim Cohen.

ESPN International, ESPN Deportes/Senior Vice President and Managing Director: Willy Burkhardt. **Vice President, Operations and International Production:** Jodi Markley.

Senior Vice President, Communications: Rosa Gatti. **Vice President, Communications:** Chris LaPlaca. **Director, Communications:** Diane Lamb. **Coordinator, Communications:** Amy Wildhack.

Commentators, Sunday Night Baseball: Play-by-play—Jon Miller. Analyst—Joe Morgan.

Other Commentators: Dave Barnett, Chris Berman, Jeff Brantley, Tom Candiotti, Bob Carpenter, Rob Dibble, Rich Eisen, Peter Gammons, Tony Gwynn, Tim Kurkjian, Karl Ravech, Harold Reynolds, Dan Shulman, Rick Sutcliffe.

FOX SPORTS

- Saturday Game of the Week
- All-Star Game, 2003-2006
- Division Series, Championship Series, World Series, 2003-2006

Mailing Address, Los Angeles: Fox Network Center, Building 101, 5th floor, 10201 West Pico Blvd., Los Angeles,

CA 90035. **Telephone:** (310) 369-6000. **FAX:** (310) 969-9467.

Mailing Address, New York: 1211 Avenue of the Americas, 2nd Floor, New York, NY 10036. **Telephone:** (212) 556-2500. **FAX:** (212) 354-6902. **Website:** www.foxsports.com.

Chairman/Chief Executive Officer, Fox Sports Television Group: David Hill. **President, Executive Producer:** Ed Goren. **Chief Operating Officer:** Larry Jones. **Executive Vice President, Production/Coordinating Studio Producer:** Scott Ackerson. **Executive VP, Marketing:** Neal Tiles. **Senior VP, Production/Senior Producer:** Bill Brown. **VP, Production:** Jack Simmons. **VP, Operations/MLB on Fox:** Jerry Steinberg. **Director, Production Services/MLB on FOX:** Lynn Gambatesa. **Studio Producer, MLB on Fox:** Gary Lang. **Studio Director, MLB on Fox:** Bob Levy.

Senior VP, Communcations: Lou D'Ermilio. **Director, Communications:** Dan Bell. **Publicists:** Tim Buckman, Ileana Pena.

Broadcasters: Thom Brennaman, Joe Buck, Josh Lewin, Kevin Kennedy, Steve Lyons, Tim McCarver, Jeanne Zelasko.

Other Television Networks

ABC SPORTS

Mailing Address: 47 West 66th St., New York, NY 10023. **Telephone:** (212) 456-4878. **FAX:** (212) 456-2877. **Website:** www.abcsports.com.

President, ABC Sports: Howard Katz. **Senior Vice President, Programming:** Loren Matthews. **VP, Media Relations:** Mark Mandel. **Publicist, Media Relations:** Adam Freifeld.

CBS SPORTS

Mailing Address: 51 W. 52nd St., New York, NY 10019. **Telephone:** (212) 975-5230. **FAX:** (212) 975-4063. **Website:** cbs.sportsline.com.

President, CBS Sports: Sean McManus. **Executive Producer:** Tony Petitti. **Senior Vice Presidents, Programming:** Mike Aresco, Rob Correa. **Vice President, Communications:** Leslie Anne Wade.

NBC SPORTS

Mailing Address: 30 Rockefeller Plaza, Suite 1558, New York, NY 10112. **Telephone:** (212) 664-2014. **FAX:** (212) 664-6365. **Website:** www.msnbc.com/news/spt-summary.asp.

Chairman, NBC Sports: Dick Ebersol. **President, NBC Sports:** Ken Schanzer.

Vice President, Sports Communications: Kevin Sullivan.

Superstations

ROGERS SPORTSNET (Canada)

Mailing Address: 9 Channel Nine Court, Scarborough, Ontario M1S 4B5. **Telephone:** (416) 332-5600. **FAX:** (416) 332-5767.

President, Rogers Media: Tony Viner. **President, Rogers Sportsnet:** Doug Beeforth. **Vice President, Communications:** Jan Innes.

THE SPORTS NETWORK (Canada)

Mailing Address: Bell Globemedia Inc., 9 Channel Nine Court, Scarborough, Ontario M1S 4B5. **Telephone:** (416) 332-5000. **FAX:** (416) 332-7658. **Website:** www.tsn.ca

Senior Vice President, General Manager: Doug Beeforth. **Managing Director, Interactive Media/Legal Services:** David Akande. **VP, Production:** Scott Moore. **Manager, Communications:** David Rashford.

TBS (Atlanta Braves)

Mailing Address: One CNN Center, P.O. Box 105366, Atlanta, GA 30348. **Telephone:** (404) 827-1700. **FAX:** (404) 827-1593. **Website:** www.superstation.com.

Executive Producer: Glenn Diamond.

WGN (Chicago Cubs, Chicago White Sox)

Mailing Address: 2501 W Bradley Pl., Chicago, IL 60618. **Telephone:** (773) 528-2311. **FAX:** (773) 528-6050. **Website:** www.wgntv.com.

Director, Programming: Bob Vorwald.

RADIO NETWORKS

ESPN RADIO

Mailing Address: ESPN Plaza, Bristol, CT 06010. **Telephone:** (860) 766-2661. **FAX:** (860) 589-5523.

General Manager: Eric Schoenfeld. **Assistant GM, Program Director:** Len Weiner. **Executive Producer:** John Martin.

Commentators: Dave Barnett, Dave Campbell, Rob Dibble, Jim Durham, Brent Musburger, Charley Steiner.

ABC SPORTS RADIO

Mailing Address: 125 West End Ave., 6th Floor, New York, NY 10023. **Telephone:** (212) 456-5185. **Studio:** (800) 221-4559. **E-Mail Address:** abcsportsradio@abc.com.

Vice President, Radio: Steve Jones. **General Manager, News/Sports:** Michael Rizzo. **Operations Manager:** Cliff Bond. **Producers:** Andrew Bogusch, Eric Duetsch, Howie Karpin, Mike Kirk, Tim McDermott, Yvette Michael, Tushar Saxena. Steve White. **Anchors:** Todd Ant, John Cloghessy, Johnny Holliday, Keith Olbermann.

SPORTING NEWS RADIO NETWORK

Mailing Address: P.O. Box 509, Techny, IL 60082. **Telephone:** (847) 509-1661. **Producers Line:** (800) 224-2004.

FAX: (847) 509-1677. **Website:** www.sportingnewsradio.com.

President: Chris Brennan. **Executive Vice President, Affiliate Relations:** Chuck Duncan. **Executive VP, Sales:** Bill Peterson. **Sports Directors:** Matt Nahigian, Ryan Williams. **Executive Producers:** Randy Merkin, Jen Williams.

SPORTS BYLINE USA

Mailing Address: 300 Broadway, Suite 8, San Francisco, CA 94133. **Telephone:** (415) 434-8300. **Guest Line:** (800) 358-4457. **Studio Line:** (800) 878-7529. **FAX:** (415) 391-2569. **E-Mail Address:** byline@pacbell.net. **Website:** www.sportsbyline.com.

President: Darren Peck. **Executive Producer:** Alex Murillo.

NEWS ORGANIZATIONS

ASSOCIATED PRESS

Mailing Address: 50 Rockefeller Plaza, New York, NY 10020. **Telephone:** (212) 621-1630. **FAX:** (212) 621-1639. **Website:** www.ap.org.

Deputy Sports Editor: Aaron Watson. **Sports Photo Editor:** Mike Feldman. **Baseball Writers:** Ron Blum, Josh Dubow, Ben Walker.

BLOOMBERG SPORTS NEWS

Address: 400 College Road East, P.O. Box 888, Princeton, NJ 08540. **Telephone:** (609) 750-4691. **FAX:** (609) 897-8397.

Sports Editor: Jay Beberman. **Deputy Sports Editor:** Mike Sillup. **National Baseball Writer:** Jerry Crasnick.

CANADIAN PRESS

Mailing Address, Toronto: 36 King St. East, Toronto, Ontario M5C 2L9. **Mailing Address, Montreal:** 215 Saint-Jacques St., Suite 100, Montreal, Quebec H2Y 1M6. **Telephone:** (416) 364-0321 (Toronto), (514) 849-3212 (Montreal). **FAX:** (416) 364-0207 (Toronto), (514) 849-7693 (Montreal). **E-Mail Address:** sports@cp.org.

Sports Editor: Neil Davidson. **Baseball Writer:** Pierre Lebrun. **Sports Writer, Montreal:** Bill Beacon.

SPORTSTICKER

Mailing Address: Harborside Financial Center, 800 Plaza Two, 8th Floor, Jersey City, NJ 07311. **Telephone:** (201) 309-1200. **FAX:** (201) 860-9742. **E-Mail Address:** newsroom@sportsticker.com.

General Manager: Jim Morganthaler. **Senior Editor, Major League Baseball:** Anthony Mormile. **Director, News:** Chris Bernucca. **Director, Newsroom/League Operations:** John Mastroberardino. **Director, New Content/Newsroom Services:** Lou Monaco.

PRESS ASSOCIATIONS

BASEBALL WRITERS ASSOCIATION OF AMERICA

Mailing Address: 78 Olive St., Lake Grove, NY 11755. **Telephone:** (631) 981-7938. **FAX:** (631) 585-4669. **E-Mail Address:** bbwaa@aol.com.

President: Paul Hagen (Philadelphia Daily News). **Vice President:** Drew Olson (Milwaukee Journal-Sentinel). **Secretary-Treasurer:** Jack O'Connell (Hartford Courant).

Board of Directors: Mike Berardino (South Florida Sun-Sentinel), Bill Center (San Diego Union-Tribune), Bob Dutton (Kansas City Star), Jason Reid (Los Angeles Times).

NATIONAL COLLEGIATE BASEBALL WRITERS ASSOCIATION

Mailing Address: 35 E. Wacker Dr., Suite 650, Chicago, IL 60601. **Telephone:** (312) 553-0483. **FAX:** (312) 553-0495.

Executive Director: Bo Carter (Big 12 Conference).

President: Rob Carolla (Big East). **First Vice President:** Jeff Hurd (WAC). **Second Vice President:** Mike Montore (Southern Mississippi). **Third Vice President:** Todd Lamb (Ohio State).

Newsletter Editor: Bo Carter, Big 12. **Telephone:** (214) 753-0102. **E-Mail Address:** bo@big12sports.com.

NEWSPAPERS/PERIODICALS

USA TODAY

Mailing Address: 7950 Jones Branch Drive, McLean, VA 22108. **Telephone/Baseball Desk:** (703) 854-5954, 854-5286, 854-3706, 854-3744, 854-3746. **FAX:** (703) 854-2072. **Website:** www.usatoday.com.

Publishing Frequency: Daily (Monday-Friday).

Baseball Editors: Cesar Brioso, Matt Cimento, Margaret McCahill, John Tkach. **Baseball Columnist:** Hal Bodley. **Baseball Writers:** Mel Antonen, Rod Beaton, Mike Dodd, Gary Graves, Chuck Johnson.

THE SPORTING NEWS

Mailing Address: 10176 Corporate Square Dr., Suite 200, St. Louis, MO 63132. **Telephone:** (314) 997-7111. **FAX:** (314) 997-0765. **Website:** www.sportingnews.com.

Publishing Frequency: Weekly.

Senior Vice President/Editorial Director: John Rawlings. **Executive Editor:** Bob Hille. **Managing Editor:** Stan McNeal. **Senior Writers:** Ken Rosenthal. **Senior Photo Editor:** Paul Nisely.

SPORTS ILLUSTRATED

Mailing Address: 135 W. 50th St., New York, NY 10020. **Telephone:** (212) 522-1212. **FAX, Editorial:** (212) 522-4543. **FAX, Public Relations:** (212) 522-4832. **Website:** www.si.com

Publishing Frequency: Weekly.

Managing Editor: Terry McDonnell. **Senior Editor:** Larry Burke. **Associate Editor:** B.J. Schecter. **Senior Writers:** Jeff Pearlman, Tom Verducci. **Staff Writer:** Danny Habib. **Writer-Reporter:** Albert Chen, Gene Menez.

Vice President, Communications: Art Berke.

USA TODAY SPORTS WEEKLY

Mailing Address: 7950 Jones Branch Drive, McLean, VA 22108. **Telephone:** (800) 872-1415; (703) 854-6319. **FAX:** (703) 854-2034. **Website:** www.usatodaysportsweekly.com.

Publishing Frequency: Weekly.

Publisher/Executive Editor: Lee Ivory. **Managing Editor:** Tim McQuay. **Deputy Managing Editor:** Scott Zucker. **Senior Editor:** Frank Cooney. **Operations Editor:** Amanda Tinkham Boltax.

Senior Writers: Bob Nightengale, Paul White, Lisa Winston. **Writers:** Chris Colston, Steve DiMeglio, Seth Livingstone.

STREET AND SMITH'S SPORTS BUSINESS JOURNAL

Mailing Address: 120 W. Morehead St., Suite 310, Charlotte, NC 28202. **Telephone:** (704) 973-1400. **FAX:** (704) 973-1401. **Website:** www.sportsbusinessjournal.com.

Publishing Frequency: Weekly.

Publisher: Richard Weiss. **Editor-in-chief:** John Genzale. **Managing Editor:** Ross Nethery.

ESPN THE MAGAZINE

Mailing Address: 19 E. 34th St., 7th Floor, New York, NY 10016. **Telephone:** (212) 515-1000. **FAX:** (212) 515-1290. **Website:** www.espnmag.com.

Publishing Frequency: Bi-weekly.

Executive Editor: Steve Wulf. **Senior Editor:** Jon Scher. **General Editor:** Ed McGregor. **Senior Writers:** Jeff Bradley, Peter Gammons, Tim Keown, Tim Kurkjian. **Writer/Reporter:** Andy Latack. **Photo Editor:** Nik Kleinberg. **Deputy Photo Editor:** John Toolan. **Manager of Communications:** Ashley Swadel. **Senior Publicist:** Danny Ferrauiola.

BASEBALL AMERICA

Address: 201 West Main St., Suite 201, Durham, NC 27702. **Mailing Address:** P.O. Box 2089, Durham, NC 27702. **Telephone:** (919) 682-9635. **FAX:** (919) 682-2880.

Publishing Frequency: Bi-weekly.

President: Catherine Silver. **Publisher:** Lee Folger. **Editor:** Allan Simpson. **Managing Editor:** Will Lingo. **Executive Editor:** Jim Callis. **Senior Writers:** John Manuel, Alan Schwarz.

BASEBALL DIGEST

Mailing Address: 990 Grove St., Evanston, IL 60201. **Telephone:** (847) 491-6440. **FAX:** (847) 491-6203. **E-Mail Address:** bkuenster@centurysports.net. **Website:** www.centurysports.net/baseball.

Publishing Frequency: Monthly.

Publisher: Norman Jacobs. **Editor:** John Kuenster. **Managing Editor:** Bob Kuenster.

COLLEGIATE BASEBALL

Mailing Address: P.O. Box 50566, Tucson, AZ 85703. **Telephone:** (520) 623-4530. **FAX:** (520) 624-5501. **E-Mail Address:** editor@baseballnews.com. **Website:** www.baseballnews.com.

Publishing Frequency: Bi-weekly, January-June; September, October.

Publisher: Lou Pavlovich. **Editor:** Lou Pavlovich Jr.

JUNIOR BASEBALL MAGAZINE

Mailing Address: P.O. Box 9099, Canoga Park, CA 91309. **Telephone:** (818) 710-1234. **Customer Service:** (888) 487-2448. **FAX:** (818) 710-1877. **E-Mail Address:** cs@juniorbaseball.com. **Website:** www.juniorbaseball.com.

Publishing Frequency: Bi-monthly.

Publisher/Editor: Dave Destler.

SPORTS ILLUSTRATED FOR KIDS

Mailing Address: 135 W. 50th St., Fourth Floor, New York, NY 10020. **Telephone:** (212) 522-1212. **FAX:** (212) 522-0120. **Website:** www.sikids.com.

Publishing Frequency: Monthly.

Managing Editor: Neil Cohen. **Assistant Managing Editor:** Peter Kay. **Senior Editor:** Michael Northrop.

BASEBALL PARENT

Mailing Address: 4437 Kingston Pike, Suite 2204, Knoxville, TN 37919. **Telephone:** (865) 523-1274. **FAX:** (865) 673-8926. **E-Mail Address:** baseparent@aol.com. **Website:** www.baseball-parent.com.

Publishing Frequency: Six issues yearly—January, March, April, May, June, July.

Publisher/Editor: Wayne Christensen.

BASEBALL ANNUALS

ATHLON SPORTS BASEBALL

Mailing Address: 220 25th Ave. N., Suite 200, Nashville, TN 37203. **Telephone:** (615) 327-0747. **FAX:** (615) 327-1149. **E-Mail Address:** info@athlonsports.com. Website: www.athlonsports.com.

Chief Executive Officer: Roger Di Silvestro. **President:** Charles Allen. **Managing Editor:** Charlie Miller. **Senior Editor:** Rob Doster. **Editor:** Mitch Light.

STREET AND SMITH'S BASEBALL YEARBOOK

Mailing Address: 120 West Morehead Street, Suite 230, Charlotte, NC 28202. **Telephone:** (704) 973-1575. **FAX:** (704) 973-1576. **E-Mail Address:** annuals@streetandsmiths.com. **Website:** www.streetandsmiths.com.

Publisher: Mike Kallay. **Managing Editor:** Scott Smith.

SPORTING NEWS BASEBALL YEARBOOK

Mailing Address: 10176 Corporate Square Dr., Suite 200, St. Louis, MO 63132. **Telephone:** (314) 997-7111. **FAX:**

(314) 997-0765.

Editor: John Rawlings. **Executive Editor:** Bob Hille. **Managing Editor:** Stan McNeal. **Senior Writers:** Ken Rosenthal. **Photo Editor:** Paul Nisely.

SPRING TRAINING BASEBALL YEARBOOK

Mailing Address: Vanguard Publications, P.O. Box 667, Chapel Hill, NC 27514. **Telephone:** (919) 967-2420. **FAX:** (919) 967-6294. **E-Mail Address:** vanguard3@mindspring.com. **Website:** www.springtrainingmagazine.com.

Publisher: Merle Thorpe. **Editor:** Myles Friedman.

Baseball Encyclopedias

TOTAL BASEBALL

The Official Encyclopedia of Major League Baseball

Mailing Address: SportClassic Books, Sport Media Publishing, 21 Carlaw Ave., Toronto, ON M4M 2R6. **Telephone:** (416) 466-0418. **FAX:** (416) 466-9530. **E-Mail Address:** info@sportclassicbooks.com. **Website:** www.sportclassicbooks.com.

Editors, Total Baseball: John Thorn, Pete Palmer, Michael Gershman.

HOBBY PUBLICATIONS

BECKETT PUBLICATIONS

Mailing Address: 15850 Dallas Pkwy., Dallas, TX 75248. **Telephone:** (800) 840-3137. **FAX:** (972) 991-8930. **Website:** www.beckett.com.

Chief Executive Officer, Publisher: James Beckett. **Editor:** Mike Payne.

KRAUSE PUBLICATIONS

Mailing Address: 700 E. State St., Iola, WI 54990. **Telephone:** (715) 445-4612. **FAX:** (715) 445-4087. **Website:** www.krause.com, www.collect.com, www.fantasysportsmag.com.

Publisher: Dean Listle. **Editor, Fantasy Sports:** Greg Ambrosius. **Editor, Sports Collectors Digest:** T.S. O'Connell. **Editor, Tuff Stuff:** Rocky Landsverk.

TEAM PUBLICATIONS

COMAN PUBLISHING

Diehard (Boston Red Sox), Mets Inside Pitch (New York Mets)

Mailing Address: P.O. Box 2331, Durham, NC 27702. **Telephone:** (919) 688-0218. **FAX:** (919) 682-1532. **Publisher:** Stuart Coman. **Managing Editor:** Steve Downey.

VINE LINE (Chicago Cubs)

Mailing Address: Chicago Cubs Publications, 1060 W. Addison St., Chicago, IL 60613. **Telephone:** (773) 404-2827. **FAX:** (773) 404-4129. **E-Mail Address:** jmcardle@cubs.com. **Managing Editor:** Lena McDonagh. **Editor:** Jim McArdle.

YANKEES MAGAZINE (New York Yankees)

Mailing Address: Yankee Stadium, Bronx, NY 10451. **Telephone:** (800) 469-2657. **Publisher/Director, Publications and Media:** Mark Mandrake. **Managing Editor:** Glenn Slavin.

INDIANS INK (Cleveland Indians)

Mailing Address: P.O. Box 539, Mentor, OH 44061. **Telephone:** (440) 953-2200. **FAX:** (440) 953-2202. **Editor:** Frank Derry.

OUTSIDE PITCH (Baltimore Orioles)

Mailing Address: P.O. Box 27143, Baltimore, MD 21230. **Telephone:** (410) 234-8888, (800) 342-4737. **FAX:** (410) 234-1029. **Website:** www.outsidepitch.com. **Publisher:** David Simone. **Editor:** David Hill.

REDS REPORT (Cincinnati Reds)

Mailing Address: Columbus Sports Publications, P.O. Box 12453, Columbus, OH 43212. **Telephone:** (614) 486-2202. **FAX:** (614) 486-3650. **Publisher:** Frank Moskowitz. **Editor:** Steve Helwagen.

FANTASY BASEBALL

DIAMOND LIBRARY PUBLICATIONS

Mailing Address: 15 Cannon Rd., Wilton, CT 06897. **Telephone:** (800) 707-9090, (203) 834-1231. **Website:** www.johnbenson.com.

Publisher: John Benson.

KRAUSE PUBLICATIONS FANTASY SPORTS

Mailing Address: 700 E. State St., Iola, WI 54990. **Telephone:** (715) 445-4612. **FAX:** (715) 445-4087. **Website:** www.fantasysportsmag.com.

Publisher: Dean Listle. **Editorial Director:** Rocky Landsverk. **Editor:** Greg Ambrosius. **Divisional Publisher:** Hugh McAloon. **Managing Editor:** Tom Kessenich. **Assistant Editors:** Scott Kelnhofer, Bert Lehman.

THE SPORTING NEWS FANTASY BASEBALL OWNERS MANUAL

Mailing Address: 10176 Corporate Square Dr., Suite 200, St. Louis, MO 63132. **Telephone:** (314) 997-7111. **FAX:** (314) 997-0765. **Website:** fantasy.sportingnews.com/baseball/.

Senior Managing Editor: Mike Nahrstedt. **Assistant Managing Editor:** Dave Darling.

OTHER
INFO

GENERAL INFORMATION

MAJOR LEAGUE BASEBALL PLAYERS ASSOCIATION

Mailing Address: 12 E. 49th St., 24th Floor, New York, NY 10017. **Telephone:** (212) 826-0808. **FAX:** (212) 752-4378. **Website:** www.bigleaguers.yahoo.com.

Year Founded: 1966.

Executive Director, General Counsel: Donald Fehr.

Associate General Counsel: Gene Orza. **Assistant General Counsel:** Doyle Pryor, Robert Lenaghan, Michael Weiner. **Counsel:** Jeff Fannell.

Special Assistants: Tony Bernazard, Phil Bradley, Steve Rogers, Allyne Price.

Director, Business Affairs/Licensing: Judy Heeter. **General Manager, Licensing:** Richard White. **Director, Communications:** Greg Bouris. **Licensing Counsel:** Evie Goldstein. **Manager, Marketing Services:** Melissa Persaud. **Category Manager, Trading Cards:** Evan Kaplan. **Category Manager, Apparel:** Nancy Willis. **Category Director, Interactive Games:** John Olshan. **Editor, Website:** Chris Dahl. **Licensing Assistant:** Heather Saks.

Executive Board: Player representatives of the 30 major league clubs.

League Representatives: American League—Rick Helling; **National League**—Tom Glavine.

SCOUTING

MAJOR LEAGUE SCOUTING BUREAU

Mailing Address: 3500 Porsche Way, Suite 100, Ontario, CA 91764. **Telephone:** (909) 980-1881. **FAX:** (909) 980-7794.

Year Founded: 1974.

Director: Frank Marcos. **Assistant Director:** Rick Oliver. **Office Coordinator:** Joanne Costanzo. **Administrative Assistant:** Debbie Keedy.

Board of Directors: Sandy Alderson (Major League Baseball), Dave Dombrowski (Tigers), Bob Gebhard (Cardinals), Roland Hemond (White Sox), Frank Marcos, Omar Minaya (Expos), Randy Smith (Padres), Jimmie Lee Solomon (Major League Baseball), Art Stewart (Royals), Kevin Towers (Padres).

Scouts: Rick Arnold (Centre Hall, PA), Andy Campbell (Chandler, AZ), Mike Childers (Lexington, KY), Dick Colpaert (Utica, MI), Craig Conklin (Cayucos, CA), Dan Cox (Santa Ana, CA), Dan Dixon (Temecula, CA), J.D. Elliby (Glen Allen, VA), Jim Elliott (Winston-Salem, NC), Mike Fiol (Dayton, NJ), Art Gardner (Walnut Grove, MS), Rusty Gerhardt (New London, TX), Dennis Haren (San Diego, CA), Doug Horning (Schererville, IN), Don Jacoby (Winter Haven, FL), Brad Kohler (Bethlehem, PA), Don Kohler (Asbury, NJ), Mike Larson (Waseca, MN), Wayne Mathis (Kansas City, MO), Jethro McIntyre (Pittsburg, CA), Paul Mirocke (Wesley Chapel, FL), Carl Moesche (Gresham, OR), Tim Osborne (Woodstock, GA), Gary Randall (Rock Hill, SC), Willie Romay (Miami Springs, FL), Kevin Saucier (Pensacola, FL), Pat Shortt (South Hempstead, NY), Craig Smajstrla (Pearland, TX), Christie Stancil (Raleigh, NC), Ed Sukla (Irvine, CA), Marv Thompson (Wickenburg, AZ), Jim Walton (Shattuck, OK).

Canadian Scouts: Walt Burrows (Brentwood Bay, BC), supervisor; Curtis Bailey (Red Deer, AB), Jason Chee-Aloy (Toronto, ON), Gerry Falk (Carman, MB), Bill Green (Vancouver, BC), Sean Gulliver (St. John's, NL), Ian Jordan (Kirkland, QC), Ken Lenihan (Bedford, NS), Dave McConnell (Kelowna, BC), Dan Mendham (Dorchester, ON), Jean Marc Mercier (Charlesbourg, QC), Todd Plaxton (Saskatoon, SK), Tony Wylie (Anchorage, AK).

Supervisor, Puerto Rico: Pepito Centeno (Bayamon, PR).

SCOUT OF THE YEAR FOUNDATION

Mailing Address: P.O. Box 211585, West Palm Beach, FL 33421. **Telephone:** (561) 798-5897. **FAX:** (561) 798-4644. **E-Mail Address:** bertmazur@aol.com.

President: Roberta Mazur. **Vice President:** Tracy Ringolsby. **Treasurer:** Ron Mazur II.

Board of Advisors: Joe L. Brown, Bob Fontaine, Pat Gillick, Roland Hemond, Gary Hughes, Tommy Lasorda, Ron Shapiro, Allan Simpson, Ted Spencer, Bob Watson.

SCOUTING SERVICES

INSIDE EDGE, INC.

Mailing Address: 5049 Emerson Ave. S., Minneapolis, MN 55419. **Telephone:** (800) 858-3343. **FAX:** (508) 526-6145. **E-Mail Address:** insideedge@aol.com. **Website:** inside-edge.com.

Partners: Jay Donchets, Randy Istre.

PROSPECTS PLUS/THE SCOUTING REPORT

(A Joint Venture of Baseball America and Perfect Game USA)

Mailing Address: Baseball America, P.O. Box 2089, Durham, NC 27702. **Telephone:** (800) 845-2726. **FAX:** (919) 682-2880. **E-Mail Addresses:** allansimpson@baseballamerica.com; pgjerry@qwest.net. **Website:** www.baseballamerica.com; www.perfectgame.org

Editor, Baseball America: Allan Simpson. **Director, Perfect Game USA:** Jerry Ford.

SKILLSHOW, INC.

Mailing Address: 290 King of Prussia Rd., Suite 122, Radnor, PA 19087. **Telephone:** (610) 687-9072. **FAX:** (610) 687-9629. **E-Mail Address:** info@skillshow.com. **Website:** www.skillshow.com.

Chief Executive Officer: Tom Koerick Jr. **President/Director, Sales:** Tom Koerick Sr. **Vice President, Marketing:** Louis Manon. **Webmaster:** Mark Rivera.

UMPIRES

WORLD UMPIRES ASSOCIATION

Mailing Address: P.O. Box 760, Cocoa, FL 32923. **Telephone:** (321) 637-3471. **FAX:** (321) 633-7018. **E-Mail Address:** wuaoffice@worldnet.att.net

Year Founded: 2000.

President: John Hirschbeck. **Vice President:** Joe Brinkman. **Secretary/Treasurer:** Tim Welke. **Labor Counsel:** Joel Smith. **Administrator:** Karen Brinkman.

PROFESSIONAL BASEBALL UMPIRE CORPORATION

Office Address: 201 Bayshore Dr. SE, St. Petersburg, FL 33701. **Mailing Address:** P.O. Box A, St. Petersburg, FL 33731. **Telephone:** (727) 822-6937. **FAX:** (727) 821-5819.

President: Mike Moore.

Treasurer/Vice President, Administration: Pat O'Conner. **Secretary/General Counsel:** Scott Poley.

Administrator: Eric Krupa. **Assistant to Administrator:** Lillian Dixon.

Executive Director, PBUC: Mike Fitzpatrick (Kalamazoo, MI).

Field Evaluators/Instructors: Dennis Cregg (Webster, MA), Mike Felt (Lansing, MI), Cris Jones (Wheat Ridge, CO), Jorge Bauza, (San Juan, PR), Larry Reveal (Chesapeake, VA).

UMPIRE DEVELOPMENT SCHOOLS

Harry Wendelstedt Umpire School

Mailing Address: 88 S St. Andrews Dr., Ormond Beach, FL 32174. **Telephone:** (386) 672-4879. **FAX:** (386) 672-3212. **E-Mail:** umpsch@aol.com. **Website:** www.umpireschool.com.

Operators: Harry Wendelstedt, Hunter Wendelstedt.

Jim Evans Academy of Professional Umpiring

Mailing Address: 12741 Research Blvd., Suite 401, Austin, TX 78759. **Telephone:** (512) 335-5959. **FAX:** (512) 335-5411. **E-Mail:** jimsacademy@earthlink.net. **Website:** www.umpireacademy.com.

Operator: Jim Evans.

TRAINERS

PROFESSIONAL BASEBALL ATHLETIC TRAINERS SOCIETY

Mailing Address: 400 Colony Square, Suite 1750, 1201 Peachtree St., Atlanta, GA 30361. **Telephone:** (404) 875-4000. **FAX:** (404) 892-8560. **E-Mail Address:** rmallernee@mallernee-branch.com. **Website:** www.pbats.org.

Year Founded: 1983.

President: Jamie Reed (Texas Rangers). **Secretary:** David Tumbas (Chicago Cubs). **Treasurer:** Paul Spicuzza (Cleveland Indians). **American League Representative:** Ned Bergert (Anaheim Angels). **American League Assistant Trainer Representative:** Brian Ebel (Baltimore Orioles). **National League Representative:** Tom Probst (Colorado Rockies). **National League Assistant Trainer Representative:** Brad Henderson (St. Louis Cardinals).

General Counsel: Rollin Mallernee.

EQUIPMENT

LENA BLACKBURN RUBBING MUD

(Official rubbing mud of Major League Baseball)

Mailing Address: 186 Forge Rd., Delran, NJ 08075. **Telephone:** (856) 764-7501. **FAX:** (856) 461-4089. **E-Mail Address:** lbrubmud@aol.com.

President: James Bintliff.

MUSEUMS

BABE RUTH BIRTHPLACE and OFFICIAL ORIOLES MUSEUM

Office Address: 216 Emory St., Baltimore, MD 21230. **Telephone:** (410) 727-1539. **FAX:** (410) 727-1652. **E-Mail Address:** info@baberuthmuseum.com. **Website:** www.baberuthmuseum.com.

Year Founded: 1973.

Executive Director: Mike Gibbons. **Curator:** Greg Schwalenberg.

Museum Hours: April-October, 10 a.m.-5 p.m. (10 a.m.-7 p.m. for Baltimore Orioles home games); November-March, 10 a.m.-4 p.m.

CANADIAN BASEBALL HALL OF FAME and MUSEUM

Museum Address: 386 Church St., St. Marys, Ontario N4X 1C2. **Mailing Address:** P.O. Box 1838, St. Marys, Ontario N4X 1C2. **Telephone:** (519) 284-1838. **FAX:** (519) 284-1234. **E-Mail Address:** baseball@baseballhalloffame.ca. **Website:** www.baseballhalloffame.ca.

Year Founded: 1983.

President/Chief Executive Officer: Tom Valcke. **Director, Operations:** Scott Crawford. **Curator:** Carl McCoomb.

Museum Hours: May—Sat. 10:30 a.m.-4:30 p.m.; Sun. noon-4 p.m.; June 1-Oct. 13—Mon.-Sat. 10:30 a.m.-4:30 p.m.; Sun noon-4 p.m. Weekends only in May.

2003 Induction Ceremonies: June 28.

Boys/Girls Week-Long Camps: June 29-July 5, July 6-12, July 13-19, July 20-26.

FIELD OF DREAMS MOVIE SITE

Address: 28963 Lansing Rd., Dyersville, IA 52040. **Telephone:** (888) 875-8404. **FAX:** (319) 875-7253. **E-Mail**

Address: info@fodmoviesite.com. **Website:** www.fodmoviesite.com.

Year Founded: 1989.

Manager, Business/Marketing: Betty Boeckenstedt.

Hours: April-November, 9 a.m.-6 p.m.

LITTLE LEAGUE BASEBALL MUSEUM

Office Address: Route 15 S., Williamsport, PA 17701. **Mailing Address:** P.O. Box 3485, Williamsport, PA 17701. **Telephone:** (570) 326-3607. **FAX:** (570) 326-2267. **E-Mail Address:** museum@littleleague.org. **Website:** www.littleleague.org/museum.

Year Founded: 1982.

Director/Curator: Michael Miller. **Business/Office Manager:** Tracey Yeagle.

Museum Hours: Memorial Day-Sept. 30, 10 a.m.-7 p.m. (Sun. noon-7 p.m.); October-May, Mon., Thurs. and Fri. 10 a.m.-5 p.m., Sat. noon-5 p.m., Sun. noon-4 p.m. Closed for Thanksgiving, Christmas Day, New Year's Day.

LOUISVILLE SLUGGER MUSEUM

Office Address: 800 W. Main St., Louisville, KY 40202. **Telephone:** (502) 588-7228. **FAX:** (502) 585-1179. **Website:** www.sluggermuseum.org.

Year Founded: 1996.

Executive Director: Bill Williams. **Director, Marketing:** Anne Jewell.

Museum Hours: Jan. 2-Dec. 23, 9 a.m.-5 p.m; Sunday (April-Nov.), noon-5 p.m.

THE NATIONAL PASTIME: MUSEUM OF MINOR LEAGUE BASEBALL

(Under Development)

Museum Address: 175 Toyota Plaza, Suite 300, Memphis, TN 38103. **Telephone:** (901) 722-0207. **FAX:** (901) 527-1642. **E-Mail Address:** dchase@memphisredbirds.com

Founders: Dean Jernigan, Kristi Jernigan.

Executive Director: Dave Chase.

NATIONAL BASEBALL HALL OF FAME AND MUSEUM

Office Address: 25 Main St., Cooperstown, NY 13326. **Mailing Address:** P.O. Box 590, Cooperstown, NY 13326. **Telephone:** (888) HALL-OF-FAME, (607) 547-7200. **FAX:** (607) 547-2044. **E-Mail Address:** info@baseballhalloffame.org. **Website:** www.baseballhalloffame.org.

Year Founded: 1939.

Chairman: Jane Forbes Clark. **Vice Chairman:** Joe Morgan. **President:** Dale Petroskey. **Senior Vice President:** Bill Haase. **VP, Communications and Education:** Jeff Idelson. **VP/Chief Curator:** Ted Spencer. **Executive Director, Retail Marketing:** Barbara Shinn. **Curator of Collections:** Peter Clark. **Librarian:** Jim Gates. **Controller:** Fran Althiser.

Museum Hours: Memorial Day Weekend-Labor Day—9 a.m.-9 p.m.; remainder of year—9 a.m.-5 p.m. Open daily except Thanksgiving, Christmas Day, New Year's Day.

2003 Hall of Fame Induction Ceremonies: July 27, 1:30 p.m., Cooperstown, NY. **Hall of Fame Game:** June 16, 2 p.m., Tampa Bay Devil Rays vs. Philadelphia Phillies.

NEGRO LEAGUES BASEBALL MUSEUM

Mailing Address: 1616 E 18th St., Kansas City, MO 64108. **Telephone:** (816) 221-1920. **FAX:** (816) 221-8424. **E-Mail Address:** nlmuseum@hotmail.com. **Website:** www.nlbm.com.

Year Founded: 1990.

Chairman: Buck O'Neil. **President:** Mark Bryant.

Executive Director: Don Motley. **Marketing Director:** Bob Kendrick. **Curator:** Raymond Doswell.

Museum Hours: Tues.-Sat. 9 a.m.-6 p.m., Sun. noon-6 p.m. Closed Monday.

TED WILLIAMS MUSEUM and HITTERS HALL OF FAME

Mailing Address: 2455 N. Citrus Hills Blvd., Hernando, FL 34442. **Telephone:** (352) 527-6566. **FAX:** (352) 527-4163. **Website:** twmuseum.com.

Executive Director: Dave McCarthy. **Museum Director:** Sandy Langley.

Museum Hours: Tues.-Sun., 10 a.m.-4 p.m.

RESEARCH

SOCIETY FOR AMERICAN BASEBALL RESEARCH

Mailing Address: 812 Huron Rd. E., Suite 719, Cleveland, OH 44115. **Telephone:** (216) 575-0500. **FAX:** (216) 575-0502. **Website:** www.sabr.org.

Year Founded: 1971.

President: Claudia Perry. **Vice President:** Stew Thornley. **Secretary:** Neil Traven. **Treasurer:** F.X. Flinn. **Directors:** Daniel Ginsburg, Rodney Johnson, Norman Macht, Andy McCue.

Executive Director: John Zajc. **Membership Services Associate:** Ryan Chamberlain. **Director, Publications:** Jim Charlton.

ALUMNI ASSOCIATIONS

MAJOR LEAGUE BASEBALL PLAYERS ALUMNI ASSOCIATION

Mailing Address: 1631 Mesa Ave., Suite C, Colorado Springs, CO 80906. **Telephone:** (719) 477-1870. **FAX:** (719) 477-1875. **E-Mail Address:** postoffice@mlbpaa.com. **Website:** www.baseball-legends.com.

President: Brooks Robinson. **Chief Executive Officer:** Dan Foster.

Board of Directors: Sandy Alderson, Nellie Briles, Jerry Dipoto, Denny Doyle, Don Fehr, Greg Gagne, Jim "Mudcat" Grant, Rich Hand, Jim Hannan (chairman), Ken Sanders, Bob Tewksbury, Jose Valdivielso, Fred Valentine (vice chairman).

Legal Counsel: Sam Moore.

Director, Special Events/Florida Operations: Chris Torgusen. **Director, Marketing/Memorabilia:** Wade Den Hartog. **Director, Special Events/Colorado Operations:** Geoffrey Hixson. **Director, Youth Baseball:** Lance James. **Director, Administration:** Chandra Van Nostrand.

ASSOCIATION OF PROFESSIONAL BASEBALL PLAYERS OF AMERICA

Mailing Address: 1820 W. Orangewood Ave., Suite 206, Orange, CA 92868. **Telephone:** (714) 935-9993. **FAX:** (714) 935-0431. **E-Mail Address:** BallPlayersAssn@aol.com. **Website:** www.apbpa.org.

Year Founded: 1924.

President: John McHale. **First Vice President:** Roland Hemond. **Second VP:** Dick Wagner. **Third VP:** Bob Kennedy. **Secretary-Treasurer:** Dick Beverage. **Administrative Assistant:** Patty Helmsworth.

Directors: Sparky Anderson, Tony Gwynn, Whitey Herzog, Tony La Russa, Tom Lasorda, Brooks Robinson, Nolan Ryan, Tom Seaver.

BASEBALL ASSISTANCE TEAM (BAT)

Mailing Address: 245 Park Ave., 34th Floor, New York, NY 10167. **Telephone:** (212) 931-7823, (866) 605-4594. **FAX:** (212) 949-5691.

Year Founded: 1986.

President, Chief Executive Officer: Earl Wilson. **Vice Presidents:** Steve Garvey, Bob Gibson, Larry Gorman, Ed Stack. **Chairman:** Bobby Murcer.

Executive Director: James Martin. **Secretary:** Thomas Ostertag. **Treasurer:** Jonathan Mariner. **Consultant:** Sam McDowell.

MINISTRY

BASEBALL CHAPEL

Mailing Address: P.O. Box 302, Springfield, PA 19064.**Telephone:** (609) 391-6444. **E-Mail Address:** office@baseballchapel.org. **Website:** www.baseballchapel.org.

Year Founded: 1973.

President: Vince Nauss.

Director, Latin America: Rich Sparling. **Assistant Director:** Kyle Abbott. **Coordinator, Baseball Family:** Coleen Endres.

Board of Directors: Don Christenson, Travis Fryman, Greg Groh, Dave Howard, Jim Lane, Mike Matheny, Chuck Murphy, Vince Nauss, Bill Sampen, Tye Waller, Walt Wiley (chairman).

TRADE, EMPLOYMENT

THE BASEBALL TRADE SHOW

Mailing Address: P.O. Box A, St. Petersburg, FL 33731. **Telephone:** (727) 822-6937, (727) 456-1718. **FAX:** (727) 825-3785.

Manager, Exhibition Services/Alumni Association: Noreen Brantner.

2003 Convention: Dec. 12-15 at New Orleans.

PROFESSIONAL BASEBALL EMPLOYMENT OPPORTUNITIES

Mailing Address: P.O. Box A, St. Petersburg, FL 33731. **Telephone:** (866) 397-7236. **FAX:** (727) 821-5819. **E-Mail:** info@pbeo.com. **Website:** www.pbeo.com.

Contact: Scott Kravchuk.

SENIOR LEAGUES

MEN'S SENIOR BASEBALL LEAGUE

(28 and Over, 38 and Over)

Mailing Address: One Huntington Quadrangle, Suite 3NO7, Mellville, NY 11747. **Telephone:** (631) 753-6725. **FAX:** (631) 753-4031.

President: Steve Sigler. **Vice President:** Gary D'Ambrisi.

E-Mail Address: info@msblnational.com. **Website:** www.msblnational.com.

2003 World Series: Oct. 12-Nov. 1, Phoenix, AZ (28-plus, 38-plus, 48-plus, 58-plus, father/son divisions). **Fall Classic:** Nov. 3-8, Clearwater, FL (28-plus, 38-plus, 47-plus).

MEN'S ADULT BASEBALL LEAGUE

(18 and Over)

Mailing Address: One Huntington Quadrangle, Suite 3NO7, Mellville, NY 11747. **Telephone:** (631) 753-6725. **FAX:** (631) 753-4031.

E-Mail Address: info@msblnational.com. **Website:** www.msblnational.com.

President: Steve Sigler. **Vice President:** Gary D'Ambrisi.

2003 World Series: Oct. 15-19, Phoenix, AZ (four divisions). **Fall Classic:** Oct. 31-Nov. 3, Clearwater, FL.

NATIONAL ADULT BASEBALL ASSOCIATION

Mailing Address: 3609 S. Wadsworth Blvd., Suite 135, Lakewood, CO 80235. **Telephone:** (800) 621-6479. **FAX:** (303) 639-6605. **E-Mail:** nabanational@aol.com. **Website:** www.dugout.org.

President/National Director: Shane Fugita.

Memorial Day Tournament: 18 and over (three divisions), 30 and over (two divisions), 40 and over (two divisions), 50 and over—May 24-26, Las Vegas, NV. **Hall of Fame Tournament:** Cooperstown, NY (wood bat)—July 3-6. **Mile High Classic:** Denver, CO—July 4-6. **California State Championship:** San Diego, CA—July 4-6. **Gold Rush Tournament:** Sacramento, CA—Aug 30-Sept 1.

World Championship Series: 18 and over (three divisions), 30 and over (two divisions), 40 and over (two divisions), 50 and over (two divisions)—Sept. 30-Oct. 11, Phoenix, AZ. **NABA Over 50 Baseball National "Fun" Tournament:** 50 and over only—Oct. 19-26, Las Vegas, NV.

ROY HOBBS BASEBALL

Open (28-Over), Veterans (38-Over), Masters (48-Over),
Legends (55-Over), Classics (58-Over), Women's open

Mailing Address: 2048 Akron Peninsula Rd., Akron, OH 44313. **Telephone:** (330) 923-3400. **FAX:** (330) 923-1967. **E-Mail Address:** royhobbs@royhobbs.com. **Website:** www.royhobbs.com.

President: Tom Giffen. **Vice President:** Ellen Giffen.

2003 World Series (all in Fort Myers, FL): Nov. 5-9—Women's Amateur National Championship; Nov. 1-8—Open Division (four divisions); Nov. 8-15—Veterans Division (four divisions); Nov. 15-22—Masters Division (three divisions), Legends Division, Classics Division.

AMATEUR ATHLETIC UNION WOMEN'S BASEBALL

Open Division (16-Over)

Mailing Address: 2048 Akron Peninsula Rd., Akron, OH 44313. **Telephone:** (330) 923-3400. **FAX:** (330) 923-1967. **Website:** www.aauwomensbaseball.com.

National Women's Baseball Chair: Tom Giffen. **Committee Members:** Adriane Adler, Tina Beining, Christi Hill,, Kari Hall Keating, John Kovach, Alison Maya, Robin Wallace.

2003 National Championship: Nov. 5-9 at Fort Myers, FL.

FANTASY CAMPS

LOS ANGELES DODGERS ADULT BASEBALL CAMP

Mailing Address: Dodgertown, P.O. Box 2887, Vero Beach, FL 32961. **Telephone:** (772) 569-4900, (800) 334-7529. **FAX:** (772) 229-6708. **E-Mail Address:** nancyg@ladodgers.com. **Website:** www.ladabc.com.

Camp Administrator: Nancy Gollnick.

RANDY HUNDLEY'S FANTASY BASEBALL CAMPS

Mailing Address: 128 S Northwest Hwy., Palatine, IL 60067. **Telephone/FAX:** (847) 991-9595. **E-Mail:** rhundley@home.com. **Website:** www.cubsfantasycamps.com.

Camp Coordinator: Barb Kozuh.

BASEBALL CARD MANUFACTURERS

DONRUSS/PLAYOFF

Mailing Address: 2300 E. Randoll Mill, Arlington, TX 76011. **Telephone:** (817) 983-0300. **FAX:** (817) 983-0400. **E-Mail Address:** info@donruss.com. **Website:** www.donruss.com.

FLEER/SKYBOX INTERNATIONAL

Mailing Address: 1120 Route 73 S., Suite 300, Mount Laurel, NJ 08054. **Telephone:** (800) 343-6816 . **FAX:** (856) 231-0383. **E-Mail Address:** info@fleer.com. **Website:** www.fleer.com.

GRANDSTAND CARDS

Mailing Address: 22647 Ventura Blvd., #192, Woodland Hills, CA 91364. **Telephone:** (818) 992-5642. **FAX:** (818) 348-9122. **E-Mail Address:** gscards1@pacbell.net. **Website:** www.grandstandcards.com.

MULTI-AD SPORTS

Mailing Address: 1720 W. Detweiller Dr., Peoria, IL 61615. **Telephone:** (800) 348-6485, ext. 5111. **FAX:** (309) 692-8378. **E-Mail Address:** bjeske@multi-ad.com. **Website:** www.multi-ad.com.

TOPPS

Mailing Address: One Whitehall St., New York, NY 10004. **Telephone:** (212) 376-0300. **FAX:** (212) 376-0623. **Website:** www.topps.com.

UPPER DECK

Mailing Address: 5909 Sea Otter Place, Carlsbad, CA 92008. **Telephone:** (800) 873-7332. **FAX:** (760) 929-6548. **E-Mail Address:** customer_service@upperdeck.com. **Website:** www.upperdeck.com.

MINOR LEAGUES

MINOR LEAGUE BASEBALL

NATIONAL ASSOCIATION OF PROFESSIONAL BASEBALL LEAGUES

Office Address: 201 Bayshore Dr. SE, St. Petersburg, FL 33701. **Mailing Address:** P.O. Box A, St. Petersburg, FL 33731. **Telephone:** (727) 822-6937. **FAX:** (727) 821-5819. **Website:** www.milb.com.

Year Founded: 1901.

President, Chief Executive Officer: Mike Moore.

Vice President: Stan Brand (Washington, D.C.).

Treasurer/Chief Operating Officer/VP, Administration: Pat O'Conner. **Assistant to VP, Administration:** Mary Wooters.

Secretary/General Counsel: Scott Poley. **Assistant to General Counsel:** Sandie Olmsted.

Executive Director, Business Operations: Misann Ellmaker.

Mike Moore

Director, Baseball Operations: Tim Brunswick.

Director, Media Relations: Jim Ferguson. **Assistant Director, Media Relations:** Steve Densa.

Director, Business/Finance: Eric Krupa. **Assistant to Director, Business/Finance:** Lillian Dixon. **Manager, Accounting:** Jeff Carrier.

Director, Information Technology: Rob Colamarino.

Official Statistician: SportsTicker-Boston, Boston Fish Pier, West Bldg. #1, Suite 302, Boston, MA 02210. Telephone: (617) 951-0070.

2003 Winter Meetings: Dec. 12-15 at New Orleans, LA.

Affiliated Members/Council of League Presidents

Class AAA

League	President	Telephone	FAX Number
International	Randy Mobley	(614) 791-9300	(614) 791-9009
Mexican	Raul Gonzalez	011-555-557-1007	011-555-395-2454
Pacific Coast	Branch Rickey	(719) 636-3399	(719) 636-1199

Class AA

League	President	Telephone	FAX Number
Eastern	Joe McEacharn	(207) 761-2700	(207) 761-7064
Southern	Don Mincher	(770) 321-0400	(770) 321-0037
Texas	Tom Kayser	(210) 545-5297	(210) 545-5298

High Class A

League	President	Telephone	FAX Number
California	Joe Gagliardi	(408) 369-8038	(408) 369-1409
Carolina	John Hopkins	(336) 691-9030	(336) 691-9070
Florida State	Chuck Murphy	(386) 252-7479	(386) 252-7495

Low Class A

League	President	Telephone	FAX Number
Midwest	George Spelius	(608) 364-1188	(608) 364-1913
South Atlantic	John Moss	(704) 739-3466	(704) 739-1974

Short-Season Class A

League	President	Telephone	FAX Number
New York-Penn	Ben Hayes	(727) 576-6300	(727) 576-6307
Northwest	Bob Richmond	(208) 429-1511	(208) 429-1525

Rookie Advanced

League	President	Telephone	FAX Number
Appalachian	Lee Landers	(704) 873-5300	(704) 873-4333
Pioneer	Jim McCurdy	(509) 456-7615	(509) 456-0136

Rookie

League	President	Telephone	FAX Number
Arizona	Bob Richmond	(208) 429-1511	(208) 429-1525
Dominican Summer	Freddy Jana	(809) 563-3233	(809) 563-3233
Gulf Coast	Tom Saffell	(941) 966-6407	(941) 966-6872
Venezuela Summer	Saul Gonzalez	011-58-41-24-0321	011-58-41-24-0321

National Association Board of Trustees

Class Triple-A (at-large)—Mike Tamburro, vice chairman (Pawtucket). **International League**—Ken Young (Norfolk). **Pacific Coast League**—Sam Bernabe (Iowa). **Mexican League**—Alvaro Ley Lopez (Saltillo).

Eastern League—Joe Finley (Trenton). **Southern League**—Frank Burke (Chattanooga). **Texas League**—Miles Prentice (Midland).

California League—Mike Ellis (Lancaster). **Carolina League**—Kelvin Bowles (Salem). **Florida State League**—Ken Carson, secretary (Dunedin). **Midwest League**—Dave Walker, chairman (Burlington). **South Atlantic League**—Ron McKee (Asheville).

New York-Penn League—Bill Gladstone (Tri-City). **Northwest League**—Bob Beban, (Eugene).

Appalachian League—Cam Bonifay (Princeton). **Pioneer League**—Dave Baggott (Ogden). **Gulf Coast League**—Bill Smith, Twins.

PROFESSIONAL BASEBALL PROMOTION CORPORATION

Office Address: 201 Bayshore Dr. SE, St. Petersburg, FL 33701. **Mailing Address:** P.O. Box A, St. Petersburg, FL 33731. **Telephone:** (727) 822-6937. **FAX/Marketing:** (727) 894-4227. **FAX/Licensing:** (727) 825-3785.

President, Chief Executive Officer: Mike Moore.

Treasurer/Chief Operating Officer/VP, Administration: Pat O'Conner. **Assistant to Chief Operating Officer:** Mary Wooters.

Executive Director, Business Operations: Misann Ellmaker. **Senior Assistant Director, Special Operations:** Kelly Ryan. **Assistant Director, Special Operations:** Scott Kravchuk.

Director, Licensing: Brian Earle. **Assistant Director, Licensing:** Tina Gust.

Director, Marketing: Rod Meadows. **Senior Manager, Marketing Administration:** Derek Johnson. **Account Managers, Marketing:** Jessica Bayer, Jen Morris.

Professional Baseball Employment Opportunities Contact: Scott Kravchuk. **Manager, Exhibition Services/Alumni Association:** Noreen Brantner. **Manager, Trademarks/Contracts:** Kiran Varma. **Club Coordinator, Marketing:** Susan Pinckney. **Assistant, Special Operations:** Jill Rusinko. **Administrative Assistant, Special Operations:** Jeannette Machicote.

PROFESSIONAL BASEBALL UMPIRE CORPORATION

Office Address: 201 Bayshore Dr. SE, St. Petersburg, FL 33701. **Mailing Address:** P.O. Box A, St. Petersburg, FL 33731. **Telephone:** (727) 822-6937. **FAX:** (727) 821-5819.

President: Mike Moore.

Treasurer/Vice President, Administration: Pat O'Conner. **Secretary/General Counsel:** Scott Poley.

Administrator: Eric Krupa. **Assistant to Administrator:** Lillian Dixon.

Executive Director, PBUC: Mike Fitzpatrick (Kalamazoo, MI).

Field Evaluators/Instructors: Dennis Cregg (Webster, MA), Mike Felt (Lansing, MI), Cris Jones (Wheat Ridge, CO), Jorge Bauza (San Juan, PR), Larry Reveal (Chesapeake, VA).

GENERAL INFORMATION

		Regular Season			All-Star Games	
	Teams	Games	Open. Day	Clos. Day	Date	Site
International	14	144	April 3	Sept. 1	*July 16	Memphis
Pacific Coast	16	144	April 3	Sept. 2	*July 16	Memphis
Eastern	12	142	April 3	Sept. 1	July 16	New Britain
Southern	10	140	April 3	Sept. 1	July 8	Jacksonville
Texas	8	140	April 3	Aug. 31	June 16	Wichita
California	10	140	April 3	Sept. 1	#June 24	Rancho Cuca.
Carolina	8	140	April 4	Sept. 1	#June 24	Rancho Cuca.
Florida State	12	140	April 3	Aug. 31	June 14	Fort Myers
Midwest	14	140	April 3	Sept. 1	June 17	West Michigan
South Atlantic	16	140	April 3	Sept. 1	June 24	Lexington
New York-Penn	14	76	June 17	Sept. 3	None	
Northwest	8	76	June 17	Sept. 4	None	
Appalachian	10	68	June 16	Aug. 25	None	
Pioneer	8	76	June 17	Sept. 5	None	
Arizona	9	56	June 23	Aug. 30	None	
Gulf Coast	12	60	June 19	Aug. 24	None	

*Triple-A All-Star Game
#California League vs. Carolina League

MINOR LEAGUES

2002 STANDINGS

Parent club in parentheses. *Split-season champion. #Wild card.

INTERNATIONAL LEAGUE — AAA

EAST	W	L	PCT	GB	Manager(s)
Scranton/Wilkes-Barre (Phillies)	91	53	.632	—	Marc Bombard
#Buffalo (Indians)	87	57	.604	4	Eric Wedge
Ottawa (Expos)	80	61	.567	9½	Tim Leiper
Syracuse (Blue Jays)	64	80	.444	27	Omar Malave
Pawtucket (Red Sox)	60	84	.417	31	Buddy Bailey
Rochester (Orioles)	55	89	.382	36	Andy Etchebarren
WEST	**W**	**L**	**PCT**	**GB**	**Manager(s)**
Toledo (Tigers)	81	63	.563	—	Bruce Fields
Louisville (Reds)	79	65	.549	2	Dave Miley
Indianapolis (Brewers)	67	76	.469	13½	Ed Romero
Columbus (Yankees)	59	83	.415	21	Brian Butterfield/Stump Merrill
SOUTH	**W**	**L**	**PCT**	**GB**	**Manager**
Durham (Devil Rays)	80	64	.556	—	Bill Evers
Richmond (Braves)	75	67	.528	4	Fredi Gonzalez
Norfolk (Mets)	70	73	.490	9½	Bobby Floyd
Charlotte (White Sox)	55	88	.385	24½	Nick Capra

GOVERNORS' CUP PLAYOFFS—Semifinals: Durham defeated Toledo 3-0 and Buffalo defeated Scranton/Wilkes-Barre 3-0 in best-of-5 series. **Finals**: Durham defeated Buffalo 3-0 in best-of-5 series.

PACIFIC COAST LEAGUE — AAA

AMERICAN CONFERENCE					
EAST	**W**	**L**	**PCT**	**GB**	**Manager**
Oklahoma (Rangers)	75	69	.521	—	Bobby Jones
New Orleans (Astros)	75	69	.521	—	Chris Maloney
Nashville (Pirates)	72	71	.503	2½	Marty Brown
Memphis (Cardinals)	71	71	.500	3	Gaylen Pitts
CENTRAL	**W**	**L**	**PCT**	**GB**	**Manager(s)**
Salt Lake (Angels)	78	66	.542	—	Mike Brumley
Omaha (Royals)	76	68	.528	2	Bucky Dent
Iowa (Cubs)	71	73	.493	7	Bruce Kimm/Pat Listach
Colorado Springs (Rockies)	58	86	.403	20	Chris Cron
PACIFIC CONFERENCE					
WEST	**W**	**L**	**PCT**	**GB**	**Manager**
Edmonton (Twins)	81	59	.579	—	John Russell
Portland (Padres)	72	71	.503	10½	Rick Sweet
Calgary (Marlins)	67	71	.486	13	Dean Treanor
Tacoma (Mariners)	65	76	.461	16½	Dan Rohn
SOUTH	**W**	**L**	**PCT**	**GB**	**Manager**
Las Vegas (Dodgers)	85	59	.590	—	Brad Mills
Tucson (Diamondbacks)	73	66	.518	10½	Al Pedrique
Sacramento (Athletics)	66	78	.458	19	Bob Geren
Fresno (Giants)	57	87	.396	28	Lenn Sakata

PLAYOFFS—Semifinals: Edmonton defeated Las Vegas 3-1 and Salt Lake defeated Oklahoma 3-0 in best-of-5 series. **Finals:** Edmonton defeated Salt Lake 3-1 in best-of-5 series.

EASTERN LEAGUE — AA

NORTH	W	L	PCT	GB	Manager(s)
Norwich (Yankees)	76	64	.543	—	Stump Merrill/Luis Sojo
#New Haven (Cardinals)	74	65	.532	1½	Mark DeJohn
Binghamton (Mets)	73	68	.518	3½	Howie Freiling
New Britain (Twins)	67	72	.482	8½	Stan Cliburn
Trenton (Red Sox)	63	77	.450	13	Ron Johnson
Portland (Marlins)	63	77	.450	13	Eric Fox
SOUTH	**W**	**L**	**PCT**	**GB**	**Manager(s)**
Akron (Indians)	93	48	.660	—	Brad Komminsk
#Harrisburg (Expos)	79	63	.556	14½	Dave Huppert
Reading (Phillies)	76	66	.535	17½	Greg Legg
Altoona (Pirates)	72	63	.511	21	Dale Sveum
Bowie (Orioles)	55	85	.393	37½	Dave Cash/Dave Stockstill
Erie (Tigers)	52	89	.369	41	Kevin Bradshaw

PLAYOFFS—Semifinals: Norwich defeated New Haven 3-0 and Harrisburg defeated Akron 3-2 in best-of-5 series. **Finals:** Norwich defeated Harrisburg 3-2 in best-of-5 series.

SOUTHERN LEAGUE — AA

EAST	W	L	PCT	GB	Manager
*Jacksonville (Dodgers)	77	62	.554	—	Dino Ebel
Greenville (Braves)	65	69	.485	9½	Brian Snitker
*Carolina (Rockies)	65	71	.478	10½	P.J. Carey
Chattanooga (Reds)	60	80	.429	17½	Phillip Wellman
Orlando (Devil Rays)	58	79	.423	18	Mako Oliveras
WEST	**W**	**L**	**PCT**	**GB**	**Manager**
*Birmingham (White Sox)	79	61	.564	—	Wally Backman
Mobile (Padres)	76	63	.547	2½	Craig Colbert
*West Tenn (Cubs)	73	67	.521	6	Bobby Dickerson
Huntsville (Brewers)	70	69	.504	8½	Frank Kremblas
Tennessee (Blue Jays)	69	71	.493	10	Rocket Wheeler

PLAYOFFS—Semifinals: Birmingham defeated West Tenn 3-2 and Jacksonville defeated Carolina 3-2 in best-of-5 series. **Finals:** Birmingham defeated Jacksonville 3-0 in best-of-5 series.

TEXAS LEAGUE — AA

EAST	W	L	PCT	GB	Manager
*Wichita (Royals)	80	59	.576	—	Keith Bodie
Midland (Athletics)	75	64	.540	5	Tony DeFrancesco
*Tulsa (Rangers)	72	67	.518	8	Tim Ireland
Arkansas (Angels)	51	89	.364	29½	Doug Sisson
WEST	**W**	**L**	**PCT**	**GB**	**Manager**
El Paso (Diamondbacks)	76	62	.551	—	Chip Hale
*Round Rock (Astros)	75	65	.536	2	Jackie Moore
*San Antonio (Mariners)	68	72	.486	9	Dave Brundage
Shreveport (Giants)	60	79	.432	16½	Mario Mendoza

PLAYOFFS—Semifinals: San Antonio defeated Round Rock 3-2 and Tulsa defeated Wichita 3-0 in best-of-5 series. **Finals:** San Antonio defeated Tulsa 4-3 in best-of-7 series.

CALIFORNIA LEAGUE — HIGH A

NORTH	W	L	PCT	GB	Manager
*Stockton (Reds)	89	51	.636	—	Jayhawk Owens
*Modesto (Athletics)	78	62	.557	11	Greg Sparks
#Visalia (Athletics)	70	71	.496	19½	Webster Garrison
Bakersfield (Devil Rays)	69	72	.489	20½	Charlie Montoyo
San Jose (Giants)	68	72	.486	21	Bill Hayes
SOUTH	**W**	**L**	**PCT**	**GB**	**Manager(s)**
*San Bernardino (Mariners)	77	63	.550	—	Daren Brown
*Lake Elsinore (Padres)	75	65	.536	2	George Hendrick
#Lancaster (Diamondbacks)	63	77	.450	14	Steve Scarsone/Bill Plummer
High Desert (Brewers)	60	80	.429	17	Mike Caldwell
Rancho Cucamonga (Angels)	52	88	.371	25	Bobby Meacham

PLAYOFFS—First Round: Modesto defeated Visalia 2-0 and Lake Elsinore defeated Lancaster 2-0 in best-of-3 series. **Semifinals:** Stockton defeated Modesto 3-0 and Lake Elsinore defeated San Bernardino 3-2 in best-of-5 series. **Finals:** Stockton defeated Lake Elsinore 3-1 in best-of-5 series.

CAROLINA LEAGUE — HIGH A

NORTH	W	L	PCT	GB	Manager
*Wilmington (Royals)	89	51	.636	—	Jeff Garber
#Lynchburg (Pirates)	87	53	.621	2	Pate Mackanin
Potomac (Cardinals)	59	81	.421	30	Joe Cunningham
Frederick (Orioles)	47	92	.338	41½	Jack Voigt
SOUTH	**W**	**L**	**PCT**	**GB**	**Manager**
*Myrtle Beach (Braves)	79	61	.564	—	Randy Ingle
*Kinston (Indians)	74	65	.532	4½	Ted Kubiak
Salem (Rockies)	74	66	.529	5	Stu Cole
Winston-Salem (White Sox)	50	90	.357	29	Razor Shines

PLAYOFFS—Semifinals: Lynchburg defeated Wilmington 2-1 and Kinston defeated Myrtle Beach 2-0 in best-of-3 series. **Final:** Lynchburg defeated Kinston 3-1 in best-of-5 series.

FLORIDA STATE LEAGUE — HIGH A

EAST	W	L	PCT	GB	Manager(s)
*Jupiter (Marlins)	81	57	.587	—	Luis Dorante
Vero Beach (Dodgers)	72	63	.533	7½	Juan Bustabad
St. Lucie (Mets)	71	69	.507	11	Ken Oberkfell
*Lakeland (Tigers)	69	70	.496	12½	Gary Green
Daytona (Cubs)	64	73	.467	16½	Dave Trembley
Brevard County (Expos)	51	85	.375	29	Bob Didier/Tony Torchia

WEST	W	L	PCT	GB	Manager(s)
*Charlotte (Rangers)	84	56	.600	—	Darryl Kennedy
Fort Myers (Twins)	77	62	.554	6½	Jose Marzan
*Tampa (Yankees)	71	62	.534	9½	Mitch Seoane
Dunedin (Blue Jays)	63	72	.467	18½	Marty Peavy
Sarasota (Red Sox)	62	74	.456	20	Billy Gardner
Clearwater (Phillies)	57	79	.419	25	John Morris/Roly DeArmas

PLAYOFFS—Semifinals: Charlotte defeated Tampa 2-0 and Lakeland defeated Jupiter 2-0 in best-of-3 series. **Finals:** Charlotte defeated Lakeland 3-2 in best-of-5 series.

MIDWEST LEAGUE — LOW A

EAST	W	L	PCT	GB	Manager
*West Michigan (Tigers)	83	57	.593	—	Phil Regan
*Michigan (Astros)	79	61	.564	4	John Massarelli
#Lansing (Cubs)	74	65	.532	8½	Julio Garcia
#Dayton (Reds)	73	67	.521	10	Donnie Scott
Fort Wayne (Padres)	69	68	.504	12	Tracy Woodson
South Bend (D'backs)	52	87	.374	30½	Dick Schofield
WEST	**W**	**L**	**PCT**	**GB**	**Manager**
*Peoria (Cardinals)	85	53	.616	—	Danny Sheaffer
*Cedar Rapids (Angels)	81	58	.583	4½	Todd Claus
#Quad City (Twins)	71	65	.522	13	Jeff Carter
#Burlington (Royals)	68	71	.489	17½	Joe Szekely
Kane County (Marlins)	64	75	.460	21½	Steve Phillips
Clinton (Expos)	61	75	.449	23	Dave Machemer
Beloit (Brewers)	57	82	.410	28½	Don Money
Wisconsin (Mariners)	53	86	.381	32½	Gary Thurman

PLAYOFFS—Quarterfinals: Peoria defeated Burlington 2-0, Lansing defeated Michigan 2-1, West Michigan defeated Dayton 2-0 and Cedar Rapids defeated Quad City 2-0 in best-of-3 series. **Semifinals:** Peoria defeated Cedar Rapids 2-0 and Lansing defeated West Michigan 2-1 in best-of-3 series. **Finals:** Peoria defeated Lansing 3-1 in best-of-5 series.

SOUTH ATLANTIC LEAGUE — LOW A

NORTH	W	L	PCT	GB	Manager
*Hickory (Pirates)	83	56	.597	—	Tony Beasley
Lexington (Astros)	81	59	.579	2½	J.J. Cannon
*Delmarva (Orioles)	76	64	.543	7½	Joe Ferguson
Greensboro (Yankees)	75	65	.536	8½	Bill Masse
Lakewood (Phillies)	69	70	.496	14	Jeff Manto
Kannapolis (White Sox)	66	74	.471	17½	John Orton
Hagerstown (Giants)	63	77	.450	20½	Mike Ramsey
Charleston, W.Va. (Blue Jays)	61	79	.436	22½	Paul Elliott
SOUTH	**W**	**L**	**PCT**	**GB**	**Manager**
*Columbus (Indians)	79	60	.568	—	Torey Lovullo
South Georgia (Dodgers)	75	63	.543	3½	Scott Little
*Capital City (Mets)	75	64	.540	4	Tony Tijerina
Augusta (Red Sox)	69	67	.507	8½	Arnie Beyeler
Macon (Braves)	66	74	.471	13½	Lynn Jones
Asheville (Rockies)	64	74	.464	14½	Joe Mikulik
Charleston, S.C. (Devil Rays)	60	76	.441	17½	Buddy Biancalana
Savannah (Rangers)	49	89	.355	29½	Paul Carey

PLAYOFFS—Semifinals: Hickory defeated Delmarva 2-0 and Columbus defeated Capital City 2-1 in best-of-3 series. **Finals:** Hickory defeated Columbus 3-2 in best-of-5 series.

NEW YORK-PENN LEAGUE — SHORT-SEASON A

McNAMARA	W	L	PCT	GB	Manager
Staten Island (Yankees)	48	26	.649	—	Derek Shelton
#Williamsport (Pirates)	48	28	.632	1	Andy Stewart
New Jersey (Cardinals)	39	37	.513	10	Tommy Shields
Brooklyn (Mets)	38	38	.500	11	Howard Johnson
Aberdeen (Orioles)	31	45	.408	18	Joe Almaraz
Hudson Valley (Devil Rays)	26	49	.347	22½	David Howard
PINCKNEY	**W**	**L**	**PCT**	**GB**	**Manager**
Auburn (Blue Jays)	47	29	.618	—	Dennis Holmberg
Mahoning Valley (Indians)	46	30	.605	1	Chris Bando
Batavia (Phillies)	34	42	.447	13	Ronnie Ortegon
Jamestown (Marlins)	32	42	.432	14	Johnny Rodriguez
STEDLER	**W**	**L**	**PCT**	**GB**	**Manager**
Oneonta (Tigers)	47	27	.635	—	Randy Ready
Lowell (Red Sox)	34	41	.453	13½	Mike Boulanger
Vermont (Expos)	30	45	.400	17½	Dave Barnett
Tri-City (Astros)	27	48	.360	20½	Ivan DeJesus

PLAYOFFS—Semifinals: Staten Island defeated Williamsport 2-0 and Oneonta defeated Auburn 2-0 in best-of-3 series. **Final:** Staten Island defeated Oneonta 2-0 in best-of-3 series.

NORTHWEST LEAGUE — SHORT-SEASON A

NORTH	W	L	PCT	GB	Manager
Boise (Cubs)	49	27	.645	—	Steve McFarland
Tri-City (Rockies)	40	36	.526	9	Ron Gideon
Spokane (Royals)	29	47	.382	20	Tom Poquette
Yakima (Diamondbacks)	23	53	.303	26	Mike Aldrete
SOUTH	**W**	**L**	**PCT**	**GB**	**Manager(s)**
Everett (Mariners)	44	32	.579	—	Omer Munoz/Roger Hansen
Salem-Keizer (Giants)	41	35	.539	3	Fred Stanley
Eugene (Padres)	41	35	.539	3	Jeff Gardner
Vancouver (Athletics)	37	39	.487	7	Orv Franchuk

PLAYOFFS—Boise defeated Everett 3-0 in best-of-5 championship series.

APPALACHIAN LEAGUE — ROOKIE ADVANCED

EAST	W	L	PCT	GB	Manager
Bluefield (Orioles)	45	23	.662	—	Joe Almaraz
Martinsville (Astros)	41	26	.612	3½	Jorge Orta
Danville (Braves)	37	31	.544	8	Ralph Henriquez
Burlington (Indians)	29	39	.426	16	Rouglas Odor
Princeton (Devil Rays)	19	49	.279	26	Edwin Rodriguez
WEST	**W**	**L**	**PCT**	**GB**	**Manager**
Bristol (White Sox)	43	25	.632	—	Nick Leyva
Elizabethton (Twins)	37	30	.552	5½	Ray Smith
Pulaski (Rangers)	34	32	.515	8	Pedro Lopez
Johnson City (Cardinals)	29	38	.433	13½	Brian Rupp
Kingsport (Mets)	23	44	.343	19½	Joey Cora

PLAYOFFS—Bristol defeated Bluefield 2-1 in best-of-3 championship series.

PIONEER LEAGUE — ROOKIE ADVANCED

NORTH	W	L	PCT	GB	Manager
*Great Falls (Dodgers)	47	28	.627	—	Dann Bilardello
*Billings (Reds)	38	37	.507	9	Rick Burleson
Medicine Hat (Blue Jays)	37	38	.493	10	Rolando Pino
Missoula (Diamondbacks)	35	41	.461	12½	Jack Howell
SOUTH	**W**	**L**	**PCT**	**GB**	**Manager**
*Ogden (Brewers)	40	35	.533	—	Tim Blackwell
*Provo (Angels)	38	38	.500	2½	Tom Kotchman
Casper (Rockies)	35	41	.461	5½	Darron Cox
Idaho Falls (Padres)	32	44	.421	8½	Don Werner

PLAYOFFS—Semifinals: Great Falls defeated Billings 2-0 and Provo defeated Ogden 2-1 in best-of-3 series. **Final:** Great Falls defeated Provo 2-1 in best-of-3 series.

ARIZONA LEAGUE — ROOKIE

	W	L	PCT	GB	Manager
*Cubs	35	21	.625	—	Carmelo Martinez
*Giants	33	23	.589	2	Bert Hunter
Athletics	28	28	.500	7	Ruben Escalera
Angels	28	28	.500	7	Brian Harper
White Sox	27	29	.482	8	Jerry Hairston
Brewers	26	30	.464	9	Carlos Lezcano
Mariners	19	37	.339	16	Darrin Garner

PLAYOFFS—Cubs defeated Giants in one-game playoff.

GULF COAST LEAGUE — ROOKIE

EAST	W	L	PCT	GB	Manager
Dodgers	33	27	.550	—	Luis Salazar
Marlins	31	29	.517	2	Jesus Campos
Expos	28	32	.467	5	Andy Skeels
Braves	28	32	.467	5	Jim Saul
NORTH	**W**	**L**	**PCT**	**GB**	**Manager**
Phillies	39	21	.650	—	Ruben Amaro Sr.
Yankees	36	24	.600	3	Manny Crespo
Tigers	23	37	.383	16	Howard Bushong
Royals	22	38	.367	17	Lloyd Simmons
WEST	**W**	**L**	**PCT**	**GB**	**Manager**
Pirates	37	23	.617	—	Woody Huyke
Twins	35	25	.585	2	Rudy Hernandez
Reds	30	30	.500	7	Edgar Caceras
Rangers	28	32	.467	9	Carlos Subero
Red Sox	26	34	.433	11	John Sanders
Orioles	24	36	.400	13	Jesus Alfaro

PLAYOFFS—Semifinals: Dodgers defeated Pirates in one-game playoff. **Final:** Phillies defeated Dodgers 2-1 in best-of-3 series.

INTERNATIONAL LEAGUE

CLASS AAA

Office Address: 55 S. High St., Suite 202, Dublin, OH 43017. **Telephone:** (614) 791-9300. **FAX:** (614) 791-9009. **E-Mail Address:** office@ilbaseball.com. **Website:** www.ilbaseball.com.

Years League Active: 1884-.

President/Treasurer: Randy Mobley.

Assistant to President: Nathan Blackmon.

Vice Presidents: Harold Cooper, Dave Rosenfield (Norfolk), Tex Simone (Syracuse), George Sisler Jr. **Corporate Secretary:** Max Schumacher (Indianapolis).

Randy Mobley

Directors: Bruce Baldwin (Richmond), Don Beaver (Charlotte), George Habel (Durham), Rick Muntean (Scranton/Wilkes-Barre), Joe Napoli (Toledo), Ray Pecor Jr. (Ottawa), Bob Rich Jr. (Buffalo), Dave Rosenfield (Norfolk), Ken Schnacke (Columbus), Max Schumacher (Indianapolis), Naomi Silver (Rochester), John Simone (Syracuse), Mike Tamburro (Pawtucket), Gary Ulmer (Louisville).

Office Manager: Loretta Holland.

2003 Opening Date: April 3. **Closing Date:** Sept. 1.

Regular Season: 144 games.

Division Structure: North—Buffalo, Ottawa, Pawtucket, Rochester, Scranton/Wilkes-Barre, Syracuse. **West**—Columbus, Indianapolis, Louisville, Toledo. **South**—Charlotte, Durham, Norfolk, Richmond.

Playoff Format: West champion plays South champion in best-of-5 series; wild-card club (non-division winner with best record) plays North champion in best-of-5 series. Winners meet in best-of-5 series for Governors' Cup championship.

All-Star Game: July 16 at Memphis (IL vs. Pacific Coast League).

Roster Limit: 23; 24 from April 5-May 4 and after Aug. 9. **Player Eligibility Rule:** No restrictions.

Brand of Baseball: Rawlings ROM-INT.

Statistician: SportsTicker-Boston, Boston Fish Pier, West Bldg. #1, Suite 302, Boston MA 02210.

Umpires: Bob Bainter (Taylorville, IL), John Bennett (Louisville, KY), Brad Cole (Jacksonville, FL), Dan Cricks (Palm Bay, FL), Dusty Dellinger (Landis, NC), Chad Fairchild (Sarasota, FL), Mike Fichter (Muster, IN), Troy Fullwood (Hampton, VA), Don Goller (East Aurora, NY), Brian Hale (Trussville, AL), Matt Hollowell (Whitehouse Station, NJ), James Hoye (Brookpark, OH), Dan Iassogna (Smyrna, GA), Justin Klemm (Brentwood, NY), Olindo Mattia (Port St. Lucie, FL), Scott Nelson (Coshocton, OH), Scott Packard (Horseheads, NY), David Riley (Neenah, WI), Andy Shultz (Lancaster, PA), Darren Spagnardi (Lexington, NC), Neil Taylor (Dunedin, FL), Webb Turner (Avon, CT), Mike VanVleet (Battle Creek, MI), Scott Walendowski (Washington, MI), Darin Williams (Beebe, AR).

STADIUM INFORMATION

		Dimensions				
Club	Stadium	LF	CF	RF	Capacity	2002 Att.
Buffalo	Dunn Tire Park	325	404	325	21,050	642,272
Charlotte	Knights	325	400	325	10,000	303,321
Columbus	Cooper	355	400	330	15,000	490,390
Durham	Durham Bulls Athletic	305	400	327	10,000	519,122
Indianapolis	Victory Field	320	402	320	15,500	571,984
Louisville	Louisville Slugger Field	325	400	340	13,200	659,340
Norfolk	Harbor Park	333	410	338	12,067	500,192
Ottawa	Lynx	325	404	325	10,332	191,305
Pawtucket	McCoy	325	400	325	10,031	615,540
Richmond	The Diamond	330	402	330	12,134	452,961
Rochester	Frontier Field	335	402	325	10,868	421,494
Scranton/WB	Lackawanna County	330	408	330	10,982	466,342
Syracuse	P&C	330	400	330	11,604	413,566
Toledo	Fifth Third Field	320	412	326	8,943	567,804

BUFFALO
Bisons

Office Address: 275 Washington St., Buffalo, NY 14203. **Mailing Address:** P.O. Box 450, Buffalo, NY 14205. **Telephone:** (716) 846-2000. **FAX:** (716) 852-6530. **E-Mail Address:** info@bisons.com. **Website:** www.bisons.com.

Affiliation (first year): Cleveland Indians (1995). **Years in League:** 1886-90, 1912-70, 1998-.

Ownership, Management

Operated by: Rich Products Corp.

Principal Owner, President: Robert Rich Jr. **Chairman:** Robert Rich Sr.

President, Rich Entertainment Group: Melinda Rich. **President, Rich Baseball Operations:** Jon Dandes. **VP/Treasurer:** David Rich. **VP/Secretary:** William Gisel.

VP/General Manager: Mike Buczkowski. **VP, Sales/Marketing:** Marta Hiczewski. **Director, Finance:** Joe Segarra. **Corporate Counsel:** Jill Bond, William Grieshober. **Director, Public Relations/Marketing:** Tom Burns. **Video Entertainment Coordinator:** Justin White. **Director, Sales/Marketing:** Christopher Hill. **Controller:** John Rupp. **Accounting Assistant:** Amy Delaney. **Accountants:** Rita Clark, Linda Gallagher, Kevin Parkinson, Nicole Winiarski. **Manager, Ticket Operations:** Mike Poreda. **Manager, Merchandise:** Kathey Wind. **Coordinators, Customer Care:** Kristen Burwell, Carole Rosenhaus. **Ticket/Sales Account Executives:** Mark Gordon, Burt Mirti, Frank Mooney, Bob O'Connor, Anthony Sprague. **Account Executives:** Kathleen Delisanti, Jim Harrington, Brendan Kelly, Jim Mack. **Director, Stadium Operations:** Tom Sciarrino. **Assistant Manager, Concessions:** Roger Buczek. **Director, Concessions/Pettibones Grille:** John Corey. **Assistant Manager, Pettibones Grille:** Mary Jo Crowe. **Equipment Manager:** Scott Lesher. **Visiting Clubhouse Manager:** Nick Birti. **Office Manager:** Margaret Russo. **Executive Assistants:** Donna Notto, Tina Sarcinelli.

Field Staff

Manager: Marty Brown. **Coach:** Carlos Garcia. **Pitching Coach:** Carl Willis. **Trainer:** Nick Paparesta.

Game Information

Radio Announcers: Jim Rosenhaus, Duke McGuire. **No. of Games Broadcast:** Home-72, Away-72. **Flagship Station:** WWKB 1520-AM.

PA Announcer: John Summers. **Official Scorers:** Mike Kelly, Kevin Lester.

Stadium Name (year opened): Dunn Tire Park (1988). **Location:** From north, take I-190 to Elm Street exit, left onto Swan Street. From east, take I-90 West to exit 51 (Route 33) to end, exit at Oak Street, right onto Swan Street. From west, take I-90 East, exit 53 to I-190 North, exit at Elm Street, left onto Swan Street. **Standard Game Times:** 7:05 p.m.; Thur. 1:05; Sat. 2:05, 7:05; Sun 2:05.

Visiting Club Hotel: Downtown Holiday Inn, 620 Delaware Ave., Buffalo, NY 14202. Telephone: (716) 886-2121.

CHARLOTTE
Knights

Office Address: 2280 Deerfield Dr., Fort Mill, SC 29715. **Telephone:** (704) 357-8071. **FAX:** (704) 329-2155. **E-Mail Address:** knights@charlotteknights.com. **Website:** www.charlotteknights.com.

Affiliation (first year): Chicago White Sox (1999). **Years in League:** 1993-.

Ownership, Management

Operated by: Knights Baseball, LLC.

Principal Owners: Bill Allen, Don Beaver, Derick Close.

President: Don Beaver.

Vice President/General Manager: Bill Blackwell. **Assistant GM, Marketing/Promotions:** Mark Viniard. **Assistant GM, Stadium Operations:** Jon Percival. **Director, Ticket Operations:** Kelly Crawford. **Director, Media/Community Relations:** Ryan Gerds. **Director, Group Sales:** Sean Owens. **Group Event Coordinators:** Ryan Brown, Sean O'Conner, Brooke Varner, Bryan Stefani. **Corporate Account Managers:** Adam Deschenes, John Watkins. **Director, Broadcasting/Team Travel:** Matt Swierad. **Director, Creative Services:** Mike Riviello. **Coordinator, Stadium Operations:** Will Leach. **Mascot Coordinator:** Billy Yandle. **Business Manager/Merchandise:** Sam Kaune. **Head Groundskeeper:** Eddie Busque. **Assistant Groundskeeper:** Brandon Landreth. **Office Manager:** Ronda Lessmeister. **Facility Maintenance Manager:** Joe Sistare. **Clubhouse Manager:** John Bare.

Field Staff

Manager: Nick Capra. **Coach:** Greg Walker. **Pitching Coach:** Curt Hasler. **Trainer:** Scott Johnson.

Game Information

Radio Announcers: Matt Swierad. **No. of Games Broadcast:** Home-72, Away-72. **Flagship Station:** WFNZ 610-AM.

PA Announcer: Unavailable. **Official Scorers:** Brent Stastny, Ed Walton.

Stadium Name (year opened): Knights Stadium (1990). **Location:** Exit 88 off I-77, east on Gold Hill Road. **Standard Game Times:** 7:15 p.m.; Sun. 2:15.

Visiting Club Hotel: Hilton Garden Inn, 425 Town Center Blvd., Pineville NC 28134. Telephone: (704) 889-3279.

COLUMBUS
Clippers

Office Address: 1155 W. Mound St., Columbus, OH 43223. **Telephone:** (614) 462-5250. **FAX:** (614) 462-3271. **E-Mail Address:** colsclippers@earthlink.net. **Website:** www.clippersbaseball.com.

Affiliation (first year): New York Yankees (1979). **Years in League:** 1955-70, 1977-.

Ownership, Management

Operated by: Columbus Baseball Team, Inc.

Principal Owner: Franklin County, Ohio.

Board of Directors: Ralph Anderson, Donald Borror, Stephen Cheek, Wayne Harer, Richard Smith, Charlotte Witkind, John Wolfe.

President, General Manager: Ken Schnacke. **Assistant GM:** Mark Warren. **Assistant GM, Consultant:** Dick Fitzpatrick. **Director, Stadium Operations:** Steve Dalin. **Director, Ticket Operations:** Scott Ziegler. **Director, Group Sales:** Ty Debevoise. **Director, Marketing:** Shawne Beck. **Director, Promotions:** Jason Kidik. **Director, Broadcasting:** Todd Bell. **Director, Advertising:** Keif Fetch. **Director, Communications:** Joe Santry. **Director, Community/Media Relations:** Neal Zaccagnini. **Director, Merchandising:** Krista Oberlander. **Director, Finance:** Bonnie Badgley. **Assistant to GM:** Judi Timmons. **Administrative Assistants:** Kelly Ryther, Leah Dittoe, Brittney Heimann.

Field Staff

Manager: Bucky Dent. **Coaches:** Hop Cassady, Sal Rende. **Pitching Coach:** Neil Allen. **Trainer:** Darren London.

Game Information

Radio Announcers: Todd Bell, Gary Richards. **No. of Games Broadcast:** Home-72, Away-72. **Flagship Station:** WSMZ 103.1-FM.

PA Announcer: Rich Hanchette. **Official Scorers:** Chuck Emmerling, Frank Fraas, Kris Hutchins.

Stadium Name (year opened): Cooper Stadium (1977). **Location:** From north/south, I-71 to I-70 West, exit at Mound Street. From west, I-70 East, exit at Broad Street, east to Glenwood, south to Mound Street. From east, I-70 West, exit at Mound Street. **Standard Game Times:** 7:05 p.m.; Fri. 7:05/7:25; Sat. 6:05/7:05; Sun. 2:05/5:05.

Visiting Club Hotels: Radisson Hotel, 7007 N. High St., Columbus, OH 43085. Telephone: (614) 436-0700; Sheraton Suites-Columbus, 201 Hutchinson Ave., Columbus, OH 43235. Telephone: (614) 781-7316.

DURHAM
Bulls

Office Address: 409 Blackwell St., Durham, NC 27701. **Mailing Address:** P.O. Box 507, Durham, NC 27702. **Telephone:** (919) 687-6500. **FAX:** (919) 687-6560. **Website:** www.durhambulls.com.

Affiliation (first year): Tampa Bay Devil Rays (1998). **Years in League:** 1998-.

Ownership, Management

Operated by: Capitol Broadcasting Co., Inc.

President, Chief Executive Officer: Jim Goodmon.

Vice President: George Habel. **VP, Legal Counsel:** Mike Hill.

General Manager: Mike Birling. **Manager, Sales:** Chip Hutchinson. **Account Executives, Sponsorship:** Enrique Casanova, Brian French, Shannon Haire. **Coordinator, Sponsorship Services:** Unavailable. **Director, Media Relations/Promotions:** Matt DeMargel. **Multimedia Operations:** Aaron Bare. **Assistant, Media Relations/Promotions:** Micah Heilicser. **Manager, Ticket Sales:** Jon Bishop. **Supervisor, Ticket Operations:** Josh Levi. **Coordinator, Group Outings:** Tim Seaton. **Supervisor, Group Sales:** Melissa Kopp. **Coordinator, Business Development:** Tadd Hall. **Group Sales Assistants:** Sheldon Leonard, Peter Strnad. **Director, Stadium Operations:** Mike Tilly. **Supervisor, Operations:** Derek Walsh. **Manager, Merchandise:** Allan Long. **General Manager, Concessions:** Jamie Jenkins. **Assistant GM, Concessions:** Tammy Scott. **Head Groundskeeper:** Jimmy Simpson. **Manager, Business:** Rhonda Carlisle. **Accountants:** Theresa Stocking, Delesia Rogers. **Director, Security:** Ed Sarvis. **Facility Superintendent:** Steve Banos. **Administrative Assistant:** Libby Hamilton. **Receptionist/Secretary:** Barbara Goss. **Box Office Sales:** Jerry Mach.

Field Staff

Manager: Bill Evers. **Coach:** Richie Hebner. **Pitching Coach:** Joe Coleman. **Trainer:** Tom Tisdale.

Game Information

Radio Announcer: Steve Barnes. **No. of Games Broadcast:** Home-72, Away-72. **Flagship Station:** WDNC 620-AM.

PA Announcer: Bill Law. **Official Scorer:** Brent Belvin.

Stadium Name (year opened): Durham Bulls Athletic Park (1995). **Location:** From Raleigh, I-40 West to Highway 147 North, exit 12B to Willard, two blocks on Willard to stadium. From I-85, Gregson Street exit to downtown, left on Chapel Hill Street, right on Mangum Street. **Standard Game Times:** 7 p.m.; Sun. 5.

Visiting Club Hotel: Durham Marriott at the Civic Center, 201 Foster St., Durham, NC 27701. Telephone: (919) 768-6000.

INDIANAPOLIS
Indians

Office Address: 501 W. Maryland St., Indianapolis, IN 46225. **Telephone:** (317) 269-3542. **FAX:** (317) 269-3541. **E-Mail Address:** indians@indyindians.com **Website:** www.indyindians.com.

Affiliation (first year): Milwaukee Brewers (2000). **Years in League:** 1963, 1998-.

Ownership, Management

Operated by: Indians, Inc.

Chairman, President: Max Schumacher.

General Manager: Cal Burleson. **Assistant GM, Marketing:** Bill Fulton. **Assistant GM, Operations:** Randy Lewandowski. **Director, Corporate Development:** Bruce Schumacher. **Director, Advertising:** Chris Herndon. **Director, Ticket Operations:** Mike Schneider. **Manager, Tickets:** Matt Guay. **Manager, Box Office:** Kerry Vick. **Director, Media Relations/Publications:** Tim Harms. **Director, Community Relations:** Traci Vernon. **Director, Merchandising:** Mark Schumacher. **Marketing Coordinator:** Nicole Luepke. **Group Sales Executive:** Michael Blackert. **Group Sales Executive:** Samantha Coghill. **Director, Broadcasting:** Howard Kellman. **Director, Business Operations:** Brad Morris. **Director, Stadium/Baseball Operations:** Scott Rubin. **Director, Suiteholder Services:** Dave McGhee. **Personnel Director:** Robin Ellet. **Facility Director:** Bill Sampson. **Director, Stadium Maintenance:** Tim Hughes. **Maintenance Assistant:** Allan Danehy. **Head Groundskeeper:** Mike Boekholder. **Assistant Groundskeeper:** Jamie Mehringer. **Administrative Assistant:** Stu Tobias. **Equipment/Clubhouse Manager:** J.R. Rinaldi. **Director, Food Services:** Carey Landis.

Field Staff

Manager: Cecil Cooper. **Coach:** Gaylen Pitts. **Pitching Coach:** Mike Caldwell. **Trainer:** Jeff Paxson.

Game Information

Radio Announcers: Howard Kellman, Brian Giffin. **No. of Games Broadcast:** Home-72, Away-72. **Flagship Station:** WXNT 1430-AM.

PA Announcer: Bruce Schumacher. **Official Scorers:** Kim Rogers, Tom Akins, Mark Walpole.

Stadium Name (year opened): Victory Field (1996). **Location:** I-70 to West Street exit, north on West Street to ballpark; I-65 to Martin Luther King and West Street exit, south on West Street to ballpark. **Standard Game Times:** 7 p.m.; Sun. 2/6.

Visiting Club Hotel: The Comfort Inn, 530 S. Capitol, Indianapolis, IN 46225. Telephone: (317) 631-9000.

LOUISVILLE
Bats

Office Address: 401 E. Main St., Louisville, KY 40202. **Telephone:** (502) 212-2287. **FAX:** (502) 515-2255. **E-Mail Address:** info@batsbaseball.com. **Website:** www.batsbaseball.com.

Affiliation (first year): Cincinnati Reds (2000). **Years in League:** 1998-.

Ownership, Management

Operated by: Louisville Baseball Club, Inc.

Board of Directors: Ed Glasscock, Jack Hillerich, Kenny Huber, Jim Morrissey, Tom Musselman, Dale Owens, Bob Stallings, Dan Ulmer, Gary Ulmer.

Chairman: Dan Ulmer. **President:** Gary Ulmer.

Vice President/General Manager: Dale Owens. **Assistant GM/Director, Marketing:** Greg Galiette. **Director, Baseball Operations:** Mary Barney. **Director, Stadium Operations:** Scott Shoemaker. **Director, Ticket Sales:** James Breeding. **Director, Broadcasting:** Jim Kelch. **Controller:** Michele Anderson. **Manager, Tickets:** George Veith. **Director, Public/Media Relations:** Svend Jansen. **Director, Suite Level Services:** Graham Honaker. **Manager, Ticket Accounting:** Earl Stubblefield. **Coordinator, Group Sales:** Bryan McBride. **Senior Account Executives:** Jason Abraham, Courtney Myers, Russell Pol. **Assistant Director, Public/Media Relations:** Megan Dimond. **Account Executives:** Jason Hartings, Hal Norwood, Denny Williams. **Manager, Community Relations:** Karrie Harper. **Assistant Manager, Tickets:** Kyle Reh. **Operations Assistants:** Doug Randol, Emily House. **Sales Representatives:** Matt Andrews, Harry Einbinder.

Administrative Assistant: Jodi Tischendorf. **Head Groundskeeper:** Tom Nielsen. **Assistant Groundskeeper:** Brad Smith.

Field Staff

Manager: Dave Miley. **Coach:** Adrian Garrett. **Pitching Coach:** Mack Jenkins. **Trainer:** John Young.

Game Information

Radio Announcer: Jim Kelch. **No. of Games Broadcast:** Home-72, Away-72. **Flagship Station:** WGTK 970-AM.

PA Announcer: Charles Gazaway. **Official Scorer:** Ken Horn.

Stadium Name (year opened): Louisville Slugger Field (2000). **Location:** I-64 and I-71 to I-65 South/North to Brook Street exit, right on Market Street, left on Jackson Street, stadium on Main Street between Jackson and Preston. **Standard Game Times:** 7:15 p.m.; Sat: 6:15; Sun: 1:15/6:15.

Visiting Club Hotel: Ramada Inn Riverside, 700 W Riverside Dr., Jeffersonville, IN 47130. Telephone: (812) 284-6711.

NORFOLK
Tides

Office Address: 150 Park Ave., Norfolk, VA 23510. **Telephone:** (757) 622-2222. **FAX:** (757) 624-9090. **E-Mail Address:** info@norfolktides.com. **Website:** www.norfolktides.com.

Affiliation (first year): New York Mets (1969). **Years in League:** 1969-.

Ownership, Management

Operated by: Tides Baseball Club, LP.

President: Ken Young.

General Manager: Dave Rosenfield. **Assistant GM:** Jay Richardson. **Director, Media Relations:** Robin Wentz. **Director, Community Relations:** Heather Harkins. **Manager, Merchandising:** Mark Kaczorowski. **Coordinator, Sales/Promotions:** Ben Giancola. **Director, Ticket Operations:** Glenn Riggs. **Director, Video Operations:** Jody Cox. **Director, Group Sales:** Dave Harrah. **Coordinators, Group Sales:** Stephanie Brammer, Brigette Langford. **Business Manager:** Mike Giedlin. **Director, Stadium Operations:** John Slagle. **Assistant, Stadium Operations:** Ethan Silverman. **Ticket Manager:** Linda Waisanen. **Administrative Assistant:** Stephanie Guilfoyle. **Equipment/Clubhouse Manager:** Stan Hunter. **Head Groundskeeper:** Ken Magner. **Assistant Groundskeeper:** Keith Collins.

Field Staff

Manager: Bobby Floyd. **Coach:** Al LeBoeuf. **Pitching Coach:** Randy Niemann. **Trainer:** Brian Chicklo.

Game Information

Radio Announcers: Jeff McCarragher, John Castleberry. **No. of Games Broadcast:** Home-72, Away-72. **Flagship Station:** ESPN Radio 1310-AM, WFOG 1050-AM.

PA Announcer: Don Bolger. **Official Scorer:** Unavailable.

Stadium Name (year opened): Harbor Park (1993). **Location:** Exit 9, 11A or 11B off I-264, adjacent to the Elizabeth River in downtown Norfolk. **Standard Game Times:** 7:15 p.m.; Sun. (April-June) 1:15, (July-Sept.) 6:15.

Visiting Club Hotels: Sheraton Waterside, 777 Waterside Dr., Norfolk, VA 23510. Telephone: (757) 622-6664; Doubletree Club Hotel, 880 N. Military Hwy., Norfolk, VA 23502. Telephone: (757) 461-9192.

OTTAWA
Lynx

Office Address: Lynx Stadium, 300 Coventry Rd., Ottawa, Ontario K1K 4P5. **Telephone:** (613) 747-5969. **FAX:** (613) 747-0003. **E-Mail Address:** lynx@ottawalynx.com. **Website:** www.ottawalynx.com.

Affiliation (first year): Baltimore Orioles (2003). **Years in League:** 1951-54, 1993-.

Ownership/Management

Operated By: Ottawa Lynx Company.

Principal Owner: Ray Pecor.

General Manager: Kyle Bostwick. **Office Administrator:** Lorraine Charrette. **Director, Corporate Support:** Mark Sluban. **Director, Marketing/Community Relations:** Marie Heikkinen Webb. **Director, Media/Public Relations:** Brian Morris. **Director, Ticket Operations/Group Sales:** Scott MacIntosh. **Assistant Director, Ticket Operations:** Melissa Rumble. **Sales Account Executives:** Don Charrette, Kevin Priddle. **Equipment Manager:** John Bryk. **Visiting Clubhouse Manager:** Jeff Keech. **Head Groundskeeper:** Peter Webb.

Field Staff

Manager: Gary Allenson. **Coach:** Dave Cash. **Pitching Coach:** Steve McCatty. **Trainer:** Homer Zulaica.

Game Information

Radio: Unavailable.

PA Announcer: Jeff Lefebvre. **Official Scorer:** Frank Calamatas.

Stadium Name (Year Opened): Lynx Stadium (1993). **Location:** Highway 417 to Vanier Parkway exit, Vanier Parkway north to Coventry Road to stadium. **Standard Game Times:** 7:05 p.m.; Sat., Sun. and holidays 1:05.

Visiting Club Hotel: Chimo Hotel, 1199 Joseph Cyr Rd., Ottawa, Ontario K1K 3P5. Telephone: (613) 744-1060.

PAWTUCKET
Red Sox

Office Address: One Ben Mondor Way, Pawtucket, RI 02860. **Mailing Address:** P.O. Box 2365, Pawtucket, RI 02861. **Telephone:** (401) 724-7300. **FAX:** (401) 724-2140. **E-Mail Address:** info@pawsox.com. **Website:** www.pawsox.com.

Affiliation (first year): Boston Red Sox (1973). **Years in League:** 1973-.

Ownership, Management

Operated by: Pawtucket Red Sox Baseball Club, Inc.

Chairman: Ben Mondor. **President:** Mike Tamburro.

Vice President/General Manager: Lou Schwechheimer. **VP, Chief Financial Officer:** Matt White. **VP, Sales/Marketing:** Michael Gwynn. **VP, Stadium Operations:** Mick Tedesco. **VP, Public Relations:** Bill Wanless. **Assistant to GM:** Daryl Jasper. **Director, Ticket Operations:** Tom Hohol. **Manager, Finance:** Kristy Batchelder. **Director, Community Relations:** Jeff Bradley. **Director, Merchandising:** Steve Napolillo. **Director, Media Services:** Jeff Quimette. **Director, Warehouse Operations:** Dave Johnson. **Director, Concession Services:** Jim Hogan. **Administrative Assistant:** Griffin Hughes. **Account Executive:** Gordon Smith. **Secretary:** Jackie Dryer. **Clubhouse Manager:** Chris Parent. **Head Groundskeeper:** Casey Erven. **Assistant Groundskeeper:** Matt McKinnon. **Facility Operations:** Kevin Galligan. **Executive Chef:** Dom Rendine.

Field Staff

Manager: Buddy Bailey. **Coach:** U.L. Washington. **Pitching Coach:** Mike Griffin. **Trainer:** Bill Coffey.

Game Information

Radio Announcers: Dave Flemming, Andy Freed. **No. of Games Broadcast:** Home-72, Away-72. **Flagship Station:** WSKO 790-AM.

PA Announcer: Jim Martin. **Official Scorer:** Bruce Guindon.

Stadium Name (year opened): McCoy Stadium (1946). **Location:** From north, Route 95 South to exit 2A in Massachusetts (Newport Ave./Pawtucket), follow Newport Ave. for 2 miles, right on Columbus Ave., follow Columbus Ave. for one mile, stadium on right. From south, Route 95 North to exit 28 (School Street), right at bottom of exit ramp, through two sets of lights, left onto Pond Street, right on Columbus Ave., stadium entrance on left. From west, (Worcester), Route 146 South to Route 295 North to Route 95 South and follow directions from north. From east (Fall River), Route 195 West to Route 95 North and follow directions from south. **Standard Game Times:** 7 p.m.; Sat. 6, Sun. 1.

Visiting Club Hotel: Comfort Inn, 2 George St., Pawtucket, RI 02860. Telephone: (401) 723-6700.

RICHMOND
Braves

Office Address: 3001 North Blvd., Richmond, VA 23230. **Mailing Address:** P.O. Box 6667, Richmond, VA 23230. **Telephone:** (804) 359-4444. **FAX:** (804) 359-0731. **E-Mail Address:** info@rbraves.com. **Website:** www.rbraves.com.

Affiliation (first year): Atlanta Braves (1966). **Years in League:** 1884, 1915-17, 1954-64, 1966-.

Ownership, Management

Operated by: Atlanta National League Baseball, Inc.

President: Stan Kasten.

General Manager: Bruce Baldwin. **Assistant GM:** Toby Wyman. **Receptionist:** Janet Zimmerman. **Manager, Stadium Operations:** Rob Bordner. **Manager, Field Maintenance:** Chad Mulholland. **Manager, Public Relations:** Todd Feagans. **Public Relations Assistant:** Noir Fowler. **Manager, Promotions/Marketing:** Jeremy Wells. **Manager, Ticket Operations:** Bobby Holland. **Assistant, Ticket Operations:** Ben Terry. **Assistant, Marketing/Promotions:** Elizabeth Snavely. **Office Manager:** Joanne Curnutt. **Clubhouse Manager:** Nicholas Leto.

Field Staff

Manager: Pat Kelly. **Coach:** Rick Albert. **Pitching Coach:** Guy Hansen. **Trainer:** Jay Williams.

Game Information

Radio Announcers: Robert Fish. **No. of Games Broadcast:** Home-72, Away-72. **Flagship Station:** Unavailable.

PA Announcer: Mike Blacker. **Official Scorers:** Leonard Alley, Roscoe Puckett.

Stadium Name (year opened): The Diamond (1985). **Location:** Exit 78 (Boulevard) at junction of I-64 and I-95, follow signs to park. **Standard Game Times:** 7 p.m., Sun. 2.

Visiting Club Hotel: Quality Inn, 8008 W. Broad St., Richmond, VA 23230. Telephone: (804) 346-0000.

ROCHESTER

Red Wings

Office Address: One Morrie Silver Way, Rochester, NY 14608. **Telephone:** (585) 454-1001. **FAX:** (585) 454-1056, (585) 454-1057. **E-Mail Address**: info@redwings-baseball.com **Website**: www.redwingsbaseball.com.

Affiliation (first year): Minnesota Twins (2003). **Years in League:** 1885-89, 1891-92, 1895-.

Ownership, Management

Operated by: Rochester Community Baseball.

Chairman, Chief Operating Officer: Naomi Silver. **President, Chief Executive Officer**: Gary Larder.

General Manager: Dan Mason. **Assistant GM**: Will Rumbold. **Controller**: Darlene Giardina. **Operations Coordinator**: Mary Goldman. **Head Groundskeeper**: Gene Buonomo. **Director, Media/Public Relations**: Chuck Hinkel. **Director, Marketing**: Nick Sciarratta. **Director Group Sales**: Parker Allen. **Director, Promotions:** Matt Cipro. **Director, Game Day Production:** Brian Golding. **Director, Ticket Sales**: Joe Ferrigno. **Director, Merchandising**: Lisa Cardilli. **Director, Human Resources**: Paula LoVerde. **APAR Manager**: Liz Ammons. **Executive Secretary:** Ginny Colbert. **Director, Food Services**: Jeff Dodge. **Manager, Suites/Catering**: Jennifer Pierce. **Manager, Concessions**: Sue King. **Business Manager, Concessions**: Dave Bills. **Clubhouse Operations**: Terry Costello. **Account Representative:** Zach Holmes. **Night Secretary**: Cathie Costello.

Field Staff

Manager: Phil Roof. **Coach**: Mike Hart. **Pitching Coach:** Bobby Cueller. **Trainer:** Dave Pruemer.

Game Information

Radio Announcers: Josh Whetzel, Joe Altobelli. **No. of Games Broadcast**: Home-72, Away-72. **Flagship Stations**: WHTK 1280-AM, WHAM 1180-AM.

PA Announcer: Pete McKenzie. **Official Scorer**: Lary Bump.

Stadium Name: Frontier Field (1997). **Location**: I-490 East to exit 12 (Brown/Broad Street) and follow signs. I-490 West to exit 14 (Plymouth Ave.) and follow signs. **Standard Game Times**: 7:05 p.m., Sun 1:35.

Visiting Club Hotel: Crown Plaza, 70 State St., Rochester, NY 14608. Telephone: (585) 546-3450.

SCRANTON/WILKES-BARRE

Red Barons

Office Address: 235 Montage Mountain Rd., Moosic, PA 18507. **Mailing Address:** P.O. Box 3449, Scranton, PA 18505. **Telephone:** (570) 969-2255. **FAX:** (570) 963-6564. **E-Mail Address:** barons@epix.net. **Website:** www.redbarons.com.

Affiliation (first year): Philadelphia Phillies (1989). **Years in League:** 1989-.

Ownership, Management

Operated by: Lackawanna County Stadium Authority.

Chairman: Bill Jenkins.

General Manager: Rick Muntean. **Director, Media/Public Relations:** Mike Cummings. **Director, Promotions:** Chris Petrewski, **Executive Assistant:** Kelly Byron. **Director, Stadium Operations:** Jeremy Ruby. **Director, Sales/Marketing:** Ron Prislupski. **Senior Account Representatives:** Ned Gavlick, Jack Gowron, Joe Shaughnessy, Travis Spencer, Tara Vanness. **Director, Ticket Sales:** Ann Marie Nocera. **Director, Merchandising:** Ray Midura. **Director, Food Services:** Rich Sweeney. **Clubhouse Operations:** Red Brower, Rich Revta. **Director, Special Projects:** Karen Healey. **Office Manager:** Donna Kunda. **Controller:** Vicki Lamberton. **Head Groundskeeper:** Bill Casterline.

Field Staff

Manager: Marc Bombard. **Coach:** Jerry Martin. **Pitching Coach:** Mike Mason. **Trainer:** Craig Strobel.

Game Information

Radio Announcer: Kent Westling. **No. of Games Broadcast:** Home-72, Away-72. **Flagship Station:** WWDL 104.9-FM.

PA Announcer: Johnny Davies. **Official Scorers:** Bob McGoff, Jeep Fanucci.

Stadium Name (Year Opened): Lackawanna County Stadium (1989). **Location:** I-81 to exit 182 (Davis Street/Montage Mountain Road), take Montage Mountain Road one mile to stadium. **Standard Game Times:** 7 p.m.; Sun. 2/6.

Visiting Club Hotel: Radisson at Lackawanna Station, 700 Lackawanna Ave., Scranton, PA 18503. Telephone: (570) 342-8300.

SYRACUSE
SkyChiefs

Office Address: P&C Stadium, One Tex Simone Dr., Syracuse, NY 13208. **Telephone:** (315) 474-7833. **FAX:** (315) 474-2658. **E-Mail Address:** baseball@skychiefs.com. **Website:** www.skychiefs.com.

Affiliation (first year): Toronto Blue Jays (1978). **Years in League:** 1885-89, 1891-92, 1894-1901, 1918, 1920-27, 1934-55, 1961-.

Ownership, Management

Operated by: Community Owned Baseball Club of Central New York, Inc.

Chairman: Richard Ryan. **President:** Donald Waful. **Vice President/Chief Operating Officer:** Anthony "Tex" Simone.

General Manager: John Simone. **Assistant GM, Sales:** Tom Van Schaack. **Director, Group Sales:** Victor Gallucci. **Director, Operations:** H.J. Refici. **Assistant GM, Business:** Don Lehtonen. **Associate Director, Group/Corporate Sales:** Mike Voutsinas. **Director, Merchandising:** Wendy Shoen. **Director, Ticket Office:** Jason Anderson. **Director, Internet/Website:** Kevin Kawa. **Team Historian:** Ron Gersbacher. **Receptionist:** Priscilla Venditti. **Field Maintenance:** Jim Jacobson.

Field Staff

Manager: Omar Malave. **Coach:** Ken Landreaux. **Pitching Coach:** Tom Filer. **Trainer:** Jon Woodworth.

Game Information

Radio Announcer: Bob McElligott. **No. of Games Broadcast:** Home-72, Away-72. **Flagship Station:** SportsRadio ESPN 1260-AM.

PA Announcer: Unavailable. **Official Scorers:** Tom Leo, Joel Marieniss.

Stadium Name (year opened): P&C Stadium (1997). **Location:** New York State Thruway to exit 36 (I-81 South), to 7th North Street exit, left on 7th North, right on Hiawatha Boulevard. **Standard Game Times:** 7 p.m., Sun. 6.

Visiting Club Hotel: Ramada Inn, 1305 Buckley Rd., Syracuse, NY 13212. Telephone: (315) 457-8670.

TOLEDO
Mud Hens

Office Address: 406 Washington St., Toledo, OH 43604. **Telephone:** (419) 725-4367. **FAX:** (419) 725-4368. **E-Mail Address:** mudhens@mudhens.com. **Website:** www.mudhens.com.

Affiliation (first year): Detroit Tigers (1987). **Years in League:** 1889, 1965-.

Ownership, Management

Operated by: Toledo Mud Hens Baseball Club, Inc.

Chairman, President: Michael Miller.

General Manager: Joseph Napoli. **Assistant GM/Director, Corporate Sales:** Scott Jeffer. **Assistant GM/Director, Marketing:** Neil Neukam. **Manager, Business Operations:** Dorothy Welniak. **Chief Financial Officer:** Bob Eldridge. **Manager, Stadium Operations:** Kirk Sausser. **Maintenance Supervisor:** L.C. Bates. **Head Groundskeeper:** Jeff Limburg. **Director, Media/Public Relations:** Jason Griffin. **Director, Promotions:** Kerri White. **Director, Ticket Sales/Operations:** Erik Ibsen. **Manager, Merchandising:** Unavailable. **Merchandise Associate:** Dan Berns. **Clubhouse Operations:** Joe Sarkisian. **Office Manager:** Carol Hamilton. **Manager, Group Sales:** Joe Barbarito. **Manager, Season Ticket Sales/Services:** Thom Townley. **Season Ticket Sales/Group Sales Associates:** Steve Dolinar, Chris Hole, Neil Stein, Brian Perkins, Greg Setola. **Manager, Box Office:** April Byers.

Field Staff

Manager: Larry Parrish. **Coach:** Leon Durham. **Pitching Coach:** Jeff Jones. **Trainer:** Matt Rankin.

Game Information

Radio Announcers: Jim Weber, Frank Gilhooley. **No. of Games Broadcast:** Home-72, Away-72. **Flagship Station:** WLQR 1470-AM.

PA Announcer: Bobb Vergeils. **Official Scorers:** Ron Kleinfelter, Guy Lammers, Jeff Bussinger.

Stadium Name (year opened): Fifth Third Field (2002). **Location:** From Ohio Turnpike 80/90, exit 54 (4A) to I-75 North, follow I-75 North to exit 201-B, left onto Erie Street, right onto Washington Street. From Detroit, I-75 South to exit 202-A, right onto Washington Street. From Dayton, I-75 North to exit 201-B, left onto Erie Street, right onto Washington Street. From Ann Arbor, Route 23 South to I-475 East, I-475 East to I-75 South, I-75 South to exit 202-A, right onto Washington Street. **Standard Game Times:** 7 p.m.; Sun. 2.

Visiting Club Hotel: Radisson, 101 North Summit, Toledo, OH 43604. Telephone: (419) 241-3000.

PACIFIC COAST LEAGUE

CLASS AAA

Mailing Address: 1631 Mesa Ave., Suite A, Colorado Springs, CO 80906. **Telephone:** (719) 636-3399. **FAX:** (719) 636-1199. **E-Mail Address:** office@pclbaseball.com. **Website:** www.pclbaseball.com.

PACIFIC COAST LEAGUE

Branch Rickey

President: Branch B. Rickey.

Vice President: Don Logan (Las Vegas).

Directors: Don Beaver (New Orleans), Sam Bernabe (Iowa), Hilary Buzas-Drammis (Salt Lake), Hugh Campbell (Edmonton), John Carbray (Fresno), George Foster (Tacoma), Al Gordon (Nashville), Bob Goughan (Colorado Springs), Dean Jernigan (Memphis), Tom Lasley (Portland), Don Logan (Las Vegas), Matt Minker (Omaha), Tim O'Toole (Oklahoma), Art Savage (Sacramento), Ken Young (Albuquerque), Jay Zucker (Tucson).

Director, Operations: George King. **Office Manager:** Melanie Fiore.

2003 Opening Date: April 3. **Closing Date:** Sept. 2.

Regular Season: 144 games.

Division Structure. American Conference—Central: Albuquerque, Colorado Springs, Iowa, Omaha. **Eastern:** Memphis, Nashville, New Orleans, Oklahoma. **Pacific Conference—Southern:** Fresno, Las Vegas, Sacramento, Tucson. **Northern:** Edmonton, Portland, Salt Lake, Tacoma.

Playoff Format: Northern champion plays Southern champion, and Central champion plays Eastern champion in best-of-5 semifinal series. Winners meet in best-of-5 series for league championship.

All-Star Game: July 16 at Memphis (International League vs. PCL).

Roster Limit: 23; 24 for first 30 days of season and after Aug. 9. **Player Eligibility Rule:** No restrictions.

Brand of Baseball: Rawlings ROM.

Umpires: Ramon Armendariz (Vista, CA), David Aschwege (Lincoln, NE), Lance Barksdale (Jackson, MS), John Bullock (Burbank, CA), Geoff Burr (Escondido, CA), Greg Chittenden (Springfield, MO), Frank Coffland (San Antonio, TX), Steve Cox (Tulsa, OK), Adam Dowdy (Pontiac, IL), Robert Drake (Buena Park, CA), Chris Guccione (Brighton, CO), Scott Higgins (Keizer, OR), Jimmy Horton (Louisville, MS), Mike Jost (Modesto, CA), Kevin Kelley (St. Louis, MO), Brian Knight (Helena, MT), Mike Mauro (San Mateo, CA), Casey Moser (Iowa Park, TX), Michael Muchlinski (Ephrata, WA), Shawn Rakos (Pacific, WA), Travis Reininger (Brighton, CO), Jack Samuels (Orange, CA), Matthew Schaeffer (Oldsmar, FL), Patrick Spieler (Omaha, NE), Kevin Sweeney (Rio Rancho, NM), Ryan West (Littleton, CO), Mark Winters (Springfield, IL), Jim Wolf (West Hills, CA).

STADIUM INFORMATION

		Dimensions				
Club	Stadium	LF	CF	RF	Capacity	2002 Att.
*Albuquerque	Albuquerque Sports	360	410	340	10,510	182,831
Colorado Springs	Sky Sox	350	400	350	9,000	267,028
Edmonton	TELUS Field	340	420	320	9,200	340,387
Fresno	Grizzly Stadium	324	402	335	12,500	563,079
Iowa	Sec Taylor	335	400	335	10,800	509,384
Las Vegas	Cashman Field	328	433	323	9,334	327,289
Memphis	AutoZone Park	319	400	322	14,200	794,550
Nashville	Herschel Greer	327	400	327	10,700	322,059
New Orleans	Zephyr Field	333	405	332	11,000	410,183
Oklahoma	Southwestern Bell	325	400	325	13,066	432,887
Omaha	Rosenblatt	332	408	332	24,000	344,718
Portland	PGE Park	319	405	321	19,810	454,197
Sacramento	Raley Field	330	405	325	14,111	817,317
Salt Lake	Franklin Covey	345	420	315	15,500	460,839
Tacoma	Cheney	325	425	325	9,600	300,910
Tucson	Tucson Electric	340	405	340	11,000	268,807

*Club operated in Calgary in 2002

ALBUQUERQUE
Isotopes

Office Address: 1601 Avenida Cesar Chavez SE, Albuquerque, NM 87106. **Telephone:** (505) 924-2255. **FAX:** (505) 242-8899. **E-Mail Address:** info@albuquerquebaseball.com. **Website:** www.albuquerquebaseball.com.

Affiliation (first year): Florida Marlins (2003). **Years in League:** 2003-.

Ownership, Management

Operated by: Albuquerque Baseball Club, LLC.

President: Ken Young.

Directors: Ken Young, Emmett Hammond.

General Manager: Mel Kowalchuk. **Director, Baseball/Business Operations:** John Traub. **Director, Sales/Marketing:** Nick LoBue. **Director, Stadium Operations:** Drew Stuart. **General Manager, Food Service:** Jay Satenspiel. **Director, Group Sales/Season Tickets:** Jennifer Steger. **Director, Accounting:** Michael Margolis. **Manager, Merchandise:** Jeff Patrick. **Coordinator, Public Relations:** David Bearman. **Coordinator, Community Relations:** Melissa Gomez. **Manager, Box Office:** Daniel Luna. **Coordinator, Hispanic Sales:** Tomas Sanchez. **Ticket Sales:** Chris Holland. **Sales Representative:** Frances Morrow. **Coordinator, Special Projects:** Paul Hartenberger. **Head Groundskeeper:** Tony Lee. **Clubhouse Operations:** Unavailable. **Office Manager:** Gloria Gallegos.

Field Staff

Manager: Dean Treanor. **Coach:** Matt Stark. **Pitching Coach:** Gary Buckels. **Trainer:** Sean Bearer.

Game Information

Radio Announcer: Bob Socci. **No. of Games Broadcast:** Home-72, Away-72. **Flagship Station:** KNML 610-AM.

PA Announcer: Unavailable. **Official Scorer:** Unavailable.

Stadium Name (year opened): Albuquerque Sports Stadium (2003). **Location:** University Boulevard to Avenida Cesar Chavez SE. **Standard Game Times:** 7:11 p.m.; Sun. (April-May) 1:35, (June-Sept.) 6:05.

Visiting Club Hotel: Holiday Inn Mountain View, 2020 Menaul SE, Albuquerque, NM 87106. Telephone: (505) 884-2511.

COLORADO SPRINGS
Sky Sox

Office Address: 4385 Tutt Blvd., Colorado Springs, CO 80922. **Telephone:** (719) 597-1449. **FAX:** (719) 597-2491. **E-Mail Address:** info@skysox.com. **Website:** www.skysox.com.

Affiliation (first year): Colorado Rockies (1993). **Years in League:** 1988-.

Ownership, Management

Operated by: Colorado Springs Sky Sox, Inc.

Principal Owner: David Elmore.

President/General Manager: Bob Goughan. **Senior Vice President, Administration:** Sam Polizzi. **Senior VP, Operations:** Dwight Hall. **Senior VP, Marketing:** Rai Henniger. **Senior VP, Stadium Operations:** Mark Leasure. **Senior VP, Advertising:** Robert Stein. **Coordinator, Special Events:** Brien Smith. **Assistant GM, Public Relations:** Gabe Ross. **Director, Finance:** Craig Levin. **Director, Broadcast Operations:** Dan Karcher. **Assistant GM, Community Relations:** Corey Wynn. **Assistant GM, Merchandise/Account Manager:** Murlin Whitten. **Group Sales Director:** Dan Schaefer. **Group Sales/Ticket Operations:** Chip Dreamer. **Promotions/Public Relations Coordinator:** Kazuhito Oki. **Home Clubhouse Manager:** Ricky Grima. **Visiting Clubhouse Manager:** Greg Grimaldo. **Marketing Representatives:** Robert Boyd, Vincent Briedis, David Cole, Jennifer Shelton, Andrea Villalpando.

Field Staff

Manager: Rick Sofield. **Coach:** Alan Cockrell. **Pitching Coach:** Bob McClure. **Trainer:** Travis Anderson.

Game Information

Radio Announcers: Dan Karcher, Dick Chase. **No. of Games Broadcast:** Home-72, Away-72. **Flagship Station:** KRDO 1240-AM.

PA Announcer: Chip Dreamer. **Official Scorer:** Marty Grantz.

Stadium Name (year opened): Sky Sox Stadium (1988). **Location:** I-25 South to Woodmen Road exit, east on Woodmen to Powers Boulevard, right on Powers to Barnes Road. **Standard Game Times:** 7:05 p.m.; Sun. 1:35.

Visiting Club Hotel: Sheraton Colorado Springs Hotel, 2886 S. Circle Dr., Colorado Springs, CO 80906. Telephone: (719) 576-5900.

EDMONTON
Trappers

Office Address: 10233 96th Ave., Edmonton, Alberta T5K 0A5. **Telephone:** (780) 414-4450. **FAX:** (780) 414-4475. **E-Mail Address:** trappers@trappersbaseball.com. **Website:** www.trappersbaseball.com.

Affiliation (first year): Montreal Expos (2003). **Years in League:** 1981-.

Ownership, Management

Operated by: Edmonton Trapper Baseball Club.

Owner: Edmonton Eskimo Football Club. **President/Chief Eexecutive Officer**: Hugh Campbell.

Chief Operating Officer: Rick LeLacheur **Assistant GM:** Dennis Henke. **Office Manager:** Nancy Yeo. **Executive Assistant to COO:** Cathy Fiss. **Accountant:** Heather Pick. **Account Executives:** Ken Charuk, Del Schjefte. **Manager, Baseball Information:** Gary Tater. **Manager, Tickets:** Heather Sayers. **Manager, Merchandise:** Darin Kowalchuk. **Manager, Marketing/Community Relations**: Karen Gurba. **Stadium Manager:** Don Benson. **Head Groundskeeper:** Fraser Murray. **Home Clubhouse Manager:** James Rosnau. **Visiting Clubhouse Manager:** Ian Rose.

Field Staff

Manager: Dave Huppert. **Coach:** Jose Castro. **Pitching Coach:** Tommy John. **Trainer:** Mike Quinn.

Game Information

Radio Announcer: Al Coates. **No. of Games Broadcast:** Unavailable. **Flagship Station:** CHQT 880-AM.

PA Announcers: Ron Rimer, Bill Cowen. **Official Scorers:** Al Coates, Gary Tater.

Stadium Name (year opened): TELUS Field (1995). **Location:** From north, 101st Street to 96th Avenue, left on 96th, one block east; From south, Calgary Trail North to Queen Elizabeth Hill, right across Walterdale Bridge, right on 96th Avenue. **Standard Game Times:** 7:05 p.m.; Sun. 1:35.

Visiting Club Hotel: Sheraton Grande, 10235 101st St., Edmonton, Alberta T5J 3E9. Telephone: (780) 428-7111.

FRESNO
Grizzlies

Office Address: 1800 Tulare St., Fresno, CA 93721. **Telephone:** (559) 442-1994. **FAX:** (559) 264-0795. **E-Mail Address:** info@fresnogrizzlies.com. **Website:** www.fresnogrizzlies.com.

Affiliation (first year): San Francisco Giants (1998). **Years in League:** 1998-.

Ownership, Management

Operated by: Fresno Diamond Group, LLC.

President: Scott Hulme. **General Manager:** Bill Gorman.

Senior Vice President: Tim Cullen. **VP, Operations:** Steve Macfadyen. **VP, Marketing:** Jeff Gardiner. **VP, Sales:** David Martin. **Chief Financial Officer:** Mike Hulme. **Financial Officer:** Susan Washburn. **Director, Sales:** Pat Cassidy. **Director, Corporate Sales:** Mike Maiorana. **Director, Stadium/Baseball Operations:** Eric Colby. **Director, Human Resources:** Theresa Graham. **Director, Public Relations:** Jesse Molina. **Director, Ticket Operations:** Keith Ford. **Director, Merchandise:** Trish Dolan. **Director, Community Development:** Gus Zernial. **Director, Promotions:** Bobby Mollison. **Director, Video Operations:** Pat McGinnis. **Director, Community Relations:** Erin Deis. **Managers, Corporate Accounts:** Wendy Kalpakoff, Heather Stephenson. **Manager, Ticket Office:** Adam O'Connell. **Manager, Booking:** Michelle Mignacca. **GM, Food/Beverage:** Scott Giddens. **Executive Chef:** Steve Kretz. **Manager, Catering/Suites:** Misty Piell. **Manager, Concessions:** Steve Patterson. **Coordinator, Operations:** Gayle Prezioso. **Head Groundskeeper:** Jim Silva. **Assistant Head Groundskeeper:** Danny Hagopian. **Manager, Warehouse:** Henry Lockwood. **Manager, Maintenance:** C.A. Althoff. **Manager, Housekeeping:** Jerry Benebides. **Administrative Assistant:** Julianna Hickerson. **Sales/Marketing Associates:** Al Batto, Jed Fritz, Mark Haupt, Brian Merrell, Shane Scott, Cynthia Wells, Jake Williams.

Field Staff

Manager: Fred Stanley. **Coach:** Steve Decker. **Pitching Coach:** Bert Bradley. **Trainer:** Mark Gruesbeck.

Game Information

Radio Announcers: Doug Greenwald, Jason Anaforian (English), Jess Gonzalez (Spanish). **No. of Games Broadcast:** Home-72, Away-72. **Flagship Stations:** KAAT 103.1-FM (English), KGST 1600-AM (Spanish).

PA Announcer: Brian Anthony. **Official Scorer:** Unavailable.

Stadium Name (year opened): Grizzlies Stadium (2002) **Location:** From 99 North, take Fresno Street exit, left on Fresno Street, left on Inyo or Tulare to stadium; from 99 South, take Fresno Street exit, left on Fresno Street, right on Broadway to H Street; from 41 North, take Van Ness exit towards downtown Fresno, left on Van Ness, left on Inyo or Tulare, stadium is straight ahead; from 41 South, take Tulare exit, stadium is located at Tulare and H Streets, or take Van Ness exit, right on Van Ness, left on Inyo or Tulare, stadium is straight ahead. **Standard Game Times:** 7:05 p.m., Sun. (April-June 15) 2:05.

Visiting Club Hotel: Unavailable.

IOWA
Cubs

Office Address: 350 SW First St., Des Moines, IA 50309. **Telephone:** (515) 243-6111. **FAX:** (515) 243-5152. **E-Mail Address:** kthrall@iowacubs.com. **Website:** www.iowacubs.com.

Affiliation (first year): Chicago Cubs (1981). **Years in League:** 1969-.

Ownership, Management

Operated by: Raccoon Baseball Inc.

Chairman, Principal Owner: Michael Gartner. **Executive Vice President:** Michael Giudicessi.

President, General Manager: Sam Bernabe. **VP, Assistant GM:** Jim Nahas. **VP, Chief Financial Officer:** Sue Tollefson. **VP/Director, Stadium Operations:** Tom Greene. **VP/Director, Broadcast Operations:** Deene Ehlis. **Director, Media Relations:** Jeff Lantz. **Coordinator, Public Relations:** Katelyn Thrall. **Director, Community Relations:** Matt Johnson. **Coordinators, Group Sales:** Jen Hoffman, Ryan Ulrich. **Director, Sales:** Rich Gilman. **Director, Luxury Suites:** Brent Conkel. **Manager, Stadium Operations:** Jeff Tilley. **Corporate Sales Executives:** Greg Ellis, Julie Lofdahl, Brett Johnson. **Corporate Relations:** Red Hollis. **Manager, Broadcast Operations:** David Raymond. **Head Groundskeeper:** Chris Schlosser. **Director, Merchandise:** Kenny Houser. **Coordinator, Merchandise:** Rick Giudicessi. **Accountant:** Lori Auten. **Manager, Cub Club:** Rick Cooper. **Office Manager**: Brenda Ballew.

Field Staff

Manager: Mike Quade. **Coach:** Pat Listach. **Pitching Coach:** Jerry Reuss. **Trainer:** Ed Halbur.

Game Information

Radio Announcers: Deene Ehlis, David Raymond. **No. of Games Broadcast:** Home-72, Away-72. **Flagship Station:** KXNO 1460-AM.

PA Announcers: Corey Coon, Mark Pierce. **Official Scorers:** Dirk Brinkmeyer, Brian Gibson.

Stadium Name (year opened): Sec Taylor Stadium (1992). **Location:** I-80 or I-35 to I-235, to Third Street exit, south on Third Street, left on Tuttle Street. **Standard Game Times:** 7:05 p.m.; Sun. 1:05.

Visiting Club Hotel: Valley West Inn, 3535 Westown Pkwy., West Des Moines, IA 50266. Telephone: (515) 225-2524.

LAS VEGAS
51s

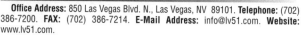

Office Address: 850 Las Vegas Blvd. N., Las Vegas, NV 89101. **Telephone:** (702) 386-7200. **FAX:** (702) 386-7214. **E-Mail Address:** info@lv51.com. **Website:** www.lv51.com.

Affiliation (first year): Los Angeles Dodgers (2001). **Years in League:** 1983-.

Ownership, Management

Operated by: Mandalay Baseball Properties.

Chief Executive Officer: Hank Stickney.

Managing Director: Ken Stickney. **Chairman:** Peter Guber. **Vice Chairman:** Paul Schaeffer. **President, MSE Teams Division:** Jon Spoelstra.

President, General Manager: Don Logan. **Executive Vice President:** Steve DeLay. **VP, Finance/Controller:** Allen Taylor. **VP, Operations/Security:** Nick Fitzenreider. **Director, Ticket Sales:** Tom D'Abruzzo. **Director, Group Events/Game Entertainment:** Derek Eige. **Director, Ticket Operations:** Mike Rodriguez. **Director, Corporate Sponsorships:** Dylan Hanahan. **Director, Sponsor Services:** Mike Hollister. **Director, Merchandise:** Laurie Wanser. **Director, Broadcasting:** Russ Langer. **Creative Director, MSE:** Aaron Artman. **Creative Manager, MSE:** Diana Poveromo. **Manager, Corporate Marketing Sales:** Brandon Raphael. **Managers, Corporate Marketing:** Scott Christiansen, Matt Amoia, Jeff Lukich. **Managers, Group Accounts:** Travis Best, Anthony Albert. **Manager, Consumer Marketing:** Jenny Kraeger. **Coordinator, Consumer Marketing:** Melissa Buxbaum. **Consumer Marketing Assistant:** Natasha Singer. **Manager, Marketing Services:** Dennis Ebbitt. **Baseball Administration:** Denise Korach. **Special Assistant to GM:** Bob Blum. **Coordinator, Mascot Marketing:** Tony Canepa. **Administrative Assistant:** Michelle Taggart.

Field Staff

Manager: John Shoemaker. **Coach:** George Hendrick. **Pitching Coach:** Shawn Barton. **Trainer:** Jason Mahnke.

Game Information

Radio Announcer: Russ Langer. **No. of Games Broadcast:** Home-72, Away-72. **Flagship Station:** KBAD 920-AM.

PA Announcer: Dan Bickmore. **Official Scorer:** Kevin Force.

Stadium Name (year opened): Cashman Field (1983). **Location:** I-15 to US 95 exit (Fremont Street), east to Las Vegas Boulevard North exit, north on Las Vegas Boulevard. **Standard Game Times:** 7:10 p.m.; Sun. 12:30, 1:30.

Visiting Club Hotel: Castaways Hotel Casino, 2800 Fremont St., Las Vegas, NV 89104. Telephone: (702) 385-9123.

MEMPHIS
Redbirds

Office Address: 175 Toyota Plaza, Suite 300, Memphis, TN 38103. **Telephone:** (901) 721-6000. **FAX:** (90)1-892-1222. **Website:** www.memphisredbirds.com.

Affiliation (first year): St. Louis Cardinals (1998). **Years in League:** 1998-.

Ownership, Management

Operated by: Memphis Redbirds Baseball Foundation, Inc. **Founders:** Dean Jernigan, Kristi Jernigan.

President/General Manager: Dave Chase **Assistant GM:** Steele Ford. **Executive Assistant to President:** Cathy Allen. **Controller:** Garry Condrey. **Accounting Manager:** Jennifer Sullivan. **Accounting Specialist:** Deborah Boyle. **Human Resources Specialist:** Pam Abney. **Manager, Information Technology:** P.J. McGhee. **GM, Ovations:** Robert Garcia. **Office Manager, Ovations:** Marianne Banks. **Manager, Catering:** Harold Goldberg. **Executive Chef:** Bob Barlow. **VP, Marketing:** Kerry Sewell. **Manager, Season Tickets:** Jennifer Brereton. **Manager, Marketing:** Kim Jackson. **Graphic Designer:** Iris Horne. **Coordinator, Publishing:** John Lambert. **Mascot Coordinator:** Chris Pegg. **Director, Entertainment:** Shawn Bennett. **Director, Broadcasting:** Tom Stocker. **Manager, Media Relations:** Jason Jones. **Senior VP, Sales:** Pete Rizzo. **Executive Assistant:** Rhonda Anderson. **Director, Retail Operations:** Dana Loughridge. **Retail Assistant:** Starr Taiani. **Manager, Group Sales:** Paige Perkins. **Coordinator, Group Sales:** Megan Tucker. **Sales Executive:** Rob Edgerton. **Sales Coordinator:** Lauren Isaacman. **Sales Representatives:** Kelly Davidson, Jason Keeling. **VP, Community Relations:** Reggie Williams. **Coordinator, Community Relations:** Emma Glover. **Program Coordinator, Community Relations:** Andres Diaz. **Director, Field Operations:** Steve Horne. **Groundskeeper:** Ed Collins. **Ticket Manager:** Phil McKay. **Assistant Ticketing Manager:** Landon Smith. **Facilities Manager:** Don Rovak. **Chief Engineer:** Danny Abbott. **Coordinator, Stadium Operations:** Asim Thomas. **Office Coordinator:** Trina Ross.

Field Staff

Manager: Tom Spencer. **Coach:** Tommy Gregg. **Pitching Coach:** Dyar Miller. **Trainer:** Aaron Bruns.

Game Information

Radio Announcers: Tom Stocker, Steve Selby. **No. of Games Broadcast:** Home-72, Away-72. **Flagship Station:** WHBQ 560-AM.

PA Announcer: Tim Van Horn. **Official Scorer:** J.J. Guinozzo.

Stadium Name (year opened): AutoZone Park (2000). **Location:** North on I-240, exit at Union Avenue West, approx. 1½ miles to park. **Standard Game Times:** 7:05 p.m.; Sat. 6:05; Sun. 2:05.

Visiting Club Hotel: Sleep Inn at Court Square, 40 N. Front, Memphis, TN 38103. Telephone: (901) 522-9700.

NASHVILLE
Sounds

Office Address: 534 Chestnut St., Nashville, TN 37203. **Telephone:** (615) 242-4371. **FAX:** (615) 256-5684. **E-Mail Address:** info@nashvillesounds.com. **Website:** www.nashvillesounds.com.

Affiliation (first year): Pittsburgh Pirates (1998). **Years in League:** 1998-.

Ownership, Management

Operated by: AmeriSports.

President/Owner: Al Gordon.

General Manager: Glenn Yaeger. **Assistant GM, Operations:** Jason Hise. **Assistant GM, Sales:** Chris Snyder. **Director, Accounting:** Barb Walker. **Director, Sales:** Joe Hart. **Director, Ticketing:** Ricki Schlabach. **Director, Media Relations:** Doug Scopel. **Director, Promotions/Public Relations:** Brandon Vonderharr. **Director, Marketing:** Samantha Snyder. **Director, Corporate Sales:** Jason Bennett. **Manager, Stadium Operations:** Ken Thomas. **Manager, Food/Beverage:** Mark Lawrence. **Manager, Church/Youth Programs:** Brent High. **Manager, Community Relations:** Sarah Barthol. **Manager, Mascot/Entertainment:** Buddy Yelton. **Manager, Ticket Sales:** Patrick Ventura. **Coordinator, Human Resources/Groups:** Andrea Mace. **Office Manager:** Sharon Ridley. **Manager, Broadcasting:** Chuck Valenches. **Clubhouse Manager:** Cory Sifford. **Head Groundskeeper:** Chris Pearl.

Field Staff

Manager: Trent Jewett. **Coach:** Jay Loviglio. **Pitching Coach:** Darold Knowles. **Trainer:** Josh Mendez.

Game Information

Radio Announcer: Chuck Valenches. **No. of Games Broadcast:** Home-72, Away-72. **Flagship Station:** WANT 98.9-FM.

PA Announcer: Unavailable. **Official Scorers:** Eric Jones, Matt Wilson.

Stadium Name (year opened): Herschel Greer Stadium (1978). **Location:** I-65 to Wedgewood exit, west to Eighth Avenue, right on Eighth to Chestnut Street, right on Chestnut. **Standard Game Times:** 7 p.m.; Wed. 12; Sat. 6; Sun. (April-May) 2, (June-Aug.) 6.

Visiting Club Hotel: Holiday Inn Select, 2613 West End Ave., Nashville, TN 37203. Telephone: (615) 327-4707.

NEW ORLEANS
Zephyrs

Office Address: 6000 Airline Dr., Metairie, LA 70003. **Telephone:** (504) 734-5155. **FAX:** (504) 734-5118. **E-Mail Address:** zephyrs@zephyrsbaseball.com. **Website:** www.zephyrsbaseball.com.

Affiliation (first year): Houston Astros (1997). **Years in League:** 1998-.

Ownership, Management

Owner/President: Don Beaver.

Vice President/General Manager: Dan Rajkowski. **VP, Business Operations:** Clyde Smoll. **Director, Finance/Accounting:** Penny Middleton. **Director, Group Sales:** Mike Schline. **Director, Community Relations**: Marc Allen. **Director, Broadcasting**: Tim Grubbs. **Director, Corporate Sales:** Marc Mouton. **Director, Merchandising:** Pattie Feder. **Director, Operations:** Jon Peterson. **Director, Special Events**: Todd Covino. **Media Relations:** John Mooney. **Media Manager:** Ron Swoboda. **Group Event Coordinators:** Scott Bogosian, Dale Gautreaux, Sam Steinmetz, Ian Dallimore. **Assistant Director, Operations:** Jay Bratschi. **Assistant to GM**: Lesa Badon. **Group Event Assistant:** Preston Gautreaux. **Administrative Support:** Alicia Berthelot. **GM, Ovations Food Services:** George Messina. **Assistant GM, Ovations Food Services:** Kristy Palermo. **Administrative Assistant, Ovations Food Services:** Pricella Arbelo. **Head Groundskeeper:** Thomas Marks. **Assistant Groundskeeper:** Craig Shaffer. **Clubhouse Operations:** Kelly Sharitt. **Operations:** Bill Rowell.

Field Staff

Manager: Chris Maloney. **Coach:** Gary Gaetti. **Pitching Coach:** Jim Hickey. **Trainer:** Mike Freer.

Game Information

Radio Announcers: Tim Grubbs, Ron Swoboda, Herman Rodriguez (Spanish). **No. of Games Broadcast:** Home-72, Away-72; Spanish: Home-30. **Flagship Station:** WTIX 690-AM/94.3-FM, WSLA 1560-AM (Spanish).

PA Announcer: Rene Nadeau. **Official Scorer:** J.L. Vangilder.

Stadium Name (year opened): Zephyr Field (1997). **Location:** I-10 to Clearview Parkway South exit, right on Airline Drive (Route 61) for 1 mile. **Standard Game Times:** 7:05 p.m.; Sun. (April-May) 2:05, (June-Sept.) 5:05.

Visiting Club Hotel: Best Western Landmark, 2601 Severn Ave., Metairie, LA 70002. Telephone: (504) 888-9500.

OKLAHOMA
RedHawks

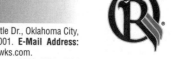

Mailing Address: SBC Bricktown Ballpark, 2 S. Mickey Mantle Dr., Oklahoma City, OK 73104. **Telephone:** (405) 218-1000. **FAX:** (405) 218-1001. **E-Mail Address:** info@oklahomaredhawks.com. **Website:** www.oklahomaredhawks.com.

Affiliation (first year): Texas Rangers (1983). **Years in League:** 1963-1968, 1998-.

Ownership, Management

Operated by: OKC Athletic Club, LP.

Principal Owner: Gaylord Entertainment Company.

President, General Manager: Tim O'Toole. **Director, Finance:** Steve McEwen. **Director, Merchandise/Guest Services:** Mike Prange. **Director, Facility Operations:** Harlan Budde. **Director, Communication:** Shara Cofer. **Director, Sales:** Robert Lavender. **Senior Accountant:** Nicole Lamb. **Accountant:** Sarah Miller. **Manager, Group Sales:** Kristin Packnett. **Manager, Baseball Operations:** Mike Pomeroy. **Manager, Corporate Sales:** Ryan O'Toole. **Senior Account Executive:** Brandon Baker. **Manager, Promotions:** Brandi Hunter. **Manager, Ticket Sales:** Jared Bullock. **Head Groundskeeper:** Monte McCoy. **Clubhouse Manager:** Joe Catalano. **Director, Administration/Special Events:** Nancy Simmons.

Field Staff

Manager: Bobby Jones. **Coach:** Bruce Crabbe. **Pitching Coach:** Glenn Abbott. **Trainer:** Unavailable.

Game Information

Radio Announcer: Jim Byers. **No. of Games Broadcast:** Home-72, Away-72. **Flagship Station:** WKY 930-AM.

PA Announcer: Randy Kemp. **Official Scorers:** Bob Colon, Mike Treps.

Stadium Name (year opened): SBC Bricktown Ballpark (1998). **Location:** At interchange of I-235 and I-40, take Reno exit, east on Reno. **Standard Game Times:** 7:05 p.m., Sun. (April-May) 2:05.

Visiting Club Hotel: Westin Hotel, One N. Broadway, Oklahoma City, OK 73102. Telephone: (405) 235-2780.

OMAHA
Royals

Office Address: Rosenblatt Stadium, 1202 Bert Murphy Ave., Omaha, NE 68107. **Telephone:** (402) 734-2550. **FAX:** (402) 734-7166. **E-Mail Address:** info@oroyals.com. **Website:** www.oroyals.com.

Affiliation (first year): Kansas City Royals (1969). **Years in League:** 1998-.

Ownership, Management

Operated by: Omaha Royals Limited Partnership.

Principal Owners: Matt Minker, Warren Buffett, Walter Scott. **Managing General Partner, President:** Matt Minker. **Vice President, General Manager:** Doug Stewart. **VP, Sales/Marketing:** Matt Brown. **Director, Business/Baseball Operations:** Kyle Fisher. **Director, Broadcasting:** Mark Nasser. **Director, Media Relations:** Kevin McNabb. **Director, Public Relations:** Bill Steckis. **Director, Group Sales:** Don Wilson. **Director, Merchandise/Promotions:** Cassie Duncan. **Director, Ticket Sales/Operations:** Erich Hover. **Sponsorship Sales Representative:** Angela Bonella. **Head Groundskeeper:** Jesse Cuevas. **General Manager, Concessions:** Ryan Slane. **Administrative Assistants:** Kay Besta, Lois Biggs. **Assistant Director, Marketing:** Rose Swenson. **Assistant Director, Group Sales:** Jenny Cheney. **Assistant Director, Ticket Operations:** Nic Laue. **Assistant, Ticket Operations:** Bob Brown.

Field Staff

Manager: Mike Jirschele. **Coach:** Kevin Long. **Pitching Coach:** Dave LaRoche. **Trainer:** Jeff Stevenson.

Game Information

Radio Announcers: Mark Nasser, Kevin McNabb. **No. of Games Broadcast:** Home-72, Away-72. **Flagship Station:** KOSR 1490-AM.

PA Announcers: Bill Jensen, Steve Roberts. **Official Scorer:** Rob White.

Stadium Name (year opened): Rosenblatt Stadium (1948). **Location:** I-80 to 13th Street exit, one block south. **Standard Game Times:** 7:05 p.m., Sun. 1:35.

Visiting Club Hotel: Red Lion, 7007 Grover St., Omaha, NE 68106. Telephone: (402) 397-7030.

PORTLAND
Beavers

Office Address: 1844 SW Morrison, Portland, OR, 97205. **Telephone:** (503) 553-5400. **FAX:** (503) 553-5405. **E-Mail Address:** info@pdxpfe.com. **Website:** www.portlandbeavers.com.

Affiliation (first year): San Diego Padres (2001). **Years in League:** 1903-1917, 1919-1972, 1978-1993, 2001-.

Ownership, Management

Operated by: Metropolitan Sports, LLC.

President/General Manager: Mark Schuster. **Special Assistant:** Jack Cain. **Director, Communications:** Chris Metz. **Director, Operations:** Ken Puckett. **Director, Finance:** Kim Veys. **Director, Promotions/Travel:** Jennifer Gartz. **Manager, Operations/Merchandise:** Jamie Cummins. **Manager, Group Sales:** Ben Hoel. **Manager, Accounting:** Karen McConkey. **Manager, Facility Maintenance:** Dave Tankersley. **Senior Account Executive:** J.D. Bigelow. **Corporate Account Executives:** Rich Burk, Jesse Ouellette. **Account Executive:** Dan Zusman. **Accounts Receivable/Payroll Administrator:** Amy Camp. **Receptionist:** Jenny Hamilton. **Head Groundskeeper:** Jessie Smith.

Field Staff

Manager: Rick Sweet. **Coach:** Rob Deer. **Pitching Coach:** Mike Couchee. **Trainer:** John Maxwell.

Game Information

Radio Announcers: Bill Schonely, Rich Burk. **No. of Games Broadcast:** Home-72, Away-72. **Flagship Station:** KUFO 970-AM.

PA Announcer: Mike Stone. **Official Scorer:** Blair Cash.

Stadium Name: PGE Park (1926). **Location:** I-405 to West Burnside exit, SW 20th Street to park. **Standard Game Times:** 7:05 p.m.; Sun. 2:05.

Visiting Club Hotel: Portland Marriott-Downtown, 1401 SW Naito Pkwy., Portland, OR 97201. Telephone: (503) 226-7600.

SACRAMENTO
River Cats

Office Address: 400 Ballpark Dr., West Sacramento, CA 95691. **Telephone:** (916) 376-4700. **FAX:** (916) 376-4710. **E-Mail Address:** info@rivercats.com. **Website:** www.rivercats.com.

Affiliation (first year): Oakland Athletics (2000). **Years in League:** 1903, 1909-11, 1918-60, 1974-76, 2000-.

Ownership, Management

Owned by: Sacramento River Cats Baseball Club, LLC.

Principal Owner, Chief Executive Officer: Art Savage. **President, Chief Operating Officer:** Alan Ledford. **Executive Vice Presidents:** Bob Hemond, Warren Smith.

Senior Vice President, General Manager: Gary Arthur. **Senior VP, Sales/Marketing:** Tom Glick. **Senior VP, Chief Financial Officer:** Dan Vistica. **General Counsel:** Matthew Re. **VP, Corporate Partnerships:** Darrin Gross. **VP, Consumer Marketing:** Ray Krise. **Director, Media Relations:** Mike Gazda. **Director, Stadium Operations:** Matt Fucile. **Director, Ticket/Parking Operations:** Scott Gephart. **Director, Guest Services/Employee Relations:** Kristi Goldby. **Director, Community Relations:** Tony Asaro. **Director, Marketing:** Bret Smith. **Director, Finance/Administration:** Rita Ward. **Manager, Merchandise:** Lori Mattson. **Manager, Special Events:** Karolen LaRose. **Manager, Ticket Sales:** Andy Fiske. **Manager, Ticket Services:** Kristen Taylor. **Manager, Game Entertainment:** Paul Flanigan. **Manager, Stadium Operations/Head Groundskeeper:** Matt LaRose. **Coordinator, Baseball Operations:** Matt Thomas. **Executive Assistant/Team Travel:** Pat Berger.

Field Staff

Manager: Tony DeFrancesco. **Coach:** Roy White. **Pitching Coach:** Curt Young. **Trainer:** Walt Horn.

Game Information

Radio Announcer: Johnny Doskow (English), Jose Reynoso (Spanish). **No. of Games Broadcast:** Home-72, Away-72 (English); 28 (Spanish). **Flagship Stations:** KSTE 650-AM (English), KSQR 1240-AM (Spanish).

PA Announcer: Greg Lawson. **Official Scorers:** Brian Berger, Mark Honbo.

Stadium Name (year opened): Raley Field (2000). **Location:** I-5 to Business 80 West, exit at Jefferson Blvd. **Standard Game Time:** 7:05 p.m.

Visiting Club Hotel: Holiday Inn, Capitol Plaza, 300 J St., Sacramento, CA 95814. Telephone: (916) 446-0100.

SALT LAKE
Stingers

Office Address: 77 W. 1300 South, Salt Lake City, UT 84115. **Mailing Address:** P.O. Box 4108, Salt Lake City, UT 84110. **Telephone:** (801) 485-3800. **FAX:** (801) 485-6818. **E-Mail Address:** info@stingersbaseball.com. **Website:** www.stingersbaseball.com.

Affiliation (first year): Anaheim Angels (2001). **Years in League:** 1915-25, 1958-65, 1970-84, 1994-.

Ownership, Management

Owned by: Buzas Baseball Inc.

Principal Owners: Joe Buzas, Helen Buzas, Hilary Buzas-Drammis, Jason Buzas.

President: Hilary Buzas-Drammis.

Vice President, Assistant General Manager: Dorsena Picknell. **VP, Sales/Marketing:** Brad Tammen. **Director, Media/Public Relations:** Michael Weisbart. **Director, Ticket Operations:** Richard Lahr. **Director, Group Sales:** Mike Daniels. **Account Executives:** Jacob Bailey, Will Erickson, Kevin Huffine, Todd Morgan, Gary Tomlinson. **Office Manager:** Julie Empey. **Special Projects:** Josh France. **Director, Food Services:** Jason Wilson.

Field Staff

Manager: Mike Brumley. **Coach:** Jim Eppard. **Pitching Coach:** Rich Bombard. **Trainer:** Adam Nevala.

Game Information

Radio Announcer: Steve Klauke. **No. of Games Broadcast:** Home-72, Away-72. **Flagship Station:** KWUN 1230-AM.

PA Announcer: Jeff Reeves. **Official Scorers:** Bruce Hilton, Howard Nakagama.

Stadium Name (year opened): Franklin Covey Field (1994). **Location:** I-15 to 1300 South exit, east to West Temple; exit TRAX at "Ball Park" station, one block east. **Standard Game Times:** 7 p.m., (April-May) 6:30; Sun. 2.

Visiting Club Hotel: Sheraton City Centre, 150 W. 500 South, Salt Lake City, UT 84101. Telephone: (801) 401-2000.

TACOMA
Rainiers

Office Address: 2502 S. Tyler St., Tacoma, WA 98405. **Telephone:** (253) 752-7707, (800) 281-3834. **FAX:** (253) 752-7135. **Website:** www.tacomarainiers.com.

Affiliation: Seattle Mariners (1995). **Years in League:** 1904-1905, 1960-.

Ownership, Management

Operated by: George's Pastime, Inc.

President: George Foster.

Board of Directors: George Foster, Jeff Foster, Jonathan Foster, Sue Foster, Mark Kanai, Jack Pless.

Community Fund President: Margaret McCormick.

General Manager: Dave Lewis. **Chief Financial Officer:** Laurie Yarbrough. **Assistant GM, Baseball Operations:** Kevin Kalal. **Assistant GM, Stadium Operations:** Philip Cowan. **Director, Marketing:** Rachel Marecle. **Director, Sales:** Tim Sexton. **Director, Promotions:** Nate Kelley. **Group Sales Coordinator:** Cory Carbary. **Account Executive:** Shane Santman. **Director, Food/Beverage:** Corey Brandt. **Director, Merchandise:** Kathy Baxter. **Manager, Tickets:** Darrin Miller. **Staff Accountant:** Jacquie Sonnenfeld. **Office Manager:** Patti Stacy. **Head Groundskeeper:** Ryan Schutt. **Maintenance Supervisor:** Jim Smith. **Clubhouse Manager:** Jeff Bopp. **Assistant Clubhouse Manager:** Jake Parker.

Field Staff

Manager: Dan Rohn. **Coach:** Gary Thurman. **Pitching Coach:** Jim Slaton. **Trainer:** Rob Nodine.

Game Information

Radio Broadcaster: Mike Curto. **No. of Games Broadcast:** Home-72, Away-72. **Flagship Station:** KHHO 850-AM.

PA Announcer: Jeff Randall. **Official Scorekeeper:** Darin Padur.

Stadium name (year opened): Cheney Stadium (1960). **Location:** From I-5, take exit 132 (Highway 16 West) for 1.2 miles to 19th Street East exit, right on Tyler St for ⅓ mile. **Standard Game Times:** 7:05 p.m., (April-May) 6:05 p.m.; Sun., holidays 1:35.

Visiting Club Hotel: La Quinta Inn, 1425 E. 27th St., Tacoma, WA 98421. Telephone (253) 383-0146.

TUCSON
Sidewinders

Office Address: 2500 E. Ajo Way, Tucson, AZ 85713. **Mailing Address:** P.O. Box 27045, Tucson, AZ 85726. **Telephone:** (520) 434-1021. **FAX:** (520) 889-9477. **E-Mail Address:** mail@tucsonsidewinders.com. **Website:** www.tucsonsidewinders.com.

Affiliation (first year): Arizona Diamondbacks (1998). **Years in League:** 1969-.

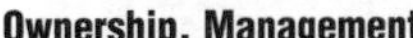

Ownership, Management

Operated by: Tucson Baseball LLC.

Principal Owner/Chief Executive Officer: Jay Zucker.

General Manager: Rick Parr. **Executive Assistant:** Deanna Ruiz. **Director, Stadium Operations:** Matthew Burke. **Director, Broadcasting:** Brett Dolan. **Director, Group Sales:** Brian Moss. **Director, Community Relations:** Sergio Pedroza. **Director, Media Relations:** Brian Simpson. **Director, Inside Sales:** Sandy Davis. **Account Executive, Sales/Marketing:** Nick Wesoky. **Coordinator, Promotions:** Linda Varella. **Group Sales Representative:** Kimberly Levin. **Administrative Assistant:** Claudia Ruiz.

Field Staff

Manager: Al Pedrique. **Coach:** Jack Howell. **Pitching Coach:** Mike Parrott. **Trainer:** Greg Barber.

Game Information

Radio Announcer: Brett Dolan. **No. of Games Broadcast:** Home-72, Away-72. **Flagship Station:** KTKT 990-AM.

PA Announcer: Dale Lopez. **Official Scorer:** Unavailable.

Stadium Name (year opened): Tucson Electric Park (1998). **Location:** From northwest, I-10 to Ajo exit, east on Ajo to stadium; from southeast, I-10 to Palo Verde exit, north to Ajo, west to stadium. **Standard Game Times:** 7 p.m., (April-May) 6:30; Sun. 6:30.

Visiting Club Hotel: Viscount Suite Hotel, 4855 E. Broadway, Tucson, AZ 85711. Telephone: (520) 745-6500.

EASTERN LEAGUE

CLASS AA

Office Address: 511 Congress St., 7th Floor, Portland, ME 04101. **Mailing Address:** P.O. Box 9711, Portland, ME 04104. **Telephone:** (207) 761-2700. **FAX:** (207) 761-7064. **E-Mail Address:** elpb@easternleague.com. **Website:** www.easternleague.com.

Joe McEacharn

Years League Active: 1923-.

President, Treasurer: Joe McEacharn.

Assistant to President: Bill Rosario.

Directors: Greg Agganis (Akron), Jon Danos (Bowie), William Dowling (New Britain), Charles Eshbach (Portland), Barry Gordon (Norwich), Chuck Greenberg (Altoona), Alan Levin (Erie), Ed Massey (New Haven), Greg Martini (Harrisburg), Dick Stanley (Trenton), Craig Stein (Reading), Mike Urda (Binghamton).

2003 Opening Date: April 3. **Closing Date:** Sept. 1.

Regular Season: 142 games.

Division Structure: North—Binghamton, New Britain, New Haven, Norwich, Portland, Trenton. South—Akron, Altoona, Bowie, Erie, Harrisburg, Reading.

Playoff Format: Top two teams in each division play best-of-5 series. Winners meet in best-of-5 series for league championship.

All-Star Game: July 16 at New Britain.

Roster Limit: 23; 24 until 30th day of season and after Aug. 9. **Player Eligibility Rule:** No restrictions.

Brand of Baseball: Rawlings ROM-EL.

Statistician: SportsTicker-Boston, Boston Fish Pier, West Bldg. #1, Suite 302, Boston, MA 02210.

Umpires: Scott Barry (Quincy, MI), Mike Belin (Niagara Falls, NY), Kevin Causey (Springdale, AR), Paul Chandler (Silverdale, WA), G.C. Fernandez (Miami, FL), Rusty Griffin (Gillsville, GA), Andy Hergesheimer (Seattle, WA), Chris Hubler (Dysart, IA), Darren Hyman (Moline, IL), Adrian Johnson (Houston, TX), Joe Judkowitz (Coral Springs, FL), Scott Letendre (Tempe, AZ), Ben Lindquist (Jamestown, NY), Keith McConkey (Thorold, Ontario), John McMasters (Tacoma, WA), Trey Nelson (Lincoln, NE), Brent Rice (Jackson, MI), Andrew Vincent (Simsbury, CT).

STADIUM INFORMATION

		Dimensions				
Club	**Stadium**	**LF**	**CF**	**RF**	**Capacity**	**2002 Att.**
Akron	Canal Park	331	400	337	9,297	400,187
Altoona	Blair County Ballpark	315	400	325	7,200	363,871
Binghamton	NYSEG	330	400	330	6,012	214,289
Bowie	Prince George's	309	405	309	10,000	341,322
Erie	Jerry Uht Park	312	400	328	6,000	211,899
Harrisburg	RiverSide	335	400	335	6,300	266,808
New Britain	New Britain	330	400	330	6,146	265,484
New Haven	Yale Field	340	405	315	6,200	182,164
Norwich	Thomas J. Dodd	309	401	309	6,275	222,134
Portland	Hadlock Field	315	400	330	6,975	382,738
Reading	FirstEnergy	330	400	330	9,000	486,570
Trenton	Waterfront Park	330	407	330	6,341	408,463

AKRON
Aeros

Office Address: 300 S. Main St., Akron, OH 44308. **Telephone:** (330) 253-5151. **FAX:** (330) 253-3300. **E-Mail Adress:** info@akronaeros.com. **Website:** www.akron-aeros.com.

Affiliation (first year): Cleveland Indians (1989). **Years in League:** 1989-.

Ownership, Management

Operated by: Akron Professional Baseball, Inc.

Principal Owners: Mike Agganis, Greg Agganis.

Chief Executive Officer: Greg Agganis. **Vice President:** Drew Cooke. **Chief Financial Officer:** Bob Larkins.

Executive VP/General Manager: Jeff Auman. **Director, Corporate Sales:** Dan Burr. **Director, Group Sales:** Kim Usselman-Fogel. **Manager, Package Sales:** Kevin Snyder. **Senior Account Representative, Group Sales:** Thomas Craven. **Assistant Director, Ticket Sales/Suites Manager:** Stephanie Ulery. **Group Sales Associate:** Bob Rich. **Director, Public Relations:** James Carpenter. **Director, Community Events:** Amanda Flood. **Associate, Corporate/Ticket Sales:** Keith Solar. **Director, Merchandising:** Kris Roukey. **Director, Field Maintenance:** Rick Izzo. **Director, Stadium Operations:** Unavailable. **Director, Player Facilities:** Fletcher Wilkes. **Office Manager:** Arlene Vidumanksy.

Field Staff

Manager: Brad Komminsk. **Coach:** Mike Sarbaugh. **Pitching Coach:** Terry Clark. **Trainer:** Todd Tomczyk.

Game Information

Radio Announcer: Jim Clark. **No. of Games Broadcast:** Home-71, Away-71. **Flagship Station:** WAPS 91.3-FM.

PA Announcer: Joe Jastrzemski. **Official Scorer:** Tom Liggett.

Stadium Name (year opened): Canal Park (1997). **Location:** From I-76 East or I-77 South, exit onto Route 59 East, exit at Exchange/Cedar, right onto Cedar, left at Main Street. From I-76 West or I-77 North, exit at Main Street/Downtown, follow exit onto Broadway Street, left onto Exchange Street, right at Main Street. **Standard Game Times:** 7:05 p.m.; Sat. (April) 2:05; Sun. 2:05.

Visiting Club Hotel: Radisson Hotel Akron City Centre, 20 W. Mill St., Akron, OH 44308. Telephone: (330) 384-1500.

ALTOONA
Curve

Office Address: 1000 Park Ave., Altoona, PA 16602. **Mailing Address:** P.O. Box 1029, Altoona, PA 16603. **Telephone:** (877) 99-CURVE, (814) 943-5400. **FAX:** (814) 942-9132, (814) 943-9050. **E-Mail Address:** frontoffice@altoonacurve.com. **Website:** www.altoonacurve.com.

Affiliation (first year): Pittsburgh Pirates (1999). **Years in League:** 1999-.

Ownership, Management

Operated by: Curve Baseball LP.

President, Managing Partner: Chuck Greenberg. **General Manager:** Todd Parnell. **Assistant GM:** Rick Janac. **Senior Director, Ticketing/Group Sales:** Brent Boznanski. **Director, Broadcasting:** Rob Egan. **Director, Media Relations:** Jason Dambach. **Director, Community Relations:** Elsie Zengel. **Director, Merchandising:** Linda Ianuzzi. **Director, Ballpark Operations:** Kirk Stiffler. **Director, Finance:** Machelle Noel. **Director, Entertainment:** Bob Masiewicz. **Sales/Marketing Specialist:** Jeff Garner. **Group Sales Associate:** Loedicia Stoltz. **Ticketing Associates:** Matt Buckley, Corey Homan, Derek Martin, Gary Marutiak, Doug Nelson, Chris Phillips. **Head Groundskeeper:** Patrick Coakley. **Assistant Groundskeeper:** Matt Neri. **Director, Food Services:** Jim Stearley. **Assistant Manager, Concessions:** Yvonne Hunter. **Clubhouse Operations:** Jake Hundt (home), Ken Thomas (visitors).

Field Staff

Manager: Dale Sveum. **Coach:** John Wehner. **Pitching Coach:** Jeff Andrews. **Trainer:** Jose Ministral.

Game Information

Radio Announcers: Rob Egan, Jason Dambach. **No. of Games Broadcast:** Home-71, Away-71. **Flagship Station:** WFBG 1290-AM.

PA Announcer: Rich DeLeo. **Official Scorer:** Ted Beam.

Stadium Name (year opened): Blair County Ballpark (1999). **Location:** I-99 to Frankstown Road exit. **Standard Game Times:** Weekdays 7:05 p.m., (April-May) 6:35; Sun. 6:35, (April-May) 3:05.

Visiting Club Hotel: Ramada Inn of Altoona, Route 220 and Plank Road, Altoona, PA 16602. Telephone: (814) 946-1631.

BINGHAMTON
Mets

Office Address: 211 Henry St., Binghamton, NY 13901. **Mailing Address:** P.O. Box 598, Binghamton, NY 13902. **Telephone:** (607) 723-6387. **FAX:** (607) 723-7779. **E-Mail Address:** bmets@bmets.com. **Website:** www.bmets.com.

Affiliation (first year): New York Mets (1992). **Years in League:** 1923-37, 1940-63, 1966-68, 1992-.

Ownership, Management

Operated by: Binghamton Mets Baseball Club, Inc.

Principal Owners: Bill Maines, David Maines, R.C. Reuteman, George Scherer, Chris Urda, Michael Urda.

President: Michael Urda.

General Manager: Bill Terlecky. **Assistant GM:** Scott Brown. **Director, Stadium Operations:** Richard Tylicki. **Director, Business Operations:** Jim Weed. **Director, Food/Beverage:** Pete Brotherton. **Director, Group Sales/Fundraising:** Robert O'Brien. **Director, Media Relations:** Joe Hecht. **Sales Representative:** Mike Catalano. **Special Events Coordinator:** Dan Abashian. **Office Manager:** Rebecca Brown. **Manager, Merchandise:** Lisa Shattuck. **Administrative Assistant:** Nancy Wiseman. **Head Groundskeeper:** Jake Tyler.

Field Staff

Manager: John Stearns. **Coach:** Edgar Alfonzo. **Pitching Coach:** Bob Ojeda, **Trainer:** Jason Wulf.

Game Information

Radio Announcer: Joe Hecht. **No. of Games Broadcast:** Home-71, Away-71. **Flagship Station:** WNBF 1290-AM.

PA Announcer: Roger Neel. **Official Scorer:** Steve Kraly.

Stadium Name (year opened): Binghamton Municipal (1992). **Location:** I-81 to exit 4S (Binghamton), Route 11 exit to Henry Street. **Standard Game Times:** 7 p.m., (April-May) 6; Sat. 6; Sun. 1:30.

Visiting Club Hotel: Holiday Inn Arena, 8 Hawley St., Binghamton, NY 13901. Telephone: (607) 722-1212.

BOWIE
Baysox

Office Address: 4101 NE Crain Hwy., Bowie, MD 20716. **Telephone:** (301) 805-6000. **FAX:** (301) 464-4911. **E-Mail Address:** info@baysox.com. **Website:** www.baysox.com.

Affiliation (first year): Baltimore Orioles (1993). **Years In League:** 1993-.

Ownership, Management

Operated by: Comcast-Spectacor.

Directors: Peter Luukko, Frank Miceli.

General Manager: Jon Danos. **Assistant GM:** Mike Munter. **Director, Ticket Operations/Group Events:** Brain Shallcross. **Director, Marketing:** Phil Wrye. **Assistant Director, Marketing:** Keri Scrivani. **Director, Communications:** Andy Frankel. **Coordinator, Community Relations:** Kristen Daffin. **Manager, Ticket Office:** Jennifer Martino. **Director, Stadium Operations:** Phil Laws. **Head Groundskeeper:** Matt Parrott. **Account Managers, Group Events:** Anthony Aspaas, Clark Baker, Stephanie Offen, Pete Sekulow, Addie Staebler. **Corporate Partnerships:** Brian Mulligan, Ryan Raley, Bill Snitcher. **Bookkeeper:** Carol Terwillger. **Receptionist:** Unavailable **Assistants, Ticket Operations:** Matt Murphy, Bill Brueske. **Assistant, Box Office:** David Durand. **Assistant, Communications:** Amy Zirkle. **Assistant, Sponsorship Sales:** Unavailable.

Field Staff

Manager: Dave Trembley. **Coach:** Butch Davis. **Pitching Coach:** Dave Schuler. **Trainer:** P.J. Mainville.

Game Information

Radio Announcer: Dave Collins. **No. of Games Broadcast:** Unavailable. **Flagship Station:** Unavailable.

PA Announcer: Unavailable. **Official Scorer:** Jeff Hertz.

Stadium Name (year opened): Prince George's Stadium (1994). **Location:** ¼ mile south of U.S. 50-U.S. 301 interchange at Bowie. **Standard Game Times:** 7:05 p.m.; Thurs. 6:35; Sun. 1:05.

Visiting Club Hotel: Best Western-Annapolis, 2520 Riva Rd., Annapolis, MD 21401. Telephone: (410) 224-2800.

ERIE
SeaWolves

Office Address: 110 E. 10th St., Erie, PA 16501. **Mailing Address:** P.O. Box 1776, Erie, PA 16507. **Telephone:** (814) 456-1300. **FAX:** (814) 456-7520. **E-Mail Address:** kerik@seawolves.com. **Website:** www.seawolves.com.

Affiliation (first year): Detroit Tigers (2001). **Years in League:** 1999-.

Ownership, Management

Operated by: Palisades Baseball Ltd.

Principal Owner: Alan Levin. **Executive Vice President:** Erik Haag. **Director, Finance:** Cheryl Case.

General Manager: John Frey. **Head Groundskeeper:** Pete Geddes. **Director, Marketing/Promotions:** Keri Haibach. **Director, Ticket Operations:** Mike Blackert. **Director, Group Sales:** Gary Nader. **Director, Concessions:** Mark Pirrello. **Assistant GM/Business Development:** Matt Bresee. **Ticket Sales Representatives:** Rob Magee, Becky Obradovic. **Accountant:** Bernadette Mulvihill. **Administrative Assistant:** Christine Brown.

Field Staff

Manager: Kevin Bradshaw. **Coach:** Matt Martin. **Pitching Coach:** Britt Burns. **Trainer:** Unavailable.

Game Information

Radio Announcer: Rob Bressler. **No. of Games Broadcast:** Home-71, Away-71. **Flagship Station:** WLKK 1400-AM.

PA Announcer: Dean Pepicello. **Official Scorer:** Les Caldwell.

Stadium Name (year opened): Jerry Uht Park (1995). **Location:** U.S. 79 North to East 12th Street exit, left on State Street, right on 10th Street. **Standard Game Times:** 7 p.m., (April-May) 6:30; Sun. 2.

Visiting Club Hotel: Avalon Hotel, 16 W. 10th St., Erie, PA 16501. Telephone: (814) 459-2220.

HARRISBURG
Senators

Office Address: RiverSide Stadium, City Island, Harrisburg, PA 17101. **Mailing Address**: P.O. Box 15757, Harrisburg, PA 17105. **Telephone:** (717) 231-4444. **FAX:** (717) 231-4445. **E-Mail Address:** hbgsenator@aol.com. **Website:** www.senatorsbaseball.com.

Affiliation (first year): Montreal Expos (1991). **Years in League:** 1924-35, 1987-.

Ownership, Management

Operated by: Harrisburg Civic Baseball Club, Inc.

Chairman: Greg Martini.

General Manager: Todd Vander Woude. **Assistant GM, Baseball Operations**: Mark Mattern. **Assistant GM, Business Operations:** Mark Clarke. **Director, Broadcasting/Media Relations**: Brad Sparesus. **Director, Facilities Operations**: Tim Foreman. **Director, Concessions Operations:** Steve Leininger. **Concession Manager:** Traci Kirkhoff. **Director, Ticket Sales:** Tom Wess. **Director, Group Sales:** Brian Egli. **Director, Picnic Operations:** Carol Baker. **Ticket Sales Associate:** Mark Brindle. **Turf Manager:** Ryan Schmidt.

Field Staff

Manager: Dave Machemer. **Coach:** Art Defreites. **Pitching Coach**: Charlie Corbell. **Trainer:** Rich Ramirez.

Game Information

Radio Announcers: Brad Sparesus, Mark Mattern. **No. of Games Broadcast**: Home-71, Away-71. **Flagship Station:** WKBO 1230-AM.

PA Announcer: Chris Andree. **Official Scorer**: Dave Wright.

Stadium Name (year opened): RiverSide Stadium (1987). **Location:** I-83, exit 23 (Second Street) to Market Street, bridge to City Island. **Standard Game Times:** 6:35 p.m.; Sat. 6:05; Sun. 1:05.

Visiting Club Hotel: Hilton Hotel, One N. Second St., Harrisburg, PA 17101. Telephone: (717) 233-6000.

NEW BRITAIN
Rock Cats

Office Address: 230 John Karbonic Way, New Britain, CT 06051. **Mailing Address:** P.O. Box 1718, New Britain, CT 06050. **Telephone:** (860) 224-8383. **FAX:** (860) 225-6267. **E-Mail Address:** rockcats@rockcats.com. **Website:** www.rockcats.com.

Affiliation (first year): Minnesota Twins (1995). **Years in League:** 1983-.

Ownership, Management

Operated by: New Britain Baseball, Inc.

Principal Owners: William Dowling, Coleman Levy.

Chairman: Coleman Levy.

President, General Manager: William Dowling. **Assistant GMs:** Evan Levy, John Willi. **Controller:** Paula Perdelwitz. **Director, Media Relations:** Chris McKibben. **Director, Broadcasting:** Jeff Dooley. **Director, Ticket Operations:** Peter Colon. **Senior Account Executive:** Alec Moore. **Account Executives:** Matt Person, Amy Schoch, L.J. Weslowki. **Coordinator, Stadium Operations/Home Clubhouse Manager:** Rich Grajewski. **Visiting Clubhouse Manager:** Jack Josefs.

Field Staff

Manager: Stan Cliburn. **Coach:** Riccardo Ingram. **Pitching Coach:** Stu Cliburn. **Trainer:** Tony Leo.

Game Information

Radio Announcer: Jeff Dooley, Dan Lovallo. **No. of Games Broadcast:** Home-71, Away-71. **Flagship Station:** WDRC 1360-AM (Hartford).

PA Announcer: Mark Douglas. **Official Scorer:** Bob Kirschner.

Stadium Name (year opened): New Britain Stadium (1996). **Location:** From I-84, take Route 72 East (exit 35) or Route 9 South (exit 39A), left at Ellis Street (exit 25), left at South Main Street, stadium one mile on right; From Route 91 or Route 5, take Route 9 North to Route 71 (exit 24), first exit. **Standard Game Times:** 7:05 p.m., (April-June) 6:35; Sun. 1:35.

Visiting Club Hotel: Super 8, 1 Industrial Park Rd., Cromwell, CT 06416. Telephone: (860) 632-8888.

NEW HAVEN
Ravens

Office Address: 252 Derby Ave., West Haven, CT 06516. **Telephone:** (203) 782-1666. **FAX:** (203) 782-3150. **E-Mail Address:** info@ravens.com. **Website:** www.ravens.com.

Affiliation (first year): Toronto Blue Jays (2003). **Years in League:** 1916-32, 1994-.

Ownership, Management

Operated By: New Haven Baseball, LP.

Principal Owner: Edward Massey. **President:** Shawn Smith. **Chief Executive Officer:** Drew Weber.

General Manager: Adam Schierholz. **Assistant GM, PR/Marketing:** Bob Garguilo. **Assistant GM, Finance/Accounting:** Tamara Nolin. **Assistant GM, Concessions:** Shawn Campbell. **Director, Broadcasting:** Bill Schweizer. **Director, Group Sales:** Erik Lesniak. **Director, Merchandise/Community Relations:** Kristian Velez. **Director, Tickets:** Unavailable. **Director, Website/Pressbox Operations:** Sam Rubin. **Director, Operations:** Casey Rasmussen. **Accounting Assistant:** Barbara Prato. **Groundskeeper:** Unavailable.

Field Staff

Manager: Marty Pevey. **Coach:** Ken Joyce. **Pitching Coach:** Dane Johnson. **Trainer:** Jeff Stay.

Game Information

Radio Announcer: Bill Schweizer. **No. of Games Broadcast:** Home-71, Away-71. **Flagship Station:** Unavailable.

PA Announcer: Unavailable. **Official Scorer:** Ron Vaccaro.

Stadium Name (year opened): Yale Field (1927). **Location:** From I-95, take eastbound exit 44 or westbound exit 45 to Route 10 and follow the Yale Bowl signs. From Merritt Parkway, take exit 57, follow to 34 East. **Standard Game Times:** 7:05 p.m., (April-June 6) 6:35; Sun. 1:05.

Visiting Club Hotel: Howard Johnson Inn, 2260 Whitney Ave. (Route 10), West Haven, CT 06518. Telephone: (203) 288-3831.

NORWICH
Navigators

Office Address: 14 Stott Ave., Norwich, CT 06360. **Mailing Address:** P.O. Box 6003, Yantic, CT 06389. **Telephone:** (860) 887-7962. **FAX:** (860) 886-5996. **E-Mail Address:** tater@gators.com. **Website:** www.gators.com.

Affiliation (first year): San Francisco Giants (2003). **Years in League:** 1995-.

Ownership, Management

Operated by: Minor League Sports Enterprises, LP.

Chairman: Barry Gordon. **President:** Hank Smith.

General Manager: Keith Hallal. **Assistant GM/ Director, Marketing:** Tom Hinsch. **Director, Finance:** Richard Darling. **Senior Director, Stadium Operations:** John Gilbert. **Managers, Group Sales:** Brad Favreau, Heather Proskey. **Director, Merchandise/Internet:** John Fleming. **Director, Ticket Sales:** Pat Quish. **Director, Media/Broadcasting:** Brett Quintyne. **Office Manager:** Michelle Sadowski. **Stadium Superintendent:** Chris Berube. **Head Groundskeeper:** Kyle Lewis. **Interns:** Katie Brunelle, Nikki Cisco, Alyssa Gerlando, Don Lemieux, Dan Pierce.

Field Staff

Manager: Shane Turner. **Coach:** Willie Upshaw. **Pitching Coach:** Ross Grimsley. **Trainer:** Rob Knepper.

Game Information

Radio Announcers: Brett Quintyne. **No. of Games Broadcast:** Home-71, Away-71. **Flagship Station:** Unavailable.

PA Announcer: Ed Weyant. **Official Scorer:** Gene Gumbs.

Stadium Name (year opened): Sen. Thomas J. Dodd Memorial Stadium (1995). **Location:** I-395 to exit 82, follow signs to Norwich Industrial Park, stadium is in back of industrial park. **Standard Game Times:** 7:05 p.m.; Mon., Tue., Thur. (April-May) 6:35; Wed. (April-May) 12:35; Sat. (April-May) 1:05; Sun. 1:05.

Visiting Club Hotel: Days Inn-Niantic, 265 Flanders Rd., Niantic, CT 06357. Telephone: (860) 739-6921.

PORTLAND
Sea Dogs

Office Address: 271 Park Ave., Portland, ME 04102. **Mailing Address:** P.O. Box 636, Portland, ME 04104. **Telephone:** (207) 874-9300. **FAX:** (207) 780-0317. **E-Mail Address:** seadogs@portlandseadogs.com. **Website:** www.seadogs.com.

Affiliation (first year): Boston Red Sox (2003). **Years in League:** 1994-.

Ownership, Management

Operated By: Portland, Maine Baseball, Inc.

Principal Owner, Chairman: Daniel Burke.

President, General Manager: Charles Eshbach. **Vice President/Assistant GM:** John Kameisha. **Assistant GM, Business Operations:** Jim Heffley. **Assistant GM, Sales/Marketing:** Jim Beaudoin. **Director, Promotions:** Kelli Heffley. **Director, Public Relations:** Chris Cameron. **Director, Group Sales:** Geoff Iacuessa. **Director, Group Sales:** Greg Hughes. **Director, Ticketing:** Dave Strong. **Manager, Box Office:** Jason Lemont. **Director, Food Services:** Mike Scorza. **Office Manager:** Judy Bray. **Administrative Assistants:** Aaron Donahue, Andrew Gosselin, Jason Lamantagne, Dennis Meehan, Amy Ouellette, Nancy Quinlan. **Clubhouse Managers:** Craig Candage Jr. (H), Craig Candage Sr. (H), Rick Goslin (V). **Head Groundskeeper**: Rick Anderson.

Field Staff

Manager: Ron Johnson. **Coach:** Mark Budaska. **Pitching Coach:** Bob Kipper. **Trainer:** Bryan Jaquette.

Game Information

Radio Announcers: Todd Jamison, Steve Pratt. **No. of Games Broadcast:** Home-71, Away-71. **Flagship Station:** WMTW 870-AM.

PA Announcer: Dean Rogers. **Official Scorer:** Mike Beveridge.

Stadium Name (year opened): Hadlock Field (1994). **Location:** From South, I-295 to exit 5, merge onto Congress Street, left at St. John Street, merge right onto Park Ave.; From North, I-295 to exit 6A, right onto Park Ave. **Standard Game Times:** 7 p.m., (April-May) 6; Sat. (April-May) 1, (June-Sept.) 6; Sun. 1.

Visiting Club Hotel: DoubleTree Hotel, 1230 Congress St., Portland, ME 04102. Telephone: (207) 774-5611.

READING
Phillies

Office Address: Rt. 61 South/1900 Centre Ave., Reading, PA 19601. **Mailing Address:** P.O. Box 15050, Reading, PA 19612. **Telephone:** (610) 375-8469. **FAX:** (610) 373-5868. **E-Mail Address:** info@readingphillies.com. **Website:** www.readingphillies.com.

Affiliation (first year): Philadelphia Phillies (1967). **Years in League:** 1933-35, 1952-61, 1963-65, 1967-.

Ownership, Management

Operated By: E&J Baseball Club, Inc.

Principal Owner, President: Craig Stein.

General Manager: Chuck Domino. **Assistant GM:** Scott Hunsicker. **Director, Stadium Operations/Concessions:** Andy Bortz. **Director, Maintenance/Game Staff Operations:** Troy Potthoff. **Director, Stadium Grounds:** Dan Douglas. **Office Manager:** Deneen Giesen. **Controller:** Kristyne Haver. **Director, Tickets/Ticket Operations:** Joe Pew. **Director, Merchandise:** Kevin Sklenarik. **Manager, Tickets:** Mike Becker. **Manager, Group Sales:** Bree Hagan. **Group Sales Specialists:** Ryan Bardi, Christie Chrisanthon, Mike Robinson. **Director, Communications:** Rob Hackash. **Communications Assistant:** Andy Kauffman. **Director, New Business Development:** Joe Bialek. **Director, Fan Development:** Ashley Forlini. **Coordinators, Fan Development:** Tonya Adams, Matt Jackson.

Field Staff

Manager: Greg Legg. **Coach:** John Morris. **Pitching Coach:** Rod Nichols. **Trainer:** Unavailable.

Game Information

Radio Announcer: Steve Degler. **No. of Games Broadcast:** Home-71, Away-71. **Flagship Station:** WIOV 1240-AM.

PA Announcer: Dave Bauman. **Official Scorer:** John Lemcke.

Stadium Name (year opened): FirstEnergy Stadium (1950). **Location:** From east, take Pennsylvania Turnpike West to Morgantown exit, to 176 North, to 422 West, to Route 12 East, to Route 61 South exit. From west, take 422 East to Route 12 East, to Route 61 South exit. From north, take 222 South to Route 12 exit, to Route 61 South exit. From south, take 222 North to 422 West, to Route 12 East exit at Route 61 South. **Standard Game Times:** 7:05 p.m., Mon.-Thurs. (April-May) 6:35; Sun. 1:05.

Visiting Club Hotel: Wellesley Inn, 910 Woodland Ave., Wyomissing, PA 19610. Telephone: (610) 374-1500.

TRENTON
Thunder

Office Address: One Thunder Rd., Trenton, NJ 08611. **Telephone:** (609) 394-3300. **FAX:** (609) 394-9666. **E-Mail Address:** office@trentonthunder.com. **Website:** www.trentonthunder.com.

Affiliation (first year): New York Yankees (2003). **Years in League:** 1994-.

Ownership, Management

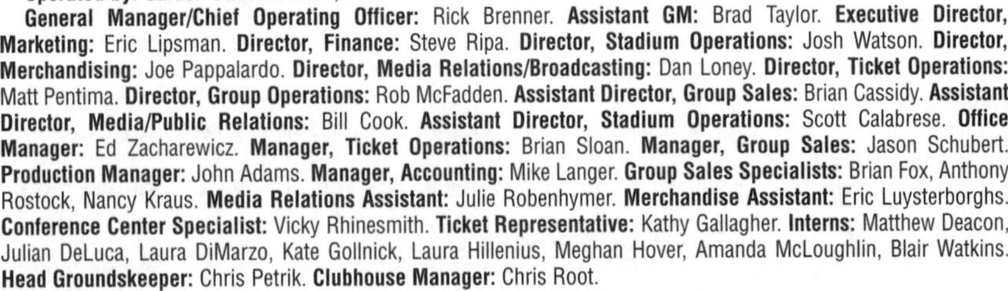

Operated by: Garden State Baseball, LLP.

General Manager/Chief Operating Officer: Rick Brenner. **Assistant GM:** Brad Taylor. **Executive Director, Marketing:** Eric Lipsman. **Director, Finance:** Steve Ripa. **Director, Stadium Operations:** Josh Watson. **Director, Merchandising:** Joe Pappalardo. **Director, Media Relations/Broadcasting:** Dan Loney. **Director, Ticket Operations:** Matt Pentima. **Director, Group Operations:** Rob McFadden. **Assistant Director, Group Sales:** Brian Cassidy. **Assistant Director, Media/Public Relations:** Bill Cook. **Assistant Director, Stadium Operations:** Scott Calabrese. **Office Manager:** Ed Zacharewicz. **Manager, Ticket Operations:** Brian Sloan. **Manager, Group Sales:** Jason Schubert. **Production Manager:** John Adams. **Manager, Accounting:** Mike Langer. **Group Sales Specialists:** Brian Fox, Anthony Rostock, Nancy Kraus. **Media Relations Assistant:** Julie Robenhymer. **Merchandise Assistant:** Eric Luysterborghs. **Conference Center Specialist:** Vicky Rhinesmith. **Ticket Representative:** Kathy Gallagher. **Interns:** Matthew Deacon, Julian DeLuca, Laura DiMarzo, Kate Gollnick, Laura Hillenius, Meghan Hover, Amanda McLoughlin, Blair Watkins. **Head Groundskeeper:** Chris Petrik. **Clubhouse Manager:** Chris Root.

Field Staff

Manager: Stump Merrill. **Coach:** Steve Braun. **Pitching Coach:** Gary Lavelle. **Trainer:** Greg Spratt.

Game Information

Radio Announcers: Dan Loney, Steve Rudensteiin. **No. of Games Broadcast:** Home-71, Away-71. **Flagship Station:** WHWH 1350-AM.

PA Announcer: Bill Bromberg. **Official Scorers:** Jay Dunn, Mike Maconi.

Stadium Name (year opened): Samuel J. Plumeri Sr. Field at Mercer County Waterfront Park (1994). **Location:** From 1-95, take Route 29 South; stadium exit just before tunnel. **Standard Game Times:** 7:05 p.m.; Sun. 1:35.

Visiting Club Hotel: McIntosh Hotel, 3270 Brunswick Pike, Lawrenceville, NJ 08648. Telephone: (609) 896-3700.

SOUTHERN LEAGUE

CLASS AA

Don Mincher

Mailing Address: 2551 Roswell Rd., Suite 330, Marietta, GA 30062. **Telephone:** (770) 321-0400. **FAX:** (770) 321-0037. **E-Mail Address:** soleague@earthlink.net. **Website:** www.southernleague.com.

Years League Active: 1964-.

President: Don Mincher.

Vice President: Steve DeSalvo. **Secretary-Treasurer:** Lori Webb.

Directors: Don Beaver (Tennessee), Peter Bragan Jr. (Jacksonville), Steve Bryant (Carolina), Frank Burke (Chattanooga), Steve DeSalvo (Greenville), Tony Ensor (Birmingham), Chuck LaMar (Orlando), Robert Lozinak (West Tenn), Miles Prentice (Huntsville), Bill Shanahan (Mobile).

Director, Administration: Lori Webb. **Director, Media Relations:** Brian Benvie.

2003 Opening Date: April 3. **Closing Date:** Sept. 1.

Regular Season: 140 games (split schedule).

Division Structure: East—Carolina, Greenville, Jacksonville, Orlando, Tennessee. **West**—Birmingham, Chattanooga, Huntsville, Mobile, West Tenn.

Playoff Format: First-half division champions play second-half division champions in best-of-5 series. Winners meet in best-of-5 series for league championship.

All-Star Game: July 8 at Jacksonville.

Roster Limit: 23 active, until midnight Aug. 10 when roster can be expanded to 24. **Player Eligibility Rule:** No restrictions.

Brand of Baseball: Rawlings.

Statistician: SportsTicker-Boston, Boston Fish Pier, West Bldg. #1, Suite 302, Boston MA 02210.

Umpires: Damien Beal (Stone Mountain, GA), Tyler Bolick (Roswell GA), Brandon Bushee (Tocsin, IL), Scot Chamberlain (Strawberry Plains, TN), Brad Cole (Sioux City, IA), Mike Estabrook (Tampa, FL), Cameron Keller (Wyoming, MI), Brian Kennedy (Greenville, NC), Scott Kennedy (Louisville, KY), Andrew Roberts (Birmingham, AL), Jamie Roebuck (Connelly Springs, NC), Ed Rogers (Thomson, GA), Jeff Spisak (Portage, MI), R.J. Thompson (Ooltewah, TN), Garrett Watson (Reno, NV), John Woods (Orlando, FL).

STADIUM INFORMATION

		Dimensions				
Club	**Stadium**	**LF**	**CF**	**RF**	**Capacity**	**2002 Att.**
Birmingham	Hoover Metropolitan	340	405	340	10,800	276,016
Carolina	Five County	330	400	330	6,500	205,812
Chattanooga	BellSouth Park	325	400	330	6,160	280,692
Greenville	Greenville Municipal	335	400	335	7,027	214,220
Huntsville	Davis Municipal	345	405	330	10,200	206,068
Jacksonville	Baseball Grounds/Jacksonville	321	420	317	11,000	230,156
Mobile	Hank Aaron	325	400	310	6,000	216,597
Orlando	Disney Complex	340	400	340	9,100	139,489
Tennessee	Smokies Park	330	400	330	6,000	268,033
West Tenn	Pringles Park	310	395	320	6,000	224,698

BIRMINGHAM
Barons

Office Address: 100 Ben Chapman Dr., Hoover, AL 35244. **Mailing Address:** P.O. Box 360007, Birmingham, AL 35236. **Telephone:** (205) 988-3200. **FAX:** (205) 988-9698. **E-Mail Address:** barons@barons.com. **Website:** www.barons.com.

Affiliation (first year): Chicago White Sox (1986). **Years in League:** 1964-65, 1967-75, 1981-.

Ownership, Management

Operated by: Elmore Sports Group, Ltd.

Principal Owner: Dave Elmore.

President, General Manager: Tony Ensor. **Assistant GM:** Jonathan Nelson. **Director, Operations:** Eric Crook. **Head Groundskeeper:** Unavailable. **Director, Broadcasting:** Curt Bloom. **Director, Media Relations:** Mike Hobson. **Director, Sales:** Martie Cordaro. **Director, Ticket Sales:** Chris Jenkins. **Director, Group Sales:** Dave Endress. **Community Event Planner:** Jim Stennett. **Director, Food Services:** Dave Gardner. **Director, Catering:** Heather Davis. **Director, Promotions:** Bill Ezrin. **Corporate Events Planners:** Michael Peppers, James Young. **Group Event Planner:** Amy Garner. **Office Manager:** Kecia Arnold. **Assistant Office Manager:** Rebecca Vickers.

Field Staff

Manager: Wally Backman. **Coach:** Gregg Ritchie. **Pitching Coach:** Juan Nieves. **Trainer:** Joe Geck.

Game Information

Radio Announcer: Curt Bloom. **No. of Games Broadcast:** Home-70, Away-70. **Flagship Station:** WYDE 101.1-FM.

PA Announcer: Unavailable. **Official Scorer:** Unavailable.

Stadium Name (year opened): Hoover Metropolitan Stadium (1988). **Location:** I-459 to Highway 150 (exit 10) in Hoover. **Standard Game Times:** 7 p.m., Wed (April-June) 11 a.m.; Sun. (April-June) 2, (July-Aug.) 6.

Visiting Club Hotel: Riverchase Inn, 1800 Riverchase Dr., Birmingham, AL 35244. Telephone: (205) 985-7500.

CAROLINA
Mudcats

Office Address: 1501 N.C. Hwy. 39, Zebulon, NC 27597. **Mailing Address:** P.O. Drawer 1218, Zebulon, NC 27597. **Telephone:** (919) 269-2287. **FAX:** (919) 269-4910. **E-Mail Address:** muddy@gomudcats.com. **Website:** www.gomudcats.com.

Affiliation (first year): Florida Marlins (2003). **Years in League:** 1991-.

Ownership, Management

Operated by: Carolina Mudcats Professional Baseball Club, Inc.

Principal Owner: Steve Bryant.

General Manager: Joe Kremer. **Assistant GM:** Eric Gardner. **Director, Broadcasting:** Patrick Kinas. **Director, Stadium Operations:** Ben Layton. **Director, Sales:** Will Barfield. **Director, Food Services:** Mike Joyner. **Director, Group Sales:** Elizabeth Henderson. **Director, Ticket Sales:** Fred Cook. **Director, Special Events:** Jonathan Jones. **Head Groundskeeper:** John Packer. **Office Manager:** Jackie DiPrimo. **Group Sales Associates:** Anna Whitehurst, Eddie Reel, Laura Bauguess, Amy Koler.

Field Staff

Manager: Tracy Woodson. **Coach:** Matt Raleigh. **Pitching Coach:** Tom Signore. **Trainer:** Gene Basham.

Game Information

Radio Announcer: Patrick Kinas. **No. of Games Broadcast:** Home-70, Away-70. **Flagship Station:** WSAY 98.5-FM.

PA Announcer: Duke Sanders. **Official Scorer:** John Hobgood.

Stadium Name (year opened): Five County Stadium (1991). **Location:** From Raleigh, U.S. 64 East to 264 East, exit at Highway 39 in Zebulon. **Standard Game Times:** 7:15 p.m.; Sun. (April-May) 2, (June-Aug.) 5.

Visiting Club Hotel: Country Inn and Suites, 2715 Capital Blvd., Raleigh, NC 27604. Telephone: (919) 872-5000.

CHATTANOOGA
Lookouts

Office Address: 201 Power Alley, Chattanooga, TN 37402. **Mailing Address:** P.O. Box 11002, Chattanooga, TN 37401. **Telephone:** (423) 267-2208. **FAX:** (423) 267-4258. **E-Mail Address:** lomktg@bellsouth.net. **Website:** www.lookouts.com.

Affiliation (first year): Cincinnati Reds (1988). **Years in League:** 1964-65, 1976-.

Ownership, Management

Operated by: Chattanooga Baseball, LLC.

Principal Owners: Daniel Burke, Frank Burke, Charles Eshbach.

President/General Manager: Frank Burke. **Assistant GM:** Brad Smith. **Director, Business Administration:** Jack Mitchell. **Director, Group Sales:** Bill Wheeler. **Director, Merchandising:** Keith Dierks. **Director, Sales/Media Relations:** John Maedel. **Director, Ticketing Operations:** Christine Vonsick-Johnson. **Director, Concessions:** Debbie Triplett. **Director, Stadium Operations:** Allen Key. **Head Groundskeeper:** Bo Henley. **Director, Special Events:** Sally Violin. **Broadcasting Assistant:** Claude Dicks.

Field Staff

Manager: Phillip Wellman. **Coaches:** Greg Grall, Alonzo Powell. **Pitching Coach:** Bill Moloney. **Trainer:** John Finley.

Game Information

Radio Announcers: Larry Ward. **No. of Games Broadcast:** Home-70, Away-70. **Flagship Station:** WDOD 1310-AM.

PA Announcer: John Maedel. **Official Scorers:** Wirt Gammon, Andy Paul

Stadium Name (year opened): BellSouth Park (2000). **Location:** From I-24, take U.S. 27 North to exit 1C (4th Street), first left onto Chestnut Street, left onto Third Street. **Standard Game Times:** 7:15 p.m.; Wed. 12:15; Sun. 2:15.

Visiting Club Hotel: Holiday Inn, 2345 Shallowford Rd., Chattanooga, TN 37412. Telephone: (423) 855-2898.

GREENVILLE
Braves

Office Address: One Braves Ave., Greenville, SC 29607. **Mailing Address:** P.O. Box 16683, Greenville, SC 29606. **Telephone:** (864) 299-3456. **FAX:** (864) 277-7369. **Website:** www.gbraves.com.

Affiliation (first year): Atlanta Braves (1984). **Years in League:** 1984-.

Ownership, Management

Operated by: Atlanta National League Baseball Club, Inc. **Principal Owner:** AOL/Time Warner. **President:** Stan Kasten.

General Manager: Steve DeSalvo. **Assistant GM:** Jim Bishop. **Director, Media/Public Relations:** Mark Hauser. **Head Groundskeeper:** Matt Taylor. **Director, Community Relations:** Brenda Yoder. **Director, Ticket Sales:** LeAnn Esmann. **Director, Food Services:** Brian Prochilo. **Office Manager:** Patti Rice.

Field Staff

Manager: Brian Snitker. **Coach:** Mel Roberts. **Pitching Coach:** Mike Alvarez. **Trainer:** Mike Graus.

Game Information

Radio Announcer: Mark Hauser. **No. of Games Broadcast:** Home-70, Away-70. **Flagship Station:** WCCP 104.9-FM.

PA Announcer: Chris Lee. **Official Scorer:** John Burton.

Stadium Name (year opened): Greenville Municipal Stadium (1984). **Location:** I-85 to exit 46 (Mauldin Road), east two miles. **Standard Game Times:** 7:15 p.m.; Sun. (April-June) 1:15, (July-Sept.) 5:15.

Visiting Club Hotel: Quality Inn, 50 Orchard Park Dr., Greenville, SC 29615. Telephone: (864) 297-9000.

HUNTSVILLE
Stars

Office Address: 3125 Leeman Ferry Rd., Huntsville, AL 35801. **Mailing Address:** P.O. Box 2769, Huntsville, AL 35804. **Telephone:** (256) 882-2562. **FAX:** (256) 880-0801. **E-Mail Address:** stars@huntsvillestars.com. **Website:** www.huntsvillestars.com.

Affiliation (first year): Milwaukee Brewers (1999). **Years In League:** 1985-.

Ownership, Management

Operated by: Huntsville Stars, LLC.

President: Miles Prentice.

General Manager: Bryan Dingo. **Assistant GM:** Clifford Pate. **Director, Broadcasting/Media Relations:** Robert Portnoy. **Director, Marketing:** Shawn Bulman. **Media Relations Assistant:** Wes Robertson. **Director, Ticketing:** Robin Bellizzi. **Director, Field Maintenance:** Andrew Wright. **Director, Stadium Operations:** Adam Davis. **Director, Food Services:** Gus Stoudemire. **Office Manager:** Earl Grilliot.

Field Staff

Manager: Frank Kremblas. **Coach:** Sandy Guerrero. **Pitching Coach:** Stan Kyles. **Trainer:** Greg Barajas.

Game Information

Radio Announcer: Robert Portnoy. **No. of Games Broadcast:** Home-70, Away-70. **Flagship Station:** WLOR 1550-AM.

PA Announcer: Todd Blass. **Official Scorer:** Don Rizzardi.

Stadium Name (year opened): Joe W. Davis Municipal Stadium (1985). **Location:** I-65 to I-565 East, south on Memorial Parkway to Drake Avenue exit, right on Don Mincher Drive. **Standard Game Times:** 7:05 p.m., Tues.-Wed. (April-June 15) 12:05; Sun. (April-June 15) 2:05, (June 22-Sept.) 6:05.

Visiting Club Hotel: La Quinta Inn, 3141 University Dr., Huntsville, AL 35805. Telephone: (256) 533-0756.

JACKSONVILLE
Suns

Mailing Address: P.O. Box 4756, Jacksonville, FL 32201. **Telephone:** (904) 358-2846. **FAX:** (904) 358-2845. **E-Mail Address:** jaxsuns@bellsouth.net. **Website:** www.jaxsuns.com.

Affiliation (first year): Los Angeles Dodgers (2002). **Years In League:** 1970-.

Ownership, Management

Operated by: Baseball Jax, Inc.

Principal Owner, President: Peter Bragan Sr. **Assistant to President:** Jerry LeMoine. **Vice President:** Bonita Bragan.

VP/General Manager: Peter Bragan Jr. **Assistant GM:** Kirk Goodman. **Director, Ticket Operations:** Karlie Evatt. **Director, Merchandise:** Andrew Squibb. **Director, Community Relations:** Tana Stavinoha. **Director, Group Sales:** Brooke Adriance. **Director, Sales/Marketing:** Mike White. **Director, Food Services:** David Leathers. **Director, Stadium Operations:** Brock Mikowski. **Manager, Food Services:** Aaron Harp. **Office Manager:** Barbara O'Berry. **Business Manager:** Craig Barnett. **Administrative Assistants:** Justin Rossi, Suzanne Stafford, Scott Taylor.

Field Staff

Manager: Dino Ebel. **Coach:** Pat Harrison. **Pitching Coach:** Marty Reed. **Trainer:** Tony Cordova.

Game Information

Radio Announcer: Joe Block. **No. of Games Broadcast:** Home-70, Away-70. **Flagship Station:** The Fox 930-AM.

PA Announcer: John Leard. **Official Scorer:** Jason Eliopulos.

Stadium Name (year opened): The Baseball Grounds of Jacksonville (2003). **Location:** I-95 North to 20th Street East exit, turn right before Alltel Stadium; I-95 South to Emerson Street exit, go right to Hart Bridge, take Sports Complex exit, left at light to stop sign, take right and quick left; From Mathews Bridge, take A. Phillip Randolph exit, straight to stadium. **Standard Game Times:** 7:05 p.m, 12:35; Sun. 3:05.

Visiting Club Hotel: Adam's Mark Jacksonville, 225 Coastline Dr., Jacksonville, FL 32202. Telephone: (904) 360-8656.

MOBILE
BayBears

Office Address: Hank Aaron Stadium, 755 Bolling Bros. Blvd., Mobile, AL 36606. **Telephone:** (251) 479-2327. **FAX:** (251) 476-1147. **E-Mail Address:** baybears@mobilebaybears.com. **Website:** www.mobilebaybears.com.

Affiliation (first year): San Diego Padres (1997). **Years in League:** 1966, 1970, 1997-.

Ownership, Management

Operated by: Cincinnati Sports Ventures.

Principal Owner: Fred Mayerson.

President/General Manager: Bill Shanahan. **Vice President/GM, Sales:** Travis Toth. **Assistant GM, Finance:** Betty Adams. **Assistant GM, Ticket Operations:** Doug Stephens. **Assistant GM, Facility Operations/Head Groundskeeper:** Pat White. **Broadcaster/Director, Media Relations:** Tom Nichols. **Director, Group Sales:** Jeff Long. **Director, Corporate Development/Sales:** Karen Cross-Blackwell. **Director, Marketing/Sales:** Kirstin Rayborn. **Sales/Telemarketing:** La Loni Taylor. **Administrative Assistant, Merchandising:** Mandy Schmitz. **Charities Coordinator/Graphic Designer:** Rebekah Robinson. **Assistant Director, Stadium Operations**: Grant Barnett. **Ticket Sales:** Nick Krause, Jason Kirksey, Jennifer Wirtz. **Media Relations**: Aaron McCreight. **Groundskeeper:** Jacob Stubbs. **Assistant, Stadium Operations:** Wade Vadakin. **Internet Liaison/Chaplain:** Lorin Barr. **Interns:** A.J. Niland, Chris Ott.

Field Staff

Manager: Craig Colbert. **Coach:** Mike Davis. **Pitching Coach:** Darren Balsley. **Trainer:** Will Sinon.

Game Information

Radio Announcer: Tom Nichols. **No. of Games Broadcast:** Home-70, Away-70. **Flagship Station:** WABB 1480-AM.

PA Announcer: Jay Hasting. **Official Scorers:** Craig Gault, Matt Smith.

Stadium Name (year opened): Hank Aaron Stadium (1997). **Location:** I-65 to exit 1A (Government Street East), right at Satchel Paige Drive, right at Bolling Bros. Boulevard. **Standard Game Time:** 7:05 p.m.

Visiting Club Hotel: Adam's Mark, 64 S. Water St., Mobile, AL 36602. Telephone: (251) 438-4000.

ORLANDO
Rays

Office Address: 700 South Victory Way, Kissimmee, FL 34747. **Mailing Address:** P.O. Box 470818, Celebration, FL 34747. **Telephone:** (407) 939-4263. **FAX:** (407) 938-3442. **Website:** www.orlandorays.com.

Affiliation (first year): Tampa Bay Devil Rays (1999). **Years in League:** 1973-.

Ownership, Management

Operated by: Orlando Rays Baseball, Inc.

Principal Owner: Tampa Bay Devil Rays, Ltd. **President, Chief Executive Officer:** Vincent Naimoli.

General Manager/Tampa Bay: Mitch Lukevics. **Assistant GM/Disney Liaison:** Kevin Reynolds. **Manager, Stadium Operations:** Dwight Door. **Coordinator, Stadium Operations:** Vinny O'Leary. **Manager, Media/Public Relations:** Brian Fling. **Media/Public Relations Intern:** Bill Mayville. **Promotions Representative:** Katherine Wu. **Sponsorship Representatives:** Michael Benn, Doug McDonald. **Sales Managers:** Amy Atchison, Michael Crawford, Brian Fling, Rick Morris, Scott St. George, Pablo Tirado. **Manager, Box Office:** Dayla Foster. **Manager, Entertainment:** Cary Brandt. **Manager, Marketing:** Courtney Ware. **Sales Intern:** Amanda Sinclair.

Field Staff

Manager: Charlie Montoyo. **Coach:** Skeeter Barnes. **Pitching Coach:** Dick Bosman. **Trainer:** Matt Lucero.

Game Information

Radio: None.

PA Announcer: Unavailable. **Official Scorer:** Unavailable.

Stadium Name (year opened): Disney's Wide World of Sports Complex (1997). **Location:** I-4 to Osceola Parkway (exit 65), left at Victory Way. **Standard Game Time:** 7:05 p.m.

Visiting Club Hotel: La Quinta at Lakeside, 7769 W. Irlo Bronson Memorial Hwy., Kissimmee, FL 34747. Telephone: (407) 396-2222.

TENNESSEE
Smokies

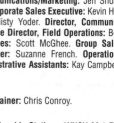

Office Address: 3540 Line Dr., Kodak, TN 37764. **Telephone:** (865) 286-2300. **FAX:** (865) 523-9913. **E-Mail Address:** info@smokiesbaseball.com. **Website:** www.smokiesbaseball.com.

Affiliation (first year): St. Louis Cardinals (2003). **Years in League:** 1964-67, 1972-.

Ownership, Management

Operated by: SPBC, LLC.

President: Doug Kirchhofer.

General Manager: Brian Cox. **Assistant GM:** Mark Seaman. **Director, Communications/Marketing:** Jeff Shoaf. **Director, Broadcasting/Media Relations:** Tom Hart. **Director, Sales:** Jon Zeitz. **Corporate Sales Executive:** Kevin Hill. **Director, Stadium Operations:** Brian Webster. **Director, Ticket Operations:** Misty Yoder. **Director, Community Relations:** Lauren Chesney. **Director, Field Operations:** Ross D'Lugos. **Assistance Director, Field Operations:** Bob Shoemaker. **Director, Group Sales:** Jon Kuka. **Assistant Director, Group Sales:** Scott McGhee. **Group Sales Representatives:** Gabe Bowden, Tom Luebbe, Keli Mayes. **Business Manager:** Suzanne French. **Operations Assistants:** Jason Adzigian, Aaron Anderson, Bryce Patton, Chris Strunk. **Administrative Assistants:** Kay Campbell, Tolena Trout.

Field Staff

Manager: Mark DeJohn. **Coach:** Steve Balboni. **Pitching Coach:** Blaise Ilsley. **Trainer:** Chris Conroy.

Game Information

Radio Announcer: Tom Hart. **No. of Games Broadcast:** Home-70, Away-70. **Flagship Stations:** WNOX 99.1-FM, WSEV 105.5-FM.

PA Announcer: George Yardley. **Official Scorers:** Paul Barger, Randy Corrado.

Stadium Name (year opened): Smokies Park (2000). **Location:** I-40 to exit 407, Highway 66 North. **Standard Game Times:** 7:15 p.m., Sun. 5.

Visiting Club Hotel: Days Inn-Exit 407, 3402 Winfield Dunn Pkwy., Kodak TN 37764. Telephone: (865) 933-4500.

WEST TENN
Diamond Jaxx

Office Address: 4 Fun Place, Jackson, TN 38305. **Telephone:** (731) 988-5299. **FAX:** (731) 988-5246. **E-Mail Address:** fun@diamondjaxx.com. **Website:** www.diamondjaxx.com.

Affiliation (first year): Chicago Cubs (1998). **Years in League:** 1998-.

Ownership, Management

Operated by: Lozinak Baseball Properties, LLC.

General Manager: Jeff Parker. **Stadium Operations/Season Tickets:** Brian Burbage. **Director, Broadcasting/Media Relations:** Ron Potesta. **Director, Sales/Marketing:** Rick Perry. **Manager, Ticketing/Merchandise:** Jason Compton. **Director, Community Relations/Publications:** Craig Stephen. **Group/Corporate Sales Associates:** Dave Jojola, John Payne. **Administrative Assistant:** Jackie Nelson. **Head Groundskeeper:** Justin Spillman. **Director, Food Services:** Unavailable. **Clubhouse Manager:** Curtis Cooksey.

Field Staff

Manager: Bobby Dickerson. **Coach:** Von Joshua. **Pitching Coach:** Alan Dunn. **Trainer:** Justin Sharpe.

Game Information

Radio Announcer: Ron Potesta. **No. of Games Broadcast:** Home-70, Away-70. **Flagship Station:** Unavailable.

PA Announcer: Unavailable. **Official Scorer:** Jason Patterson.

Stadium Name (year opened): Pringles Park (1998). **Location:** From I-40, take exit 85 South to F.E. Wright Drive, left onto Ridgecrest Extended. **Standard Game Times:** 7:35 p.m., (April-May) 6:35; Sun. 2:05.

Visiting Club Hotel: Garden Plaza Hotel, 1770 Hwy. 45 Bypass, Jackson, TN 38305. Telephone: (731) 664-6900.

TEXAS LEAGUE

CLASS AA

Mailing Address: 2442 Facet Oak, San Antonio, TX 78232. **Telephone:** (210) 545-5297. **FAX:** (210) 545-5298. **E-Mail Address:** tkayser@iamerica.net. **Website:** www.texas-league.com.

TEXAS LEAGUE™ OF PROFESSIONAL BASEBALL CLUBS

Years League Active: 1888-1890, 1892, 1895-1899, 1902-1942, 1946-.

President, Treasurer: Tom Kayser.

Vice President: Monty Hoppel. **Corporate Secretary:** Steve Shaad. **Administrative Assistant:** Eric Doennig.

Directors: Bobby Brett (El Paso), Chuck Lamson (Tulsa), Jay Miller (Round Rock), Miles Prentice (Midland), Steve Shaad (Wichita), Hank Stickney (Frisco), Bill Valentine (Arkansas), Burl Yarbrough (San Antonio).

Tom Kayser

2003 Opening Date: April 3. **Closing Date:** Aug. 31.

Regular Season: 140 games (split schedule).

Division Structure: East—Arkansas, Frisco, Tulsa, Wichita. **West**—El Paso, Midland, Round Rock, San Antonio.

Playoff Format: First-half division champions play second-half division champions in best-of-5 series. Winners meet in best-of-7 series for league championship.

All-Star Game: June 16 at Wichita.

Roster Limit: 23 active, except during the first 30 days of the season and from midnight Aug. 10, when roster can be expanded to 24. **Player Eligibility Rule:** No restrictions.

Brand of Baseball: Rawlings.

Statistician: SportsTicker-Boston, Boston Fish Pier, West Bldg. #1, Suite 302, Boston, MA 02210.

Umpires: Angel Campos (Ontario, CA), Ben Clanton (Nesbit, MS), Delfin Colon (Houston, TX), Peter Durfee (Tucson, AZ), Chad Galloway (Roanoke, AL), Ray Gregson (River Ridge, LA), Jason Kiser (Paris, MO), Cale Smith (Kenmore, WA), Todd Tichenor (Holcomb, KS), Hitoshi Uchikawa (Osaka, Japan), A.J. Wendel (Carrollton, TX).

STADIUM INFORMATION

		Dimensions				
Club	**Stadium**	**LF**	**CF**	**RF**	**Capacity**	**2002 Att.**
Arkansas	Ray Winder Field	330	390	345	6,083	192,237
El Paso	Cohen	340	410	340	9,725	234,971
*Frisco	Dr Pepper/Seven-Up Ballpark	330	410	322	10,000	24,560
Midland	First America Bank Ballpark	330	410	322	6,669	276,380
Round Rock	The Dell Diamond	330	400	325	10,000	670,176
San Antonio	Nelson Wolff Municipal	310	402	340	6,200	316,983
Tulsa	Drillers	335	390	340	11,003	306,705
Wichita	Lawrence-Dumont	344	401	312	6,055	142,265

*Club operated in Shreveport in 2002

ARKANSAS
Travelers

Office Address: Ray Winder Field at War Memorial Park, Little Rock, AR 72205. **Mailing Address:** P.O. Box 55066, Little Rock, AR 72215. **Telephone:** (501) 664-1555. **FAX:** (501) 664-1834. **E-Mail Address:** travs@travs.com. **Website:** www.travs.com.

Affiliation (first year): Anaheim Angels (2001). **Years In League:** 1966-.

Ownership/Management

Operated by: Arkansas Travelers Baseball Club, Inc.

President: Bert Parke.

Executive Vice President, General Manager: Bill Valentine. **Assistant GM:** Hap Seliga. **Assistant GM, Concessions:** Pete Laven. **Director, Stadium Operations:** George Reynolds. **Director, Media Relations/Broadcasting:** Phil Elson. **Office Manager:** Annie Bahr. **Park Superintendent:** Greg Johnston. **Assistant Park Superintendent:** Reggie Temple. **Bookkeeper:** Nena Valentine.

Field Staff

Manager: Tyrone Boykin. **Coach:** Wes Clements. **Pitching Coach:** Keith Comstock. **Trainer:** Jamie Welch.

Game Information

Radio Announcer: Phil Elson. **No. of Games Broadcast:** Home-70, Away-70. **Flagship Station:** KDRE 101.1-FM

PA Announcer: Bill Downs. **Official Scorers:** Tim Cooper.

Stadium Name (year opened): Ray Winder Field (1932). **Location:** I-630 to Fair Park Boulevard exit, north off exit, right after zoo. **Standard Game Times:** 7:10 p.m., 6:30 DH; Sun. 2.

Visiting Club Hotel: La Quinta Inn, 4100 East McCain Blvd. North Little Rock, AR 72117. Telephone: (501) 945-0808.

EL PASO
Diablos

Office Address: 9700 Gateway North Blvd., El Paso, TX 79924. **Telephone:** (915) 755-2000. **FAX:** (915) 757-0671. **E-Mail Address:** awheeler@diablos.com. **Website:** www.diablos.com.

Affiliation (first year): Arizona Diamondbacks (1999). **Years in League:** 1962-70, 1972-.

Ownership, Management

Operated by: Brett Sports.

Principal Owners: Bobby Brett, Peter Gray, Bill Pereira.

Vice President, General Manager: Andrew Wheeler. **Vice President, Sales/Marketing:** Ken Schrom. **Director, Ticket Sales:** Angela Martinez. **Manager, Group Sales:** Manuel Gomez. **Manager, Box Office:** Tina Arrambide. **Director, Broadcasting:** Matt Hicks. **Controller:** Melissa Wachter. **Head Groundskeeper:** Tony Lee. **Assistant Operations Director/Manager, Merchandise:** Heather Smith. **Director, Stadium Operations:** Jimmy Hicks. **Director, Spanish Broadcasting:** Miguel Flores. **Public Relations/Account Executive:** Brett Pollock. **Coordinator, Promotions:** Kathy Sarver. **Account Representatives:** Miguel Flores, Matt Hicks, Bernie Ricono.

Field Staff

Manager: Scott Coolbaugh. **Coaches:** Lorenzo Bundy. **Pitching Coach:** Claude Osteen. **Trainer:** Roger Fleming.

Game Information

Radio Announcers: Matt Hicks, Brett Pollock (English); Miguel Flores (Spanish). **No. of Games Broadcast:** Home-70, Away-70. **Flagship Station:** KHEY 1380-AM (English), KAMA 750-AM (Spanish).

PA Announcer: Unavailable. **Official Scorer:** Bernie Olivas.

Stadium Name (year opened): Cohen Stadium (1990). **Location:** I-10 to U.S. 54 (Patriot Freeway), east to Diana exit to Gateway North Boulevard. **Standard Game Time:** 6:30 p.m.

Visiting Club Hotel: Best Western Airport Inn, 7144 Gateway Blvd. E., El Paso, TX 79915. Telephone: (915) 779-7700.

FRISCO
RoughRiders

Office Address: 7725 Gaylord Pkwy., Frisco, TX 75034. **Telephone:** (972) 731-9200. **FAX:** (972-731-7455). **E-Mail Address:** info@ridersbaseball.com. **Website:** www.ridersbaseball.com.

Affiliation (first year): Texas Rangers (2003). **Years in League:** 2003-.

Ownership, Management

Operated by: Mandalay Sports Entertainment.

Principal Owners: Mandalay Sports Entertainment, Southwest Sports Group.

President, General Manager: Mike McCall. **Senior VP, Sponsorships:** Kevin Rochlitz. **VP, Marketing:** Lynn Wittenburg. **VP, Ticket Sales:** Matt Cornell. **VP, Communications:** Shellie Johnson. **VP, Development:** Dennis Burbank. **VP, Stadium Operations:** Mike deMaine. **Director, Group Sales:** Marcia Steinberg. **Director, Finance:** Sally Morris. **Director, Customer Service:** Marty Whitaker. **Director, Special Projects:** Rebecca King. **Sponsor Service Managers:** Tara Bent, Jennifer Livingston. **Managers, Corporate Marketing:** Michael Byrnes, Flavil Hampsten, Steve Hobbs, Miles McCune, Will Rhodes, Susan Scott. **Customer Account Managers:** Shannon Agnew, Carrie Caldwell, Neil Carey. **Receptionist:** Jennifer Jimenez. **Head Groundskeeper:** Blake Shinn. **Director, Broadcasting:** Unavailable. **Executive Assistant to President:** Jennifer Lavery.

Field Staff

Manager: Tim Ireland. **Coach:** Paul Carey. **Pitching Coach:** Steve Luebber. **Trainer:** Unavailable.

Game Information

Radio Announcer: Unavailable. **No. of Games Broadcast:** Home-70, Away-70. **Radio Station:** KBTK 1700-AM.

PA Announcer: Unavailable. **Official Scorer:** Unavailable.

Stadium Name (year opened): Dr. Pepper/Seven-Up Ballpark (2003). **Location:** Dallas North Tollway to State Highway 121. **Standard Game Times:** 7 p.m.; Fri.-Sat. 7:30; Sun. (April-May) 2, (June-Aug.) 6.

Visiting Club Hotel: Hampton Inn & Suites, 3199 Parkwood Blvd., Frisco, TX 75034. Telephone: (972) 712-8400.

MIDLAND
RockHounds

Office Address: 5514 Champions Dr., Midland, TX 79706. **Mailing Address:** P.O. Box 9580, Midland, TX 79708. **Telephone:** (915) 520-2255. **FAX:** (915) 520-8326. **Website:** www.midlandrockhounds.org.

Affiliation (first year): Oakland Athletics (1999). **Years in League:** 1972-.

Ownership, Management

Operated By: Midland Sports, Inc.

Principal Owners: Miles Prentice, Bob Richmond.

President: Miles Prentice. **Executive Vice President:** Bob Richmond.

General Manager: Monty Hoppel. **Assistant GM:** Jeff VonHolle. **Assistant GM, Marketing/Tickets:** Jamie Richardson. **Assistant GM, Corporate Sales:** Harold Fuller. **Director, Broadcasting/Publications:** Bob Hards. **Director, Advertising:** Erick Chapman. **Executive Director, Midland Concessions:** Dave Baur. **Concessions Assistant:** Edwin White. **Director, Merchandising/Manager, Stadium Facilities:** Ray Fieldhouse. **Director, Business Operations:** Eloisa Galvan. **Manager, Season Ticket Sales:** Kevin Smith. **Director, Group Sales:** Bob Flannery. **Box Office Ticket Manager:** Stacy Fielding. **Director, Team Operations:** Joe Harrell. **Head Groundskeeper:** Monty Sowell. **Administrative Assistant:** Brittney Holum.

Field Staff

Manager: Greg Sparks. **Coach:** Dave Joppie. **Pitching Coach:** Craig Lefferts. **Trainer:** Brian Thorson.

Game Information

Radio Announcer: Bob Hards. **No. of Games Broadcast:** Home-70, Away-70. **Flagship Station:** KCRS 550-AM.

PA Announcer: Ace O'Connel. **Official Scorer:** Bobby Dunn.

Stadium Name (year opened): First American Bank Ballpark (2002). **Location:** From I-20, exit Loop 250 North to intersection with Highway. 191. **Standard Game Times:** 7 p.m.; Sunday (April-May) 2, (June-Aug.) 6.

Visiting Club Hotel: Holiday Inn Hotel and Suites, 4300 W. Hwy. 80, Midland, TX 79703. Telephone: (915) 697-3181.

ROUND ROCK
Express

Office Address: 3400 Palm Valley Blvd., Round Rock, TX 78664. **Mailing Address:** P.O. Box 5309, Round Rock, TX 78683. **Telephone:** (512) 255-2255. **FAX:** (512) 255-1558. **E-Mail Address:** info@rrexpress.com. **Website:** www.roundrockexpress.com.

Affiliation (first year): Houston Astros (2000). **Years in League:** 2000-.

Ownership, Management

Operated by: Round Rock Baseball, Inc.

Principal Owners: Rich Hollander, Eddie Maloney, J. Con Maloney, Nolan Ryan, Reid Ryan, Don Sanders.

Chairman, President: Reid Ryan.

Vice President, General Manager: Jay Miller. **Chief Financial Officer:** Reese Ryan. **Assistant GM, Sales/Marketing:** Dave Fendrick. **Controller:** Debbie Coughlin. **Assistant GM, Promotions/Stadium Entertainment:** Derrick Grubbs. **Assistant GM, Media/Public Relations:** J.J. Gottsch. **Director, Merchandising:** Sue Denny. **Director, Ticket Operations:** Ross Scott. **Director, United Heritage Center:** Scott Allen. **Assistant Director, United Heritage Center:** Laura Whatley. **Director, Community Relations:** Elisa Macias. **Director, Group Sales:** Henry Green. **Director, Sales:** Gary Franke. **Director, Customer Relations:** George Smith. **Account Executives:** Clint Bell, LaBaron Graham, Jillian Purdue. **Receptionist:** Wendy Gordon. **Head Groundskeeper:** Dennis Klein. **Director, Broadcasting:** Mike Capps. **Clubhouse Manager:** Unavailable.

Field Staff

Manager: Jackie Moore. **Coaches:** Spike Owen, Sean Berry. **Pitching Coach:** Joe Slusarski. **Trainer:** Unavailable.

Game Information

Radio Announcer: Mike Capps. **No. of Games Broadcast:** Home-70, Away-70. **Flagship Station:** 107.7-FM The End.

PA Announcer: Derrick Grubbs. **Official Scorer:** Mike Hemker.

Stadium Name (year opened): The Dell Diamond (2000). **Location:** I-35 North to exit 253 (Hwy. 79 East/Taylor), stadium on left approx. 3½ miles. **Standard Game Times:** 7:05 p.m.; Sun. (April-May) 2:05, (June-Sept.) 6:05.

Visiting Club Hotel: Hilton Garden Inn, 2310 N. IH-35, Round Rock, TX 78681. Telephone: (512) 341-8200.

SAN ANTONIO
Missions

Office Address: 5757 Hwy. 90 W., San Antonio, TX 78227. **Telephone:** (210) 675-7275. **FAX:** (210) 670-0001. **E-Mail Address:** missionspr@samissions.com. **Website:** www.samissions.com.

Affiliation (third year): Seattle Mariners (2001). **Years In League:** 1888, 1892, 1895-99, 1907-42, 1946-64, 1968-.

Ownership, Management

Operated by: Elmore Sports Group.

Principal Owner: Dave Elmore.

President, General Manager: Burl Yarbrough. **Assistant GMs:** Jeff Long, Jeff Windle. **Controller:** John Sharp. **Stadium Manager:** Tom McAfee. **Director, Media Relations:** Woody Hinkel. **Community Relations:** Wesley Ratliff. **Manager, Group Sales:** Bill Gerlt. **Coordinator, Group Sales:** Mac Brown. **Director, Ticket Operations:** Russell Stehling. **Director, Season Ticket Sales:** Charles Smith. **Director, Broadcasting:** Roy Acuff. **Account Executives:** Mickey Holt, Andy Peal. **President, Diamond Concessions:** Doug Campbell. **Office Manager:** Delia Rodriguez. **Merchandising:** Karen Sada. **Clubhouse Operations:** Matt Martinez (home), Jim Vasaldua (visitors).

Field Staff

Manager: Dave Brundage. **Coach:** Terry Pollreisz. **Pitching Coach:** Rafael Chaves. **Trainer:** Chris Gorosics.

Game Information

Radio Announcers: Roy Acuff. **No. of Games Broadcast:** Home-70, Away-70. **Flagship Station:** KKYX 680-AM.

PA Announcer: Stan Kelly. **Official Scorer:** David Humphrey.

Stadium Name (year opened): Nelson W. Wolff Municipal Stadium (1994). **Location:** From I-10, I-35 or I-37, take U.S. 90 West to Callaghan Road exit, stadium is on right. **Standard Game Times:** 7:05 p.m.; Sun. 6:05.

Visiting Club Hotel: Unavailable.

TULSA
Drillers

Office Address: 4802 E. 15th St., Tulsa, OK 74112. **Telephone:** (918) 744-5998. **FAX:** (918) 747-3267. **E-Mail Address:** mail@tulsadrillers.com. **Website:** www.tulsadrillers.com.

Affiliation (first year): Colorado Rockies (2003). **Years in League:** 1933-42, 1946-65, 1977-.

Ownership, Management

Operated by: Tulsa Baseball, Inc.

Principal Owner, President: Went Hubbard.

Executive Vice President, General Manager: Chuck Lamson. **Assistant GM:** Mike Melega. **Bookkeeper:** Cheryll Couey. **Office Manager:** D.D. Bristol. **Director, Promotions/Merchandise:** Jason George. **Director, Ticket Sales:** Belinda Shepherd. **Director, Public Relations:** Brian Carroll. **Director, Stadium Operations/Group Sales:** Mark Hilliard. **Head Groundskeeper:** Gary Shepherd. **Corporate Sales Associate:** Seth Alberg. **Assistant Director, Group Ticket Sales/Promotions:** Brian Worsham. **Assistant Director, Ticket Sales:** Valerie Cain. **Assistant Director, Operations:** Cary Stidham.

Field Staff

Manager: Marv Foley. **Coach:** Theron Todd. **Pitching Coach:** Bo McLaughlin. **Trainer:** Jeremy Moeller.

Game Information

Radio Announcer: Mark Neely. **No. of Games Broadcast:** Home-70, Away-70. **Flagship Station:** KAKC 1300-AM.

PA Announcer: Kirk McAnany. **Official Scorers:** Bruce Howard, Larry Lewis.

Stadium Name (year opened): Drillers Stadium (1981). **Location:** Three miles north of I-44 and 1½ miles south of I-244 at 15th Street and Yale Avenue. **Standard Game Times:** 7:05 p.m.; Sun. (April-June) 2:05, (July-Aug.) 6:05.

Visiting Club Hotel: Hampton Inn, 3209 S. 79th E. Ave., Tulsa, OK 74145. Telephone: (918) 663-1000.

WICHITA
Wranglers

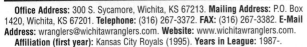

Office Address: 300 S. Sycamore, Wichita, KS 67213. **Mailing Address:** P.O. Box 1420, Wichita, KS 67201. **Telephone:** (316) 267-3372. **FAX:** (316) 267-3382. **E-Mail Address:** wranglers@wichitawranglers.com. **Website:** www.wichitawranglers.com.

Affiliation (first year): Kansas City Royals (1995). **Years in League:** 1987-.

Ownership, Management

Operated by: Wichita Baseball, Inc. **Principal Owner:** Rich Products Corp.

Chairman: Robert Rich Sr. **President:** Robert Rich Jr. **Executive Vice President:** Melinda Rich.

VP/General Manager, National Baseball Congress: Steve Shaad. **Assistant GM/Director, Sales and Marketing:** Kyle Ebers. **Assistant GM, Stadium/Baseball Operations:** Josh Robertson. **Director, Business Operations:** Tobin Acebedo. **Manager, Marketing:** Matt Rogers. **Assistant, Media Relations/Marketing:** Staci Flinchbaugh. **Senior Account Executive/Coordinator, Sponsorship, Advertising and Promotions:** Tim Frasco. **Senior Account Executive/Group Sales Coordinator:** Craig Jenkins. **Senior Account Executive, Ticket/SAP Sales:** Robert Slaughter. **Business Manager:** Mary Luce. **Ticket Manager:** Stephanie White. **Associate, Baseball/Stadium Operations:** Mike Quick. **Gameday Operations/Coordinator, Merchandise:** Ryanne Rogers.

Field Staff

Manager: Keith Bodie. **Coach:** Nelson Liriano. **Pitching Coach:** Larry Carter. **Trainer:** Trent Stratton.

Game Information

Radio Announcers: Rick Page, Brian Goldberg. **No. of Games Broadcast:** Home-68, Away-72. **Flagship Station:** WKME 93.5-FM.

PA Announcer: Scott Stocki. **Official Scorer:** Ted Woodward.

Stadium Name (year opened): Lawrence-Dumont Stadium (1934). **Location:** I-35 to Kellogg Avenue West, north on Broadway, west on Lewis. **Standard Game Times:** 7 p.m.; Sun. (April-May) 2, (June-August) 6.

Visiting Club Hotel: La Quinta, 7700 E. Kellogg, Wichita, KS 67207. Telephone: (316) 681-2881.

CALIFORNIA LEAGUE

CLASS A ADVANCED

Office Address: 2380 S. Bascom Ave., Suite 200, Campbell, CA 95008. **Telephone:** (408) 369-8038. **FAX:** (408) 369-1409. **E-Mail Address:** cabaseball@aol.com. **Website:** www.californialeague.com.

Joe Gagliardi

Years League Active: 1941-1942, 1946-.

President/Treasurer: Joe Gagliardi.

Vice President: Mike Ellis (Lancaster). **Corporate Secretary/League Historian:** Bill Weiss.

Directors: Bobby Brett (High Desert), Chris Chen (Modesto), Mike Ellis (Lancaster), Gary Jacobs (Lake Elsinore), Jack Patton (Bakersfield), Tom Seidler (Visalia), Harry Stavrenos (San Jose), Hank Stickney (Rancho Cucamonga), Donna Tuttle (Inland Empire), Tom Volpe (Stockton).

Director, Marketing: Pete Thureson. **League Administrator:** Kathleen Kelly. **Director, Umpire Development:** John Oldham.

2003 Opening Date: April 3. **Closing Date:** Sept. 1.

Regular Season: 140 games (split schedule).

Division Structure: North—Bakersfield, Modesto, San Jose, Stockton, Visalia. **South**—High Desert, Lake Elsinore, Lancaster, Rancho Cucamonga, San Bernardino.

Playoff Format: Six teams. First-half champions in each division earn first-round bye; second-half champions meet wild card with next best overall record in best-of-3 quarterfinals. Winners meet first-half champions in best-of-5 semifinals. Winners meet in best-of-5 series for league championship.

All-Star Game: June 24 at Rancho Cucamonga (California League vs. Carolina League).

Roster Limit: 25 active. **Player Eligibility Rule:** No more than two players and one player-coach on active list may have more than six years experience.

Brand of Baseball: Rawlings ROM-CAL.

Statistician: Howe Sportsdata, Boston Fish Pier, West Bldg. #1, Suite 302, Boston MA 02210; P.O. Box 5061, San Mateo, CA 94402.

Umpires: John Brammer (Marlow, OK), Chris Griffith (Fort Worth, TX), Robert Hansen (Aberdeen, SD), Jeffrey Latter (Lincoln, NE), Brandon Leopoldus (Colorado Springs, CO), Thadd Prince (Lafayette, LA), Jason Stein (Arlington, TX), Arthur Stewart (Frankport, IL), Jacob Uhlenhopp (Nevada, IA), Todd Waters (Coppell, TX).

STADIUM INFORMATION

		Dimensions				
Club	**Stadium**	**LF**	**CF**	**RF**	**Capacity**	**2002 Att.**
Bakersfield	Sam Lynn Ballpark	328	354	328	4,200	101,377
High Desert	Mavericks	340	401	340	3,808	139,348
*Inland Empire	Arrowhead Credit Union	330	410	330	5,000	222,881
Lake Elsinore	The Diamond	330	400	310	7,866	230,957
Lancaster	Lancaster Municipal	350	410	350	4,500	181,007
Modesto	Thurman Field	312	400	319	4,000	155,171
R. Cucamonga	Epicenter	335	400	335	6,615	293,150
San Jose	Municipal	340	390	340	4,000	154,322
Stockton	Billy Hebert Field	325	392	335	3,500	71,333
Visalia	Recreation Park	320	405	320	1,647	58,734

*Team known as San Bernardino in 2002

BAKERSFIELD
Blaze

Office Address: 4009 Chester Ave., Bakersfield, CA 93301. **Mailing Address:** P.O. Box 10031, Bakersfield, CA 93389. **Telephone:** (661) 322-1363. **FAX:** (661) 322-6199. **E-Mail Address:** blaze1@bakersfieldblaze.com. **Website:** www.bakersfield-blaze.com.

Affiliation: Tampa Bay Devil Rays (2001). **Years In League:** 1941-42, 1946-75, 1978-79, 1982-.

Ownership, Management

Principal Owner/President: Pat Patton.

Vice President, General Manager: Jack Patton. **Assistant GMs:** Brian Thomas, Susan Wells. **Director, Baseball Operations:** Joe Foye. **Head Groundskeeper:** Leon Williams. **Director, Community Relations:** Paul Sheldon. **Director, Special Projects:** Cricket Whitaker. **Office Manager:** Rev. Seve Niron. **Director, Radio Broadcasting:** Mark Roberts.

Field Staff

Manager: Omer Munoz. **Coach:** Ramon Ortiz. **Pitching Coach:** Marty DeMerritt. **Trainer:** Chris Tomashoff.

Game Information

Radio Announcers: Mark Roberts, Brian Thomas. **No. of Games Broadcast:** Home-70, Away-70. **Flagship Station:** KGEO 1230-AM.

PA Announcer: John Bryan. **Official Scorer:** Tim Wheeler.

Stadium Name (year opened): Sam Lynn Ballpark (1941). **Location:** Highway 99 to California Avenue, east three miles to Chester Avenue, north two miles to stadium. **Standard Game Time:** 7:15 p.m.

Visiting Club Hotel: Unavailable.

HIGH DESERT
Mavericks

Office Address: 12000 Stadium Way, Adelanto, CA 92301. **Telephone:** (760) 246-6287. **FAX:** (760) 246-3197. **E-Mail Address:** mavsinfo@hdmavs.com. **Website:** www.hdmavs.com.

Affiliation (first year): Milwaukee Brewers (2001). **Years in League:** 1991-.

Ownership, Management

Operated by: High Desert Mavericks, Inc.

Principal Owner: Bobby Brett. **President:** Andy Billig.

General Manager/Vice President: Brent Miles. **Director, Season Tickets:** Annie Montgomery. **Director, Group Tickets:** S.P. Manson. **Account Executive:** Kary Wallace. **Director, Sponsorships:** Bruce Mann. **Director, Broadcasting:** Mike Lindskog. **Office Manager:** Robin Buckles. **Head Groundskeeper:** Tino Gonzales. **Clubhouse Manager:** Unavailable.

Field Staff

Manager: Tim Blackwell. **Coach:** Rich Morales. **Pitching Coach:** Bill Champion. **Trainer:** Matt Toth.

Game Information

Radio Announcer: Mike Lindskog. **No. of Games Broadcast:** Home-70, Away-70. **Flagship Station:** KRAK 910-AM.

PA Announcer: Unavailable. **Official Scorer:** Jack Tucker.

Stadium Name (year opened): Mavericks Stadium (1991). **Location:** I-15 North to Highway 395 to Adelanto Road. **Standard Game Times:** 7:05 p.m.; Sun. (April-May) 3:05, (June-Aug.) 5:05.

Visiting Club Hotel: Red Roof Inn-Victorville, 13409 Mariposa Rd., Victorville, CA 92392. Telephone: (760) 241-1577.

INLAND EMPIRE
66ers

Office Address: 280 South E St., San Bernardino, CA 92401. **Telephone:** (909) 888-9922. **FAX:** (909) 888-5251. **E-Mail Address:** mail@ie66ers.com. **Website:** www.ie66ers.com.

Affiliation (first year): Seattle Mariners (2001). **Years in League:** 1941, 1987-.

Ownership, Management

Operated by: Inland Empire 66ers Baseball Club of San Bernardino.

Principal Owners: David Elmore, Donna Tuttle.

President/General Manager: Dave Oldham. **Assistant GM:** Paul Stiritz. **Chief Financial Officer:** Brett Tyndale. **Director, Broadcasting:** Mike Saeger. **Director, Special Events**: Seneca Manzo. **Director, Food and Beverage/Stadium Manager**: Joe Henderson. **Assistant Stadium Manager**: Cody Hutchins. **Director, Ticketing:** Mitchell Sadowsky. **Director, Corporate Communications:** Laura Tolbirt. **Manager, Corporate Sales:** Rob Kasprzyk. **Director, Community Relations:** Danielle Harsh. **Account Executives:** Ryan English, Steve James, Ryan Seeberg. **Receptionist:** Unavailable. **Head Groundskeeper:** Jessie Sandoval.

Field Staff

Manager: Steve Roadcap . **Coach:** Henry Cotto. **Pitching Coach:** Scott Budner. **Trainer:** Nathan Peck.

Game Information

Radio Announcer: Mike Saeger. **No. of Games Broadcast:** Unavailable. **Flagship Stations:** KVCR 91.9-FM.

PA Announcer: J.J. Gould. **Official Scorer:** Unavailable.

Stadium Name (year opened): Arrowhead Credit Union Park (1996). **Location:** From south, I-215 to 2nd Street exit, east on 2nd, right on G Street. From north, I-215 to 3rd Street exit, left on Rialto, right on G Street. **Standard Game Times:** 7:05 p.m.; Sun. (April-May) 2:05, (June-Aug.) 6:05.

Visiting Club Hotel: Radisson Hotel, 295 North E St., San Bernardino, CA 92401. Telephone: (909) 381-6181.

LAKE ELSINORE
Storm

Office Address: 500 Diamond Dr., Lake Elsinore, CA 92530. **Mailing Address:** P.O. Box 535, Lake Elsinore, CA 92531. **Telephone:** (909) 245-4487. **FAX:** (909) 245-0305. **E-Mail Address:** info@stormbaseball.com. **Website:** www.stormbaseball.com.

Affiliation (first year): San Diego Padres (2001). **Years in League:** 1994-.

Ownership, Management

Operated by: Storm, LLC.

Principal Owner: Gary Jacobs.

President/General Manager: Dave Oster. **Assistant GM:** Chris Jones. **Special Assistant to President:** Kathy Mair. **VP, Stadium Operations:** Bruce Kessman. **Director, Business Administration:** Yvonne Hunneman. **Director, Broadcasting:** Sean McCall. **VP, Sales/Marketing:** Willie Wong. **Office Manager:** Jo Equila. **Director, Community Development:** Tracy Beskid. **Director, Graphic Communications:** Mark Beskid. **Director, Field Maintenance:** Francisco Castaneda. **Director, Corporate Sales:** Paul Engl. **Director, Food/Beverage:** Steven Wassman. **Director, Media/Public Relations:** Jon Fusco. **Assistant Director, Food/Beverage:** Jordan Beldner. **Director, Group Sales:** Robyn Wassman. **Assistant Director, Ticket Operations:** Corrine Roberge. **Assistant Director, Stadium Operations**: Jake Burch. **Clubhouse Manager:** Kyle Ross.

Field Staff

Manager: Jeff Gardner. **Coach:** Rick Renteria. **Pitching Coach:** Gary Lance. **Trainer:** Jason Haeussinger.

Game Information

Radio Announcer: Sean McCall. **No. of Games Broadcast:** Home-70, Away-70. **Flagship Station:** Unavailable.

PA Announcer: Unavailable. **Official Scorers:** Dennis Bricker, Nelda Bricker.

Stadium Name (year opened): The Diamond (1994). **Location:** From I-15, exit at Diamond Drive, west one mile to stadium. **Standard Game Times:** 7:05 p.m.; Sun. (first half) 2:05, (second half) 6:05.

Visiting Club Hotel: Lake Elsinore Hotel and Casino, 20930 Malaga St., Lake Elsinore, CA 92530. Telephone: (909) 674-3101.

LANCASTER
JetHawks

Office Address: 45116 Valley Central Way, Lancaster, CA 93536. **Telephone:** (661) 726-5400. **FAX:** (661) 726-5406. **E-Mail Address:** ljethawks@qnet.com. **Website:** www.jethawks.com.

Affiliation (first year): Arizona Diamondbacks (2001). **Years in League:** 1996-.

Ownership, Management

Operated By: Clutch Play Baseball, LLC.

Chairman: Horn Chen. **President:** Mike Ellis. **Vice President:** Matt Ellis.

VP/General Manager: Mark Helminiak. **Director, Broadcasting/Public Relations:** Tim O'Sullivan. **Office Administrator:** Bonnie Ward. **Director, Stadium Operations:** John Laferney. **Director, Ticketing:** Steve Resa. **Director, Special Promotions:** Chris Hogan. **Accounting Executive:** Joe Reinch. **Administrative Assistant, Merchandising/Tickets:** Mary Helminiak. **Head Groundskeeper:** Dave Phatenhaur.

Field Staff

Manager: Mike Aldrete. **Coach:** Damon Mashore. **Pitching Coach:** Mel Stottlemyre Jr. **Trainer:** Rodger Fleming.

Game Information

Radio Announcer: Tim O'Sullivan. **No. of Games Broadcast:** Home-70, Away-70. **Flagship Station:** Unavailable.

PA Announcer: Unavailable. **Official Scorer:** Unavailable.

Stadium Name (year opened): Lancaster Municipal Stadium (1996). **Location:** Highway 14 in Lancaster to Avenue I exit, west one block to stadium. **Standard Game Times:** 7:15 p.m.; Sun. (April-June 15) 2, (June 22-Sept.) 5.

Visiting Club Hotel: The Desert Inn, 44219 N. Sierra Hwy., Lancaster, CA 93536. Telephone: (661) 942-8401.

MODESTO
A's

Office Address: 601 Neece Dr., Modesto, CA 95351. **Mailing Address:** P.O. Box 883, Modesto, CA 95353. **Telephone:** (209) 572-4487. **FAX:** (209) 572-4490. **E-Mail Address:** fun@modestoathletics.com. **Website:** www.modestoathletics.com.

Affiliation (first year): Oakland Athletics (1975). **Years in League:** 1946-64, 1966-.

Ownership, Management

Operated by: Modesto A's Baseball Club, Inc.

Principal Owner, President: Chris Chen.

Vice President, Business Development: Tim Marting.

General Manager: Greg Coleman. **Assistant GM, Public Relations:** Michael Gorrasi. **Assistant GM, Sales/Marketing:** Mike Malinas. **Director, Food Service:** Alan Day. **Director, Group Sales:** Daniel Plantier. **Director, Broadcasting:** Paul Chiofar. **Director, Tickets:** Bob Angus. **Office/Accounting Manager:** Debra Baucom. **Manager, Sales:** Mike Shaw. **Director, Operations:** Les Groscup. **Client Service Manager:** Callie Brown.

Field Staff

Manager: Rick Rodriguez **Coach:** Brian McArn. **Pitching Coach:** Scott Emerson. **Trainer:** Chris Lessner.

Game Information

Radio Announcer: Paul Chiofar. **No. of Games Broadcast:** Home-50, Away-50. **Flagship Station:** KESP 970-AM.

PA Announcer: Unavailable. **Official Scorer:** Unavailable.

Stadium Name (year opened): John Thurman Field (1952). **Location:** Highway 99 in Southwest Modesto to Tuolomne Boulevard exit, west on Tuolomne for one block to Neece Drive, left for ¼ mile to stadium. **Standard Game Times:** 7:05 p.m.; Sun. (April-June) 1:05, (July-Aug.) 5:05.

Visiting Club Hotel: Vagabond Inn, 1525 McHenry Ave., Modesto, CA 95350. Telephone: (209) 521-6340.

RANCHO CUCAMONGA
Quakes

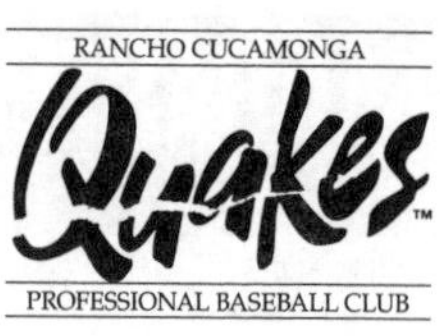

Office Address: 8408 Rochester Ave., Rancho Cucamonga, CA 91730. **Mailing Address:** P.O. Box 4139, Rancho Cucamonga, CA 91729. **Telephone:** (909) 481-5000. **FAX:** (909) 481-5005. **E-Mail Address:** rcquakes@aol.com. **Website:** www.rcquakes.com.

Affiliation (first year): Anaheim Angels (2001). **Years in League:** 1993-.

Ownership, Management

Operated by: Valley Baseball Inc.

Principal Owners: Jack Cooley, Mark Harmon, Hank Stickney.

Chairman: Hank Stickney.

General Manager: Pat Filippone. **Assistant GM/Director, Ticket Sales:** Andrew Stuebner. **Director, Finance:** Kristen Streit. **Head Groundskeeper:** Rex Whitney. **Director, Broadcasting/Media Relations:** Rob Brender. **Director, Community Relations:** Heather Williams. **Director, Group Sales:** Chris Bitters. **Director, Stadium Operations:** Jason Lehr. **Assistant Director, Stadium Operations:** Ryan Ross. **Manager, Marketing:** Matt Abt. **Client Services:** Brandon Tanner. **Manager, Group Sales:** Scott Carter. **Manager, Corporate Marketing:** Andrew Guidi. **Ticket Manager:** Heather Lint. **Ticket Sales Representative:** Jan Selasky. **Administrative Assistant:** Stacey Lord.

Field Staff

Manager: Bobby Meacham. **Coach:** Todd Takayoshi. **Pitching Coach:** Zeke Zimmerman. **Trainer:** Armando Rivas.

Game Information

Radio Announcer: Rob Brender. **No. of Games Broadcast:** Home-70, Away-70. **Flagship Station:** KWRM 1370-AM.

PA Announcer: Matt Abt. **Official Scorer:** Larry Kavanaugh.

Stadium Name (year opened): The Epicenter (1993). **Location:** I-10 to I-15 North, exit at Foothill Boulevard, left on Foothill, left on Rochester to stadium. **Standard Game Times:** 7:15 p.m.; Sun. (first half) 2:15, (second half) 6:15.

Visiting Club Hotel: Best Western Heritage Inn, 8179 Spruce Ave., Rancho Cucamonga, CA 91730. Telephone: (909) 466-1111.

SAN JOSE
Giants

Office Address: 588 E. Alma Ave., San Jose, CA 95112. **Mailing Address:** P.O. Box 21727, San Jose, CA 95151. **Telephone:** (408) 297-1435. **FAX:** (408) 297-1453. **E-Mail Address:** sanjosegiants@sjgiants.com **Website:** www.sjgiants.com.

Affiliation (first year): San Francisco Giants (1988). **Years in League:** 1942, 1947-58, 1962-76, 1979-.

Ownership, Management

Operated by: Progress Sports Management.

Principal Owners: Heidi Cox, Richard Beahrs.

President: Harry Stavrenos.

General Manager: Mark Wilson. **Assistant GM:** Dave Moudry. **Director, Marketing/Promotions:** Mike McCarroll. **Director, Public Relations:** Erik Holland. **Director, Sales:** Linda Pereira. **Director, Guest Services:** Zach Walter. **Ticket Director/Group Sales:** Chris DiGiorgio. **Director, BBQ/Stadium Operations:** Jeremy Tobin.

Field Staff

Manager: Bill Hayes. **Coach:** F.P. Santangelo. **Pitching Coach:** Jerry Cram. **Trainer:** Ben Downing.

Game Information

Radio Announcer: Rocky Koplik. **No. of Games Broadcast:** Home-23, Away-27. **Flagship Station:** KSFB 1220-AM.

PA Announcers: Brian Burkett. **Official Scorer:** John Pletsch.

Stadium Name (year opened): Municipal Stadium (1942). **Location:** From I-280, 10th Street exit to Alma, left on Alma, stadium on right. From U.S. 101, Tully Road exit to Senter, right on Senter, left on Alma, stadium on left. **Standard Game Times:** 7 p.m.; Sat. 5; Sun. (first half) 1, (second half) 5.

Visiting Club Hotel: Wyndham Hotel, 1350 N. First St., San Jose, CA 95112. Telephone: (408) 453-6200.

STOCKTON
Ports

Office Address: Billy Hebert Field at Oak Park, Alpine and Sutter Streets, Stockton, CA 95204. **Mailing Address:** P.O. Box 8365, Stockton, CA 95208. **Telephone:** (209) 644-1900. **FAX:** (209) 644-1931. **E-Mail Address:** info@stocktonports.com. **Website:** www.stocktonports.com.

Affiliation (first year): Texas Rangers (2003). **Years in League:** 1941, 1946-72, 1978-.

Ownership, Management

Operated by: 7th Inning Stretch, LLC.

Chairman, Chief Executive Officer: Tom Volpe.

Vice President, General Manager: John Katz. **Assistant GM:** Trevor Fawcett. **Director, Sales/Marketing:** Jamie Brown. **Account Executive:** Brandon Winslow. **Clubhouse Manager:** Ted Neal.

Field Staff

Manager: Arnie Beyeler. **Coach:** Joe Ayrault. **Pitching Coach:** Fred Dabney. **Trainer:** Mark Vinson.

Game Information

Radio Announcer: Steve Wendt. **No. of Games Broadcast:** Away-70. **Flagship Station:** Unavailable.

PA Announcer: Steve Wendt. **Official Scorer:** Unavailable.

Stadium Name (year opened): Billy Hebert Field (1927). **Location:** From I-5/99, take Crosstown Freeway (Highway 4) to El Dorado Street, north on El Dorado to Alpine, right on Alpine Street, left on Alvarado into Oak Park, first left to stadium. **Standard Game Times:** 7:05 p.m.; Sun. (first half) 1:05, (second half) 5:05.

Visiting Club Hotel: Hampton Inn and Suites, 5045 S. Highway 99, Stockton, CA 95215. Telephone: (209) 946-1234.

VISALIA
Oaks

Office Address: 440 N. Giddings Ave., Visalia, CA 93291. **Telephone:** (559) 625-0480. **FAX:** (559) 739-7732. **E-Mail Address:** oaksbaseball@hotmail.com. **Website:** www.oaksbaseball.com.

Affiliation (first year): Colorado Rockies (2003). **Years in League:** 1946-62, 1968-75, 1977-.

Ownership, Management

Operated by: Top of the Third, Inc.

Principal Owners: Tom Seidler, Kevin O'Malley.

General Manager: Jennifer Whiteley. **Director, Broadcasting/Media Relations:** David Skoczen. **Group Sales Executive:** John Drigotas. **Director, Concessions:** Don Cary. **Head Groundskeeper:** Ken Peterson.

Field Staff

Manager: Stu Cole. **Coach:** Don Reynolds. **Pitching Coach:** Jim Bennett. **Trainer:** Beau Clay.

Game Information

Radio Announcer: David Skoczen. **No. of Games Broadcast:** Home-70, Away-70. **Flagship Station:** KJUG 1270-AM.

PA Announcer: Chris White. **Official Scorer:** Harry Kargenian.

Stadium Name (year opened): Recreation Park (1946). **Location:** From Highway 99, take 198 East to Mooney Boulevard exit, left on Giddings Avenue. **Standard Game Times:** 6:35 p.m.; Fri.-Sat. 7:05; Sun. 1:35.

Visiting Club Hotel: Radisson Hotel, 300 S. Court St. Visalia, CA 93291 Telephone: (559) 636-1111.

CAROLINA LEAGUE

CLASS A ADVANCED

John Hopkins

Office Address: 1806 Pembroke Rd., Greensboro, NC 27408. **Mailing Address:** P.O. Box 9503, Greensboro, NC 27429. **Telephone:** (336) 691-9030. **FAX:** (336) 691-9070. **E-Mail Address:** office@carolinaleague.com. **Website:** www.carolinaleague.com.

Years League Active: 1945-.

President/Treasurer: John Hopkins.

Vice Presidents: Kelvin Bowles (Salem), Calvin Falwell (Lynchburg). **Corporate Secretary:** Matt Minker (Wilmington).

Directors: Don Beaver (Winston-Salem), Kelvin Bowles (Salem), Calvin Falwell (Lynchburg), George Habel (Myrtle Beach), North Johnson (Kinston), Peter Luukko (Frederick), Matt Minker (Wilmington), Art Silber (Potomac).

Administrative Assistants: Michael Albrecht, Marnee Larkins.

2003 Opening Date: April 4. **Closing Date:** Sept. 1.

Regular Season: 140 games (split schedule).

Division Structure: North—Frederick, Lynchburg, Potomac, Wilmington. **South**—Kinston, Myrtle Beach, Salem, Winston-Salem.

Playoff Format: First-half division champions play second-half division champions in best-of-3 series (team that wins both halves plays wild-card). Division champions meet in best-of-5 series for Mills Cup.

All-Star Game: June 24 at Rancho Cucamonga, CA (Carolina League vs. California League).

Roster Limit: 25 active. **Player Eligibility Rule:** No age limit. No more than two players and one player-coach on active list may have six or more years of prior minor league service.

Brand of Baseball: Rawlings.

Statistician: SportsTicker-Boston, Boston Fish Pier, West Bldg. #1, Suite 302, Boston MA 02210.

Umpires: John Blackburn (Brick, NJ), Francis Burke (Apex, NC), Chris Conroy (Williamstown, MA), Brandon Cooper (Louisville, KY), Jason Klein (Orange, CT), Stephen McMullen (Hainesport, NJ), Karreem Mebane (Hamden, CT), Joseph Stegner (Boise, ID).

STADIUM INFORMATION

		Dimensions				
Club	**Stadium**	**LF**	**CF**	**RF**	**Capacity**	**2002 Att.**
Frederick	Harry Grove	325	400	325	5,400	305,950
Kinston	Grainger	335	390	335	3,800	106,472
Lynchburg	City	325	390	325	4,000	127,916
Myrtle Beach	Coastal Federal	325	405	328	4,324	200,463
Potomac	Pfitzner	315	400	315	6,000	182,059
Salem	Salem Memorial	325	401	325	6,300	196,347
Wilmington	Frawley	325	400	325	6,532	331,545
Winston-Salem	Ernie Shore	325	400	325	6,000	136,302

FREDERICK
Keys

Office Address: 6201 New Design Rd., Frederick, MD 21703. **Mailing Address:** P.O. Box 3169, Frederick, MD 21705. **Telephone:** (301) 662-0013. **FAX:** (301) 662-0018. **E-Mail Address:** info@frederickkeys.com **Website:** www.frederickkeys.com.

Affiliation (first year): Baltimore Orioles (1989). **Years in League:** 1989-.

Ownership, Management

Operated by: Comcast-Spectacor.

Directors: Peter Luukko, Frank Miceli.

General Manager: Joe Pinto. **Assistant GM:** Gina Stepoulos. **Director, Marketing:** Mark Fine. **Marketing Assistant:** Sharine Iacono. **Director, Public Relations:** Cory Cox. **Public Relations Assistant:** Bryan Burns. **Director, Stadium Operations:** Dave Wisner. **Senior Account Manager:** Mark Zeigler. **Account Managers:** Shaun O'Neal, Ernie Stepoulos, Jimmy Sweet. **Ticket Operations:** Ed Maurer. **Box Office Manager:** Mike McAtee. **Events Coordinators:** Kelly Crum, Kevin DeLauter, Josh Passman. **Administrative Assistants:** Barb Freund, Katy Hampson. **Bookkeeper:** Tami Hetrick. **Clubhouse Manager:** George Bell. **GM, Ovations Food Services:** Mike Brulatour. **Assistant GM, Ovations Food Services:** Shannon Roppolo. **Head Groundskeeper:** Tommy Long.

Field Staff

Manager: Tom Lawless. **Coach:** Moe Hill. **Pitching Coach:** Scott McGregor. **Trainer:** Mark Shires.

Game Information

Radio: None.

PA Announcer: Unavailable. **Official Scorer:** George Richardson.

Stadium Name (year opened): Harry Grove Stadium (1990). **Location:** From I-70, take exit 54 (Market Street), left at light. From I-270, take exit 32 (I-70 Baltimore/Hagerstown) towards Baltimore (I-70 East), to exit 54, left at Market Street. **Standard Game Times:** 7:05 p.m.; Sun. 1:05.

Visiting Club Hotel: Comfort Inn, 420 Prospect Blvd., Frederick, MD 21701. Telephone: (301) 695-6200.

KINSTON
Indians

Office Address: 400 E. Grainger Ave., Kinston, NC 28501. **Mailing Address:** P.O. Box 3542, Kinston, NC 28502. **Telephone:** (252) 527-9111. **FAX:** (252) 527-2328. **E-Mail Address:** info@kinstonindians.com. **Website:** www.kinstonindians.com.

Affiliation (first year): Cleveland Indians (1987). **Years in League:** 1956-57, 1962-74, 1978-.

Ownership, Management

Operated by: Slugger Partners, LP.

Principal Owners: Cam McRae, North Johnson.

Chairman: Cam McRae.

President, General Manager: North Johnson. **Assistant GM:** Shari Massengill. **Director, Community Relations:** Chrystal Bowen. **Director, Food/Beverage:** Sarah Frazier. **Head Groundskeeper:** Tommy Walston. **Clubhouse Operations:** Robert Smeraldo. **Interns:** Patrick Robertson, Stephen Poe, Brian Queen.

Field Staff

Manager: Torey Lovullo. **Coach:** Lou Frazier. **Pitching Coach:** Steve Lyons. **Trainer:** Lee Slagle.

Game Information

Radio Announcer: Brian Collins, Todd Bartley. **No. of Games Broadcast:** Home-70, Away-70. **Flagship Station:** WLNR 1230-AM.

PA Announcer: Jeff Diamond. **Official Scorers:** Chris Kline.

Stadium Name (year opened): Grainger Stadium (1949). **Location:** From west, take US 70 Business (Vernon Avenue), left on East Street; from east, take US 70 W, right on Highway 58, right on Vernon Avenue, right on East Street. **Standard Game Times:** 7 p.m.; Sun. (April-June 22) 2, (June 29-Aug.) 6.

Visiting Club Hotel: Hampton Inn, Highway 70 Bypass, Kinston NC 28504. Telephone: (252) 523-1400.

LYNCHBURG
Hillcats

Office Address: Lynchburg City Stadium, 3180 Fort Ave., Lynchburg, VA 24501. **Mailing Address:** P.O. Box 10213, Lynchburg, VA 24506. **Telephone:** (434) 528-1144. **FAX:** (434) 846-0768. **E-Mail Address:** hillcatsbb@aol.com. **Website:** www.lynchburg-hillcats.com.

Affiliation (first year): Pittsburgh Pirates (1995). **Years in League:** 1966-.

Ownership, Management

Operated by: Lynchburg Baseball Corp.

President: Calvin Falwell.

General Manager: Paul Sunwall. **Assistant GM:** Ronnie Roberts. **Director, Group Sales/Promotions:** Kevin Donahue. **Head Groundskeeper/Sales:** Darren Johnson. **Director, Broadcasting/Publications:** Matt Provence. **Assistant Director, Broadcasting:** Josh Hummel. **Media Relations Assistant:** Jon Schaeffer. **Office Manager:** Diane Tucker.

Field Staff

Manager: Dave Clark. **Coach:** Jeff Livesey. **Pitching Coach:** Scott Lovekamp. **Trainer:** Jason Palmer.

Game Information

Radio Announcers: Matt Provence, Josh Hummel, Jon Schaeffer. **No. of Games Broadcast:** Home-70, Away-70. **Flagship Station:** WZZU 97.9-FM.

PA Announcer: Chuck Young. **Official Scorers:** Malcolm Haley, Chuck Young.

Stadium Name (year opened): Lynchburg City Stadium (1940). **Location:** US 29 South to The Merritt Hutchinson Stadium (exit 6); US 29 North to The Merritt Hutchinson Stadium (exit 4). **Standard Game Times:** 7:05 p.m.; Sun. (first half) 2:05, (second half) 6:05.

Visiting Club Hotel: Best Western, 2815 Candlers Mountain Rd., Lynchburg, VA 24502. Telephone: (434) 237-2986.

MYRTLE BEACH
Pelicans

Office Address: 1251 21st Ave. N., Myrtle Beach, SC 29577. **Telephone:** (843) 918-6002. **FAX:** (843) 918-6001. **E-Mail Address:** info@myrtlebeachpelicans.com. **Website:** www.myrtlebeachpelicans.com.

Affiliation (first year): Atlanta Braves (1999). **Years in League:** 1999-.

Ownership, Management

Operated by: Capitol Broadcasting Company.

Principal Owner: Jim Goodmon. **Vice President:** George Habel.

Vice President, General Manager: Matt O'Brien. **Senior Director, Sales:** Tony Zefiretto. **Senior Director, Operations:** David Frost. **Director, Corporate Sales:** Robert Stockhausen. **Manager, Corporate Sales/Promotions:** Chris Millar. **Coordinator, Group Sales/Community Relations:** Debbie Drutar. **Coordinator, Group Sales:** Ody Perez. **Director, Broadcasting:** Garry Griffith. **Accounting Manager:** Anne Frishmuth. **Director, Ticket Operations:** Scott Tanfield. **Manager, Ticket Sales:** Glenn Fallon. **Ticket Sales Representative:** Frank Coppola. **Retail Manager:** Richard Graves. **Director, Ballpark Operations:** Tricia Keala. **Administrative/Media Assistant:** Angela Barwick. **Director, Field Operations:** Chris Ball. **Assistant Groundskeeper:** Tracy Schneweis. **Clubhouse Manager:** Mark Conrad.

Field Staff

Manager: Randy Ingle. **Coaches:** Jack Maloof, Edison Renteria. **Pitching Coach:** Bruce Dal Canton. **Trainer:** Mike Dart.

Game Information

Radio Announcer: Garry Griffith. **No. of Games Broadcast:** Home-70, Away-70. **Flagship Station:** WRNN 99.5-FM.

PA Announcer: Unavailable. **Official Scorer:** Unavailable.

Stadium Name (year opened): Coastal Federal Field (1999). **Location:** US Highway 17 Bypass to 21st Avenue North, 1/2 mile to stadium. **Standard Game Time:** 7:05 p.m.

Visiting Club Hotel: Holiday Inn Express-Broadway at the Beach, U.S. Highway 17 Bypass & 29th Avenue North; Myrtle Beach, SC 29578. Telephone: (843) 916-4993.

POTOMAC
Cannons

Office Address: 7 County Complex Ct., Woodbridge, VA 22192. **Mailing Address:** P.O. Box 2148, Woodbridge, VA 22195. **Telephone:** (703) 590-2311. **FAX:** (703) 590-5716. **E-Mail Address:** cannonswin@aol.com. **Website:** www.potomaccannons.com.

Affiliation (first year): Cincinnati Reds (2003). **Years in League:** 1978-.

Ownership, Management

Operated by: Prince William Professional Baseball Club, Inc.

Principal Owner: Art Silber. **President:** Lani Silber.

Vice President, General Manager: Max Baker. **Director, Operations:** Lyle Mattson. **Director, Marketing:** Erik Hernquist. **Director, Ticket Operations:** Eric Fiscus. **Director, Community Relations:** Liz Braswell. **Director, Group Sales:** Nicole Palmieri. **Ticket Account Sales Executive:** Wesley Hall. **Director, Food Services:** Kristian Hawkins. **Director, Broadcasting:** Unavailable. **Outside Sales Representative:** Don Wallace. **Head Groundskeeper:** Mike Lundy.

Field Staff

Manager: Jayhawk Owens. **Coach:** Jamie Dismuke. **Pitching Coach:** Larry Pierson. **Trainer:** Chris LaPole.

Game Information

Radio: Unavailable.

PA Announcer: Dave Sher. **Official Scorer:** Dave Vincent.

Stadium Name (year opened): G. Richard Pfitzner Stadium (1984). **Location:** From I-95, take exit 158B and continue on Prince William Parkway for 5 miles, right into County Complex Court. **Standard Game Times:** 7:05 p.m.; Sun. (April-June) 1:35, (July-Sept.) 6:05.

Visiting Club Hotel: Best Western Potomac Mills, 14619 Potomac Mills Rd., Woodbridge, VA 22192. Telephone: (703) 494-4433.

SALEM
Avalanche

Office Address: 1004 Texas St., Salem, VA 24153. **Mailing Address:** P.O. Box 842, Salem, VA 24153. **Telephone:** (540) 389-3333. **Fax:** (540) 389-9710. **E-Mail Address:** info@salemavalanche.com. **Website:** www.salemavalanche.com. **Affiliation (first year):** Houston Astros (2003). **Years in League:** 1968-.

Ownership/Management

Operated by: Salem Professional Baseball Club, Inc.

Principal Owner/President: Kelvin Bowles.

General Manager: Stan Macko. **Assistant GM:** Todd Lange. **Director, Finance:** Brian Bowles. **Director, Group Sales:** Tim Schuster. **Director, Stadium Operations:** Phillip Spencer. **Director, Tickets:** Matt Barnes. **Director, Merchandising:** Page Griffin. **Director, Food Service:** Allen Lawrence. **Director, Broadcasting:** Kevin Reiter. **Head Groundskeeper:** Unavailable. **Interns:** Chris Broadus, Amber Byer, Tommy Chambers.

Field Staff

Manager: John Massarelli. **Coach:** Pete Rancont. **Pitching Coach:** Stan Borowski. **Trainer:** Mike Smith.

Game Information

Radio Announcer: Kevin Reiter. **No. of Games Broadcast:** Home-70, Away-70. **Flagship Stations:** WGMN 1240-AM, WVGM 1320-AM.

PA Announcer: Adam Ranzer. **Official Scorer:** Bob Teitlebaum.

Stadium Name (year opened): Salem Memorial Baseball Stadium (1995). **Location:** I-81 to exit 141 (Route 419), follow signs to Salem Civic Center Complex. **Standard Game Times:** 7:05 p.m.; Sun. (April-June) 2:05, (July-Aug) 6:05.

Visiting Club Hotel: Comfort Inn Airport, 5070 Valley View Blvd., Roanoke VA 24012. Telephone: (540) 527-2020.

WILMINGTON
Blue Rocks

Office Address: 801 S. Madison St., Wilmington, DE 19801. **Telephone:** (302) 888-2015. **FAX:** (302) 888-2032. **E-Mail Address:** info@bluerocks.com. **Website:** www.bluerocks.com.

Affiliation (first year): Kansas City Royals (1993). **Years in League:** 1993-.

Ownership, Management

Operated by: Wilmington Blue Rocks, LP.

President: Matt Minker. **Vice President:** Tom Palmer. **Secretary/Treasurer:** Bob Stewart.

General Manager: Chris Kemple. **Assistant GM:** Andrew Layman. **Director, Finance:** Craig Bailey. **Director, Merchandising:** Jim Beck. **Head Groundskeeper:** Steve Gold. **Director, Broadcasting/Media Relations:** Steve Lenox. **Assistant Director, Media Relations:** Kevin Linton. **Director, Sales/Marketing:** Chris Parise. **Director, Group Sales:** Jen Francis. **Director, Publications/Promotions:** Tripp Baum. **Director, Tickets:** Jared Forma. **Director, Community Relations:** Dave Brown. **GM, Food Services:** Bobby Dichiaro. **Assistant Director, Group Sales:** Melissa Golden. **Office Manager:** Terra Crump. **Community Relations Assistant:** Matthew Broomall. **Merchandising Assistant:** Frank Chimera. **Ticket Assistants:** Ethan Jacoby, Lawrence Levine. **Marketing Assistants:** Ray Cotrufo, Jen Krebs. **Visiting Clubhouse Manager:** Len Zito. **Home Clubhouse Manager:** Marvin Brittingham. **Assistant Home Clubhouse Manager:** Kenny Brown.

Field Staff

Manager: Billy Gardner Jr. **Coach:** Terry Bradshaw. **Pitching Coach:** Bill Slack. **Trainer:** Ken Forth.

Game Information

Radio Announcer: Steve Lenox. **No. of Games Broadcast:** Home-70, Away-70. **Flagship Station:** WJBR 1290-AM.

PA Announcer: John McAdams. **Official Scorers:** E.J. Casey, Jay Dunn, Dick Shute.

Stadium Name (year opened): Judy Johnson Field at Daniel S. Frawley Stadium (1993). **Location:** I-95 North to Maryland Ave. (exit 6), right onto Maryland Ave., right on Read Street, right on South Madison Street to ballpark; I-95 South to Maryland Ave. (exit 6), left at Martin Luther King Blvd., right on South Madison Street. **Standard Game Times:** 7:05 p.m.; Sun. 1:35.

Visiting Club Hotel: Quality Inn-Skyways, 147 N. DuPont Hwy., New Castle, DE 19720. Telephone: (302) 328-6666.

WINSTON-SALEM
Warthogs

Office Address: 401 Deacon Blvd., Winston-Salem, NC 27105. **Mailing Address:** P.O. Box 4488, Winston-Salem, NC 27115. **Telephone:** (336) 759-2233. **FAX:** (336) 759-2042. **E-Mail Address:** warthogs@warthogs.com. **Website:** www.warthogs.com.

Affiliation (first year): Chicago White Sox (1997). **Years in League:** 1945-.

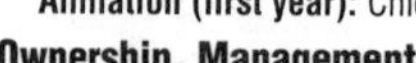

Ownership, Management

Principal Owner, President: Unavailable.

General Manager: Peter Fisch. **Assistant GM:** Ryan Manuel. **Special Assistant to GM:** David Beal. **Director, Broadcast/Media Relations:** Alan York. **Director, Community Relations:** Wil Loftis. **Director, Merchandise:** Amanda Williams. **Account Executive:** Shaun McElhinny. **Sales Associates:** Sarcanda Bellissimo, Greg Jordanoff, Vinny Pannutti.

Field Staff

Manager: Razor Shines. **Coach:** Ken Dominguez. **Pitching Coach:** J.R Perdew. **Trainer:** Josh Fallin.

Game Information

Radio Announcer: Alan York. **No. of Games Broadcast:** Home-70, Away-70. **Flagship Station:** Unavailable.

PA Announcer: Unavailable. **Official Scorer:** Scott Strickland.

Stadium Name (year opened): Ernie Shore Field (1956). **Location:** I-40 Business to Cherry Street exit, north through downtown, right on Deacon Boulevard, park on left. **Standard Game Times:** 7:15 p.m.; Sun. 2:05.

Visiting Club Hotel: Ramada Plaza, 3050 University Pkwy., Winston-Salem, NC 27106. Telephone: (336) 723-2911.

FLORIDA STATE LEAGUE

CLASS A ADVANCED

Chuck Murphy

Street Address: 103 E. Orange Ave., Daytona Beach, FL 32114. **Mailing Address:** P.O. Box 349, Daytona Beach, FL 32115. **Telephone:** (386) 252-7479. **FAX:** (386) 252-7495. **E-Mail Address:** fslbaseball@cfl.rr.com. **Website:** www.fslbaseball.com.

Years League Active: 1919-1927, 1936-1941, 1946-.

President, Treasurer: Chuck Murphy.

Vice Presidents: Ken Carson (Dunedin), Rob Rabenecker (Jupiter).

Corporate Secretary: David Hood.

Directors: Sammy Arena (Tampa), Brian Barnes (Jupiter), Ken Carson (Dunedin), Ben Cherington (Sarasota), Andy Dunn (Brevard County), Chris Easom (Palm Beach), Marvin Goldklang (Fort Myers), Trevor Gooby (Vero Beach), Don Miers (Lakeland), Andrew Rayburn (Daytona), Paul Taglieri (St. Lucie), John Timberlake (Clearwater).

Office Secretary: Peggy Catigano.

2003 Opening Date: April 3. **Closing Date:** Aug. 31.

Regular Season: 140 games (split schedule).

Division Structure: East—Brevard County, Daytona, Jupiter, Palm Beach, St. Lucie, Vero Beach. **West**—Clearwater, Dunedin, Fort Myers, Lakeland, Sarasota, Tampa.

Playoff Format: First-half division champions play second-half champions in best-of-3 series. Winners meet in best-of-5 series for league championship.

All-Star Game: June 14 at Fort Myers.

Roster Limit: 25. **Player Eligibility Rule:** No age limit. No more than two players and one player-coach on active list may have six or more years of prior minor league service.

Brand of Baseball: Rawlings.

Statistician: SportsTicker-Boston, Boston Fish Pier, West Bldg. #1, Suite 302, Boston, MA 02210.

Umpires: John Coons (Streator, IL), Eric Eckert (Ballwin, MO), Robert Healey (Cranston, RI), Matt Kaylor (Blue Springs, MO), Brian Martin (Mooresville, NC), Josh Miller (Coral Springs, FL), Maria Papageorgiou (Rock Island, IL), Brent Persinger (Lexington, KY), Daniel Reyburn (DeWitt, MI), Chris Tiller (Carthage, TX).

STADIUM INFORMATION

		Dimensions				
Club	**Stadium**	**LF**	**CF**	**RF**	**Capacity**	**2002 Att.**
Brevard County	Space Coast	340	404	340	7,500	89,480
Clearwater	Jack Russell Memorial	330	400	330	6,917	78,459
Daytona	Jackie Robinson Ballpark	317	400	325	4,000	72,655
Dunedin	Dunedin	335	400	315	6,106	47,717
Fort Myers	Hammond	330	405	330	7,500	109,293
Jupiter	Roger Dean	330	400	325	6,871	103,640
Lakeland	Joker Marchant	340	420	340	7,100	21,503
*Palm Beach	Roger Dean	330	400	325	6,871	23,998
St. Lucie	Thomas J. White	338	410	338	7,500	78,564
Sarasota	Ed Smith	340	400	340	7,500	57,365
Tampa	Legends Field	318	408	314	10,386	75,061
Vero Beach	Holman	340	400	340	6,500	53,088

*Franchise operated in Charlotte in 2002

BREVARD COUNTY
Manatees

Office Address: 5800 Stadium Pkwy., Melbourne, FL 32940. **Telephone:** (321) 633-9200. **FAX:** (321) 633-9210. **E-Mail Address:** brevardoperations@spacecoast-stadium.com. **Website:** www.bcmanatees.com.

Affiliation (first year): Montreal Expos (2002). **Years in League:** 1994-.

Ownership, Management

Operated by: Montreal Expos.

Vice President, Brevard Operations: Andy Dunn. **Assistant General Manager:** Trey Fraser. **Director, Sales/Marketing:** Tim Bawmann. **Manager, Group Sales/Public Relations:** Eliza Folsom. **Manager, Sales/Promotions:** Calvin Funkhouser. **Manager, Tickets:** Jeff Weinhold. **Account Executives:** Jamie Brooks, Kim Capogreca. **Executive Assistant:** Susie Palm. **Office Manager:** Lilya McAtee. **Head Groundskeeper:** Doug Lopas. **Assistant Groundskeeper:** Roger Manuel. **Facilities Engineers:** Charles Bunch, Kevin Seidell. **Director, Brevard Concessions:** Roy Lake. **Manager, Concessions:** Doug Rand. **Office Manager, Concessions:** Siv Donovan.

Field Staff

Manager: Doug Sisson. **Coach:** Joe Marchese. **Pitching Coach:** Mark Grater. **Trainer:** Steve Gober.

Game Information

Radio: None.

PA Announcer: Pat Hernan. **Official Scorer:** Ron Jernick.

Stadium Name (year opened): Space Coast Stadium (1994). **Location:** I-95 North to Wickham Road (exit 73), left on Wickham, right on Lake Andrew Drive, left onto Judge Fran Jameson Way, right on Stadium Parkway; I-95 South to Fiske Boulevard (exit 74), left on Fiske, follow Fiske/Stadium Parkway to ballpark. **Standard Game Times:** 7:05 p.m., Sun. 1:05.

Visiting Club Hotel: Baymont Inn & Suites, 7200 George T. Edwards Dr., Melbourne, FL 32940. Telephone: (321) 242-9400.

CLEARWATER
Phillies

Office Address: 800 Phillies Dr., Clearwater, FL 33755. **Mailing Address:** P.O. Box 10336, Clearwater, FL 33757. **Telephone:** (727) 441-8638. **FAX:** (727) 447-3924. **Website:** www.clearwaterphillies.com.

Affiliation (first year): Philadelphia Phillies (1985). **Years in League:** 1985-.

Ownership, Management

Operated by: The Philadelphia Phillies.

Chairman: Bill Giles. **President:** David Montgomery.

Director, Florida Operations: John Timberlake. **Assistant Director, Florida Operations:** Lee McDaniel. **Business Manager:** Dianne Gonzalez.

General Manager: John Cook. **Director, Sales:** Dan McDonough. **Coordinator, Ticketing/Media:** Jason Adams. **Manager, Food/Beverage:** Tim Arseneau. **Coordinator, Merchandising/Special Events:** Carrie Jenkins. **Office Manager:** De De Angelillis. **Head Groundskeeper:** Opie Cheek. **Clubhouse Operations:** Cliff Armbruster.

Field Staff

Manager: Roly de Armas. **Coach:** Manny Amador. **Pitching Coach:** Rich Dubee. **Trainer:** Joel Kennedy.

Game Information

Radio: None.

PA Announcer: Don Guckian. **Official Scorer:** Larry Wiederecht.

Stadium Name (year opened): Jack Russell Memorial Stadium (1955). **Location:** US 19 North to Drew Street, west to Greenwood Avenue, north to Seminole Street, right to park. **Standard Game Times:** 7 p.m., Sun. 2.

Visiting Club Hotel: Econo Lodge, 21252 US 19 N., Clearwater, FL 33765. Telephone: (727) 796-3165.

DAYTONA
Cubs

Office Address: 105 East Orange Ave., Daytona Beach, FL 32114. **Telephone:** (386) 257-3172. **FAX:** (386) 257-3382. **E-Mail Address:** info@daytonacubs.com. **Website:** www.daytonacubs.com.

Affiliation (first year): Chicago Cubs (1993). **Years in league:** 1920-24, 1928, 1936-41, 1946-73, 1977-87, 1993-.

Ownership/Management

Operated by: Big Game Florida, LLC.

Principal Owner/President: Andrew Rayburn.

General Manager: Buck Rogers. **Assistant GM:** Michael Swope. **Director, Sales/Marketing:** Babs Rogers. **Director, Media:** Mike Cichowicz. **Director, Stadium Operations:** Eddie Fisher. **Merchandise Manager:** Heather Swartz.

Field Staff

Manager: Rick Kranitz. **Coach:** Trey Forkerway. **Pitching Coach:** Tom Pratt. **Trainer:** Steve Melendez.

Game Information

Radio Announcer: Mike Johnson. **No. of Games Broadcast:** Home-70, Away-70. **Flagship Station:** WELE 1380-AM.

PA Announcer: Tim Lecras. **Official Scorer:** Lyle Fox.

Stadium Name (year opened): Jackie Robinson Ballpark (1930). **Location:** I-95 to International Speedway Blvd. exit (Route 92), east to Beach Street, south to Orange Ave., east to ballpark; A1A North/South to Orange Ave., west to ballpark. **Standard Game Times:** 6:45 p.m.; Sun. 1:45.

Visiting Club Hotel: Treasure Island Resort, 2025 S. Atlantic Ave., Daytona Beach Shores, FL 32118. Telephone: (386) 255-8371.

DUNEDIN
Blue Jays

Office Address: 373-A Douglas Ave., Dunedin, FL 34698. **Telephone:** (727) 733-9302. **FAX:** (727) 734-7661. **E-Mail Address:** feedback@dunedinbluejays.com. **Website:** www.dunedinbluejays.com.

Affiliation (first year): Toronto Blue Jays (1987). **Years in League:** 1978-79, 1987-.

Ownership, Management

Operated by: Toronto Blue Jays.

Director, Florida Operations/General Manager: Ken Carson. **Assistant GM:** Carrie Johnson. **Manager, Sales/Marketing:** Bill Berger. **Manager, Group Sales/Tickets:** Jay Eylward. **Office Manager:** Pat Smith. **Administrative Assistant:** Carol Borish. **Sales Representative:** Lizz Curll. **Head Groundskeeper:** Eddie Rivera. **Clubhouse Operations:** Mickey McGee.

Field Staff

Manager: Mike Basso. **Coach:** Gary Cathcart. **Pitching Coach:** Rick Langford. **Trainer:** Mike Frostad.

Game Information

Radio: None.

PA Announcers: Ed Groth, Dave Bell. **Official Scorer:** Bobby Porter.

Stadium Name (year opened): Dunedin Stadium (1977). **Location:** From I-275, north on Highway 19, left on Sunset Point Road for 4½ miles, right on Douglas Avenue, stadium is ½ mile on right. **Standard Game Times:** 7 p.m.; Sun. 5.

Visiting Club Hotel: Red Roof Inn, 32000 US Hwy. 19 N., Palm Harbor, FL 34684. Telephone: (727) 786-2529.

FORT MYERS
Miracle

Office Address: 14400 Six Mile Cypress Pkwy., Fort Myers, FL 33912. **Telephone:** (239) 768-4210. **FAX:** (239) 768-4211. **E-Mail Address:** miracle@miraclebaseball.com. **Website:** www.miraclebaseball.com.

Affiliation: Minnesota Twins (1993) **Years in League:** 1926, 1978-87, 1991-.

Ownership, Management

Operated by: Greater Miami Baseball Club, LP.

Principal Owner/Chairman: Marvin Goldklang. **Chief Executive Officer:** Mike Veeck. **President:** Linda McNabb.

General Manager: Dave Burke. **Assistant GM:** Andrew Seymour. **Director, Business Operations:** Suzanne Reaves. **Manager, Sales/Marketing:** Terry Simon. **Head Groundskeeper:** Keith Blasingim. **Manager, Media Relations:** Sean Aronson. **Manager, Special Projects:** Vincent Mitchell. **Ticket Sales Representatives:** Ben Lynch, John Pezzente. **Manager, Food/Beverage:** John Acquavella.

Field Staff

Manager: Jose Marzan. **Coach:** Mike Tosar. **Pitching Coach:** Eric Rasmussen. **Trainer:** Larry Bennese.

Game Information

Radio/Internet Broadcaster: Sean Aronson. **No of Games Broadcast:** Home-70, Away-70. **Flagship Stations:** ESPN 770-AM, www.sportsjuice.com (Internet).

PA Announcer: Ted Fitzgeorge. **Official Scorer:** Benn Norton.

Stadium Name (year opened): William H. Hammond (1991). **Location:** Exit 131 off I-75, west on Daniels Parkway, left on Six Mile Cypress Parkway. **Standard Game Times:** 7:05 p.m.; Sun. 1:05.

Visiting Club Hotel: Wellesley Inn and Suites, 4400 Ford St. Extension, Fort Myers, FL 33909. Telephone: (239) 278-3949.

JUPITER
Hammerheads

Office Address: 4751 Main St., Jupiter, FL 33458. **Telephone:** (561) 775-1818. **FAX:** (561) 691-6886. **E-Mail Address:** info@rogerdeanstadium.com. **Website:** www.jupiterhammerheads.com.

Affiliation (first year): Florida Marlins (2002). **Years in League:** 1998-

Ownership, Management

Owned by: Florida Marlins.

Operated by: Jupiter Stadium, LTD.

General Manager: Rob Rabenecker. **Executive Assistant to GM**: Carol McAteer. **Director, Hammerheads/Event Operations:** Brian Barnes. **Associate Director, Hammerheads Operations:** Chris Easom. **Director, Sales/Marketing:** Jennifer Brown. **Manager, Merchandise:** Kristy Garcia. **Manager, Stadium Building:** Jorge Toro. **Manager, Facility Operations:** Steve Peeler. **Assistant Managers, Facility Operations:** Marshall Jennings, Johnny Simmons. **Office Manager:** Susan Provinzano. **Ticket Manager:** Tim Stoyle. **Manager, Marketing:** Matt McKenna. **Marketing Sales Executive:** George Linley. **Senior Sales Representative:** Holly Myers. **Sales Representative:** Mauricio Hernandez. **Interns:** Jonathan Frost, Doug Fugate, Matthew Grosso, Jennifer Nevius, Matthew Payne, Lainey Ruskay, Ryan Smith, Brett Stewart, Chris Tunno.

Field Staff

Manager: Luis Dorante. **Coach:** Paul Sanagorski. **Pitching Coach:** Gil Lopez. **Trainer:** Jason Barela.

Game Information

Radio: None.

PA Announcers: John Frost, Dick Sanford. **Official Scorer:** Ted Colton.

Stadium Name (year opened): Roger Dean Stadium (1998). **Location:** I-95 to exit 83, east on Donald Ross Road for ¼ mile. **Standard Game Times:** 7:05 p.m.; Sun. 1:05.

Visiting Club Hotel: Waterford Hotel & Conference Center, 11360 US Hwy. One, North Palm Beach, FL 33408. Telephone: (561) 624-7186.

LAKELAND
Tigers

Office Address: 2125 N. Lake Ave., Lakeland, FL 33805. **Mailing Address:** P.O. Box 90187, Lakeland, FL 33804. **Telephone:** (863) 686-8075. **FAX:** (863) 688-9589. **E-Mail Address:** ryan.black@detroittigers.com.

Affiliation (first year): Detroit Tigers (1967). **Years in League:** 1919-26, 1953-55, 1960, 1962-64, 1967-.

Ownership, Management

Operated by: Detroit Tigers.

Principal Owner: Mike Ilitch. **President:** Dave Dombrowski. **Director, Florida Operations:** Don Miers.

General Manager: Todd Pund. **Assistant GM:** Ryan Black. **Ticket Operations:** Jason Elias. **Director, Merchandising/Concessions:** Kay LaLonde. **Director, Tiger Town Cafeteria:** Agnes Proctor. **Clubhouse Operations:** Tab Kolehouse. **Head Groundskeeper:** Bryan French.

Field Staff

Manager: Gary Green. **Coach:** Basilio Cabrera. **Pitching Coach:** Joe Boever. **Trainer:** Chris McDonald.

Game Information

Radio: None.

PA Announcer: Unavailable. **Official Scorer:** Sandy Shaw.

Stadium Name (year opened): Joker Marchant Stadium (1966). **Location:** I-4 to Exit 33, left 1½ miles. **Standard Game Times:** 7 p.m.; Sun. 1.

Visiting Club Hotel: Baymont Inns and Suites, 4315 Lakeland Park Dr., Lakeland, FL 33809. Telephone: (863) 815-0606.

PALM BEACH
Cardinals

Office Address: 4751 Main St., Jupiter, FL 33458. **Telephone:** (561) 775-1818. **FAX:** (561) 691-6886. **E-Mail Address:** info@rogerdeanstadium.com. **Website:** www.palmbeachcardinals.com.

Affiliation (first year): St. Louis Cardinals (2003). **Years in League:** 2003-.

Ownership, Management

Owned by: St. Louis Cardinals.

Operated by: Jupiter Stadium, LTD.

General Manager, JSL: Rob Rabenecker. **Executive Assistant to GM, JSL**: Carol McAteer. **Director, Cardinals Operations:** Chris Easom. **Associate Director, Cardinals Operations:** Brian Barnes. **Director, Sales/Marketing:** Jennifer Brown. **Manager, Merchandising:** Kristy Garcia. **Manager, Stadium Building:** Jorge Toro. **Manager, Facility Operations:** Steve Peeler. **Assistant Managers, Facility Operations:** Marshall Jennings, Johnny Simmons. **Office Manager:** Susan Provinzano. **Manager, Tickets:** Tim Stoyle. **Manager, Marketing:** Matt McKenna. **Marketing Sales Executive:** George Linley. **Senior Sales Representative:** Holly Myers. **Sales Representative:** Mauricio Hernandez. **Interns:** Jonathan Frost, Doug Fugate, Matthew Grosso, Jennifer Nevius, Matthew Payne, Lainey Ruskay, Ryan Smith, Brett Stewart, Chris Tunno.

Field Staff

Manager: Tom Nieto. **Coach:** Todd Steverson. **Pitching Coach:** Rich DeLucia. **Trainer:** Kevin Crawmer.

Game Information

Radio: None.

PA Announcers: John Frost, Dick Sanford. **Official Scorer:** Ted Colton.

Stadium Name (year opened): Roger Dean Stadium (1998). **Location:** I-95 to exit 83, east on Donald Ross Road for ¼ mile. **Standard Game Times:** 7:05 p.m., Sun. 1:05.

Visiting Club Hotel: Waterford Hotel & Conference Center, 11360 US Hwy. One, North Palm Beach, FL 33408. Telephone: (561) 624-7186.

ST. LUCIE
Mets

Office Address: 525 NW Peacock Blvd., Port St. Lucie, FL 34986. **Telephone:** (772) 871-2100. **FAX:** (772) 878-9802. **Website:** www.stluciemets.com.

Affiliation (first year): New York Mets (1988). **Years in League:** 1988-.

Ownership, Management

Operated by: Sterling Mets, LP.

Chairman: Fred Wilpon. **President:** Saul Katz. **Executive Vice President/Chief Operating Officer:** Jeff Wilpon.

Director, Florida Operations/General Manager: Paul Taglieri. **Assistant GM, Stadium Operations:** Traer Van Allen. **Assistant GM, Marketing/Public Relations:** Ari Skalet. **Director, Food Services:** Chip Wheeler. **Office Assistant:** Cynthia Malaspino. **Account Executive:** Brian Paupeck. **Administrative Assistant:** Paula Sloan. **Head Groundskeeper:** Tommy Bowes. **Clubhouse Manager:** Jack Brenner.

Field Staff

Manager: Ken Oberkfell. **Coach:** Howard Johnson. **Pitching Coach:** Dan Warthen. **Trainer:** Mike Lopriore.

Game Information

Radio: None.

PA Announcer: Kevin Driscoll. **Official Scorer:** Bob Adams.

Stadium Name (year opened): Thomas J. White Stadium (1988). **Location:** Exit 121 (St. Lucie West Blvd.) off I-95, east ½ mile, left on NW Peacock Blvd. **Standard Game Times:** 7 p.m.; Sun 1.

Visiting Club Hotel: Holiday Inn, 10120 S. Federal Hwy., Port St. Lucie, FL 34952. Telephone: (772) 337-2200.

SARASOTA
Red Sox

Office Address: 2700 12th St., Sarasota, FL 34237. **Mailing Address:** P.O. Box 2816, Sarasota, FL 34230. **Telephone:** (941) 365-4460. **FAX:** (941) 365-4217.

Affiliation (first year): Boston Red Sox (1994). **Years in League:** 1927, 1961-65, 1989-.

Ownership, Management

Operated by: Red Sox of Florida, Inc. **Principal Owner:** Boston Red Sox.

General Manager: Todd Stephenson. **Assistant GM:** Jon Haley. **Director, Operations/Marketing:** Brandon Kuhn. **Manager, Ticketing:** Mike Chasanoff. **Clubhouse Manager:** Unavailable.

Field Staff

Manager: Tim Leiper. **Coach:** Chad Epperson. **Pitching Coach:** Ace Adams. **Trainer:** Jeff Gorden.

Game Information

Radio: None.

PA Announcer: Joe Mercurio. **Official Scorer:** Howard Spungen.

Stadium Name (year opened): Ed Smith Stadium (1989). **Location:** I-75 to exit 210, three miles west to Tuttle Avenue, right on Tuttle ½ mile to 12th Street, stadium on left. **Standard Game Times:** 7:05 p.m.; Sun. 1.

Visiting Club Hotel: AmericInn and Suites, 5931 Fruitville Rd, Sarasota, FL 34232. Telephone: (941) 342-8778.

TAMPA Yankees

Office Address: One Steinbrenner Dr., Tampa, FL 33614. **Telephone:** (813) 875-7753. **FAX:** (813) 673-3174. **E-Mail Address:** sarena@yankees.com.

Affiliation (first year): New York Yankees (1994). **Years in League:** 1919-27, 1957-1988, 1994-.

Ownership, Management

Operated by: New York Yankees, LP.

Principal Owner: George Steinbrenner.

General Manager: Sammy Arena. **Assistant GM:** Patrick Scanlon. **Director, Stadium Operations:** Dean Holbert. **Director, Sales/Marketing:** Howard Grosswirth. **Account Representative:** Heath Hardin. **Director, Ticket Sales:** Vance Smith. **Head Groundskeeper:** Ritchie Anderson.

Field Staff

Manager: Bill Masse. **Coach:** Joe Breeden. **Pitching Coach:** Greg Pavlick. **Trainer:** Mike Wickland.

Game Information

Radio: None.

PA Announcer: Steve Hague. **Official Scorer:** Dan Casey.

Stadium Name (year opened): Legends Field (1996). **Location:** I-275 to Martin Luther King, west on Martin Luther King to Dale Mabry. **Standard Game Times:** 7 p.m.; Sun. 1.

Visiting Club Hotel: Holiday Inn Express, 4732 N. Dale Mabry Hwy., Tampa, FL 33614. Telephone: (813) 877-6061.

VERO BEACH Dodgers

Office Address: 4101 26th St., Vero Beach, FL 32960. **Mailing Address:** P.O. Box 2887, Vero Beach, FL 32961. **Telephone:** (772) 569-4900. **FAX:** (772) 567-0819. **E-Mail Address:** info@vbdodgers.com. **Website:** www.vbdodgers.com.

Affiliation (first year): Los Angeles Dodgers (1980). **Years in League:** 1980-.

Ownership, Management

Operated by: Los Angeles Dodgers.

President: Bob Daly.

General Manager: Trevor Gooby. **Assistant GM:** Jeff Singer. **Head Groundskeeper:** Steve Carlsward. **Director, Ticket Sales:** Louise Boissy. **Manager, Concessions/Souvenirs:** Kathy Bond. **Secretary:** Joann Lane. **Advertising Secretary:** Betty Rollins. **Administrative Assistants:** Geoff Freedman, A.J. Grant, Chris Jett.

Field Staff

Manager: Scott Little. **Coach:** Brian Traxler. **Pitching Coach:** Ken Howell. **Trainer:** Chris Hiatt.

Game Information

Radio Announcer: Scott Lauer. **No. of Games Broadcast:** Home-70, Away-70. **Flagship Station:** WTTB 1490-AM.

PA Announcers: Joe Sanchez, Steve Stone. **Official Scorer:** Randy Phillips.

Stadium Name (year opened): Holman Stadium (1953). **Location:** I-95 to Route 60 East, left on 43rd Avenue, right on Aviation Boulevard. **Standard Game Times:** 7 p.m.; Sun. (April-June) 1, (July-Aug.) 5.

Visiting Club Hotel: Key West Inn, 1580 US 1, Sebastian, FL 32958. Telephone: (772) 388-8588.

MIDWEST LEAGUE

CLASS A

Office Address: 1118 Cranston Rd., Beloit, WI 53511. **Mailing Address:** P.O. Box 936, Beloit, WI 53512. **Telephone:** (608) 364-1188. **FAX:** (608) 364-1913. **E-Mail Address:** mwl@midwestleague.com. **Website:** www.midwestleague.com.

Years League Active: 1947-.

President, Treasurer: George Spelius.

Vice President: Ed Larson. **Legal Counsel/Secretary:** Richard Nussbaum.

Directors: Andrew Appleby (Fort Wayne), Sam Bernabe (Battle Creek), Lew Chamberlin (West Michigan), Dennis Conerton (Beloit), Tom Dickson (Lansing), Kevin Krause (Quad City), Wally Krouse (Cedar Rapids), Alan Levin (South Bend), Robert Murphy (Dayton), Doug Smith (Clinton), Rocky Vonachen (Peoria), Dave Walker (Burlington), Mike Woleben (Kane County), Rob Zerjav (Wisconsin).

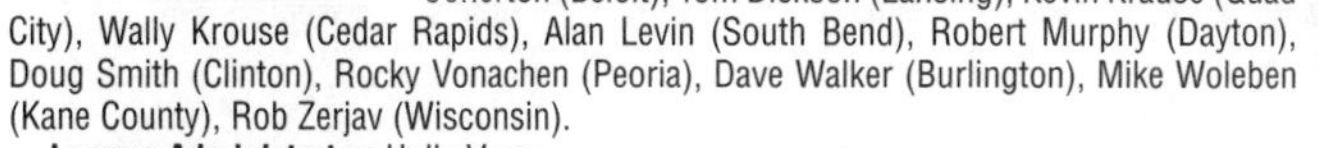

George Spelius

League Administrator: Holly Voss.

2003 Opening Date: April 3. **Closing Date:** Sept. 1.

Regular Season: 140 games (split-schedule).

Division Structure: East—Battle Creek, Dayton, Fort Wayne, Lansing, South Bend, West Michigan. **West**—Beloit, Burlington, Cedar Rapids, Clinton, Kane County, Peoria, Quad City, Wisconsin.

Playoff Format: Eight teams qualify. First-half and second-half division champions, and wild-card teams, meet in best-of-3 quarterfinal series. Winners meet in best-of-3 series for division championship. Division champions meet in best-of-5 final for league championship.

All-Star Game: June 17 at West Michigan.

Roster Limit: 25 active. **Player Eligibility Rule:** No age limit. No more than two players and one player-coach on active list may have more than five years experience.

Brand of Baseball: Rawlings ROM-MID.

Statistician: SportsTicker-Boston, Boston Fish Pier, West Bldg. #1, Suite 302, Boston MA 02210.

Umpires: Jeremy Barbe (Wichita, KS), Steven Bretz (St. Johns, MI), Josh Carlisle (New Philadelphia, OH),Jason Day (Carlyle, IL), Russell Dunn (Caruthersville, MO),Barry Larson (Lewiston, ID), Joe Maiden (West Hills, CA), Bojo Morris (Texarkana, AR), Brian Reilly (Lansing, MI), Will Robinson (Jonesboro, AR), Jeremy Sparling (El Segundo, CA), Chris Thomas (Versailles, KY), David Uyl (Caledonia, MI).

STADIUM INFORMATION

		Dimensions				
Club	**Stadium**	**LF**	**CF**	**RF**	**Capacity**	**2002 Att.**
Battle Creek	C.O. Brown	322	402	333	6,000	84,723
Beloit	Pohlman Field	325	380	325	3,500	74,096
Burlington	Community Field	338	403	315	3,500	58,511
Cedar Rapids	Veterans Memorial	325	385	325	6,000	196,066
Clinton	Riverview	335	390	325	2,500	78,550
Dayton	Fifth Third Field	320	400	320	7,230	571,094
Fort Wayne	Memorial	330	400	330	6,516	260,166
Kane County	Philip B. Elfstrom	335	400	335	7,400	510,390
Lansing	Oldsmobile Park	305	412	305	11,000	380,820
Peoria	O'Brien Field	310	400	310	6,500	254,407
Quad City	John O'Donnell	340	390	340	5,200	117,559
South Bend	Coveleski Regional	336	405	336	5,000	181,021
West Michigan	Fifth Third Ballpark	327	402	327	10,900	400,166
Wisconsin	Fox Cities	325	405	325	5,500	199,210

BATTLE CREEK
Yankees

Office Address: 1392 Capital Ave. NE, Battle Creek MI 49017. **Telephone:** (269) 660-2287. **FAX:** (269) 660-2288. **E-Mail Address:** info@battlecreekyankees.com. **Website:** www.battlecreekyankees.com

Affiliation (first year): New York Yankees (2003). **Years in League:** 1995-.

Ownership, Management

Operated by: Riverside Baseball, LLC.

Executive Director: Sam Bernabe.

General Manager: Tony DaSilveira. **Director, Stadium Operations:** Luke Kuboushek. **Director, Media Relations:** Scott Sailor. **Director, Community Relations:** David Darkey. **Director, Corporate Sales:** Tim Wilson. **Director, Baseball Operations:** Jacob Bolton. **Director, Technology:** Michael Gartner. **Sports Turf Manager:** Len Matthews.

Field Staff

Manager: Mitch Seoane. **Coach:** Ty Hawkins. **Pitching Coach:** Steve Renko. **Trainer:** Zac Womack.

Game Information

Radio: Unavailable.

PA Announcer: Unavailable. **Official Scorer:** Unavailable.

Stadium Name (year opened): C.O. Brown Stadium (1990). **Location:** I-94 to exit 98B (downtown), to Capital Avenue and continue five miles to stadium. **Standard Game Times:** 7 p.m., (April-May) 6; Sun. 2.

Visiting Club Hotel: Comfort Inn, 165 Capital Ave. SW, Battle Creek MI 49017. Telephone: (269) 965-3201.

BELOIT
Snappers

Office Address: 2301 Skyline Dr., Beloit, WI 53511. **Mailing Address:** P.O. Box 855, Beloit, WI 53512. **Telephone:** (608) 362-2272. **FAX:** (608) 362-0418. **E-Mail Address:** snappy@snappersbaseball.com. **Website:** www.snappersbaseball.com.

Affiliation (first year): Milwaukee Brewers (1982). **Years in League:** 1982-.

Ownership, Management

Operated by: Beloit Professional Baseball Association, Inc.

Chairman: Dennis Conerton. **President:** Marcy Olsen.

General Manager: Brian Schackow. **Director, Public Relations/Promotions:** Dave Costello. **Director, Corporate Sales/Gameday Operations:** Brian Barkowski. **Director, Ticket Operations/Merchandise/Concessions**: Jeff Vohs.

Field Staff

Manager: Don Money. **Coach:** Unavailable. **Pitching Coach:** Rich Sauveur. **Trainer:** Alan Diamond.

Game Information

Radio: Unavailable.

PA Announcer: Dave Costello. **Official Scorer:** Unavailable.

Stadium Name (year opened): Pohlman Field (1982). **Location:** I-90 to exit 185-A, right at Cranston Road; I-43 to Wisconsin 81 to Cranston Road, right at Cranston. **Standard Game Times:** 7 p.m., (April-May) 6:30; Sun. 2.

Visiting Club Hotel: Econo Lodge, 2956 Milwaukee Rd., Beloit, WI 53511. Telephone: (608) 364-4000.

BURLINGTON
Bees

BURLINGTON Bees TM

Office Address: 2712 Mt. Pleasant St., Burlington, IA 52601. **Mailing Address:** P.O. Box 824, Burlington, IA 52601. **Telephone:** (319) 754-5705. **FAX:** (319) 754-5882. **E-Mail Address:** staff@gobees.com. **Website:** www.gobees.com.

Affiliation (first year): Kansas City Royals (2001). **Years in League:** 1962-.

Ownership, Management

Operated by: Burlington Baseball Association, Inc.

President: Dave Walker.

General Manager: Chuck Brockett. **Director, Media/Public Relations:** Randy Wehofer. **Head Groundskeeper:** Chad Kluesner. **Director, Stadium Operations/Marketing Assistant:** Heath Thomas. **Office Manager:** Lisa Siefken.

Field Staff

Manager: Joe Szekely. **Coach:** Patrick Anderson. **Pitching Coach:** Tom Burgmeier. **Trainer:** Mark Stubblefield.

Game Information

Radio Announcer: Randy Wehofer. **No. of Games Broadcast:** Home-70, Away-70. **Flagship Stations:** KBUR 1490-AM, KBKB 1360-AM.

PA Announcer: Bob Engberg. **Official Scorer:** Scott Logas.

Stadium Name (year opened): Community Field (1947). **Location:** From US 34, take US 61 North to Mt. Pleasant Street, east ⅛ mile. **Standard Game Times:** 7 p.m.; Sat. (April-May) 6; Sun. 2.

Visiting Club Hotel: Pzazz Best Western, 3001 Winegard Dr., Burlington, IA 52601. Telephone: (319) 753-2223.

CEDAR RAPIDS
Kernels

Office Address: 950 Rockford Rd. SW, Cedar Rapids, IA 52404. **Mailing Address:** P.O. Box 2001, Cedar Rapids, IA 52406. **Telephone:** (319) 363-3887. **FAX:** (319) 363-5631. **E-Mail Address:** kernels@kernels.com. **Website:** www.kernels.com.

Affiliation (first year): Anaheim Angels (1993). **Years in League:** 1962-.

Ownership, Management

Operated by: Cedar Rapids Baseball Club, Inc.

President: Wally Krouse.

General Manager: Jack Roeder. **Director, Merchandising:** Nancy Cram. **Head Groundskeeper:** Rob Schulte. **Director, Ticket/Group Sales:** Kelly O'Brien. **Director, Marketing/Public Relations:** Mike Koolbeck. **Director, Finance/Human Resources:** Charlie Patrick. **Director, Stadium Operations/Sales:** Alan Bernard. **Director, Graphics/Technology:** Andrew Pantini. **Assistant to GM:** Casey Haakinson. **Clubhouse Operations:** Ron Plein.

Field Staff

Manager: Todd Claus. **Coach:** James Rowson. **Pitching Coach:** Erik Bennett. **Trainer:** Tyler Waltz.

Game Information

Radio Announcer: John Rodgers. **No. of Games Broadcast:** Home-70, Away-70. **Flagship Station:** KCRG 1600-AM.

PA Announcer: Dale Brodt. **Official Scorer:** Al Gruwell.

Stadium Name (year opened): Veterans Memorial Stadium (2002). **Location:** I-380 to Wilson Ave. exit, west to Rockford Road, right one mile to corner of 8th Ave. and 15th Street SW. **Standard Game Times:** 7 p.m., (April-May, Sept.) 6:30 p.m.; Sat. (April-May) 5, (June-Aug.) 7; Sun. 2.

Visiting Club Hotel: Best Western Village Inn, 100 F Ave. NW, Cedar Rapids, IA 52405. Telephone: (319) 366-5323.

CLINTON
LumberKings

Office Address: Alliant Energy Field, Sixth Avenue and First Street, Clinton, IA 52732. **Mailing Address:** P.O. Box 1295, Clinton, IA 52733. **Telephone:** (563) 242-0727. **FAX:** (563) 242-1433. **E-Mail Address:** lumberkings@lumberkings.com. **Website:** www.lumberkings.com.

Affiliation (first year): Texas Rangers (2003). **Years in League:** 1956-.

Ownership, Management

Operated by: Clinton Baseball Club, Inc.

Chairman: Don Roode. **President:** Doug Smith.

General Manager: Ted Tornow. **Director, Sales/Promotions:** Troy Russell. **Groundskeeper:** Unavailable.

Field Staff

Manager: Carlos Subero. **Coach:** Mike Boulanger. **Pitching Coach:** Andy Hawkins. **Trainer:** Mark Ryan.

Game Information

Radio Announcer: Chris Lake. **No. of Games Broadcast:** Home-70, Away-70. **Flagship Station:** KCLN 1390-AM.

PA Announcer: Morty Kriner. **Official Scorer:** Spike Tuss.

Stadium Name (year opened): Alliant Energy Field (1937). **Location:** Highway 30 East to Sixth Avenue North, right on Sixth, cross railroad tracks, stadium on right. **Standard Game Times:** 7 p.m.; Sat. (April-May) 2; Sun. 2.

Visiting Club Hotel: Super 8 Motel, 1711 Lincoln Way, Clinton, IA 52732. Telephone: (563) 242-8870.

DAYTON
Dragons

Office Address: Fifth Third Field, 220 N. Patterson Blvd., Dayton, OH 45402. **Mailing Address:** P.O. Box 2107, Dayton, OH 45401. **Telephone:** (937) 228-2287.

FAX: (937) 228-2284. **E-Mail Address:** dragons@daytondragons.com. **Website:** www.daytondragons.com.
Affiliate (first year): Cincinnati Reds (2000). **Years in League:** 2000-.

Ownership, Management

Operated by: Dayton Professional Baseball, LLC.

Owners: Hank Stickney, Ken Stickney, Peter Guber, Paul Schaeffer, Earvin "Magic" Johnson, Archie Griffin.

President: Robert Murphy. **Executive Vice President:** Eric Deutsch.

VP, Baseball/Stadium Operations: Gary Mayse. **VP, Sponsorships:** Mark Clayton. **Director, Ticket Sales:** Deron Marchant. **Director, Team Accounting:** Jim Goodrich. **Staff Accountant:** Dorothy Day. **Director, Entertainment:** Shari Sharkins. **Director, Marketing:** Jim Francis. **Director, Media Relations/Broadcasting:** Mike Vander Wood. **Corporate Sales:** Jeff Forthofer, Jeff Thompson. **Corporate Marketing Managers:** Michael Blanton, Brian Brinck, Jermaine Gage, Laura Rose, Mark Wilhelm. **Marketing Managers:** Brad Eaton, Shannon Johnson, Damon Swenson. **Manager, Box Office:** Sally Ledford. **Operations Manager:** Joe Eaglowski. **Facilities Manager:** Joe Elking. **Operations Associate:** Mitch Heaton. **Head Groundskeeper:** Ryan Kaspitzke. **Office Administrator:** Leslie Stuck. **Administrative Assistant:** Lisa Rike. **Receptionist:** Barbara Van Schaik.

Field Staff

Manager: Donnie Scott. **Coach:** Billy White. **Pitching Coach:** Jaime Garcia. **Trainer:** Randy Brackney.

Game Information

Radio Announcer: Mike Vander Wood. **No. of Games Broadcast:** Home-70, Away-70. **Flagship Station:** WHIO 1290-AM.

PA Announcer: Unavailable. **Official Scorers:** Matt Lindsay, Jim Scott.

Stadium Name (year opened): Fifth Third Field (2000). **Location:** I-75 South to downtown Dayton, left at First Street; I-75 North, right at First Street exit. **Standard Game Times:** 7 p.m.; Sun. 2.

Visiting Club Hotel: Fairfield Inn-Dayton North, 6960 Miller Lane, Dayton, OH 45414. Telephone: (937) 898-1120.

FORT WAYNE
Wizards

Office Address: 1616 E. Coliseum Blvd., Fort Wayne, IN 46805. **Telephone:** (260) 482-6400. **FAX:** (260) 471-4678. **E-Mail:** info@wizardsbaseball.com. **Website:** www.wizardsbaseball.com.

Affiliation (first year): San Diego Padres (1999). **Years in League:** 1993-.

Ownership/Management

Operated by: General Sports and Entertainment, LLC.

Owner: Andrew Appleby.

General Manager: Mike Nutter. **Vice President, Business Operations:** Tracy Marek. **Senior Assistant GM:** David Lorenz. **Director, Business Development:** Randy Newell. **Director, Marketing/Graphic Design:** Michael Limmer. **Director, Ticket Operations:** Michael Moody. **Director, Broadcasting:** Terry Byrom. **Community/Media Relations:** Jared Parcell. **Group Sales Representative:** Michael Donohoo. **Group Sales Representative/Coordinator, Reading Program:** Jeff Bierly. **Office Manager:** Lisa Lorenz.

Field Staff

Manager: Gary Jones. **Coach:** Tom Tornincasa. **Pitching Coach:** Mike Harkey. **Trainer:** Brian Komprood.

Game Information

Radio Announcers: Terry Byrom, Kent Hormann. **No. of Games Broadcast:** Home-70, Away-70. **Flagship Station:** WONO 1380-AM.

PA Announcer: Unavailable. **Official Scorer:** Unavailable.

Stadium Name (year opened): Memorial Stadium (1993). **Location:** Exit 112A (Coldwater Road South) off I-69 to Coliseum Blvd., left to stadium. **Standard Game Times:** 6 p.m., (June-July) 7; Wed. 11, (June-July) 12; Sat. 4, (June-July) 6; Sun. 2.

Visiting Club Hotel: Best Western Luxbury, 5501 Coventry Lane, Fort Wayne, IN 46804. Telephone: (260) 436-0242.

KANE COUNTY
Cougars

Office Address: 34W002 Cherry Lane, Geneva, IL 60134. **Telephone:** (630) 232-8811. **FAX:** (630) 232-8815. **E-Mail Addresses:** info@kccougars.com. **Website:** www.kccougars.com.

Affiliation (first year): Oakland Athletics (2003). **Years in League:** 1991-.

Ownership, Management

Operated by: Cougars Baseball Partnership/American Sports Enterprises, Inc.

President: Mike Woleben. **Vice President:** Mike Murtaugh.

VP/General Manager: Jeff Sedivy. **Assistant GMs:** Curtis Haug, Jeff Ney. **Business Manager:** Mary Almlie. **Comptroller:** Doug Czurylo. **Director, Ticket Operations:** Amy Mason. **Coordinator, Season Tickets:** Kelle Renninger. **Ticket Operations:** Mike Gilreath, Brandi Hagen. **Director, Ticket Sales:** Michael Patterson. **Account Executives:** Mike Antonellis, David Edison, Kristen Gorski, Marty Henry, Greg Hofer, Patti Savage, Brock Shaw. **Director, Food/Beverage:** Rich Essegian. **Director, Catering:** Mike Klafehn. **Personnel Manager:** Sam Rasmussen. **Manager, Public Relations:** Kari Kuefler. **Public Relations Assistant:** Denise Cromer. **Manager, Advertising:** Bill Baker. **Head Groundskeeper:** Ryan Nieuwsma. **Assistant Groundskeeper:** Brad Anderson. **Design/Graphics:** Emmet Broderick, Todd Koenitz. **Office Manager:** Carol Huppert. **Facilities Management:** Bill Hutchens, Jeff Snyder. **Head of Security:** Dan Klinkhammer. **Clubhouse Manager:** Unavailable.

Field Staff

Manager: Webster Garrison. **Coach:** Eddie Williams. **Pitching Coach:** Jim Coffman. **Trainer:** Justin Whitehouse.

Game Information

Radio Announcer: Mike Antonellis. **No. of Games Broadcast:** Home-70, Away-70. **Flagship Station:** WBIG 1280-AM.

PA Announcer: Kevin Sullivan. **Official Scorer:** Bill Baker.

Stadium Name (year opened): Philip B. Elfstrom Stadium (1991). **Location:** From east or west, I-88 (East-West Tollway) to Farnsworth Road North exit, north five miles to Cherry Lane, left into stadium complex; from north, Route 59 south to Route 64 (North Ave.), west to Kirk Road, south past Route 38 to Cherry Lane, right into stadium complex; from northwest, I-90 to Randall Road South exit, south to Fabyan Parkway, east to Kirk Road, north to Cherry Lane, left into stadium complex. **Standard Game Times:** 7 p.m., (April-May 22) 6; Sat. (April-May 17) 4, (May 24-Sept.) 6; Sun. 2.

Visiting Club Hotel: Best Western Naperville, 1617 Naperville Rd., Naperville, IL 60563. Telephone: (630) 505-0200.

LANSING
Lugnuts

Office Address: 505 E. Michigan Ave., Lansing, MI 48912. **Telephone:** (517) 485-4500. **Fax:** (517) 485-4518. **E-Mail Address:** info@lansinglugnuts.com. **Website:** www.lansinglugnuts.com.

Affiliation (first year): Chicago Cubs (1999). **Years In League:** 1996-.

Ownership, Management

Operated by: Take Me Out to the Ballgame, LLC.

Principal Owners: Tom Dickson, Sherrie Myers.

General Manager: Greg Rauch. **Vice President, Sales:** Jeff Calhoun. **Director, Marketing:** Darla Bowen. **Director, Finance/Human Resources:** Kimberly Hengesbach. **Director, Operations:** Jeremy Knuckman. **Manager, Food Service:** Dave Parker. **Manager, Marketing:** Elizabeth Klatt. **Manager, Tickets:** Chris Troub. **Director, Retail:** Cherie Hargitt. **Marketing Assistant:** Seth VanHoven. **Head Groundskeeper:** Russ Washegesic. **Managers, Group Sales:** Nick Grueser, Shawn Mortensen. **Group Sales Representative:** Jessica Fergesen. **Sponsorship Account Executive:** Bill Kennedy. **Sponsorship Service Representative:** Valerie Claus. **Coordinator, Sponsorship:** Marla Terranova. **Business Manager:** Suzanne Brock. **Front Desk Administrator:** Sharon Jackson.

Field Staff

Manager: Julio Garcia. **Coach:** Mike Micucci. **Pitching Coach:** Mike Anderson. **Trainer:** Jason Palmateer.

Game Information

Radio Announcer: Jim Tocco. **No. of Games Broadcast:** Home-64, Away-67 (no weekday day games). **Flagship Station:** WVFN 730-AM.

PA Announcer: J.J. Wright. **Official Scorer:** Mike Clark.

Stadium Name (year opened): Oldsmobile Park(1996). **Location:** I-96 East/West to U.S. 496, exit at Larch Street. **Standard Game Times:** 7:05 p.m., (April-May) 6:05; Sun. 2:05.

Visiting Club Hotel: Holiday Inn South, 6820 S. Cedar St., Lansing, MI 48911. Telephone: (517) 694-8123.

PEORIA
Chiefs

Office Address: 730 SW Jefferson, Peoria, IL 61605. **Telephone:** (309) 680-4000. **FAX:** (309) 680-4080. **Website:** www.peoriachiefs.com.

Affiliation (first year): St. Louis Cardinals (1995). **Years in League:** 1983-.

Ownership/Management

Operated by: Peoria Chiefs Community Baseball Club, LLC.

President, General Manager: Rocky Vonachen. **Vice President:** Mark Moehlenkamp. **Assistant GM, Operations:** Mark Vonachen. **Director, Administration/Finance:** Angie Riley. **Manager, Media/Marketing:** Jay Allen. **Director,**

Guest Services/Account Executive: Howard Yates. **Manager, Box Office:** Ryan Sivori. **Manager, Entertainment/Events:** Autum Vorhees. **Account Executives:** Jennifer Blackorby, Kelley Currier, Brian Finn, Joel Peterson, Andrew Tyra. **Office Manager:** Barb Lindberg.

Field Staff

Manager: Joe Cunningham. **Coach:** Tony Diggs. **Pitching Coach:** Derek Lilliquist. **Trainer:** R.J. Romero.

Game Information

Radio: Unavailable.

PA Announcer: Seth Treptow. **Official Scorers:** Jeff Morris, Jim Rea.

Stadium Name (year opened): O'Brien Field (2002). **Location:** From South/East, I-74 to exit 93 (Jefferson Street), west one mile, stadium is one block west of Kumpf Blvd. on left. From North/West, I-74 to exit 91 (Glendale Avenue), straight through stoplight and follow Kumpf Blvd. left for five blocks, right on Jefferson Street, stadium on left. **Standard Game Times:** 7 p.m., (April-May) 6:30; Sun. 2, (April-May) 5.

Visiting Club Hotel: Holiday Inn City Centre, 500 Hamilton Blvd., Peoria, IL 61602. Telephone: (309) 674-2500.

QUAD CITY
River Bandits

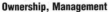

Office Address: 209 S. Gaines St., Davenport, IA 52802. **Mailing Address:** P.O. Box 3496, Davenport, IA 52808. **Telephone:** (563) 324-3000. **FAX:** (563) 324-3109. **E-Mail Address:** bandit@riverbandits.com. **Website:** www.riverbandits.com.

Affiliation (first year): Minnesota Twins (1999). **Years in League:** 1960-.

Ownership, Management

Operated by: Seventh Inning Stretch, LLC.

Principal Owner, President: Kevin Krause.

General Manager: Dave Ziedelis. **Assistant GM:** Josh Krueger. **Manager, Tickets:** Keith Vaske. **Manager, Group Sales:** Michael Corrigan. **Manager, Concessions:** Unavailable. **Director, Broadcasting/Media Relations:** Andrew Rudnik. **Office Manager:** Carrie Brus. **Head Groundskeeper:** Andy Duyvejonck.

Field Staff

Manager: Jeff Carter. **Coach:** Floyd Rayford. **Pitching Coach:** Gary Lucas. **Trainer:** Cory Andrews.

Game Information

Radio Announcer: Andrew Rudnik. **No. of Games Broadcast:** Home-70, Away-70. **Flagship Station:** WKBF 1270-AM.

PA Announcer: Jaimie Jorgenson. **Official Scorer:** Andy Duyvejonck.

Stadium Name (year opened): John O'Donnell Stadium (1931). **Location:** From I-74, take State Street exit, west onto River Drive, south on Gaines Street. From I-80, take Brady/Harrison Street exit south, west onto River Drive, south on Gaines Street. **Standard Game Times:** 7 p.m., (April) 6; Sat. (April) 2; Sun. 2.

Visiting Club Hotel: Clarion Hotel, 227 LeClaire St., Davenport, IA 52801. Telephone: (563) 324-1921.

SOUTH BEND
Silver Hawks

Office Address: 501 W. South St., South Bend, IN 46601. **Mailing Address:** P.O. Box 4218, South Bend, IN 46634. **Telephone:** (574) 235-9988. **FAX:** (574) 235-9950. **E-Mail Address:** hawks@silverhawks.com. **Website:** www.silverhawks.com.

Affiliation (first year): Arizona Diamondbacks (1997). **Years in League:** 1988-.

Ownership, Management

Operated by: Palisades Baseball, Ltd.

Principal Owner: Alan Levin. **Executive Vice President:** Erik Haag. **Chief Financial Officer:** Mick Rauch. **Director, Finance:** Cheryl Case. **Staff Accountant:** Rose Rendek.

General Manager: Christian Carlson. **Manager, Operations:** Mike Cook. **Director, Ticket Sales:** Tony Wittrock. **Manager, Marketing:** Greg Boyd. **Manager, Box Office:** Brian Kost. **Account Executives:** Stephen Hinkel, Ian Zelenski. **Office Manager:** Brandy Beehler. **Head Groundskeeper:** Joel Reinebold.

Field Staff

Manager: Von Hayes. **Coach:** Hector De la Cruz. **Pitching Coach:** Dan Carlson. **Trainer:** Scott Jones.

Game Information

Radio Announcer: Michael Lockert. **No. of Games Broadcast:** Home-70, Away-70. **Flagship Station:** WDND 1620-AM.

PA Announcer: Mark Yarrish. **Official Scorers:** Wade Coulter, Scott Wortman.

Stadium Name (year opened): Stanley Coveleski Regional Stadium (1988). **Location:** I-80/90 toll road to exit 77, take US 31/33 south to South Bend, to downtown (Main Street), to Western Avenue, right on Western, left on Taylor. **Standard Game Times:** 7 p.m., (April-May) 6:30; Sun. 1:30.

Visiting Club Hotel: Holiday Inn-University Area, 515 Dixie Way North, South Bend, IN 46637. Telephone: (574) 272-6600.

WEST MICHIGAN
Whitecaps

Office Address: 4500 W. River Dr., Comstock Park, MI 49321. **Mailing Address:** P.O. Box 428, Comstock Park, MI 49321. **Telephone:** (616) 784-4131. **FAX:** (616) 784-4911. **E-Mail Address:** playball@whitecaps-baseball.com. **Website:** www.whitecaps-baseball.com.

Affiliation (first year): Detroit Tigers (1997). **Years in League:** 1994-.

Ownership, Management

Operated by: Whitecaps Professional Baseball Corp.

Principal Owners: Lew Chamberlin, Dennis Baxter.

Chief Executive Officer, Managing Partner: Lew Chamberlin. **President:** Scott Lane.

Vice President, Operations: Jim Jarecki. **VP, Sales/Marketing:** John Guthrie. **Chief Financial Officer:** Denny Baxter. **Director, Sales:** Dan McCrath. **Director, Food/Beverage:** Tim Restall. **Director, Ticket Sales:** Steve McCarthy. **Manager, Ticket Operations:** Bruce Radley. **Manager, Group Sales:** Kerri Troyer. **Manager, Operations:** Matt Costello. **Manager, Human Resources:** Ellen Chamberlin. **Head Groundskeeper:** Kari Briggs. **Manager, Facility Maintenance:** Dutch VanSingel. **Coordinator, Media Relations:** Jamie Farber. **Coordinator, Community Relations:** Beth Mitchell. **Coordinator, Promotions:** Mickey Graham. **Corporate Sales:** Rick Berkey, Trevor Tkach. **Ticket Sales Consultants:** Jenny Borg, Jason Lewandowski, Scott Lutz. **Facility Maintenance Assistant:** Brian Hammond. **Accounts Receivable Assistant:** Barb Renteria. **Receptionists:** Sarah Doyle, Susie Former. **Ticket Sales Interns:** Josh Eling, Erin Williams. **Public Relations Intern:** Dewayne Hankins.

Field Staff

Manager: Phil Regan. **Coaches:** Barbaro Garbey, Brent Gates. **Pitching Coach:** A.J. Sager. **Trainer:** Rob Sonnenberg.

Game Information

Radio Announcer: Rick Berkey. **No. of Games Broadcast:** Home-70, Away-70. **Flagship Station:** WOOD 1300-AM.

PA Announcers: Bob Wells, Mike Newell. **Official Scorers:** Mike Dean, Don Thomas.

Stadium Name (year opened): Fifth Third Ballpark (1994). **Location:** U.S. 131 North from Grand Rapids to exit 91 (West River Drive). **Standard Game Times:** 7 p.m., (April-May) 6:35; Sat. (April-May) 2; Sun. 2.

Visiting Club Hotel: Days Inn-Downtown, 310 Pearl St. NW, Grand Rapids, MI 49504. Telephone: (616) 235-7611.

WISCONSIN
Timber Rattlers

Office Address: 2400 N. Casaloma Dr., Appleton, WI 54915. **Mailing Address:** P.O. Box 7464, Appleton, WI 54912. **Telephone:** (920) 733-4152. **FAX:** (920) 733-8032. **E-Mail Address:** info@timberrattlers.com. **Website:** www.timberrattlers.com.

Affiliation (first year): Seattle Mariners (1993). **Years in League:** 1962-.

Ownership, Management

Operated by: Appleton Baseball Club, Inc.

Chairman: Mike Weller.

President, General Manager: Rob Zerjav. **Director, Operations:** Tom Kulczewski. **Director, Marketing:** Scott Grall. **Controller:** Cathy Spanbauer. **Community/Media Relations:** Nikki Becker. **Manager, Promotions/Merchandise:** Angela Ceranski. **Manager, Ticket Sales:** Andrew Podlasik. **Managers, Group Sales:** Darren Feller, Lisa Nortman, Peter Schueppert. **Director, Corporate Sales:** Laurie Schill. **Managers, Corporate Sales:** Nicole DeBoth, David Katzenmaier, Chris Mehring. **Office Manager:** Mary Robinson. **Head Groundskeeper:** Jesse Mallmann.

Field Staff

Manager: Daren Brown. **Coach:** Dana Williams. **Pitching Coach:** Brad Holman. **Trainer:** Jeremy Clipperton.

Game Information

Radio Announcer: Chris Mehring. **No. of Games Broadcast:** Home-70, Away-70. **Flagship Station:** WECB 104.3-FM.

PA Announcer: Matt Wittlin. **Official Scorer:** Dan Huber.

Stadium Name (year opened): Fox Cities Stadium (1995). **Location:** Highway 41 to Northand Avenue exit, west to Casaloma Drive, left to stadium. **Standard Game Times:** 7:05 p.m., (April-May) 6:35; Wed. (May) 12:05; Sat. (April-May) 1:05; Sun. 1:05, 5:05.

Visiting Club Hotel: Fairfield Inn, 132 N. Mall Dr., Appleton, WI 54913. Telephone: (920) 954-0202.

SOUTH ATLANTIC LEAGUE

CLASS A

Office Address: 504 Crescent Hill, Kings Mountain, NC 28086. **Mailing Address:** P.O. Box 38, Kings Mountain, NC 28086. **Telephone:** (704) 739-3466. **FAX:** (704) 739-1974. **E-Mail Address:** saleague@bellsouth.net. **Website:** www.southatlanticleague.com.

John Moss

Years League Active: 1904-1964, 1979 -.

President/Secretary-Treasurer: John Moss.

Vice President: Ron McKee (Asheville).

Directors: Don Beaver (Hickory), Cooper Brantley (Greensboro), Rita Carfagna (Lake County), Tom Dickson (Charleston, WV), Joseph Finley (Lakewood), Marv Goldklang (Charleston, SC), Larry Hedrick (Kannapolis), David Heller (South Georgia), Peter Luukko (Delmarva), Ron McKee (Asheville), Chip Moore (Rome), Rich Mozingo (Capital City), Andrew Rayburn (Hagerstown), Michael Savit (Augusta), Ken Silver (Savannah), Alan Stein (Lexington).

Director, Administration: Elaine Moss. **Administrative Assistant:** Patrick Heavner.

2003 Opening Date: April 3. **Closing Date:** Sept. 1.

Regular Season: 140 games (split-schedule).

Division Structure: North—Charleston WV, Delmarva, Greensboro, Hagerstown, Kannapolis, Lake County, Lakewood, Lexington. **South**—Asheville, Augusta, Capital City, Charleston SC, Hickory, Rome, Savannah, South Georgia.

Playoff Format: First-half and second-half division champions meet in best-of-3 semifinal series. Winners advance in best-of-5 series for league championship.

All-Star Game: June 24 at Lexington.

Roster Limit: 25 active. **Player Eligibility Rule:** No age limit. No more than two players and one player-coach on active list may have more than five years of experience.

Brand of Baseball: Rawlings.

Statistician: SportsTicker-Boston, Boston Fish Pier, West Bldg. #1, Suite 302, Boston, MA 02210.

Umpires: John Bennett (Sarasota, FL), Charlie Carillo (Staten Island, NY), Scott Childers (Augusta, GA),Bill Coble (Graham, NC), Brandon Coony (Andrews, TX), Steven Cummings (Pomona Park, FL), Ryan Drake (Oklahoma City, OK), Mike Edwards (Chesapeake, VA), Steve Fritz (Montclair, CA), Edwin Hickox (Daytona Beach, FL), Nathan Huber (Louisville, KY), James Leonard (Port St. Lucie, FL), Jonathan Merry (Gainesville, GA), Billy Parker (Rochester Hills, MI), James Pearson (Mansfield, LA), J.D. Robertson (Hampton, GA).

STADIUM INFORMATION

			Dimensions			
Club	**Stadium**	**LF**	**CF**	**RF**	**Capacity**	**2002 Att.**
Asheville	McCormick Field	328	402	300	4,000	145,065
Augusta	Lake Olmstead	330	400	330	4,322	127,314
Capital City	Capital City	330	395	320	6,000	111,349
Charleston, SC	Riley Ballpark	306	386	336	5,800	242,143
Charleston, WV	Watt Powell Park	340	406	330	4,500	95,187
Delmarva	Perdue	309	402	309	5,200	253,171
Greensboro	War Memorial	327	401	327	7,500	179,393
Hagerstown	Municipal	335	400	330	4,600	103,188
Hickory	L.P. Frans	330	401	330	5,062	182,800
Kannapolis	Fieldcrest Cannon	330	400	310	4,700	105,873
*Lake County	Eastlake Ballpark	320	400	320	7,273	52,103
Lakewood	FirstEnergy Park	325	400	325	6,588	466,474
Lexington	Legends	320	401	318	6,033	428,840
#Rome	Floyd County	335	401	330	5,100	84,001
Savannah	Grayson	290	410	310	8,000	119,223
South Georgia	Paul Eames Sports Complex	310	400	335	4,000	72,025

*Club operated in Columbus, GA, in 2002
#Club operated in Macon, GA, in 2002

ASHEVILLE
Tourists

Office Address: McCormick Field, 30 Buchanan Pl., Asheville, NC 28801. **Mailing Address:** P.O. Box 1556, Asheville, NC 28802. **Telephone:** (828) 258-0428. **FAX:** (828) 258-0320. **E-Mail Address:** touristsbb@mindspring.com. **Website:** www.theashevilletourists.com.

Affiliation (first year): Colorado Rockies (1994). **Years in League:** 1976-.

Ownership, Management

Operated by: Asheville Tourists Baseball, Inc.

Principal Owners: Peter Kern, Ron McKee.

President: Peter Kern.

General Manager: Ron McKee. **Assistant GMs:** Chris Smith, Larry Hawkins. **Director, Business Operations:** Carolyn McKee. **Director, Media Relations:** Bill Ballew. **Director, Tickets/Merchandising:** Margarita Turner. **Concessions Manager:** Ben Ashby. **Head Groundskeeper:** Patrick Schrimplin.

Field Staff

Manager: Joe Mikulik. **Coach:** Darron Cox. **Pitching Coach:** Mike Arner. **Trainer:** Heath Townsend.

Game Information

Radio: None.

PA Announcer: Rick Diggler. **Official Scorers:** Wilt Browning, Mike Gore.

Stadium Name (year opened): McCormick Field (1992). **Location:** I-240 to Charlotte Street South exit, south one mile on Charlotte, left on McCormick Place. **Standard Game Times:** 7 p.m.; Sun. 2.

Visiting Club Hotel: Holiday Inn East, 1450 Tunnel Rd., Asheville, NC 28805. Telephone: (828) 298-5611.

AUGUSTA
GreenJackets

Office Address: 78 Milledge Rd., Augusta, GA 30904. **Mailing Address:** P.O. Box 3746, Augusta, GA 30904. **Telephone:** (706) 736-7889. **FAX:** (706) 736-1122. **E-Mail Address:** grnsox@aol.com. **Website:** www.greenjackets.net.

Affiliation (first year): Boston Red Sox (1999). **Years in League:** 1988-.

Ownership, Management

Operated by: H.W.S. Baseball, LLC.

Chief Executive Officer: Michael Savit. **Chief Operating Officer:** Jeffrey Savit. **Executive Vice President:** Chris Scheuer.

General Manager: David Van Lenten. **Assistant GM:** Nick Brown. **Business Manager:** Jenny Mercer. **Assistant, Stadium Operations:** David Ryther. **Assistant, Promotions:** Larry Lichtenfeld. **Assistant, Media Relations:** Unavailable. **Groundskeeper:** Unavailable.

Field Staff

Manager: Russ Morman. **Pitching Coach:** Dave Tomlin. **Hitting Coach:** John Malzone. **Trainer:** Chris Sheheane.

Game Information

Radio: None.

PA Announcer: Scott Skadan. **Official Scorer:** Steve Cain.

Stadium Name (year opened): Lake Olmstead Stadium (1995). **Location:** I-20 to exit 199 (Washington Road), east to Broad Street, left onto Milledge Road, stadium on right. **Standard Game Times:** 7:15 p.m., Sun. 2:15.

Visiting Club Hotel: Holiday Inn-West, 1075 Stevens Creek Rd., Augusta, GA 30907. Telephone: (706) 738-8811.

CAPITAL CITY
Bombers

Office Address: 301 S. Assembly St., Columbia, SC 29201. **Mailing Address:** P.O. Box 7845, Columbia, SC 29202. **Telephone:** (803) 256-4110. **FAX:** (803) 256-4338. **E-Mail Address:** info@bomberball.com. **Website:** www.bomberball.com.

Affiliation (first year): New York Mets (1983). **Years in League:** 1960-61, 1983-.

Ownership, Management

Operated by: RB3, LLC

President: Rich Mozingo.

General Manager: Tim Swain. **Assistant GM/Director, Media:** Mark Bryant. **Assistant GM, Ticket Operations:**

Brian Kenna. **Director, Stadium Operations/Head Groundskeeper:** Bob Hook. **Director, Corporate Ticket Sales:** Henry Chastain. **Director, Group Sales:** Pete Ehmke. **Account Executives:** Scott Ehrlich, Elizabeth Gibbons.

Field Staff

Manager: Tony Tijerina. **Coach:** Donovan Mitchell. **Pitching Coach:** Blaine Beatty. **Trainer:** Victor Trasoff-Jilg.

Game Information

Radio: None.

PA Announcer: Unavailable. **Official Scorer:** Julian Gibbons.

Stadium Name (year opened): Capital City Stadium (1991). **Location:** I-26 East to Columbia, Elmwood Avenue to Assembly Street, right on Assembly for four miles; I-77 South to Columbia, exit at State Road 277 (Bull Street), right on Elmwood, left on Assembly. **Standard Game Times:** 7:05 p.m., Sun. (April-May) 2:05, (June-Aug.) 6:05.

Visiting Club Hotel: Travelodge, 2210 Bush River Rd., Columbia, SC 29210. Telephone: (803) 798-9665.

CHARLESTON, S.C.

RiverDogs

Office Address: 360 Fishburne St., Charleston, SC 29403. **Mailing Address:** P.O. Box 20849, Charleston, SC 29413. **Telephone:** (843) 723-7241. **FAX:** (843) 723-2641. **E-Mail Address:** dogsrus@riverdogs.com. **Website:** www.riverdogs.com.

Affiliation (first year): Tampa Bay Devil Rays (1997). **Years in League:** 1973-78, 1980-.

Ownership, Management

Operated by: The Goldklang Group/South Carolina Baseball Club, LP.

Principal Owners: Marv Goldklang, Mike Veeck, Bill Murray.

General Manager: Derek Sharrer. **Assistant GM:** Jim Lucas. **Director, Stadium Operations:** Ben Danosky. **Director, Promotions/Merchandise:** Stacy Wagner. **Coordinator, Sales:** Joe Hauhn. **Coordinator, Sponsorship:** Andy Lange. **Business Manager:** Aubra Carlton. **Office Manager:** Kristal Lessington. **Director, Special Events:** Dale Stickney. **Director, Food/Beverage:** Nick Fleming. **Ticket Manager:** Chris Ginnett. **Coordinator, Media Relations:** Dan Lehv. **Coordinator, Internet:** Will Cobb. **Director, Community Relations:** Danielle Swigart. **Manager, Food/Beverage:** Amy Ferris. **Assistant Manager, Food/Beverage:** Darnell Aiken. **Manager, Sales:** Harold Craw. **Promotions Assistant:** Kristi Tolley. **Intern, Broadcast/Media:** Darren Goldwater.

Field Staff

Manager: Mako Oliveras. **Coach:** Steve Livesey. **Pitching Coach:** Xavier Hernandez. **Trainer:** Dan Plante.

Game Information

Radio Announcers: Dan Lehv, Jim Lucas. **No. of Games Broadcast:** Home-70, Away-70. **Flagship Station:** WQSC 1340-AM.

PA Announcer: Ken Carrington. **Official Scorer:** Chuck Manka.

Stadium Name (year opened): Joseph P. Riley Jr. Ballpark (1997). **Location:** From U.S. 17, take Lockwood Drive North, right on Fishburne Street. **Standard Game Times:** 7:05 p.m.; Sun. 5:05.

Visiting Club Hotel: Howard Johnson Riverfront, 250 Spring St., Charleston, SC 29403. Telephone: (843) 722-4000.

CHARLESTON, W.VA.

Alley Cats

Office Address: 3403 MacCorkle Ave. SE, Charleston, WV 25304. **Telephone:** (304) 344-2287. **FAX:** (304) 344-0083. **E-Mail Address:** team@charlestonalleycats.com. **Website:** www.charlestonalleycats.com.

Affiliation (first year): Toronto Blue Jays (2001). **Years in League:** 1987-.

Ownership, Management

Operated by: Charleston Professional Baseball Club, LLC.

Principal Owners: Tom Dickson, Sherrie Myers.

General Manager: Megan Frazer. **Assistant GM:** Patrick Day. **Business Manager:** Krystal Trent. **Director, Concessions:** Doug Prosperi. **Director, Ticketing/Operations:** Chad Hodson. **Group Sales Intern:** Gretchen Smith. **Group Sales Representative:** Christopher Hahn. **Manager, Marketing:** Jordan Welsh.

Field Staff

Manager: Mark Meleski. **Coach:** Charles Poe. **Pitching Coach:** James Keller. **Trainer:** Voon Chong.

Game Information

Radio Announcer: Dan Peterson. **No. of Games Broadcast:** Home-70, Away-70. **Flagship Station:** WBES 1240-AM.

PA Announcer: Unavailable. **Official Scorer:** Unavailable.

Stadium Name (year opened): Watt Powell Park (1949). **Location:** From north/west, I-64/77 to exit 98 (35th Street

Bridge), cross bridge, ballpark is at MacCorkle; From south/east, I-64/77 to exit 95 (MacCorkle Avenue), take MacCorkle Avenue West ramp (Route 61 North), stadium is 21/2 miles on left. **Standard Game Times:** 6:15 p.m./7:15; Sun. 2:15.

Visiting Club Hotel: TraveLodge of Charleston, 2 Kanawha Blvd. East, Charleston, WV 25301. Telephone: (304) 343-4521.

DELMARVA
Shorebirds

Office Address: 6400 Hobbs Rd., Salisbury, MD 21804. **Mailing Address:** P.O. Box 1557, Salisbury, MD 21802. **Telephone:** (410) 219-3112. **FAX:** (410) 219-9164. **E-Mail Address:** information@theshorebirds.com. **Website:** www.theshorebirds.com.

Affiliation (first year): Baltimore Orioles (1997). **Years in League:** 1996-.

Ownership, Management

Operated by: Comcast-Spectacor.

Directors: Peter Luukko, Frank Miceli.

General Manager: Jim Terrill. **Assistant GM:** Martin Ward. **Director, Stadium Operations:** Deandre Ewell. **Head Groundskeeper:** Chris Farner. **Director, Media/Public Relations:** Keli Wright. **Director, Broadcasting:** Shane Griffin. **Director, Marketing:** Ryan Murray. **Corporate Account Representatives:** Chris Ouellet, Charlie Shahan. **Manager, Accounting:** Gail Potts. **Ticket Manager:** Randy Brown. **Director, Ticket Operations:** Brad Sims. **Assistant Director, Ticket Operations:** Kristi Thompson. **Ticket Sales Representatives:** Jason Hall, John Perdue, Kris Rutledge, Norb Sadilek. **Office Manager:** Dana Holyfield.

Field Staff

Manager: Stan Hough. **Coach:** Don Werner. **Pitching Coach:** Larry McCall. **Trainer:** Trek Schuler.

Game Information

Radio Announcer: Shane Griffin. **No. of Games Broadcast:** Home-70, Away-70. **Flagship Station:** WTDK 107.1-FM.

PA Announcer: Jim Whittemore. **Official Scorer:** Unavailable.

Stadium Name (year opened): Arthur W. Perdue Stadium (1996). **Location:** From U.S. 50 East, right on Hobbs Road; From U.S. 50 West, left on Hobbs Road. **Standard Game Times:** 6:35 p.m.; Sun. 1:05.

Visiting Club Hotel: Ramada Inn and Convention Center, 300 S. Salisbury Blvd., Salisbury, MD 21801. Telephone: (410) 546-4400.

GREENSBORO
Bats

Office Address: 510 Yanceyville St., Greensboro, NC 27405. **Telephone:** (336) 333-2287. **FAX:** (336) 273-7350. **E-Mail Address:** bats@greensborobats.com. **Website:** www.greensborobats.com.

Affiliation (first year): Florida Marlins (2003). **Years in League:** 1979-.

Ownership, Management

Operated by: Greensboro Baseball, LLC.

Principal Owners: Cooper Brantley, Bill Lee, Pat Pittard, Len White.

President, General Manager: Donald Moore **Assistant GM:** Tom Howe. **Director, Stadium Operations/Head Groundskeeper:** Jake Holloway. **Director, Broadcasting /Media Relations:** Josh Flickinger. **Director, Finance:** Lesley Burnette. **Office Manager/Director, Merchandise:** Sue DeRocco. **Executive Assistant to GM**: Rosalee Brewer.

Field Staff

Manager: Steve Phillips. **Coach:** Tom Donovan. **Pitching Coach:** Scott Mitchell. **Trainer**: Steve Miller.

Game Information

Radio Announcer: Josh Flickinger. **No. of Games Broadcast:** Home-70, Away-70. **Flagship Station:** WPET 950-AM.

PA Announcer: Jim Scott. **Official Scorer:** Joe Cristy.

Stadium Name (year opened): War Memorial Stadium (1926). **Location:** I-40/I-85 to Highway 29, north to Lee Street, west to Bennett Avenue, right on Bennett. **Standard Game Times:** 7 p.m.; Sun. 2.

Visiting Club Hotel: Howard Johnson Hotel, 3030 High Point Rd., Greensboro, NC 27403. Telephone: (336) 294-4920.

HAGERSTOWN
Suns

Office Address: 274 E. Memorial Blvd., Hagerstown, MD 21740. **Telephone:** (301) 791-6266. **FAX:** (301) 791-6066. **E-Mail Address:** info@hagerstownsuns.com. **Website:** www.hagerstownsuns.com.

Affiliation (first year): San Francisco Giants (2001). **Years in League:** 1993-.

Ownership, Management

Operated by: Mandalay Sports Entertainment.

Principal Owners: Hank Stickney, Ken Stickney, Peter Guber, Paul Schaeffer.

General Manager: Kurt Landes. **Assistant GM:** Bill Papierniak. **Director, Business Operations:** Carol Gehr. **Director, Stadium Operations:** Mike Showe. **Director, Ticket Sales/Merchandise:** Will Smith. **Director, Group Sales/Concessions:** Chris Matthias. **Manager, Media Relations:** Loren Foxx. **Clubhouse Manager:** Mike Dickinson.

Field Staff

Manager: Mike Ramsey. **Hitting Coach:** Willie Aviles. **Pitching Coach:** Bob Stanley. **Trainer:** Katsu Masumoto.

Game Information

Radio Announcer: Loren Foxx. **No. of Games Broadcast:** Home-70, Away-70. **Flagship Station:** WHAG 1410-AM.

PA Announcer: Unavailable. **Official Scorer:** Unavailable.

Stadium Name (year opened): Municipal Stadium (1931). **Location:** Exit 32B (US 40 West) on I-70 West, left at Eastern Blvd.; Exit 6A (US 40 East) on I-81 South, right at Cleveland Ave. **Standard Game Times:** 7:05 p.m.; Sun. 1:35.

Visiting Club Hotel: Clarion Hotel, 901 Dual Hwy., Hagerstown, MD 21740. Telephone: (301) 733-5100.

HICKORY
Crawdads

Office Address: 2500 Clement Blvd. NW, Hickory, NC 28601. **Mailing Address:** P.O. Box 1268, Hickory, NC 28603. **Telephone:** (828) 322-3000. **FAX:** (828) 322-6137. **E-Mail Address:** crawdad@hickorycrawdads.com. **Website:** www.hickorycrawdads.com.

Affiliation (first year): Pittsburgh Pirates (1999). **Years in League:** 1952, 1960, 1993-.

Ownership, Management

Operated by: Hickory Baseball, Inc.

Principal Owners: Don Beaver, Luther Beaver, Charles Young.

President: Don Beaver.

General Manager: David Haas. **Ticket Manager:** Brad Dail. **Director, Operations:** Matt Davis. **Director, Merchandise**: Barbara Beatty. **Office Manager/Special Events:** Jeanna Homesley. **Director, Broadcasting/Media Relations:** Canio Costanzo. **Director, Community Relations:** Jeremy Neisser. **Account Executive:** Jason Deans.

Field Staff

Manager: Tony Beasley. **Coach:** Matt Winters. **Pitching Coach:** Bob Milacki. **Trainer:** Thomas Pribyl.

Game Information

Radio Announcer: Canio Costanzo. **No. of Games Broadcast:** Home-70, Away-70. **Flagship Station:** WMNC 92.1-FM.

PA Announcers: JuJu Phillips, Steve Fisher. **Official Scorers:** Gary Olinger.

Stadium Name (year opened): L.P. Frans Stadium (1993). **Location:** I-40 to exit 123 (Lenoir North), 321 North to Clement Blvd., left for 1/2 mile. **Standard Game Times:** 7 p.m., 6:30 (school nights); Sun. (April-May) 2, (June-Aug.) 6.

Visiting Club Hotel: Red Roof Inn, 1184 Lenoir Rhyne Blvd., Hickory, NC 28602. Telephone: (828) 323-1500.

KANNAPOLIS
Intimidators

Office Address: 2888 Moose Rd., Kannapolis, NC 28083. **Mailing Address**: P.O. Box 64, Kannapolis, NC 28082. **Telephone**: (704) 932-3267. **FAX**: (704) 938-7040. **E-Mail Address**: info@intimidatorsbaseball.com. **Website**: www.intimidatorsbaseball.com.

Affiliation (first year): Chicago White Sox (2001). **Years in League**: 1995-.

Ownership, Management

Operated by: Carolina Baseball, Inc.

Principal Owners: Larry Hedrick, Bruton Smith, estate of Dale Earnhardt. **President:** Billy Raines. **Vice President**:

Craig Detwiler.

General Manager: Tim Mueller. **Associate GM**: Randy Long. **Assistant GM, Stadium Operations**: Jaime Pruitt. **Director, Media Relations/Broadcasting**: Michael Pacheco. **Director, Tickets/Group Sales/Community Relations**: Tracy Snelbaker. **Director, Merchandise**: Sean Feeney.

Field Staff

Manager: John Orton. **Coach**: Brandon Moore. **Pitching Coach**: Sean Snedeker. **Trainer**: Kevin Pillifant.

Game Information

Radio Announcer: Mike Pacheco. **No. of Games Broadcast:** Home-70, Away-70. **Flagship Station:** WRKB 1460-AM.

PA Announcer: Unavailable. **Official Scorer**: Unavailable.

Stadium Name (year opened): Fieldcrest Cannon Stadium (1995). **Location**: Exit 63 on I-85, west on Lane Street to Stadium Drive. **Standard Game Times**: 7:05 p.m.; Sun. 5.

Visiting Club Hotel: Hampton Inn, 612 Dickens Place NE, Concord, NC 28025. Telephone: (704) 793-9700.

LAKE COUNTY
Captains

Office Address: 35300 Vine St., Eastlake, OH 44095. **Mailing Address:** P.O. Box 7129, Eastlake, OH 44095. **Telephone:** (440) 975-8085. **FAX:** (440) 975-8958. **E-Mail Address:** info@captainsbaseball.com. **Website:** www.captainsbaseball.com.

Affiliation (first year): Cleveland Indians (2003). **Years in League:** 2003-.

Ownership, Management

Operated by: Cascia, LLC.

Principal Owner, President: Rita Murphy Carfagna. **Vice President:** Ray Murphy.

Vice President, Baseball Operations/General Manager: Mike Edwards. **Assistant GM, Sales/Marketing:** Gary Thomas. **Assistant GM, Operations:** Paul Siegwarth. **Assistant GM, Public/Community Relations:** Katie Dannemiller. **Assistant GM/Tickets:** Bill Levy. **Director, Merchandise:** Scott Beaman. **Director, Ticket Sales:** Kevin Brodzinski. **Sports Turf Manager:** Greg Elliott. **Director, Community Relations:** Kate Furman. **Controller:** Tony Hormanski. **Business Manager:** Priscilla Hyclak. **Director, Promotions:** Joel Koch. **Account Executives**: Kelly Kuczynski, John Murphy. **Administrative Assistant:** Julia LaManna. **Director, Stadium Operations:** Rob LoPresti. **Manager, Executive Marketing:** Steven Minner. **Director, Client Services:** Josh Myers. **Coordinator, Executive Suite:** Mike Radey. **Manager, Marketing:** Becki Rath. **Manager, Food Service:** Linda Stringham. **Director, Group Sales:** Casey Stump. **Director, Broadcasting/Media Relations:** Dave Wilson. **Interns:** Tiffany Bell, Dan Brokos, Jeff Hull, Travis Hunter, Arica Kress, Mike Mazzone, Matt Phillips, Beth West.

Field Staff

Manager: Luis Rivera. **Coach:** Wayne Kirby. **Pitching Coach:** Tony Arnold. **Trainer:** Jeff Desjardins.

Game Information

Radio Announcer: Dave Wilson. **No. of Games Broadcast:** Home-70, Away-70. **Flagship Station:** WELW 1330-AM.

PA Announcer: Unavailable. **Official Scorer:** Unavailable.

Stadium Name (year opened): Eastlake Ballpark (2003). **Location:** From Route 2 East, exit at Ohio 91, stadium is ½ mile north. **Standard Game Times:** 7:05 p.m.; Sat. (April-May): 2:05; Sun. 2:05.

Visiting Club Hotel: Hampton Inn-Wickliffe, 28611 Euclid Ave., Wickliffe, OH 44092. Telephone: (440) 944-4030.

LAKEWOOD
BlueClaws

Office Address: 2 Stadium Way, Lakewood, NJ 08701. **Telephone:** (732) 901-7000. **FAX:** (732) 901-3967. **E-Mail Address:** info@lakewoodblueclaws.com. **Website:** www.lakewoodblueclaws.com.

Affiliation: Philadelphia Phillies (2001). **Years In League:** 2001-.

Ownership, Management

Operated by: American Baseball Company, LLC.

General Manager: Geoff Brown. **Assistant GM:** John Clark. **Director, Media/Public Relations:** Neil Solondz. **Executive Director, Marketing:** Eric Lipsman. **Director, Marketing:** Mike Ryan. **Director, Production:** Clint Wulfekotte. **Manager, Merchandising:** Brian Rieder. **Director, Ticket Sales:** Jeremy Fishman. **Ticket Manager:** Hal Hansen. **Director, Group Sales:** Keri Conway. **Managers, Group Sales:** Annette Ballina, Zak Boenig, Michelle Casserly, Jim DeAngelis, Adam King. **Director, Operations:** Brandon Marano. **Assistant, Operations:** Joe Scalise. **Director, Finance:** Steve Ripa. **Assistant Controller:** Denise Casazza. **Office Manager:** Eric Finkel. **Head Groundskeeper:** Bill Butler. **Assistant Groundskeeper:** Ben Strouse.

Field Staff

Manager: Buddy Biancalana. **Coach:** Tony Barron. **Pitching Coach:** Ken Westray. **Trainer:** Sean Fcasni.

Game Information

Radio Announcer: Neil Solondz. **No. of Games Broadcast:** Home-70, Road- 70. **Flagship Station:** WOBM 1160-AM.

PA Announcer: Jack Aponte. **Official Scorer:** Kevin Clark.

Stadium Name (year opened): FirstEnergy Park (2001). **Location:** Route 70 to New Hampshire Ave., north on New Hampshire for 2½ miles to ballpark. **Standard Game Times:** 7:05 p.m.; Mon.-Thur. (April-May) 6:35, Sat. (April) 1:05; Sun 1:05, (July-Aug.) 5:05.

Visiting Team Hotel: Super 8, 2016 Hwy. 37 W., Manchester Township, NJ. Telephone: (732) 657-7100.

LEXINGTON
Legends

Office Address: 207 Legends Lane, Lexington, KY 40505. **Mailing Address:** P.O. Box 11458, Lexington, KY 40575. **Telephone:** (859) 252-4487. **FAX:** (859) 252-0747. **E-Mail Address:** lglover@lexingtonlegends.com. **Website:** www.lexingtonlegends.com.

Affiliation (first year): Houston Astros (2001). **Years in League:** 2001-.

Ownership, Management

Operated by: Lexington Professional Baseball Company.

Principal Owner: Brad Redmon. **President, Chief Executive Officer:** Alan Stein. **Chief Financial Officer:** Stacy Martin.

General Manager/Baseball Operations: Gary Durbin. **Director, Human Resources**: Shannon Kidd. **Director, Client Services/Creative Services:** Christi Clay. **Director, Event Services:** Rick Bryant. **Director, Field Maintenance:** Steve Kundick. **Director, Merchandise:** Missy Carl. **Director, Group Sales:** Beth Goldenberg. **Director, Broadcasting/Media Relations:** Larry Glover. **Director, Marketing/Promotions:** Eliza Olinger. **Comptroller:** Jeff Black. **Manager, Tickets:** Micki Wright.

Field Staff

Manager: Russ Nixon. **Coach:** Gregg Langbehn. **Pitching Coach:** Charley Taylor. **Trainer:** Eric Montague.

Game Information

Radio Announcer: Larry Glover. **No. of Games Broadcast:** Home-70, Away-70. **Flagship Station:** WLXG-AM 1300-AM.

PA Announcer: Unavailable. **Official Scorer:** Kenny Bourne.

Stadium Name (year opened): Applebee's Park (2001). **Location:** From I-64/75, take exit 113, right onto North Broadway toward downtown Lexington for 1.2 miles, past New Circle Road (Highway 4), right into stadium, located adjacent to Northland Shopping Center. **Standard Game Times:** 7:05 p.m.; Sun. (April-May) 2:05, (June-Aug.) 6:05.

Visiting Club Hotel: Ramada Inn and Conference Center, 2143 N. Broadway, Lexington, KY 40505. Telephone: (859) 299-1261.

ROME
Braves

Office Address: Floyd County Stadium, 755 Braves Blvd, Rome, GA 30161. **Mailing Address:** P.O. Box 5515, Rome, GA 30162. **Telephone:** (706) 368-9388. **FAX:** (706) 368-6525.

E-Mail Address: rome.braves@turner.com. **Website:** www.romebraves.com.

Affiliation (first year): Atlanta Braves (2003). **Years in League:** 2003-.

Ownership, Management

Operated by: Atlanta National League Baseball Club, Inc.

Principal Owner: AOL/Time Warner. **President:** Stan Kasten.

General Manager: Michael Dunn. **Assistant GM:** Jim Jones. **Stadium Operations Manager:** Eric Almond. **Ticket Manager:** Terry Morgan. **Administrative Manager**: Kristie Hancock. **Manager, Community Relations:** Erin White. **Account Representatives**: Jennifer Adams, Dave Butler. **Manager, Food/Beverage:** Dave Atwood. **Head Groundskeeper:** Andrew Wright. **Interns:** Rana Fraley, Jay Stephenson.

Field Staff

Manager: Rocket Wheeler. **Coach:** Bobby Moore. **Pitching Coach:** Kent Willis. **Trainer:** Drew Van Dam.

Game Information

Radio Announcers: Bryan Evans. **No. of Games Broadcast:** Home-70, Away-70. **Flagship Stations:** WLAQ 1410-AM, WATG 95.7-FM.

PA Announcer: Unavailable. **Official Scorer:** Unavailable.

Stadium Name (year opened): Floyd County Stadium (2003). **Location:** I-75 North to exit 290 (Rome/Canton), left off exit and follow Highway 411/Highway 20 to Rome; at intersection of Highway 411 and Highway 1 (Veterans Memorial Highway, go right, stadium is at intersection of Veterans Memorial Highway and Riverside Parkway.

Standard Game Times: 7 p.m.; Sun. 2.

Visiting Club Hotel: Days Inn, 840 Turner McCall Blvd., Rome, GA 30161. Telephone: (706) 295-0400.

SAVANNAH
Sand Gnats

Office Address: 1401 E. Victory Dr., Savannah, GA 31404. **Mailing Address:** P.O. Box 3783, Savannah, GA 31414. **Telephone:** (912) 351-9150. **Fax:** (912) 352-9722. **E-Mail Address:** sandgnts@bellsouth.net. **Website:** www.sandgnats.com.

Affiliation (first year): Montreal Expos (2003). **Years in League:** 1962, 1984 -.

Ownership, Management

Operated by: Savannah Big Time Baseball, LLC.

President: Kenneth Silver.

Chief Operating Officer, General Manager: Ken Shepard. **Assistant GM, Sales/Marketing:** Marty Wheeler. **Director, Merchandising:** Chrissy Baines. **Director, Media Relations:** Jody Wells. **Director, Promotions/Public Relations:** Rebecca Blow. **Assistant Director, Promotions/Public Relations:** Jessica Rohlik. **Assistant, Marketing/Client Services:** Nicky King. **Assistants, Promotions/Public Relations:** Crystal Caines, Cody Hetzel, Brian DeWine, Melissa Wright. **Director, Ticket Operations:** Austin Leonard. **Ticket Manager:** Ryan Eason. **Managers, Group Sales:** Jessica Adkins, Alex Beekman. **Director, Field Operations/Groundskeeper:** Chuck Cannon. **Clubhouse Manager:** Marcus Commander. **Office Manager:** Deleah Garcia. **Director, Food/Beverage:** Debbie Kessler. **Assistants, Food/Beverage:** Matt Barry, John Penington.

Field Staff

Manager: Joey Cora. **Coach:** Andy Skeels. **Pitching Coach:** Reggie Jackson. **Trainer:** Beth Jarrett.

Game Information

Radio: None.

PA Announcer: Unavailable. **Official Scorer:** Marcus Holland.

Stadium Name (year opened): Grayson Stadium (1941). **Location:** From I-16 to 37th Street exit, left on 37th, right on Abercorn Street, left on Victory Drive; From I-95 to exit 16 (Savannah/Pembroke), east on 204, right on Victory Drive, stadium is on right in Daffin Park. **Standard Game Times:** 7 p.m.; Mon.-Thurs. (April-May) 6:35; Sun. (April-May) 2, (June-Sept.) 5.

Visiting Club Hotel: Days Inn–Oglethorpe Mall, 114 Mall Blvd., Savannah, GA 31406. Telephone: (912) 352-4455.

SOUTH GEORGIA
Waves

Office Address: Paul Eames Sports Complex, 1130 Ballpark Lane, Albany, GA 31705. **Telephone:** (229) 420-5924. **FAX:** (229) 420-5925. **E-Mail Address:** info@sgwaves.com. **Website:** www.sgwaves.com.

Affiliation (second year): Los Angeles Dodgers (2002). **Years in League:** 2002-.

Ownership, Management

Operated by: Main Street Baseball, LLC.

Owner: David Heller.

General Manager: Gerry McKearney. **Director, Ticket Operations:** Lou Brzozowski. **Director, Group Sales:** Tasha Guglik. **Director, Community Relations:** Jenn Ely. **Director, Stadium Operations:** Brian Sheets. **Director, Media Relations/Broadcasting:** Tim Becwar. **Director, Concessions:** Tim Tierney.

Field Staff

Manager: Dann Bilardello. **Coach:** Garey Ingram. **Pitching Coach:** Roger McDowell. **Trainer:** Carlos Olivas.

Game Information

Radio Announcer: Tim Becwar. **No. of Games Broadcast:** Home-70, Away-70. **Flagship Station:** WGNP 90.7-FM.

Stadium Name (year opened): Paul Eames Stadium (1992). **Location:** Highway 82 to Blaylock Street, north to Ballpark Lane, turn left, stadium on left. **Standard Game Times:** 7:05 p.m.; Sun. (April-June) 2:05, (July-Aug.) 6:05.

Visiting Club Hotel: Ramada Inn, 2505 N. Slappey Blvd., Albany, GA 31701. Telephone: (229) 883-3211.

NEW YORK-PENN LEAGUE

SHORT-SEASON CLASS A

Ben Hayes

Mailing Address: 9410 International Court N., St. Petersburg, FL 33716. **Telephone:** (727) 576-6300. **FAX:** (727) 576-6307. **E-Mail Address:** Unavailable. **Website:** www.nypennleague.com.

Years League Active: 1939-.

President: Ben Hayes.

Vice President: Sam Nader (Oneonta). **Treasurer:** Bill Gladstone (Tri-City). **Corporate Secretary:** Tony Torre (New Jersey).

Directors: Eric Edelstein (Jamestown), Jeff Eiseman (Aberdeen), Joshua Getzler (Staten Island), Bill Gladstone (Tri-City), Steve Gliner (Hudson Valley), Barry Gordon (New Jersey), Alan Levin (Mahoning Valley), Paul Marriott (Batavia), Sam Nader (Oneonta), Ray Pecor (Vermont), Leo Pinckney (Auburn), R.C. Reuteman (Brooklyn), Shawn Smith (Lowell), Paul Velte (Williamsport).

League Administrator: Debbie Carlisle. **Umpire Supervisor:** Joe Milazzo. **League Historian:** Charles Wride.

2003 Opening Date: June 17. **Closing Date:** Sept. 3.

Regular Season: 76 games.

Division Structure: McNamara—Aberdeen, Brooklyn, Hudson Valley, New Jersey, Staten Island, Williamsport. **Pinckney**—Auburn, Batavia, Jamestown, Mahoning Valley. **Stedler**—Lowell, Oneonta, Tri-City, Vermont.

Playoff Format: Division champions and wild-card team meet in best-of-3 semifinals. Winners meet in best-of-3 series for league championship.

All-Star Game: None. **Hall of Fame Game:** July 27 at Cooperstown, NY (Auburn vs. Oneonta).

Roster Limit: 30 active, but only 25 may be in uniform and eligible to play in any given game. **Player Eligibility Rule:** No more than four players who are 23 or older. No more than three players on active list may have four or more years of prior service.

Brand of Baseball: Rawlings.

Statistician: SportsTicker-Boston, Boston Fish Pier, West Bldg. #1, Suite 302, Boston MA 02210.

Umpires: Unavailable.

STADIUM INFORMATION

		Dimensions				
Club	**Stadium**	**LF**	**CF**	**RF**	**Capacity**	**2002 Att.**
Aberdeen	Ripken	310	400	310	6,000	231,935
Auburn	Falcon Park	330	400	330	2,800	62,419
Batavia	Dwyer	325	400	325	2,600	43,494
Brooklyn	KeySpan Park	315	412	325	7,500	317,124
Hudson Valley	Dutchess	325	400	325	4,494	162,724
Jamestown	Diethrick Park	335	410	353	3,324	56,545
Lowell	LeLacheur Park	337	400	302	5,000	185,000
Mahoning Valley	Cafaro Field	335	405	335	6,000	160,107
New Jersey	Skylands Park	330	392	330	4,356	129,607
Oneonta	Damaschke Field	350	406	350	4,200	56,602
Staten Island	Richmond County Bank	325	400	325	6,500	181,936
Tri-City	Joseph L. Bruno	325	400	325	5,000	108,409
Vermont	Centennial Field	330	405	323	4,400	108,081
Williamsport	Bowman Field	345	405	350	4,200	82,006

ABERDEEN
IronBirds

Office Address: 923 Gilbert Rd., Aberdeen, MD 21001. **Telephone:** (410) 297-9292. **FAX:** (410) 297-6653. **E-Mail Address:** info@ironbirdsbaseball.com. **Website:** www.ironbirdsbaseball.com.

Affiliation (first year): Baltimore Orioles (2002). **Years in League:** 2002-.

Ownership, Management

Operated by: Ripken Professional Baseball, LLC.

Principal Owner: Cal Ripken.

General Manager: Jeff Eiseman. **Assistant GM:** Aaron Moszer. **Director, Sales:** Amy Venuto. **Manager, Public Relations/Broadcasting:** Steve Spafadino.

Field Staff

Manager: Joe Almaraz. **Coaches:** Gary Kendall, Cedric Landrum. **Pitching Coach:** Doc Watson. **Trainer:** Joe Benge.

Game Information

Radio Announcer: Steve Spafadino. **No. of Games Broadcast:** Home-38, Away-30. **Flagship Station:** WAMD 970-AM.

PA Announcer: Unavailable. **Official Scorers:** Doug Young, Joe Stetka.

Stadium Name (year opened): Ripken Stadium (2002). **Location:** I-95 to exit 85 (Route 22), left on Route 22, first right on Gilbert Road, stadium 1/4 mile on right. **Standard Game Times:** 7:05 p.m., Sun. 1:05.

Visiting Club Hotel: Wingate Inn, Riverside Parkway, Aberdeen, MD 21001. Telephone: (410) 272-2929.

AUBURN
Doubledays

Office Address: 130 N. Division St., Auburn, NY 13021. **Telephone:** (315) 255-2489. **FAX:** (315) 255-2675. **E-Mail Address:** ddays@auburndoubledays.com. **Website:** www.auburndoubledays.com.

Affiliation (first year): Toronto Blue Jays (2001). **Years in League:** 1958-80, 1982-.

Ownership, Management

Operated by: Auburn Community Non-Profit Baseball Association, Inc.

Chairman: Tom Ganey. **President:** Leo Pinckney.

General Manager: Jason Smorol. **Assistant GM:** Carl Gutelius. **Head Groundskeeper:** Rich Wild. **Director, Media/Public Relations:** Unavailable.

Field Staff

Manager: Dennis Holmberg. **Coach:** Dave Pano. **Pitching Coach:** Tom Bradley. **Trainer:** Tommy Craig.

Game Information

Radio Announcer: Unavailable. **No of Games Broadcast:** Away-38. **Flagship Station:** WDWN 89.1-FM

PA Announcer: Unavailable. **Official Scorer:** Unavailable.

Stadium Name (year opened): Falcon Park (1995). **Location:** I-90 to exit 40, right on Route 34 for 8 miles to York Street, right on York, left on North Division Street. **Standard Game Times:** 7 p.m., Sun. 6.

Visiting Club Hotel: Microtel, 12 Seminary Ave., Auburn, NY 13021. Telephone: (315) 253-5000.

BATAVIA
Muckdogs

Office Address: Dwyer Stadium, 299 Bank St., Batavia, NY 14020. **Telephone:** (585) 343-5454. **FAX:** (585) 343-5620. **E-Mail Address:** info@muckdogs.com. **Website:** www.muckdogs.com.

Affiliation (first year): Philadelphia Phillies (1988). **Years in League:** 1939-53, 1957-59, 1961-.

Ownership, Management

Operated by: Genesee County Baseball Club.

President: Dennis Dwyer.

General Manager: Paul Marriott. **Assistant GM:** Jon Blumenthal. **Director, Business Operations:** Melissa Meeder. **Director, Media/Public Relations:** Matt Ridley. **Director, Community Relations:** Linda Crook. **Director, Stadium Operations:** Ryan Liddell. **Clubhouse Operations:** Tony Pecora.

Field Staff

Manager: Luis Melendez. **Coach:** Jim Morrison. **Pitching Coach:** Warren Brusstar. **Trainer:** Jason Kirkman.

Game Information

Radio Announcer: Matt Ridley, Ryan Liddell. **No. of Games Broadcast:** Away-38. **Flagship Station:** WBSU 89.1-FM.

PA Announcer/Official Scorer: Wayne Fuller.

Stadium Name (year opened): Dwyer Stadium (1996). **Location:** I-90 to exit 48, left on Route 98 South, left on Richmond Avenue, left on Bank Street. **Standard Game Times:** 7:05 p.m., Sun. 6:05.

Visiting Club Hotel: Days Inn of Batavia, 200 Oak St., Batavia, NY 14020. Telephone: (585) 343-1440.

BROOKLYN
Cyclones

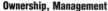

Office/Mailing Address: 1904 Surf Ave., Brooklyn, NY 11224. **Telephone:** (718) 449-8497. **FAX:** (718) 449-6368. **E-Mail Address:** info@brooklyncyclones.com. **Website:** www.brooklyncyclones.com.

Affiliation (first year): New York Mets (2001). **Years in League:** 2001-.

Ownership, Management

Operated by: Brooklyn Baseball Co., LLC.

Managing Member: Fred Wilpon.

Executive Vice President/Chief Operating Officer: Jeff Wilpon. **Senior VP, Business Affairs:** R.C. Reuteman.

General Manager: Steve Cohen. **Assistant GM/Manager, Tickets:** Kevin Mahoney. **Director, Sales/Marketing:** Vince Bulik. **Manager, Media Relations:** Dave Campanaro. **Manager, Community Relations:** Gary Perone. **Manager, Merchandise:** Kevin Jimenez. **Manager, Marketing:** Holly Esposito. **Manager, Promotions/Entertainment:** Howie Wolpoff. **Account Executives:** Vic Christopher, Robert Field, Marty Haber. **Manager, Brooklyn Baseball Gallery:** Anna Isaacson. **Head Groundskeeper:** Mike Procops. **Administrative Assistant:** Barbara Spina. **Receptionist:** Sharon Ross.

Field Staff

Manager: Tim Teufel. **Coach:** Roger LaFrancois. **Pitching Coach:** Hector Berrios. **Trainer:** Reuben Barrera.

Game Information

Radio Announcer: Warner Fusselle. **No. of Games Broadcast:** Home-38, Away-38. **Flagship Station:** WSNR 620-AM.

PA Announcer: Dominick Alagia. **Official Scorer:** David Freeman.

Stadium Name (year opened): KeySpan Park (2001). **Location:** Belt Parkway to Cropsey Avenue South, continue on Cropsey until it becomes West 17th Street, continue to Surf Avenue, stadium on south side of Surf Ave. By subway— West to Stillwell Avenue/Coney Island Station. **Standard Game Times:** 7 p.m., Sat. 6, Sun. 5.

Visiting Club Hotel: Comfort Inn, 8315 Fourth Ave., Brooklyn, NY 11209. Telephone: (718) 238-3737.

HUDSON VALLEY
Renegades

Office Address: Dutchess Stadium, Route 9D, Wappingers Falls, NY 12590. **Mailing Address:** P.O. Box 661, Fishkill, NY 12524. **Telephone:** (845) 838-0094. **FAX:** (845) 838-0014. **E-Mail Address:** info@hvrenegades.com. **Website:** www.hvrenegades.com.

Affiliation (first year): Tampa Bay Devil Rays (1996). **Years in League:** 1994-.

Ownership, Management

Operated by: Keystone Professional Baseball Club, Inc.

Principal Owner: Marv Goldklang.

President, General Manager: Steve Gliner. **Vice President/Assistant GM:** Kathy Butsko. **Director, Ticket Operations:** Bonnie Johnson. **Director, Operations:** Derek Sharp. **Director, Food Services:** Joe Ausanio. **Director, Business Operations:** Jennifer Vitale. **Director, Entertainment:** Stephen Colvin. **Director, Special Events/Renegades Charitable Fund:** Rick Zolzer. **Head Groundskeeper/Director, Stadium Maintenance:** Tom Hubmaster. **Director, Client Services/Media Relations:** Tom Butkier. **Director, Community Relations:** Danielle Wachter. **Director, Ticket Sales:** Jessica Ball. **Administrative Assistant, Tickets:** Unavailable. **Administrative Assistant, Marketing:** Corey Whitted. **Assistant Director, Food Services:** Unavailable. **Assistant Groundskeeper:** Stephen Cunningham. **Clubhouse Manager:** Chris Campassi.

Field Staff

Manager: Dave Howard. **Coach:** Jorge Robles. **Pitching Coach:** Rafael Montalvo. **Trainer:** Nate Shaw.

Game Information

Radio Announcer: Sean Ford. **No. of Games Broadcast:** Home-38, Away-38. **Flagship Stations:** WBNR 1260-AM, WLNA 1420-AM.

PA Announcer: Rick Zolzer. **Official Scorer:** Bob Beretta.

Stadium Name (year opened): Dutchess Stadium (1994). **Location:** I-84 to exit 11 (Route 9D North), north one mile to stadium. **Standard Game Times:** 7:15 p.m., Sun. 5:15.

Visiting Club Hotel: Unavailable.

JAMESTOWN
Jammers

Office Address: 485 Falconer St., Jamestown, NY 14702. **Mailing Address:** P.O. Box 638, Jamestown, NY 14702. **Telephone:** (716) 664-0915. **FAX:** (716) 664-4175. **E-Mail Address:** email@jamestownjammers.com. **Website:** www.jamestownjammers.com.

Affiliation (first year): Florida Marlins (2002). **Years in League:** 1939-57, 1961-73, 1977-.

Ownership, Management

Operated by: Rich Baseball Operations.

Principal Owner, President: Robert Rich Jr. **Chairman:** Robert Rich Sr. **President, Rich Baseball Operations:** Jonathon Dandes.

General Manager: Eric Edelstein. **Assistant GM, Sales/Marketing:** Matthew Drayer. **Director, Baseball Operations:** Brianne Tieff. **Head Groundskeeper:** Jamie Bloomquist. **Director, Food Services:** Rich Ruggerio.

Field Staff

Manager: Benny Castillo. **Coach:** Brandon Hyde. **Pitching Coach:** Reid Cornelius. **Trainer:** Unavailable.

Game Information

Radio Announcer: Andrew Barch. **No. of Games Broadcast:** Away-38. **Flagship Station:** WKSN 1340-AM.

PA Announcer: Andrew Barch. **Official Scorer:** Jim Riggs.

Stadium Name (year opened): Russell E. Diethrick Jr. Park (1941). **Location:** From I-90, south on Route 60, left on Buffalo Street, left on Falconer Street. **Standard Game Times:** 7:05 p.m., Sun. 6:05.

Visiting Club Hotel: Red Roof Inn, 1980 E. Main St., Falconer, NY 14733. Telephone: (716) 665-3670.

LOWELL
Spinners

Office Address: 450 Aiken St., Lowell, MA 01854. **Telephone:** (978) 459-2255. **FAX:** (978) 459-1674. **E-Mail Address:** generalinfo@lowellspinners.com. **Website:** www.lowellspinners.com.

Affiliation (first year): Boston Red Sox (1996). **Years in League:** 1996-.

Ownership, Management

Operated by: Diamond Action, Inc.

Chief Executive Officer: Drew Weber.

President, General Manager: Shawn Smith. **Assistant GM:** Brian Lindsay. **Controller:** Priscilla Harbour. **Director, Stadium Operations:** Dan Beaulieu. **Assistant Director, Stadium Operations:** Gareth Markey. **Director, Corporate Sales:** John Egan. **Director, Media Relations:** Jon Goode. **Director, Merchandising:** Joann Weber. **Director, Ticket Operations:** Jeff Tagliaferro. **Assistant Director, Ticket Operations:** Jon Healy. **Director, Stadium Services:** Mike Biagini. **Head Groundskeeper:** Rick Walker. **Clubhouse Manager:** Del Christman.

Field Staff

Manager: Jon Deeble. **Coach:** Randy Phillips. **Pitching Coach:** Darryl Milne. **Trainer:** David Cohen.

Game Information

Radio Announcer: Bob Ellis, Chaz Scoggins. **No. of Games Broadcast:** Home-38, Away-38. **Flagship Station:** WUML 91.5-FM.

PA Announcers: Jack Baldwin, Matt Steinberg. **Official Scorers:** Dave Rourke, Rusty Eggen, Bob Ellis.

Stadium Name (year opened): Edward LeLacheur Park (1998). **Location:** From Routes 495 and 3, take exit 35C (Lowell Connector), follow connector to exit 5B (Thorndike Street) onto Dutton Street, past city hall, left onto Father Morrissette Boulevard, right on Aiken Street. **Standard Game Times:** 7:05 p.m.; Sat.-Sun. 5:05.

Visiting Club Hotel: Doubletree Inn, 50 Warren St., Lowell, MA 01852. Telephone: (978) 452-1200.

MAHONING VALLEY
Scrappers

Office Address: 111 Eastwood Mall Blvd., Niles, OH 44446. **Mailing Address:** P.O. Box 1357, Niles, OH 44446. **Telephone:** (330) 505-0000. **FAX:** (330) 505-9696. **E-Mail Address:** mvscrappers@onecom.com. **Website:** www.mvscrappers.com.

Affiliation (first year): Cleveland Indians (1999). **Years in League:** 1999-.

Ownership, Management

Operated by: Palisades Baseball, Ltd.

Managing General Partner: Alan Levin. **Executive Vice President:** Erik Haag. **Director, Finance:** Cheryl Case.

General Manager: Andy Milovich. **Assistant GM:** Dave Smith. **Director, Stadium Operations:** Matt Duncan. **Director, Ticket Operations:** Mike Uden. **Manager, Box Office:** Heather Safarek. **Accountant:** Debbie Primmer. **Director, Promotions/Marketing:** Jim Riley. **Sponsorship Sales Representative:** Jordan Taylor. **Ticket Sales Representatives:** Jeff Meehan, John Muszkewycz. **Director, Concessions:** Unavailable. **Client Services Representative:** Mike Brent.

Field Staff

Manager: Ted Kubiak. **Coach:** Chris Bando. **Pitching Coach:** Ken Rowe. **Trainer:** Michael Salazar.

Game Information

Radio Announcer: Unavailable. **No. of Games Broadcasts:** Home-38, Away-38. **Flagship Station:** WNIO 1390-AM.

PA Announcer: Ed Byers. **Official Scorer:** Al Thorne.

Stadium Name (year opened): Cafaro Field (1999). **Location:** I-80 to 11 North to 82 West to 46 South, stadium located behind Eastwood Mall. **Standard Game Times:** 7 p.m.; Sun. 2.

Visiting Club Hotel: Unavailable.

NEW JERSEY
Cardinals

Office Address: 94 Championship Pl., Suite 2, Augusta, NJ 07822. **Telephone:** (973) 579-7500. **FAX:** (973) 579-7502. **E-Mail Address:** office@njcards.com. **Website:** www.njcards.com.

Affiliation (first year): St. Louis Cardinals (1994). **Years in League:** 1994-.

Ownership, Management

Operated by: Minor League Heroes, LP.

Chairman: Barry Gordon. **President:** Marc Klee.

Vice President, General Manager: Tony Torre. **Assistant GM:** Herm Sorcher. **Head Groundskeeper:** Ralph Naife. **Director, Marketing/Merchandising**: Bob Commentucci. **Director, Ticket Operations:** Bob Mischler. **Director, Group Sales:** Matt Millet. **Director, Sponsorships/Group Sales:** Gregg Kubala. **Promotions/Group Sales:** Jody Sellers. **Director, Community Relations/Group Sales:** Lisa Howell. **Director, Finance:** Jeff Marsden.

Field Staff

Manager: Tommy Shields. **Coach:** Ron Warner. **Pitching Coach:** Sid Monge. **Trainer:** James Spinale.

Game Information

Radio Announcers: Phil Pepe, Joel Konya. **No. of Games Broadcast:** Unavailable. **Flagship Station:** WNNJ 1360-AM.

PA Announcer: Mike Rowpone. **Official Scorer:** Ken Hand.

Stadium Name (year opened): Skylands Park (1994). **Location:** In New Jersey, I-80 to exit 34B (Route 15 North) to Route 565 East; In Pennsylvania, I-84 to Route 6 (Matamoras) to Route 206 North to Route 565 East. **Standard Game Times:** 7:15 p.m., Sat.-Sun. 5.

Visiting Club Hotel: Wellesley Inn, 1255 Route 10, Whippany, NJ 07981. Telephone: (973) 539-8350.

ONEONTA
Tigers

Office Address: 95 River St., Oneonta, NY 13820. **Telephone:** (607) 432-6326. **FAX:** (607) 432-1965. **E-Mail Address:** naderas@telenet.net. **Website:** www.oneontatigers.com.

Affiliation (first year): Detroit Tigers (1999). **Years in League:** 1966-.

Ownership, Management

Operated by: Oneonta Athletic Corp., Inc.

President, General Manager: Sam Nader. **Director, Business/Stadium Operations:** John Nader. **Controller:** Sidney Levine. **Head Groundskeepers:** Dan Obergufell, Mike Dunn. **Director, Media/Public Relations:** Alice O'Conner. **Director, Marketing/Merchandising:** Suzanne Longo. **Director, Special Projects:** Mark Nader. **Director, Operations/Ticket Sales:** Bob Zeh. **Director, Food Services:** Brad Zeh.

Field Staff

Manager: Randy Ready. **Coach:** Joe Alvarez. **Pitching Coach:** Bill Monbouquette. **Trainer:** Chris Vernon.

Game Information

Radio: None.

PA Announcer: John Horne. **Official Scorer:** Tom Heitz.

Stadium Name (year opened): Damaschke Field (1940). **Location:** Exit 15 off I-88. **Standard Game Times:** 7 p.m., Sun. 6.

Visiting Club Hotels: Town House Motor Inn, 318 Main St., Oneonta, NY 13820. Telephone: (607) 432-1313. Oasis Motor Inn, 366 Chestnut St., Oneonta, NY 13820. Telephone: (607) 432-6041.

STATEN ISLAND
Yankees

Stadium/Mailing Address: 75 Richmond Terrace, Staten Island, NY 10301. **Telephone:** (718) 720-9265. **FAX:** (718) 273-5763. **E-Mail Address:** siyanks@siyanks.com. **Website:** www.siyanks.com.

Affiliation (first year): New York Yankees (1999). **Years in League:** 1999-.

Ownership, Management

Operated by: Staten Island Minor League Holdings, LLC.

Principal Owners: Josh Getzler, Phyllis Getzler, Stan Getzler.

Chairman: Stan Geltzer. **President:** Henry Steinbrenner. **Chief Operating Officer:** Josh Getzler.

General Manager: Jeff Dumas. **Assistant GM:** Jane Rogers. **Director, Media Relations:** Rose DeInnocentiis. **Bookkeeper:** Ruth Rizzo. **Director, Tickets:** Dominic Costantino. **Technical Director:** John Davison. **Director, Group Sales:** Dan Yaeger. **Director, Stadium Operations:** Greg LaPlaca. **Director, Concessions:** Carlos Lemus. **Director, Concerts/Stadium Events:** Joe Ricciutti. **Head Groundskeeper:** Sean Mantucca.

Field Staff

Manager: Andy Stankiewicz. **Coach:** Kevin Higgins. **Pitching Coach:** Rick Tomlin. **Trainer:** Liam Frawley.

Game Information

Radio Announcer: Unavailable. **No. of Games Broadcast:** Home-38, Away-38. **Flagship Station:** Unavailable.

PA Announcer: Unavailable. **Official Scorer:** Richard Senzel.

Stadium Name (year opened): Richmond County Bank Ballpark at St. George (2001). **Location:** St. George located in Staten Island, next to Staten Island Ferry Terminal. **Standard Game Times:** 7:15 p.m., Sun. 5:15.

Visiting Club Hotel: The Navy Lodge, Bldg. 408, North Path Road, Staten Island, NY 10305. Telephone: (718) 442-0413.

TRI-CITY
ValleyCats

Stadium Address: 80 Vandenburgh Ave., Troy, NY 12180. **Mailing Address:** P.O. Box 694, Troy, NY 12181. **Telephone:** (518) 629-2287. **FAX:** (518) 629-2299. **E-Mail Address:** info@tcvalleycats.com. **Website:** www.tcvalleycats.com.

Affiliation: Houston Astros (2001). **Years in League:** 2002-.

Ownership, Management

Operated by: National Pastime Corporation.

Principal Owners: Martin Barr, John Burton, William Gladstone, Richard Murphy, Alfred Roberts, Stephen Siegel.

President: William Gladstone.

General Manager: Richard Murphy. **Director, Sales/Marketing:** Peter Rosenberg **Account Executives:** Dave Bestle, Craig Couture, Brett Gilmore, Lynne Soltysiak, Mike Sousa. **Administrative Assistant:** Terry Rusik. **Director, Community Relations**: Eileen McCarthy.

Field Staff

Manager: Ivan DeJesus. **Coach:** Brian Dayett. **Pitching Coach:** Bill Ballou. **Trainer:** Adam Thomas.

Game Information

Radio Announcer: Unavailable. **No. of Games Broadcast:** Home-38, Away-38. **Flagship Station:** Unavailable.

PA Announcer: Unavailable. **Official Scorer:** Unavailable.

Stadium Name (year opened): Hudson Valley Community College (2002). **Location:** From north, I-87 to exit 7 (Route 7), go east approximately 1½ miles to I-787 South, to Route 378 East, go over bridge to Route 4, right to Route

4 south, one mile to Hudson Valley Community College campus on left. From south, I-87 to exit 23 (I-787), I-787 north six miles to exit for Route 378 east, Route 378 over bridge to Route 4, go right to Route 4 South, one mile to Hudson Valley Community College campus on left. From east, Massachusetts Turnpike to exit B-1 (I-90), go nine miles to Exit 8 (Defreestville), left off ramp to Route 4 North, Route 4 North for five miles, Hudson Valley Community College on right. From West, I-90 to exit 24 (I-90 East), I-90 east for six miles to I-787 North (Troy), take I-787 North for 2.2 miles to exit for Route 378 East, take Route 378 over bridge to Route 4,, right to Route 4 south for one mile to Hudson Valley Community College campus on left. **Standard Game Times:** 7 p.m.; Sun. 6.

Visiting Club Hotel: Unavailable.

VERMONT
Expos

Office Address: 1 Main St., Suite 4, Winooski, VT 05404. **Telephone:** (802) 655-4200. **FAX:** (802) 655-5660. **E-Mail Address:** mail@vermontexpos.com. **Website:** www.vermontexpos.com.

Affiliation (first year): Montreal Expos (1994). **Years in League:** 1994-.

Ownership, Management

Operated by: Vermont Expos, Inc.

Principal Owner, President: Ray Pecor. **Vice President:** Kyle Bostwick.

General Manager: C.J. Knudsen. **Assistant GM:** Mike Simpson. **Director, Stadium Operations:** Jim O'Brien. **Head Groundskeeper:** Chris Baker. **Director, Public Relations/Promotions:** Adrienne Wilson. **Director, Media Relations:** Paul Stanfield. **Director, Sales:** Shawn Quinn. **Director, Ticket Operations/Design:** Nate Cloutier. **Director, Food Services:** Steve Bernard. **Director, Special Projects:** Onnie Matthews. **Clubhouse Operations:** Phil Schelzo. **Group Sales Representative:** Dan Winters. **Quality Control:** Ron Citorik.

Field Staff

Manager: Dave Barnett. **Coach:** Steve Allyn. **Pitching Coach:** Craig Bjornson. **Trainer:** Unavailable.

Game Information

Radio Announcer: George Commo. **No. of Games Broadcast:** Home-25, Away-25. **Flagship Station:** WVAA 1390-AM.

PA Announcer: Rich Haskell. **Official Scorer:** Ev Smith.

Stadium Name (year opened): Centennial Field (1922). **Location:** I-89 to exit 14W, right on East Avenue for one mile, right at Colchester Avenue. **Standard Game Times:** 7:05 p.m., Sun. 5:05.

Visiting Club Hotel: University Inn & Suites, 5 Dorset St., South Burlington, VT 05403. Telephone: (802) 863-5541.

WILLIAMSPORT
Crosscutters

Office Address: Bowman Field, 1700 W. Fourth St., Williamsport, PA 17701. **Mailing Address:** P.O. Box 3173, Williamsport, PA 17701. **Telephone:** (570) 326-3389. **FAX:** (570) 326-3494. **E-Mail Address:** mail@crosscutters.com. **Website:** www.crosscutters.com.

Affiliation (first year): Pittsburgh Pirates (1999). **Years in League:** 1968-72, 1994-.

Ownership, Management

Operated by: Geneva Cubs Baseball, Inc.

Principal Owners: Paul Velte, John Schreyer. **President:** Paul Velte. **Vice President:** John Schreyer.

General Manager: Doug Estes. **Director, Marketing/Public Relations:** Gabe Sinicropi. **Director, Food/Beverage:** Kris Smaldone. **Director, Ticket Operations/Community Relations:** Adriane Schlachter. **Ticket Operations Assistant:** Sarah Budd. **Public Relations Assistant**: Chris MacLean. **Stadium Operations Assistant:** Greg Davis. **Head Groudskeeper:** Melissa Slingerland. **Clubhouse Manager:** John White.

Field Staff

Manager: Andy Stewart. **Coach:** Jeff Branson. **Pitching Coach:** Ray Searage. **Trainer:** Bryan Housand.

Game Information

Radio: Unavailable.

PA Announcer: Rob Thomas. **Official Scorers:** Rob Dietrich, Kenny Myers.

Stadium Name (year opened): Bowman Field (1923). **Location:** From south, Route 15 to Maynard Street, right on Maynard, left on Fourth Street for one mile; From north, Route 15 to Fourth Street, left on Fourth. **Standard Game Time:** 7:05 p.m.

Visiting Club Hotel: Holiday Inn, 1840 E. Third St., Williamsport, PA 17701. Telephone: (570) 326-1981.

NORTHWEST LEAGUE

SHORT-SEASON CLASS A

Bob Richmond

Office Address: 910 Main St., Suite 351, Boise, ID 83702. **Mailing Address:** P.O. Box 1645, Boise, ID 83701. **Telephone:** (208) 429-1511. **FAX:** (208) 429-1525. **E-Mail Address:** bobrichmond@worldnet.att.net.

Years League Active: 1954-.

President, Treasurer: Bob Richmond.

Vice President: Fred Herrmann (Vancouver). **Corporate Secretary:** Jerry Walker (Salem-Keizer).

Directors: Bob Beban (Eugene), Bobby Brett (Spokane), Fred Herrmann (Vancouver), Mike McMurray (Yakima), Mark Schuster (Tri-City), Mark Sperandio (Everett), Dan Walker (Boise), Jerry Walker (Salem-Keizer).

Administrative Assistant: Rob Richmond.

2003 Opening Date: June 17. **Closing Date:** Sept. 4.

Regular Season: 76 games.

Division Structure: East—Boise, Spokane, Tri-City, Yakima. **West**—Eugene, Everett, Salem-Keizer, Vancouver.

Playoff Format: Division winners play best-of-5 series for league championship.

All-Star Game: None.

Roster Limit: 30 active, 35 under control. **Player Eligibility Rule:** No more than four players 23 or older. No more than three players on active list may have four or more years of prior service.

Brand of Baseball: Rawlings.

Statistician: SportsTicker-Boston, Boston Fish Pier, West Bldg. #1, Suite 302, Boston MA 02210.

Umpires:

STADIUM INFORMATION

		Dimensions				
Club	**Stadium**	**LF**	**CF**	**RF**	**Capacity**	**2002 Att.**
Boise	Memorial	335	405	335	4,500	109,646
Eugene	Civic	335	400	328	6,800	123,389
Everett	Everett Memorial	330	395	330	3,682	110,373
Salem-Keizer	Volcanoes	325	400	325	4,100	122,334
Spokane	Seafirst	335	398	335	7,162	161,570
Tri-City	Pasco	335	400	335	3,730	69,824
Vancouver	Nat Bailey	335	395	335	6,500	127,099
Yakima	Yakima County	295	406	295	3,000	56,404

BOISE
Hawks

Office Address: 888 N. Cole Rd., Boise, ID 83704. **Telephone:** (208) 322-5000. **FAX:** (208) 322-7432. **E-Mail Address:** info@boisehawks.com. **Website:** www.boise-hawks.com.

Affiliation (first year): Chicago Cubs (2001). **Years in League:** 1975-76, 1978, 1985-.

Ownership, Management

Operated by: Horizon Broadcasting Group.

Chairman: Bill Ackerley. **Presidents:** Dan Walker, Keith Shipman.

General Manager: Jeff Walker. **Controller:** Lee Ryan. **Stadium Operations/Head Groundskeeper:** Boyd Mauer. **Corporate Account Executives:** Brent Moore, Mick Skinner. **Director, Customer Service/Administrative Assistant:** Dina Duncan. **Director, Marketing/Media Relations:** Dan Peterson. **Director, Ticket Sales:** Ernie Plutt. **Director, Ticketing:** Torin Oberlindacher. **Ticketing Account Executive:** Dorothy Gutierrez.

Field Staff

Manager: Steve McFarland. **Coach:** Tom Beyers. **Pitching Coach:** David Haas. **Trainer:** Matt Johnson.

Game Information

Radio Announcer: Dan Peterson. **No. of Games Broadcast:** Home-38, Away-38. **Flagship Station:** KTIK 1350-AM.

PA Announcer: Dave Hahn. **Official Scorer:** Todd Miles.

Stadium Name (year opened): Memorial Stadium (1989). **Location:** I-84 to Cole Road, north to Western Idaho Fairgrounds at 5600 North Glenwood Street. **Standard Game Times:** 7:05 p.m., Sun. 6:05.

Visiting Club Hotel: Holiday Inn, 3300 Vista Ave., Boise, ID 83705. Telephone: (208) 344-8365.

EUGENE
Emeralds

Office Address: 2077 Willamette St., Eugene, OR 97405. **Mailing Address:** P.O. Box 5566, Eugene, OR 97405. **Telephone:** (541) 342-5367. **FAX:** (541) 342-6089. **E-Mail Address:** ems@go-ems.com. **Website:** www.go-ems.com.

Affiliation (first year): San Diego Padres (2001). **Years in League:** 1955-68, 1974-.

Ownership, Management

Operated by: Elmore Sports Group, Ltd.

Principal Owner: David Elmore.

President, General Manager: Bob Beban. **Assistant GM:** Dennis Higgins. **Business Manager:** Eileen Beban. **Director, Food Services:** Jeph Mitchell. **Director, Special Events:** Sergio Apodaca. **Facilities Director:** David Puente. **Grounds Superintendent:** Peter Lockwood.

Field Staff

Manager: Roy Howell. **Coach:** Ben Oglivie. **Pitching Coach:** Dave Rajsich. **Trainer:** Wade Yamasaki.

Game Information

Radio Announcer: Unavailable. **No. of Games Broadcast:** Home-38, Away-38. **Flagship Station:** KPNW 1120-AM.

PA Announcer: Steve Brown. **Official Scorer:** Unavailable.

Stadium Name (year opened): Civic Stadium (1938). **Location:** From I-5, take I-105 to Exit 2, stay left and follow to downtown, cross over Ferry Street Bridge to Eighth Avenue, left on Pearl Street, south to 20th Avenue. **Standard Game Times:** 7:05 p.m., Sun. 5:05.

Visiting Club Hotel: Doubletree Inn, 3280 Gateway Rd., Springfield, OR 97477. Telephone: (541) 726-8181.

EVERETT
Aquasox

Mailing Address: 3802 Broadway, Everett, WA 98201. **Telephone:** (425) 258-3673. **FAX:** (425) 258-3675. **E-Mail Address:** aquasox@aquasox.com. **Website:** www.aquasox.com.

Affiliation (first year): Seattle Mariners (1995). **Years in League:** 1984-.

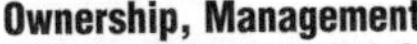

Ownership, Management

Operated by: Farm Club Sports, Inc.

President: Mark Sperandio. **Vice President:** Joan Sperandio.

Director, Operations: Dan Lewis. **Director, Corporate Sales:** Brian Sloan. **Director, Broadcasting/Advertising Sales Associate:** Pat Dillon. **Director, Ballpark Operations:** Jason Jarett. **Director, Ticket Services:** Dave Roberts. **Director, Information Systems/Group Sales Associate:** Matt Nystrom. **Manager, Food and Beverage/Group Sales Associate:** Cathy Bierman. **Group Sales Associate:** George Schaefer. **Director, Media Relations:** Amy Randall.

Field Staff

Manager: Pedro Grifol. **Coach:** Darrin Garner. **Pitching Coach:** Gary Wheelock. **Trainer:** Spyder Webb.

Game Information

Radio Announcer: Pat Dillon. **No. of Games Broadcast:** Home-38, Away-38. **Flagship Station:** KSER 90.7-FM.

PA Announcer: Tom Lafferty. **Official Scorer:** Pat Castro.

Stadium Name (year opened): Everett Memorial Stadium (1984). **Location:** I-5, exit 192. **Standard Game Times:** 7:05 p.m., Sun 4:05.

Visiting Club Hotel: Best Western Cascadia Inn, 2800 Pacific Ave., Everett, WA 98201. Telephone: (425) 258-4141.

SALEM-KEIZER
Volcanoes

Street Address: 6700 Field of Dreams Way NE, Keizer, OR 97307. **Mailing Address:** P.O. Box 20936, Keizer, OR 97307. **Telephone:** (503) 390-2225. **FAX:** (503) 390-2227. **E-Mail Address:** probasebal@aol.com. **Website:** www.volcanoesbaseball.com.

Affiliation (first year): San Francisco Giants (1997). **Years in League:** 1997-.

Ownership, Management

Operated By: Sports Enterprises, Inc.

Principal Owners: Jerry Walker, Bill Tucker.

President, General Manager: Jerry Walker. **Vice President, Operations:** Rick Nelson. **Manager, Corporate Sales/Director, Promotions:** Lisa Walker. **Corporate Sponsorships:** Patrick Garcia. **Director, Sales/Media Relations:** Pat Lafferty. **Director, Community Relations:** Steve Davies. **Director, Ticket/Group Sales:** Greg Herbst. **Manager, Corporate Sales:** Scott Clem. **Director, Merchandising:** Anna Marie Stephens,

Field Staff

Manager: Jack Lind. **Coach:** Joe Strain. **Pitching Coach:** Trevor Wilson. **Trainer:** Rene Velazquez.

Game Information

Radio Announcer: Pat Lafferty. **No. of Games Broadcast:** Home-38, Away-38. **Flagship Station:** KYKN 1430-AM.

PA Announcer: Dave Jarvis. **Official Scorer:** Dawn Hills.

Stadium Name (year opened): Volcanoes Stadium (1997). **Location:** I-5 at exit 260 (Chemawa Road), west one block to Radiant Drive, north six blocks to stadium. **Standard Game Time:** 7:05 p.m.

Visiting Club Hotel: Holiday Inn Express, 890 Hawthorne Ave. SE, Salem, OR 97301. Telephone: (503) 391-7000.

SPOKANE
Indians

Office Address: 602 N. Havana, Spokane, WA 99202. **Mailing Address:** P.O. Box 4758, Spokane, WA 99220. **Telephone:** (509) 535-2922. **FAX:** (509) 534-5368. **E-Mail Address:** mail@spokaneindiansbaseball.com. **Website:** www.spokaneindians-baseball.com.

Affiliation (first year): Texas Rangers (2003). **Years in League:** 1972, 1983-.

Ownership, Management

Operated by: Longball, Inc.

Principal Owners: Bobby Brett, George Brett, J.B. Brett, Ken Brett.

President: Andrew Billig.

Vice President, General Manager: Paul Barbeau. **VP, Sponsorships:** Otto Klein. **Director, Accounting:** Greg Sloan. **Director, Ticket Sales:** Paul Zilm. **Director, Stadium Operations:** Trevor Kettrick. **Director, Promotions:** Chris Duff. **Director, Concessions/Administration:** Lesley DeHart. **Executive Administrative Assistant:** Barbara Klante. **Controller:** Carol Dell. **Account Executives:** Scott Litle, Randy Schwaegler. **Group Sales Coordinators:** Brian Burton, Aaron Hill. **Director, Public Relations:** Unavailable. **Manager, Ticket Office:** Unavailable. **Manager, Merchandise:** Unavailable. **Head Groundskeeper:** Bret Whiteman. **Assistant Director, Stadium Operations:** Larry Blumer.

Field Staff

Manager: Darryl Kennedy. **Coach:** Derek Lee. **Pitching Coach:** David Chavarria. **Trainer:** Brian Bobier.

Game Information

Radio Announcer: Bob Robertson. **No. of Games Broadcast:** Home-38, Away-38. **Flagship Station:** KFAN 790-AM.

PA Announcer: Unavailable. **Official Scorer:** Unavailable.

Stadium Name (year opened): Avista Stadium at Spokane County Fair and Expo Center (1958). **Location:** From west, I-90 to exit 283B (Thor/Freya), east on 3rd Avenue, left onto Havana; from east, I-90 to Broadway exit, right onto Broadway, left onto Havana. **Standard Game Time:** 6:30 p.m.

Visiting Club Hotel: West Coast Ridpath Hotel, 515 W. Sprague, Spokane, WA 99201. Telephone: (509) 838-2711.

TRI-CITY
Dust Devils

Office Address: 6200 Burden Rd., Pasco, WA 99301. **Telephone:** (509) 544-8789. **FAX:** (509) 547-9570. **E-Mail Address:** info@dustdevilsbaseball.com. **Website:** www.dustdevilsbaseball.com.

Affiliation (first year): Colorado Rockies (2001). **Years in League:** 1955-1974, 1983-1986, 2001-.

Ownership, Management

Operated by: Metropolitan Sports, LLC.

President: Mark Schuster.

General Manager: Brian Rogers. **Director, Corporate Sales:** Unavailable. **Director, Group Sales:** Brian Sherrill. **Director, Ticket Sales:** Unavailable. **Office Manager:** Unavailable.

Field Staff

Manager: Ron Gideon. **Coach:** Freddie Ocasio. **Pitching Coach:** Mike Snyder. **Trainer:** Scott Murayama.

Game Information

Radio Announcer: Unavailable. **No. of Games Broadcast:** Home-38, Away-38. **Flagship Station:** KALE 970-AM.

PA Announcer: Unavailable. **Official Scorer:** Unavailable.

Stadium Name (year opened): Pasco Stadium (1995). **Location:** I-182 to exit 9 (Road 68), north to Burden Rd., right to stadium. **Standard Game Times:** 7:05, 6:05 Sun.

Visiting Club Hotel: West Coast Tri-Cities Hotel, 1101 N. Columbia Center Blvd., Kennewick, WA 99336. Telephone: (509) 783-0611.

VANCOUVER
Canadians

Office Address: 4601 Ontario St., Vancouver, British Columbia V5V 3H4. **Telephone:** (604) 872-5232. **FAX:** (604) 872-1714. **E-Mail Address:** staff@canadiansbaseball.com. **Website:** www.canadiansbaseball.com.

Affiliation (first year): Oakland Athletics (2000). **Years in League:** 2000-.

Ownership, Management

Operated by: National Sports Organization, Inc.

Principal Owners: Dwain Cross, Fred Herrmann, Bud Kaufman.

President: Dan Kilgras.

General Manager: Jason Rowland. **Account Executives:** Delany Dunn, Ben Ekren. **Head Groundskeeper:** Bill Posthumus. **Clubhouse Manager:** Trevor Reid. **Office Manager:** Carol Miner.

Field Staff

Manager: Dennis Rogers. **Coach:** Juan Dilone. **Pitching Coach:** Ed Vosberg. **Trainer:** Blake Bowers.

Game Information

Radio: Unavailable.

PA Announcer: Delany Dunn. **Official Scorer:** Pat Karl.

Stadium Name (year opened): Nat Bailey Stadium (1951). **Location:** From downtown, take Cambie Street Bridge, left on East 29th Avenue, left on Clancy Loringer Way, right to stadium; from south, take Highway 99 to Oak Street, right on 41st Avenue, left on Ontario to 30th Avenue. **Standard Game Times:** 7:05 p.m.; Wed. 12:15; Sun. 1:30.

Visiting Club Hotel: Rosedale on Robson Suite Hotel, 838 Hamilton St., Vancouver, B.C. V6B 6A2. Telephone: (800) 661-8870, (604) 689-8033.

YAKIMA
Bears

Office Address: 8 N. 2nd St., Yakima, WA 98901. **Mailing Address:** P.O. Box 483, Yakima, WA 98907. **Telephone:** (509) 457-5151. **FAX:** (509) 457-9909. **E-Mail Address:** info@yakimabears.com. **Website:** www.yakimabears.com.

Affiliation (first year): Arizona Diamondbacks (2001). **Years in League:** 1955-66, 1990-.

Ownership, Management

Operated by: Short Season, LLC.

President: Mike Ellis. **Managing Partner:** Mike McMurray.

General Manager: Bob Romero. **Office Manager:** Louise Adams. **Director, Operations:** K.L. Wombacher. **Ticket/Group Sales:** Teddi Fowler. **Head Groundskeeper:** Bob Garretson. **Clubhouse Operations:** Paul Romero. **Administrative Assistant:** Unavailable.

Field Staff

Manager: Bill Plummer. **Coach:** Jay Gainer. **Pitching Coach:** Jeff Pico. **Trainer:** Unavailable.

Game Information

Radio Announcer: John Klima. **No. of Games Broadcast:** Home-38, Away-38. **Flagship Station:** KUTI 1460-AM.

PA Announcer: Todd Lyons. **Official Scorers:** Doug Evans, Gene Evans.

Stadium Name (year opened): Yakima County Stadium (1993). **Location:** I-82 to exit 34 (Nob Hill Boulevard), west to Fair Avenue, right on Fair, right on Pacific Avenue. **Standard Game Times:** 7:05 p.m., Sun. 6:05.

Visiting Club Hotel: Best Western Ahtanum Inn, 2408 Rudkin Rd., Union Gap, WA 98903. Telephone: (509) 248-9700.

APPALACHIAN LEAGUE

ROOKIE ADVANCED CLASSIFICATION

Mailing Address: 283 Deerchase Circle, Statesville, NC 28625. **Telephone:** (704) 873-5300. **FAX:** (704) 873-4333. **E-Mail Address:** appyleague@direcway.com.

Years League Active: 1921-25, 1937-55, 1957-.

President, Treasurer: Lee Landers. **Corporate Secretary:** Jim Holland (Princeton).

Directors: Cam Bonifay (Princeton), John Farrell (Burlington), Bob Fontaine (Bristol), Len Johnston (Bluefield), Bruce Manno (Johnson City), Dayton Moore (Danville), Kevin Morgan (Kingsport), Tim Purpura (Martinsville), Jim Rantz (Elizabethton), Dick Scott (Pulaski).

Lee Landers

League Administrator: Bobbi Landers.

2003 Opening Date: June 16. **Closing Date:** Aug. 25.

Regular Season: 68 games.

Division Structure: East—Bluefield, Burlington, Danville, Martinsville, Princeton. **West**—Bristol, Elizabethton, Johnson City, Kingsport, Pulaski.

Playoff Format: Division winners meet in best-of-3 series for league championship.

All-Star Game: None.

Roster Limit: 35 active. **Player Eligibility Rule:** No more than two years of prior minor league service. No more than 12 players 21 years of age or older, provided no more than two of the 12 may be 23 years of age or older.

Brand of Baseball: Rawlings.

Statistician: SportsTicker-Boston, Boston Fish Pier, West Bldg. #1, Suite 302, Boston, MA 02210.

Umpires: Unavailable.

STADIUM INFORMATION

		Dimensions				
Club	**Stadium**	**LF**	**CF**	**RF**	**Capacity**	**2002 Att.**
Bluefield	Bowen Field	335	365	335	2,250	29,462
Bristol	DeVault Memorial	325	400	310	2,000	21,921
Burlington	Burlington Athletic	335	410	335	3,000	36,481
Danville	Dan Daniel Memorial	330	400	330	2,588	32,981
Elizabethton	Joe O'Brien Field	335	414	326	1,500	24,959
Johnson City	Howard Johnson	320	410	320	2,500	37,786
Kingsport	Hunter Wright	330	410	330	2,500	21,911
Martinsville	Hooker Field	330	402	330	3,200	32,148
Princeton	Hunnicutt Field	330	396	330	1,950	29,336
Pulaski	Calfee Park	335	405	310	2,500	25,492

BLUEFIELD
Orioles

Office Address: 2003 Stadium Dr., Bluefield, WV 24701. **Mailing Address:** P.O. Box 356, Bluefield, WV 24701. **Telephone:** (276) 326-1326. **FAX:** (276) 326-1318.

Affiliation (first year): Baltimore Orioles (1958). **Years in League:** 1946-55, 1957-.

Ownership, Management

Operated by: Bluefield Baseball Club, Inc.

Director: Len Johnston (Baltimore Orioles).

Vice President: Cecil Smith. **Secretary:** K.K. Burton. **Counsel:** David Kersey.

President, General Manager: George McGonagle. **Controller:** Charles Peters. **Director, Special Projects:** Tuillio Ramella.

Field Staff

Manager: Don Buford. **Coaches:** Len Johnston, Hensley Meulens. **Pitching Coach:** Andre Rabouin. **Trainer:** Unavailable.

Game Information

Radio Announcer: Unavailable. **No. of Games Broadcast:** Away-34. **Flagship Station:** WHIS 1440-AM.

PA Announcer: Unavailable. **Official Scorer:** Will Prewitt.

Stadium Name (year opened): Bowen Field (1939). **Location:** I-77 to Bluefield exit, Route 290 to Route 460 West, right onto Leatherwood Lane, left at first light, past Chevron station and turn right, stadium 1¼ mile on left. **Standard Game Times:** 7 p.m., DH 6; Sun. 6, DH 5.

Visiting Club Hotel: Ramada Inn-East River, 3175 E. Cumberland Rd., Bluefield, WV 24701. Telephone: (276) 325-5421.

BRISTOL
White Sox

Office Address: 1501 Euclid Ave., Bristol, VA 24201. **Mailing Address:** P.O. Box 1434, Bristol, VA 24203. **Telephone:** (540) 645-7275. **FAX:** (540) 669-7686. **E-Mail Address:** bwsox@3wave.com. **Website:** www.bristolsox.com.

Affiliation (first year): Chicago White Sox (1995). **Years in League:** 1921-25, 1940-55, 1969-.

Ownership, Management

Operated by: Bristol Baseball, Inc.

Director: Bob Fontaine (Chicago White Sox).

President: Boyce Cox. **General Manager:** Robert Childress.

Field Staff

Manager: Jerry Hairston. **Coaches:** Chet DeMidio, Ryan Long. **Pitching Coach:** Bill Kinneberg. **Trainer:** Tomas Vera.

Game Information

Radio: None.

PA Announcer: Boyce Cox. **Official Scorer:** Allen Shepherd.

Stadium Name (year opened): DeVault Memorial Stadium (1969). **Location:** I-81 to exit 3 onto Commonwealth Ave., right on Euclid Ave. for ½ mile. **Standard Game Time:** 7 p.m.

Visiting Club Hotel: Ramada Inn, 2122 Euclid Ave., Bristol, VA 24201. Telephone: (540) 669-7171.

BURLINGTON
Indians

Office Address: 1450 Graham St., Burlington, NC 27217. **Mailing Address:** P.O. Box 1143, Burlington, NC 27217. **Telephone:** (336) 222-0223. **FAX:** (336) 226-2498. **E-Mail Address:** info@btribebaseball.com. **Website:** www.btribebaseball.com.

Affiliation (first year): Cleveland Indians (1986). **Years in League:** 1986-.

Ownership, Management

Operated by: Burlington Baseball Club, Inc.

Director: John Farrell (Cleveland Indians).

President: Miles Wolff. **Vice President:** Dan Moushon.

General Manager: Mark Cryan. **Assistant GM:** Melissa Kesterson. **Director, Media Relations:** Stephen Gates.

Field Staff

Manager: Rouglas Odor. **Coach:** Jack Mull. **Pitching Coach:** Ruben Niebla. **Trainer:** Teddy Blackwell.

Game Information

Radio Announcer: Stephen Gates. **No. of Games Broadcast:** Home-34, Away-34. **Flagship Station:** WBAG 1150-AM.

PA Announcer: Byron Tucker. **Official Scorer:** David Williams.

Stadium Name (year opened): Burlington Athletic Stadium (1960). **Location:** I-40/85 to exit 145, north on Route 100 (Maple Avenue) for 1½ miles, right on Mebane Street for 1½ miles, right on Beaumont, left on Graham. **Standard Game Time:** 7 p.m.

Visiting Club Hotel: Holiday Inn-Outlet Center, 2444 Maple Ave., Burlington, NC 27215. Telephone: (336) 229-5203.

DANVILLE
Braves

Office Address: Dan Daniel Memorial Park, 302 River Park Dr., Danville, VA 24540. **Mailing Address:** P.O. Box 378, Danville, VA 24543. **Telephone:** (434) 797-3792. **FAX:** (434) 797-3799. **E-Mail Address:** info@dbraves.com. **Website:** www.dbraves.com.

Affiliation (first year): Atlanta Braves (1993). **Years in League:** 1993-.

Ownership, Management

Operated by: Atlanta National League Baseball Club, Inc.

Director: Dayton Moore (Atlanta Braves).

General Manager: David Cross. **Assistant GM:** Bob Kitzmiller. **Head Groundskeeper:** Richard Gieselman. **Office Manager:** Shelby Tate.

Field Staff

Manager: Kevin McMullan. **Coach:** Billy Best. **Pitching Coach:** Jim Czajkowski. **Trainer:** Tyson Burton.

Game Information

Radio: None.

PA Announcer: Unavailable. **Official Scorer:** Unavailable.

Stadium Name (first year): Legion Field at Dan Daniel Memorial Park (1993). **Location:** US 58 to US 29 S. bypass, follow signs to park; US 29 bypass to Dan Daniel Park exit (River Park Drive), follow signs. **Standard Game Times:** 7 p.m.; Sun. 4.

Visiting Club Hotel: Innkeeper-West, 3020 Riverside Dr., Danville, VA 24541. Telephone: (434) 799-1202.

ELIZABETHTON
Twins

Office Address: 208 N. Holly Lane, Elizabethton, TN 37643. **Mailing Address:** 136 S. Sycamore St., Elizabethton, TN 37643. **Telephone:** (423) 547-6440, (423) 547-6443. **FAX:** (423) 547-6442. **E-Mail Address:** etwins@preferred.com. **Website:** www.elizabethtontwins.com.

Affiliation (first year): Minnesota Twins (1974). **Years in League:** 1937-42, 1945-51, 1974-.

Ownership, Management

Operated by: City of Elizabethton.

Director: Jim Rantz (Minnesota Twins).

President: Harold Mains.

General Manager: Mike Mains. **Clubhouse Operations:** David McQueen. **Head Groundskeeper:** David Nanney. **Director, Promotions:** Jim Jones. **Director, Ticket Sales:** Sherri Campbell. **Director, Group Sales:** Harold Ray. **Director, Merchandising:** Linda Church. **Director, Food Services:** Jane Hardin.

Field Staff

Manager: Ray Smith. **Coach:** Jeff Reed. **Pitching Coach:** Jim Shellenback. **Trainer:** Chad Jackson.

Game Information

Radio Announcer: Frank Santore. **No. of Games Broadcast:** Home-35, Away-6. **Flagship Station:** WBEJ 1240-AM.

PA Announcer: Tom Banks. **Official Scorer:** Bill Crow.

Stadium Name (year opened): Joe O'Brien Field (1974). **Location:** I-81 to I-181, exit at Highway 321/67, left at Holly Lane. **Standard Game Times:** 7 p.m., DH 6.

Visiting Club Hotel: Days Inn, 505 W. Elk Ave., Elizabethton, TN 37643. Telephone: (423) 543-3344.

JOHNSON CITY
Cardinals

Office Address: 111 Legion St., Johnson City, TN 37601. **Mailing Address:** P.O. Box 179, Johnson City, TN 37605. **Telephone:** (423) 461-4866. **FAX:** (423) 461-4864. **E-Mail Address:** jccardinalsbb@aol.com. **Website:** www.jccardinals.com.

Affiliation (first year): St. Louis Cardinals (1974). **Years in League:** 1911-13, 1921-24, 1937-55, 1957-61, 1964-.

Ownership, Management

Operated by: City of Johnson City.

Director: Bruce Manno (St. Louis Cardinals).

General Manager: Vance Spinks. **Assistant GM:** Chuck Flannagan. **Groundskeeper:** Michael Whitson.

Field Staff

Manager: Danny Sheaffer. **Coach:** Tommy Kidwell. **Pitching Coach:** Al Holland. **Trainer:** Kevin Crawmer.

Game Information

Radio: Unavailable.

PA Announcer: Unavailable. **Official Scorer:** Unavailable.

Stadium Name (year opened): Howard Johnson Field (1956). **Location:** I-181 to exit 32, left on East Main, through light onto Legion Street. **Standard Game Time:** 7 p.m.

Visiting Club Hotel: Holiday Inn, 101 W. Springbrook Dr., Johnson City, TN 37601. Telephone: (423) 282-4611.

KINGSPORT
Mets

Office Address: 433 E. Center St., Kingsport, TN 37664. **Mailing Address:** P.O. Box 1128, Kingsport, TN 37662. **Telephone:** (423) 378-3744. **FAX:** (423) 392-8538. **E-Mail Address:** kingsportmets@chartertn.net. **Website:** www.kmets.com.

Affiliation (first year): New York Mets (1980). **Years in League:** 1921-25, 1938-52, 1957, 1960-63, 1969-82, 1984-.

Ownership, Management

Operated by: S&H Baseball, LLC.

Director: Kevin Morgan (New York Mets).

President: Rick Spivey. **Vice President:** Steve Harville.

General Manager: Myra McEntire. **Director, Housing:** Peggy Lozier.

Field Staff

Manager: Mookie Wilson. **Coach:** Luis Natera. **Pitching Coach:** Rick Mahler. **Trainer:** Michael Suski.

Game Information

Radio: None.

PA Announcer: Don Spivey. **Official Scorer:** Eddie Durham.

Stadium Name (year opened): Hunter Wright Stadium (1995). **Location:** I-81 to I-181 North, exit 11E (Stone Drive), left on West Stone Drive (US 11W), right on Granby Road. **Standard Game Times:** 7 p.m., DH 6.

Visiting Club Hotel: Ramada Inn, 2005 Lamasa Dr., Kingsport, TN 37660. Telephone: (423) 245-0271.

MARTINSVILLE
Astros

Office Address: Hooker Field, 450 Commonwealth Blvd., Martinsville, VA 24112. **Mailing Address:** P.O. Box 3614, Martinsville, VA 24115. **Telephone:** (276) 666-2000. **FAX:** (276) 666-2139. **E-Mail Address:** info@martinsvilleastros.com. **Website:** www.martinsvilleastros.com.

Affiliation (first year): Houston Astros (1999). **Years in League:** 1988-.

Ownership, Management

Operated by: Houston Astros Baseball Club.

Director: Tim Purpura (Houston Astros). **Director, Baseball Operations:** Jay Edmiston.

General Manager: Charlie Norton. **Assistant GM:** Lynsi House. **Head Groundskeeper:** Sammy Pickeral. **Clubhouse Operations:** Troy Wells.

Field Staff

Manager: Jorge Orta. **Coach:** Marc Ronan. **Pitching Coach:** Jack Billingham. **Trainer:** Unavailable.

Game Information

Radio Announcer: Unavailable. **No. of Games Broadcast:** Home-34. **Flagship Station:** WHEE 1320 AM.

PA Announcer: Unavailable. **Official Scorer:** Micheal Nemec.

Stadium Name (year opened): Hooker Field (1988). **Location:** US 220 Business to Commonwealth Boulevard, east for three miles; US 58 to Chatham Heights Road, north two blocks, stadium at intersection of Commonwealth and Chatham Heights. **Standard Game Times:** 7 p.m, Sun. 6.

Visiting Club Hotel: Dutch Inn, 2360 Virginia Ave., Collinsville, VA 24078. Telephone: (276) 647-3721.

PRINCETON
Devil Rays

Office Address: Hunnicutt Field, Old Bluefield Road, Princeton, WV 24740. **Mailing Address:** P.O. Box 5646, Princeton, WV 24740. **Telephone:** (304) 487-2000. **FAX:** (304) 487-8762. **E-Mail Address:** raysball@sunlitsurf.com. **Website:** www.princetondevilrays.com.

Affiliation (first year): Tampa Bay Devil Rays (1997). **Years in League:** 1988-.

Ownership, Management

Operated by: Princeton Baseball Association, Inc.

Director: Cam Bonifay (Tampa Bay Devil Rays).

President: Dewey Russell.

General Manager: Jim Holland. **Director, Stadium Operations:** Mick Bayle. **Head Groundskeeper:** Frankie Bailey. **Account Representative:** Paul Lambert. **Clubhouse Manager:** Matt Gallant.

Field Staff

Manager: Jamie Nelson. **Coach:** Manny Castillo. **Pitching Coach:** Brad Woodall. **Trainer:** Unavailable.

Game Information

Radio Announcer: Robert Langpaap. **No. of Games Broadcast:** Away-34. **Flagship Station:** WAEY 1490-AM.

PA Announcer: Dave Ebert. **Official Scorer:** Dick Daisey.

Stadium Name (year opened): Hunnicutt Field (1988). **Location:** Exit 9 off I-77, US 460 West to downtown exit, left on Stafford Drive, stadium located behind Mercer County Technical Education Center. **Standard Game Times:** 7 p.m., DH 5:30; Sun. 4.

Visiting Club Hotel: Days Inn, I-77 and Ambrose Lane, Princeton, WV 24740. Telephone: (304) 425-8100.

PULASKI
Blue Jays

Mailing Address: P.O. Box 676, Pulaski, VA 24301. **Telephone:** (540) 980-1070. **FAX:** (540) 980-1850. **E-Mail Address:** mail@pulaskibluejays.com. **Website:** www.pulaskibluejays.com.

Affiliation (first year): Toronto Blue Jays (2003). **Years in League:** 1946-50, 1952-55, 1957-58, 1969-77, 1982-92, 1997-.

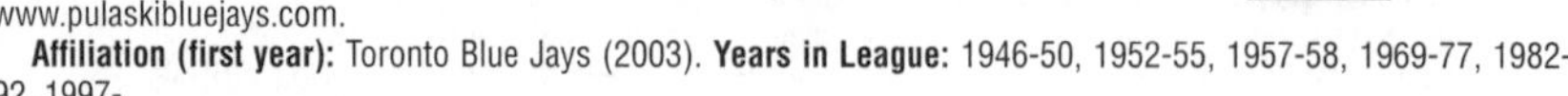

Ownership, Management

Operated by: Pulaski Baseball, Inc.

General Manager: Tom Compton. **Assistant GM:** Shawn Hite.

Field Staff

Manager: Paul Elliott. **Coach:** Unavailable. **Pitching Coach:** Lee Guetterman. **Trainer:** Unavailable.

Game Information

Radio: None.

PA Announcer: Andy French. **Official Scorer:** Unavailable.

Stadium Name (year opened): Calfee Park (1935). **Location:** I-81 to exit 89 (Route 11), north to Pulaski, right on Pierce Avenue. **Standard Game Time:** 7 p.m.

Visiting Club Hotel: Comfort Inn, 4424 Cleburne Blvd., Dublin, VA 24084. Telephone: (540) 674-1100.

PIONEER LEAGUE

ROOKIE ADVANCED CLASSIFICATION

Jim McCurdy

Office Address: 157 S. Lincoln Ave., Spokane, WA 99201. **Mailing Address:** P.O. Box 2564, Spokane, WA 99220. **Telephone:** (509) 456-7615. **FAX:** (509) 456-0136. **E-Mail Address:** fanmail@pioneerleague.com. **Website:** www.pioneerleague.com.

Years League Active: 1939-42, 1946-.

President/Secretary-Treasurer: Jim McCurdy.

Vice President: Mike Ellis (Missoula).

Directors: Dave Baggott (Ogden), Mike Ellis (Missoula), D.G. Elmore (Helena), Larry Geske (Great Falls), Kevin Greene (Idaho Falls), Kevin Haughian (Casper), Rob Owens (Provo), Bob Wilson (Billings).

Administrative Assistant: Teryl MacDonald.

2003 Opening Date: June 17. **Closing Date:** Sept. 5.

Regular Season: 76 games (split schedule).

Division Structure: North—Billings, Great Falls, Helena, Missoula. **South**—Casper, Idaho Falls, Ogden, Provo.

Playoff Format: First-half division winners play second-half division winners in best-of-3 series. Winners meet in best-of-3 series for league championship.

All-Star Game: None.

Roster Limit: 35 active, 30 dressed for each game. **Player Eligibility Rule:** No more than 17 players 21 and older, provided that no more than two are 23 or older. No player on active list may have more than three years of prior service.

Brand of Baseball: Rawlings.

Statistician: SportsTicker-Boston, Boston Fish Pier, West Bldg. #1, Suite 302, Boston, MA 02210.

Umpires: Unavailable.

STADIUM INFORMATION

		Dimensions				
Club	**Stadium**	**LF**	**CF**	**RF**	**Capacity**	**2002 Att.**
Billings	Cobb Field	335	405	325	4,200	98,345
Casper	Mike Lansing Field	355	400	345	2,500	50,573
Great Falls	Legion Park	335	414	335	3,800	90,079
*Helena	Kendrick Legion Field	335	400	325	1,700	26,285
Idaho Falls	McDermott Field	340	400	350	2,928	63,192
Missoula	Lindborg-Cregg	320	400	320	2,200	55,268
Ogden	Lindquist Field	335	396	334	5,000	126,700
Provo	Larry H. Miller Field	345	400	345	2,000	55,050

*Club operated in Medicine Hat in 2002

BILLINGS
Mustangs

Office Address: Cobb Field, 901 N. 27th St., Billings, MT 59101. **Mailing Address:** P.O. Box 1553, Billings, MT 59103. **Telephone:** (406) 252-1241. **FAX:** (406) 252-2968. **E-Mail Address:** mustangs@billingsmustangs.com. **Website:** www.billingsmustangs.com.

Affiliation (first year): Cincinnati Reds (1974). **Years in League:** 1948-63, 1969-.

Ownership, Management

Operated by: Billings Pioneer Baseball Club, Inc.

Chairman: Ron May.

President, General Manager: Bob Wilson. **Assistant GM:** Gary Roller. **Head Groundskeeper:** Dave Graves. **Director, Sales:** Allen Reynolds. **Director, Broadcasting:** Mike Cappello. **Director, Clubhouse Operations:** George Kimmet.

Field Staff

Manager: Rick Burleson. **Coach:** Jay Sorg. **Pitching Coach:** Ed Hodge. **Trainer:** Unavailable.

Game Information

Radio Announcer: Mike Cappello. **No. of Games Broadcast:** Home-38, Away-38. **Flagship Station:** KBUL 970-AM.

PA Announcer: Adam Bryant. **Official Scorer:** Matt Bender.

Stadium Name (year opened): Cobb Field (1948). **Location:** I-90 to 27th Street North exit, north to Ninth Avenue North. **Standard Game Times:** 7 p.m., Sun. 4.

Visiting Club Hotel: Rimrock Inn, 1203 N. 27th St., Billings, MT 59101. Telephone: (406) 252-7107.

CASPER
Rockies

Office Address: 907 N. Poplar, No. 140, Casper, WY 82601 (until June 1, 2003); 330 Kati Lane, Casper, WY 82601 (after June 1, 2003). **Mailing Address:** P.O. Box 1293, Casper, WY 82602. **Telephone:** (307) 232-1111. **FAX:** (307) 265-7867. **E-Mail Address:** baseball@casperrockies.com. **Website:** www.casperrockies.com.

Affiliation (first year): Colorado Rockies (2001).

Years in League: 2001-.

Ownership, Management

Operated by: Casper Professional Baseball Club, LLC.

Principal Owner, Chief Executive Officer: Kevin Haughian.

President, General Manager: Mary Stanley. **Assistant GM/Director, Operations:** Todd Titus. **Assistant GM/Manager, Corporate Sales:** Danny Tetzlaff. **Director, Ticket Operations:** Abi Gerhard.

Field Staff

Manager: P.J. Carey. **Coach:** Tony Diaz. **Pitching Coach:** Richard Palacios. **Trainer:** Jason Skolnick.

Game Information

Radio: Unavailable.

PA Announcer: Unavailable. **Official Scorer:** Unavailable.

Stadium Name (year opened): Mike Lansing Field (2002). **Location:** I-25 to Poplar Street exit, north on Poplar Street, right into Crossroads Park. **Standard Game Times:** 7:05 p.m., Sun. 5:05.

Visiting Club Hotel: Parkway Plaza, 123 W. "E" St., Casper, WY 82601. Telephone (307) 235-1777.

GREAT FALLS
White Sox

Office Address: 12 Third St. NW, Suite 150, Great Falls, MT 59403 (until June 1, 2003); 1015 25th St. North, Great Falls, MT 59401 (after June 1, 2003). **Mailing Address:** P.O. Box 1621, Great Falls, MT 59403. **Telephone:** (406) 452-5311. **FAX:** (406) 454-0811. **E-Mail Address:** whitesox@greatfallswhitesox.com. **Website:** www.greatfallswhitesox.com.

Affiliation (first year): Chicago White Sox (2003). **Years in League:** 1948-1963, 1969-.

Ownership/Management

Operated by: Great Falls Baseball Club, Inc.

President: Larry Geske.

General Manager: Jim Keough. **Assistant GM:** Ginger Burcham. **Head Groundskeeper:** Carl Christofferson.

Field Staff

Manager: Chris Cron. **Coach:** Mark Haley. **Pitching Coach:** Richard Dotson. **Trainer:** Mark Snow.

Game Information

Radio Announcers: Michael Purpura, Ben Adler. **No. of Games Broadcast:** Home-38, Away-38. **Flagship Station:** KMON 560-AM.

PA Announcer/Official Scorer: Tim Paul.

Stadium Name (Year Opened): Legion Park (1956). **Location:** From I-15, take 10th Ave. South (exit 281) for four miles to 26th Street, left to 8th Ave. North, left to 25th Street North, right to ballpark. **Standard Game Times:** 7 p.m., Sun. 4.

Visiting Club Hotel: Midtown Hotel, 526 Second Ave. N., Great Falls, MT 59401. Telephone: (406) 453-2411.

HELENA
Brewers

Office Address: 1300 N. Ewing, Helena, MT 59601. **Mailing Address:** P.O. Box 6756, Helena, MT 59604. **Telephone:** (406) 495-0500. **FAX:** (406) 495-0900. **E-Mail Address:** helenabrewers@hotmail.com. **Website:** www.helenabrewers.net.

Affiliation (first year): Milwaukee Brewers (2003). **Years in League:** 2003-.

Ownership, Management

Operated by: Helena Baseball Club LLC.

Principal Owner: D.G. Elmore.

General Manager: Paul Fetz. **Assistant GM:** Melissa Dudek. **Director, Broadcasting/Media Relations:** Rob Sinclair.

Field Staff

Manager: Ed Sedar. **Coach:** Andy Tomberlin. **Pitching Coach:** Mark Littell. **Trainer:** Masa Koyanagi.

Game Information

Radio Announcer: Rob Sinclair. **No. of Games Broadcast:** Home-38, Away-38. **Flagship Station:** KCAP 1340-AM.

PA Announcer: Unavailable. **Official Scorer:** Unavailable.

Stadium Name (year opened): Kindrick Field (1939). **Location:** Cedar Street exit off I-15, west to Main Street, left at Memorial Park. **Standard Game Time:** 7:05 p.m.

Visiting Club Hotel: Unavailable.

IDAHO FALLS
Padres

Office Address: 568 W. Elva, Idaho Falls, ID 83402. **Mailing Address:** P.O. Box 2183, Idaho Falls, ID 83403. **Telephone:** (208) 522-8363. **FAX:** (208) 522-9858. **E-Mail Address:** padres@ifpadres.com. **Website:** www.ifpadres.com.

Affiliation (first year): San Diego Padres (1995). **Years in League:** 1940-42, 1946-.

Ownership, Management

Operated by: The Elmore Group.

Principal Owner: David Elmore.

President, General Manager: Kevin Greene. **Assistant GM, Merchandise:** Marcus Loyola. **Director, Public Relations/Concessions:** Nathaniel Peck. **Director, Corporate Sales/Operations:** Travis Brower. **Head Groundskeeper:** Dan Guthrie.

Field Staff

Manager: Carlos Lezcano. **Coach:** Jake Molina. **Pitching Coach:** Jerry Nyman. **Trainer:** Paul Navarro.

Game Information

Radio Announcers: John Balginy, Jim Garshow. **No. of Games Broadcast:** Home-38, Away-38. **Flagship Station:** KUPI 980-AM.

PA Announcer: Unavailable. **Official Scorer:** John Balginy.

Stadium Name (year opened): McDermott Field (1976). **Location:** I-15 to West Broadway exit, left onto Memorial Drive, right on Mound Avenue, 1/4 mile to stadium. **Standard Game Times:** 7:15 p.m., Sun. 5.

Visiting Club Hotel: Unavailable.

MISSOULA
Osprey

Office Address: 137 E. Main St., Missoula, MT 59802. **Telephone:** (406) 543-3300. **FAX:** (406) 543-9463. **E-Mail Address:** generalmgr@missoulaosprey.com. **Website:** www.missoulaosprey.com.

Affiliation (first year): Arizona Diamondbacks (1999). **Years in League:** 1956-60, 1999-.

Ownership, Management

Operated by: Mountain Baseball, LLC.

President: Mike Ellis. **Executive Vice President:** Judy Ellis.

VP/General Manager: Matt Ellis. **Assistant GM:** Chris Hale. **Director, Finance/Human Resources:** Shelly Ellis. **Director, Stadium Operations:** Jared Amoss. **Manager, Group Sales:** Mari Raney. **Director, Merchandise:** Lori Hale. **Office Administrator:** Traci Gilman. **Clubhouse Manager:** Unavailable.

Field Staff

Manager: Tony Perezchica. **Coach:** Jason Bates. **Pitching Coach:** Wellington Cepeda. **Trainer:** Unavailable.

Game Information

Radio Announcer: Tim Boulware. **No. of Games Broadcast:** Home-38, Away-38. **Flagship Station:** Unavailable.

PA Announcer: Patrick Nikolay. **Official Scorer:** Unavailable.

Stadium Name (year opened): Missoula Civic Stadium (2003). **Location:** West on Orange to Craig, north on Craig, stadium west of McCormick Park. **Standard Game Times:** 7:05 p.m., Sun. 5:05.

Visiting Club Hotel: Campus Inn, 744 E. Broadway, Missoula, MT 59802. Telephone: (406) 549-5134.

OGDEN
Raptors

Office Address: 2330 Lincoln Ave., Ogden, UT 84401. **Telephone:** (801) 393-2400. **FAX:** (801) 393-2473. **E-Mail Address:** homerun@ogden-raptors.com. **Website:** www.ogden-raptors.com.

Affiliation (first year): Los Angeles Dodgers (2003). **Years in League:** 1939-42, 1946-55, 1966-74, 1994-.

Ownership, Management

Operated by: Ogden Professional Baseball, Inc.

Principal Owners: Dave Baggott, John Lindquist.

Chairman, President: Dave Baggott. **General Manager:** Joe Stein. **Controller:** Carol Spickler. **Head Groundskeeper:** Ken Kopinski. **Director, Merchandising:** Geri Kopinski.

Field Staff

Manager: Travis Barbary. **Coach:** Juan Bustabad. **Pitching Coach:** Tim Kelly. **Trainer:** Robert Picard.

Game Information

Radio Announcer: Unavailable. **No. of Games Broadcast:** Home-38, Away-38. **Flagship Station:** KSOS 800-AM.

PA Announcer: Pete Diamond. **Official Scorer:** Dennis Kunimura.

Stadium Name (year opened): Lindquist Field (1997). **Location:** I-15 North to 21st Street exit, east to Lincoln Avenue, south three blocks to park. **Standard Game Times:** 7 p.m., Sun. 1.

Visiting Club Hotel: Marriott, 247 24th St., Odgen, UT 84401. Telephone: (801) 627-1190.

PROVO
Angels

Office Address: One E. Center St, Suite 205, Provo, UT 84606. **Telephone:** (801) 377-2255. **FAX:** (801) 377-2345. **Website:** www.provoangels.com.

Affiliation: Anaheim Angels (2001) **Years in League:** 2001-.

Ownership/Management

Operated by: Never Say Never, Inc.

Principal Owners: Rob Owens, Linda Gach Ray.

Chairman: Linda Gach Ray. **President:** Rob Owens.

General Manager: John Stein. **Director, Sales/Marketing:** John Stein. **Director, Public Relations:** Becky Vallett. **Manager, Stadium Operations:** Curtis Malone.

Field Staff

Manager: Tom Kotchman. **Coach:** Kevin Ham. **Pitching Coach:** Kernan Ronan. **Trainer:** Unavailable.

Game Information

Radio Announcer: Unavailable. **No. of Games Broadcast:** Home-38, Away-38. **Flagship Station:** Unavailable.

PA Announcer: Kelly Newbold. **Official Scorer:** Todd Fairbourne.

Stadium Name (year opened): Larry H. Miller Field at Miller Park (2001). **Location:** Exit 272 (University Parkway) off 1-15, east four miles to Brigham Young University campus, stadium on right. **Standard Game Times:** 7:05 p.m., DH 6:05; Mon. 5:05.

Visiting Club Hotel: Provo Days Inn, 1675 N. 200 West, Provo, UT 84604. Telephone: (801) 375-8600.

ARIZONA LEAGUE

ROOKIE CLASSIFICATION

Office Address: 910 Main St., Suite 351, Boise, ID 83702. **Mailing Address:** P.O. Box 1645, Boise, ID 83701. **Telephone:** (208) 429-1511. **FAX:** (208) 429-1525. **E-Mail Address:** bobrichmond@worldnet.att.net.

Years League Active: 1988-.

President/Treasurer: Bob Richmond.

Vice President: Bobby Evans (Giants). **Corporate Secretary:** Ted Polakowski (Athletics).

Administrative Assistant: Rob Richmond.

2003 Opening Date: June 23. **Closing Date:** Aug. 30. **Standard Game Times:** 10:30 a.m.; night games—7 p.m.

Division Structure: None. **Teams:** Angels, Athletics, Brewers, Cubs, Giants, Mariners, Rangers, Royals I, Royals II.

Regular Season: 56 games (split schedule).

Playoff Format: First-half winner meets second-half winner in one-game championship.

All-Star Game: None.

Roster Limit: 35 active, 35 under control. **Player Eligibility Rule:** No more than eight players 20 or older, and no more than six players 21 or older, including four players not selected in most recent first-year draft. At least 10 pitchers. No more than two years of prior service, excluding Rookie leagues outside the United States and Canada.

Brand of Baseball: Rawlings.

Statistician: SportsTicker-Boston, Boston Fish Pier, West Bldg. #1, Suite 302, Boston, MA 02210.

Clubs	Playing Site	Manager	Coach	Pitching Coach
Angels	Gene Autry Park, Mesa	Brian Harper	Bobby Magallanes	Jack Uhey
Athletics	Papago Park Sports Complex, Phoenix	Ruben Escalera	F. Arroyo/B. Owens	Fernando Arroyo
Brewers	Maryvale Baseball Complex, Phoenix	Hector Torres	George McPherson	Steve Cline
Cubs	Fitch Park, Mesa	Carmelo Martinez	Ricardo Medina	Rick Tronerud
Giants	Scottsdale Stadium, Scottsdale	Bert Hunter	Leonardo Garcia	Maximino Molina
Mariners	Peoria Sports Complex, Peoria	Scott Steinmann	T. Cruz/A. Bottin	Marcos Garcia
Rangers	Surprise Recreation Campus	Pedro Lopez	B. Jacoby/K. Dattola	Aris Tirado
Royals I	Surprise Recreation Campus	Kevin Boles	Pookie Wilson	Jose Bautista
Royals II	Surprise Recreation Campus	Lloyd Simmons	Tom Poquette	Royal Clayton

GULF COAST LEAGUE

ROOKIE CLASSIFICATION

Mailing Address: 1503 Clower Creek Dr., Suite H-262, Sarasota, FL 34231. **Telephone:** (941) 966-6407. **FAX:** (941) 966-6872.

Years League Active: 1964-.

President/Secretary-Treasurer: Tom Saffell.

First Vice President: Steve Noworyta (Phillies). **Second Vice President:** Jim Rantz (Twins).

Administrative Assistant: Bill Ventolo.

2003 Opening Date: June 19. **Closing Date:** Aug. 24.

Regular Season: 60 games.

Division Structure: East—Braves, Dodgers, Expos, Marlins. **North**—Phillies, Pirates, Tigers, Yankees. **South**—Orioles, Reds, Red Sox, Twins.

Playoff Format: Division winner with best regular season record plays winner of one-game playoff between other two division winners in best-of-3 series for championship.

Roster Limit: 35 active, but only 30 eligible for each game. **Player Eligibility Rule:** No more than eight players 20 or older, and no more than two players 21 or older. Four players of any age who were eligible but passed over in the 2001 draft. No more than two years of prior service, excluding Rookie leagues outside the United States and Canada. A third year is allowed for players under 20.

Brand of Baseball: Rawlings.

Statistician: SportsTicker-Boston, Boston Fish Pier, West Bldg. #1, Suite 302, Boston, MA 02210.

Clubs	Playing Site	Manager	Coach(es)	Pitching Coach
Braves	Disney's Wide World of Sports, Orlando	Ralph Henriquez	S. Lezcano/J. Saul	D. Botelho/G. Luckert
Dodgers	Dodgertown, Vero Beach	Luis Salazar	Tony Harris	George Culver
Expos	Carl Barger Baseball Complex, Melbourne	Bobby Henley	Jose Alguacil	Doug White
Marlins	Roger Dean Stadium, Jupiter	Tim Cossins	Johnny Rodriguez	Jeff Schwarz
Orioles	Twin Lakes Park, Sarasota	Jesus Alfaro	Joe Tanner/Mike Felder	Larry Jaster
Phillies	Carpenter Complex, Clearwater	Ruben Amaro Sr.	Ramon Aviles	Carlos Arroyo
Pirates	Pirate City Complex, Bradenton	Woody Huyke	Greg Briley	Miguel Bonilla
Reds	Ed Smith Stadium, Sarasota	Edgar Caceres	B. Williams/M. Davalillo	Jeff Gray
Red Sox	Red Sox minor league complex, Fort Myers	Ralph Treuel	Walter Miranda	Alan Mauthe
Tigers	Tigertown, Lakeland	Howard Bushong	Scott Makarewicz	Greg Sabat
Twins	Lee County Stadium, Fort Myers	Rudy Hernandez	J. Pont/M. Cuyler	Steve Mintz
Yankees	Yankee Complex, Tampa	Dan Radison	Bill Mosiello	Dave Eiland

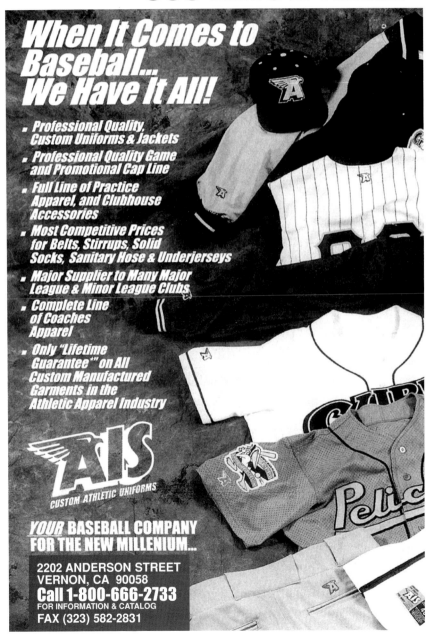

MINOR LEAGUE SCHEDULES

CLASS AAA
INTERNATIONAL LEAGUE

Buffalo

APRIL

3-4-5-6 .... Pawtucket
7-8-9 .... Syracuse
10-11-12-13 .... at Ottawa
14-15-16 ..... at Syracuse
17 .... at Rochester
18-19-20 .... Ottawa
21-22-23 ...... at Scranton
24-25 .... at Pawtucket
26-27 .... Scranton
29-30 .... at Rochester

MAY

1-2-3-4 .... Louisville
5-6-7-8 .... Toledo
9-10-11-12 .... at Indy
13-14-15-16 .... at Toledo
17-18-19-20 .... Indy
22-23-24-25 ... Richmond
26-27-28-29 ...... at L'ville
30-31 .... at Columbus

JUNE

1-2 .... at Columbus
3-4-5-6 .... Norfolk
7-8-9-10 .... Rochester
12-13-14-15 ...... at Rich.
16-17-18-19 ... at Norfolk
20-21-21-22 .... Charlotte
24-25-26-27 ... Columbus
28-29 .... Scranton
30 .... at Ottawa

JULY

1 .... at Ottawa
2-3 .... Ottawa
4-5-6-7 .... at Charlotte
8-9-10-11 ...... at Durham
12-13 .... at Syracuse
17-18-19-20 ...... Durham
21-22 .... Syracuse
23-24 .... at Syracuse
25-26-27 .... at Pawtucket
29-30-31 .... Syracuse

AUGUST

1-2-3-4 .... Pawtucket
5-6 .... at Rochester
7 .... Rochester
8-9-10 .... at Pawtucket
11-12-13 ...... at Scranton
15 .... at Syracuse
16-17-18-19 .... Scranton
20-21-22 .... Ottawa
23-24 .... Rochester
25-26 .... at Rochester
27-28 .... at Scranton
29-30 .... at Ottawa
31 .... at Rochester

SEPTEMBER

1 .... Rochester

Charlotte

APRIL

3-4-5-6 .... Richmond
7-8 .... Norfolk
9-10 .... at Louisville
11-12-13 .... at Indy
15-16 .... Louisville
17-18-19-20 .... Indy
21-22 .... Durham
23-24-25 .... at Richmond
26-27 .... at Norfolk
28-29 .... Durham

MAY

1-2-3-4 .... Rochester
5-6-7-8 .... Syracuse
9-10-11-12 ...... at Toledo
13-14-15-16 .... at Col.
17-18-18-20 .... Scranton
21-22-23-24 .... Toledo
26-27 .... at Durham
28-29 .... Durham
30-31 .... at Scranton

JUNE

1-2 .... at Scranton
3-4-5-6 ...... at Rochester
7-8-9-10 .... at Ottawa
12-13-14-15 ... Columbus
16-17-18-19 .... Ottawa
20-21-21-22 ... at Buffalo
24-25-26-27 .... at Syr.
28-29-30 .... Pawtucket

JULY

1 .... Pawtucket
2-3 .... Toledo
4-5-6-7 .... Buffalo
8-9-10-11 ... at Pawtucket
12-13 .... Richmond
17-18 .... Norfolk
19-20 .... at Norfolk
21-22 .... at Richmond
23-24 .... Columbus
25-26-27-28 ...... at L'ville
29-30 .... at Columbus
31 .... Norfolk

AUGUST

1 .... Norfolk
2-3-4-5 .... Louisville
6-7 .... at Norfolk
8-9-10 ..... at Indianapolis
11-12 .... at Toledo
14-15 .... Indianapolis
16-17 .... Richmond
18-19 .... Durham
20-21-22 .... at Richmond
23-24 .... at Norfolk
25-26-27 .... at Durham
28-29 .... Norfolk
30-31 .... at Durham

SEPTEMBER

1 .... at Durham

Columbus

APRIL

3-4-5-6 .... Indianapolis
7-8 .... at Louisville
9-10 .... at Norfolk
11-12-13-14 ...... at Rich.
15-16 .... Toledo
17-18 .... Norfolk
19-19-21-22 ... Richmond
24-25 .... at Louisville
26-27 ...... at Indianapolis
28-29 .... at Toledo

MAY

1-2-3-4 .... Scranton
5-6-7-8 .... at Ottawa
9-10-11-12 .... at Roch.
13-14-15-16 .... Charlotte
17-18-19-20 ... Rochester
22-23-24-25 .... at Paw.
26-27-28-29 .... at Scr.
30-31 .... Buffalo

JUNE

1-2 .... Buffalo
3-4-5-6 .... Durham
7-8-9-10 .... at Durham
12-13-14-15 ...... at Char.
16-17 .... at Louisville
18-19 .... Louisville
20-21-22-23 .... Norfolk
24-25-26-27 ... at Buffalo
28-29-30 ..... at Syracuse

JULY

1 .... at Syracuse
2-3 .... Indianapolis
4-5-6-7 .... Ottawa
8-9-10-11 .... Syracuse
12-13 .... at Toledo
17-18-19-20 ... Pawtucket
21-22 ...... at Indianapolis
23-24 .... at Charlotte
25-26-27-28 ... at Norfolk
29-30 .... Charlotte
31 .... Richmond

AUGUST

1 .... Richmond
2-3 .... at Toledo
4-5 .... at Indianapolis
6-7 .... Durham
8-9-10 .... Toledo
12-13-14-15 .... Louisville
16-17 .... at Durham
18-19 .... at Richmond
20-21 .... Indianapolis
22-23 .... at Toledo
24-25-26 .... Toledo
27-28 .... Louisville
29-30 ...... at Indianapolis
31 .... at Louisville

SEPTEMBER

1 .... at Louisville

Durham

APRIL

3-4-5-6 .... Norfolk
7-8 .... Richmond
9-10 .... at Indianapolis
11-12-13 ..... at Louisville
15-16 .... Indianapolis
17-18-19-20 .... Louisville
21-22 .... at Charlotte
23-24-25 .... at Norfolk
26-27 .... at Richmond
28-29 .... at Charlotte

MAY

1-2-3-4 .... Syracuse
5-6-7-8 .... Rochester
9-10-11-12 .. at Syracuse
13-14-15-16 ..... at Roch.
17-18-19-20 .... Toledo
22-23-24-25 .... Scranton
26-27 .... Charlotte
28-29 .... at Charlotte
30-31 .... at Toledo

JUNE

1-2 .... at Toledo
3-4-5-6 ...... at Columbus
7-8-9-10 .... Columbus
12-13-14-15 .... Ottawa
16-17-18-19 .... at Paw.
20-20-21-22 .... at Scr.
24-25-26-27 ... Pawtucket
28-29 .... Louisville
30 .... Toledo

JULY

1 .... Toledo
2-3 .... at Norfolk
4-5-6-7 ...... at Richmond
8-9-10-11 .... Buffalo
12-13 .... Norfolk
17-18-19-20 ... at Buffalo
21-22-23-24 .... at Ottawa
25-26-27-28 .... Indy
29-30 .... Norfolk
31 .... at Indianapolis

AUGUST

1-2-3 .... at Indianapolis
4-5 .... at Toledo
6-7 .... at Columbus
8-9-10 .... at Louisville
12-13-14-15 ... Richmond
16-17 .... Columbus
18-19 .... at Charlotte
20-21-22 .... at Norfolk
23-24 .... at Richmond
25-26-27 .... Charlotte
28-29 .... Richmond
30-31 .... Charlotte

SEPTEMBER

1 .... Charlotte

Indianapolis

APRIL

3-4-5-6 ...... at Columbus
7-8 .... at Toledo
9-10 .... Durham
11-12-13 .... Charlotte
15-16 .... at Durham
17-18-19-20 ...... at Char.
21-22-23 ..... at Louisville
24-25 .... Toledo
26-27 .... Columbus
29-30 .... Louisville

MAY

1-2-3-4 ...... at Richmond
5-6-7-8 .... at Norfolk
9-10-11-12 .... Buffalo
13-14-15-16 ... Pawtucket
17-18-19-20 ... at Buffalo
22-23-24-25 .... at Ottawa
26-27-28-29 ... Rochester

30-31 .... Ottawa

JUNE

1-2 .... Ottawa
3-4 .... at Toledo
5-6 .... Toledo
7-8-9-10 ...... at Syracuse
12-13-14-15 .... Scranton
16-17-18-19 .... Syracuse
20-21-22-23 .... at Paw.
24-25-26-27 .... at Scr.
28-29-30 .... Richmond

JULY

1 .... Richmond
2-3 .... at Columbus
4-5-6-7 .... Louisville
8-9-10-11 .... Norfolk
12-13 .... at Louisville
17-18-19-20 ..... at Roch.
21-22 .... Columbus
23-24 .... at Richmond
25-26-27-28 ... at Durham
29-30 .... Richmond
31 .... Durham

AUGUST

1-2-3 .... Durham
4-5 .... Columbus
6-7 .... at Toledo
8-9-10 .... Charlotte
12-13 .... at Norfolk
14-15 .... at Charlotte
16-17 .... Norfolk
18-19 .... Toledo
20-21 .... at Columbus
22-23-24 ..... at Louisville
25-26 .... Louisville
27-28 .... Toledo
29-30 .... Columbus
31 .... at Toledo

SEPTEMBER

1 .... at Toledo

Louisville

APRIL

3-4-5-6 .... at Toledo
7-8 .... Columbus
9-10 .... Charlotte
11-12-13 .... Durham
15-16 .... at Charlotte
17-18-19-20 ... at Durham
21-22-23 ..... Indianapolis
24-25 .... Columbus
26-27 .... Toledo
29-30 ...... at Indianapolis

MAY

1-2-3-4 .... at Buffalo
5-6-7-8 .... Scranton
9-10-11-12 .... Pawtucket
13-14-15-16 ... at Scranton
17-18-19-20 .... at Paw.
22-23-24-25 ... Rochester
26-27-28-29 .... Buffalo
30-31 .... at Syracuse

JUNE

1-2 .... at Syracuse
3-4-5-6 .... Richmond
7-8-9-10 .... at Richmond
12-13-14-15 ... at Norfolk
16-17 .... Columbus
18-19 .... at Columbus
20-21-22-23 .... Syracuse
24-25-26-27 .... Norfolk
28-29 .... at Durham
30 .... at Norfolk

JULY

1 .... at Norfolk
2-3 .... Richmond
4-5-6-7 ... at Indianapolis
8-9-10-11 .... Ottawa
12-13 .... Indianapolis
17-18-19-20 .... at Ottawa
21-22-23-24 ..... at Roch.
25-26-27-28 .... Charlotte
29-30-31 .... Toledo

AUGUST

1 .... Toledo
2-3-4-5 .... at Charlotte
6-7 .... at Richmond
8-9-10 .... Durham
12-13-14-15 .... at Col.
16-17 .... Toledo
18-19 .... Norfolk
20-21 .... at Toledo
22-23-24 ..... Indianapolis
25-26 ...... at Indianapolis
27-28 .... at Columbus
29-30 .... at Toledo
31 .... Columbus

SEPTEMBER

1 .... Columbus

Norfolk

APRIL

3-4-5-6 .... at Durham
7-8 .... at Charlotte
9-10 .... Columbus
11-12-13-14 .... Toledo
15-16 .... at Richmond
17-18 .... at Columbus
19-20-21-22 .... at Toledo
23-24-25 .... Durham
26-27 .... Charlotte
28-29 .... Richmond

MAY

1-2-3-4 ...... at Pawtucket
5-6-7-8 .... Indianapolis
9-10-11-12 .... Ottawa
13-14-15-16 .... at Syr.
17-18-19-20 .... at Ottawa
22-23-24-25 .... Syracuse
26-27-28-29 ... Pawtucket
30-31 .... at Rochester

JUNE

1-2 .... at Rochester
3-4-5-6 .... at Buffalo
7-8-9-10 ...... at Scranton
12-13-14-15 .... Louisville
16-17-18-19 .... Buffalo
20-21-22-23 .... at Col.
24-25-26-27 ...... at L'ville
28-29 .... Toledo
30 .... Louisville

JULY

1 .... Louisville
2-3 .... Durham
4-5-6-7 .... Rochester
8-9-10-11 .... at Indy
12-13 .... at Durham
17-18 .... at Charlotte
19-20 .... Charlotte
21-22-23-24 .... Scranton
25-26-27-28 ... Columbus
29-30 .... at Durham
31 .... at Charlotte

AUGUST

1 .... at Charlotte
2-3-4-5 ..... at Richmond
6-7 .... Charlotte
8-9-10 .... Richmond
12-13 .... Indianapolis
14-15 .... at Toledo
16-17 ...... at Indianapolis
18-19 .... at Louisville
20-21-22 .... Durham
23-24 .... Charlotte
26 .... Richmond
27 .... at Richmond
28-29 .... at Charlotte
30-31 .... Richmond

SEPTEMBER

1 .... at Richmond

Ottawa

APRIL

3-4-5-6 .... at Scranton
7-8-9 .... at Pawtucket
10-11-12-13 .... Buffalo
14-15-16-17 ... Pawtucket
18-19-20 .... at Buffalo
21-22 .... Rochester
24-25 .... Scranton
26-27 .... at Rochester
28-29-30 ..... at Syracuse

MAY

1-2-3-4 .... Toledo
5-6-7-8 .... Columbus
9-10-11-12 ..... at Norfolk
13-14-15-16 ...... at Rich.
17-18-19-20 .... Norfolk
22-23-24-25 .... Indy
26-27-28-29 .... at Toledo
30-31 ...... at Indianapolis

JUNE

1-2 .... at Indianapolis
3-4-5-6 .... Syracuse
7-8-9-10 .... Charlotte
12-13-14-15 ... at Durham
16-17-18-19 ...... at Char.
20-21-22-23 ... Richmond
25-26-27 .... at Rochester
28-29 .... Rochester
30 .... Buffalo

JULY

1 .... Buffalo
2-3 .... at Buffalo
4-5-6-7 ...... at Columbus
8-9-10-11 .... at Louisville
12-13 .... Scranton
17-18-19-20 .... Louisville
21-22-23-24 ...... Durham
25-26-27-28 .... at Scr.
29-30-31 .... at Pawtucket

AUGUST

1-2-3-4 .... Rochester
5-6 .... Scranton
8-9-10 .... at Rochester
11-12-13 ..... at Syracuse
14-15 .... Pawtucket
16-17-18-19 .... Syracuse
20-21-22 .... at Buffalo
23-24 .... Pawtucket
25-26 .... at Syracuse
27-28 .... at Pawtucket
29-30 .... Buffalo
31 .... Scranton

SEPTEMBER

1 .... Scranton

Pawtucket

APRIL

3-4-5-6 .... at Buffalo
7-8-9 .... Ottawa
10-11-12-13 ... Rochester
14-15-16-17 .... at Ottawa
18-19-20 .... at Rochester
22-23 .... Syracuse
24-25 .... Buffalo
26-27 .... at Syracuse
28-29 .... at Scranton

MAY

1-2-3-4 .... Norfolk
5-6-7-8 .... Richmond
9-10-11-12 .. at Louisville
13-14-15-16 .... at Indy
17-18-19-20 .... Louisville
22-23-24-25 ... Columbus
26-27-28-29 ... at Norfolk
30-31 .... at Richmond

JUNE

1-2 .... at Richmond
3-4-5-6 .... Scranton
7-8-9-10 .... Toledo
12-13-14-15 at Syracuse
16-17-18-19 ...... Durham
20-21-22-23 .... Indy
24-25-26-27 ... at Durham
28-29-30 ...... at Charlotte

JULY

1 .... at Charlotte
2-3 .... Scranton
4-5-6-7 .... at Scranton
8-9-10-11 .... Charlotte
12-13-14 .... at Rochester
17-18-19-20 .... at Col.
21-22-23-24 .... at Toledo
25-26-27 .... Buffalo
29-30-31 .... Ottawa

AUGUST

1-2-3-4 .... at Buffalo
5-6-7 .... Syracuse
8-9-10 .... Buffalo
12-13 .... at Rochester
14-15 .... at Ottawa
16-17-18-19 ... Rochester
20-21-22 .... Syracuse
23-24 .... at Ottawa
25-26 .... at Scranton
27-28 .... Ottawa
29-30 .... Scranton
31 .... at Syracuse

SEPTEMBER

1 .... at Syracuse

Richmond

APRIL

3-4-5-6 .... at Charlotte
7-8 .... at Durham
9-10 .... Toledo
11-12-13-14 ... Columbus
15-16 .... Norfolk
17-18 .... at Toledo
19-19-21-22 .... at Col.

23-24-25 .... Charlotte
26-27 .... Durham
28-29 .... at Norfolk

MAY

1-2-3-4 .... Indianapolis
5-6-7-8 ...... at Pawtucket
9-10-11-12 ... at Scranton
13-14-15-16 .... Ottawa
17-18-19-20 .... Syracuse
22-23-24-25 ... at Buffalo
26-27-28-29 .... at Syr.
30-31 .... Pawtucket

JUNE

1-2 .... Pawtucket
3-4-5-6 .... at Louisville
7-8-9-10 .... Louisville
12-13-14-15 .... Buffalo
16-17-18-19 ..... at Roch.
20-21-22-23 .... at Ottawa
25-25-26-27 .... Toledo
28-29-30 .... at Indy

JULY

1 .... at Indianapolis
2-3 .... at Louisville
4-5-6-7 .... Durham
8-9-10-11 ...... Rochester
12-13 .... at Charlotte
17-18-19-20 .... Scranton
21-22 .... Charlotte
23-24 .... Indianapolis
25-26-27-28 .... at Toledo
29-30 ...... at Indianapolis
31 .... at Columbus

AUGUST

1 .... at Columbus
2-3-4-5 .... Norfolk
6-7 .... Louisville
8-9-10 .... at Norfolk
12-13-14-15 ... at Durham
16-17 .... at Charlotte
18-19 .... Columbus
20-21-22 .... Charlotte
23-24 .... Durham
26 .... at Norfolk
27 .... Norfolk
28-29 .... at Durham
30-31 .... at Norfolk

SEPTEMBER

1 .... Norfolk

Rochester

APRIL

3-4 .... at Syracuse
5-6 .... Syracuse
7-8-9 .... at Scranton
10-11-12-13 .... at Paw.
14-15-16 .... Scranton
17 .... Buffalo
18-19-20 .... Pawtucket
21-22 .... at Ottawa
24 .... at Syracuse
25 .... Syracuse
26-27 .... Ottawa
29-30 .... Buffalo

MAY

1-2-3-4 .... at Charlotte
5-6-7-8 .... at Durham
9-10-11-12 .... Columbus
13-14-15-16 ...... Durham
17-18-19-20 .... at Col.
22-23-24-25 at Louisville
26-27-28-29 .... at Indy
30-31 .... Norfolk

JUNE

1-2 .... Norfolk
3-4-5-6 .... Charlotte
7-8-9-10 .... at Buffalo
12-13-14-15 .... Toledo
16-17-18-19 ... Richmond
20-21-22-23 .... at Toledo
25-26-27 .... Ottawa
28-29 .... at Ottawa
30 .... Scranton

JULY

1 .... Scranton
2-3 .... Syracuse
4-5-6-7 .... at Norfolk
8-9-10-11 .. at Richmond
12-13-14 .... Pawtucket
17-18-19-20 .... Indy
21-22-23-24 .... Louisville
25-26-27-28 .... at Syr.
29-30-31 ...... at Scranton

AUGUST

1-2-3-4 .... at Ottawa
5-6 .... Buffalo
7 .... at Buffalo
8-9-10 .... Ottawa
12-13 .... Pawtucket
14-15 .... at Scranton
16-17-18-19 .... at Paw.
20-21-22 .... Scranton
23-24 .... at Buffalo
25-26 .... Buffalo
27 .... at Syracuse
28-29-30 .... Syracuse
31 .... Buffalo

SEPTEMBER

1 .... at Buffalo

Scranton/W-B

APRIL

3-4-5-6 .... Ottawa
7-8-9 .... Rochester
10-11-12-13 .... at Syr.
14-15-16 .... at Rochester
18-19-20 .... Syracuse
21-22-23 .... Buffalo
24-25 .... at Ottawa
26-27 .... at Buffalo
28-29 .... Pawtucket

MAY

1-2-3-4 ...... at Columbus
5-6-7-8 .... at Louisville
9-10-11-12 .... Richmond
13-14-15-16 .... Louisville
17-18-18-20 ...... at Char.
22-23-24-25 ... at Durham
26-27-28-29 ... Columbus
30-31 .... Charlotte

JUNE

1-2 .... Charlotte
3-4-5-6 ...... at Pawtucket
7-8-9-10 .... Norfolk
12-13-14-15 .... at Indy
16-17-18-19 .... at Toledo
20-20-21-22 ...... Durham
24-25-26-27 .... Indy
28-29 .... at Buffalo
30 .... at Rochester

JULY

1 .... at Rochester
2-3 .... at Pawtucket
4-5-6-7 .... Pawtucket
8-9-10-11 .... Toledo
12-13 .... at Ottawa
17-18-19-20 ...... at Rich.
21-22-23-24 ... at Norfolk
25-26-27-28 .... Ottawa
29-30-31 .... Rochester

AUGUST

1-2-3-4 .... at Syracuse
5-6 .... at Ottawa
8-9-10 .... Syracuse
11-12-13 .... Buffalo
14-15 .... Rochester
16-17-18-19 ... at Buffalo
20-21-22 .... at Rochester
23-24 .... Syracuse
25-26 .... Pawtucket
27-28 .... Buffalo
29-30 .... at Pawtucket
31 .... at Ottawa

SEPTEMBER

1 .... at Ottawa

Syracuse

APRIL

3-4 .... Rochester
5-6 .... at Rochester
7-8-9 .... at Buffalo
10-11-12-13 .... Scranton
14-15-16 .... Buffalo
18-19-20 ...... at Scranton
22-23 .... at Pawtucket
24 .... Rochester
25 .... at Rochester
26-27 .... Pawtucket
28-29-30 .... Ottawa

MAY

1-2-3-4 .... at Durham
5-6-7-8 .... at Charlotte
9-10-11-12 .... Durham
13-14-15-16 .... Norfolk
17-18-19-20 ...... at Rich.
22-23-24-25 ... at Norfolk
26-27-28-29 ... Richmond
30-31 .... Louisville

JUNE

1-2 .... Louisville
3-4-5-6 .... at Ottawa
7-8-9-10 ..... Indianapolis
12-13-14-15 ... Pawtucket
16-17-18-19 .... at Indy
20-21-22-23 ...... at L'ville
24-25-26-27 .... Charlotte
28-29-30 .... Columbus

JULY

1 .... Columbus
2-3 .... at Rochester
4-5-6-7 .... at Toledo
8-9-10-11 ... at Columbus
12-13 .... Buffalo
17-18-19-20 .... Toledo
21-22 .... at Buffalo
23-24 .... Buffalo
25-26-27-28 ... Rochester
29-30-31 .... at Buffalo

AUGUST

1-2-3-4 .... Scranton
5-6-7 .... at Pawtucket
8-9-10 .... at Scranton
11-12-13 .... Ottawa
15 .... Buffalo
16-17-18-19 .... at Ottawa
20-21-22 .... at Pawtucket
23-24 .... at Scranton
25-26 .... Ottawa
27 .... Rochester
28-29-30 .... at Rochester
31 .... Pawtucket

SEPTEMBER

1 .... Pawtucket

Toledo

APRIL

3-4-5-6 .... Louisville
7-8 .... Indianapolis
9-10 .... at Richmond
11-12-13-14 ... at Norfolk
15-16 .... at Columbus
17-18 .... Richmond
19-20-21-22 .... Norfolk
24-25 ...... at Indianapolis
26-27 .... at Louisville
28-29 .... Columbus

MAY

1-2-3-4 .... at Ottawa
5-6-7-8 .... at Buffalo
9-10-11-12 ...... Charlotte
13-14-15-16 .... Buffalo
17-18-19-20 ... at Durham
21-22-23-24 ... at Charlotte
26-27-28-29 .... Ottawa
30-31 .... Durham

JUNE

1-2 .... Durham
3-4 .... Indianapolis
5-6 .... at Indianapolis
7-8-9-10 .... at Pawtucket
12-13-14-15 ..... at Roch.
16-17-18-19 .... Scranton
20-21-22-23 ... Rochester
25-25-26-27 ...... at Rich.
28-29 .... at Norfolk
30 .... at Durham

JULY

1 .... at Durham
2-3 .... at Charlotte
4-5-6-7 .... Syracuse
8-9-10-11 .... at Scranton
12-13 .... Columbus
17-18-19-20 .... at Syr.
21-22-23-24 ... Pawtucket
25-26-27-28 ... Richmond
29-30-31 ..... at Louisville

AUGUST

1 .... at Louisville
2-3 .... Columbus
4-5 .... Durham
6-7 .... Indianapolis
8-9-10 .... at Columbus
11-12 .... Charlotte
14-15 .... Norfolk
16-17 .... at Louisville
18-19 ...... at Indianapolis
20-21 .... Louisville
22-23 .... Columbus
24-25-26 .... at Columbus
27-28 ...... at Indianapolis
29-30 .... Louisville
31 .... Indianapolis

SEPTEMBER

1 .... Indianapolis

PACIFIC COAST LEAGUE

Albuquerque

APRIL

3-4-5-6 .... at Memphis
7-8-9-10 ...... at Nashville
11-12-13-14 ... Oklahoma
15-16-17-18 ... Colo. Spr.
19-20-21-22 .... at Okla.
24-25-26-27 .... at C.S.
28-29-30 .... Iowa

MAY

1 .... Iowa
2-3-4-5 .... Salt Lake
6-7-8-9 .... at Tucson
10-11-12-13 .... Iowa
15-16-17-18 .... Nashville
19-20-21-22 .... at N.O.
23-24-25-26 ..... at Mem.
27-28-29-30 ... Colo. Spr.
31 .... at Fresno

JUNE

1-2-3 .... at Fresno
5-6-7-8 .... at Sacramento
9-10-11-12 ..... Oklahoma
13-14-15-16 ..... Portland
17-18-19-20 .... at C.S.
21-22-23-24 ... Edmonton
26-27-28-29 .... at N.O.
30 .... Omaha

JULY

1-2-3 .... Omaha
4-5-6 .... at Iowa
7-8-9 .... at Omaha
10-11-12-13 .... Memphis
17-18-19-20 .... Tacoma
21-22-23-24 .... N.O.
25-26-27-28 .... at L.V.
29-30-31 ...... at Nashville

AUGUST

1 .... at Nashville
2-3-4-5 .... Memphis
7-8-9-10 .... New Orleans
11-12-13-14 .... at Okla.
15-16-17-18 .... Omaha
19-20-21-22-23 .. at Iowa
24-25-26-27-28 .. at Omaha
29-30-31 .... Nashville

SEPTEMBER

1 .... Nashville

Colo. Springs

APRIL

3-4-5-6 .... at Oklahoma
7-8-9-10 ... at New Orleans
11-12-13-14 .... Memphis
15-16-17-18 .... at Alb.
19-20-21-22 ..... at Mem.
24-25-26-27 .... Alb.
28-29-30 .... at Sacra.

MAY

1 .... at Sacramento
2-3-4-5 ...... New Orleans
6-7-8-9 .... Tacoma
10-11-12-13 .... at Fresno
15-16-17-18 ... at Tucson
19-20-21-22 .... Iowa
23-24-25-26 ... Edmonton
27-28-29-30 .... at Alb.
31 .... at Oklahoma

JUNE

1-2-3 .... at Oklahoma
5-6-7-8 .... Oklahoma
9-10-11-12 .... Portland
13-14-15-16 .... at N.O.
17-18-19-20 .... Alb.
21-22-23-24 ..... at Nash.
26-27-28-29 ... Oklahoma
30 .... Iowa

JULY

1-2-3 .... Iowa
4-5-6 .... at Omaha
7-8-9 .... at Iowa
10-11-12-13 ... at Salt Lake
17-18-19-20 .... at L.V.
21-22-23-24 ..... at Mem.
25-26-27-28 .... Nashville
29-30-31 .... New Orleans

AUGUST

1 .... New Orleans
2-3-4-5 .... at Nashville
7-8-9-10 .... Nashville
11-12-13-14 .... Omaha
15-16-17-18 .... Memphis
19-20-21-22-23 .. at Omaha
24-25-26-27-28 ... at Alb.
29-30-31 .... Omaha

SEPTEMBER

1 .... Omaha

Edmonton

APRIL

3-4-5-6 .... at Tucson
7-8-9-10 .... at Las Vegas
11-12-13-14 .... Sacra.
15-16-17-18 .... Fresno
19-20-21-22 ..... at Sacra.
24-25-26-27 .... at Fresno
28-29-30 .... Nashville

MAY

1 .... Nashville
2-3-4-5 .... Tucson
6-7-8-9 ...... at Las Vegas
10-11-12-13 ..... Portland
15-16-17-18 ...... Tacoma
19-20-21-22 .... at Fresno
23-24-25-26 .... at C.S.
27-28-29-30 .... N.O.
31 .... Memphis

JUNE

1-2-3 .... Memphis
5-6-7-8 .... at Omaha
9-10-11-12 .... at Iowa
13-14-15-16 .... Sacra.
17-18-19-20 ... Las Vegas
21-22-23-24 .... at Alb.
26-27-28-29 ...... Tacoma
30 .... Salt Lake

JULY

1-2-3 .... Salt Lake
4-5-6 .... at Portland
7-8-9 .... at Salt Lake
10-11-12-13 .... Fresno
17-18-19-20 ... at Tucson
21-22-23-24 ... Las Vegas
25-26-27-28 .... Tucson
29-30-31 .... at Tacoma

AUGUST

1 .... at Tacoma
2-3-4-5 .... Oklahoma
7-8-9-10 ... at Sacramento
11-12-13-14 ... at Tacoma
15-16-17-18 .... Salt Lake
19-20-21-22-23 ... at Port.
24-25-26-27-28 ..... at S.L.
29-30-31 .... Portland

SEPTEMBER

1 .... Portland

Fresno

APRIL

3-4-5-6 .... Tacoma
7-8-9-10 .... Portland
11-12-13-14 .... at S.L.
15-16-17-18 ...... at Edm.
19-20-21-22 .... Salt Lake
24-25-26-27 ... Edmonton
28-29-30 .... at Tacoma

MAY

1 .... at Tacoma
2-3-4-5 .... at Portland
6-7-8-9 .... at Salt Lake
10-11-12-13 ... Colo. Spr.
15-16-17-18 .... at N.O.
19-20-21-22 ... Edmonton
23-24-25-26 ..... at Sacra.
27-28-29-30 ...... Tacoma
31 .... Albuquerque

JUNE

1-2-3 .... Albuquerque
5-6-7-8 .... at Nashville
9-10-11-12 ... at Memphis
13-14-15-16 .... Salt Lake
17-18-19-20 .... Omaha
21-22-23-24 ... at Tucson
26-27-28-29 .... Sacra.
30 .... at Las Vegas

JULY

1-2-3 .... at Las Vegas
4-5-6 .... Tucson
7-8-9 .... Las Vegas
10-11-12-13 ...... at Edm.
17-18-19-20 ..... at Sacra.
21-22-23-24 .... Iowa
25-26-27-28 ..... Portland
29-30-31 .... at Las Vegas

AUGUST

1 .... at Las Vegas
2-3-4-5 .... at Portland
7-8-9-10 .... at Tacoma
11-12-13-14 .... Sacra.
15-16-17-18 .... at Okla.
19-20-21-22-23 ... Tucson
24-25-26-27-28 .... L.V.
29-30-31 .... at Tucson

SEPTEMBER

1 .... at Tucson

Iowa

APRIL

3-4-5-6 .... at Nashville
7-8-9-10 ...... at Memphis
11-12-13-14 .... Nashville
15-16-17-18 ... at Omaha
19-20-21-22 .... N.O.
24-25-26-27 ..... Portland
28-29-30 .... at Alb.

MAY

1 .... at Albuquerque
2-3-4-5 .... Tacoma
6-7-8-9 .... Memphis
10-11-12-13 .... at Alb.
15-16-17-18 .... Omaha
19-20-21-22 .... at C.S.
23-24-25-26 ... Oklahoma
27-28-29-30 .... Nashville
31 .... at New Orleans

JUNE

1-2-3 ...... at New Orleans
5-6-7-8 ...... New Orleans
9-10-11-12 .... Edmonton
13-14-15-16 ..... at Mem.
17-18-19-20 ..... at Nash.
21-22-23-24 ... Oklahoma
26-27-28-29 ... at Omaha
30 .... at Colo. Springs

JULY

1-2-3 .... at Colo. Springs
4-5-6 .... Albuquerque
7-8-9 .... Colo. Springs
10-11-12-13 .... at L.V.
17-18-19-20 .... Memphis
21-22-23-24 .... at Fresno
25-26-27-28 ..... at Sacra.
29-30-31 .... Omaha

AUGUST

1 .... Omaha
2-3-4-5 .... at Tucson
7-8-9-10 ..... at Oklahoma
11-12-13-14 .... Salt Lake
15-16-17-18 .... at N.O.
19-20-21-22-23 .... Alb.
24-25-26-27-28 .... C.S.
29-30-31 .... at Oklahoma

SEPTEMBER

1 .... at Oklahoma

Las Vegas

APRIL

3-4-5-6 .... Salt Lake
7-8-9-10 .... Edmonton
11-12-13-14 ... at Tacoma
15-16-17-18 ... at Portland
19-20-21-22 ...... Tacoma
24-25-26-27 .... Sacra.
28-29-30 .... at Oklahoma

MAY

1 .... at Oklahoma
2-3-4-5 .... at Nashville
6-7-8-9 .... Edmonton
10-11-12-13 .... Tucson
15-16-17-18 .... at S.L.
19-20-21-22 ... at Tucson
23-24-25-26 ..... Portland
27-28-29-30 .... Salt Lake
31 .... at Portland

JUNE

1-2-3 .... at Portland
5-6-7-8 .... at Tacoma
9-10-11-12 .... Omaha
13-14-15-16 ...... Tacoma
17-18-19-20 ...... at Edm.
21-22-23-24 .... at S.L.

26-27-28-29 .... Tucson
30 .... Fresno

JULY

1-2-3 .... Fresno
4-5-6 .... at Sacramento
7-8-9 .... at Fresno
10-11-12-13 .... Iowa
17-18-19-20 .... Colo. Spr.
21-22-23-24 ...... at Edm.
25-26-27-28 .... Alb.
29-30-31 .... Fresno

AUGUST

1 .... Fresno
2-3-4-5 ... at New Orleans
7-8-9-10 .... at Tucson
11-12-13-14 ..... at Mem.
15-16-17-18 ..... Portland
19-20-21-22-23 .. at Sacra.
24-25-26-27-28 .... at Fres.
29-30-31 ..... Sacramento

SEPTEMBER

1 .... Sacramento

Memphis

APRIL

3-4-5-6 ...... Albuquerque
7-8-9-10 .... Iowa
11-12-13-14 .... at C.S.
15-16-17-18 ... at Nashville
19-20-21-22 ... Colo. Spr.
24-25-26-27 .... Omaha
28-29-30 at New Orleans

MAY

1 .... at New Orleans
2-3-4-5 .... Sacramento
6-7-8-9 .... at Iowa
10-11-12-13 .... Nashville
15-16-17-18 .... at Okla.
19-20-21-22 ..... at Nash.
23-24-25-26 .... Alb.
27-28-29-30 .... Omaha
31 .... at Edmonton

JUNE

1-2-3 .... at Edmonton
5-6-7-8 .... at Salt Lake
9-10-11-12 .... Fresno
13-14-15-16 .... Iowa
17-18-19-20 ... at Tacoma
21-22-23-24 ... at Portland
26-27-28-29 .... Nashville
30 .... at Oklahoma

JULY

1-2-3 .... at Oklahoma
4-5-6 .... New Orleans
7-8-9 .... Oklahoma
10-11-12-13 .... at Alb.
17-18-19-20 .... at Iowa
21-22-23-24 ... Colo. Spr.
25-26-27-28 ... at Omaha
29-30-31 .... Tucson

AUGUST

1 .... Tucson
2-3-4-5 ... at Albuquerque
7-8-9-10 .... at Omaha
11-12-13-14 ... Las Vegas
15-16-17-18 .... at C.S.
19-20-21-22-23 .... N.O.
24-25-26-27-28 ...... Okla.
29-30-31 .... at N.O.

SEPTEMBER

1 .... at N.O.

Nashville

APRIL

3-4-5-6 .... Iowa
7-8-9-10 .... Albuquerque
11-12-13-14 .... at Iowa
15-16-17-18 .... Memphis
19-20-21-22 .... Omaha
24-25-26-27 .... at S.L.
28-29-30 .... at Edmonton

MAY

1 .... at Edmonton
2-3-4-5 .... Las Vegas
6-7-8-9 .... Sacramento
10-11-12-13 ..... at Mem.
15-16-17-18 .... at Alb.
19-20-21-22 .... Memphis
23-24-25-26 .... Omaha
27-28-29-30 .... at Iowa
31 .... at Omaha

JUNE

1-2-3 .... at Omaha
5-6-7-8 .... Fresno
9-10-11-12 .... at N.O.
13-14-15-16 .... at Okla.
17-18-19-20 .... Iowa
21-22-23-24 ... Colo. Spr.
26-27-28-29 ..... at Mem.
30 .... at New Orleans

JULY

1-2-3 ...... at New Orleans
4-5-6 .... Oklahoma
7-8-9 .... New Orleans
10-11-12-13 .... Tucson
17-18-19-20 .... at Omaha
21-22-23-24 .... at Okla.
25-26-27-28 .... at C.S.
29-30-31 .... Albuquerque

AUGUST

1 .... Albuquerque
2-3-4-5 ..... Colo. Springs
7-8-9-10 .... at C.S.
11-12-13-14 ... at Portland
15-16-17-18 ... at Tacoma
19-20-21-22-23 ..... Okla.
24-25-26-27-28 ...... N.O.
29-30-31 .... at Alb.

SEPTEMBER

1 .... at Albuquerque

New Orleans

APRIL

3-4-5-6 .... Omaha
7-8-9-10 ... Colo. Springs
11-12-13-14 ... at Omaha
15-16-17-18 .... at Okla.
19-20-21-22 .... at Iowa
24-25-26-27 ... Oklahoma
28-29-30 .... Memphis

MAY

1 .... Memphis
2-3-4-5 ...... at Colo. Spr.
6-7-8-9 .... Omaha
10-11-12-13 ... at Omaha
15-16-17-18 .... Fresno
19-20-21-22 .... Alb.
23-24-25-26 .... at S.L.
27-28-29-30 ...... at Edm.
31 .... Iowa

JUNE

1-2-3 .... Iowa
5-6-7-8 .... at Iowa
9-10-11-12 ...... Nashville
13-14-15-16 ... Colo. Spr.
17-18-19-20 ... at Portland
21-22-23-24 ... at Tacoma
26-27-28-29 .... Alb.
30 .... Nashville

JULY

1-2-3 .... Nashville
4-5-6 .... at Memphis
7-8-9 .... at Nashville
10-11-12-13 .... Sacra.
17-18-19-20.... Oklahoma
21-22-23-24 .... at Alb.
25-26-27-28 .... at Okla.
29-30-31 .... at Colo. Spr.

AUGUST

1 .... at Colo. Springs
2-3-4-5 .... Las Vegas
7-8-9-10 .... at Alb.
11-12-13-14 .... Tucson
15-16-17-18 .... Iowa
19-20-21-22-23 ... at Mem.
24-25-26-27-28 ... at Nash.
29-30-31 .... Memphis

SEPTEMBER

1 .... Memphis

Oklahoma

APRIL

3-4-5-6 ..... Colo. Springs
7-8-9-10 .... Omaha
11-12-13-14 .... at Alb.
15-16-17-18 .... N.O.
19-20-21-22 .... Alb.
24-25-26-27 .... at N.O.
28-29-30 .... Las Vegas

MAY

1 .... Las Vegas
2-3-4-5 .... at Omaha
6-7-8-9 .... at Portland
10-11-12-13 ... at Tacoma
15-16-17-18 .... Memphis
19-20-21-22 ... at Omaha
23-24-25-26 .... at Iowa
27-28-29-30 .... Sacra.
31 .... Colorado Springs

JUNE

1-2-3 .... Colorado Springs
5-6-7-8 ... at Colo. Springs
9-10-11-12 .... at Alb.
13-14-15-16 .... Nashville
17-18-19-20 .... Tucson
21-22-23-24 .... at Iowa
26-27-28-29 .... at C.S.
30 .... Memphis

JULY

1-2-3 .... Memphis
4-5-6 .... at Nashville
7-8-9 .... at Memphis
10-11-12-13 .... Omaha
17-18-19-20......... at N.O.
21-22-23-24 .... Nashville
25-26-27-28 .... N.O.
29-30-31 ..... at Salt Lake

AUGUST

1 .... at Salt Lake
2-3-4-5 ...... at Edmonton
7-8-9-10 .... Iowa
11-12-13-14 .... Alb.
15-16-17-18 .... Fresno
19-20-21-22-23 ... at Nash.
24-25-26-27-28 ... at Mem.
29-30-31 .... Iowa

SEPTEMBER

1 .... Iowa

Omaha

APRIL

3-4-5-6 .... at New Orleans
7-8-9-10 ..... at Oklahoma
11-12-13-14 .... N.O.
15-16-17-18 .... Iowa
19-20-21-22 ..... at Nash.
24-25-26-27 ..... at Mem.
28-29-30 .... Portland

MAY

1 .... Portland
2-3-4-5 .... Oklahoma
6-7-8-9 .... at New Orleans
10-11-12-13 .... N.O.
15-16-17-18 .... at Iowa
19-20-21-22 ... Oklahoma
23-24-25-26 ..... at Nash.
27-28-29-30 ..... at Mem.
31 .... Nashville

JUNE

1-2-3 .... Nashville
5-6-7-8 .... Edmonton
9-10-11-12 .... at L.V.
13-14-15-16 ... at Tucson
17-18-19-20 .... at Fresno
21-22-23-24 ..... at Sacra.
26-27-28-29 .... Iowa
30 .... at Albuquerque

JULY

1-2-3 ...... at Albuquerque
4-5-6 .... Colo. Springs
7-8-9 .... Albuquerque
10-11-12-13 .... at Okla.
17-18-19-20 ..... Nashville
21-22-23-24 ...... Tacoma
25-26-27-28 .... Memphis
29-30-31 .... at Iowa

AUGUST

1 .... at Iowa
2-3-4-5 .... Salt Lake
7-8-9-10 .... Memphis
11-12-13-14 .... at C.S.
15-16-17-18 .... at Alb.
19-20-21-22-23 .... C.S.
24-25-26-27-28 .... Alb.
29-30-31 .... at Colo. Spr.

SEPTEMBER

1 .... Colorado Springs

Portland

APRIL

3-4-5-6 .... at Sacramento
7-8-9-10 .... at Fresno
11-12-13-14 .... Tucson
15-16-17-18 ... Las Vegas
19-20-21-22 ... at Tucson
24-25-26-27 .... at Iowa
28-29-30 .... at Omaha

MAY

1 .... at Omaha
2-3-4-5 .... Fresno
6-7-8-9 .... Oklahoma
10-11-12-13 ...... at Edm.
15-16-17-18 Sacramento

19-20-21-22 .... Salt Lake
23-24-25-26 .... at L.V.
27-28-29-30 ... at Tucson
31 .... Las Vegas

JUNE

1-2-3 .... Las Vegas
5-6-7-8 .... Tucson
9-10-11-12 ... at Colo. Spr.
13-14-15-16 .... at Alb.
17-18-19-20 .... N.O.
21-22-23-24 .... Memphis
26-27-28-29 .... at S.L.
30 .... at Tacoma

JULY

1-2-3 .... at Tacoma
4-5-6 .... Edmonton
7-8-9 .... Tacoma
10-11-12-13 ... at Tacoma
17-18-19-20..... Salt Lake
21-22-23-24 ..... at Sacra.
25-26-27-28 .... at Fresno
29-30-31 ..... Sacramento

AUGUST

1 .... Sacramento
2-3-4-5 .... Fresno
7-8-9-10 ...... at Salt Lake
11-12-13-14 .... Nashville
15-16-17-18 .... at L.V.
19-20-21-22-23 ..... Edm.
24-25-26-27-28 ... Tacoma
29-30-31 .... at Edmonton

SEPTEMBER

1 .... at Edmonton

Sacramento

APRIL

3-4-5-6 .... Portland
7-8-9-10 .... Tacoma
11-12-13-14 ...... at Edm.
15-16-17-18 ... at Salt Lake
19-20-21-22 ... Edmonton
24-25-26-27 .... at L.V.
28-29-30 ... Colo. Springs

MAY

1 .... Colorado Springs
2-3-4-5 .... at Memphis
6-7-8-9 .... at Nashville
10-11-12-13 .... Salt Lake
15-16-17-18 ... at Portland
19-20-21-22 ... at Tacoma
23-24-25-26 .... Fresno
27-28-29-30 .... at Okla.
31 .... at Tacoma

JUNE

1-2-3 .... at Tacoma
5-6-7-8 ...... Albuquerque
9-10-11-12 ... at Salt Lake
13-14-15-16 ...... at Edm.
17-18-19-20 .... Salt Lake
21-22-23-24 .... Omaha
26-27-28-29 .... at Fresno
30 .... at Tucson

JULY

1-2-3 .... at Tucson
4-5-6 .... Las Vegas
7-8-9 .... Tucson
10-11-12-13 .... at N.O.
17-18-19-20......... Fresno
21-22-23-24 ..... Portland
25-26-27-28 .... Iowa
29-30-31 ...... at Portland

AUGUST

1 .... at Portland
2-3-4-5 .... Tacoma
7-8-9-10 .... Edmonton
11-12-13-14 .... at Fresno
15-16-17-18 ... at Tucson
19-20-21-22-23 .... L.V.
24-25-26-27-28 ... Tucson
29-30-31 .... at Las Vegas

SEPTEMBER

1 .... at Las Vegas

Salt Lake

APRIL

3-4-5-6 ...... at Las Vegas
7-8-9-10 .... at Tucson
11-12-13-14 .... Fresno
15-16-17-18 .... Sacra.
19-20-21-22 .... at Fresno
24-25-26-27 .... Nashville
28-29-30 .... Tucson

MAY

1 .... Tucson
2-3-4-5 ... at Albuquerque
6-7-8-9 .... Fresno
10-11-12-13 ..... at Sacra.
15-16-17-18 ... Las Vegas
19-20-21-22 ... at Portland
23-24-25-26 .... N.O.
27-28-29-30 .... at L.V.
31 .... at Tucson

JUNE

1-2-3 .... at Tucson
5-6-7-8 .... Memphis
9-10-11-12 ... Sacramento
13-14-15-16 .... at Fresno
17-18-19-20 ..... at Sacra.
21-22-23-24 ... Las Vegas
26-27-28-29 ..... Portland
30 .... at Edmonton

JULY

1-2-3 .... at Edmonton
4-5-6 .... Tacoma
7-8-9 .... Edmonton
10-11-12-13 .... at C.S.
17-18-19-20... at Portland
21-22-23-24 .... Tucson
25-26-27-28 ... at Tacoma
29-30-31 .... Oklahoma

AUGUST

1 .... Oklahoma
2-3-4-5 .... at Omaha
7-8-9-10 .... Portland
11-12-13-14 .... at Iowa
15-16-17-18 ...... at Edm.
19-20-21-22-23 ... Tacoma
24-25-26-27-28 ..... Edm.
29-30-31 .... at Tacoma

SEPTEMBER

1 .... at Tacoma

Tacoma

APRIL

3-4-5-6 .... at Fresno
7-8-9-10 ... at Sacramento
11-12-13-14 ... Las Vegas
15-16-17-18 .... Tucson
19-20-21-22 .... at L.V.
24-25-26-27 ... at Tucson
28-29-30 .... Fresno

MAY

1 .... Fresno
2-3-4-5 .... at Iowa
6-7-8-9 .... at Colo. Spr.
10-11-12-13 ... Oklahoma
15-16-17-18 ...... at Edm.
19-20-21-22 .... Sacra.
23-24-25-26 .... Tucson
27-28-29-30 .... at Fresno
31 .... Sacramento

JUNE

1-2-3 .... Sacramento
5-6-7-8 .... Las Vegas
9-10-11-12 ..... at Tucson
13-14-15-16 .... at L.V.
17-18-19-20 .... Memphis
21-22-23-24 .... N.O.
26-27-28-29 ...... at Edm.
30 .... Portland

JULY

1-2-3 .... Portland
4-5-6 .... at Salt Lake
7-8-9 .... at Portland
10-11-12-13 ..... Portland
17-18-19-20 .... at Alb.
21-22-23-24 ... at Omaha
25-26-27-28 .... Salt Lake
29-30-31 .... Edmonton

AUGUST

1 .... Edmonton
2-3-4-5 .... at Sacramento
7-8-9-10 .... Fresno
11-12-13-14 ... Edmonton
15-16-17-18 .... Nashville
19-20-21-22-23 ... at S.L.
24-25-26-27-28 ... at Port.
29-30-31 .... Salt Lake

SEPTEMBER

1 .... Salt Lake

Tucson

APRIL

3-4-5-6 .... Edmonton
7-8-9-10 .... Salt Lake
11-12-13-14 ... at Portland
15-16-17-18 ... at Tacoma
19-20-21-22 ..... Portland
24-25-26-27 ...... Tacoma
28-29-30 ..... at Salt Lake

MAY

1 .... at Salt Lake
2-3-4-5 ...... at Edmonton
6-7-8-9 ...... Albuquerque
10-11-12-13 .... at L.V.
15-16-17-18 ... Colo. Spr.
19-20-21-22 ... Las Vegas
23-24-25-26 ... at Tacoma
27-28-29-30 ..... Portland
31 .... Salt Lake

JUNE

1-2-3 .... Salt Lake
5-6-7-8 .... at Portland
9-10-11-12 .... Tacoma
13-14-15-16 .... Omaha
17-18-19-20 .... at Okla.
21-22-23-24 .... Fresno
26-27-28-29 .... at L.V.
30 .... Sacramento

JULY

1-2-3 .... Sacramento
4-5-6 .... at Fresno
7-8-9 .... at Sacramento
10-11-12-13 ..... at Nash.
17-18-19-20 ... Edmonton
21-22-23-24 .... at S.L.
25-26-27-28 ...... at Edm.
29-30-31 ..... at Memphis

AUGUST

1 .... at Memphis
2-3-4-5 .... Iowa
7-8-9-10 .... Las Vegas
11-12-13-14 .... at N.O.
15-16-17-18 .... Sacra.
19-20-21-22-23 ... at Fres.
24-25-26-27-28 ... at Sacra.
29-30-31 .... Fresno

SEPTEMBER

1 .... Fresno

CLASS AA
EASTERN LEAGUE

Akron

APRIL
3-4-5-6 ... at Erie
7-8-9 ... Harrisburg
10-11-12-13 ... Erie
14-15-16-17 ... at Reading
18-19-20 ... at Harrisburg
21-22-23 ... Bowie
25-26-27 ... at Altoona
28-29-30 ... at New Britain

MAY
1 ... at New Britain
2-3-4 ... at Norwich
6-7-8 ... Altoona
9-10-11 ... Norwich
12-13-14 ... at Bowie
15-16-17-18 ... at N.H.
19-20-21-22 ... Binghamton
23-24-25-26 ... Reading
27-28-29 ... at Altoona
30-31 ... at Bowie

JUNE
1 ... at Bowie
3-4-5 ... Trenton
6-7-8 ... Reading
9-10-11 ... at Erie
13-14-15 ... Portland
16-17-18 ... at Reading
19-20-21-22 ... at Bing.
23-24-25 ... at Portland
27-28-29 ... Erie
30 ... at Bowie

JULY
1-2-3 ... at Bowie
4-5-6 ... Harrisburg
7-8-9-10 ... Bowie
11-12-13-14 ... at Altoona
17-18-19-20 ... New Haven
21-22-23-24 ... Harrisburg
25-26-27 ... at Erie
28-29-30 ... Bowie
31 ... Altoona

AUGUST
1-2-3 ... Altoona
5-6-7 ... at Erie
8-9-10 ... at Reading
11-12-13-14 ... at H'burg
15-16-17 ... Altoona
18-19-20 ... Reading
22-23-24 ... at Harrisburg
26-27-28 ... at Trenton
29-30-31 ... New Britain

SEPTEMBER
1 ... New Britain

Altoona

APRIL
3-4-5-6 ... at Reading
7-8-9 ... at Erie
10-11-12-13 ... Reading
15-16-17 ... at Harrisburg
18-19-20 ... Bowie
21-22-23 ... at Erie
25-26-27 ... Akron
29-30 ... at Bowie

MAY
1 ... at Bowie
2-3-4 ... at Reading
6-7-8 ... at Akron
9-10-11 ... Erie
12-13-14 ... Reading
15-16-17-18 ... at Bing.
19-20-21-22 ... at N.H.
23-24-25-26 ... Binghamton
27-28-29 ... Akron
30-31 ... at Trenton

JUNE
1 ... at Trenton
2-3-4 ... Portland
6-7-8 ... Harrisburg
9-10-11 ... at New Britain
12-13-14-15 ... at H'burg
16-17-18 ... Trenton
19-20-21-22 ... Harrisburg
24-25-26 ... at Reading
27-28-29 ... at Portland
30 ... at Norwich

JULY
1-2-3 ... at Norwich
4-5-6 ... Erie
7-8-9-10 ... Norwich
11-12-13-14 ... Akron
18-19-20 ... at Erie
21-22-23-24 ... New Haven
25-26-27 ... at Bowie
28-29-30 ... New Britain
31 ... at Akron

AUGUST
1-2-3 ... at Akron
5-6-7 ... at Harrisburg
8-9-10 ... Harrisburg
11-12-13-14 ... Bowie
15-16-17 ... at Akron
18-19-20 ... Bowie
21-22-23-24 ... at Bowie
25-26-27 ... Reading
29-30-31 ... Erie

SEPTEMBER
1 ... Erie

Binghamton

APRIL
3-4-5-6 ... at Norwich
7-8-9 ... at New Haven
10-11-12-13 ... Norwich
14-15-16 ... at Portland
18-19-20 ... Trenton
22-23-24 ... Portland
25-26-27 ... at Norwich
28-29-30 ... New Haven

MAY
1 ... New Haven
2-3-4 ... Bowie
6-7-8 ... at Trenton
9-10-11 ... at Harrisburg
12-13-14 ... New Britain
15-16-17-18 ... Altoona
19-20-21-22 ... at Akron
23-24-25-26 ... at Altoona
27-28-29 ... New Haven
30-31 ... Portland

JUNE
1 ... Portland
3-4-5 ... at Norwich
6-7-8 ... at Portland
9-10-11 ... Harrisburg
13-14-15 ... at Reading
16-17-18 ... at New Haven
19-20-21-22 ... Akron
23-24-25 ... New Britain
27-28-29 ... at Trenton
30 ... at New Britain

JULY
1-2-3 ... at New Britain
4-5-6 ... Norwich
7-8-9-10 ... Erie
11-12-13-14 ... at N.H.
17-18-19-20 ... New Britain
21-22-23-24 ... at Erie
25-26-27 ... at New Britain
28-29-30 ... Norwich
31 ... Portland

AUGUST
1-2-3 ... Portland
4-5-6 ... at Bowie
7-8-9-10 ... at Portland
11-12-13 ... Trenton
15-16-17 ... Reading
18-19-20 ... New Haven
21-22-23-24 ... at Trenton
25-26-27 ... at New Britain
29-30-31 ... Trenton

SEPTEMBER
1 ... Trenton

Bowie

APRIL
3-4-5-6 ... at Harrisburg
7-8-9 ... at Reading
10-11-12-13 ... Harrisburg
15-16-17 ... Erie
18-19-20 ... at Altoona
21-22-23 ... at Akron
25-26-27 ... Erie
29-30 ... Altoona

MAY
1 ... Altoona
2-3-4 ... at Binghammton
5-6-7 ... at Erie
9-10-11 ... Reading
12-13-14 ... Akron
15-16-17-18 ... at Trenton
19-20-21-22 ... at Portland
23-24-25-26 ... at N.B.
27-28-29 ... Norwich
30-31 ... Akron

JUNE
1 ... Akron
3-4-5 ... at New Haven
6-7-8 ... at Norwich
9-10-11 ... Reading
12-13-14-15 ... Erie
16-17-18 ... Harrisburg
19-20-21-22 ... at Erie
24-25-26 ... New Haven
27-28-29 ... at Harrisburg
30 ... Akron

JULY
1-2-3 ... Akron
4-5-6 ... at Reading
7-8-9-10 ... at Akron
11-12-13-14 ... Trenton
17-18-19-20 ... at Reading
21-22-23-24 ... Portland
25-26-27 ... Altoona
28-29-30 ... at Akron
31 ... New Britain

AUGUST
1-2-3 ... New Britain
4-5-6 ... Binghamton
8-9-10 ... at Erie
11-12-13-14 ... at Altoona
15-16-17 ... Harrisburg
18-19-20 ... at Altoona
21-22-23-24 ... Altoona
25-26-27 ... at Harrisburg
29-30-31 ... Reading

SEPTEMBER
1 ... Reading

Erie

APRIL
3-4-5-6 ... at Harrisburg
7-8-9 ... at Reading
10-11-12-13 ... Harrisburg
15-16-17 ... Erie
18-19-20 ... at Altoona
21-22-23 ... at Akron
25-26-27 ... Erie
29-30 ... Altoona

MAY
1 ... Altoona
2-3-4 ... at Binghamton
5-6-7 ... at Erie
9-10-11 ... Reading
12-13-14 ... Akron
15-16-17-18 ... at Trenton
19-20-21-22 ... at Portland
23-24-25-26 ... at N.B.
27-28-29 ... Norwich
30-31 ... Akron

JUNE
1 ... Akron
3-4-5 ... at New Haven
6-7-8 ... at Norwich
9-10-11 ... Reading
12-13-14-15 ... Erie
16-17-18 ... Harrisburg
19-20-21-22 ... at Erie
24-25-26 ... New Haven
27-28-29 ... at Harrisburg

30 .... Akron

JULY

1-2-3 .... Akron
4-5-6 .... at Reading
7-8-9-10 .... at Akron
11-12-13-14 .... Trenton
17-18-19-20 ... at Reading
21-22-23-24 .... Portland
25-26-27 .... Altoona
28-29-30 .... at Akron
31 .... New Britain

AUGUST

1-2-3 ....New Britain
4-5-6 .... Binghamton
8-9-10 .... at Erie
11-12-13-14 .... at Altoona
15-16-17 .... Harrisburg
18-19-20 .... at Altoona
21-22-23-24 .... Altoona
25-26-27 .... at Harrisburg
29-30-31 .... Reading

SEPTEMBER

1 .... Reading

Harrisburg

APRIL

3-4-5-6 .... Bowie
7-8-9 .... at Akron
10-11-12-13 ...... at Bowie
15-16-17 .... Altoona
18-19-20 .... Akron
22-23-24 .... at Reading
25-26-27 .... Reading
28-29-30 .... Erie

MAY

1 .... Erie
2-3-4 .... at Erie
6-7-8 .... at Reading
9-10-11 .... Binghamton
12-13-14 .... New Haven
15-16-17-18 .... at Erie
19-20-21-22 .... Trenton
23-24-25-26 ... at Portland
27-28-29 ... at New Britain
30-31 .... Erie

JUNE

1 .... Erie
3-4-5 .... New Britain
6-7-8 .... at Altoona
9-10-11 .... at Binghamton
12-13-14-15 .... Altoona
16-17-18 .... at Bowie
19-20-21-22 .... at Altoona
24-25-26 .... Erie
27-28-29 .... Bowie
30 .... Portland

JULY

1-2-3 .... Portland
4-5-6 .... at Akron
7-8-9-10 .... at Reading
11-12-13-14 .... Reading
17-18-19-20 .... at Trenton
21-22-23-24 .... at Akron
25-26-27 .... Reading
28-29-30 ... at New Haven
31 .... Norwich

AUGUST

1-2-3 .... Norwich
5-6-7 .... Altoona
8-9-10 .... at Altoona
11-12-13-14 .... Akron
15-16-17 .... at Bowie
18-19-20 .... at Erie
22-23-24 .... Akron
25-26-27 .... Bowie
29-30-31 .... at Norwich

SEPTEMBER

1 .... at Norwich

New Britain

APRIL

4-5 .... New Haven
6 .... at New Haven
7-8-9 .... Portland
10-11-12 .... at New Haven
13 .... New Haven
14-15-16-17 .... at Trenton
18-19-20 .... at Portland
22-23-24 .... Norwich
25-26-27 .... at Trenton
28-29-30 .... Akron

MAY

1 .... Akron
2-3-4 .... Trenton
6-7-8 .... at New Haven
9-10-11 .... at Portland
12-13-14 ... at Binghamton
15-16-17-18 .... Portland
19-20-21-22 ... at Norwich
23-24-25-26 .... Bowie
27-28-29 .... Harrisburg
30-31 .... Norwich

JUNE

1 .... Norwich
3-4-5 .... at Harrisburg
6-7-8 .... at New Haven
9-10-11 .... Altoona
13-14-15 .... New Haven
16-17-18 .... at Norwich
19-20-21-22 .... Trenton
23-24-25 ... at Binghamton
27-28-29 .... at Norwich
30 .... Binghamton

JULY

1-2-3 .... Binghamton
4-5-6 .... at Trenton
7-8-9-10 .... at Portland
11-12-13-14 .... Erie
17-18-19-20 .... at Bing.
21-22-23-24 .... Norwich
25-26-27 ...... Binghamton
28-29-30 .... at Altoona
31 .... at Bowie

AUGUST

1-2-3 .... at Bowie
5-6-7 .... Reading
8-9-10 .... New Haven
11-12-13-14 .... at Erie
15-16-17 .... Portland
18-19-20 .... Trenton
21 .... New Haven
22-23-24 .... at Reading
25-26-27 ...... Binghamton
29-30-31 .... at Akron

SEPTEMBER

1 .... at Akron

New Haven

APRIL

4-5 .... at New Britain
6 .... New Britain
7-8-9 .... Binghamton
10-11-12 .... New Britain
13 .... at New Britain
14-15-16-17 ... at Norwich
18-19-20 .... Norwich
21-22-23 .... Trenton
25-26-27 .... at Portland
28-29-30 ... at Binghamton

MAY

1 .... at Binghamton
2-3-4 .... Portland
6-7-8 .... New Britain
9-10-11 .... at Trenton
12-13-14 ..... at Harrisburg
15-16-17-18 .... Akron
19-20-21-22 .... Altoona
23-24-25-26 .... at Erie
27-28-29 ... at Binghamton
30-31 .... at Reading

JUNE

1 .... at Reading
3-4-5 .... Bowie
6-7-8 .... New Britain
10-11-12 .... at Trenton
13-14-15 ... at New Britain
16-17-18 ...... Binghamton
19-20-21-22 .... Portland
24-25-26 .... at Bowie
27-28-29 .... Reading
30 .... Trenton

JULY

1-2-3 .... Trenton
4-5-6 .... at Portland
7-8-9-10 .... at Trenton
11-12-13-14 .... Bing.
17-18-19-20 .... at Akron
21-22-23-24 .... at Altoona
25-26-27 .... Trenton
28-29-30 .... Harrisburg
31 .... Erie

AUGUST

1-2-3 .... Erie
4-6-7 .... at Norwich
8-9-10 .... at New Britain
11-12-13-14 .... Norwich
15-16-17 .... at Norwich
18-19-20 ... at Binghamton
21 .... at New Britain
22-23-24 .... Norwich
26-27-28 .... Portland
29-30-31 .... at Portland

SEPTEMBER

1 .... at Portland

Norwich

APRIL

3-4-5-6 .... Binghamton
7-8-9 .... Trenton
10-11-12-13 .... at Bing.
14-15-16-17 ... New Haven
18-19-20 .... at New Haven
21-22-23 ... at New Britain
25-26-27 ...... Binghamton
28-29-30 .... at Trenton

MAY

1 .... at Trenton
2-3-4 .... Akron
5-6-7 .... Portland
9-10-11 .... at Akron
12-13-14 .... at Erie
15-16-17-18 ... at Reading
19-20-21-22 ... New Britain
23-24-25-26 .... Trenton
27-28-29 .... at Bowie
30-31 .... at New Britain

JUNE

1 .... at New Britain
3-4-5 .... Binghamton
6-7-8 .... Bowie
9-10-11 .... at Portland
13-14-15 .... at Trenton
16-17-18 .... New Britain
19-20-21-22 .... Reading
24-25-26 .... at Trenton
27-28-29 .... New Britain
30 .... Altoona

JULY

1-2-3 .... Altoona
4-5-6 .... at Binghamton
7-8-9-10 .... at Altoona
11-12-13-14 .... Portland
17-18-19-20 ... at Portland
21-22-23-24 .... at N.B.
25-26-27 .... Portland
28-29-30 ... at Binghamton
31 .... at Harrisburg

AUGUST

1-2-3 .... at Harrisburg
4-6-7 .... New Haven
8-9-10 .... Trenton
11-12-13-14 .... at N.H.
15-16-17 .... New Haven
19-20-21 .... at Portland
22-23-24 .... at New Haven
25-26-27 .... Erie
29-30-31 .... Harrisburg

SEPTEMBER

1 .... Harrisburg

Portland

APRIL

3-4-5-6 .... Trenton
7-8-9 .... at New Britain
10-11-12-13 .... at Trenton
14-15-16 ...... Binghamton
18-19-20 .... New Britain
22-23-24 ... at Binghamton
25-26-27 .... New Haven
28-29-30 .... Reading

MAY

1 .... Reading
2-3-4 .... at New Haven
5-6-7 .... at Norwich
9-10-11 .... New Britain
12-13-14 .... Trenton
15-16-17-18 .... at N.B.
19-20-21-22 .... Bowie
23-24-25-26 ... Harrisburg
27-28-29 .... at Trenton
30-31 .... at Binghamton

JUNE

1 .... at Binghamton
2-3-4 .... at Altoona
6-7-8 .... Binghamton
9-10-11 .... Norwich

13-14-15 .... at Akron
16-17-18 .... at Erie
19-20-21-22 .... at N.H.
23-24-25 .... Akron
27-28-29 .... Altoona
30 .... at Harrisburg

JULY

1-2-3 .... at Harrisburg
4-5-6 .... New Haven
7-8-9-10 .... New Britain
11-12-13-14 ... at Norwich
17-18-19-20 .... Norwich
21-22-23-24 ...... at Bowie
25-26-27 .... at Norwich
28-29-30 .... Trenton
31 .... at Binghamton

AUGUST

1-2-3 .... at Binghamton
4-5-6 .... at Trenton
7-8-9-10 .... Binghamton
11-12-13-14 ... at Reading
15-16-17 ... at New Britain
19-20-21 .... Norwich
22-23-24 .... Erie
26-27-28 ... at New Haven
29-30-31 .... New Haven

SEPTEMBER

1 .... New Haven

Reading

APRIL

3-4-5-6 .... Altoona
7-8-9 .... Bowie
10-11-12-13 .... at Altoona
14-15-16-17 .... Akron
18-19-20 .... at Erie
22-23-24 .... Harrisburg
25-26-27 ..... at Harrisburg
28-29-30 .... at Portland

MAY

1 .... at Portland
2-3-4 .... Altoona
6-7-8 .... Harrisburg
9-10-11 .... at Bowie
12-13-14 .... at Altoona
15-16-17-18 .... Norwich
19-20-21-22 .... Erie
23-24-25-26 .... at Akron
27-28-29 .... at Erie
30-31 .... New Haven

JUNE

1 .... New Haven
2-3-4 .... Erie
6-7-8 .... at Akron
9-10-11 .... at Bowie
13-14-15 ...... Binghamton
16-17-18 .... Akron
19-20-21-22 ... at Norwich
24-25-26 .... Altoona
27-28-29 .... at New Haven
30 .... at Erie

JULY

1-2-3 .... at Erie
4-5-6 .... Bowie
7-8-9-10 .... Harrisburg
11-12-13-14 ..... at H'burg
17-18-19-20 .... Bowie
21-22-23-24 .... at Trenton
25-26-27 ..... at Harrisburg
28-29-30 .... Erie
31 .... Trenton

AUGUST

1-2-3 .... Trenton
5-6-7 .... at New Britain
8-9-10 .... Akron
11-12-13-14 .... Portland
15-16-17 ... at Binghamton
18-19-20 .... at Akron
22-23-24 .... New Britain
25-26-27 .... at Altoona
29-30-31 .... at Bowie

SEPTEMBER

1 .... at Bowie

Trenton

APRIL

3-4-5-6 .... at Portland
7-8-9 .... at Norwich
10-11-12-13 .... Portland
14-15-16-17 ... New Britain
18-19-20 ... at Binghamton
21-22-23 .... at New Haven
25-26-27 .... New Britain
28-29-30 .... Norwich

MAY

1 .... Norwich
2-3-4 .... at New Britain
6-7-8 .... Binghamton
9-10-11 .... New Haven
12-13-14 .... at Portland
15-16-17-18 .... Bowie
19-20-21-22 ..... at H'burg
23-24-25-26 ... at Norwich
27-28-29 .... Portland
30-31 .... Altoona

JUNE

1 .... Altoona
3-4-5 .... at Akron
6-7-8 .... at Erie
10-11-12 .... New Haven
13-14-15 .... Norwich
16-17-18 .... at Altoona
19-20-21-22 .... at N.B.
24-25-26 .... Norwich
27-28-29 ...... Binghamton
30 .... at New Haven

JULY

1-2-3 .... at New Haven
4-5-6 .... New Britain
7-8-9-10 .... New Haven
11-12-13-14 .... at Bowie
17-18-19-20 ... Harrisburg
21-22-23-24 .... Reading
25-26-27 .... at New Haven
28-29-30 .... at Portland
31 .... at Reading

AUGUST

1-2-3 .... at Reading
4-5-6 .... Portland
8-9-10 .... at Norwich
11-12-13 ... at Binghamton
15-16-17 .... Erie
18-19-20 ... at New Britain
21-22-23-24 .... Bing.
26-27-28 .... Akron
29-30-31 ... at Binghamton

SEPTEMBER

1 .... at Binghamton

SOUTHERN LEAGUE

Birmingham

APRIL

3-4-5-6 .... at Greenville
7-8-9 .... at West Tenn
11-12-13 .... Caronlina
14-15-16-17 .... Mobile
18-19-20-21 .... at H'ville
22-23-24-25 .... Orlando
26-27-28-29 .... at J'ville

MAY

1-2-3-4 .... at Orlando
6-7-8-9 .... Jacksonville
10-11-12-13 ... West Tenn
15-16-17-18 ... at Carolina
19-20-21-22 .... at Tenn.
23-24-25-26 ..... at Mobile
27-28-29-30 .... Huntsville
31 .... West Tenn

JUNE

1-2-3 .... West Tenn
5-6-7-8 .... at West Tenn
9-10-11-12 .... Huntsville
13-14-15-16 .... Chatt.
18-19-20-21 .... at Orlando
22-23-24 .... at Mobile
26-27-28 ... at Jacksonville
29-30 .... at Huntsville

JULY

1 .... at Huntsville
2-3 .... Huntsville
4-5-6 .... Jacksonville
10-11 .... Mobile
12-13 .... at Mobile
14-15-16-17 .... at Chatt.
18-19-20-21 .... Tennessee
22-23-24-25 .... Chatt.
26-27 .... Mobile
28-29 .... at Mobile
30-31 .... at Huntsville

AUGUST

2-3 .... Huntsville
4-5-6-7 .... Jacksonville
8-9-10-11 .... at Chatt.
12-13-14-15 .... Mobile
16-17-18-19 .... Chatt.
21-22-23-24 .... at W.T.
25-26-27-28 .... at H'ville
29-30-31 .... Greenville

SEPTEMBER

1 .... Greenville

Carolina

APRIL

3-4-5-6 .... Chattanooga
7-8-9 .... Mobile
11-12-13 ... at Birmingham
14-15-16-17 .... at Chatt.
18-19-20-21 .... J'ville
22-23-24-25 .... at G;ville
26-27-28-29 ... West Tenn

MAY

1-2-3-4 ..... at Jacksonville
6-7-8-9 .... at Orlando
10-11-12-13 ..... at Mobile
15-16-17-18 .... Birm.
19-20-21-22 .... Orlando
23-24-25-26 .... at J'ville
27-28-29-30 .... Tennessee
31 .... Greenville

JUNE

1-2-3 .... Greenville
5-6-7-8 .... at Tennessee
9-10-11-12 .... at Chatt.
13-14-15-16 .... Tennessee
18-19-20-21 .... at W.T.
22-23-24 ...... at Huntsville
26-27-28-29 .... Mobile
30 .... at Tennessee

JULY

1-2-3 .... at Tennessee
4-5-6 .... Orlando
10-11-12-13 .... at G'ville
14-15-16-17 .... West Tenn
18-19-20-21 .... at J'ville
22-23-24-25 ... at Orlando
26-27-28-29 .... J'ville
31 .... Greenville

AUGUST

1-2-3 .... Greenville
4-5-6-7 .... at Tennessee
8-9-10-11 .... Orlando
12-13-14-15 ..... Greenville
16-17-18-19 .... at G'ville
21-22-23-24 ..... Huntsville
25-26-27-28 .... Tennessee
29-30-31 .... at Orlando

SEPTEMBER

1 .... at Orlando

Chattanooga

APRIL

3-4-5-6 .... at Carolina
7-8-9 .... at Greenville
11-12-13 .... West Tenn
14-15-16-17 .... Carolina
18-19-20-21 .... at W.T.
22-23-24-25 .... J'ville
26-27-28-29 .... Mobile

MAY

1-2-3-4 .... at Huntsville
6-7-8-9 .... Huntsville
10-11-12-13 ..... Greenville
15-16-17-18 .... at Tenn.
19-20-21-22 .... at W.T.
23-24-25-26 .... Tennessee
27-28-29-30 ..... at Mobile

31 .... at Orlando

JUNE

1-2-3 .... at Orlando
5-6-7-8 .... at Huntsville
9-10-11-12 .... Carolina
13-14-15-16 .... at Birm.
18-19-20-21 .... Mobile
22-23-24-25 .... at W.T.
26-27-28 .... Huntsville
30 .... Orlando

JULY

1-2-3 .... Orlando
4-5-6 .... at West Tenn
10-11-12-13 ... West Tenn
14-15-16-17 .... Birm.
18-19-20-21 ..... at Mobile
22-23-24-25 .... at Birm.
26-27-28-29 .... Huntsville
31 .... at Jacksonville

AUGUST

1-2-3 .... at Jacksonville
4-5-6-7 .... West Tenn
8-9-10-11 ..... Birmingham
12-13-14-15 .... at H'ville
16-17-18-19 .... at Birm.
21-22-23-24 .... Mobile
25-26-27-28 ..... at Mobile
29-30-31 .... Huntsville

SEPTEMBER

1 .... Huntsville

Greenville

APRIL

3-4-5-6 .... Birmingham
7-8-9 .... Chattanooga
11-12-13 .... at Mobile
14-15-16-17 .... at W.T.
18-19-20-21 .... Tennessee
22-23-24-25 .... Carolina
26-27-28-29 at Huntsville

MAY

1-2-3-4 .... Mobile
6-7-8-9 .... at Tennessee
10-11-12-13 .... at Chatt.
15-16-17-18 .... J'ville
19-20-21-22 .... Huntsville
23-24-25-26 .... at Orlando
27-28-29-30 ... West Tenn
31 .... at Carolina

JUNE

1-2-3 .... at Carolina
5-6-7-8 .... Orlando
9-10-11-12 ... at Tennessee
13-14-15-16 .... at J'ville
18-19-20-21 .... Huntsville
22-23-24-25 .... Tennessee
27-28-29 ..... at Tennessee
30 .... at Jacksonville

JULY

1-2-3 .... at Jacksonville
4-5-6 .... Tennessee
10-11-12-13 .... Carolina
14-15-16-17 at Tennessee
18-19-20-21 .... Orlando
22-23-24-25 .... J'ville
26-27-28-29 .... at W.T.
31 .... at Carolina

AUGUST

1-2-3 .... at Carolina
4-5-6-7 .... Orlando
8-9-10-11 ..... Jacksonville
12-13-14-15 ... at Carolina
16-17-18-19 .... Carolina
20-21-22-23 .... at J'ville
25-26-27-28 .... at Orlando
29-30-31 ... at Birmingham

SEPTEMBER

1 .... at Birmingham

Huntsville

APRIL

1-2-3-4 .... Jacksonville
7-8-9 .... Orlando
11-12-13 ... at Jacksonville
14-15-16-17 .... at Orlando
18-19-20-21 .... Birm.
22-23-24-25 ..... at Mobile
26-27-28-29 ..... Greenville

MAY

1-2-3-4 .... Chattanooga
6-7-8-9 .... at Chattanooga
10-11-12-13 .... Tennessee
15-16-17-18 .... at W.T.
19-20-21-22 .... at G'ville
23-24-25-26 ... West Tenn
27-28-29-30 .... at Birm.
31 .... Mobile

JUNE

1-2-3 .... Mobile
5-6-7-8 .... Chattanooga
9-10-11-12 .... at Birm.
13-14-15-16 ... West Tenn
18-19-20-21 .... at G'ville
22-23-24 .... Carolina
26-27-28 ... at Chattanooga
29-30 .... Birmingham

JULY

1 .... Birmingham
2-3 .... at Birmingham
4-5-6 .... Mobile
10-11-12-13 .... at Tenn.
14-15-16-17 ..... at Mobile
18-19-20-20 ... West Tenn
22-23-24-25 .... Tennessee
26-27-28-29 .... at Chatt.
31 .... Birmingham

AUGUST

1 .... Birmingham
2-3 .... at Birmingham
4-5-6-7 .... Mobile
8-9-10-11 .... at West Tenn
12-13-14-15 .... Chatt.
16-17-18-19 ..... at Mobile
21-22-23-24 ... at Carolina
25-26-27-28 .... Birm.
29-30-31 ... at Chattanooga

SEPTEMBER

1 .... at Chattanooga

Jacksonville

APRIL

3-4-5-6 .... at Huntsville
7-8-9 .... at Tennessee
11-12-13 .... Huntsville
14-15-16-17 .... Tennessee
18-19-20-21 ... at Carolina
22-23-24-25 .... at Chatt.
26-27-28-29 .... Birm.

MAY

1-2-3-4 .... Carolina
6-7-8-9 ..... at Birmingham
10-11-12-13 .... Orlando
15-16-17-18 .... at G'ville
19-20-21-22 .... Mobile
23-24-25-26 .... Carolina
27-28-29-30 .... at Orlando
31 .... Tennessee

JUNE

1-2-3 .... Tennessee
5-6-7-8 .... at Mobile
9-10-11-12 ...... at Orlando
13-14-15-16 ..... Greenville
18-19-20-21 .... at Tenn.
22-23-24-25 .... Orlando
26-27-28 ...... Birmingham
30 .... Greenville

JULY

1-2-3 .... Greenville
4-5-6 .... at Birmingham
10-11-12-13 .... at Orlando
14-15-16-17 .... Orlando
18-19-20-21 .... Carolina
22-23-24-25 .... at G'ville
26-27-28-29 ... at Carolina
31 .... Chattanooga

AUGUST

1-2-3 .... Chattanooga
4-5-6-7 ..... at Birmingham
8-9-10-11 ..... at Greenville
12-13-14-15 ... West Tenn
16-17-18-19 .... Tennessee
20-21-22-23 ..... Greenville
25-26-27-28 .... at W.T.
29-30-31 ..... at Tennessee

SEPTEMBER

1 .... at Tennessee

Mobile

APRIL

3-4-5-6 .... at Tennessee
7-8-9 .... at Carolina
11-12-13 .... Greenville
14-15-16-17 .... at Birm.
18-19-20-21 .... Orlando
22-23-24-25 ..... Huntsville
26-27-28-29 .... at Chatt.

MAY

1-2-3-4 .... at Greenville
6-7-8-9 .... West Tenn
10-11-12-13 .... Carolina
15-16-17-18 .... at Orlando
19-20-21-22 .... at J'ville
23-24-25-26 .... Birm.
27-28-29-30 .... Chatt.
31 .... at Huntsville

JUNE

1-2-3 .... at Huntsville
5-6-7-8 .... Jacksonville
9-10-11-12 .... at W.T.
13-14-15-16 .... Orlando
18-19-20-21 .... at Chatt.
22-23-24 ...... Birmingham
26-27-28-29 ... at Carolina

JULY

1-2-3 .... West Tenn
4-5-6 .... at Huntsville
10-11 .... at Birmingham
12-13 .... Birmingham
14-15-16-17 ..... Huntsville
18-19-20-21 .... Chatt.
22-23-24-25 .... at W.T.
26-27 .... at Birmingham
28-29 .... Birmingham
31 .... West Tenn

AUGUST

1-2-2-3 .... West Tenn
4-5-6-7 .... at Huntsville
8-9-10-11 .... Tennessee
12-13-14-15 .... at Birm.
16-17-18-19 ..... Huntsville
21-22-23-24 .... at Chatt.
25-26-27-28 .... Chatt.
29-30-31 ..... at West Tenn

SEPTEMBER

1 .... at West Tenn

Orlando

APRIL

3-4-5-6 .... at West Tenn
7-8-9 .... at Huntsville
11-12-13 .... Tennessee
14-15-16-17 ..... Huntsville
18-19-20-21 ..... at Mobile
22-23-24-25 .... at Birm.
26-27-28-29 .... at Tenn.

MAY

1-2-3-4 .... Birmingham
6-7-8-9 .... Carolina
10-11-12-13 .... at J'ville
15-16-17-18 .... Mobile
19-20-21-22 ... at Carolina
23-24-25-26 ..... Greenville
27-28-29-30 .... J'ville
31 .... Chattanooga

JUNE

1-2-3 .... Chattanooga
5-6-7-8 .... at Greeville
9-10-11-12 ... Jacksonville
13-14-15-16 ..... at Mobile
18-19-20-21 .... Birm.
22-23-24-25 .... at J'ville
27-28-29 .... West Tenn
30 .... at Chattanooga

JULY

1-2-3 .... at Chattanooga
4-5-6 .... at Carolina
10-11-12-13 .... J'ville
14-15-16-17 .... at J'ville
18-19-20-21 .... at G'ville
22-23-24-25 .... Carolina
26-27-28-29 .... Tennessee
31 .... at Tennessee

AUGUST

1-2-3 .... at Tennessee
4-5-6-7 .... at Greenville
8-9-10-11 .... at Carolina
12-13-14-15 .... Tennessee
16-17-18-19 ... West Tenn
21-22-23-24 .... at Tenn.

25-26-27-28 .... Greenville
29-30-31 .... Carolina

SEPTEMBER

1 .... Carolina

Tennessee

APRIL

3-4-5-6 .... Mobile
7-8-9 .... Jacksonville
11-12-13 .... at Orlando
14-15-16-17 .... at J'ville
18-19-20-21 .... at G'ville
22-23-24-25 ... West Tenn
26-27-28-29 .... Orlando

MAY

1-2-3-4 .... at West Tenn
6-7-8-9 .... Greenville
10-11-12-13 .... at H'ville
15-16-17-18 .... Chatt.
19-20-21-22 .... Birm.
23-24-25-26 .... at Chatt.
27-28-29-30 ... at Carolina
31 .... at Jacksonville

JUNE

1-2-3 .... at Jacksonville
5-6-7-8 .... Carolina
9-10-11-12 .... Greenville
13-14-15-16 ... at Carolina
18-19-20-21 .... J'ville
22-23-24-25 .... at G'ville
27-28-29 .... Greenville
30 .... Carolina

JULY

1-2-3 .... Carolina
4-5-6 .... at Greenville
10-11-12-13 ..... Huntsville
14-15-16-17 ..... Greenville
18-19-20-21 .... at Birm.
22-23-24-25 .... at H'ville
26-27-28-29 .... at Orlando
31 .... Orlando

AUGUST

1-2-3 .... Orlando
4-5-6-7 .... Carolina
8-9-10-11 .... at Mobile
12-13-14-15 .... at Orlando
16-17-18-19 .... at J'ville
21-22-23-24 .... Orlando
25-26-27-28 ... at Carolina
29-30-31 ...... Jacksonville

SEPTEMBER

1 .... Jacksonville

West Tenn

APRIL

3-4-5-6 .... Orlando
7-8-9 .... Birmingham
11-12-13 ... at Chattanooga
14-15-16-17 ..... Greenville
18-19-20-21 .... Chatt.
22-23-24-25 .... at Tenn.
26-27-28-29 ... at Carolina

MAY

1-2-3-4 .... Tennessee
6-7-8-9 .... at Mobile
10-11-12-13 .... at Birm.
15-16-17-18 ..... Huntsville
19-20-21-22 .... Chatt.
23-24-25-26 .... at H'ville
27-28-29-30 .... at G'ville
31 .... at Birmingham

JUNE

1-2-3 .... at Birmingham
5-6-7-8 .... Birmingham
9-10-11-12 .... Mobile
13-14-15-16 .... at H'ville
18-19-20-21 .... Carolina
22-23-24-25 .... Chatt.
27-28-29 .... at Orlando

JULY

1-2-3 .... at Mobile
4-5-6 .... Chattanooga
10-11-12-13 .... at Chatt.
14-15-16-17 ... at Carolina
18-19-20-20 .... at H'ville
22-23-24-25 .... Mobile
26-27-28-29 ..... Greenville
31 .... at Mobile

AUGUST

1-2-2-3 .... at Mobile
4-5-6-7 .... at Chattanooga
8-9-10-11 .... Huntsville
12-13-14-15 .... at J'ville
16-17-18-19 .... at Orlando
21-22-23-24 .... Birm.
25-26-27-28 .... J'ville
29-30-31 .... Mobile

SEPTEMBER

1 .... Mobile

TEXAS LEAGUE

Arkansas

APRIL

3-4-5-6-7-8 .... Wichita
9-10-11-12 .... Tulsa
13-14-15-16 .... at Wichita
17-18-19-20 .... at Tulsa
22-23-24-25 .... Midland
26-27-28-29 .... El Paso

MAY

1-2-3-4 .... at Midland
5-6-7-8 .... at El Paso
9-10-11-12 .... Tulsa
13-14-15-16 .... at Frisco
17-18-19-20 .... at Wichita
21-22-23-24 .... Frisco
26-27-28-29 .... Wichita
30-31 .... at San Antonio

JUNE

1-2 .... at San Antonio
3-4-5-6 .... at Round Rock
7-8-9-10 .... San Antonio
11-12-13-14 .... R.R.
18-19-20-21 .... Tulsa
23-24-25-26 .... at S.A.
27-28-29-30 .... at R.R.

JULY

1-2-3-4 .... Wichita
5-6-7-8 .... at Tulsa
9-10-11-12 .... at Frisco
14-15-16-17 .... S.A.
18-19-19-21 .... R.R.
22-23-24-25 .... Frisco
26-27-28-29 .... at Wichita
31 .... Frisco

AUGUST

1-2-2 .... Frisco
5-6-7-8-9-10 .... at Tulsa
11-12-13-14 .... El Paso
15-16-16-17 .... Midland
20-21-22-23 .... at El Paso
24-25-26-27 ... at Midland
28-29-30-31 .... at Frisco

El Paso

APRIL

3-4-5-6-7-8 .... at S.A.
9-10-11-12 .... at R.R.
13-14-15-16 .... S.A.
17-18-19-20 .... R.R.
22-23-24-25 .... at Frisco
26-27-28-29 ... at Arkansas

MAY

1-2-3-4 .... Frisco
5-6-7-8 .... Arkansas
9-10-11-12 .... at R.R.
13-14-15-16 ... at Midland
17-18-19-20 .... at S.A.
22-23-24-25 .... Midland
26-27-28-29 .... S.A.
30-31 .... at Wichita

JUNE

1-2 .... at Wichita
3-4-5-6 .... at Tulsa
7-8-9-10 .... Wichita
11-12-13-14 .... Tulsa
19-20-21-22 .... R.R.
23-24-25-26 .... at Wichita
27-28-29-30 .... at Tulsa

JULY

1-2-3-4 .... Round Rock
5-6-7-8 ..... at San Antonio
10-11-12-13 .... Midland
14-15-16-17 .... Tulsa
18-19-20-21 .... Wichita
22-23-24-25 ... at Midland
26-27-28-29 .... at R.R.
31 .... at Midland

AUGUST

1-2-3 .... at Midland
5-6-7-8-9-10 .... S.A.
11-12-13-14 ... at Arkansas
15-16-17-18 .... at Frisco
20-21-22-23 ...... Arkansas
24-25-26-27 .... Frisco
28-29-30-31 .... Midland

Frisco

APRIL

3-4-5-6-7-8 .... Tulsa
9-10-11-12 .... Wichita
13-14-15-16 .... at Tulsa
17-18-19-20 .... at Wichita
22-23-24-25 .... El Paso
26-27-28-29 .... Midland

MAY

1-2-3-4 .... at El Paso
5-6-7-8 .... at Midland
9-10-11-12 .... Wichita
13-14-15-16 ...... Arkansas
17-18-19-20 .... at Tulsa
21-22-23-24 ... at Arkansas
26-27-28-29 .... Tulsa
30-31 ..... at Round Roock

JUNE

1-2 .... at Round Rock
3-4-5-6 ..... at San Antonio
7-8-9-10 ...... Round Rock
11-12-13-14 .... S.A.
18-19-20-21 .... at Wichita
23-24-25-26 .... at R.R.
27-28-29-30 .... at S.A.

JULY

1-2-3-4 .... Tulsa
5-6-7-8 .... at Wichita
9-10-11-12 .... Arkansas
14-15-16-17 .... R.R.
18-19-20-21 .... S.A.
22-23-24-25 ... at Arkansas
26-27-28-29 .... at Tulsa
31 .... at Arkansas

AUGUST

1-2-2 .... at Arkansas
4-5-6-7-8-9 .... Wichita
11-12-13-14 .... Midland
15-16-17-18 .... El Paso
20-21-22-23 ... at Midland
24-25-26-27 .... at El Paso
28-29-30-31 ...... Arkansas

Midland

APRIL

3-4-5-6-7-8 .... at R.R.
9-10-11-12 .... at S.A.
13-14-15-16 .... R.R.
17-18-19-20 .... S.A.
22-23-24-25 ... at Arkansas
26-27-28-29 .... at Frisco

MAY

1-2-3-4 .... Arkansas
5-6-7-8 .... Frisco
9-10-11-12 .... at S.A.
13-14-15-16 .... El Paso
17-18-19-20 .... R.R.
22-23-24-25 .... at El Paso
26-27-28-29 .... at R.R.
30-31 .... at Tulsa

JUNE

1-2 .... at Tulsa
3-4-5-6 .... at Wichita
7-8-9-10 .... Tulsa
11-12-13-14 .... Wichita
18-19-20-21 .... S.A.
23-24-25-26 .... at Tulsa
27-28-29-30 .... at Wichita

JULY

1-2-3-4 .... San Antonio
5-6-7-8 .... at Round Rock

10-11-12-13 .... at El Paso
14-15-16-17 .... Wichita
18-19-20-21 .... Tulsa
22-23-24-25 .... El Paso
26-27-28-29 .... at S.A.
31 .... El Paso

AUGUST

1-2-3 .... El Paso
4-5-6-7-8-9 ... Round Rock
11-12-13-14 .... at Frisco
15-16-16-17 ... at Arkansas
20-21-22-23 .... Frisco
24-25-26-27 ...... Arkansas
28-29-30-31 .... at El Paso

Round Rock

APRIL

3-4-5-6-7-8 .... Midland
9-10-11-12 .... El Paso
13-14-15-16 ... at Midland
17-18-19-20 .... at El Paso
22-23-24-25 .... Tulsa
26-27-28-29 .... Wichita

MAY

1-2-3-4 .... at Tulsa
5-6-7-8 .... at Wichita
9-10-11-12 .... El Paso
13-14-15-16 .... S.A.
17-18-19-20 ... at Midland
21-22-23-24 .... at S.A.
26-27-28-29 .... Midland
30-31 .... Frisco

JUNE

1-2 .... Frisco
3-4-5-6 .... Arkansas
7-8-9-10 .... at Frisco
11-12-13-14 ... at Arkansas
19-20-21-22 .... at El Paso
23-24-25-26 .... Frisco
27-28-29-30 ...... Arkansas

JULY

1-2-3-4 .... at El Paso
5-6-7-8 .... Midland
9-10-11-12 ... San Antonio
14-15-16-17 .... at Frisco
18-19-19-21 ... at Arkansas
22-23-24-25 .... at S.A.
26-27-28-29 .... El Paso
31 .... at San Antonio

AUGUST

1-2-3 .... at San Antonio
4-5-6-7-8-9 ..... at Midland
11-12-13-14 .... Tulsa
15-16-17-18 .... Wichita
20-21-22-23 .... at Tulsa
24-25-26-27 .... at Wichita
28-29-30-31 .... S.A.

San Antonio

APRIL

3-4-5-6-7-8 .... El Paso
9-10-11-12 .... Midland
13-14-15-16 .... at El Paso
17-18-19-20 ... at Midland
22-23-24-25 .... Wichita
26-27-28-29 .... Tulsa

MAY

1-2-3-4 .... at Wichita
5-6-7-8 .... at Tulsa
9-10-11-12 .... Midland
13-14-15-16 .... at R.R.
17-18-19-20 .... El Paso
21-22-23-24 .... R.R.
26-27-28-29 .... at El Paso
30-31 .... Arkansas

JUNE

1-2 .... Arkansas
3-4-5-6 .... Frisco
7-8-9-10 .... at Arkansas
11-12-13-14 .... at Frisco
18-19-20-21 ... at Midland
23-24-25-26 ...... Arkansas
27-28-29-30 .... Frisco

JULY

1-2-3-4 .... at Midland
5-6-7-8 .... El Paso
9-10-11-12 .... at R.R.
14-15-16-17 ... at Arkansas
18-19-20-21 .... at Frisco
22-23-24-25 .... R.R.
26-27-28-29 .... Midland
31 .... Round Rock

AUGUST

1-2-3 .... Round Rock
5-6-7-8-9-10 .... at El Paso
11-12-13-14 .... Wichita
15-16-17-18 .... Tulsa
20-21-22-23 .... at Wichita
24-25-26-27 .... at Tulsa
28-29-30-31 .... at R.R.

Tulsa

APRIL

3-4-5-6-7-8 .... at Frisco
9-10-11-12 .... at Arkansas
13-14-15-16 .... Frisco
17-18-19-20 ...... Arkansas
22-23-24-25 .... at R.R.
26-27-28-29 .... at S.A.

MAY

1-2-3-4 .... Round Rock
5-6-7-8 .... San Antonio
9-10-11-12 .... at Arkansas
13-14-15-16 .... at Wichita
17-18-19-20 .... Frisco
22-23-24-25 .... Wichita
26-27-28-29 .... at Frisco
30-31 .... Midland

JUNE

1-2 .... Midland
3-4-5-6 .... El Paso
7-8-9-10 .... at Midland
11-12-13-14 .... at El Paso
18-19-20-21 ... at Arkansas
23-24-25-26 .... Midland
27-28-29-30 .... El Paso

JULY

1-2-3-4 .... at Frisco
5-6-7-8 .... Arkansas
9-10-11-12 .... Wichita
14-15-16-17 .... at El Paso
18-19-20-21 ... at Midland
23-23-24-25 .... at Wichita
26-27-28-29 .... Frisco
31 .... Wichita

AUGUST

1-2-3 .... Wichita
5-6-7-8-9-10 ..... Arkansas
11-12-13-14 .... at R.R.
15-16-17-18 .... at S.A.
20-21-22-23 .... R.R.
24-25-26-27 .... S.A.
28-29-30-31 .... at Wichita

Wichita

APRIL

3-4-5-6-7-8 ... at Arkansas
9-10-11-12 .... at Frisco
13-14-15-16 ...... Arkansas
17-18-19-20 .... Frisco
22-23-24-25 .... at S.A.
26-27-28-29 .... at R.R.

MAY

1-2-3-4 .... San Antonio
5-6-7-8 .... Round Rock
9-10-11-12 .... at Frisco
13-14-15-16 .... Tulsa
17-18-19-20 ...... Arkansas
22-23-24-25 .... at Tulsa
26-27-28-29 ... at Arkansas
30-31 .... El Paso

JUNE

1-2 .... El Paso
3-4-5-6 .... Midland
7-8-9-10 .... at El Paso
11-12-13-14 ... at Midland
18-19-20-21 .... Frisco
23-24-25-26 .... El Paso
27-28-29-30 .... Midland

JULY

1-2-3-4 .... at Arkansas
5-6-7-8 .... Frisco
9-10-11-12 .... at Tulsa
14-15-16-17 ... at Midland
18-19-20-21 .... at El Paso
23-23-24-25 .... Tulsa
26-27-28-29 ...... Arkansas
31 .... at Tulsa

AUGUST

1-2-3 .... at Tulsa
4-5-6-7-8-9 .... at Frisco
11-12-13-14 .... at S.A.
15-16-17-18 .... at R.R.
20-21-22-23 .... S.A.
24-25-26-27 .... R.R.
28-29-30-31 .... Tulsa

CLASS A
CALIFORNIA LEAGUE

Bakersfield

APRIL
4-5-6 .... R.Cucamonga
7-8-9-10 .... Stockton
11-12-13 .... at Visalia
14-15-16-17 ...... San Jose
18-19-20 .... at Modesto
22-23-24 .... Modesto
25-26-27 .... Visalia
28-29-30 .... at Visalia

MAY
1 .... at Visalia
2-3-4 .... at San Jose
5-6-7-8 .... at Modesto
9-10-11 .... San Jose
13-14-15 .... Lancaster
16-17-18 .... Stockton
19-20-21-22 ... at San Jose
23-24-25 .... at Stockton
26-27-28 .... Modesto
29-30-31 .... at Stockton

JUNE
1 .... at Stockton
2-3-4-5 .... Visalia
6-7-8 .... at R. Cucamonga
9-10-11 ... at Lake Elsinore
13-14-15 ...... at Lancaster
16-17-18-19 ...... Stockton
20-21-22 .... San Jose
26-27-28-29 ... at San Jose
30 .... at Modesto

JULY
1-2-3 .... at Modesto
4-5-6 .... Stockton
8-9-10 .... Lake Elsinore
11-12-13 .... at Visalia
14-15-16-17 ...... Modesto
18-19-20 .... Visalia
22-23-24 .... at Modesto
25-26-27 ... Inland Empire
28-29-30-31 ... at Stockton

AUGUST
1-2-3 .... Modesto
4-5-6 .... at Visalia
7-8-9-10 .... Visalia
12-13-14 .... at I.E.
15-16-17 ... at High Desert
19-20-21 .... High Desert
22-23-24 .... at Stockton
25-26-27 .... at San Jose
29-30-31 .... San Jose

SEPTEMBER
1 .... San Jose

High Desert

APRIL
3-4-5-6 ... at Lake Elsinore
8-9-10 .... Modesto
11-12-13 .... Lake Elsinore
14-15-16 .... at R.C.
17-18-19-20 ..... Lancaster
21-22-23-24 .... I.E.
25-26-27 .... at L.E.
28-29-30 ...... at Lancaster

MAY
1 .... at Lancaster
2-3-4 .... R. Cucamonga
6-7-8 ..... at Inland Empire
9-10-11 .... Stockton
12-13-14-15 .... L.E.
16-17-18-19 .... at R.C.
20-21-22 ... R. Cucamonga
23-24-25 .... Lancaster
26-27-28 .... at Stockton
30 .... at San Jose

JUNE
1-2 .... at San Jose
3-4-5 .... at Lancaster
6-7-8 .... Lake Elsinore
10-11-12 .... Visalia
13-14-14-15 .... at I.E.
16-17-18 .... Lancaster
20-21-22 ... Inland Empire
26-27-28-29 .... at L.E.

JULY
1-2-3 .... Lake Elsinore
4-5-6 ...... at Lake Elsinore
8-9-10 ... at Inland Empire
11-12-13 ... R. Cucamonga
14-15-16 .... at Visalia
17-18-19-20 .... I.E.
21-22-23-24 ...... San Jose
25-26-27 .... at R.C.
28-29-30-31 .... at I.E.

AUGUST
1-2-3 .... at Lancaster
4-5-6-7 ..... R. Cucamonga
8-9-10 ... at R. Cucamonga
11-12-13-14 .... at Lanc.
15-16-17 .... Bakersfield
19-20-21 .... at Bakersfield
22-23-24 .... at Modesto
26-27-28 .... Lancaster
29-30-31 .... Lake Elsinore

SEPTEMBER
1 .... Lake Elsinore

Inland Empire

APRIL
3 ...... Rancho Cucamonga
4-5-6 .... at Lancaster
9-10 ... Rancho Cucamonga
11-12-13 .... at R.C.
15-16 .... Lancaster
17-18-19-20 .... R.C.
21-22-23-24 .... at H.D.
25-26-27 .... San Jose
29-30 .... at San Jose

MAY
1 .... at San Jose
2-3-4 .... at Modesto
6-7-8 .... High Desert
9-10-11 ... at Lake Elsinore
12-13-14-15 .... at R.C.
16-17-17-18 .... L.E.
19-20-21-22 .... at L.E.
23-24-25 .... Visalia
26-28-29 .... Lake Elsinore
30-31 ... at R. Cucamonga

JUNE
1 ... at Rancho Cucamonga
3-4-5 .... Stockton
6-7-7-8-9 .... Lancaster
10-11-12 ...... at Lancaster
13-14-14-15 .... H.D.
16-17-18 .... Lake Elsinore
20-21-22 ... at High Desert
26-27-28-29 ..... Lancaster

JULY
1-2-3 .... at R. Cucamonga
4-4-5-6 ...... R. Cucamonga
8-9-10 .... High Desert
11-12-13 ...... at Lancaster
14-15-16 .... at Stockton
17-18-19-20 .... at H.D.
22-23-24 .... at Visalia
25-26-27 .... at Bakersfield
28-29-30-31 .... H.D.

AUGUST
1-2-3 .... R. Cucamonga
4-5-6-7 ... at Lake Elsinore
8-9-10 .... Lake Elsinore
12-13-14 .... Bakersfield
15-16-17-18 .... at Lanc.
19-20-21 .... at L.E.
22-23-24 .... Lancaster
26-27-28 .... Modesto
29-30-31 .... at R.C.

SEPTEMBER
1 ... at Rancho Cucamonga

Lake Elsinore

APRIL
3-4-5-6 .... High Desert
7-8-9-10 .... Lancaster
11-12-13 ... at High Desert
15-16-17 .... at Visalia
18-19-20 .... at Stockton
22-23-24 .... San Jose
25-26-27 .... High Desert
28-29-30 .... at R.C.

MAY
1 ... at Rancho Cucamonga
2-3-4 .... at Lancaster
6-7-8 .... Lancaster
9-10-11 ..... Inland Empire
12-13-14-15 .... at H.D.
16-17-18 .... at I.E.
19-20-21-22 .... I.E.
23-24-25 ... R. Cucamonga
26-28-29 .... at I.E.
30-31 .... at Lancaster

JUNE
1-2 .... at Lancaster
3-4-5 .... R. Cucamonga
6-7-8 .... at High Desert
9-10-11 .... Bakersfield
13-14-15 .... Modesto
16-17-18 .... at I.E.
19-20-21-22 ..... Lancaster
26-27-28-29 .... H.D.

JULY
1-2-3 .... at High Desert
4-5-6 .... High Desert
8-9-10 .... at Bakersfield
11-12-13 .... at Modesto
14-15-16 .... at San Jose
18-19-20 ...... at Lancaster
22-23-24 .... Stockton
25-26-27 .... Lancaster
28-29-30-31 .... at Lanc.

AUGUST
1-2-3 .... Visalia
4-5-6-7 ...... Inland Empire
8-9-10 ... at Inland Empire
11-12-13-14 .... at R.C.
15-16-17 ... R. Cucamonga
19-20-21 ... Inland Empire
22-23-24 .... at R.C.
25-26-27-28 .... R.C.
29-30-31 ... at High Desert

SEPTEMBER
1 .... at High Desert

Lancaster

APRIL
4-5-6 .... Inland Empire
7-8-9-10 .... at L.E.
11-12-13 .... Modesto
15-16 ..... at Inland Empire
17-18-19-20 .... at H.D.
21-22-23-24 .... R.C.
25-26-27 .... at R.C.
28-29-30 .... High Desert

MAY
1 .... High Desert
2-3-4 .... Lake Elsinore
6-7-8 ...... at Lake Elsinore
9-10-11 .... R. Cucamonga
13-14-15 .... at Bakersfield
16-17-18 .... at Visalia
20-21-22 .... Visalia
23-24-25 ... at High Desert
26-27-28-29 .... at R.C.
30-31 .... Lake Elsinore

JUNE
1-2 .... Lake Elsinore
3-4-5 .... High Desert
6-7-8-9 ... at Inland Empire
10-11-12 ... Inland Empire
13-14-15 .... Bakersfield
16-17-18 ... at High Desert
19-20-21-22 .... at L.E.
26-27-28-29 .... at I.E.

JULY
1-2-3 .... San Jose
4-5-6 .... at San Jose
8-9-10 ...... R. Cucamonga
11-12-13 ... Inland Empire
14-15-16-17 .... at R.C.
18-19-20 .... Lake Elsinore
21-22-23-24 .... R.C.
25-26-27 .... at L.E.
28-29-30-31 .... L.E.

AUGUST
1-2-3 .... High Desert
5-6-7 .... at Modesto

8-9-10 .... at Stockton
11-12-13-14 .... H.D.
15-16-17-18 .... I.E.
19-20-21 .... at R.C.
22-23-24 .... at I.E.
26-27-28 ... at High Desert
29-30-31 .... Stockton

Modesto

APRIL

3-4-5-6 .... Visalia
8-9-10 .... at High Desert
11-12-13 ...... at Lancaster
15-16-17 .... at Stockton
18-19-20 .... Bakersfield
22-23-24 .... at Bakersfield
25-26-27 .... Stockton
29-30 .... at Stockton

MAY

1-1 .... at Stockton
2-3-4 .... Inland Empire
5-6-7-8 .... Bakersfield
9-10-11 .... at Visalia
12-13-14 .... San Jose
15-16-17-18 ... at San Jose
20-21-22-22 ...... Stockton
23-24-25 .... San Jose
26-27-28 .... at Bakersfield
29-30-31 .... at Visalia

JUNE

1 .... at Visalia
3-4-5 .... San Jose
6-7-8 .... Visalia
9-10-11-12 .... R.C.
13-14-15 .... at L.E.
17-18-19 .... at San Jose
20-21-22 .... Visalia
27-28-29 .... at R.C.
30 .... Bakersfield

JULY

1-2-3 .... Bakersfield
4-5-6 .... at Visalia
7-8-9-10 .... Stockton
11-12-13 .... Lake Elsinore
14-15-16-17 .... at Bak.
18-19-20 .... at Stockton
22-23-24 .... Bakersfield
25-26-27 .... Stockton
28-29-30-31 ... at San Jose

AUGUST

1-2-3 .... at Bakersfield
5-6-7 .... Lancaster
8-9-10 .... San Jose
11-12-13-14 ... at Stockton
15-16-17 .... at San Jose
18-19-20-21 .... Visalia
22-23-24 .... High Desert
26-27-28 .... at I.E.
29-30-31 .... at Visalia

SEPTEMBER

1 .... at Visalia

Rancho Cucamonga

APRIL

3 .... at Inland Empire
4-5-6 .... at Bakersfield
9-10 .... at Inland Empire
11-12-13 ... Inland Empire
14-15-16 .... High Desert
17-18-19-20 .... at I.E.
21-22-23-24 .... at Lanc.
25-26-27 .... Lancaster
28-29-30 .... Lake Elsinore

MAY

1 .... Lake Elsinore
2-3-4 .... at High Desert
6-7-8 .... Stockton
9-10-11 .... at Lancaster
12-13-14-15 .... I.E.
16-17-18-19 .... H.D.
20-21-22 ... at High Desert
23-24-25 .... at L.E.
26-27-28-29 ..... Lancaster
30-31 .... Inland Empire

JUNE

1 .... Inland Empire
3-4-5 ...... at Lake Elsinore
6-7-8 .... Bakersfield
9-10-11-12 .... at Modesto
13-14-15 .... at San Jose
17-18-19 .... at Visalia
20-21-22 .... at Stockton
27-28-29 .... Modesto

JULY

1-2-3 .... Inland Empire
4-4-5-6 ... at Inland Empire
8-9-10 .... at Lancaster
11-12-13 ... at High Desert
14-15-16-17 ..... Lancaster
18-19-20 .... San Jose
21-22-23-24 .... at Lanc.
25-26-27 .... High Desert
29-30-31 .... Visalia

AUGUST

1-2-3 ..... at Inland Empire
4-5-6-7 ..... at High Desert
8-9-10 .... High Desert
11-12-13-14 .... L.E.
15-16-17 .... at L.E.
19-20-21 .... Lancaster
22-23-24 .... Lake Elsinore
25-26-27-28 .... at L.E.
29-30-31 ....Inland Empire

SEPTEMBER

1 .... Inland Empire

San Jose

APRIL

3-4-5-6 .... at Stockton
7-8-9-10 .... Visalia
11-12-13 .... Stockton
14-15-16-17 .... at Bak.
18-19-20 .... Visalia
22-23-24 at Lake Elsinore
25-26-27 .... at I.E.
29-30 .... Inland Empire

MAY

1 .... Inland Empire
2-3-4 .... Bakersfield
6-7-8 .... at Visalia
9-10-11 ...... at Bakersfield
12-13-14 .... at Modesto
15-16-17-18 ...... Modesto
19-20-21-22 ... Bakersfield
23-24-25 .... at Modesto
26-26-27-28 ...... at Visalia
30 .... High Desert

JUNE

1-2 .... High Desert
3-4-5 .... at Modesto
6-7-8-9 .... Stockton
10-11-12 .... at Stockton
13-14-15 ... R. Cucamonga
17-18-19 .... Modesto
20-21-22 .... at Bakersfield
26-27-28-29 ... Bakersfield

JULY

1-2-3 .... at Lancaster
4-5-6 .... Lancaster
7-8-9-10 .... Visalia
11-12-13 .... at Stockton
14-15-16 .... Lake Elsinore
18-19-20 .... at R.C.
21-22-23-24 .... at H.D.
25-26-27 .... Visalia
28-29-30-31 ...... Modesto

AUGUST

1-2-3-3 .... at Stockton
5-6-7 .... Stockton
8-9-10 .... at Modesto
11-12-13-14 ...... at Visalia
15-16-17 .... Modesto
19-20-21 .... Stockton
22-23-24 .... at Visalia
25-26-27 .... Bakersfield
29-30-31 .... at Bakersfield

SEPTEMBER

1 .... at Bakersfield

Stockton

APRIL

3-4-5-6 .... San Jose
7-8-9-10 ..... at Bakersfield
11-12-13 .... at San Jose
15-16-17 .... Modesto
18-19-20 .... Lake Elsinore
21-22-23-24 ...... at Visalia
25-26-27 .... at Modesto
29-30 .... Modesto

MAY

1-1 .... Modesto
2-3-4 .... Visalia
6-7-8 .... at R. Cucamonga
9-10-11 ..... at High Desert
13-14-15 .... Visalia
16-17-18 .... at Bakersfield
20-21-22-22 ... at Modesto
23-24-25 .... Bakersfield
26-27-28 .... High Desert
29-30 .... Bakersfield

JUNE

1 .... Bakersfield
3-4-5 ..... at Inland Empire
6-7-8-9 .... at San Jose
10-11-12 .... San Jose
13-14-15 .... at Visalia
16-17-18-19 .... at Bak.
20-21-22 ... R. Cucamonga
26-27-28-29 ...... at Visalia
30 .... Visalia

JULY

1-2-3 .... Visalia
4-5-6 .... at Bakersfield
7-8-9-10 .... at Modesto
11-12-13 .... San Jose
14-15-16 ... Inland Empire
18-19-20 .... Modesto
22-23-24 .... at L.E.
25-26-27 .... at Modesto
28-29-30-31 ... Bakersfield

AUGUST

1-2-3-3 .... San Jose
5-6-7 .... at San Jose
8-9-10 .... Lancaster
11-12-13-14 ...... Modesto
15-16-17 .... at Visalia
19-20-21 .... at San Jose
22-23-24 .... Bakersfield
26-27-28 .... Visalia
29-30-31 ...... at Lancaster

Visalia

APRIL

3-4-5-6 .... at Modesto
7-8-9-10 .... at San Jose
11-12-13 .... Bakersfield
15-16-17 .... Lake Elsinore
18-19-20 .... at San Jose
21-22-23-24 .... Stockton
25-26-27 .... at Bakersfield
28-29-30 .... Bakersfield

MAY

1 .... Bakersfield
2-3-4 .... at Stockton
6-7-8 .... San Jose
9-10-11 .... Modesto
13-14-15 .... at Stockton
16-17-18 .... Lancaster
20-21-22 ...... at Lancaster
23-24-25 .... at I.E.
26-26-27-28 ...... San Jose
29-30-31 .... Modesto

JUNE

1 .... Modesto
2-3-4-5 .... at Bakersfield
6-7-8 .... at Modesto
10-11-12 ... at High Desert
13-14-15 .... Stockton
17-18-19 ... R. Cucamonga
20-21-22 .... at Modesto
26-27-28-29 ...... Stockton
30 .... at Stockton

JULY

1-2-3 .... at Stockton
4-5-6 .... Modesto
7-8-9-10 .... at San Jose
11-12-13 .... Bakersfield
14-15-16 .... High Desert
18-19-20 .... at Bakersfield
22-23-24 ... Inland Empire
25-26-27 .... at San Jose
29-30-31 .... at R.C.

AUGUST

1-2-3 ...... at Lake Elsinore
4-5-6 .... Bakersfield
7-8-9-10 ..... at Bakersfield
11-12-13-14 ...... San Jose
15-16-17 .... Stockton
18-19-20-21 ... at Modesto
22-23-24 .... San Jose
26-27-28 .... at Stockton
29-30-31 .... Modesto

SEPTEMBER

1 .... Modesto

CAROLINA LEAGUE

Frederick

APRIL

4-5-6 .... Lynchburg
8-9-10 .... at Kinston
11-12-13 .... at M.B.
14-15-16 .... Salem
17-18-19-20 .... at W-S
21-22-23 .... Wilmington
25-26-27 .... Potomac
28-29-30 ... at Wilmington

MAY

1-2-3-4 .... at Potomac
5-6-7 .... Kinston
8-9-10-11 ... at Lynchburg
12-13-14-15 ...... at Salem
16-17-18 .... Lynchburg
20-21-22 .... W-S
23-24-25 ..... Myrtle Beach
26-27-28-29 .... at Kinston
30-31 ...... at Myrtle Beach

JUNE

1 .... at Myrtle Beach
2-3-4-5 .... Salem
6-7-8 ... at Winston-Salem
9-10-11 .... Wilmington
12-13-14-15 ...... Potomac
17-18-19 ... at Wilmington
20-21-22 .... at Potomac
26-27-28 .... Kinston
29-30 .... Myrtle Beach

JULY

1 .... Myrtle Beach
2-3-4 ... at Winston-Salem
5-6-7 .... at Lynchburg
9-10-11 ... Winston-Salem
12-13-14-15 .... M.B.
17-18-19 .... at Kinston
20-21-22-23 .... at M.B.
25-26-27 .... Potomac
28-29-30 .... at Salem
31 .... Wilmington

AUGUST

1-2-3 .... Wilmington
4-5-6 .... Salem
7-8-9-10 .... at Wilmington
11-12-13 .... at Potomac
14-15-16-17 .... Kinston
18-19-20-21 ... Lynchburg
22-23-24 .... at Salem
25-26-27 ..... at Lynchburg
29-30-31 .... W-S

SEPTEMBER

1 .... Winston-Salem

Kinston

APRIL

4-5-6 .... Winston-Salem
8-9-10 .... Frederick
11-12-13 .... at Potomac
14-15-16 ... at Wilmington
17-18-19-20 .... M.B.
21-22-23 .... Salem
24-25-26 ..... at Lynchburg
28-29-30 .... at Salem

MAY

1-2-3-4 .... Lynchburg
5-6-7 .... at Frederick
8-9-10-11 ...... at Potomac
12-13-14-15 ... Wilmington
16-17-18 .... at W-S
20-21-22 .... at M.B.
23-24-25 .... W-S
26-27-28-29 ...... Frederick
30-31 .... at Potomac

JUNE

1 .... at Potomac
2-3-4-5 ..... at Wilmington
6-7-8 .... Myrtle Beach
9-10-11 .... at Salem
12-13-14-15 ...... at Lynch.
17-18-19 .... Lynchburg
20-21-22 .... Salem
26-27-28 .... at Frederick
29-30 .... Potomac

JULY

1 .... Potomac
2-3-4 .... Wilmington
5-6-7 ... at Winston-Salem
9-10-11 .... at Lynchburg
12-13-14-15 .... W-S
17-18-19 .... Frederick
21-22-23-24 ... at Potomac
25-26-27 ... at Wilmington
28-29-30 ..... Myrtle Beach
31 .... at Salem

AUGUST

1-2-3 .... at Salem
4-5-6 .... at Myrtle Beach
7-8-9-10 .... Salem
11-12-13 .... Lynchburg
14-15-16-17 ... at Frederick
18-19-20 .... Potomac
21-22-23 .... Wilmington
25-26-27-28 .... at W-S
29-30-31 .... at M.B.

SEPTEMBER

1 .... at Myrtle Beach

Lynchburg

APRIL

4-5-6 .... at Frederick
8-9-10 .... at W-S
11-12-13 .... Wilmington
14-15-16 .... Potomac
17-18-19-20 ...... at Salem
21-22-23 .... at M.B.
24-25-26 .... Kinston
28-29-30 ..... Myrtle Beach

MAY

1-2-3-4 .... at Kinston
5-6-7 .... Winston-Salem
8-9-10-11 .... Frederick
12-13-14-15 .... at W-S
16-17-18 .... at Frederick
20-21-22 .... Salem
23-24-25 ... at Wilmington
26-27-28-29 ... at Potomac
30-31 .... Wilmington

JUNE

1 .... Wilmington
2-3-4-5 .... Potomac
6-7-8 .... at Salem
9-10-11 ... at Myrtle Beach
12-13-14-15 .... Kinston
17-18-19 .... at Kinston
20-21-22 ..... Myrtle Beach
26-27-28 .... W-S
29-30 .... at Wilmington

JULY

1 .... at Wilmington
2-3-4 .... Salem
5-6-7 .... Frederick
8-9-10 .... Kinston
12-13-14-15 .... at Wilm.
17-18-19 .... at Potomac
20-21-22-23 ... Wilmington
25 .... Salem
26 .... at Salem
27 .... Salem
28-29-30 .... at W-S
31 .... at Myrtle Beach

AUGUST

1-2-3 .... at Myrtle Beach
4-5-6 .... Potomac
7-8-9-10 ..... Myrtle Beach
11-12-13 .... at Kinston
14-15-16-17 .... W-S
18-19-20-21 ... at Frederick
22-23-24 .... at Potomac
25-26-27 .... Frederick
29 .... at Salem
30-31 .... Salem

SEPTEMBER

1 .... at Salem

Myrtle Beach

APRIL

4-5-6-7 ...... at Wilmington
8-9-10 .... at Potomac
11-12-13 .... Frederick
14-15-16 .... W-S
17-18-19-20 .... at Kinston
21-22-23 .... Lynchburg
24-25-26 .... Salem
28-29-30 ..... at Lynchburg

MAY

1-2-3-4 .... at Salem
5-6-7 .... Potomac
9-10-11 ..... at Wilmington
12-13-14-15 ... at Potomac
16-17-18 .... Wilmington
20-21-22 .... Kinston
23-24-25 .... at Frederick
26-27-28-29 .... at W-S
30-31 .... Frederick

JUNE

1 .... Frederick
2-3-4-5 .... Winston-Salem
6-7-8 .... at Kinston
9-10-11 .... Lynchburg
12-13-14-15 .... Salem
17-18-19 .... at Salem
20-21-22 ..... at Lynchburg
26-27-28 .... Potomac
29-30 .... at Frederick

JULY

1 .... at Frederick
2-3-4 .... at Potomac
5-6-7 .... Wilmington
9-10-11 .... Salem
12-13-14-15 ... at Frederick
17-18-19 .... at W-S
20-21-22-23 ...... Frederick
25-26-27 .... W-S
28-29-30 .... at Kinston
31 .... Lynchburg

AUGUST

1-2-3 .... Lynchburg
4-5-6 .... Kinston
7-8-9-10 ..... at Lynchburg
11-12-13 .... at Salem
14-15-16-17 ...... Potomac
18-19-20 ... at Wilmington
21-22-23 .... at W-S
24-25-26-27 ... Wilmington
29-30-31 .... Kinston

SEPTEMBER

1 .... Kinston

Potomac

APRIL

4-5-6 .... at Salem
8-9-10 .... Myrtle Beach
11-12-13 .... Kinston
14-15-16 ..... at Lynchburg
17-18-19-20 ... Wilmington
21-22-23 .... at W-S
25-26-27 .... at Frederick
28-29-30 .... W-S

MAY

1-2-3-4 .... Frederick
5-6-7 .... at Myrtle Beach
8-9-10-11 .... at Kinston
12-13-14-15 .... M.B.
16-17-18 .... at Salem
20-21-22 ... at Wilmington
23-24-25 .... Salem
26-27-28-29 ... Lynchburg
30-31 .... Kinston

JUNE

1 .... Kinston
2-3-4-5 .... at Lynchburg
6-7-8 .... Wilmington
9-10-11 ... Winston-Salem
12-13-14-15 ... at Frederick
17-18-19 .... at W-S
20-21-22 .... Frederick
26-27-28 .... at M.B.
29-30 .... at Kinston

JULY

1 .... at Kinston
2-3-4 .... Myrtle Beach
5-6-7 .... Salem
9-10-11 ..... at Wilmington
12-13-14-15 ...... at Salem
17-18-19 .... Lynchburg
21-22-23-24 .... Kinston
25-26-27 .... at Frederick

28-29-30 .... Wilmington
31 .... Winston-Salem

AUGUST

1-2-3 .... Winston-Salem
4-5-6 .... at Lynchburg
7-8-9-10 .... at W-S
11-12-13 .... Frederick
14-15-16-17 .... at M.B.
18-19-20 .... at Kinston
22-23-24 .... Lynchburg
25-26-27-28 .... Salem
29-30-31 ... at Wilmington

SEPTEMBER

1 .... at Wilmington

Salem

APRIL

4-5-6 .... Potomac
8-9-10 .... Wilmington
11-12-13 .... at W-S
14-15-16 .... at Frederick
17-18-19-20 ... Lynchburg
21-22-23 .... at Kinston
24-25-26 .... at M.B.
28-29-30 .... Kinston

MAY

1-2-3-4 .... Myrtle Beach
5-6-7 .... at Wilmington
8 .... Winston-Salem
9-10-11 .... at W-S
12-13-14-15 ...... Frederick
16-17-18 .... Potomac
20-21-22 ..... at Lynchburg
23-24-25 .... at Potomac
26-27-28-29 ... Wilmington
30-31 ...... Winston-Salem

JUNE

1 .... Winston-Salem
2-3-4-5 .... at Frederick
6-7-8 .... Lynchburg
9-10-11 .... Kinston
12-13-14-15 .... at M.B.
17-18-19 ..... Myrtle Beach
20-21-22 .... at Kinston
26-27-28 ... at Wilmington
29-30 ...... Winston-Salem

JULY

1 .... Winston-Salem
2-3-4 .... at Lynchburg
5-6-7 .... at Potomac
9-10-11 ... at Myrtle Beach
12-13-14-15 ...... Potomac
17-18-19 .... Wilmington
21-22-23-24 .... at W-S
25 .... at Lynchburg
26 .... Lynchburg
27 .... at Lynchburg
28-29-30 .... Frederick
31 .... Kinston

AUGUST

1-2-3 .... Kinston
4-5-6 .... at Frederick
7-8-9-10 .... at Kinston
11-12-13 ..... Myrtle Beach
14-15-16-17 .... at Wilm.
18-19-20 .... W-S
22-23-24 .... Frederick
25-26-27-28 ... at Potomac
29 .... Lynchburg
30-31 .... at Lynchburg

SEPTEMBER

1 .... Lynchburg

Wilmington

APRIL

4-5-6-7 .... Myrtle Beach
8-9-10 .... at Salem
11-12-13 ..... at Lynchburg
14-15-16 .... Kinston
17-18-19-20 ... at Potomac
21-22-23 .... at Frederick
25-26-27 .... W-S
28-29-30 .... Frederick

MAY

1-2-3-4 .... at W-S
5-6-7 .... Salem
9-10-11 .... Myrtle Beach
12-13-14-15 .... at Kinston
16-17-18 .... at M.B.
20-21-22 .... Potomac
23-24-25 .... Lynchburg
26-27-28-29 ...... at Salem
30-31 .... at Lynchburg

JUNE

1 .... at Lynchburg
2-3-4-5 .... Kinston
6-7-8 .... at Potomac
9-10-11 .... at Frederick
12-13-14-15 .... W-S
17-18-19 .... Frederick
20-21-22 .... at W-S
26-27-28 .... Salem
29-30 .... Lynchburg

JULY

1 .... Lynchburg
2-3-4 .... at Kinston
5-6-7 .... at Myrtle Beach
9-10-11 .... Potomac
12-13-14-15 ... Lynchburg
17-18-19 .... at Salem
20-21-22-23 ...... at Lynch.
25-26-27 .... Kinston
28-29-30 .... at Potomac
31 .... at Frederick

AUGUST

1-2-3 .... at Frederick
4-5-6 .... Winston-Salem
7-8-9-10 .... Frederick
11-12-13 .... at W-S
14-15-16-17 .... Salem
18-19-20 ..... Myrtle Beach
21-22-23 .... at Kinston
24-25-26-27 .... at M.B.
29-30-31 .... Potomac

SEPTEMBER

1 .... Potomac

Winston-Salem

APRIL

4-5-6 .... at Kinston
8-9-10 .... Lynchburg
11-12-13 .... Salem
14-15-16 .... at M.B.
17-18-19-20 ...... Frederick
21-22-23 .... Potomac
25-26-27 ... at Wilmington
28-29-30 .... at Potomac

MAY

1-2-3-4 .... Wilmington
5-6-7 .... at Lynchburg
8 .... at Salem
9-10-11 .... Salem
12-13-14-15 ... Lynchburg
16-17-18 .... Kinston
20-21-22 .... at Frederick
23-24-25 .... at Kinston
26-27-28-29 .... M.B.
30-31 .... at Salem

JUNE

1 .... at Salem
2-3-4-5 ... at Myrtle Beach
6-7-8 .... Frederick
9-10-11 .... at Potomac
12-13-14-15 .... at Wilm.
17-18-19 .... Potomac
20-21-22 .... Wilmington
26-27-28 ..... at Lynchburg
29-30 .... at Salem

JULY

1 .... at Salem
2-3-4 .... Frederick
5-6-7 .... Kinston
9-10-11 .... at Frederick
12-13-14-15 .... at Kinston
17-18-19 ..... Myrtle Beach
21-22-23-24 .... Salem
25-26-27 .... at M.B.
28-29-30 .... Lynchburg
31 .... at Potomac

AUGUST

1-2-3 .... at Potomac
4-5-6 .... at Wilmington
7-8-9-10 .... Potomac
11-12-13 .... Wilmington
14-15-16-17 ...... at Lynch.
18-19-20 .... at Salem
21-22-23 ..... Myrtle Beach
25-26-27-28 .... Kinston
29-30-31 .... at Frederick

SEPTEMBER

1 .... at Frederick

FLORIDA STATE LEAGUE

Brevard County

APRIL

3 .... at St. Lucie
4 .... St. Lucie
5-6 .... at St. Lucie
7-8 .... at Jupiter
9-10 .... Daytona
11-12-13-14 .... Dunedin
15-16-17-18 ... at Sarasota
19-20 .... Palm Beach
21-22 .... Jupiter
23-24 .... at Vero Beach
25-26-27 .... at Daytona
28 .... Daytona
29-30 .... at Palm Beach

MAY

1 .... at Vero Beach
2-3-3 .... Vero Beach
5-6 .... at Vero Beach
7 .... Palm Beach
8-9-10-11 ... at Fort Myers
12-13-14-15 ... Clearwater
16-17-18-19 ... at Lakeland
20-21-22-23 .... Tampa
24-26 .... St. Lucie
27-28 .... Jupiter
29-30 .... at Jupiter
31 .... St. Lucie

JUNE

1 .... at Daytona
2 .... Daytona
3 .... at Daytona
4-5 .... at Palm Beach
6-7 .... Vero Beach
8 .... Palm Beach
9 .... St. Lucie
10-11 .... at St. Lucie
12 .... Daytona
16-17-18-19 .... Jupiter
20 .... at St. Lucie
21 .... St. Lucie
23 .... at St. Lucie
24-25-26-27 .... at C'water
28-29-30 .... Fort Myers

JULY

1 .... Fort Myers
2 .... St. Lucie
3 .... at St. Lucie
4 .... Vero Beach
5 .... at Vero Beach
7-8-9-10 .... at Daytona
11-12-13-14 ...... Lakeland
16-17 .... at Jupiter
18 .... at Vero Beach
19 .... Vero Beach
20-21 .... St. Lucie
22-23 .... Palm Beach
24-25 .... at Palm Beach
26-27-28-29 ...... Sarasota
30-31 .... at Tampa

AUGUST

1-2 .... at Tampa
4-5 .... Daytona
6-7 .... Vero Beach
8 .... at Daytona
9 .... Daytona
11-12 .... at Vero Beach
13-14-15-16 ... at Dunedin
18-19 .... at Palm Beach
20 .... Vero Beach
21 .... at Vero Beach
22-23 .... Vero Beach
24 .... at St. Lucie
25 .... St. Lucie
26 .... at St. Lucie
27-28 .... Daytona
29-30 .... at Jupiter

Clearwater

APRIL

3 .... Dunedin

4 .... at Dunedin
5 .... Dunedin
6 .... at Dunedin
7-8 .... at Tampa
9-10 .... at Lakeland
11-12-13-14 .... Jupiter
15-16 .... St. Lucie
17-18 .... at St. Lucie
19-20-21-22 .... at F.M.
23-24 .... Sarasota
25-26 .... at Sarasota
27 .... Tampa
28 .... at Tampa
29 .... Tampa
30 .... at Tampa

MAY

1-2 .... at Lakeland
3-3 .... Lakeland
5 .... at Dunedin
6-7 .... Dunedin
8-9-10-11 ... at Vero Beach
12-13-14-15 .... at Brevard
16-17-18-19 .. Palm Beach
20-21-22-23 ... at Daytona
24-25 .... Fort Myers
27-28 .... Lakeland
29 .... at Dunedin
30 .... Dunedin
31 .... at Dunedin

JUNE

1 .... at Dunedin
2-3 .... at Sarasota
4-5-6 .... Tampa
7 .... at Tampa
8-9 .... Sarasota
10 .... Dunedin
11-12 .... Fort Myers
16 .... at Tampa
17-18-19 .... Tampa
20-21-22 .... at Fort Myers
24-25-26-27 .... Brevard
28-29-30 .... Daytona

JULY

1 .... Daytona
2-3 .... at Lakeland
4-5 .... Lakeland
7-8 .... at Sarasota
9-10 .... Sarasota
11-12 .... St. Lucie
13-14 .... at St. Lucie
16-17-18-19 ... Fort Myers
20-21 .... at Tampa
22-23 .... Dunedin
24-25 .... at Dunedin
26-27-28-29 ... Vero Beach
30-31 .... at Palm Beach

AUGUST

1-2 .... at Palm Beach
4-5 .... at Dunedin
6-7 .... Dunedin
8-9 .... at Lakeland
11-12 .... Lakeland
13-14-15-16 ..... at Jupiter
18-19 .... Dunedin
20-21 .... Tampa
22-23 .... Sarasota
25-26 .... at Tampa
27-28 .... at Dunedin
29-30 .... at Sarasota
31 .... at Fort Myers

Daytona

APRIL

3-4 .... Vero Beach
5-6 .... at Vero Beach
7-8 .... Palm Beach
9-10 .... at Brevard County
11-12-13-14 .... Tampa
15-16-17-18 ... at Lakeland
19-20 .... at Jupiter
21-22 .... St. Lucie
23-24 .... at Palm Beach
25-26-27 ...... Brevard Cty.
28 .... at Brevard County
29-30 .... Jupiter

MAY

1-2 .... at St. Lucie
3-3 .... St. Lucie
5-6 .... Palm Beach
7 .... at Vero Beach
8-9-10-11 ...... at Sarasota
12-13-14-15 .... Dunedin
16-17-18-19 .... at F.M.
20-21-22-23 ... Clearwater
24-25 .... Jupiter
27-28 .... Vero Beach
29-30 .... at St. Lucie
31 .... at Palm Beach

JUNE

1 .... Brevard County
2 .... at Brevard County
3 .... Brevard County
4-5 .... Vero Beach
6 .... at Palm Beach
7-8 .... at Jupiter
9-10-11 ...... at Vero Beach
12 .... at Brevard County
16-17-18-19 .... at P.B.
20-21-22 .... Vero Beach
24-25-26-27 ... Fort Myers
28-29-30 ..... at Clearwater

JULY

1 .... at Clearwater
2-3 .... Vero Beach
4-5 .... at St. Lucie
7-8-9-10 ... Brevard County
11-12-13-14 ... at Dunedin
16-17 .... Palm Beach
18-19 .... at Jupiter
20-21 .... at Vero Beach
22-23 .... St. Lucie
24-25 .... Vero Beach
26-27-28-29 ...... at Tampa
30-31 .... Sarasota

AUGUST

1-2 .... Sarasota
4-5 ...... at Brevard County
6-7 .... at Jupiter
8 .... Brevard County
9 .... at Brevard County
11-12 .... St. Lucie
13-14-15-16 ...... Lakeland
17-18-19 ... at Vero Beach
20-21 .... Palm Beach
22-23 .... at St. Lucie
25-26 .... Jupiter
27-28 ... at Brevard County
29 .... Vero Beach
30 .... at Vero Beach

Dunedin

APRIL

3 .... at Clearwater
4 .... Clearwater
5 .... at Clearwater
6 .... Clearwater
7-8 .... Sarasota
9-10 .... Tampa
11-12-13-14 .... at Brevard
15-16-17-18 .... at V.B.
19-20 .... Lakeland
21-22 .... Sarasota
23-24-25-26 ... at Lakeland
27-28 .... at Sarasota
29-30 .... Fort Myers

MAY

1-2 .... at Tampa
3-3 .... Tampa
5 .... Clearwater
6-7 .... at Clearwater
8-9-10-11 .... Jupiter
12-13-14-15 ... at Daytona
16-17-18-19 ...... St. Lucie
20-21-22-23 .... P.B.
24-25 .... at Sarasota
27-28 .... at Tampa
29 .... Clearwater
30 .... at Clearwater
31 .... Clearwater

JUNE

1 .... Clearwater
2 .... Tampa
3 .... at Tampa
4-5-6-7 .... at Fort Myers
8-9 .... Fort Myers
10 .... at Clearwater
11-12 .... Lakeland
16-17 .... at Lakeland
18-19 .... Lakeland
20-21-22 .... at Tampa
24-25-26-27 .... at P.B.
28-29-30 .... Vero Beach

JULY

1 .... Vero Beach
2-3-4-5 .... at Fort Myers
7-8 .... Tampa
9-10 .... at Tampa
11-12-13-14 .... Daytona
16-17-18-19 ... at Sarasota
20-21 .... Lakeland
22-23 .... at Clearwater
24-25 .... Clearwater
26-27-28-29 ..... at Jupiter
30-31 .... at St. Lucie

AUGUST

1-2 .... at St. Lucie
4-5 .... Clearwater
6-7 .... at Clearwater
8-9-11-12 .... Sarasota
13-14-15-16 .... Brevard
18-19 .... at Clearwater
20-21-22-23 ... Fort Myers
25-26 .... at Lakeland
27-28 .... Clearwater
29-30-31 .... Tampa

Fort Myers

APRIL

3 .... Sarasota
4 .... at Sarasota
5 .... Sarasota
6 .... at Sarasota
7-8 .... Lakeland
9-10 .... Sarasota
11-12-13-14 .... at P.B.
15-16-17-18 ..... at Jupiter
19-20-21-22 ... Clearwater
23-24-25-26 .... Tampa
27-28 .... at Lakeland
29-30 .... at Dunedin

MAY

1-2-3-3 .... at Sarasota
5 .... Lakeland
6-7 .... at Lakeland
8-9-10-11 ..... Brevard Cty.
12-13-14-15 ... at St. Lucie
16-17-18-19 .... Daytona
20-21-22-23 ... Vero Beach
24-25 .... at Clearwater
27-28 .... Sarasota
29-30-31 .... at Tampa

JUNE

1 .... at Tampa
2-3 .... Lakeland
4-5-6-7 .... Dunedin
8-9 .... at Dunedin
10 .... at Lakeland
11-12 .... at Clearwater
16-17 .... at Sarasota
18-19 .... Sarasota
20-21-22 .... Clearwater
24-25-26-27 ... at Daytona
28-29-30 ... at Brevard Cty.

JULY

1 .... at Brevard County
2-3-4-5 .... Dunedin
7-8-9-10 .... at Lakeland
11-12-13-14 .... Jupiter
16-17-18-19 .... at C'water
20-21 .... Sarasota
22-23 .... at Tampa
24-25 .... Tampa
26-27-28-29 ...... St. Lucie
30-31 .... at Vero Beach

AUGUST

1-2 .... at Vero Beach
4-5-6-7 .... Lakeland
8-9 .... at Tampa
11-12 .... Tampa
13-14-15-16 .... P.B.
18-19 .... Sarasota
20-21-22-23 ... at Dunedin
25-26-27-28 ... at Sarasota
29 .... Lakeland
30 .... at Lakeland
31 .... Clearwater

Jupiter

APRIL

3-4 .... Palm Beach
5-6 .... at Palm Beach
7-8 .... Brevard County

9-10 .... St. Lucie
11-12-13-14 .... at C'water
15-16-17-18 ... Fort Myers
19-20 .... Daytona
21-22 ... at Brevard County
23-24 .... at St. Lucie
25-26 .... at Vero Beach
27-28 .... Vero Beach
29-30 .... at Daytona

MAY

1-2 .... Palm Beach
3-3 .... at Palm Beach
5-6-7 .... St. Lucie
8-9-10-11 .... at Dunedin
12-13-14-15 ...... at Tampa
16-17-18-19 ...... Sarasota
20-21-22-23 ...... Lakeland
24-25 .... at Daytona
27-28 ... at Brevard County
29-30 ...... Brevard County
31 .... at Vero Beach

JUNE

1 .... at Vero Beach
2-3 .... Vero Beach
4-5-6 .... at St. Lucie
7-8 .... Daytona
9-10 .... Palm Beach
11-12 .... at Palm Beach
16-17-18-19 .... at Brevard
20-21-22 .... Palm Beach
24-25-26-27 ... at Sarasota
28-29-30 .... Tampa

JULY

1 .... Tampa
2-3 .... at Palm Beach
4-5 .... Palm Beach
7-8 .... at Vero Beach
9-10 .... St. Lucie
11-12-13-14 .... at F.M.
16-17 ...... Brevard County
18-19 .... Daytona
20-21 .... at Palm Beach
22-23 .... Vero Beach
24-25 .... at St. Lucie
26-27-28-29 .... Dunedin
30-31 .... at Lakeland

AUGUST

1-2 .... at Lakeland
4-5 .... at Vero Beach
6-7 .... Daytona
8-9 .... Palm Beach
11-12 .... at Palm Beach
13-14-15-16 ... Clearwater
18-19 .... at St. Lucie
20-21 .... St. Lucie
22 .... Palm Beach
23 .... at Palm Beach
25-26 .... at Daytona
27 .... St. Lucie
28 .... at St. Lucie
29-30 ...... Brevard County
31 .... at Palm Beach

Lakeland

APRIL

3 .... Tampa
4 .... at Tampa
5 .... Tampa
6 .... at Tampa
7-8 .... at Fort Myers
9-10 .... Clearwater
11-12-13-14 ... at St. Lucie
15-16-17-18 .... Daytona
19-20 .... at Dunedin
21-22 .... at Tampa
23-24-25-26 .... Dunedin
27-28 .... Fort Myers
29-30 .... Sarasota

MAY

1-2 .... Clearwater
3-3 .... at Clearwater
5 .... at Fort Myers
6-7 .... Fort Myers
8-9-10-11 .... at P.B.
12-13-14-15 ... Vero Beach
16-17-18-19 .... Brevard
20-21-22-23 ..... at Jupiter
24-25 .... Tampa
27-28 .... at Clearwater
29-30 .... at Sarasota
31 .... Sarasota

JUNE

1 .... Sarasota
2-3 .... at Fort Myers
4 .... Sarasota
5-6-7 .... at Sarasota
8 .... at Tampa
9 .... Tampa
10 .... Fort Myers
11-12 .... at Dunedin
16-17 .... Dunedin
18-19 .... at Dunedin
20-21-22 .... Sarasota
24-25-26-27 .... at V.B.
28-29-30 .... St. Lucie

JULY

1 .... St. Lucie
2-3 .... Clearwater
4-5 .... at Clearwater
7-8-9-10 .... Fort Myers
11-12-13-14 .... at Brevard
16-17-18-19 .... Tampa
20-21 .... at Dunedin
22-23-24-25 ... at Sarasota
26-27-28-29 .... P.B.
30-31 .... Jupiter

AUGUST

1-2 .... Jupiter
4-5-6-7 .... at Fort Myers
8-9 .... Clearwater
11-12 .... at Clearwater
13-14-15-16 ... at Daytona
18-19 .... at Tampa
20-21 .... Sarasota
22-23 .... at Tampa
25-26 .... Dunedin
27 .... Tampa
28 .... at Tampa
29 .... at Fort Myers
30 .... Fort Myers
31 .... at Sarasota

Palm Beach

APRIL

3-4 .... at Jupiter
5-6 .... Jupiter
7-8 .... at Daytona
9-10 .... at Vero Beach
11-12-13-14 ... Fort Myers
15-16-17-18 ...... at Tampa
19-20 ... at Brevard County
21-22 .... Vero Beach
23-24 .... Daytona
25-26 .... St. Lucie
27-28 .... at St. Lucie
29-30 ...... Brevard County

MAY

1-2 .... at Jupiter
3-3 .... Jupiter
5-6 .... at Daytona
7 .... at Brevard County
8-9-10-11 .... Lakeland
12-13-14-15 ...... Sarasota
16-17-18-19 .... at C'water
20-21-22-23 ... at Dunedin
24-25 .... Vero Beach
27-28 .... St. Lucie
29-30 .... at Vero Beach
31 .... Daytona

JUNE

1 .... St. Lucie
2-3 .... at St. Lucie
4-5 .... Brevard County
6 .... Daytona
7 .... at St. Lucie
8 .... at Brevard County
9-10 .... at Jupiter
11-12 .... Jupiter
16-17-18-19 .... Daytona
20-21-22 .... at Jupiter
24-25-26-27 .... Dunedin
28-29-30 .... at Sarasota

JULY

1 .... at Sarasota
2-3 .... Jupiter
4-5 .... at Jupiter
7-8 .... St. Lucie
9-10 .... at Vero Beach
11-12-13-14 .... Tampa
16-17 .... at Daytona
18-19 .... at St. Lucie
20-21 .... Jupiter
22-23 ... at Brevard County
24-25 ...... Brevard County
26-27-28-29 ... at Lakeland
30-31 .... Clearwater

AUGUST

1-2 .... Clearwater
4-5 .... St. Lucie
6-7 .... at St. Lucie
8-9 .... at Jupiter
11-12 .... Jupiter
13-14-15-16 .... at F.M.
18-19 ...... Brevard County
20-21 .... at Daytona
22 .... at Jupiter
23 .... Jupiter
25-26 .... Vero Beach
27-28 .... at Vero Beach
29 .... St. Lucie
30 .... at St. Lucie
31 .... Jupiter

St. Lucie

APRIL

3 .... Brevard County
4 .... at Brevard County
5-6 .... Brevard County
7-8 .... Vero Beach
9-10 .... at Jupiter
11-12-13-14 ...... Lakeland
15-16 .... at Clearwater
17-18 .... Clearwater
19-20 .... at Vero Beach
21-22 .... at Daytona
23-24 .... Jupiter
25-26 .... at Palm Beach
27-28 .... Palm Beach
29-30 .... Vero Beach

MAY

1-2 .... Daytona
3-3 .... at Daytona
5-6-7 .... at Jupiter
8-9-10-11 .... at Tampa
12-13-14-15 ... Fort Myers
16-17-18-19 ... at Dunedin
20-21 .... at Sarasota
22-23 .... Sarasota
24-26 ... at Brevard County
27-28 .... at Palm Beach
29-30 .... Daytona
31 .... at Brevard County

JUNE

1 .... at Palm Beach
2-3 .... Palm Beach
4-5-6 .... Jupiter
7 .... Palm Beach
8 .... at Vero Beach
9 .... at Brevard County
10-11 ...... Brevard County
12 .... at Vero Beach
16-17-18 ... at Vero Beach
19 .... Vero Beach
20 .... Brevard County
21 .... at Brevard County
23 .... Brevard County
24-25-26-27 .... Tampa
28-29-30 .... at Lakeland

JULY

1 .... at Lakeland
2 .... at Brevard County
3 .... Brevard County
4-5 .... Daytona
7-8 .... at Palm Beach
9-10 .... at Jupiter
11-12 .... at Clearwater
13-14 .... Clearwater
16-17 .... Vero Beach
18-19 .... Palm Beach
20-21 ... at Brevard County
22-23 .... at Daytona
24-25 .... Jupiter
26-27-28-29 .... at F.M.
30-31 .... Dunedin

AUGUST

1-2 .... Dunedin
4-5 .... at Palm Beach
6-7 .... Palm Beach
8 .... Vero Beach
9 .... at Vero Beach
11-12 .... at Daytona

13-14 .... Sarasota
15-16 .... at Sarasota
18-19 .... Jupiter
20-21 .... at Jupiter
22-23 .... Daytona
24 .... Brevard County
25 .... at Brevard County
26 .... Brevard County
27 .... at Jupiter
28 .... Jupiter
29 .... at Palm Beach
30 .... Palm Beach

Sarasota

APRIL

3 .... at Fort Myers
4 .... Fort Myers
5 .... at Fort Myers
6 .... Fort Myers
7-8 .... at Dunedin
9-10 .... at Fort Myers
11-12-13-14 ... Vero Beach
15-16-17-18 .... Brevard
19-20 .... at Tampa
21-22 .... at Dunedin
23-24 .... at Clearwater
25-26 .... Clearwater
27-28 .... Dunedin
29-30 .... at Lakeland

MAY

1-2-3-3 .... Fort Myers
5-6 .... Tampa
7 .... at Tampa
8-9-10-11 .... Daytona
12-13-14-15 .... at P.B.
16-17-18-19 ..... at Jupiter
20-21 .... St. Lucie
22-23 .... at St. Lucie
24-25 .... Dunedin
27-28 .... at Fort Myers
29-30 .... Lakeland
31 .... at Lakeland

JUNE

1 .... at Lakeland
2-3 .... Clearwater
4 .... at Lakeland
5-6-7 .... Lakeland
8-9 .... at Clearwater
10 .... at Tampa
11-12 .... Tampa
16-17 .... Fort Myers
18-19 .... at Fort Myers
20-21-22 .... at Lakeland
24-25-26-27 .... Jupiter
28-29-30 .... Palm Beach

JULY

1 .... Palm Beach
2-3-4 .... Tampa
5 .... at Tampa
7-8 .... Clearwater
9-10 .... at Clearwater
11-12-13-14 .... at V.B.
16-17-18-19 .... Dunedin
20-21 .... at Fort Myers
22-23-24-25 ...... Lakeland
26-27-28-29 .... at Brevard
30-31 .... at Daytona

AUGUST

1-2 .... at Daytona
4 .... Tampa
5-6-7 .... at Tampa
8-9-11-12 .... at Dunedin
13-14 .... at St. Lucie
15-16 .... St. Lucie
18-19 .... at Fort Myers
20-21 .... at Lakeland
22-23 .... at Clearwater
25-26-27-28 ... Fort Myers
29-30 .... Clearwater
31 .... Lakeland

Tampa

APRIL

3 .... at Lakeland
4 .... Lakeland
5 .... at Lakeland
6 .... Lakeland
7-8 .... Clearwater
9-10 .... at Dunedin
11-12-13-14 ... at Daytona
15-16-17-18 .... P.B.
19-20 .... Sarasota
21-22 .... Lakeland
23-24-25-26 .... at F.M.
27 .... at Clearwater
28 .... Clearwater
29 .... at Clearwater
30 .... Clearwater

MAY

1-2 .... Dunedin
3-3 .... at Dunedin
5-6 .... at Sarasota
7 .... Sarasota
8-9-10-11 .... St. Lucie
12-13-14-15 .... Jupiter
16-17-18-19 .... at V.B.
20-21-22-23 .... at Brevard
24-25 .... at Lakeland
27-28 .... Dunedin
29-30-31 .... Fort Myers

JUNE

1 .... Fort Myers
2 .... at Dunedin
3 .... Dunedin
4-5-6 .... at Clearwater
7 .... Clearwater
8 .... Lakeland
9 .... at Lakeland
10 .... Sarasota
11-12 .... at Sarasota
16 .... Clearwater
17-18-19 ..... at Clearwater
20-21-22 .... Dunedin
24-25-26-27 ... at St. Lucie
28-29-30 .... at Jupiter

JULY

1 .... at Jupiter
2-3-4 .... at Sarasota
5 .... Sarasota
7-8 .... at Dunedin
9-10 .... Dunedin
11-12-13-14 .... at P.B.
16-17-18-19 ... at Lakeland
20-21 .... Clearwater
22-23 .... Fort Myers
24-25 .... at Fort Myers
26-27-28-29 .... Daytona
30-31 ...... Brevard County

AUGUST

1-2 .... Brevard County
4 .... at Sarasota
5-6-7 .... Sarasota
8-9 .... Fort Myers
11-12 .... at Fort Myers
13-14-15-16 ... Vero Beach
18-19 .... Lakeland
20-21 .... at Clearwater
22-23 .... Lakeland
25-26 .... Clearwater
27 .... at Lakeland
28 .... Lakeland
29-30-31 .... at Dunedin

Vero Beach

APRIL

3-4 .... at Daytona
5-6 .... Daytona
7-8 .... at St. Lucie
9-10 .... Palm Beach
11-12-13-14 ... at Sarasota
15-16-17-18 .... Dunedin
19-20 .... St. Lucie
21-22 .... at Palm Beach
23-24 ...... Brevard County
25-26 .... Jupiter
27-28 .... at Jupiter
29-30 .... at St. Lucie

MAY

1 .... Brevard County
2-3-3 ... at Brevard County
5-6 .... Brevard County
7 .... Daytona
8-9-10-11 .... Clearwater
12-13-14-15 ... at Lakeland
16-17-18-19 .... Tampa
20-21-22-23 .... at F.M.
24-25 .... at Palm Beach
27-28 .... at Daytona
29-30 .... Palm Beach
31 .... Jupiter

JUNE

1 .... Jupiter
2-3 .... at Jupiter
4-5 .... at Daytona
6-7 ...... at Brevard County
8 .... St. Lucie
9-10-11 .... Daytona
12 .... St. Lucie
16-17-18 .... St. Lucie
19 .... at St. Lucie
20-21-22 .... at Daytona
24-25-26-27 ...... Lakeland
28-29-30 .... at Dunedin

JULY

1 .... at Dunedin
2-3 .... at Daytona
4 .... at Brevard County
5 .... Brevard County
7-8 .... Jupiter
9-10 .... Palm Beach
11-12-13-14 ...... Sarasota
16-17 .... at St. Lucie
18 .... Brevard County
19 .... at Brevard County
20-21 .... Daytona
22-23 .... at Jupiter
24-25 .... at Daytona
26-27-28-29 .... at C'water
30-31 .... Fort Myers

AUGUST

1-2 .... Fort Myers
4-5 .... Jupiter
6-7 ...... at Brevard County
8 .... at St. Lucie
9 .... St. Lucie
11-12 ...... Brevard County
13-14-15-16 ...... at Tampa
17-18-19 .... Daytona
20 .... at Brevard County
21 .... Brevard County
22-23 ... at Brevard County
25-26 .... at Palm Beach
27-28 .... Palm Beach
29 .... at Daytona
30 .... Daytona

MIDWEST LEAGUE

Battle Creek

APRIL

3-4-5-6 .... at W.M.
7-8-9 .... at Lansing
11-12-13-14 .... W.M.
15-16-17-18 ..... Quad City
19-20-21-22 .... at K.C.
24-25 .... at Fort Wayne
26-27 .... Fort Wayne
28-29-30 .... Lansing

MAY

1-2-3-4 .... Cedar Rapids
5-6-7-8 .... at Peoria
9-10-11-12 ... at Wisconsin
13-14-15-16 ... Fort Wayne
17-18-19-20 Kane County
22-23-24-25 .... at S.B.
26-27-28-29 .... Beloit
30-31 .... at Burlington

JUNE

1-2 .... at Burlington
3-4-5-6 .... Peoria
7-8-9-10 .... Dayton
12-13-14-15 ..... at Dayton
19-20-21-22 .... at C.R.
23-24-25-26 .... S.B.
27-28-29 .... Lansing
30 .... at Beloit

JULY

1-2-3 .... at Beloit
4-5-6 .... at Lansing
7-8-9-10 .... Burlington
11-12-13-14 .... Dayton
17-18-19-20 .... at S.B.
21-22-23-24 .... at W.M.
25-26-27-28 .... Clinton

29-30-31 .... at Dayton

AUGUST

1 .... at Dayton
2-3-4-5 .... South Bend
7-8-9-10 .... at Clinton
12-13-14-15 .... W.M.
16-17-18-19 ... Wisconsin
21-22-23-24 .... at Q.C.
25-26-27-28 .... at F.W.
29-30 .... Fort Wayne
31 .... at Fort Wayne

SEPTEMBER

1 .... at Fort Wayne

Beloit

APRIL

3-4-5-6 .... at Wisconsin
8-9-10 .... at Quad City
11-12-13-14 ..... Kane Cty.
15-16-17-18 ... Wisconsin
19-20-21-22 .... at F.W.
24-25-26-27 .... at Lansing
28-29-30 .... Quad City

MAY

1-2-3-4 .... West Michigan
5-6-7-8 .... at W.M.
9-10-11-12 .... at S.B.
13-14-15-16 .... S.B.
17-18-19-20 .... Lansing
22-23-24-25 .... at K.C.
26-27-28-29 .... at B.C.
30-31 .... Cedar Rapids

JUNE

1-2 .... Cedar Rapids
3-4-5-6 .... Kane County
7-8-9-10 .... at Clinton
12-13-14-15 .... Clinton
19-20-21-22 .... Peoria
23-24-25-26 ... Fort Wayne
27-28-29 ...... at Quad City
30 .... Battle Creek

JULY

1-2-3 .... Battle Creek
4-5-6 .... Quad City
7-8-9-10 .... at C.R.
11-12-13-14 .... Burlington
17-18-19-20 .... Peoria
21-22-23-24 .... at Burl.
25-26-27-28 .... at K.C.
29-30-31 .... at Peoria

AUGUST

1 .... at Peoria
2-3-4-5 .... Dayton
7-8-9-10 ...... at Wisconsin
12-13-14-15 ... Wisconsin
16-17-18-19 .... at Burl.
21-22-23-24 .... at C.R.
25-26-27-28 .... Clinton
29-30-31 .... at Dayton

SEPTEMBER

1 .... at Dayton

Burlington

APRIL

3-4-5-6 .... at Peoria
8-9-10 ..... at Kane County
11-12-13-14 ... Wisconsin
15-16-17-18 .... Lansing
19-20-22-23 .... at Q.C.
24-25-26-27 .... at W.M.
28-29-30 ..... Kane County

MAY

1-2-3-4 .... Fort Wayne
5-6-7-8 ...... at Fort Wayne
9-10-11-12 ...... at Lansing
13-14-15-16 ..... Quad City
17-18-19-20 .... Clinton
22-23-24-25 ...... at Peoria
26-27-28-29 ..... at Clinton
30-31 .... Battle Creek

JUNE

1-2 .... Battle Creek
3-4-5-6 .... South Bend
7-8 .... at Cedar Rapids
9 .... Cedar Rapids
10 .... at Cedar Rapids
12-13-14 .... Cedar Rapids
15 .... at Cedar Rapids
19-20-21-22 .... at Wisc.
23-24-25-26 ..... at Dayton
27-28-29 ..... Kane County
30 .... Clinton

JULY

1-2-3 .... Clinton
4-5-6 .... at Kane County
7-8-9-10 ... at Battle Creek
11-12-13-14 .... at Beloit
17-18-19-20 .... C.R.
21-22-23-24 .... Beloit
25-26-27-28 ..... Quad City
29-30-31 .... at Clinton

AUGUST

1 .... at Clinton
2-3-4-5 .... Peoria
7-8-9-10 .... Dayton
12-13-14-15 .... at C.R.
16-17-18-19 .... Beloit
21-22-23-24 .... at Wisc.
25-26-27-28 .... W.M.
29-30-31 ... at South Bend

SEPTEMBER

1 .... at South Bend

Cedar Rapids

APRIL

3-4-5-6 .... at Quad City
7-8-9 .... at Peoria
11-12-13-14 ..... Quad City
15-16-17-18 ... Fort Wayne
19-20-21-22 .... at Wisc.
24-25-26-27 .... K.C.
28-29-30 .... Peoria

MAY

1-2-3-4 ..... at Battle Creek
5-6-7-8 .... Dayton
9-10-11-12 .... W.M.
13-14-15-16 ..... at Dayton
17-18-19-20 .... S.B.
22-23-24-25 .... Clinton
26-27-28-29 .... at K.C.
30-31 .... at Beloit

JUNE

1-2 .... at Beloit
3-4-5-6 .... at W.M.
7-8 .... Burlington
9 .... at Burlington
10 .... Burlington
12-13-14 ..... at Burlington
15 .... Burlington
19-20-21-22 .... B.C.
23-24-25-26 .... at Lansing
27-28-29 .... at Peoria
30 .... at Fort Wayne

JULY

1-2-3 .... at Fort Wayne
4-5-6 .... Peoria
7-8-9-10 .... Beloit
11-12-13-14 .... at K.C.
17-18-19-20 .... at Burl.
21-22-23-24 ..... Quad City
25-26-27-28 .... at Wisc.
29-30-31 .... Wisconsin

AUGUST

1 .... Wisconsin
2-3-4-5 .... Clinton
7-8-9-10 .... at South Bend
12-13-14-15 .... Burlington
16-17-18-19 ..... at Clinton
21-22-23-24 .... Beloit
25-26-27-28 .... Lansing
29-30-31 .... at Clinton

SEPTEMBER

1 .... at Clinton

Clinton

APRIL

3-4-5-6 .... at Kane County
7-8-9 .... at Wisconsin
11-12-13-14 ... Fort Wayne
15-16-17-18 .... Peoria
19-20-21-22 .... at W.M.
24-25-26-27 ...... at Peoria
28-29-30 .... Wisconsin

MAY

1-2-3-4 .... Lansing
5-6-7-8 .... at Quad City
9-10-11-12 .... Dayton
13-14-15-16 .... Peoria
17-18-19-20 .... at Burl.
22-23-24-25 .... at C.R.
26-27-28-29 .... Burlington
30-31 .... South Bend

JUNE

1-2 .... South Bend
3-4-5-6 .... at Dayton
7-8-9-10 .... Beloit
12-13-14-15 .... at Beloit
19-20-21-22 .... at Q.C.
23-24-25-26 .... W.M.
27-28-29 .... Wisconsin
30 .... at Burlington

JULY

1-2-3 .... at Burlington
4-5-6 .... at Wisconsin
7-8-9-10 ...... Kane County
11-12-13-14 ..... Quad City
17-18-19-20 .... K.C.
21-22-23-24 .... at S.B.
25-26-27-28 .... at B.C.
29-30-31 .... Burlington

AUGUST

1 .... Burlington
2-3-4-5 ... at Cedar Rapids
7-8-9-10 .... Battle Creek
12-13-14-15 .... at F.W.
16-17-18-19 .... C.R.
21-22-23-24 .... at Lansing
25-26-27-28 .... at Beloit
29-30-31 .... Cedar Rapids

SEPTEMBER

1 .... Cedar Rapids

Dayton

APRIL

3-4-5-6 ...... at Fort Wayne
7-8-9 .... at West Michigan
11-12-13-14 .... Peoria
15-16-17-18 .... K.C.
19-20-21-22 .... at Lansing
24-25-26-27 .... at Q.C.
28-29-30 ... West Michigan

MAY

1-2-3-4 .... Wisconsin
5-6-7-8 ... at Cedar Rapids
9-10-11-12 .... at Clinton
13-14-15-16 .... C.R.
17-18-19-20 ... Fort Wayne
22-23-24-25 .... at Lansing
26-27 .... at South Bend
28-29 .... South Bend
30-31 .... Lansing

JUNE

1-2 .... Lansing
3-4-5-6 .... Clinton
7-8-9-10 ... at Battle Creek
12-13-14-15 .... B.C.
19-20-21-22 ... Fort Wayne
23-24-25-26 .... Burlington
27-28-29 ... at W. Michigan
30 .... at South Bend

JULY

1-2-3 .... at South Bend
5-5-6 .... West Michigan
7-8-9-10 ...... at Wisconsin
11-12-13-14 .... at B.C.
17-18-19-20 .... Lansing
21-22-23-24 .... at K.C.
25-26-27-28 ...... at Peoria
29-30-31 .... Battle Creek

AUGUST

1 .... Battle Creek
2-3-4-5 .... at Beloit
7-8-9-10 ...... at Burlington
11-12-13-14 ..... Quad City
16-17-18-19 .... at F.W.
21-22-23-24-25-26 ... S.B.
27-28 .... at South Bend
29-30-31 .... Beloit

SEPTEMBER

1 .... Beloit

Fort Wayne

APRIL

3-4-5-6 .... Dayton
7-8-9 .... South Bend
11-12-13-14 ..... at Clinton
15-16-17-18 .... at C.R.
19-20-21-22 .... Beloit
24-25 .... Battle Creek
26-27 .... at Battle Creek
28-29-30 ... at South Bend

MAY

1-2-3-4 .... at Burlington

5-6-7-8 .... Burlington
9-10-11-12 ... Kane County
13-14-15-16 .... at B.C.
17-18-19-20 ..... at Dayton
22-23-24-25 ..... Quad City
26-27-28-29 ... Wisconsin
30-31 .... at Peoria

JUNE

1-2 .... at Peoria
3-4-5-6 .... at Wisconsin
7-8-9-10 .... Peoria
12-13-14-15 .... Lansing
19-20-21-22 ..... at Dayton
23-24-25-26 .... at Beloit
27-28-29 .... South Bend
30 .... Cedar Rapids

JULY

1-2-3 .... Cedar Rapids
4-5-6 .... at South Bend
7-8-9-10 .... at Quad City
11-12-13-14 .... Lansing
17-18-19-20 .... W.M.
21-22-23-24 .... at Lansing
25-26-27-28 .... at W.M.
29-30-31 ... West Michigan

AUGUST

1 .... West Michigan
2-3-4-5 .... at Kane County
7-8-9-10 .... at Lansing
12-13-14-15 .... Clinton
16-17-18-19 .... Dayton
21-22-23-24 .... at W.M.
25-26-27-28 .... B.C.
29-30 .... at Battle Creek
31 .... Battle Creek

SEPTEMBER

1 .... Battle Creek

Kane County

APRIL

3-4-5-6 .... Clinton
8-9-10 .... Burlington
11-12-13-14 .... at Beloit
15-16-17-18 ..... at Dayton
19-20-21-22 .... B.C.
24-25-26-27 .... at C.R.
28-29-30 ..... at Burlington

MAY

1-2-3-4 .... Peoria
5-6-7-8 .... South Bend
9-10-11-12 at Fort Wayne
13-14-15-16 .... W.M.
17-18-19-20 .... at B.C.
22-23-24-25 .... Beloit
26-27-28-29 .... C.R.
30-31 .... at Quad City

JUNE

1-2 .... at Quad City
3-4-5-6 .... at Beloit
7-8-9-10 .... at W.M.
12-13-14-15 ... Wisconsin
19-20-21-22 .... at Lansing
23-24-25-26 ..... Quad City
27-28-29 ..... at Burlington
30 .... at Peoria

JULY

1-2-3 .... at Peoria
4-5-6 .... Burlington
7-8-9-10 .... at Clinton
11-12-13-14 .... C.R.
17-18-19-20 ..... at Clinton
21-22-23-24 .... Dayton
25-26-27-28 .... Beloit
29-30-31 ...... at Quad City

AUGUST

1 .... at Quad City
2-3-4-5 .... Fort Wayne
7-8-9-10 .... Quad City
11-12-13-14 .... at S.B.
16-17-18-19 .... Lansing
21-22-23-24 ...... at Peoria
25-26-27-28 .... at Wisc.
29-30-31 .... Wisconsin

SEPTEMBER

1 .... Wisconsin

Lansing

APRIL

3-4-5-6 .... South Bend
7-8-9 .... Battle Creek
11-12-13-14 .... at S.B.
15-16-17-18 .... at Burl.
19-20-21-22 .... Dayton
24-25-26-27 .... Beloit
28-29-30 ... at Battle Creek

MAY

1-2-3-4 .... at Clinton
5-6-7-8 .... Wisconsin
9-10-11-12 ...... Burlington
13-14-15-16 .... at Wisc.
17-18-19-20 .... at Beloit
22-23-24-25 .... Dayton
26-27-28-29 .... Peoria
30-31 .... at Dayton

JUNE

1-2 .... at Dayton
3-4-5-6 .... at Quad City
7-8-9-10 .... Quad City
12-13-14-15 .... at F.W.
19-20-21-22 .... K.C.
23-24-25-26 .... C.R.
27-28-29 ... at Battle Creek
30 .... at West Michigan

JULY

1-2-3 .... at West Michigan
4-5-6 .... Battle Creek
7-8-9-10 ... West Michigan
11-12-13-14 .... at F.W.
17-18-19-20 ..... at Dayton
21-22-23-24 ... Fort Wayne
25-26-27-28 .... S.B.
29-30-31 ... at South Bend

AUGUST

1 .... at South Bend
2-3-4-5 .... at W.M.
7-8-9-10 .... Fort Wayne
12-13-14-15 ...... at Peoria
16-17-18-19 .... at K.C.
21-22-23-24 .... Clinton
25-26-27-28 .... at C.R.
29-30-31 ... West Michigan

SEPTEMBER

1 .... West Michigan

Peoria

APRIL

3-4-5-6 .... Burlington
7-8-9 .... Cedar Rapids
11-12-13-14 ..... at Dayton
15-16-17-18 ..... at Clinton
19-20 .... at South Bend
21-22 .... South Bend
24-25-26-27 .... Clinton
28-29-30 .... at C.R.

MAY

1-2-3-4 .... at Kane County
5-6-7-8 .... Battle Creek
9-10-11-12 ... at Quad City
13-14-15-16 ..... at Clinton
17-18-19-20 .... Wisconsin
22-23-24-25 .... Burlington
26-27-28-29 .... at Lansing
30-31 .... Fort Wayne

JUNE

1-2 .... Fort Wayne
3-4-5-6 ..... at Battle Creek
7-8-9-10 .... at Fort Wayne
12-13-14-15 ..... Quad City
19-20-21-22 .... at Beloit
23-24-25-26 .... at Wisc.
27-28-29 .... Cedar Rapids
30 .... Kane County

JULY

1-2-3 .... Kane County
4-5-6 ...... at Cedar Rapids
7-8 .... at South Bend
9-10 .... South Bend
11-12-13-14 .... Wisconsin
17-18-19-20 .... at Beloit
21-22-23-24 .... at Wisc.
25-26-27-28 .... Dayton
29-30-31 .... Beloit

AUGUST

1 .... Beloit
2-3-4-5 .... at Burlington
7-8-9-10 ... West Michigan
12-13-14-15 .... Lansing
16-17-18-19 .... at W.M.
21-22-23-24 .... K.C.
25-26-27-28 ..... Quad City
29-30-31 ...... at Quad City

SEPTEMBER

1 .... at Quad City

Quad City

APRIL

3-4-5-6 .... Cedar Rapids
8-9-10 .... Beloit
11-12-13-14 .... at C.R.
15-16-17-18 .... at B.C.
19-20-22-23 .... Burlington
24-25-26-27 .... Dayton
28-29-30 .... at Beloit

MAY

1-2-3-4 ...... at South Bend
5-6-7-8 .... Clinton
9-10-11-12 .... Peoria
13-14-15-16 .... at Burl.
17-18-19-20 .... W.M.
22-23-24-25 .... at F.W.
26-27-28-29 .... at W.M.
30-31 .... Kane County

JUNE

1-2 .... Kane County
3-4-5-6 .... Lansing
7-8-9-10 .... at Lansing
12-13-14-15 ...... at Peoria
19-20-21-22 .... Clinton
23-24-25-26 .... at K.C.
27-28-29 .... Beloit
30 .... Wisconsin

JULY

1-2-3 .... Wisconsin
4-5-6 .... at Beloit
7-8-9-10 .... Fort Wayne
11-12-13-14 ..... at Clinton
17-18-19-20 .... Wisconsin
21-22-23-24 .... at C.R.
25-26-27-28 .... at Burl.
29-30-31 ..... Kane County

AUGUST

1 .... Kane County
2-3-4-5 .... at Wisconsin
7-8-9-10 ... at Kane County
11-12-13-14 ..... at Dayton
15-16-17-18 .... S.B.
21-22-23-24 .... B.C.
25-26-27-28 ...... at Peoria
29-30-31 .... Peoria

SEPTEMBER

1 .... Peoria

South Bend

APRIL

3-4-5-6 .... at Lansing
7-8-9 .... at Fort Wayne
11-12-13-14 .... Lansing
15-16-17-18 .... W.M.
19-20 .... Peoria
21-22 .... at Peoria
24-25-26-27 .... at Wisc.
28-29-30 .... Fort Wayne

MAY

1-2-3-4 .... Quad City
5-6-7-8 .... at Kane County
9-10-11-12 .... Beloit
13-14-15-16 .... at Beloit
17-18-19-20 .... at C.R.
22-23-24-25 .... B.C.
26-27 .... Dayton
28-29 .... at Dayton
30-31 .... at Clinton

JUNE

1-2 .... at Clinton
3-4-5-6 .... at Burlington
7-8-9-10 .... Wisconsin
12-13-14-15 .... W.M.
19-20-21-22 .... at W.M.
23-24-25-26 .... at B.C.
27-28-29 ... at Fort Wayne
30 .... Dayton

JULY

1-2-3 .... Dayton
4-5-6 .... Fort Wayne
7-8 .... Peoria
9-10 .... at Peoria
11-12-13-14 .... at W.M.
17-18-19-20 .... B.C.
21-22-23-24 .... Clinton
25-26-27-28 .... at Lansing
29-30-31 .... Lansing

AUGUST

1 .... Lansing

2-3-4-5 ..... at Battle Creek
7-8-9-10 ..... Cedar Rapids
11-12-13-14 .... K.C.
15-16-17-18 .... at Q.C.
21-22-23-24-25-26 . at Day.
27-28 .... Dayton
29-30-31 .... Burlington

SEPTEMBER

1 .... Burlington

West Michigan

APRIL

3-4-5-6 .... Battle Creek
7-8-9 .... Dayton
11-12-13-14 .... at B.C.
15-16-17-18 .... at S.B.
19-20-21-22 .... Clinton
24-25-26-27 .... Burlington
28-29-30 .... at Dayton

MAY

1-2-3-4 .... at Beloit
5-6-7-8 .... Beloit
9-10-11-12 .... at C.R.
13-14-15-16 .... at K.C.
17-18-19-20 .... at Q.C.
22-23-24-25 ... Wisconsin
26-27-28-29 ..... Quad City
30-31 .... at Wisconsin

JUNE

1-2 .... at Wisconsin
3-4-5-6 .... Cedar Rapids
7-8-9-10 .... Kane County
12-13-14-15 .... at S.B.
19-20-21-22 .... S.B.
23-24-25-26 ..... at Clinton
27-28-29 .... Dayton
30 .... Lansing

JULY

1-2-3 .... Lansing
5-5-6 .... at Dayton
7-8-9-10 .... at Lansing
11-12-13-14 .... S.B.
17-18-19-20 .... at F.W.
21-22-23-24 .... B.C.
25-26-27-28 ... Fort Wayne
29-30-31 ... at Fort Wayne

AUGUST

1 .... at Fort Wayne
2-3-4-5 .... Lansing
7-8-9-10 .... at Peoria
12-13-14-15 .... at B.C.
16-17-18-19 .... Peoria
21-22-23-24 ... Fort Wayne
25-26-27-28 .... at Burl.
29-30-31 .... at Lansing

SEPTEMBER

1 .... at Lansing

Wisconsin

APRIL

3-4-5-6 .... Beloit
7-8-9 .... Clinton
11-12-13-14 .... at Burl.
15-16-17-18 .... at Beloit
19-20-21-22 .... C.R.
24-25-26-27 .... S.B.
28-29-30 .... at Clinton

MAY

1-2-3-4 .... at Dayton
5-6-7-8 .... at Lansing
9-10-11-12 ... Battle Creek
13-14-15-16 .... Lansing
17-18-19-20 ...... at Peoria
22-23-24-25 .... at W.M.
26-27-28-29 .... at F.W.
30-31 .... West Michigan

JUNE

1-2 .... West Michigan
3-4-5-6 .... Fort Wayne
7-8-9-10 .... at South Bend
12-13-14-15 .... at K.C.
19-20-21-22 .... Burlington
23-24-25-26 .... Peoria
27-28-29 .... at Clinton
30 .... at Quad City

JULY

1-2-3 .... at Quad City
4-5-6 .... Clinton
7-8-9-10 .... Dayton
11-12-13-14 ...... at Peoria
17-18-19-20 .... at Q.C.
21-22-23-24 .... Peoria
25-26-27-28 .... C.R.
29-30-31 .... at C.R.

AUGUST

1 .... at Cedar Rapids
2-3-4-5 .... Quad City
7-8-9-10 .... Beloit
12-13-14-15 .... at Beloit
16-17-18-19 .... at B.C.
21-22-23-24 .... Burlington
25-26-27-28 .... K.C.
29-30-31 .... at K.C.

SEPTEMBER

1 .... at Kane County

SOUTH ATLANTIC LEAGUE

Asheville

APRIL

3-4-5-6 .... Capital City
7-8-9 .... Hickory
10-11-12-13 ... at Cap. City
14-15-16 .... at Hickory
17-18-19 ...... at South Ga.
21-22-23-24 .... Lexington
25-26-27-28 .... Char., WV
30 .... at Savannah

MAY

1-2 .... at Savannah
3-4-5 .... at Charleston, SC
6-7-8 .... Rome
9-10-11 ..... South Georgia
12-13-14-15 ..... at G'boro
16-17-18-19 .... at Kann.
21-22-23 .... Savannah
24-25-26 .... Hickory
27-28-29-30 ... at Augusta
31 .... at Hickory

JUNE

1-2 .... at Hickory
3-4-5-6 .... Augusta
7-8-9-10 .... at Rome
12-13-14-15 ..... Char., SC
17-18-19 ...... at South Ga.
20-21-22 .... Rome
26-27-28-29 ... Capital City
30 .... Hickory

JULY

1-2-3 .... Hickory
4-5-6-7 ...... at Capital City
9-10-11 .... Charleston, SC
12-13-14 ...... at Savannah
15-16-17 ... South Georgia
18-19-20 .... at Rome
21-22 .... at Hickory
23 .... Hickory
24-25-26 .... Savannah
28-29-30-31 ..... at L'wood

AUGUST

1-2-3-4 .... at Delmarva
6-7-8-9 .... Lake County
10-11-12-13 ... Hagerstown
15-16-17 .... at Char., SC
18-19-20 .... at Hickory
21-22-23-24 .... Augusta
25-26 .... at Hickory
27-28 .... Hickory
29-30-31 .... at Augusta

SEPTEMBER

1 .... at Augusta

Augusta

APRIL

3-4-5-6 .... Hickory
7-8-9 .... at Capital City
10-11-12-13 .... at Hickory
14-15-16 .... Capital City
17-18-19 .... at Char., SC
21-22-23-24 .... G'boro
25-26-27-28 ... Kannapolis
30 .... at Rome

MAY

1-2 .... at Rome
3-4-5 ..... at South Georgia
6-7-8 .... Savannah
9-10-11 .... Charleston, SC
12-13-14-15 .... at Lex.
16-17-18-19 ... at Char., WV
21-22-23 .... Rome
24 .... Capital City
25-26 .... at Capital City
27-28-29-30 ...... Asheville
31 .... Capital City

JUNE

1-2 .... Capital City
3-4-5-6 .... at Asheville
7-8-9-10 .... at Savannah
12-13-14-15 .... South Ga.
17-18-19 ...... at Savannah
20-21-22 ... Charleston, SC
26-27-28-29 .... Hickory
30 .... Capital City

JULY

1-2 .... Capital City
3 .... at Capital City
4-5-6-7 .... at Hickory
9-10-11 .... Rome
12-13-14 ...... at South Ga.
15-16-17 .... Savannah
18-19-20 .... at Char., SC
21-22-23 .... at Capital City
24-25-26 ... South Georgia
28-29-30-31 ... at Lake Cty.

AUGUST

1-2-3-4 ..... at Hagerstown
6-7-8-9 .... Lakewood
10-11-12-13 ..... Delmarva
14-15-16 .... at Rome
18-19 .... Capital City
20 .... at Capital City
21-22-23-24 ... at Asheville
25-26-27 .... at Capital City
28 .... Capital City
29-30-31 .... Asheville

SEPTEMBER

1 .... Asheville

Capital City

APRIL

3-4-5-6 .... at Asheville
7-8-9 .... Augusta
10-11-12-13 ...... Asheville
14-15-16 .... at Augusta
17-18-19 .... at Rome
21-22-23-24 ... Kannapolis
25-26-27-28 .... G'boro
30 .... at Charleston, SC

MAY

1-2 .... at Charleston, SC
3-4-5 .... at Savannah
6-7-8 .... South Georgia
9-10-11 .... Rome
12-13-14-15 ... at Char., WV
16-17-18-19 .... at Lex.
21-22-23 .... Char., SC
24 .... at Augusta
25-26 .... Augusta
27-28-29-30 .... at Hickory
31 .... at Augusta

JUNE

1-2 .... at Augusta
3-4-5-6 .... Hickory
7-8-9-10 ...... at South Ga.
12-13-14-15 ..... Savannah
17-18-19 .... at Rome
20-21-22 ... South Georgia
26-27-28-29 ... at Asheville
30 .... at Augusta

JULY

1-2 .... at Augusta
3 .... Augusta
4-5-6-7 .... Asheville
9-10-11 .... Savannah
12-13-14 .... at Char., SC
15-16-17 .... Rome
18-19-20 ...... at Savannah
21-22-23 .... Augusta
24-25-26 .... Char., SC

28-29-30-31 .... at Hag.

AUGUST

1-2-3-4 .... at Lake County
6-7-8-9 .... Delmarva
10-11-12-13 .... Lakewood
15-16-17 ...... at South Ga.
18-19 .... at Augusta
20 .... Augusta
21-22-23-24 .... Hickory
25-26-27 .... Augusta
28 .... at Augusta
29-30-31 .... at Hickory

SEPTEMBER

1 .... at Hickory

Charleston, SC

APRIL

3-4-5-6 ..... South Georgia
7-8-9 .... at Savannah
10-11-12-13 ... at South Ga.
14-15-16 .... Savannah
17-18-19 .... Augusta
21-22-23-24 .... at Hag.
25-26-27-28 ... at Lake Cty.
30 .... Capital City

MAY

1-2 .... Capital City
3-4-5 .... Asheville
6-7-8 .... at Hickory
9-10-11 .... at Augusta
12-13-14-15 ..... Delmarva
16-17-18-19 .... Lakewood
21-22-23 .... at Capital City
24-25-26 ...... at Savannah
27-28-29-30 .... Rome
31 .... Savannah

JUNE

1-2 .... Savannah
3-4-5-6 .... at Rome
7-8-9-10 .... Hickory
12-13-14-15 ... at Asheville
17-18-19 .... Hickory
20-21-22 .... at Augusta
26-27-28-29 .... at Rome
30 .... at South Georgia

JULY

1-2-3 ..... at South Georgia
4-5-6-7 .... Rome
9-10-11 .... at Asheville
12-13-14 .... Capital City
15-16-17 .... at Hickory
18-19-20 .... Augusta
21-22-23 .... Rome
24-25-26 .... at Capital City
28-29-30-31 .... G'boro

AUGUST

1-2-3-4 .... Kannapolis
6-7-8-9 .... at Lexington
10-11-12-13 ... at Char., WV
15-16-17 .... Asheville
18-19-20 .... at Rome
21-22-23-24 ..... Savannah
25-26-27-28 .... South Ga.
29-30-31 ...... at Savannah

SEPTEMBER

1 .... at Savannah

Charleston, WV

APRIL

3-4-5-6 .... Delmarva
7-8-9 .... Lakewood
10-11-12-13 ... at Lake Cty.
14-15 .... at Lexington
17-18-19-20 .. Hagerstown
21-22-23-24 .... at Hickory
25-26-27-28 ... at Asheville
29-30 .... Lake County

MAY

1-2 .... Lake County
3-4-5-6 .... at Lakewood
7-8-9-10 .... at Delmarva
12-13-14-15 ... Capital City
16-17-18-19 .... Augusta
21-22-23 ... at Hagerstown
24-25 .... Lexington
26-27-28-29 .... G'boro
30-31 .... at Kannapolis

JUNE

1-2 .... at Kannapolis
3-4-5-6 ...... at Greensboro
7-8-9 .... at Lexington
10-11 .... Lexington
12-13-14-15 ... Kannapolis
16-17 .... at Lexington
20-21-22 .... Kannapolis
26-27-28-29 .... at Hag.
30 .... at Lake County

JULY

1-2-3 .... at Lake County
4-5-6-7 .... Lakewood
9-10 .... at Greensboro
11-12-13-14 .... at Kann.
15-16-17-18 .... Lexington
19-20-21-22 .... G'boro
24-25-26-27 ...... Lake Cty.
28-29-30-31 .... at Rome

AUGUST

1-2-3-4 .... at South Ga.
6-7-8-9 .... Savannah
10-11-12-13 ..... Char., SC
15-16-17-18 ... at Delmarva
19-20-21-22 ... at L'wood
23-24 .... at Greensboro
25-26-27-28 ... Hagerstown
29-30-31 .... Delmarva

SEPTEMBER

1 .... Delmarva

Delmarva

APRIL

3-4-5-6 .... at Char., WV
7-8-9 .... at Greensboro
10-11-12-13 ... Kannapolis
14-15 .... at Lake County
16-17-18-19 .... at Lex.
21-22-23-24 .... South Ga.
25-26-27-28 .... Rome
29-30 .... at Kannapolis

MAY

1-2 .... at Kannapolis
3-4-5-6 .... Greensboro
7-8-9-10 .... Char., WV
12-13-14-15 ... at Char., SC
16-17-18-19 ... at Savannah
21-22-23 .... Lexington
24-25-26-27 ... Hagerstown
28-29 .... at Lake County
30 .... at Hagerstown

JUNE

1-2 .... at Hagerstown
3-4-5-6 .... Lakewood
7-8-9-10 .... Lake County
12-13-14-15 ..... at L'wood
17-18 .... at Lake County
19-20-21-22 ...... Lake Cty.
26-27-28-29 .... G'boro
30 .... Kannapolis

JULY

1-2-3 .... Kannapolis
4-5-6-7 ...... at Greensboro
9-10-11 .... Hagerstown
12-13-14-15 ..... at L'wood
16-17-18 ... at Hagerstown
19-20-21-22 .... Lakewood
24-25-26-27 .... at Kann.
28-29-30-31 .... Hickory

AUGUST

1-2-3-4 .... Asheville
6-7-8-9 .... at Capital City
10-11-12-13 ... at Augusta
15-16-17-18 .... Char., WV
19-20-21-22 .... Lexington
23-24 .... at Lake County
25-26-27-28 .... at Lex.
29-30-31 ...... at Char., WV

SEPTEMBER

1 .... at Charleston, WV

Greensboro

APRIL

3-4-5-6 .... Hagerstown
7-8-9 .... Delmarva
10-11-12-13 ..... at L'wood
14-15 .... Kannapolis
17-18-19-20 ...... Lake Cty.
21-22-23-24 ... at Augusta
25-26-27-28 ... at Cap. City
29-30 .... Lakewood

MAY

1-2 .... Lakewood
3-4-5-6 .... at Delmarva
7-8-9-10 ... at Hagerstown
12-13-14-15 ...... Asheville
16-17-18-19 .... Hickory
21-22-23 ... at Lake County
24-25 .... Kannapolis
26-27-28-29 ... at Char., WV
30-31 .... at Lexington

JUNE

1-2 .... at Lexington
3-4-5-6 ... Charleston, WV
7-8-9-10 ..... at Kannapolis
12-13-14-15 .... Lexington
17-18-19 .... at Kannapolis
20-21-22 .... Lexington
26-27-28-29 ... at Delmarva
30 .... at Lakewood

JULY

1-2-3 .... at Lakewood
4-5-6-7 .... Delmarva
9-10 .... Charleston, WV
11-12-13-14 .... at Lex.
15-16-17-18 ... Kannapolis
19-20-21-22 ... at Char., WV
23-24-25-26 .... Lakewood
28-29-30-31 ... at Char., SC

AUGUST

1-2-3-4 .... at Savannah
6-7-8-9 ..... South Georgia
10-11-12-13 .... Rome
15-16-17-18 .... at Hag.
19-20-21-22 ... at Lake Cty.
23-24 ...... Charleston, WV
25-26-27-28 .... Lakewood
29-30-31 ...... Hagerstown

SEPTEMBER

1 .... Hagerstown

Hagerstown

APRIL

3-4-5-6 ...... at Greensboro
7-8-9 .... at Kannapolis
10-11-12-13 .... Lexington
14-15 .... Lakewood
17-18-19-20 ... at Char., WV
21-22-23-24 ..... Char., SC
25-26-27-28 ..... Savannah
29-30 .... at Lexington

MAY

1-2 .... at Lexington
3-4-5-6 .... Kannapolis
7-8-9-10 .... Greensboro
12-13-14-15 .... at Rome
16-17-18-19 ... at South Ga.
21-22-23 .... Char., WV
24-25-26-27 ... at Delmarva
28-29 .... Lakewood
30 .... Delmarva

JUNE

1-2 .... Delmarva
3-4-5-6 .... Lake County
7-8-9-10 ...... at Lakewood
12-13-14-15 ... at Lake Cty.
17-18-19-20 ...... at L'wood
21-22 .... Lakewood
26-27-28-29 .... Char., WV
30 .... Lexington

JULY

1-2-3 .... Lexington
4-5-6-7 .... at Kannapolis
9-10-11 .... at Delmarva
12-13-14-15 ...... Lake Cty.
16-17-18 .... Delmarva
19-20-21-22 ... at Lake Cty.
23-24-25-26 .... at Lex.
28-29-30-31 ... Capital City

AUGUST

1-2-3-4 .... Augusta
6-7-8-9 .... at Hickory
10-11-12-13 ... at Asheville
15-16-17-18 .... G'boro
19-20-21-22 ... Kannapolis
23-24 .... Lakewood
25-26-27-28 ... at Char., WV
29-30-31 ... at Greensboro

SEPTEMBER

1 .... at Greensboro

Hickory

APRIL

3-4-5-6 .... at Augusta
7-8-9 .... at Asheville
10-11-12-13 .... Augusta
14-15-16 .... Asheville

17-18-19 ...... at Savannah
21-22-23-24 .... Char., WV
25-26-27-28 .... Lexington
30 .... at South Georgia

MAY

1-2 .... at South Georgia
3-4-5 .... at Rome
6-7-8 .... Charleston, SC
9-10-11 .... Savannah
12-13-14-15 .... at Kann.
16-17-18-19 ..... at G'boro
21-22-23 ... South Georgia
24-25-26 .... at Asheville
27-28-29-30 ...... Cap. City
31 .... Asheville

JUNE

1-2 .... Asheville
3-4-5-6 ...... at Capital City
7-8-9-10 .... at Char., SC
12-13-14-15 .... Rome
17-18-19 .... at Char., SC
20-21-22 .... Savannah
26-27-28-29 ... at Augusta
30 .... at Asheville

JULY

1-2-3 .... at Asheville
4-5-6-7 .... Augusta
9-10-11 .... at South Ga.
12-13-14 .... at Rome
15-16-17 ... Charleston, SC
18-19-20 ... South Georgia
21-22 .... Asheville
23 .... at Asheville
24-25-26 .... Rome
28-29-30-31 ... at Delmarva

AUGUST

1-2-3-4 .... at Lakewood
6-7-8-9 .... Hagerstown
10-11-12-13 ...... Lake Cty.
15-16-17 ...... at Savannah
18-19-20 .... Asheville
21-22-23-24 ... at Cap. City
25-26 .... Asheville
27-28 .... at Asheville
29-30-31......... Capital City

SEPTEMBER

1 .... Capital City

Kannapolis

APRIL

3-4-5-6 .... Lake County
7-8-9 .... Hagerstown
10-11-12-13 ... at Delmarva
14-15 .... at Greensboro
16-17-18-19 .... Lakewood
21-22-23-24 ... at Cap. City
25-26-27-28 ... at Augusta
29-30 .... Delmarva

MAY

1-2 .... Delmarva
3-4-5-6 ..... at Hagerstown
7-8-9-10 ... at Lake County
12-13-14-15 .... Hickory
16-17-18-19 ...... Asheville
21-22-23 ..... at Lakewood
24-25 .... at Greensboro
26-27-28-29 .... Lexington
30 .... Charleston, WV

JUNE

1-2 .... Charleston, WV
3-4-5-6 .... at Lexington
7-8-9-10 .... Greensboro
12-13-14-15 ... at Char., WV
17-18-19 .... Greensboro
20-21-22 ...... at Char., WV
26-27-28-29 .... Lexington
30 .... at Delmarva

JULY

1-2-3 .... at Delmarva
4-5-6-7 .... Hagerstown
9-10 .... Lexington
11-12-13-14 .... Char., WV
15-16-17-18 ..... at G'boro
19-20-21-22 .... at Lex.
24-25-26-27 ..... Delmarva
28-29-30-31 .. at Savannah

AUGUST

1-2-3-4 .... at Char., SC
6-7-8-9 .... Rome
10-11-12-13 .... South Ga.
15-16-17-18 ... at Lake Cty.
19-20-21-22 .... at Hag.
23-24 .... Lexington
25-26-27-28 ...... Lake Cty.
29-30-31 .... at Lakewood

SEPTEMBER

1 .... at Lakewood

Lake County

APRIL

3-4-5-6 .... at Kannapolis
7-8-9 .... at Lexington
10-11-12-13 .... Char., WV
14-15 .... Delmarva
17-18-19-20 ..... at G'boro
21-22-23-24 ..... Savannah
25-26-27-28 ..... Char., SC
29-30 ... at Charleston, WV

MAY

1-2 ...... at Charleston, WV
3-4-5-6 .... Lexington
7-8-9-10 .... Kannapolis
12-13-14-15 ... at South Ga.
16-17-18-19 .... at Rome
21-22-23 .... Greensboro
24-25-26-27 ..... at L'wood
28-29 .... Delmarva
30 .... Lakewood

JUNE

1-2 .... Lakewood
3-4-5-6 ..... at Hagerstown
7-8-9-10 .... at Delmarva
12-13-14-15 ... Hagerstown
17-18 .... Delmarva
19-20-21-22 ... at Delmarva
26-27-28-29 .... Lakewood
30 .... Charleston, WV

JULY

1-2-3 .... Charleston, WV
4-5-6-7 .... at Lexington
9-10-11 .... Lakewood
12-13-14-15 .... at Hag.
16-17-18 ..... at Lakewood
19-20-21-22 ... Hagerstown
24-25-26-27 ... at Char., WV
28-29-30-31 .... Augusta

AUGUST

1-2-3-4 .... Capital City
6-7-8-9 .... at Asheville
10-11-12-13 .... at Hickory
15-16-17-18 ... Kannapolis
19-20-21-22 ... Greensboro
23-24 .... Delmarva
25-26-27-28 .... at Kann.
29-30-31 ...... at Lexington

SEPTEMBER

1 .... at Lexington

Lakewood

APRIL

3-4-5-6 .... at Lexington
7-8-9 ... at Charleston, WV
10-11-12-13 ... Greensboro
14-15 .... at Hagerstown
16-17-18-19 .... at Kann.
21-22-23-24 .... Rome
25-26-27-28 .... South Ga.
29-30 .... at Greensboro

MAY

1-2 .... at Greensboro
3-4-5-6 ... Charleston, WV
7-8-9-10 .... Lexington
12-13-14-15 ... at Savannah
16-17-18-19 ... at Char., SC
21-22-23 .... Kannapolis
24-25-26-27 ...... Lake Cty.
28-29 .... at Hagerstown
30-31 .... at Lake County

JUNE

1-2 .... at Lake County
3-4-5-6 .... at Delmarva
7-8-9-10 .... Hagerstown
12-13-14-15 ..... Delmarva
17-18-19-20 ... Hagerstown
21-22 .... at Hagerstown
26-27-28-29 ... at Lake Cty.
30 .... Greensboro

JULY

1-2-3 .... Greensboro
4-5-6-7 .... at Char., WV
9-10-11 .... at Lake County
12-13-14-15 ..... Delmarva
16-17-18 ...... Lake County
19-20-21-22 ... at Delmarva
23-24-25-26 ..... at G'boro
28-29-30-31 ....Asheville

AUGUST

1-2-3-4 .... Hickory
6-7-8-9 .... at Augusta
10-11-12-13 ... at Cap. City
15-16-17-18 .... Lexington
19-20-21-22 .... Char., WV
23-24 .... at Hagerstown
25-26-27-28 ..... at G'boro
29-30-31 .... Kannapolis

SEPTEMBER

1 .... Kannapolis

Lexington

APRIL

3-4-5-6 .... Lakewood
7-8-9 .... Lake County
10-11-12-13 .... at Hag.
14-15 ...... Charleston, WV
16-17-18-19 ..... Delmarva
21-22-23-24 ... at Asheville
25-26-27-28 .... at Hickory
29-30 .... Hagerstown

MAY

1-2 .... Hagerstown
3-4-5-6 ..... at Lake County
7-8-9-10 ...... at Lakewood
12-13-14-15 .... Augusta
16-17-18-19 ...... Cap. City
21-22-23 ...... at Delmarva
24-25 ... at Charleston, WV
26-27-28-29 .... at Kann.
30 .... Greensboro

JUNE

1-2 .... Greensboro
3-4-5-6 .... Kannapolis
7-8-9 .... Charleston, WV
10-11 ... at Charleston, WV
12-13-14-15 ..... at G'boro
16-17 ...... Charleston, WV
20-21-22 ... at Greensboro
26-27-28-29 .... at Kann.
30 .... at Hagerstown

JULY

1-2-3 .... at Hagerstown
4-5-6-7 .... Lake County
9-10 .... at Kannapolis
11-12-13-14 ... Greensboro
15-16-17-18 ... at Char., WV
19-20-21-22 ... Kannapolis
23-24-25-26 ... Hagerstown
28-29-30-31 ... at South Ga.

AUGUST

1-2-3-4 .... at Rome
6-7-8-9 .... Char., SC
10-11-12-13 ..... Savannah
15-16-17-18 ..... at L'wood
19-20-21-22 ... at Delmarva
23-24 .... at Kannapolis
25-26-27-28 ..... Delmarva
29-30-31 ...... Lake County

SEPTEMBER

1 .... Lake County

Rome

APRIL

3-4-5-6 .... at Savannah
7-8-9 ..... at South Georgia
11-12-13 .... Savannah
14-15-16 ... South Georgia
17-18-19 .... Capital City
21-22-23-24 ..... at L'wood
25-26-27-28 ... at Delmarva
30 .... Augusta

MAY

1-2 .... Augusta
3-4-5 .... Hickory
6-7-8 .... at Asheville
9-10-11 ...... at Capital City
12-13-14-15 ... Hagerstown
16-17-18-19 ...... Lake Cty.
21-22-23 .... at Augusta
24-25-26 ... South Georgia
27-28-29-30 ... at Char., SC
31 .... at South Georgia

JUNE

1-2 .... at South Georgia

3-4-5-6 ..... Charleston, SC
7-8-9-10 .... Asheville
12-13-14-15 .... at Hickory
17-18-19 .... Capital City
20-21-22 .... at Asheville
26-27-28-29 ..... Char., SC
30 .... Savannah

JULY

1-2-3 .... Savannah
4-5-6-7 .... at Char., SC
9-10-11 .... at Augusta
12-13-14 .... Hickory
15-16-17 .... at Capital City
18-19-20 .... Asheville
21-22-23 .... at Char., SC
24-25-26 .... at Hickory
28-29-30-31 .... Char., WV

AUGUST

1-2-3-4 .... Lexington
6-7-8-9 .... at Kannapolis
10-11-12-13 ..... at G'boro
14-15-16 .... Augusta
18-19-20 ... Charleston, SC
21-22-23-24 .. at South Ga.
25-26-27-28 .. at Savannah
29-30-31 ... South Georgia

SEPTEMBER

1 .... South Georgia

Savannah

APRIL

3-4-5-6 .... Rome
7-8-9 .... Charleston, SC
11-12-13 .... at Rome
14-15-16 .... at Char., SC
17-18-19 .... Hickory
21-22-23-24 ... at Lake Cty.
25-26-27-28 .... at Hag.
30 .... Asheville

MAY

1-2 .... Asheville
3-4-5 .... Capital City
6-7-8 .... at Augusta
9-10-11 .... at Hickory
12-13-14-15 .... Lakewood
16-17-18-19 ..... Delmarva
21-22-23 .... at Asheville
24-25-26 .... Char., SC
27-28-29-30 at South Ga.
31 .... at Charleston, SC

JUNE

1-2 .... at Charleston, SC
3-4-5-6 ..... South Georgia
7-8-9-10 .... Augusta
12-13-14-15 ... at Cap. City
17-18-19 .... Augusta
20-21-22 .... at Hickory
26-27-28-29 .. at South Ga.
30 .... at Rome

JULY

1-2-3 .... at Rome
4-5-6-7 ..... South Georgia
9-10-11 ...... at Capital City
12-13-14 .... Asheville
15-16-17 .... at Augusta
18-19-20 .... Capital City
21-22-23 ...... at South Ga.
24-25-26 .... at Asheville
28-29-30-31 ... Kannapolis

AUGUST

1-2-3-4 .... Greensboro
6-7-8-9 .... at Char., WV
10-11-12-13 at Lexington
15-16-17 .... Hickory
18-19-20 ... South Georgia
21-22-23-24 ... at Char., SC
25-26-27-28 .... Rome
29-30-31 .... Char., SC

SEPTEMBER

1 .... Charleston, SC

South Georgia

APRIL

3-4-5-6 .... at Char., SC
7-8-9 .... Rome
10-11-12-13 ..... Char., SC
14-15-16 .... at Rome
17-18-19 .... Asheville
21-22-23-24 ... at Delmarva
25-26-27-28 ..... at L'wood
30 .... Hickory

MAY

1-2 .... Hickory
3-4-5 .... Augusta
6-7-8 .... at Capital City
9-10-11 .... at Asheville
12-13-14-15 ...... Lake Cty.
16-17-18-19 ... Hagerstown
21-22-23 .... at Hickory
24-25-26 .... at Rome
27-28-29-30 ..... Savannah
31 .... Rome

JUNE

1-2 .... Rome
3-4-5-6 .... at Savannah
7-8-9-10 .... Capital City
12-13-14-15 ... at Augusta
17-18-19 .... Asheville
20-21-22 .... at Capital City
26-27-28-29 ..... Savannah
30 .... Charleston, SC

JULY

1-2-3 .... Charleston, SC
4-5-6-7 .... at Savannah
9-10-11 .... Hickory
12-13-14 .... Augusta
15-16-17 .... at Asheville
18-19-20 .... at Hickory
21-22-23 .... Savannah
24-25-26 .... at Augusta
28-29-30-31 .... Lexington

AUGUST

1-2-3-4 ... Charleston, WV
6-7-8-9 ...... at Greensboro
10-11-12-13 .... at Kann.
15-16-17 .... Capital City
18-19-20 ...... at Savannah
21-22-23-24 .... Rome
25-26-27-28 ... at Char., SC
29-30-31 .... at Rome

SEPTEMBER

1 .... at Rome

SHORT-SEASON CLASS A

NEW YORK-PENN LEAGUE

Aberdeen

JUNE
17-18-19 .... Brooklyn
20-21 ... at Hudson Valley
22-23-24 .... H.V.
25-26-27 .... at J'town
28-29 .... Staten Island
30 .... at Williamsport

JULY
1-2 .... at Williamsport
3-4 .... at Brooklyn
5-6-7 .... at Tri-City
9-10-11 .... W'port
12-13-14 .... Oneonta
15-16-17 .... at H.V.
18-19-20 ... Staten Island
21-22 .... New Jersey
23-24-25 .... Lowell
26-27-28 .... at N.J.
30-31 .... Brooklyn

AUGUST
1-2-3 .... New Jersey
4-5-6 .... at Brooklyn
7-8 .... Hudson Valley
9-10-11 .... Batavia
12-13-14 .... at W'port
15-16-17 .... at Auburn
18-19 .... at Staten Island
21-22-23 ...... at Vermont
24-25-26 .... at S.I.
27-28 .... at New Jersey
29-30-31 .... M.V.

SEPTEMBER
1-2-3 .... Williamsport

Auburn

JUNE
17-18-19 ...... Jamestown
20-21-22 .... at M.V.
23-24 .... at Jamestown
25-26-27 .... Vermont
28-29-30 .... at M.V.

JULY
1-2 .... Mahoning Valley
3 .... Batavia
4 .... at Batavia
5-6-7 .... Hudson Valley
9-10-11 .... at Tri-City
12-13-14 ...... at Brooklyn
15-16-17 ...... Jamestown
18 .... Batavia
19 .... at Batavia
20 .... Batavia
21-22 .... at M.V.
23-24-25 .... at S.I.
26 .... at Batavia
27 .... Batavia
28 .... at Batavia
30-31 .... at Jamestown

AUGUST
1 .... at Jamestown
2-3-4 .... Mahoning Valley
5 .... Batavia
6 .... at Batavia
7-8 .... Jamestown
9-10-11 .... at W'port
12-13-14 .... Oneonta
15-16-17 .... Aberdeen
18-19 .... at Jamestown
21-22-23 ...... New Jersey
24 .... Batavia
25 .... at Batavia
26 .... Batavia
27-28 ... Mahoning Valley
29-30-31 .... at Lowell

SEPTEMBER
1 .... at Batavia
2 .... Batavia
3 .... at Batavia

Batavia

JUNE
17-18-19 .... M.V.
20 .... Jamestown
21 .... at Jamestown
22 .... Jamestown
23-24 .... at M.V.
25-26-27 .... W'port
28 .... Jamestown
29 .... at Jamestown
30 .... Jamestown

JULY
1 .... at Jamestown
2 .... Jamestown
3 .... at Auburn
4 .... Auburn
5-6-7 .... at Lowell
9-10-11 ..... Staten Island
12-13-14 .... at H.V.
15-16-17 .... M.V.
18 .... at Auburn
19 .... Auburn
20 .... at Auburn
21-22 .... at Jamestown
23-24-25 .... Brooklyn
26 .... Auburn
27 .... at Auburn
28 .... Auburn
30-31 .... at M.V.

AUGUST
1 ...... at Mahoning Valley
2 .... at Jamestown
3 .... Jamestown
4 .... at Jamestown
5 .... at Auburn
6 .... Auburn
7-8 .... at M.V.
9-10-11 .... at Aberdeen
12-13-14 .... Tri-City
15-16-17 .... Vermont
18-19 ... Mahoning Valley
21-22-23 .... at Oneonta
24 .... at Auburn
25 .... Auburn
26 .... at Auburn
27 .... at Jamestown
28 .... Jamestown
29-30-31 ... at New Jersey

SEPTEMBER
1 .... Auburn
2 .... at Auburn
3 .... Auburn

Brooklyn

JUNE
17-18-19 ..... at Aberdeen
20-21 .... at New Jersey
22 .... at Staten Island
23 .... Staten Island
24 .... at Staten Island
25-26-27 .... Tri-City
28 .... at New Jersey
29 .... New Jersey
30 .... Staten Island

JULY
1 .... at Staten Island
2 .... Staten Island
3-4 .... Aberdeen
5-6-7 .... at Oneonta
9 .... New Jersey
10 .... at New Jersey
11 .... New Jersey
12-13-14 .... Auburn
15 .... at Staten Island
16 .... Staten Island
17 .... at Staten Island
18-19-20-21-22 .. at W'port
23-24-25 .... at Batavia
26-27-28 .... W'port
30-31 .... at Aberdeen

AUGUST
1 .... Staten Island
2 .... at Staten Island
3 .... Staten Island
4-5-6 .... Aberdeen
7-8 .... Williamsport
9-10-11 .... at Lowell
12-13-14 ...... Jamestown
15-16-17 .... H.V.
18-19 .... at H.V.
21-22-23 .... at M.V.
24 .... at New Jersey
25-26 .... New Jersey
27-28 .... Hudson Valley
29-30-31 .... Vermont

SEPTEMBER
1-2-3 ... at Hudson Valley

Hudson Valley

JUNE
17 .... New Jersey
18 .... at New Jersey
19 .... New Jersey
20-21 .... Aberdeen
22-23-24 ..... at Aberdeen
25-26-27 .... M.V.
28-29 .... Williamsport
30 .... at New Jersey

JULY
1 .... New Jersey
2 .... at New Jersey
3-4 .... Williamsport
5-6-7 .... at Auburn
9-10-11 .... at Vermont
12-13-14 .... Batavia
15-16-17 .... Aberdeen
18 .... New Jersey
19 .... at New Jersey
20 .... New Jersey
21 .... at Staten Island
22 .... Staten Island
23-24-25 .... at Tri-City
26 .... at Staten Island
27 .... Staten Island
28 .... at Staten Island
30 .... Staten Island
31 .... at Staten Island

AUGUST
1-2-3 ...... at Williamsport
4 .... at New Jersey
5 .... New Jersey
6 .... at New Jersey
7-8 .... at Aberdeen
9-10-11 .... Oneonta
12-13-14 .... Lowell
15-16-17 ...... at Brooklyn
18-19 .... Brooklyn
21 .... at Staten Island
22-23 .... Staten Island
24 .... Williamsport
25-26 ..... at Williamsport
27-28 .... at Brooklyn
29-30-31 .. at Jamestown

SEPTEMBER
1-2-3 .... Brooklyn

Jamestown

JUNE
17-18-19 .... at Auburn
20 .... at Batavia
21 .... Batavia
22 .... at Batavia
23-24 .... Auburn
25-26-27 .... Aberdeen
28 .... at Batavia
29 .... Batavia
30 .... at Batavia

JULY
1 .... Batavia
2 .... at Batavia
3-4 ... at Mahoning Valley
5-6-7 ...... at Williamsport
9-10-11 .... Lowell
12-13-14 ...... New Jersey
15-16-17 .... at Auburn
18-19-20 .... M.V.
21-22 .... Batavia
23-24-25 .... at Oneonta
26-27-28 .... M.V.
30-31 .... Auburn

AUGUST
1 .... Auburn
2 .... Batavia
3 .... at Batavia
4 .... Batavia

5-6 .... Mahoning Valley
7-8 .... at Auburn
9-10-11 .... at Vermont
12-13-14 ...... at Brooklyn
15-16-17 .... at S.I.
18-19 .... Auburn
21-22-23 .... Tri-City
24-25-26 .... at M.V.
27 .... Batavia
28 .... at Batavia
29-30-31 .... H.V.

SEPTEMBER

1-2-3 .... at M.V.

Lowell

JUNE

17-18-19 .... Tri-City
20-21-22 ...... at Vermont
23-24 .... Vermont
25-26-27 .... S.I.
28-29-30 .... at Oneonta

JULY

1-2 .... Oneonta
3-4 .... at Tri-City
5-6-7 .... Batavia
9-10-11 .... at Jamestown
12-13-14 .... at M.V.
15-16-17 .... at Oneonta
18-19-20 .... Tri-City
21-22 .... Oneonta
23-24-25 ..... at Aberdeen
26-27-28 .... Vermont
30-31 .... at Tri-City

AUGUST

1 .... at Tri-City
2-3-4 .... Vermont
5-6 .... at Oneonta
7-8 .... Tri-City
9-10-11 .... Brooklyn
12-13-14 .... at H.V.
15-16-17 .... at N.J.
18-19 .... at Tri-City
21-22-23 .... W'port
24-25-26 .... Oneonta
27-28 .... at Vermont
29-30-31 .... Auburn

SEPTEMBER

1-2-3 .... at Vermont

Mahoning Valley

JUNE

17-18-19 .... at Batavia
20-21-22 .... Auburn
23-24 .... Batavia
25-26-27 .... at H.V.
28-29-30 .... Auburn

JULY

1-2 .... at Auburn
3-4 .... Jamestown
5-6-7 .... at Vermont
9-10-11 .... Oneonta
12-13-14 .... Lowell
15-16-17 .... at Batavia
18-19-20 ... at Jamestown
21-22 .... Auburn
23-24-25 .... W'port
26-27-28 .... at J'town
30-31 .... Batavia

AUGUST

1 .... Batavia
2-3-4 .... at Auburn
5-6 .... at Jamestown
7-8 .... Batavia
9-10-11 ..... Staten Island
12-13-14 .... at N.J.
15-16-17 .... at Tri-City
18-19 .... at Batavia
21-22-23 .... Brooklyn
24-25-26 ...... Jamestown
27-28 .... at Auburn
29-30-31 ..... at Aberdeen

SEPTEMBER

1-2-3 .... Jamestown

New Jersey

JUNE

17 .... at Hudson Valley
18 .... Hudson Valley
19 .... at Hudson Valley
20-21 .... Brooklyn
22-23-24 .... at W'port
25-26-27 .... Oneonta
28 .... Brooklyn
29 .... at Brooklyn
30 .... Hudson Valley

JULY

1 .... at Hudson Valley
2 .... Hudson Valley
3 .... at Staten Island
4-5-6 .... Staten Island
7 .... at Staten Island
9 .... at Brooklyn
10 .... Brooklyn
11 .... at Brooklyn
12-13-14 ... at Jamestown
15-16-17 .... W'port
18 .... at Hudson Valley
19 .... Hudson Valley
20 .... at Hudson Valley
21-22 .... at Aberdeen
23-24-25 ...... at Vermont
26-27-28 .... Aberdeen
30-31 ..... at Williamsport

AUGUST

1-2-3 .... at Aberdeen
4 .... Hudson Valley
5 .... at Hudson Valley
6 .... Hudson Valley
7 .... Staten Island
8 .... at Staten Island
9-10-11 .... at Tri-City
12-13-14 .... M.V.
15-16-17 .... Lowell
18-19 .... Williamsport
21-22-23 .... at Auburn
24 .... Brooklyn
25-26 .... at Brooklyn
27-28 .... Aberdeen
29-30-31 .... Batavia

SEPTEMBER

1 .... at Staten Island
2 .... Staten Island
3 .... at Staten Island

Oneonta

JUNE

17-18-19 .... Vermont
20-21-22-23 ... at Tri-City
24 .... Tri-City
25-26-27 ... at New Jersey
28-29-30 .... Lowell

JULY

1-2 .... at Lowell
3-4 .... Vermont
5-6-7 .... Brooklyn
9-10-11 .... at M.V.
12-13-14 ..... at Aberdeen
15-16-17 .... Lowell
18-19-20 ...... at Vermont
21-22 .... at Lowell
23-24-25 ...... Jamestown
26-27-28 .... Tri-City
30-31 .... at Vermont

AUGUST

1 .... at Vermont
2 .... Tri-City
3 .... at Tri-City
4 .... Tri-City
5-6 .... Lowell
7-8 .... at Vermont
9-10-11 .... at H.V.
12-13-14 .... at Auburn
15-16-17 .... W'port
18-19 .... Vermont
21-22-23 .... Batavia
24-25-26 .... at Lowell
27 .... Tri-City
28 .... at Tri-City
29-30-31 ... Staten Island

SEPTEMBER

1-2 .... at Tri-City
3 .... Tri-City

Staten Island

JUNE

17-18-19 .... at W'port
20-21 .... Williamsport
22 .... Brooklyn
23 .... at Brooklyn
24 .... Brooklyn
25-26-27 .... at Lowell
28-29 .... at Aberdeen
30 .... at Brooklyn

JULY

1 .... Brooklyn
2 .... at Brooklyn
3 .... New Jersey
4-5-6 .... at New Jersey
7 .... New Jersey
9-10-11 .... at Batavia
12-13-14 .... Tri-City
15 .... Brooklyn
16 .... at Brooklyn
17 .... Brooklyn
18-19-20 ..... at Aberdeen
21 .... Hudson Valley
22 .... at Hudson Valley
23-24-25 .... Auburn
26 .... Hudson Valley
27 .... at Hudson Valley
28 .... Hudson Valley
30 .... at Hudson Valley
31 .... Hudson Valley

AUGUST

1 .... at Brooklyn
2 .... Brooklyn
3 .... at Brooklyn
4-5-6 .... Williamsport
7 .... at New Jersey
8 .... New Jersey
9-10-11 .... at M.V.
12-13-14 .... Vermont
15-16-17 ...... Jamestown
18-19 .... Aberdeen
21 .... Hudson Valley
22-23 ... at Hudson Valley
24-25-26 .... Aberdeen
27-28 .... at W'port
29-30-31 .... at Oneonta

SEPTEMBER

1 .... New Jersey
2 .... at New Jersey
3 .... New Jersey

Tri-City

JUNE

17-18-19 .... at Lowell
20-21-22-23 ..... Oneonta
24 .... at Oneonta
25-26-27 ...... at Brooklyn
28-29-30 ...... at Vermont

JULY

1-2 .... at Vermont
3-4 .... Lowell
5-6-7 .... Aberdeen
9-10-11 .... Auburn
12-13-14 .... at S.I.
15-16-17 .... Vermont
18-19-20 .... at Lowell
21-22 .... Vermont
23-24-25 .... H.V.
26-27-28 .... at Oneonta
30-31 .... Lowell

AUGUST

1 .... Lowell
2 .... at Oneonta
3 .... Oneonta
4 .... at Oneonta
5-6 .... at Vermont
7-8 .... at Lowell
9-10-11 .... New Jersey
12-13-14 .... at Batavia
15-16-17 .... M.V.
18-19 .... Lowell
21-22-23 ... at Jamestown
24-25-26 .... Vermont
27 .... at Oneonta
28 .... Oneonta
29-30-31 .... at W'port

SEPTEMBER

1-2 .... Oneonta
3 .... at Oneonta

Vermont

JUNE

17-18-19 .... at Oneonta
20-21-22 .... Lowell
23-24 .... at Lowell
25-26-27 .... at Auburn
28-29-30 .... Tri-City

JULY

1-2 .... Tri-City
3-4 .... at Oneonta
5-6-7 .... Mahoning Valley
9-10-11 ... Hudson Valley
12-13-14 .... at W'port

15-16-17 .... at Tri-City
18-19-20 .... Oneonta
21-22 .... at Tri-City
23-24-25 ...... New Jersey
26-27-28 .... at Lowell
30-31 .... Oneonta

AUGUST

1 .... Oneonta
2-3-4 .... at Lowell
5-6 .... Tri-City
7-8 .... Oneonta
9-10-11 .... Jamestown
12-13-14 .... at S.I.
15-16-17 .... at Batavia
18-19 .... at Oneonta
21-22-23 .... Aberdeen
24-25-26 .... at Tri-City
27-28 .... Lowell
29-30-31 ...... at Brooklyn

SEPTEMBER

1-2-3 .... Lowell

Williamsport

JUNE

17-18-19 ... Staten Island
20-21 .... at S.I.
22-23-24 ...... New Jersey
25-26-27 .... at Batavia
28-29 ... at Hudson Valley
30 .... Aberdeen

JULY

1-2 .... Aberdeen
3-4 .... at Hudson Valley
5-6-7 .... Jamestown
9-10-11 .... at Aberdeen
12-13-14 .... Vermont
15-16-17 ... at New Jersey
18-19-20-21-22 ... Brook.
23-24-25 .... at M.V.
26-27-28 ...... at Brooklyn
30-31 .... New Jersey

AUGUST

1-2-3 .... Hudson Valley
4-5-6 ..... at Staten Island
7-8 .... at Brooklyn
9-10-11 .... Auburn
12-13-14 .... Aberdeen
15-16-17 .... at Oneonta
18-19 .... at New Jersey
21-22-23 .... at Lowell
24 .... at Hudson Valley
25-26 .... Hudson Valley
27-28 .... Staten Island
29-30-31 .... Tri-City

SEPTEMBER

1-2-3 .... at Aberdeen

NORTHWEST LEAGUE

Boise

JUNE

17-18 .... Tri-City
19-20 ....at Tri-City
21-22-23-24-25 ... Spokane
26-27-28-29-30 .. at Everett

JULY

1-2-3 .... at Spokane
4-5-6-7 .... Tri-City
9 .... at Tri-City
10-11-12-13-14 .... at Van.
16-17-18-19-20 ... Eugene
21-22-23 ...... at Spokane
24-25-26-27-28 .... Van.
30-31 .... at Yakima

AUGUST

1 .... at Yakima
2-3-4-5-6 .... at S-K
7-8-9-10-11 .... Everett
12-13-14 .... Yakima
15-16-17-18-19 .... at Eug.
21-22-23 .... at Tri-City
24-25-26 .... Spokane
27-28-29 .... Yakima
30-31 .... at Yakima

SEPTEMBER

1 .... at Yakima
2-3-4 .... Spokane

Eugene

JUNE

18-19-20 .... at S-K
21-22-23-24-25 ... Tri-City
26-27-28-29-30 ..... at Yak.

JULY

1-2-3 .... Spokane
4-5-6 .... at Everett
7-8-9 .... at Vancouver
10-11-12-13-14 ... Yakima
16-17-18-19-20 ... at Boise
21-22-23 .... Everett
24-25-26-27-28 ... at Spo.
30-31 .... Everett

AUGUST

1 .... Everett
2-3-4-5-6 .... at Tri-City
7-8-9-10-11 ...... Spokane
12-13-14 .... at Everett
15-16-17-18-19 .... Boise
21-22 .... at S-K
23 .... S-K
24-25-26 .... Vancouver
27-28-29 ... at Vancouver
30-31 .... S-K

SEPTEMBER

1 .... at S-K
2-3-4 .... Vancouver

Everett

JUNE

18-19-20 .... Vancouver
21-22-23-24-25 ... at Spo.
26-27-28-29-30 .... Boise

JULY

1-2-3 .... at Vancouver
4-5-6 .... Eugene
7-8-9 .... at S-K
10-11-12-13-14 .... at T-C
16-17-18-19-20 ...... Spo.
21-22-23 .... at Eugene
24-25-26-27-28 ... Tri-City
30-31 .... at Eugene

AUGUST

1 .... at Eugene
2-3-4-5-6 .... Yakima
7-8-9-10-11 ...... at Boise
12-13-14 .... Eugene
15-16-17-18-19 ... at Yak.
21-22-23 .... Vancouver
24-25-26 .... S-K
27-28-29 .... at S-K
30-31 .... at Vancouver

SEPTEMBER

1 .... at Vancouver
2-3-4 .... S-K

Salem-Keizer

JUNE

18-19-20 .... Eugene
21-22-23-24-25 ... at Boise
26-27-28-29-30 ...... Spo.

JULY

1-2-3 .... at Eugene
4-5-6 .... Vancouver
7-8-9 .... Everett
10-11-12-13-14 ... at Spo.
16-17-18-19-20 ... Tri-City
21-22-23 ... at Vancouver
24-25-26-27-28 ... Yakima
30-31 .... at Vancouver

AUGUST

1 .... at Vancouver
2-3-4-5-6 .... Boise
7-8-9-10-11 .... at Yakima
12-13-14 .... Vancouver
15-16-17-18-19 .... at T-C
21-22 .... Eugene
23 .... at Eugene
24-25-26 .... at Everett
27-28-29 .... Everett
30-31 .... at Eugene

SEPTEMBER

1 .... Eugene
2-3-4 .... at Everett

Spokane

JUNE

18-19-20 .... at Yakima
21-22-23-24-25 ... Everett
26-27-28-29-30 ... at S-K

JULY

1-2-3 .... Boise
4-5-6 .... Yakima
7-8-9 .... at Yakima
10-11-12-13-14 .... S-K
16-17-18-19-20 ... at Eve.
21-22-23 .... Boise
24-25-26-27-28 ... Eugene
30-31 .... at Tri-City

AUGUST

1 .... at Tri-City
2-3-4-5-6 .... Vancouver
7-8-9-10-11 .... at Eugene
12-13-14 .... Tri-City
15-16-17-18-19 ... at Van.
21-22-23 .... Yakima
24-25-26 .... at Boise
27-28-29 .... at Tri-City
30-31 .... Tri-City

SEPTEMBER

1 .... Tri-City
2-3-4 .... at Boise

Tri-City

JUNE

17-18 .... at Boise
19-20 .... Boise
21-22-23-24-25 ... at Eug.
26-27-28-29-30 ...... Van.

JULY

1 .... Yakima
2 .... at Yakima
3 .... Yakima
4-5-6-7 .... at Boise
9 .... Boise
10-11-12-13-14 ... Everett
16-17-18-19-20 ... at S-K
21-22-23 .... Yakima
24-25-26-27-28 ... at Eve.
30-31 .... Spokane

AUGUST

1 .... Spokane
2-3-4-5-6 .... Eugene
7-8-9-10-11 .... at Van.
12-13-14 ...... at Spokane
15-16-17-18-19 .... S-K
21-22-23 .... Boise
24-25-26 .... at Yakima
27-28-29 .... Spokane
30-31 .... at Spokane

SEPTEMBER

1 .... at Spokane
2 .... Yakima
3-4 .... at Yakima

Vancouver

JUNE

18-19-20 .... at Everett
21-22-23-24-25 ... Yakima
26-27-28-29-30 .... at T-C

JULY

1-2-3 .... Everett
4-5-6 .... at S-K
7-8-9 .... Eugene
10-11-12-13-14 .... Boise
16-17-18-19-20 ... at Yak.
21-22-23 .... S-K
24-25-26-27-28 ... at Boise
30-31 .... S-K

AUGUST

1 .... S-K
2-3-4-5-6 ...... at Spokane
7-8-9-10-11 .... Tri-City
12-13-14 .... at S-K
15-16-17-18-19 ...... Spo.
21-22-23 .... at Everett
24-25-26 .... at Eugene
27-28-29 .... Eugene
30-31 .... Everett

SEPTEMBER

1 .... Everett
2-3-4 .... at Eugene

Yakima

JUNE

18-19-20 .... Spokane
21-22-23-24-25 ... at Van.
26-27-28-29-30 ... Eugene

JULY

1 .... at Tri-City
2 .... Tri-City
3 .... at Tri-City
4-5-6 .... at Spokane
7-8-9 .... Spokane
10-11-12-13-14 ... at Eug.
16-17-18-19-20 ...... Van.
21-22-23 .... at Tri-City
24-25-26-27-28 ... at S-K
30-31 .... Boise

AUGUST

1 .... Boise
2-3-4-5-6 .... at Everett
7-8-9-10-11 .... S-K
12-13-14 .... at Boise
15-16-17-18-19 ... Everett
21-22-23 ...... at Spokane
24-25-26 .... Tri-City
27-28-29 .... at Boise
30-31 .... Boise

SEPTEMBER

1 .... Boise
2 .... at Tri-City
3-4 .... Tri-City

ROOKIE LEAGUES
APPALACHIAN LEAGUE

Bluefield

JUNE
16 .... at Princeton
17-18-19 .... Princeton
20-21-22 ... at Elizabethton
23-24-25 .... Pulaski
26 .... Princeton
27 .... at Princeton
28 .... Princeton
29-30 .... at Burlington

JULY
1 .... at Burlington
3 .... Pulaski
4 .... at Pulaski
5-6 .... Danville
7-8 .... at Danville
9-10-11 ...... at Kingsport
12-13-14 ...... Martinsville
16-17-18 ..... Elizabethton
19-20-21 .... at Bristol
22-23-24 .... at J.C.
25-26-27 .... Danville
28 .... Pulaski
29-30 .... at Pulaski
31 .... Burlington

AUGUST
1-2 .... Burlington
3-4-5 .... at Princeton
7 .... Princeton
8 .... at Princeton
9-10-11 .... Kingsport
12-13-14 ... at Martinsville
15-16-17 .... at Danville
18-19-20 .... Bristol
21-22-23 ... Johnson City
24-25 .... at Pulaski

Bristol

JUNE
16 .... Elizabethton
17 .... at Elizabethton
18-19 .... at Kingsport
20-21-22 .... Burlington
23-24-25 .... Danville
26-27-28 .... at Pulaski
29-30 .... at Princeton

JULY
1 .... at Princeton
3 .... Kingsport
4 .... at Kingsport
5 .... Elizabethton
6 .... at Elizabethton
7 .... at Kingsport
8 .... Kingsport
9-10-11 ..... Johnson City
12-13-14 ... at Elizabethton
16-17-18 ... at Burlington
19-20-21 .... Bluefield
22-23 .... at Kingsport
24 .... Kingsport
25-26-27 ... at Martinsville
28-29-30 .... at Danville
31 .... Princeton

AUGUST
1-2 .... Princeton
3-4-5 .... Pulaski
7-8 .... at Kingsport
9-10-11 .... at J.C.
12-13-14 ..... Elizabethton
15-16-17 ...... Martinsville
18-19-20 ...... at Bluefield
21-22-23 .... Kingsport
24-25 .... Johnson City

Burlington

JUNE
16 .... at Danville
17 .... Danville
18 .... at Danville
19 .... Danville
20-21-22 .... at Bristol
23-24-25 .... at Kingsport
26-27-28 ...... Martinsville
29-30 .... Bluefield

JULY
1 .... Bluefield
3-4 .... Princeton
5-6 .... at Martinsville
7-8 .... Martinsville
9-10-11 .... at Princeton
12-13-14 .... at Danville
16-17-18 .... Bristol
19-20-21 ... Johnson City
22-23-24 .... at Pulaski
25-26-27 ..... Elizabethton
28-29-30 .... Kingsport
31 .... at Bluefield

AUGUST
1-2 .... at Bluefield
3-4-5 .... at Martinsville
7-8 .... Danville
9-10-11 .... Princeton
12 .... at Danville
13-14 .... Danville
15-16-17 ... at Elizabethton
18-19-20 .... at J.C.
21-22-23 .... Pulaski
24-25 .... at Princeton

Danville

JUNE
16 .... Burlington
17 .... at Burlington
18 .... Burlington
19 .... at Burlington
20-21-22 ..... at Princeton
23-24-25 .... at Bristol
26-27-28 .... Kingsport
29-30 .... Johnson City

JULY
1 .... Johnson City
3 .... Martinsville
4 .... at Martinsville
5-6 .... at Bluefield
7-8 .... Bluefield
9-10-11 .... at Martinsville
12-13-14 .... Burlington
16-17-18 .... Princeton
19-20-21 .... Pulaski
22-23-24 ... at Elizabethton
25-26-27 ...... at Bluefield
28-29-30 .... Bristol
31 .... at Johnson City

AUGUST
1-2 .... at Johnson City
3-4-5 .... at Kingsport
7-8 .... at Burlington
9-10-11 .... Martinsville
12 .... Burlington
13-14 .... at Burlington
15-16-17 .... Bluefield
18-19-20 .... at Pulaski
21-22-23 ..... Elizabethton
24 .... at Martinsville
25 .... Martinsville

Elizabethton

JUNE
16 .... at Bristol
17 .... Bristol
18 .... at Kingsport
19 .... Kingsport
20-21-22 .... Bluefield
23-24-25 ... at Martinsville
26 .... Johnson City
27-28 .... at Johnson City
29-30 .... at Kingsport

JULY
1 .... Kingsport
3 .... Johnson City
4 .... at Johnson City
5 .... at Bristol
6 .... Bristol
7 .... Johnson City
8 .... at Johnson City
9-10-11 .... Pulaski
12-13-14 .... Bristol
16-17-18 ...... at Bluefield
19-20-21 ..... at Princeton
22-23-24 .... Danville
25-26-27 ... at Burlington
28-29-30 ...... Martinsville
31 .... Kingsport

AUGUST
1-2 .... Kingsport
3 .... at Johnson City
4-5 .... Johnson City
7 .... at Johnson City
8 .... Johnson City
9-10-11 .... at Pulaski
12-13-14 .... at Bristol
15-16-17 .... Burlington
18-19-20 .... Princeton
21-22-23 .... at Danville
24-25 .... at Kingsport

Johnson City

JUNE
16 .... at Kingsport
17 .... Kingsport
18-19 .... Bristol
20-21-22 ... at Martinsville
23-24-25 .... Princeton
26 .... at Elizabethton
27-28 .... Elizabethton
29-30 .... at Danville

JULY
1 .... at Danville
3 .... at Elizabethton
4 .... Elizabethton
5 .... at Kingsport
6 .... Kingsport
7 .... at Elizabethton
8 .... Elizabethton
9-10-11 .... at Bristol
12-13-14 .... at Pulaski
16-17-18 ...... Martinsville
19-20-21 ... at Burlington
22-23-24 .... Bluefield
25 .... at Kingsport
26-27 .... Kingsport
28-29-30 ..... at Princeton
31 .... Danville

AUGUST
1-2 .... Danville
3 .... Elizabethton
4-5 .... at Elizabethton
7 .... Elizabethton
8 .... at Elizabethton
9-10-11 .... Bristol
12-13-14 .... Pulaski
15 .... at Kingsport
16 .... Kingsport
17 .... at Kingsport
18-19-20 .... Burlington
21-22-23 ...... at Bluefield
24-25 .... at Bristol

Kingsport

JUNE
16 .... Johnson City
17 .... at Johnson City
18 .... Elizabethton
19 .... at Elizabethton
20-21-22 .... Pulaski
23-24-25 .... Burlington
26-27-28 .... at Danville
29-30 .... Elizabethton

JULY
1 .... at Elizabethton
3 .... at Bristol
4 .... Bristol
5 .... Johnson City
6 .... at Johnson City
7 .... Bristol
8 .... at Bristol
9-10-11 .... Bluefield

12-13-14 .... Princeton
16-17-18 .... at Pulaski
19-20-21 ... at Martinsville
22-23 .... Bristol
24 .... at Bristol
25 .... Johnson City
26-27 .... at Johnson City
28-29-30 ... at Burlington
31 .... at Elizabethton

AUGUST

1-2 .... at Elizabethton
3-4-5 .... Danville
7-8 .... Bristol
9-10-11 .... at Bluefield
12-13-14 ..... at Princeton
15 .... Johnson City
16 .... at Johnson City
17 .... Johnson City
18-19-20 ...... Martinsville
21-22-23 .... at Bristol
24-25 .... Elizabethton

Martinsville

JUNE

16 .... Pulaski
17-18-19 .... at Pulaski
20-21-22 ... Johnson City
23-24-25 ..... Elizabethton
26-27-28 ... at Burlington
29-30 .... at Pulaski

JULY

1 .... at Pulaski
3 .... at Danville
4 .... Danville
5-6 .... Burlington
7-8 .... at Burlington
9-10-11 .... Danville
12-13-14 ...... at Bluefield
16-17-18 .... at J.C.
19-20-21 .... Kingsport
22-23-24 ..... at Princeton
25-26-27 .... Bristol
28-29-30 ... at Elizabethton
31 .... Pulaski

AUGUST

1-2 .... Pulaski
3-4-5 .... Burlington
7-8 .... Pulaski
9-10-11 .... at Danville
12-13-14 .... Bluefield
15-16-17 .... at Bristol
18-19-20 .... at Kingsport
21-22-23 .... Princeton
24 .... Danville
25 .... at Danville

Princeton

JUNE

16 .... Bluefield
17-18-19 ...... at Bluefield
20-21-22 .... Danville
23-24-25 .... at J.C.
26 .... at Bluefield
27 .... Bluefield
28 .... at Bluefield
29-30 .... Bristol

JULY

1 .... Bristol
3-4 .... at Burlington
5-6 .... at Pulaski
7-8 .... Pulaski
9-10-11 .... Burlington
12-13-14 .... at Kingsport
16-17-18 .... at Danville
19-20-21 ..... Elizabethton
22-23-24 ...... Martinsville
25-26-27 .... at Pulaski
28-29-30 ... Johnson City
31 .... at Bristol

AUGUST

1-2 .... at Bristol
3-4-5 .... Bluefield
7 .... at Bluefield
8 .... Bluefield
9-10-11 ..... at Burlington
12-13-14 .... Kingsport
15-16-17 .... Pulaski
18-19-20 ... at Elizabethton
21-22-23 ... at Martinsville
24-25 .... Burlington

Pulaski

JUNE

16 .... at Martinsville
17-18-19 ...... Martinsville
20-21-22 .... at Kingsport
23-24-25 ...... at Bluefield
26-27-28 .... Bristol
29-30 .... Martinsville

JULY

1 .... Martinsville
3 .... at Bluefield
4 .... Bluefield
5-6 .... Princeton
7-8 .... at Princeton
9-10-11 ... at Elizabethton
12-13-14 ... Johnson City
16-17-18 .... Kingsport
19-20-21 .... at Danville
22-23-24 .... Burlington
25-26-27 .... Princeton
28 .... at Bluefield
29-30 .... Bluefield
31 .... at Martinsville

AUGUST

1-2 .... at Martinsville
3-4-5 .... at Bristol
7-8 .... at Martinsville
9-10-11 .... Elizabethton
12-13-14 .... at J.C.
15-16-17 ..... at Princeton
18-19-20 .... Danville
21-22-23 ... at Burlington
24-25 .... Bluefield

Billings

JUNE

17-18 .... at Great Falls
19-20-21 .... Helena
23-24-25-26 ..... at Provo
27-28-29 .... at Ogden

JULY

1-2-3 .... Provo
4-5-6-7 .... Ogden
9-10-11 .... at Missoula
12-13-14 ... at Great Falls
15-16-17 .... Great Falls
18-19-20-21 .... at Helena
22-23-24-25 .... Missoula
26-27 .... Great Falls
28-29-30 ...... at Missoula
31 .... Helena

AUGUST

1 .... Helena
2-3-4-5 .... Missoula
6-7-8-9 .... at Helena
11-12-13-14 ... Idaho Falls
15-16-17 .... Casper
18-19-20 ... at Idaho Falls
21-22-23-24 .... at Casper
26-27-28 .... Helena
29-30-31 ... at Great Falls

SEPTEMBER

1-2 .... at Missoula
3-4-5 .... Great Falls

PIONEER LEAGUE

Casper

JUNE

17-18-19 ... at Idaho Falls
20-21-22 .... Ogden
23-24-25-26 .... at Helena
27-28-29 ...... at Missoula

JULY

1-2-3 .... Helena
4-5-6-7 .... Missoula
9-10-11-12 .... at Provo
14-15-16-17 .... Provo
18-19-20 ... at Idaho Falls
21-22-23-24 .... at Ogden
25-26-27 .... Idaho Falls
28-29 .... Ogden
30-31 .... at Provo

AUGUST

1-2 .... at Provo
3-4-5-6 .... Provo
7-8-9 .... Ogden
11-12-13-14 .... at G.F.
15-16-17 .... at Billings
18-19-20 .... Great Falls
21-22-23-24 .... Billings
26-27-28-29 .... at Ogden
30-31 .... at Idaho Falls

SEPTEMBER

1-2-3-4-5 ...... Idaho Falls

Great Falls

JUNE

17-18 .... Billings
19-20-21 .... Missoula
23-24-25-26 .... at Ogden
27-28-28 .... at Provo

JULY

1-2-3 .... Ogden
4-5-6-7 .... Provo
9-10-11 .... at Helena
12-13-14 .... Billings
15-16-17 .... at Billings
18-19-20-21 ... at Missoula
22-23-24-25 .... Helena
26-27 .... at Billings
28-29-30 .... at Helena
31 .... Missoula

AUGUST

1 .... Missoula
2-3-4-5 .... Helena
6-7-8-9 .... at Missoula
11-12-13-14 .... Casper
15-16-17 .... Idaho Falls
18-19-20 .... at Casper
21-22-23-24 .... at I.F.
26-27-28 .... Missoula
29-30-31 .... Billings

SEPTEMBER

1-2 .... at Helena
3-4-5 .... at Billings

Helena

JUNE

17-18 .... Missoula
19-20-21 .... at Billings
23-24-25-26 .... Casper
27-28-29 .... Idaho Falls

JULY

1-2-3 .... at Casper
4-5-6-7 ..... at Idaho Falls
9-10-11 .... Great Falls
12-13-14 .... Missoula
15-16-17 ...... at Missoula
18-19-20-21 .... Billings
22-23-24-25 .... at G.F.
26-27 .... at Missoula
28-29-30 .... Great Falls
31 .... at Billings

AUGUST

1 .... at Billings
2-3-4-5 ...... at Great Falls
6-7-8-9 .... Billings
11-12-13-14 ..... at Provo
15-16-17 .... at Ogden
18-19-20-21 .... Ogden
22-23-24 .... Provo
26-27-28 .... at Billings
29-30-31 .... Missoula

SEPTEMBER

1-2 .... Great Falls
3-4-5 .... at Missoula

Idaho Falls

JUNE

17-18-19 .... Casper
20-21-22 .... Provo
23-24-25-26 ... at Missoula
27-28-29 .... at Helena

JULY

1-2-3 .... Missoula
4-5-6-7 .... Helena
9-10-11-12 ...... at Ogden
14-15-16-17 .... Ogden
18-19-20 .... Casper

21-22-23-24 ..... at Provo
25-26-27 .... at Casper
28-29 .... Provo
30-31 .... Ogden

AUGUST

1-2 .... Ogden
3-4-5-6 .... at Ogden
7-8-9 .... Provo
11-12-13-14 ... at Billings
15-16-17 ... at Great Falls
18-19-20 .... Billings
21-22-23-24 ... Great Falls
25-26-27-29 ..... at Provo
30-31 .... Casper

SEPTEMBER

1-2-3-4-5 .... at Casper

Missoula

JUNE

17-18 .... at Helena
19-20-21 ... at Great Falls
23-24-25-26 ... Idaho Falls
27-28-29 .... Casper

JULY

1-2-3 .... at Idaho Falls
4-5-6-7 .... at Casper
9-10-11 .... Billings
12-13-14 .... at Helena
15-16-17 .... Helena
18-19-20-21 ... Great Falls
22-23-24-25 ... at Billings
26-27 .... Helena
28-29-30 .... Billings
31 .... at Great Falls

AUGUST

1 .... at Great Falls
2-3-4-5 .... at Billings
6-7-8-9 .... Great Falls
11-12-13-14 .... at Ogden
15-16-16 .... at Provo
18-19-20-21 .... Provo
22-23-24 .... Ogden
26-27-28 ... at Great Falls
29-30-31 .... at Helena

SEPTEMBER

1-2 .... Billings
3-4-5 .... Helena

Ogden

JUNE

17-18-19 .... at Provo
20-21-22 .... at Casper
23-24-25-26 ... Great Falls
27-28-29 .... Billings

JULY

1-2-3 .... at Great Falls
4-5-6-7 .... at Billings
9-10-11-12 ... Idaho Falls
14-15-16-17 .... at I.F.
18-19-20 .... Provo
21-22-23-24 .... Casper
25-26 .... at Provo
27 .... Provo
28-29 .... at Casper
30-31 .... at Idaho Falls

AUGUST

1-2 .... at Idaho Falls
3-4-5-6 .... Idaho Falls
7-8-9 .... at Casper
11-12-13-14 .... Missoula
15-16-17 .... Helena
18-19-20-21 .... at Helena
22-23-24 ...... at Missoula
26-27-28-29 .... Casper
30-31 .... Provo

SEPTEMBER

1-2-3 .... at Provo
4-5 .... Provo

Provo

JUNE

17-18-19 .... Ogden
20-21-22 ... at Idaho Falls
23-24-25-26 .... Billings
27-28-28 .... Great Falls

JULY

1-2-3 .... at Billings
4-5-6-7 ...... at Great Falls
9-10-11-12 .... Casper
14-15-16-17 .... at Casper
18-19-20 .... at Ogden
21-22-23-24 ... Idaho Falls
25-26 .... Ogden
27 .... at Ogden
28-29 .... at Idaho Falls
30-31 .... Casper

AUGUST

1-2 .... Casper
3-4-5-6 .... at Casper
7-8-9 .... at Idaho Falls
11-12-13-14 .... Helena
15-16-16 .... Missoula
18-19-20-21 at Missoula
22-23-24 .... at Helena
25-26-27-29 ... Idaho Falls
30-31 .... at Ogden

SEPTEMBER

1-2-3 .... Ogden
4-5 .... at Ogden

INDEPENDENT LEAGUES

INDEPENDENT LEAGUES

*Split-season champion

2002 STANDINGS

#Wild-card

ATLANTIC LEAGUE

NORTH	W	L	PCT	GB
*Bridgeport	71	55	.563	—
Long Island	65	61	.512	6
Nashua	54	71	.432	16½
Pennsylvania	34	91	.272	36½
SOUTH	**W**	**L**	**PCT**	**GB**
*Atlantic City	71	53	.573	—
#Camden	71	54	.568	½
#Newark	69	55	.556	2
Somerset	65	60	.520	6½

PLAYOFFS: Semifinals—Newark defeated Atlantic City 2-1 and Bridgeport defeated Camden 2-1 in best-of-3 series. **Finals**—Newark defeated Bridgeport 3-0 in best-of-5 series.

CENTRAL LEAGUE

EAST	W	L	PCT	GB
*Alexandria	59	36	.621	—
*Jackson	49	46	.516	10
Springfield/Ozark	45	51	.469	14½
Fort Worth	36	60	.375	23½
WEST	**W**	**L**	**PCT**	**GB**
*Edinburg	54	42	.563	—
*San Angelo	50	42	.543	2
Amarillo	46	50	.479	8
Rio Grande Valley	44	52	.458	10

PLAYOFFS: Semifinals—Jackson defeated Alexandria 3-1 and San Angelo defeated Edinburg 3-1 in best-of-5 series. **Finals**—San Angelo defeated Jackson 3-2 in best-of-5 series.

FRONTIER LEAGUE

EAST	W	L	PCT	GB
Washington	56	28	.667	—
#Richmond	53	31	.631	3
#Kalamazoo	46	38	.548	10
Canton	41	43	.488	15
Chillicothe	35	49	.417	21
Johnstown	30	54	.357	26
WEST	**W**	**L**	**PCT**	**GB**
Dubois County	52	32	.619	—
Rockford	45	39	.536	7
Cook County	40	44	.476	12
River City	39	45	.464	13
Gateway	34	50	.405	18
Evansville	33	51	.393	19

PLAYOFFS: Semifinals—Richmond defeated Dubois County 2-1 and Washington defeated Kalamazoo 2-0 in best-of-3 series. **Finals**—Richmond defeated Washington 3-1 in best-of-5 series.

NORTHERN LEAGUE

CENTRAL DIVISION

NORTH	W	L	PCT	GB
*Winnipeg	56	33	.629	—
Fargo-Moorhead	52	37	.584	4
Sioux Falls	41	49	.456	15½
St. Paul	39	50	.438	17
Duluth-Superior	36	54	.400	19½
SOUTH	**W**	**L**	**PCT**	**GB**
#Lincoln	55	36	.604	—
*Joliet	54	38	.587	1½
*Sioux City	46	43	.517	8
Schaumburg	35	53	.398	18½
Gary	35	55	.389	19½

PLAYOFFS: First Round—Sioux City defeated Joliet 3-0 and Winnipeg defeated Lincoln 3-2 in best-of-5 series. **Semifinals**—Winnipeg defeated Sioux City 3-1 in best-of-5 series. **Finals**—New Jersey (Eastern Division) defeated Winnipeg 3-1 in best-of-5 series.

EASTERN DIVISION

NORTH	W	L	PCT	GB
*Adirondack	52	38	.578	—
*Quebec	52	38	.578	—
Albany-Colonie	46	43	.517	5½
Berkshire	24	65	.270	27½
SOUTH	**W**	**L**	**PCT**	**GB**
*New Jersey	62	27	.697	—
#Elmira	54	36	.600	8½
Brockton	42	47	.472	20
Allentown	26	64	.289	36½

PLAYOFFS: First Round—New Jersey defeated Elmira 3-2 and Adirondack defeated Quebec 3-2 in best-of-5 series. **Semifinals**—New Jersey defeated Adirondack 3-2 in best-of-5 series. **Finals**—New Jersey defeated Winnipeg (Central Division) 3-1 in best-of-5 series.

SOUTHEASTERN LEAGUE

	W	L	PCT	GB
Pensacola	40	28	.588	—
Baton Rouge	39	29	.574	1
Montgomery	36	32	.529	4
Selma	31	35	.470	8
^Americus	10	17	.370	
$Ozark	8	23	.258	

^Suspended operations July 15
$Suspended operations July 18

PLAYOFFS: Pensacola 3-1, Montgomery 3-2, Baton Rouge 1-2, Selma 0-2 in double-elimination tournament; Pensacola defeated Montgomery in one-game championship final.

WESTERN LEAGUE

NORTH	W	L	PCT	GB
*Chico	55	35	.611	—
#Sonoma County	49	41	.544	6
Yuba-Sutter	43	47	.478	12
SOUTH	**W**	**L**	**PCT**	**GB**
*Long Beach	44	46	.489	—
Solano	42	48	.467	2
*Yuma	37	53	.411	7

PLAYOFFS: Semifinals—Long Beach defeated Yuma 3-2 and Chico defeated Sonoma County 3-1 in best-of-5 series. **Finals**—Chico defeated Long Beach 3-1 in best-of-5 series.

ARIZONA-MEXICO LEAGUE

Office Addresses: 105 E. San Antonio St., No. 377, El Paso, TX 79901; Carta Blanca Estadio, Avienda Reforma y Uruguay, Calle Reforma #1688, Colonia Barral, Ciudad Juarez, Chihuahua, Mexico 32032. **Telephone**: (623) 826-0174. **FAX**: (623) 321-7837. **E-Mail Address**: indyproball@aol.com. **Website**: www.arizonamexicoleague.com.

Year Founded: 2003.

President/Treasurer: Bob Lipp. **Vice President**: John Guy. **Secretary/Counsel:** Hank Lacey. **Secretary:** Alicia Barboza. **Office Manager:** Unavailable.

Directors: Alicia Barboza (Juarez), David Delk (Nogales), Abe Erdman Jr. (Cananea), John Guy (Bisbee-Douglas).

Regular Season: 72 games (split schedule).

Division Structure: None.

Member Clubs: Bisbee-Douglas (Arizona); Cananea (Sonora, Mexico); Juarez (Chihuahua, Mexico), Nogales (Arizona).

2003 Opening Date: May 30. **Closing Date**: Aug. 19.

Playoff Format: Top two teams meet in best-of-5 series for league championship.

All-Star Game: Unavailable.

Roster Limit: 25 total, 23 active. **Player Eligibility Rule**: No restrictions.

Brand of Baseball: Rawlings.

Official Statistician: SportsTicker-Boston, Boston Fish Pier, West Bldg. #1, Suite 302, Boston, MA 02210.

ATLANTIC LEAGUE

Mailing Address: 401 N. Delaware Ave., Camden, NJ 08102. **Telephone:** (856) 541-9400. **FAX:** (856) 541-9410. **E-Mail Address:** atllge@aol.com. **Website:** www.atlanticleague.com.

Year Founded: 1998.

Chief Executive Officer: Frank Boulton.

Executive Director: Joe Klein.

Vice Presidents: Rick Cerone (Newark), Mickey Herbert (Bridgeport).

Directors: Frank Boulton (Long Island), Rick Cerone (Newark), Chris English (Nashua), Mickey Herbert (Bridgeport), Steve Kalafer (Somerset), Peter Kirk (Keystone Baseball/Pennsylvania), Tony Rosenthal (Atlantic City), Steve Shilling (Camden).

2003 Opening Date: May 1. **Closing Date:** Sept. 14.

Regular Season: 126 games (split schedule).

Division Structure: North—Bridgeport, Long Island, Nashua, Pennsylvania. **South**—Atlantic City, Camden, Newark, Somerset.

Playoff Format: First-half division winners meet second-half winners in best-of-3 series. Winners meet in best-of-5 final for league championship.

All-Star Game: July 9 at Nashua.

Roster Limit: 25. **Eligibility Rule:** No restrictions.

Brand of Baseball: Rawlings.

Statistician: SportsTicker—Boston, Boston Fish Pier, West Bldg. #1, Suite 302, Boston, MA 02210.

ATLANTIC CITY
Surf

Office Address: 545 N. Albany Ave., Atlantic City, NJ 08401. **Telephone:** (609) 344-8873. **FAX:** (609) 344-7010. **E-Mail Address:** surf@acsurf.com. **Website:** www.acsurf.com.

Operated by: Jersey Shore Professional Baseball, Inc.

General Manager/Baseball Operations: Mario Perrucci. **Assistant GM/Director, Group Sales:** John Kiphorn. **Director, Media Relations/Marketing:** Chuck Betson. **Director, Ticket Sales:** Joe Harrington. **Director, Merchandising/Stadium Operations:** Danny Petrazzolo. **Director, Promotions/Community Relations:** Carl Grider. **Clubhouse Operations:** Unavailable.

Manager: Mitch Williams. **Coaches:** Tim Lindecamp, Pete Incaviglia.

Game Information

Radio Announcer: Unavailable. **No. of Games Broadcast:** Home-72, Away-54. **Flagship Station:** WUSS 1490-AM.

PA Announcer: Greg Maiuro. **Official Scorer:** Brian McCormick.

Stadium Name (year opened): The Sandcastle (1998). **Location:** Atlantic City Expressway to exit 2, east on Routes

40/322. **Standard Game Times:** 6:35 p.m.; Sun. 1:35, (May-June, Sept.) 5:05.
Visiting Club Hotel: Unavailable.

BRIDGEPORT
Bluefish

Office Address: 500 Main St., Bridgeport, CT 06604. **Telephone:** (203) 345-4800. **FAX:** (203) 345-4830. **E-Mail Address:** cromano@bridgeportbluefish.com. **Website:** www.bridgeportbluefish.com.

Operated by: Bridgeport Bluefish Professional Baseball Club, LLC.

Owners: Charlie Dowd, Mickey Herbert, Ken Paul.

President, Chief Executive Officer: Mickey Herbert. **Senior Vice President:** Ken Paul.

General Manager: Charlie Dowd. **Assistant GM:** Rick DelVecchio. **Senior Account Executive:** John Harris. **Account Executive:** Ian Boyle. **Manager, Community Relations/Merchandising:** John Farrell. **Manager, Public Relations/Marketing:** Chris Romano. **Manager, Ticketing:** Joe Skarupa. **Coordinator, Ticketing:** Rebecca Ramos. **Ticketing Assistant:** John Williams. **Manager, Group Sales:** Jennifer Davis. **Group Sales Coordinators:** Chris Domans, Megan Watson. **Controller:** Tony Scott. **Director, Operations:** John Cunningham. **Coordinator, Accounting:** Alison Mester. **Head Groundskeeper:** Craig Veeder.

Manager: Duffy Dyer. **Coaches:** Unavailable. **Trainer:** Pat LeGault.

Game Information

Radio Announcer: Jeff Holtz. **No. of Games Broadcast:** Unavailable. **Flagship Station:** WVOF 88.5-FM.

PA Announcer: Bill Jensen. **Official Scorer:** Al Carbone.

Stadium Name (year opened): The Ballpark at Harbor Yard (1998). **Location:** I-95 to exit 27, Route 8/25 to exit 1. **Standard Game Times:** 6:35 p.m., Sun. 1:35.

Visiting Club Hotel: Holiday Inn Bridgeport, 1070 Main St., Bridgeport, CT 06604. Telephone: (203) 334-1234.

CAMDEN
Riversharks

Office Address: 401 N. Delaware Ave., Camden, NJ 08102. **Telephone:** (856) 963-2600. **FAX:** (856) 963-8534. **E-Mail Address:** riversharks@riversharks.com. **Website:** www.riversharks.com.

Operated by: Camden Baseball, LLC.

Principal Owner: Steve Shilling.

General Manager: John Brandt. **Assistant GM, Operations:** Matt Kastel. **Assistant GM, Marketing:** David Brady. **Controller:** Ed Skomsky. **Community Relations:** Bree Maddocks. **Office Manager:** Patty MacLuckie. **Accounting:** Mary Anne Callan, Shannon Sloan. **Receptionist:** Dolores Rozier. **Ticket Operations:** Jason Marshall. **Director, Community Partnerships:** Sean Baedke. **Director, Corporate Partnerships:** Adam Lorber. **Senior Account Executives:** Chris Somers, Brad Strauss. **Marketing Operations:** Leslie Surden. **Operations:** Eric Enders. **Group Sales:** Robert Nehring, Danielle Martinez. **Head Groundskeeper:** Chris Walsh.

Manager: Wayne Krenchicki. **Coach:** Victor Torres. **Pitching Coach:** Steve Foucault.

Game Information

Radio: Unavailable.

PA Announcer: Kevin Casey. **Official Scorer:** Unavailable.

Stadium Name (year opened): Campbell's Field (2001). **Location:** From Philadelphia, go right on 6th Street, right after Ben Franklin Bridge toll booth, right on Cooper Street until it ends at Delaware Ave. From Camden, I-676 to exit 5B, follow signs to field. **Standard Game Times:** 6:35 p.m., Sun. 1:35.

Visiting Club Hotel: Holiday Inn, Route 70 and Sayer Ave., Cherry Hill, NJ 08002. Telephone: (856) 663-5300.

LONG ISLAND
Ducks

Mailing Address: 3 Court House Dr., Central Islip, NY 11722. **Telephone:** (631) 940-3825. **FAX:** (631) 940-3800. **E-Mail Address:** info@liducks.com. **Website:** www.liducks.com.

Operated by: Long Island Ducks Professional Baseball.

Principal Owner, Chief Executive Officer: Frank Boulton. **Owner/Senior Vice President, Baseball Operations:** Bud Harrelson.

General Manager: Michael Hirsch. **Assistant GM:** Doug Cohen. **Controller:** Alex Scannella. **Manager, Media

Relations: Michael Pfaff. **Manager, Group Sales:** Mike Pacella. **Manager, Promotions:** Chris Lombardo. **Manager, Ticket Sales:** Ben Harper. **Manager, Community Relations:** Jaslyn Alicea. **Manager, Operations:** Andrew Washington. **Business Manager:** Gerry Anderson. **Manager, Clubhouse Operations:** Tom Kitz. **Assistant Manager, Tickets:** Ron Varrichio. **Coordinator, Administration:** Michele Connizzo. **Facilities:** George Harrison.

Field Manager: Don McCormack. **Coach:** Bud Harrelson. **Pitching Coach:** Dave LaPoint. **Trainers:** Mike Moran, Tony Amin.

Game Information

Radio Announcers: Chris King, David Weiss. **No. of Games Broadcast:** 60. **Flagship Station:** WLIE 540-AM.

PA Announcers: Pitt Schultz, Bob Ottone. **Official Scorers:** Joe Donnelly, Red Foley.

Stadium Name (year opened): Citibank Park (2000). **Location:** Southern State Parkway east to Carleton Avenue North (exit 43 south), right onto Courthouse Drive, stadium behind Federal Courthouse Complex. **Standard Game Times:** 7:05 p.m.; Sat.-Sun. 1:35.

Visiting Club Hotel: Huntington Hilton, 598 Broad Hollow Rd., Melville, NY 11747. Telephone: (631) 845-1000.

NASHUA
Pride

Office Address: Holman Stadium, 67 Amherst St., Nashua, NH 03064. **Telephone:** (603) 883-2255. **FAX:** (603) 883-0880. **E-Mail Address:** lionsden@nashuapride.com. **Website:** www.nashuapride.com.

Operated by: Nashua Pride Professional Baseball, LLC.

Principal Owner, President: Chris English.

General Manager: Todd Marlin. **Assistant GM:** Andy Crossley. **Director, Business Development:** Mark Sousa. **Manager, Operations:** Steve Cox. **Manager, Tickets:** Jeff Farrar. **Manager, Media Relations:** Kristen Johnson. **Manager, Merchandise:** Kelly Stevens. **Office Manager:** Bev Taylor.

Manager: Butch Hobson. **Pitching Coach:** Unavailable.

Game Information

Radio: Unavailable.

PA Announcer: Ken Cail. **Official Scorer:** Roger Pepin.

Stadium Name (year opened): Holman Stadium (1937). **Location:** Route 3 to exit 7E (Amherst Street), one mile on left. **Standard Game Times:** 7:05 p.m.; Mon.-Tue. 6:35; Sun. (May-June, Sept.) 6:35, (July-Aug.) 2:05.

Visiting Club Hotel: Sheraton of Nashua, 11 Tara Blvd., Nashua, NH 03062. Telephone: (603) 888-9970.

NEWARK
Bears

Office Address: 450 Broad St., Newark, NJ 07102. **Telephone:** (973) 848-1000. **FAX:** (973) 621-0095. **Website:** www.newarkbears.com.

Operated by: Newark Bears Baseball Club, Inc.

Owner: Steven Kalafer. **Owner/Founder:** Rick Cerone. **Chief Financial Officer:** Jack Cust.

Vice President/General Manager: Chris Bryan. **Assistant GM:** Dean Rivera. **Director, Player Personnel:** Victor Rojas. **Director, Marketing:** Richard Hawkinson. **Director, Stadium Operations:** John LoRusso. **Director, Public Relations:** Ross Blacker. **Business Manager:** Jerry Glover. **Manager, Office/Marketing Partnerships:** Kimberly Rojas. **Director, Ticket Operations:** Ken Skrypek. **Director, Ticket Sales:** Dave Rosoff. **Group Sales:** Nelson Constantino. **Head Groundskeeper:** Unavailable.

Manager: Unavailable. **Coaches:** Unavailable.

Game Information

Radio Announcer: Victor Rojas. **No. of Games Broadcast:** Home-60, Away-40. **Flagship Station:** WSOU 89.5-FM.

PA Announcer: Unavailable. **Official Scorer:** John Nolan.

Stadium Name (year opened): Bears & Eagles Riverfront Stadium (1999). **Location:** New Jersey Parkway North/South to exit 145 (280 East), to exit 15; New Jersey Turnpike North/South to 280 West, to exit 15A. **Standard Game Times:** 7:05 p.m., Sat. 6:05, Sun. 1:35.

Visiting Club Hotel: Ramada Conference Center, 130 Route 10 West, East Hanover, NJ 07936. Telephone: (973) 386-5622.

PENNSYLVANIA
Road Warriors

The franchise will be operated by the Atlantic League as a road team during the 2003 season.

Manager: Bert Pena. **Coaches:** Unavailable.

SOMERSET
Patriots

Office Address: One Patriots Park, Bridgewater, NJ 08807. **Telephone:** (908) 252-0700. **FAX:** (908) 252-0776. **Website:** www.somersetpatriots.com.

Operated by: Somerset Patriots Baseball Club, LLC.

Principal Owners: Steven Kalafer, Jack Cust, Byron Brisby, Don Miller.

Chairman: Steven Kalafer.

Vice President, General Manager: Patrick McVerry. **Assistant GMs:** Brendan Fairfield, Dave Marek. **Controller:** Wayne Seguin. **Head Groundskeeper:** Ray Cipperly. **Director, Media Relations:** Marc Russinoff. **Director, Sales:** Dave Gambrill. **Director, Operations:** Rob Lukachyk. **Account Representatives:** Chris Bates, Kenny Blattenbauer, Cary Stanek. **Director, Community Relations:** Rich Reitman. **Director, Ticket Sales:** Bryan Iwicki. **Group Sales:** Adam Altman, Jen Goddard, Chris Grundman. **Assistant Director, Tickets:** Dan Neville. **Executive Assistant to GM:** Michele DaCosta. **Accountants:** Stephanie Diez, Ari Gall. **Receptionist:** Lorraine Ott.

Director, Player Procurement: Jim Frey. **Manager:** Sparky Lyle. **Pitching Coach:** John Montefusco. **Trainer:** Paul Kolody.

Game Information

Radio Announcer: David Schultz. **No. of Games Broadcast:** Home-72, Away-54. **Flagship Station:** WCTC 1450-AM.

PA Announcers: Paul Spychala. **Official Scorer:** Unavailable.

Stadium Name (year opened): Commerce Bank Ballpark (1999). **Location:** Route 287 North to exit 13B/Route 287 South to exit 13 (Somerville Route 28 West); at second light take jughandle on right and cross over Route 28 to Chimney Rock Road to Foothill Road. **Standard Game Times:** 7:05 p.m., Sun. 2:05.

Visiting Club Hotel: Somerset Ramada, 60 Cottontail Lane, Somerset, NJ 08873. Telephone: (732) 560-9880.

CENTRAL LEAGUE

Mailing Address/Baseball Operations: P.O. Box 1282, Durham, NC 27702. **Telephone:** (919) 956-8150. **FAX:** (919) 683-2693. **Mailing Address/Business Operations:** P.O. Box 2712, Colorado Springs, CO 87901. **Telephone:** (719) 520-0060. **FAX:** (719) 520-0221. **E-Mail Address:** info@centralleaguebaseball.com. **Website:** www.centralleaguebaseball.com.

Year Founded: 1994.

Commissioner: Miles Wolff. **Vice President, Baseball Operations:** Dan Moushon. **Director, Media Relations:** Stephen Gates. **Supervisor, Umpires:** Kevin Winn.

2003 Opening Date: May 7. **Closing Date:** Aug. 23.

Regular Season: 96 games (split schedule).

Division Structure: East—Alexandria, Fort Worth, Jackson, Shreveport, Springfield/Ozark. **West**—Amarillo, Coastal Bend, Edinburg, Rio Grande Valley, San Angelo.

All-Star Game: July 14 at Edinburg.

Playoff Format: First-half division winners meet second-half division winners in best-of-5 series. Winners meet in best-of-5 series for league championship.

Roster Limit: 22. **Player Eligibility Rule:** Minimum of five first-year players, maximum of four veterans (at least four years of professional experience).

Brand of Baseball: Rawlings.

Statistician: SportsTicker-Boston, Boston Fish Pier, West Bldg. #1, Suite 302, Boston, MA 02210.

ALEXANDRIA
Aces

Office Address: 1 Babe Ruth Dr., Alexandria, LA 71301. **Mailing Address:** P.O. Box 6005, Alexandria, LA 71307. **Telephone:** (318) 473-2237. **FAX:** (318) 473-2229. **E-Mail Address:** acesbaseball@centurytel.net. **Website:** www.acesbaseball.com.

President: Steve Spielman. **Vice President:** John Dittrich.

General Manager: Lydia Bergeron. **Director, Community Relations:** Amanda Holzhauser.

Manager: Unavailable. **Coaches:** Unavailable. **Trainer:** Chris Brister.

Game Information

Radio Announcer: Lyn Rollins. **No. of Games Broadcast:** Unavailable. **Flagship Station:** Unavailable.

PA Announcer: Rich Dupree. **Official Scorer:** Jim Smilie.

Stadium Name (year opened): Bringhurst Field (1933). **Location:** One mile east of Alexandria Mall on 165 Business (Masonic Drive), left on Babe Ruth Drive. **Standard Game Times:** 7:05 p.m., Sun. 6:05.

Visiting Club Hotel: Travelodge, 2211 N. MacArthur Dr., Alexandria, LA 71301. Telephone: (318) 443-2561.

AMARILLO
Dillas

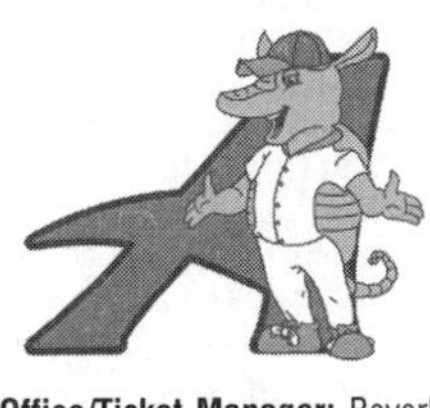

Mailing Address: P.O. Box 31241, Amarillo, TX 79120. **Telephone:** (806) 342-3455. **FAX:** (806) 467-9894. **Website:** www.dillas.com.

General Manager: Ric Sisler. **Director, Sales/Marketing:** Mark Lee. **Director, Corporate Sales/Special Events:** Amy Koffel. **Director, Ticket Sales:** Nick Barkley. **Office/Ticket Manager:** Beverly Sanders. **Manager, Grounds/Operations:** Jeff Schenck.

Manager: John Harris. **Coaches:** Unavailable.

Game Information

Radio Announcer: Unavailable. **No. of Games Broadcast:** Home-48, Away-48. **Flagship Station:** KPUR 1440-AM.

PA Announcer: Joe Frank Wheeler. **Official Scorer:** Jeff Schenck.

Stadium Name: Amarillo National Dilla Villa. **Location:** I-40 to Grand Ave. North exit, left at 3rd Ave. **Standard Game Times:** 7:05 p.m., Sun. 2:05.

Visiting Club Hotel: Homegate Studios & Suites, 6800 W. Interstate 40, Amarillo, TX 79106. Telephone: (806) 358-7943.

COASTAL BEND
Aviators

Mailing Address: 1150 E. Main Ave., Robstown, TX 78380. **Telephone:** (361) 387-8585. **FAX:** (361) 387-3535. **Website:** coastalbendprobaseball.com.

General Manager: George Stavrenos. **Assistant GM:** Shane Tritz. **Director, Stadium Operations:** Leroy Gonzalez. **Director, Media/Community Relations:** Elizabeth Schrader. **Office Manager:** Carolyn Booth. **Sales Executives:** Tracy Games, Javier Limon.

Manager: Les Lancaster. **Coach:** Eric Gonzalez. **Pitching Coach:** Brett Black.

Game Information

Radio: Unavailable.

PA Announcer: Unavailable. **Official Scorer:** Unavailable.

Stadium Name (year opened): Unavailable (2003). **Location:** 12 miles west of downtown Corpus Christi at junction of Highway 77 and Highway 44. **Standard Game Times:** 7:05 p.m.; Sun. 6:05.

Visiting Club Hotel: Unavailable.

EDINBURG
Roadrunners

Office Address: 920 N. Sugar Rd., Edinburg, TX 78539. **Mailing Address:** P.O. Box 4119, Edinburg, TX 78540. **Telephone:** (956) 289-8800. **FAX:** (956) 289-8833. **E-Mail Address:** winstonayala@yahoo.com. **Website:** www.roadrunnersbaseball.com.

General Manager: Winston Ayala. **Director, Sales/Marketing:** Bob Flanagan. **Director, Business Operations:** Rudy

Rodriguez. **Manager, Sales:** Mike Patrick. **Sales Executive:** Jeremy Martin. **Director, Public Relations**: George Aboud. **Office Manager:** Imelda Palacios.

Manager: Chad Tredaway. **Coach:** Shawn Moes.

Game Information

Radio: Unavailable.

PA Announcer: Tony Forina. **Official Scorer:** Carlos Cavazos.

Stadium Name (year opened): Edinburg Stadium (2001). **Location:** Highway 281, left at Schuinor Street to Sugar Road, stadium on right. **Standard Game Time:** 7:05 p.m.

Visiting Club Hotel: University Inn, 1400 University Dr., Edinburg, TX 78539. Telephone: (956) 381-5400.

FORT WORTH
Cats

Mailing Address: P.O Box 4411, Fort Worth, TX 76106. **Telephone:** (817) 226-2287. **FAX:** (817) 534-4620. **Email:** marty.scott@fwcats.com. **Website:** www.fwcats.com.

Operated By: Texas Independent Baseball.

Principal Owner: Carl Bell.

President, Chief Operating Officer: Marty Scott. **Vice President, General Manager:** Monty Clegg. **VP/Director, Sales and Marketing:** Brant Ringler. **VP, Special Projects:** Maury Wills. **Assistant GM:** Kevin Forrester. **Director, Media Relations:** Unavailable. **Operations Manager:** John Bilbow. **Manager, Special Projects:** Kyle Smith. **Manager, Merchandise:** Mike Barron. **Manager, Group Sales:** Jeff Carman. **Office Manager:** Stacy Navarro. **Manager, Community Relations:** Candiss Caudle. **Head Groundskeeper:** Bobby Gonzalez.

Director, Player Development: Barry Moss.

Manager: Wayne Terwilliger. **Coach:** Toby Harrah. **Pitching Coach:** Dan Smith. **Trainer:** Unavailable.

Game Information

Radio Announcers: John Nelson, David Hatchett. **No. of Games Broadcast:** Home-48, Away-48. **Flagship Station:** Unavailable.

PA Announcer: Frankie Gasca. **Official Scorer:** Bruce Unrue.

Stadium Name (year opened): LaGrave Field (2002). **Location:** From 1-30, take 1-35 North to North Side Drive exit, left (west) off exit to Main Street, left (south) on Main, left (east) onto NE Sixth Street. **Standard Game Times:** 7:05 p.m.; Sun. 2:05

Visiting Club Hotel: Clarion Hotel, 600 Commerce St., Fort Worth, TX 76102. Telephone: (871) 332-6900.

JACKSON
Senators

Office Address: 1200 Lakeland Dr., Jackson, MS 39216. **Mailing Address:** P.O. Box 4934, Jackson, MS 39296. **Telephone:** (601) 362-2294. **FAX:** (601) 362-9577. **E-Mail Address:** info@jacksonsenators.com. **Website:** www.jacksonsenators.com.

Operated By: Texas Independent Baseball.

Principal Owner: Carl Bell.

President, Chief Operating Officer: Marty Scott. **Vice President, General Manager:** Craig Brasfield. **Assistant GM/Director, Sales and Marketing:** Chet Carey. **Assistant GM/Director, Baseball Operations:** Andrew Aguilar. **Office Manager/Director, Merchandising:** Carrie Brasfield. **Director, Group Sales:** Amanda Stringer. **Director, Ticket Operations:** Tammy Starkey. **Director, Food/Beverage:** Gary Starkey. **Account Executive:** Jeremy McClain.

Manager: Dan Schwam. **Coach:** Lonnie Maclin. **Trainer:** Jeff Martinez.

Game Information

Radio Announcer: Andrew Aguilar. **No. of Games Broadcast:** Home-48, Away-48. **Flagship Station:** WSLI 930-AM.

PA Announcer: Glen Waddle. **Official Scorer:** Denny Hales.

Stadium Name (year opened): Smith-Wills Stadium (1975). **Location:** I-55 to Lakeland Drive, left at Cool Papa Bell Drive. **Standard Game Times:** 7:05 p.m.; Sun. 2:05, 6:05.

Visiting Club Hotel: Unavailable.

RIO GRANDE VALLEY
WhiteWings

Mailing Address: 1216 Fair Park Blvd., Harlingen, TX 78550. **Telephone:** (956) 412-9464. **FAX:** (956) 412-9479. **E-Mail Address:** grandslam2425@yahoo.com.

Website: www.rgvwhitewings.com.

General Manager: Jason Driskell. **Director, Business Operations:** Jody Lane. **Director, Sales/Marketing:** Bob Flanagan. **Head Groundskeeper:** Jeff Lisi. **Office Manager:** Marilyn Farley.

Manager: James Frisbee. **Coach:** Unavailable.

Game Information

Radio: None.

PA Announcer: Unavailable. **Official Scorer:** Unavailable.

Stadium Name (year opened): Harlingen Field (1951). **Location:** Expressway 83 to Lewis Lane exit, stadium behind auditorium. **Standard Game Times:** 7:05 p.m.

Visiting Club Hotel: Howard Johnson, Expressway 83 and Stuart Place Road, Harlingen, TX 78550. Telephone: (956) 425-7070.

SAN ANGELO
Colts

Office Address: 1600 University Ave., San Angelo, TX 76904. **Telephone:** (915) 942-6587. **FAX:** (915) 947-9480. **E-Mail Address:** colts@wcc.net. **Website:** www.sanangelocolts.com.

Operated by: San Angelo Colts Baseball Club, LLC.

President, Executive General Manager: Harlan Bruha. **GM:** Paula Dowler. **Director, Community Relations:** Paige Jackson. **Account Representative:** Gary Kelton. **Assistant GM, Sales/Ticket Manager:** Kathleen Quanz.

Manager: Steve Maddock. **Coach:** Tom Waelchli. **Trainer:** Jeff Mann.

Game Information

Radio Announcer: Unavailable. **No. of Games Broadcast:** Home-48, Away-48. **Flagship Station:** KKSA 1260-AM.

PA Announcer: John Flint. **Official Scorer:** Kirby Poss.

Stadium Name (year opened): Colts Stadium (2000). **Location:** From north/south, take US 87 to Knickerbocker Road, west to stadium; From east/west, take US 67 to US 87 South, to Knickerbocker Road, west to stadium. **Standard Game Time:** 7:05 p.m.

Visiting Club Hotel: Howard Johnson, 415 W. Beauregard Blvd., San Angelo, TX 76903. Telephone: (915) 653-2995.

SHREVEPORT
Sports

Mailing Address: 2901 Pershing Blvd, Shreveport, LA 71109. **Telephone:** (318) 636-5555. **FAX:** (318) 636-5670. **Website:** www.shreveportbaseballclub.com.

General Manager: Brian Viselli. **Assistant GM:** Jeff Stewart. **Account Executives:** Nicholas Criscuolo, Zach Viselli. **Media Relations:** Dave Nitz. **Corporate Sales:** Sam Wilbur.

Manager: Terry Bevington. **Coach:** Unavailable.

Game Information

Radio Announcer: Dave Nitz. **No. of Games Broadcast:** Home-48, Away-48. **Flagship Station:** Unavailable.

PA Announcer: Unavailable. **Official Scorer:** Unavailable.

Stadium Name (year opened): Fair Grounds Field (1986). **Location:** Hearne Ave. (US 171) exit off I-20 at Louisiana State Fairgrounds. **Standard Game Times:** 7:05 p.m., Sun. 4:05.

Visiting Club Hotel: Unavailable.

SPRINGFIELD/OZARK
Mountain Ducks

Office Address: 4400 N. 19th St., Ozark, MO 65721. **Mailing Address:** P.O. Box 1472, Ozark, MO 65721. **Telephone:** (417) 581-2868. **FAX:** (417) 581-8342. **E-Mail Address:** info@mountainducksbaseball.com. **Website:** www.mountainducksbaseball.com.

General Manager: Phil Wilson. **Vice President, Sales/Marketing:** Todd Rahr. **Business Operations:** Jim Metcalf. **Stadium Operations:** Brock Phipps. **Ticket Sales:** Eric Day. **Office Manager:** Carolina Gold.

Manager: Phil Wilson. **Coaches:** Unavailable. **Trainer:** Gary Turbak.

Game Information

Radio Announcer: Jim Metcalf. **No. of Games Broadcast:** Home-48, Away-48. **Flagship Station:** KWTO 98.7-FM.

PA Announcer: Unavailable. **Official Scorer:** Unavailable.

Stadium Name (year opened): Price Cutter Park (1999). **Location:** Highway 65 to CC&J exit, right on 17th Street, follow signs to stadium. **Standard Game Times:** Unavailable.

Visiting Club Hotel: Clarion Hotel, 3333 S. Glenstone Ave., Springfield, MO 65804. Telephone: (417) 883-6550.

FRONTIER LEAGUE

Office Address: 45 N. 4th St., Zanesville, OH 43701. **Mailing Address:** P.O. Box 2662, Zanesville, OH 43702. **Telephone:** (740) 452-7400. **FAX:** (740) 452-2999. **E-Mail Address:** office@frontierleague.com. **Website:** www.frontierleague.com.

Year Founded: 1993.

Commissioner: Bill Lee.

President: Chris Hanners (Chillicothe). **Vice Presidents:** John Swiatek (Washington), Duke Ward (Richmond).

Corporate Secretary/Treasurer: Bob Wolfe. **Legal Counsel/Deputy Commissioner:** Kevin Rouch.

Directors: David Arch (Cook County), Bill Bussing (Evansville), Dave Ciarrachi (Rockford), Gary Enzweiler (Florence), Chris Hanners (Chillicothe), Mike Hayes (Kenosha), Rich Sauget (Gateway), John Swiatek (Washington), Duke Ward (Richmond), Gary Wendt (Mid-Missouri), Ken Wilson (River City), Bill Wright (Kalamazoo).

2003 Opening Date: May 23. **Closing Date:** Aug. 31.

Regular Season: 90 games.

Division Structure: East—Chillicothe, Evansville, Florence, Kalamazoo, Richmond, Washington. **West**—Cook County, Gateway, Kenosha, Mid-Missouri, River City, Rockford.

Playoff Format: Division winners plus next two best overall finishers meet in best-of-3 semifinals. Winners meet in best-of-5 series for league championship.

All-Star Game: July 16 at Gateway.

Roster Limit: 24. **Eligibility Rule:** Minimum of 10 first-year players; maximum of seven players with one year professional experience; maximum of two players with two years of experience and maximum of three players with three or more years of experience. No player may be 27 prior to May 30.

Brand of Baseball: Wilson.

Statistician: SportsTicker-Boston, Boston Fish Pier, West Bldg. #1, Suite 302, Boston, MA 02210.

CHILLICOTHE
Paints

Office Address: 59 N. Paint St., Chillicothe, OH 45601. **Telephone:** (740) 773-8326. **FAX:** (740) 773-8338. **E-Mail Address:** paints@bright.net. **Website:** www.chillicothepaints.com.

Operated by: Chillicothe Paints Professional Baseball Association, Inc.

Principal Owner: Chris Hanners. **President:** Shirley Bandy.

Vice President, General Manager: Bryan Wickline. **Stadium Superintendent:** Jim Miner. **Director, Finance:** Maleine Davis. **Office Manager:** Patrick Davidson. **Director, Sales/Marketing:** John Wend. **Director, Tickets/Group Sales:** Morgan West. **Director, Merchandise:** Logan Hanners. **Director, Souvenirs/Concessions:** Jody Clary. **Head Groundskeeper:** Isaac Hanners.

Field Manager: Jamie Keefe. **Coaches:** Marty Dunn, Rick Blanc. **Trainer:** Aaron Schreiner.

Game Information

Radio Announcer: Unavailable. **No. of Games Broadcast:** Home-45, Away-45. **Flagship Station:** WXIZ 100.9-FM.

PA Announcer: John Wend. **Official Scorer:** Aaron Lemaster.

Stadium Name (year opened): V.A. Memorial Stadium (1993). **Location:** Route 23 to Bridge Street, west on Route 35, north on Route 104. **Standard Game Times:** 7:05 p.m., Sun. 6:05.

Visiting Club Hotel: Days Inn of Chillicothe, 1250 N. Bridge St., Chillicothe, OH 45601. Telephone: (740) 775-7000.

COOK COUNTY
Cheetahs

Office Address: 13152 S. Cicero Ave., Suite 281, Crestwood, IL 60445. **Telephone:** (708) 489-2255. **FAX:** (708) 489-2999. **E-Mail Address:** cheetahsbaseball@aol.com. **Website:** www.gocheetahs.com.

Operated by: Cheetah Professional Sports II LLC.

Chairman: David Arch. **President:** Leon Steinberg.

General Manager: Chuck Heeman. **Director, Administration:** Pat Rusthoven. **Director, Ticket Sales:** Erin Hanson. **Manager:** Mike Moore. **Coaches:** Ross Kott, Greg Beck, Carlos May. **Trainer:** Aaron Brossett.

Game Information

Radio: None.

PA Announcer: Kevin O'Connor. **Official Scorer:** Joe Stillwell.

Stadium Name (year opened): Hawkinson Ford Field (1999). **Location:** I-294 to Cicero Ave. exit (Route 50), south for 1½ miles, left at Midlothian Turnpike, right on Kenton Ave. **Standard Game Times:** 7:05 p.m., Sun. 1:05.

Visiting Club Hotel: Georgio's Comfort Inn, 8800 W. 159th St., Orland Park, IL 60462. Telephone: (708) 403-1100.

EVANSVILLE
Otters

Office Address: 1701 N. Main St., Evansville, IN 47711. **Mailing Address:** P.O. Box 3565, Evansville, IN 47734. **Telephone:** (812) 435-8686. **FAX:** (812) 435-8688. **E-Mail Address:** ottersbb@evansville.net. **Website:** www.evansvilleotters.com.

Operated by: Evansville Baseball, LLC.

President: Bill Bussing.

Vice President, General Manager: Jim Miller. **VP/Director, Baseball Operations:** Gary Jones. **Assistant GM/Director, Business Operations:** Steve Tahsler. **Director, Promotions:** Andrew Aldenderfer. **Administrative Assistant:** Andi Speer. **Director, Special Projects:** Bryan Williams. **Director, Government Relations:** Mike Duckworth. **Account Executive:** Don Hess. **Head Groundskeeper:** Andy Miller.

Manager: Greg Jelks. **Coaches:** Ron Ryan, J.R. Seymour. **Pitching Coach:** Jeff Pohl. **Trainer:** Unavailable.

Game Information

Radio Announcer: Unavailable. **No. of Games Broadcast:** Home-45, Away-45. **Flagship Station:** Unavailable.

PA Announcer: Eric Stone. **Official Scorer:** Steve Rhoads.

Stadium Name (year opened): Bosse Field (1915). **Location:** US 41 to Diamond Ave. West, left at Heidelbach Ave. **Standard Game Times:** 7:05 p.m., Sun. 6:05.

Visiting Club Hotel: Unavailable.

FLORENCE
Freedom

Office Address: P.O. Box 6691, Florence, KY 41022. **Telephone:** (859) 380-9610. **FAX:** Unavailable. **Website:** Unavailable.

Operated by: Northern Kentucky Professional Baseball.

President, Managing Partner: Gary Enzweiler. **General Manager:** Jeff Hollis. **Director, Food Services:** Joe Peeno. **Director, Stadium Operations:** Dan Jordan. **Clubhouse Operations:** Unavailable.

Manager: Chris Sabo. **Coach:** Eric Minshall. **Pitching Coach:** Steve Merriman. **Trainer:** Unavailable.

Game Information

Radio Announcer: Unavailable. **No. of Games Broadcast:** Home-45, Away-45. **Flagship Station:** Unavailable.

PA Announcer: Unavailable. **Official Scorer:** Unavailable.

Stadium: Unavailable. **Standard Game Time:** 7:05 p.m.

Visiting Club Hotel: Unavailable.

GATEWAY
Grizzlies

Mailing Address: 2301 Grizzlie Bear Blvd., Sauget, IL 62206. **Telephone:** (618) 337-3000. **FAX:** (618) 332-3625. **E-Mail Address:** grizzlies@accessus.net. **Website:** www.gatewaygrizzlies.com.

Operated by: Gateway Baseball, LLC. **Managing Officer:** Richard Sauget.

General Manager: Tony Funderburg. **Director, Ticket Sales:** Steven Gomric. **Director, Corporate Sales:** Brady Bruhn. **Office Operations/Ticket Sales Associate:** Brent Pownall. **Corporate Sales Associate/Broadcaster:** Joe Pott. **Ticket Sales Associate/Promotions:** Jackie Marko. **Director, Ticket Operations:** Matt Wilson. **Corporate Sales Associate/Stadium Operations:** C.J. Hendrickson. **Ticket Sales Associate/Merchandise:** Kelly Kicielinski. **Corporate Sales Associate/Head Groundskeeper:** Craig Kuhl. **Communities Relations Associate/Clubhouse Manager:** John Aebischer. **Interns:** Andrew Collmeyer, Marlena Huenefeld, Eric Wittenauer.

Manager: Danny Cox. **Coaches:** Tim Mueth, Neil Fiala. **Trainer:** Greg Williams.

Game Information

Radio Announcer: Joe Pott. **No of Games Broadcast:** Home-45, Away-45. **Flagship Station:** WSMI 106.1-FM.

Network Stations: WNSV 104.7-FM, KJFF 1400-AM.

PA Announcer: Unavailable. **Official Scorer:** Unavailable.

Stadium Name (year opened): GMC Stadium (2002). **Location:** I-255 at exit 15 (Mousette Lane). **Standard Game Times:** 7:05 p.m.; Sun. 6:05.

Visiting Club Hotel: The Crown Hotel at the Casino Queen, 200 Front St., East St. Louis, IL 62201. Telephone: (618) 874-5000.

KALAMAZOO
Kings

Mailing Address: 251 Mills St., Kalamazoo, MI 49001. **Telephone:** (269) 388-8326. **FAX:** (269) 388-8333. **E-Mail Address:** kalamazookings@kalamazookings.com. **Website:** www.kalamazookings.com.

Operated by: Team Kalamazoo, LLC.

Owners: Bill Wright, Mike Seelye, Pat Seelye, Joe Rosenhagen, Ed Bernard, Scott Hocevar.

General Manager/Managing Partner: Joe Rosenhagen. **Business Manager/Fundraising Coordinator:** Linda Wright. **Account Executive:** Jim Lefler. **Administrative Assistant:** Lucille Comartin. **Marketing/Community Relations:** Melanie Grewe.

Director, Baseball Operations/Field Manager: Woody Sorrell. **Pitching Coach:** Stephen Byrd.

Game Information

Radio Announcer: Unavailable. **No. of Games Broadcast:** Home-45, Away-45. **Flagship Station:** Unavailable.

PA Announcers: Jim Lefler, Tom Dukesherer. **Official Scorer:** Jason Zerban.

Stadium Name (year opened): Homer Stryker Field (1995). **Location:** I-94 to Sprinkle Road (exit 80), north on Sprinkle Road, left on Business Loop 94, left on Kings Highway, right on Mills Street, park on right. **Standard Game Times:** 6:35 p.m., Sun. 5:35 p.m.

Visiting Club Hotel: Days Inn Airport Hotel, 3522 Sprinkle Rd., Kalamazoo, MI 49002. Telephone: (269) 381-7070.

KENOSHA

Office Address: 7817 Sheridan Rd., Kenosha, WI 53143. **Telephone:** Unavailable. **FAX:** Unavailable. **E-Mail Address:** Unavailable. **Website:** Unavailable.

Operated By: Redcoats Baseball, Inc.

Principal Owner/President/General Manager: Bill Larsen. **Director, Marketing/Promotions:** Ray Gross. **Director, Media Relations:** Chris Diserio.

Manager: Greg Tagert. **Pitching Coach:** Unavailable. **Trainer:** Unavailable.

Game Information

Radio Announcer: Unavailable. **No. of Games Broadcast:** Home-45. **Flagship Station:** Unavailable.

PA Announcer: Unavailable. **Official Scorer:** Unavailable.

Stadium Name (year opened): Simmons Field (1933). **Location:** I-94 to exit 50, east to Sheridan Rd., right to ballpark. **Standard Game Times:** 7 p.m.; Sat. 6; Sun. 2, 4.

Visiting Club Hotel: Unavailable.

MID-MISSOURI
Mavericks

Mailing Address: 810 E. Walnut, Columbia, MO 65201. **Telephone:** (573) 256-4004. **FAX:** (573) 256-4003. **E-Mail Address:** homerun@socket.net. **Website:** Unavailable.

Operated by: Columbia Professional Baseball LLC.

President: Gary Wendt.

Vice President, General Manager: Patrick Daly. **Director, Community Relations:** Ann Wilhelm. **Director, Office/Ticket Operations:** Karen Watson.

Manager: Unavailable. **Coach:** Unavailable. **Trainer:** Unavailable.

Game Information

Radio Announcer: Unavailable. **No. of Games Broadcast:** Home-45, Away-45. **Flagship Station:** KTGR 1580-AM.

PA Announcer: Unavailable. **Official Scorer:** Unavailable.

Stadium Name (year opened): Taylor Stadium (2000). **Location:** I-70 to Providence Road exit, south to Research

Park Drive, right to stadium. **Standard Game Times:** 7:05 p.m., Sun. 6:05.
Visiting Club Hotel: Unavailable.

RICHMOND
Roosters

Mailing Address: 201 NW 13th St., Richmond, IN 47374. **Telephone:** (765) 935-7529. **FAX:** (765) 962-7047. **E-Mail Address:** staff@richmondroosters.com. **Website:** www.richmondroosters.com.

Operated by: Richmond Roosters Baseball, LLC.

Owners: Allen Brady, Rob Quigg. **President:** Allen Brady.

General Manager: Deanna Beaman. **Director, Baseball Operations:** John Cate. **Sales:** Robert Jones. **Head Groundskeeper:** Cindy Cate. **Clubhouse Operations:** Unavailable. **Office Manager:** LaDonna White.

Manager: Chris Mongiardo. **Coach:** Jeremiah Klosterman, Bryan Needle. **Trainer:** Mark Colston.

Game Information

Radio Announcer: Gary Kitchel. **No. of Games Broadcast:** Home-42, Away-42. **Flagship Stations:** WKBV 1490-AM, WCNB 1580-AM, Star 98.3-FM.

PA Announcer: Scott Beaman. **Official Scorer:** Josh Amyx.

Stadium Name (year opened): McBride Stadium (1936). **Location:** I-70 to exit 149A (Williamsburg Pike), right on West Main Street, right on NW 13th Street. **Standard Game Times:** 6:35 p.m.; Sun. 4:35.

Visiting Club Hotel: Unavailable.

RIVER CITY
Rascals

Office Address: T.R. Hughes Ballpark, 900 Ozzie Smith Dr., O'Fallon, MO 63366. **Mailing Address:** P.O. Box 662, O'Fallon, MO 63366. **Telephone:** (636) 240-2287. **FAX:** (636) 240-7313. **E-Mail Address:** info@rivercityrascals.com. **Website:** www.rivercityrascals.com.

Operated by: Missouri River Baseball, LLC.

Managing Partner: Ken Wilson.

General Manager: Matt Jones. **Assistant GM:** Steve Chanez. **Director, Corporate Sales:** Allen Gossett. **Director, Merchandising:** Bobby Rhoden. **Director, Ticket Sales/Operations:** Bryan Goodall. **Director, Community/Media Relations:** Wendy Rackovan. **Director, Group Sales:** Alan Jackson. **Group Sales Coordinators:** Phil Giubileo, Grant Wilson, Travis Young. **Extra Event Coordinator:** Scott Morel. **Head Groundskeeper:** Chris Young.

Manager: Marc Hill. **Coaches:** Randy Martz, Mike Barger, Grant Wilson. **Trainer:** Unavailable.

Game Information

Radio Announcer: Phil Giubileo. **No. of Games Broadcast:** Home-45, Away-45. **Flagship Station:** KSLQ 104.5-FM.

PA Announcer: Unavailable. **Official Scorer:** Unavailable.

Stadium Name (year opened): T.R. Hughes Ballpark (1999). **Location:** I-70 to K and M exits, right on Tom Ginnever Ave. **Standard Game Times:** 7:05 p.m., Sun. 6:05.

Visiting Club Hotel: Holiday Inn Select, 4221 South Outer Rd., St. Peters, MO 63376. Telephone: (636) 928-2927.

ROCKFORD
RiverHawks

Office Address: 101 15th Ave., Rockford, IL 61104. **Telephone:** (815) 964-2255. **FAX:** (815) 964-2462. **E-Mail Address:** playball@rockfordriverhawks.com. **Website:** www.rockfordriverhawks.com.

Operated by: Rockford Baseball, LLC.

Managing Partner: Dave Ciarrachi.

General Manager, Business/Operations: Kristan Dolan. **GM, Sales/Operations:** Mike Babcock. **Director, Finance:** Todd Fulk. **Director, Community Relations/Manager, Merchandise:** Dawn Plock. **Director, Media Relations:** Brian Ciarrachi. **Director, Sales:** Cory Dirksen. **Sales Manager:** Bill Shaw. **Head Groundskeeper:** Justin Kees.

Manager: Bob Koopmann. **Coaches:** J.D. Arndt, Sam Knaack.

Game Information

Radio Announcer: Bill Czaja. **No. of Games Broadcast:** Home-45, Away-45. **Flagship Station:** WRHL 102.3-FM.

PA Announcer: Scott Bentley. **Official Scorer:** Aaron Nester.

Stadium Name: Marinelli Field (1988). **Location:** From north, I-90 South to I-39 South (US 51 South exit), continue on US 20 West for six miles to Illinois Highway 2 (North Main), north on North Main for two miles, right on 15th Ave. From east, I-90 North to US 20 West to Illinois Highway 2 (North Main), north on North Main for two miles, right on 15th Ave. **Standard Game Times:** 7:05 p.m., Sun 3:05.

Visiting Club Hotel: Sweden House Lodge, 4605 E. State St., Rockford, IL 61107. Telephone: (815) 398-4130.

WASHINGTON
Wild Things

Office Address: Falconi Field, One Washington Federal Way, Washington, PA 15301. **Telephone:** (724) 250-9555. **FAX:** (724) 250-2333. **E-Mail Address:** info@washingtonwildthings.com. **Website:** www.washingtonwildthings.com.

Owned by: Sports Facilites, L.L.C. **Managing Partner:** Stu Williams.

Operated by: Washington Frontier League Baseball, LLC. **Managing Partners:** Jeff Coury, John Swiatek. **President/Chief Executive Officer:** John Swiatek.

General Manager: Ross Vecchio. **Director, Marketing:** Christine Blaine. **Director, Merchandise:** Scott Eafrati. **Director, Sales/Service:** Jeff Ptak. **Director, Baseball Operations:** Kent Tekulve. **Director, Stadium Operations:** Steve Zavacky. **Account Representative:** Ricci Rich.

Manager: Jeff Isom. **Coach:** Joe Charboneau. **Pitching Coach:** Mark Mason. **Trainer:** Craig Castor.

Game Information

Radio Announcers: Bob Gregg, Ned Bowdern. **No. of Games Broadcast:** Home-45, Away-45. **Flagship Station:** WJPA 95.3-FM.

PA Announcer: Bill DiFabio. **Official Scorer:** Skip Hood.

Stadium Name (year opened): Falconi Field (2002). **Location:** I-70 to exit 3 (Chesnut Street), right on Chesnut Street, to Washington Crown Center Mall, right at mall entrance and right on to Mall Drive to stadium. **Standard Game Times:** 7:05 p.m., Sun. 6:05.

Visiting Club Hotel: Ramada Inn, 1170 W. Chesnut St., Washington, PA 15301. Telephone: (724) 223-2912.

NORTHEAST LEAGUE

Office Address: 524 S. Duke St., Durham, NC 27701. **Mailing Address:** P.O. Box 1282, Durham, NC 27702. **Telephone:** (919) 956-8150. **FAX:** (919) 683-2693. **E-Mail Address:** info@northeastleague.com. **Website:** www.northeastleague.com.

Year Founded: 1995.

Commissioner: Miles Wolff. **President:** Dan Moushon. **Director, Media Relations:** Stephen Gates.

Supervisor, Umpires: Tony Carilli.

2003 Opening Date: May 22. **Closing Date:** Sept. 1.

Regular Season: 92 games (split schedule).

Division Structure: North—Bangor, Brockton, North Shore, Québec. **South**—Allentown, Berkshire, Elmira, New Jersey.

All-Star Game: July 29 at Québec.

Playoff Format: First-half division winners meet second-half division winners in best-of-5 series. Winners meet in best-of-5 series for league championship.

Roster Limit: 22. **Eligibility Rule:** Minimum of five first-year players; maximum of four veterans (at least four years of professional experience).

Brand of Baseball: Rawlings.

Statistician: SportsTicker-Boston, Boston Fish Pier, West Bldg. #1, Suite 302, Boston, MA 02210.

ALLENTOWN
Ambassadors

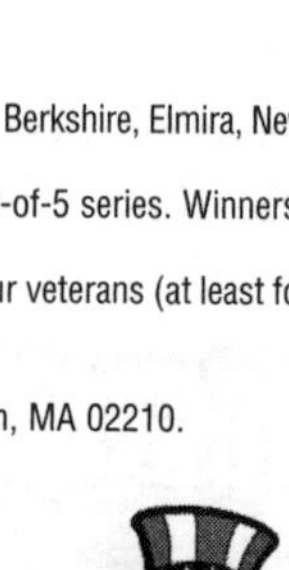

Office Address: 1511-1525 Hamilton St., Allentown, PA 18102. **Telephone:** (610) 437-6800. **FAX:** (610) 437-6804. **E-Mail Address:** info@ambassadorbaseball.com. **Website:** www.ambassadorbaseball.com.

Operated by: Allentown Ambassadors Professional Baseball, Inc.

Principal Owners: Peter Karoly, Lauren Angstadt.

General Manager: Michael Jermain. **Director, Operations:** Ralph Wasiakowski. **Director, Public Relations:** Unavailable. **Office Manager:** Unavailable. **Assistant to GM:** Unavailable.

Director, Player Personnel: Vic Davilla.

Manager: Ed Ott. **Coaches:** Dean Lackantosh, Denton Lackantosh. **Pitching Coach:** Rick Wise.

Game Information

Radio Announcer: Unavailable. **No. of Games Broadcast:** Home-46, Road-46. **Flagship Station:** Unavailable.

PA Announcer: Unavailable. **Official Scorer:** Unavailable.

Stadium Name (year opened): Bicentennial Park (1930). **Location:** I-78 to Lehigh Street, north on Lehigh for two miles toward downtown. **Standard Game Times:** 7:05 p.m., Sun. 5:05.

Visiting Club Hotel: Unavailable.

BANGOR
Lumberjacks

Office Address: 663 Stillwater Ave., Bangor, ME 04401. **Telephone:** (207) 947-1900. **FAX:** (207) 947-9900. **E-Mail Address:** info@bangorlumberjacks.com. **Website:** www.bangorlumberjacks.com.

Operated by: Lumberjack Baseball, LLC.

Principal Owner: Chip Hutchins.

General Manager: Curt Jacey. **Business Manager:** Sueann Robinson. **Sales:** Ryan Conley, Jessica Perkins, Lesile Trott. **Game Day Operations:** Doug Collyer.

Director, Player Procurement: Nick Belmonte.

Manager: Kash Beauchamp. **Coach:** Unavailable.

Game Information

Stadium Name (year opened): Mahaney Diamond (1984). **Location:** I-95 to exit 51, right onto Stillwater Ave., right at fourth light onto College Ave., left after one mile into Alfond Sports Arena lot, past football stadium. **Standard Game Times:** 7 p.m., Sun. 2.

Visiting Club Hotel: Best Western Black Bear Inn, 4 Godfrey Dr., Orono, ME 04473. Telephone: (207) 866-7120.

BERKSHIRE
Black Bears

Office Address: 2 South St., Suite 120, Pittsfield, MA 01201. **Mailing Address:** P.O. Box 646, Pittsfield, MA 01202. **Telephone:** (413) 448-2255. **FAX:** (413) 445-5500. **E-Mail:** info@berkshireblackbears.com. **Website:** www.berkshireblackbears.com.

Ownership, Management

Operated by: Flyball, LLC.

Principal Owner: Jonathan Fleisig.

President, General Manager: Mike Kardamis. **Director, Ticket Operations:** Chris Aubertin. **Director, Group Sales:** Tom Linehan.

Manager: Darren Bush. **Coach:** Unavailable. **Trainer:** Unavailable.

Game Information

Radio Announcer: Eric Kopf. **No. of Games Broadcast:** Home-46, Away-46. **Flagship Station:** WBRK 101.7-FM.

PA Announcer: Curt Preisser. **Official Scorer:** Unavailable.

Stadium Name (year opened): Wahconah Park (1919). **Directions:** Massachusetts Turnpike/I-90 to exit 2, follow signs for Route 7/20 North to Pittsfield; Route 7 (South Street) to North Street, follow North Street to Wahconah Street, left to ballpark. **Standard Game Times:** 7:05 p.m., Sun. 2:05.

Visiting Club Hotel: Holiday Inn of the Berkshires, 40 Main St., North Adams, MA 01247. Telephone: (413) 663-6500.

BROCKTON
Rox

Office Address: 1 Lexington Ave, Brockton, MA 02301. **Mailing Address:** P.O. Box 7547, Brockton, MA 02303. **Telephone:** (508) 559-7000. **FAX:** (508) 587-2802. **Website:** www.brocktonrox.com.

Principal Owner: Van Schley. **President:** Tom Whaley.

General Manager: Dave Echols. **Assistant GM:** David Sacchetti. **Corporate Sales:** Gwen Pointer, Gary MacKinnon. **Ticket Manager:** Bret Richards. **Ticket Sales:** John Gibson, Shawn Malenfant. **Bookkeeper:** Mary Scarlett. **Director, Food Services:** John Schumacher. **Promotions/Merchandise:** Jim Pfander. **Media Relations:** Ryan Smith. **Groundskeeper:** Tom Hassett. **Receptionist:** Dawn Brunetti.

Manager: Ed Nottle. **Coach:** Unavailable. **Trainer:** Unavailable.

Game Information

Radio Announcer: Larry Blucher. **No. of Games Broadcast:** Home-42, Away-40. **Flagship Station:** WBET 1460-AM.

PA Announcer: John Dolan. **Official Scorer:** Unavailable.

Stadium name (year opened): Campanelli Stadium (2002). **Directions:** Route 24 North/South to Route 123 East, stadium 2 miles on right. **Standard Game Times:** 7:11 p.m.; Sun. (May-June) 2:05, (July-Sept.) 5:05.

Visiting Club Hotel: Residence Inn, 124 Liberty St., Brockton, MA 02301. Telephone: (508) 583-3600.

ELMIRA
Pioneers

Office Address: 546 Luce St., Elmira, NY 14904. **Telephone:** (607) 734-1270. **FAX:** (607) 734-0891. **E-Mail Address:** pioneers@elmirapioneers.com. **Website:** www.elmirapioneers.com.

Operated by: Elmira Baseball, LLC.

President: Phil Kramer.

General Manager: Patrick McKernan. **Director, Business Operations:** Steve Ervin. **Director, Sales/Marketing:** George Bessey. **Head Groundskeeper:** Dale Storch. **Director, Ticket Operations:** Ferrell Butler. **Director, Concessions:** Matt McKernan.

Manager: Mitch Lyden. **Coach:** Unavailable. **Director, Player Procurement:** Jeff Kunion.

Game Information

Radio: Unavailable.

PA Announcer: Unavailable. **Official Scorer:** Unavailable.

Stadium Name (year opened): Dunn Field (1939). **Location:** I-86 (Route 17) to exit 56 (Church Street), left on Madison Ave., left on Maple Ave., left on Luce Street. **Standard Game Times:** 7:05 p.m., Sun. 1:05.

Visiting Club Hotel: Holiday Inn Elmira-Riverview, 760 E. Water, Elmira, NY 14901. Telephone: (607) 734-4211.

NEW JERSEY
Jackals

Office Address: One Hall Dr., Little Falls, NJ 07424. **Telephone:** (973) 746-7434. **FAX:** (973) 655-8021. **E-Mail Address:** njjackals@aol.com. **Website:** www.jackals.com.

Operated by: Floyd Hall Enterprises, LLC.

Principal Owner, Chairman: Floyd Hall. **President:** Greg Lockard.

General Manager: Larry Hall. **Assistant GM:** Elisabeth Unley. **Director, Business Operations:** Jennifer Fertig. **Director, Media/Public Relations:** Jim Cerny. **Head Groundskeeper:** Aldo Licitra. **Director, Sales/Marketing:** Kenneth Yudman. **Director, Ticket Sales:** Keri Mackie. **Sales Representative:** Matt Abel. **Clubhouse Operations:** Wally Brackett.

Manager: Joe Calfapietra. **Coach:** Unavailable. **Pitching Coach:** Brain Draham. **Trainer:** Katie Whitehead.

Game Information

Radio Announcers: Jim Cerny. **No. of Games Broadcast:** Home-46, Away-46. **Flagship Station:** Unavailable.

PA Announcer: Unavailable. **Official Scorer:** Kim DeRitter.

Stadium Name (year opened): Yogi Berra Stadium (1998). **Location:** Route 80 or Garden State Parkway to Route 46, take Valley Road exit to Montclair State University. **Standard Game Times:** 7:05 p.m.; Sun. (May-June) 2:05, (July-Sept.) 5:05.

Visiting Club Hotel: Ramada Inn, Route 3 East, Clifton, NJ 07014. Telephone: (973) 778-6500.

NORTH SHORE
Spirit

Office Address: 365 Western Ave, Lynn, MA 01904. **Mailing Address:** P.O. Box 8120, Lynn, MA 01904. **Telephone:** (781) 592-0007. **FAX:** (781) 592-0004. **E-Mail Address:** info@northshorespirit.com. **Website:** www.northshorespirit.com.

Ownership, Management

Operated by: Spirit of New England Baseball Club, LLC.

Principal Owner: Nicholas Lopardo.

General Manager: Ben Wittkowski. **Executive Assistant/Director, Fan Services:** Dawna Dombroski. **Director, Sales/Marketing:** Brent Connolly. **Director, Ticket Sales:** Andy Seguin. **Account Executive:** Bryce Scottron. **Media Relations:** Nicki Reilly. **Group Sales:** Luis Breazeale. **Director, Baseball Administration:** Heather Pellegrini.

Manager: John Kennedy. **Coaches:** Rich Gedman, Frank Carey, Jim Tgettis. **Pitching Coach:** Dick Radatz. **Strength/Conditioning Coach:** Paul Melanson.

Game Information

Radio Announcer: Don Boyle. **No. of Games Broadcast:** Home-46, Away-46. **Flagship Station:** WESX 1230-AM.

PA Announcer: Unavailable. **Official Scorer:** Unavailable.

Stadium Name (year opened): Fraser Field (1940). **Location:** Route 129 (Lynn exit) into Lynn on Lynnfield Street), left at Chestnut Street; right at Western Ave. (Route 107), stadium on right. **Standard Game Times:** 7 p.m., Sun. 1:30.

Visiting Club Hotel: Sheraton Colonial Hotel, 1 Audubon Rd., Wakefield, MA 01880. Telephone: (781) 245-9300.

QUEBEC
Les Capitales

Office Address: 100 Rue du Cardinal Maurice-Roy, Quebec City, Quebec G1K 8Z1. **Telephone:** (418) 521-2255. **FAX:** (418) 521-2266. **E-Mail Address:** baseball@capitalesdequebec.com. **Website:** www.capitalesdequebec.com.

President: Miles Wolff.

General Manager: Nicolas Labbé. **Director, Business Operations:** Rémi Bolduc. **Director, Media/Public Relations:** Alain Garon. **Director, Sales/Marketing:** Léo St. Jacques. **Director, Ticket Sales:** Nathalie Gauthier.

Manager: Unavailable. **Coach:** Stéphan Bédard.

Game Information

Radio: Unavailable.

PA Announcer: François Therrien. **Official Scorer:** Stéphan Lévesque.

Stadium Name (year opened): Stade Municipal de Québec (1938). **Location:** Highway 40 to Highway 173 (Centre-Ville) exit, two miles to Parc Victoria. **Standard Game Times:** 7:05 p.m., Sun. 1:05.

Visiting Club Hotel: Hotel du Nord, 640 St. Vallier W., Quebec City, Quebec G1N 1C5. Telephone: (418) 522-1554.

NORTHERN LEAGUE

Office Address: 3220 N. Freeway, Suite 100, Fort Worth, TX 76111. **Telephone:** (817) 378-9898. **FAX:** (817) 378-9805. **E-Mail Address:** info@northernleague.com. **Website:** www.northernleague.com.

Commissioner: Mike Stone. **Director, Baseball Operations:** Mike Marshall.

Directors: Jim Abel (Lincoln), John Ehlert (Kansas City), Rich Ehrenreich (Schaumburg), Marv Goldklang (St. Paul), Michael Hansen (Joliet), Sam Katz (Winnipeg), Jeff Loebl (Sioux Falls), John Roost (Sioux City), Mike Tatoian (Gary), Bruce Thom (Fargo-Moorhead).

Supervisor, Umpires: Butch Fisher.

2003 Opening Date: May 23. **Closing Date:** Aug. 31.

Regular Season: 90 games (split schedule).

Division Structure: West—Fargo-Moorhead, Kansas City, Lincoln, Sioux City, Sioux Falls. **East**—Gary, Joliet, Schaumburg, St. Paul, Winnipeg.

All-Star Game: July 22 at Lincoln.

Playoff Format: First-half division winners play second-half division winners in best-of-5 series. Winners meet in best-of-5 series for league championship.

Roster Limit: 22. **Eligibility Rule:** Minimum of five first-year players; maximum of four veterans (at least four years of professional experience).

Brand of Baseball: Rawlings.

Statistician: Sports Ticker-Boston, Boston Fish Pier, West Bldg. #1, Suite 302, Boston, MA 02210.

FARGO-MOORHEAD
RedHawks

Office Address: 1515 15th Ave. N., Fargo, ND 58102. **Telephone:** (701) 235-6161. **FAX:** (701) 297-9247. **E-Mail Address:** redhawks@fmredhawks.com. **Website:** www.fmredhawks.com.

Operated by: Fargo Baseball, LLC.

Ownership: Otter Tail Corporation.

President: Bruce Thom. **Vice President:** Brad Thom.

General Manager: Lee Schwartz. **Director, Baseball Operations:** Josh Buchholz. **Senior Accountant:** Sue Wild.

Assistant Manager, Accounting: Sara Dobervich. **Director, Sales:** Mara Pierce. **Director, Ticket Sales:** Paula Cihla. **Director, Stadium Operations/Head Groundskeeper:** Blair Tweet. **Director, Graphic Design/Advertising:** Rhianna O'Shea. **Director, Promotions:** Kristie Schwan. **Director, Game Day Operations/Special Events:** Sara Garaas. **Office Manager:** Jenny Vangerud. **Director, Fan Services:** Brian Heim. **Clubhouse Operations:** Brent Tehven.

Manager/Director, Player Procurement: Doug Simunic. **Pitching Coach/Assistant Director, Player Procurement:** Jeff Bittiger. **Coach:** Bucky Burgau. **Trainer:** Don Bruenjes.

Game Information

Radio Announcers: Jack Michaels, Maury Wills. **No. of Games Broadcast:** Home-45, Away-45. **Flagship Station:** WDAY 970-AM.

PA Announcer: Merrill Piepkorn. **Official Scorer:** Rob Olson.

Stadium Name (year opened): Newman Outdoor Field (1996). **Location:** I-29 North to exit 67, right on 19th Ave. North, right on Albrecht Blvd. **Standard Game Times:** 7:05 p.m., Sun. 2:05.

Visiting Club Hotel: Comfort Inn West, 3825 9th Ave. SW, Fargo, ND 58103. Telephone: (701) 282-9596.

GARY SOUTHSHORE
RailCats

Office Address: One Stadium Plaza, Gary, IN 46402. **Telephone:** (219) 882-2255. **FAX:** (219) 882-2259. **E-Mail Address:** info@railcatsbaseball.com. **Website:** www.railcatsbaseball.com.

Operated by: SouthShore Baseball LLC.

Principal Owners: Timothy Haffner, Richard Hill, George Huber, Mike Tatoian, Tony Zirille.

Chairman: George Huber. **President, Chief Executive Officer:** Mike Tatoian.

Vice President, General Manager: Roger Wexelberg. **Assistant GM:** Kevin Spudic. **Director, Public/Community Relations:** Aukesha Henry. **Director, Marketing/Promotions:** Jim Smith. **Director, Media/Broadcasting:** Alan Garrett. **Director, Ticket Operations:** Carrie Butterfield. **Director, Ticket Sales:** Camille Cooke. **Director, Facilities:** Mike Figgs. **Manager, Group Sales:** Sierra Foster. **Manager, Merchandise:** Dannie Barrall. **Groundskeeper:** Mike Faust. **Executive Assistant:** Patricia Richards.

Manager: Garry Templeton. **Pitching Coach:** Scott May.

Game Information

Radio Announcers: Alan Garrett. **No. of Games Broadcast:** Home-45, Away-45. **Flagship Station:** Unavailable.

Stadium Name (year opened): RailCats Stadium (2003). **Location:** I-65 to I-90 W (toll), one mile to Broadway south, left on Fifth Street. **Standard Game Times:** 7 p.m.; Sat. 6; Sun. 1.

Visiting Club Hotel: Trump Hotel, 21 Buffington Harbor Dr., Gary, IN 46406. Telephone: (219) 977-9999.

JOLIET
JackHammers

Office Address: 1 Mayor Art Schultz Dr., Joliet, IL 60432. **Telephone:** (815) 726-2255. **FAX:** (815) 726-9223. **E-Mail Address:** info@jackhammerbaseball.com. **Website:** www.jackhammerbaseball.com.

Operated by: Joliet Professional Baseball Club, LLC.

Chairman: Peter Ferro. **Vice Chairman:** Charles Hammersmith. **Chief Executive Officer/General Counsel:** Michael Hansen. **Chief Financial Officer/President:** John Costello.

Executive Vice President/General Manager: Steve Malliet. **Director, Ticket Operations:** Rick Mickel. **Ticket Sales Representatives:** Kyle Kreger, Rich Kuchar. **Manager, Box Office:** Chad Therrien. **Director, Broadcasting/Media Relations:** Bryan Dolgin. **Director, Corporate Sales:** John Kuhn. **Director, Retail:** Kelly Sufka. **Coordinator, Community Relations/Promotions:** Sarah Heth. **Director, Accounting/Human Resources:** Penny Roach. **Administrative Assistant:** Teresa Dyer. **Head Groundskeeper:** Jeff Eckert.

Manager: Matt Nokes. **Coaches:** Les Norman, Mike Pinto. **Pitching Coach:** Greg Hibbard, **Trainer:** Unavailable.

Game Information

Radio Announcers: Bryan Dolgin, Mark Vasko. **No. of Games Broadcast:** Home-45, Away-45. **Flagship Stations:** WJOL 1340-AM, WYKT 105.5-FM.

PA Announcer: Irwin Fletcher. **Official Scorers:** Brian Berg, Dave Laketa.

Stadium Name (year opened): Silver Cross Field (2002). **Location:** I-80 to Chicago Street/Route 53 North exit, go ½ mile on Chicago Street until it dead ends into Washington Street, right on Washington to Jefferson Street/US 52, right on Jefferson, ballpark on left. **Standard Game Times:** 7:05 p.m., Sun. 6:05.

Visiting Club Hotel: Hampton Inn, 3555 Mall Loop Dr., Joliet, IL 60431. Telephone: (815) 439-9500.

KANSAS CITY
T-Bones

Office Address: 11865 S. Conley, Olathe KS 66061. **Mailing Address:** P.O. Box 13365, Kansas City, KS 66113. **Telephone:** (913) 328-2255. **FAX:** (913) 685-3642. **E-Mail Address:** batterup@tbonesbaseball.com. **Website:** www.tbonesbaseball.com.

Operated By: T-Bones Baseball Club, LLC.

Owner, President: John Ehlert.

General Manager: Adam Ehlert. **Director, Ticket Operations**: Craig Pronske. **Vice President, Sales:** Kevin Battle. **Director, Stadium Operations:** Chris Browne. **Manager, Sales:** Scott Steckly. **Marketing/Corporate Sponsorship:** Margaret Doughty. **Team Concierge:** Andy Vanassee. **Interns:** Diedre Bieber, Matt Pellant, Brandon Smith, Justin Stancil.

Manager: Al Gallagher. **Coaches:** Darryl Motley, Ray Brown. **Pitching Coach:** Chris White. **Trainer:** Rodney Johnson.

Game Information

Radio Announcer: Danny Clinkscale. **No. of Games Broadcast:** Home-45, Away-45. **Flagship Station:** WHB 810-AM.

PA Announcer: Unavailable. **Official Scorer:** Unavailable.

Stadium Name (year opened): Community America Ballpark (2003). **Location:** State Ave. west off I-435, corner of 110th and State Ave. **Standard Game Times:** 7:05 p.m., Sun. 5:05.

Visiting Club Hotel: Hilton Garden Inn, 520 Minnesota Ave, Kansas City, KS 66101. Telephone: (913) 342-7900.

LINCOLN
Saltdogs

Office Address: 403 Line Dr., Suite A, Lincoln, NE 68508. **Telephone:** (402) 474-2255. **FAX:** (402) 474-2254. **E-Mail Address:** info@saltdogs.com. **Website:** www.saltdogs.com.

Owner: Jim Abel. **President:** Charlie Meyer.

Vice President, General Manager: Tim Utrup. **Assistant GM/Director, Ticketing:** Bret Beer. **Director, Media Relations:** Jason Wostrel. **Director, Marketing:** Jamie Von Sossan. **Director, Merchandising:** Unavailable. **Assistant Directors, Sales:** Stephanie Erwin, Tim Petersen. **Director, Stadium Operations:** Ryan Lockhart. **Athletic Turf Management:** Dan Bergstom. **Office Manager:** Jeanette Eagleton.

Manager: Tim Johnson. **Coaches:** Unavailable.

Game Information

Radio Announcers: Bill Doleman, John Baylor. **No. of Games Broadcast:** Home-45, Away-45. **Flagship Station:** KFOR 1240-AM.

PA Announcer: Chris Lofgren. **Official Scorer:** Unavailable.

Stadium Name (year opened): Haymarket Park (2001). **Location:** I-80 to Cornhusker Highway West, left on First Street, right on Sun Valley Blvd., left on Line Drive. **Standard Game Times:** 7:05 p.m., Sun. 5:05.

Visiting Club Hotel: Embassy Suites, 1040 P St., Lincoln, NE 68508. Telephone: (402) 474-1111.

ST. PAUL
Saints

Office Address: 1771 Energy Park Dr., St. Paul, MN 55108. **Telephone:** (651) 644-3517. **FAX:** (651) 644-1627. **E-Mail Address:** funsgood@saintsbaseball.com. **Website:** www.saintsbaseball.com.

Operated By: St. Paul Saints Baseball Club, Inc.

Principal Owners: Marv Goldklang, Mike Veeck, Bill Murray.

Chairman: Marv Goldklang. **President:** Mike Veeck.

Executive Vice President, General Manager: Bill Fanning. **Executive VP, Operations:** Tom Whaley. **Assistant GM, Operations:** Bill Fisher. **Director, Community Relations:** Paul Tarnowski. **Director, Media/Public Relations:** Dave Wright. **Ticket Manager:** Shane Anderson. **Coordinator, Group Sales:** Dave Wojkowski. **Coordinator, Promotions:** Matt Hansen. **Office Manager:** Teresa Schmit. **Controller:** Wayne Engel. **Director, Stadium Operations:** Bob Klepperich. **Head Groundskeeper:** Connie Rudolph. **Director, Food Service:** Tom Farrell.

Manager: George Tsamis. **Coaches:** Jarvis Brown, Jackie Hernandez, Lamarr Rogers, T.J. Wiesner. **Trainer:** Unavailable.

Game Information

Radio Announcer: Kris Atteberry. **No. of Games Broadcast:** Home-45, Away-45. **Flagship Station:** KCCO 950AM.

PA Announcer: Eric Webster. **Official Scorer:** Unavailable.

Stadium Name (year opened): Midway Stadium (1982). **Location:** From I-94, take Snelling Avenue exit, north on

Snelling, west onto Energy Park Drive. **Standard Game Times:** 7:05 p.m., Sun. 1:05.

Visiting Club Hotel: Holiday Inn North, 1201 West County Rd. E., St. Paul, MN 55112. Telephone: (651) 636-4123.

SCHAUMBURG
Flyers

Office Address: 1999 S. Springinsguth Rd., Schaumburg, IL 60193. **Telephone:** (847) 891-2255. **FAX:** (847) 891-6441. **E-Mail Address:** info@flyersbaseball.com. **Website:** www.flyersbaseball.com.

Principal Owners: Richard Ehrenreich, John Hughes, Gregory Smith. **Managing Partner/President:** Richard Ehrenreich.

General Manager: Rick Rungaitis. **Assistant GM, Sales/Marketing:** Tom O'Reilly. **Director, Media Relations:** Matt McLaughlin. **Manager, Group Sales:** Brett Fata. **Ticket Manager:** Scott Boor. **Director, Baseball Operations:** Eric Tholen. **Director, Graphics/Publications:** Shannan Kelly. **Director, Stadium Operations:** Kirk Bana. **Director, Community Relations:** Kristy Paukner. **Director, Merchandising/Promotions:** Lindsay Wells. **Suite Sales/Schaumburg Club:** Angela Burg. **Head Groundskeeper:** Eric Fasbender. **Director, Business Development:** Ron Kittle. **Human Resources-Corporate Sales:** Ben Burke. **Clubhouse Manager:** Greg Garofalo.

Manager: Andy McCauley. **Coach:** Unavailable. **Pitching Coach:** Jim Boynewicz. **Trainer:** Mike Hickey.

Game Information

Radio Announcer: Matt McLaughlin. **No. of Games Broadcast:** Home-45, Away-45. **Flagship Station:** WONC 89.1-FM.

PA Announcer: Unavailable. **Official Scorer:** Unavailable.

Stadium Name (year opened): Alexian Field (1999). **Location:** From north, I-290 to Elgin-O'Hare Expressway (Thorndale), west on expressway to Irving Park Road exit, left on Springinsguth under expressway, stadium on left; From south, US 20 West (Lake Street) to Elgin-O'Hare Expressway (Thorndale), east on expressway, right on Springinsguth Road. **Standard Game Times:** 7:05 p.m.; Sat. 6:20; Sun. 1:20.

Visiting Club Hotel: Baymont Inn and Suites, 2075 Barrington Rd., Hoffman Estates, IL 60195. Telephone: (847) 882-8848.

SIOUX CITY
Explorers

SIOUX CITY X's EXPLORERS

Office Address: 3400 Line Dr., Sioux City, IA 51106. **Telephone:** (712) 277-9467. **FAX:** (712) 277-9406. **E-Mail Address:** siouxcityxs@yahoo.com. **Website:** www.xsbaseball.com.

Operated by: Sioux City Explorers Baseball Club, LLC.

General Manager: Chuck Robbins. **Office Manager:** Kris McElroy. **Director, Media Relations:** Luke Nielsen. **Director, Stadium Operations:** Jesse Underwood. **Director, Broadcasting/Community Relations:** Paul Guggenheimer. **Player Procurement:** Harry Stavrenos.

Manager: Jay Kirkpatrick. **Pitching Coach:** Joe Georger. **Trainer:** Brandon Marreel.

Game Information

Radio Announcer: Paul Guggenheimer. **No. of Games Broadcast:** Home-45, Away-45. **Flagship Station:** KSCJ 1360-AM.

PA Announcer: Lew Roberts. **Official Scorer:** Randy Krascht.

Stadium Name (year opened): Lewis and Clark Park (1993). **Location:** I-29 to Singing Hills North, right on Line Drive. **Standard Game Times:** 7:05 p.m., Sun. 5:05.

Visiting Club Hotel: Best Western, 130 Nebraska St., Sioux City, IA 51101. Telephone: (712) 277-1550.

SIOUX FALLS
Canaries

Office Address: 1001 N. West Ave., Sioux Falls, SD 57104. **Mailing Address:** 1001 N. West Ave, Sioux Falls, SD 57104. **Telephone:** (605) 333-0179. **FAX:** (605) 333-0139. **E-Mail Address:** canaries@canariesbaseball.com. **Website:** www.canariesbaseball.com.

Operated by: Sioux Falls Canaries Professional Baseball Club, LLC.

Principal Owner, Chairman: Ben Zuraw. **President:** Jeff Loebl.

General Manager: Brad Seymour. **Assistant GM:** Larry McKenney. **Manager, Communications:** Greg Detter. **Manager, Marketing/Promotions:** Amber Grayson. **Manager, Sales:** Barb Lien. **Office/Ticket Manager:** Katie DeJean. **Account Executive:** Leif Peterson. **Fun Manager:** Dan Christopherson. **Administrative Assistant:** Rachel Weirsma.

Clubhouse Manager: Tom Whaley.

Manager/Director, Player Personnel: Doc Edwards. **Coaches:** Javier DeJesus, Billy Williams. **Trainer:** Jason Nelson.

Game Information

Radio Announcer: Greg Detter. **No. of Games Broadcast:** Home-45, Away-45. **Flagship Station:** KWSN 1230-AM.

PA Announcer: Dan Christopherson. **Official Scorer:** Unavailable.

Stadium Name (year opened): Sioux Falls Stadium (1964). **Location:** I-29 to Russell Street, south one mile, right on West Avenue. **Standard Game Times:** 7:03 p.m., Sun. 5:03.

Visiting Club Hotel: Baymont Inn, 3200 Meadow Ave., Sioux Falls, SD 57106. Telephone: (605) 362-0835.

WINNIPEG
Goldeyes

Office Address: One Portage Ave. E., Winnipeg, Manitoba R3B 3N3. **Telephone:** (204) 982-2273. **FAX:** (204) 982-2274. **E-Mail Address:** goldeyes@goldeyes.com. **Website:** www.goldeyes.com.

Operated by: Winnipeg Goldeyes Baseball Club, Inc.

Principal Owner, President: Sam Katz.

General Manager: Andrew Collier. **Director, Marketing:** Dan Chase. **Director, Communications:** Jonathan Green. **Director, Promotions:** Barb McTavish. **Director, Sales:** Lorraine Maciboric. **Director, Group Sales:** Tracy Smith. **Account Representatives:** Trevor Franzmann, Regan Katz, Dave Loat, Dennis McLean, Kevin Moore, Tom Thiessen. **Director, Merchandising:** Tracy Nanka. **Comptroller:** Judy Jemson. **Facility Manager:** Scott Horn. **Administrative Assistant**: Heather Mann-O'Hara. **Head Groundskeeper:** Don Ferguson.

Manager/Director, Player Procurement: Hal Lanier. **Pitching Coach:** Rick Forney. **Trainer:** Patrick Smith.

Game Information

Radio Announcer: Paul Edmonds. **No. of Games Broadcast:** Home-33, Road-33. **Flagship Station:** CJOB 680-AM.

PA Announcer: Ron Arnst. **Official Scorer:** Steve Eitzen.

Stadium Name (year opened): CanWest Global Park (1999) **Location:** Pembina Highway (Route 75), east on River Ave., north on Main Street, east on Water Ave. **Standard Game Times:** 7:05 p.m., Sun. 1:35.

Visiting Club Hotel: Ramada Marlborough, 331 Smith St., Winnipeg, Manitoba R3B 2G9 Telephone: (204) 942-6411.

Stadium Name (year opened): CanWest Global Park (1999) **Location:** Pembina Highway (Route 75), east on River Ave., north on Main Street, east on Water Ave. **Standard Game Times:** 7:05 p.m., Sun. 1:35.

SOUTHEASTERN LEAGUE

Office Address: 227 Southeast Blvd, Suite 7, Morgan City, LA 70380. **Telephone**: (985) 385-9195. **FAX**: (985) 385-9155. **E-Mail Address**: admin@southeasternleague.com. **Website**: www.southeasternleague.com.

Year Founded: 2002.

President: L.J. Dupuy. **Commissioner**: James Gamble.

Directors: Gus Brown Jr. (Houma), Noopie Cosby (Montgomery), Joel Robison (Baton Rouge), Quint Studer (Pensacola), Gary Wilson (Selma).

Regular Season: 72 games (split schedule).

Member Clubs: Baton Rouge (La.) River Bats, Houma (La.) Hawks, Montgomery (Ala.) Wings, Pensacola (Fla.) Pelicans, Selma (Ala.) Cloverleafs.

Division Structure: None.

2003 Opening Date: May 30. **Closing Date**: Unavailable.

Playoff Format: Top four teams meet in best-of-3 series; winners meet in best-of-5 series for league championship.

All-Star Game: Unavailable.

Roster Limit: 24 total, 21 active. **Player Eligibility Rule**: Minimum of two first-year professionals.

Brand of Baseball: Kazuma.

Official Statistician: Sports Ticker-Boston, Boston Fish Pier, West Bldg. #1, Suite 302, Boston, MA 02210.

INDEPENDENT
ATLANTIC LEAGUE

Atlantic City

MAY

9-10-11 .... Long Island
13-14-15 .... Somerset
20-21-22 ..... Pennsylvania
23-24-25 .... Newark
26-27-28 ..... Pennsylvania

JUNE

1-2-3 .... Bridgeport
10-11-12 .... Nashua
13-14-15 .... Camden
23-24-25 .... Long Island
26-27-28 .... Somerset

JULY

2-3-4 .... Pennsylvania
5-6-7 .... Newark
14-15-16 ..... Pennsylvania
23-24-25 .... Bridgeport
26-27-28 .... Nashua
29-30-31 .... Newark

AUGUST

8-9-10 .... Long Island
12-13-14 .... Somerset
18-19-20 ..... Pennsylvania
21-22-23 .... Camden
24-25-26 ..... Pennsylvania
30-31 .... Bridgeport

SEPTEMBER

1 .... Bridgeport
9-10-11 .... Nashua
12-13-14 .... Camden

Bridgeport

MAY

6-7-8 .... Atlantic City
9-10-11 .... Camden
13-14-15 ..... Pennsylvania
16-17-18 .... Nashua
20-21-22 .... Somerset

JUNE

7-8-9 .... Atlantic City
13-14-15 .... Nashua
17-18-19 .... Newark
20-21-22 ..... Pennsylvania
23-24-25 .... Camden
26-27-28 ..... Pennsylvania

JULY

2-3-4 .... Somerset
5-6-7 .... Long Island
14-15-16 .... Long Island
17-18-19 .... Atlantic City
26-27-28 .... Newark

AUGUST

5-6-7 .... Pennsylvania
8-9-10 .... Camden
15-16-17 .... Nashua
18-19-20 .... Somerset
21-22-23 ..... Pennsylvania
27-28-29 .... Long Island

SEPTEMBER

5-6-7 .... Pennsylvania
9-10-11 .... Newark

Camden

MAY

1-2-3-4 .... Somerset
6-7-8 .... Long Island
16-17-18 .... Atlantic City
20-21-22 .... Newark
23-24-25 ..... Pennsylvania
29-30-31 ..... Pennsylvania

JUNE

4-5-6 .... Bridgeport
7-8-9 .... Nashua
18-19 .... Somerset
20-21-22 .... Long Island
29-30 .... Atlantic City

JULY

1 .... Atlantic City
5-6-7 .... Pennsylvania
11-12-13 ..... Pennsylvania
14-15-16 .... Newark
20-21-22 .... Bridgeport
23-24-25 .... Nashua
29-30-31 ..... Pennsylvania

AUGUST

1-2-3 .... Somerset
5-6-7 .... Long Island
15-16-17 .... Atlantic City
24-25-26 .... Newark
27-28-29 ..... Pennsylvania

SEPTEMBER

2-3-4 .... Bridgeport
5-6-7 .... Nashua

Long Island

MAY

1-2-3-4 .... Pennsylvania
13-14-15 .... Newark
20-21-22 .... Nashua
23-24-25 .... Bridgeport
29-30-31 .... Bridgeport

JUNE

1-2-3 .... Camden
4-5-6 .... Pennsylvania
11-12 .... Pennsylvania
13-14-15 .... Somerset
17-18-19 .... Atlantic City
26-27-28 .... Newark

JULY

2-3-4 .... Nashua
17-18-19 .... Camden
20-21-22 .... Atlantic City
26-27-28 ..... Pennsylvania
29-30-31 .... Somerset

AUGUST

1-2-3 .... Atlantic City
12-13-14 .... Bridgeport
18-19-20 .... Nashua
21-22-23 .... Newark
30-31 .... Camden

SEPTEMBER

1 .... Camden
2-3-4 .... Pennsylvania
9-10-11 .... Pennsylvania
12-13-14 .... Somerset

Nashua

MAY

1-2-3-4 .... Atlantic City
9-10-11 .... Pennsylvania
13-14-15 .... Camden
23-24-25 .... Somerset
26-27-28 .... Long Island

JUNE

1-2-3 .... Newark
5-6 .... Atlantic City
17-18-19 ..... Pennsylvania
23-24-25 ..... Pennsylvania
26-27-28 .... Camden
29-30 .... Bridgeport

JULY

1 .... Bridgeport
5-6-7 .... Somerset
11-12-13 .... Long Island
17-18-19 .... Newark
20-21-22 ..... Pennsylvania
29-30-31 .... Bridgeport

AUGUST

1-2-3 .... Pennsylvania
8-9-10 .... Pennsylvania
12-13-14 .... Camden
21-22-23 .... Somerset
24-25-26 .... Long Island
30-31 .... Newark

SEPTEMBER

1 .... Newark
2-3-4 .... Atlantic City
12-13-14 .... Bridgeport

Newark

MAY

1-2-3-4 .... Bridgeport
6-7-8 .... Nashua
16-17-18 ..... Pennsylvania
26-27-28 .... Camden
29-30-31 .... Atlantic City

JUNE

4-5-6 .... Somerset
7-8-9 .... Long Island
11-12 .... Bridgeport
13-14-15 ..... Pennsylvania
20-21-22 .... Nashua
29-30 .... Pennsylvania

JULY

1 .... Pennsylvania
2-3-4 .... Camden
11-12-13 .... Atlantic City
20-21-22 .... Somerset
23-24-25 ..... Pennsylvania

AUGUST

1-2-3 .... Bridgeport
5-6-7 .... Nashua
12-13-14 ..... Pennsylvania
15-16-17 .... Long Island
18-19-20 .... Camden
27-28-29 .... Atlantic City

SEPTEMBER

2-3-4 .... Somerset
5-6-7 .... Long Island
12-13-14 ..... Pennsylvania

Pennsylvania

No home dates

Somerset

MAY

6-7-8 .... Pennsylvania
9-10-11 .... Newark
16-17-18 .... Long Island
26-27-28 .... Bridgeport
29-30-31 .... Nashua

JUNE

1-2-3 .... Pennsylvania
7-8-9 .... Pennsylvania
10-11-12 .... Camden
20-21-22 .... Atlantic City
23-24-25 .... Newark
29-30 .... Long Island

JULY

1 .... Long Island
11-12-13 .... Bridgeport
14-15-16 .... Newark
17-18-19 ..... Pennsylvania
23-24-25 .... Long Island
26-27-28 .... Camden

AUGUST

5-6-7 .... Atlantic City
8-9-10 .... Newark
15-16-17 ..... Pennsylvania
24-25-26 .... Bridgeport
27-28-29 .... Nashua
30-31 .... Pennsylvania

SEPTEMBER

1 .... Pennsylvania
5-6-7 .... Atlantic City
9-10-11 .... Camden

NOTE: Home games only.

CENTRAL LEAGUE

Alexandria

MAY

8-9-10-11 .... Jackson
19-20-21-22 ... Rio Grande
26-27-28 .... Amarillo

JUNE

2-3-4 .... Shreveport
9-10-11 .... Fort Worth
21-22-23-24 .... Ozark
25-26-27 ..... Coastal Bend

JULY

9-10-11-12 ..... Fort Worth
16-17-18-19 ... San Angelo
21-22-23-24 ...... Edinburg

AUGUST

1-2-3 .... Shreveport
4-5-6 .... Rio Grande
11-12-13 .... Jackson
15-16-17 .... Ozark

Amarillo

MAY

15-16-17-18 ... Shreveport
19-20-21-22 ... Coast. Bend
30-31 .... Fort Worth

JUNE

1 .... Fort Worth
10-11-12 .... Edinburg
13-14-15 .... Jackson
21-22-23 .... San Angelo
26-27-28-29 ... Rio Grande

JULY

1-2-3-4 .... Coastal Bend
16-17-18-19 ... Fort Worth
25-26-27 .... Ozark
28-29-30 .... Shreveport

AUGUST

7-8-9-10 .... Alexandria
14-15-16 .... Rio Grande
17-18-19 .... San Angelo

Coastal Bend

MAY

15-16-17-18 .... Alexandria
23-24-25 .... Jackson
26-27-28 .... Shreveport

JUNE

2-3-4 .... Amarillo
6-7-8-9 .... Ozark
13-14-15 .... San Angelo
17-18-19-20 ...... Edinburg

JULY

5-6-7-8 .... Edinburg
16-17-18-19 ... Rio Grande
20-21-22-23 .... Amarillo
28-29-30 .... Alexandria

AUGUST

8-9-10 .... San Angelo
11-12-13 .... Edinburg
21-22-23 .... Fort Worth

Edinburg

MAY

12-13-14 .... Alexandria
19-20-21-22 .... Jackson
23-24-25 .... Ozark

JUNE

2-3-4 .... San Angelo
5-6-7-8 .... Fort Worth
13-14-15 .... Rio Grande
26-27-28-29 ... San Angelo

JULY

1-2-3-4 .... Alexandria
10-11 .... Rio Grande
16-17-18-19 ... Shreveport
28-29-30 .... Jackson
31 .... San Angelo

AUGUST

1-2 .... San Angelo
9-10 .... Rio Grande
18-19-20 ..... Coastal Bend
21-22-23 .... Amarillo

Fort Worth

MAY

7-8-9-10 ..... Coastal Bend
19-20-21 .... Shreveport
23-24-25 .... Alexandria

JUNE

2-3-4 .... Rio Grande
13-14-15 .... Shreveport
17-18-19-20 .... Amarillo
25-26-27-28 .... Ozark

JULY

1-2-3-4 .... Jackson
5-6-7-8 .... San Angelo
21-22-23-24 .... Ozark
25-26-27 .... Alexandria

AUGUST

4-5-6 .... Edinburg
11-12-13 .... Amarillo
14-15-16 ..... Coastal Bend

Jackson

MAY

12-13-14 .... Ozark
16-17-18 .... Rio Grande
27-28-29 .... Edinburg
30-31 .... Alexandria

JUNE

1 .... Alexandria
5-6-7-8 .... Shreveport
17-18-19-20 .... Alexandria
21-22-23-24 ... Fort Worth

JULY

5-6-7-8 .... Ozark
9-10-11-12 .... Amarillo
20-21-22-23 ... San Angelo

AUGUST

1-2-3 .... Fort Worth
4-5-6 .... Coastal Bend
14-15-16 .... Shreveport
18-19-20 .... Ozark

Rio Grande Valley

MAY

8-9-10-11 ...... San Angelo
12-13-14 ..... Coastal Bend
23-24-25 .... Amarillo
26-27-28 .... Ozark

JUNE

5-6-7-8 .... Amarillo
10-11-12 ..... Coastal Bend
21-22-23-24 ...... Edinburg

JULY

5-6-7-8 .... Alexandria
9 .... Edinburg
12 .... Edinburg
20-21-22-23 ... Shreveport
25-26-27 .... Jackson

AUGUST

1-2-3 .... Amarillo
7-8 .... Edinburg
11-12-13 .... San Angelo
18-19-20 .... Fort Worth

San Angelo

MAY

12-13-14 .... Amarillo
15-16-17 .... Edinburg
26-27-28-29 ... Fort Worth
30-31 .... Coastal Bend

JUNE

1 .... Coastal Bend
5-6-7-8 .... Alexandria
10-11-12 .... Jackson
17-18-19-20 ... Rio Grande

JULY

1-2-3-4 .... Shreveport
9-10-11-12 .... Ozark
24-25-26-27 ... Coast. Bend
28-29-30 .... Rio Grande

AUGUST

4-5-6 .... Amarillo
14-15-16 .... Edinburg
21-22-23 .... Rio Grande

Shreveport

MAY

8-9-10-11 .... Edinburg
12-13-14 .... Fort Worth
22-23-24 .... San Angelo
30-31 .... Rio Grande

JUNE

1 .... Rio Grande
10-11-12 .... Ozark
21-22-23-24 ... Coast. Bend
25-26-27-28 .... Jackson

JULY

5-6-7-8 .... Amarillo
9-10-11-12 .... Coastal Bend
25-26-27 .... Edinburg

AUGUST

4-5-6 .... Ozark
7-8-9-10 .... Fort Worth
18-19-20 .... Alexandria
21-22-23 .... Jackson

Springfield-Ozark

MAY

8-9-10-11 .... Amarillo
15-16-17 .... Fort Worth
18-19-20-21 ... San Angelo
30-30-31 .... Edinburg

JUNE

2-3-4 .... Jackson
13-14-15 .... Alexandria
17-18-19-20 ... Shreveport
30 .... Rio Grande

JULY

1-2-3 .... Rio Grande
16-17-18-19 .... Jackson
29-30-31 .... Fort Worth

AUGUST

1-2-3 .... Coastal Bend
7-8-9-10 .... Jackson
11-12-13 .... Shreveport
21-22-23 .... Alexandria

FRONTIER LEAGUE

Chillicothe

MAY

23-24-25 .... Florence
28-29-30 .... Evansville

JUNE

6-7-8 .... Kalamazoo
14-15 .... River City
17-18 .... Gateway
19-20 .... Mid-Missouri
27-28-29 .... Evansville
30 .... Florence

JULY

1-2 .... Florence
6-7-8 .... Richmond
21-22-23 .... Washington
24-25-26 .... Florence
31 .... Cook County

AUGUST

1 .... Cook County
2-3 .... Kenosha
4-5 .... Rockford
14-15-16 .... Richmond
17-18-19 .... Washington
26-27-28 .... Kalamazoo

Cook County

MAY

23-24-25 .... Rockford

JUNE

3-4-5 .... River City
6-7-8 .... Mid-Missouri
17-18 .... Richmond
19-20 .... Kalamazoo
21-22 .... Washington
30 .... Mid-Missouri

JULY

1-2 .... Mid-Missouri
3-4-5 .... Rockford
12-13-14 .... Kenosha
18-19-20 .... Gateway
27-28-29 .... River City

AUGUST

7-8 .... Chillicothe
9-10 .... Evansville
11-12 .... Florence
17-18-19 .... Gateway
23-24-25 .... Kenosha
29-30-31 .... Rockford

Evansville

MAY

24-25-26 .... Richmond
31 .... Florence

JUNE

1-2 .... Florence
6-7-8 .... Washington
17-18 .... Mid-Missouri
19-20 .... River City
21-22 .... Gateway
30 .... Richmond

JULY

1-2 .... Richmond
6-7-8 .... Kalamazoo
12-13-14 .... Chillicothe
18-19-20 .... Kalamazoo
24-25-26 .... Richmond
31 .... Rockford

AUGUST

1 .... Rockford
2-3 .... Cook County
4-5 .... Kenosha
14-15-16 ...... Washington
23-24-25 .... Chillicothe
26-27-28 .... Florence

Florence

JUNE

3-4-5 .... Washington
6-7-8 .... Richmond
17-18 .... River City
19-20 .... Gateway
21-22 .... Mid-Missouri
27-28-29 .... Kalamazoo

JULY

3-4-5 .... Evansville
6-7-8 .... Washington
9-10-11 .... Chillicothe
21-22-23 .... Evansville
31 .... Kenosha

AUGUST

1 .... Kenosha
2-3 .... Rockford
4-5 .... Cook County
14-15-16 .... Kalamazoo
17-18-19 .... Richmond
20-21-22 .... Chillicothe
29-30-31 .... Chillicothe

Gateway

MAY

23-24-25 .... River City
31 .... Cook County

JUNE

1-2 .... Cook County
3-4-5 .... Mid-Missouri
10-11 .... Chillicothe
12-13 .... Florence
14-15 .... Evansville
24-25-26 .... Kenosha

JULY

3-4-5 .... River City
6-7-8 .... Cook County
21-22-23 .... Rockford
24-25-26 .... River City
31 .... Richmond

AUGUST

1 .... Richmond
2-3 .... Kalamazoo
4-5 .... Washington
14-15-16 .... Kenosha
23-24-25 .... Mid-Missouri
26-27-28 .... Rockford

Kalamazoo

MAY

23-24-25 .... Washington
28-29-30 .... Florence

JUNE

3-4-5 .... Evansville
10-11 .... Rockford
12-13 .... Cook County
14-15 .... Kenosha
24-25-26 .... Chillicothe

JULY

3-4-5 .... Richmond
9-10-11 .... Washington
12-13-14 .... Florence
27-28-29 .... Chillicothe

AUGUST

7-8-9-10 .... Gateway
11-12 .... River City
17-18-19 .... Evansville
23-24-25 .... Richmond
29-30-31 .... Washington

Kenosha

MAY

28-29-30 ..... Cook County

JUNE

3-4-5 .... Rockford
6-7-8 .... Gateway
17-18 .... Washington
19-20 .... Richmond
21-22 .... Kalamazoo
27-28-29 ..... Cook County

JULY

6-7-8 .... Rockford
9-10-11 ...... Mid-Missouri
21-22-23 .... River City
27-28-29 .... Gateway

AUGUST

7-8 .... Florence
9-10 .... Chillicothe
11-12 .... Evansville
20-21-22 .... Mid-Missouri
26-27-28 .... River City
29-30-31 .... Mid-Missouri

Mid-Missouri

MAY

23-24-25 .... Kenosha

JUNE

10-11 .... Evansville
12-13 .... Chillicothe
14-15 .... Florence
24-25-26 .... Rockford
27-28-29 .... Gateway

JULY

3-4-5 .... Kenosha
6-7-8 .... River City
12-13-14 .... Gateway
21-22-23 ..... Cook County
24-25-26 .... Kenosha
31 .... Kalamazoo

AUGUST

1 .... Kalamazoo
2-3 .... Washington
4-5 .... Richmond
14-15-16 .... Rockford
17-18-19 .... River City
26-27-28 ..... Cook County

Richmond

MAY

31 .... Kalamazoo

JUNE

1-1 .... Kalamazoo
3-4-5 .... Chillicothe
10-11 .... Cook County
12-13 .... Kenosha
14-15 .... Rockford
24-25-26 .... Florence
27-28-29 ...... Washington

JULY

9-10-11 .... Evansville
18-19-20 .... Chillicothe
21-22-23 .... Kalamazoo
27-28-29 .... Florence

AUGUST

7-8 .... Gateway
9-10 .... River City
11-12 .... Mid-Missouri
20-21-22 .... Evansville
26-27-28 .... Washington
29-30-31 .... Evansville

River City

MAY

28-29-30 .... Mid-Missouri
31 .... Kenosha

JUNE

1-2 .... Kenosha
10-11 .... Florence
12-13 .... Evansville
21-22 .... Chillicothe
24-25-26 ..... Cook County
30 .... Kenosha

JULY

1-2 .... Kenosha
9-10-11 .... Gateway
12-13-14 .... Rockford
18-19-20 .... Mid-Missouri
31 .... Washington

AUGUST

1 .... Washington
2-3 .... Richmond
4-5 .... Kalamazoo
14-15-16 ..... Cook County
20-21-22 .... Gateway
23-24-25 .... Rockford
29-30-31 .... Gateway

Rockford

MAY

28-29-30 .... Gateway
31 .... Mid-Missouri

JUNE

1-2 .... Mid-Missouri
6-7-8 .... River City
17-18 .... Kalamazoo
19-20 .... Washington
21-22 .... Richmond
27-28-29 .... River City
30 .... Gateway

JULY

1-2 .... Gateway
9-10-11 .... Cook County
18-19-20 .... Kenosha
24-25-26 ..... Cook County
27-28-29 .... Mid-Missouri

AUGUST

7-8 .... Evansville
9-10 .... Florence
11-12 .... Chillicothe
17-18-19 .... Kenosha
20-21-22 ..... Cook County

Washington

MAY

28-29-30 .... Richmond
31 .... Chillicothe

JUNE

1-2 .... Chillicothe
10-11 .... Kenosha
12-13 .... Rockford
14-15 .... Cook County
24-25-26 .... Evansville
30 .... Kalamazoo

JULY

1-2 .... Kalamazoo
3-4-5 .... Chillicothe
12-13-14 .... Richmond
18-19-20 .... Florence
24-25-26 .... Kalamazoo
27-28-29 .... Evansville

AUGUST

7-8 .... River City
9-10 .... Mid-Missouri
11-12 .... Gateway
20-21-22 .... Kalamazoo
23-24-25 .... Florence

NORTHEAST LEAGUE

Allentown

MAY
22-23-24-25 .... Bangor
30-31 .... Berkshire

JUNE
1 .... Berkshire
2-3-4 .... Brockton
13-14-15 .... Elmira
16-17-18-19 ... New Jersey
27-28-29 ...... North Shore
30 .... Quebec

JULY
1-2 .... Quebec
11-12-13 .... Bangor
21-22-23-24 ...... Brockton
25-26-27 .... Berkshire

AUGUST
4-5-6-7 .... Elmira
10 .... New Jersey
15-16 .... New Jersey
18-19-20 ...... North Shore
21-22-23 .... Quebec

Bangor

MAY
30-31 .... New Jersey

JUNE
1 .... New Jersey
2-3-4 .... Elmira
13-14-15 .... Brockton
16-17-18-19 ..... Berkshire
27-28-29 .... Quebec

JULY
4-5-6 .... Allentown
7-8-9 .... North Shore
18-19-20 .... New Jersey
21-22-23-24 .... Elmira

AUGUST
3-4-5-6 .... Brockton
8-9-10 .... Berkshire
18-19-20 .... Quebec
26-27-28 .... Allentown
29-30-31 ...... North Shore

SEPTEMBER
1 .... North Shore

Berkshire

JUNE
2-3-4 .... Quebec
5-6-7-8 .... Allentown
13-14-15 ...... North Shore
23-24-25-26 .... Bangor
27-28-29 .... Elmira

JULY
4-5-6 .... New Jersey
7-8-9 .... Brockton
18-19-20 .... Allentown
21-22-23-24 .... Quebec

AUGUST
4-5-6 .... North Shore
14-15-16 .... Bangor
18-19-20 .... Elmira
25-26-27 .... New Jersey
29-30-31 .... Brockton

SEPTEMBER
1 .... Brockton

Brockton

MAY
22-23-24-25 ... North Shore
26 .... Bangor
27-28-29 .... Berkshire

JUNE
9-10-11 .... New Jersey
16-17-18-19 .... Quebec
20-21-22 .... Allentown

JULY
1-2 .... Bangor
3-4-5-6 .... Elmira
15-16-17 .... Berkshire
18-19-20 ...... North Shore
30-31 .... New Jersey

AUGUST
1-2 .... New Jersey
7 .... New Jersey
8-9 .... Quebec
11-12-13 .... Allentown
22-23-24 .... Bangor
26-27-28 .... Elmira

Elmira

MAY
22-23-24-25 .... Quebec
26-27-28 .... Allentown

JUNE
5-6-7 .... Brockton
9-10-11 .... Berkshire
16-17-18-19 ... North Shore
20-21-22 .... Bangor
30 .... New Jersey

JULY
1-2 .... New Jersey
11-12-13 .... Brockton
14-15-16-17 .... Allentown
25-26-27 .... Quebec
30-31 .... Berkshire

AUGUST
1-2 .... Berkshire
11-12-13 .... Bangor
15-16-17 ...... North Shore
22-23-24 .... New Jersey

New Jersey

MAY
22-23-24-25 ..... Berkshire

JUNE
2-3-4 .... North Shore
5-6-7-8 .... Bangor
13-14-15 .... Quebec
23-24-25-26 .... Allentown
27-28-29 .... Brockton

JULY
7-8-9 .... Elmira
11-12-13 .... Berkshire
21-22-23-24 ... North Shore
25-26-27 .... Bangor

AUGUST
4-5-6-7 .... Quebec
8-9 .... Allentown
18-19-20 .... Brockton
29-30-31 .... Elmira

SEPTEMBER
1 .... Elmira

North Shore

MAY
28-29 .... Bangor
30-31 .... Brockton

JUNE
1 .... Brockton
5-6-7-8 .... Quebec
9-10-11 .... Allentown
20-21-22 .... New Jersey
23-24-25-26 .... Elmira
30 .... Bangor

JULY
1-2-3 .... Berkshire
11-12-13 .... Quebec
14-15-16 .... Bangor
25-26-27 .... Brockton
30-31 .... Allentown

AUGUST
1-2 .... Allentown
8-9 .... Elmira
11-12-13 .... New Jersey
21-22-23-24 ..... Berkshire

Quebec

MAY
27-28-29 .... New Jersey
30-31 .... Elmira

JUNE
1 .... Elmira
10-11-12 .... Bangor
20-21-22 .... Berkshire
23-24-25-26 ...... Brockton

JULY
4-5-6 .... North Shore
7-8-9 .... Allentown
14-15-16-17 ... New Jersey
18-19-20 .... Elmira
30-31 .... Bangor

AUGUST
1-2 .... Bangor
11-12-13 .... Berkshire
14-15-16 .... Brockton
26-27-28 ...... North Shore
29-30-31 .... Allentown

SEPTEMBER
1 .... Allentown

NORTHERN LEAGUE

Fargo-Moorhead

MAY
23-24-25 .... Winnipeg
30-31 .... Schaumburg

JUNE
1 .... Schaumburg
2-3-4 .... St. Paul
6-7-8 .... Sioux Falls
13-14-15 .... Gary

JULY
1-2-3 .... Sioux Falls
7-8-9-10 .... Sioux City
15-16-17 .... Winnipeg

AUGUST
1-2-3 .... Kansas City
8-9-10 .... Lincoln
11-12-13-14 .... Joliet
22-23-24-25 ... Kansas City
26-27-28 .... Lincoln
29-30-31 .... Sioux City

Gary

MAY
26-27-28 ..... Schaumburg
30-31 .... Kansas City

JUNE
1 .... Kansas City
3-4-5 .... Sioux City
20-21-22 ..... Schaumburg
23-24-25-26 .... F-M
30 .... Joliet

JULY
1-2-3 .... Joliet
4-5-6 .... Winnipeg
11-12-13 .... Joliet
24-25-26-27 ...... Schaum.
28-29-30 .... St. Paul

AUGUST
1-2-3 .... Lincoln
8-9-10 .... Sioux Falls
15-16-17 .... Winnipeg
18-19-20 .... St. Paul

Joliet

MAY
23-24-25 .... Gary
26-27-28 .... Kansas City

JUNE
2-3-4 .... Sioux Falls
13-14-15 .... Lincoln
16-17-18 .... Sioux City
19-20-21-22 .... F-M
27-28-29 .... Winnipeg

JULY
4-5-6 .... Schaumburg
14-15-16-17 ...... Schaum.
18-19-20 .... Gary
24-25-26-27 .... St. Paul

AUGUST
4-5-6 .... Sioux Falls
18-19-20 .... Winnipeg
22-23-24 .... St. Paul

Kansas City

JUNE

6-7-8 .... Sioux City
9-10-11 .... F-M
12-13-14 .... Winnipeg
23-24-25-26 .... Joliet
27-28-29 .... Gary

JULY

4-5-6 .... St. Paul
11-12-13 .... F-M
15-16-17 .... Lincoln
24-25-26-27 .... Lincoln

AUGUST

5-6-7 .... Gary
8-9-10 .... Sioux City
11-12-13-14 ... Sioux Falls
18-19-20 ..... Schaumburg
29-30-31 .... Sioux Falls

Lincoln

MAY

23-24-25 .... Sioux City
26-27-28 .... Winnipeg

JUNE

2-3-4-5 .... Kansas City
6-7-8 .... Gary
16-17-18 ..... Schaumburg
20-21-22 .... Kansas City

JULY

4-5-6 .... F-M
8-9-10 .... Joliet
11-12-13 .... Sioux Falls
28-29-30-31 .... Sioux City

AUGUST

5-6-7 .... St. Paul
15-16-17 .... Kansas City
18-19-20 .... F-M
21-22-23-24 ... Sioux Falls

St. Paul

MAY

23-24-25 .... Kansas City

JUNE

6-7-8 .... Schaumburg
9-10-11 .... Joliet
16-17-18 .... F-M
23-24-25 .... Sioux City
26-27-28-29 ... Sioux Falls

JULY

1-2-3 .... Lincoln
8-9-10 .... Winnipeg
14-15-16-17 .... Gary

AUGUST

1-2-3 .... Joliet
8-9-10 .... Schaumburg
11-12-13-14 ..... Winnipeg
15-16-17 .... Joliet
29-30-31 .... Gary

Schaumburg

MAY

23-24-25 .... Sioux Falls

JUNE

9-10-11-12 .... Lincoln
13-14-15 .... Sioux City
23-24-25 .... Lincoln
27-28-29 .... F-M
30 .... Winnipeg

JULY

1-2-3 .... Winnipeg
8-9-10 .... Gary
11-12-13 .... St. Paul
18-19-20 .... Kansas City
29-30-31 .... Joliet

AUGUST

11-12-13 .... Gary
21-22-23-24 ..... Winnipeg
26-27-28 .... St. Paul
29-30-31 .... Joliet

Sioux City

MAY

26-27-28-29 .... St. Paul
30-31 .... Joliet

JUNE

1 .... Joliet
9-10-11 .... Winnipeg
20-21-22 .... Sioux Falls
26-27-28-29 .... Lincoln

JULY

1-2-3 .... Kansas City
6 .... Sioux Falls
15-16-17 .... Sioux Falls
18-19-20 .... F-M

AUGUST

1-2-3 .... Schaumburg
4-5-6 .... F-M
12-13-14 .... Lincoln
15-16-17 .... F-M
22-23-24-25 .... Gary
26-27-28 .... Kansas City

Sioux Falls

MAY

26-27-28 .... F-M
29-30-31 .... Lincoln

JUNE

9-10-11-12 .... Gary
13-14-15 .... St. Paul
16-17-18 .... Kansas City

JULY

4-5 .... Sioux City
7-8-9-10 .... Kansas City
18-19-20 .... Lincoln
24-25-26-27 .... Sioux City
29-30-31 .... F-M

AUGUST

1-2-3 .... Winnipeg
15-16-17 ..... Schaumburg
18-19-20 .... Sioux City
26-27-28 .... Joliet

Winnipeg

MAY

30-31 .... St. Paul

JUNE

1 .... St. Paul
2-3-4-5 .... Schaumburg
6-7-8 .... Joliet
16-17-18 .... Gary
19-20-21-22 .... St. Paul
23-24-25 .... Sioux Falls

JULY

11-12-13 .... Sioux Citiy
18-19-20 .... St. Paul
24-25-26-27 .... F-M
29-30-31 .... Kansas City

AUGUST

5-6-7 .... Schaumburg
8-9-10 .... Joliet
26-27-28 .... Gary
29-30-31 .... Lincoln

INTERNATIONAL LEAGUES

FOREIGN LEAGUES

2002 STANDINGS

AMERICAS

MEXICAN LEAGUE

TRIPLE-A CLASSIFICATION

EAST	W	L	PCT	GB
*Mexico City Red Devils	74	36	.673	—
#Saltillo	66	43	.606	7½
Two Laredos	62	48	.564	12
Monterrey	60	43	.550	13½
Monclova	56	54	.509	18
Union Laguna	44	65	.404	29½
Reynosa	43	67	.391	31
Puebla	38	70	.352	35
CENTRAL	**W**	**L**	**PCT**	**GB**
*Oaxaca	62	45	.579	—
#Yucatan	60	47	.561	2
Mexico Tigers	57	49	.538	4½
Veracruz	55	53	.509	7½
Cancun	53	54	.495	9
Campeche	52	55	.486	10
Tabasco	48	61	.440	15
Cordoba	37	71	.343	25½

*First-half champion
#Second-half champion

PLAYOFFS: Quarterfinals (best-of-7)—Mexico City Red Devils defeated Monclova 4-1; Mexico Tigers defeated Yucatan 4-3; Oaxaca defeated Veracruz 4-0; Two Laredos defeated Saltillo 4-2. **Semifinals** (best-of-7)—Mexico City Red Devils defeated Two Laredos 4-3; Mexico Tigers defeated Oaxaca 4-3. **Finals** (best-of-7)—Mexico City Red Devils defeated Mexico Tigers 4-3.

DOMINICAN SUMMER LEAGUE

ROOKIE CLASSIFICATION

SANTO DOMINGO EAST/East	W	L	PCT	GB
Red Sox	41	31	.569	—
Cardinals	36	32	.529	3
Giants	37	35	.514	4
Rockies	34	37	.479	6½
Expos	29	40	.420	10½
Diamondbacks	30	42	.417	11
SANTO DOMINGO EAST/Central	**W**	**L**	**PCT**	**GB**
Phillies	49	22	.690	—
Brewers	48	24	.667	1½
Dodgers I	38	33	.535	11
Tigers	34	37	.479	15
Athletics East	31	40	.437	18
Mariners	31	41	.431	18½
Yankees II	24	48	.333	25½
SANTO DOMINGO WEST	**W**	**L**	**PCT**	**GB**
Yankees I	42	28	.600	—
Padres	38	31	.551	3½
Indians II	39	33	.542	4
Mets	37	33	.529	5
Dodgers II	34	34	.500	7
Athletics West	34	35	.493	7½
Twins	29	40	.420	12½
Reds	25	44	.362	16½
SAN PEDRO de MACORIS	**W**	**L**	**PCT**	**GB**
Blue Jays	46	25	.648	—
Astros	39	32	.549	7
Angels	39	33	.542	7½
Cubs	37	34	.521	9
Pirates	36	36	.500	10½
Orioles	33	39	.458	13½
Rangers	31	40	.437	15
Marlins	25	47	.347	21½
CIBAO	**W**	**L**	**PCT**	**GB**
Indians	49	19	.721	—
White Sox	47	21	.691	2
Braves II	32	35	.478	16½
Braves I	24	44	.353	25
Royals	17	50	.254	31½

PLAYOFFS: **Quarterfinals** (one-game playoff)—Phillies defeated Red Sox 1-0. **Semifinals** (best-of-3)—Blue Jays defeated Phillies 2-1; Indians defeated Yankees I 2-1. **Finals** (best-of-5)—Indians defeated Blue Jays 3-0.

VENEZUELAN SUMMER LEAGUE

ROOKIE CLASSIFICATION

BARQUISIMETO	W	L	PCT	GB
San Felipe	42	16	.717	—
Chivacoa	29	28	.508	12½
Carora	26	31	.458	15½
Cabudare	18	40	.317	24
VALENCIA	**W**	**L**	**PCT**	**GB**
Aguirre	41	17	.703	—
Cagua	33	26	.558	8½
Venoco	32	26	.551	9
Ciudad Alianza	31	29	.517	11
Puerto Cabello	28	29	.492	12½
San Joaquin	25	32	.441	15½
Mariara	24	36	.400	18
Universidad Carabobo	19	38	.333	21½

PLAYOFFS: **Finals** (best-of-3)—Aguirre defeated San Felipe 2-0.

CUBA

GROUP A	W	L	PCT	GB
Pinar del Rio	64	26	.711	—
Isla de la Juventud	51	39	.567	13
Matanzas	48	42	.533	16
Metropolitanos	31	59	.344	33
GROUP B	**W**	**L**	**PCT**	**GB**
Sancti Spiritus	53	37	.589	—
Industriales	49	41	.544	4
Havana	45	45	.500	8
Cienfuegos	33	57	.367	20
GROUP C	**W**	**L**	**PCT**	**GB**
Villa Clara	54	36	.600	—
Camaguey	44	46	.489	10
Ciego de Avila	42	48	.467	12
Las Tunas	23	67	.256	31

GROUP D	W	L	PCT	GB
Holguin	55	35	.611	—
Santiago de Cuba	54	36	.600	1
Granma	38	52	.422	17
Guantanamo	36	54	.400	19

PLAYOFFS—Quarterfinals (best-of-5): Holguin defeated Camaguey 3-1; Sancti Spiritus defeated Isla de la Juventud 3-2; Villa Clara defeated Santiago 3-1; Pinar del Rio defeated Industriales 3-1. **Semifinals** (best-of-7): Holguin defeated Villa Clara 4-2; Sancti Spiritus defeated Pinar del Rio 4-2. **Finals** (best-of-7): Holguin defeated Sancti Spiritus 4-2.

ASIA

JAPANESE LEAGUES

CENTRAL	W	L	PCT	GB
Yomiuri	86	52	.623	—
Yakult	74	62	.544	11
Chunichi	69	66	.511	15½
Hanshin	66	70	.485	19
Hiroshima	64	72	.471	21
Yokohama	49	86	.363	35½
PACIFIC	**W**	**L**	**PCT**	**GB**
Seibu	90	49	.647	—
Osaka Kintetsu	73	65	.529	16½
Fukuoka	73	65	.529	16½
Chiba Lotte	67	72	.482	23
Nippon Ham	61	76	.445	28
Orix	50	87	.365	39

PLAYOFFS: Finals (best-of-7)—Yomiuri defeated Seibu 4-0.

KOREA BASEBALL ORGANIZATION

	W	L	PCT	GB
Samsung	82	47	.636	—
Kia	78	51	.605	4
Hyundai	70	58	.547	11½
LG	66	61	.520	15
Doosan	66	65	.504	17
SK	61	69	.469	21½
Hanwha	59	69	.461	22½
Lotte	35	97	.265	48½

PLAYOFFS: Quarterfinals (best-of-3)—LG defeated Hyundai 2-0. **Semifinals** (best-of-5)—LG defeated Kia 3-2. **Finals** (best-of-7)—Samsung defeated LG 4-2.

TAIWANESE LEAGUES

CPBL	W	L	PCT	GB
*Brother	53	33	.616	—
China	45	42	.517	8½
Sinon	44	45	.494	10½
President	32	54	.372	20

*First- and second-half champion

PLAYOFFS: Finals (best-of-7)—Brother defeated China Trust 4-0.

TAIWAN MAJOR

	W	L	PCT	GB
Taichung	47	24	.662	—
Kaohsiung	34	37	.479	13
Taipei	31	39	.443	15½
Chiayi	29	41	.414	17½

PLAYOFFS: Finals (best-of-7)—Taichung defeated Kaohsiung 4-2.

EUROPE

ITALY

	W	L	PCT	GB
Rimini	39	15	.722	—
Bologna	39	15	.722	—
Nettuno	37	17	.685	2
Grosseto	35	19	.648	4
Parma	30	24	.556	9
Modena	27	27	.500	12
Anzio	21	32	.396	17½
Firenze	20	34	.370	19
Codogno	14	40	.259	25
Paterno	7	46	.132	31½

PLAYOFFS: Finals (best-of-7)—Rimini defeated Nettuno 4-1.

NETHERLANDS

PLAYOFF POOL	W	L	PCT	GB
Neptunus	38	7	.830	—
Kinheim	31	15	.670	7½
HCAW	29	16	.638	9
Hoofddorp	21	22	.489	16
PSV Eindhoven	20	24	.457	17½
Hague	20	24	.457	17½
PROMOTION/RELEGATION POOL	**W**	**L**	**PCT**	**GB**
Sparta/Feyenoord	15	5	.750	—
Amsterdam Pirates	12	7	.625	2½
Almere	12	8	.600	3
Oosterhout	10	10	.500	5
RCH	6	13	.325	6
Alcmaria	4	16	.250	11

PLAYOFFS: Finals (best-of-5)—Neptunus defeated HCAW 3-0.

AMERICAS

MEXICO

MEXICAN LEAGUE

Member, National Association

Class AAA

NOTE: *The Mexican League is a member of the National Association of Professional Baseball Leagues and has a Triple-A classification. However, its member clubs operate largely independent of the 30 major league teams, and for that reason the league is listed in the international and winter league section.*

Mailing Address: Angel Pola No. 16, Col. Periodista, CP 11220, Mexico, D.F. **Telephone:** (555) 557-1007, (555) 557-1408. **FAX:** (555) 395-2454. **E-Mail Address:** mbl@prodigy.net.mx. **Website:** www.lmb.com.mx.

Years League Active: 1955-.

President: Raúl González Rodríguez. **Operations Manager:** Nestor Alba Brito.

2003 Opening Date: March 18. **Closing Date:** July 27.

Regular Season: 110 games.

Division Structure: North—Laguna, Mexico City Red Devils, Monclova, Monterrey, Puebla, Reynosa, Saltillo, Two Laredos. **South**—Angelopolis Tigers, Campeche, Cancún, Cordoba, Oaxaca, Tabasco, Veracruz, Yucatan.

Playoff Format: Eight teams qualify; the first-fourth place teams in each division. First and second round playoffs are best-of-7 series. Division finalists meet in best 4 of 7 series for league championship.

Roster Limit: 28. **Roster Limit, Imports:** 5.

Statistician: Ana Luisa Perea Talarico, Angel Pola No. 16, Col. Periodista, CP 11220, Mexico, D.F.

ANGELOPOLIS TIGERS

Office Address: Blvd. Díaz Ordaz, #811 Mezzanine A Plaza Dorada, Col. Anzures, CP 72530 Puebla, Puebla. **Telephone:** (222) 237-0148. **FAX:** (222) 237-1670. **E-Mail Address:** tigres@tigrescapitalinos.com.mx. **Website:** www.tigrescapitalinos.com.mx.

President: Cuauhtémoc Rodriguez. **General Manager:** Iram Campos Lara.

Manager: Lee Sigman.

CAMPECHE PIRATES

Office Address: Unidad Deportiva 20 de Noviembre, Local 4, CP 24000, Campeche, Campeche. **Telephone:** (981) 816-6071. **FAX:** (981) 816-3807. **E-Mail Address:** piratasc@prodigy.net.mx.

President: Gabriel Escalante Castillo. **General Manager:** Maria del Socorro Morales.

Manager: Manuel Cazarin.

CANCUN LOBSTERMEN

Office Address: Av. De la Costa #40 S.M. L27, Mza. 11, CP 77500, Cancún, Quintana Roo. **Telephone:** (998) 892-3783. **FAX:** (998) 887-8863. **E-Mail Address:** clublangosteros@hotmail.com. **Website:** www.langosteros.com.

President: Francisco Villanueva. **General Manager:** Luisa Vanessa Villanueva Vargas.

Manager: Unavailable.

CORDOBA COFFEEGROWERS

Office Address: Av. 1 Esquina Calle 24, CP 94560, Córdoba, Veracruz. **Telephone:** (271) 716-5411, 716-5535. **FAX:** (271) 716-5570. **E-Mail Address:** cafeteros@prodigy.net.mx. **Website:** www.cafeterosdecordoba.com.mx.

President: Jean Paul Mansur Beltrán. **General Manager:** Antelmo Hernandez Quirasco.

Manager: Eddie Diaz.

MEXICO CITY RED DEVILS

Office Address: Av. Cuauhtemoc #451-101, Col. Narvarte, CP 03020, Mexico DF **Telephone:** (555) 639-8722. **FAX:** (555) 639-9722. **E-Mail Address:** diablos@diablos-rojos.com.mx. **Website:** www.diablos.com.mx.

President: Roberto Mansur Galán. **General Manager:** Eduardo de la Cerda.

Manager: Bernie Tatis.

MONCLOVA STEELERS

Office Address: Av. Ciudad Deportiva y Av. Cuauhtemoc s/n Interior Estadio Monclova, Col. Ciudad Deportiva, CP 25750, Monclova, Coahuila. **Telephone:** (866) 636-2334. **FAX:** (866) 636-2688. **E-Mail Address:** acereros@gan.com.mx. **Website:** www.acereros.com.mx.

President: Manuel Ancira Elizondo. **General Manager:** Arturo Rodriguez Peña.

Manager: Derek Bryant.

MONTERREY SULTANS

Office Address: Av. Manuel Barragan s/n, Estadio Monterrey, CP 66460, Monterrey, Nuevo Leon. **Telephone:** (818) 351-8022, (818) 351-9467. **FAX:** (818) 351-9186. **E-Mail Address:** sultanes@sultanes.com.mx.

President: José Maiz García. **General Manager:** Roberto Magdaleno Ramírez.

Manager: Dan Firova.

OAXACA WARRIORS

Office Address: Privada del Chopo #105, Fraccionamiento El Chopo, CP 68050, Oaxaca, Oaxaca. **Telephone:** (951) 515-5522. **FAX:** (951) 515-4966. **E-Mail Addresses:** guerreros@infosel.net.mex, guerreros@guerrerosdeoaxaca.com. **Website:** www.guerrerosdeoaxaca.com.

President: Vicente Pérez Avellá Villa. **General Manager:** Guillermo Rodriguez Velazquez.

Manager: Houston Jimenez.

PUEBLA PARROTS

Office Address: Parque Hermanos Serdán, Unidad Deportiva 5 de Mayo s/n, Col. Maravillas, CP 72220, Puebla, Puebla. **Telephone:** (222) 222-2116. **FAX:** (222) 222-2117. **E-Mail Address:** oficina@pericosdepuebla.com.mx. **Website:** www.pericosdepuebla.com.mx.

President: Samuel Lozano Molina. **General Manager:** Jorge Calvo Lara.

Manager: Unavailable.

REYNOSA BRONCOS

Office Address: Blvd. Hidalgo Km. 102, Col. Adolfo López Mateos, CP 88650, Reynosa, Tamaulipas. **Telephone:** (899) 924-1750, (899) 925-2808. **FAX:** (899) 924-2695. **E-Mail Address:** broncos1@prodigy.net.mx. **Website:** www.losbroncos.com.mx.

President: César Villanueva Cuellar. **General Manager:** Leo Clayton.

Manager: Unavailable.

SALTILLO SARAPE MAKERS

Office Address: Blvd. Nazario Ortiz Garza Esquina con Blvd. Jesus Sanchez, Col. Ciudad Deportiva, CP 25280, Saltillo, Coahuila. **Telephone:** (667) 713-3369, 712-2446. **FAX:** (667) 715-6828. **E-Mail Address:**

aley@grupoley.com. **Website:** www.saraperos.com.mx.

President: Juan Manuel Ley López. **General Manager:** Carlos de la Garza Barajas.

Manager: Raul Cano.

TABASCO CATTLEMEN

Office Address: Explanada de la Ciudad Deportiva, Parque de Beisbol Centenario del 27 de Febrero, Col. Atasta de Serra, CP 86100, Villahermosa, Tabasco. **Telephone:** (993) 352-2787. **FAX:** (993) 352-2788. **E-Mail Address:** olmecastab@prodigy.net.mx.

President: Rafael Duran Lili. **General Manager:** Juan Antonio Balmaceda.

Manager: Sergio Borges Suarez.

TWO LAREDOS OWLS

Office Address: Av. Santos Degollado #235-G, Col. Independencia, CP 88020, Nuevo Laredo, Tamaulipas. **Telephone:** (867) 712-2299. **FAX:** (867) 712-0736. **E-Mail Address:** tecolotes@globalpc.net. **Website:** www.tecolotes.com.mx.

President: Martín Reyes Madrigal. **General Manager:** Francisco Reyes Madrigal.

Manager: Unavailable.

LAGUNA COWBOYS

Office Address: Juan Gutenberg s/n, Col. Centro, CP 27000, Torreon, Coahuila. **Telephone:** (871) 718-5515. **FAX:** (871) 717-4335. **E-Mail Address:** unionlag@prodigy.net.mx. **Website:** www.unionlaguna.com.mx.

President: Jose Antonio Mansur Beltran. **General Manager:** Carlos Gomez del Campo.

Manager: Unavailable.

VERACRUZ REDS

Office Address: Av. Jacarandas s/n, Esquina España, Fraccionamiento Virginia, CP 94294, Boca del Rio, Veracruz. **Telephone:** (229) 935-5004. **FAX:** (229) 935-5008. **E-Mail Address:** rojosdelaguila@terra.com.mx. **Website:** www.rojosdelaguila.com.mx.

President: Gustavo Sousa Escamilla. **General Manager:** Carlos Nahun Hernández.

Manager: Andres Mora.

YUCATAN LIONS

Office Address: Calle 50 #406-B, Entre 35 y 37, Col. Jesus Carranza, CP 97109, Merida, Yucatán. **Telephone:** (999) 926-3022. **FAX:** (999) 926-3631. **E-Mail Addresses:** leonesy@sureste.com, leonesy@cablered.net.mx. **Website:** www.leones.yucatan.com.mx.

President: Gustavo Ricalde Durán. **General Manager:** Jose Rivero Ancona.

Manager: Francisco Estrada Soto.

DOMINICAN REPUBLIC

DOMINICAN SUMMER LEAGUE

Member, National Association

Rookie Classification

Mailing Address: Calle Segunda No. 14, Reparto Antilla, Santo Domingo, Dominican Republic. **Telephone:** (809) 532-3619. **FAX:** (809) 532-3619.

Years League Active: 1985-.

President: Freddy Jana. **Administrative Assistant:** Orlando Diaz.

2003 Member Clubs: Angels, Diamondbacks, Braves I, Braves II, Orioles, Red Sox, Cubs, White Sox, Reds, Indians, Rockies, Tigers, Marlins, Astros, Royals, Dodgers I, Dodgers II, Brewers, Twins, Expos, Mets, Yankees I, Yankees II, Athletics I, Athletics II, Phillies, Pirates, Cardinals, Padres, Giants, Mariners, Rangers, Blue Jays.

2003 Opening Date: June 7. **Closing Date:** Aug. 31.

Regular Season: 70-72 games, depending on divisions.

Playoff Format: Unavailable.

Roster Limit: 30 active. **Player Eligibility Rule:** No more than eight players 20 or older and no more than two players 21 or older. At least 10 players must be pitchers. No more than two years of prior service, excluding Rookie leagues outside the U.S. and Canada.

VENEZUELA

VENEZUELAN SUMMER LEAGUE

Member, National Association

Rookie Classification

Mailing Address: C.C. Caribbean Plaza Modulo 8, P.A. Local 173-174, Valencia, Carabobo, Venezuela. **Telephone:** 011-58-241-8240321 or 8240980. **FAX:** 011-58-241-8240705. **Website:** www.venezuelansummerleague.com.

Years League Active: 1997-.

Administrator: Saul Gonzalez. **Coordinator, Valencia:** Ramon Fereira. **Coordinator, Barquisimeto:** Jose Rafael Ramos. **Statistics, Barquisimeto:** Diego Matheus. **Statistics, Valencia:** Franklin Moreno Celis.

2003 Member Clubs, Division Structure: Barquisimeto—Carora, Cabudare, Chivacoa, San Felipe. **Valencia**—Aguirre, Cagua, Ciudad Alianza, La Pradera, Mariana, San Joaquin, Universidad, Venoco.

2003 Opening Date: June 1. **Closing Date:** Aug. 22.

Regular Season: 60 games.

Playoffs: Best-of-3 series between division champions for league championship.

Roster Limit: 30 active. **Player Eligibility Rule:** No player on active list may have more than three years of minor league service. Open to players from all Latin American Spanish-speaking countries except Mexico, the Dominican Republic and Puerto Rico.

CANADA

CANADIAN BASEBALL LEAGUE

Office Address: Suite 440-1140 W. Pender St., Vancouver, B.C. V6E 4G1. **Telephone:** (604) 689-1566. **FAX:** (604) 689-1531. **E-Mail Address:** info@canadianbaseballleague.com. **Website**: www.canadianbaseballleague.com.

Years League Active: 2003.

Commissioner: Ferguson Jenkins. **Chairman/Chief Strategist:** Tony Riviera. **President/Chief Executive Officer:** Charlton Lui. **Director, Baseball Operations:** John Haar. **Director, Communications:** Alex Klenman.

2003 Opening Date: May 21. **Closing Date:** Sept. 21.

Regular Season: 72 games (split schedule)

Division Structure: West—Victoria (B.C.) Capitals, Kelowna (B.C.) Heat, Calgary Outlaws, Saskatoon (Sask.) Legends. **East**—London (Ont.) Monarchs, Niagara (Ont.) Stars, Trois-Rivieres (Quebec) Saints, Montreal Royales.

Playoff Format: First-half division winners meet second-half division winners in best-of-5 series. Winners meet in best-of-7 series for league championship.

All-Star Game: July 23 at Calgary.

Roster Limit: 25. **Player Eligibility Rule:** Minimum of five Canadian-born players per team.

Brand of Baseball: Rawlings.

Statistician: Unavailable.

ASIA

CHINA

CHINA BASEBALL LEAGUE

Mailing Address: 5, Tiyuguan Road, Beijing 100763, Peoples Republic of China. **Telephone:** 86-10-85826002. **FAX:** 86-10-85825994. **E-Mail Address:** Cga_cra@263.net.

Years League Active: 2002-.

Commissioner/Executive Director: Yang Jie. **Secretary General, CBL/China Baseball Association:** Shen Wei. **Vice Chairman:** Tom McCarthy.

Member Clubs: Beijing Tigers, Shanghai Golden Eagles, Tianjin Lions, Guangdong Leopards.

Regular Season: 24 games.

2003 Opening Date: March 15. **Closing Date:** June 8. (playoffs through June 29)

Import Rule: Only three import players may be active at any time.

JAPAN

Mailing Address: Imperial Tower, 14F, 1-1-1 Uchisaiwai-cho, Chiyoda-ku, Tokyo 100-0011. **Telephone:** 03-3502-0022. **FAX:** 03-3502-0140.

Commissioner: Hiromori Kawashima.

Executive Secretary: Kazuo Hasegawa. **Executive Director, Public Relations:** Kunio Shimoda. **Executive Director, Baseball Operations:** Masaru Madate. **Assistant Directors, International Affairs:** Nobuhisa "Nobby" Ito, Tack Nakajima.

Japan Series: Best-of-7 series between Central and Pacific League champions, begins Oct. 18 at home of Pacific League club.

All-Star Series: July 15 at Osaka Dome; July 16 at Chiba.

Roster Limit: 70 per organization (one major league club, one minor league club). Major league club is permitted to register 28 players at a time, though just 25 may be available for each game. **Roster Limit, Imports:** 4 (2 position players and 2 pitchers or 3 position players and 1 pitcher or 3 pitchers and 1 position player) in majors; unlimited in minors.

CENTRAL LEAGUE

Mailing Address: Asahi Bldg. 3F, 6-6-7 Ginza, Chuo-ku, Tokyo 104-0061. **Telephone:** 03-3572-1673. **FAX:** 03-3571-4545.

President: Hajime Toyokura. **Secretary General:** Hideo Okoshi. **Planning Department:** Masaaki Nagino. **Public Relations:** Kazu Ogaki.

2003 Opening Date: March 28. **Closing Date:** Sept. 21.

Regular Season: 140 games.

Playoff Format: None.

CHUNICHI DRAGONS

Mailing Address: Chunichi Bldg. 6F, 4-1-1 Sakae, Naka-ku, Nagoya 460-0008. **Telephone:** 052-252-5226. **FAX:** 052-263-7696.

Chairman: Bungo Shirai. **President:** Junnosuke Nishikawa. **General Manager:** Kazumasa Ito. **Field Manager:** Hisashi Yamada.

2003 Foreign Players: Ivan Cruz, Eddie Gaillard, Omar Linares (Cuba), Marc Valdes, Martin Vargas.

HANSHIN TIGERS

Mailing Address: 1-47 Koshien-cho, Nishinomiya-shi, Hyogo-ken 663-8152. **Telephone:** 0798-46-1515. **FAX:** 0798-40-0934.

Chairman: Shunjiro Kuma. **President:** Katsuyoshi Nozaki. **General Manager:** Kunio Takeda. **Field Manager:** Senichi Hoshino.

2003 Foreign Players: George Arias, Trey Moore, Lou Pote, Jeff Williams. **Coach:** Tom O'Malley.

HIROSHIMA TOYO CARP

Mailing Address: 5-25 Motomachi, Naka-ku, Hiroshima 730-8508. **Telephone:** 082-221-2040. **FAX:** 082-228-5013.

President: Hajime Matsuda. **General Manager:** Junro Anan. **Field Manager:** Koji Yamamoto.

2003 Foreign Players: Jimmy Hurst, Dave Lundquist, Alan Newman, Ramon Ramirez, Andy Sheets.

YAKULT SWALLOWS

Mailing Address: Shimbashi MCV Bldg. 5F, 5-13-5 Shimbashi, Minato-ku, Tokyo 105-0004. **Telephone:** 03-5470-8915. **FAX:** 03-5470-8916.

Chairman: Naomi Matsuzono. **President:** Yoshikazu Tagiku. **General Manager:** Kesatoku Kurashima. **Field Manager:** Tsutomu Wakamatsu.

2003 Foreign Players: Todd Betts, Kevin Hodges, Daniel Matsumoto (Brazil), Alex Ramirez, Leonardo Sato (Brazil).

YOKOHAMA BAYSTARS

Mailing Address: Kannai Arai Bldg, 7F, 1-8 Onoe-cho, Naka-ku, Yokohama 231-0015. **Telephone:** 045-681-0811. **FAX:** 045-661-2500.

Chairman: Yukio Sunahara. **President:** Takashi Ohori. **General Manager:** Yoshio Noguchi. **Field Manager:** Daisuke Yamashita.

2003 Foreign Players: Steve Cox, Domingo Guzman, Chris Holt, Matt Whiteside, Tyrone Woods. **Coach:** John Turney.

YOMIURI GIANTS

Mailing Address: Takebashi 3-3 Bldg., 3-3 Kanda Nishiki-cho, Chiyoda-ku, Tokyo 101-8462. **Telephone:** 03-3295-7711. **FAX:** 03-3295-7708.

Chairman: Tsuneo Watanabe. **General Manager:** Makoto Doi. **Field Manager:** Tatsunori Hara.

2003 Foreign Players: Cory Bailey, Rodney Pedraza, Roberto Petagine, Matt Randel, Gary Rath.

PACIFIC LEAGUE

Mailing Address: Asahi Bldg. 9F, 6-6-7 Ginza, Chuo-ku, Tokyo 104-0061. **Telephone:** 03-3573-1551. **FAX:** 03-3572-5843.

President: Tadao Koike. **Secretary General:** Shigeru Murata. **Administration Department:** Katsuhisa Matsuzaki.

2003 Opening Date: March 28. **Closing Date:** Sept. 30.

Regular Season: 140 games.

Playoff Format: None.

CHIBA LOTTE MARINES

Mailing Address: WBG Marive West 26F, 2-6 Nakase, Mihama-ku, Chiba-shi, Chiba-ken 261-8587. **Telephone:** 043-297-2101. **FAX:** 043-297-2181.

Chairman: Takeo Shigemitsu. **General Manager:** Tomoichi Kawakita. **Field Manager:** Koji Yamamoto.

2003 Foreign Players: Derrick May, Nate Minchey, Bobby Rose, Rick Short, Brian Sikorski.

FUKUOKA DAIEI HAWKS

Mailing Address: Fukuoka Dome, 2-2-2 Jigyohama, Chuo-ku, Fukuoka 810-0065. **Telephone:** 092-844-1189. **FAX:** 092-844-4600.

Chairman: Tadashi Nakauchi. **President:** Takeshi Kotsuka. **General Manager:** Ryuzo Setoyama. **Field Manager:** Sadaharu Oh.

2003 Foreign Players: Anderson Gomez, Brandon Knight, Bryant Nelson, Matt Skrmetta, Pedro Valdes, Chen Wen-bin (Taiwan).

NIPPON HAM FIGHTERS

Mailing Address: Roppongi Denki Bldg. 6F, 6-1-20 Roppongi, Minato-ku, Tokyo 106-0032. **Telephone:** 03-3403-9131. **FAX:** 03-3403-9143.

President: Junji Iwamura. **General Manager:** Takeshi Kojima. **Field Manager:** Trey Hillman.

2003 Foreign Players: D.T. Cromer. Angel Echevarria, Carlos Mirabal, Chris Seelbach. **Coach:** Gary Denbo.

ORIX BLUEWAVE

Mailing Address: Green Stadium Kobe, Midoridai, Suma-ku, Kobe 654-0163. **Telephone:** 078-795-1203. **FAX:** 078-795-1505.

Chairman: Yoshihiko Miyauchi. **President:** Yutaka Okazoe. **General Manager:** Kiyoshi Yano. **Field Manager:** Hiromichi Ishige.

2003 Foreign Players: Roosevelt Brown, Jose Ortiz, Koo Dae Sung (Korea), Scott Sheldon. **Coach:** Leon Lee.

OSAKA KINTETSU BUFFALOES

Mailing Address: Midosuji Grand Bldg. 2-2-3 Namba, Chuo-ku, Osaka 542-0076. **Telephone:** 06-6212-9744. **FAX:** 06-6212-6834.

Chairman: Wa Tashiro. **President:** Mitsuru Nagai. **General Manager:** Tetsuya Kobayashi. **Field Manager:** Masataka Nashida.

2003 Foreign Players: Kevin Beirne, Jeremy Powell, Tuffy Rhodes.

SEIBU LIONS

Mailing Address: 2135 Kami-Yamaguchi, Tokorozawa-shi, Saitama-ken 359-1189. **Telephone:** 042-924-1155. **FAX:** 042-928-1919.

Chairman: Yoshiaki Tsutsumi. **General Manager:** Kenji Ono. **Field Manager:** Haruki Ihara.

2003 Foreign Players: Alex Cabrera, Chang Chi-Chie (Taiwan), Scott McClain, Hsu Ming-chieh (Taiwan).

KOREA

KOREA BASEBALL ORGANIZATION

Mailing Address: 946-16 Dokokdong, Kangnam-gu, Seoul, Korea. **Telephone:** (02) 3460-4643. **FAX:** (02) 3460-4649.

Years League Active: 1982-.

Commissioner: Park Yong-oh. **Secretary General:** Choi Young-eun. **Manager, International Affairs/Public Relations:** Lee Sang-hyun. **Assistant Manager:** Park Chan-keun.

2003 Opening Date: April 5. **Closing Date:** Unavailable.

Regular Season: 132 games.

Division Structure: None.

Korean Series: Regular-season champion automatically goes to the Korean Series. Fourth- and third-place teams meet in best-of-3 series with winner advancing to meet second-place team in best-of-5 series, with winner meeting first-place team in best-of-7 championship.

Roster Limit: 27 active through Sept. 1, when rosters expand to 32. **Imports:** 3 active.

DOOSAN BEARS

Mailing Address: Chamsil Baseball Stadium, 10 Chamsil-1 dong, Songpa-ku, Seoul, Korea 138-221. **Telephone:** (02) 2240-1777. **FAX:** (02) 2240-1788.

General Manager: Kun Koo Kang.

KIA TIGERS

Mailing Address: Kwangju Shi, Seo-gu, Daebang-dong 266, 2nd floor, Zip 502-807.**Telephone:** (062) 370-1878. **FAX:** (062) 525-5350.

General Manager: Jeong Jae-kong.

HANHWA EAGLES

Mailing Address: 22-1 Youngjeon-dong, Dong-ku, Taejeon, Korea 300-200. **Telephone:** (042) 637-6001. **FAX:** (042) 632-2929.

General Manager: Kyung Yon Hwang.

HYUNDAI UNICORNS

Mailing Address: Hyundai Haesang Bldg., 9th Floor, 1014 Kwonseon-dong, Kwonseon-ku, Suwon, Kyung Ki, Korea 441-390. **Telephone:** (032) 433-7979. **FAX:** (032) 435-3108.

General Manager: Jeong Jae-ho.

LG TWINS

Mailing Address: Chamsil Baseball Stadium, 10 Chamsil-1 dong, Songpa-ku, Seoul, Korea 138-221. **Telephone:** (02) 2005-5760, (02) 2005-5801.

General Manager: You Song-min.

LOTTE GIANTS

Mailing Address: 930 Sajik-Dong Dongrae-Ku, Pusan, Korea. **Telephone:** 51-505-7422-3.**FAX:** 51-506-0090.

General Manager: Chul Hwa Lee.

SAMSUNG LIONS

Mailing Address: 184-3, Sunhwari, Jinryangyup, Kyungsan, Kyung Buk, Korea 712-830. **Telephone:** (053) 859-3114. **FAX:** (053) 859-3117.

General Manager: Jong Man Kim.

SK WYVERNS

Mailing Address: 1456-1 Kuwol-dong, Namdong-ku, Inchon, Korea 405-220. **Telephone:** (032) 422-7949. **FAX:** (032) 429-4565.

General Manager: Myung Yung-chul.

TAIWAN

CHINESE PROFESSIONAL BASEBALL LEAGUE

Mailing Address: 2F, No. 32, Pateh Road, Sec. 3, Taipei, Taiwan. **Telephone:** 886-2-2577-6992. **FAX:** 886-2-2577-2606. **Website:** www.cpbl.com.tw.

Years League Active: 1990-.

Commissioner: Harvey Tung. **Secretary General:** Wayne Lee.

Member Clubs: Brother Elephants (Taipei), China Trust Whales (Chiayi City), President Lions (Tainan), Sinon Bulls (Taichung), plus two teams from the former Taiwan Major League.

Regular Season: 100 games (split schedule).

2003 Opening Date: March 1. **Closing Date:** October 4.

Championship Series: Top two teams meet in best-of-7 series, Oct. 10-18.

Import Rule: Only three import players may be active, and only two may be on the field at the same time.

EUROPE

ITALY

ITALTIAN SERIE A/1

Mailing Address: Federazione Italiana Baseball/Softball, Viale Tiziano 70, 00196 Roma, Italy. **Telephone:** 39-06-36858297. **FAX:** 39-06-36858201. **Website:** www.baseball-softball.it.

President: Riccardo Fraccari. **General Secretary:** Marcello Standoli.

ANZIO

Mailing Address: Via delle Felci 4, 00040 Lavinio (Roma). **Telephone:** 39-06-981-9087. **Website:** www.anziobc.it.

President: Roberto Monaco. **Manager:** Carlo Morville.

BOLOGNA

Mailing Address: Piazzale Atleti Azzurri d'Italia, 40122 Bologna. **Telephone:** 39-051-479618. **FAX:** 39-051-554000. **E-Mail Address:** fortitudobaseball@tin.it. **Website:** fortitudobaseball.com.

President: Stefano Michelini. **Manager:** Mauro Mazzotti.

CODOGNO

Mailing Address: Casella Postale 13, 26845 Codogno. **Telephone:** 39-0377-430601. **E-Mail Address:** codogno@codognobaseball.it. **Website:** www.codogno baseball.it.

President: Salvatore Della Monica. **Manager**: Daniele Carelli.

FIRENZE

Mailing Address: Unavailable. **Telephone:** 39-055-422-0872. **E-Mail Address:** info@fiorentinabaseball.it. **Website:** www.fiorentinabaseball.it.

President: Pier Paulo Vita. **Manager**: Alberto Martinez.

GROSSETO

Mailing Address: Via della Repubblica 2, 58100 Grosseto. **Telephone:** 39-0564-494149. **FAX:** 39-0564-476750. **Website:** www.gol.grosseto.it/asso/golzine/arazzi/bbc.htm.

President: Claudio Banchi. **Manager:** Marco Mazzieri.

MODENA

Mailing Address: Casella Postale 69, 41010 Saliceto Panaro, Modena. **Telephone:** 39-059-371655. **FAX:** 39-059-365300. **E-Mail Address:** modenabc@tin.it **Website:** modenabc.tripod.com.

President: Giovanni Tinti. **Manager:** Juan Castro.

NETTUNO

Mailing Address: Stadio Steno Borghese, Via Scipione Borghese, 00048 Nettuno (Roma). **Telephone/FAX:** 39-06-9854966. **Website:** www.nettunobaseball.com.

President: Cesare Augusto Spigoni. **Manager:** Ruggero Bagialemani.

PARMA

Mailing Address: Via Donatore 4, Collecchio, 43044 Parma. **Telephone:** 39-335-604-8969. **FAX:** 39-0521-802601. **E-Mail Address:** parmabaseball@hotmail.com. **Website:** www.eteamz.com/cusparma.

President: Rossano Rinaldi. **Manager:** Sandro Rizzi.

PATERNO

Mailing Address: Unavailable. **Telephone:** Unavailable. **FAX:** 39-095-623590. **E-Mail Address:** team@warriorspaterno.com. **Website:** www.warriorspaterno.com.

President: Nunzio Botta. **Manager:** Alejandro Duret.

RIMINI

Mailing Address: Via Monaco 2, 47900 Rimini. **Telephone/FAX:** 39-0541-741761. **E-Mail Address:** info@baseballrimini.com. **Website:** www.baseballrimini.com.

President: Cesare Zangheri. **Manager:** Michele Romano.

NETHERLANDS

DUTCH MAJOR LEAGUE

Mailing Address: Koninklijke Nederlandse Baseball en Softball Bond (Royal Dutch Baseball and Softball Association), "Twinstate II", Perkinsbaan 15, 3439 ND Nieuwegein, Holland. **Telephone:** 31-(0) 30- 607-6070. **FAX:** 31-30-294-3043. **Website:** www.knbsb.nl.

President: Hans Meijer.

ALMERE '90

Mailing Address: Fanny Blankers Koen Sportpark, Almere. **Telephone:** +31 (0) 36-549 95 40. **Website:** www.almere90.nl.

AMSTERDAM PIRATES

Mailing Address: Sportpark Ookmeer, Herman Bonpad 5, 1067 SN Amsterdam. **Telephone:** +31 (0) 20-616 21 51. **Website:** www.amsterdam-pirates.nl.

DEN HAAG TORNADOS

Mailing Address: Steenwijklaan 500, 2541 RL Den Haag. **Telephone:** +31 (0) 70-366 97 22. **Website:** www.svado.nl.

HCAW

Mailing Address: Mr. Cocker HCAW, Postbus 1321, 1400 BH Bussum. **Telephone:** +31 (0) 35-693- 14 30. **Website:** www.hcaw.nl.

HOOFDDORP PIONIERS

Mailing Address: Postbus 475, 2130 AL Hoofddorp. **Telephone:** +31 (0) 23-561 35 57. **Website:** www.hoofddorp-pioniers.nl.

KINHEIM

Mailing Address: Gemeentelijk Sportpark, Badmintonpad, 2023 BT Haarlem. **Telephone:** +31 (0) 23-526 00 21. **Website:** www.kinheim.net.

NEPTUNUS

Mailing Address: Sportclub Neptunus, Postbus 35064, 3005 DB Rotterdam. **Telephone:** +31 (0) 10-437 53 69. **Website:** www.neptunussport.com.

PSV

Mailing Address: PSV Honkbal, Postbus 4057, 5604 EB Eindhoven. **Telephone:** +31 (0) 40-211 19 84. **Website:** www.psv-honk-softbal.nl.

RCH

Mailing Address: Heemsteedse Sportparken, Ringvaartlaan, 2103 XV Heemstede. **Telephone:** +31 (0) 23-528 43 88. **Website:** www.rch-pinguins.nl/.

SPARTA/FEYENOORD

Mailing Address: Postbus 9211, 3007 AE Rotterdam. **Telephone:** +31 (0) 10-479-04 83. **Website:** www.diertens.myweb.nl/.

WINTER
LEAGUES

2002-2003 STANDINGS

CARIBBEAN SERIES

	W	L	Pct.	GB
Dominican Republic	6	1	.857	—
Puerto Rico (Mayaguez)	5	2	.714	1
Puerto Rico (Caguas)	2	4	.333	3½
Mexico	0	6	.000	5½

DOMINICAN LEAGUE

	W	L	Pct.	GB
Aguilas	33	17	.660	—
Estrellas	28	22	.560	5
Gigantes	27	23	.540	6
Escogido	26	24	.520	7
Licey	20	30	.400	13
Azucareros	16	34	.320	17
Round-Robin	**W**	**L**	**Pct.**	**GB**
Aguilas	11	5	.688	—
Escogido	10	8	.556	2
Estrellas	8	9	.471	3½
Gigantes	5	12	.294	6½

PLAYOFFS: Finals (best-of-7)—Aguilas def. Escogido 4-0.

MEXICAN PACIFIC LEAGUE

	W	L	Pct.	GB
*Mexicali	37	29	.561	—
Hermosillo	36	30	545	1
*Obregon	37	31	.544	1
Culiacan	35	30	.538	1½
Mazatlan	31	34	.477	5½
Navojoa	31	36	.463	6½
Guasave	30	37	.448	7½
Los Mochis	28	38	.424	9

*Split season champion

PLAYOFFS: Quarterfinals (best-of-7)—Los Mochis def. Hermosillo 4-1; Mazatlan def. Mexicali 4-2; Obregon def. Culiacan 4-2. **Semifinals** (best-of-7)—Los Mochis def. Mazatlan 4-1; Obregon def. Mexicali 4-3. **Finals** (best-of-7)—Los Mochis def. Obregon 4-1.

PUERTO RICAN LEAGUE

	W	L	Pct.	GB
Caguas	32	18	.640	—
Mayaguez	29	21	.580	3
Bayamon	27	23	.540	5
Ponce	24	26	.480	8
Carolina	20	30	.400	12
Santurce	18	32	.360	14

PLAYOFFS: Semifinals (best-of-7)—Mayaguez def. Bayamon 4-1; Caguas def. 4-2. **Finals** (best-of-9)—Mayaguez def. Caguas 5-1.

VENEZUELAN LEAGUE

EAST	**W**	**L**	**Pct.**	**GB**
Caracas	23	16	.590	—
La Guaira	23	17	.575	½
Magallanes	18	21	.447	5
Oriente	18	24	.429	6½
WEST	**W**	**L**	**Pct.**	**GB**
Aragua	28	11	.718	—
Lara	21	20	.512	8
Zulia	17	24	.425	11
Pastora	12	27	.308	16

NOTE: Remainder of regular season and playoffs cancelled Dec. 2 due to national strike in Venezuela.

ARIZONA FALL LEAGUE

EAST	**W**	**L**	**Pct.**	**GB**
Scottsdale	29	15	.659	—
Phoenix	25	19	.568	4
Mesa	19	24	.442	9½
WEST	**W**	**L**	**Pct.**	**GB**
Peoria	26	17	.605	—
Grand Canyon	20	23	.465	6
Maryvale	11	32	.256	15

PLAYOFFS: Finals (one game)—Peoria def. Scottsdale 1-0.

WINTER BASEBALL

CARIBBEAN BASEBALL CONFEDERATION

(Confederacion de Beisbol Profesional del Caribe)

Mailing Address: Frank Feliz Miranda, No. 1, Naco, Santo Domingo, Dominican Republic. **Telephone:** (809) 562-4737, 562-4715. **FAX:** (809) 565-4654.

Commissioner: Juan Fco. Puello Herrera. **Secretary:** Benny Agosto.

Year Founded: 1949.

Member Countries: Dominican Republic, Mexico, Puerto Rico, Venezuela.

2004 Caribbean Series: Feb. 1-8 in Dominican Republic.

DOMINICAN LEAGUE

(Liga de Beisbol Profesional de la Republica Dominicana)

Office Address: Estadio Quisqueya, 2da. Planta, Ens. La Fe, Santo Domingo, D.N., Dominican Republic. **Mailing Address:** Apartado Postal 1246, Santo Domingo, D.N., Dominican Republic. **Telephone:** (809) 567-6371, (809) 563-5085. **FAX:** (809) 567-5720. **E-Mail Address:** info@besiboldominicano.com. **Website:** www.beisboldominicano.com.

Years League Active: 1951-.

President: Dr. Leonardo Matos Berrido. **Administrator:** Marcos Rodriguez. **Director, Public Relations:** Jorge Torres.

2002-2003 Opening Date: Oct. 18. **Closing Date:** Dec 27.

Regular Season: 50 games.

Playoff Format: Top four teams meet in 18-game round-robin (if fifth-place team is three games or less out of fourth place, fourth-place and fifth-place teams meet in best-of-3 playoff to determine fourth playoff team). Top two teams advance to best-of-7 series for league championship. Winner advances to Caribbean Series.

Roster Limit: 30. **Roster Limit, Imports:** 7.

AGUILAS CIBAEÑAS

Office Address: Estadio Cibao, Ave. Imbert, Santiago, Dom. Rep. **Mailing Address:** EPS B-225, P.O. Box 02-5360, Miami, FL 33102. **Telephone:** (809) 575-4310, (809) 575-8250. **FAX:** (809) 575-0865. **E-Mail Address:** a.cibaenas@codetel.net.do. **Website:** www.lasaguilas.com.

President: Winston Llenas. **General Manager:** Reynaldo Bisono.

2002-2003 Manager: Felix Fermin.

AZUCAREROS DEL ESTE

Mailing Address: Estadio Francisco Micheli, La Romana, Dom. Rep. **Telephone:** (809) 556-4955, (809) 556-6188. **FAX:** (809) 550-1550. **E-Mail Address:** arturo.miguel@codetel.net.do.

President: Arturo Gil. **General Manager:** Carlos Juan Bernhardt.

2002-2003 Managers: Bobby Jones, Jorge Bell.

LIONES DEL ESCOGIDO

Office Address: Estadio Quisqueya, Ens. la Fe, Santo Domingo, Dom. Rep. **Mailing Address:** P.O. Box 1287, Santo Domingo, Dom. Rep. **Telephone:** (809) 565-1910. **FAX:** (809) 567-7643. **E-Mail Address:** info@escogido.com. **Website:** www.escogido.com.do.

President: Daniel Aquino Mendez. **General Manager:** Felipe Alou Rojas.

2002-2003 Managers: Bruce Fields, Mako Oliveras.

ESTRELLAS ORIENTALES

Office Address: Av. Lope de Vega No. 45, Ens. Piantini, Santo Domingo, Dom. Rep. **Telephone:** (809) 529-3618, (809) 246-4077. **FAX:** (809) 529-7752. **E-Mail Address:** info@estrellasdeoriente.com.

President: Carlos Juan Musa-Hazim. **General Manager:** Pablo Peguero.

2002-2003 Manager: Manny Acta.

TIGRES DEL LICEY

Office Address: Estadio Quisqueya, Santo Domingo, Dom. Rep. **Mailing Address:** P.O. Box 1321, Santo Domingo, Dom. Rep. **Telephone:** (809) 567-3090. **FAX:** (809) 542-7714. **E-Mail Address:** licey.club@codetel.net.do. **Website:** www.licey.com.

President: Emigdio Garrido. **General Manager:** Fernando Ravelo Jana.

2002-2003 Manager: Dave Jauss.

GIGANTES DEL CIBAO

Office Address: Estadio Julian Javier, San Francisco de Macoris, Dom. Rep. **Mailing Address:** Ave. Luperon No. 25, Zona Industrial de Herrera, Santo Domingo, Dom. Rep. **U.S. Mailing Address:** EPS No. F-1447, P.O. Box 02-5301, Miami, FL 33102. **Telephone:** (809) 566-4882. **FAX:** (809) 566-1628. **Website:** www.gigantesdelcibao.com.

President: Stanley Javier. **General Manager:** Nelson Silverio.

2002-2003 Manager: Joe Shoemaker.

MEXICAN PACIFIC LEAGUE

(Liga Mexicana del Pacifico)

Mailing Address: Av. Insurgentes No. 847 Sur, Interior 402, Col. Centro, CP 80120, Culiacan, Sinaloa. **Telephone/FAX:** 011-52 (667) 761-25-70, 011-52 (667) 761-25-71. **E-Mail Address:** ligadelpacifico@imparcial.com.mx. **Website:** www.ligadelpacifico.com.mx.

Years League Active: 1958-.

President: Renato Vega Alvarado. **General Manager:** Oviel Dennis Gonzalez.

2002-2003 Opening Date: Oct. 11. **Closing Date:** Dec. 30.

Regular Season: 68 games.

Playoff Format: Six teams advance to best-of-7 quarterfinals. Three winners and losing team with best record advance to best-of-7 semifinals. Winners meet in best-of-7 series for league championship. Winner advances to Caribbean World Series.

Roster Limit: 30. **Roster Limit, Imports:** 5.

TOMATEROS DE CULIACAN

Street Address: Av. Alvaro Obregon 348 Sur, Col. Jorge Almada, CP 80200, Culiacan, Sinaloa, Mexico. **Telephone/FAX:** 011-52 (667) 713-39-69, 011-52 (667) 712-24-46.

President: Juan Manuel Ley Lopez. **General Manager:** Luis Carlos Joffroy.

2002-2003 Manager: Paquin Estrada.

ALGODONEROS DE GUASAVE

Mailing Address: Av. Obregon No. 43, Col. Centro, CP 81000, Guasave, Sinaloa, Mexico. **Telephone:** 011-52 (687) 872-29-98. **FAX:** 011-52 (687) 872-14-31.

President: Carlos Chavez. **General Manager:** Joaquin Valenzuela.

2002-2003 Manager: Raul Cano.

NARANJEROS DE HERMOSILLO

Mailing Address: Blvd. Solidaridad S/N, Col. Pimentel, CP 83188, Hermosillo, Sonora, Mexico. **Telephone:** 011-52 (662) 260-69-32, 011-52 (662) 260-69-33. **FAX:** 011-52 (662) 260-69-31.

President: Enrique Mazon Rubio. **General Manager:** Marco Antonio Manzo.

2002-2003 Manager: Derek Bryant.

CANEROS DE LOS MOCHIS

Mailing Address: Francisco I. Madero No. 116 Oriente, Col. Centro, CP 81200, Los Mochis, Sinaloa, Mexico. **Telephone:** 011-52 (668) 812-86-02. **FAX:** 011-52 (668) 812-67-40.

President: Mario Lopez Valdez. **General Manager:** Antonio Castro Chavez.

2002-2003 Manager: Mario Mendoza.

VENADOS DE MAZATLAN

Mailing Address: Gutierrez Najera No. 821, Col. Montuosa, CP 82000, Mazatlan, Sinaloa, Mexico. **Telephone:** 011-52 (669) 981-17-10. **FAX:** 011-52 (669) 981-17-11.

President: Jesus Ismael Barros Cebreros. **General Manager:** Alejandro Lizarraga Osuna.

2002-2003 Manager: Dan Firova.

AGUILAS DE MEXICALI

Mailing Address: Pesqueira No. 401-R, Sur Altos, CP 85800, Navojoa, Sonora, Mexico. **Telephone:** 011-52 (686) 567-0040. **FAX:** 011-52 (686) 567-5129.

President: Dio Alberto Murrillo. **General Manager:** Jesus Sommers.

2002-2003 Manager: Lorenzo Bundy.

MAYOS DE NAVOJOA

Mailing Address: Rosales No. 102, Col. Reforma, CP 85830, Navojoa, Sonora, Mexico. **Telephone:** 011-52 (642) 422-14-33, 011-52 (642) 422-37-64. **FAX:** 011-52 (642) 422-89-97.

President: Victor Cuevas Garibay. **General Manager:** Lauro Villalobos.

2002-2003 Manager: Alfonso Jimenez.

YAQUIS DE OBREGON

Mailing Address: Calle Guerrero y Michoacan, Estadio de Beisbol Tomas Oroz Gaytan, CP 85130, Ciudad Obregon, Sonora, Mexico. **Telephone:** 011-52 (644) 413-77-66. **FAX:** 011-52 (644) 414-11-56.

President: Hector Bernetche. **General Manager:** Roberto Diaz Gonzalez.

2002-2003 Manager: Tim Johnson.

PUERTO RICAN LEAGUE

(Liga de Beisbol Profesional de Puerto Rico)

Office Address: Avenida Munoz Rivera 1056, Edificio First Federal, Suite 501, Rio Piedras, PR 00925. **Mailing Address:** P.O. Box 191852, San Juan, PR 00019. **Telephone:** (787) 765-6285, 765-7285. **FAX:** (787) 767-3028.

Years League Active: 1938-.

President: Enrique Cruz Colon. **Vice President:** Jose Santiago. **Executive Director:** Benny Agosto.

2002-2003 Opening Date: Oct. 29. **Closing Date:** Jan. 6.

Regular Season: 50 games.

Playoff Format: Top four teams meet in best-of-7 semifinal series. Winners meet in best-of-9 series for league championship. Winner advances to Caribbean World Series.

Roster Limit: 28. **Roster Limit, Imports:** 9.

VAQUEROS DE BAYAMON

Mailing Address: P.O. Box 1667, Bayamon, PR 00960. **Telephone:** (787) 269-3531, 269-3296. **FAX:** (787) 269-3874.

Owner, President: Carlos Baerga. **General Manager:** Candy Maldonado.

2002-2003 Manager: Carmelo Martinez.

CRIOLLOS DE CAGUAS

Mailing Address: P.O. Box 1415, Caguas, PR 00726. **Telephone:** (787) 258-2222. **FAX:** (787) 743-0545.

President: Jose Guillermo Santiago. **Vice President:** Jenaro Marchand. **General Manager:** Ronquito Garcia.

2002-2003 Manager: Oscar Acosta.

GIGANTES DE CAROLINA

Mailing Address: Roberto Clemente Stadium, P.O. Box 366246, San Juan, PR 00936. **Telephone:** (787) 643-4351, 643-2511. **FAX:** (787) 731-7051.

President: Benjamin Rivera. **Vice President:** Heli Rivera. **General Manager:** Edwin Rodriguez.

2002-2003 Managers: Jose Oquendo, Ramon Aviles.

INDIOS DE MAYAGUEZ

Mailing Address: 3089 Marina Station, Mayaguez, PR 00681. **Telephone:** (787) 834-6111, 834-5211. **FAX:** (787) 834-7480.

President: Daniel Aquino. **General Manager:** Carlos Pieve.

2002-2003 Manager: Nick Leyva.

LIONES DE PONCE

Mailing Address: P.O. Box 363148, San Juan, PR 00936. **Telephone:** (787) 848-8884. **FAX:** (787) 848-0050.

President: Antonio Munoz Jr. **General Manager:** Ramon Conde.

2002-2003 Manager: Jose Cruz Sr.

CANGREGEROS DE SANTURCE

Mailing Address: P.O. Box 1077, Hato Rey, PR 00919. **Telephone:** (787) 772-9573. **FAX:** (787) 772-9574.

President: Julio Hazim. **General Manager:** Hector Otero.

2002-2003 Manager: Mako Oliveras.

VENEZUELAN LEAGUE

(Liga Venezolana de Beisbol Profesional)

Mailing Address: Avenida Casanova, Centro Comercial "El Recreo," Torre Sur, Piso 3, Oficinas 6 y 7, Sabana Grande, Caracas, Venezuela. **Telephone:** (011-58) 212-761-4932. **FAX:** (011-58) 212-761-7661. **Website:** www.lvbp.com.

Years League Active: 1946-.

President: Ramon Guillermo Aveledo. **General Manager:** Jose Domingo Alvarez.

Division Structure: **East**—Caracas, La Guaira, Magallanes, Oriente. **West**—Aragua, Lara, Pastora, Zulia.

2002-2003 Opening Date: Oct. 16. **Closing Date:** Dec. 30.

Regular Season: 62 games.

Playoff Format: Top two teams in each division, plus a wild-card team, meet in 16-game round-robin series. Top two finishers meet in best-of-7 series for league championship. Winner advances to Caribbean Series.

Roster Limit: 26. **Roster Limit, Imports:** 7.

TIGRES DE ARAGUA

Mailing Address: Estadio Jose Perez Colmenares, Calle Campo Elias, Barrio Democratico, Maracay, Aragua, Venezuela. **Telephone:** (011-58) 243-554-4134. **FAX:** (011-58) 243-253-8655. **Website:** www.tigresdearagua.com.ve.

President, General Manager: Rafael Rodriguez.

2002-2003 Manager: Buddy Bailey.

LIONES DE CARACAS

Mailing Address: Edificio Centro Seguros La Paz, Oficina 42-C, La California Norte, Caracas, Venezuela. **Telephone:** (011-58) 212-238-0691. **Website:** www.leones.com.

President: Ariel Prat. **General Manager:** Oscar Prieto.

2002-2003 Manager: Tim Tolman.

TIBURONES DE LA GUAIRA

Mailing Address: Primera Transversal, Urbanizacion Miramar Pariata, Maiquetia, Vargas, Venezuela. **Telephone:** (011-58) 212-332-5579. **FAX:** (011-58) 212-332-3116. **Website:** www.tiburones.com.

President: Percy Chacin. **General Manager:** Armando Arratia.

2002-2003 Manager: Luis Salazar.

CARDINALES DE LARA

Mailing Address: Av. Rotaria, Estadio Antonio Herrera Gutiérrez, Barquisimeto, Lara, Venezuela. **Telephone:** (011-58) 251-442- 4543. **FAX:** (011-58) 251-442-8321. **E-Mail Address:** cardenal@cardenales.org. **Website:** www.cardenalesdelara.com.

President: Adolfo Alvarez. **General Manager:** Humberto Oropeza.

2002-2003 Manager: Dan Rohn.

NAVEGANTES DE MAGALLANES

Mailing Address: Centro Comercial Caribbean Plaza, Modulo 8, Local 173, Valencia, Carabobo, Venezuela. **Telephone:** (011-58) 241-824-0321 or 0980. **FAX:** (011-58) 241-824-0705. **E-Mail address:** Magallanes@telcel.net.ve. **Website:** www.magallanes.com

President, General Manager: Juan Jose Avila.

2002-2003 Manager: Phil Regan.

PASTORA DE LOS LLANOS

Mailing Address: Estadio Bachiller Julio Hernandez Molina, Avenida Romulo Gallegos, Aruare, Portuguesa, Venezuela. **Telephone:** (011-58) 255-622-2945. **FAX:** (011-58) 255-621-8595.

President, General Manager: Enrique Finol.

2002-2003 Manager: Luis Dorante.

CARIBES DE ORIENTE

Mailing Address: Avenida Estadio Alfonso Carrasquel, Oficina Caribes de Oriente, Centro Comercial Novocentro, Piso 2, Local 2-4, Puerto la Cruz, Anzoategui, Venezuela. **Telephone:** (011-58) 281-266-2536. **FAX:** (011-58) 281-266-7054. **Website:** caribesbbc.com

President: Aurelio Fernandez-Concheso. **Vice President:** Pablo Ruggeri.

2002-2003 Manager: Omar Malave.

AGUILAS DE ZULIA

Mailing Address: Avenida 8 con Calle 81, Urb. Santa Rita, Edificio Las Carolinas, Mezzanine Local M-3, Maracaibo, Zulia, Venezuela. **Telephone:** (011-58) 261-798-0541 or 9835. **FAX:** (011-58) 261-798-0579. **Website:** aguilas.com.

President: Lucas Rincon Colmenares. **General Manager:** Luis Rodolfo Machado Silva.

2002-2003 Manager: Ruben Amaro Sr.

OTHER WINTER LEAGUES

ARIZONA FALL LEAGUE

Mailing Address: 10201 S. 51st St., Suite 230, Phoenix, AZ 85044. **Telephone:** (480) 496-6700. **FAX:** (480) 496-6384. **E-Mail Address:** afl@mlb.com. **Website:** www.mlb.com.

Years League Active: 1992-.

Operated by: Major League Baseball.

Executive Vice President: Steve Cobb. **Seasonal Assistant:** Joan McGrath.

2003 Opening Date: Sept. 30. **Closing Date:** Nov. 13.

Regular Season: 39 games.

Playoff Format: Division champions meet in one-game championship.

Roster Limit: 30. Players with less than one year of major league service are eligible.

GRAND CANYON RAFTERS

Mailing Address: See league address.

Affiliates: Atlanta Braves, Philadelphia Phillies, San Francisco Giants, Tampa Bay Devil Rays, Toronto Blue Jays.

2002 Manager: Lenn Sakata (Giants).

MARYVALE SAGUAROS

Mailing Address: See league address.

Affiliates: Baltimore Orioles, Milwaukee Brewers, Montreal Expos, New York Yankees, St. Louis Cardinals.

2002 Manager: Tommy John (Expos).

MESA SOLAR SOX

Mailing Address: See league address.

Affiliates: Chicago Cubs, Colorado Rockies, Detroit Tigers, Florida Marlins, Houston Astros.

2002 Manager: Bobby Dickerson (Cubs).

PEORIA JAVELINAS

Mailing Address: See league address.

Affiliates: Chicago White Sox, Los Angeles Dodgers, San Diego Padres, Seattle Mariners, Texas Rangers.

2002 Manager: Razor Shines (White Sox).

PHOENIX DESERT DOGS

Mailing Address: See league address.

Affiliates: Cleveland Indians, Minnesota Twins, New York Mets, Oakland Athletics, Pittsburgh Pirates.

2002 Manager: John Russell (Twins).

SCOTTSDALE SCORPIONS

Mailing Address: See league address.

Affiliates: Anaheim Angels, Arizona Diamondbacks, Boston Red Sox, Cincinnati Reds, Kansas City Royals.

2002 Manager: Al Pedrique (Diamondbacks).

COLLEGES

COLLEGE BASEBALL

NATIONAL COLLEGIATE ATHLETIC ASSOCIATION

Mailing Address: P.O. Box 6222, Indianapolis, IN 46206. **Telephone:** (317) 917-6222. **FAX:** (317) 917-6826 , 917-6857. **E-Mail Addresses:** dpoppe@ncaa.org (Dennis Poppe), rbuhr@ncaa.org (Randy Buhr), jimwright@ncaa.org (Jim Wright), sstraziscar@ncaa.org (Sean Straziscar). **Websites:** www.ncaa.org, www.ncaabaseball.com.

President: Myles Brand. **Managing Director, Baseball:** Dennis Poppe. **Assistant Director, Championships:** Randy Buhr. **Media Contact, College World Series:** Jim Wright. **Contact, Statistics:** Sean Straziscar.

Chairman, Division I Baseball Committee: Charlie Carr (senior associate athletic director, Florida State). **Division I Baseball Committee:** Skip Bertman (athletic director, Louisiana State), Rudy Davalos (AD, New Mexico), Mike Gaski (baseball coach, UNC Greensboro), Dan Guerrero (AD, UCLA), Gothard Lane (AD, St. Bonaventure), Tom Jurich (AD, Louisville), Chris Monasch (commissioner, America East Conference), Bill Rowe (AD, Southwest Missouri State), Bob Todd (baseball coach, Ohio State).

Chairman, Division II Baseball Committee: Gary Rundles (baseball coach, West Alabama). **Chairman, Division III Baseball Committee:** Matt McDonald (baseball coach, St. Olaf, Minn.).

2004 National Convention: Jan. 10-12 at Nashville

2003 Championship Tournaments
NCAA Division I

57th College World Series .... Omaha, NE, June 13-22/23
Super Regionals (8) .... June 6-9
Regionals (16) .... May 30-June 1

NCAA Division II

36th World Series .... Montgomery, AL, May 24-31
Regionals (8) .... Campus sites, May 15-17

NCAA Division III

28th World Series .... Appleton, WI, May 23-27
Regionals (8) .... Campus sites, May 15-18

NATIONAL ASSOCIATION OF INTERCOLLEGIATE ATHLETICS

Mailing Address: 23500 W. 105th St., P.O. Box 1325, Olathe, KS 66051. **Telephone:** (913) 791-0044. **FAX:** (913) 791-9555. **Website:** www.naia.org.

Chief Executive Officer: Steve Baker. **Director, Championship Events:** Natalie Cronkhite. **Director, Sports Information:** Dawn Harmon.

2003 Championship Tournament

NAIA World Series .... Lewiston, ID, May 23-30

NATIONAL JUNIOR COLLEGE ATHLETIC ASSOCIATION

Mailing Address: P.O. Box 7305, Colorado Springs, CO 80933. **Telephone:** (719) 590-9788. **FAX:** (719) 590-7324. **Website:** www.njcaa.org.

Executive Director: George Killian. **Director, Division I Baseball Tournament:** Jamie Hamilton. **Director, Division II Tournament:** John Daigle. **Director, Division III Tournament:** Barry Bower.

2003 Championship Tournaments
Division I

World Series .... Grand Junction, CO, May 24-31

Division II

World Series .... Millington, TN, May 24-31

Division III

World Series .... Batavia, NY, May 17-23

CALIFORNIA COMMUNITY COLLEGE COMMISSION ON ATHLETICS

Mailing Address: 2017 O St., Sacramento, CA 95814. **Telephone:** (916) 444-1600. **FAX:** (916) 444-2616. **E-Mail Address:** info@coasports.org. **Website:** www.coasports.org.

Commissioner of Athletics: Joanne Fortunato. **Associate Commissioner, Athletics:** Stuart Van Horn. **Director, Sports Information:** David Eadie.

2003 Championship Tournament

State Championship .... Fresno City College, May 24-26

AMERICAN BASEBALL COACHES ASSOCIATION

Office Address: 108 S. University Ave., Suite 3, Mount Pleasant, MI 48858. **Telephone:** (989) 775-3300. **FAX:** (989) 775-3600. **E-Mail Address:** abca@abca.org. **Website:** www.abca.org.

Executive Director: Dave Keilitz. **Assistant to Executive Director:** Betty Rulong. **Membership/Convention Coordinator:** Nick Phillips. **Assistant Coordinator:** Juahn Clark.

Chairman: Carroll Land (Point Loma Nazarene U., CA). **President:** David Altopp (Lee University, Cleveland, TN).

2004 National Convention: Jan. 2-5 at San Antonio (Marriott Rivercenter).

NCAA DIVISION I CONFERENCES

AMERICA EAST CONFERENCE

Mailing Address: 10 High St., Suite 860, Boston, MA 02110. **Telephone:** (617) 695-6369. **FAX:** (617) 695-6385. **E-Mail Address:** bourque@americaeast.com. **Website:** www.americaeast.com.

Baseball Members (First Year): Albany (2002), Binghamton (2002), Hartford (1990), Maine (1990), Northeastern (1990), Stony Brook (2002), Vermont (1990).

Assistant Commissioner/Communications: Matt Bourque.

2003 Tournament: Four teams, double-elimination. May 22-24 at Burlington, VT (University of Vermont).

ATLANTIC COAST CONFERENCE

Office Address: 4512 Weybridge Lane, Greensboro, NC 27407. **Mailing Address:** P.O. Drawer ACC, Greensboro, NC 27417. **Telephone:** (336) 851-6062. **FAX:** (336) 854-8797. **E-Mail Address:** ayakola@theacc.org. **Website:** www.theacc.com.

Baseball Members (First Year): Clemson (1953), Duke (1953), Florida State (1992), Georgia Tech (1980), Maryland (1953), North Carolina (1953), North Carolina State (1953), Virginia (1953), Wake Forest (1953).

Assistant Director, Media Relations: Amy Moore Yakola.

2003 Tournament: Nine teams, double-elimination. May 20-25 at Salem, VA (Salem Memorial Stadium).

ATLANTIC SUN CONFERENCE

Mailing Address: 3370 Vineville Ave., Suite 108-B, Macon, GA 31204. **Telephone:** (478) 474-3394. **FAX:** (478) 474-4272. **E-Mail Address:** sid@atlanticsun.org. **Website:** www.atlanticsun.org.

Baseball Members (First Year): Belmont (2002), Campbell (1994), Central Florida (1992), Florida Atlantic (1993), Gardner-Webb (2003), Georgia State (1983), Jacksonville (1999), Jacksonville State (1996), Mercer (1978), Samford (1978), Stetson (1985), Troy State (1998).

Assistant Commissioner, Media/Championships: Devlin Pierce. **Assistant Director, Media Relations:** Jo-Anne Gonzalez.

2003 Tournament: Six teams, double-elimination. May 21-24 at DeLand, FL (Stetson University).

ATLANTIC-10 CONFERENCE

Mailing Address: 230 S. Broad St., Suite 1700, Philadelphia, PA 19102. **Telephone:** (215) 545-6678. **FAX:** (215) 545-3342. **E-Mail Address:** shaug@atlantic10.org. **Website:** www.atlantic10.org.

Baseball Members (First Year): Dayton (1996), Duquesne (1977), Fordham (1996), George Washington (1977), LaSalle (1996), Massachusetts (1977), Rhode Island (1981), Richmond (2002), St. Bonaventure (1980), Saint Joseph's (1983), Temple (1983), Xavier (1996).

Director, Baseball Communications: Stephen Haug.

2003 Tournament: Six teams, double-elimination. May 15-17 at Norwich, CT (Thomas J. Dodd Memorial Stadium). Top two teams meet in best-of-3 series, May 22-24 at campus of highest seed.

BIG EAST CONFERENCE

Mailing Address: 222 Richmond St., Suite 110, Providence, RI 02903. **Telephone:** (401) 272-9108. **FAX:** (401) 751-8540. **E-Mail Address:** rcarolla@bigeast.org. **Website:** www.bigeast.org.

Baseball Members (First Year): Boston College (1985), Connecticut (1985), Georgetown (1985), Notre Dame (1996), Pittsburgh (1985), Rutgers (1996), St. John's (1985), Seton Hall (1985), Villanova (1985), Virginia Tech (2001), West Virginia (1996).

Director, Communications: Rob Carolla.

2003 Championship: Four teams, double-elimination. May 22-24 at Bridgewater, NJ (Commerce Bank Ballpark).

BIG SOUTH CONFERENCE

Mailing Address: 6428 Bannington Dr., Suite A, Charlotte, NC 28226. **Telephone:** (704) 341-7990. **FAX:** (704) 341-7991. **E-Mail Address:** drewd@bigsouth.org. **Website:** www.bigsouthsports.com.

Baseball Members (First Year): Charleston Southern (1983), Coastal Carolina (1983), Elon (1999), High Point (1999), Liberty (1991), UNC Asheville (1985), Radford (1983), Winthrop (1983).

Assistant Commissioner: Drew Dickerson.

2003 Tournament: Six teams, double-elimination. May 22-25 at Rock Hill, SC (Winthrop University).

BIG TEN CONFERENCE

Mailing Address: 1500 W. Higgins Rd., Park Ridge, IL 60068. **Telephone:** (847) 696-1010. **FAX:** (847) 696-1110. **E-Mail Address**: schipman@bigten.org. **Website:** www.bigten.org.

Baseball Members (First Year): Illinois (1896), Indiana (1906), Iowa (1906), Michigan (1896), Michigan State (1950), Minnesota (1906), Northwestern (1898), Ohio State (1913), Penn State (1992), Purdue (1906).

Associate Director, Communications: Scott Chipman.

2003 Tournament: Six teams, double-elimination. May 21-24 at regular-season champion.

BIG 12 CONFERENCE

Mailing Address: 2201 Stemmons Freeway, 28th Floor, Dallas, TX 75207. **Telephone:** (214) 753-0102. **FAX:** (214) 753-0145. **E-Mail Address:** bo@big12sports.com. **Website:** www.big12sports.com.

Baseball Members (First Year): Baylor (1997), Kansas (1997), Kansas State (1997), Missouri (1997), Nebraska (1997), Oklahoma (1997), Oklahoma State (1997), Texas (1997), Texas A&M (1997), Texas Tech (1997).

Assistant Commissioner, Media Relations: Bo Carter.

2003 Tournament: Eight teams, double-elimination. May 21-25 at Oklahoma City, OK (SBC Bricktown Ballpark).

BIG WEST CONFERENCE

Mailing Address: 2 Corporate Park, Suite 206, Irvine, CA 92606. **Telephone:** (949) 261-2525. **FAX:** (949) 261-2528. **E-Mail Address:** cramos@bigwest.org. **Website:** www.bigwest.org.

Baseball Members (First Year): Cal Poly (1997), UC Irvine (2002), UC Riverside (2002), UC Santa Barbara (1970), Cal State Fullerton (1975), Cal State Northridge (2001), Long Beach State (1970), Pacific (1972).

Assistant Director, Information: Chris Ramos.

2003 Tournament: None.

COLONIAL ATHLETIC ASSOCIATION

Mailing Address: 8625 Patterson Ave., Richmond, VA 23229. **Telephone:** (804) 754-1616. **FAX:** (804) 754-

1830. **E-Mail Address:** rwashburn@caasports.com. **Website:** www.caasports.com.

Baseball Members (First Year): Delaware (2002), Drexel (2002), George Mason (1986), Hofstra (2002), James Madison (1986), UNC Wilmington (1986), Old Dominion (1992), Towson (2002), Virginia Commonwealth (1996), William & Mary (1986).

Sports Information Director: Rob Washburn.

2003 Tournament: Six teams, double-elimination. May 21-24 at Manteo, NC (Coy Tillet Field).

CONFERENCE USA

Mailing Address: 35 E. Wacker Dr., Suite 650, Chicago, IL 60601. **Telephone:** (312) 553-0483. **FAX:** (312) 553-0495. **E-Mail Address:** rdanderson@c-usa.org. **Website:** www.c-usasports.com.

Baseball Members (First Year): Alabama-Birmingham (1996), Charlotte (1996), Cincinnati (1996), East Carolina (2002), Houston (1997), Louisville (1996), Memphis (1996), Saint Louis (1996), South Florida (1996), Southern Mississippi (1996), Texas Christian (2002), Tulane (1996).

Director, Media Relations: Russell Anderson.

2003 Tournament: Eight teams, double-elimination. May 21-25 at New Orleans (Tulane University).

HORIZON LEAGUE

Mailing Address: 201 S. Capitol Ave., Suite 500, Indianapolis, IN 46225. **Telephone:** (317) 237-5622 . **FAX:** (317) 237-5620. **E-Mail Address:** mingberg@horizonleague.org. **Website:** www.horizonleague.org.

Baseball Members (First Year): Butler (1979), Cleveland State (1994), Detroit (1980), Illinois-Chicago (1994), Wisconsin-Milwaukee (1994), Wright State (1994), Youngstown State (2002).

Director, Communications: Michael Ingberg.

2003 Tournament: Seven teams, double-elimination. May 21-25 at Dayton, OH (Wright State University).

IVY LEAGUE

Mailing Address: 330 Alexander Rd., First Floor, Princeton, NJ 08544. **Telephone:** (609) 258-6426. **FAX:** (609) 258-1690. **E-Mail Address:** ivygroup@princeton.edu. **Website:** www.ivyleaguesports.com.

Baseball Members (First Year): Rolfe—Brown (1948), Dartmouth (1930), Harvard (1948), Yale (1930). **Gehrig**—Columbia (1930), Cornell (1930), Pennsylvania (1930), Princeton (1930).

Assistants, Public Information: Kevin Anderson, LaKesha Walker.

2003 Tournament: Best-of-3 series between division champions. May 10-11 at Rolfe Division champion.

METRO ATLANTIC ATHLETIC CONFERENCE

Mailing Address: 712 Amboy Ave., Edison, NJ 08837. **Telephone:** (732) 738-5455. **FAX:** (732) 738-8366. **E-Mail Address:** jill.skotarczak@maac.org. **Website:** www.maacsports.com.

Baseball Members (First Year): Canisius (1990), Fairfield (1982), Iona (1982), LeMoyne (1990), Manhattan (1982), Marist (1998), Niagara (1990), Rider (1998), St. Peter's (1982), Siena (1990).

Director, Media Relations: Jill Skotarczak

2003 Tournament: Four teams, double-elimination. May 22-24 at Fishkill, NY (Dutchess Stadium).

MID-AMERICAN CONFERENCE

Mailing Address: 24 Public Square, 15th Floor, Cleveland, OH 44113. **Telephone:** (216) 566-4622. **FAX:** (216) 858-9622. **E-Mail Address:** bmcgowan@mac-sports.com. **Website:** www.mac-sports.com.

Baseball Members (First Year): East—Akron (1992), Buffalo (2001), Kent State (1951), Marshall (1997), Miami (1947), Ohio (1946). **West**—Ball State (1973), Bowling Green State (1952), Central Michigan (1971), Eastern Michigan (1971), Northern Illinois (1997), Toledo (1950), Western Michigan (1947).

Associate Director, Media Relations: Bryan McGowan.

2003 Tournament: Six teams (top two in each division, two wild-card teams with next best conference winning percentage), double-elimination. May 21-24 at team with best conference winning percentage.

MID-CONTINENT CONFERENCE

Mailing Address: 340 W. Butterfield Rd., Suite 3-D, Elmhurst, IL 60126. **Telephone:** (630) 516-0661. **FAX:** (630) 516-0673. **E-Mail Address:** hamilton@mid-con.com. **Website:** www.mid-con.com.

Baseball Members (First Year): Chicago State (1994), Oakland (2000), Oral Roberts (1998), Southern Utah (2000), Valparaiso (1984), Western Illinois (1984).

Director, Media Relations: Tony Hamilton.

2003 Tournament: Four teams, double-elimination. May 22-24 at Tulsa, OK (Oral Roberts University).

MID-EASTERN ATHLETIC CONFERENCE

Mailing Address: 102 N. Elm St., Suite 401, P.O. Box 21205, Greensboro, NC 27420. **Telephone:** (336) 275-9961. **FAX:** (336) 275-9964. **E-Mail Address:** conawayl@themeac.com. **Website:** www.meacsports.com.

Baseball Members (First Year): North—Coppin State (1985), Delaware State (1970), Maryland-Eastern Shore (1970). **South**—Bethune-Cookman (1979), Florida A&M (1979), Norfolk State (1998), North Carolina A&T (1970).

Director, Media Relations: LeCounte Conaway.

2003 Tournament: Seven teams, double-elimination. May 8-11 at Orlando, FL (Disney Wide World of Sports Complex).

MISSOURI VALLEY CONFERENCE

Mailing Address: 1818 Chouteau Ave., St. Louis, MO 63103. **Telephone:** (314) 421-0339. **FAX:** (314) 421-3505. **E-Mail Address:** watkins@mvc.org. **Website:** www.mvc.org.

Baseball Members (First Year): Bradley (1955), Creighton (1976), Evansville (1994), Illinois State (1980), Indiana State (1976), Northern Iowa (1991), Southern Illinois (1974), Southwest Missouri State (1990), Wichita State (1945).

Assistant Commissioner: Jack Watkins.

2003 Tournament: Six teams, double-elimination. May 21-24 at Wichita, KS (Wichita State University).

MOUNTAIN WEST CONFERENCE

Mailing Address: 15455 Gleneagle Dr., Suite 200B, Colorado Springs, CO 80921. **Telephone:** (719) 488-4040. **FAX:** (719) 487-7241. **E-Mail Address:** rchristian@TheMWC.com. **Website:** www.TheMWC.com.

Baseball Members (First Year): Air Force (2000), Brigham Young (2000), Nevada-Las Vegas (2000), New Mexico (2000), San Diego State (2000), Utah (2000).

Assistant Director, Communications: Ron Christian.

2003 Tournament: Six teams, double-elimination. May 21-24 at Albuquerque, NM (Albuquerque Sports Stadium).

NORTHEAST CONFERENCE

Mailing Address: 200 Cottontail Lane, Vantage Court North, Somerset, NJ 08873. **Telephone:** (732) 469-0440. **FAX:** (732) 469-0744. **E-Mail Address:**

rratner@northeastconference.org. **Website:** www.northeastconference.org.

Baseball Members (First Year): Central Connecticut State (1999), Fairleigh Dickinson (1981), Long Island (1981), Maryland-Baltimore County (1999), Monmouth (1985), Mount St. Mary's (1989), Quinnipiac (1999), Sacred Heart (2000), St. Francis, N.Y. (1981), Wagner (1981).

Associate Commissioner: Ron Ratner.

2003 Tournament: Four teams, double-elimination. May 16-18 at Lakewood, NJ (First Energy Park).

OHIO VALLEY CONFERENCE

Mailing Address: 278 Franklin Rd., Suite 103, Brentwood, TN 37027. **Telephone:** (615) 371-1698. **FAX:** (615) 371-1788. **E-Mail Address:** kmelcher@ovc.org. **Website:** www.ovcsports.com.

Baseball Members (First Year): Austin Peay State (1962), Eastern Illinois (1996), Eastern Kentucky (1948), Morehead State (1948), Murray State (1948), Southeast Missouri State (1991), Tennessee-Martin (1992), Tennessee Tech (1949).

Assistant Commissioner: Kim Melcher.

2003 Tournament: Six teams, double-elimination. May 21-24 at Paducah, KY (Brooks Stadium).

PACIFIC-10 CONFERENCE

Mailing Address: 800 S. Broadway, Suite 400, Walnut Creek, CA 94596. **Telephone:** (925) 932-4411. **FAX:** (925) 932-4601. **E-Mail Address:** bniemi@pac-10.org. **Website:** www.pac-10.org.

Baseball Members (First Year): Arizona (1979), Arizona State (1979), California (1916), UCLA (1928), Oregon State (1916), Southern California (1922), Stanford (1917), Washington (1916), Washington State (1917).

Public Relations Intern: Bri Niemi.

2003 Tournament: None.

PATRIOT LEAGUE

Mailing Address: 3773 Corporate Parkway, Suite 190, Center Valley, PA 18034. **Telephone:** (610) 289-1950. **FAX:** (610) 289-1952. **E-Mail Address:** kpetersen@patriotleague.com. **Website:** www.patriotleague.com.

Baseball Members (First Year): Army (1993), Bucknell (1991), Holy Cross (1991), Lafayette (1991), Lehigh (1991), Navy (1993).

Assistant Director, Media Relations: Kristina Petersen.

2003 Tournament: Top three teams; No. 2 plays No. 3 in one-game playoff. Winner faces No. 1 team in best-of-3 series at No. 1 seed, May 10-11.

SOUTHEASTERN CONFERENCE

Mailing Address: 2201 Richard Arrington Blvd. N., Birmingham, AL 35203. **Telephone:** (205) 458-3000. **FAX:** (205) 458-3030. **E-Mail Address:** cdunlap@sec.org. **Website:** www.secsports.com.

Baseball Members (First Year): East—Florida (1933), Georgia (1933), Kentucky (1933), South Carolina (1992), Tennessee (1933), Vanderbilt (1933). **West**—Alabama (1933), Arkansas (1992), Auburn (1933), Louisiana State (1933), Mississippi (1933), Mississippi State (1933).

Media Relations Assistant: Chuck Dunlap.

2003 Tournament: Eight teams, modified double-elimination. May 21-25 at Birmingham, AL (Hoover Metropolitan Stadium).

SOUTHERN CONFERENCE

Mailing Address: 905 E. Main Street, Spartanburg, SC 29302. **Telephone:** (864) 591-5100. **FAX:** (864) 591-3448. **E-Mail Address:** sshutt@socon.org. **Website:** www.soconsports.com.

Baseball Members (First Year): Appalachian State (1971), Charleston (1998), The Citadel (1936), Davidson (1991), East Tennessee State (1978), Furman (1936), Georgia Southern (1991), UNC Greensboro (1997), Virginia Military Institute (1924), Western Carolina (1976), Wofford (1997).

Assistant Commissioner, Public Affairs: Steve Shutt.

2003 Tournament: Eight teams, double-elimination. May 21-24 at Charleston, SC (The Citadel).

SOUTHLAND CONFERENCE

Mailing Address: 1700 Alma Dr., Suite 550, Plano, TX 75075. **Telephone:** (972) 422-9500. **FAX:** (972) 422-9225. **E-Mail Address:** bludlow@southland.org. **Website:** www.southland.org.

Baseball Members (First Year): Lamar (1999), Louisiana-Monroe (1983), McNeese State (1973), Nicholls State (1992), Northwestern State (1988), Sam Houston State (1988), Southeastern Louisiana (1998), Southwest Texas State (1988), Texas-Arlington (1964), Texas-San Antonio (1992).

Baseball Contact/Assistant Commissioner: Bruce Ludlow.

2002 Tournament: Six teams, double-elimination. May 21-24 at Hammond, LA (Southeastern Louisiana University).

SOUTHWESTERN ATHLETIC CONFERENCE

Mailing Address: A.G. Gaston Building, 1527 Fifth Ave. N., Birmingham, AL 35203. **Telephone:** (205) 252-7573, ext. 111. **FAX:** (205) 252-9997. **E-Mail Address:** wdooley@swac.org. **Website:** www.swac.org.

Baseball Members (First Year): East—Alabama A&M (2000), Alabama State (1982), Alcorn State (1962), Jackson State (1958), Mississippi Valley State (1968). **West**—Arkansas-Pine Bluff (1999), Grambling State (1958), Prairie View A&M (1920), Southern (1934), Texas Southern (1954).

Assistant Commissioner, Media Relations: Wallace Dooley.

2003 Tournament: Six teams, double-elimination. May 1-4 at Baton Rouge, LA (Southern University).

SUN BELT CONFERENCE

Mailing Address: 601 Poydras St., Suite 2355, New Orleans, LA 70130. **Telephone:** (504) 299-9066. **FAX:** (504) 299-9068. **E-Mail Address:** willson@sunbeltsports.org. **Website:** www.sunbeltsports.org.

Baseball Members (First Year): Arkansas-Little Rock (1991), Arkansas State (1991), Florida International (1999), Louisiana-Lafayette (1991), Middle Tennessee (2001), New Mexico State (2001), New Orleans (1976), South Alabama (1976), Western Kentucky (1982).

Director, Service Bureau: Judy Willson.

2003 Tournament: Eight teams, double-elimination. May 21-24 at Lafayette, LA. (University of Louisiana-Lafayette).

WEST COAST CONFERENCE

Mailing Address: 1200 Bayhill Dr., Suite 302, San Bruno, CA 94066. **Telephone:** (650) 873-8622. **FAX:** (650) 873-7846. **E-Mail Addresses:** bwalker@westcoast.org, jdouglas@westcoast.org. **Website:** www.wccsports.com.

Baseball Members (First Year): Coast—Gonzaga (1996), Pepperdine (1968), Saint Mary's (1968), Santa Clara (1968). **West**—Loyola Marymount (1968),

Portland (1996), San Diego (1979), San Francisco (1968).

Assistant Commissioner: Brad Walker. **Communications Assistant:** Jae Wilson.

2003 Tournament: Division champions meet in best-of-3 series, May 23-25.

WESTERN ATHLETIC CONFERENCE

Mailing Address: 9250 East Costilla Ave., Suite 300, Englewood, CO 80112. **Telephone:** (303) 799-9221. **FAX:** (303) 799-3888. **E-Mail Address:** wac@wac.org. **Website:** www.wacsports.com.

Baseball Members (First Year): Fresno State (1993), Hawaii (1980), Louisiana Tech (2002), Nevada (2001), Rice (1997), San Jose State (1997).

Commissioner: Karl Benson. **Senior Associate Commissioner:** Jeff Hurd. **Director, Sports Information:** Dave Chaffin.

2003 Tournament: None.

NCAA DIVISION II CONFERENCES

CALIFORNIA COLLEGIATE ATHLETIC ASSOCIATION

Mailing Address: 800 S. Broadway, Suite 309, Walnut Creek, CA 94596. **Telephone:** (925) 472-8299. **FAX:** (925) 472-8887. **Website:** www.goccaa.org.

Baseball Members: UC Davis, UC San Diego, Cal State Bakersfield, Cal State Chico, Cal State Dominguez Hills, Cal State San Bernardino, Cal State Stanislaus, San Francisco State, Sonoma State.

CAROLINAS-VIRGINIA ATHLETIC CONFERENCE

Mailing Address: 26 Cub Dr., Thomasville, NC 27360. **Telephone:** (336) 884-0482. **FAX:** (336) 884-0315. **E-Mail Address:** CVAC@triad.rr.com. **Website:** www.cvac.net.

Baseball Members: Anderson, Barton, Belmont Abbey, Coker, Erskine, Limestone, Longwood, Mount Olive, Pfeiffer, St. Andrews Presbyterian.

CENTRAL ATLANTIC COLLEGIATE CONFERENCE

Mailing Address: c/o NJIT Sports Information, University Heights, Newark, NJ 07102. **Telephone:** (973) 596-8324. **FAX:** (973) 596-8440. **E-Mail Address:** mentone@adm.njit.edu. **Website:** www.caccathletics.org.

Baseball Members: Bloomfield, Caldwell, Dominican (N.Y.), Felician, New Jersey Tech, Nyack, Philadelphia University of Sciences, Teikyo Post, Wilmington (Del.).

CENTRAL INTERCOLLEGIATE ATHLETIC ASSOCIATION

Mailing Address: 303 Butler Farm Rd., Suite 102, Hampton, VA 23666. **Telephone:** (757) 865-0071. **FAX:** (757) 865-8436. **E-Mail Address**: TheCiaa@aol.com. **Website**: www.theciaa.com.

Baseball Members: Elizabeth City State, Saint Augustine's, Saint Paul's, Shaw, Virginia State.

GREAT LAKES INTERCOLLEGIATE ATHLETIC CONFERENCE

Mailing Address: 1110 Washington Ave., Bay City, MI 48708. **Telephone:** (989) 894-2529. **FAX:** (989) 894-2825. **E-Mail Address:** tomjb@gliac.org. **Website:** www.gliac.org.

Baseball Members: Ashland, Findlay, Gannon, Grand Valley State, Hillsdale, Mercyhurst, Northwood, Saginaw Valley State, Wayne State (Mich.).

GREAT LAKES VALLEY CONFERENCE

Mailing Address: Pan Am Plaza, Suite 560, 201 S. Capitol Ave., Indianapolis, IN 46225. **Telephone:** (317) 237-5636. **FAX:** (317) 237-5632. **E-Mail Address**: jnglvc@aol.com. **Website**: www.glvcsports.com.

Baseball Members: Bellarmine, Indianapolis, Kentucky Wesleyan, Lewis, Missouri-Saint Louis, Northern Kentucky, Quincy, Saint Joseph's (Ind.), Southern Illinois-Edwardsville, Southern Indiana, Wisconsin-Parkside.

GULF SOUTH CONFERENCE

Mailing Address: 4 Office Park Circle, Suite 218, Birmingham, AL 25223. **Telephone:** (205) 870-9750. **FAX:** (205) 870-4723. **E-Mail Address:** gcsid@mindspring.com. **Website:** www.gulfsouthconference.org.

Baseball Members: Alabama-Huntsville, Arkansas-Monticello, Arkansas Tech, Central Arkansas, Christian Brothers, Delta State, Harding, Henderson State, Lincoln Memorial, Montevallo, North Alabama, Ouachita Baptist, Southern Arkansas, Valdosta State, West Alabama, West Florida, West Georgia.

LONE STAR CONFERENCE

Mailing Address: 1221 W. Campbell Rd., No. 245, Richardson, TX 75080. **Telephone:** (972) 234-0033. **FAX:** (972) 234-4110. **E-Mail Address**: tinderj@lonestarconference.org. **Website**: www.lonestarconference.org.

Baseball Members: Abilene Christian, Cameron, Central Oklahoma, East Central, Eastern New Mexico, Northeastern State, Southeastern Oklahoma State, Southwestern Oklahoma State, Tarleton State, Texas A&M-Kingsville, West Texas A&M.

MID-AMERICA INTERCOLLEGIATE ATHLETICS ASSOCIATION

Mailing Address: 10551 Barkley, Suite 501, Overland Park, KS 66212. **Telephone:** (913) 341-3839/3080. **FAX:** (913) 341-5887/2995. **E-Mail Address:** rmcfillen@themiaa.com. **Website:** www.themiaa.com.

Baseball Members: Central Missouri State, Emporia State, Missouri-Rolla, Missouri Southern State, Missouri Western State, Northwest Missouri State, Pittsburg State, Southwest Baptist, Truman State, Washburn.

NEW YORK COLLEGIATE ATHLETIC CONFERENCE

Mailing Address: 320 Sea Cliff Ave., Sea Cliff, NY 11579. **Telephone:** (516) 609-2714. **FAX:** (516) 609-0881. **E-Mail**: gonycac@hotmail.com. **Website:** www.nycac.net.

Baseball Members: Adelphi, Bridgeport, Concordia (N.Y.), Dowling, Mercy, Molloy, Philadelphia, Queens, St. Thomas Aquinas.

NORTH CENTRAL INTERCOLLEGIATE ATHLETIC CONFERENCE

Mailing Address: 2400 N. Louise, Ramkota Inn, Sioux Falls, SD 57107. **Telephone:** (605) 338-0907. **FAX:** (605) 373-9018. **E-Mail Address:** info@northcentralconference.org. **Website:** www.northcentralconference.org.

Baseball Members: Augustana (S.D.), Minnesota State-Mankato, Morningside, Nebraska-Omaha, North

Dakota, North Dakota State, Northern Colorado, St. Cloud State, South Dakota, South Dakota State.

NORTHEAST-10 CONFERENCE

Mailing Address: 16 Belmont St., South Easton, MA 02375. **Telephone:** (508) 230-9844. **FAX:** (508) 230-9845. **E-Mail**: kbelbin@northeast10.org. **Website**: www.northeast10.org.

Baseball Members: American International, Assumption, Bentley, Bryant, Franklin Pierce, Massachusetts-Lowell, Merrimack, Saint Anselm, Saint Rose, Southern Connecticut State, Southern New Hampshire, Stonehill.

NORTHERN SUN INTERCOLLEGIATE CONFERENCE

Mailing Address: 2331 University Ave., Suite 122, Minneapolis, MN 55414. **Telephone:** (612) 627-6831. **FAX:** (612) 627-6830. **E-Mail**: lockr100@hotmail.com. **Website:** www.northernsun.org.

Baseball Members: Bemidji State, Concordia-St. Paul, Minnesota-Crookston, Minnesota-Duluth, Minnesota-Morris, Northern State, Southwest State, Wayne State (Neb.), Winona State.

PEACH BELT CONFERENCE

Mailing Address: P.O. Box 204290, Augusta, GA 30917. **Telephone:** (706) 860-8499. **FAX:** (706) 650-8113. **E-Mail Address:** mediarelations@peachbelt.com. **Website:** www.peachbelt.com.

Baseball Members: Armstrong Atlantic State, Augusta State, Columbus State, Francis Marion, Georgia College & State, Kennesaw State, Lander, UNC Pembroke, North Florida, South Carolina-Aiken, South Carolina-Spartanburg.

PENNSYLVANIA STATE ATHLETIC CONFERENCE

Mailing Address: 204 Annex Building, Susquehanna Ave., Lock Haven, PA 17745. **Telephone:** (570) 893-2780. **FAX:** (570) 893-2206. **E-Mail Address:** wadair@lhup.edu. **Website:** www.psacsports.org.

Baseball Members: Bloomsburg, California (Pa.), Clarion, Edinboro, Indiana (Pa.), Kutztown, Lock Haven, Mansfield, Millersville, Shippensburg, Slippery Rock, West Chester.

ROCKY MOUNTAIN ATHLETIC CONFERENCE

Mailing Address: 219 West Colorado Ave., Suite 110, Colorado Springs, CO 80903. **Telephone:** (719) 471-0066. **FAX:** (719) 471-0088. **E-Mail Address:** tkrmac@qwest.net. **Website:** www.rmacsports.org.

Baseball Members: Colorado School of Mines, Fort Hays State, Mesa State, Metro State, Nebraska-Kearney, New Mexico Highlands, Regis, Southern Colorado.

SOUTH ATLANTIC CONFERENCE

Mailing Address: Gateway Plaza, Suite 130, 226 N. Park Dr., Rock Hill, SC 29730. **Telephone:** (803) 981-5240. **FAX:** (803) 981-9444. **E-Mail Address:** thesac@comporium.net. **Website:** www.thesac.com.

Baseball Members: Carson-Newman, Catawba, Lenoir-Rhyne, Mars Hill, Newberry, Presbyterian, Tusculum, Wingate.

SOUTHERN INTERCOLLEGIATE ATHLETIC CONFERENCE

Mailing Address: 3469 Lawrenceville Highway, Suite 103, Tucker, GA 30084. **Telephone:** (770) 908-0482. **FAX:** (770) 408-2772. **Website:** www.thesiac.com.

Baseball Members: Albany State (Ga.), Clark Atlanta, Kentucky State, Lane, LeMoyne-Owen, Miles, Paine, Tuskegee.

SUNSHINE STATE CONFERENCE

Mailing Address: 7061 Grand National Dr., Suite 140, Orlando, FL 32819. **Telephone:** (407) 248-8460. **FAX:** (407) 248-8325. **E-Mail Address:** info@ssconference.org. **Website:** www.ssconference.org.

Baseball Members: Barry, Eckerd, Florida Southern, Florida Tech, Lynn, Rollins, Saint Leo, Tampa.

WEST VIRGINIA INTERCOLLEGIATE ATHLETIC CONFERENCE

Mailing Address: 1422 Main St., Princeton, WV 24740. **Telephone:** (304) 487-6298. **FAX:** (304) 487-6299. **E-Mail Address:** will@wviac.org. **Website:** www.wviac.org.

Baseball Members: Alderson-Broaddus, Bluefield State, Charleston, Concord, Davis & Elkins, Fairmont State, Ohio Valley, Salem International, Shepherd, West Liberty State, West Virginia State, West Virginia University Tech, West Virginia Wesleyan.

NCAA DIVISION I TEAMS

*Recruiting coordinator

AIR FORCE ACADEMY Falcons

Conference: Mountain West.

Mailing Address: 2169 Field House Dr., USAF Academy, CO 80840. **Website:** www.airforcesports.com.

Head Coach: Reed Peters. **Assistant Coaches:** Mark Breeding, *Greg Brummett, Chris Humphrey. **Telephone:** (719) 333-7898. ■ **Baseball SID:** Dave Toller. **Telephone:** (719) 333-3478. **FAX:** (719) 333-3798.

AKRON Zips

Conference: Mid-American (East).

Mailing Address: 178 JAR Arena, Akron, OH 44325. **Website:** www.gozips.com.

Head Coach: Tim Berenyi. **Assistant Coaches:** *Scott Demetral, Trent McIlvain, Don Thorley. **Telephone:** (330) 972-7290. ■ **Baseball SID:** Shawn Nestor. **Telephone:** (330) 972-6292. **FAX:** (330) 374-8844.

ALABAMA Crimson Tide

Conference: Southeastern (West).

Mailing Address: P.O. Box 870391, Tuscaloosa, AL 35487. **Website:** www.rolltide.com.

Head Coach: Jim Wells. **Assistant Coaches:** Brent Boyd, *Jim Gatewood, Danny Watkins. **Telephone:** (205) 348-4029. ■ **Baseball SID:** Barry Allen. **Telephone:** (205) 348-6084. **FAX:** (205) 348-8841.

Home Field: Sewell-Thomas Stadium. **Seating Capacity:** 6,118. **Outfield Dimensions:** LF—325, CF—400, RF—325. **Press Box Telephone:** (205) 348-4927.

ALABAMA-BIRMINGHAM Blazers

Conference: Conference USA.

Mailing Address: 1530 3rd Ave. S., Birmingham, AL 35294. **Website:** www.UABSports.com.

Head Coach: Larry Giangrosso. **Assistant Coaches:** Nick Dumas, *Frank Walton. **Telephone:** (205) 934-5181. ■ **Baseball SID:** Mark Crawford. **Telephone:** (205) 934-0722. **FAX:** (205) 934-7505.

Home Field: Jerry D. Young Memorial Field. **Seating Capacity:** 1,000. **Outfield Dimensions:** LF—330, CF—400, RF—330. **Press Box Telephone:** (205) 934-0200.

ALABAMA A&M Bulldogs

Conference: Southwestern Athletic (East).

Mailing Address: P.O. 1597, Normal, AL 35762.

Head Coach: Thomas Wesley. **Telephone:** (256) 851-4004. ■ **Baseball SID**: Steve Underwood. **Telephone:** (256) 858-4005. **FAX:** (256) 372-5919.

ALABAMA STATE Hornets

Conference: Southwestern Athletic (East).

Mailing Address: 915 S. Jackson St., Montgomery, AL 36101.

Head Coach: Larry Watkins. **Telephone:** (334) 229-4228. ■ **Baseball SID**: Laytonia Thurston. **Telephone:** (334) 229-4511. **FAX:** (334) 262-2971.

ALBANY Great Danes

Conference: America East.

Mailing Address: P.E. 125, 1400 Washington Ave., Albany, NY 12222. **Website:** www.albany.edu/sports.

Head Coach: Jon Mueller. **Assistant Coaches:** Mark Lavenia, Mike Oliva. **Telephone:** (518) 442-3014. ■ **Baseball SID**: Gene Brtalik. **Telephone:** (518) 442-3359. **FAX:** (518) 442-3139.

ALCORN STATE Braves

Conference: Southwestern Athletic (East).

Mailing Address: 1000 ASU Drive, No. 510, Alcorn State, MS 39096. **Website:** www.alcorn.edu/athletics.

Head Coach: Willie McGowan. **Assistant Coach:** Nathan Kennedy. **Telephone:** (601) 877-6279. ■ **Baseball SID:** Peter Forest. **Telephone:** (601) 877-6466. **FAX:** (601) 877-3821.

APPALACHIAN STATE Mountaineers

Conference: Southern.

Mailing Address: Broome-Kirk Gym, Boone, NC 28608. **Website:** www.goasu.com.

Head Coach: Troy Huestess. **Assistant Coaches:** Ski Chernisky, Robbie Huffstetter. **Telephone:** (828) 262-6097. ■ **Baseball SID:** Kelby Siler. **Telephone:** (828) 262-2268. **FAX:** (828) 262-6106.

ARIZONA Wildcats

Conference: Pacific-10.

Mailing Address: Room 106, McKale Center, Tucson, AZ 85721. **Website:** www.arizonaathletics.com.

Head Coach: Andy Lopez. **Assistant Coaches:** Jeff Morris, *Mark Wasikowski. **Telephone:** (520) 621-4102. ■ **Baseball SID:** Matt Rector. **Telephone:** (520) 621-0914. **FAX:** (520) 621-2681.

Home Field: Frank Sancet Field. **Seating Capacity:** 6,500. **Outfield Dimensions:** LF—360, CF—400, RF—360. **Press Box Telephone:** (520) 621-4440.

ARIZONA STATE Sun Devils

Conference: Pacific-10.

Mailing Address: Arizona State University, Tempe, AZ 85287. **Website:** www.TheSunDevils.com.

Head Coach: Pat Murphy. **Assistant Coaches:** Mike Rooney, *Jay Sferra, Chris Sinacori. **Telephone:** (480) 965-3677. ■ **Baseball SID:** Jeff Evans. **Telephone:** (480) 965-6594. **FAX:** (480) 965-9309.

Home Field: Packard Stadium (Bobby Winkles Field). **Seating Capacity:** 4,000. **Outfield Dimensions:** LF—340, CF—395, RF—340. **Press Box Telephone:** (480) 727-7253.

ARKANSAS Razorbacks

Conference: Southeastern (West).

Mailing Address: P.O. Box 7777, Fayetteville, AR 72702. **Website:** www.hogwired.com.

Head Coach: Dave Van Horn. **Assistant Coaches:** *Matt Deggs, Dave Jorn. **Telephone:** (479) 575-3655. ■ **Baseball SID:** Bob Grant. **Telephone:** (479) 575-2751. **FAX:** (479) 575-7481.

Home Field: Baum Stadium. **Seating Capacity:** 5,900. **Outfield Dimensions:** LF—320, CF—400, RF—320. **Press Box Telephone:** (501) 444-0031.

ARKANSAS-LITTLE ROCK Trojans

Conference: Sun Belt.

Mailing Address: 2801 S. University Ave., Little Rock, AR 72204. **Website:** www.ualrtrojans.com.

Head Coach: Brian Rhees. **Assistant Coaches:** Patrick Kircher, *Karl Kuhn, Damien Stambersky. **Telephone:** (501) 663-8095. ■ **Baseball SID:** John Evans. **Telephone:** (501) 569-3077. **FAX:** (501) 683-7002.

ARKANSAS-PINE BLUFF Golden Lions

Conference: Southwestern Athletic (West).

Mailing Address: 1200 University Drive, Pine Bluff, AR 71601. **Website**: www.uapb.edu.

Head Coach: Elbert Bennett. **Assistant Coach:** *Michael Bumpers, Carlos James. **Telephone:** (870) 575-8938. ■ **Baseball SID:** Tamara Williams. **Telephone:** (870) 575-7174. **FAX:** (870) 543-8017.

ARKANSAS STATE Indians

Conference: Sun Belt.

Mailing Address: P.O. Box 1000, State University, AR 72467. **Website:** www.asuindians.com.

Head Coach: Keith Kessinger. **Assistant Coaches:** Brad Henderson, *Christian Ostrander. **Telephone:** (870) 972-2700. ■ **Baseball SID:** David Wilson. **Telephone:** (870) 972-2541. **FAX:** (870) 972-3367.

ARMY Cadets

Conference: Patriot.

Mailing Address: 639 Howard Rd., West Point, NY 10996. **Website:** www.goarmysports.com.

Head Coach: Joe Sottolano. **Assistant Coach:** Capt. Dave Borowicz, Fritz Hamburg, *Victor Solis. **Telephone:** (845) 938-3712. ■ **Baseball SID:** Bob Beretta. **Telephone:** (845) 938-6416. **FAX:** (845) 446-2556.

AUBURN Tigers

Conference: Southeastern (West).

Mailing Address: P.O. Box 351, Auburn, AL 36830. **Website:** www.auburntigers.com.

Head Coach: Steve Renfroe. **Assistant Coaches:** Chris Finwood, Mark Fuller. **Telephone:** (334) 844-4975. ■ **Baseball SID:** Kirk Sampson. **Telephone:** (334) 844-9803. **FAX:** (334) 844-9807.

Home Field: Hitchcock Field at Plainsman Park. **Seating Capacity:** 4,096. **Outfield Dimensions:** LF—315, CF—385, RF—331. **Press Box Telephone:** (334) 844-4138.

AUSTIN PEAY STATE Governors

Conference: Ohio Valley.

Mailing Address: P.O. Box 4515, Clarksville, TN 37044. **Website:** www.apsu.edu/athletics.

Head Coach: Gary McClure. **Assistant Coaches:** *Brian Hetland, Greg Troy. **Telephone:** (931) 221-6266. ■ **Baseball SID:** Cody Bush. **Telephone:** (931) 221-7561. **FAX:** (931) 221-7562.

BALL STATE Cardinals

Conference: Mid-American (West).

Mailing Address: HP 120, Muncie, IN 47306. **Website**: www.ballstatesports.com.

Head Coach: Greg Beals. **Assistant Coaches:** *Clint Albert, Jason Taulman. **Telephone:** (765) 285-8226. ■ **Baseball SID:** Brad Caudill. **Telephone:** (765) 285-8242. **FAX:** (765) 285-8929.

Home Field: Ball Diamond. **Seating Capacity:** 1,700. **Outfield Dimensions:** LF—330, CF—400, RF—330. **Press Box Telephone:** (765) 285-8932.

BAYLOR Bears

Conference: Big 12.

Mailing Address: Baylor Ballpark, 1612 S. University Parks Dr., Waco, TX 76706. **Website:** www.BaylorBears.com.

Head Coach: Steve Smith. **Assistant Coaches:** Chris Berry, Steve Johnigan, *Mitch Thompson. **Telephone:** (254) 710-3029. ■ **Baseball SID:** Jeff Brown. **Telephone:** (254) 710-3065. **FAX:** (254) 710-1369.

Home Field: Ferrell Field at Baylor Ballpark. **Seating Capacity:** 3,000. **Outfield Dimensions:** LF—325, CF—400, RF—325. **Press Box Telephone:** (254) 754-5546.

BELMONT Bruins

Conference: Atlantic Sun.

Mailing Address: 1900 Belmont Blvd., Nashville, TN 37212. **Website:** www.belmont.edu/athletics.

Head Coach: Dave Jarvis. **Assistant Coaches:** Matt Barnett, *Jason Stein. **Telephone:** (615) 460-6166. ■ **Baseball SID:** Matt Wilson. **Telephone:** (615) 460-6000. **FAX:** (615) 460-5584.

BETHUNE-COOKMAN Wildcats

Conference: Mid-Eastern Athletic (South).

Mailing Address: 640 Dr. Mary McLeod Bethune Blvd., Daytona Beach, FL 32114. **Website:** www.cookman.edu/athletics/baseball.

Head Coach: Mervyl Melendez. **Assistant Coaches:** Willie Brown, Matt Knox, *Joel Sanchez. **Telephone:** (386) 481-2224. ■ **Baseball SID:** Devon Quash. **Telephone:** (386) 481-2206. **FAX:** (386) 481-2219.

BINGHAMTON Bearcats

Conference: America East.

Mailing Address: P.O. Box 6000, Binghamton, NY 13902. **Website:** athletics.binghamton.edu.

Head Coach: Tim Sinicki. **Assistant Coaches:** *Mike Collins, Tim Harkness. **Telephone:** (607) 777-2525. **Baseball SID:** John Hartrick. **Telephone:** (607) 777-6800. **FAX:** (607) 777-4597.

BIRMINGHAM-SOUTHERN Panthers

Conference: Big South (not eligible for 2003 championship).

Mailing Address: 900 Arkadelphia Rd., Birmingham, AL 35254. **Website:** www.bscsports.net.

Head Coach: Brian Shoop. **Assistant Coaches:** *Matt Bragga, Bob Keller. **Telephone:** (205) 226-4797. **Baseball SID:** Will Chandler. **Telephone:** (205) 226-7736. **FAX:** (205) 226-3049.

BOSTON COLLEGE Eagles

Conference: Big East.

Mailing Address: 140 Commonwealth Ave., Chestnut Hill, MA 02467. **Website**: www.bceagles.com.

Head Coach: Pete Hughes. **Assistant Coaches:** Rob Carpentier, Steve Englert, *Dave Turgeon. **Telephone:** (617) 552-1131. ■ **Baseball SID:** Mickey Brown. **Telephone:** (617) 552-4508. **FAX:** (617) 552-4903.

Home Field: Commander Shea Field. **Seating Capacity:** 1,000. **Outfield Dimensions:** LF—330, CF—400, RF—320. **Press Box Telephone:** None.

BOWLING GREEN STATE Falcons

Conference: Mid-American (East).

Mailing Address: 201 Doyt Perry Stadium East, Bowling Green, OH 43403. **Website:** www.bgsufalcons.com.

Head Coach: Danny Schmitz. **Assistant Coaches:** *Tod Brown, Chris Hoiles, Dave Whitmire. **Telephone:** (419) 372-7065. ■ **Baseball SID:** Kris Kamann. **Telephone:** (419) 372-7077. **FAX:** (419) 372-6015.

Home Field: Warren Steller Field. **Seating Capacity:** 1,100. **Outfield Dimensions:** LF—340, CF—400, RF—340. **Press Box Telephone:** (419) 372-1234.

BRADLEY Braves

Conference: Missouri Valley.

Mailing Address: 1501 West Bradley Ave., Peoria, IL 61625. **Website:** www.bubraves.com.

Head Coach: Dewey Kalmer. **Assistant Coaches:** Mike Dunne, John Dyke, *John Young. **Telephone:** (309) 677-2684. ■ **Baseball SID:** Bobby Parker. **Telephone:** (309) 677-2624. **FAX:** (309) 677-2626.

Home Field: O'Brien Field. **Seating Capacity:** 7,500. **Outfield Dimensions:** LF—310, CF—400, RF—310. **Press Box Telephone:** (309) 680-4045.

BRIGHAM YOUNG Cougars

Conference: Mountain West.

Mailing Address: 111 Miller Park, Provo, UT 84602. **Website:** www.byucougars.com.

Head Coach: Vance Law. **Assistant Coaches:** *Mike Karpel, Ryan Roberts. **Telephone:** (801) 378-5047. ■ **Baseball SID:** Ralph Zobell. **Telephone:** (801) 422-9769. **FAX:** (801) 422-0633.

Home Field: Larry Miller Field. **Seating Capacity:** 2,300. **Outfield Dimensions:** LF—345, CF—400, RF—

345. **Press Box Telephone:** (801) 378-4041.

BROWN Bears

Conference: Ivy League (Rolfe).

Mailing Address: P.O. Box 1932, Providence, RI 02912. **Website:** www.BrownBears.com.

Head Coach: Marek Drabinski. **Assistant Coaches:** *Raphael Cerrato, Jim Foster. **Telephone:** (401) 863-3090. ■ **Baseball SID:** Meghan Moore. **Telephone:** (401) 863-2219. **FAX:** (401) 863-1436.

BUCKNELL Bison

Conference: Patriot.

Mailing Address: Moore Ave., Lewisburg, PA 17837. **Website:** www.bucknellbison.com.

Head Coach: Gene Depew. **Assistant Coaches:** *Rick Ciccione, Brian Hoyt. **Telephone:** (570) 577-3593. ■ **Baseball SID:** Niki DeSantis. **Telephone:** (570) 577-3068. **FAX:** (570) 577-1660.

BUFFALO Bisons

Conference: Mid-American (East).

Mailing Address: 102 Alumni Arena, Buffalo, NY 14260. **Website:** www.buffalobulls.com.

Head Coach: Bill Breene. **Assistant Coaches:** Dave Borsuk, *Ron Torgalski. **Telephone:** (716) 645-6808. ■ **Baseball SID:** John Fuller. **Telephone:** (716) 645-6762. **FAX:** (716) 645-6840.

BUTLER Bulldogs

Conference: Horizon.

Mailing Address: 510 W. 49th St., Indianapolis, IN 46208. **Website:** www.butlersports.com.

Head Coach: Steve Farley. **Assistant Coach:** Bob Keeney. **Telephone:** (317) 940-9721. ■ **Baseball SID:** Jim McGrath. **Telephone:** (317) 940-9414. **FAX:** (317) 940-9808.

CALIFORNIA Golden Bears

Conference: Pacific-10.

Mailing Address: 210 Memorial Stadium, Berkeley, CA 94720. **Website:** www.calbears.com.

Head Coach: David Esquer. **Assistant Coaches:** *Dan Hubbs, Mike Teijeiro, Ron Witmeyer. **Telephone:** (510) 643-6006. ■ **Baseball SID:** Scott Ball. **Telephone:** (510) 643-1741. **FAX:** (510) 643-7778.

Home Field: Evans Diamond. **Seating Capacity:** 2,500. **Outfield Dimensions:** LF—320, CF—395, RF—320. **Press Box Telephone:** (510) 642-3098.

UCLA Bruins

Conference: Pacific-10.

Mailing Address: 325 Westwood Plaza, Los Angeles, CA 90095. **Website:** www.uclabruins.com.

Head Coach: Gary Adams. **Assistant Coaches:** Gary Adcock, *Vince Beringhele. **Telephone:** (310) 794-8210. ■ **Baseball SID:** Neila Matheny. **Telephone:** (310) 206-4008. **FAX:** (310) 825-8664.

Home Field: Jackie Robinson Stadium. **Seating Capacity:** 1,250. **Outfield Dimensions:** LF—365, CF—390, RF—365. **Press Box Telephone:** (310) 794-8213.

UC IRVINE Anteaters

Conference: Big West.

Mailing Address: 1394 Crawford Hall, Irvine, CA 92697. **Website:** www.athletics.uci.edu.

Head Coach: John Savage. **Assistant Coaches:** Joe DeMarco, *Jason Gill, *Pat Shine. **Telephone:** (949) 824-4292. ■ **Baseball SID:** Fumi Kimura. **Telephone:** (949) 824-9474. **FAX:** (949) 824-5260.

Home Field: Anteater Stadium. **Seating Capacity:** 3,200. **Outfield Dimensions:** LF—335, CF—405, RF—335. **Press Box Telephone:** (949) 824-9905.

UC RIVERSIDE Highlanders

Conference: Big West.

Mailing Address: 900 University Ave., Riverside, CA 92521. **Website:** www.athletics.ucr.edu.

Head Coach: Jack Smitheran. **Assistant Coach:** Andrew Checketts, *Doug Smith. **Telephone:** (909) 787-5441. ■ **Baseball SID:** Thomas LaRocca. **Telephone:** (909) 787-5438. **FAX:** (909) 787-5889.

Home Field: Riverside Sports Complex. **Seating Capacity:** 2,500. **Outfield Dimensions:** LF—330, CF—400, RF—330. **Press Box Telephone:** (909) 787-6415.

UC SANTA BARBARA Gauchos

Conference: Big West.

Mailing Address: Robertson Gym, Santa Barbara, CA 93106. **Website:** www.ucsbgauchos.com.

Head Coach: Bob Brontsema. **Assistant Coaches:** *Dan Ricabal, Bob Townsend. **Telephone:** (805) 893-3690. ■ **Baseball SIDs:** Tony LaTorra, Andy Nicolai. **Telephone:** (805) 893-3428. **FAX:** (805) 893-4537.

Home Field: Caesar Uyesaka Stadium. **Seating Capacity:** 1,000. **Outfield Dimensions:** LF—335, CF—400, RF—335. **Press Box Telephone:** (805) 893-4671.

CAL POLY Mustangs

Conference: Big West.

Mailing Address: One Grand Ave., San Luis Obispo, CA 93407. **Website:** www.gopoly.com.

Head Coach: Larry Lee. **Assistant Coaches:** *Chal Fanning, Jerry Weinstein. **Telephone:** (805) 756-6367. ■ **Baseball SID:** Eric Burdick. **Telephone:** (805) 756-6550. **FAX:** (805) 756-2650.

Home Field: Robin Baggett Stadium. **Seating Capacity:** 1,534. **Outfield Dimensions:** LF—335, CF—405, RF—335. **Press Box Telephone:** (805) 756-7456.

CAL STATE FULLERTON Titans

Conference: Big West.

Mailing Address: 800 N. State College Blvd., Fullerton, CA 92834. **Website:** www.titansports.org.

Head Coach: George Horton. **Assistant Coaches:** Chad Baum, *Dave Serrano, Rick Vanderhook. **Telephone:** (714) 278-3780. ■ **Baseball SID:** Ryan Ermeling. **Telephone:** (714) 278-3081. **FAX:** (714) 278-3141.

Home Field: Goodwin Field. **Seating Capacity:** 3,500. **Outfield Dimensions:** LF—330, CF—400, RF—330. **Press Box Telephone:** (714) 278-5327.

CAL STATE NORTHRIDGE Matadors

Conference: Big West.

Mailing Address: 18111 Nordhoff St., Northridge, CA 91330. **Website:** www.gomatadors.com.

Head Coach: Steve Rousey. **Assistant Coaches:** *Grant Hohman, Mark Kertenian, Rob McKinley. **Telephone:** (818) 677-7055. ■ **Baseball SID:** Aaron Meier. **Telephone:** (818) 677-3243. **FAX:** (818) 677-4950.

Home Field: Matador Field. **Seating Capacity:** 1,200. **Outfield Dimensions:** LF—325, CF—400, RF—330. **Press Box Telephone:** (818) 677-4293.

CAL STATE SACRAMENTO Hornets

Conference: Independent.

Mailing Address: 6000 J St., Sacramento, CA 95819. **Website:** www.hornetsports.com.

Head Coach: John Smith. **Assistant Coaches:** Jim Barr, Paul Martinez, Rusty McLain. **Telephone:** (916) 278-7225. ■ **Baseball SID:** Brian Berger. **Telephone:** (916) 278-4313. **FAX:** (916) 278-5429.

CAMPBELL Fighting Camels

Conference: Atlantic Sun.

Mailing Address: P.O. Box 10, Buies Creek, NC 27506. **Website:** www.campbell.edu/athletics.

Head Coach: Chip Smith. **Assistant Coaches:** *Jeff Bock, Kent Cox. **Telephone:** (910) 893-1354. ■ **Baseball SID:** Chris Kilcoyne. **Telephone:** (910) 814-4367. **FAX:** (910) 893-1330.

CANISIUS Golden Griffins

Conference: Metro Atlantic (North).

Mailing Address: 2001 Main St., Buffalo, NY 14208. **Website:** www.gogriffs.com.

Head Coach: *Mark Notaro. **Assistant Coaches:** Don Bell, Tim Smith. **Telephone:** (716) 888-3762. ■ **Baseball SID:** Marc Gignac. **Telephone:** (716) 888-2978. **FAX:** (716) 888-3178.

CENTENARY Gents

Conference: Independent.

Mailing Address: 2911 Centenary Blvd., Shreveport, LA 71134. **Website**: www.centenary.edu.

Head Coach: Ed McCann. **Assistant Coaches**: Ben Adams, Jeremy Cantrell, Aaron Vorcheck. **Telephone**: (318) 869-5095. ■ **Baseball SID**: David Pratt. **Telephone**: (318) 869-5092. **FAX**: (318) 869-5128.

CENTRAL CONNECTICUT STATE Blue Devils

Conference: Northeast.

Mailing Address: 1615 Stanley St., New Britain, CT 06050. **Website:** www.ccsubluedevils.com.

Head Coach: Charlie Hickey. **Assistant Coaches:** *Paul LaBella, Jim Ziogas. **Telephone:** (860) 832-3074. ■ **Baseball SID:** Tom Pincince. **Telephone:** (860) 832-3089. **FAX:** (860) 832-3084.

CENTRAL FLORIDA Golden Knights

Conference: Atlantic Sun.

Mailing Address: P.O. Box 163555, Orlando, FL 32816. **Website:** www.ucfathletics.com.

Head Coach: Jay Bergman. **Assistant Coaches:** Craig Cozart, *Greg Frady, Derek Wolfe. **Telephone:** (407) 823-0140. ■ **Baseball SID:** Jason Baum. **Telephone:** (407) 823-0994. **FAX:** (407) 823-5266.

Home Field: Jay Bergman Field. **Seating Capacity:** 1,980. **Outfield Dimensions:** LF—325, CF—400, RF—325. **Press Box Telephone:** (407) 823-4487.

CENTRAL MICHIGAN Chippewas

Conference: Mid-American (West).

Mailing Address: 108 West Hall, Central Michigan, Mount Pleasant, MI 48859. **Website:** www.cmuchippewas.com.

Head Coach: Steve Jaksa. **Assistant Coaches:** Brian Kalczynski, *Matt MacDonald, Jeff Siler. **Telephone:** (989) 774-4392. ■ **Baseball SID:** Fred Stabley. **Telephone:** (989) 774-3277. **FAX:** (989) 774-7324.

CHARLESTON Cougars

Conference: Southern.

Mailing Address: 30 George St., Charleston, SC 29424. **Website:** www.cougars.cofc.edu.

Head Coach: John Pawlowski. **Assistant Coaches:** *Scott Foxhall, Stuart Lake. **Telephone:** (843) 953-5916. ■ **Baseball SID:** Tony Ciuffo. **Telephone:** (843) 953-953-6722. **FAX:** (843) 953-6534.

Home Field: Patriots Point. **Seating Capacity:** 2,000. **Outfield Dimensions:** LF—330, CF—405, RF—330. **Press Box Telephone:** (843) 953-9141.

CHARLESTON SOUTHERN Buccaneers

Conference: Big South.

Mailing Address: P.O. Box 118087, Charleston, SC 29423. **Website:** www.csusports.com.

Head Coach: Gary Murphy. **Assistant Coaches:** Michael Bayne, David Kolhagen, Dirk Thomas. **Telephone:** (843) 863-7591. ■ **Baseball SID:** David Shelton. **Telephone:** (843) 863-7688. **FAX:** (843) 863-7676.

CHARLOTTE 49ers

Conference: Conference USA.

Mailing Address: 9201 University City Blvd., Charlotte, NC 28223. **Website:** www.charlotte49ers.com.

Head Coach: Loren Hibbs. **Assistant Coaches:** Bo Durkac, *Brandon Hall, Jason Hill. **Telephone:** (704) 689-3933. ■ **Baseball SID:** Brent Stastny. **Telephone:** (704) 687-6313. **FAX:** (704) 687-4918.

Home Field: Tom and Lib Phillips Field. **Seating Capacity:** 2,000. **Outfield Dimensions:** LF—335, CF—390, RF—335. **Press Box Telephone:** (704) 687-3148.

CHICAGO STATE Cougars

Conference: Mid-Continent.

Mailing Address: 9501 S. King Dr., Chicago, IL 60628. **Website:** www.csu.edu/athletics.

Head Coach: Terrence Jackson. **Assistant Coaches:** *Dennis Bonebreak, Dwight Litzsey. **Telephone:** (773) 995-3659. ■ **Baseball SID:** Mark Johnson. **Telephone:** (773) 995-2217. **FAX:** (773) 995-3656.

CINCINNATI Bearcats

Conference: Conference USA.

Mailing Address: 309 Laurence Hall, Cincinnati, OH 45221. **Website:** www.ucbearcats.com.

Head Coach: Brian Cleary. **Assistant Coaches:** Kyle DiEduardo, *Jeff Ditch, Brad Meador. **Telephone:** (513) 556-0571. ■ **Baseball SID:** Shawn Sell. **Telephone:** (513) 556-5191. **FAX:** (513) 556-0619.

THE CITADEL Bulldogs

Conference: Southern.

Mailing Address: 171 Moultrie St., Charleston, SC 29409. **Website:** www.citadelsports.com.

Head Coach: Fred Jordan. **Assistant Coaches:** David Beckley, Chris Gibson, *Chris Lemonis. **Telephone:** (843) 953-5285. ■ **Baseball SID:** Kevin Rhodes. **Telephone:** (843) 953-5120. **FAX:** (843) 953-5058.

Home Field: Joseph P. Riley Park. **Seating Capacity:** 6,000. **Outfield Dimensions:** LF—343, CF—398, RF—315. **Press Box Telephone:** (843) 965-4151.

CLEMSON Tigers

Conference: Atlantic Coast.

Mailing Address: P.O. Box 31, 100 Perimeter Rd., Clemson, SC 29634. **Website:** www.clemsontigers.com.

Head Coach: Jack Leggett. **Assistant Coaches:** Bradley LeCroy, *Kevin O'Sullivan, Tom Riginos. **Telephone:** (864) 656-1947. ■ **Baseball SID**: Brian Hennessy. **Telephone:** (864) 656-1921. **FAX:** (864) 656-0299.

Home Field: Doug Kingsmore Stadium. **Seating Capacity:** 5,000. **Outfield Dimensions:** LF—320, CF—400, RF—330. **Press Box Telephone:** (864) 656-7731.

CLEVELAND STATE Vikings

Conference: Horizon.

Mailing Address: 2000 Prospect Ave., Cleveland, OH 44115. **Website:** www.csuvikings.com.

Head Coach: Jay Murphy. **Assistant Coaches:** Brian Donohew, Dave Sprochi, Larry Straub. **Telephone:** (216) 687-4822. ■ **Baseball SID:** Alan Ashby. **Telephone:** (216) 687-5288. **FAX:** (216) 523-7257.

Home Field: Memorial Field. **Seating Capacity:** 1,500. **Outfield Dimensions:** LF—300, CF—395, RF—300. **Press Box Telephone:** (440) 562-5438.

COASTAL CAROLINA Chanticleers

Conference: Big South.

Mailing Address: P.O. Box 261954, Conway, SC 29526. **Website:** www.coastal.edu.

Head Coach: Gary Gilmore. **Assistant Coaches:** Eric Filipek, *Bill Jarman, Kevin Schnall. **Telephone:** (843) 349-2816. ■ **Baseball SID:** Matt Hogue. **Telephone:**

(843) 349-2809. **FAX:** (843) 349-2819.

Home Field: Watson Stadium. **Seating Capacity:** 3,000. **Outfield Dimensions:** LF—320, CF—390, RF—320. **Press Box Telephone:** (843) 347-7453.

COLUMBIA Lions

Conference: Ivy League (Gehrig).

Mailing Address: 3030 Broadway, M.C. 1914, New York, NY 10027. **Website:** www.gocolumbialions.com.

Head Coach: *Mik Aoki. **Assistant Coaches:** Bryan Haley, Matt Rush. **Telephone:** (212) 854-7772. ■ **Baseball SID:** Rachel Hitchcock. **Telephone:** (212) 854-2534. **FAX:** (212) 854-8168.

CONNECTICUT Huskies

Conference: Big East.

Mailing Address: 2111 Hillside Road, U-78, Storrs, CT 06269. **Website:** www.uconnhuskies.com.

Head Coach: Andy Baylock. **Assistant Coaches:** Jerry LaPenta, *Jim Penders, Shaun Skeffington. **Telephone:** (860) 486-2458. ■ **Baseball SID:** Mike Enright. **Telephone:** (860) 486-3531. **FAX:** (860) 486-5085.

Home Field: J.O. Christian Field. **Seating Capacity:** 2,500. **Outfield Dimensions:** LF—340, CF—405, RF—340. **Press Box Telephone:** (860) 486-2018.

COPPIN STATE Eagles

Conference: Mid-Eastern Athletic (North).

Mailing Address: 2500 W. North Ave., Baltimore, MD 21216. **Website:** www.coppin.edu/athletics.

Head Coach: *Guy Robertson. **Assistant Coaches:** Ruffin Bell, Peter Buck. **Telephone:** (410) 951-3740. ■ **Baseball SID:** Kevin Paige. **Telephone:** (410) 951-3729. **FAX:** (410) 951-3718.

CORNELL Big Red

Conference: Ivy League (Rolfe).

Mailing Address: Teagle Hall, Campus Road, Ithaca, NY 14853. **Website:** www.cornellbigred.com.

Head Coach: Tom Ford. **Assistant Coach:** Scott Marsh. **Telephone:** (607) 255-6604. ■ **Baseball SID:** Laura Stange. **Telephone:** (607) 255-5627. **FAX:** (607) 255-9791.

CREIGHTON Blue Jays

Conference: Missouri Valley.

Mailing Address: 2500 California Plaza, Omaha, NE 68178. **Website:** www.gocreighton.com.

Head Coach: Jack Dahm. **Assistant Coaches:** C.J. Keating, *Ed Servais. **Telephone:** (402) 280-5545. ■ **Baseball SID:** Jeffrey Seals. **Telephone:** (402) 280-5544. **FAX:** (402) 280-2495.

Home Field: Creighton Sports Complex. **Seating Capacity:** 1,000. **Outfield Dimensions:** LF—332, CF—402, RF—332. **Press Box Telephone:** (402) 490-4454.

DARTMOUTH Big Green

Conference: Ivy League (Rolfe).

Mailing Address: 6083 Alumni Gym, Hanover, NH 03755. **Website:** www.dartmouth.edu.

Head Coach: Bob Whalen. **Assistant Coach:** *Tony Baldwin, Brian Bishop. **Telephone:** (603) 646-2477. ■ **Baseball SID:** Mike Vietti. **Telephone:** (603) 646-2468. **FAX:** (603) 646-3348.

DAVIDSON Wildcats

Conference: Southern.

Mailing Address: P.O. Box 1750, Davidson, NC 28035. **Website:** www.davidson.edu.

Head Coach: Dick Cooke. **Assistant Coaches:** Stephen Aldrich, Mike McAlpin, *Andrew Riepe. **Telephone:** (704) 894-2368. ■ **Baseball SID:** Rick Bender. **Telephone:** (704) 894-2123. **FAX:** (704) 894-2636.

DAYTON Flyers

Conference: Atlantic-10 (West).

Mailing Address: 300 College Park, Dayton, OH 45469. **Website:** www.daytonflyers.com.

Head Coach: Tony Vittorio. **Assistant Coaches:** Terry Bell, Todd Linklater, Shane Pool. **Telephone:** (937) 229-4456. ■ **Baseball SID:** John Popelar. **Telephone:** (937) 229-4390. **FAX:** (937) 229-4461.

DELAWARE Fightin' Blue Hens

Conference: Colonial Athletic.

Mailing Address: 112 Delaware Field House, Newark, DE 19716. **Website:** www.udel.edu/sportsinfo

Head Coach: Jim Sherman. **Assistant Coaches:** Tim Hamberger, Dan Hammer, *Greg Mamula. **Telephone:** (302) 831-8596. ■ **Baseball SID:** Mark Kimmell. **Telephone:** (302) 831-2186. **FAX:** (302) 831-8653.

Home Field: Bob Hannah Stadium. **Seating Capacity:** 1,300. **Outfield Dimensions:** LF—330, CF—400, RF—330. **Press Box Telephone:** (302) 831-4122.

DELAWARE STATE Hornets

Conference: Mid-Eastern Athletic (North).

Mailing Address: 1200 N. DuPont Hwy., Dover, DE 19901. **Website:** www.dsc.edu/athletics.

Head Coach: J.P. Blandin. **Assistant Coaches:** Michael August, *Clint Ayers, Rich Szvitich. **Telephone:** (302) 857-6035. ■ **Baseball SID:** Dennis Jones. **Telephone:** (302) 857-6065. **FAX:** (302) 857-6069.

DETROIT Titans

Conference: Horizon.

Mailing Address: 4001 W. McNichols Rd., Detroit, MI 48221. **Website:** www.detroittitans.com.

Head Coach: Chris Czarnik. **Assistant Coaches:** *Mark Van Ameyde, Al Willett. **Telephone:** (313) 993-1725. ■ **Baseball SID:** Sean Palchick. **Telephone:** (313) 993-1745. **FAX:** (313) 993-1765.

DREXEL Dragons

Conference: Colonial Athletic.

Mailing Address: 3141 Chestnut St., Philadelphia, PA 19104. **Website:** www.drexel.edu.

Head Coach: Don Maines. **Assistant Coaches:** Blaine Brown, Paul McGloin, *Zeke Mitchem. **Telephone:** (215) 895-1782. ■ **Baseball SID:** Jim Mack. **Telephone:** (215) 895-1570. **FAX:** (215) 895-2038.

DUKE Blue Devils

Conference: Atlantic Coast.

Mailing Address: P.O. Box 90557, Durham, NC 27708. **Website:** www.GoDuke.com.

Head Coach: Bill Hillier. **Assistant Coaches:** Bill Hillier Jr., John Yurkow. **Telephone:** (919) 668-0255. ■ **Baseball SID:** Melanie McCullough. **Telephone:** (919) 684-2668. **FAX:** (919) 684-2489.

Home Field: Jack Coombs Stadium. **Seating Capacity:** 2,000. **Outfield Dimensions:** LF—330, CF—400, RF—330. **Press Box Telephone:** (919) 684-6074.

DUQUESNE Dukes

Conference: Atlantic-10 (West).

Mailing Address: A.J. Palumbo Center, 600 Forbes Ave., Pittsburgh, PA 15282. **Website:** www.GoDukes.duq.edu.

Head Coach: Mike Wilson. **Assistant Coaches:** *Marc Marrizaldi, Will Swisher. **Telephone:** (412) 396-5245. ■ **Baseball SID:** George Nieman. **Telephone:** (412) 396-5376. **FAX:** (412) 396-6210.

EAST CAROLINA Pirates

Conference: Conference USA.

Mailing Address: 320 Ward Sports Medicine Bldg.,

Greenville, NC 27858. **Website:** www.ecupirates.com.

Head Coach: Randy Mazey. **Assistant Coaches:** Tommy Eason, Eddie Loesner, *Allen Osborne. **Telephone:** (252) 328-4604. ■ **Baseball SID:** Jody Jones. **Telephone:** (252) 328-4522. **FAX:** (252) 328-4528.

Home Field: Harrington Field. **Seating Capacity:** 2,500. **Outfield Dimensions:** LF—320, CF—410, RF—320. **Press Box Telephone:** (252) 328-0068.

EAST TENNESSEE STATE Buccaneers

Conference: Southern.

Mailing Address: P.O. Box 70707, Johnson City, TN 37614. **Website:** www.ETSUBucs.com.

Head Coach: Tony Skole. **Assistant Coaches:** *Nate Goulet, Dave Shelton. **Telephone:** (423) 439-4496. ■ **Baseball SID:** Matt Snellings. **Telephone:** (423) 439-4220. **FAX:** (423) 439-6138.

Home Field: Cardinal Park. **Seating Capacity:** 2,000. **Outfield Dimensions:** LF—330, CF—430, RF—330. **Press Box Telephone:** (425) 461-4865.

EASTERN ILLINOIS Panthers

Conference: Ohio Valley.

Mailing Address: 600 W. Lincoln, Charleston, IL 61920. **Website:** www.eiu.edu/panthers.

Head Coach: Jim Schmitz. **Assistant Coach:** *Matt Husted. **Telephone:** (217) 581-2522. ■ **Baseball SID:** Patrick Osterman. **Telephone:** (217) 581-7020. **FAX:** (217) 581-6434.

EASTERN KENTUCKY Colonels

Conference: Ohio Valley.

Mailing Address: Alumni Coliseum, Rm. 115, Richmond, KY 40475. **Website:** www.ekusports.com.

Head Coach: Elvis Dominguez. **Assistant Coach:** John Corbin, *Rick Court. **Telephone:** (859) 622-2128. ■ **Baseball SID:** Amy Ratliff. **Telephone:** (859) 622-1253. **FAX:** (859) 622-1230.

Home Field: Turkey Hughes Field. **Seating Capacity:** 1,200. **Outfield Dimensions:** LF—340, CF—415, RF—335. **Press Box Telephone:** None.

EASTERN MICHIGAN Eagles

Conference: Mid-American (West).

Mailing Address: Room 307, Convocation Center, Ypsilanti, MI 48197. **Website:** www.emich.edu/goeagles.

Head Coach: Roger Coryell. **Assistant Coach:** Jake Boss. **Telephone:** (734) 487-0315. ■ **Baseball SID:** Bernadette Vielhaber. **Telephone:** (734) 487-0317. **FAX:** (734) 485-3840.

Home Field: Oestrike Stadium. **Seating Capacity:** 2,500. **Outfield Dimensions:** LF—330, CF—390, RF—330. **Press Box Telephone:** (734) 481-9328.

ELON Phoenix

Conference: Big South.

Mailing Address: Elon College, 2500 Campus Box, NC 27244. **Website:** www.elon.edu/athletics.

Head Coach: Mike Kennedy. **Assistant Coaches:** Austin Alexander, *Greg Starbuck. **Telephone:** (336) 278-6741. ■ **Baseball SID:** Matt Eviston. **Telephone:** (336) 278-6711. **FAX:** (336) 278-6768.

EVANSVILLE Purple Aces

Conference: Missouri Valley.

Mailing Address: 1800 Lincoln Ave., Evansville, IN 47722. **Website:** www.gopurpleaces.com.

Head Coach: Dave Schrage. **Assistant Coaches:** Tyler Herbst, Kevin Koch, *Scott Lawler. **Telephone:** (812) 479-2059. ■ **Baseball SID:** Tom Benson. **Telephone:** (812) 488-1152. **FAX:** (812) 479-2090.

Home Field: Braun Stadium. **Seating Capacity:** 1,200. **Outfield Dimensions:** LF—330, CF—400, RF—330. **Press Box Telephone:** (812) 479-2587.

FAIRFIELD Stags

Conference: Metro Atlantic (South).

Mailing Address: 1073 N. Benson Rd., Fairfield, CT 06430. **Website:** www.fairfieldstags.com.

Head Coach: John Slosar. **Assistant Coach:** Bill Consiglio, Dennis Whalen. **Telephone:** (203) 254-4000, ext. 2605. ■ **Baseball SID:** Patrick Moran. **Telephone:** (203) 254-4000, ext. 2877. **FAX:** (203) 254-4117.

FAIRLEIGH DICKINSON Knights

Conference: Northeast.

Mailing Address: 1000 River Rd., Teaneck, NJ 07666. **Website:** www.fdu.edu/athletics.

Head Coach: Dennis Sasso Sr. **Assistant Coaches:** Don Hahn, John Kroeger, Dennis Sasso. **Telephone:** (201) 692-2245. ■ **Baseball SID:** Drew Brown. **Telephone:** (201) 692-2204. **FAX:** (201) 692-9361.

FLORIDA Gators

Conference: Southeastern (East).

Mailing Address: P.O. Box 14485, Gainesville, FL 32604. **Website:** www.gatorzone.com.

Head Coach: Pat McMahon. **Assistant Coaches:** John Cohen, Brian Fleetwood, *Ross Jones. **Telephone:** (352) 375-4683, ext. 4457. ■ **Baseball SID:** Brian Dietz. **Telephone:** (352) 375-4683, ext. 6130. **FAX:** (352) 375-4809.

Home Field: McKethan Stadium. **Seating Capacity:** 5,000. **Outfield Dimensions:** LF—330, CF—400, RF—325. **Press Box Telephone:** (352) 375-4683, ext. 4355/4356.

FLORIDA A&M Rattlers

Conference: Mid-Eastern Athletic (South).

Mailing Address: Room 205, Gaither Athletic Center, Tallahassee, FL 32307. **Website:** www.famu.edu/athletics.

Head Coach: Joe Durant. **Assistant Coaches:** K.C. Carter, *Brett Richardson, Derrick Richardson. **Telephone:** (850) 599-3202. ■ **Baseball SID:** Alvin Hollins. **Telephone:** (850) 599-3200. **FAX:** (850) 599-3206.

FLORIDA ATLANTIC Owls

Conference: Atlantic Sun.

Mailing Address: 777 Glades Rd., Boca Raton, FL 33431. **Website:** www.fausports.com.

Head Coach: Kevin Cooney. **Assistant Coaches:** Dickie Hart, *John McCormack, George Roig. **Telephone:** (561) 297-3956. ■ **Baseball SID:** Dawn Elston. **Telephone:** (561) 297-3513. **FAX:** (561) 297-3499.

Home Field: FAU Field. **Seating Capacity:** 2,000. **Dimensions:** LF—330, CF—400, RF—330. **Press Box Telephone:** (561) 297-3455.

FLORIDA INTERNATIONAL Golden Panthers

Conference: Sun Belt.

Mailing Address: 11200 SW 8th St., Miami, FL 33199. **Website:** www.fiu.edu/~athletic/basehome.

Head Coach: Danny Price. **Assistant Coaches:** Marc Calvi, *Rolando Casanova, Keith Shives. **Telephone:** (305) 348-3166. ■ **Baseball SID:** David Gladow. **Telephone:** (305) 348-6024. **FAX:** (305) 348-2963.

Home Field: University Park. **Seating Capacity:** 2,000. **Outfield Dimensions:** LF—325, CF—400, RF—325. **Press Box Telephone:** (305) 554-8694.

FLORIDA STATE Seminoles

Conference: Atlantic Coast.

Mailing Address: P.O. Box 2195, Tallahassee, FL 32316. **Website:** www.seminoles.com.

Head Coach: Mike Martin. **Assistant Coaches:** Link Jarrett, Mike Martin Jr., *Jamey Shouppe. **Telephone:**

(850) 644-1073. ■ **Baseball SID:** Jeff Purinton. **Telephone:** (850) 644-0615. **FAX:** (850) 644-3820.

Home Field: Dick Howser Stadium. **Seating Capacity:** 5,000. **Outfield Dimensions:** LF—340, CF—400, RF—320. **Press Box Telephone:** (850) 644-1553.

FORDHAM Rams

Conference: Atlantic-10 (East).

Mailing Address: 441 E. Fordham Rd., Bronx, NY 10458. **Website:** www.fordham.edu.

Head Coach: Dan Gallagher. **Assistant Coaches:** Bob Caputo, Tony Mellaci, *Nick Restaino. **Telephone:** (718) 817-4290. ■ **Baseball SID:** Scott Kwiatkowski. **Telephone:** (718) 817-4242. **FAX:** (718) 817-4278.

FRESNO STATE Bulldogs

Conference: Western Athletic.

Mailing Address: 5305 N. Campus Dr., Room 153, Fresno, CA 93740. **Website:** www.gobulldogs.com.

Head Coach: Mike Batesole. **Assistant Coaches:** Matt Curtis, *Tim Montez. **Telephone:** (559) 278-2178. ■ **Baseball SID:** Darren Moradian. **Telephone:** (559) 278-6187. **FAX:** (559) 278-4689.

Home Field: Beiden Field. **Seating Capacity:** 6,575. **Outfield Dimensions:** LF—330, CF—400, RF—330. **Press Box Telephone:** (559) 278-7678.

FURMAN Paladins

Conference: Southern.

Mailing Address: 3300 Poinsett Hwy., Greenville, SC 29613. **Website:** www.furmanpaladins.com.

Head Coach: Ron Smith. **Assistant Coaches:** Jon Placko, *Jeff Young. **Telephone:** (864) 294-2146. ■ **Baseball SID:** Robby Campbell. **Telephone:** (864) 294-3062. **FAX:** (864) 294-3061.

GARDNER-WEBB Runnin' Bulldogs

Conference: Atlantic Sun.

Mailing Address: P.O. Box 877, Boiling Springs, NC 28017. **Website:** www.gwusports.com.

Head Coach: Rusty Stroupe. **Assistant Coaches:** Todd Interdonato, *Dan Roszel, Donnie Suttles. **Telephone:** (704) 406-4421. ■ **Baseball SID:** Marc Rabb. **Telephone:** (704) 406-4355. **FAX:** (704) 406-4739.

GEORGE MASON Patriots

Conference: Colonial Athletic.

Mailing Address: MSN 3A5, 4400 University Dr., Fairfax, VA 22030. **Website:** www.GMUsports.com.

Head Coach: Bill Brown. **Assistant Coaches:** *Joe Raccuia, Shawn Stiffler. **Telephone:** (703) 993-3282. ■ **Baseball SID:** Ben Trittipoe. **Telephone:** (703) 993-3263. **FAX:** (703) 993-3259.

Home Field: Hap Spuhler Field. **Seating Capacity:** 900. **Outfield Dimensions:** LF—320, CF—400, RF—320. **Press Box Telephone:** (571) 228-3819.

GEORGE WASHINGTON Colonials

Conference: Atlantic-10 (West).

Mailing Address: 600 22nd St. NW, Washington, DC 20037. **Website:** www.gwsports.com.

Head Coach: Tom Walter. **Assistant Coaches:** Chris Ebrahimoff, *Dennis Healy, Tag Montague. **Telephone:** (202) 994-7399. ■ **Baseball SID:** Lars Thorn. **Telephone:** (202) 994-0339. **FAX:** (202) 994-2713.

GEORGETOWN Hoyas

Conference: Big East.

Mailing Address: McDonough Arena, 37th & O Streets NW, Washington, DC 20057. **Website:** www.guhoyas.com.

Head Coach: Pete Wilk. **Assistant Coaches:** *Doc Beeman, Matt Daily. **Telephone:** (202) 687-2462. ■ **Baseball SID:** Rich Comstove. **Telephone:** (202) 687-5366. **FAX:** (202) 687-2491.

Home Field: Shirley Povich Field. **Seating Capacity:** 1,500. **Outfield Dimensions:** LF—330, CF—375, RF—330. **Press Box Telephone:** None.

GEORGIA Bulldogs

Conference: Southeastern (East).

Mailing Address: P.O. Box 1472, Athens, GA 30603. **Website:** www.georgiadogs.com.

Head Coach: David Perno. **Assistant Coaches:** Rick Eckstein, Jason Eller, *Butch Thompson. **Telephone:** (706) 542-7971. ■ **Baseball SID:** Christopher Lakos. **Telephone:** (706) 542-1621. **FAX:** (706) 542-7993.

Home Field: Foley Field. **Seating Capacity:** 3,291. **Outfield Dimensions:** LF—350, CF—410, RF—320. **Press Box Telephone:** (706) 542-6162/6161.

GEORGIA SOUTHERN Eagles

Conference: Southern.

Mailing Address: P.O. Box 8085, Statesboro, GA 30460. **Website:** www.georgiasoutherneagles.com.

Head Coach: Rodney Hennon. **Assistant Coaches:** Matthew Boggs, Sean Teague, *Mike Tidick. **Telephone:** (912) 486-7360. ■ **Baseball SID:** Ricky Ray. **Telephone:** (912) 681-5071. **FAX:** (912) 681-0046.

Home Field: J.I. Clements Stadium. **Seating Capacity:** 2,000. **Outfield Dimensions:** LF—330, CF—380, RF—330. **Press Box Telephone:** (912) 681-2508.

GEORGIA STATE Panthers

Conference: Atlantic Sun.

Mailing Address: 125 Decatur St., Suite 201, Atlanta, GA 30303. **Website:** www.gsu.edu.

Head Coach: Mike Hurst. **Assistant Coaches:** David Hartley, Josh Hopper, Shane West. **Telephone:** (404) 244-5804. ■ **Baseball SID:** Steven Ericson. **Telephone:** (404) 651-4629. **FAX:** (404) 651-3204.

Home Field: Panthersville. **Seating Capacity:** 1,000. **Outfield Dimensions:** LF—334, CF—385, RF—338. **Press Box Telephone:** (404) 244-5801/5802/5803.

GEORGIA TECH Yellow Jackets

Conference: Atlantic Coast.

Mailing Address: 150 Bobby Dodd Way, Atlanta, GA 30332. **Website:** www.ramblinwreck.com.

Head Coach: Danny Hall. **Assistant Coaches:** Bobby Moranda, Jon Palmieri, *Scott Stricklin. **Telephone:** (404) 894-5471. ■ **Baseball SID:** Chris Capo. **Telephone:** (404) 894-5445. **FAX:** (404) 894-1248.

Home Field: Russ Chandler Stadium. **Seating Capacity:** 4,100. **Outfield Dimensions:** LF—328, CF—400, RF—334. **Press Box Telephone:** (404) 894-3167.

GONZAGA Bulldogs

Conference: West Coast.

Mailing Address: E. 502 Boone Ave., Spokane, WA 99258. **Website:** www.gozags.com.

Head Coach: Steve Hertz. **Assistant Coaches:** Scott Asan, *Mark Machtolf, Chris Sheehan. **Telephone:** (509) 323-4226. ■ **Baseball SID:** Rich Moser. **Telephone:** (509) 323-5484. **FAX:** (509) 323-5730.

GRAMBLING STATE Tigers

Conference: Southwestern Athletic (West).

Mailing Address: P.O. Box 868, Grambling, LA 71245. **Website:** www.gram.edu.

Head Coach: Wilbert Ellis. **Assistant Coach:** James Randall. **Telephone:** (318) 274-2218. ■ **Baseball SID:** Roderick Mosley. **Telephone:** (318) 274-6199. **FAX:** (318) 274-2761.

HARTFORD Hawks

Conference: America East.

Mailing Address: 200 Bloomfield Ave., West Hartford,

CT 06117. **Website:** www.HartfordHawks.com.

Head Coach: Harvey Shapiro. **Assistant Coaches:** Al Furrow, Mike Susi. **Telephone:** (860) 768-4656. ■ **Baseball SID:** Mike Vigneux. **Telephone:** (860) 768-4501. **FAX:** (860) 768-4068.

HARVARD Crimson

Conference: Ivy League (Rolfe).

Mailing Address: Murr Center, 65 N. Harvard St., Boston, MA 02163. **Website:** www.athletics.harvard.edu.

Head Coach: Joe Walsh. **Assistant Coaches:** Gary Donovan, *Matt Hyde. **Telephone:** (617) 495-2629. ■ **Baseball SID:** Cassie Lawton. **Telephone:** (617) 495-2206. **FAX:** (617) 495-2130.

HAWAII Rainbows

Conference: Western Athletic.

Mailing Address: 1337 Lower Campus Rd., Honolulu, HI 96822. **Website:** www.uhathletics.hawaii.edu.

Head Coach: Mike Trapasso. **Assistant Coaches:** Brian Green, *Chad Konishi, Keith Komeiji. **Telephone:** (808) 956-6247. ■ **Baseball SID:** Pakalani Bello. **Telephone:** (808) 956-7506. **FAX:** (808) 956-4470.

Home Field: Les Murakami Stadium. **Seating Capacity:** 5,000. **Outfield Dimensions:** LF—325, CF—390, RF—325. **Press Box Telephone:** (808) 956-6253.

HAWAII-HILO Vulcans

Conference: Independent.

Mailing Address: 200 W. Kawili St., Hilo, HI 96720. **Website:** www.vulcans.uhh.hawaii.edu.

Head Coach: Joey Estrella. **Assistant Coaches:** Onan Masaoka, David Miller, Darin Miyake. **Telephone:** (808) 974-7700. ■ **Baseball SID:** Kelly Leong. **Telephone:** (808) 974-7606. **FAX:** (808) 974-7711.

HIGH POINT Panthers

Conference: Big South.

Mailing Address: 833 Montlieu Ave., High Point, NC 27262. **Website**: www.highpointpanthers.com.

Head Coach: Sal Bando Jr. **Assistant Coaches:** John Eberle, Michael Lowman, Phil Maier. **Telephone:** (336) 841-9190. ■ **Baseball SID:** Lee Owen. **Telephone:** (336) 841-4605. **FAX:** (336) 841-9182.

HOFSTRA Flying Dutchmen

Conference: Colonial Athletic.

Mailing Address: Physical Fitness Center, 230 Hofstra University, Hempstead, NY 11549. **Website:** www.hofstra.edu/sports.

Head Coach: Chris Dotolo. **Assistant Coaches:** *Mike Fahid, Pete Graham. **Telephone:** (516) 463-5065. ■ **Baseball SID:** Stephen Gorchov. **Telephone:** (516) 463-4933. **FAX:** (516) 463-5033.

Home Field: University Field. **Seating Capacity:** 500. **Outfield Dimensions:** LF—335, CF—390, RF—335.

HOLY CROSS Crusaders

Conference: Patriot.

Mailing Address: One College St., Worcester, MA 01610. **Website:** www.holycross.edu.

Head Coach: Fran O'Brien. **Assistant Coaches:** Craig Najarian. **Telephone:** (508) 793-2221. ■ **Baseball SID:** Kara McGillicuddy. **Telephone:** (508) 793-2780. **FAX:** (508) 793-2309.

HOUSTON Cougars

Conference: Conference USA.

Mailing Address: 3100 Cullen Rd., Houston, TX 77204. **Website:** www.uhcougars.com.

Head Coach: Rayner Noble. **Assistant Coaches:** Sean Allen, *Todd Whitting. **Telephone:** (713) 743-9396. ■ **Baseball SID:** Jeff Conrad. **Telephone:** (713) 743-9404. **FAX:** (713) 743-9411.

Home Field: Cougar Field. **Seating Capacity:** 3,500. **Outfield Dimensions:** LF—330, CF—390, RF—330. **Press Box Telephone:** (713) 743-0840.

ILLINOIS Fighting Illini

Conference: Big Ten.

Mailing Address: 1700 S. Fourth St., Champaign, IL 61820. **Website:** www.fightingillini.com.

Head Coach: Richard "Itch" Jones. **Assistant Coaches:** *Dan Hartleb, Eric Snider. **Telephone:** (217) 333-8605. ■ **Baseball SID:** Michelle Warner. **Telephone:** (217) 333-1391. **FAX:** (217) 333-5540.

Home Field: Illinois Field. **Seating Capacity:** 1,500. **Outfield Dimensions:** LF—330, CF—400, RF—330. **Press Box Telephone:** (217) 333-1227.

ILLINOIS-CHICAGO Flames

Conference: Horizon.

Mailing Address: 839 W. Roosevelt Rd., Chicago, IL 60608. **Website:** www.uicflames.com.

Head Coach: Mike Dee. **Assistant Coaches:** *Sean McDermott, Scott Stahoviak, Troy Stein. **Telephone:** (312) 996-8645. ■ **Baseball SID:** Matt Brendich. **Telephone:** (312) 996-5881. **FAX:** (312) 996-5882.

ILLINOIS STATE Redbirds

Conference: Missouri Valley.

Mailing Address: Campus Box 7130, Normal, IL 61790. **Website:** www.redbirds.org.

Head Coach: Jim Brownlee. **Assistant Coaches:** *Tim Brownlee, Seth Kenny. **Telephone:** (309) 438-5151. ■ **Baseball SID:** Rob Huizenga. **Telephone:** (309) 438-3598. **FAX:** (309) 438-5634.

Home Field: Redbird Field. **Seating Capacity:** 1,500. **Outfield Dimensions:** LF—375, CF—400, RF—375. **Press Box Telephone:** (309) 438-3504.

INDIANA Hoosiers

Conference: Big Ten.

Mailing Address: 1001 E. 17th St., Assembly Hall, Bloomington, IN 47408. **Website:** www.iuhoosiers.com.

Head Coach: Bob Morgan. **Assistant Coaches:** Jeff Calcaterra, *Tony Kestranek. **Telephone:** (812) 855-1680. ■ **Baseball SID:** Christy Tolin. **Telephone:** (812) 856-0146. **FAX:** (812) 855-9401.

Home Field: Sembower Field. **Seating Capacity:** 3,500. **Outfield Dimensions:** LF—333, CF—400, RF—333. **Press Box Telephone:** (812) 855-4787.

INDIANA-PURDUE UNIVERSITY Mastodons

Conference: Independent.

Mailing Address: 2101 Coliseum Blvd., Fort Wayne, IN 46805. **Website:** www.ipfw.edu/athletics.

Head Coach: William Gernon. **Assistant Coach:** Blaine McFerrin. **Telephone:** (260) 481-5480. ■ **Baseball SID:** Michael Jewell. **Telephone:** (260) 481-6646. **FAX:** (260) 481-6002.

INDIANA STATE Sycamores

Conference: Missouri Valley.

Mailing Address: Fourth and Chestnut Streets, Terre Haute, IN 47809. **Website:** www.indstate.edu/athletics.

Head Coach: Bob Warn. **Assistant Coach:** Jim Fredwell, Jason Ronai, *Nick Zumsande,. **Telephone:** (812) 237-4051. ■ **Baseball SID:** Adam Rouse. **Telephone:** (812) 237-4158. **FAX:** (812) 237-4157.

Home Field: Sycamore Field. **Seating Capacity:** 2,000. **Outfield Dimensions:** LF—340, CF—402, RF—340. **Press Box Telephone:** (812) 237-4187.

IONA Gaels

Conference: Metro Atlantic (South).

Mailing Address: 715 North Ave., New Rochelle, NY 10801. **Website:** www.iona.edu.

Head Coach: Al Zoccolillo. **Assistant Coaches:** John Barone, *Chris Lombardo. **Telephone:** (914) 633-2319. ■ **Baseball SID:** Joe Formisano. **Telephone:** (914) 633-2334. **FAX:** (914) 633-2072.

IOWA Hawkeyes

Conference: Big Ten.

Mailing Address: 232 Carver-Hawkeye Arena, Iowa City, IA 52242. **Website:** www.hawkeyesports.com.

Head Coach: Scott Broghamer. **Assistant Coaches:** Tim Evans, *Travis Wyckoff. **Telephone:** (319) 335-9390. ■ **Baseball SID:** Chris Brewer. **Telephone:** (319) 335-9411. **FAX:** (319) 335-9417.

Home Field: Duane Banks Field. **Seating Capacity:** 3,000. **Outfield Dimensions:** LF—330, CF—400, RF—330. **Press Box Telephone:** (319) 335-9520.

JACKSON STATE Tigers

Conference: Southwestern Athletic (East).

Mailing Address: 1400 John R. Lynch St., Jackson, MS 39217. **Website:** www.jsums.edu.

Head Coach: Mark Salter. **Assistant Coach**: *Omar Johnson. **Telephone:** (601) 979-3928. ■ **Baseball SID:** Deidra Jones. **Telephone:** (601) 979-2273. **FAX:** (601) 979-2000.

JACKSONVILLE Dolphins

Conference: Atlantic Sun.

Mailing Address: 2800 University Blvd. N., Jacksonville, FL 32211. **Website:** www.judolphins.com.

Head Coach: Terry Alexander. **Assistant Coaches:** John Howard, *Bob Shepherd, Les Wright. **Telephone:** (904) 256-7476. ■ **Baseball SID:** Russell Reneau. **Telephone:** (904) 256-7402. **FAX:** (904) 256-7179.

Home Field: Alexander Brest Field. **Seating Capacity:** 1,500. **Outfield Dimensions:** LF—340, CF—405, RF—340. **Press Box Telephone:** (904) 256-7422.

JACKSONVILLE STATE Gamecocks

Conference: Atlantic Sun.

Mailing Address: 700 Pelham Road N., Jacksonville, AL 36265. **Website:** www.jsugamecocksports.com.

Head Coach: Jim Case. **Assistant Coaches:** Steve Gillespie, Matt Ishee. **Telephone:** (256) 782-5367. ■ **Baseball SID:** Greg Seitz. **Telephone:** (256) 782-5377. **FAX:** (256) 782-5958.

JAMES MADISON Dukes

Conference: Colonial Athletic.

Mailing Address: MSC 2301 Godwin Hall, Harrisonburg, VA 22807. **Website:** www.jmusports.edu.

Head Coach: Spanky McFarland. **Assistant Coaches:** *Chuck Bartlett, Ryan Brownlee, Jay Sullenger. **Telephone:** (540) 568-6467. ■ **Baseball SID:** Curt Dudley. **Telephone:** (540) 568-6154. **FAX:** (540) 568-3703.

Home Field: Long Field/Mauck Stadium. **Seating Capacity:** 1,200. **Outfield Dimensions:** LF—340, CF—400, RF—320. **Press Box Telephone:** (540) 568-6545.

KANSAS Jayhawks

Conference: Big 12.

Mailing Address: 1651 Naismith Dr, Lawrence, KS 66047. **Website:** www.kuathletics.com.

Head Coach: Ritch Price. **Assistant Coaches:** Steve Abney, Reggie Christiansen, *Ryan Graves. **Telephone:** (785) 864-7907. ■ **Baseball SID:** Mason Logan. **Telephone:** (785) 864-3420. **FAX:** (785) 864-7944.

Home Field: Hoglund Ballpark. **Seating Capacity:** 2,500. **Outfield Dimensions:** LF—350, CF—400, RF—350. **Press Box Telephone:** (785) 864-4037.

KANSAS STATE Wildcats

Conference: Big 12.

Mailing Address: 1800 College Ave., Bramlage Coliseum, Manhattan, KS 66503. **Website:** www.kstatesports.com.

Head Coach: Mike Clark. **Assistant Coaches:** *Mike Hensley, Steve Miller. **Telephone:** (785) 532-5723. ■ **Baseball SID:** Tom Gilbert. **Telephone:** (785) 532-7979. **FAX:** (785) 532-6093.

Home Field: Tointon Family Stadium. **Seating Capacity:** 2,331. **Outfield Dimensions:** LF—340, CF—400, RF—325. **Press Box Telephone:** (785) 532-5801.

KENT STATE Golden Flashes

Conference: Mid-American (East).

Mailing Address: 234 Mac Center, Kent, OH 44242. **Website:** www.kent.edu/athletics.

Head Coach: Rick Rembielak. **Assistant Coaches:** *Mike Birkbeck, Jeff Waggoner. **Telephone:** (330) 672-8432. ■ **Baseball SID:** Kent Reichert. **Telephone:** (330) 672-2110. **FAX:** (330) 672-2112.

Home Field: Gene Michael Field. **Seating Capacity:** 2,000. **Outfield Dimensions:** LF—330, CF—400, RF—330. **Press Box:** (330) 672-2036.

KENTUCKY Wildcats

Conference: Southeastern (East).

Mailing Address: Memorial Coliseum, Room 23, Lexington, KY 40506. **Website:** www.ukathletics.com.

Head Coach: Keith Madison. **Assistant Coaches:** Greg Goff, *Jan Weisberg, Corey Whitby. **Telephone:** (859) 257-1419. ■ **Baseball SID:** Doug Rentz. **Telephone:** (859) 257-3838. **FAX:** (859) 323-4310.

Home Field: Cliff Hagan Stadium. **Seating Capacity:** 3,000. **Outfield Dimensions:** LF—340, CF—390, RF—310. **Press Box Telephone:** (859) 257-9013.

LAFAYETTE Leopards

Conference: Patriot.

Mailing Address: Kirby Sports Center, Pierce and Hamilton Streets, Easton, PA 18042. **Website:** www.goleopards.com.

Head Coach: *Joe Kinney. **Assistant Coaches:** Gregg Durrah, Paul Englehardt, Scott Stewart. **Telephone:** (610) 330-5476. ■ **Baseball SIDs:** Alison Hischak, Philip LaBella. **Telephone:** (610) 330-5176. **FAX:** (610) 330-5519.

LAMAR Cardinals

Conference: Southland.

Mailing Address: Box 10066, Beaumont, TX 77710. **Website:** www.athletics.lamar.edu.

Head Coach: Jim Gilligan. **Assistant Coaches:** Scott Hatten, *Jim Ricklefsen. **Telephone:** (409) 880-8315. ■ **Baseball SID:** Daucy Crizer. **Telephone:** (409) 880-2319. **FAX:** (409) 880-2338.

Home Field: Vincent-Beck Stadium. **Seating Capacity:** 3,500. **Outfield Dimensions:** LF—325, CF—380, RF—325. **Press Box Telephone:** (409) 880-8327.

LA SALLE Explorers

Conference: Atlantic-10 (West).

Mailing Address: 1900 W. Olney Ave., Philadelphia, PA 19141. **Website:** www.lasalle.edu/athletic

Head Coach: Larry Conti. **Assistant Coaches:** Jordan Nicgorski, Lee Saverio. **Telephone:** (215) 951-1995. ■ **Baseball SID:** Tom Emberly. **Telephone:** (215) 951-1633. **FAX:** (215) 951-1694.

LEHIGH Mountain Hawks

Conference: Patriot.

Mailing Address: 641 Taylor St., Bethlehem, PA 18015. **Website:** www.lehigh.edu.

Head Coach: *Sean Leary. **Assistant Coaches:** Dave Cerminaro, Gerry Mack. **Telephone:** (610) 758-4315. ■ **Baseball SID:** Jeff Tourial. **Telephone:** (610) 758-3158.

FAX: (610) 758-4407.

LE MOYNE Dolphins

Conference: Metro Atlantic (North).

Mailing Address: 1419 Salt Springs Rd., Syracuse, NY 13214. **Website:** www.lemoyne.edu/athletics.

Head Coach: Steve Owens. **Assistant Coaches:** *Pete Hoy, Bob Nandin. **Telephone:** (315) 445-4415. ■ **Baseball SID:** Mike Donlin. **Telephone:** (315) 445-4412. **FAX:** (315) 445-4678.

LIBERTY Flames

Conference: Big South.

Mailing Address: 1971 University Blvd., Lynchburg, VA 24502. **Website:** www.liberty.edu/athletics.

Head Coach: Matt Royer. **Assistant Coaches:** Reggie Reynolds, *Randy Tomlin, Terry Weaver. **Telephone:** (434) 582-2103. ■ **Baseball SID:** Joey Mullins. **Telephone:** (434) 582-2292. **FAX:** (434) 582-2076.

Home Field: Worthington Stadium. **Seating Capacity:** 1,000. **Outfield Dimensions:** LF—325, CF—390, RF—325. **Press Box Telephone:** (434) 582-2914.

LIPSCOMB Bisons

Conference: Southern (not eligible for 2003 championship).

Mailing Address: 3901 Granny White Pike, Nashville, TN 37204. **Website:** www.lipscombsports.com.

Head Coach: Wynn Fletcher. **Assistant Coach:** Jay Chittam. **Telephone:** (615) 279-5716. ■ **Baseball SID:** Kevin Farris. **Telephone:** (615) 279-5862. **FAX:** (615) 269-1806.

LONG BEACH STATE 49ers

Conference: Big West.

Mailing Address: 1250 Bellflower Blvd., Long Beach, CA 90840. **Website:** www.longbeachstate.com.

Head Coach: Mike Weathers. **Assistant Coaches:** Don Barbara, *Troy Buckley. **Telephone:** (562) 985-7548. ■ **Baseball SID:** Niall Adler. **Telephone:** (562) 985-7565. **FAX:** (562) 985-1549.

Home Field: Blair Field. **Seating Capacity:** 3,000. **Outfield Dimensions:** LF—348, CF—400, RF—348. **Press Box Telephone:** (562) 433-8605.

LONG ISLAND Blackbirds

Conference: Northeast.

Mailing Address: One University Plaza, Brooklyn, NY 11201. **Website:** www.liu.edu.

Head Coach: Frank Giannone. **Assistant Coaches:** *Chris Bagley, Mike Ryan. **Telephone:** (718) 488-1538. ■ **Baseball SID:** Greg Fox. **Telephone:** (718) 488-1420. **FAX:** (718) 488-3302.

LOUISIANA-LAFAYETTE Ragin' Cajuns

Conference: Sun Belt.

Mailing Address: 201 Reinhardt Dr., Lafayette, LA 70506. **Website:** www.ragincajuns.com.

Head Coach: Tony Robichaux. **Assistant Coaches:** Anthony Babineaux, John Szefc. **Telephone:** (337) 482-6093. ■ **Baseball SID:** Trey Franchebois. **Telephone:** (337) 482-6331. **FAX:** (337) 482-6649.

Home Field: Moore Field. **Seating Capacity:** 4,000. **Outfield Dimensions:** LF—330, CF—400, RF—330. **Press Box Telephone:** (337) 482-6331.

LOUISIANA-MONROE Indians

Conference: Southland.

Mailing Address: 308 Stadium Dr., Monroe, LA 71209. **Website**: www.ulmathletics.com.

Head Coach: Brad Holland. **Assistant Coaches:** *Steve Johnson, Britten Oubre, Jeremy Talbot. **Telephone:** (318) 342-5396. ■ **Baseball SID:** Troy Mitchell. **Telephone:** (318) 342-5460. **FAX:** (318) 342-5464.

Home Field: Indian Field. **Seating Capacity:** 3,000. **Outfield Dimensions:** LF—330, CF—400, RF—330. **Press Box Telephone:** (318) 342-5476.

LOUISIANA STATE Tigers

Conference: Southeastern (West).

Mailing Address: P.O. Box 25095, Baton Rouge, LA 70894. **Website:** www.LSUsports.net

Head Coach: Smoke Laval. **Assistant Coaches:** Jody Autery, *Turtle Thomas, Brady Wiederhold. **Telephone:** (225) 578-4148. ■ **Baseball SID:** Bill Franques. **Telephone:** (225) 578-8226. **FAX:** (225) 578-1861.

Home Field: Alex Box Stadium. **Seating Capacity:** 7,760. **Outfield Dimensions:** LF—330, CF—405, RF—330. **Press Box Telephone:** (225) 578-4149.

LOUISIANA TECH Bulldogs

Conference: Western Athletic.

Mailing Address: P.O. Box 3046, Ruston, LA 71272. **Website:** www.latechsports.com.

Head Coach: Wade Simoneaux. **Assistant Coaches:** Fran Andermann, *Brian Rountree. **Telephone:** (318) 257-4111. ■ **Baseball SID:** Robby Lockwood. **Telephone:** (318) 257-3144. **FAX:** (318) 257-3757.

LOUISVILLE Cardinals

Conference: Conference USA.

Mailing Address: 2100 S. Floyd St., Room E203, Louisville, KY 40208. **Website:** www.uoflsports.com.

Head Coach: Lelo Prado. **Assistant Coaches:** *Brian Mundorf, Bobby Perez, Jim Zerilla. **Telephone:** (502) 852-0103. ■ **Baseball SID:** Sean Moth. **Telephone:** (502) 852-2159. **FAX:** (502) 852-7401.

Home Field: Cardinal Stadium. **Seating Capacity:** 33,000. **Outfield Dimensions:** LF—360, CF—405, RF—305.

LOYOLA MARYMOUNT Lions

Conference: West Coast (West).

Mailing Address: One LMU Drive, Los Angeles, CA 90045. **Website:** www.lmulions.com.

Head Coach: Frank Cruz. **Assistant Coaches:** Robbie Moen, Hon Strauss. **Telephone:** (310) 338-2949. ■ **Baseball SID:** Scott Johnson. **Telephone:** (310) 338-7638. **FAX:** (310) 338-2703.

Home Field: Page Stadium. **Seating Capacity:** 600. **Outfield Dimensions:** LF—326, CF—413, RF—330. **Press Box Telephone:** (310) 338-3046.

MAINE Black Bears

Conference: America East.

Mailing Address: 5747 Memorial Gym, Orono, ME 04469. **Website:** www.goblackbears.com.

Head Coach: Paul Kostacopoulos. **Assistant Coach:** *Scott Friedholm. **Telephone:** (207) 581-1096. ■ **Baseball SID:** Julia Eberhart. **Telephone:** (207) 581-1086. **FAX:** (207) 581-3297.

MANHATTAN Jaspers

Conference: Metro Atlantic (South).

Mailing Address: 4513 Manhattan College Pkwy., Riverdale, NY 10471. **Website:** www.gojaspers.com.

Head Coach: Steve Trimper. **Assistant Coaches:** Kevin Leighton, Tom Sowinski. **Telephone:** (718) 862-7486. ■ **Baseball SID:** Adrienne Mullikin. **Telephone:** (718) 862-7228. **FAX:** (718) 862-8020.

MARIST Red Foxes

Conference: Metro Atlantic (North).

Mailing Address: 3399 North Rd., Poughkeepsie, NY 12601. **Website:** www.GoRedFoxes.com.

Head Coach: Jim Tyrrell. **Assistant Coaches:** Matt Brennie, *Sean Moran. **Telephone:** (914) 575-3699. ■ **Baseball SID:** Chris O'Connor. **Telephone:** (914) 575-

3321. **FAX:** (914) 471-0466.

MARSHALL Thundering Herd

Conference: Mid-American (East).

Mailing Address: P.O. Box 1360, Huntington, WV 25715. **Website:** www.herdzone.com.

Head Coach: Dave Piepenbrink. **Assistant Coaches:** *Tom Carty, Chad Miller, Brad Stromdahl. **Telephone:** (304) 696-5277. ■ **Baseball SID:** Brandon Parro. **Telephone:** (304) 696-4660. **FAX:** (304) 696-2325.

MARYLAND Terrapins

Conference: Atlantic Coast.

Mailing Address: Comcast Center, Terrapin Trail, College Park, MD 20742. **Website:** www.umterps.com.

Head Coach: Terry Rupp. **Assistant Coaches:** Ben Bachmann, *Gregg Kilby, J.C. Nolan. **Telephone:** (301) 314-7122. ■ **Baseball SID:** Mark Fratto. **Telephone:** (301) 314-8052. **FAX:** (301) 314-9094.

Home Field: Shipley Field. **Seating Capacity:** 3,000. **Outfield Dimensions:** LF—320, CF—380, RF—320. **Press Box Telephone:** (301) 314-0379.

MARYLAND-BALTIMORE COUNTY Retrievers

Conference: Northeast.

Mailing Address: 1000 Hilltop Circle, Baltimore, MD 21250. **Website:** www.umbcretrievers.com.

Head Coach: John Jancuska. **Assistant Coaches:** Matt Barry, *Bob Mumma. **Telephone:** (410) 455-2239. ■ **Baseball SID:** David Gansell. **Telephone:** (410) 455-2197. **FAX:** (410) 455-3994.

MARYLAND-EASTERN SHORE Fighting Hawks

Conference: Mid-Eastern Athletic (North).

Mailing Address: William P. Hytch Athletic Center, Backbone Road, Princess Anne, MD 21853. **Website:** www.umes.edu/athletics.

Head Coach: Kirkland Hall. **Assistant Coaches:** Allen Davenport, Ephraim Hall, Dave Tyler. **Telephone:** (410) 651-6708. ■ **Baseball SID:** Stan Bradley. **Telephone:** (410) 651-6499. **FAX:** (410) 651-7514.

MASSACHUSETTS Minutemen

Conference: Atlantic-10 (East).

Mailing Address: Baseball Office, 7 Boyden Building, Amherst, MA 01003. **Website:** www.umassathletics.com.

Head Coach: Mike Stone. **Assistant Coaches:** *Tim Laurita, Ernie May. **Telephone:** (413) 545-3120. ■ **Baseball SID**: Charles Bare. **Telephone:** (413) 545-2439. **FAX:** (413) 545-1556.

McNEESE STATE Cowboys

Conference: Southland.

Mailing Address: 615 Bienville St., Lake Charles, LA 70607. **Website:** www.geaucowboys.com.

Head Coach: Todd Butler. **Assistant Coaches**: *Chad Clement, Mike Trahan. **Telephone:** (337) 475-5484/5482. ■ **Baseball SID:** Todd Butler. **Telephone:** (337) 475-5207. **FAX:** (337) 475-5202.

MEMPHIS Tigers

Conference: Conference USA.

Mailing Address: 570 Normal, A.O.B. Rm. 203, Memphis, TN 38152. **Website:** www.gotigersgo.com.

Head Coach: Dave Anderson. **Assistant Coaches:** Mitch Dunn, George Holt, *Larry Owens. **Telephone:** (901) 678-2452. ■ **Baseball SID:** Ryan Powell. **Telephone:** (901) 678-2444. **FAX:** (901) 678-4134.

Home Field: Nat Buring Stadium. **Seating Capacity:** 2,000. **Outfield Dimensions:** LF—320, CF—380, RF—320. **Press Box Telephone:** (901) 678-1721.

MERCER Bears

Conference: Atlantic Sun.

Mailing Address: 1400 Coleman Ave., Macon, GA 31207. **Website:** www.merceruniversity.edu.

Head Coach: Barry Myers. **Assistant Coach:** *Craig Gibson, Jeff Nebel. **Telephone:** (478) 301-2738. ■ **Baseball SID:** Craig Gibson. **Telephone:** (478) 301-2396. **FAX:** (478) 301-2061.

MIAMI Hurricanes

Conference: Independent.

Mailing Address: 6201 San Amaro Dr., Coral Gables, FL 33146. **Website:** www.hurricanesports.com.

Head Coach: Jim Morris. **Assistant Coaches:** Lazaro Collazo, *Gino DiMare, Greg Lovelady. **Telephone:** (305) 284-4171. ■ **Baseball SID:** Josh Maxson. **Telephone:** (305) 284-3244. **FAX:** (305) 284-3227.

Home Field: Mark Light Stadium. **Seating Capacity:** 5,000. **Outfield Dimensions:** LF—330, CF—400, RF—330. **Press Box Telephone:** (305) 284-5626.

MIAMI Redskins

Conference: Mid-American (East).

Mailing Address: 230 Millett Hall, Oxford, OH 45056. **Website:** www.MURedHawks.com.

Head Coach: Tracy Smith. **Assistant Coaches:** Bill Doran, Scott Googins, *Dan Simonds. **Telephone:** (513) 529-6631. ■ **Baseball SID:** Ryan Erb. **Telephone:** (513) 529-1601. **FAX:** (513) 529-6729.

Home Field: Stanley G. McKie Field. **Seating Capacity:** 1,000. **Outfield Dimensions:** LF—332, CF—400, RF—343. **Press Box Telephone:** (513) 529-4331.

MICHIGAN Wolverines

Conference: Big Ten.

Mailing Address: 1000 S. State St., Ann Arbor, MI 48109. **Website:** www.mgoblue.com.

Head Coach: Rich Maloney. **Assistant Coaches**: John Lowery, Scott Mallernee, *Jason Murray. **Telephone:** (734) 647-4550. ■ **Baseball SID:** Jim Schneider. **Telephone:** (734) 763-4423. **FAX:** (734) 647-1188.

Home Field: Ray Fisher Stadium. **Seating Capacity:** 4,000. **Outfield Dimensions:** LF—330, CF—400, RF—330. **Press Box Telephone:** (734) 647-1283.

MICHIGAN STATE Spartans

Conference: Big Ten.

Mailing Address: 304 Jenison Field House, East Lansing, MI 48824. **Website:** www.msuspartans.com.

Head Coach: Ted Mahan. **Assistant Coaches:** Cory Mee, Dylan Putnam. **Telephone:** (517) 355-4486. ■ **Baseball SID:** Ben Phlegar. **Telephone:** (517) 355-2271. **FAX:** (517) 353-9636.

Home Fields Kob Field. **Seating Capacity:** 3,000. **Outfield Dimensions:** LF—340, CF—410, RF—309. **Press Box Telephone:** (517) 353-3009.

MIDDLE TENNESSEE STATE Blue Raiders

Conference: Sun Belt.

Mailing Address: 1301 E. Main St., Murfreesboro, TN 37132. **Website:** www.goblueraiders.com.

Head Coach: Steve Peterson. **Assistant Coaches:** Kevin Erminio, Andy Haines, *Jim McGuire. **Telephone:** (615) 898-2450. ■ **Baseball SID:** JoJo Freeman. **Telephone:** (615) 898-5270. **FAX:** (615) 898-5626.

Home Field: Reese Smith Field. **Seating Capacity:** 2,600. **Outfield Dimensions:** LF—325, CF—390, RF—325. **Press Box Telephone:** (615) 898-2117.

MINNESOTA Golden Gophers

Conference: Big Ten.

Mailing Address: 244 Bierman Field Athletic Building, 516 15th Ave. SE, Minneapolis, MN 55455. **Website:** www.gophersports.com.

Head Coach: John Anderson. **Assistant Coaches:**

*Rob Fornasiere, Todd Oakes. **Telephone:** (612) 625-1060. ■ **Baseball SID:** Steve Geller. **Telephone:** (612) 624-9396. **FAX:** (612) 625-0359.

Home Fields (Seating Capacity): Siebert Field (1,100), Metrodome (55,000). **Outfield Dimensions:** Siebert Field/LF—330, CF—380, RF—330; Metrodome/LF—343, CF—408, RF—327. **Press Box Telephones:** Siebert Field/(612) 625-4031; Metrodome/(612) 627-4400.

MISSISSIPPI Rebels

Conference: Southeastern (West).

Mailing Address: P.O. Box 217, University, MS 38677. **Website:** www.OleMissSports.com.

Head Coach: Mike Bianco. **Assistant Coaches:** Kyle Bunn, Clint Carver, *Dan McDonnell. **Telephone:** (662) 915-6643. ■ **Baseball SID:** Rick Stupak. **Telephone:** (662) 915-7522. **FAX:** (662) 915-7006.

Home Field: Oxford-University Stadium/Swayze Field. **Seating Capacity:** 3,500. **Outfield Dimensions:** LF—330, CF—400, RF—330. **Press Box Telephone:** (662) 236-2478.

MISSISSIPPI STATE Bulldogs

Conference: Southeastern (West).

Mailing Address: P.O. Box 5327, Starkville, MS 39762. **Website:** www.mstateathletics.com.

Head Coach: Ron Polk. **Assistant Coaches:** Russ McNickle, Tommy Raffo, *Daron Schoenrock. **Telephone:** (662) 325-3597. ■ **Baseball SID:** Joe Dier. **Telephone:** (662) 325-8040. **FAX:** (662) 325-3654.

Home Field: Dudy Noble Field/Polk-DeMent Stadium. **Seating Capacity:** 15,000. **Outfield Dimensions:** LF—325, CF—390, RF—325. **Press Box Telephone:** (662) 325-3776.

MISSISSIPPI VALLEY STATE Delta Devils

Conference: Southwestern Athletic (East).

Mailing Address: 14000 Hwy. 82 W., No. 7246, Itta Bena, MS 38941. **Website:** www.mvsu.edu/athletics.

Head Coach: Doug Shanks. **Assistant Coaches:** Aaron Stevens. **Telephone:** (662) 254-3834. ■ **Baseball SID:** Jay Philley. **Telephone:** (662) 254-3551. **FAX:** (662) 254-3639.

MISSOURI Tigers

Conference: Big 12.

Mailing Address: 370 Hearnes Center, Columbia, MO 65211. **Website:** www.mutigers.com.

Head Coach: Tim Jamieson. **Assistant Coaches:** *Sean McCann, Evan Pratte, Tony Vitello. **Telephone:** (573) 884-0731. ■ **Baseball SID:** Kevin Fletcher. **Telephone:** (573) 882-7826. **FAX:** (573) 882-4729.

Home Field: Taylor Stadium. **Seating Capacity:** 2,200. **Outfield Dimensions:** LF—340, CF—400, RF—340. **Press Box Telephone:** (573) 884-8912.

MONMOUTH Hawks

Conference: Northeast.

Mailing Address: 400 Cedar Ave., West Long Branch, NJ 07764. **Website:** www.monmouth.edu.

Head Coach: Dean Ehehalt. **Assistant Coaches:** *Jeff Barbalinardo, Dan Coia, Tim Davis. **Telephone:** (732) 263-5186. ■ **Baseball SID:** Chris Tobin. **Telephone:** (732) 571-4447. **FAX:** (732) 571-3535.

MOREHEAD STATE Eagles

Conference: Ohio Valley.

Mailing Address: 154 Academic-Athletic Center Morehead, KY 40351. **Website:** www.msueagles.com.

Head Coach: John Jarnagin. **Assistant Coach:** Rob Taylor, *Marc Wagner. **Telephone:** (606) 783-2882. ■ **Baseball SID:** Randy Stacy. **Telephone:** (606) 783-2500. **FAX:** (606) 783-2550.

MORRIS BROWN Wolverines

Conference: Independent.

Mailing Address: 643 Martin Luther King Jr. Dr., Atlanta, GA 30314. **Website:** www.morrisbrown.edu.

Head Coach: Barry Cross. **Assistant Coach:** *Marqus Johnson. **Telephone:** (404) 739-4548. **Baseball SID:** Marqus Johnson. **Telephone:** (404) 739-1622. **FAX:** (404) 739-1621.

MOUNT ST. MARY'S Mountaineers

Conference: Northeast.

Mailing Address: 16300 Old Emmitsburg Rd., Emmitsburg, MD 21727. **Website:** www.mountathletics.com.

Head Coach: Scott Thomson. **Assistant Coaches:** Steve Mott, Steve Thomson. **Telephone:** (301) 447-3806. ■ **Baseball SID:** Mark Vandergrift. **Telephone:** (301) 447-5384. **FAX:** (301) 447-5300.

MURRAY STATE Thoroughbreds

Conference: Ohio Valley.

Mailing Address: 218 Stewart Stadium, Murray, KY 42071. **Website:** www.goracers.com.

Head Coach: Mike Thieke. **Assistant Coach:** Bart Osborne. **Telephone:** (270) 762-4892. ■ **Baseball SID:** David Snow. **Telephone:** (270) 762-4271. **FAX:** (270) 762-6814.

NAVY Midshipmen

Conference: Patriot.

Mailing Address: 566 Brownson Rd., Annapolis, MD 21402. **Website:** www.navysports.com.

Head Coach: Steve Whitmyer. **Assistant Coaches:** *Chris Murphy, Dan Nellum. **Telephone:** (410) 293-5571. ■ **Baseball SID:** Price Atkinson. **Telephone:** (410) 293-2700. **FAX:** (410) 293-8954.

NEBRASKA Cornhuskers

Conference: Big 12.

Mailing Address: 116 S. Stadium, Lincoln, NE 68588. **Website:** www.huskers.com.

Head Coach: Mike Anderson. **Assistant Coaches:** *Rob Childress, Andy Sawyers, Brandt Vlieger. **Telephone:** (402) 472-2263. ■ **Baseball SID:** Shamus McKnight. **Telephone:** (402) 472-7772. **FAX:** (402) 472-2005.

Home Field: Hawks Field at Haymarket Park. **Seating Capacity:** 6,000. **Outfield Dimensions:** LF—335, CF—395, RF—325. **Press Box Telephone:** (402) 434-6861.

NEVADA Wolf Pack

Conference: Western Athletic.

Mailing Address: 1664 N. Virginia, Reno, NV 89557. **Website:** www.nevadawolfpack.com.

Head Coach: Gary Powers. **Assistant Coaches:** *Stan Stolte, Jay Uhlman. **Telephone:** (775) 784-6900, ext. 252. ■ **Baseball SID:** Jack Kuestermeyer. **Telephone:** (775) 784-6900, ext. 244. **FAX:** (775) 784-4386.

Home Field: Peccole Park. **Seating Capacity:** 3,000. **Outfield Dimensions:** LF—340, CF—400, RF—340. **Press Box Telephone:** (775) 784-1585.

NEVADA-LAS VEGAS Rebels

Conference: Mountain West.

Mailing Address: 4505 Maryland Pkwy., Las Vegas, NV 89154. **Website:** www.unlvrebels.com.

Head Coach: Jim Schlossnagle. **Assistant Coaches:** *Buddy Gouldsmith, Matt Siegel, Kevin Smoot. **Telephone:** (702) 895-3499. ■ **Baseball SID:** Brian Albertson. **Telephone:** (702) 895-3764. **FAX:** (702) 895-0989.

Home Field: Earl E. Wilson Stadium. **Seating Capacity:** 3,000. **Outfield Dimensions:** LF—335, CF—400, RF—335. **Press Box Telephone:** (702) 895-1595.

NEW MEXICO Lobos

Conference: Mountain West.

Mailing Address: 1414 University Blvd., Albuquerque, NM 87131. **Website:** www.GoLobos.com.

Head Coach: Rich Alday. **Assistant Coaches:** Ryan Beggs, *Mark Martinez. **Telephone:** (505) 925-5720. ■ **Baseball SID:** Ron Gonzalez. **Telephone:** (505) 925-5528. **FAX:** (505) 925-5529.

Home Field: Lobo Field. **Seating Capacity:** 2,000. **Outfield Dimensions:** LF—337, CF—412, RF—337. **Press Box Telephone:** (505) 925-5722.

NEW MEXICO STATE Aggies

Conference: Sun Belt.

Mailing Address: P.O. Box 30001, Las Cruces, NM 88003. **Website:** www.nmstatesports.com.

Head Coach: Rocky Ward. **Assistant Coaches:** Brad Dolejsi, Mike Pietrack, *Chad Wolff. **Telephone:** (505) 646-5813. ■ **Baseball SID:** Sean Johnson. **Telephone:** (505) 646-1805. **FAX:** (505) 646-2425.

Home Field: Presley Askew Field. **Seating Capacity:** 1,000. **Outfield Dimensions:** LF—345, CF—400, RF—345. **Press Box Telephone:** (505) 646-5700. **Press Box Telephone:** (505) 646-5700

NEW ORLEANS Privateers

Conference: Sun Belt.

Mailing Address: 6801 Franklin Ave., New Orleans, LA 70148. **Website:** www.unoprivateers.com.

Head Coach: Randy Bush. **Assistant Coaches:** *Kenny Bonura, Joe Slusarski. **Telephone:** (504) 280-7021. ■ **Baseball SID:** Bob Boyle. **Telephone:** (504) 280-7027. **FAX:** (504) 280-7240.

Home Field: Privateer Park. **Seating Capacity:** 4,200. **Outfield Dimensions:** LF—330, CF—400, RF—330. **Press Box Telephone:** (504) 280-7027.

NEW YORK TECH Bears

Conference: Independent.

Mailing Address: Northern Blvd., Old Westbury, NY 11568. **Website:** www.nyit.edu.

Head Coach: Bob Hirschfield. **Assistant Coaches:** Ray Giannelli, *Jim Shevlin, Joe Thomas. **Telephone:** (516) 686-7513. ■ **Baseball SID:** Ben Arcuri. **Telephone:** (516) 686-7504. **FAX:** (516) 686-1219.

NIAGARA Purple Eagles

Conference: Metro Atlantic (North).

Mailing Address: P.O. Box 2009, Niagara University, NY 14109. **Website:** www.purpleeagles.com.

Head Coach: Mike McRae. **Assistant Coach:** Bryan Dean, Mike Kunigonis. **Telephone:** (716) 286-8624. ■ **Baseball SID:** Ryan Hoyle. **Telephone:** (716) 286-8588. **FAX:** (716) 286-8609.

NICHOLLS STATE Colonels

Conference: Southland.

Mailing Address: P.O. Box 2032, Thibodaux, LA 70310. **Website:** www.nicholls.edu/athletics.

Head Coach: B.D. Parker. **Assistant Coaches:** *Gerald Cassard, Jeff McCannon. **Telephone:** (985) 448-4808. ■ **Baseball SID:** Bobby Galinsky. **Telephone:** (985) 448-4281. **FAX:** (985) 448-4924.

NORFOLK STATE Spartans

Conference: Mid-Eastern Athletic (South).

Mailing Address: 700 Park Ave., Norfolk, VA 23504. **Website:** www.nsu.edu.

Head Coach: Marty Miller. **Assistant Coach:** Enrique Mendieta. **Telephone:** (757) 823-9539. ■ **Baseball SID:** Matt Machlec. **Telephone:** (757) 823-2628. **FAX:** (757) 823-8218.

NORTH CAROLINA Tar Heels

Conference: Atlantic Coast.

Mailing Address: P.O. Box 2126, Chapel Hill, NC 27515. **Website:** www.tarheelblue.com.

Head Coach: Mike Fox. **Assistant Coaches:** Ned French, *Chad Holbrook, Roger Williams. **Telephone:** (919) 962-2351. ■ **Baseball SID:** David Tinson. **Telephone:** (919) 962-0084. **FAX:** (919) 962-0612.

Home Field: Boshamer Stadium. **Seating Capacity:** 2,500. **Outfield Dimensions:** LF—330, CF—400, RF—330. **Press Box Telephone:** (919) 962-3509.

UNC ASHEVILLE Bulldogs

Conference: Big South.

Mailing Address: One University Heights, Justice Center, Asheville, NC 28804. **Website:** www.unca.edu/athletics/baseball.

Head Coach: Matt Myers. **Assistant Coach:** Fore Rembert, Willie Stewart. **Telephone:** (828) 251-6920. ■ **Baseball SID:** Mike Gore. **Telephone:** (828) 251-6923. **FAX:** (828) 251-6386.

UNC GREENSBORO Spartans

Conference: Southern.

Mailing Address: P.O. Box 26168, Greensboro, NC 27402. **Website:** www.uncgspartans.com.

Head Coach: Mike Gaski. **Assistant Coaches:** *Neil Avent, Mike Rodriguez. **Telephone:** (336) 334-3247. ■ **Baseball SID:** Michael Bertsch. **Telephone:** (336) 334-5615. **FAX:** (336) 334-3182.

Home Field: UNCG Baseball Stadium. **Seating Capacity:** 3,000. **Outfield Dimensions:** LF—340, CF—405, RF—340. **Press Box Telephone:** (336) 334-3885.

UNC WILMINGTON Seahawks

Conference: Colonial Athletic.

Mailing Address: 601 S. College Rd., Wilmington, NC 28403. **Website:** www.uncwsports.com.

Head Coach: Mark Scalf. **Assistant Coaches:** *Randy Hood, Scott Jackson. **Telephone:** (910) 962-3570. ■ **Baseball SID:** Tom Riordan. **Telephone:** (910) 962-4099. **FAX:** (910) 392-3686.

Home Field: Brooks Field. **Seating Capacity:** 3,000. **Outfield Dimensions:** LF—340, CF—380, RF—340. **Press Box Telephone:** (910) 395-5141.

NORTH CAROLINA A&T Aggies

Conference: Mid-Eastern Athletic (South).

Mailing Address: 1601 E. Market St., Moore Gym, Greensboro, NC 27411. **Website**: www.ncat.edu.

Head Coach: *Keith Shumate. **Assistant Coach:** Rod Gorham. **Telephone:** (336) 334-7371. ■ **Baseball SIDs:** Kia Mason, Tyler Ball. **Telephone:** (336) 334-7141. **FAX:** (336) 334-7181.

Home Field: War Memorial Stadium. **Seating Capacity:** 7,500. **Outfield Dimensions:** LF—330, CF—401, RF—327. **Press Box Telephone:** (336) 333-2287.

NORTH CAROLINA STATE Wolfpack

Conference: Atlantic Coast.

Mailing Address: P.O. Box 8501, Raleigh, NC 27695. **Website:** www.gopack.com.

Head Coach: Elliott Avent. **Assistant Coaches:** Billy Jones, *Bill Kernen. **Telephone:** (919) 515-3613. ■ **Baseball SID:** Bruce Winkworth. **Telephone:** (919) 515-1182. **FAX:** (919) 515-2898.

Home Field: Doak Field. **Seating Capacity:** 3,000. **Outfield Dimensions:** LF—340, CF—400, RF—340. **Press Box Telephone:** (919) 515-7643.

NORTHEASTERN Huskies

Conference: America East.

Mailing Address: 360 Huntington Ave., Boston, MA

02115. **Website:** www.gonu.com/baseball.

Head Coach: Neil McPhee. **Assistant Coaches:** *Greg DiCenzo, Mike Grant, Tim Trovill. **Telephone:** (617) 373-3657. ■ **Baseball SID:** Adam Polgren. **Telephone:** (617) 373-4154. **FAX:** (617) 373-3152.

NORTHERN ILLINOIS Huskies

Conference: Mid-American (West).

Mailing Address: 1525 W. Lincoln Hwy., DeKalb, IL 60115. **Website:** www.niuhuskies.com.

Head Coach: Ed Mathey. **Assistant Coaches:** Steve Joslyn, *Tim McDonough, Luke Sabers. **Telephone:** (815) 753-2225. ■ **Baseball SID:** Michael Smoose. **Telephone:** (815) 753-1706. **FAX:** (815) 753-9540.

NORTHERN IOWA Panthers

Conference: Missouri Valley.

Mailing Address: UNI-Dome, NW Upper, Cedar Falls, IA 50614. **Website:** www.unipanthers.com.

Head Coach: Rick Heller. **Assistant Coaches:** *Dan Davis, Dan Heefner, Ryan Jacobs. **Telephone:** (319) 273-6323. ■ **Baseball SID:** Jill Gansemer. **Telephone:** (319) 273-5455. **FAX:** (319) 273-3602.

Home Field: Waterloo Riverfront Stadium. **Seating Capacity:** 4,277. **Outfield Dimensions:** LF—335, CF—380, RF—335. **Press Box Telephone:** (319) 287-6395.

NORTHWESTERN Wildcats

Conference: Big Ten.

Mailing Address: 1501 Central St., Evanston, IL 60208. **Website:** www.nusports.com.

Head Coach: Paul Stevens. **Assistant Coaches:** Joe Keenan, Ron Klein, *Tim Stoddard. **Telephone:** (847) 491-4652. ■ **Baseball SID:** Aaron Bongle. **Telephone:** (847) 491-7503. **FAX:** (847) 491-8818.

Home Field: Rocky Miller Park. **Seating Capacity:** 1,000. **Outfield Dimensions:** LF—330, CF—400, RF—330. **Press Box Telephone:** (847) 491-4200.

NORTHWESTERN STATE Demons

Conference: Southland.

Mailing Address: Athletic Fieldhouse, Natchitoches, LA 71497. **Website:** www.nsudemons.com.

Head Coach: Mitch Gaspard. **Assistant Coaches:** *J.P. Davis, Travis Jansen. **Telephone:** (318) 357-4139. ■ **Baseball SID:** Kenny Lannon. **Telephone:** (318) 357-6468. **FAX:** (318) 357-4515.

NOTRE DAME Fighting Irish

Conference: Big East.

Mailing Address: 112 Joyce Center, Notre Dame, IN 46556. **Website:** www.und.com.

Head Coach: Paul Mainieri. **Assistant Coaches:** *David Grewe, Brian O'Connor, Wally Widelski. **Telephone:** (574) 631-6366. ■ **Baseball SID:** Pete LaFleur. **Telephone:** (574) 631-7516. **FAX:** (574) 631-7941.

Home Field: Frank Eck Stadium. **Seating Capacity:** 2,500. **Outfield Dimensions:** LF—331, CF—401, RF—331. **Press Box Telephone:** (574) 631-9018.

OAKLAND Golden Grizzlies

Conference: Mid-Continent.

Mailing Address: Athletic Center Bldg., Rochester, MI 48309. **Website:** www.ougrizzlies.com.

Head Coach: Mark Avery. **Assistant Coaches:** Ben DiPonio, Chris Newell, *Mike Villano. **Telephone:** (248) 370-4059. ■ **Baseball SID:** Phil Hess. **Telephone:** (248) 370-4008. **FAX:** (248) 370-4056.

OHIO Bobcats

Conference: Mid-American (East).

Mailing Address: Convocation Center, Richland Ave., Athens, OH 45701. **Website:** www.ohiobobcats.com.

Head Coach: Joe Carbone. **Assistant Coach:** Bill Toadvine. **Telephone:** (740) 593-1180. ■ **Baseball SID:** Paul Warner. **Telephone:** (740) 597-1837. **FAX:** (740) 597-1838.

Home Field: Bob Wren Stadium. **Seating Capacity:** 6,000. **Outfield Dimensions:** LF—340, CF—405, RF—340. **Press Box Telephone:** None.

OHIO STATE Buckeyes

Conference: Big Ten.

Mailing Address: Room 124 St. John Arena, 410 Woody Hayes Dr., Columbus, OH 43210. **Website:** www.ohiostatebuckeyes.com.

Head Coach: Bob Todd. **Assistant Coaches:** Pat Bangston, *Greg Cypret, Erik Hagen. **Telephone:** (614) 292-1075. ■ **Baseball SID:** Todd Lamb. **Telephone:** (614) 688-0343. **FAX:** (614) 292-8547.

Home Field: Bill Davis Stadium. **Seating Capacity:** 4,450. **Outfield Dimensions:** LF—330, CF—400, RF—330. **Press Box Telephone:** (614) 292-0021.

OKLAHOMA Sooners

Conference: Big 12.

Mailing Address: 401 W. Imhoff, Norman, OK 73019. **Website:** www.soonersports.com.

Head Coach: Larry Cochell. **Assistant Coaches:** *Ray Hayward, Rich Hills, Aric Thomas. **Telephone:** (405) 325-8354. ■ **Baseball SID:** Danielle Felter. **Telephone:** (405) 325-8372. **FAX:** (405) 325-7623.

Home Field: L. Dale Mitchell Park. **Seating Capacity:** 2,700. **Outfield Dimensions:** LF—335, CF—411, RF—335. **Press Box Telephone:** (405) 325-8363.

OKLAHOMA STATE Cowboys

Conference: Big 12.

Mailing Address: 220 OSU Athletics Center, Stillwater, OK 74075. **Website:** www.okstate.com.

Head Coach: Tom Holliday. **Assistant Coaches:** Jason Bell, *Josh Holliday, *Robbie Wine. **Telephone:** (405) 744-5849. ■ **Baseball SID:** Thomas Samuel. **Telephone:** (405) 744-7714. **FAX:** (405) 744-7754.

Home Field: Allie P. Reynolds Stadium. **Seating Capacity:** 4,000. **Outfield Dimensions:** LF—390, CF—400, RF—385.

OLD DOMINION Monarchs

Conference: Colonial Athletic.

Mailing Address: Athletic Administration Bldg., Norfolk, VA 23529. **Website:** www.odusports.com.

Head Coach: Tony Guzzo. **Assistant Coaches:** *Shohn Doty, Eric Folmar, Jeff Sziksai. **Telephone:** (757) 683-4230. ■ **Baseball SID:** Carol Hudson, Jr. **Telephone:** (757) 683-3372. **FAX:** (757) 683-3119.

Home Field: Bud Metheny Stadium. **Seating Capacity:** 2,500. **Outfield Dimensions:** LF—320, CF—395, RF—320. **Press Box Telephone:** (757) 683-5036/4142.

ORAL ROBERTS Golden Eagles

Conference: Mid-Continent.

Mailing Address: 7777 S Lewis Ave., Tulsa, OK 74171. **Website:** www.orugoldeneagles.com.

Head Coach: Sunny Golloway. **Assistant Coaches:** Justin Timmerman, James Vilade, *Rob Walton. **Telephone:** (918) 495-7131. ■ **Baseball SID:** Cris Belvin. **Telephone:** (918) 495-7094. **FAX:** (918) 495-7142.

Home Field: J.L. Johnson Stadium. **Seating Capacity:** 2,418. **Outfield Dimensions:** LF—330, CF—400, RF—330. **Press Box Telephone:** (918) 495-7165.

OREGON STATE Beavers

Conference: Pacific-10.

Mailing Address: Gill Coliseum, Room 127, Corvallis, OR 97331. **Website:** www.osubeavers.com.

Head Coach: Pat Casey. **Assistant Coaches:** *Gary

Henderson, Marty Lees, Dan Spencer. **Telephone:** (541) 737-2825. ■ **Baseball SID:** Kip Carlson. **Telephone:** (541) 737-7472. **FAX:** (541) 737-3072.

Home Field: Goss Stadium at Coleman Field. **Seating Capacity:** 2,000. **Outfield Dimensions:** LF—330, CF—400, RF—330. **Press Box Telephone:** (541) 737-7475.

PACE Setters

Conference: Independent.

Mailing Address: 861 Bedford Rd., Pleasantville, NY 10570. **Website:** www.pace.edu.

Head Coach: Hank Manning. **Assistant Coaches:** *Trevor Brown, Jerry DeFabbia. **Telephone:** (914) 773-3413. ■ **Baseball SID:** Brian Mundy. **Telephone:** (914) 773-3411. **FAX:** (914) 773-3491.

PACIFIC Tigers

Conference: Big West.

Mailing Address: 3601 Pacific Ave., Stockton, CA 95211. **Website Address:** www.pacifictigers.com.

Head Coach: Quincey Noble. **Assistant Coaches:** Tim Dixon, *Denny Peterson. **Telephone:** (209) 946-2709. ■ **Baseball SID:** Mike Millerick. **Telephone:** (209) 946-2289. **FAX:** (209) 946-2757.

Home Field: Billy Hebert Field. **Seating Capacity:** 3,500. **Outfield Dimensions:** LF—325, CF—390, RF—330. **Press Box Telephone:** (209) 644-1916.

PENNSYLVANIA Quakers

Conference: Ivy League (Gehrig).

Mailing Address: 235 S. 33rd St., James D. Donning Center, Philadelphia, PA 19104. **Website:** www.penn athletics.com.

Head Coach: *Bob Seddon. **Assistant Coaches:** Bill Wagner, Dan Young. **Telephone:** (215) 898-6282. ■ **Baseball SID:** Don Delaney. **Telephone:** (215) 898-1748. **FAX:** (215) 898-1747.

PENN STATE Nittany Lions

Conference: Big Ten.

Mailing Address: 112 Bryce Jordan Center, University Park, PA 16802. **Website:** www.GoPSUsports.com.

Head Coach: Joe Hindelang. **Assistant Coaches:** *Randy Ford, Dave Jameson, Jon Ramsey. **Telephone:** (814) 863-0239. ■ **Baseball SID:** Bob Volkert. **Telephone:** (814) 865-1757. **FAX:** (814) 863-3165.

Home Field: Beaver Field. **Seating Capacity:** 1,000. **Outfield Dimensions:** LF—350, CF—405, RF—350. **Press Box Telephone:** (814) 865-2552.

PEPPERDINE Waves

Conference: West Coast (Coast).

Mailing Address: 24255 Pacific Coast Hwy., Malibu, CA 90263. **Website:** www.pepperdine.edu.

Head Coach: Frank Sanchez. **Assistant Coaches:** *Rick Hirtensteiner, Steve Rodriguez. **Telephone:** (310) 506-4199. ■ **Baseball SID:** Al Barba. **Telephone:** (310) 506-4455. **FAX:** (310) 506-4322.

Home Field: Eddy D. Field Stadium. **Seating Capacity:** 2,200. **Outfield Dimensions:** LF—330, CF—400, RF—330. **Press Box Telephone:** (310) 506-4598.

PITTSBURGH Panthers

Conference: Big East.

Mailing Address: P.O. Box 7436, Pittsburgh, PA 15213. **Website**: www.pitt.edu.

Head Coach: Joe Jordano. **Assistant Coaches:** Joel Dombkowski, *Dan Ninemire. **Telephone:** (412) 648-8208. ■ **Baseball SID:** Burt Lauten. **Telephone:** (412) 648-8244. **FAX:** (412) 648-8248.

Home Field: Trees Field. **Seating Capacity:** 200. **Outfield Dimensions:** LF—300, CF—400, RF—320. **Press Box Telephone:** None.

PORTLAND Pilots

Conference: West Coast (West).

Mailing Address: 5000 N. Willamette Blvd., Portland, OR 97203. **Website:** www.portlandpilots.com.

Head Coach: Chris Sperry. **Assistant Coaches:** Brian Graham, Gary Van Tol. **Telephone:** (503) 943-7707. ■ **Baseball SID:** Loren Wohlgemuth. **Telephone:** (503) 943-7439. **FAX:** (503) 943-7242.

Home Field: Pilot Stadium. **Seating Capacity:** 1,500. **Outfield Dimensions:** LF—350, CF—385, RF—348. **Press Box Telephone:** (503) 943-7253.

PRAIRIE VIEW A&M Panthers

Conference: Southwestern Athletic (West).

Mailing Address: P.O. Box 97, Prairie View, TX 77446. **Website:** www.pvamu.edu/sports.

Head Coach: Michael Robertson. **Assistant Coach:** Adrian Adams, *Alicia Pete. **Telephone:** (936) 857-4290. ■ **Baseball SID:** Harlan Robinson. **Telephone:** (936) 857-2114. **FAX:** (936) 857-2395.

PRINCETON Tigers

Conference: Ivy League (Gehrig).

Mailing Address: P.O. Box 71, Jadwin Gym, Princeton, NJ 08544. **Website:** www.goprinceton-tigers.com.

Head Coach: Scott Bradley. **Assistant Coaches:** Lloyd Brewer, Pete Silletti. **Telephone:** (609) 258-5059. ■ **Baseball SID:** Yariv Amir. **Telephone:** (609) 258-5701. **FAX:** (609) 258-2399.

PURDUE Boilermakers

Conference: Big Ten.

Mailing Address: 302C Mollenkopf, West Lafayette, IN 47907. **Website:** www.purduesports.com.

Head Coach: Doug Schreiber. **Assistant Coaches:** Todd Hode, *Todd Murphy, Rob Smith. **Telephone:** (765) 494-3998. ■ **Baseball SID:** Mark Leddy. **Telephone:** (765) 494-3201. **FAX:** (765) 494-5447.

Home Field: Lambert Field. **Seating Capacity:** 1,100. **Outfield Dimensions:** LF—340, CF—408, RF—340. **Press Box Telephone:** (765) 494-1522.

QUINNIPIAC Braves

Conference: Northeast.

Mailing Address: 275 Mount Carmel Ave., Hamden, CT 06518. **Website:** www.qunnipiacbobcats.com.

Head Coach: Dan Gooley. **Assistant Coaches:** *Dan Scarpa, Marc Stonaha Jr., Mickey White. **Telephone:** (203) 582-8966. ■ **Baseball SID:** Christine Graziano. **Telephone:** (203) 582-5387. **FAX:** (203) 582-8716.

RADFORD Highlanders

Conference: Big South.

Mailing Address: P.O. Box 6913, Radford, VA 24142. **Website:** www.radford.edu/athletics.

Head Coach: Lew Kent. **Assistant Coach:** Ryan Brittle, Robert Brown. **Telephone:** (540) 831-5881. ■ **Baseball SID:** Aaron Barter. **Telephone:** (540) 831-5726. **FAX:** (540) 831-5556.

RHODE ISLAND Rams

Conference: Atlantic-10 (East).

Mailing Address: 3 Keaney Rd., Suite One, Kingston, RI 02881. **Website:** www.gorhody.com.

Head Coach: Frank Leoni. **Assistant Coaches:** *Jim Mason, Mike Santay. **Telephone:** (401) 874-4550. ■ **Baseball SID:** Dan Booth. **Telephone:** (401) 874-5356. **FAX:** (401) 874-5354.

RICE Owls

Conference: Western Athletic.

Mailing Address: 6100 Main St., Houston, TX 77005.

Website: www.RiceOwls.com.

Head Coach: Wayne Graham. **Assistant Coaches:** Zane Curry, *David Pierce, Mike Taylor. **Telephone:** (713) 348-6022. ■ **Baseball SID:** Bill Cousins. **Telephone:** (713) 348-5775. **FAX:** (713) 348-6019.

Home Field: Reckling Park. **Seating Capacity:** 3,500. **Outfield Dimensions:** LF—330, CF—400, RF—330. **Press Box Telephone:** (713) 348-4931.

RICHMOND Spiders

Conference: Atlantic 10.

Mailing Address: Baseball Office, Robins Center, Richmond, VA 23173. **Website:** www.richmondspiders.com.

Head Coach: Ron Atkins. **Assistant Coaches:** *Curtis Brown, Mike Loyd, Adam Taylor. **Telephone:** (804) 289-1933. ■ **Baseball SID:** Jennifer Arnette. **Telephone:** (804) 289-6313. **FAX:** (804) 289-8820.

RIDER Broncs

Conference: Metro Atlantic (South).

Mailing Address: 2083 Lawrenceville Rd., Lawrenceville, NJ 08648. **Website:** www.gobroncs.com.

Head Coach: Sonny Pittaro. **Assistant Coaches:** *Rick Freeman, Tom Petroff, Jeff Plunkett. **Telephone:** (609) 896-5055. ■ **Baseball SID:** Bud Focht. **Telephone:** (609) 896-5138. **FAX:** (609) 896-0341.

RUTGERS Scarlet Knights

Conference: Big East.

Mailing Address: 83 Rockefeller Rd., Piscataway, NJ 08854. **Website:** www.scarletknights.com.

Head Coach: Fred Hill. **Assistant Coaches:** Tom Baxter, Jay Blackwell, *Glen Gardner. **Telephone:** (732) 445-7833. ■ **Baseball SID:** Pat McBride. **Telephone:** (732) 445-4200. **FAX:** (732) 445-3063.

Home Field: Class of '53 Baseball Complex. **Seating Capacity:** 1,500. **Outfield Dimensions:** LF—330, CF—410, RF—320. **Press Box Telephone:** (732) 794-1207.

SACRED HEART Pioneers

Conference: Northeast.

Mailing Address: 5151 Park Ave., Fairfield, CT 06825. **Website:** www.sacredheartpioneers.com.

Head Coach: Nick Giaquinto. **Assistant Coaches:** Brian Brunckhorst, *Seth Kaplan. **Telephone:** (203) 365-7632. ■ **Baseball SID:** Gene Gumbs. **Telephone:** (203) 396-8127. **FAX:** (203) 371-7889.

ST. BONAVENTURE Bonnies

Conference: Atlantic-10 (East).

Mailing Address: Reilly Center, St. Bonaventure, NY 14778. **Website:** www.gobonnies.com.

Head Coach: Larry Sudbrook. **Assistant Coaches:** *Mark Evers, Kyle Stark. **Telephone:** (716) 375-2641. ■ **Baseball SID:** Steve Mest. **Telephone:** (716) 375-2319. **FAX:** (716) 375-2280.

ST. FRANCIS Terriers

Conference: Northeast.

Mailing Address: 180 Remsen St., Brooklyn Heights, NY 11201. **Website:** www.stfranciscollege.edu.

Head Coach: Frank Del George. **Assistant Coaches:** Tony Barone, *Mike Lopiparo. **Telephone:** (718) 489-5490. ■ **Baseball SID:** Angela Merlino. **Telephone:** (718) 489-5369. **FAX:** (718) 797-2140.

ST. JOHN'S Red Storm

Conference: Big East.

Mailing Address: 8000 Utopia Pkwy., Jamaica, NY 11439. **Website:** www.redstormsports.com.

Head Coach: Ed Blankmeyer. **Assistant Coaches:** Mike Fahid, *Mike Hampton, Mike Maerten. **Telephone:** (718) 990-6148. ■ **Baseball SID:** Mike Carey. **Telephone:** (718) 990-1521. **FAX:** (718) 969-8468.

Home Field: The Ballpark at St. John's. **Seating Capacity:** 3,500. **Outfield Dimensions:** LF—325, CF—390, RF—325. **Press Box Telephone:** (718) 990-6057.

ST. JOSEPH'S Hawks

Conference: Atlantic-10 (East).

Mailing Address: 5600 City Ave., Philadelphia, PA 19131. **Website:** www.sjuhawks.com.

Head Coach: Jim Ertel. **Assistant Coaches:** *Ken Krsolovic, Jack Stanczak, Joe Tremoglie. **Telephone:** (610) 660-1718. ■ **Baseball SID:** Phil Denne. **Telephone:** (610) 660-1738. **FAX:** (610) 660-1724.

SAINT LOUIS Billikens

Conference: Conference USA.

Mailing Address: 3672 W. Pine Blvd., St. Louis, MO 63108. **Website:** www.slubillikens.com.

Head Coach: Bob Hughes. **Assistant Coaches:** Dan Nicholson, *Todd Whaley. **Telephone:** (314) 977-3172. ■ **Baseball SID:** Diana Koval. **Telephone:** (314) 977-3463. **FAX:** (314) 977-7193.

Home Field: Billiken Sports Center. **Seating Capacity:** 500. **Outfield Dimensions:** LF—330, CF—395, RF—330. **Press Box Telephone:** (314) 402-8655.

ST. MARY'S Gaels

Conference: West Coast (West).

Mailing Address: 1928 St. Mary's Rd., Moraga, CA 94575. **Website:** www.smcgaels.com.

Head Coach: John Baptista. **Assistant Coaches:** J.J. Brock, *Ted Turkington, Eric Valenzuela. **Telephone:** (925) 631-4637. ■ **Baseball SID:** Jason Santos. **Telephone:** (925) 631-4950. **FAX:** (925) 631-4405.

Home Field: Louis Guisto Field. **Seating Capacity:** 500. **Outfield Dimensions:** LF—340, CF—415, RF—340. **Press Box Telephone:** (925) 376-3906.

ST. PETER'S Peacocks

Conference: Metro Atlantic (South).

Mailing Address: 2641 John F. Kennedy Blvd., Jersey City, NJ 07306. **Website:** www.spc.edu.

Head Coach: Jimmy Walsh. **Telephone:** (201) 915-9459. ■ **Baseball SID:** Tim Camp. **Telephone:** (201) 915-9101. **FAX:** (201) 915-9102.

SAM HOUSTON STATE Bearkats

Conference: Southland.

Mailing Address: P.O. Box 2268, Huntsville, TX 77341. **Website:** www.shsu.edu/~ath_www/baseball.

Head Coach: Chris Rupp. **Assistant Coaches:** Josh Blunt, Phillip Ghutzman. **Telephone:** (936) 294-1731. ■ **Baseball SID:** Paul Ridings. **Telephone:** (936) 294-1764. **FAX:** (936) 294-3538.

SAMFORD Bulldogs

Conference: Atlantic Sun.

Mailing Address: 800 Lakeshore Dr., Birmingham, AL 35229. **Website:** www.samfordsports.com.

Head Coach: Tim Parenton. **Assistant Coaches:** Todd Buczek, Gerald Tuck. **Telephone:** (205) 726-2134. ■ **Baseball SID:** Kerwin Lonzo. **Telephone:** (205) 726-2799. **FAX:** (205) 726-2545.

SAN DIEGO Toreros

Conference: West Coast (Coast).

Mailing Address: 5998 Alcala Park, San Diego, CA 92110. **Website:** usdtoreros.com.

Head Coach: Rich Hill. **Assistant Coaches:** Craig deLuz, *Sean Kenny, Mike Kramer. **Telephone:** (619) 260-5953. ■ **Baseball SID:** Nick Mirkovich. **Telephone:** (619) 260-4745. **FAX:** (619) 260-2990.

Home Field: Cunningham Stadium. **Seating**

Capacity: 2,000. **Outfield Dimensions:** LF—309, CF—395, RF—335. **Press Box Telephone:** None.

SAN DIEGO STATE Aztecs

Conference: Western Athletic.

Mailing Address: Department of Athletics, San Diego, CA 92182. **Website:** www.goaztecs.com.

Head Coach: Tony Gwynn. **Assistant Coaches:** *Rusty Filter, Anthony Johnson, Jay Martel. **Telephone:** (619) 594-6889. ■ **Baseball SID:** Dave Kuhn. **Telephone:** (619) 594-5242. **FAX:** (619) 582-6541.

Home Field: Tony Gwynn Stadium. **Seating Capacity:** 3,000. **Outfield Dimensions:** LF—340, CF—410, RF—340. **Press Box Telephone:** (619) 594-4103.

SAN FRANCISCO Dons

Conference: West Coast (Coast).

Mailing Address: Memorial Gym, 2130 Fulton St., San Francisco, CA 94117. **Website:** www.usfdons.com.

Head Coach: Nino Giarratano. **Assistant Coaches:** *Greg Moore, Dutch Mendenhall, Troy Nakamura. **Telephone:** (415) 422-2393. ■ **Baseball SID:** Ryan McCrary. **Telephone:** (415) 422-6162. **FAX:** (415) 422-2510.

Home Field: Benedetti Diamond. **Seating Capacity:** 1,000. **Outfield Dimensions:** LF—312, CF—442, RF—323. **Press Box Telephone:** None.

SAN JOSE STATE Spartans

Conference: Western Athletic.

Mailing Address: One Washington Square, San Jose, CA 95192. **Website:** www.sjsuspartans.com.

Head Coach: Sam Piraro. **Assistant Coaches:** Brian Kohndrow, *Dean Madsen, *Doug Thurman. **Telephone:** (408) 924-1255. ■ **Baseball SID:** Brian Blank. **Telephone:** (408) 924-1211. **FAX:** (408) 924-1291.

Home Field: Municipal Stadium. **Seating Capacity:** 5,000. **Outfield Dimensions:** LF—330, CF—400, RF—330. **Press Box Telephone:** (408) 924-7276.

SANTA CLARA Broncos

Conference: West Coast (West).

Mailing Address: 500 El Camino Real, Santa Clara, CA 95053. **Website:** www.santaclarabroncos.com.

Head Coach: Mark O'Brien. **Assistant Coaches:** Scott Kidd, Tom Myers, Mike Oakland. **Telephone:** (408) 554-4680. ■ **Baseball SID:** David Wahlstrom. **Telephone:** (408) 554-4670. **FAX:** (408) 554-6942.

Home Field: Buck Shaw Stadium. **Seating Capacity:** 6,800. **Outfield Dimensions:** LF—360, CF—400, RF—340. **Press Box Telephone:** (408) 554-4752.

SAVANNAH STATE Tigers

Conference: Independent.

Mailing Address: 312 College St. Savannah, GA 31404. **Website:** www.savstate.edu.

Head Coach: Jamie Rigdon. **Assistant Coaches:** Robert Lampkin, Luis Marquez. **Telephone:** (912) 356-2801. ■ **Baseball SID:** Lee Pearson. **Telephone:** (912) 353-4670. **FAX:** (912) 353-3073.

SETON HALL Pirates

Conference: Big East.

Mailing Address: 400 S. Orange Ave., South Orange, NJ 07079. **Website:** www.shupirates.com.

Head Coach: Mike Sheppard. **Assistant Coaches:** Phil Cundari, Charlie Killeen, *Rob Sheppard. **Telephone:** (973) 761-9557. ■ **Baseball SID:** Kevin Fischer. **Telephone:** (973) 761-7507. **FAX:** (973) 761-9061.

Home Field: Owen T. Carroll Field. **Seating Capacity:** 500. **Outfield Dimensions:** LF—320, CF—400, RF—320. **Press Box Telephone:** None.

SIENA Saints

Conference: Metro Atlantic (North).

Mailing Address: 515 New Loudon Rd., Loudonville, NY 12211. **Website:** www.sienasaints.com.

Head Coach: Tony Rossi. **Assistant Coaches:** Bill Cilento, Tony Curro, Paul Thompson. **Telephone:** (518) 786-5044. ■ **Baseball SID:** Jason Rich. **Telephone:** (518) 783-2411. **FAX:** (518) 783-2992.

SOUTH ALABAMA Jaguars

Conference: Sun Belt.

Mailing Address: 1209 Mitchell Center, Mobile, AL 36688. **Website:** www.usajaguars.com.

Head Coach: Steve Kittrell. **Assistant Coaches:** Ronnie Powell, *Scot Sealy, Tom Whitehurst. **Telephone:** (251) 460-6876. ■ **Baseball SID:** Matt Smith. **Telephone:** (251) 460-7035. **FAX:** (251) 460-7297.

Home Field: Eddie Stanky Field. **Seating Capacity:** 3,500. **Outfield Dimensions:** LF—330, CF—400, RF—330. **Press Box Telephone:** (251) 460-7126.

SOUTH CAROLINA Gamecocks

Conference: Southeastern (East).

Mailing Address: 1300 Rosewood Dr., Columbia, SC 29208. **Website:** www.uscsports.com.

Head Coach: Ray Tanner. **Assistant Coaches:** Monty Lee, Jerry Meyers, *Jim Toman. **Telephone:** (803) 777-0116. ■ **Baseball SID**: Andrew Kitick. **Telephone:** (803) 777-5257. **FAX:** (803) 777-2967.

Home Field: Sarge Frye Field. **Seating Capacity:** 6,000. **Outfield Dimensions:** LF—325, CF—390, RF—320. **Press Box Telephone:** (803) 777-6648.

SOUTH FLORIDA Bulls

Conference: Conference USA.

Mailing Address: 4202 E. Fowler Ave., Tampa, FL 33620. **Website:** www.GoUSFBulls.com.

Head Coach: Eddie Cardieri. **Assistant Coaches:** Nelson North, *Bryan Peters. **Telephone:** (813) 974-2504. ■ **Baseball SID:** Fred Huff. **Telephone:** (813) 974-4087. **FAX:** (813) 974-5328.

Home Field: Red McEwen Field. **Seating Capacity:** 1,500. **Outfield Dimensions:** LF—340, CF—400, RF—340. **Press Box Telephone:** (813) 974-3604.

SOUTHEAST MISSOURI STATE Indians

Conference: Ohio Valley.

Mailing Address: One University Plaza, MS0200, Cape Girardeau, MO 63701. **Website:** www.gosoutheast.com.

Head Coach: Mark Hogan. **Assistant Coaches:** Conan Horton, Scott Southard, *Jeremy Tyson. **Telephone:** (573) 651-2645. ■ **Baseball SID:** Justin Maskus. **Telephone:** (573) 651-2937. **FAX:** (573) 651-2810.

Home Field: Capaha Field. **Seating Capacity:** 2,000. **Outfield Dimensions:** LF—335, CF—400, RF—335. **Press Box Telephone:** (573) 651-9139.

SOUTHEASTERN LOUISIANA Lions

Conference: Southland.

Mailing Address: SLU Station 10309, Hammond, LA 70402. **Website:** www.LionSports.net.

Head Coach: Dan Canevari. **Assistant Coaches:** Fred Burnside, *Bill Daily, Rusty Miller. **Telephone:** (985) 549-2896. ■ **Baseball SID:** Matt Sullivan. **Telephone:** (985) 549-3774. **FAX:** (985) 549-3773.

Home Field: Alumni Field. **Seating Capacity:** 3,000. **Outfield Dimensions:** LF—320, CF—400, RF—320. **Press Box Telephone:** None.

SOUTHERN Jaguars

Conference: Southwestern Athletic (West).

Mailing Address: P.O. Box 10850, Baton Rouge, LA 70813. **Website:** www.subr.edu/baseball.

Head Coach: Roger Cador. **Assistant Coaches:** Arnold Brathwaite, *Barret Rey. **Telephone:** (225) 771-2513. ■ **Baseball SID:** Christopher Jones. **Telephone:** (225) 771-2601. **FAX:** (225) 771-4400.

SOUTHERN CALIFORNIA Trojans

Conference: Pacific-10.

Mailing Address: HER-103, Los Angeles, CA 90089. **Website:** www.usctrojans.com.

Head Coach: Mike Gillespie. **Assistant Coaches:** Rob Klein, *Dave Lawn, Andy Nieto. **Telephone:** (213) 740-5762. ■ **Baseball SID:** Jason Pommier. **Telephone:** (213) 740-8480. **FAX:** (213) 740-7584.

Home Field: Dedeaux Field. **Seating Capacity:** 2,500. **Outfield Dimensions:** LF—335, CF—395, RF—335. **Press Box Telephone:** (213) 748-3449.

SOUTHERN ILLINOIS Salukis

Conference: Missouri Valley.

Mailing Address: 128 Lingle Hall, Carbondale, IL 62901. **Website:** www.siusalukis.com.

Head Coach: Dan Callahan. **Assistant Coaches:** *Ken Henderson, Kevin Kimball, Ty Neal. **Telephone:** (618) 453-2802. ■ **Baseball SID:** Jeff Honza. **Telephone:** (618) 453-5470. **FAX:** (618) 453-2648.

Home Field: Abe Martin Field. **Seating Capacity:** 2,000. **Outfield Dimensions:** LF—340, CF—390, RF—340. **Press Box Telephone:** (618) 453-3794.

SOUTHERN MISSISSIPPI Golden Eagles

Conference: Conference USA.

Mailing Address: P.O. Box 5017, Hattiesburg, MS 39406. **Website:** www.southernmiss.com.

Head Coach: Corky Palmer. **Assistant Coaches:** Scott Berry, *Lane Burroughs. **Telephone:** (601) 266-5427. ■ **Baseball SID:** Mike Montoro. **Telephone:** (601) 266-5947. **FAX:** (601) 266-4507.

Home Field: Pete Taylor Park. **Seating Capacity:** 3,678. **Outfield Dimensions:** LF—340, CF—400, RF—340. **Press Box Telephone:** (601) 266-5684.

SOUTHERN UTAH Thunderbirds

Conference: Mid-Continent.

Mailing Address: 351 W. Center St., Cedar City, UT 84720. **Website:** www.suu.edu/athletics.

Head Coach: Kurt Palmer. **Assistant Coach:** Jason Jacobsen. **Telephone:** (435) 586-7932. ■ **Baseball SID:** Steve Johnson. **Telephone:** (435) 586-7752. **FAX:** (435) 865-8037.

SOUTHWEST MISSOURI STATE Bears

Conference: Missouri Valley.

Mailing Address: 901 S. National Ave., Springfield, MO 65804. **Website:** www.smsbears.net.

Head Coach: Keith Guttin. **Assistant Coaches:** *Paul Evans, Brent Thomas. **Telephone:** (417) 836-5242. ■ **Baseball SIDs**: Jeff Williams. **Telephone:** (417) 836-5402. **FAX:** (417) 836-4868.

Home Field: Price Cutter Park. **Seating Capacity:** 6,000. **Outfield Dimensions:** LF—330, CF—400, RF—330. **Press Box Telephone:** (417) 581-9819.

SOUTHWEST TEXAS STATE Bobcats

Conference: Southland.

Mailing Address: 601 University, San Marcos, TX 78666. **Website:** www.swtbobcats.com.

Head Coach: Ty Harrington. **Assistant Coaches:** Jon Choate, Gene Salazar, *Travis Waldin. **Telephone:** (512) 245-7566. ■ **Baseball SID:** Travis Tholen. **Telephone:** (512) 245-2988. **FAX:** (512) 245-2967.

Home Field: Bobcat Field. **Seating Capacity:** 1,800. **Outfield Dimensions:** LF—330, CF—404, RF—330. **Press Box Telephone:** (512) 245-3654.

STANFORD Cardinal

Conference: Pacific-10.

Mailing Address: Arrillaga Family Sports Center, Stanford, CA 94305. **Website:** www.gostanford.com.

Head Coach: Mark Marquess. **Assistant Coaches:** Tom Kunis, David Nakama, *Dean Stotz. **Telephone:** (650) 723-4528. ■ **Baseball SID:** Kyle McRae. **Telephone:** (650) 725-2959. **FAX:** (650) 725-2957.

Home Field: Sunken Diamond. **Seating Capacity:** 4,000. **Outfield Dimensions:** LF—335, CF—400, RF—335. **Press Box Telephone:** (650) 723-4629.

STETSON Hatters

Conference: Atlantic Sun.

Mailing Address: P.O. Box 8359, 421 N. Woodland Blvd., DeLand, FL 32723. **Website:** www.stetson.edu/offices/athletics.

Head Coach: Pete Dunn. **Assistant Coaches:** Mitch Markham, Frank Martello, *Terry Rooney. **Telephone:** (386) 822-8730. ■ **Baseball SID:** Jaime Bataille. **Telephone:** (386) 822-8130. **FAX:** (386) 822-8132.

Home Field: Melching Field at Conrad Park. **Seating Capacity:** 2,500. **Outfield Dimensions:** LF—335, CF—403, RF—335. **Press Box Telephone:** (386) 736-7360.

STONY BROOK Seawolves

Conference: America East.

Mailing Address: USB Sports Complex, Stony Brook, NY 11794. **Website:** www.goseawolves.org.

Head Coach: Matt Senk. **Assistant Coaches:** Tom Nielsen, Gerry Sputo. **Telephone:** (631) 632-9226. ■ **Baseball SID:** Tim Szlosek. **Telephone:** (631) 632-7125. **FAX:** (631) 632-8841.

TEMPLE Owls

Conference: Atlantic-10 (East).

Mailing Address: Vivacqua Hall, 1700 N. Broad St., Philadelphia, PA 19122. **Website:** www.owlsports.com.

Head Coach: Skip Wilson. **Assistant Coaches:** Rob Kell, John McArdle. **Telephone:** (215) 424-7670. ■ **Baseball SID:** Chet Zukowski. **Telephone:** (215) 204-6912. **FAX:** (215) 204-7499.

TENNESSEE Volunteers

Conference: Southeastern (East).

Mailing Address: P.O. Box 15016, Knoxville, TN 37901. **Website:** www.utsports.com.

Head Coach: Rod Delmonico. **Assistant Coaches:** Fred Corral, Larry Simcox. **Telephone:** (865) 974-2057. ■ **Baseball SID:** Jeff Muir. **Telephone:** (865) 974-1212. **FAX:** (865) 974-1269.

Home Field: Lindsey Nelson Stadium. **Seating Capacity:** 4,000. **Outfield Dimensions:** LF—335, CF—404, RF—330. **Press Box Telephone:** (865) 974-3376.

TENNESSEE-MARTIN Skyhawks

Conference: Ohio Valley.

Mailing Address: 1037 Elam Center, Martin, TN 38238. **Website:** www.utm.edu.

Head Coach: *Bubba Cates. **Assistant Coach:** David Hogue, Brandon Nolen. **Telephone:** (731) 587-7337. ■ **Baseball SID:** Joe Lofaro. **Telephone:** (731) 587-7632. **FAX:** (731) 587-7624.

TENNESSEE TECH Golden Eagles

Conference: Ohio Valley.

Mailing Address: P.O. Box 5057, Cookeville, TN 38505. **Website:** www.tntech.edu.

Head Coach: Aaron Carroll. **Assistant Coach:** *Ryan Edwards, Tommy Jackson. **Telephone:** (931) 372-3925. ■ **Baseball SID:** Scott Wilson. **Telephone:** (931) 372-3088. **FAX:** (931) 372-6139.

TEXAS Longhorns

Conference: Big 12.

Mailing Address: P.O. Box 7399, Austin, TX 78713. **Website:** www.TexasSports.com.

Head Coach: Augie Garrido. **Assistant Coaches:** Frank Anderson, *Tommy Harmon. **Telephone:** (512) 471-5732. ■ **Baseball SID:** Mike Forcucci. **Telephone:** (512) 471-6039. **FAX:** (512) 471-6040.

Home Field: Disch-Falk Field. **Seating Capacity:** 6,649. **Outfield Dimensions:** LF—340, CF—400, RF—325. **Press Box Telephone:** (512) 471-1146.

TEXAS-ARLINGTON Mavericks

Conference: Southland.

Mailing Address: P.O. Box 19079, Arlington, TX 76019. **Website:** www.utamavs.edu.

Head Coach: Jeff Curtis. **Assistant Coaches:** Mike Dilley, Scott Malone, *Darin Thomas. **Telephone:** (817) 272-2060. ■ **Baseball SID:** John Brush. **Telephone:** (817) 272-5706. **FAX:** (817) 272-2254.

TEXAS-PAN AMERICAN Broncs

Conference: Independent.

Mailing Address: 1201 W. University Dr., Edinburg, TX 78541. **Website:** www.panam.edu.

Head Coach: Willie Gawlik. **Assistant Coaches:** John Johnson, Kiki Trevino. **Telephone:** (956) 381-2235. ■ **Baseball SID:** Dave Geringer. **Telephone:** (956) 381-2240. **FAX:** (956) 381-2398.

Home Field: Edinburg Baseball Stadium. **Seating Capacity:** 4,000. **Outfield Dimensions:** LF—325, CF—400, RF—325. **Press Box Telephone:** Unavailable.

TEXAS-SAN ANTONIO Roadrunners

Conference: Southland.

Mailing Address: 6900 N. Loop 1604 W., San Antonio, TX 78249. **Website:** www.utsa.edu.

Head Coach: Sherman Corbett. **Assistant Coaches:** Jim Blair, *Jason Marshall. **Telephone:** (210) 458-4805. ■ **Baseball SID:** Erin Molina. **Telephone:** (210) 458-4930. **FAX:** (210) 458-4569.

TEXAS A&M Aggies

Conference: Big 12.

Mailing Address: P.O. Box 30017, College Station, TX 77842. **Website:** www.aggieathletics.com.

Head Coach: Mark Johnson. **Assistant Coaches:** David Coleman, Jason Hutchins, *Jim Lawler. **Telephone:** (979) 845-4810. ■ **Baseball SID:** Chuck Glenewinkel. **Telephone:** (979) 845-3239. **FAX:** (979) 845-0564.

Home Field: Olsen Field. **Seating Capacity:** 7,053. **Outfield Dimensions:** LF—330, CF—400, RF—330. **Press Box Telephone:** (979) 845-4810.

TEXAS A&M-CORPUS CHRISTI Islanders

Conference: Independent.

Mailing Address: 6300 Ocean Dr., Corpus Christi, TX 78412. **Website:** www.goislanders.com.

Head Coach: Hector Salinas. **Assistant Coach:** *Jorge Hernandez. **Telephone:** (361) 825-3252. ■ **Baseball SID:** John Gilger. **Telephone:** (361) 825-3410. **FAX:** (361) 825-3218.

TEXAS CHRISTIAN Horned Frogs

Conference: Conference USA.

Mailing Address: TCU Box 297600, Fort Worth, TX 76129. **Website:** www.gofrogs.com.

Head Coach: Lance Brown. **Assistant Coaches:** Glenn Dishman, Josh Stewart, *Donnie Watson. **Telephone:** (817) 257-5354. ■ **Baseball SID:** Mike Flynn. **Telephone:** (817) 257-7969. **FAX:** (817) 257-7964.

Home Field: Lupton Stadium. **Seating Capacity:** 2,500. **Outfield Dimensions:** LF—330, CF—400, RF—330. **Press Box Telephone:** (817) 257-7966.

TEXAS SOUTHERN Tigers

Conference: Southwestern Athletic (West).

Mailing Address: 3100 Cleburne St., Houston, TX 77004. **Website:** www.tsu.edu.

Head Coach: Candy Robinson. **Assistant Coach:** Brian White. **Telephone:** (713) 313-7993. ■ **Baseball SID:** Erwin Hall. **Telephone:** (713) 313-6826. **FAX:** (713) 313-1045.

TEXAS TECH Red Raiders

Conference: Big 12.

Mailing Address: P.O. Box 43021, Lubbock, TX 79409. **Website:** www.texastech.com.

Head Coach: Larry Hays. **Assistant Coaches:** *Greg Evans, Daren Hays, Brian Strickland. **Telephone:** (806) 742-3355. ■ **Baseball SID:** Blayne Beal. **Telephone:** (806) 742-2770. **FAX:** (806) 742-1970.

Home Field: Dan Law Field. **Seating Capacity:** 5,050. **Outfield Dimensions:** LF—330, CF—405, RF—330. **Press Box Telephone:** (806) 742-3688.

TOLEDO Rockets

Conference: Mid-American (West).

Mailing Address: 2801 W. Bancroft St., Toledo, OH 43606. **Website:** www.utrockets.com.

Head Coach: Joe Kruzel. **Assistant Coaches:** Junie Melendez, Steve Parrill. **Telephone:** (419) 530-6264. ■ **Baseball SID:** Brian DeBenedictis. **Telephone:** (419) 530-4919. **FAX:** (419) 530-4930.

TOWSON Tigers

Conference: Colonial Athletic.

Mailing Address: 8000 York Rd., Towson, MD 21252. **Website:** www.towsontigers.com.

Head Coach: *Mike Gottlieb. **Assistant Coaches:** Mel Bacon, Liam Healy. **Telephone:** (410) 704-3775. ■ **Baseball SID:** Dan O'Connell. **Telephone:** (410) 704-3102. **FAX:** (410) 704-3861.

Home Field: John Schuerholz Park. **Seating Capacity:** 1,000. **Outfield Dimensions:** LF—312, CF—424, RF—302. **Press Box Telephone:** (410) 704-5810.

TROY STATE Trojans

Conference: Atlantic Sun.

Mailing Address: Davis Field House, 100 George Wallace Dr., Troy, AL 36082. **Website:** www.troyst.edu/athletics.

Head Coach: Bobby Pierce. **Assistant Coaches:** Todd Lamberth, *Mark Smartt. **Telephone:** (334) 670-3489. ■ **Baseball SID:** Brian Henry. **Telephone:** (334) 670-3229. **FAX:** (334) 670-5665.

Home Field: Riddle-Pace Field. **Seating Capacity:** 2,000. **Outfield Dimensions:** LF—330, CF—400, RF—310. **Press Box Telephone:** (334) 670-5701.

TULANE Green Wave

Conference: Conference USA.

Mailing Address: Wilson Center, Ben Weiner Drive, New Orleans, LA 70118. **Website:** www.tulanegreenwave.com.

Head Coach: Rick Jones. **Assistant Coaches:** Chris Burr, *Mark Kingston, Chad Sutter. **Telephone:** (504) 862-8239. ■ **Baseball SID:** Richie Weaver. **Telephone:** (504) 865-5506. **FAX:** (504) 865-5512.

Home Field: Turchin Stadium. **Seating Capacity:** 3,600. **Outfield Dimensions:** LF—325, CF—400, RF—325. **Press Box Telephone:** (504) 862-8224.

UTAH Utes

Conference: Mountain West.

Mailing Address: 1825 E. South Campus Dr., Salt Lake City, UT 84112. **Website:** www.utahutes.com.

Head Coach: Tim Esmay. **Assistant Coaches:** *Matt Eeles, John Flores, Chris Simonsen. **Telephone:** (801)

581-3526. ■ **Baseball SID:** Hope Wagner. **Telephone:** (801) 581-3771. **FAX:** (801) 581-4358.

Home Field: Franklin Covey Field. **Seating Capacity:** 15,500. **Outfield Dimensions:** LF—345, CF—420, RF—315. **Press Box Telephone:** (801) 464-6969.

VALPARAISO Crusaders

Conference: Mid-Continent.

Mailing Address: Athletic Recreation Center, Valparaiso, IN 46383. **Website:** www.valpo.edu/athletics.

Head Coach: Paul Twenge. **Assistant Coaches:** Mike Nall, John Olson. **Telephone:** (219) 464-5239. ■ **Baseball SID:** Bill Rogers. **Telephone:** (219) 464-6953. **FAX:** (219) 464-5762.

VANDERBILT Commodores

Conference: Southeastern (East).

Mailing Address: 2601 Jess Neely Dr., Nashville, TN 37212. **Website:** www.vucommodores.com.

Head Coach: Tim Corbin. **Assistant Coaches:** *Erik Bakich, Derek Johnson. **Telephone:** (615) 322-7725. ■ **Baseball SID:** Andre Foushee. **Telephone:** (615) 322-4121. **FAX:** (615) 343-7064.

Home Field: Hawkins Field. **Seating Capacity:** 1,575. **Outfield Dimensions:** LF—310, CF—400, RF—330. **Press Box Telephone:** (615) 320-0436.

VERMONT Catamounts

Conference: America East.

Mailing Address: 226 Patrick Gym, Burlington, VT 05405. **Website:** www.uvmathletics.com.

Head Coach: Bill Currier. **Assistant Coaches:** Jim Carter, Mike Cole, *Anthony DeCicco. **Telephone:** (802) 656-7701. ■ **Baseball SID:** Bruce Bosley. **Telephone:** (802) 656-1109. **FAX:** (802) 656-8328.

VILLANOVA Wildcats

Conference: Big East.

Mailing Address: Jake Nevin Field House, 800 Lancaster Ave., Villanova, PA 19085. **Website:** www.villanova.com.

Head Coach: Joe Godri. **Assistant Coaches:** Rick Clagett, Rod Johnson, Doc Kennedy. **Telephone:** (610) 519-4529. ■ **Baseball SID:** Jonathan Gust. **Telephone:** (610) 519-4122. **FAX:** (610) 519-7323.

Home Field: Villanova Ballpark at Plymouth Community Center. **Seating Capacity:** 750. **Outfield Dimensions:** LF—320, CF—400, RF—320. **Press Box Telephone:** None.

VIRGINIA Cavaliers

Conference: Atlantic Coast.

Mailing Address: P.O. Box 400853, Charlottesville, VA 22904. **Website:** www.virginiasports.com.

Head Coach: Dennis Womack. **Assistant Coaches:** *Steve Heon, Chip Schaffner, Neil Schaffner. **Telephone:** (434) 982-5775. ■ **Baseball SID:** Adam Jones. **Telephone:** (434) 982-5131. **FAX:** (434) 982-5525.

Home Field: Virginia Baseball Field. **Seating Capacity:** 2,000. **Outfield Dimensions:** LF—352, CF—408, RF—352. **Press Box Telephone:** (434) 295-9262.

VIRGINIA COMMONWEALTH Rams

Conference: Colonial Athletic.

Mailing Address: 1300 W. Broad St., Richmond, VA 23284. **Website:** www.vcurams.vcu.edu.

Head Coach: Paul Keyes. **Assistant Coaches:** Tim Haynes, *Mark McQueen, Ryan Morris. **Telephone:** (804) 828-4820. ■ **Baseball SID:** Scott Garbarini. **Telephone:** (804) 828-7000. **FAX:** (804) 828-9428.

Home Field: The Diamond. **Seating Capacity:** 12,134. **Outfield Dimensions:** LF—330, CF—402, RF—330. **Press Box Telephone:** (804) 359-1565.

VIRGINIA MILITARY INSTITUTE Keydets

Conference: Southern.

Mailing Address: Main Street, Cameron Hall, Lexington, VA 24450. **Website:** www.vmi.edu.

Head Coach: Tom Slater. **Assistant Coaches:** *Marlin Ikenberry, Andrew Slater. **Telephone:** (540) 464-7609. ■ **Baseball SID:** Bradley Damron. **Telephone:** (540) 464-7015. **FAX:** (540) 464-7583.

VIRGINIA TECH Hokies

Conference: Big East.

Mailing Address: 210 Cassell Coliseum, Blacksburg, VA 24061. **Website:** www.hokiesports.com.

Head Coach: Chuck Hartman. **Assistant Coaches:** Jon Hartness, *Jay Phillips. **Telephone:** (540) 231-3671. ■ **Baseball SID:** Dave Smith. **Telephone:** (540) 231-6726. **FAX:** (540) 231-6984.

Home Field: English Field. **Seating Capacity:** 1,500. **Outfield Dimensions:** LF—330, CF—400, RF—330. **Press Box Telephone:** (540) 231-4013.

WAGNER Seahawks

Conference: Northeast.

Mailing Address: One Campus Road, Staten Island, NY 10301. **Website:** www.wagner.edu/athletics.

Head Coach: *Joe Litterio. **Assistant Coach:** Jim Agnello, Mike Seel, Jeff Toth. **Telephone:** (718) 390-3154. ■ **Baseball SID:** Todd Vatter. **Telephone:** (718) 390-3215. **FAX:** (718) 390-3347.

WAKE FOREST Demon Deacons

Conference: Atlantic Coast.

Mailing Address: 203 Manchester Athletic Center, Winston-Salem, NC 27109. **Website:** www.wakeforest sports.com.

Head Coach: George Greer. **Assistant Coaches:** Scott Daeley, Michael Holmes, *Jamie Mabe. **Telephone:** (336) 758-5570. ■ **Baseball SID:** Mike Vest. **Telephone:** (336) 758-5640. **FAX:** (336) 758-5140.

Home Field: Hooks Stadium. **Seating Capacity:** 2,500. **Outfield Dimensions:** LF—340, CF—400, RF—315. **Press Box Telephone:** (336) 759-9711.

WASHINGTON Huskies

Conference: Pacific-10.

Mailing Address: Graves Bldg., Box 354070, Seattle, WA 98195. **Website:** www.gohuskies.com.

Head Coach: Ken Knutson. **Assistant Coaches:** Travis Jewett, *Joe Ross, Gregg Swenson. **Telephone:** (206) 616-4335. ■ **Baseball SID:** Jeff Bechthold. **Telephone:** (206) 543-2230. **FAX:** (206) 543-5000.

Home Field: Husky Ballpark. **Seating Capacity:** 1,500. **Outfield Dimensions:** LF—327, CF—395, RF—317. **Press Box Telephone:** (206) 685-1994.

WASHINGTON STATE Cougars

Conference: Pacific-10.

Mailing Address: P.O Box 641602, Pullman, WA 99164. **Website:** www.wsucougars.com.

Head Coach: *Tim Mooney. **Assistant Coaches:** Mike Cummins, Gary Picone. **Telephone:** (509) 335-0211. ■ **Baseball SID:** Jon Naito. **Telephone:** (509) 335-5785. **FAX:** (509) 335-0267.

Home Field: Bailey-Brayton Field. **Seating Capacity:** 3,500. **Outfield Dimensions:** LF—330, CF—400, RF—375. **Press Box Telephone:** (509) 335-8291.

WEST VIRGINIA Mountaineers

Conference: Big East.

Mailing Address: P.O. Box 0877, Morgantown, WV 26507. **Website:** www.MSNSportsnet.com.

Head Coach: Greg Van Zant. **Assistant Coaches:** *Bruce Cameron, Ernie Galusky, Joe McNamee.

Telephone: (304) 293-2308. ■ **Baseball SID:** Adam Zundell. **Telephone:** (304) 293-2821. **FAX:** (304) 293-4105.

Home Field: Hawley Field. **Seating Capacity:** 1,500. **Outfield Dimensions:** LF—325, CF—390, RF—325. **Press Box Telephone:** (304) 293-5988.

WESTERN CAROLINA Catamounts

Conference: Southern.

Mailing Address: Ramsey Center, Cullowhee, NC 28723. **Website:** www.catamountsports.com.

Head Coach: Todd Raleigh. **Assistant Coaches:** Paul Menhart, Chris Roberts, Bergin Tatham. **Telephone:** (828) 227-7338. ■ **Baseball SID:** Mike Cawood. **Telephone:** (828) 227-2339. **FAX:** (828) 227-7688.

Home Field: Childress Field at Hennon Stadium. **Seating Capacity:** 1,500. **Outfield Dimensions:** LF—325, CF—390, RF—325. **Press Box Telephone:** (828) 227-7020.

WESTERN ILLINOIS Leathernecks

Conference: Mid-Continent.

Mailing Address: 204 Western Hall, 1 University Circle, Macomb, IL 61455. **Website:** www.wiuathletics.com.

Head Coach: Stan Hyman. **Assistant Coaches:** *Dan Duffy, Tom Radz. **Telephone:** (309) 298-1521. ■ **Baseball SID:** Shana Daniels. **Telephone:** (309) 298-1133. **FAX:** (309) 298-3366.

WESTERN KENTUCKY Hilltoppers

Conference: Sun Belt.

Mailing Address: One Big Red Way, Bowling Green, KY 42101. **Website:** www.wkusports.com.

Head Coach: Joel Murrie. **Assistant Coaches:** Mike McLaury, Dan Mosier. **Telephone:** (270) 745-6496. ■ **Baseball SID:** Aaron Ames. **Telephone:** (270) 745-4298. **FAX:** (270) 745-3444.

Home Field: Nick Denes Field. **Seating Capacity:** 1,050. **Outfield Dimensions:** LF—330, CF—400, RF—330. **Press Box Telephone:** (270) 745-6941/6456.

WESTERN MICHIGAN Broncos

Conference: Mid-American (West).

Mailing Address: 218 Read Field House, Kalamazoo, MI 49008. **Website**: www.wmubroncos.com.

Head Coach: Fred Decker. **Assistant Coaches:** Mike Diaz, Mike Hodgins, *Ken Jones. **Telephone:** (616) 387-8149. ■ **Baseball SID:** Daniel Jankowski. **Telephone:** (616) 387-4122. **FAX:** (616) 387-4139.

WICHITA STATE Shockers

Conference: Missouri Valley.

Mailing Address: 1845 Fairmount St., Campus Box 18, Wichita, KS 67260. **Website:** www.goshockers.com.

Head Coach: Gene Stephenson. **Assistant Coaches:** *Brent Kemnitz, Matt Patrick, Jim Thomas. **Telephone:** (316) 978-3636. ■ **Baseball SID:** Tami Capek. **Telephone:** (316) 978-5559. **FAX:** (316) 978-3336.

Home Field: Tyler Field-Eck Stadium. **Seating Capacity:** 7,851. **Outfield Dimensions:** LF—330, CF—390, RF—330. **Press Box Telephone:** (316) 978-3390.

WILLIAM & MARY Tribe

Conference: Colonial Athletic.

Mailing Address: P.O. Box 399, Williamsburg, VA 23188. **Website:** www.tribeathletics.com.

Head Coach: Jim Farr. **Assistant Coaches:** Jason Aquilante, *Ryan Wheeler. **Telephone:** (757) 221-3399. ■ **Baseball SID**: Chris Poore. **Telephone:** (757) 221-3370. **FAX:** (757) 221-3412.

Home Field: Plumeri Park. **Seating Capacity:** 1,000. **Outfield Dimensions:** LF—320, CF—400, RF—320. **Press Box Telephone:** (757) 221-3562.

WINTHROP Eagles

Conference: Big South.

Mailing Address: Winthrop Coliseum, Rock Hill, SC 29733. **Website:** www.winthropeagles.com.

Head Coach: Joe Hudak. **Assistant Coaches:** Chris Cook, Scott Forbes, *Jeremy Keller. **Telephone:** (803) 323-2129, ext. 6235. ■ **Baseball SID:** John Verser. **Telephone:** (803) 323-2129, ext. 6245. **FAX:** (803) 323-2433.

Home Field: Winthrop Ballpark. **Seating Capacity:** 2,000. **Outfield Dimensions:** LF—325, CF—390, RF—325. **Press Box Telephone:** (803) 323-2114/2155.

WISCONSIN-MILWAUKEE Panthers

Conference: Horizon.

Mailing Address: Athletic Dept., North Bldg., P.O. Box 413, Milwaukee, WI 53201. **Website:** www.uwmpanthers.com.

Head Coach: Jerry Augustine. **Assistant Coach:** Scott Doffek. **Telephone:** (414) 229-5670. ■ **Baseball SID:** Kevin O'Connor. **Telephone:** (414) 229-5674. **FAX:** (414) 229-6759.

WOFFORD Terriers

Conference: Southern.

Mailing Address: 429 N. Church St., Spartanburg, SC 29303. **Website:** www.wofford.edu/athletics.

Head Coach: Steve Traylor. **Assistant Coaches:** Scott Brickman, *Brandon McKillop. **Telephone:** (864) 597-4126. ■ **Baseball SID:** Mark Cohen. **Telephone:** (864) 597-4093. **FAX:** (864) 597-4129.

WRIGHT STATE Raiders

Conference: Horizon.

Mailing Address: 3640 Col. Glenn Hwy., Dayton, OH 45435. **Website:** www.wsuraiders.com.

Head Coach: Ron Nischwitz. **Assistant Coaches:** *Bo Bilinski, Jake Long. **Telephone:** (937) 775-2771. ■ **Baseball SID:** Matt Zircher. **Telephone:** (937) 775-2816. **FAX:** (937) 775-2818.

XAVIER Musketeers

Conference: Atlantic-10 (West).

Mailing Address: 3800 Victory Pkwy., Cincinnati, OH 45207. **Website:** athletics.xavier.edu.

Head Coach: John Morrey. **Assistant Coaches:** J.D. Heilmann, *Joe Regruth. **Telephone:** (513) 745-2890. ■ **Baseball SID:** Bill Thomas. **Telephone:** (513) 745-3416. **FAX:** (513) 745-2825.

YALE Bulldogs

Conference: Ivy League (Rolfe).

Mailing Address: P.O. Box 208216, New Haven, CT 06520. **Website:** www.yale.edu/athletics.

Head Coach: John Stuper. **Assistant Coaches:** Bill Asermely, Glenn Lungarini. **Telephone:** (203) 432-1466. ■ **Baseball SID:** Michelle Whyte. **Telephone:** (203) 432-1457. **FAX:** (203) 432-1454.

YOUNGSTOWN STATE Penguins

Conference: Horizon.

Mailing Address: One University Plaza, Youngstown, OH 44555. **Website:** www.ysu.edu/sports

Head Coach: *Mike Florak. **Assistant Coaches:** Craig Antush, *Dan Stricko, Mark Thomas. **Telephone:** (330) 941-3485. ■ **Baseball SID:** John Vogel. **Telephone:** (330) 941-3192. **FAX:** (330) 941-3191.

Home Field: Cofaro Field. **Seating Capacity:** 6,500. **Outfield Dimensions:** LF—335, CF—405, RF—335. **Press Box Telephone:** (330) 505-0000, ext. 229.

SMALL COLLEGES

NCAA DIVISION II • NCAA DIVISION III • NAIA

School	Mailing Address	Head Coach	Telephone
Abilene Christian U.	ACU Box 27916, Abilene, TX 79699	Britt Bonneau	(915) 674-2325
Adelphi U.	South Ave., Garden City, NY 11530	Ron Davies	(516) 877-4240
Adrian College	110 S. Madison St., Adrian, MI 49221	Craig Rainey	(517) 264-3977
Alabama-Huntsville, U. of	205 Spragins Hall, Huntsville, AL 35899	David Keel	(256) 824-2206
Albany State U.	504 College Dr., Albany, GA 31705	Edward Taylor	(229) 430-1829
Albertson College	2112 Cleveland Blvd., Caldwell, ID 83605	Shawn Humberger	(208) 459-5862
Albertus Magnus College	700 Prospect St., New Haven, CT 06511	Joe Tonelli	(203) 773-8578
Albion College	4830 Kellogg Center, Albion, MI 49224	Jim Conway	(517) 629-0500
Albright College	P.O. Box 15234, Reading, PA 19612	Jeff Feiler	(610) 921-7828
Alderson-Broaddus Coll.	Campus Box 2062, Philippi, WV 26416	Brian Sutphin	(304) 457-6265
Alice Lloyd College	100 Purpose Rd., Pippa Passes, KY 41844	Scott Cornett	(606) 368-6121
Allegheny College	P.O. Box AC, Meadville, PA 16335	Mike Ferris	(814) 332-2830
Allen U.	1530 Harden St., Columbia, SC 29204	Bob Smith	(803) 376-5770
Alma College	614 W. Superior St., Alma, MI 48801	John Leister	(517) 463-7276
Alvernia College	400 Saint Bernardine St., Reading, PA 19607	Yogi Lutz	(610) 796-8476
American Int'l Coll.	1000 State St., Springfield, MA 01109	Chuck Lelas	(413) 205-3574
Amherst College	P.O. Box 5000, Amherst, MA 01002	Bill Thurston	(413) 542-2284
Anderson College	316 Boulevard St., Anderson, SC 29621	Joe Miller	(864) 231-2013
Anderson U.	1100 E. 5th St., Anderson, IN 46012	Don Brandon	(765) 641-4488
Anna Maria College	Sunset Lane, Paxton, MA 01612	Rich Coleman	(508) 849-3446
Aquinas College	1607 Robinson Rd. SE, Grand Rapids, MI 49506	Doug Greenslate	(616) 459-8281
Arcadia University	450 S. Easton Rd., Glenside, PA 19038	Stan Exeter	(215) 572-2976
Arkansas Tech	1604 Coliseum Dr., Russellville, AR 72801	Billy Goss	(479) 968-0648
Arkansas-Monticello, U. of	UAM Box 3066, Monticello, AR 71656	Kevin Downing	(870) 460-1257
Armstrong Atlantic State U.	11935 Abercorn St., Savannah, GA 31419	Joe Roberts	(912) 921-5686
Asbury College	1 Macklem Dr., Wilmore, KY 40390	Joe Reed	(859) 858-3511
Ashland U.	401 College Ave., Ashland, OH 44805	John Schaly	(419) 289-5444
Assumption College	500 Salisbury St., Worcester, MA 01609	Jim Vail	(508) 767-7232
Atlanta Christian College	2605 Ben Hill Rd., East Point, GA 30344	Alan Wilson	(404) 761-8861
Auburn U.-Montgomery	7300 University Dr., Montgomery, AL 36117	Q.V. Lowe	(334) 244-3237
Augsburg College	2211 Riverside Ave., Minneapolis, MN 55454	Doug Schildgen	(612) 330-1395
Augusta State U.	2500 Walton Way #10, Augusta, GA 30904	Stanley Fite	(706) 731-7917
Augustana College	3500 5th Ave., Rock Island, IL 61201	Greg Wallace	(309) 794-7527
Augustana College	2001 S. Summit Ave, Sioux Falls, SD 57197	Jeff Holm	(605) 274-5541
Aurora U.	347 S. Gladstone Ave, Aurora, IL 60506	Shaun Neitzel	(630) 844-6515
Austin College	900 N. Grand Ave, Suite 6A, Sherman, TX 75090	Bruce Mauppin	(903) 813-2516
Averett University	420 W. Main St., Danville, VA 24541	Ed Fulton	(434) 791-5030
Avila College	11901 Wornall Rd., Kansas City, MO 64145	Ryan Howard	(816) 501-3739
Azusa Pacific U.	901 E. Alosta Ave., Azusa, CA 91702	Paul Svagdis	(626) 815-6000
Babson College	Webster Center, Babson Park, MA 02457	Frank Millerick	(781) 239-4528
Bacone College	2299 Old Bacone Rd., Muskogee, OK 74403	Matt Cloud	(918) 781-7237
Baker U.	P.O. Box 65, Baldwin City, KS 66006	Phil Hannon	(785) 594-8493
Baldwin-Wallace College	275 Eastland Rd., Berea, OH 44017	Bob Fisher	(440) 826-2182
Barry U.	11300 NE 2nd Ave., Miami, FL 33161	Juan Ranero	(305) 899-3558
Barton College	401 Rountree St., Wilson, NC 27893	Todd Wilkinson	(252) 399-6552
Baruch College	One Bernard Baruch Way, New York, NY 10010	Basil Tarasko	(616) 312-5040
Bates College	130 Central Ave., Lewiston, ME 04240	Craig Vandersea	(207) 786-6063
Becker College	964 Main St., Leicester, MA 01524	Walter Beede	(508) 791-9241
Belhaven College	1500 Peachtree St., Jackson, MS 39202	Hill Denson	(601) 968-8898
Bellarmine College	2001 Newburg Rd., Louisville, KY 40205	Scott Wiegandt	(502) 452-8496
Bellevue U.	1000 Galvin Rd. S., Bellevue, NE 68005	Mike Evans	(402) 293-3782
Belmont Abbey College	100 Belmont-Mount Holly Rd., Belmont, NC 28012	Kermit Smith	(704) 825-6804
Beloit College	700 College St., Beloit, WI 53511	Dave DeGeorge	(608) 363-2039
Bemidji State U.	1500 Birchmont Dr. NE, Bemidji, MN 56601	Chris Brown	(218) 755-2958
Benedict College	1600 Harden St., Columbia, SC 29204	Yancy King	(803) 253-5075
Benedictine College	1020 N. 2nd St., Atchison, KS 66002	Dan Griggs	(913) 367-5340
Benedictine U.	5700 College Rd., Lisle, IL 60532	John Ostrowski	(630) 829-6147
Bentley College	175 Forest St., Waltham, MA 02452	Bob DeFelice	(781) 891-2332
Berea College	CPO 2187, Berea, KY 40404	Ryan Hess/Todd Morris	(859) 985-3429
Berry College	P.O. Box 172, Mount Berry, GA 30149	David Beasley	(706) 236-1743
Bethany College	Hummel Fieldhouse, Bethany, WV 26032	Rick Carver	(304) 829-7246
Bethany College	800 Bethany Dr., Scotts Valley, CA 95066	Giuseppe Chiaramonte	(831) 438-3800

Bethel College	1001 McKinley Ave, Mishawaka, IN 46545	Mike Hutcheon	(574) 257-3287
Bethel College	3900 Bethel Dr., St. Paul, MN 55112	Ken Neuhaus	(651) 638-6143
Bethel College	325 Cherry St., McKenzie, TN 38201	Glenn Hayes	(731) 352-4206
Biola U.	13800 Biola Ave, La Mirada, CA 90639	John Verhoeven	(562) 944-0351
Blackburn College	700 College Ave., Carlinville, IL 62626	Mike Neal	(217) 854-3231
Bloomfield College	467 Franklin St., Bloomfield, NJ 07003	Matt Belford	(973) 748-9000
Bloomsburg U.	400 E. 2nd St., Bloomsburg, PA 17815	Matt Haney	(570) 389-4375
Bluefield College	3000 College Dr., Bluefield, VA 24605	Greg Stewart	(276) 326-4477
Bluefield State College	219 Rock St., Bluefield, WV 24701	Geoff Hunter	(304) 327-4084
Bluffton College	280 West College Ave, Bluffton, OH 45817	Greg Brooks	(419) 358-3225
Bowdoin College	9000 College Station, Brunswick, ME 04011	Michael Connolly	(207) 725-3734
Brandeis U.	415 South St., Waltham, MA 02454	Pete Varney	(781) 736-3639
Brescia U.	717 Frederica St., Owensboro, KY 42301	Jason Vittone	(270) 686-4207
Brevard College	400 N. Broad St., Brevard, NC 28712	Gil Payne	(828) 884-8273
Brewton Parker College	Hwy. 280, Mt. Vernon, GA 30445	Chad Parker	(912) 583-3274
Briar Cliff College	P.O. Box 2100, Sioux City, IA 51104	Boyd Pitkin	(712) 279-5553
Bridgeport, U. of	120 Waldemere Ave., Bridgeport, CT 06601	Dick Jeynes	(203) 576-4229
Bridgewater College	402 E. College St., Bridgewater, VA 22812	Curt Kendall	(540) 828-5407
Bridgewater State College	Room 200, Bridgewater, MA 02325	Rick Smith	(508) 531-1352
British Columbia, U. of	6081 University Blvd., Vancouver, B.C. V6T 1Z1	Terry McKaig	(604) 822-4720
Bryant College	1150 Douglas Pike, Smithfield, RI 02917	Jon Sjogren	(401) 232-6397
Buena Vista U.	610 West 4th St., Storm Lake, IA 50588	Steve Eddie	(712) 749-2253
C.W. Post/Long Island U.	720 Northern Blvd., Brookville, NY 11548	Dick Vining	(718) 423-2913
Caldwell College	9 Ryerson Ave., Caldwell, NJ 07006	Chris Reardon	(973) 618-3462
UC Davis	One Shields Ave., Davis, CA 95616	Rex Peters	(530) 752-7513
UC San Diego	9500 Gilman Dr., La Jolla, CA 92093	Dan O'Brien	(858) 534-4211
Cal Poly Pomona	3801 West Temple Ave., Pomona, CA 91768	Mike Ashman	(909) 869-2829
Cal State Chico	1st & Orange Sts., Chico, CA 95929	Lindsay Meggs	(530) 898-4374
Cal State Dominguez Hills	1000 E. Victoria St., Carson, CA 90747	George Wing	(310) 243-3765
Cal State Hayward	25800 Carlos Bee Blvd., Hayward, CA 94542	Dirk Morrison	(510) 885-3046
Cal State Los Angeles	5151 State University Dr., Los Angeles, CA 90032	John Herbold	(323) 343-3093
Cal State San Bernardino	5500 University Pwy., San Bernardino, CA 92407	Don Parnell	(909) 880-5021
Cal State Stanislaus	801 W. Monte Vista Ave., Turlock, CA 95382	Kenny Leonesio	(209) 667-3272
Cal Tech	1201 E. California Blvd., Pasadena, CA 91125	John D'Auria	(626) 395-3263
California Baptist U.	8432 Magnolia Ave., Riverside, CA 92504	Paul Kumamoto	(909) 343-4382
California Lutheran U.	60 W. Olsen Rd., Thousand Oaks, CA 91360	Marty Slimak	(805) 493-3398
California U. (Pa.)	250 University Ave., California, PA 15419	Mike Conte	(724) 938-5837
Calvin College	3201 Burton St. SE, Grand Rapids, MI 49546	Jeff Pettinga	(616) 957-6021
Cameron U.	2800 West Gore Blvd., Lawton, OK 73505	Ron Ihler	(580) 581-2479
Campbellsville U.	One University Dr., Campbellsville, KY 42718	Beauford Sanders	(270) 789-5056
Capital U.	2199 E. Main St., Columbus, OH 43209	Steve Shoemaker	(614) 236-6203
Cardinal Stritch U.	6801 N. Yates Rd., Milwaukee, WI 53217	Joseph Zolecki	(414) 410-4519
Carleton College	1 N. College St., Northfield, MN 55057	Bill Nelson	(507) 646-4051
Carroll College	100 N. East Ave, Waukesha, WI 53186	Stephen Dannhoff	(262) 524-7105
Carson-Newman College	P.O. Box 72009, Jefferson City, TN 37760	Brent Achord	(865) 471-3465
Carthage College	2001 Alford Park Dr., Kenosha, WI 53140	Augie Schmidt	(262) 551-5935
Case Western Reserve U.	10900 Euclid Ave., Cleveland, OH 44106	Jerry Seimon	(216) 368-5379
Castleton State College	Glennbrook Rd., Castleton, VT 05735	Ted Shipley	(802) 468-1491
Catawba College	2300 W. Innes St., Salisbury, NC 28144	Jim Gantt	(704) 637-4469
Catholic U.	3606 McCormack Rd. NE, Washington, DC 20064	Ross Natoli	(202) 319-6092
Cazenovia College	Liberty Street, Cazenovia, NY 13035	Peter Liddell	(315) 655-7141
Cedarville U.	251 N. Main St., Cedarville, OH 45314	Greg Hughes	(937) 766-3246
Centenary College	400 Jefferson St., Hackettstown, NJ 07840	Dave Swaicki	(908) 852-1400
Central Arkansas, U. of	314 Western Ave., Conway, AR 72032	Willie Gawlik	(501) 450-3407
Central Christian College	P.O. Box 1403, McPherson, KS 67460	Jared Hamilton	(620) 241-0723
Central College	812 University St., Pella, IA 50219	Matt Ballou/Dave Baker	(641) 628-5226
Central Methodist College	411 CMC Square, Fayette, MO 65248	Jim Dapkus	(660) 248-6352
Central Missouri State U.	500 Washington St., Warrensburg, MO 64093	Brad Hill	(660) 543-4800
Central Oklahoma, U. of	100 N. University Dr., Edmond, OK 73034	Wendell Simmons	(405) 974-2506
Central Washington U.	400 E. 8th Ave., Ellensburg, WA 98926	Desi Storey	(509) 963-3018
Centre College	600 W. Walnut St., Danville, KY 40422	Ed Rall	(859) 238-5489
Chapman U.	One University Dr., Orange, CA 92866	Tom Tereschuk	(714) 997-6662
Charleston, U. of	2300 MacCorkle Ave. SE, Charleston, WV 25304	Tom Nozica	(304) 357-4823
Chicago, U. of	5734-A S. University Ave., Chicago, IL 60637	Brian Baldea	(773) 702-4643
Chowan College	200 Jones Dr., Murfreesboro, NC 27855	Steve Flack	(252) 398-6228
Christian Brothers U.	650 E. Parkway South, Memphis, TN 38104	Phil Goodwin	(901) 321-3375
Christopher Newport U.	1 University Place, Newport News, VA 23606	John Harvell	(757) 594-7054
Circleville Bible Coll.	1476 Lancaster Pike, Circleville, OH 43113	Larry Olson	(740) 477-7761
Claremont-Mudd-Scripps Coll	500 E. 9th St., Claremont, CA 91711	Randy Town	(909) 607-3796
Clarion U.	238 Tippin Gym, Clarion, PA 16214	Scott Feldman	(814) 393-1651
Clark Atlanta U.	223 Brawley Dr., Atlanta, GA 30314	Antonio Grissom	(404) 880-8123

Clark U.	950 Main St., Worcester, MA 01610	Jason Falcon	(508) 793-7729
Clarke College	1550 Clarke Dr., Dubuque, IA 52001	Eric Frese	(563) 588-6601
Clarkson U.	Box 5830, Alumni Gym, Potsdam, NY 13699	Jim Kane	(315) 268-3759
Clearwater Christian	3400 Gulf-to-Bay Blvd., Clearwater, FL 33759	Mark Bates	(727) 726-1153
Coe College	1220 First Ave. NE, Cedar Rapids, IA 52402	Steve Cook	(319) 399-8849
Coker College	300 E. College Ave., Hartsville, SC 29550	Dave Schmotzer	(843) 383-8105
Colby College	4900 Mayflower Hill, Waterville, ME 04901	Tom Dexter	(207) 872-3369
Colby-Sawyer College	100 Main St., New London, NH 03257	Jim Broughton	(603) 526-3607
Colorado School of Mines	1500 Illinois St., Golden, CO 80401	Mike Mulvaney	(303) 273-3367
Columbia Union College	7600 Flower Ave., Takoma Park, MD 20912	Brad Durby	(301) 891-4481
Columbus State U.	4225 University Ave., Columbus, GA 31907	Greg Appleton	(706) 568-2444
Concord College	Campus Box 77, Athens, WV 24712	Kevin Garrett	(304) 384-5340
Concordia College (Ala.)	1804 Green St., Selma, AL 36703	Frank Elliott	(334) 874-7143
Concordia College (Minn.)	901 8th Street S., Moorhead, MN 56562	Don Burgau	(218) 299-3209
Concordia College (N.Y.)	171 White Plains Rd., Bronxville, NY 10708	Bob Greiner	(914) 337-9300
Concordia U. (Calif.)	1530 Concordia West, Irvine, CA 92612	Shannon Blansette	(949) 854-8002
Concordia U. (Ill.)	7400 Augusta St., River Forest, IL 60305	Spiro Lempesis	(708) 209-3125
Concordia U. (Mich.)	4090 Geddes Rd., Ann Arbor, MI 48105	Tim Taylor	(734) 995-7579
Concordia U. (Minn.)	275 Syndicate St. N., St. Paul, MN 55104	Mark McKenzie	(651) 603-6208
Concordia U. (Neb.)	800 N. Columbia Ave, Seward, NE 68434	Jeremy Geidel	(402) 643-7233
Concordia U. (Ore.)	2811 NE Holman St., Portland, OR 97211	Rob Vance	(503) 280-8691
Concordia U. (Texas)	3400 I-35 North, Austin, TX 78705	Mike Gardner	(512) 452-7662
Concordia U. (Wis.)	12800 N. Lake Shore Dr., Mequon, WI 53097	Val Keiper	(262) 243-4266
Cornell College	600 1st Street W., Mount Vernon, IA 52314	Frank Fisher	(319) 895-4257
Cortland State	P.O. Box 2000, Cortland, NY 13045	Joe Brown	(607) 753-4950
Crown College	6425 County Road 30, St. Bonafacius, MN 55375	Kelly Spann	(952) 446-4146
Culver-Stockton College	One College Hill, Canton, MO 63435	Doug Bletcher	(217) 231-6374
Cumberland College	7028 College Station Dr., Williamsburg, KY 40769	Brad Shelton	(606) 539-4387
Cumberland U.	One Cumberland Sq., Lebanon, TN 37087	Woody Hunt	(615) 444-2562
Curry College	1071 Blue Hill Ave., Miller Gym, Milton, MA 02186	Dave Perdios	(617) 333-2055
D'Youville College	320 Porter Ave., Buffalo, NY 14201	Mike Webster	(716) 984-7676
Dakota State U.	820 N. Washington Ave, Madison, SD 57042	Pat Dolan	(605) 256-5232
Dakota Wesleyan U.	1200 W. University Ave, Mitchell, SD 57301	Adam Neisius	(605) 995-2853
Dallas Baptist U.	3000 Mountain Creek Pkwy., Dallas, TX 75211	Mike Bard	(214) 333-5326
Dallas, U. of	1845 E. Northgate Dr., Irving, TX 75062	Sam Blackmon	(972) 721-5117
Dana College	2848 College Dr., Blair, NE 68008	Damon Day	(402) 426-7374
Daniel Webster College	20 University Dr., Nashua, NH 03063	Brian Aloia	(603) 577-6491
Davis & Elkins College	100 Campus Dr., Elkins, WV 26241	Ryan Brisbin	(304) 637-1342
Defiance College	701 N. Clinton St., Defiance, OH 43512	Chad Donsbach	(419) 783-2341
Delaware Valley College	700 E. Butler Ave., Doylestown, PA 18901	Bob Altieri	(215) 489-2379
Delta State U.	P.O. Box 3161, Cleveland, MS 38733	Mike Kinnison	(662) 846-4291
Denison U.	100 Livingston Ave., Granville, OH 43023	Barry Craddock	(740) 587-6714
De Pauw U.	702 S. College St., Greencastle, IN 46135	Matt Walker	(765) 658-4939
DeSales U.	2755 Station Ave., Center Valley, PA 18034	Tim Nieman	(610) 282-1100
Dickinson College	P.O. Box 1773, High Street, Carlisle, PA 17013	Todd Melisaukas	(717) 245-1320
Dickinson State U.	291 Campus Dr., Dickinson, ND 58601	Duane Monlux	(701) 483-2735
Doane College	1014 Boswell Ave., Crete, NE 68333	Jack Hudkins	(402) 826-8204
Dominican College	470 Western Hwy., Orangeburg, NY 10962	Rick Giannetti	(845) 398-3008
Dominican U.	7900 W. Division St., River Forest, IL 60305	Tom Uraski	(708) 524-6542
Dordt College	498 4th Ave. NE, Sioux Center, IA 51250	Tom Visker	(712) 722-6232
Dowling College	150 Idle Hour Blvd., Oakdale, NY 11769	Carmen Carcone	(631) 244-3229
Drew U.	36 Madison Ave., Madison, NJ 07940	Vince Masco	(973) 408-3443
Dubuque, U. of	2000 University Ave., Dubuque, IA 52001	Dennis Rima	(563) 589-3229
Earlham College	801 National Rd. W., Richmond, IN 47374	Tom Parkevich	(765) 983-1237
East Central U.	1100 East 14th St., Ada, OK 74820	Ron Hill	(580) 436-4940
East Stroudsburg U.	Smith & Normal Streets, East Stroudsburg, PA 18301	Roger Barren	(570) 422-3263
East Texas Baptist U.	1209 N. Grove St., Marshall TX 75670	Robert Riggs	(903) 935-7963
Eastern U.	1300 Eagle Rd., St. Davids, PA 19087	Don Hare	(610) 341-1735
Eastern Connecticut State U.	83 Windham St., Willimantic, CT 06226	Bill Holowaty	(860) 465-5185
Eastern Mennonite U.	1200 Park Rd., Harrisonburg, VA 22802	Rob Roeschley	(540) 432-4333
Eastern Nazarene College	23 East Elm Ave., Quincy, MA 02170	Todd Reid	(617) 745-3648
Eastern New Mexico U.	Greyhound Arena, Station 17, Portales, NM 88130	Phil Clabaugh	(505) 562-2889
Eastern Oregon U.	One University Blvd., La Grande, OR 97850	Wes McAllaster	(541) 962-3110
Eckerd College	4200 54th Ave. S., St. Petersburg, FL 33711	Bill Mathews	(727) 864-8253
Edgewood College	1000 Edgewood College Dr., Madison, WI 53711	Al Brisack	(608) 663-3289
Edinboro U.	McComb Fieldhouse, Edinboro, PA 16444	Mitch House	(814) 732-2776
Edward Waters College	1658 Kings Rd., Jacksonville, FL 32209	Carl Burden	(904) 366-2796
Elizabeth City State U.	1704 Weeksville Rd., Elizabeth City, NC 27909	Terrance Whittle	(252) 335-3392
Elizabethtown College	One Alpha Dr., Elizabethtown, PA 17022	Matt Jones	(717) 361-1463
Elmhurst College	190 Prospect Ave., Elmhurst, IL 60126	Clark Jones	(630) 617-3143

Embry-Riddle U.	600 S. Clyde Morris Blvd., Daytona Beach, FL 32114	Greg Guilliams	(386) 323-5010
Emerson College of Art	100 Boylston St., Boston, MA 02116	Michael Burns	(617) 824-8122
Emmanuel College	P.O. Box 129, Franklin Springs, GA 30639	Robbie Jones	(706) 245-9721
Emory & Henry College	King Athletic Center, Emory, VA 24327	Dewey Lusk	(276) 944-6855
Emory U.	600 Asbury Circle, Atlanta, GA 30322	Mike Twardoski	(404) 727-0877
Emporia State U.	12th & Commercial Streets, Emporia, KS 66801	Brian Embery	(620) 341-5930
Endicott College	376 Hale St., Beverly, MA 01915	Larry Hiser	(978) 232-2304
Erskine College	2 Washington St., Due West, SC 29639	Kevin Nichols	(864) 379-8777
Eureka College	300 E. College Ave., Eureka, IL 61530	Airren Nylin	(309) 467-6376
Evangel U.	1111 North Glenstone Ave, Springfield, MO 65802	Al Poland	(417) 865-2815
Fairleigh Dickinson U.-Madison	285 Madison Ave., M130A, Madison, NJ 37940	Doug Radziewicz	(973) 443-8826
Fairmont State College	1201 Locust Ave., Fairmont, WV 26554	Ray Bonnett	(304) 367-4220
Faulkner U.	5345 Old Atlanta Hwy., Montgomery, AL 36109	Brent Barker	(334) 386-7318
Felician College	262 S. Main St., Lodi, NJ 07644	Steve Svenson	(201) 559-3509
Ferrum College	P.O. Box 1000, Route 40 W., Ferrum, VA 24088	Abe Naff	(540) 365-4488
Findlay, U. of	1000 N. Main St., Findlay, OH 45840	Jim Givens	(419) 434-4793
Fisk U.	17 Avenue N., Nashville, TN 37208	Phillip Kimbro	(615) 329-8782
Fitchburg State College	160 Pearl St., Fitchburg, MA 01420	Pete Egbert	(978) 665-4681
Flagler College	74 King St., St. Augustine, FL 32084	Dave Barnett	(904) 829-6481
Florida Gulf Coast U.	10501 FGCU Blvd., South, Fort Myers, FL 33965	Dave Tollett	(941) 590-7051
Florida Memorial College	15800 NW 42nd Ave., Opa Locka, FL 33054	Robert Smith	(305) 626-3690
Florida Southern College	111 Lake Hollingsworth Dr., Lakeland, FL 33801	Pete Meyer	(863) 680-4264
Florida Tech	150 W. University Blvd., Melbourne, FL 32901	Paul Knight	(321) 674-8193
Fontbonne College	6800 Wydown St., St. Louis, MO 63105	Scott Cooper	(314) 719-8064
Fort Hays State U.	600 Park St., Hays, KS 67601	Bob Fornelli	(785) 628-4357
Framingham State College	100 State St., Framingham, MA 01701	Mike Sarno	(508) 626-4566
Francis Marion U.	P.O. Box 100547, Florence, SC 29501	Art Inabinet	(843) 661-1242
Franklin & Marshall College	P.O. Box 3003, College Ave., Lancaster, PA 17608	Brett Boretti	(717) 399-4530
Franklin College	501 E. Monroe St., Franklin, IN 46131	Lance Marshall	(317) 738-8136
Franklin Pierce College	P.O. Box 60, Rindge, NH 03461	Jayson King	(603) 899-4084
Fredonia State U.	Dods Hall, Fredonia, NY 14063	Matt Palisin	(716) 673-3743
Freed-Hardeman U.	158 E. Main St., Henderson, TN 38340	Chuck Box	(731) 989-6904
Friends U.	2100 W. University St., Wichita, KS 67213	Mark Carvalho	(316) 295-5769
Frostburg State U.	101 Braddock Rd, Frostburg, MD 21532	Chris McKnight	(301) 687-4273
Gallaudet U.	800 Florida Ave. NE, Washington, DC 20002	Kris Gould	(202) 651-5603
Gannon U.	109 University Square, Erie, PA 16541	Rick Iacobucci	(814) 871-5846
Geneva College	3200 College Ave., Beaver Falls, PA 15010	Alan Sumner	(724) 847-6647
George Fox U.	414 N. Meridian St., Newberg, OR 97132	Pat Bailey	(503) 554-2914
Georgetown College	400 E. College St., Georgetown, KY 40324	Jim Hinerman	(502) 863-8207
Georgia College & State U.	Campus Box 65, Milledgeville, GA 31061	Steve Mrowka	(478) 445-5319
Georgia Southwestern	800 Wheatley St., Americus, GA 31709	Barry Davis	(229) 931-2220
Gettysburg College	300 N. Washington St, Gettysburg, PA 17325	John Campo	(717) 337-6413
Gordon College	255 Grapevine Rd., Wenham, MA 01984	Bob Dickerman	(978) 927-2306
Goshen College	1700 S. Main St., Goshen, IN 46526	Brent Hoober	(574) 535-7495
Grace College	200 Seminary Dr., Winona Lake, IN 46590	Dennis Boyd	(574) 372-5719
Graceland U.	One University Pl., Lamoni, IA 50140	Brady McKillip	(515) 784-5351
Grand Canyon U.	P.O. Box 11097, Phoenix, AZ 85017	Dave Stapleton	(602) 589-2817
Grand Valley State U.	1 Campus Dr., Allendale, MI 49401	Steve Lyon	(616) 895-3584
Grand View College	1200 Grandview Ave., Des Moines, IA 50316	Lou Yacinich	(515) 263-2897
Greensboro College	815 W. Market St., Greensboro, NC 27401	Ken Carlyle	(336) 272-7102
Greenville College	P.O. Box 159, Greenville, IL 62246	Lynn Carlson	(618) 664-6623
Grinnell College	P.O. Box 805, Grinnell, IA 50112	Tim Hollibaugh	(641) 269-3822
Grove City College	100 Campus Dr., Grove City, PA 16127	Rob Skaricich	(724) 458-3836
Guilford College	5800 W. Friendly Ave., Greensboro, NC 27410	Gene Baker	(336) 316-2161
Gustavus Adolphus College	800 W. College Ave., St. Peter, MN 56082	Mike Carroll	(507) 933-6297
Gwynedd Mercy College	1325 Sumneytown Pike, Gwynedd Valley, PA 19437	Paul Murphy	(215) 646-7300
Hamilton College	198 College Hill Rd., Clinton, NY 13323	John Keady	(315) 859-4763
Hamline U.	1536 Hewitt Ave., St. Paul, MN 55104	Jason Verdugo	(651) 523-2035
Hampden-Sydney College	Kirby Field House, Hampden-Sydney, VA 23943	Todd Lampman	(434) 223-6981
Hannibal-LaGrange College	2800 Palmyra Rd., Hannibal, MO 63401	Scott Ashton	(573) 221-3675
Hanover College	P.O. Box 108, Hanover, IN 47243	Dick Naylor	(812) 866-7374
Hardin-Simmons U.	2200 Hickory Rd., Abilene, TX 79698	Steve Coleman	(915) 670-1493
Harding U.	Box 12281, Searcy, AR 72149	Shane Fullerton	(501) 279-4344
Harris-Stowe State College	3026 Laclede Ave., St. Louis, MO 63103	Tony Dattoli	(314) 340-3530
Hartwick College	Binder PE Center, Oneonta, NY 13820	Barry Shelton	(607) 431-4706
Hastings College	7th & Turner, Hastings, NE 68902	Jim Boeve	(402) 461-7468
Haverford College	370 Lancaster Ave., Haverford, PA 19041	Dave Beccaria	(610) 896-1172
Hawaii Pacific U.	1060 Bishop St., Honolulu, HI 96813	Allan Sato	(808) 543-8021
Heidelberg College	310 E. Market St., Tiffin, OH 44883	Matt Palm	(419) 448-2009
Henderson State U.	P.O. Box 7630, Arkadelphia, AR 71999	Pete Southall	(870) 230-5071

Hendrix College	1600 Washington Ave., Conway, AR 72032	Greg Baxendale	(501) 450-3898
Hilbert College	5200 S. Park Ave, Hamburg, NY 14075	Matt Palisin	(716) 649-7900
Hillsdale College	201 Oak St., Hillsdale, MI 49242	Paul Noce	(517) 607-3146
Hillsdale Freewill Baptist	P.O. Box 6343, Moore, OK 73153	Tim Lisenbee	(330) 569-5348
Hiram College	P.O. Box 1777, Hiram, OH 44234	Howard Jenter	(330) 569-5348
Hope College	137 E. 12th St., Holland, MI 49422	Stuart Fritz	(616) 395-7692
Houston Baptist U.	7502 Fondren Rd., Houston, TX 77074	Brian Huddleston	(281) 649-3332
Howard Payne U.	508 2nd St., Brownwood, TX 76801	Mike Kennemer	(915) 649-8103
Huntingdon College	1500 E. Fairview Ave, Montgomery, AL 36106	Scot Patterson	(334) 833-4501
Huntington College	2303 College Ave., Huntington, IN 46750	Mike Frame	(219) 359-4082
Huron U.	333 9th Street SW, Huron, SD 57350	Dean Berry	(605) 352-8721
Husson College	1 College Circle, Bangor, ME 04401	John Kolasinski	(207) 941-7700
Huston-Tillotson College	900 Chicon St., Austin, TX 78702	Alvin Moore	(512) 505-3069
Illinois College	1101 W. College Ave., Jacksonville, IL 62650	Jay Eckhouse	(217) 245-3387
Illinois Tech	3300 S. Federal St., Chicago, IL 60616	Jim Darrah	(312) 567-3298
Illinois Wesleyan U.	P.O. Box 2900, Bloomington, IL 61702	Dennis Martel	(309) 556-3335
Incarnate Word, U. of the	4301 Broadway St., San Antonio, TX 78209	Danny Heep	(210) 829-3830
Indiana Tech	1600 E. Washington Blvd., Fort Wayne, IN 46803	Steve Devine	(260) 422-5561
Indiana U. (Pa.)	660 South 11th St., Indiana, PA 15705	Tom Kennedy	(724) 357-7830
Indiana U.-Southeast	4201 Grant Line Rd., New Albany, IN 47150	Rick Parr	(812) 941-2450
Indiana Wesleyan U.	4201 S. Washington St., Marion, IN 46953	Mark DeMichael	(765) 677-2324
Indianapolis, U. of	1400 E. Hanna Ave., Indianapolis, IN 46227	Gary Vaught	(317) 788-3414
Iowa Wesleyan College	601 N. Main St., Mount Pleasant, IA 52641	Todd Huckabone	(319) 385-6349
Ithaca College	Ceracche Athletics Center, Ithaca, NY 14850	George Valesente	(607) 274-3749
Jamestown College	P.O. Box 6088, Jamestown, ND 58405	Tom Hager	(701) 252-3467
Jarvis Christian College	P.O. Box G, Hawkins, TX 75765	Robert Thomas	(903) 769-5763
John Carroll U.	20700 N. Park Blvd., University Heights, OH 44118	Marc Thibeault	(216) 397-4660
John Jay College	899 10th Ave., New York, NY 10019	Rudy Piccinillo	(212) 237-8371
Johns Hopkins U.	3400 N. Charles St., Baltimore, MD 21218	Bob Babb	(410) 516-7485
Johnson & Wales U.	8 Abbott Park Pl., Providence, RI 02903	John LaRose	(401) 598-1609
Johnson Bible College	7900 Johnson Dr., Knoxville, TN 37998	Doug Karnes	(865) 251-2210
Judson College	1151 N. State St., Elgin, IL 60123	Shawn Summe	(847) 628-2523
Juniata College	1700 Moore St., Huntingdon, PA 16652	George Zanic	(814) 641-3515
Kalamazoo College	1200 Academy St., Kalamazoo, MI 49006	Steve Wideen	(616) 337-7287
Kansas Wesleyan U.	100 E. Claflin Ave, Salina, KS 67401	Tim Bellew	(785) 827-5541
Kean U.	1000 Morris Ave., Union, NJ 07083	Neil Ioviero	(908) 737-5452
Keene State College	229 Main St., Keene, NH 03435	Ken Howe	(603) 358-2809
Kennesaw State U.	1000 Chastain Rd. NW, Kennesaw, GA 30144	Mike Sansing	(770) 423-6264
Kentucky State U.	400 E. Main St., Frankfort, KY 40601	Elwood Johnson	(502) 597-6018
Kentucky Wesleyan College	P.O. Box 1039, Owensboro, KY 42302	Todd Lillpop	(270) 683-4795
Kenyon College	Athletic Dept., Duff Street, Gambier, OH 43022	Matt Burdette	(740) 427-5810
Keuka College	Weed Physical Arts Center, Keuka Park, NY 14478	Jeff Cleanthes	(315) 279-5687
King College	1350 King College Rd., Bristol, TN 37620	Craig Kleinmann	(423) 652-6017
King's College	133 N. River St., Wilkes-Barre, PA 18711	Jerry Greeley	(570) 208-5855
Knox College	2 E. South St., Galesburg, IL 61401	Jami Isaacson	(309) 341-7456
Knoxville College	901 College St., Knoxville, TN 37921	Gene Hill	(423) 524-6689
Kutztown U.	Keystone Hall, Kutztown, PA 19530	Chris Blum	(610) 683-4063
LaGrange College	601 Broad St., La Grange, GA 30240	Kevin Howard	(706) 880-8295
Lake Erie College	391 W. Washington St., Painesville, OH 44077	Jeff Davison	(440) 639-7958
Lakeland College	P.O. Box 359, Sheboygan, WI 53082	John Weber	(920) 565-1411
Lakewood College	P.O. Box 521, Lakewood, OH 44107	Richard Manning	
Lambuth U.	705 Lambuth Blvd., Jackson, TN 38301	Wayne Albury	(731) 425-3385
Lancaster Bible College	901 Eden Rd., Lancaster, PA 17601	Peter Beers	(717) 560-8267
Lander U.	320 Stanley Ave., Greenwood, SC 29649	Mike McGuire	(864) 388-8961
Lane College	545 Lane Ave., Jackson, TN 38301	Anthony Sawyer	(731) 426-7571
La Roche College	9000 Babcock Blvd., Pittsburgh, PA 15237	Rich Pasquaze	(412) 536-1046
La Verne, U. of	1950 3rd St., La Verne, CA 91750	Scott Winterburn	(909) 593-3511
Lawrence U.	1100 E. South River St., Appleton, WI 54912	Korey Krueger	(920) 832-7346
Lebanon Valley College	101 N. College Ave., Annville, PA	Jim Hoar	(717) 867-6260
Lee U.	1120 Ocoee St., Cleveland, TN 37311	Dave Altopp	(423) 614-8445
Lehman College	250 Bedford Park Blvd. W., Bronx, NY 10468	Kiko Reyes	(718) 960-7746
LeMoyne-Owen College	807 Walker Ave., Memphis, TN 38126	Willie Patterson	(901) 942-7325
Lenoir-Rhyne College	P.O. Box 7356, Hickory, NC 28603	Frank Pait	(828) 328-7136
LeTourneau U.	P.O. Box 7001, Longview, TX 75602	Robert Riggs	(903) 233-3372
Lewis & Clark College	0615 SW Palatine Hill Rd., Portland, OR 97219	Reed Rainey	(503) 768-7059
Lewis U.	One University Pkwy, Romeoville, IL 60446	Irish O'Reilly	(815) 836-5255
Lewis-Clark State College	500 8th Ave., Lewiston, ID 83501	Ed Cheff	(208) 792-2272
Limestone College	1115 College Dr., Gaffney, SC 29340	Anthony Lombardo	(864) 488-4565
Lincoln Christian College	100 Campus View Dr., Lincoln, IL 62656	Clint Mustain	(217) 732-3168

Lincoln Memorial U.	P.O. Box 2028, Harrogate, TN 37752	Eddie Graham	(423) 869-6345
Lincoln U.	820 Chestnut St., Jefferson City, MO 65102	Earl Wheeler	(573) 681-5334
Lincoln U.	P.O. Box 179, Lincoln University, PA 19352	Paul Johnson	(610) 932-8300
Lindenwood U.	209 S. Kings Highway, St. Charles, MO 63301	Tommy Broyles	(636) 949-4946
Lindsey Wilson College	210 Lindsey Wilson St., Columbia, KY 42728	Mike Talley	(270) 384-8074
Linfield College	900 SE Baker St., McMinnville, OR 97128	Scott Carnahan	(503) 434-2229
Lock Haven U.	Thomas Fieldhouse, Lock Haven, PA 17745	Smokey Stover	(570) 893-2245
Longwood College	201 High St., Farmville, VA 23909	Buddy Bolding	(434) 395-2352
Loras College	1450 Alta Vista St., Dubuque, IA 52004	Carl Tebon	(563) 588-7732
Louisiana College	1140 College Dr., Pineville, LA 71360	Mike Byrnes	(318) 487-7322
Loyola U.	6363 St. Charles Ave., New Orleans, LA 70118	Gregg Mucerino	(504) 864-7225
LSU-Shreveport	One University Place, Shreveport, LA 71115	Rocke Musgraves	(318) 798-4107
Lubbock Christian U.	5601 W. 19th St., Lubbock, TX 79407	Bobby Sherrard	(806) 720-7281
Luther College	700 College Dr., Decorah, IA 52101	Brian Gillogly	(563) 387-1590
Lynchburg College	1501 Lakeside Dr., Lynchburg, VA 24501	Percy Abell	(434) 544-8496
Lyndon State College	P.O. Box 919, Lyndonville, VT 05851	Skip Pound	(802) 626-6477
Lynn U.	3601 N. Military Trail, Boca Raton, FL 33431	Rudy Garbalosa	(561) 237-7242
Lyon College	2400 Highland Ave., Batesville, AR 72501	Kirk Kelley	(870) 698-4337
Macalester College	1600 Grand Ave., St. Paul, MN 55105	Matt Parrington	(651) 696-6774
Mac Murray College	447 E. College Ave, Jacksonville, IL 62650	Kevin Vest	(217) 479-7153
Madonna U.	36600 Schoolcraft Rd., Livonia, MI 48150	Greg Haeger	(734) 432-5609
Maine-Farmington, U. of	111 South St., Farmington, ME 04938	Richard Meader	(207) 778-7148
Maine-Presque Isle, U. of	181 Main St., Presque Isle, ME 04769	Leo Saucier	(207) 768-9421
Malone College	515 25th St. NW, Canton, OH 44709	Jay Martin	(330) 471-8286
Manchester College	604 E. College Ave., North Manchester, IN 46962	Rick Espeset	(260) 982-5390
Manhattanville College	2900 Purchase St., Purchase, NY 10577	Joe Ferraro	(914) 323-7284
Mansfield U.	Academy St., Mansfield, PA 16933	Harry Hillson	(570) 662-4457
Maranatha Baptist College	745 W. Main St., Watertown, WI 53094	Jerry Terrill	(920) 206-2380
Marian College	45 S. National Ave., Fond du Lac, WI 54935	Jason Bartelt	(920) 923-8090
Marian College	3200 Cold Spring Rd., Indianapolis, IN 46222	Kurt Guldner	(317) 955-6310
Marietta College	215 5th St., Marietta, OH 45750	Don Schaly	(740) 376-4673
Mars Hill College	100 Athletic St., Mars Hill, NC 28754	Daniel Taylor	(828) 689-1173
Martin Luther College	1995 Luther Court, New Ulm, MN 56073	Drew Buck	(507) 354-8221
Martin Methodist College	433 W. Madison St., Pulaski, TN 38478	Jeff Dodson	(931) 363-9827
Mary, U. of	7500 University Dr., Bismarck, ND 58504	Van Vanatta	(701) 255-7500
Mary Hardin-Baylor U.	UMHB Box 8010, 9th & College, Belton, TX 76513	Micah Wells	(254) 295-4619
Mary Washington College	Goolrick Gymnasium, Fredericksburg, VA 22401	Tom Sheridan	(540) 654-1882
Maryville College	502 E. Lamar Alexander Pkwy., Maryville, TN 37804	Eric Etchison	(865) 981-8283
Maryville U.-St. Louis	13550 Conway Rd., St. Louis, MO 63141	Tracy Schmidt	(314) 529-9483
Marywood U.	2300 Adams Ave., Scranton, PA 18509	Joe Ross	(570) 961-4724
Mass College of Liberal Arts	375 Church St., North Adams, MA 01247	Jeff Puleri	(413) 662-5403
Mass Institute of Technology	P.O. Box 397404, Cambridge, MA 02139	Mac Singleton	(617) 258-7310
Mass Maritime Academy	101 Academy Dr., Buzzards Bay, MA 02532	Bob Corradi	(508) 830-5055
Mass-Boston Harbor, U. of	100 Morrissey Blvd., Boston, MA 02125	Mark Bettencourt	(617) 287-7817
Mass-Dartmouth, U. of	285 Old Wesport Rd., North Dartmouth, MA 02747	Bruce Wheeler	(508) 999-8721
Mass-Lowell, U. of	1 University Ave, Costello Gym, Lowell, MA 01854	Jim Stone	(978) 934-2344
Master's College, The	21726 Placerita Canyon Rd., Santa Clarita, CA 91321	Monte Brooks	(661) 259-3540
Mayville State U.	330 3rd St. NE, Mayville, ND 58257	Scott Berry	(701) 786-2301
McDaniel College	2 College Hill, Westminster, MD 21157	David Seibert	(410) 857-2583
McKendree College	701 College Rd., Lebanon, IL 62254	Jim Boehne	(618) 537-6906
McMurry U.	South 14th St. & Sayles Blvd., Abilene, TX 79697	Lee Driggers	(951) 793-4650
Medaille College	18 Agassiz Circle, Buffalo, NY 14214	Jim Koernehead	(716) 884-3281
Menlo College	1000 El Camino Real, Atherton, CA 94027	Reggie Christiansen	(650) 543-3775
Mercy College	555 Broadway, Dobbs Ferry, NY 10522	Billy Sullivan	(914) 674-7566
Mercyhurst College	501 E. 38th St., Erie, PA 16546	Joe Spano	(814) 824-2441
Merrimack College	315 Turnpike St., North Andover, MA 01845	Barry Rosen	(978) 837-5000
Mesa State College	1100 North Ave., Grand Junction, CO 81501	Chris Hanks	(970) 248-1891
Messiah College	One College Ave., Grantham, PA 17027	Frank Montgomery	(717) 766-2511
Methodist College	5400 Ramsey St., Fayetteville, NC 28311	Tom Austin	(910) 630-7176
Metropolitan State U.	P.O. Box 173362, Campus Box 9, Denver, CO 80217	Vince Porreco	(303) 556-3301
Mid-America Bible College	3500 SW 119th St., Oklahoma City, OK 73170	Gerre Griffin	(405) 692-3141
Mid-America Nazarene	2030 E. College Way, Olathe, KS 66062	Todd Garrett	(913) 782-3750
Mid-Continent College	99 Powell Rd. E., Mayfield, KY 42066	Seth Zartman	(207) 247-8521
Middlebury College	Memorial Fieldhouse, Middlebury, VT 05753	Robert Smith	(802) 443-5264
Midland Lutheran College	900 N. Clarkson St., Fremont, NE 68025	Jeff Field	(402) 941-6371
Miles College	5500 Myron Massey Blvd., Birmingham, AL 35208	Willie Patterson	(205) 929-1617
Millersville U.	P.O. Box 1002, Millersville, PA 17551	Glenn Gallagher	(717) 871-2411
Milligan College	P.O. Box 500, Milligan College, TN 37682	Danny Clark	(423) 461-8722
Millikin U.	1184 W. Main St., Decatur, IL 62522	Josh Manning	(217) 424-3608
Millsaps College	1701 N. State St., Jackson, MS 39210	Jim Page	(601) 974-1196
Milwaukee Engineering	1025 N. Broadway, Milwaukee, WI 53202	Len VandenBoom	(414) 277-7154

Minnesota Bible College	920 Mayowood Road SW, Rochester, MN 55902	Mark Comeaux	(507) 288-4563
Minnesota-Crookston, U. of	Sports Center, Crookston, MN 56716	Steve Olson	(218) 281-8419
Minnesota-Duluth, U. of	1216 Ordean Court, Duluth, MN 55812	Scott Hanna	(218) 726-7563
Minnesota-Morris, U. of	E. 2nd St., Morris, MN 56267	Mark Fohl	(320) 589-6421
Minnesota State U.-Mankato	135 Myers Fieldhouse, Mankato, MN 56001	Dean Bowyer	(507) 389-2689
Minot State U.	500 University Ave. W., Minot, ND 58707	Ian Shoemaker	(701) 858-3833
Misericordia College	301 Lake St., Dallas, PA 18612	Chuck Edkins	(570) 674-6397
Mississippi College	P.O. Box 4049, Clinton, MS 39058	Lee Kuyrkendall	(601) 925-3346
Missouri Baptist College	1 College Park Dr., St. Louis, MO 63141	Eddie Uschold	(314) 392-2384
Missouri Southern State Coll.	3950 E. Newman Rd, Joplin, MO 64801	Warren Turner	(417) 625-9312
Missouri-Rolla, U. of	Athletic Dept., Rolla, MO 65409	Travis Boulware	(573) 341-4191
Missouri-St. Louis, U. of	8001 Natural Bridge Rd., St. Louis, MO 63141	Jim Brady	(314) 516-5647
Missouri Valley College	500 E. College St., Marshall, MO 65340	Elliott Sampley	(660) 831-4113
Missouri Western State	4525 Downs Dr., St. Joseph, MO 64507	Buzz Verduzco	(816) 271-4484
Mobile, U. of	5735 College Pkwy, Mobile, AL 36663	Mike Jacobs	(334) 442-2278
Molloy College	1000 Hempstead Ave., Rockville Centre, NY 11570	Bernie Havern	(251) 256-2228
Monmouth College	700 E. Broadway, Monmouth, IL 61462	Roger Sander	(309) 457-2176
Montclair State U.	One Normal Ave., Upper Montclair, NJ 07043	Norm Schoenig	(973) 655-5281
Montevallo, U. of	Station 6600, Montevallo, AL 35115	Bob Riesener	(205) 665-6760
Montreat College	405 Assemly Dr., Montreat, NC 28757	Darin Chaplain	(828) 669-8012
Moravian College	1200 Main St., Bethlehem, PA 18018	Ed Little	(610) 861-1536
Morningside College	1501 Morningside Ave, Sioux City, IA 51106	Jim Scholten	(712) 274-5258
Morris College	N. Main St., Sumter, SC 29150	Clarence Houck	(803) 775-9371
Mount Marty College	1105 West 8th St., Yankton, SD 57078	Kelly Heller	(605) 668-1548
Mount Mercy College	1330 Elmhurst Drive NE, Cedar Rapids, IA 52402	Justin Schulte	(319) 363-1323
Mount Olive College	634 Henderson St., Mount Olive, NC 28365	Carl Lancaster	(919) 658-7669
Mount St. Clare College	400 N. Bluff Blvd., Clinton, IA 52732	Desi Druschel	(563) 242-4023
Mount St. Joseph College	5701 Delhi Rd., Cincinnati, OH 45233	Chuck Murray	(513) 244-4402
Mount St. Mary College	330 Powell Ave., Newburgh, NY 12550	Matt Dembinsky	(845) 569-3287
Mount Senario College	1500 College Ave. W., Ladysmith, WI 54848	Darren Vanderheyden	(715) 532-5511
Mount Union College	1972 Clark Ave., Alliance, OH 44601	Paul Hesse	(330) 823-4878
Mount Vernon Nazarene Coll.	800 Martinsburg Rd., Mt. Vernon, OH 43050	Keith Veale	(740) 392-6868
Muhlenberg College	2400 W. Chew St., Allentown, PA 18104	Bob Macaluso	(484) 664-3684
Muskingum College	163 Stormont St., New Concord, OH 43762	Gregg Thompson	(740) 826-8318
Nebraska-Kearney, U. of	Hwy 30 & 15th Ave., Kearney, NE 68849	Tony Murray	(308) 865-8022
Nebraska-Omaha, U. of	6001 Dodge St., Omaha, NE 68182	Bob Herold	(402) 554-3388
Nebraska Wesleyan U.	5000 St. Paul Ave., Lincoln, NE 68504	Mark Mancuso	(402) 465-2171
Neumann College	One Neumann Dr., Aston, PA 19014	Len Schuler	(610) 558-5625
New England College	Clement Arena, 24 Bridge St., Henniker, NH 03242	Dave Anderson	(603) 428-2407
New Haven, U. of	300 Orange Ave., West Haven, CT 06516	Frank Vieira	(203) 932-7018
New Jersey City U.	2039 Kennedy Blvd., Jersey City, NJ 07305	Ken Heaton	(201) 200-3079
New Jersey Tech	323 Martin Luther King Blvd., Newark, NJ 07102	Brian Callahan	(973) 596-5827
New Jersey, College of	P.O. Box 7718, Ewing, NJ 08628	Rick Dell	(609) 771-2374
New Mexico Highlands U.	Athletic Dept Fieldhouse, Las Vegas, NM 87701	Steve Jones	(505) 425-3587
Newberry College	2100 College St., Newberry, SC 29108	Tim Medlin	(803) 321-5162
Newman U.	3100 McCormick St., Wichita, KS 67213	Kevin Ulwelling	(316) 942-4884
Nichols College	P.O. Box 5000, Dudley, MA 01571	Steve Nadeau	(508) 213-2363
North Alabama, U. of	Box 5072, Florence, AL 35632	Mike Lane	(256) 765-4615
North Carolina Wesleyan	3400 Wesleyan Blvd., Rocky Mount, NC 27804	Charlie Long	(252) 985-5219
North Carolina-Pembroke, U. of	P.O. Box 1510, Pembroke, NC 28372	Paul O'Neil	(910) 521-6810
North Central College	30 N. Brainard St., Naperville, IL 60540	Brian Michalak	(630) 637-5512
North Dakota State U.	1600 N. University Dr., Fargo, ND 58105	Mitch McLeod	(701) 231-8853
North Dakota, U. of	P.O. Box 9013, Grand Forks, ND 58203	Kelvin Ziegler	(701) 777-4038
North Florida, U. of	4567 St. Johns Bluff Rd. S., Jacksonville, FL 32224	Dusty Rhodes	(904) 620-2556
North Georgia College	State Hwy 60 S., Dahlonega, GA 30597	Tom Cantrell	(706) 867-2754
North Greenville College	P.O. Box 1892, Tigerville, SC 29688	Tim Nihart	(864) 977-7156
North Park U.	3225 W. Foster Ave, Chicago, IL 60625	Steve Vanden Branden	(773) 244-5675
Northeastern State U.	600 N. Grand Ave., Tahlequah, OK 74464	Sergio Espinal	(918) 456-5511
Northern Colorado, U. of	251 Butler-Hancock Hall, Greeley, CO 80639	Kevin Smallcomb	(970) 351-1714
Northern Kentucky U.	1 Nunn Drive, Highland Heights, KY 41099	Todd Asalon	(859) 572-6474
Northern State U.	1200 South Jay St., Aberdeen, SD 57401	Curt Fredrickson	(605) 626-7735
Northland College	1411 Ellis Ave., Ashland, WI 54806	Joel Barta	(715) 682-1387
Northwest Missouri State	800 University Dr., Maryville, MO 64468	Darin Loe	(660) 562-1304
Northwest Nazarene U.	623 Holly St., Nampa, ID 83686	Tim Onofrei	(208) 467-8351
Northwestern College	101 7th St. SW, Orange City, IA 51041	Derrion Hardie	(712) 737-7310
Northwestern College	3003 Snelling Ave. N., St. Paul, MN 55113	Dave Hieb	(651) 631-5345
Northwestern Okla. State	709 Oklahoma Blvd., Alva, OK 73717	Joe Phillips	(580) 327-8635
Northwood U.	4000 Whiting Drive, Midland, MI 48640	Joe DiBenedetto	(989) 837-4427
Northwood U.	1114 West FM 1382, Cedar Hill, TX 75104	Pat Malcheski	(972) 293-5439
Norwich U.	158 Harmon Dr., Northfield, VT 05663	Bill Barrale	(802) 485-2239
Nova Southeastern U.	3301 College Ave., Fort Lauderdale, FL 33314	Michael Mominey	(954) 262-8259

Nyack College	1 South Blvd., Nyack, NY 10960	Jason Beck	(845) 358-1710
Oakland City U.	143 Lucretia St., Oakland City, IN 47660	Ray Fletcher	(812) 749-1576
Oberlin College	200 Woodland Ave., Oberlin, OH 44074	Eric Lahetta	(440) 775-8502
Occidental College	1600 Campus Rd., Los Angeles, CA 90041	Jeff Henderson	(323) 259-2683
Oglethorpe U.	4484 Peachtree Rd. NE, Atlanta, GA 30319	Bill Popp	(404) 364-8417
Ohio College	P.O. Box 450640, Westlake, OH 44145	Bob Cooke	(440) 555-1212
Ohio Dominican College	1216 Sunbury Rd., Columbus, OH 43219	Paul Page	(614) 251-4535
Ohio Northern U.	525 S. Main, Ada, OH 45810	Milan Rasic	(419) 772-2442
Ohio Valley College	1 Campus View Dr., Vienna, WV 26105	Bob Crawford	(304) 865-6048
Ohio Wesleyan U.	61 S. Sandusky St., Delaware, OH 43015	Roger Ingles	(740) 368-3738
Oklahoma Baptist U.	500 W. University St., Shawnee, OK 74804	Bobby Cox	(405) 878-2139
Oklahoma City U.	2501 N. Blackwelder, Oklahoma City, OK 73106	Denny Crabaugh	(405) 521-5156
Oklahoma Wesleyan Coll.	2201 Silverlake Rd., Bartlesville, OK 74006	Jason Zielenski	(918) 335-6848
Olivet College	320 S. Main St., Olivet, MI 49076	Carlton Hardy	(269) 749-4184
Olivet Nazarene U.	One University Ave., Bourbonnais, IL 60914	Elliot Johnson	(815) 939-5119
Oneonta State U.	Ravine Pkwy., Oneonta, NY 13820	Rick Ferchen	(607) 436-2661
Oregon Tech	3201 Campus Dr., Klamath Falls, OR 97601	Pete Whisler	(541) 885-1722
Ottawa U.	1001 South Cedar St., Ottawa, KS 66067	Jarrod Titus	(785) 242-5200
Otterbein College	160 Center St., Westerville, OH 43081	George Powell	(614) 823-3521
Ouachita Baptist U.	410 Ouachita, Arkadelphia, AR 71998	B.J. Brown	(870) 245-5083
Ozarks, College of the	P.O. Box 17, Point Lookout, MO 65726	Patrick McGaha	(417) 334-6411
Ozarks, U. of the	415 College Ave., Clarksville, AR 72830	Jimmy Clark	(501) 979-1409
Pacific Lutheran U.	12180 Park Ave. S., Tacoma, WA 98447	Geoff Loomis	(253) 535-8789
Pacific U.	2043 College Way, Forest Grove, OR 97116	Greg Bradley	(503) 359-2142
Paine College	1235 15th St., Augusta, GA 30901	Stanley Stubbs	(706) 821-8228
Palm Beach Atlantic Coll.	901 S. Flagler Dr., West Palm Beach, FL 33416	Kyle Forbes	(561) 803-2523
Panhandle State U.	P.O. Box 430, Goodwell, OK 73939	Ron Clark	(580) 349-1340
Park U.	8700 NW River Park Dr., Parkville, MO 64152	Dan Backhaus	(816) 584-6746
Penn State U.-Altoona	3000 Ivyside Park, Altoona, PA 16601	Joe Piotti	(814) 949-5226
Penn State Behrend Coll.	5091 Station Rd., Erie, PA 16563	Paul Benim	(814) 898-6322
Peru State College	P.O. Box 10, Peru, NE 68421	Mark Bayliss	(402) 872-2443
Pfeiffer U.	P.O. Box 960, Misenheimer, NC 28109	Chris Pollard	(704) 463-1360
Philadelphia, U. of Sciences	600 S. 43rd St., Philadelphia, PA 19104	Jack Bilbee	(215) 895-1109
Philadelphia U.	School House Lane & Henry Ave., Philadelphia, PA 19144	Don Flynn	(215) 951-2630
Philadelphia Biblical U.	200 Manor Ave., Langhorne, PA 19047	Bill Marshall	(215) 702-4405
Piedmont College	P.O. Box 10, Demorest, GA 30535	Jim Peeples	(706) 778-3000
Pikeville College	147 Sycamore St., Pikeville, KY 41501	Johnnie LeMaster	(606) 218-5370
Pittsburg State U.	1701 S. Broadway, Pittsburg, KS 66762	Steve Bever	(620) 232-7951
Pittsburgh-Bradford, U. of	300 Campus Dr., Bradford, PA 16701	Bret Butler	(814) 362-5271
Pittsburgh-Greensburg, U. of	1150 Mt. Pleasant Rd., Greensburg, PA 15601	Joe Hill	(724) 836-7185
Pittsburgh-Johnstown, U. of	450 School House Rd., Johnstown, PA 15904	Todd Williams	(814) 269-7170
Plymouth State College	PE Center #32, Holderness Rd., Plymouth, NH 03264	Dennis McManus	(603) 535-2756
Point Loma Nazarene U.	3900 Lomaland Dr., San Diego, CA 92106	Scott Sarver	(619) 849-2615
Point Park College	201 Wood St., Pittsburgh, PA 15222	Al Liberi	(412) 392-3845
Polytechnic U.	6 Metro Tech Ctr., Brooklyn, NY 11201	Roger Perez	(718) 875-6083
Pomona-Pitzer College	220 E. 6th St., Claremont, CA 91711	Paul Svagdis	(909) 621-8422
Presbyterian College	105 Ashland, Clinton, SC 29325	Doug Kovash	(864) 833-8236
Principia College	1 Maybeck Place, Elsah, IL 62028	Mike Barthelmen	(618) 374-5036
Puget Sound, U. of	1500 N. Warner St., Tacoma, WA 98416	Brian Billings	(253) 879-3414
Purdue U.-North Central	1401 U.S. Hwy. 421 S., Westville, IN 46391	Ryan Brown	(219) 785-5273
Queens College	65-30 Kissena Blvd., Flushing, NY 11367	Frank Battaglia	(718) 997-2781
Quincy U.	1800 College Ave., Quincy, IL 62301	Greg McVey	(217) 228-5268
Ramapo College	505 Ramapo Valley Rd., Mahwah, NJ 07430	Rich Martin	(201) 684-7098
Randolph-Macon College	P.O. Box 5005, Ashland, VA 23005	Gregg Waters	(804) 752-7303
Redlands, U. of	P.O. Box 3080, Redlands, CA 92373	Scott Laverty	(909) 335-4005
Regis U.	Athletic Dept., Denver, CO 80221	Dan McDermott	(303) 458-3519
Rensselaer Poly Institute	110 8th St., Troy, NY 12180	Karl Steffen	(518) 276-6185
Rhode Island College	600 Mt. Pleasant Ave., Providence, RI 02908	Jay Grenier	(401) 456-8641
Rhodes College	2000 N. Parkway, Memphis, TN 38112	Alan Reynolds	(901) 843-3456
Richard Stockton College	P.O. Box 195, Pomona, NJ 08240	Marty Kavanagh	(609) 652-4217
Rio Grande, U. of	218 N. College Ave, Rio Grande, OH 45674	Brad Warnimont	(740) 245-7486
Ripon College	300 Seward St., Ripon, WI 54971	Gordon Gillespie	(920) 748-8776
Rivier College	420 Main St., Nashua, NH 03060	Scott Thomas	(603) 888-1311
Roanoke College	221 College Lane, Salem, VA 24153	Richard Morris	(540) 378-5147
Robert Morris College	401 S. State St., Chicago, IL 60605	Woody Urchak	(312) 838-9965
Rochester, U. of	Goergen Athletic Center, Rochester, NY 14627	Joe Reina	(716) 275-6027
Rochester College	800 W. Avon Rd., Rochester Hills, MI 48307	Virgil Smith	(248) 218-2135
Rochester Tech	51 Lomb Memorial Dr., Rochester, NY 14623	Rob Grow	(716) 475-2210
Rockford College	5050 E. State St., Rockford, IL 61108	William Langston	(815) 226-4048

Rockhurst U.	1100 Rockhurst Rd., Kansas City, MO 64110	Gary Burns	(816) 501-4130
Roger Williams U.	One Old Ferry Rd., Bristol, RI 02809	Derek Carlson	(401) 254-3050
Rollins College	1000 Holt Ave, Winter Park, FL 32789	Bob Rikeman	(407) 646-2328
Rose-Hulman Tech	5500 Wabash Ave., Terre Haute, IN 47803	Jeff Jenkins	(812) 877-8209
Rowan U.	201 Mullica Hill Rd., Glassboro, NJ 08028	John Cole	(856) 256-4687
Rust College	150 E. Rust Ave., Holly Springs, MS 38635	Avery Mason	(662) 252-4661
Rutgers U.-Camden	3rd & Linden Streets, Camden, NJ 08102	Keith Williams	(856) 225-6197
Rutgers U.-Newark	42 Warren St., Newark, NJ 07102	Mark Rizzi	(973) 353-5474
Saginaw Valley State	7400 Bay Rd., University Center, MI 48710	Walt Head	(989) 964-7334
St. Ambrose U.	518 W. Locust St., Davenport, IA 52803	Jim Callahan	(563) 333-6237
St. Andrews Presbyterian	1700 Dogwood Mile St., Laurinburg, NC 28352	Bobby Simmons	(910) 277-5426
St. Anselm College	100 St. Anselm Dr., Manchester, NH 03102	Ken Harring	(603) 656-6016
St. Augustine's College	1315 Oakwood Ave., Raleigh, NC 27610	Henry White	(919) 516-4174
St. Cloud State U.	720 4th Ave. S., St. Cloud, MN 56301	Denny Lorsung	(320) 255-3208
St. Edwards U.	3001 S. Congress Ave., Austin, TX 78704	Jerry Farber	(512) 448-8497
St. Francis, U. of	500 Wilcox St., Joliet, IL 60435	Tony Delgado	(815) 740-3406
St. Francis, U. of	2701 Spring St., Fort Wayne, IN 46808	Doug Coate	(260) 434-7414
St. Gregory's U.	1900 W. MacArthur Dr., Shawnee, OK 74804	Jay Moore	(405) 878-5151
St. John Fisher College	3690 East Ave., Rochester, NY 14618	Dan Pepicelli	(716) 385-8419
St. John's U.	P.O. Box 7277, Collegeville, MN 56321	Jerry Haugen	(320) 363-2756
St. Joseph's College	P.O. Box 875, Rensselaer, IN 47978	Rick O'Dette	(219) 866-6399
St. Joseph's College	278 Whites Bridge Rd., Standish, ME 04084	Will Sanborn	(207) 893-6675
St. Joseph's College	155 Roe Blvd., Patchogue, NY 11772	Randy Caden	(631) 447-3349
St. Lawrence U.	Park Street, Canton, NY 13617	Tom Fay	(315) 229-5882
St. Leo U.	P.O. Box 6665, St. Leo, FL 33574	Ed Stabile	(352) 588-8227
St. Louis Christian College	1360 Grandview Dr., Florissant, MO 63033	Mike Pabarcus	(314) 837-6777
St. Martin's College	5300 Pacific Ave. SE, Lacey, WA 98503	Joe Dominiak	(360) 438-4531
St. Mary College	4100 S. 4th St., Leavenworth, KS 66048	Erik Lehman	(913) 758-4341
St. Mary's College	Somerset Hall, St. Mary's City, MD 20686	Lew Jenkins	(240) 895-4312
St. Mary's U.	700 Terrace Heights #47, Winona, MN 55987	Nicholas Whaley	(507) 457-1577
St. Mary's U.	1 Camino Santa Maria St., San Antonio, TX 78228	Charlie Migl	(210) 436-3034
St. Michael's College	One Winooski Park, Colchester, VT 05439	Perry Bove	(802) 654-2725
St. Norbert College	100 Grant St., De Pere, WI 54115	Tom Winske	(920) 403-3545
St. Olaf College	1520 St. Olaf Ave., Northfield, MN 55057	Matt McDonald	(507) 646-3638
St. Paul's College	115 College Dr., Lawrenceville, VA 23868	Oliver Harrison	(804) 848-3111
St. Rose, College of	432 Western Ave., Albany, NY 12203	Bob Bellizzi	(518) 458-2040
St. Scholastica, College of	1200 Kenwood Ave., Duluth, MN 55811	John Baggs	(218) 723-6298
St. Thomas, U. of	3800 Montrose Blvd., Houston, TX 77006	John Goebel	(713) 525-3874
St. Thomas, U. of	2115 Summit Ave., St. Paul, MN 55105	Dennis Denning	(651) 962-5924
St. Thomas Aquinas	125 Route 340, Sparkill, NY 10976	Scott Muscat	(845) 398-4027
St. Thomas U.	16400 NW 32nd Ave., Miami, FL 33054	Manny Mantrana	(305) 628-6730
St. Vincent College	300 Fraser Purchase Rd., Latrobe, PA 15650	Mick Janosko	(724) 539-9761
St. Xavier U.	3700 W. 103rd St., Chicago, IL 60655	Mike Dooley	(773) 298-3103
Salem-International U.	223 W. Main St., Salem, WV 26426	Rich Leitch	(304) 782-5632
Salem State College	352 Lafayette St., Salem, MA 01970	Ken Perrone	(978) 542-7260
Salisbury U.	1101 Camden Ave., Salisbury, MD 21801	Doug Fleetwood	(410) 543-6034
Salve Regina U.	100 Ochre Point Ave., Newport, RI 02840	Steve Cirella	(401) 341-2267
San Francisco State U.	1600 Holloway Ave., San Francisco, CA 94132	Matt Markovich	(415) 338-1226
Savannah Art & Design	P.O. Box 3146, Savannah, GA 31402	Doug Wollenburg	(912) 525-4800
Schreiner College	2100 Memorial Blvd., Kerrville, TX 78028	Joe Castillo	(830) 792-7292
Scranton, U. of	John J. Long Center, Scranton, Pa. 18510	Mike Bertoletti	(570) 941-7440
Shaw U.	118 E. South St., Raleigh, NC 27601	Bobby Sanders	(919) 546-8281
Shawnee State U.	940 2nd St., Portsmouth, OH 45662	Tom Brogan	(740) 351-3537
Shenandoah U.	1460 University Dr., Winchester, VA 22601	Justin Cronk	(540) 665-4531
Shepherd College	James Butcher Center, Shepherdstown, WV 25443	Wayne Riser	(304) 876-5472
Shippensburg U.	1871 Old Main Dr., Shippensburg, PA 17257	Bruce Peddie	(717) 477-1508
Shorter College	315 Shorter Ave., Rome, GA 30165	Ricci Lattanzi	(706) 233-7347
Siena Heights U.	1247 E. Siena Heights Dr., Adrian, MI 49221	Gordie Theisen	(517) 264-7872
Simpson College	2211 College View Dr., Redding, CA 96003	Jon Mason	(530) 226-4157
Simpson College	701 North C St., Indianola, IA 50125	John Sirianni	(515) 961-1620
Sioux Falls, U. of	1101 W. 22nd St., Sioux Falls, SD 57105	Luke Langenfeld	(605) 331-6638
Skidmore College	North Broadway, Saratoga Springs, NY 12866	Ron Plourde	(518) 580-5380
Slippery Rock U.	102 Morrow Fieldhouse, Slippery Rock, PA 16057	Jeff Messer	(724) 738-2813
Sonoma State U.	1801 E. Cotati Ave., Rohnert Park, CA 94928	John Goelz	(707) 664-2524
South Carolina-Aiken, U. of	471 University Parkway, Aiken, SC 29801	Kenny Thomas	(803) 641-3410
South Carolina-Spartanburg, U. of	800 University Way, Spartanburg, SC 29303	Matt Fincher	(864) 503-5135
South Dakota, U. of	414 E. Clark St., Vermillion, SD 57069	Brian Atchison	(605) 677-6259
South Dakota State U.	16th Ave. & 11th St., Brookings, SD 57007	Mark Ekeland	(605) 688-5027
South, U. of the	735 University Ave., Sewanee, TN 37383	Scott Baker	(931) 598-1545
Southeastern College	1000 Longfellow Blvd, Lakeland, FL 33801	John Anderson	(863) 667-5138
Southeastern Oklahoma State	1405 N. 4th, PMB 4049, Durant, OK 74701	Mike Metheny	(580) 745-2478

Southern Arkansas U.	100 E. University St., Magnolia, AR 71753	Steve Goodheart	(870) 235-4127
Southern Colorado, U .of	2200 N. Bonforte Blvd., Pueblo, CO 81001	Stan Sanchez	(719) 549-2065
Southern Connecticut State	125 Wintergreen Ave., New Haven, CT 06515	Tim Shea	(203) 392-6021
Southern Illinois U.-Edwardsville	SIUE Box 1129, Edwardsville, IL 62026	GaryCollins	(618) 650-2872
Southern Indiana, U. of	8600 University Blvd, Evansville, IN 47712	Mike Goedde	(812) 464-1943
Southern Maine, U. of	37 College Ave., Gorham, ME 04038	Ed Flaherty	(207) 780-5474
Southern Nazarene U.	6729 NW 39th Expy., Bethany, OK 73008	Scott Selby	(405) 491-6630
Southern New Hampshire U.	2500 N. River Rd., Manchester, NH 03106	Bruce Joyce	(603) 645-9637
Southern Tech	1100 S. Marietta Pkwy., Marietta, GA 30060	Tommy Knight	(770) 528-5445
Southern Vermont College	982 Mansion Dr., Bennington, VT 05201	Ryan Marks	(802) 447-4658
Southern Virginia College	1 College Hill Dr., Buena Vista, VA 24416	Jerry Schlegelmilch	(540) 261-4092
Southern Wesleyan U.	1 Wesleyan Dr., Central, SC 29630	Mike Gillespie	(864) 639-5035
Southwest, College of the	6610 N. Lovington Hwy., Hobbs, NM 88240	Jim Marshall	(505) 392-6561
Southwest Baptist U.	1600 University Ave., Bolivar, MO 65613	Sam Berg	(417) 328-1794
Southwest State U.	1501 State St., Marshall, MN 56258	Paul Blanchard	(507) 537-7268
Southwestern Adventist U.	P.O. Box 567, Keene, TX 76059	Bruce Norman	(817) 645-3921
Southwestern Oklahoma State	100 Campus Dr., Weatherford, OK 73096	Charles Teasley	(580) 774-3263
Southwestern U.	1001 E. University, Georgetown, TX 78626	Jim Mallon	(512) 863-1383
Spalding U.	851 S. 4th St., Louisville, KY 40203	Kevin Kocks	(502) 585-9911
Spring Arbor College	106 E. Main St., Spring Arbor, MI 49283	Sam Riggleman	(517) 750-6503
Spring Hill College	4000 Dauphin St., Mobile, AL 36608	Frank Sims	(251) 380-3486
Springfield College	263 Alden St., Springfield, MA 01109	Mark Simeone	(413) 748-3274
Staten Island, College of	2800 Victory Blvd., Staten Island, NY 10314	Bill Cali	(718) 982-3171
Sterling College	Gleason Center, Sterling, KS 67579	Scott Norwood	(620) 278-4227
Stevens Tech	Castle Point on Hudson, Hoboken, NJ 07030	John Crane	(201) 216-8033
Stillman College	3600 Stillman Blvd., Tuscaloosa, AL 35401	Bobby Parker	(205) 366-8915
Stonehill College	320 Washington St., North Easton, MA 02357	Patrick Boen	(508) 565-1351
Suffolk U.	41 Temple St., Boston, MA 02114	Cary McConnell	(617) 573-8379
Sul Ross State U.	Box C-17, Hwy. 90 E., Alpine, TX 79832	Mike Pallanez	(915) 837-8231
SUNY Brockport	350 New Campus Dr., Brockport, NY 14420	Mark Rowland	(716) 395-5329
SUNY Farmingdale	Rte. 110 & Melville Rd., Farmingdale, NY 11735	Ken Rocco	(631) 420-2253
SUNY Maritime College	6 Pennyfield Ave., Bronx, NY 10465	Frank Menna	(718) 409-7331
SUNY New Paltz	75 S. Manheim Blvd., New Paltz, NY 12561	Mike Juhl	(845) 257-3915
SUNY Old Westbury	P.O. Box 210, Old Westbury, NY 11568	John Lonardo	(516) 876-3241
SUNY Oswego	Route 104, Oswego, NY 13126	Frank Paino	(315) 312-2405
SUNY Plattsburg	101 Broad St., Plattsburg, NY 12901	Kris Doorey	(518) 564-4136
SUNY Utica-Rome	P.O. Box 3050, Utica, NY 13504	Kevin Edick	(315) 792-7520
Susquehanna U.	514 University Ave., Selinsgrove, PA 17870	Tim Briggs	(570) 372-4417
Swarthmore College	500 College Ave., Swarthmore, PA 19081	Frank Agovino	(610) 328-8216
Tabor College	400 S. Jefferson St., Hillsboro, KS 67063	John Sparks	(620) 947-3121
Talladega College	627 Battle Street W., Talladega, AL 35160	Rodney Lipscomb	(256) 761-6238
Tampa, U. of	401 W. Kennedy Blvd., Tampa, FL 33606	Joe Urso	(813) 253-6240
Tarleton State U.	Box T-80, Stephenville, TX 76402	Trey Felan	(254) 968-9528
Taylor U.	236 W. Reade Ave, Upland, IN 46989	Mark Raikes	(765) 998-4635
Teikyo-Post U.	800 Country Club Rd., Waterbury, CT 06723	Wayne Mazzoni	(203) 596-4517
Tennessee Temple U.	1815 Union Ave., Chattanooga, TN 37404	Kevin Templeton	(423) 493-4220
Tennessee Wesleyan College	40 Green St., Athens, TN 37371	Ashley Lawson	(423) 746-5277
Texas A&M-Kingsville	MSC 202, Kingsville, TX 78363	Russell Stockton	(361) 593-3487
Texas College	P.O. Box 4500, Tyler, TX 75712	Malcolm Walker	(903) 593-8311
Texas-Dallas, U. of	Box 830688 AB 10, Richardson, TX 75083	Shane Shewmake	(972) 883-2392
Texas Lutheran U.	1000 W. Court St., Seguin, TX 78155	Bill Miller	(830) 372-8124
Texas Wesleyan U.	1201 Wesleyan St., Fort Worth, TX 76105	Mike Jeffcoat	(817) 531-7547
Thiel College	75 College Ave., Greenville, PA 16125	Joe Schaly	(724) 589-2139
Thomas College	West River Rd., Waterville, ME 04901	Greg King	(207) 859-1208
Thomas U.	1501 Millpond Rd., Thomasville, GA 31792	Mike Lee	(229) 226-1621
Thomas More College	333 Thomas More Pkwy., Crestview Hills, KY 41017	Jeff Hetzer	(859) 344-3532
Tiffin U.	155 Miami St., Tiffin, OH 44883	Lonny Allen	(419) 448-3359
Toccoa Falls College	P.O. Box 800818, Toccoa Falls, GA 30598	Joel Johnson	(706) 886-6831
Transylvania U.	300 N. Broadway, Lexington, KY 40508	Shayne Stock	(859) 233-8699
Trevecca Nazarene U.	333 Murfreesboro Rd., Nashville, TN 37210	Jeff Forehand	(615) 248-1276
Tri-State U.	1 University Ave., Angola, IN 46703	Greg Perschke	(260) 665-4135
Trinity Christian College	6601 W. College Dr., Palos Heights, IL 60463	Rich Cook	(708) 239-4780
Trinity College	Ferris Center, Summit St., Hartford, CT 06106	William Decker	(860) 297-2066
Trinity International U.	500 NE 1st Ave., Miami, FL 33132	Jud Damon	(305) 577-4600
Trinity International U.	2065 Half Day Rd., Deerfield, IL 60015	Mark Landvick	(847) 317-7093
Trinity U.	715 Stadium Dr., San Antonio, TX 78212	Tim Scannell	(210) 999-8287
Truman State U.	100 E. Normal St., Kirksville, MO 63501	Larry Scully	(660) 785-6003
Tufts U.	161 College Ave., Medord, MA 02155	John Casey	(617) 627-5218
Tusculum College	P.O. Box 5090, Greenville, TN 37743	Doug Jones	(423) 636-7322
Tuskegee U.	321 James Center, Tuskegee, AL 36088	Reggie Ruffin	(334) 724-4229

Union College	310 College St., Barbourville, KY 40906	Darin Wilson	(606) 546-1355
Union College	Alumni Gym, Union Ave., Schenectady, NY 12308	Gary Reynolds	(518) 388-6548
Union U.	1050 Union University Dr., Jackson, TN 38305	Andy Rushing	(901) 661-5333
U.S. Coast Guard Academy	15 Mohegan Ave., New London, CT 06320	Pete Barry	(860) 701-6132
U.S. Merchant Marine	300 Steamboat Rd., Kings Point, NY 11024	Dennis Gagnon	(516) 773-5620
Upper Iowa U.	Box 1857, Fayette, IA 52142	Mark Danker	(563) 425-5290
Urbana U.	579 College Way, Urbana, OH 43078	Al Fulk	(937) 484-1325
Ursinus College	Main St., Collegeville, PA 19426	Brian Thomas	(610) 409-3606
Utica College	1600 Burnstone Rd., Utica, NY 13502	Don Guido	(315) 752-3378
Valdosta State U.	1500 N. Patterson St, Valdosta, GA 31698	Tommy Thomas	(229) 259-5562
Valley City State U.	101 College St. SW, Valley City, ND 58072	Cory Anderson	(701) 845-7413
Valley Forge Christian	1401 Charlestown Rd., Phoenixville, PA 19460	John News	(610) 917-1479
Vanguard U.	55 Fair Dr., Costa Mesa, CA 92626	Kevin Kasper	(714) 556-3610
Vassar College	124 Raymond Ave., Poughkeepsie, NY 12604	Andy Barlow	(845) 437-5344
Vermont Tech	Randolph Center, VT 05061	Aaron Hill	(802) 728-1382
Villa Julie College	1525 Greenspring Valley Rd., Stevenson, MD 21153	Ray Kosmicky	(410) 602-7334
Virginia Intermont	1013 Moore St., Bristol, VA 24201	Chris Holt	(276) 466-7945
Virginia State U.	P.O. Box 9058, Petersburg, VA 23806	Herb Wheat	(804) 524-5816
Virginia Wesleyan College	1584 Wesleyan Dr., Norfolk, VA 23502	Nick Boothe	(757) 455-3348
Virginia-Wise, U. of	1 College Ave., Wise, VA 24293	Hank Banner	(276) 328-0207
Viterbo College	815 9th St. S., La Crosse, WI 54601	Larry Lipker	(608) 796-3824
Voorhees College	P.O. Box 678, Voorhees Rd., Denmark, SC 29042	Adrian West	(803) 703-7142
Wabash College	301 West Wabash Ave., Crawfordsville, IN 47933	Bill Boone	(765) 361-6209
Walsh U.	2020 Easton St. NW, North Canton, OH 44720	Tim Mead	(330) 490-7013
Warner Southern College	13895 Hwy. 27, Lake Wales, FL 33853	Jeff Sikes	(863) 638-7259
Wartburg College	100 Wartburg Blvd., Waverly, IA 50677	Joel Holst	(319) 352-8532
Washburn U.	1700 SW College Ave., Topeka, KS 66621	Steve Anson	(785) 231-1010
Washington & Jefferson College	60 S. Lincoln, Washington, PA 15301	Mark Mason	(724) 250-3306
Washington & Lee U.	P.O. Drawer 928, Lexington, VA 24450	Jeff Stickley	(540) 463-8680
Washington Bible College	6511 Princess Garden Pkwy., Lanham, MD 20706	Dave Gough	(301) 552-1400
Washington College	300 Washington Ave, Chestertown, MD 21620	Al Streelman	(410) 778-7239
Washington U.	Campus Box 1067, St. Louis, MO 63130	Ric Lessmann	(314) 935-5945
Wayland Baptist U.	1900 W.7th St., Plainview, TX 79072	Brad Bass	(806) 291-1132
Wayne State College	1111 Main St., Wayne, NE 68787	John Manganaro	(402) 375-7499
Wayne State U.	5101 Lodge Dr., Detroit, MI 48202	Jay Alexander	(313) 577-4280
Waynesburg College	51 W. College St., Waynesburg, PA 15370	Duane Lanzy	(724) 852-3229
Webber College	1201 N. Scenic Hwy. 27 South, Babson Park, FL 33827	Brad Niethammer	(863) 638-2951
Webster U.	470 E. Lockwood Ave, Webster Groves, MO 63119	Marty Hunsucker	(314) 961-2660
Wentworth Tech	550 Huntington Ave., Boston, MA 02115	Tom Randolph	(617) 989-4824
Wesley College	120 N. State St., Dover, DE 19901	Matt Addonizio	(302) 735-5939
Wesleyan U.	Freeman Athletic Center, Middletown, CT 06459	Mark Woodworth	(860) 685-2924
West Alabama, U. of	UWA Station 5, Livingston, AL 35470	Gary Rundles	(205) 652-3870
West Chester U.	Sturzebecker Center, West Chester, PA 19383	Chris Calciano	(610) 436-2152
West Florida, U. of	11000 University Pkwy., Pensacola, FL 32514	Jim Spooner	(850) 474-2488
West Georgia, State U. of	1600 Maple St., Carrollton, GA 30118	Doc Fowlkes	(770) 836-6533
West Liberty State College	Bartell Fieldhouse, West Liberty, WV 26074	Bo McConnaughy	(304) 336-8235
West Texas A&M U.	WTAMU Box 60049, Canyon, TX 79016	Mark Jones	(806) 651-2676
West Virginia State College	Campus Box 181, Institute, WV 25112	Cal Bailey	(304) 766-3208
West Virginia Tech	405 Fayette Pike, Route 61, Montgomery, WV 25136	Tim Epling	(304) 442-3121
West Virginia Wesleyan	College Ave., Buckhannon, WV 26201	Randy Tenney	(304) 473-8054
Western Baptist College	5000 Deer Park Drive SE, Salem, OR 97301	Paul Gale	(503) 589-8183
Western Connecticut State	181 White St., Danbury, CT 06810	John Susi	(203) 837-8608
Western New England College	1215 Wilbraham Rd., Springfield, MA 01119	Matt LaBranche	(413) 782-1792
Western Oregon U.	345 Monmouth Ave N., Monmouth, OR 97361	Terry Baumgartner	(503) 838-8448
Westfield State College	577 Western Ave., Westfield, MA 01086	Tom LoRicco	(413) 572-5633
Westminster College	501 Westminster Ave, Fulton, MO 65251	Scott Pritchard	(573) 592-5333
Westminster College	Market St., New Wilmington, PA 16172	Sean Kelly	(724) 946-7311
Westmont College	955 La Paz Rd., Santa Barbara, CA 93108	Warren Dickey	(805) 565-6012
Wheaton College	501 East College Ave, Wheaton, IL 60187	Bobby Elder	(630) 752-7164
Wheaton College	Haas Athletic Center, Norton, MA 02766	Eric Podbelski	(508) 286-3988
Whitman College	345 Boyer Ave., Walla Walla, WA 99362	Travis Feezell	(509) 527-4931
Whittier College	13406 E. Philadelphia St., Whittier, CA 90608	Mike Rizzo	(562) 907-4967
Whitworth College	300 W. Hawthorne Rd., Spokane, WA 99251	Keith Ward	(509) 777-4394
Widener U.	1 University Place, Chester, PA 19013	Sean Matkowski	(610) 499-4446
Wiley College	711 Wiley Ave., Marshall, TX 75670	Eddie Watson	(903) 927-3292
Wilkes U.	P.O. Box 111, Wilkes-Barre, PA 18703	Joe Folek	(570) 408-4020
Willamette U.	900 State St., Salem, OR 97301	David Wong	(503) 370-6011
William Carey Col	498 Tuscan Ave., Hattiesburg, MS 39401	Bobby Halford	(601) 582-6110
William Jewell Col	500 College Hill, Liberty, MO 64068	Mike Stockton	(816) 781-7700
William Paterson U.	300 Pompton Rd., Wayne, NJ 07470	Jeff Albies	(973) 720-2210

William Penn College	201 Trueblood Ave., Oskaloosa, IA 52577	Mike Laird	(641) 673-1023
William Woods U.	1 University Drive, Fulton, MO 65251	Tom Vodnansky	(573) 592-1187
Williams College	22 Spring St., Williamstown, MA 01267	Dave Barnard	(413) 597-3326
Wilmington College	320 N. DuPont Highway, New Castle, DE 19720	Matt Brainard	(302) 328-9435
Wilmington College	251 Ludovic St., Wilmington, OH 45177	Tony Haley	(937) 382-6661
Wingate U.	P.O. Box 3054, Wingate, NC 28174	Bill Nash	(704) 233-8242
Winona State U.	P.O. Box 5838, Winona, MN 55987	Kyle Poock	(507) 457-2332
Wisconsin Lutheran College	8800 W. Bluemound Rd., Milwaukee, WI 53226	Brook Smith	(414) 443-8990
Wisconsin-La Crosse, U. of	Mitchell Hall, La Crosse, WI 54601	George Williams	(608) 785-6540
Wisconsin-Oshkosh, U. of	800 Algoma Blvd., Oshkosh, WI 54901	Tom Lechnir	(920) 424-0374
Wisconsin-Parkside, U. of	900 Wood Rd., Kenosha, WI 53141	Tracy Archuleta	(262) 595-2317
Wisconsin-Platteville, U. of	1 University Plaza, Platteville, WI 53818	Jamie Sailors	(608) 342-1843
Wisconsin-Stevens Point, U. of	134 HEC, Stevens Point, WI 54481	Brian Nelson	(715) 346-4412
Wisconsin-Stout, U. of	Johnson Fiedhouse, Menomonie, WI 54751	Craig Walter	(715) 232-1459
Wisconsin-Superior, U. of	1800 Grand Ave., Superior, WI 54880	James Stukel	(715) 394-8272
Wisconsin-Whitewater, U. of	800 W. Main St., Whitewater, WI 53190	Jim Miller	(262) 472-5649
Wittenberg U.	P.O. Box 720, Springfield, OH 45501	Jay Lewis	(937) 327-6494
Wooster, College of	1189 Beall Ave., Wooster, OH 44691	Tim Pettorini	(330) 263-2180
Worcester State College	486 Chandler St., Worcester, MA 01602	Dirk Baker	(508) 929-8852
Worcester Tech	100 Institute Rd., Worcester, MA 01609	Chris Robertson	(508) 831-5624
York College	1125 E. 8th St., York, NE 68467	Jerry Laird	(402) 363-5736
York College	Country Club Road, York, PA 17405	Paul Saikia	(717) 815-1245

JUNIOR COLLEGE

School	Address	Coach	Telephone
Abraham Baldwin College	ABAC 41, Tifton, GA 31794	Steve Janousek	(229) 386-7217
Adirondack CC	Bay Road, Queensbury, NY 12804	Mike Leonbrund	(518) 743-2269
Alabama Southern CC	P.O. Box 2000, Monroeville, AL 36461	Mike Jeffcoat	(251) 575-3156
Alfred State Col	Orvis Center, Alfred, NY 14802	Tom Kenney	(607) 587-4369
Allan Hancock Col	800 S. College Dr., Santa Maria, CA 93454	Chris Stevens	(805) 922-6966
Allegany College	12401 Willowbrook Rd., Cumberland, MD 21502	Steve Bazarnic	(301) 784-5267
Allegheny CCAC	808 Ridge Ave., Pittsburgh, PA 15212	Bob Janeda	(412) 237-2563
Allegheny County CC -Boyce	595 Beatty Rd., Monroeville, PA 15146	Bill Holmes	(724) 325-6621
Allegheny County CC -South	1750 Clairton Rd., West Mifflin, PA 15122	Jeff Minick	(412) 469-4304
Allen County CC	1801 N. Cottonwood St., Iola, KS 66749	Val McLean	(620) 365-5116
Alvin CC	3110 Mustang Rd., Alvin, TX 77511	Bryan Alexander	(281) 756-3694
American River Col	4700 College Oak Dr., Sacramento, CA 95841	Kevin Higgins	(916) 484-8294
Ancilla College	9601 S. Union Rd., Donaldson, IN 46513	Gene Reese	(574) 936-8898
Andrew College	413 College St., Cuthbert, GA 31740	Chip Reese	(229) 732-5953
Angelina College	P.O. Box 1768, Lufkin, TX 75902	Jeff Livin	(936) 633-5282
Anne Arundel CC	101 College Parkway, Arnold, MD 21012	Lou DiMenna	(410) 777-2034
Anoka-Ramsey CC	11200 Mississippi Blvd. NW, Coon Rapids, MN 55433	Tom Yelle	(763) 422-3521
Antelope Valley Col	3041 W. Avenue K, Lancaster, CA 93536	Jeffrey Leonard	(661) 722-6449
Arapahoe CC	5900 S. Santa Fe Dr., Littleton, CO 80160	Buzz Banda	(303) 797-5853
Arizona Western College	P.O. Box 929, Yuma, AZ 85366	John Stratton	(928) 344-7542
Arkansas-Fort Smith	5210 Grand Ave., Fort Smith, AR 72913	Dale Harpenau	(479) 788-7591
Bakersfield College	1801 Panorama Dr., Bakersfield, CA 93305	Tim Painton	(805) 395-4261
Baltimore CC-Liberty	2901 Liberty Heights Ave, Baltimore, MD 21215	Lance Mauch	(410) 462-8320
Barstow CC	2700 Barstow Rd., Barstow, CA 92311	Mike Gorman	(760) 252-7296
Barton County CC	245 NE 30th Rd., Great Bend, KS 67530	Mike Warren	(620) 792-9373
Bellevue CC	3000 Landerholm Circle SE, Bellevue, WA 98007	Mark Yoshino	(425) 564-2356
Bergen CC	400 Paramus Rd., Paramus, NJ 07652	Manny Del Rosario	(201) 447-7183
Bethany Lutheran Col	700 Luther Dr., Mankato, MN 56001	Derek Woodley	(507) 344-7375
Bevill State CC- Fayette	2631 Temple Ave N., Fayette, AL 35555	Joey May	(205) 932-3221
Bevill State CC- Sumiton	P.O. Box 800, Sumiton, AL 35148	Ed Langham	(205) 648-3271
Big Bend CC	7662 Chanute St., Moses Lake, WA 98837	Don Lindgren	(509) 762-5351
Bishop State CC	351 N. Broad St., Mobile, AL 36603	Johnny Watkins	(334) 690-6807
Bismarck State Col	P.O. Box 5587, Bismarck, ND 58506	Buster Gillis	(701) 224-5480
Black Hawk College	6600 34th Ave., Moline, IL 61265	Tim McChesney	(309) 796-5602
Blinn College	902 College Ave., Brenham, TX 77833	Brian Roper	(979) 830-4171
Blue Mountain CC	P.O. Box 100, Pendleton, OR 97801	Brett Bryan	(541) 278-5900
Blue Ridge CC	College Drive, Flat Rock, NC 28731	Damon Towe	(828) 694-1778
Bossier Parish CC	2719 Airline Dr., Bossier City, LA 71111	Jay Artigues	(318) 746-9851
Briarcliffe College	1055 Stewart Ave., Bethpage, NY 11714	Jack Bryant	(516) 918-3731
Brigham Young U.-Idaho	Hart Bldg., 264 Athletic Office, Rexburg, ID 83460	Don Schiess	(208) 356-2127
Bronx CC	W. 181st & University, Bronx, NY 10453	Adolfo DeJesus	(718) 289-5274
Brookdale CC	765 Newman Springs Rd., Lincroft, NJ 07738	Johnny Johnson	(732) 224-2542
Brookhaven College	3939 Valley View Lane, Farmers Branch, TX 75244	Denny Dixon	(972) 860-4121
Broome CC	P.O. Box 1017, Binghamton, NY 13902	Scott Landers	(607) 778-5003
Broward CC-Downtown	3501 SW Davie Rd., Davie, FL 33314	Mike Silvestri	(954) 475-6949

Broward CC-Central	3501 Davie Rd., Davie, FL 33314	Bob Detchsman	(954) 475-6995
Brown Mackie Col	2106 S. Ninth, Salina, KS 67401	Steve Bartow	(785) 825-5422
Bucks County CC	Gym Office #102, Swamp Rd, Newton, PA 18940	Lou Pacchioli	(215) 504-8551
Bunker Hill CC	250 New Rutherford Ave, Charlestown, MA 02129	David Treska	(617) 228-2088
Burlington County Col	Pemberton-Browns Mills Rd, Pemberton, NJ 08068	John Holt	(609) 894-9311
Butler County CC	901 S. Haverhill Rd., El Dorado, KS 67042	Trent Nesmith	(316) 322-3201
Butler County CC	P.O. Box 1203, Butler, PA 16003	Tom Roper	(724) 287-8711
Butte College	3536 Butte Campus Dr., Oroville, CA 95965	Wendell Bolar	(530) 895-2521
Cabrillo College	6500 Soquel Dr., Aptos, CA 95003	Rich Weidinger	(831) 479-6594
Camden County College	P.O. Box 200, Blackwood, NJ 08012	Frank Angeloni	(856) 227-7200
Canada College	4200 Farm Hill Blvd., Redwood City, CA 94061	Mike Garcia	(650) 306-3275
Canyons, College of the	26455 Rockwell Canyon Rd., Santa Clarita, CA 91355	Chris Cota	(661) 259-7800
Carl Albert State College	1507 S. McKenna St., Poteau, OK 74953	Mark Pollard	(918) 647-1376
Carl Sandburg College	2400 Tom L. Wilson Blvd., Galesburg, IL 61401	Mike Bailey	(309) 341-5227
CCBC-Catonsville	800 S. Rolling Rd., Catonsville, MD 21228	Pat Crouse	(410) 455-6996
CCBC-Dundalk	7200 Sollers Point Rd., Baltimore, MD 21222	Scott Roane	(410) 285-9714
CCBC-Essex	7201 Rossville Blvd., Baltimore, MD 21237	George Henderson	(410) 780-6346
Cecil CC	One Seahwack Dr., North East, MD 21901	Charlie O'Brien	(410) 287-6060
Cedar Valley College	3030 N. Dallas Ave., Lancaster, TX 75134	Kyle Koehler	(972) 860-8177
Central Alabama CC	1675 Cherokee Rd., Alexander City, AL 35010	Don Ingram	(256) 215-4320
Central Arizona College	8470 N. Overfield Rd., Coolidge, AZ 85228	Clint Myers	(520) 426-4336
Central Florida CC	3001 SW College Rd., Ocala, FL 34471	Marty Smith	(352) 237-2111
Central Lakes College	501 W. College Dr., Brainerd, MN 56401	Warren Mertens	(218) 855-8211
Centralia College	600 W. Locust St., Centralia, WA 98531	Bruce Pocklington	(360) 736-9391
Cerritos College	11110 East Alondra Blvd., Norwalk, CA 90650	Geraldo Perez	(562) 860-2451
Cerro Coso CC	3000 College Heights Blvd., Ridgecrest, CA 93555	Dick Adams	(760) 384-6386
Chabot College	25555 Hesperian Blvd., Hayward, CA 94545	Steve Friend	(510) 723-6935
Chaffey College	5885 Haven Ave., Rancho Cucamonga, CA 91737	Chuck Deagle	(909) 941-2345
Chandler-Gilbert CC	2626 E. Pecos Rd., Chandler, AZ 85225	Doyle Wilson	(480) 732-7177
Chattahoochee Valley CC	2602 College Dr., Phenix City, AL 36869	Adam Thomas	(334) 291-4908
Chattanooga State Tech CC	4501 Amnicola Hwy., Chattanooga, TN 37406	Skip Shook	(423) 697-3397
Chemeketa CC	4000 Lancaster Dr. NE, Salem, OR 97305	John Doran	(503) 339-5081
Chesapeake College	P.O. Box 8, Wye Mills, MD 21679	Frank Szymanski	(410) 827-5828
Chipola JC	3094 Indian Circle, Marianna, FL 32446	Jeff Johnson	(850) 718-2237
Citrus College	1000 W. Foothill Blvd., Glendora, CA 91741	Skip Claprood	(626) 914-8656
Clackamas CC	19600 S. Molalla Ave., Oregon City, OR 97045	Robin Robinson	(503) 657-6958
Clarendon College	P.O. Box 968, Clarendon, TX 79226	Trent Petrie	(806) 874-3571
Clark State CC	P.O. Box 570, Springfield, OH 45501	Tim Riger	(937) 328-6027
Cleveland State CC	P.O. Box 3570, Cleveland, TN 37320	Mike Policastro	(423) 478-6219
Clinton CC	136 Clinton Point Dr., Plattsburgh, NY 12901	Tom Neale	(518) 562-4220
Cloud County CC	Box 1002, Concordia, KS 66901	Bryan Conger	(785) 243-1435
Coahoma JC	3240 Friars Point Rd., Clarksdale, MS 38614	Billy Fields	(662) 621-4231
Cochise County CC	4190 W. Hwy. 80, Douglas, AZ 85607	Todd Inglehart	(520) 417-4095
Coffeyville CC	400 W. 11th St., Coffeyville, KS 67337	Matt Ranson	(620) 252-7095
Colby CC	1255 S. Range Ave, Colby, KS 67701	Ryan Carter	(785) 462-3984
Collin County CC	2800 E. Spring Creek Pkwy., Plano, TX 75074	Greg Dennis	(972) 881-5150
Colorado Northwestern CC	500 Kennedy Dr., Rangely, CO 81648	George Fortunato	(970) 675-3317
Columbia Basin CC	2600 N. 20th Ave., Pasco, WA 99301	Scott Rogers	(509) 547-0511
Columbia State CC	P.O. Box 1315, Columbia, TN 38402	Jim Painter	(931) 540-2632
Columbia-Greene CC	4400 Route 23, Hudson, NY 12534	Bob Godlewski	(518) 828-4181
Columbus State CC	550 E. Spring St., Columbus, OH 43215	Greg Weyrich	(614) 287-2616
Compton CC	111 East Artesia Blvd., Compton, CA 90221	Simon Peters	(310) 900-1600
Connecticut-Avery Point, U. of	1084 Shennescossett Rd., Groton, CT 06340	Roger Bidwell	(860) 405-9183
Connors State College	Rt. 1, Box 1000, Warner, OK 74469	Perry Keith	(918) 463-6218
Contra Costa College	2600 Mission Bell Dr., San Pablo, CA 94806	Marvin Webb	(510) 235-7800
Copiah-Lincoln JC	P.O. Box 649, Wesson, MS 39191	Keith Case	(601) 643-8381
Corning CC	1 Academic Dr., Corning, NY 14830	Brian Hall	(607) 962-9383
Cosumnes River Col	8401 Center Pkwy., Sacramento CA 95823	Tony Bloomfield	(916) 691-7397
Cowley County CC	125 S. 2nd St., Arkansas City, KS 67005	Dave Burroughs	(620) 441-5246
Crowder College	601 Laclede Ave., Neosho, MO 64850	Chip Durban	(417) 455-5480
Cuesta College	P.O. Box 8106, San Luis Obispo, CA 93403	Bob Miller	(805) 546-3100
Cumberland County College	P.O. Box 1500, Vineland, NJ 08362	Don Robbins	(856) 691-8600
Cuyahoga CC-West	2900 Community College Ave., Cleveland, OH 44130	Brian Harrison	(216) 987-3623
Cypress College	9200 Valley View St., Cypress, CA 90630	Scott Pickler	(714) 821-7870
Danville Area CC	2000 E. Main St., Danville, IL 61832	Tim Bunton	(217) 443-8807
Darton College	2400 Gillionville Rd., Albany, GA 31707	Glenn Eames	(229) 430-6788
Dawson CC	P.O. Box 421, Glendive, MT 59330	Brent Diegel	(406) 377-9450
Daytona Beach CC	P.O. Box 2811, Daytona Beach, FL 32120	Tim Touma	(386) 254-4486
Dean College	99 Main St., Franklin, MA 02038	Kevin Burr	(508) 541-1814
De Anza College	21250 Stevens Creek Blvd., Cupertino, CA 95014	Scott Hertler	(408) 864-8741

Delaware County CC	901 S. Media Line Rd., Media, PA 19063	Paul Motta	(610) 353-8584
Delaware Tech & CC-Owens	P.O. Box 610, Route 18, Georgetown, DE 19947	Curtis Brock	(302) 855-1636
Delgado CC	615 City Park Ave., New Orleans, LA 70119	Joe Scheuermann	(504) 483-4381
Des Moines Area CC-Boone	1125 Hancock Dr., Boone, IA 50036	John Smith	(515) 433-5050
Desert, College of the	43500 Monterey Ave., Palm Desert, CA 92260	David Buttles	(760) 773-2585
Diablo Valley College	321 Golf Club Rd., Pleasant Hill, CA 94523	Larry Quirico	(925) 685-1230
Dixie State College	225 S. 700 E., St. George, UT 84770	Mike Littlewood	(435) 652-7530
Dodge City CC	2501 N. 14th Ave., Dodge City, KS 67801	Erick Wright	(620) 227-9347
DuPage, College of	425 Fawell Blvd., Glen Ellyn, IL 60137	Dan Kusinski	(630) 942-2734
Dutchess CC	53 Pendell Rd., Poughkeepsie, NY 12601	Joe DeRosa	(845) 431-8468
Dyersburg State CC	1510 Lake Rd., Dyersburg, TN 38024	Eliseo Herrera	(731) 286-3259
East Central CC	P.O. Box 129, Decatur, MS 39327	Jake Yarborough	(601) 635-2111
East Central College	P.O. Box 529, Union, MO 63084	Gale Wallis	(314) 583-5195
East Los Angeles College	1301 Avenida Cesar Chavez, Monterey Park, CA 91754	James Hines	(323) 265-8650
East Mississippi JC	P.O. Box 158, Scooba, MS 39358	Bill Baldner	(662) 476-5128
Eastern Arizona JC	3714 Church St., Thatcher, AZ 85552	Jim Bagnall	(928) 428-8414
Eastern Oklahoma State	1301 W. Main St., Wilburton, OK 74578	Todd Shelton	(918) 465-2361
Eastern Utah, College of	451 E. 400 N., Price, UT 84501	Eric Madsen	(435) 613-5357
Eastfield College	3737 Motley Dr., Mesquite, TX 75150	Michael Martin	(972) 860-7643
Edison CC	College Pkwy., Fort Myers, FL 33907	John Cedarburg	(941) 489-9486
Edmonds CC	20000 68th Ave. W., Lynnwood, WA 98036	Don Marbut	(425) 640-1507
El Camino College	16007 Crenshaw Blvd., Torrance, CA 90506	Nick Van Lue	(310) 660-3679
El Paso CC	P.O. Box 20500, El Paso, TX 79998	Ken Jacome	(915) 831-2277
Elgin CC	1700 Spartan Dr., Elgin, IL 60123	Bill Angelo	(847) 214-7552
Ellsworth CC	1100 College Ave., Iowa Falls, IA 50126	Joel Lueken	(641) 648-4611
Enterprise State JC	600 Plaza Dr., Enterprise, AL 36330	Tim Hulsey	(334) 347-2623
Erie CC	21 Oak St., Buffalo, NY 14221	Joe Bauth	(716) 851-1220
Everett CC	2000 Tower St., Everett, WA 98201	Levi Lacey	(425) 388-9322
Faulkner State CC	1900 Hwy. 31 South, Bay Minette, AL 36507	Wayne Larker	(334) 580-2160
Fergus Falls CC	1414 College Way, Fergus Falls, MN 56357	Kent Bothwell	(218) 739-7538
Finger Lakes CC	4355 Lakeshore Dr., Canandaigua, NY 14424	Jason Rich	(585) 394-3500
Florida CC	11901 Beach Blvd., Jacksonville, FL 32216	Chris Blaquiere	(904) 646-2205
Florida College	119 N. Glen Arven Ave., Temple Terrace, FL 33617	Kerry Keenan	(813) 899-6789
Forest Park JC	5600 Oakland Ave., St. Louis, MO 63110	Darin Hendrickson	(314) 644-9688
Fort Scott CC	2108 S. Horton St., Fort Scott, KS 66701	Ryan McCune	(620) 223-2700
Frank Phillips College	P.O. Box 5118, Borger, TX 79008	Guy Simmons	(806) 274-5961
Frederick CC	7932 Opossumtown Pike, Frederick, MD 21702	Rodney Bennett	(301) 846-2501
Fresno City College	1101 E. University Ave., Fresno, CA 93741	Ron Scott	(559) 237-8974
Fullerton College	321 E. Chapman Ave., Fullerton, CA 92832	Nick Fuscardo	(714) 992-7401
Fulton-Montgomery CC	2805 State Highway 67, Johnstown, NY 12095	Mike Mulligan	(518) 762-4651
Gadsden State CC	P.O. Box 227, Gadsden, AL 35902	Bill Lockridge	(256) 549-8331
Galveston College	4015 Avenue Q, Galveston, TX 77550	Ruben Felix	(409) 763-6551
Garden City CC	801 Campus Dr., Garden City, KS 67846	Rick Sabath	(620) 276-9595
Garrett CC	687 Mosser Rd., McHenry, MD 21541	Ed Wildesen	(301) 387-3052
Gateway Tech CC	60 Sargent Dr., New Haven, CT 06511	Darryl Morhardt	(203) 285-2213
Gavilan College	5055 Santa Teresa Blvd., Gilroy, CA 95020	Mike McCormick	(408) 848-4916
Genesee CC	1 College Rd., Batavia, NY 14021	Barry Carigen	(585) 345-6898
George C. Wallace CC	1141 Wallace Dr., Dothan, AL 36303	Mackey Sasser	(334) 983-3521
George C. Wallace State	P.O. Drawer 1049, Selma, AL 36702	Todd Alford	(334) 876-9227
Georgia Perimeter College	3251 Panthersville Rd., Decatur, GA 30034	David Stephenson	(404) 244-5765
Glen Oaks CC	62249 Shimmel Rd., Centreville, MI 49032	Chad Newhard	(269) 467-9945
Glendale CC	6000 W. Olive Ave., Glendale, AZ 85302	David Grant	(623) 845-3046
Glendale College	1500 N. Verdugo Rd., Glendale, CA 91208	Jon Strauss	(818) 240-1000
Globe Tech	291 Broadway, New York, NY 10007	Chris Carminucci	(212) 349-4330
Gloucester County College	1400 Tanyard Rd., Sewell, NJ 08080	Rob Valli	(856) 415-2213
Golden West College	15744 Golden West St., Huntington Beach, CA 92647	Roberto Villarreal	(714) 895-8260
Gordon College	419 College Dr., Barnesville, GA 30204	Travis McClanahan	(770) 358-5037
Grand Rapids CC	143 Bostwick Ave. NE, Grand Rapids, MI 49503	Doug Wabeke	(616) 234-4271
Grays Harbor College	1620 Edward P. Smith Dr., Aberdeen, WA 98520	Shon Schreiber	(360) 538-4207
Grayson County College	6101 Grayson Dr., Denison, TX 75020	Tim Tadlock	(903) 463-8719
Green River CC	12401 SE 320th St., Auburn, WA 98092	Matt Acker	(253) 833-9111
Grossmont College	8800 Grossmont College Dr., El Cajon, CA 92020	Ed Olsen	(619) 644-7447
Gulf Coast CC	5230 W. Highway 98, Panama City, FL 32401	Darren Mazeroski	(850) 872-3830
Hagerstown CC	11400 Robinwood Dr., Hagerstown, MD 21742	Scott Jennings	(301) 790-2800
Harford CC	401 Thomas Run Rd., Bel Air, MD 21015	John Cephalis	(410) 836-4321
Harper College	1200 W. Algonquin Rd., Palatine, IL 60067	Norm Garrett	(847) 925-6957
Hartnell CC	156 Homestead Ave., Salinas, CA 93901	Dan Teresa	(831) 755-6840
Henry Ford CC	5101 Evergreen Rd., Dearborn, MI 48128	Stuart Rose	(313) 845-9647
Herkimer County CC	100 Reservoir Rd., Herkimer, NY 13350	Henry Testa	(315) 866-0300

Hesston College	325 S. College Dr., Hesston, KS 67062	Art Mullet	(620) 327-8278
Hibbing CC	1515 E. 25th St., Hibbing, MN 55746	Mike Turnbull	(218) 262-6749
Highland CC	2998 W. Pearl City Rd., Freeport, IL 61032	Mike Edmonds	(815) 599-3465
Highland CC	606 W. Main, Highland, KS 66035	Rick Eberly	(785) 442-6039
Hill JC	P.O. Box 619, Hillsboro, TX 76645	Gary Benton	(254) 582-2555
Hillsborough CC	P.O. Box 30030, Tampa, FL 33630	Gary Calhoun	(813) 253-7446
Hinds CC	P.O. Box 1100, Raymond, MS 39154	Rick Clarke	(601) 857-3520
Hiwassee College	225 Hiwassee College Dr., Madisonville, TN 37354	Jerry Edwards	(423) 442-2001
Holmes CC	P.O. Box 369, Goodman, MS 39079	Kenny Dupont	(662) 472-9024
Holyoke CC	303 Homestead Ave., Holyoke, MA 01040	Pat Consedine	(413) 552-2163
Hostos CC	500 Grand Concourse, Bronx, NY 10451	John Sanchez	(718) 518-6879
Howard College	1001 Birdwell Lane, Big Spring, TX 79720	Justin Hays	(915) 264-5195
Hudson Valley CC	80 Vandenburg Ave., Troy, NY 12180	Tom Reinisch	(518) 629-7328
Hutchinson CC	1300 N. Plum St., Hutchinson, KS 67501	Jon Wente	(316) 665-3441
Illinois Central College	One College Dr., East Peoria, IL 61635	Brett Kelley	(309) 694-5429
Illinois Valley CC	815 N. Orlando Smith St., Oglesby, IL 61348	Bob Koopman	(815) 224-0471
Imperial Valley College	P.O. Box 158, Imperial, CA 92251	Dave Drury	(760) 355-6323
Independence CC	P.O. Box 708, Independence, KS 67301	Jon Olsen	(620) 331-4100
Indians Hills CC	721 N. 1st St., Centerville, IA 52544	Cam Walker	(515) 856-2143
Indian River CC	3209 Virginia Ave., Fort Pierce, FL 34981	Mike Easom	(772) 462-4772
Iowa Central CC	330 Avenue M, Fort Dodge, IA 50501	Rick Sandquist	(515) 576-7201
Iowa Lakes CC	300 S. 18th St., Estherville, IA 51334	Jason Nell	(712) 362-7903
Iowa Western CC	2700 College Rd., Council Bluffs, IA 51503	Therron Brockish	(712) 325-3402
Irvine Valley College	5500 Irvine Center Dr., Irvine, CA 92620	Kent Madole	(949) 451-5763
Itasca CC	1851 E. Hwy. 169, Grand Rapids, MN 55744	Justin Lamppa	(218) 327-4226
Itawamba CC	602 W. Hill St., Fulton, MS 38843	Rick Collier	(662) 862-8122
Jackson State CC	2046 N. Parkway, Jackson, TN 38301	Steve Cornelison	(731) 425-2649
Jamestown CC	525 Falconer St., Jamestown, NY 14701	Kerry Kellogg	(716) 665-5220
Jefferson CC	1220 Coffeen St., Watertown, NY 13601	Paul Alteri	(315) 786-2248
Jefferson College	1000 Viking Dr., Hillsboro, MO 63050	Dave Oster	(636) 797-3000
Jefferson Davis CC	P.O. Box 958, Brewton, AL 36427	Mark Jackson	(251) 809-1622
Jefferson State CC	2601 Carson Rd., Birmingham, AL 35215	Ben Short	(205) 856-7879
John A. Logan College	700 Logan College Rd., Carterville, IL 62918	Jerry Halstead	(618) 985-2828
Johnson County CC	12345 College Blvd., Overland Park, KS 66210	Kent Shelley	(913) 469-3820
John C. Calhoun CC	P.O. Box 2216, Decatur, AL 35609	Gary Redus	(205) 306-2854
John Wood CC	150 S. 48th St., Quincy, IL 62301	Greg Wathen	(217) 641-4308
Joliet JC	1215 Houbolt Rd., Joliet, IL 60431	Wayne King	(815) 280-2210
Jones County JC	900 S. Court St., Ellisville, MS 39437	Bobby Glaze	(601) 477-4087
Kalamazoo Valley CC	P.O. Box 4070, Kalamazoo, MI 49003	Dave Koren	(616) 372-5393
Kankakee CC	P.O. Box 888, River Rd., Kankakee, IL 60901	Todd Post	(815) 933-0228
Kansas City CC	7250 State Ave., Kansas City, KS 66112	Steve Burleson	(913) 288-7150
Kaskaskia CC	27210 College Rd., Centralia, IL 62801	Brad Tuttle	(618) 545-3146
Kellogg CC	450 North Ave., Battle Creek, MI 49017	Russ Bortell	(269) 965-4151
Kemper Military JC	701 3rd St., Boonville, MO 65233	Jayson Campbell	(660) 882-5623
Keystone College	One College Green, La Plume, PA 18440	Jamie Shevchik	(570) 945-5141
Kingsborough CC	2001 Oriental Blvd., Brooklyn, NY 11235	Jim Ryan	(718) 368-5737
Kirkwood CC	P.O. Box 2068, Cedar Rapids, IA 52406	John Lewis	(319) 398-5589
Kishwaukee College	21193 Malta Rd., Malta, IL 60150	Mike Davenport	(815) 825-2086
Labette CC	200 S. 14th St., Parsons, KS 67357	Tom Hilton	(620) 820-1011
Lackawanna JC	500 Jefferson Ave., Scranton, PA 18509	Mike Bartoletti	(570) 961-0700
Lake City CC	RR 19, Box 1030, Lake City, FL 32025	Tom Clark	(386) 754-4363
Lake County, College of	19351 W. Washington St., Grayslake, IL 60030	Gene Hanson	(847) 543-2046
Lake Land College	5001 Lake Land Blvd., Mattoon, IL 61938	Jim Jarrett	(217) 234-5496
Lake Michigan College	2755 E. Napier Ave., Benton Harbor, MI 49022	Keith Schreiber	(269) 927-8165
Lake Sumter CC	9501 US Hwy. 441, Leesburg, FL 32788	Mike Matulia	(352) 323-3643
Lakeland CC	7700 Clocktower Dr., Kirtland, OH 44094	Howie Krause	(440) 953-7350
Lamar CC	2401 S. Main St., Lamar, CO 81052	Scott Crampton	(719) 336-1681
Lane CC	4000 E. 30th Ave., Eugene, OR 97405	Donny Harrel	(541) 463-5599
Laney College	900 Fallon St., Oakland, CA 94607	Francisco Zapata	(510) 464-3476
Lansing CC	P.O. Box 40010, Lansing, MI 48901	Frank Deak	(517) 483-1622
Laredo CC	West End, Washington St., Laredo, TX 78040	Ruben Lozano	(956) 721-5326
Lassen College	P.O. Box 3000, Susanville, CA 96130	Glen Yonan	(530) 251-8815
Lenoir CC	P.O. Box 188, Kinston, NC 28502	Lind Hartsell	(252) 527-6223
Lewis & Clark CC	5800 Godfrey Rd., Godfrey, IL 62035	Randy Martz	(618) 468-6230
Lincoln College	300 Keokuk St., Lincoln, IL 62656	Tony Thomas	(217) 732-3155
Lincoln Land CC	5250 Shepherd Rd., Springfield, IL 62794	Ron Riggle	(217) 786-2581
Lincoln Trail College	11220 State Hwy. 1, Robinson, IL 62454	Mitch Hannahs	(618) 544-8657
Linn-Benton CC	6500 Pacific Blvd. SW, Albany, OR 97321	Greg Hawk	(541) 917-4242
Lon Morris College	800 College Ave., Jacksonville, TX 75766	Barry Hoffpauir	(903) 589-4000

Long Beach City College	4901 E. Carson St., Long Beach, CA 90808	Casey Crook	(562) 938-4242
Longview CC	500 SW Longview Rd., Lee's Summit, MO 64081	Mark Lyford	(816) 672-2440
Los Angeles City College	855 N. Vermont Ave., Los Angeles, CA 90029	Robert McKinley	(323) 953-4000
Los Angeles Harbor College	1111 Figueroa Pl., Wilmington, CA 90744	Jay Uhlman	(310) 522-8464
Los Angeles Pierce College	6201 Winnetka Ave., Woodland Hills, CA 91371	Bob Lofrano	(818) 710-2823
Los Angeles Valley College	5800 Fulton Ave., Valley Glen, CA 91401	Chris Johnson	(818) 947-2509
Los Medanos College	2700 E. Leland Rd., Pittsburg, CA 94565	Carl Fraticelli	(925) 439-2185
Louisburg College	501 N. Main St., Louisburg, NC 27549	Billy Godwin	(919) 497-3266
Lower Columbia College	P.O. Box 3010, Longview, WA 98632	Kelly Smith	(360) 442-2870
LSU-Eunice	P.O. Box 1129, Eunice, LA 70535	David Russo	(337) 550-1394
Lurleen B. Wallace State JC	P.O. Box 1418, Andalusia, AL 36420	Steve Helms	(334) 222-6591
Macomb CC	14500 E. 12 Mile Rd., Warren, MI 48093	Mike Kaczmarek	(586) 445-7119
Madison Area Tech	3550 Anderson St., Madison, WI 53704	Leo Kalinowski	(608) 246-6099
Manatee CC	5840 26th St. W, Bradenton, FL 34207	Tim Hill	(941) 752-5261
Manchester CC	P.O. Box 1046, Manchester, CT 06045	Chris Strahowski	(860) 512-3353
Manhattan CC	199 Chambers St., New York, NY 10007	Juan Colon	(212) 346-8279
Maple Woods CC	2601 NE Barry Rd., Kansas City, MO 64156	Chris Mihlfeld	(816) 437-3175
Marin CC	835 College Ave., Kentfield, CA 94904	Steve Berringer	(415) 485-9589
Marion Military Institute	1101 Washington St., Marion, AL 36756	Gerry Lewis	(334) 683-2359
Marshalltown CC	3700 S. Center St., Marshalltown, IA 50158	Kevin Benzing	(641) 752-7106
Massachusetts Bay CC	50 Oakland St., Wellesley Hills, MA 02481	Alan Harrison	(508) 270-4065
Massasoit CC	1 Massasoit Blvd., Brockton, MA 02302	Thomas Frizzell	(508) 588-9100
McCook CC	1205 E. 3rd St., McCook, NE 69001	Ryan Jones	(308) 345-6303
McHenry County College	8900 U.S. Hwy. 14, Crystal Lake, IL 60012	Kim Johnson	(815) 455-8547
McLennan CC	1400 College Dr., Waco, TX 76708	David Wrzesinski	(254) 299-8811
Mendocino CC	1000 Hensley Creek Rd, Ukiah, CA 95482	Matthew Gordon	(707) 468-3142
Merced College	3600 M St., Merced, CA 95348	Chris Pedretti	(209) 384-6028
Mercer County CC	1200 Old Trenton Rd., Trenton, NJ 08690	Randy Voorhees	(609) 586-4800
Mercyhurst-North East	16 W. Division St., North East, PA 16428	Mike Folga	(814) 725-6390
Meridian CC	910 Hwy. 19 N., Meridian MS 39307	Mike Federico	(601) 484-8670
Mesa CC	1833 W. Southern Ave., Mesa, AZ 85202	Tony Cirelli	(480) 461-7562
Mesabi Range College	1001 Chestnut St W., Virginia, MN 55792	Brad Scott	(218) 748-2424
Miami-Dade CC	11011 SW 104 St., Miami, FL 33176	Steve Hertz	(305) 237-0730
Miami U.-Middletown	4200 E. University Blvd., Middletown, OH 45042	Kenneth Prichard	(513) 727-3273
Middle Georgia College	1100 2nd St. SE, Cochran, GA 31014	Craig Young	(478) 934-3044
Middlesex County College	2600 Woodbridge Ave., Edison, NJ 08817	Michael Lepore	(732) 906-2558
Midland College	3600 N. Garfield St., Midland, TX 79705	Steve Ramharter	(915) 685-5561
Miles CC	2715 Dickinson St., Miles City, MT 59301	Rob Bishop	(406) 234-3536
Milwaukee Area Tech	700 W. State St., Milwaukee, WI 53233	Chris Merritt	(414) 297-7872
Mineral Area JC	5270 Flat River Rd., Park Hills, MO 63601	Jim Komar	(573) 518-2104
Minnesota West Comm. & Tech	1450 College Way, Worthington, MN 56187	Brian Iverson	(507) 372-3409
Minot State U.	105 Simrall Blvd., Bottineau, ND 58318	Ian Shoemaker	(701) 228-5457
Mission College	3000 Mission College Blvd., Santa Clara, CA 95054	Todd Eagen	(408) 855-5366
Mississippi Delta CC	P.O. Box 668, Moorhead, MS 38761	Terry Thompson	(662) 246-6303
Mississippi Gulf Coast JC	Box 548, Perkinston, MS 39573	Cooper Farris	(601) 928-6224
Mitchell College	437 Pequot Ave., New London, CT 06320	Len Farquhar	(860) 701-5047
Modesto JC	435 College Ave., Modesto, CA 95350	Paul Aiello	(209) 575-6274
Mohawk Valley CC	1101 Sherman Dr., Utica, NY 13501	Dave Warren	(315) 792-5570
Monroe CC	1000 E. Henrietta Rd., Rochester, NY 14623	Skip Bailey	(585) 292-2088
Monterey Peninsula College	980 Fremont St., Monterey, CA 93940	Kenny Leonesio	(831) 646-4223
Montgomery College-Rockville	51 Mannakee St., Rockville, MD 20850	Tom Shaffer	(301) 251-7985
Montgomery-Germantown	20200 Observation Dr., Germantown, MD 20876	Tom Cassera	(301) 353-7727
Moorpark College	7075 Campus Rd., Moorpark, CA 93021	Mario Porto	(805) 378-1457
Moraine Valley CC	10900 S. 88th Ave., Palos Hills, IL 60465	Al Budding	(708) 974-5213
Morris, County College of	214 Center Grove Rd., Randolph, NJ 07869	Ed Moskal	(973) 328-5252
Morton College	3801 S. Central Ave., Cicero, IL 60804	Tony Hubbard	(708) 656-8000
Motlow State CC	P.O. Box 8500, Lynchburg, TN 37352	Don Rhoton	(931) 393-1615
Mott CC	1401 E. Court St., Flint, MI 48503	Dan LaNoue	(810) 762-0419
Mount Hood CC	26000 SE Stark St., Gresham, OR 97030	Gabe Sandy	(503) 491-7352
Mount San Antonio College	1100 N. Grand Ave., Walnut, CA 91789	Stacy Parker	(909) 594-5611
Mount San Jacinto CC	1499 N. State St., San Jacinto, CA 92583	Steve Alonzo	(909) 487-6752
Murray State College	1 Murray Campus, Tishomingo, OK 73460	Mike McBrayer	(580) 371-2371
Muscatine CC	152 Colorado St., Muscatine, IA 52761	Bob Allison	(563) 288-6001
Muskegon CC	221 S. Quarterline Rd., Muskegon, MI 49442	Cap Pohlman	(231) 777-0381
Napa Valley College	2277 Napa-Vallejo Hwy., Napa, CA 94558	Bob Freschi	(707) 253-3232
Nassau CC	One Education Dr., Garden City, NY 11530	Larry Minor	(516) 572-7522
Naugatuck Valley Tech	750 Chase Pkwy., Waterbury, CT 06708	Steve Baldwin	(203) 575-8073
Navarro College	3200 W. 7th Ave., Corsicana, TX 75110	Skip Johnson	(903) 875-7487
Neosho County CC	800 W. 14th St., Chanute, KS 66720	Steve Murry	(620) 431-2820
New Hampshire Tech	11 Institute Dr., Concord, NH 03301	Tom Neal	(603) 271-6426

New Mexico JC	5317 N. Lovington Hwy., Hobbs, NM 88240	Ray Birmingham	(505) 392-5503
New Mexico Military Inst.	101 W. College Blvd., Roswell, NM 88201	Marty Zeller	(505) 624-8271
Niagara County CC	3111 Saunders Settlement Rd., Sanborn, NY 14132	Dave Nemi	(716) 614-6271
North Arkansas Tech	1515 Pioneer Dr., Harrison, AR 72601	Phil Wilson	(870) 391-3287
North Central Missouri College	1301 Main St.., Trenton, MO 64683	Steve Richman	(660) 359-3948
North Central Texas College	1525 W. California St., Gainesville, TX 76240	Kevin Darwin	(940) 668-7731
North Florida CC	1000 Turner Davis Dr., Madison, FL 32340	Steve Givens	(850) 973-1609
North Hennepin CC	7411 85th Ave. N., Brooklyn Park, MN 55445	Greg Thorstad	(763) 424-0796
North Iowa Area CC	500 College Dr., Mason City, IA 50401	Todd Rima	(641) 422-4281
North Lake CC	5001 N. MacArthur Blvd., Irving, TX 75038	Steve Cummings	(972) 273-3518
North Shore CC	One Ferncroft Rd., Danvers, MA 01923	Charles Lyttle	(781) 477-2123
Northampton CC	3835 Green Pond Rd., Bethlehem, PA 18020	John Sweeney	(610) 861-5369
Northeast Mississippi CC	101 Cunningham Blvd., Booneville, MS 38829	Ray Scott	(662) 720-7309
Northeast Texas CC	P.O. Box 1307, Mount Pleasant, TX 75456	Chad Tidwell	(903) 572-1911
Northeastern JC	100 College Dr., Sterling, CO 80751	Danny Drum	(970) 521-6746
Northeastern Oklahoma A&M	200 I Street NE, Miami, OK 74354	Roger Ward	(918) 540-6323
Northern Oklahoma-Enid	P.O. Box 2300, Enid, OK 73701	Raydon Leaton	(580) 628-6760
Northern Essex CC	100 Elliot Way, Haverhill, MA 01830	Kerry Quinlan	(978) 548-2329
Northland Tech	1101 Highway 1 E., Thief River Falls, MN 56701	Guy Finstrom	(218) 681-0739
Northern Oklahoma College	1220 E. Grand Ave., Tonkawa, OK 74653	Terry Ballard	(580) 628-6218
Northwest Mississippi CC	4975 Hwy. 51 N., Senatobia, MS 38668	Donny Castle	(662) 562-3422
Northwest Shoals JC	800 George Wallace Blvd., Muscle Shoals, AL 35661	David Langston	(256) 331-5291
Norwalk CC	188 Richards Ave., Norwalk, CT 06854	Mark Lambert	(203) 857-7155
Oakton CC	1600 E. Golf Rd., Des Plaines, IL 60016	Mike Pinto	(847) 635-1753
Ocean County College	P.O. Box 2001, Toms River, NJ 08754	Ernie Leta	(732) 255-0345
Odessa College	201 W. University Blvd., Odessa, TX 79764	Rick Zimmerman	(915) 335-6850
Ohio State U.-Lima Tech	4240 Campus Dr., Lima, OH 45804	Robert Livchak	(419) 221-1641
Ohlone College	43600 Mission Blvd., Fremont, CA 94539	Paul Moore	(510) 659-6056
Okaloosa-Walton CC	100 College Blvd., Niceville, FL 32578	Keith Griffin	(850) 729-5379
Olive-Harvey	10001 S. Woodlawn Ave., Chicago, IL 60628	Mike Mayden	(773) 291-6272
Olney Central College	305 West St., Olney, IL 62450	Dennis Conley	(618) 395-7777
Olympic College	1600 Chester Ave., Bremerton, WA 98337	Michael Reese	(360) 475-7460
Onondaga CC	4941 Onondaga Rd., Syracuse, NY 13215	Joe Autanio	(315) 498-2492
Orange Coast College	P.O. Box 5005, Costa Mesa, CA 92628	John Altobelli	(714) 432-5892
Orange County CC	115 South St., Middletown, NY 10940	Wayne Smith	(845) 341-4211
Otero JC	1802 Colorado Ave., La Junta, CO 81050	Mark Priegnitz	(719) 384-6833
Owens CC	P.O. Box 10000, Toledo, OH 43699	Robert Schultz	(419) 661-7974
Oxnard College	4000 S. Rose Ave., Oxnard, CA 93033	Jon Larson	(805) 986-5800
Palm Beach CC	4200 S. Congress Ave., Lake Worth, FL 33461	Craig Gero	(561) 868-3007
Palomar College	1140 W. Mission Rd., San Marcos, CA 92069	Bob Vetter	(760) 744-1150
Panola College	1109 W. Panola St., Carthage, TX 75633	Don Clinton	(903) 693-2062
Paris JC	2400 Clarksville St., Paris, TX 75460	Deron Clark	(903) 782-0218
Parkland College	2400 W. Bradley Ave., Champaign, IL 61820	Dave Seifert	(217) 351-2297
Pasadena City College	1570 E. Colorado Blvd., Pasadena, CA 91106	Mike Scolinos	(626) 585-7789
Pasco-Hernando CC	10230 Ridge Rd., New Port Richey, FL 34654	Steve Winterling	(727) 816-3340
Pearl River CC	101 Hwy. 11 N., Poplarville, MS 39470	Jay Artigues	(601) 403-1217
Penn State-Abington	1600 Woodland Rd., Abington, PA 19001	Bobby Spratt	(215) 881-7440
Penn State-Beaver	100 University Dr., Monaca, PA 15061	Ronald Nichols	(724) 773-3879
Penn State-Berks/Lehigh	P.O. Box 7009, Reading, PA 19610	William Sutherland	(610) 396-6154
Penn State-Delaware	25 Yearsley Mill Rd., Media, PA 19063	Jeff Vickers	(610) 892-1470
Penn State-Fayette	P.O. Box 519, Uniontown, PA 15401	Joe Gessner	(724) 430-4271
Penn State-Hazleton	Highacres, Hazelton, PA 18201	Cy Falatko	(570) 450-3164
Penn State-McKeesport	4000 University Dr., McKeesport, PA 15131	Mike Cherepko	(412) 675-9483
Penn State-Mont Alto	Campus Dr., Mount Alto, PA 17237	Jim Brown	(717) 749-6172
Penn State-New Kensington	3550 7th Street Rd., New Kensington, PA 15068	Robert Darby	(724) 339-6044
Penn State-Wilkes-Barre	P.O. Box PSU, Lehman, PA 18627	Gerry Greely	(717) 675-9259
Penn State-Worthington	120 Ridgeview Dr., Dunmore, PA 18512	Jeff Mallas	(570) 963-2611
Pennsyvania Tech	One College Ave., Williamsport, PA 17701	Michael Stanzione	(570) 327-4763
Pensacola JC	1000 College Blvd., Pensacola, FL 32504	Bill Hamilton	(850) 484-1304
Philadelphia CC	1700 Spring Garden St., Philadelphia, PA 19130		(215) 751-8964
Phoenix College	1202 W. Thomas Rd., Phoenix, AZ 85013	Mike Poplin	(602) 285-7122
Pierce College	9401 Farwest Dr. SW, Lakewood, WA 98498	Brett Muche	(253) 964-6613
Pima CC	2202 W. Anklam Rd., Tucson, AZ 85709	Edgar Soto	(520) 206-6005
Pitt CC	P.O. Drawer 7007, Greenville, NC 27835	Monte Little	(252) 321-4633
Polk CC	999 Avenue H NE, Winter Haven, FL 33881	Johnny Wiggs	(863) 297-1017
Porterville College	100 E. College Ave., Porterville, CA 93257	Bret Davis	(559) 791-2335
Potomac State College	101 Fort Ave., Keyser, WV 26726	Craig Rotruck	(304) 788-6879
Prairie State College	202 S. Halstead St., Chicago Heights, IL 60411	Michael Pohlman	(708) 709-3950
Pratt CC	348 NE Hwy. 61, Pratt, KS 67124	Jeff Brewer	(620) 672-5641
Prince George's CC	301 Largo Rd., Largo, MD 20774	William Vaughan	(301) 322-0513

Queensborough CC	22205 56th Ave., Flushing, NY 11364	Craig Everett	(718) 631-6322
Quinsigamond CC	670 W. Boylston St., Worcester, MA 01606	Barry Glinski	(508) 854-4266
Ranger College	1100 College Circle, Ranger, TX 76470	Don Flowers	(254) 647-3234
Raritan Valley CC	P.O. Box 3300, Route 28, Sommerville, NJ 08876	George Repetz	(908) 526-1200
Redlands CC	1300 S. Country Club Rd., El Reno, OK 73036	Don Brown	(405) 422-1280
Redwoods, College of the	7351 Tompkins Hill Rd., Eureka, CA 95501	Bob Brown	(707) 476-4239
Reedley College	Reed & Manning Ave, Reedley, CA 93654	Jack Hacker	(559) 638-0303
Rend Lake JC	468 N. Ken Gray Pkwy., Ina, IL 62846	Greg Moddlemog	(618) 437-5321
Rhode Island, CC of	400 East Ave. Warwick, RI 02886	Jay Grenier	(401) 825-2114
Richland College	12800 Abrams Rd., Dallas, TX 75243	Bill Wharton	(972) 238-6261
Ridgewater College	2101 15th Ave. NW, Willmar, MN 56201	Dwight Kotila	(320) 231-5124
Rio Hondo College	3600 Workman Mill Rd., Whittier, CA 90601	Mike Salazar	(562) 692-0921
Riverland CC	1900 8th Ave. SW, Austin, MN 55912	Lee Brand	(507) 433-0543
Riverside CC	4800 Magnolia Ave., Riverside, CA 92506	Dennis Rogers	(909) 222-8333
Roane State CC	276 Patton Lane, Harriman, TN 37748	Larry Works	(865) 882-4583
Rochester Tech CC	851 30th Ave. SE, Rochester, MN 55904	Brian LaPlante	(507) 285-7106
Rockingham CC	P.O. Box 38, Wentworth, NC 27375	John Barrow	(336) 342-4261
Rock Valley College	3301 N. Mulford Rd., Rockford, IL 61114	Jeremy Warren	(815) 921-3802
Rockland CC	145 College Rd., Suffern, NY 10901	Dan Keeley	(845) 574-4452
Rose State College	6420 SE 15th St., Midwest City, OK 73110	Lloyd Cummings	(405) 733-7350
Roxbury CC	1234 Columbus Ave., Roxbury Crossing, MA 02120	Ed Neal	(617) 541-2477
Sacramento City College	3835 Freeport Blvd., Sacramento, CA 95822	Andy McKay	(916) 558-2684
Saddleback CC	28000 Marguerite Pkwy., Mission Viejo, CA 92692	Jack Hodges	(949) 582-4642
St. Catharine College	2735 Bardstown Rd., St. Catharine, KY 40061	Brad Shelton	(859) 336-5082
St. Charles CC	4601 Mid Rivers Mall Dr., St. Peters, MO 63376	Chris Gober	(636) 922-8211
St. Clair County CC	323 Erie St., Port Huron, MI 48060	Rick Smith	(810) 989-5671
St. Johns River CC	5001 St. Johns Ave., Palatka, FL 32177	Sam Rick	(386) 312-4162
St. Louis CC-Florissant Valley	3400 Pershall Rd., St. Louis, MO 63135	Donnie Hillerman	(314) 595-4534
St. Louis CC-Meramec	11333 Big Bend Rd., St. Louis, MO 63122	Joe Swiderski	(314) 984-7786
St. Petersburg CC	P.O. Box 13489, St. Petersburg, FL 33733	Dave Pano	(727) 341-4777
Salem CC	460 Hollywood Ave., Carney's Point, NJ 08069	Joe Houghton	(856) 351-2693
Salt Lake CC	4600 S. Redwood Rd., Salt Lake City, UT 84130	Bill Groves	(801) 957-4861
San Bernardino Valley JC	701 S. Mt. Vernon Ave., San Bernardino, CA 92410	Bill Mierzwik	(909) 384-8643
San Diego City College	1313 12th Ave., San Diego, CA 92101	Chris Brown	(619) 388-3705
San Diego Mesa College	7250 Mesa College Dr., San Diego, CA 92111	Kevin Hazlett	(619) 388-5804
San Francisco, City College of	50 Phelan Ave., San Francisco, CA 94112	John Vanocini	(415) 239-3811
San Jacinto College-North	5800 Uvalde Rd., Houston, TX 77049	Tom Arrington	(281) 459-7107
San Joaquin Delta College	5151 Pacific Ave., Stockton, CA 95207	Jim Yanko	(209) 954-5189
San Jose City College	2100 Moorpark Ave., San Jose, CA 95128	Doug Robb	(408) 288-3730
San Mateo, College of	1700 W. Hillsdale Blvd., San Mateo, CA 94402	Doug Williams	(650) 358-6875
Santa Ana College	1530 W. 17th St., Santa Ana, CA 92706	Don Sneddon	(714) 564-6911
Santa Barbara City College	721 Cliff Dr., Santa Barbara, CA 93109	Teddy Warrecker	(805) 965-0581
Santa Fe CC	3000 NW 83rd St., Gainesville, FL 32606	Harry Tholen	(352) 395-5536
Santa Rosa JC	1501 Mendocino Ave., Santa Rosa, CA 95401	Ron Myers	(707) 527-4389
Sauk Valley CC	173 State Route 2, Dixon, IL 61021	Terry Cox	(815) 288-5511
Schenectady County CC	78 Washington Ave., Schenectady, NY 12305	Tim Andi	(518) 381-1356
Scottsdale CC	9000 E. Chaparral Rd., Scottsdale, AZ 85256	Ed Yeager	(480) 423-6616
Seminole CC	100 Weldon Blvd., Sanford, FL 32773	Mike Nicholson	(407) 328-2148
Seminole State College	2701 Boren Blvd., Seminole, OK 74868	Eric Myers	(405) 382-9201
Sequoias, College of the	915 S. Mooney Blvd., Visalia, CA 93277	Jody Allen	(559) 737-6196
Seward County CC	1801 N. Kansas, Liberal, KS 67905	Galen McSpadden	(620) 629-2730
Shasta College	P.O. Box 496006, Redding, CA 96049	Brad Rupert	(530) 225-4919
Shawnee College	8364 Shawnee College Rd., Ullin, IL 62992	Greg Sheppard	(618) 634-3253
Shelby State CC	P.O. Box 40568, Memphis, TN 38174	Doug Darnall	(901) 333-5143
Shoreline CC	16101 Greenwood Ave. N., Seattle, WA 98133	Matt Barker	(206) 546-4740
Sierra College	5000 Rocklin Rd., Rocklin, CA 95677	Rob Wilson	(916) 781-0583
Shelton State	9500 old Greensboro Rd., Tuscaloosa, AL 35405	Bobby Sprowl	(205) 391-2206
Sinclair CC	444 W. 3rd St., Dayton, OH 45402	Mike Goldschmidt	(937) 512-3039
Siskiyous, College of the	800 College Ave., Weed, CA 96094	Steve Neel	(530) 938-5231
Skagit Valley College	2405 E. College Way, Mount Vernon, WA 98273	Mark Linden	(360) 416-7690
Skyline College	3300 College Dr., San Bruno, CA 94066	Dino Nomicos	(650) 738-4197
Snead State CC	220 N. Walnut St., Boaz, AL 35957	Gerry Ledbetter	(256) 593-5120
Solano CC	4000 Suisun Valley Rd., Suisun City, CA 94585	Scott Stover	(707) 864-7000
South Carolina-Salkehatchie	P.O. Box 617, Allendale, SC 29810	Joe Baxter	(803) 584-3446
South Florida CC	600 W. College Dr., Avon Park, FL 33825	Rick Hitt	(863) 453-6661
South Georgia College	100 W. College Park Dr., Douglas, GA 31533	Scott Sims	(912) 389-4231
South Mountain CC	7050 S. 24th St., Phoenix, AZ 85040	George Lopez	(602) 243-8236
South Suburban College	15800 S. State St., South Holland, IL 60473	Steve Ruzich	(708) 596-2000
Southeastern CC	P.O. Box 151, Whiteville, NC 28472	Chuck Baldwin	(910) 642-7141
Southeastern CC	1500 W. Agency Rd., West Burlington, IA 52655	Lonnie Winston	(319) 752-2731

Southeastern Illinois College	3575 College Rd., Harrisburg, IL 62946	Adam Hines	(618) 252-5400
Southern Idaho, College of	315 Falls Ave., Twin Falls, ID 83303	Jim Walker	(208) 732-6650
Southern Maine Tech	Fort Rd., South Portland, ME 04106	Philip Desjardins	(207) 839-6563
Southern Maryland, Col of	P.O. Box 910, La Plata, MD 20646	Joe Blandford	(301) 934-7761
Southern Nevada, CC of	700 College Dr., Henderson, NV 89015	Tim Chambers	(702) 651-3013
Southern Union State CC	P.O. Box 1000, Wadley, AL 36726	Joe Jordan	(256) 395-2211
Southwest Mississippi CC	100 College Drive, Summit, MS 39666	Larry Holmes	(601) 276-2000
Southwest Tennessee CC	P.O. Box 780, Memphis, TN 38101	Douglas Darnell	(901) 333-5145
Southwestern CC	1501 W. Townline Rd., Creston, IA 50801	Mike Cook	(641) 782-1459
Southwestern College	900 Otay Lakes Rd., Chula Vista, CA 91910	Jerry Bartow	(619) 482-6370
Southwestern Illinois College	2500 Carlyle Ave., Belleville, IL 62221	Neil Fiala	(618) 222-5371
Southwestern Oregon CC	1988 Newmark Ave., Coos Bay, OR 97420	Corky Franklin	(541) 888-7348
Spartanburg Methodist JC	1200 Textile Rd., Spartanburg, SC 29301	Tim Wallace	(864) 587-4237
Spokane CC	1810 N. Greene St., Spokane, WA 99217	David Keller	(509) 533-3639
Spoon River College	23235 N. County Rd 22, Canton, IL 61520	Joe Moore	(309) 649-6303
Springfield College	1500 N. 5th St., Springfield, IL 62702	Steve Torricelli	(217) 525-1420
Springfield Tech CC	1 Armory Sq., Springfield, MA 01105	J.C. Fernandes	(413) 755-4061
Suffolk CC-West	Crooked Hill Road, Brentwood, NY 11717	Mike Utnowski	(631) 851-6785
Suffolk County CC-Selden	533 College Rd., Selden, NY 11784	Eric Brown	(631) 732-2929
SUNY Cobleskill	Route 7, Cobleskill, NY 12043	Shawn Noel	(518) 255-5127
SUNY Morrisville	P.O. Box 901, Morrisville, NY 13408	Carl Lohman	(315) 684-6072
Surry CC	P.O. Box 304, Dobson, NC 27017	Mark Tucker	(336) 386-3217
Sussex County CC	1 College Hill Rd., Newton, NJ 07860	Todd Poltersdorf	(973) 300-2230
Taft College	29 Emmers Park Dr., Taft, CA 93268	Tony Thompson	(661) 763-7740
Tallahassee CC	444 Appleyard Dr., Tallahassee, FL 32304	Mike McLeod	(850) 201-8588
Temple College	2600 S. First St., Temple, TX 76504	Craig McMurtry	(254) 298-8524
Texarkana College	2500 N. Robison Rd., Texarkana, TX 75599	Matt Deggs	(903) 832-5565
Texas-Brownsville, U. of	80 Fort Brown, Brownsville, TX 78520	Eliseo Herrera	(956) 544-5134
Three Rivers CC	2080 Three Rivers Blvd., Poplar Bluff, MO 63901	Stacey Burkey	(573) 840-9613
Treasure Valley CC	650 College Blvd., Ontario, OR 97914	Rick Baumann	(503) 889-6493
Trinidad State JC	600 Prospect St., Trinidad, CO 81082	Scott Douglas	(719) 846-5510
Triton College	2000 N. 5th Ave., River Grove, IL 60171	Bob Symonds	(708) 456-0300
Truett McConnell College	100 Alumni Dr., Cleveland, GA 30528	Jim Waits	(706) 865-2136
Tyler JC	P.O. Box 9020, Tyler, TX 75711	Jon Groth	(903) 510-2320
Ulster County CC	Stone Ridge, NY 12484	Ryan Snair	(845) 687-5278
Union County College	1033 Springfield Ave., Cranford, NJ 07016	Mark Domashinski	(908) 709-7093
Utah Valley State College	800 W. University Pkwy., Orem, UT 84058	Steve Gardner	(801) 863-8998
Ventura College	4667 Telegraph Rd., Ventura, CA 93003	Don Adams	(805) 654-6348
Vermilion CC	1900 E. Camp St., Ely, MN 55731	Ray Podominick	(218) 365-7276
Vernon Regional JC	4400 College Dr., Vernon, TX 76384	Kevin Lallman	(940) 552-6291
Victor Valley CC	18422 Bear Valley Rd., Victorville, CA 92392	Nate Lambdin	(760) 245-4271
Vincennes University	1002 N. 1st St., Vincennes, IN 47591	Jerry Blemker	(812) 888-4478
Volunteer State CC	1480 Nashville Pike, Gallatin, TN 37066	Jeff Smith	(615) 230-3248
Wabash Valley College	2200 College Dr., Mount Carmel, IL 62863	Rob Fournier	(618) 263-4999
Waldorf College	206 John K. Hanson Dr., Forest City, IA 50436	Brian Grunzke	(641) 585-8183
Walla Walla CC	500 Tausick Way, Walla Walla, WA 99362	Chad Miltenberger	(509) 527-4494
Wallace CC Selma	3000 Earl Goodwin Pkwy., Selma, AL 36702	E.J. Brophy	(334) 876-9340
Wallace State CC Hanceville	P.O. Box 2000, Hanceville, AL 35077	Randy Putman	(256) 352-8121
Walters State CC	500 S. Davy Crockett Pkwy., Morristown, TN 37813	Ken Campbell	(423) 585-6759
Waubonsee College	Route 47 at Waubonsee Dr., Sugar Grove, IL 60554	Dave Randall	(630) 466-2527
Waukesha County Tech	800 Main St., Pewaukee, WI 53072	Roy Jeske	(262) 691-5545
Wenatchee Valley CC	1300 5th St., Wenatchee, WA 98801	Bob Duda	(509) 664-2584
West Hills College	300 W. Cherry Lane, Coalinga, CA 93210	Paul Hodsdon	(559) 934-2458
West Valley College	14000 Fruitvale Ave., Saratoga, CA 95070	Mike Perez	(408) 741-2176
Westchester CC	75 Grasslands Rd., Valhalla, NY 10595	Larry Massanori	(914) 785-6150
Western Nebraska CC	1601 E. 27th St., Scottsbluff, NE 69361	Mike Jones	(308) 635-6198
Western Oklahoma State	2801 N. Main St., Altus, OK 73521	James Luetjen	(580) 477-7800
Western Texas College	6200 S. College Ave., Snyder, TX 79549	James King	(915) 573-8511
Western Wisconsin Tech	304 North Sixth St., La Crosse, WI 54602	Aaron Boyer	(608) 785-9442
Westmoreland County CC	400 Armburst Rd., Youngwood, PA 15697	Mike Draghi	(724) 925-4129
Wharton County JC	911 E. Boling Hwy., Wharton, TX 77488	Bob Nottebart	(979) 532-6369
Wilkes CC	P.O. Box 120, Wilkesboro, NC 28697	Tim Lackey	(336) 838-6189
Williamson Free School	106 S. New Middletown Rd., Media, PA 19063	Sal Intelisano	(610) 566-1776
Williston State College	P.O. Box 1326, Williston, ND 58802	Dave Richter	(701) 744-4242
Wisconsin, U. of-Barron	1800 College Dr., Rice Lake, WI 54868	Brad Randle	(715) 234-8176
Yakima Valley CC	P.O. Box 22520, Yakima, WA 98907	Bob Garretson	(509) 574-4724
Yavapai College	1100 E. Sheldon St., Prescott, AZ 86301	Sky Smeltzer	(928) 776-2292
Young Harris College	1 College St., Young Harris, GA 30582	Rick Robinson	(706) 379-4311
Yuba CC	2088 N. Beale Rd., Marysville, CA 95901	Tim Gloyd	(530) 634-7725

AMATEUR

INTERNATIONAL

INTERNATIONAL OLYMPIC COMMITTEE

Mailing Address: Chateau de Vidy, 1007 Lausanne, Switzerland.
Telephone: (41-21) 621-6111. **FAX:** (41-21) 621-6216. **Website:** www.olympic.org.
President: Jacques Rogge. **Director, Communications:** Giselle Davies.
Games of the XXVIII Olympiad: Aug. 13-29, 2004 at Athens, Greece.

U.S. OLYMPIC COMMITTEE

Mailing Address: One Olympic Plaza, Colorado Springs, CO 80909. **Telephone:** (719) 866-4500. **FAX:** (719) 866-4654.
Chief Executive Officer: Lloyd Ward. **Chief Communications Officer:** Darryl Seibel.
Games of the XXVIII Olympiad: Aug. 13-29, 2004 at Athens, Greece.

PAN AMERICAN GAMES SOCIETY, INC.

XIV Pan American Games, 2003 (baseball competition): Aug. 1-15, 2003 at Santo Domingo, Dominican Republic.

INTERNATIONAL BASEBALL FEDERATION

Mailing Address: Avenue de Mon-Repos 24, Case Postale 131, 1000 Lausanne 5, Switzerland. **Telephone:** (41-21) 318-8240. **FAX:** (41-21) 318-8241. **E-Mail Address:** ibaf@baseball.ch. **Website:** www.baseball.ch.
Year Founded: 1938.
President: Aldo Notari (Italy). **Secretary General:** Eduardo De Bello (Panama). **Executive Director:** Miquel Ortin.

2003 Events

XXXV World Cup (senior) .... Havana, Cuba, Oct. 12-25
XI World Youth AA Championship .... Kaohsiung, Taiwan, Aug. 8-17
XIV World Children's Baseball Fair .... Yamaguchi, Japan, Aug. 11-18

CONFEDERATION PAN AMERICANA DE BEISBOL (COPABE)

Mailing Address: Cerro Patacon, Kilometro 3, Estadio Nacional, Panama. **Telephone:** (507) 230-5399. **FAX:** (507) 230-4524/4525. **E-Mail Address:** copabe@sinfo.net.
President: Eduardo De Bello (Panama).

2003 Events

*Pan American Championship .... Panama City, Panama, Oct. 30-Nov. 11
**Americas Junior Championship .... Willemstad, Curacao, July 15-25
*Qualifying tournament for 2004 Olympics
**Qualifying tournament for 2004 World Junior Championship

BASEBALL CANADA

Mailing Address: 2212 Gladwin Cres., Suite A7, Ottawa, Ontario K1B 5N1. **Telephone:** (613) 748-5606. **FAX:** (613) 748-5767. **E-Mail Address:** info@baseball.ca. **Website:** www.baseball.ca.
Director General: Jim Baba. **Head Coach/Director, National Teams:** Greg Hamilton. **Program Coordinator:** Kelly Benoit.
Baseball Canada Cup (17 and under): Aug. 13-18 at Windsor, Ontario.

AFRICAN BASEBALL/SOFTBALL ASSOCIATION

Mailing Address: Paiko Road, Changaga, Minna, Niger State, PMB 150, Nigeria. **Telephone:** (234-66) 224-555, (234-66) 224-711. **FAX:** (234-66) 224-555. **E-Mail Address**: absa@mlstn.com.
President: Ishola Williams (Nigeria).

2003 Events

*All Africa Games .... Abuja, Nigeria, Oct. 4-10

BASEBALL FEDERATION OF ASIA

Mailing Address: Mainichi Palaceside Bldg., 1-1-1, Hitotsubahi, Chiyoda-ku, Tokyo 100, Japan. **Telephone:** (81-3) 320-11155, (81-3) 321-36776. **FAX:** (81-3) 320-10707.
President: Eiichiro Yamamoto (Japan).

2003 Events

*Asian Championship .... Sapporo, Japan, Oct. 31-Nov. 7
**Asian Junior Championship .... Bangkok, Thailand, Aug. 30-Sept. 5

EUROPEAN BASEBALL CONFEDERATION

Mailing Address: Thonatlaan 52, Antwerp 2050, Belgium. **Telephone:** (32-3) 219-0440. **FAX:** (32-3) 219-0440. **E-Mail Address:** info@baseballeurope.com.
President: Aldo Notari (Italy).

2003 Events

*European Olympic Qualifier .... July 23-27, Rotterdam/Haarlem, The Netherlands
***European Pool A Championship .... July 11-19, Rotterdam/Haarlem, The Netherlands
**European Junior Championship .... July 7-13, Capelle/Ijssel, The Netherlands
***Qualifier for 2005 World Cup

BASEBALL CONFERERATION OF OCEANIA

Mailing Address: 48 Partridge Way, Mooroolbark, Victoria 3138, Australia. **Telephone:** (61-3) 9727-1779. **FAX:** (61-3) 9727-5959. **E-Mail Address**: chetg@ozemail.com.au.

President: Mark Peters (Australia).

2003 Events

%Oceania Championship .... April 22-30, Guam
**Oceania Junior Championship .... April 26-30, Guam
South Pacific Games .... June 28-July 12

%Qualifier for 2003 World Cup

INTERNATIONAL SPORTS GROUP

Mailing Address: 142 Shadowood Dr., Pleasant Hill, CA 94523. **Telephone:** (925) 798-4591. **FAX:** (925) 680-1182. **E-Mail Address:** ISGbaseball@aol.com.

President: Bill Arce. **Secretary/Treasurer:** Jim Jones.

NATIONAL

USA BASEBALL

Mailing Address, Corporate Headquarters: P.O. Box 1131, Durham, NC 27702. **Telephone:** Unavailable. **FAX:** Unavailable. **E-Mail Address:** info@usabaseball.com. **Website:** www.usabaseball.com.

Chairman: Lindsay Burbage. **President:** Mike Gaski. **Executive Vice President:** Steve Shaad. **Secretary:** Jack Kelly. **Treasurer:** Abraham Key. **Executive Officer:** Stephen Keener.

Executive Director, Chief Executive Officer: Paul Seiler. **Director, National Teams:** Steve Cohen. **Director, Finance:** Miki Partridge. **Director, Marketing/Licensing:** David Perkins. **Director, Communications:** Dave Fanucchi. **Associate Directors, National Teams:** Eric Campbell, Ray Darwin.

National Members: Amateur Athletic Union (AAU), American Amateur Baseball Congress (AABC), American Baseball Coaches Association (ABCA), American Legion Baseball, Babe Ruth Baseball, Dixie Baseball, Little League Baseball, National Amateur Baseball Federation (NABF), National Association of Intercollegiate Athletics (NAIA), National Baseball Congress (NBC), National Collegiate Athletic Association (NCAA), National Federation of State High School Athletic Associations, National High School Baseball Coaches Association, National Junior College Athletic Association (NJCAA), Police Athletic League (PAL), PONY Baseball, YMCAs of the USA.

2003 Events

Team USA—Professional Level

Olympic Qualifying/Team Training Camp .... Durham, NC, October
Athens Olympics Qualifier .... Panama City, Panama, Oct. 30-Nov. 11

Team USA—Collegiate Level

Team Trials .... Durham, NC, June 21-27
Team USA-Japan Exhibition Series .... United States, July 2-7
USA Red, White and Blue Tour .... United States, July 9-28
Pan American Games .... Santo Domingo, Dominican Republic, Aug. 1-15

Team USA—Junior Level (18 and under)

USA Baseball Tournament of Stars .... Joplin, MO, June 15-23
Junior National Team Training .... Site unavailable, July
COPABE Pan Am Championship .... Willemstad, Curacao, July 14-24

Team USA—Youth Level (16 and under)

Junior Olympic Championship—West .... Tucson, AZ, June 20-28
Junior Olympic Championship—East .... Jupiter, FL, June 20-28
National Team Trials .... Site unavailable, July
IBAF World Youth Championship .... Kaohsiung, Taiwan, Aug. 8-17

AMERICAN BASEBALL FOUNDATION

Mailing Address: 1313 13th St. S., Birmingham, AL 35205. **Telephone:** (205) 558-4235. **FAX:** (205) 918-0800. **E-Mail Address:** abf@asmi.org. **Website:** www.americanbaseball.org.

Executive Director: David Osinski.

NATIONAL BASEBALL CONGRESS

Mailing Address: P.O. Box 1420, Wichita, KS 67201. **Telephone:** (316) 267-3372. **FAX:** (316) 267-3382.

Year Founded: 1931.

President: Robert Rich Jr.

Vice President/General Manager: Steve Shaad. **Assistant GM/Stadium Operations Manager:** Josh Robertson. **Tournament Director:** Jerry Taylor. **Stadium Manager:** Teressa Hackworth. **Director, Marketing:** Matt Rogers.

2003 NBC World Series (collegiate, ex-professional, unlimited): Aug. 2-16 at Wichita, KS (Lawrence Dumont Stadium).

ATHLETES IN ACTION

Mailing Address: 651 Taylor Dr., Xenia, OH 45385. **Telephone:** (937) 352-1000. **FAX:** (937) 352-1245. **E-Mail Address:** baseball@athletesinaction.org. **Website:** www.aiabaseball.org.

Director: Jason Lester. **Staff:** Chris Beck, J.D. Bickle, Eric Trevino.

SUMMER COLLEGE LEAGUES

NATIONAL ALLIANCE OF COLLEGIATE SUMMER BASEBALL

Mailing Address: 85 Willow Glen Circle, Warwick, RI 02889. **Telephone:** (401) 739-7875. **FAX:** (401) 739-9789.

Executive Director: Thomas Hutton. **Deputy Executive Director:** Rick Gesualdi. **Secretary:** Roger Ingles.

NCAA Sanctioned Leagues: Atlantic Collegiate League, Cape Cod League, Central Illinois Collegiate League, Coastal Plain League, Great Lakes League, New England Collegiate League, New York Collegiate League, Northwoods League, Southern Collegiate League, Valley League.

ALASKA BASEBALL LEAGUE

Mailing Address: 207 E. Northern Lights Blvd., Suite 106, Anchorage, AK 99503. **Telephone:** (907) 274-3627. **FAX:** (907) 274-3628.

Year Founded: 1969 (reunited, 1998).

President: Chuck Shelton. **First Vice President:** Bill Bartholemew. **Vice President, Marketing:** Dennis Mattingly.

Division Structure: None.

2003 Opening Date: June 9. **Closing Date:** Aug. 1.

Regular Season: 35 league games.

Playoff Format: None. Top two teams advance to National Baseball Congress World Series.

Roster Limit: 22, plus exemption for Alaska residents. **Player Eligibility Rule:** Players with college eligibility, except drafted seniors.

ALASKA GOLDPANNERS

Mailing Address: P.O. Box 71154, Fairbanks, AK 99707. **Telephone:** (907) 451-0095. **FAX:** (907) 456-6429. **E-Mail Address:** todd@goldpanners.com. **Website:** www.goldpanners.com.

President: Bill Stroecker. **General Manager:** Don Dennis. **Assistant GM:** Todd Dennis. **Head Coach:** Ed Cheff (Lewis-Clark State, Idaho).

ANCHORAGE BUCS

Mailing Address: P.O. Box 240061, Anchorage, AK 99524. **Telephone:** (907) 561-2827. **FAX:** (907) 561-2920. **E-Mail Address:** ad.om@anchoragebucs.com. **Website:** www.anchoragebucs.com.

President: Eugene Furman. **General Manager:** Dennis Mattingly. **Head Coach:** Jim Yanko (San Joaquin Delta, Calif., JC).

ANCHORAGE GLACIER PILOTS

Mailing Address: 207 E. Northern Lights Blvd., Suite 106, Anchorage, AK 99503. **Telephone:** (907) 274-3627. **FAX:** (907) 274-3628. **E-Mail Address:** gpilots@alaska.net. **Website:** www.glacierpilots.com.

President: David Foreman. **General Manager:** Chuck Shelton. **Head Coach:** Kris Didion.

ATHLETES IN ACTION-ALASKA

Mailing Address: 651 Taylor Dr., Xenia, OH 45385. **Telephone:** (937) 352-1000. **FAX:** (937) 352-1245. **E-Mail Address:** chris.beck@aia.com. **Website:** www.aiabaseball.org.

General Manager: Chris Beck. **Head Coach:** Perry Roth (Birmingham-Southern).

MAT-SU MINERS

Mailing Address: P.O. Box 2690, Palmer, AK 99645. **Telephone:** (907) 746-4914. **FAX:** (907) 746-5068. **E-Mail Address:** pdkkc@gci.net. **Website:** www.matsuminers.org.

President: Bill Bartholomew. **General Manager:** Pete Christopher. **Vice President:** Mark Alger. **Head Coach:** Gerard Pineda (El Paso, Texas, CC).

PENINSULA OILERS

Mailing Address: 601 S. Main St., Kenai, AK 99611. **Telephone:** (907) 283-7133. **FAX:** (907) 283-3390. **E-Mail Address:** info@oilersbaseball.com. **Website:** www.oilersbaseball.com.

President: Karen Kester. **General Manager:** Mike Baxter. **Head Coach:** Kyle DiEduardo (Cincinnati).

ATLANTIC COLLEGIATE LEAGUE

Mailing Address: 401 Timber Dr., Berkeley Heights, NJ 07922. **Telephone/FAX:** (908) 464-8042. **E-Mail Address:** acbl@vs-inc.com. **Website:** www.acbl-online.org.

Year Founded: 1967.

Commissioner: Robert Pertsas. **Acting President:** Tom Bonekemper. **Vice President/Treasurer:** Jerry Valonis. **Secretary/Public Relations:** Ben Smookler.

Member Clubs, Division Structure: Wolff—Delaware Valley (Pa.) Gulls, Lehigh Valley (Pa.) Catz, Jersey (N.J.) Pilots, Quakertown (Pa.) Blazers, Scranton (Pa.) Red Soxx. **Kaiser**—Long Island (N.Y.) Collegians, Metro New York Cadets, New York Generals, New Jersey Colts, Stamford (Conn.) Robins.

2003 Opening Date: June 1. **Closing Date:** July 31.

Regular Season: 40 games.

Playoff Format: Top two teams in each division meet in best-of-3 semifinals. Winners meet in one-game championship.

Roster Limit: 23 (college-eligible players only).

Member Clubs, Division Structure: Wolff—Delaware Valley (Pa.) Gulls, Lehigh Valley (Pa.) Catz, Jersey (N.J.) Pilots, Quakertown (Pa.) Blazers, Scranton (Pa.) Red Soxx. **Kaiser**—Long Island (N.Y.) Collegians, Metro New York Cadets, New York Generals, New Jersey Colts, Stamford (Conn.) Robins.

CALIFORNIA COASTAL LEAGUE

Mailing Address: 4299 Carpinteria Ave., Suite 201, Carpinteria, CA 93013. **Telephone:** (805) 684-0657. **FAX:** (805) 684-8596. **E-Mail Address:** whc1@mindspring.com.

Year Founded: 1993.

Directors: Tim Golden, Dave Holt, Bill Pintard.

Member Clubs: Kern County Merchants, Salinas Packers, San Luis Obispo Blues, Santa Barbara Foresters, Yuba-Sutter Gold Sox. **Division Structure:** None.

Playoff Format: League champion advances to National Baseball Congress World Series.

2003 Opening Date: June 1. **Closing Date:** Aug. 5.

Regular Season: 40 games.

Roster Limit: 33.

CAPE COD LEAGUE

Mailing Address: P.O. Box 266, Harwich Port, MA 02646. **Telephone:** (508) 385-6260. **FAX**: (508) 385-6322. **E-Mail Address:** info@capecodbaseball.org. **Website:** www.capecodbaseball.org.

Year Founded: 1885.

Commissioner: Bob Stead. **President:** Judy Scarafile. **Vice Presidents:** Jim Higgins, Phil Edwards, Peter Ford.

Deputy Commissioners: Sol Yaz, Gary Lombard. **Treasurer:** Steve Wilson. **Director, Public Relations/Broadcast Media:** John Garner. **League Communications:** Jim McGonigle.

Division Structure: East—Brewster, Chatham, Harwich, Orleans, Yarmouth-Dennis. **West**—Bourne, Cotuit, Falmouth, Hyannis, Wareham.

2003 Opening Date: June 13. **Closing Date:** Aug. 6.

Regular Season: 44 games.

All-Star Game: July 26 at Falmouth.

Playoff Format: Top two teams in each division meet in best-of-3 semifinals. Winners meet in best-of-3 series for league championship.

Roster Limit: 23 (college-eligible players only).

BOURNE BRAVES

Mailing Address: P.O. Box 895, Monument Beach, MA 02553. **Telephone:** (508) 888-5080. **FAX:** (508) 833-9250. **E-Mail Address:** lynn.ladetto@verizon.net. **Website:** www.bournebraves.org.

President: Lynn Ladetto. **General Manager:** Unavailable.

Head Coach: Harvey Shapiro (U. of Hartford).

BREWSTER WHITE CAPS

Mailing Address: P.O. Box 2349, Brewster, MA 02631. **Telephone:** (617) 835-7130. **FAX:** (781) 934-0506. **E-Mail Address:** dpmfs@aol.com

President: Hester Grue. **General Manager:** Dave Porter.

Head Coach: Bob Macaluso (Muhlenberg, Pa., College).

CHATHAM A's

Mailing Address: P.O. Box 428, Chatham, MA 02633. **Telephone:** (508) 945-3841. **FAX:** (508) 945-4787. **E-Mail Address:** cthoms@comcast.net. **Website:** www.chathamas.com

President: Peter Troy. **General Manager:** Charles Thoms.

Head Coach: John Schiffner (Plainville, Conn., HS).

COTUIT KETTLEERS

Mailing Address: P.O. Box 411, Cotuit, MA 02635. **Telephone:** (508) 428-3358. **FAX:** (508) 420-5584. **E-Mail Address:** kettleers@hotmail.com. **Website:** www.kettleers.org.

President: Martha Johnson. **General Manager:** Bruce Murphy.

Head Coach: Garrett Quinn (St. Thomas, Fla., U.).

FALMOUTH COMMODORES

Mailing Address: 33 Wintergreen Rd., Mashpee, MA 02646. **Telephone:** (508) 477-5724. **FAX:**(508) 564-7643. **E-Mail Address:** chuckhs@comcast.net. **Website:** www.falcommodores.org.

President: Steve Spitz. **General Manager:** Chuck Sturtevant.

Head Coach: Jeff Trundy (The Gunnery School, Conn.).

HARWICH MARINERS

Mailing Address: P.O. Box 201, Harwich Port, MA 02646. **Telephone:** (508) 432-2000. **FAX:** (508) 432-5357. **Website:** www.harwichmariners.org.

President: Mary Henderson. **General Manager:** Mike DeAnzeris.

Head Coach: Steve Englert (Boston College).

HYANNIS METS

Mailing Address: P.O. Box 852, Hyannis, MA 02601. **Telephone:** (508) 420-0962. **FAX:** (508) 428-8199. **E-Mail Address:** jhowitt932@comcast.net. **Website:** www.hyannismets.org.

President: Randy Shepard. **General Manager:** John Howitt.

Head Coach: Keith Stohr (Mashpee, Mass., HS).

ORLEANS CARDINALS

Mailing Address: P.O. Box 504, Orleans, MA 02653. **Telephone/FAX:** (508) 255-0793. **FAX:** (508) 255-2237. **Website:** www.orleanscardinals.com.

President: Mark Hossfeld. **General Manager:** Sue Horton.

Head Coach: Carmen Carcone (Dowling, N.Y., College).

WAREHAM GATEMEN

Mailing Address: 71 Towhee Rd., Wareham, MA 02571. **Telephone:** (508) 295-3956. **FAX:** (508) 295-8821. **Website:** www.gatemen.org.

President, General Manager: John Wylde.

Head Coach: Cooper Farris (Mississippi Gulf Coast CC).

YARMOUTH-DENNIS RED SOX

Mailing Address: P.O. Box 814, South Yarmouth, MA 02664. **Telephone:** (508) 394-9387. **FAX:** (508) 398-2239. **E-Mail Address:** jf.martin@verizon.net. **Website:** ydredsox.org.

President: Bob Mayo. **General Manager:** Jim Martin.

Head Coach: Scott Pickler (Cypress, Calif., CC).

CENTRAL ILLINOIS COLLEGIATE LEAGUE

Mailing Address: 200 Glasgow, Springfield, IL 62702. **Telephone:** (217) 793-6538. **FAX:** (217) 786-2788. **E-Mail Address:** commissioner@ciclbaseball.com, infor@ciclbaseball.com. **Website:** www.ciclbaseball.com.

Year Founded: 1963.

Commissioner: Ron Riggle. **President:** Duffy Bass. **Administrative Assistant:** Mike Woods.

Division Structure: East—Danville, Decatur, Twin City. **West**—Bluff City, Quincy, Springfield.

2003 Opening Date: June 3. **Closing Date:** Aug. 6.

Regular Season: 48 games.

All-Star Game: July 9 at Bluff City.

Playoff Format: Top two teams in each division meet in double-elimination tournament.

Roster Limit: 23 (college-eligible players only).

BLUFF CITY BOMBERS

Mailing Address: P.O. Box 141, Bethalto, IL 62010. **Telephone:** (618) 377-7789. **E-Mail Address**: actjac@hotmail.com. **Website:** www.leaguelineup.com/bluffcity bombers.

General Manager: Jack Tracz. **Head Coach:** Unavailable.

DANVILLE DANS

Mailing Address: 138 E. Raymond, Danville, IL 61832. **Telephone:** (217) 446-5521. **FAX:** (217) 442-2137. **E-Mail Address:** jc@soltec.net. **Website:** www.soltec.net/dansbaseball.

General Manager: Rick Kurth. **Assistant GM**: Jeanie Cooke. **Head Coach:** Greg Moore.

DECATUR BLUES

Mailing Address: 3619 Northhaven Court, No. 2B, Decatur, IL 62526. **Telephone:** (217) 875-0933. **FAX:** (217)362-6414. **E-Mail Address:** jmanning@mail.millikin.edu.

General Manager/Head Coach: Josh Manning.

QUINCY GEMS

Mailing Address: 300 Civic Center Plaza, Quincy, IL 62301. **Telephone:** (217) 223-1000. **FAX:** (217) 223-1330. **E-Mail Address**: jjansen@quincygems.com. **Website:** www.quincygems.com.

Executive Director: Jeff Jansen. **Head Coach:**

Unavailable.

SPRINGFIELD RIFLES

Mailing Address: 7501 Southport Lane, Springfield, IL 62707. **Telephone:** (217) 786-2425.

General Manager: Claude Kracik. **Head Coach:** Chris Barney.

TWIN CITY STARS

Mailing Address: 907 N. School St., Normal, IL 61761. **Telephone:** (309) 452-3317. **FAX:** (217) 452-0377. **E-Mail Address:** duffybass@aol.com.

General Manager: Duffy Bass. **Head Coach:** Tim Siegworth.

CLARK GRIFFITH COLLEGIATE LEAGUE

Mailing Address: 8010 Towers Crescent Dr., 3rd Floor, Vienna, VA 22182. **Telephone:** (703) 760-1684. **FAX:** (703) 821-8949. **E-Mail Address:** dkc57@aol.com. **Website:** www.clarkgriffithbaseball.com.

Year Founded: 1945.

President: Bill Dolan. **Vice President:** Frank Fannan. **Executive Director/PR:** Debbie Casey. **VP/Rules Enforcement:** Byron Zeigler. **Statistics:** Ben Trittipoe.

Division Structure: None.

2003 Opening Date: June 6. **Closing Date:** July 26.

All-Star Game: July 1 at Bethesda, MD (Shirley Povich Field.

Regular Season: 40 games (split schedule).

Playoff Format: Winners of each half meet in best-of-5 league championship. Winner advances to All-America Amateur Baseball Association World Series.

Roster Limit: 25 (players 20 and under).

ARLINGTON SENATORS

Mailing Address: 3298 Wilson Blvd., Arlington, VA 22201. **Telephone:** (703) 247-3065. **FAX:** (703) 247-3070. **E-Mail Address:** cburr17@hotmail.com. **Website:** www.arlingtonsenator.org.

President: Bill McGillicuddy. **General Manager:** Chris Burr. **Manager:** Tag Montague (George Washington U.).

BALTIMORE PRIDE

Mailing Address: The Baseball Factory, 9176 Red Branch Rd., Suite M, Columbia, MD 21045. **Telephone:** (800) 641-4487. **FAX:** (410) 715-1975. **E-Mail Address:** smcdonnell@baseballfactory.com. **Website:** www.baseball factory.com.

President: Steve Sclafani. **General Manager:** Seth McDonnell. **Manager:** Bob Mumma (U. of Maryland-Baltimore County).

BETHESDA BIG TRAIN

Mailing Address: Bethesda Community Baseball Club, P.O. Box 30306, Bethesda, MD 20824. **Telephone:** (301) 652-4019. **FAX:** (301) 652-0691. **E-Mail Address:** bruce@greaterwash.org. **Website:** www.bigtrain.org.

President: Bruce Adams. **General Manager:** Elda Hacopian. **Assistant GM:** Alex Thompson. **Manager:** Derek Hacopian.

FAUQUIER GATORS

Mailing Address: 345 Winchester St., Warrenton, VA 20189. **Telephone:** (540) 347-0194. **FAX:** (540) 341-3478. **E-Mail Address:** hootbil@aol.com. **Website:** www.fauquiergators.com.

President: Steve Athey. **General Manager:** Sam Johnson. **Manager:** Paul Koch.

GERMANTOWN BLACK ROX

Mailing Address: 841-J Quince Orchard Blvd, Gaithersburg, MD 20878. **Telephone:** (301) 527-0640. **FAX:** (301) 963-2426. **E-Mail Address:** gibsonj4@nationwide.com. **Website:** www.blackrox.com.

President/General Manager: Buddy Gibson. **Manager:** Chuck Devereux.

HERNDON BRAVES

Mailing Address: 2044 Royal Fern Court, 11-A, Reston, VA 20191. **Telephone:** (703) 648-9254. **FAX:** Unavailable. **E-Mail Address:** cfaris@farisbaseball.com. **Website:** www.farisbaseball.com.

President: Chuck Faris. **General Manager:** Paul Foley. **Manager:** Chuck Faris.

RESTON HAWKS

Mailing Address: 12606 Magna Carta Rd., Herndon, VA 20171. **Telephone:** (703) 860-4780. **FAX:** (703) 860-0143. **E-Mail Address:** fannanfj@erols.com. **Website:** Unavailable.

General Manager: Frank Fannan. **Manager:** Mike Torres.

SILVER SPRING-TAKOMA THUNDERBOLTS

Mailing Address: 326 Lincoln Ave., Takoma Park, MD 20912. **E-Mail Address:** tboltsoconn@aol.com. **Website:** www.tbolts.org.

President/General Manager: Richard O'Connor. **VP, Development/Recruiting:** Fred Rodriguez. **Manager:** Nate Harvey.

VIENNA MUSTANGS

Mailing Address: 2800 Chariton St., Oakton, VA 22124. **Telephone:** (703) 851-7330. **FAX:** (703) 519-7208. **E-Mail Address:** scott.rowland@fcps.edu. **Website:** Unavailable.

President: Fred Haden. **General Manager:** Scott Rowland. **Manager:** Shawn Stiffler (George Mason U.).

COASTAL PLAIN LEAGUE

Mailing Address: 4900 Waters Edge Dr., Suite 201, Raleigh, NC 27606. **Telephone:** (919) 852-1960. **FAX:** (919) 852-1973. **Website:** www.coastalplain.com.

Year Founded: 1997.

Chairman/Chief Executive Officer: Jerry Petitt. **President:** Pete Bock. **Director, Administration:** Jay Snead. **Media Relations:** Justin Sellers.

Division Structure: **North**—Edenton, Outer Banks, Peninsula, Petersburg. **South**—Durham, Fayetteville, Florence, Wilmington, Wilson. **West**—Asheboro, Gastonia, Spartanburg, Thomasville.

2003 Opening Date: May 30. **Closing Date:** Aug. 6.

Regular Season: 52 games (split schedule).

All-Star Game: July 22 at Gastonia.

Playoff Format: Eight-team, double-elimination tournament, Aug. 8-10 in Hampton, VA.

Roster Limit: 22 (college-eligible players only).

ASHEBORO COPPERHEADS

Mailing Address: P.O. Box 4425, Asheboro, NC 27204. **Telephone:** (336) 636-5796. **FAX:** (336) 636-5400. **E-Mail Address:** baseball@asheboro.com.

President/General Manager: Pat Brown. **Head Coach:** Willie Stewart (UNC Asheville).

DURHAM AMERICANS

Mailing Address: P.O. Box 126, Durham, NC 27704. **Telephone:** (919) 956-9555. **FAX:** (919) 667-0612.

President: Joe Glasson. **Vice President:** Mike Sayeau. **Head Coach:** Chris Cook (Lander, S.C., U.).

EDENTON STEAMERS

Mailing Address: P.O. Box 86, Edenton, NC 27932. **Telephone:** (252) 482-4080. **FAX:** (252) 482-1717. **Website:** www.edentonsteamers.com.

General Manager: Todd Hunter. **Head Coach:** Steve

Hay (Webber International).

FAYETTEVILLE SWAMPDOGS

Mailing Address: P.O. Box 64691, Fayetteville, NC 28306. **Telephone:** (910) 426-5900. **FAX:** (910) 426-3544. **Website:** www.fayettevilleswampdogs.com.

General Manager: Jack Thompson. **Assistant GM:** Steve Belcher. **Head Coach:** Tommy Atkinson (Louisburg, N.C., JC).

FLORENCE REDWOLVES

Mailing Address: P.O. Box 809, Florence, SC 29503. **Telephone:** (843) 629-0700. **FAX:** (843) 629-0703.

President: Kevin Barth. **General Manager:** Todd Whitehead. **Head Coach:** Unavailable.

GASTONIA GRIZZLIES

Mailing Address: P.O. Box 177, Gastonia, NC 28053. **Telephone:** (704) 866-8622.

President: Ken Silver. **Vice Presidents:** Dr. Michael Silver, Kevin Silver. **General Manager:** Clay Battin. **Head Coach:** Travis Little (Bethany, Kan., College).

OUTER BANKS DAREDEVILS

Mailing Address: 1014 Jefferson Ave., Newport News, VA 23607. **Telephone:** (757) 719-2473. **FAX:** (757) 244-3557.

President: Warren Spivey. **General Manager:** Joe McGowan. **Head Coach:** Jeff Sziksai (Old Dominion).

PENINSULA PILOTS

Mailing Address: 1889 W. Pembroke Ave., Hampton, VA 23661. **Telephone:** (757) 245-2222. **FAX:** (757) 245-8032. **Website:** www.peninsulapilots.com.

President: Henry Morgan. **General Manager, Operations:** Hank Morgan Jr. **GM, Sales:** Jason Matlock. **Head Coach:** Greg Lovelady (U. of Miami, Fla.).

PETERSBURG GENERALS

Mailing Address: 1981 Midway Ave., Petersburg, VA 23803. **Telephone:** (804) 722-0141. **FAX:** (804) 733-7370.

President: Larry Toombs. **General Managers:** Jeff Roemer, Jeremy Toombs. **Head Coach:** Tim Haynes (Virginia Commonwealth U.).

SPARTANBURG STINGERS

Mailing Address: P.O. Box 5493, Spartanburg, SC 29304. **Telephone:** (864) 591-2250. **FAX:** (864) 591-2131.

General Manager: Lenny Mathis. **Head Coach:** Brandon McKillop (Wofford U.).

THOMASVILLE HI-TOMS

Mailing Address: P.O. Box 3035, Thomasville, NC 27361. **Telephone:** (336) 472-8667. **FAX:** (336) 472-7198.

President: Greg Suire. **General Manager:** Roman Stout. **Head Coach:** Mike Kramer (U. of San Diego).

WILMINGTON SHARKS

Mailing Address: P.O. Box 15233, Wilmington, NC 28412. **Telephone:** (910) 343-5621. **FAX:** (910) 343-8932. **Website:** www.wilmingtonsharks.com.

President: Jim Morrison. **General Manager:** Curt Vanderzee. **Assistant GM:** Amanda Yerdon. **Head Coach:** Clint Ayers (Delaware State U.).

WILSON TOBS

Mailing Address: P.O. Box 633, Wilson, NC 27894. **Telephone:** (252) 291-8627. **FAX:** (252) 291-1224. **Website:** www.tobs.bbnp.com.

President: Greg Turnage. **General Manager:** Chris Allen. **Head Coach:** Brad Stromdahl (Marshall U.).

FLORIDA COLLEGIATE INSTRUCTIONAL LEAGUE

Mailing Address: IMG Academies/Bollettieri Campus, 5500 34th St. W., Bradenton, FL 34210. **Telephone:** (941) 727-0303. **FAX:** (941) 727-2962. **E-Mail Address:** tpluto@gte.net. **Website:** www.zonebaseball.com.

Year Founded: 2001.

President: Tom Pluto. **Secretary:** Flody Suarez.

2003 Opening Date: June 14. **Closing Date:** Aug. 3.

Regular Season: 40 games (split schedule).

All-Star Game: July 6 at Sarasota, FL (Smith Stadium).

Playoff Format: One-game playoff between first- and second-half winners.

Roster Limit: Open. **Player Eligibility Rule:** (college-eligible players only).

GREAT LAKES LEAGUE

Mailing Address: 690 Bunty Station Rd., Delaware, OH 43015. **Telephone:** (740) 368-3738. **FAX:** (740) 368-3799. **E-Mail Address:** RDIngles@owu.edu. **Website:** www.greatlakesleague.org.

Year Founded: 1986.

President, Commissioner: Roger Ingles. **Assistant Commissioner:** Kim Lance.

Division Structure: None.

2003 Opening Date: June 12. **Closing Date:** Aug. 5.

Regular Season: 44 games.

All-Star Game: July 13 at Delaware, OH.

Playoff Format: Top eight teams meet in modified double-elimination format.

Roster Limit: 27 (college-eligible players only).

COLUMBUS ALL-AMERICANS

Mailing Address: 3800 Municipal Way, Hilliard, OH 43026. **Telephone**: (614) 876-7361, ext. 500.

General Manager: Rodney Garnett. **Head Coach:** Brian Mannino

DELAWARE COWS

Mailing Address: 3800 Criswell Dr., Columbus, OH 43220. **Telephone:** (614) 451-7070. **FAX:** (614) 771-7078.

General Manager, Head Coach: Bruce Heine.

GRAND LAKE MARINERS

Mailing Address: 717 W. Walnut St., Coldwater, OH 45828. **Telephone:** (419) 678-3607. **FAX:** (419) 586-4735.

General Manager: Wayne Miller. **Head Coach:** Matt Palm.

INDIANAPOLIS ONE CROWN SERVANTS

Mailing Address: 8888 Fitness Lane, Fishers, IN 46038. **Telephone:** (317) 842-2555. **FAX:** (317) 558-1162.

General Manager, Coach: Greg Lymberopoulos.

LIMA LOCOS

Mailing Address: 3700 S. Dixie Hwy., Lima, OH 45806. **Telephone:** (419) 991-4296. **FAX:** (419) 999-4586.

General Manager: Barry Ruben. **Head Coach:** Robert Livchak.

MURRYSVILLE MIGHTY EAGLES

Mailing Address: 709 Stonehaven Dr., Greensburg, PA 15601. **Telephone:** (724) 934-7238. **FAX:** (724) 934-7296.

General Manager, Head Coach: Bob Bozzuto.

NORTHERN OHIO BASEBALL

Mailing Address: 14675 Foltz Industrial Pkwy., Strongsville, OH 44136. **Telephone:** (440) 846-0200. **FAX:** (440) 846-0606.

General Manager: Don Mills. **Head Coach:** Guido Aspeitia.

PITTSBURGH PANDAS

Mailing Address: 118 Hetherton Dr., Pittsburgh, PA 15237. **Telephone:** (412) 759-4444. **FAX:** (412) 366-2064.

General Manager: Frank Gilbert. **Head Coach:** Mark

Schmidt.

SOUTHERN OHIO BASEBALL

Mailing Address: Grover E 146, Ohio University, Athens, OH 45701. **Telephone:** (740) 593-4666. **FAX:** (740) 0539.

General Manager: Andrew Kreutzer. **Head Coach:** Scott Googins.

STARK COUNTY TERRIERS

Mailing Address: 1019 35th St. NW, Canton, OH 44709. **Telephone:** (330) 492-9220. **FAX:** (330) 492-9236.

General Manager: Greg Trbovich. **Head Coach:** Joe Gilhousen.

YOUNGSTOWN EXPRESS

Mailing Address: 945 Windham Ct., Suite 5, Boardman, OH 44512. **Telephone:** (330) 726-8028. **FAX:** (330) 726-6384.

General Managers: Chuck Whitman. **Head Coach:** Unavailable.

JAYHAWK LEAGUE

Mailing Address: 5 Adams Pl., Halstead, KS 67056. **Telephone/FAX:** (316) 755-1285.

Year Founded: 1976.

Commissioner: Bob Considine. **President:** Don Carlile. **Vice President:** Laverne Schumacher.

2003 Opening Date: June 8. **Closing Date:** July 24.

Regular Season: 30 games.

Playoff Format: Top two teams advance to National Baseball Congress World Series.

Roster Limit: 25.

EL DORADO BRONCOS

Mailing Address: 865 Fabrique, Wichita, KS 67218. **Telephone:** (316) 687-2309. **FAX:** (316) 942-2009. **Website:** www.eldoradobroncos.com.

General Manager: J.D. Schneider.

ELKHART DUSTERS

Mailing Address: P.O. Box 793, Elkhart, KS 67950. **Telephone:** (620) 697-2095. **FAX**: (620) 697-2826. **Website**: www.my.elkhart.com/dusters.

General Manager: Brian Elsen.

HAYS LARKS

Mailing Address: 3409 Summer Lane, Hays, KS 67601. **Telephone:** (785) 628-6703. **FAX**: (785) 623-2609.

General Manager: Frank Leo.

LIBERAL BEEJAYS

Mailing Address: P.O. Box 352, Liberal, KS 67901. **Telephone:** (316) 624-1904. **FAX:** 316-624-1906.

General Manager: Kim Snell.

NEVADA GRIFFONS

Mailing Address: Box 601, Nevada, MO 64772. **Telephone:** (417) 667-8308. **FAX:** (417) 667-8108.

General Manager: Dr. Jason Meisenheimer.

TOPEKA CAPITOLS

Mailing Address: 2005 SW Sims, Topeka, KS 66604. **Telephone:** (785) 234-5881.

General Manager: Don Carlile.

NEW ENGLAND COLLEGIATE LEAGUE

Mailing Address: 48 Palmer Rd. Candia, NH 03034. **Telephone:** (603) 483-0241. **FAX:** Unavailable. **E-Mail Address:** commissioner@necbl.com. **Website:** www.necbl.com.

Year Founded: 1993.

President: Fay Vincent Jr.. **Commissioner:** Kevin MacIlvane. **Deputy Commissioner:** Kurt Svoboda. **Treasurer:** Ed Slegeski. **Secretary:** Rich Rossiter. **Director, Public Relations:** Colleen Carlisi.

Division Structure: North—Concord, Keene, Mill City, North Adams, Sanford, Vermont. **South**—Danbury, Manchester, Middletown, Newport, Riverpoint, Thread City, Torrington.

2003 Opening Date: June 7. **Closing Date:** Aug. 3.

Regular Season: 42 games.

All-Star Game: July 27 at Concord.

Playoff Format: Top four teams in each division meet in best-of-3 qurterfinals; winners meet in best-of-3 semifinals; winners meet in best-of-3 finals.

Roster Limit: 25 (college-eligible players only).

CONCORD QUARRY DOGS

Mailing Address: 48 Palmer Rd., Candia, NH 03034. **Telephone:** (603) 483-0241. **Website:** www.quarrydogs.org

President: Curtis Barry. **General Manager:** Pete Dupuis. **Head Coach:** Dennis McManus (Plymouth State, N.H.).

DANBURY WESTERNERS

Mailing Address: 37 Grammar School Dr., Danbury, CT 96811. **Telephone/FAX:** (203) 744-5874. **Website:** www.danburywesterners.com

General Manager: Mario Tiani. **Head Coach:** Moe Morhardt.

KEENE SWAMP BATS

Mailing Address: 31 W. Surry Rd., Keene, NH 03431. **Telephone:** (603) 352-5120. **FAX:** (603) 352-1860.

General Manager: Vicki Bacon. **Head Coach:** Mike Sweeney (Amherst U.).

MANCHESTER SILKWORMS

Mailing Address: 16 West St., Manchester, CT 06040. **Telephone:** (860) 559-3126. **FAX:** (860) 649-8487. **Website:** www.manchestersilkworms.org

General Manager: Ed Slegeski. **Head Coach:** Anthony DiCicco (U. of Vermont).

MIDDLETOWN GIANTS

Mailing Address: 115 Azaelea Dr., Middletown, CT 06457. **Telephone:** (877) MID-GIANTS. **FAX:** (203) 688-3264. **Website:** www.middletowngiants.com

President: Ronald Lucia. **General Manager:** Jeff Clark. **Head Coach:** Brian Cain (Cal State Fullerton).

MILL CITY All-AMERICANS

Mailing Address: P.O. Box 218, Chelmsford, MA 01863. **Telephone:** (978) 251-8852, (978) 251-1000. **FAX:** (978) 251-1211. **E-Mail Address:** mcallamericans@hotmail.com.

General Manager: Harry Ayotte. **Head Coach:** Chip Forrest.

NEWPORT GULLS

Mailing Address: P.O. Box 777, Newport, RI 02840. **Telephone:** (877) 774-8557. **FAX: Website:** www.newportgulls.com

President/General Manager: Chuck Paiva. **Head Coach:** Terry Rupp (U. of Maryland).

NORTH ADAMS STEEPLECATS

Mailing Address: P.O. Box 812, North Adams, MA 01247. **Telephone:** (413) 664-7227. **Website:** www.steeplecats.com

President: General Manager: Jon Watterson. **Head Coach:** Kevin Winterrowd.

RIVERPOINT ROYALS

Mailing Address: P.O. Box 206, West Warwick, RI 02893. **Telephone/FAX:** (401) 736-4108.

President/General Manager: Pete Fontaine. **Head Coach:** Jon Palmieri (Georgia Tech).

SANFORD MAINERS

Mailing Address: 924 Main St., Sanford, ME 04073. **Telephone:** (207) 324-0010. **FAX:** (207) 875-5805.

General Manager: Neil Olson. **Head Coach:** Scott Brown (SUNY-Cortland).

THREAD CITY TIDES

Mailing Address: 902 East St., Andover, CT 06232. **Telephone:** (860) 463-9530.

General Manager: Joe Cerreto. **Head Coach:** Trevor Brown (Pace U.).

TORRINGTON TWISTERS

Mailing Address: 4 Blinkoff Ct., Torrington, CT 06790. **Telephone/FAX:** (860) 482-0450.

General Manager: Kirk Fredriksson. **Head Coach:** Gregg Hunt.

VERMONT MOUNTAINEERS

Mailing Address: P.O. Box 586, Montpelier, VT 05602. **Telephone:** (802) 223-5224.

President: Ed Walbridge. **General Manager:** Brian Gallagher. **Head Coach:** Chris Jones (St. John's U.).

NEW YORK COLLEGIATE LEAGUE

Summer Address: 28 Dunbridge Heights, Fairport, NY 14450. **Winter Address:** P.O. Box 2516, Tarpon Springs, FL 34688. **Telephone:** (585) 223-2328, (727) 942-9120.

Year Founded: 1986.

Commissioner: Dave Chamberlain. **President:** Bob Belizzi. **Treasurer:** Dan Russo.

Member Clubs: Alfred Athletes in Action, Geneva Lakes, Hornell Dodgers, Plattsburgh Thunder, Schenectady Mohawks, Wayne County Raptors, Watertown Wizards, Wellsville Nitros.

2003 Opening Date: June 10. **Closing Date:** July 31.

Regular Season: 42 games.

All Star Game: Unavailable.

Playoff Format: Top four teams meet in best-of-3 series. Winners meet in best-of-3 series for league championship.

Roster Limit: 24 (college-eligible players only).

NORTHWOODS LEAGUE

Office Address: 403 E. Center St., Rochester, MN 55904. **Mailing Address:** P.O. Box 12, Rochester, MN 55903. **Telephone:** (507) 536-4579. **FAX:** (507) 289-1866. **E-Mail Address:** nwl@chartermi.net. **Website:** www.northwoodsleague.com.

Year Founded: 1994.

President: Dick Radatz Jr. **Director of Operations:** Jon Olson.

Division Structure: North—Alexandria, Duluth, Mankato, St. Cloud, Thunder Bay. **South**—La Crosse, Madison, Rochester, Waterloo, Wisconsin.

2003 Opening Date: June 2. **Closing Date:** Aug. 15.

Regular Season: 64 games (split schedule).

All-Star Game: July 16 at Madison.

Playoff Format: First-half and second-half division winners meet in best-of-3 series. Winners meet in best-of-3 series for league championship.

Roster Limit: 25 (college-eligible players only).

ALEXANDRIA BEETLES

Mailing Address: 418 3rd Ave. E., Suite 111, Alexandria, MN 56308. **Telephone:** (320) 763-8151. **FAX:** (320) 763-8152. **E-Mail Address**: beetles@alexandriabeetles.com. **Website**: www.alexandriabeetles.com.

General Manager: Ron Voz. **Head Coach:** Matt Jones (Los Medanos, Calif., JC).

DULTUH HUSKIES

Mailing Address: 226 West 1st Street, Duluth, MN 55802. **Telephone:** (218) 786-9909. **FAX:** (218) 786-9001. **E-Mail Address:** smithdlh@chartermi.net. **Website**: www.duluthhuskies.com.

General Manager: Craig Smith.

LA CROSSE LOGGERS

Mailing Address: 1223 Caledonia St., La Crosse, WI 54601. **Telephone:** (608) 796-9553. **FAX:** (608) 796-9032. **E-Mail Address:** info@lacrosseloggers.com. **Website**: www.lacrosseloggers.com.

General Manager: Chris Goodell. **Head Coach:** Estevan Valencia (UC Riverside).

MADISON MALLARDS

Mailing Address: 2920 N. Sherman Ave., Madison, WI 53704. **Telephone:** (608) 246-4277. **FAX:** (608) 246-4163. **E-Mail Address:** vern@mallardsbaseball.com. **Website**: www.mallardsbaseball.com.

Director, Marketing/Baseball Operations: Vern Stenman. **Head Coach:** Darrell Handelsman.

MANKATO MOONDOGS

Mailing Address: 310 Belle Ave., Suite L-10, Mankato, MN 56001. **Telephone:** (507) 625-7047. **FAX:** (507) 625-7059. **E-Mail Address:** office@mankatomoondogs.com. **Website**: www.mankatomoondogs.com.

General Manager: Joe Schwei. **Head Coach:** Brad Ruppert (Shasta, Calif., JC).

ROCHESTER HONKERS

Office Address: Mayo Field, 403 E. Center St., Rochester, MN 55904. **Mailing Address:** P.O. Box 482, Rochester, MN 55903. **Telephone:** (507) 289-1170. **FAX:** (507) 289-1866. **E-Mail Address:** honkers@rochesterhonkers.com. **Website:** www.rochesterhonkers.com.

General Manager: Dan Litzinger. **Head Coach:** Dave Parra (Neosho County, KS, CC).

ST. CLOUD RIVER BATS

Office Address: Athletic Park, 5001 8th St. N., St. Cloud, MN 56303. **Mailing Address:** P.O. Box 5059, St. Cloud, MN 56302. **Telephone:** (320) 240-9798. **FAX:** (320) 255-5228. **E-Mail Address:** riverbat@cloudnet.com. **Website:** www.riverbats.com.

General Manager: Scott Schreiner. **Head Coach:** Tom Fleenor (U. of South Carolina-Spartanburg).

THUNDER BAY

Office Address: 403 E. Center St., Rochester, MN 55904. **Mailing Address:** P.O. Box 12, Rochester, MN 55903. **Telephone:** (507) 536-4579. **FAX:** (507) 289-1866. **E-Mail Address:** nwl@chartermi.net.

General Manager: Dan Wolfert. **Head Coach:** Mitch Dunn (Memphis U.).

WATERLOO BUCKS

Office Address: Riverfront Stadium, 850 Park Rd., Waterloo, IA 50703. **Mailing Address:** P.O. Box 4124, Waterloo, IA 50704. **Telephone:** (319) 232-0500. **FAX:** (319) 232-0700. **E-Mail Address:** garyrima23@hotmail.com. **Website:** www.waterloobucks.com.

General Manager: Gary Rima. **Head Coach:** Andy Haines (Middle Tennessee State U.).

WISCONSIN WOODCHUCKS

Office Address: Washington Square, 300 Third St., L4, Wausau, WI 54402. **Telephone:** (715) 845-5055. **FAX:** (715) 845-5015. **E-Mail Address:** info@woodchucks.com.

General Manager: Clark Eckhoff. **Head Coach:** Steve Foster.

PACIFIC INTERNATIONAL LEAGUE

Mailing Address: 504 Yale Ave. N., Seattle, WA 98109. **Telephone:** (206) 623-8844. **FAX:** (206) 623-8361. **E-Mail Address:** spotter@potterprinting.com. **Website:** pacificinternationalleague.com.

Year Founded: 1992.

President: Steve Konek Jr. **Commissioner:** Seth Dawson. **Vice President:** Mark Dow. **Secretary:** Steve Potter.

Member Clubs: North—Bellingham (Wash.) Bells, Everett (Wash.) Merchants, Kelowna (British Columbia) Falcons, Wenatchee (Wash.) Apple Sox, Spokane (Wash.) River Hawks. **South**—Aloha (Ore.) Knights, Bend (Ore.) Elks, Gresham (Ore.) Kings, Kirkland (Wash.) Kodiaks, Seattle Studs, Yakima (Wash) Paladin Knights.

2003 Opening Date: June 1. **Closing Date:** Aug. 4.

Regular Season: 30 games.

Playoff Format: Division champions and two wild-card teams meet in double elimination tournament; winner advances to National Baseball Congress World Series.

Roster Limit: 25.

SOUTHERN COLLEGIATE LEAGUE

Mailing Address: 49300 Fairway Ridge Dr., Charlotte, NC 28277. **Telephone:** (704) 847-5037. **Fax**: (704) 847-1455. **E-Mail Address:** WSScout@aol.com. **Website:** www.sbl.org.

Year Founded: 1999.

Commissioner: Bill Capps. **President:** Lyn Jeffers. **Vice President:** Brian Swords.

Member Clubs: North—Asheville (N.C.) Thunder, Carolina Sox (Belmont, N.C.), Johnson City (Tenn.) Redbirds, Kernersville (N.C.) Bulldogs, Lenoir (N.C.) Oilers, Salisbury (N.C.) Pirates. **South Division:** Carolina Chaos (Clemson, S.C.), Carolina Copperheads (Davidson, N.C.), Carolina Warriors (Greenville, S.C.), Charleston (S.C.) Clippers, Newberry (S.C.) Indians, Spartanburg (S.C.) Crickets.

2003 Opening Date: May 31. **Closing Date:** July 31.

Regular Season: 38 games.

Playoff Format: Top two teams from each division advance to championship tournament.

Roster Limit: 25 (college-eligible players only).

VALLEY LEAGUE

Mailing Address: 58 Bethel Green Rd., Staunton, VA 24401. **Telephone:** (540) 885-8901. **FAX:** (540) 885-2068. **E-Mail Addresses:** dudleycm@jmu.edu, davidb@fisher-autoparts.com. **Website:** www.valleyleaguebaseball.com.

Year Founded: 1961.

President: David Biery. **Executive Vice President:** Warren Shand. **Director, Public Relations:** Curt Dudley. **League Statistician:** Mark Hoskins.

2003 Opening Date: June 6. **Closing Date:** July 27.

Regular Season: 40 games.

All-Star Game: July 13 at New Market.

Division Structure: North—Front Royal, Luray, New Market, Winchester. **South**—Covington, Harrisonburg, Staunton, Waynesboro.

Playoff Format: Top two teams in each division meet in best-of-5 semifinal series. Winners meet in best-of-5 series for league championship.

Roster Limit: 25 (college eligible student-athletes only).

COVINGTON LUMBERJACKS

Mailing Address: P.O. Box 171, Covington, VA 24457. **Telephone/FAX:** (540) 863-5225. **E-Mail Address:** jacks-baseball28@aol.com. **Website:** www.jacksbaseball.com.

Owners: Clyde Helmintoller, Jason Helmintoller. **General Manager/Recruiting Coordinator:** Doug Gibson. **Head Coach:** Unavailable.

FRONT ROYAL CARDINALS

Mailing Address: P.O. Box 995, Front Royal, VA 22630. **Telephone:** (540) 636-1882. **FAX:** (540) 635-6498. **E-Mail Address:** sminkeen@shentel.net. **Website:** www.frcardinalbaseball.com.

President: Linda Keen. **Recruiting Coordinator/Manager:** Robbie Jones (Emmanuel College, GA).

HARRISONBURG TURKS

Mailing Address: 1489 S. Main St., Harrisonburg, VA 22801. **Telephone:** (540) 434-5919. **E-Mail Address:** hbg-turks@vaix.net. **Website:** www.harrisonburgturks.com.

General Manager/Head Coach: Bob Wease. **Operations Manager:** Teresa Wease. **Public Relations:** Curt Dudley.

LURAY WRANGLERS

Mailing Address: 1203 E. Main St., Luray, VA 22835. **Telephone:** (540) 743-3338. **E-Mail Addresses:** bturn-er@shentel.net, luraywranglers@hotmail.com.

President: Bill Turner. **General Manager:** Greg Moyer. **Head Coach:** Scott Feldman (Clarion U.).

NEW MARKET REBELS

Mailing Address: P.O. Box 902, New Market, VA 22844. **Telephone:** (540) 740-4247, (540) 740-8569. **E-Mail Address:** nmrebels@shentel.net. **Website:** www.shentel.net/nmrebels.

General Manager: Bruce Alger. **Public Relations:** Dick Golden. **Secretary/Treasurer:** Lynn Alger. **Recruiting Coordinator/Manager:** Ray Hedrick (UNC Pembroke).

STAUNTON BRAVES

Mailing Address: 14 Shannon Pl., Staunton, VA 24401. **Telephone:** (540) 886-0987. **FAX:** (540) 886-0905. **E-Mail Address:** sbraves@hotmail.com. **Website:** www.stauntonbraves.com.

Director, Operations: Kay Snyder. **Comptroller:** Boyd Snyder. **General Manager/Recruiting Coordinator:** Steve Cox. **Head Coach:** Lawrence Nesselrodt (West Virginia State U.).

WAYNESBORO GENERALS

Mailing Address: P.O. Box 615, Waynesboro, VA 22980. **Telephone:** (540) 949-0370, (540) 942-2474. **FAX:** (540) 949-0653. **E-Mail Address:** jim_critzer@hotmail.com.

Owner: Jim Critzer. **President:** Rennie Dobbins. **General Manager:** Dale Coffey. **Assistant GM:** Jim Stohlmann. **Recruiting Coordinator/Head Coach:** Derek McDaniel.

WINCHESTER ROYALS

Mailing Address: P.O. Box 2485, Winchester, VA 22604. **Telephone:** (540) 667-9227, (540) 662-4466. **FAX:** (540) 662-3299. **E-Mail Addresses:** tgt@shentel.net, jimphill@shentel.net. **Website:** www.winchesterroyals.com.

President: Todd Thompson. **Vice President:** Jim Phillips. **Public Relations:** Mark Sawyer. **Baseball Operations:** Brian Burke. **Recruiting Coordinator/Head Coach:** Jason Johnson.

HIGH SCHOOL/ YOUTH

HIGH SCHOOL BASEBALL

NATIONAL FEDERATION OF STATE HIGH SCHOOL ASSOCIATIONS

Mailing Address: P.O. Box 690, Indianapolis, IN 46206. **Telephone:** (317) 972-6900. **FAX:** (317) 822-5700. **E-Mail Address:** baseball@nfhs.org. **Website:** www.nfhs.org.

Executive Director: Robert Kanaby. **Chief Operating Officer:** Bob Gardner. **Assistant Director/Baseball Rules Editor:** Elliot Hopkins. **Director, Publications/Communications:** Bruce Howard.

NATIONAL HIGH SCHOOL BASEBALL COACHES ASSOCIATION

Mailing Address: P.O. Box 5128, Bella Vista, AR 72714. **Telephone:** (479) 876-2591. **FAX:** (479) 876-2596. **E-Mail Address:** homeplate@baseballcoaches.org. **Website:** www.baseballcoaches.org.

Executive Director: Jerry Miles. **Administrative Assistant:** Elaine Miles. **President:** Dave Demarest, La Quinta HS, Westminster, CA.

2003 National Convention: Dec. 4-7 at Albuquerque, NM.

GATORADE CIRCLE OF CHAMPIONS

(National High School Player of the Year Award)

Mailing Address: The Gatorade Company, 321 N. Clark St., Suite 24-3, Chicago, IL 60610. **Telephone:** (312) 553-1240. **Website:** www.gatorade.com.

Mailing Address, Scholastic Coach and Athletic Director: 557 Broadway, NY 10012. **Telephone:** (212) 343-6370. **FAX:** (212) 343-6376. **E-Mail Address:** mwallace@scholastic.com. **Website:** coachadguide.com. **Publisher:** Bruce Weber. **Marketing Manager:** Mike Wallace.

NATIONAL TOURNAMENTS

In-Season

HORIZON NATIONAL INVITATIONAL

Mailing Address: Horizon High School, 5601 E. Greenway Rd., Scottsdale, AZ 85254. **Telephone:** (602) 867-9003.

Tournament Director: Eric Kibler.

2003 Tournament: March 24-27 (16 teams).

LIONS INVITATIONAL

Mailing Address: 6626 Airoso Ave., San Diego CA 92120. **Telephone:** (619) 583-2633, (619) 444-3190. **FAX:** (619) 583-6605.

Tournament Director: Jim Gordon. **Assistant Director:** Bob Hinshaw.

2003 Tournament: April 14-17 (80 teams).

NATIONAL CLASSIC

Mailing Address: P.O. Box 338, Placentia, CA 92870. **Telephone:** (714) 993-2838. **FAX:** (714) 993-5350. **E-Mail Address:** placentiamustang@aol.com.

Tournament Director: Todd Rogers.

2003 Tournament: April 14-17 at Cal State Fullerton, UC-Irvine (16 teams).

NIKE NATIONAL BASEBALL CLASSIC

Mailing Address: Tate High School, 1771 Tate Road, Cantonment, FL 32533. **Telephone:** (850) 968-5755. **FAX:** (850) 937-2328. **E-Mail Address:** tateaggies@aol.com.

Tournament Director: Greg Blackmon.

2003 Tournament: March 31-April 3 (16 teams).

SARASOTA CLASSIC

Mailing Address: 2384 Seattle Slew Dr., Sarasota, FL 34240. **Telephone:** (941) 955-0181. **FAX:** (941) 378-5853.

Tournament Director: Clyde Metcalf.

2003 Tournament: April 14-17 at Sarasota, FL (16 teams).

USA CLASSIC

Mailing Address: 5900 Walnut Grove Rd., Memphis, TN 38120. **Telephone:** (901) 872-8326. **FAX:** (901) 681-9443. **Website:** www.usabaseballstadium.org.

Tournament Organizers: John Daigle, Buster Kelso.

2003 Tournament: April 1-5 at USA Baseball Stadium, Millington, TN (16 teams).

WEST COAST CLASSIC

Mailing Address: 5000 Mitty Way, San Jose, CA 95129. **Telephone:** (408) 252-6610. **E-Mail Address:** hutton@mitty.com.

Tournament Director: Bill Hutton.

2003 Tournament: April 22-24 (16 teams) at Archbishop Mitty HS, San Jose, CA.

WESTMINSTER SPRING BREAK SHOOTOUT

Mailing Address: Westminster Academy, 5601 N. Federal Hwy., Fort Lauderdale, FL 33308. **Telephone:** (954) 735-1841. **FAX:** (954) 735-1858.

Tournament Director: Rich Hofman.

2003 Tournament: March 17-21 (16 teams).

WESTMINSTER CLASSIC

Mailing Address: Westminster Academy, 5601 N. Federal Hwy., Fort Lauderdale, FL 33308. **Telephone:** (954) 735-1841. **FAX:** (954) 735-1858.

Tournament Director: Rich Hofman.

2003 Tournament: April 12-17 (16 teams).

Postseason

SUNBELT BASEBALL CLASSIC SERIES

Mailing Address: 505 North Blvd., Edmond, OK 73034. **Telephone:** (405) 348-3839. **FAX:** (405) 340-7538.

Chairman: Gordon Morgan. **Director:** John Schwartz.

2003 Senior Series: Dale, Seminole, Shawnee and Tecumseh, OK, June 18-23 (8 teams: Arizona, California, Florida, Georgia, Maryland, Ohio, Oklahoma, Texas).

2003 Junior Series: McAlester and Hartshorne, OK, June 6-11 (10 teams: Arizona, California, Canada, Georgia, Mississippi, Missouri, Oklahoma Blue, Oklahoma Gold, Tennessee, Texas).

2002 Sophomore Series: Edmond, OK, May 30-June 1 (4 teams: Oklahoma Red, Oklahoma White, Tennessee, Texas).

NATIONAL HIGH SCHOOL CHAMPIONSHIP

Mailing Address: c/o Champions Baseball Academy, 10701 Plantside Dr., Louisville, KY 40299. **Telephone:** (502) 261-9200. **FAX:** (502) 261-9278. **E-Mail Address:**

champ8@aol.com. **Website:** championsbaseball.com.

Tournament Directors: John Marshall, Bill Miller, Tim Brown, Justin Duncan.

2003 Tournament (high school/open): July 10-13 (64 teams).

PERFECT GAME USA/ WORLD WOOD BAT ASSOCIATION

Mailing Address: 1203 Rockford Road SW, Cedar Rapids, IA 52404. **Telephone**: (319) 298-2923. **FAX**: (319) 298-2924. **E-Mail Address**: pgjerry@qwest.net. **Website**: www.perfectgame.org.

President/Director: Jerry Ford. **National Supervisor:** Andy Ford. **National Coordinators:** Jason Gerst, Tyson Kimm. **WWBA Senior National Championship:** July 7-13 at Marietta, GA (East Cobb Baseball Complex). **WWBA Junior National Championship:** July 15-20 at Marietta, GA (East Cobb Baseball Complex). **WWBA Freshman National Championship:** Aug. 5-10 at Marietta, GA (East Cobb Baseball Complex). **WWBA Pre-High School National Championship:** Aug. 5-10 at Marietta, GA (East Cobb Baseball Complex).

Perfect Game/Baseball America WWBA Underclassmen Championship (16 and under/fall): Oct. 4-6 at Fort Myers, FL (City of Palms Complex).

Perfect Game/Baseball America WWBA Championship (fall): Oct. 24-27 at Jupiter, FL (Roger Dean Stadium).

SHOWCASE EVENTS

ALL-AMERICAN BASEBALL TALENT SHOWCASES

Mailing Address: 6 Bicentennial Ct., Erial, NJ 08081. **Telephone:** (856) 354-0201. **FAX:** (856) 354-0818. **Website:** thehitdoctor@hitdoctor.com.

National Director: Joe Barth.

AREA CODE GAMES

Mailing Address: P.O. Box 213, Santa Rosa, CA 95402. **Telephone:** (707) 975-7894. **FAX:** (707) 525-0214. **E-Mail Address:** rwilliams@areacodebaseball.org. **Website:** www.areacodebaseball.org.

President, Goodwill Series, Inc.: Bob Williams.

2003 Area Code Games: Aug. 4-9 at Long Beach, CA (Blair Field). **Regional Scouting Combines:** Cleveland Indians tryouts—June 1 at Phoenix (Chandler-Gilbert JC); June 7 at Salt Lake City (Salt Lake CC); June 9 at Denver, CO (Regis College). Milwaukee Brewers tryouts—June 16 at Fresno, CA (Fresno State U.); June 23 at Los Angeles, CA (Loyola Marymount U.); July 1 at Los Angeles, CA (Loyola Marymount U.). Montreal Expos tryouts—Harrisburg, PA (RiverSide Stadium); Melbourne, FL (Expos spring training complex). Texas Rangers tryout—June 30 at Houston (U. of Houston). Chicago White Sox tryouts—July 7-8 at Naperville, IL (North Central College).

13th International Friendship Series: Aug. 9-18 at Beijing, China. **Australia Goodwill Series VIII:** Dec. 16-31 at Adelaide, Canberra and Perth, Australia.

ARIZONA FALL CLASSIC

Mailing Address: 6102 W. Maui Lane, Glendale, AZ 85306. **Telephone:** (602) 978-2929. **FAX:** (602) 439-4494. **E-Mail Address:** azbaseballted@msn.com. **Website:** www.fallclassic.com.

Director: Ted Heid.

2003 Events: Four Corner Classic, May 30-June 1 at Peoria Sports Complex, Peoria, AZ. Senior Fall Classic (high school seniors), Oct. 10-12 at Peoria Sports Complex, Peoria, AZ. Junior Fall Classic (high school sophomores/juniors), Oct. 24-26 at Peoria Sports Complex, Peoria, AZ.

BASEBALL FACTORY

Office Address: 9176 Red Branch Rd., Suite M, Columbia, MD 21045. **Telephone:** (800) 641-4487, (410) 715-5080. **FAX:** (410) 715-1975. **E-Mail Address:** info@baseballfactory.com. **Website:** www.baseballfactory.com.

Chief Executive Officer: Steve Sclafani. **President:** Rob Naddelman. **Vice President, Baseball Operations:** Steve Bernhardt.

B.A.T.S. Program: April-October, various locations.

BLUE-GREY CLASSIC

Mailing Address: Pro-Motion Sports, 83 E. Bluff Rd., Ashland, MA 01721. **Telephone:** (508) 881-2782. **E-Mail Address:** gus@impactprospects.com. **Website:** www.impactprospects.com

Director: Gus Bell.

2003 Showcases: July 11-13 at Fort Worth, TX (Texas Christian University); July 22-24 at Jacksonville, FL (Jacksonville University); July 25-27 at St. Petersburg, FL (Devil Rays complex); Aug. 13-15 at Winston-Salem, NC (Wake Forest University); Aug. 18-20 at Williamsburg, VA (College of William & Mary); Aug. 22-24 at Conway, SC (Coastal Carolina University); Oct. 31-Nov. 2 at St. Petersburg, FL (Devil Rays complex); Dec. 6-7 at Clearwater, FL (Jack Russell Stadium).

COLLEGE SELECT SHOWCASE

Mailing Address: P.O. Box 783, Manchester, CT 06040. **Telephone:** (800) 782-3672. **E-Mail Address:** TRhit@msn.com. **Website:** www.collegeselect.org.

Consulting Director: Tom Rizzi.

2003 Showcases: July 5-7 at Norwich, CT (Thomas Dodd Memorial Stadium); Aug. 14-17 at East Hartford, CT; Aug. 22-24 at Binghamton, NY (NYSEG Stadium); Oct. 4-5 at Lakewood, NJ (GPU Energy Park).

DOYLE BASEBALL SELECT SHOWCASES

Mailing Address: P.O. Box 9156, Winter Haven, FL 33883. **Telephone:** (863) 439-1000. **FAX:** (863) 439-7086. **E-Mail Address:** doyleinfo@doylebaseball.com. **Website:** www.doylebaseball.com.

EAST COAST PROFESSIONAL BASEBALL SHOWCASE

Mailing Address: 601 S. College Rd., Wilmington, NC 28403. **Telephone:** (910) 962-3570.

Facility Directors: Mark Scalf, Randy Hood, Scott Jackson.

2002 Showcase: July 30-Aug. 2 at Wilmington, NC (UNC Wilmington).

FIVE STAR BASEBALL SHOWCASE

Mailing Address: Champions Baseball Academy, 10701 Plantside Dr., Louisville, KY 40299. **Telephone:** (502) 261-9200. **FAX:** (502) 261-9278. **E-Mail Address:** champ8@aol.com.

President: John Marshall.

2003 Showcases: July 14-16 at Louisville, KY (Louisville Slugger Field, showcase director: Torry Zerilla); July 21-23 at Cincinnati, OH (showcase director: Bill Doran).

IMPACT BASEBALL

Mailing Address: P.O. Box 71619, Durham, NC 27722. **E-Mail Address:** andypartin@aol.com. **Website:** www.impactbaseball.com.

Operator: Andy Partin.

2003 Showcases: July 1-2 at Columbia, SC (University of South Carolina); July 23-25 at Chapel Hill, NC (University of North Carolina), Aug. 11-12 at Lynchburg, VA (Liberty University); November at Hickory, NC (L.P. Frans Stadium); Dec. 6-7 at Wilmington, NC (UNC-Wilmington).

MIDWEST PROSPECTS SHOWCASE

Mailing Address: P.O. Box 12208, Oklahoma City, OK 73157. **Telephone:** (405) 942-5455. **FAX:** (405) 942-3012. **E-Mail Address:** midwestprospects@cox.net. **Website:** www.midwestprospects.com.

Director: Brian Rupe.

2003 Camps: June 20-22 at Waco, TX (Baylor University); June 27-29 at Norman, OK (University of Oklahoma); Aug. 8-10 at Arlington, TX (U. of Texas-Arlington).

PACIFIC NORTHWEST CHAMPIONSHIP

Mailing Address: 20170 SW Avery Court, Tualatin, OR 97062. **Telephone:** (503) 885-1126. **E-Mail Address**: mckay@baseballnorthwest.com. **Website:** www.baseball northwest.com.

Tournament Organizer: Jeff McKay.

2003 Events: Aug. 19-22 at Tacoma, WA (Cheney Stadium). **Oregon Prospect Games:** June 30-1 at Corvallis, OR (Oregon State University). **Washington Prospect Games:** East—June 23-24 at Pasco, WA (Pasco Stadium); West—June 25-26 at Tacoma (Cheney Stadium). **Idaho Selection Games:** Unavailable.

PERFECT GAME USA

Mailing Address: 1203 Rockford Road SW, Cedar Rapids, IA 52404. **Telephone**: (319) 298-2923, (800) 447-9362. **FAX**: (319) 298-2924. **E-Mail Address**: pgjerry@qwest.net. **Website**: www.perfectgame.org.

President, Director: Jerry Ford. **National Supervisor:** Andy Ford. **National Coordinators:** Jason Guest, Tyson Kimm. **National Scouting:** Tom Battista. **International Director:** Kentaro Yasutake.

Business Manager: Don Walser. **Office Manager:** Betty Ford. **Marketing Director:** Dick Vaske. **Facilities Director:** Tom Jackson. **Softball Director:** Wendi Krejca. **Leagues Director:** Jim Arp. **Directors, Instruction:** Bruce Kimm, Jim VanScoyac.

Spring Showcase: May 3-4 at Cedar Rapids, IA. **National Pre-Draft Camp**: May 14 at Cedar Rapids, IA (Veterans Memorial Stadium). **Sunshine West Showcase:** June 7-8 at Peoria, AZ (Peoria Sports Complex). **Sunshine East Showcase:** June 7-8 at Fort Myers, FL (City of Palms complex). **Perfect Game National Showcase:** June 13-15 at Lincoln, NE (University of Nebraska). **South Underclassmen Showcase**: July 23-25 at Waco, TX (Baylor University). **South Top Prospect Showcase**: July 27-29 at Waco, TX (Baylor University). **Northeast Underclassmen Showcase**: Aug. 11-13 at Massachusetts (site unavailable). **Northeast Top Prospect Showcase:** Aug. 15-17 at Wareham, MA (Clem Spillane Field). **Midwest Top Prospect Showcase**: Sept. 20-21 at Cedar Rapids, IA (Veterans Memorial Stadium). **Western Underclassmen Showcase:** Sept. 27-28 at Peoria, AZ (Peoria Sports Complex). **World Underclassmen Showcase:** Jan. 2-4, 2004 at Fort Myers, FL (City of Palms complex). **World Showcase**: Jan. 10-11, 2004 at Fort Myers, FL (City of Palms complex).

WWBA Senior National Championship: July 7-13 at Marietta, GA (East Cobb Baseball Complex). **WWBA Junior National Championship:** July 15-20 at Marietta, GA (East Cobb Baseball Complex). **WWBA Freshman National Championship:** Aug. 5-10 at Marietta, GA (East Cobb Baseball Complex). **WWBA Pre-High School National Championship:** Aug. 5-10 at Marietta, GA (East Cobb Baseball Complex).

Perfect Game/Baseball America WWBA Underclassmen Championship (16 and under/fall): Oct. 4-6 at Fort Myers, FL (City of Palms Complex).

Perfect Game/Baseball America WWBA Championship (fall): Oct. 24-27 at Jupiter, FL (Roger Dean Stadium).

PREMIER BASEBALL

Mailing Address: 2411 Teal Ave., Sarasota, FL 34237. **Telephone:** (941) 371-0989. **FAX:** (941) 371-0917.

Camp Directors: John Crumbley, Rich Hofman, Clyde Metcalf.

2003 Showcase: June 5-7 at Sarasota, FL.

PRO SELECT BASEBALL

Mailing Address: P.O. Box 36, Franklin Lakes, NJ 07417. **Telephone:** (201) 337-7440. **E-Mail Address:** proselectbb@aol.com.

Director: Jerry McMahon.

SELECTFEST BASEBALL

Mailing Address: 60 Franklin Place, Morris Plains, NJ 07950. **Telephone:** (973) 539-4781. **E-Mail Address:** selectfest@optonline.net.

Camp Directors: Brian Fleury, Bruce Shatel.

2003 Showcase: June 27-28 at Piscataway, NJ (Rutgers University).

TEAM ONE SHOWCASES

Mailing Address: P.O. Box 8843, Cincinnati, OH 45208. **Telephone:** (859) 466-8326. **E-Mail Address:** TeamOneBB@aol.com. **Website:** www.teamonebase ball.com.

President, Team One Sports: Jeff Spelman. **Assistant Director:** Stan Brzezicki. Telephone: (814) 899-8407. E-Mail Address: Tricky023@aol.com. **Scouting Director:** Anup Sinha. Telephone: (813) 571-1979. E-Mail Address: Nupester@aol.com. **West Coast Scout:** Scott Zilmer. E-Mail Address: Scottzilmer@hotmail.com.

2003 Team One National Showcase: September at Las Vegas, NV (UNLV).

2003 Regional Showcases: West—June 28-30 at Tempe, AZ (Diablo Stadium); Central—July 5-6, site unavailable; South—July 20-22 at Atlanta (Georgia Tech); North—July 28-30 at South Bend, IN (University of Notre Dame).

TOP 96 INVITATIONAL SHOWCASE

Mailing Address: P.O. Box 5481, Wayland, MA 01778. **Telephone:** (508) 651-0165. **E-Mail Address:** kennethp50@attbi.com. **Website:** www.top96.com.

Showcase Organizers: Dave Callum, Doug Henson, Ken Hill.

2003 Showcase: Aug. 8-9 at Lowell, MA (Alumni Field).

TOP GUNS SHOWCASE

Mailing Address: 7890 N. Franklin Rd., Suite 2, Coeur d'Alene, ID 83815. **Telephone/FAX:** (208) 762-1100. **E-Mail Address:** topgunsbss@hotmail.com. **Website:** www.topgunsbaseball.com.

President: Larry Rook. **National Director, Field Operations:** Gary Ward. **Assistant Director, National**

Scouting: Nick Rook. **Scouting/Field Operations:** Cody Rook, Jason Rook.

2003 High School National Showcase: June 23-25 at Las Vegas, NV (University of Nevada-Las Vegas).

Regional Showcases: Desert/Mountain—July 7-8 at Prescott, AZ (Yavapai CC); Southern—June 9-10 at Poplarville, MS (Pearl JC); Northeast—June 12-13 at Scranton, PA (Lackawanna County Stadium); South Central—June 14-15 at Arlington, TX (Seguin HS); Rocky Mountain—June 15-16 at Denver, CO (Regis U.); Upper Midwest—June 26-27 at Indianapolis, IN (U. of Indianapolis); Southern California—July 19-21 at Mission Viejo, Calif. (Saddleback CC); Southeast—July 29-30 at Atlanta, GA (Georgia Tech); Pacific Northwest—Aug. 8-10 at Seattle, WA (U. of Washington); Carolinas—Aug. 10-11 at Kannapolis, NC (Fieldcrest Cannon Stadium), Aug. 10-11.

SCOUTING SERVICES/HIGH SCHOOL, COLLEGE

BASEBALL FACTORY

Office Address: 9176 Red Branch Rd., Suite M, Columbia, MD 21045. **Telephone:** (800) 641-4487, (410) 715-5080. **FAX:** (410) 715-1975. **E-Mail Address:** info@baseballfactory.com. **Website:** www.baseballfactory.com.

Chief Executive Officer: Steve Sclafani. **President:** Rob Naddelman. **Vice President, Baseball Operations:** Steve Bernhardt.

PROSPECTS PLUS/THE SCOUTING REPORT

(A Joint Venture of Baseball America and Perfect Game USA)

Mailing Address: Baseball America, P.O. Box 2089, Durham, NC 27702. **Telephone:** (800) 845-2726. **FAX:** (919) 682-2880. **E-Mail Addresses:** allansimpson@baseballamerica.com; pgjerry@qwest.net. **Website:** www.baseballamerica.com; www.perfectgame.org

Editor, Baseball America: Allan Simpson. **Director, Perfect Game USA:** Jerry Ford.

SKILLSHOW, INC.

Mailing Address: 290 King of Prussia Rd., Suite 122, Radnor, PA 19087. **Telephone:** (610) 687-9072. **FAX:** (610) 687-9629. **E-Mail Address:** info@skillshow.com. **Website:** www.skillshow.com.

Chief Executive Officer: Tom Koerick Jr. **President/Director, Sales:** Tom Koerick Sr. **Vice President, Marketing:** Louis Manon. **Webmaster:** Mark Rivera.

TEAM ONE SHOWCASES

Mailing Address: P.O. Box 8843, Cincinnati, OH 45208. **Telephone:** (859) 466-8326. **E-Mail Address:** TeamOneBB@aol.com. **Website:** www.teamonebaseball.com.

President, Team One Sports: Jeff Spelman.

NATIONAL ORGANIZATIONS

ALL AMERICAN AMATEUR BASEBALL ASSOCIATION (AAABA)

Mailing Address: 331 Parkway Dr., Zanesville, OH 43701. **Telephone:** (740) 453-8531. **FAX:** (740) 453-3978. **E-Mail Address:** clw@aol.com. **Website:** www.aaaba.com.

Year Founded: 1944.

President: Robert Mingo. **Executive Director:** Bob Wolfe.

2003 National Tournament (21 and under): Aug. 4-9 at Johnstown, PA (16 teams). **AAABA Regionals:** July 29-Aug. 1 at Altoona, PA and Zanesville, OH.

AMATEUR ATHLETIC UNION OF THE UNITED STATES, INC. (AAU)

Mailing Address: P.O. Box 10000, Lake Buena Vista, FL 32803. **Telephone:** (407) 934-7200. **FAX:** (407) 934-7242. **Website:** www.aaubaseball.org.

Year Founded: 1982.

Senior Sports Manager/Baseball: Jeremy Bullock.

DIVISION I

Age Classifications, National Championships

8 and under	Concord, NC, July 10-13
9 and under	*Orlando, July 11-19
10 and under (46/60 foot)	Des Moines, IA, July 18-26
10 and under (48/65 foot)	Knoxville, TN, July 18-26
11 and under	*Orlando, July 18-26
12 and under	Burnsville/Lakeville, MN, July 25-Aug. 2
13 and under (54/80 foot)	Amarillo, TX, July 18-26
13 and under (60/90 foot)	Kinston, NC, July 25-Aug. 2
14 and under (60/90 foot)	Sarasota, FL, July 25-Aug. 2
15 and under	Kingsport, TN, July 26-Aug. 3
Junior Olympics (16 and under)	Detroit, July 24-Aug. 2
17 and under	*Orlando, July 18-26
18 and under	Fort Myers, FL, July 11-19

DIVISION II

Age Classifications, National Championships

10 and under (46/60 foot)	Des Moines, IA, July 18-26
11 and under	*Orlando, July 18-26
12 and under	Burnsville/Lakeville, MN, July 25-Aug. 2
13 and under (54/80 foot)	Amarillo, TX, July 18-26
13 and under (60/90 foot)	Kinston, NC, July 25-Aug. 2
14 and under (60/90 foot)	*Orlando, July 25-Aug. 2
15 and under	Knoxville, TN, July 25-Aug. 2
16 and under	Knoxville, TN, July 25-Aug. 2

International Championships

10 and under (46/60 foot)	*Orlando, June 13-19
12 and under	*Orlando, June 13-19

*Disney's Wide World of Sports Complex, Lake Buena Vista.

AMERICAN AMATEUR BASEBALL CONGRESS (AABC)

National Headquarters: 118-119 Redfield Plaza, P.O. Box 467, Marshall, MI 49068. **Telephone:** (269) 781-2002. **FAX:** (269) 781-2060. **E-Mail Address:** aabc@voyager.net. **Website:** www.aabc.us.

Year Founded: 1935.

President: Joe Cooper.

Age Classifications, World Series

Roberto Clemente (8 and under)	McDonough, GA, July 24-27
Willie Mays (10 and under)	Catano, PR, July 31-Aug. 4
Pee Wee Reese (12 and under)	Toa Baja, PR, Aug. 7-11
Sandy Koufax (14 and under)	Gurnee, IL, Aug. 7-10
Mickey Mantle (16 and under)	McKinney, TX, July 30-Aug. 3
Connie Mack (18 and under)	Farmington, NM, Aug. 1-7
Stan Musial (unlimited)	Battle Creek, MI, Aug. 8-12

AMERICAN AMATEUR YOUTH BASEBALL ALLIANCE

Mailing Address: P.O. Box 560, Bonne Terre, MO 63628. **Telephone:** (573) 518-0319. **FAX:** (314) 822-4974. **E-Mail Address:** clwjr28@aol.com. **Website:** www.aayba.com.

President, Baseball Operations: Carroll Wood.

Age Classifications, Open World Series

10 and under .... St. Louis, July 4-11
11 and under .... St. Louis, July 12-19
12 and under .... St. Louis, July 4-11
13 and under .... St. Louis, July 12-19
14 and under (60/90 foot) .... St. Louis, July 4-11

Age Classifications, Tournament of Champions Qualifier World Series

10 and under Gold/Silver .... Morganton, NC, July 4-12
11 and under Gold/Silver .... Austin, TX, July 4-12
12 and under Gold .... Chicago Heights, IL, July 5-12
12 and under Silver .... Chicago Heights, IL, July 13-20
13 and under Gold .... Morganton/Hickory, NC, July 4-12
13 and under Silver .... Millington, TN, July 19-26
14 and under Gold/Silver (54/80 foot) .... Columbus, GA, dates unavailable
14 and under Gold (60/90 foot) .... Millington, TN, July 19-26
14 and under Silver (60/90 foot) .... Dayton, OH, July 11-18

All-Star Nationals

9 and under .... Chicago Heights, IL, Aug. 3-10
10 and under .... Chicago Heights, IL, July 26-Aug. 2
11 and under .... St. Louis, MO, July 26-Aug. 2
12 and under .... St. Louis, MO, Aug. 3-10
13 and under .... St. Louis, MO, July 26-Aug. 2
14 and under .... St. Louis, MO, Aug. 3-10
15 and under .... Austin, TX, July 26-Aug. 2
16 and under .... Austin, TX, July 26-Aug. 2
17 and under .... Wichita, KS, July 26-Aug. 2

AMERICAN LEGION BASEBALL

National Headquarters: National Americanism Commission, P.O. Box 1055, Indianapolis, IN 46206. **Telephone:** (317) 630-1213. **FAX:** (317) 630-1369. **E-Mail Address:** acy@legion.org. **Website:** www.baseball.legion.org.

Year Founded: 1925.

Program Coordinator: Jim Quinlan.

2003 World Series (19 and under): Aug. 22-26 at Donges Stadium, Bartlesville, OK (8 teams).

2003 Regional Tournaments (Aug. 14-18, 8 teams)**: Northeast**—Torrington, CT; **Mid-Atlantic**—Newburgh, NY; **Southeast**—Rock Hill, SC; **Mid-South**—Blue Springs, MO; **Great Lakes**—Midland, MI; **Central Plains**—New Ulm, MN; **Northwest**—Whitefish, MT; **Western**—Lodi, CA.

BABE RUTH BASEBALL

International Headquarters: 1770 Brunswick Pike, P.O. Box 5000, Trenton, NJ 08638. **Telephone:** (609) 695-1434. **FAX:** (609) 695-2505. **Website:** www.baberuthleague.org.

Year Founded: 1951.

President, Chief Executive Officer: Ron Tellefsen.

Executive Vice President/Chief Financial Officer: Rosemary Schoellkopf. **Vice President, Operations/Marketing:** Joe Smiegocki. **Vice President, Planning/Development:** Debra Horn. **Commissioners:** Robert Faherty, Jamie Horn, Steven Tellefsen.

Age Classifications, World Series

10 and under .... Williamsburg, VA, Aug. 2-9
Cal Ripken (11-12) .... Aberdeen, MD, Aug. 16-24
13 .... Pine Bluff, AR, Aug. 9-16
14 .... Quincy, MA, Aug. 15-23
13-15 .... Williston, ND, Aug. 16-23
16 .... Jamestown, NY, Aug. 9-16
16-18 .... Weimar, TX, Aug. 9-16

CONTINENTAL AMATEUR BASEBALL ASSOCIATION (CABA)

Mailing Address: 82 University St., Westerville, OH 43081. **Telephone:** (740) 382-4620. **E-Mail Address:** rtremaine@cababaseball.com. **Website:** www.cababaseball.com.

Year Founded: 1984.

Commissioner: John Mocny. **President:** Carl Williams. **Vice President:** Larry Redwine. **Executive Director:** Roger Tremaine.

Age Classifications, Ultimate World Series

9 and under .... Charles City, IA, July 25-Aug. 3
10 and under .... Aurelia/Cherokee, IA, July 25-Aug. 3
11 and under .... Marion, OH, July 18-25
12 and under .... Cincinnati, July 25-Aug. 1
13 and under .... Broken Arrow, OK, July 25-Aug. 1
14 and under .... Dublin, OH, July 18-25

15 and under .... Crystal Lake, IL, July 25-Aug. 3
16 and under .... Marietta, GA, Aug. 2-10
High school age .... Euclid, OH, July 18-26
18 and under .... Houston, July 25-Aug. 1
College age .... Schenectady, NY, July 18-25
Unlimited age .... Bourbonnais, IL, Aug. 5-10

Age Classifications, Quality World Series

9 and under .... Marietta, GA, July 26-Aug. 2
10 and under .... Marietta, GA, July 26-Aug. 2
11 and under .... Broken Arrow, OK, July 25-Aug. 1
12 and under .... Marion, OH, July 25-Aug. 1
13 and under .... Cincinnati, July 25-Aug. 2
14 and under .... Mentor, OH, July 25-Aug. 2
15 and under .... Bourbonnais, IL, July 26-Aug. 2

DIXIE BASEBALL, INC.

Mailing Address: P.O. Box 877, Marshall, TX 36123. **Telephone:** (903) 927-2255. **FAX:** (903) 927-1846. **Website:** www.dixie.org.

Year Founded: 1956.

Executive Director: P.L. Corley, P.O. Box 231536, Montgomery, AL 36123. Telephone: (334) 242-8395. **Office Manager:** Rhonda Skelton.

Age Classifications, World Series

Dixie Youth (9-10) .... Florence, SC, Aug. 11-16
Dixie Youth (12 and under) .... Florence, SC, Aug. 11-16
Dixie 13 .... Jackson, TN, Aug. 2-7
Dixie Boys (13-14) .... Jackson, TN, Aug. 2-7
Dixie Pre-Majors (15-16) .... Thomasville, AL, July 26-31
Dixie Majors (15-18) .... Laurel, MS, July 26-31

DIZZY DEAN BASEBALL, INC.

Mailing Address: P.O. Box 856, Hernando, MS 38632. **Telephone:** (662) 429-4365, (850) 455-8827. **Website:** dizzydeanbbinc.org.

Year Founded: 1977.

Commissioner: Danny Phillips. **Treasurer/Administrator:** D.B. Stewart.

Age Classifications, World Series

9 and under .... Southhaven, MS, July 25-30
10 and under .... Huffman, AL, July 18-23
11 and under .... Coal Mountain, GA, July 18-23
12 and under .... Bartow, GA, July 18-23
Sophomore (13-14) .... Southaven, MS, July 25-30
Junior (15-16) .... Southaven, MS, July 25-30
Senior (17-18) .... Southaven, MS, July 25-30
High school .... Hixson, TN, July 17-22

HAP DUMONT YOUTH BASEBALL

(A Division of the National Baseball Congress)

Mailing Address: 1325 N. Westlink, Wichita, KS 67212. **Telephone:** (316) 721-1779. **FAX:** (316) 721-8054. **Website:** hapdumontbaseball.com.

Year Founded: 1974.

National Chairman: Jerry Crowell. **Vice Chairman:** Jerald Vogt. **Executive Director:** Jim Barr.

Age Classifications, World Series

8 and under .... Kearney, MO, July 25-30
9 and under .... Bartlett, TN, July 25-30
10 and under .... Roswell, GA, July 25-30
11 and under .... Oklahoma City, July 25-30
12 and under .... Harrison, AR, July 25-30
13 and under .... Casper, WY, July 25-30
14 and under .... Brainerd, MN, July 25-30
15 and under .... Greenfield, IN, July 25-30
16 and under .... Oklahoma City, July 25-30
18 and under .... Wichita, July 25-30

LITTLE LEAGUE BASEBALL, INC.

International Headquarters: P.O. Box 3485, Williamsport, PA 17701. **Telephone:** (570) 326-1921. **FAX:** (570) 326-1074. **Website:** www.littleleague.org.

Year Founded: 1939.

Chairman: Dwight Raiford.

President/Chief Executive Officer: Steve Keener. **Director, Media Relations/Communications:** Lance Van Auken. **Director, Publications:** Scott Miller. **Director, Special Projects:** Scott Rosenberg.

Age Classifications, World Series

Little League (11-12) .... Williamsport, PA, Aug. 15-24
Junior League (13-14) .... Taylor, MI, Aug. 10-16
Senior League (14-16) .... Bangor, ME, Aug. 10-16
Big League (16-18) .... Easley, SC, Aug. 2-9

NATIONAL AMATEUR BASEBALL FEDERATION (NABF)

Mailing Address: P.O. Box 705, Bowie, MD 20718. **Telephone:** (301) 464-5460. **FAX:** (301) 352-0214. **E-Mail Address:** nabf1914@aol.com. **Website:** www.nabf.com.

Year Founded: 1914.

Executive Director: Charles Blackburn. **Special Events Coordinator:** Wanda Rutledge.

Age Classifications, World Series

Rookie (10 and under) .... Southaven, MS, July 6-7
Freshman (12 and under) .... Hopkinsville, KY, July 15-20
Sophomore (14 and under) .... Joplin, MO, July 16-20
Junior (16 and under) .... Northville, MI, July 23-27
High School (17 and under) .... Millington, TN, July 24-28
Senior (18 and under) .... Welland, Ontario, July 30-Aug. 3
College (22 and under) .... Springfield, OH, Aug. 6-10
Major (unlimited) .... Louisville, KY, Aug. 13-16

NABF Classics (Invitational)

9 and under .... Southaven, MS, July 6-12
11 and under .... Southaven, MS, July 6-12
13 and under .... Southaven, MS, July 6-12
15 and under .... Nashville, July 22-27
Unlimited .... Orlando, dates unavailable

NATIONAL ASSOCIATION OF POLICE ATHLETIC LEAGUES

Mailing Address: 618 U.S. Highway 1, Suite 201, North Palm Beach, FL 33408. **Telephone:** (561) 844-1823. **FAX:** (561) 863-6120. **E-Mail Address:** copnkid@nationalpal.org. **Website:** www.nationalpal.org.

Year Founded: 1914.

Executive Director: Brad Hart. **National Program Manager:** Jeremy Phillips.

Age Classifications, World Series

14 and under .... Kissimmee, FL, July 12-18
16 and under .... Kissimmee, FL, July 12-18

PONY BASEBALL, INC.

International Headquarters: P.O. Box 225, Washington, PA 15301. **Telephone:** (724) 225-1060. **FAX:** (724) 225-9852. **E-Mail Address:** pony@pulsenet.com. **Website:** www.pony.org.

Year Founded: 1951.

President, Chief Executive Officer: Abraham Key. **Director, Baseball Operations:** Don Clawson.

Age Classifications, World Series

Shetland (5-6) .... No National Tournament
Pinto (7-8) .... No National Tournament
Mustang (9-10) .... Irving, TX, Aug. 6-9
Bronco (11-12) .... Monterey, CA, Aug. 7-13
Pony (13-14) .... Washington, PA, Aug. 9-16
Colt (15-16) .... Lafayette, IN, Aug. 5-12
Palomino (17-18) .... Santa Clara, CA, Aug. 8-11

REVIVING BASEBALL IN INNER CITIES (RBI)

Mailing Address: 245 Park Ave., New York, NY 10167. **Telephone:** (212) 931-7897. **FAX:** (212) 949-5695.

Year Founded: 1989.

Founder: John Young. **Vice President, Community Affairs:** Thomas Brasuell. **Marketing:** Kathleen Fineout.

Age Classifications, World Series

Junior Boys (13-15) .... Houston, TX, Aug. 6-13
Senior Boys (16-18) .... Houston, TX, Aug. 6-13

SUPER SERIES BASEBALL OF AMERICA

National Headquarters: 4036 East Grandview St., Mesa, AZ 85205. **Telephone:** (480) 664-2998. **FAX:** (480) 664-29997. **E-Mail Address:** info@superseriesbaseball.com. **Website:** www.superseriesbaseball.com.

President: Mark Mathew.

Age Classifications, World Series

8 and under .... Moreno Valley, CA, dates unavailable
8 and under (Coach pitch) .... Houston, TX, July 7-13
8 and under (Machine pitch) .... St. Louis, MO, July 19-27
9 and under .... Houston, TX, July 13-20
10 and under .... Colorado Springs, CO, July 19-27
11 and under (National/All-Star) .... Aurora, CO, July 12-20

11 and under (American) .... Sherwood, AR, July 25-Aug. 2
12 and under (National/All-Star) .... Kansas City, MO, July 26-Aug. 3
12 and under (American) .... St. Louis, MO, July 19-27
13 and under (National/All-Star) .... Aurora, CO, July 12-20
13 and under (American) .... Tulsa, OK, July 12-20
14 and under (National, 54/80) .... Houston, TX, July 7-13
14 and under (American/All-Star, 54/80) .... St. Louis, MO, July 12-20
14 and under (National/American, 60/90) .... Peoria, AZ, July 27-Aug. 3
15 and under .... Peoria, AZ, July 12-20
16 and under .... Peoria, AZ, July 19-26
17-18 .... Peoria, AZ, July 19-26

T-BALL USA ASSOCIATION, INC.

Office Address: 2499 Main St., Stratford, CT 06615. **Telephone:** (203) 381-1449. **FAX:** (203) 381-1440. **E-Mail Address:** teeballusa@aol.com. **Website:** www.teeballusa.org.

Year Founded: 1993.

President: Bing Broido. **Executive Vice President:** Lois Richards.

TRIPLE CROWN SPORTS

Mailing Address: 3930 Automation Way, Fort Collins, CO 80525. **Telephone:** (970) 223-6644. **FAX:** (970) 223-3636. **Websites:** www.triplecrownsports.com, www.usasportsrankings.com

Executive Director: Michael Peterson.

Age Classifications, National Championships

9, 12, 15, 16 World Series .... Steamboat Springs, CO, July 23-27
10, 12, 14, 16 World Series .... Steamboat Springs, CO, July 24-28
10, 14, 18 World Series .... Steamboat Springs, CO, July 30-Aug. 3
11, 13 World Series .... Steamboat Springs, Aug. 6-10
10, 12, 14, 15, 16 Fall Nationals .... St. Augustine, FL, Oct. 17-19
9, 11, 13, 18 Fall Nationals .... St. Augustine, FL, Oct. 24-26

U.S. AMATEUR BASEBALL ASSOCIATION (USABA)

Mailing Address: 7101 Lake Ballinger Way, Edmonds, WA 98026. **Telephone/FAX:** (425) 776-7130. **E-Mail Address:** usaba@usaba.com. **Website:** www.usaba.com.

Year Founded: 1969.

Executive Director: Al Rutledge. **Secretary:** Roberta Engelhart.

Age Classifications, World Series

11 and under .... site/dates unavailable
12 and under .... site/dates unavailable
13 and under .... site/dates unavailable
14 and under .... Pasco, WA, Aug. 10-17
15 and under .... Mianer, NV, July 27-Aug. 2
16 and under .... Richland, WA, Aug. 10-17
17 and under .... Boise, ID, Aug. 2-9
18 and under .... Reno, NV, July 20-27

U.S. AMATEUR BASEBALL FEDERATION (USABF)

Mailing Address: 1111 Orange Ave., Suite A, Coronado, CA 92118. **Telephone:** (619) 435-2831. **FAX:** (619) 435-3148. **E-Mail Address:** usabf@cox.net. **Website:** www.usabf.com.

Year Founded: 1997.

Senior CEO/President: Tim Halbig.

Age Classifications, World Series

10 and under .... San Diego, July 30-Aug. 3
11 and under .... San Diego, July 30-Aug. 3
12 and under .... San Diego, July 30-Aug. 3
13 and under .... San Diego, July 30-Aug. 3
14 and under .... San Diego, July 31-Aug. 9
15 and under .... San Diego, July 31-Aug. 9
16 and under .... San Diego, July 31-Aug. 9
18 and under .... San Diego, July 31-Aug. 9
Open .... San Diego, July 23-27

UNITED STATES SPECIALTY SPORTS ASSOCIATION (USSSA)

Executive Vice President, Baseball: Rick Fortuna, 6324 N. Chatham Ave., No. 136, Kansas City, MO 64151. **Telephone:** (816) 587-4545. **FAX:** (816) 587-4549. **E-Mail Address:** linda@kcsports.org. **Website:** kcsports.org.

Year Founded: (1965)/Baseball (1996).

Age Classifications, World Series

7 and under (Machine pitch) .... Oklahoma City, July 15-20
7 and under (Coach pitch) .... Sulphur, LA, July 15-20
8 and under (Machine pitch) .... Oklahoma City, July 15-20

8 and under (Machine pitch) .... Thomson, GA, July 15-20
8 and under (Coach pitch) .... Sulphur, LA, July 15-20
8 and under .... Chino Hills, CA, July 15-20
8 and under .... Kansas City, MO, July 15-20
9 and under (Major) .... Baton Rouge, LA, July 13-20
9 and under (AAA) .... St. Louis, July 13-20
10 and under (Major) .... Henderson, NV, July 13-20
10 and under (AAA) .... Southaven, MS, July 13-20
11 and under (Major) .... Gulfport, MS, July 20-27
11 and under (AAA) .... Overland Park, KS, July 13-20
12 and under (Major) .... Chino Hills, CA, July 20-27
12 and under (AAA) .... Hutchinson, KS, July 20-27
13 and under (Major) .... High Point, NC, July 20-27
13 and under (AAA) .... Broken Arrow, OK, July 13-20
14 and under (Major, 54/80) .... San Antonio, July 20-27
14 and under (AAA, 54/80) .... Canton, MI, July 20-27
14 and under (Major, 60/90) .... Orlando, FL, July 27-Aug. 3
15 and under (Major/AAA) .... Murfreesboro, TN, July 20-27
16 and under (Major) .... Orlando, FL, July 25-31
16 and under (AAA) .... Orlando, FL, July 24-30
17 and under (Major/AAA) .... Oklahoma City, July 20-27
18 and under (Major/AAA) .... Nicholasville, KY, July 27-Aug. 3

USA JUNIOR OLYMPIC BASEBALL CHAMPIONSHIP

Mailing Address: USA Baseball, 3400 E. Camino Campestre, Tucson, AZ 85716. **Telephone:** (520) 327-9700. **FAX:** (520) 327-9221. **E-Mail Address:** RayDarwin@aol.com. **Website:** www.usabaseball.com.

Director, Youth National Team: Ray Darwin.

Age Classifications, Championships

16 and under (West) .... Tucson, AZ, June 20-28
16 and under (East) .... Palm Beach County, FL, June 20-28

YOUTH BASEBALL TOURNAMENT CENTERS

BASEBALL USA

Mailing Address: 2626 W. Sam Houston Pkwy. N., Houston, TX 77043. **Telephone:** (713) 690-5055. **FAX:** (713) 690-9448. **E-Mail Address:** info@baseballusa.com. **Website:** www.baseballusa.com.

President: Charlie Maiorana. **Tournament Director:** Ron Mathis. **Building Manager, Accounting:** Ken Ahrens. **Director, Marketing/Development:** Trip Couch. **League Baseball:** Kevin Nichols. **Pro Shop Manager:** Don Lewis.

Activities: Camps, leagues, instruction, youth tournaments.

COCOA EXPO SPORTS CENTER

Mailing Address: 500 Friday Rd., Cocoa, FL 32926. **Telephone:** (321) 639-3976. **FAX:** (321) 639-0598. **E-Mail Address:** athleticdirector@cocoaexpo.com. **Website:** www.cocoaexpo.com.

Executive Director: Jeff Biddle.

Activities: Spring training program, instructional camps, team training camps, youth tournaments.

2003 Events/Tournaments (ages 10-18): **First Pitch Festival**, May 30-June 1. **Cocoa Expo Internationale**, July 1-6. **Cocoa Expo Summer Classic**, July 29-Aug. 3. **Labor Day Challenge**, Aug. 29-Sept. 1. **Cocoa Expo Fall Classic**, Oct. 17-19.

COOPERSTOWN BASEBALL WORLD

Mailing Address: P.O. Box 398, Bergenfield, NJ 07621. **Telephone:** (888) CBW-8750. **FAX:** (888) CBW-8720. **E-Mail Address:** cbw@cooperstownbaseballworld.com. **Website:** www.cooperstownbaseballworld.com.

Complex Address: Cooperstown Baseball World, SUNY-Oneonta, Ravine Parkway, Oneonta, NY 13820.

President/Chairman: Eddie Einhorn. **Vice President:** Debra Sirianni. **Senior Coordinator, Special Events:** Jennifer Einhorn.

Invitational Tournaments: 12 and under, 13 and under, 15 and under: June 28-July 4, July 19-25. 12 and under, 13 and under, 14 and under: July 5-11, July 12-18, July 26-Aug. 1, Aug. 2-8, Aug. 9-15.

COOPERSTOWN DREAMS PARK

Mailing Address: 101 E. Fisher St., 3rd Floor, Salisbury, NC 28144. **Telephone:** (704) 630-0050. **FAX:** (704) 630-0737. **E-Mail Address:** info@cooperstowndreamspark.com. **Website:** www.cooperstowndreamspark.com.

Complex Address: 4450 State Highway 28, Cooperstown, NY 13807.

Chief Executive Officer: Lou Presutti, **Program Director:** Phil Kehr.

Invitational Tournaments (64 teams per week): 10 and under—June 14-20; 12 and under—June 21-27, June 28-July 4, July 5-11, July 12-18, July 19-25, July 26-Aug. 1, Aug. 2-8, Aug. 9-15, Aug. 16-22.

National American Tournament of Champions: 12 and under—Aug. 23-29.

DISNEY'S WIDE WORLD OF SPORTS

Mailing Address: P.O. Box 10000, Lake Buena Vista, FL 32830. **Telephone:** (407) 938-3802. **FAX:** (407) 938-3412. **E-Mail Address:** wdw.sports.baseball@disney.com. **Website:** www.disneyworldsports.com.

Sports Manager: Kevin Russell. **Tournament Director:** Al Schlazer. **Baseball Sales Manager:** Christine Asay.

Program Coordinator, Baseball: Nick Montenegro.

2003 Events/Tournaments: Disney's Sun & Surf Baseball Bash (10 and under, 11, 12, 14, 16, 18), May 23-26. **Disney's Salute to Baseball Festival** (10 and under, 11, 12, 14, 16, 18), July 5-11. **Disney's Turn Back the Clock Weekend**(10 and under, 11, 12, 14, 16, 18), Aug. 28-Sept. 1. **Disney's New Year's Baseball Classic** (10 and under, 11, 12, 14, 16, 18), Dec. 28-Jan. 1, 2004

KC SPORTS TOURNAMENTS

Mailing Address: KC Sports, 6324 N. Chatham Ave., No. 136, Kansas City, MO 64151. **Telephone:** (816) 587-4545. **FAX:** (816) 587-4549. **E-Mail Addresses:** rick@kcsports.org, wally@kcsports.org, angelo@kcsports.org, linda@kcsports.org. **Website:** www.kcsports.org.

Activities: Youth tournaments (ages 6-18).

Tournament Organizers: Rick Fortuna, Wally Fortuna, Angela Giacalone, Linda Hottovy.

U.S. AMATEUR BASEBALL FEDERATION (USABF)

Mailing Address: 1111 Orange Ave., Suite A, Coronado, CA 92118. **Telephone:** (619) 435-2831. **FAX:** (619) 435-3148. **E-Mail Address:** usabf@cox.net. **Website:** www.usabf.com.

Senior Chief Executive Officer/President: Tim Halbig.

INSTRUCTIONAL SCHOOLS/PRIVATE CAMPS

ACADEMY OF PRO PLAYERS

Mailing Address: 317 Midland Ave., Garfield, NJ 07026. **Telephone:** (973) 772-3355. **FAX:** (973) 772-4839. **Website:** www.academypro.com.

Camp Director: Lar Gilligan.

ALDRETE BASEBALL ACADEMY

Office Address: P.O. Box 4048, Monterey, CA 93942. **Telephone:** (831) 884-0400. **FAX:** (831) 884-0800. **E-Mail Address:** aldretebaseball@aol.com. **Website:** www.aldretebaseball.com.

Camp Director: Rich Aldrete.

ALL-AMERICAN BASEBALL ACADEMY

Mailing Address: 9937 Walker St., Cypress, CA 90630. **Telephone:** (714) 995-9273. **FAX:** (714) 995-2357. **E-Mail Address:** info@all-americanbaseball.com. **Website:** www.all-americanbaseball.com.

Manager: Dave Snow.

ALL-STAR BASEBALL ACADEMY

Mailing Address: 650 Parkway Blvd., Broomall, PA 19008. **Telephone:** (610) 355-2411. **FAX:** (610) 355-2414. **E-Mail Address:** info@allstarbaseballacademy.com. **Website:** www.allstarbaseballacademy.com.

Director: Mike Manning.

THE BASEBALL ACADEMY

Mailing Address: c/o IMG Academies, 5500 34th St. W., Bradenton, FL 34210. **Telephone:** (800) 872-6425, (941) 755-1000. **FAX:** (941) 752-2531. **E-Mail Address:** net-sales@imgworld.com. **Website:** www.imgacademies.com.

Camp Director: Ken Bolek.

BUCKY DENT BASEBALL SCHOOL

Mailing Address: 490 Dotterel Rd., Delray Beach, FL 33444. **Telephone:** (561) 265-0280. **FAX:** (561) 278-6679. **E-Mail Address:** staff@dentbaseball.com. **Website:** www.dentbaseball.com.

Vice President: Larry Hoskin.

DIAMOND INDOOR SPORTS

Mailing Address: 23409 Detroit Road, Westlake, OH 44145. **Telephone:** (440) 333-9420. **FAX:** (440) 333-1115. **Website:** www.diamondndoorsports.com.

Director, Baseball Operations: Danny Allie. **Assistant, Baseball Operations:** Dave Pastors. **Hitting Coordinator:** Pete Berrios.

DOYLE BASEBALL SCHOOL

Mailing Address: P.O. Box 9156, Winter Haven, FL 33883. **Telephone:** (863) 439-1000. **FAX:** (863) 439-7086. **E-Mail Address:** doyleinfo@doylebaseball.com. **Website:** www.doylebaseball.com.

President: Denny Doyle. **Chief Executive Officer:** Blake Doyle. **On-Field Director:** Brian Doyle. **Director, Satellite School:** Rick Siebert.

FROZEN ROPES TRAINING CENTERS

Mailing Address: 31 Jonathan Bourne Dr., Pocasset, MA 02559. **Telephone:** (508) 563-1860. **FAX:** (508) 563-1875. **E-Mail Address:** info@frozenropes.com. **Website:** www.frozenropes.com.

Corporate Director: Tony Abbatine. **Camp Director:** Mike Coutts.

GRAND SLAM USA

Mailing Address: 4995 Varsity Drive, Lisle, IL 60532. **Telephone:** (630) 271-9999. **FAX:** (630) 271-0112. **E-Mail Address:** awallace@grandslamusa.com, marco@grandslamusa.com. **Website:** www.grandslamusa.com.

Operations Manager: Anthony Wallace. **General Manager:** Marco Fajardo.

MARK CRESSE BASEBALL SCHOOL

Mailing Address: P.O. Box 4041, Seal Beach, CA 90740. **Telephone:** (714) 892-6145. **FAX:** (714) 892-1881. **E-Mail Address:** info@markcresse.com. **Website:** www.markcresse.com.

Owner/Founder: Mark Cresse. **Executive Director:** Jeff Pressman.

MICKEY OWEN BASEBALL SCHOOL

Mailing Address: P.O. Box 88, Miller, MO 65707. **Telephone:** (800) 999-8369, (417) 882-2799. **FAX:** (417) 889-6978. **E-Mail Address:** info@mickeyowen.com. **Website:** www.mickeyowen.com.

President: Ken Rizzo. **General Manager:** Mark Daniel. **Camp Director:** Bobby Doe. **Clinician:** Joe Fowler. **Advisor:** Howie Bedell.

NORTH CAROLINA BASEBALL ACADEMY

Mailing Address: 1137 Pleasant Ridge Rd., Greensboro, NC 27409. **Telephone:** (336) 931-1118. **E-Mail Address:** ncba@att.net. **Website:** www.ncbaseball.com.

Owner/Director: Scott Bankhead. **Assistant Director:** Stony Wine. **Academy Director:** Tommy Jackson.

PENNSYLVANIA DIAMOND BUCKS BASEBALL CAMP

Mailing Address: 2320 Whitetail Court, Hellertown, PA 18055. **Telephone:** (610) 838-2119. **E-Mail Address:** jciganick@moravian.edu.

Camp Director: Chuck Ciganick.

PERFECT GAME USA

Mailing Address: 1203 Rockford Rd. SW, Cedar

Rapids, IA 52404. **Telephone:** (319) 298-2923. **FAX:** (319) 298-2924. **E-Mail Address:** services@perfectgame.org. **Website:** www.perfectgame.org.

President, Director: Jerry Ford. **National Supervisor:** Andy Ford. **Directors, Instruction:** Bruce Kimm, Jim VanScoyac.

PLAYBALL BASEBALL ACADEMY

Mailing Address: P.O. Box 4898, Fort Lauderdale, FL 33338. **Telephone:** (954) 776-6217. **FAX:** (954) 772-4510. **E-Mail Address:** playball@webtv.net. **Website:** www.playballbaseballacademy.com.

Camp Director: Fred Ferreira.

PROFESSIONAL BASEBALL INSTRUCTION

Mailing Address: 107 Pleasant Ave., Upper Saddle River, NJ 07458. **Telephone:** (800) 282-4638 (NY/NJ), (877) 448-2220 (rest of U.S.). **FAX:** (201) 760-8820. **E-Mail Address:** info@baseballclinics.com. **Website:** www.baseballclinics.com.

President: Doug Cinnella.

RIPKEN BASEBALL CAMPS

Mailing Address: 10801 Tony Dr., Suite A, Lutherville, MD 21093. **Telephone:** (800) 486-0850. **E-Mail Address:** information@ripkenbaseball.com. **Website:** www.ripkenbaseball.com.

Director, Operations: Bill Ripken.

ROOKIES BASEBALL

Mailing Address: P.O. Box 422, Towaco, NJ 07082. **Telephone:** (973) 872-6789. **FAX:** (973) 872-2533. **E-Mail Address:** info@rookiesbaseball.com. **Website:** www.rookiesbaseball.com.

Founders: Pat Byrnes, Joe Huffman.

SAN DIEGO SCHOOL OF BASEBALL

Mailing Address: P.O. Box 1492, La Mesa, CA 91944. **Telephone:** (619) 491-4000. **FAX:** (619) 469-5572. **E-Mail Address:** sdsbb@aol.com. **Website:** www.sandiegoschoolofbaseball.com.

Chief Executive Officer: Bob Cluck. **Vice Presidents:** Dave Smith, Alan Trammell, Reggie Waller. **Consultants:** Steve Finley, Luis Gonzalez.

SCHOOL OF SWING

Mailing Address: 2212 Fairmont, Clovis, CA 93611. **Telephone:** (559) 270-4487. **E-Mail Address:** howard@schoolofswing.com. **Website:** www.schoolofswing.com.

Camp Director: Howard McNair.

SHO-ME BASEBALL CAMP

Mailing Address: P.O. Box 2270, Branson West, MO 65737. **Telephone:** (800) 993-2267, (417) 338-5838. **FAX:** (417) 338-2610. **E-Mail Address:** info@shomebaseball.com. **Website:** www.shomebaseball.com.

Camp Director: Christopher Schroeder. **Head of Instruction:** Dick Birmingham.

SOUTHWEST PROFESSIONAL BASEBALL SCHOOL

Mailing Address: 462 S. Gilbert Rd., Mesa, AZ 85204. **Telephone:** (888) 830-8031. **FAX:** (480) 830-7455. **E-Mail Address:** leonard@swpbs.com. **Website:** www.swpbs.com

Camp Directors: Leonard Garcia, Joe Maddon.

UTAH BASEBALL ACADEMY

Mailing Address: 8385 South Allen St., Suite 103, Sandy, UT 84070. **Telephone:** (801) 561-1700. **FAX:** (801) 561-1762. **E-Mail Address:** info@utahbaseballacademy.com. **Website:** www.utahbaseballacademy.com.

CLYDE WRIGHT PITCHING SCHOOL

Mailing Address: 711 S. Beach Blvd., Anaheim, CA 92804. **Telephone:** (714) 828-5860. **FAX:** (714) 630-8003.

Owner: Clyde Wright.

COLLEGE CAMPS

Almost all of the elite college baseball programs have summer/holiday instructional camps. Please consult the college section, Pages 303-323 for listings.

AGENT
DIRECTORY

SERVICE
DIRECTORY

INDEX

AGENT DIRECTORY

Aces Inc.
Seth Levinson, Esq.; Sam Levinson; Keith Miller; Andrew Lowenthal, Esq.; Peter Pedalino, Esq.
188 Montague Street 6th Floor
Brooklyn NY 11201
718-237-2900
fax: 718-522-3906
acesinc2@aol.com

ADA Financial Inc.
3838 Camino Del Rio North
San Diego CA 92108
619-282-7661
fax: 619-282-8341
adafinancial.com

Anslow & Jaclin LLP
Richard I. Anslow, Esq.
4400 Route 9 South
Freehold NJ 07728
732-409-1212
fax: 732-577-1188
anslowlaw.com
ranslow@anslowlaw.com

Baseball Management International
Jesse Frescas Jr.
53-805 Martinez Ave.
La Quinta CA 92253
760-771-5109
fax: 760-771-5143
jessefrescas@netscape.net

Barry Axelrod, Attorney At Law
2236 Encinitas Blvd. Suite A
Encinitas CA 92024
760-753-0088
fax: 760-632-8273
baxy@msn.com

Barry P. Meister Ltd.
1200 Shermer Road
Northbrook IL 60062
847-559-8420
fax: 847-559-8434
bhbameis@aol.com

DRM Brothers Sports Management Group
William S. Rose, Denny Doyle, Blake Doyle, Brian Doyle, Todd Middlebrooks, Esq.
31 Compass Lane
Ft. Lauderdale FL 33308
954-609-1505
fax: 954-267-0336
ltdnyy@aol.com
drmsportsmgmt.com

Focus Management Inc.
Frank A. Blandino
P.O. Box 5777
Hillsborough NJ 08844
908-217-3226
fax: 908-281-0596
focusmanagementinc.com
focusmanagement@rcn.com

Golden Gate Sports Firm
Dr. Miles McAfee PhD.
Marcus Leazer, Miles E. McAfee, Esq.
7677 Oakport Street Suite 1050
Oakland CA 94621
510-567-1390
fax: 510-567-1395
goldengatesports1.com
milesmcafee@aol.com

Jennings Taylor Wheeler & Bouwkamp, Attorneys At Law
David L. Taylor
11711 N. Pennsylvania St. Suite 250
Carmel IN 46032
317-575-7979
fax: 317-575-7977
jtwblaw.com
dave_taylor@jtwblaw.com

Law Office of James R. Kauffman
877 Balboa Lane
Foster City CA 94404
650-377-0815
fax: 650-377-0885
jrklaw@pacbell.net

Law Offices of Randell A. Monaco
610 Newport Center Drive Suite 450
Newport Beach CA 92660
949-719-2669
fax: 949-719-2607
lawscout@pacbell.net

Legends Mangement Group
Tom O'Connell, Rob Fredricks
101 E. Kennedy Blvd. Suite 1790
Tampa FL 33602
813-223-5505
fax: 813-223-5402
legendsmanagement.com
toclegends1@aol.com

Northstar Sports Management
Barry Praver
105 Angelfish Lane
Jupiter FL 33477
561-775-6313
fax: 561-775-7633
northstarsports@aol.com

Peter E. Greenberg & Associates
200 Madison Avenue Suite 2225
New York NY 10016
212-334-6880
fax: 212-334-8695

Pro Agents Inc.
David Pepe, Billy Martin Jr.
90 Woodbridge Center Dr.
Woodbridge NJ 07095
800-795-3454
fax: 732-855-6117
pepeda@wilentz.com

Professional Sports Management
Alan Meersand
865 Manhattan Beach Blvd. Suite 205
Manhattan Beach CA 90226
310-546-3400
fax: 310-546-4046
meersand@aol.com

Pro Star Management Inc.
Joe Bick
250 East Fifth Street
Suite 1500
Cincinnati OH 45202
513-762-7676
fax: 513-721-4628
prostar@fuse.net

PROSPORT MANAGEMENT INC.
1831 N. Belcher Road G-3
Clearwater FL 33765
727-791-7556
fax: 727-791-1489
vkrivacs@tampabay.rr.com

Pro-Talent Inc.
Christopher Fanta, Eduardo Diaz, Jason Browning, Larry Hisle Jr.
3753 North Western Avenue
Chicago IL 60618
773-583-3411
fax: 773-583-4277
protalentchicago@aol.com

Reich, Katz & Landis Baseball Group
2370 One PPG Place
Pittsburgh PA 15222
412-391-2626
fax: 412-391-2613

Riverfront Sports Management
Brian M. Goldberg
4300 Carew Tower
441 Vine Street
Cincinnati OH 45202
513-721-3111
fax: 513-721-3077

Reynolds Sports Management
3880 Lemon St. Suite 200
Riverside CA 92501
909-784-6333
fax: 909-784-1451
ReynoldsSports@aol.com

RMG Sports Management
Robert Garber, Esq., Brett Laurvick, Robert Lisanti
115 South Vine St. Suite 1E
Hinsdale IL 60521
630-986-2500
fax: 630-986-0171

SKA Sports and Entertainment
499 North Cannon Drive Suite 403
Beverly Hills CA 90210
310-551-0381
fax: 310-551-0386
skasports@aol.com

SMI Sports Management International
P.O. Box 61190
Seattle WA 98121
800-860-8182
fax: 425-787-8423
smisports.com
eddie@smisports.com

Sosnick Cobbe Sports
1601 North California 150
Walnut Creek CA 94596
925-482-2319
fax: 925-944-0361
mattsoz@aol.com

Tanzer Sports Consultants Inc.
Tommy Tanzer, Steve Alexander, Jeff Kahn, Jamie Appel, Kenny Felder, Bob Rischitelli, Brian James
P.O. Box 680340
Park City UT 84068
435-649-7603
fax: 435-649-6464
tanzrball@aol.com

Thomas Connelly, Attorney At Law
Beus Gilbert PLLC
4800 N. Scottsdale Rd. Suite 6000
Scottsdale AZ 85251
480-429-3000
fax: 480-429-3100
tconnelly@beusgilbert.com

Torborg Sports Ltd.
Drew Seccafico, Rich Bier, Esq.
Renson Delossantos
33 Eleventh Avenue
Huntington Station NY 11746
800-431-4323
fax: 631-423-8286
dsaxon25@aol.com

Turner-Gary Sports Inc.
Jim Turner, Rex Gary, Chris Wimmer
101 S. Hanley Road Ste. 1720
St. Louis MO 63105
314-863-6611
fax: 314-863-9911

West Coast Sports Management LLC
1723 Fairmont Ave
La Canada CA 91011
323-854-4001
fax: 818-952-1527
proballfirm.com
bills@proballfirm.com

SERVICE DIRECTORY

ACCESSORIES

Akadema
317 Midland Ave.
Garfield NJ 07026
973-772-7669
fax: 973-772-4839
akademapro.com
akadema@akademapro.com

JKP Sports JUGS
19333 S.W. 118th Ave.
Tualatin OR 97062
800-547-6843
fax: 503-691-1100
jugsports.com
stevec@jkpsports.com

ART

Homefield Heroes
2618 Baybridge St.
Sacramento CA 95833
877-335-0779
fax: 916-923-1171
homefieldheroes.com
bob@homefieldheroes.com

ARTIFICIAL TURF

Sporturf
P.O. Box 2008
Dalton GA 30722
800-798-1056
fax: 706-259-8000
sporturf.com
info@sporturf.com

APPAREL

Akadema
317 Midland Ave.
Garfield NJ 07026
973-772-7669
fax: 973-772-4839
akademapro.com
akadema@akademapro.com

All Pro Sports
16919 Ventura Blvd.
Encino CA 91316
818-981-5264
fax: 818-981-3020
allprosportsshoes.com
allprosports@social.rr.com

Minor Leagues, Major Dreams
P.O. Box 6098
Anaheim CA 92816
800-345-2421
fax: 714-939-0655
minorleagues.com
mlmd@minorleagues.com

Uniforms Express
2284 Old Middlefield Way 11
Mountian View CA 94043
888-661-7044
fax: 888-661-7045
uniformsexpress.com
geoff@uniformsexpress.com

ATHLETIC INSURANCE

Francis L. Dean & Associates Inc.
2800 South Hullen St. Suite 200
Fort Worth TX 76109
800-375-0552
fax: 817-924-7884
jwjenkin@flash.net

K&K Insurance Group Inc.
1712 Magnavox Way
P.O. Box 2338
Fort Wayne IN 46801
800-441-3994
fax: 260-459-5120
kandkinsurance.com
kathy_beaver@kandkinsurance.com

BAGS

Akadema
317 Midland Ave.
Garfield NJ 07026
973-772-7669
fax: 973-772-4839
akademapro.com
akadema@akademapro.com

Brett Bros. Sports International
E 9514 Montgomery Bldg. 25
Spokane WA 99206
509-891-6435
fax: 509-891-4156
brettbats.com
brettbats@aol.com

BASEBALLS

JKP Sports JUGS
19333 S.W. 118th Ave.
Tualatin OR 97062
800-547-6843
fax: 503-691-1100
jugsports.com
stevec@jkpsports.com

Markwort Sporting Goods
4300 Forest Park Ave.
St. Louis MO 63117
314-652-3757
fax: 314-652-6241
markwort.com
sales@markwort.com

Phoenix Sports Inc.
113 Bell St. Suite 102
Seattle WA 90121
800-776-9229
fax: 800-776-4422
phoesports@aol.com

BASEBALL CARDS

Grandstand Cards
22647 Ventura BL 192
Woodland Hills CA 91364
818-992-5642
fax: 818-348-9122
gscards@aol.com

BATS

Akadema
317 Midland Ave.
Garfield NJ 07026
973-772-7669
fax: 973-772-4839
akademapro.com
akadema@akademapro.com

All Pro Sports
16919 Ventura Blvd.
Encino CA 91316
818-981-5264
fax: 818-981-3020
allprosportsshoes.com
allprosports@social.rr.com

Barnstable Bat Company
40 Pleasant Pines Avenue
Centerville MA 02632
888-549-8046
fax: 508-362-2983
barnstablebat.com

Big Bats
11361 E. Raleigh Ave.
Mesa AZ 85212
480-215-7017
fax: 480-984-0620
bigbatsaz.com

Brett Bros. Sports International
E 9514 Montgomery Bldg. 25
Spokane WA 99206
509-891-6435
fax: 509-891-4156
brettbats.com
brettbats@aol.com

BWP Bats
Rd. 1 Box 409-A
Brookville PA 15825
814-849-0089
fax: 814-849-8584
bwpbats.com
sales@bwpbats.com

D-Bat
1400 Preston Rd. Suite 110
Plano TX 75093
888-398-3393
dbatinc.com
batsales@dbatinc.com

Glomar Bats
116 W. Walnut Ave.
Fullerton CA 92832
714-871-5956
fax: 714-871-5958
glomarbats.com

Hoosier Bat Company
P.O. Box 432
4511 Evans Ave.
Valparaiso IN 46384
800-228-3787
fax: 219-465-0877
hoosierbat.com
baseball@netnitco.net

Old Hickory Bat Co.
1735 Hwy 31 W
Goodlettsville TN 37072
615-285-0588
fax: 615-331-8345
oldhickorybats.com
copley@oldhickorybats.com

Phoenix Bat Company
P.O. Box 921
Hilliard OH 43026
877-598-BATS
fax: 614-851-9448
phoenixbats.com

Sono Sports, LLC
123 Water Street
South Norwalk CT 06854
203-853-9077
fax: 203-857-0554
sonosports.com
sonosports@aol.com

The Original Maple Bat Company
202 Rochester Street
Ottawa Ontario Canada K1R 7M6
613-724-2421
fax: 613-725-3299
sambat.com
bats@sambat.com

Zinger-X Professional Bats
939 W. Center A
Lindon UT 84042
801-372-1117
fax: 801-226-5448
zingerx.com

BATTING CAGES

Batting Cages
206 S. Three Notch St.
Andalusia AL 26420
800-716-9189
fax: 334-222-3323
alaweb.com/~battingcages

C&H Baseball Inc.
2215 60th Drive East
Bradenton FL 34203
941-727-1533
fax: 941-727-0588
chbaseball.com
info@chbaseball.com

JKP Sports JUGS
19333 S.W. 118th Ave.
Tualatin OR 97062
800-547-6843
fax: 503-691-1100
jugsports.com
stevec@jkpsports.com

Miller Net Company Inc.
P.O. Box 18787
Memphis TN 38181
800-423-6603
901-774-3804
fax: 901-743-6580
millernets.com
miller@millernets.com

National Batting Cages Inc.
P.O. Box 250
Forest Grove OR 97116-0250
800-547-8800
fax: 503-357-3727
nationalbattingcages.com
fred@nationalbattingcages.com

Russell Batting Cages
2045 Hickory Rd.
Birmingham AL 35216
888-RBC-CAGE
205-822-0111
russellbattingcages.com

Vantage Products International
7895 Stage Hills Blvd. 105
Memphis TN 38133
800-244-4457
fax: 800-321-5882
vpisports.com
vpisports@aol.com

T.L.I. Sports
1452 Crestview St.
Clearwater FL 22755
727-442-2570
fax: 727-443-5462
tlisports.com
gmeeks1@tampabay.rr.com

BATTING GLOVES

Cutters Gloves
4515 N 32nd Street Suite 110
Phoenix AZ 85018
800-821-0231
fax: 602-381-5658
cuttersgloves.com
chris@cuttersgloves.com

See our ad on Page 3

BOBBLE HEADS

Exclamation Marketing Inc.
3717 Del Prado Blvd. Suite 6
Cape Coral FL 33904
239-945-7772
fax: 239-945-7776
exmktg.com
sales@exmktg.com

CAMPS/SCHOOLS

Mickey Owen Baseball School Inc.
P.O. Box 4504
Springfield MO 65808
417-882-2799
fax: 417-889-6978
mickeyowen.com

Professional Baseball Instruction
107 Pleasant Avenue
Upper Saddle River NJ 07458
877-448-2220
fax: 201-760-8820
baseballclinics.com
info@baseballclinics.com

Ripken Baseball
10801 Tony Drive Suite A
Lutherville MD 21093
800-486-0850
fax: 410-823-0850
ripkenbaseball.com
information@ripkenbaseball.com

San Diego School of Baseball
P.O. Box 1492
La Mesa CA 91944
619-491-4000
fax: 619-469-5572
sandiegoschoolofbaseball.com
sdsbb@aol.com

Sho-Me Baseball Camp
P.O. Box 2270
Branson West MO 65737
800-993-2267
fax: 417-338-2610
shomebaseball.com

The Baseball Academy
5500 34th Street West
Bradenton FL 34210
800-993-2267
fax: 941-752-2531
imgacadimes.com
netsales@imgworld.com

Wendelstedt School for Umpires
88 S. St. Andrew Drive
Ormond Beach FL 32174
386-672-4879
fax: 619-260-4185
umpireschool.com

CAPS/HEADWARE

Minor Leagues, Major Dreams
P.O. Box 6098
Anaheim CA 92816
800-345-2421
fax: 714-939-0655
minorleagues.com
mlmd@minorleagues.com

Uniforms Express
2284 Old Middlefield Way 11
Mountian View CA 94043
888-661-7044
fax: 888-661-7045
uniformsexpress.com
geoff@uniformsexpress.com

CHAMPIONSHIP RINGS

Balfour Sports
7211 Circle S Road
Austin TX 78745
512-440-2017
fax: 512-440-2661
kirk.attwood@cbi-rings.com

CLEATS/FOOTWEAR

All Pro Sports
16919 Ventura Blvd.
Encino CA 91316
818-981-5264
fax: 818-981-3020
allprosportsshoes.com
allprosports@social.rr.com

CUPHOLDERS

Caddy Products
10501 Florida Avenue South
Minneapolis, MN 55438
952-903-0110
Fax: 952-903-5020
www.caddyproducts.com
peter@caddieproducts.com

See our ad on Page 15

EDUCATIONAL ASSOCIATONS

Sports Turf Managers Association
1027 S. 3rd Street
Council Bluff IA 51503-6875
800-323-3875
fax: 712-366-9119
sportsturfmanager.com
stmahq@st.omhcoxmail.com

EMPLOYMENT

Work In Sports LLC
7335 E. Acoma Dr.
Suite 201
Scottsdale AZ 85260
480-905-7221
fax: 480-905-7231
WorkInSports.com
info@WorkInSports.com

ENTERTAINMENT

Airwave Dave! as Austin Powers
2935 Thousand Oaks 6-132
San Antonio TX 78247
888-224-5885
fax: 512-396-3120
airwavedave.com
airwave@airwavedave.com

Elvis Himselvis
1918 Jeanette Lane 5
Springfield IL 62702
888-784-5587

Gameops.com
15183 SW Walker Rd. Suite D
Beaverton OR 97006
503-626-1959
fax: 978-418-0058
gameops.com
cudo@gameops.com

World Famous Monkey Boy
Jim Cardello
VP Business Development
75 Gilcreast Rd. Suite 200
Londonderry NH 03053
603-421-1783
fax: 603-432-3371
worldfamousmonkeyboy.com
monkeyboy@worldfamousmonkeyboy.com

FIELD CONSTRUCTION/RENOVATION

Alpine Services Inc.
5313 Brookeville Rd.
Gaithersburg, MD 20882
800-292-8420
fax: 301-963-7901
alpineservices.com
asi@alpineservices.com

FIELD COVERS/TARPS

C&H Baseball Inc.
2215 60th Drive East
Bradenton FL 34203
941-727-1533
fax: 941-727-0588
chbaseball.com
info@chbaseball.com

Covermaster inc.
100 Westmore Dr. 11D
Rexdale Ontario M9V 5C3
800-387-5808
fax: 800-691-1181
covermaster.com
info@covermaster.com

Reef Industries Inc.
P.O. Box 750250
Houston TX 77275-0250
800-231-6074
fax: 713-502-4295
reefindustries.com
ri@reefindustries.com

FIELD WALL PADDING

C&H Baseball Inc.
2215 60th Drive East
Bradenton FL 34203
941-727-1533
fax: 941-727-0588
chbaseball.com
info@chbaseball.com

Covermaster inc.
100 Westmore Dr. 11D
Rexdale Ontario M9V 5C3
800-387-5808
fax: 800-691-1181
covermaster.com
info@covermaster.com

Promats Inc.
P.O. Box 508
Fort Collins CO 80522
800-678-6787
fax: 970-482-7740
promats.com
promats@aol.com

FIREWORKS

Fireworks Productions Inc.
P.O. Box 294
Maryland Line MD 21105
800-765-2264
fax: 410-357-0187
fireworksproductionsinc.com
larry@fireworksproductionsinc.com

Melrose Pyrotechnics Inc.
4652 Catawba River Rd.
Catawba SC 29704
800-771-7976
fax: 800-775-7976
melrosepyro.com
tom@melrosepyro.com

Pyrotecnico
302 Wilson Road
P.O. Box 149
New Castle PA 16103
800-854-4705
fax: 724-652-1288
pyrotecnico.com
svitale@pyrotecnico.com

FOOD SERVICE

Concession Solutions Inc.
16022-26th Ave. NE
Shoreline WA 98155
206-440-9023
Fax: 206-440-9213
concessionsolutions.com
Theresa@concessionsolutions.com

DiGiovanni's Food Service Inc.
4773 Hunters Run
Sarasota FL 34241
941-923-3663
fax: 941-922-8122
digifoods@aol.com

Houston's Peanuts
P.O. Box 160
Dublin NC 28332
800-334-8383
fax: 910-862-8076
houstonpeanuts.com

GLOVES

Akadema
317 Midland Ave.
Garfield NJ 07026
973-772-7669
fax: 973-772-4839
akademapro.com
akadema@akademapro.com

All Pro Sports
16919 Ventura Blvd.
Encino CA 91316
818-981-5264
fax: 818-981-3020
allprosportsshoes.com
allprosports@social.rr.com

Barraza BBG
P.O. Box 522
Buena Park CA 90622-5222
714-828-8874
barrazapro.com

Brett Bros. Sports International
E 9514 Montgomery Bldg. 25
Spokane WA 99206
509-891-6435
fax: 509-891-4156
brettbats.com
brettbats@aol.com

Guerrero Gloves
5859 W. Saginaw 269
Lansing MI 48917
800-826-1464
fax: 517-886-8035
guerrerogloves.com

GRAPHIC DESIGN

Low and Inside
P.O. Box 290228
Minneapolis MN 55429
612-701-2799
lowandinside.com
creative@lowandinside.com

INFLATABLES

Inflatable Images
2880 Interstate Parkway
Brunswick OH 44212
800-783-5717 ext. 134
fax: 330-273-3212
inflatableimages.com
m.yates@scherba.com

JEWELRY

Sportnecks
P.O. Box 326
Casco ME 04015
207-627-4710
fax: 207-627-4710
sportnecks@yahoo.com

MARKETING

Modern Postcard
1675 Faraday Ave
Carlsbad, CA 92008
www.modernpostcard.com
carterg@modernpostcard.com

See our ad on Page 13

MASCOTS

Street Characters Inc.
#2 2828 18 Street NE
Calgary Alberta T2E 7B1
888-Mascots
fax: 403-250-3846
mascots.com

Olympus Flag and Banner
9000 West Heather Ave.
Milwaukee WI 53224
414-355-2010
fax: 414-355-1931
olympus-flag.com
tracy.jones@olympus-flag.com

MUSIC/SOUND EFFECTS

Portland Trail Blazers Game Ops Commander
1 Center Court Suite 200
Portland OR 97227
800-346-8037
fax: 503-736-5066
gameopscommander.com
info@gameopscommander.com

Sound Creations
2820 Azalea Place
Nashville, TN 37204
615-460-7330
Fax: 615-460-7331
www.clickeffects.com
fran2nz@aol.com

See our ad on Page 17

NETTING/POSTS

C&H Baseball Inc.
2215 60th Drive East
Bradenton FL 34203
941-727-1533
fax: 941-727-0588
chbaseball.com
info@chbaseball.com

Miller Net Company Inc.
P.O. Box 18787
Memphis TN 38181
800-423-6603
901-774-3804
fax: 901-743-6580
millernets.com
miller@millernets.com

Russell Batting Cages
2045 Hickory Rd.
Birmingham AL 35216
888-RBC-CAGE
205-822-0111
russellbattingcages.com

T.L.I. Sports
1452 Crestview St.
Clearwater FL 22755
727-442-2570
fax: 727-443-5462
tlisports.com
gmeeks1@tampabay.rr.com

PITCHING MACHINES

C&H Baseball Inc.
2215 60th Drive East
Bradenton FL 34203
941-727-1533
fax: 941-727-0588
chbaseball.com
info@chbaseball.com

JKP Sports JUGS
19333 S.W. 118th Ave.
Tualatin OR 97062
800-547-6843
fax: 503-691-1100
jugsports.com
stevec@jkpsports.com

Miller Net Company Inc.
P.O. Box 18787
Memphis TN 38181
800-423-6603
901-774-3804
fax: 901-743-6580
millernets.com
miller@millernets.com

ProBatter Sports
92 Woodmont Road
Milford CT 06460
800-256-0153
fax: 203-878-9019
probatter.com
info@probatter.com

PLAYING FIELD PRODUCTS

Diamond Pro (TXI)
1341 West Mockingbird Lane
Dallas TX 75247
800-228-2987
fax: 800-640-8735
diamondpro.com

Midwest Athletic Surfaces
1125 West State St.
Marshfield WI 54449
715-384-7027
fax: 715-384-7027
webpages.charter.net/warningtrack
warningtrack@charter.net

Southwest Recreational Industries Inc.
701 Leander Drive
Leander, TX 78641
www.southwestrec.com
contact@southwestrec.com
512-259-0080
Fax: 512-528-2301

See our ad on Page 23

Sporturf
P.O. Box 2008
Dalton GA 30722
800-798-1056
fax: 706-259-8000
sporturf.com
info@sporturf.com

Stabilizer Solutions Inc.
205 South 28th St.
Phoenix AZ 85034
800-336-2468
fax: 602-225-5902
stabilizersolutions.com
lphubbs@stablilizersolutions.com

Partac Peat Corporation/ Beam Clay
Kelsey Park
Great Meadows, NJ 07838
908-637-4191
Fax: 908-637-8421

See our ad on Page 384

TURFACE
750 Lake Cook Rd. Suite 440
Buffalo Grove IL 60089
800-207-6457
fax: 718-583-1652
turface.com

T.L.I. Sports
1452 Crestview St.
Clearwater FL 22755
727-442-2570
fax: 727-443-5462
tlisports.com
gmeeks1@tampabay.rr.com

PRINTING

Low and Inside
P.O. Box 290228
Minneapolis MN 55429
612-701-2799
lowandinside.com
creative@lowandinside.com

Altoona Mirror Commercial Printing
Kel Cooper
Baseball Program Coordinator
301 Cayuga Ave
P.O. Box 930
Altoona PA 16603
570-584-4612
fax: 814-946-7410

See our ad after Page 32

Worldwide Ticket and Label
1673 SW 1st Way A-1
Deerfield Beach FL 33441
954-426-5754
fax: 954-426-5761
wwticket.com
erick@wwticket.com

PROMOTIONAL ITEMS

Exclamation Marketing Inc.
3717 Del Prado Blvd., Suite 6
Cape Coral FL 33904
239-945-7772
fax: 239-945-7776
exmktg.com
sales@exmktg.com

Rico Industries/Tag Express
1712 South Michigan Ave.
Chicago IL 60616
800-423-5856
fax: 312-427-0190
ricoinc.com
jimz@ricoinc.com

The Creativity Warehouse inc. "Values Bat"
631 Conestoga Trail
Chanhassen MN 55317
952-949-3063
fax: 952-949-3063
kdhtcw@bigfoot.com

Market Identity
2290 Agate Ct.
Simi Valley CA 93065
800-927-8070 ext. 8230
fax: 805-579-6066
nbleier@iagtm.com

PROMOTIONAL PRIZE COVERAGE

SCA Promotions Inc.
8300 Douglas Ave, 6th Floor
Dallas TX 75225
888-860-3700
fax: 214-860-3723
scapromotions.com
info@scapromo.com

PUBLICATIONS

Team Marketing Report Inc.
900 North Michigan Ave
Suite 2100
Chicago, IL 60611
312-202-6550
Fax: 312-733-4071
www.teammarketing.com

See our ad on Page 9

RADAR EQUIPMENT

JKP Sports JUGS
19333 S.W. 118th Ave.
Tualatin OR 97062
800-547-6843
fax: 503-691-1100
jugsports.com
stevec@jkpsports.com

RECRUITING SERVICES

Skillshow Inc.
927 North 78th Street
Seattle, WA 98103
610-687-9072
Fax: 610-687-9629
www.skillshow.com
info@skillshow.com

See our ad on Page 11

SCOREBOARDS

Action Graphix
2623 Commerce Drive
Jonesboro AR 72401
870-931-7440
fax: 870-931-7528
actiongraphix.com
action@actiongraphics.com

All American Scoreboards
401 S. Main St.
Pardeeville WI 53954
800-356-8146
fax: 608-429-9216
allamericanscoreboards.com
socre@everbrite.com

Nevco Scoreboard Company
301 East Harris Avenue
Greenville IL 62246
618-664-0360
fax: 618-664-0398
nevcoscoreboards.com
nevco@nevcoscoreboards.com

Sportable Scoreboards
106 Max Hurt Drive
Murray KY 42071
800-323-7745
fax: 270-759-4112
sportablescoreboards.com
sales@sportablescoreboards.com

SCOUTING

Baseball Factory
9`76 Red Branch Road Ste. M
Columbia MD 21045
800-641-4487
fax: 410-715-1975
baseballfactory.com
info@baseballfactory.com

Independent Scouting Bureau
James L. Gamble CEO
Claudio Reilsono GM
P.O. Box 524
Sewickley PA 15143
412-749-0912
protryouts.com
inscouting.com

SEATING

Seating Services Inc.
P.O. Box 4
Angola, NY 14006
716-549-9003
Fax: 716-549-9011
www.seatingservices.com
seatingdcc@msn.com

See our ad on Page 21

Sturdisteel
P.O. Box 2655
Waco, TX 76702-2655
254-666-5155
Fax: 254-666-4472
www.sturdisteel.com
rgroppe@sturdisteel.com

See our ad on Page 19

Southern Bleacher Company
P.O. Box One
Graham TX 76450
800-433-0912
fax: 940-549-1365
southernbleacher.com
sobco@wf.net

SHOWCASE EVENTS

Baseball Factory
9`76 Red Branch Road Ste. M
Columbia MD 21045
800-641-4487
fax: 410-715-1975
baseballfactory.com
info@baseballfactory.com

SOFT TOSS MACHINES

Batter Up Sports Tech Ltd.
P.O. Box 69 Arcadia
Yarmouth County Nova Scotia
BOW 1B0
902-742-3155
fax: 902-742-3155
batterup.ws
teresa.mcenaney@batterup.ws

SPORTS MEDICINE PRODUCTS

Cho-Pat Inc.
P.O. Box 293
Hainesport NJ 08036
609-261-1336
fax: 609-261-7593
cho-pat.com
sales@cho-pat.com

STADIUM ARCHITECTS

Astorino & Associates
227 Fort Pitt Blvd.
Pittsburgh, PA 15222
412-765-1700
Fax: 412-765-1711
www.ldastorino.com
bhanick@ldasorino.com

See our ad on Page 7

Clarke Caton Hintz Architects
400 Sullivan Way
Trenton NJ 80628
609-883-8323
fax: 609-883-4044
ccharchitects.com
ghibbs@cchnj.com

DLR Group
601 West Swann Avenue
Tampa, FL 33606-2727
813-254-9811
Fax: 813-254-4230
www.dlrgroup.com
tampa@dlrgroup.com

See our ad on Inside Back Cover

Ellerbe Becket
4600 Madison Ave. Suite 1000
Kansas City MO 64112
816-561-4443
fax: 816-561-2863
ellerbebecket.com
jim_ritchie@ellerbebecket.com

Gould Evans Associates
5405 West Cypress Street Suite 112
Tampa FL 33607
813-288-0729
fax: 813-288-0231
www.gouldevans.com
john.curran@gouldevans.com

HOK Sport + Venue + Event
323 West 8th Street Suite 700
Kansas City, MO 64105
816-329-1576
Fax: 816-221-1578
www.hok.com/sport
bruce.miller@hok.com

See our ad on Inside Front Cover

Tetra Tech Inc.
56 West Main Street Suite 400
Christiana, DE 19702
302-738-7551
Fax: 302-454-5980
www.tetratech.com
william.netta@tetratech.com

See our ad on Page 5

STANCE MATS

Sporturf
P.O. Box 2008
Dalton GA 30722
800-798-1056
fax: 706-259-8000
sporturf.com
info@sporturf.com

STATISTICAL SOFTWARE

More Than ERA
11038 Hildreth Ct
Camarillo CA 93012
805-491-3379
fax: 805-491-2229
morethanera.com

SOUVENIRS

Market Identity
2290 Agate Ct.
Simi Valley CA 93065
800-927-8070 ext. 8230
fax: 805-579-6066
nbleier@iagtm.com

SPORTING GOODS

All Pro Sports
16919 Ventura Blvd.
Encino CA 91316
818-981-5264
fax: 818-981-3020
allprosportsshoes.com
allprosports@social.rr.com

Better Baseball
1050 Mt. Paran Rd.
Atlanta GA 30327
800-997-4233
fax: 404-467-4573
betterbaseball.com
glen@betterbaseball.com

Frank's Sport Shop
430 East Tremont Avenue
New York, NY 10457
718-299-9628
Fax: 718-583-1652
www.frankssportshop.com

See our ad after Page 128

TICKETS

Broach Baseball Tours
5821 Fairview Road, Suite 118
Charlotte NC 28209
800-849-6345
fax: 704-365-3800
broachtours.com
broachtour@aol.com

Etix.com
5171 Glenwood Ave.
Raleigh NC 27612
919-782-5010
fax: 919-782-7727
etix.com
ben@etix.com

Ticketcraft
1390 Jerusalem Ave.
Merrick NY 11566
800-645-4944
fax: 516-538-4860
ticketcraft.com
tickets@ticketcraft.com

TRAINING EQUIPMENT

Funtastic Sports
277 Thornecliffe Dr.
State Road NC 28676
336-874-4937
fax: 336-874-4952
funtasticsports.com

QHI Sports
36-A North Research Drive
Pueblo West CO 81007
719-547-0010
fax: 719-547-4414
qhisports.com

TRAVEL

Broach Baseball Tours
5821 Fairview Road, Suite 118
Charlotte NC 28209
800-849-6345
fax: 704-365-3800
broachtours.com
broachtour@aol.com

Minor League Baseball Road Trips
P.O. Box 50
60 Main St.
Hatfield MA 01038
866-933-TRIP
fax: 413-247-5700
baseballroadtrips.com/minor
info@baseballroadtrips.com

Sports Travel and Tours
P.O. Box 50
60 Main St.
Hatfield MA 01038
866-933-TRIP
fax: 413-247-5700
baseballroadtrips.com
info@baseballroadtrips.com

TRAVEL, TEAM

World Sports International Sports Tours
P.O. Box 661624
Los Angeles CA 90405
800-496-8687
fax: 310-314-8872
worldsport-tours.com

TURNSTILE ADVERTISING

Entry Media
127 West Fairbanks Avenue 417
Winter Park FL 32788
407-678-4446
fax: 407-679-3590
entrymedia.com
entrymedia@worldnet.att.net

UNIFORMS

AIS Custom Uniforms
2202 Anderson Street
Vernon CA 90058
310-559-3999
Fax: 323-582-2831

See our ad after Page 224

Uniforms Express
2284 Old Middlefield Way 11
Mountian View CA 94043
888-661-7044
fax: 888-661-7045
uniformsexpress.com
geoff@uniformsexpress.com

WINDSCREENS

Covermaster inc.
100 Westmore Dr. 11D
Rexdale Ontario M9V 5C3
800-387-5808
fax: 800-691-1181
covermaster.com
info@covermaster.com

Miller Net Company Inc.
P.O. Box 18787
Memphis TN 38181
800-423-6603
901-774-3804
fax: 901-743-6580
millernets.com
miller@millernets.com

Promats Inc.
P.O. Box 508
Fort Collins CO 80522
800-678-6787
fax: 970-482-7740
promats.com
promats@aol.com

T.L.I. Sports
1452 Crestview St.
Clearwater FL 22755
727-442-2570
fax: 727-443-5462
tlisports.com
gmeeks1@tampabay.rr.com

2003 DIRECTORY INDEX

MAJOR LEAGUE TEAMS

American League

National League

MINOR LEAGUE TEAMS

189	Cedar Rapids	Midwest	319-363-3887	319-363-5631
196	Charleston, SC	SAL	843-723-7241	843-723-2641
196	Charleston, WV	SAL	304-344-2287	304-344-0083
136	Charlotte	IL	704-357-8071	704-329-2155
161	Chattanooga	Southern	423-267-2208	423-267-4258
182	Clearwater	FSL	727-441-8638	727-447-3924
189	Clinton	Midwest	563-242-0727	563-242-1433
144	Colorado Springs	PCL	719-597-1449	719-597-2491
137	Columbus	IL	614-462-5250	614-462-3271
216	Danville	Appy	434-797-3792	434-797-3799
189	Dayton	Midwest	937-228-2287	937-228-2284
182	Daytona	FSL	386-257-3172	386-257-3382
197	Delmarva	SAL	410-219-3112	410-219-9164
183	Dunedin	FSL	727-733-9302	727-734-7661
137	Durham	IL	919-687-6500	919-687-6560
145	Edmonton	PCL	780-414-4450	780-414-4475
216	Elizabethton	Appy	423-547-6440	423-547-6442
166	El Paso	Texas	915-755-2000	915-757-0671
155	Erie	Eastern	814-456-1300	814-456-7520
210	Eugene	Northwest	541-342-5367	541-342-6089
211	Everett	Northwest	425-258-3673	425-258-3675
183	Fort Myers	FSL	239-768-4210	239-768-4211
190	Fort Wayne	Midwest	260-482-6400	260-471-4678
177	Frederick	Carolina	301-662-0013	301-662-0018
145	Fresno	PCL	559-442-1994	559-264-0795
167	Frisco	Texas	972-731-9200	972-731-7455
221	Great Falls	Pioneer	406-452-5311	406-454-0811
197	Greensboro	SAL	336-333-2287	336-273-7350
161	Greenville	Southern	864-299-3456	864-277-7369
198	Hagerstown	SAL	301-791-6266	301-791-6066
155	Harrisburg	Eastern	717-231-4444	717-231-4445
221	Helena	Pioneer	406-495-0500	406-495-0900
198	Hickory	SAL	828-322-3000	828-322-6137
171	High Desert	Cal	760-246-6287	760-246-3197
204	Hudson Valley	NY-P	845-838-0094	845-838-0014
162	Huntsville	Southern	256-882-2562	256-880-0801
222	Idaho Falls	Pioneer	208-522-8363	208-522-9858
138	Indianapolis	IL	317-269-3542	317-269-3541
172	Inland Empire	Cal	909-888-9922	909-888-5251
146	Iowa	PCL	515-243-6111	515-243-5152
162	Jacksonville	Southern	904-358-2846	904-358-2845
205	Jamestown	NY-P	716-664-0915	716-664-4175
217	Johnson City	Appy	423-461-4866	423-461-4864
184	Jupiter	FSL	561-775-1818	561-691-6886
190	Kane County	Midwest	630-232-8811	630-232-8815
198	Kannapolis	SAL	704-932-3267	704-938-7040
217	Kingsport	Appy	423-378-3744	423-392-8538
177	Kinston	Carolina	252-527-9111	252-527-2328
199	Lake County	SAL	440-975-8085	440-975-8958
172	Lake Elsinore	Cal	909-245-4487	909-245-0305
184	Lakeland	FSL	863-686-8075	863-688-9589
199	Lakewood	SAL	732-901-7000	732-901-3967
173	Lancaster	Cal	661-726-5400	661-726-5406
191	Lansing	Midwest	517-485-4500	517-485-4518
146	Las Vegas	PCL	702-386-7200	702-386-7214
200	Lexington	SAL	859-252-4487	859-252-0747
138	Louisville	IL	502-212-2287	502-515-2255
205	Lowell	NY-P	978-459-2255	978-459-1674
178	Lynchburg	Carolina	434-528-1144	434-846-0768
206	Mahoning Valley	NY-P	330-505-0000	330-505-9696
217	Martinsville	Appy	276-666-2000	276-666-2139
147	Memphis	PCL	901-721-6000	901-892-1222
167	Midland	Texas	915-520-2255	915-520-8326
222	Missoula	Pioneer	406-543-3300	406-543-9463
163	Mobile	Southern	251-479-2327	251-476-1147
173	Modesto	Cal	209-572-4487	209-572-4490
178	Myrtle Beach	Carolina	843-918-6002	843-918-6001
147	Nashville	PCL	615-242-4371	615-256-5684
156	New Britain	Eastern	860-224-8383	860-225-6267
156	New Haven	Eastern	203-782-1666	203-782-3150
206	New Jersey	NY-P	973-579-7500	973-579-7502
148	New Orleans	PCL	504-734-5155	504-734-5118
139	Norfolk	IL	757-622-2222	757-624-9090

Page	Club	League	Phone	FAX
157	Norwich	Eastern	860-887-7962	860-886-5996
223	Ogden	Pioneer	801-393-2400	801-393-2473
148	Oklahoma	PCL	405-218-1000	405-218-1001
149	Omaha	PCL	402-734-2550	402-734-7166
206	Oneonta	NY-P	607-432-6326	607-432-1965
163	Orlando	Southern	407-939-4263	407-938-3442
139	Ottawa	IL	613-747-5969	613-747-0003
185	Palm Beach	FSL	561-775-1818	561-691-6886
140	Pawtucket	IL	401-724-7300	401-724-2140
191	Peoria	Midwest	309-680-4000	309-680-4080
157	Portland, ME	Eastern	207-874-9300	207-780-0317
149	Portland, OR	PCL	503-553-5400	503-553-5405
179	Potomac	Carolina	703-590-2311	703-590-5716
218	Princeton	Appy	304-487-2000	304-487-8762
223	Provo	Pioneer	801-377-2255	801-377-2345
218	Pulaski	Appy	540-980-1070	540-980-1850
192	Quad City	Midwest	563-324-3000	563-324-3109
174	Rancho Cucamonga	Cal	909-481-5000	909-481-5005
158	Reading	Eastern	610-375-8469	610-373-5868
140	Richmond, VA	IL	804-359-4444	804-359-0731
141	Rochester	IL	585-454-1001	585-454-1056
200	Rome	SAL	706-368-9388	706-368-6525
168	Round Rock	Texas	512-255-2255	512-255-1558
185	St. Lucie	FSL	772-871-2100	772-878-9802
150	Sacramento	PCL	916-376-4700	916-376-4710
179	Salem	Carolina	540-389-3333	540-389-9710
211	Salem-Keizer	Northwest	503-390-2225	503-390-2227
150	Salt Lake	PCL	801-485-3800	801-485-6818
168	San Antonio	Texas	210-675-7275	210-670-0001
174	San Jose	Cal	408-297-1435	408-297-1453
185	Sarasota	FSL	941-365-4460	941-365-4217
201	Savannah	SAL	912-351-9150	912-352-9722
141	Scranton/Wilkes-Barre	IL	570-969-2255	570-963-6564
192	South Bend	Midwest	574-235-9988	574-235-9950
201	South Georgia	SAL	229-420-5924	229-420-5925
212	Spokane	Northwest	509-535-2922	509-534-5368
207	Staten Island	NY-P	718-720-9265	718-273-5763
175	Stockton	Cal	209-644-1900	209-644-1931
142	Syracuse	IL	315-474-7833	315-474-2658
151	Tacoma	PCL	253-752-7707	253-752-7135
186	Tampa	FSL	813-875-7753	813-673-3174
164	Tennessee	Southern	865-286-2300	865-523-9913
142	Toledo	IL	419-725-4367	419-725-4368
158	Trenton	Eastern	609-394-3300	609-394-9666
207	Tri-City, NY	NY-P	518-629-2287	518-629-2299
212	Tri-City, WA	Northwest	509-544-8789	509-547-9570
151	Tucson	PCL	520-434-1021	520-889-9477
169	Tulsa	Texas	918-744-5998	918-747-3267
213	Vancouver	Northwest	604-872-5232	604-872-1714
208	Vermont	NY-P	802-655-4200	802-655-5660
186	Vero Beach	FSL	772-569-4900	772-567-0819
175	Visalia	Cal	559-625-0480	559-739-7732
193	West Michigan	Midwest	616-784-4131	616-784-4911
164	West Tenn	Southern	731-988-5299	731-988-5246
169	Wichita	Texas	316-267-3372	316-267-3382
208	Williamsport	NY-P	570-326-3389	570-326-3494
180	Wilmington	Carolina	302-888-2015	302-888-2032
180	Winston-Salem	Carolina	336-759-2233	336-759-2042
193	Wisconsin	Midwest	920-733-4152	920-733-8032
213	Yakima	Northwest	509-457-5151	509-457-9909

Phone and FAX numbers for minor league offices can be found on page 129.

INDEPENDENT LEAGUE TEAMS

Page	Club	League	Phone	FAX
263	Alexandria	Central	318-473-2237	318-473-2229
270	Allentown	Northeast	610-437-6800	610-437-6804
263	Amarillo	Central	806-342-3455	806-467-9894
259	Atlantic City	Atlantic	609-344-8873	609-344-7010
271	Bangor	Northeast	207-947-1900	207-947-9900
271	Berkshire	Northeast	413-448-2255	413-445-5500
260	Bridgeport	Atlantic	203-345-4800	203-345-4830
271	Brockton	Northeast	508-559-7000	508-587-2802

260	Camden	Atlantic	856-963-2600	856-963-8534
266	Chillicothe	Frontier	740-773-8326	740-773-8338
263	Coastal Bend	Central	361-387-8585	361-387-3535
266	Cook County	Frontier	708-489-2255	708-489-2999
263	Edinburg	Central	956-289-8800	956-289-8833
272	Elmira	Northeast	607-734-1270	607-734-0891
267	Evansville	Frontier	812-435-8686	812-435-8688
273	Fargo-Moorhead	Northern	701-235-6161	701-297-9247
267	Florence	Frontier	859-380-9610	Unavailable
264	Fort Worth	Central	817-226-2287	817-534-4620
274	Gary Southshore	Northern	219-882-2255	219-882-2259
267	Gateway	Frontier	618-337-3000	618-332-3625
264	Jackson	Central	601-362-2294	601-362-9577
274	Joliet	Northern	815-726-2255	815-726-9223
268	Kalamazoo	Frontier	269-388-8326	269-388-8333
275	Kansas City	Northern	913-328-2255	913-685-3642
268	Kenosha	Frontier	Unavailable	Unavailable
275	Lincoln	Northern	402-474-2255	402-474-2254
260	Long Island	Atlantic	631-940-3825	631-940-3800
268	Mid-Missouri	Frontier	573-256-4004	573-256-4003
261	Nashua	Atlantic	603-883-2255	603-883-0880
272	New Jersey	Northeast	973-746-7434	973-655-8021
261	Newark	Atlantic	973-848-1000	973-621-0095
273	North Shore	Northeast	781-592-0007	781-592-0004
262	Pennsylvania	Atlantic	—	—
273	Quebec	Northeast	418-521-2255	418-521-2266
269	Richmond, IN	Frontier	765-935-7529	765-962-7047
264	Rio Grande Valley	Central	956-412-9464	956-412-9479
269	River City	Frontier	636-240-2287	636-240-7313
269	Rockford	Frontier	815-964-2255	815-964-2462
275	St. Paul	Northern	651-644-3517	651-644-1627
265	San Angelo	Central	915-942-6587	915-947-9480
276	Schaumburg	Northern	877-891-2255	847-891-6441
265	Shreveport	Central	318-636-5555	318-636-5670
276	Sioux City	Northern	712-277-9467	712-277-9406
276	Sioux Falls	Northern	605-333-0179	605-333-0139
265	Springfield/Ozark, MO	Central	417-581-2868	417-581-8342
262	Somerset	Atlantic	908-252-0700	908-252-0776
270	Washington	Frontier	724-250-9555	724-250-2333
277	Winnipeg	Northern	204-982-2273	204-982-2274

INDEPENDENT LEAGUE OFFICES

Page	League	Phone	FAX
259	Arizona-Mexico League	623-826-0174	623-321-7837
259	Atlantic League	856-541-9400	856-541-9410
262	Central League	919-956-8150	919-683-2693
266	Frontier League	740-452-7400	740-452-2999
270	Northeast League	919-956-8150	919-683-2693
273	Northern League	817-378-9898	817-378-9805
277	Southeastern League	985-385-9195	985-385-9155

OTHER ORGANIZATIONS

Page	Organization	Phone	FAX
128	AAU Women's Baseball	330-923-3400	330-923-1967
119	ABC Sports Radio	212-456-5185	—
119	ABC-TV	212-456-4878	212-456-2877
364	Academy of Pro Players	973-772-3355	973-772-4839
344	African Baseball/Softball Association	234-66-224-711	234-66-224-555
346	Alaska Baseball League	907-274-3627	907-274-3628
364	Aldrete Baseball Academy	831-884-0400	831-884-0800
358	All-American Amateur Baseball Association	740-453-8531	740-453-3978
364	All-American Baseball Academy	714-995-9273	714-995-2357
355	All-American Baseball Talent Showcases	856-354-0201	856-354-0818
364	All-Star Baseball Academy	610-355-2411	610-355-2414
358	Amateur Athletic Union	407-934-7200	407-934-7242
358	American Amateur Baseball Congress	616-781-2002	616-781-2060
358	American Amateur Youth Baseball Alliance	573-518-0319	314-822-4974
297	American Baseball Coaches Association	989-775-3300	989-775-3600
345	American Baseball Foundation	205-558-4235	205-918-0800
359	American Legion Baseball	317-630-1213	317-630-1369
355	Area Code Games	707-975-7894	707-525-0214
355	Arizona Fall Classic	602-978-2929	602-439-4494

295	Arizona Fall League	480-496-6700	480-496-6384
120	Associated Press	212-621-1630	212-621-1639
127	Association of Professional Baseball Players	714-935-9993	714-935-0431
345	Athletes In Action	937-352-1000	937-352-1245
121	Athlon Sports Baseball	615-327-0747	615-327-1149
346	Atlantic Collegiate League	908-464-8042	908-464-8042
359	Babe Ruth Baseball	609-695-1434	609-695-2505
125	Babe Ruth Birthplace/Orioles Museum	410-727-1539	410-727-1652
364	The Baseball Academy	800-872-6425	941-752-2531
121	Baseball America	919-682-9635	919-682-2880
127	Baseball Assistance Team	212-931-7823	212-949-5691
344	Baseball Canada	613-748-5606	613-748-5767
127	Baseball Chapel	609-391-6444	—
344	Baseball Confederation of Oceania	61-3-9727-1779	61-3-9727-5959
121	Baseball Digest	847-491-6440	847-491-6203
355	Baseball Factory	410-715-5080	410-715-1975
344	Baseball Federation of Asia	81-3-320-11155	81-3-320-10707
121	Baseball Parent	865-523-1274	865-673-8926
127	Baseball Trade Show	727-822-6937	727-825-3785
363	Baseball USA	713-690-5055	713-690-9448
120	Baseball Writers Association of America	631-981-7938	631-585-4669
122	Beckett Publications	800-840-3137	972-991-8930
120	Bloomberg Sports News	609-750-4691	609-897-8397
355	Blue-Grey Classic	508-881-2782	—
364	Bucky Dent Baseball School	561-265-0280	561-278-6679
119	CBS Sports	212-975-5230	212-975-4063
344	COPABE	507-230-5399	507-230-4524
346	California Coastal League	805-684-0657	805-684-8596
297	California Community College Commission on Athletics	916-444-1600	916-444-2616
125	Canadian Baseball Hall of Fame	519-284-1838	519-284-1234
287	Canadian Baseball League	604-689-1566	604-689-1531
120	Canadian Press	416-364-0321	416-364-0207
346	Cape Cod League	508-385-6260	508-385-6322
293	Caribbean BB Confederation	809-562-4737	809-565-4654
347	Central Illinois Collegiate League	217-793-6538	217-786-2788
288	China Baseball League	86-10-8582-6002	86-10-8582-5994
289	Chinese Pro Baseball League	886-2-2577-6992	886-2-2577-2606
348	Clark Griffith League	703-760-1684	703-821-8949
365	Clyde Wright Pitching School	714-828-5860	714-630-8003
348	Coastal Plain League	919-852-1960	919-852-1973
363	Cocoa Expo Sports Center	321-639-3976	321-639-0598
355	College Select Baseball Showcase	800-782-3672	—
121	Collegiate Baseball	520-623-4530	520-624-5501
122	Coman Publishing	919-688-0218	919-682-1532
359	Continental Amateur Baseball Association	740-382-4620	—
363	Cooperstown Baseball World	888-CBW-8750	888-CBW-8720
363	Cooperstown Dreams Park	704-630-0050	704-630-0737
364	Diamond Indoor Sports	440-333-9420	440-333-1115
122	Diamond Library Publications	203-834-1231	—
363	Disney's Wide World of Sports	407-938-3802	407-938-3412
360	Dixie Baseball, Inc.	903-927-2255	903-927-1846
360	Dizzy Dean Baseball	662-429-4365	—
287	Dominican League	809-567-6371	809-567-5720
293	Dominican Summer League	809-532-3619	809-532-3619
128	Donruss/Playoff Trading Cards	817-983-0300	817-983-0400
355	Doyle Baseball Select Showcases	863-439-1000	863-439-7086
290	Dutch Major League	31-30-607-6070	31-30-294-3043
118	ESPN/ESPN2-TV	860-766-2000	860-766-2213
121	ESPN The Magazine	212-515-1000	212-515-1290
119	ESPN Radio	860-766-2661	860-589-5523
355	East Coast Pro Baseball Showcase	910-962-3570	—
118	Elias Sports Bureau	212-869-1530	212-354-0980
344	European Baseball Confederation	32-3-219-0440	32-3-219-0440
125	Field of Dreams Movie Site	888-875-8404	319-875-7253
355	Five Star Baseball Showcase	502-261-9200	502-261-9278
128	Fleer/Skybox Trading Cards	800-343-6816	856-231-0383
349	Florida Collegiate Instructional League	941-727-0303	941-727-2962
118	FOX Sports	212-556-2500	212-354-6902
364	Frozen Ropes Training Centers	508-563-1860	508-563-1875
354	Gatorade Circle of Champions	312-553-1240	—
364	Grand Slam USA	630-271-9999	630-271-0112
128	Grandstand Cards	818-992-5642	818-348-9122
349	Great Lakes League	740-368-3738	740-368-3799

360	Hap Dumont Youth Baseball	316-721-1779	316-721-8054
125	Harry Wendelstedt Umpire School	386-672-4879	386-672-3212
354	Horizon National HS Invitational	602-867-9003	—
356	Impact Baseball Showcase	—	—
122	Indians Ink	440-953-2200	440-953-2202
124	Inside Edge Scouting	800-858-3343	508-526-6145
344	International Baseball Federation	41-21-318-8240	41-21-318-8241
344	International Olympic Committee	41-21-621-6111	41-21-621-6216
345	International Sports Group	925-798-4591	925-680-1182
290	Italian Serie A/1	39-06-36858297	39-06-36858201
288	Japan League	03-3502-0022	03-3502-0140
350	Jayhawk League	316-755-1285	316-755-1285
125	Jim Evans Academy of Professional Umpiring	512-335-5959	512-335-5411
121	Junior Baseball Magazine	818-710-1234	818-710-1877
364	KC Sports Tournaments	816-587-4545	816-587-4549
289	Korea Baseball Organization	02-3460-4643	02-3460-4649
122	Krause Publications	715-445-4612	715-445-4087
125	Lena Blackburn Rubbing Mud	856-764-7501	856-461-4089
360	Little League Baseball, Inc.	570-326-1921	570-326-1074
126	Little League Baseball Museum	570-326-3607	570-326-2267
354	Lions High School Invitational	619-583-2633	619-583-6605
128	Los Angeles Dodgers Adult Baseball Camp	800-334-7529	772-229-6708
126	Louisville Slugger Museum	502-588-7228	502-585-1179
34	MLB Advanced Media (MLB.com)	212-485-3444	212-485-3456
33	MLB Commissioner's Office	212-931-7800	—
34	MLB International	212-931-7500	212-949-5795
126	MLB Players Alumni Association	719-477-1870	719-477-1875
124	MLB Players Association	212-826-0808	212-752-4378
34	MLB Productions	212-931-7777	212-931-7788
124	Major League Scouting Bureau	909-980-1881	909-980-7794
364	Mark Cresse Baseball School	714-892-6145	714-892-1881
127	Men's Adult Baseball League	631-753-6725	631-753-4031
127	Men's Senior Baseball League	631-753-6725	631-753-4031
286	Mexican League	555-557-1007	555-395-2454
293	Mexican Pacific League	667-761-25-70	667-761-25-71
364	Mickey Owen Baseball School	800-999-8369	417-889-6978
356	Midwest Prospects Showcase	405-942-5455	405-942-3012
129	Minor League Baseball	727-822-6937	727-821-5819
128	Multi-Ad Sports	800-348-6485	309-692-8378
126	Museum of Minor League Baseball	901-722-0207	901-527-1642
297	NAIA	913-791-0044	913-791-9555
119	NBC-TV	212-664-2014	212-664-6365
297	NCAA	317-917-6222	317-917-6826
297	NJCAA	719-590-9788	719-590-7324
127	National Adult Baseball Association	800-621-6479	303-639-6605
346	National Alliance of Coll. Summer Baseball	401-739-7875	401-739-9789
361	National Amateur Baseball Federation	301-464-5460	301-352-0214
345	National Baseball Congress	316-267-3372	316-267-3382
126	National Baseball Hall of Fame	607-547-7200	607-547-2044
354	National Classic High School Tournament	714-993-2838	714-993-5350
120	National Collegiate Baseball Writers	312-553-0483	312-553-0495
354	National Federation of State High School Association	317-972-6900	317-822-5700
354	National HS Baseball Coaches Association	479-876-2591	479-876-2596
354	National High School Championship	502-261-9200	502-261-9278
126	Negro Leagues Baseball Museum	816-221-1920	816-221-8424
350	New England Collegiate League	603-483-0241	—
351	New York Collegiate League	585-223-2328	—
354	Nike National Baseball Classic	850-968-5755	850-937-2328
364	North Carolina Baseball Academy	336-931-1118	—
351	Northwoods League	507-536-4579	507-289-1866
122	Outside Pitch (Orioles)	410-234-8888	410-234-1029
352	Pacific International League	206-623-8844	602-623-8361
356	Pacific Northwest Championship	503-885-1126	—
364	Pennsylvania Diamond Bucks Camp	610-838-2119	—
355	Perfect Game USA	800-447-9362	319-298-2924
365	Playball Baseball Academy	954-776-6217	954-772-4510
361	Police Athletic Leagues	561-844-1823	561-863-6120
361	PONY Baseball, Inc.	724-225-1060	724-225-9852
356	Premier Baseball	941-371-0989	941-371-0917
125	Pro Baseball Athletic Trainers Society	404-875-4000	404-892-8560
127	Pro Baseball Employment Opportunities	866-397-7236	727-821-5819
365	Pro Baseball Instruction	877-448-2220	201-760-8820
125	Pro Baseball Umpire Corporation	727-822-6937	727-821-5819

356	Pro Select Baseball	201-337-7440	—
124	Prospects Plus/The Scouting Report	800-845-2726	919-682-2880
294	Puerto Rican League	787-765-6285	787-767-3028
361	RBI	212-931-7897	212-949-5695
128	Randy Hundley's Fantasy Baseball Camps	847-991-9595	847-991-9595
122	Reds Report	614-486-2202	614-486-3650
365	Ripken Baseball Camps	800-486-0850	—
119	Rogers SportsNet	416-332-5000	416-332-5767
365	Rookies Baseball	973-872-6789	973-872-2533
128	Roy Hobbs Baseball	330-923-3400	330-923-1967
126	SABR	216-575-0500	216-575-0502
365	San Diego School of Baseball	619-491-4000	619-469-5572
354	Sarasota High School Baseball Classic	941-955-0181	941-378-5853
365	School of Swing	559-270-4487	—
124	Scout of the Year Foundation	561-798-5897	561-798-4644
356	Selectfest Baseball	973-539-4781	—
365	Sho-Me Baseball Camp	800-993-2267	417-338-2610
124	Skillshow, Inc.	610-687-9072	610-687-9629
352	Southern Collegiate League	704-847-5037	704-847-1455
365	Southwest Professional Baseball School	888-830-8031	480-830-7455
120	The Sporting News	314-997-7111	314-997-0765
119	Sporting News Radio Network	847-509-1661	847-509-1677
120	Sports Byline USA	415-434-8300	415-391-2569
120	SportsTicker	201-309-1200	201-860-9742
118	SportsTicker-Boston	617-951-0070	617-737-9960
120	Sports Illustrated	212-522-1212	212-522-4543
121	Sports Illustrated for Kids	212-522-1212	212-522-0120
119	The Sports Network	416-332-5000	416-332-7658
122	Spring Training Yearbook	919-967-2420	919-967-6294
118	STATS, INC.	847-583-2100	847-470-9160
121	Street and Smith's Baseball Yearbook	704-973-1575	704-973-1576
121	Street and Smith's Sports Business Journal	704-973-1400	704-973-1401
354	Sunbelt High School Baseball Classic Series	405-348-3839	405-340-7538
361	Super Series Baseball of America	480-664-2998	480-664-2997
362	T-Ball USA Association, Inc.	203-381-1449	203-381-1440
119	TBS	404-827-1700	404-827-1593
356	Team One Showcases	859-466-8326	—
126	Ted Williams Museum/Hitters Hall of Fame	352-527-6566	352-527-4163
356	Top 96 Showcase	508-651-0165	—
356	Top Guns Showcase	208-762-1100	208-762-1100
128	Topps	212-376-0300	212-376-0623
122	Total Baseball	416-466-0418	416-466-9530
362	Triple Crown Sports	970-223-6644	970-223-3636
362	United States Amateur Baseball Association	425-776-7130	425-776-7130
362	United States Amateur Baseball Federation	619-435-2831	619-435-3148
362	United States Specialty Sports Association	816-587-4545	816-587-4549
344	United States Olympic Committee	719-866-4500	719-866-4654
128	Upper Deck	800-873-7332	760-929-6548
345	USA Baseball	Unavailable	Unavailable
354	USA HS Classic	901-872-8326	901-681-9443
120	USA Today	703-854-5954	703-854-2072
121	USA Today Sports Weekly	703-854-6319	703-854-2034
365	Utah Baseball Academy	801-561-1700	801-561-1762
352	Valley League	540-885-8901	540-886-2068
294	Venezuelan League	58-212-761-4932	58-212-761-7661
287	Venezuelan Summer League	58-241-824-0321	58-241-824-0705
122	Vine Line (Cubs)	773-404-2827	773-404-4129
119	WGN	773-528-2311	773-528-6050
354	West Coast Classic	408-252-6670	—
354	Westminster National High School Classic	954-735-1841	954-735-1858
125	World Umpires Association	321-637-3471	321-633-7018
122	Yankees Magazine	800-469-2657	—